Lecture Notes in Computer Science 12370

More information about this subseries at http://www.springer.com/series/7412

Andrea Vedaldi · Horst Bischof ·
Thomas Brox · Jan-Michael Frahm (Eds.)

Computer Vision – ECCV 2020

16th European Conference
Glasgow, UK, August 23–28, 2020
Proceedings, Part XXV

Springer

Editors
Andrea Vedaldi 🆔
University of Oxford
Oxford, UK

Horst Bischof 🆔
Graz University of Technology
Graz, Austria

Thomas Brox 🆔
University of Freiburg
Freiburg im Breisgau, Germany

Jan-Michael Frahm
University of North Carolina at Chapel Hill
Chapel Hill, NC, USA

ISSN 0302-9743   ISSN 1611-3349   (electronic)
Lecture Notes in Computer Science
ISBN 978-3-030-58594-5   ISBN 978-3-030-58595-2   (eBook)
https://doi.org/10.1007/978-3-030-58595-2

LNCS Sublibrary: SL6 – Image Processing, Computer Vision, Pattern Recognition, and Graphics

This Springer imprint is published by the registered company Springer Nature Switzerland AG
The registered company address is: Gewerbestrasse 11, 6330 Cham, Switzerland

Foreword

Hosting the European Conference on Computer Vision (ECCV 2020) was certainly an exciting journey. From the 2016 plan to hold it at the Edinburgh International Conference Centre (hosting 1,800 delegates) to the 2018 plan to hold it at Glasgow's Scottish Exhibition Centre (up to 6,000 delegates), we finally ended with moving online because of the COVID-19 outbreak. While possibly having fewer delegates than expected because of the online format, ECCV 2020 still had over 3,100 registered participants.

Although online, the conference delivered most of the activities expected at a face-to-face conference: peer-reviewed papers, industrial exhibitors, demonstrations, and messaging between delegates. In addition to the main technical sessions, the conference included a strong program of satellite events with 16 tutorials and 44 workshops.

Furthermore, the online conference format enabled new conference features. Every paper had an associated teaser video and a longer full presentation video. Along with the papers and slides from the videos, all these materials were available the week before the conference. This allowed delegates to become familiar with the paper content and be ready for the live interaction with the authors during the conference week. The live event consisted of brief presentations by the oral and spotlight authors and industrial sponsors. Question and answer sessions for all papers were timed to occur twice so delegates from around the world had convenient access to the authors.

As with ECCV 2018, authors' draft versions of the papers appeared online with open access, now on both the Computer Vision Foundation (CVF) and the European Computer Vision Association (ECVA) websites. An archival publication arrangement was put in place with the cooperation of Springer. SpringerLink hosts the final version of the papers with further improvements, such as activating reference links and supplementary materials. These two approaches benefit all potential readers: a version available freely for all researchers, and an authoritative and citable version with additional benefits for SpringerLink subscribers. We thank Alfred Hofmann and Aliaksandr Birukou from Springer for helping to negotiate this agreement, which we expect will continue for future versions of ECCV.

August 2020

Vittorio Ferrari
Bob Fisher
Cordelia Schmid
Emanuele Trucco

Preface

Welcome to the proceedings of the European Conference on Computer Vision (ECCV 2020). This is a unique edition of ECCV in many ways. Due to the COVID-19 pandemic, this is the first time the conference was held online, in a virtual format. This was also the first time the conference relied exclusively on the Open Review platform to manage the review process. Despite these challenges ECCV is thriving. The conference received 5,150 valid paper submissions, of which 1,360 were accepted for publication (27%) and, of those, 160 were presented as spotlights (3%) and 104 as orals (2%). This amounts to more than twice the number of submissions to ECCV 2018 (2,439). Furthermore, CVPR, the largest conference on computer vision, received 5,850 submissions this year, meaning that ECCV is now 87% the size of CVPR in terms of submissions. By comparison, in 2018 the size of ECCV was only 73% of CVPR.

The review model was similar to previous editions of ECCV; in particular, it was double blind in the sense that the authors did not know the name of the reviewers and vice versa. Furthermore, each conference submission was held confidentially, and was only publicly revealed if and once accepted for publication. Each paper received at least three reviews, totalling more than 15,000 reviews. Handling the review process at this scale was a significant challenge. In order to ensure that each submission received as fair and high-quality reviews as possible, we recruited 2,830 reviewers (a 130% increase with reference to 2018) and 207 area chairs (a 60% increase). The area chairs were selected based on their technical expertise and reputation, largely among people that served as area chair in previous top computer vision and machine learning conferences (ECCV, ICCV, CVPR, NeurIPS, etc.). Reviewers were similarly invited from previous conferences. We also encouraged experienced area chairs to suggest additional chairs and reviewers in the initial phase of recruiting.

Despite doubling the number of submissions, the reviewer load was slightly reduced from 2018, from a maximum of 8 papers down to 7 (with some reviewers offering to handle 6 papers plus an emergency review). The area chair load increased slightly, from 18 papers on average to 22 papers on average.

Conflicts of interest between authors, area chairs, and reviewers were handled largely automatically by the Open Review platform via their curated list of user profiles. Many authors submitting to ECCV already had a profile in Open Review. We set a paper registration deadline one week before the paper submission deadline in order to encourage all missing authors to register and create their Open Review profiles well on time (in practice, we allowed authors to create/change papers arbitrarily until the submission deadline). Except for minor issues with users creating duplicate profiles, this allowed us to easily and quickly identify institutional conflicts, and avoid them, while matching papers to area chairs and reviewers.

Papers were matched to area chairs based on: an affinity score computed by the Open Review platform, which is based on paper titles and abstracts, and an affinity score computed by the Toronto Paper Matching System (TPMS), which is based on the paper's full text, the area chair bids for individual papers, load balancing, and conflict avoidance. Open Review provides the program chairs a convenient web interface to experiment with different configurations of the matching algorithm. The chosen configuration resulted in about 50% of the assigned papers to be highly ranked by the area chair bids, and 50% to be ranked in the middle, with very few low bids assigned.

Assignments to reviewers were similar, with two differences. First, there was a maximum of 7 papers assigned to each reviewer. Second, area chairs recommended up to seven reviewers per paper, providing another highly-weighed term to the affinity scores used for matching.

The assignment of papers to area chairs was smooth. However, it was more difficult to find suitable reviewers for all papers. Having a ratio of 5.6 papers per reviewer with a maximum load of 7 (due to emergency reviewer commitment), which did not allow for much wiggle room in order to also satisfy conflict and expertise constraints. We received some complaints from reviewers who did not feel qualified to review specific papers and we reassigned them wherever possible. However, the large scale of the conference, the many constraints, and the fact that a large fraction of such complaints arrived very late in the review process made this process very difficult and not all complaints could be addressed.

Reviewers had six weeks to complete their assignments. Possibly due to COVID-19 or the fact that the NeurIPS deadline was moved closer to the review deadline, a record 30% of the reviews were still missing after the deadline. By comparison, ECCV 2018 experienced only 10% missing reviews at this stage of the process. In the subsequent week, area chairs chased the missing reviews intensely, found replacement reviewers in their own team, and managed to reach 10% missing reviews. Eventually, we could provide almost all reviews (more than 99.9%) with a delay of only a couple of days on the initial schedule by a significant use of emergency reviews. If this trend is confirmed, it might be a major challenge to run a smooth review process in future editions of ECCV. The community must reconsider prioritization of the time spent on paper writing (the number of submissions increased a lot despite COVID-19) and time spent on paper reviewing (the number of reviews delivered in time decreased a lot presumably due to COVID-19 or NeurIPS deadline). With this imbalance the peer-review system that ensures the quality of our top conferences may break soon.

Reviewers submitted their reviews independently. In the reviews, they had the opportunity to ask questions to the authors to be addressed in the rebuttal. However, reviewers were told not to request any significant new experiment. Using the Open Review interface, authors could provide an answer to each individual review, but were also allowed to cross-reference reviews and responses in their answers. Rather than PDF files, we allowed the use of formatted text for the rebuttal. The rebuttal and initial reviews were then made visible to all reviewers and the primary area chair for a given paper. The area chair encouraged and moderated the reviewer discussion. During the discussions, reviewers were invited to reach a consensus and possibly adjust their ratings as a result of the discussion and of the evidence in the rebuttal.

After the discussion period ended, most reviewers entered a final rating and recommendation, although in many cases this did not differ from their initial recommendation. Based on the updated reviews and discussion, the primary area chair then made a preliminary decision to accept or reject the paper and wrote a justification for it (meta-review). Except for cases where the outcome of this process was absolutely clear (as indicated by the three reviewers and primary area chairs all recommending clear rejection), the decision was then examined and potentially challenged by a secondary area chair. This led to further discussion and overturning a small number of preliminary decisions. Needless to say, there was no in-person area chair meeting, which would have been impossible due to COVID-19.

Area chairs were invited to observe the consensus of the reviewers whenever possible and use extreme caution in overturning a clear consensus to accept or reject a paper. If an area chair still decided to do so, she/he was asked to clearly justify it in the meta-review and to explicitly obtain the agreement of the secondary area chair. In practice, very few papers were rejected after being confidently accepted by the reviewers.

This was the first time Open Review was used as the main platform to run ECCV. In 2018, the program chairs used CMT3 for the user-facing interface and Open Review internally, for matching and conflict resolution. Since it is clearly preferable to only use a single platform, this year we switched to using Open Review in full. The experience was largely positive. The platform is highly-configurable, scalable, and open source. Being written in Python, it is easy to write scripts to extract data programmatically. The paper matching and conflict resolution algorithms and interfaces are top-notch, also due to the excellent author profiles in the platform. Naturally, there were a few kinks along the way due to the fact that the ECCV Open Review configuration was created from scratch for this event and it differs in substantial ways from many other Open Review conferences. However, the Open Review development and support team did a fantastic job in helping us to get the configuration right and to address issues in a timely manner as they unavoidably occurred. We cannot thank them enough for the tremendous effort they put into this project.

Finally, we would like to thank everyone involved in making ECCV 2020 possible in these very strange and difficult times. This starts with our authors, followed by the area chairs and reviewers, who ran the review process at an unprecedented scale. The whole Open Review team (and in particular Melisa Bok, Mohit Unyal, Carlos Mondragon Chapa, and Celeste Martinez Gomez) worked incredibly hard for the entire duration of the process. We would also like to thank René Vidal for contributing to the adoption of Open Review. Our thanks also go to Laurent Charling for TPMS and to the program chairs of ICML, ICLR, and NeurIPS for cross checking double submissions. We thank the website chair, Giovanni Farinella, and the CPI team (in particular Ashley Cook, Miriam Verdon, Nicola McGrane, and Sharon Kerr) for promptly adding material to the website as needed in the various phases of the process. Finally, we thank the publication chairs, Albert Ali Salah, Hamdi Dibeklioglu, Metehan Doyran, Henry Howard-Jenkins, Victor Prisacariu, Siyu Tang, and Gul Varol, who managed to compile these substantial proceedings in an exceedingly compressed schedule. We express our thanks to the ECVA team, in particular Kristina Scherbaum for allowing open access of the proceedings. We thank Alfred Hofmann from Springer who again serve as the publisher. Finally, we thank the other chairs of ECCV 2020, including in particular the general chairs for very useful feedback with the handling of the program.

August 2020   Andrea Vedaldi
                                                                                      Horst Bischof
                                                                                      Thomas Brox
                                                                              Jan-Michael Frahm

Organization

General Chairs

Vittorio Ferrari	Google Research, Switzerland
Bob Fisher	University of Edinburgh, UK
Cordelia Schmid	Google and Inria, France
Emanuele Trucco	University of Dundee, UK

Program Chairs

Andrea Vedaldi	University of Oxford, UK
Horst Bischof	Graz University of Technology, Austria
Thomas Brox	University of Freiburg, Germany
Jan-Michael Frahm	University of North Carolina, USA

Industrial Liaison Chairs

Jim Ashe	University of Edinburgh, UK
Helmut Grabner	Zurich University of Applied Sciences, Switzerland
Diane Larlus	NAVER LABS Europe, France
Cristian Novotny	University of Edinburgh, UK

Local Arrangement Chairs

Yvan Petillot	Heriot-Watt University, UK
Paul Siebert	University of Glasgow, UK

Academic Demonstration Chair

Thomas Mensink	Google Research and University of Amsterdam, The Netherlands

Poster Chair

Stephen Mckenna	University of Dundee, UK

Technology Chair

Gerardo Aragon Camarasa	University of Glasgow, UK

Tutorial Chairs

Carlo Colombo   University of Florence, Italy
Sotirios Tsaftaris   University of Edinburgh, UK

Publication Chairs

Albert Ali Salah   Utrecht University, The Netherlands
Hamdi Dibeklioglu   Bilkent University, Turkey
Metehan Doyran   Utrecht University, The Netherlands
Henry Howard-Jenkins   University of Oxford, UK
Victor Adrian Prisacariu   University of Oxford, UK
Siyu Tang   ETH Zurich, Switzerland
Gul Varol   University of Oxford, UK

Website Chair

Giovanni Maria Farinella   University of Catania, Italy

Workshops Chairs

Adrien Bartoli   University of Clermont Auvergne, France
Andrea Fusiello   University of Udine, Italy

Area Chairs

Lourdes Agapito   University College London, UK
Zeynep Akata   University of Tübingen, Germany
Karteek Alahari   Inria, France
Antonis Argyros   University of Crete, Greece
Hossein Azizpour   KTH Royal Institute of Technology, Sweden
Joao P. Barreto   Universidade de Coimbra, Portugal
Alexander C. Berg   University of North Carolina at Chapel Hill, USA
Matthew B. Blaschko   KU Leuven, Belgium
Lubomir D. Bourdev   WaveOne, Inc., USA
Edmond Boyer   Inria, France
Yuri Boykov   University of Waterloo, Canada
Gabriel Brostow   University College London, UK
Michael S. Brown   National University of Singapore, Singapore
Jianfei Cai   Monash University, Australia
Barbara Caputo   Politecnico di Torino, Italy
Ayan Chakrabarti   Washington University, St. Louis, USA
Tat-Jen Cham   Nanyang Technological University, Singapore
Manmohan Chandraker   University of California, San Diego, USA
Rama Chellappa   Johns Hopkins University, USA
Liang-Chieh Chen   Google, USA

Yung-Yu Chuang	National Taiwan University, Taiwan
Ondrej Chum	Czech Technical University in Prague, Czech Republic
Brian Clipp	Kitware, USA
John Collomosse	University of Surrey and Adobe Research, UK
Jason J. Corso	University of Michigan, USA
David J. Crandall	Indiana University, USA
Daniel Cremers	University of California, Los Angeles, USA
Fabio Cuzzolin	Oxford Brookes University, UK
Jifeng Dai	SenseTime, SAR China
Kostas Daniilidis	University of Pennsylvania, USA
Andrew Davison	Imperial College London, UK
Alessio Del Bue	Fondazione Istituto Italiano di Tecnologia, Italy
Jia Deng	Princeton University, USA
Alexey Dosovitskiy	Google, Germany
Matthijs Douze	Facebook, France
Enrique Dunn	Stevens Institute of Technology, USA
Irfan Essa	Georgia Institute of Technology and Google, USA
Giovanni Maria Farinella	University of Catania, Italy
Ryan Farrell	Brigham Young University, USA
Paolo Favaro	University of Bern, Switzerland
Rogerio Feris	International Business Machines, USA
Cornelia Fermuller	University of Maryland, College Park, USA
David J. Fleet	Vector Institute, Canada
Friedrich Fraundorfer	DLR, Austria
Mario Fritz	CISPA Helmholtz Center for Information Security, Germany
Pascal Fua	EPFL (Swiss Federal Institute of Technology Lausanne), Switzerland
Yasutaka Furukawa	Simon Fraser University, Canada
Li Fuxin	Oregon State University, USA
Efstratios Gavves	University of Amsterdam, The Netherlands
Peter Vincent Gehler	Amazon, USA
Theo Gevers	University of Amsterdam, The Netherlands
Ross Girshick	Facebook AI Research, USA
Boqing Gong	Google, USA
Stephen Gould	Australian National University, Australia
Jinwei Gu	SenseTime Research, USA
Abhinav Gupta	Facebook, USA
Bohyung Han	Seoul National University, South Korea
Bharath Hariharan	Cornell University, USA
Tal Hassner	Facebook AI Research, USA
Xuming He	Australian National University, Australia
Joao F. Henriques	University of Oxford, UK
Adrian Hilton	University of Surrey, UK
Minh Hoai	Stony Brooks, State University of New York, USA
Derek Hoiem	University of Illinois Urbana-Champaign, USA

Timothy Hospedales	University of Edinburgh and Samsung, UK
Gang Hua	Wormpex AI Research, USA
Slobodan Ilic	Siemens AG, Germany
Hiroshi Ishikawa	Waseda University, Japan
Jiaya Jia	The Chinese University of Hong Kong, SAR China
Hailin Jin	Adobe Research, USA
Justin Johnson	University of Michigan, USA
Frederic Jurie	University of Caen Normandie, France
Fredrik Kahl	Chalmers University, Sweden
Sing Bing Kang	Zillow, USA
Gunhee Kim	Seoul National University, South Korea
Junmo Kim	Korea Advanced Institute of Science and Technology, South Korea
Tae-Kyun Kim	Imperial College London, UK
Ron Kimmel	Technion-Israel Institute of Technology, Israel
Alexander Kirillov	Facebook AI Research, USA
Kris Kitani	Carnegie Mellon University, USA
Iasonas Kokkinos	Ariel AI, UK
Vladlen Koltun	Intel Labs, USA
Nikos Komodakis	Ecole des Ponts ParisTech, France
Piotr Koniusz	Australian National University, Australia
M. Pawan Kumar	University of Oxford, UK
Kyros Kutulakos	University of Toronto, Canada
Christoph Lampert	IST Austria, Austria
Ivan Laptev	Inria, France
Diane Larlus	NAVER LABS Europe, France
Laura Leal-Taixe	Technical University Munich, Germany
Honglak Lee	Google and University of Michigan, USA
Joon-Young Lee	Adobe Research, USA
Kyoung Mu Lee	Seoul National University, South Korea
Seungyong Lee	POSTECH, South Korea
Yong Jae Lee	University of California, Davis, USA
Bastian Leibe	RWTH Aachen University, Germany
Victor Lempitsky	Samsung, Russia
Ales Leonardis	University of Birmingham, UK
Marius Leordeanu	Institute of Mathematics of the Romanian Academy, Romania
Vincent Lepetit	ENPC ParisTech, France
Hongdong Li	The Australian National University, Australia
Xi Li	Zhejiang University, China
Yin Li	University of Wisconsin-Madison, USA
Zicheng Liao	Zhejiang University, China
Jongwoo Lim	Hanyang University, South Korea
Stephen Lin	Microsoft Research Asia, China
Yen-Yu Lin	National Chiao Tung University, Taiwan, China
Zhe Lin	Adobe Research, USA

Haibin Ling	Stony Brooks, State University of New York, USA
Jiaying Liu	Peking University, China
Ming-Yu Liu	NVIDIA, USA
Si Liu	Beihang University, China
Xiaoming Liu	Michigan State University, USA
Huchuan Lu	Dalian University of Technology, China
Simon Lucey	Carnegie Mellon University, USA
Jiebo Luo	University of Rochester, USA
Julien Mairal	Inria, France
Michael Maire	University of Chicago, USA
Subhransu Maji	University of Massachusetts, Amherst, USA
Yasushi Makihara	Osaka University, Japan
Jiri Matas	Czech Technical University in Prague, Czech Republic
Yasuyuki Matsushita	Osaka University, Japan
Philippos Mordohai	Stevens Institute of Technology, USA
Vittorio Murino	University of Verona, Italy
Naila Murray	NAVER LABS Europe, France
Hajime Nagahara	Osaka University, Japan
P. J. Narayanan	International Institute of Information Technology (IIIT), Hyderabad, India
Nassir Navab	Technical University of Munich, Germany
Natalia Neverova	Facebook AI Research, France
Matthias Niessner	Technical University of Munich, Germany
Jean-Marc Odobez	Idiap Research Institute and Swiss Federal Institute of Technology Lausanne, Switzerland
Francesca Odone	Università di Genova, Italy
Takeshi Oishi	The University of Tokyo, Tokyo Institute of Technology, Japan
Vicente Ordonez	University of Virginia, USA
Manohar Paluri	Facebook AI Research, USA
Maja Pantic	Imperial College London, UK
In Kyu Park	Inha University, South Korea
Ioannis Patras	Queen Mary University of London, UK
Patrick Perez	Valeo, France
Bryan A. Plummer	Boston University, USA
Thomas Pock	Graz University of Technology, Austria
Marc Pollefeys	ETH Zurich and Microsoft MR & AI Zurich Lab, Switzerland
Jean Ponce	Inria, France
Gerard Pons-Moll	MPII, Saarland Informatics Campus, Germany
Jordi Pont-Tuset	Google, Switzerland
James Matthew Rehg	Georgia Institute of Technology, USA
Ian Reid	University of Adelaide, Australia
Olaf Ronneberger	DeepMind London, UK
Stefan Roth	TU Darmstadt, Germany
Bryan Russell	Adobe Research, USA

Mathieu Salzmann	EPFL, Switzerland
Dimitris Samaras	Stony Brook University, USA
Imari Sato	National Institute of Informatics (NII), Japan
Yoichi Sato	The University of Tokyo, Japan
Torsten Sattler	Czech Technical University in Prague, Czech Republic
Daniel Scharstein	Middlebury College, USA
Bernt Schiele	MPII, Saarland Informatics Campus, Germany
Julia A. Schnabel	King's College London, UK
Nicu Sebe	University of Trento, Italy
Greg Shakhnarovich	Toyota Technological Institute at Chicago, USA
Humphrey Shi	University of Oregon, USA
Jianbo Shi	University of Pennsylvania, USA
Jianping Shi	SenseTime, China
Leonid Sigal	University of British Columbia, Canada
Cees Snoek	University of Amsterdam, The Netherlands
Richard Souvenir	Temple University, USA
Hao Su	University of California, San Diego, USA
Akihiro Sugimoto	National Institute of Informatics (NII), Japan
Jian Sun	Megvii Technology, China
Jian Sun	Xi'an Jiaotong University, China
Chris Sweeney	Facebook Reality Labs, USA
Yu-wing Tai	Kuaishou Technology, China
Chi-Keung Tang	The Hong Kong University of Science and Technology, SAR China
Radu Timofte	ETH Zurich, Switzerland
Sinisa Todorovic	Oregon State University, USA
Giorgos Tolias	Czech Technical University in Prague, Czech Republic
Carlo Tomasi	Duke University, USA
Tatiana Tommasi	Politecnico di Torino, Italy
Lorenzo Torresani	Facebook AI Research and Dartmouth College, USA
Alexander Toshev	Google, USA
Zhuowen Tu	University of California, San Diego, USA
Tinne Tuytelaars	KU Leuven, Belgium
Jasper Uijlings	Google, Switzerland
Nuno Vasconcelos	University of California, San Diego, USA
Olga Veksler	University of Waterloo, Canada
Rene Vidal	Johns Hopkins University, USA
Gang Wang	Alibaba Group, China
Jingdong Wang	Microsoft Research Asia, China
Yizhou Wang	Peking University, China
Lior Wolf	Facebook AI Research and Tel Aviv University, Israel
Jianxin Wu	Nanjing University, China
Tao Xiang	University of Surrey, UK
Saining Xie	Facebook AI Research, USA
Ming-Hsuan Yang	University of California at Merced and Google, USA
Ruigang Yang	University of Kentucky, USA

Kwang Moo Yi	University of Victoria, Canada
Zhaozheng Yin	Stony Brook, State University of New York, USA
Chang D. Yoo	Korea Advanced Institute of Science and Technology, South Korea
Shaodi You	University of Amsterdam, The Netherlands
Jingyi Yu	ShanghaiTech University, China
Stella Yu	University of California, Berkeley, and ICSI, USA
Stefanos Zafeiriou	Imperial College London, UK
Hongbin Zha	Peking University, China
Tianzhu Zhang	University of Science and Technology of China, China
Liang Zheng	Australian National University, Australia
Todd E. Zickler	Harvard University, USA
Andrew Zisserman	University of Oxford, UK

Technical Program Committee

Sathyanarayanan N. Aakur	Samuel Albanie	Pablo Arbelaez
Wael Abd Almgaeed	Shadi Albarqouni	Shervin Ardeshir
Abdelrahman Abdelhamed	Cenek Albl	Sercan O. Arik
Abdullah Abuolaim	Hassan Abu Alhaija	Anil Armagan
Supreeth Achar	Daniel Aliaga	Anurag Arnab
Hanno Ackermann	Mohammad S. Aliakbarian	Chetan Arora
Ehsan Adeli	Rahaf Aljundi	Federica Arrigoni
Triantafyllos Afouras	Thiemo Alldieck	Mathieu Aubry
Sameer Agarwal	Jon Almazan	Shai Avidan
Aishwarya Agrawal	Jose M. Alvarez	Angelica I. Aviles-Rivero
Harsh Agrawal	Senjian An	Yannis Avrithis
Pulkit Agrawal	Saket Anand	Ismail Ben Ayed
Antonio Agudo	Codruta Ancuti	Shekoofeh Azizi
Eirikur Agustsson	Cosmin Ancuti	Ioan Andrei Bârsan
Karim Ahmed	Peter Anderson	Artem Babenko
Byeongjoo Ahn	Juan Andrade-Cetto	Deepak Babu Sam
Unaiza Ahsan	Alexander Andreopoulos	Seung-Hwan Baek
Thalaiyasingam Ajanthan	Misha Andriluka	Seungryul Baek
Kenan E. Ak	Dragomir Anguelov	Andrew D. Bagdanov
Emre Akbas	Rushil Anirudh	Shai Bagon
Naveed Akhtar	Michel Antunes	Yuval Bahat
Derya Akkaynak	Oisin Mac Aodha	Junjie Bai
Yagiz Aksoy	Srikar Appalaraju	Song Bai
Ziad Al-Halah	Relja Arandjelovic	Xiang Bai
Xavier Alameda-Pineda	Nikita Araslanov	Yalong Bai
Jean-Baptiste Alayrac	Andre Araujo	Yancheng Bai
	Helder Araujo	Peter Bajcsy
		Slawomir Bak

Kwok-Ping Chan
Siddhartha Chandra
Sharat Chandran
Arjun Chandrasekaran
Angel X. Chang
Che-Han Chang
Hong Chang
Hyun Sung Chang
Hyung Jin Chang
Jianlong Chang
Ju Yong Chang
Ming-Ching Chang
Simyung Chang
Xiaojun Chang
Yu-Wei Chao
Devendra S. Chaplot
Arslan Chaudhry
Rizwan A. Chaudhry
Can Chen
Chang Chen
Chao Chen
Chen Chen
Chu-Song Chen
Dapeng Chen
Dong Chen
Dongdong Chen
Guanying Chen
Hongge Chen
Hsin-yi Chen
Huaijin Chen
Hwann-Tzong Chen
Jianbo Chen
Jianhui Chen
Jiansheng Chen
Jiaxin Chen
Jie Chen
Jun-Cheng Chen
Kan Chen
Kevin Chen
Lin Chen
Long Chen
Min-Hung Chen
Qifeng Chen
Shi Chen
Shixing Chen
Tianshui Chen

Weifeng Chen
Weikai Chen
Xi Chen
Xiaohan Chen
Xiaozhi Chen
Xilin Chen
Xingyu Chen
Xinlei Chen
Xinyun Chen
Yi-Ting Chen
Yilun Chen
Ying-Cong Chen
Yinpeng Chen
Yiran Chen
Yu Chen
Yu-Sheng Chen
Yuhua Chen
Yun-Chun Chen
Yunpeng Chen
Yuntao Chen
Zhuoyuan Chen
Zitian Chen
Anchieh Cheng
Bowen Cheng
Erkang Cheng
Gong Cheng
Guangliang Cheng
Jingchun Cheng
Jun Cheng
Li Cheng
Ming-Ming Cheng
Yu Cheng
Ziang Cheng
Anoop Cherian
Dmitry Chetverikov
Ngai-man Cheung
William Cheung
Ajad Chhatkuli
Naoki Chiba
Benjamin Chidester
Han-pang Chiu
Mang Tik Chiu
Wei-Chen Chiu
Donghyeon Cho
Hojin Cho
Minsu Cho

Nam Ik Cho
Tim Cho
Tae Eun Choe
Chiho Choi
Edward Choi
Inchang Choi
Jinsoo Choi
Jonghyun Choi
Jongwon Choi
Yukyung Choi
Hisham Cholakkal
Eunji Chong
Jaegul Choo
Christopher Choy
Hang Chu
Peng Chu
Wen-Sheng Chu
Albert Chung
Joon Son Chung
Hai Ci
Safa Cicek
Ramazan G. Cinbis
Arridhana Ciptadi
Javier Civera
James J. Clark
Ronald Clark
Felipe Codevilla
Michael Cogswell
Andrea Cohen
Maxwell D. Collins
Carlo Colombo
Yang Cong
Adria R. Continente
Marcella Cornia
John Richard Corring
Darren Cosker
Dragos Costea
Garrison W. Cottrell
Florent Couzinie-Devy
Marco Cristani
Ioana Croitoru
James L. Crowley
Jiequan Cui
Zhaopeng Cui
Ross Cutler
Antonio D'Innocente

Rozenn Dahyot
Bo Dai
Dengxin Dai
Hang Dai
Longquan Dai
Shuyang Dai
Xiyang Dai
Yuchao Dai
Adrian V. Dalca
Dima Damen
Bharath B. Damodaran
Kristin Dana
Martin Danelljan
Zheng Dang
Zachary Alan Daniels
Donald G. Dansereau
Abhishek Das
Samyak Datta
Achal Dave
Titas De
Rodrigo de Bem
Teo de Campos
Raoul de Charette
Shalini De Mello
Joseph DeGol
Herve Delingette
Haowen Deng
Jiankang Deng
Weijian Deng
Zhiwei Deng
Joachim Denzler
Konstantinos G. Derpanis
Aditya Deshpande
Frederic Devernay
Somdip Dey
Arturo Deza
Abhinav Dhall
Helisa Dhamo
Vikas Dhiman
Fillipe Dias Moreira
   de Souza
Ali Diba
Ferran Diego
Guiguang Ding
Henghui Ding
Jian Ding

Mingyu Ding
Xinghao Ding
Zhengming Ding
Robert DiPietro
Cosimo Distante
Ajay Divakaran
Mandar Dixit
Abdelaziz Djelouah
Thanh-Toan Do
Jose Dolz
Bo Dong
Chao Dong
Jiangxin Dong
Weiming Dong
Weisheng Dong
Xingping Dong
Xuanyi Dong
Yinpeng Dong
Gianfranco Doretto
Hazel Doughty
Hassen Drira
Bertram Drost
Dawei Du
Ye Duan
Yueqi Duan
Abhimanyu Dubey
Anastasia Dubrovina
Stefan Duffner
Chi Nhan Duong
Thibaut Durand
Zoran Duric
Iulia Duta
Debidatta Dwibedi
Benjamin Eckart
Marc Eder
Marzieh Edraki
Alexei A. Efros
Kiana Ehsani
Hazm Kemal Ekenel
James H. Elder
Mohamed Elgharib
Shireen Elhabian
Ehsan Elhamifar
Mohamed Elhoseiny
Ian Endres
N. Benjamin Erichson

Jan Ernst
Sergio Escalera
Francisco Escolano
Victor Escorcia
Carlos Esteves
Francisco J. Estrada
Bin Fan
Chenyou Fan
Deng-Ping Fan
Haoqi Fan
Hehe Fan
Heng Fan
Kai Fan
Lijie Fan
Linxi Fan
Quanfu Fan
Shaojing Fan
Xiaochuan Fan
Xin Fan
Yuchen Fan
Sean Fanello
Hao-Shu Fang
Haoyang Fang
Kuan Fang
Yi Fang
Yuming Fang
Azade Farshad
Alireza Fathi
Raanan Fattal
Joao Fayad
Xiaohan Fei
Christoph Feichtenhofer
Michael Felsberg
Chen Feng
Jiashi Feng
Junyi Feng
Mengyang Feng
Qianli Feng
Zhenhua Feng
Michele Fenzi
Andras Ferencz
Martin Fergie
Basura Fernando
Ethan Fetaya
Michael Firman
John W. Fisher

Matthew Fisher
Boris Flach
Corneliu Florea
Wolfgang Foerstner
David Fofi
Gian Luca Foresti
Per-Erik Forssen
David Fouhey
Katerina Fragkiadaki
Victor Fragoso
Jean-Sébastien Franco
Ohad Fried
Iuri Frosio
Cheng-Yang Fu
Huazhu Fu
Jianlong Fu
Jingjing Fu
Xueyang Fu
Yanwei Fu
Ying Fu
Yun Fu
Olac Fuentes
Kent Fujiwara
Takuya Funatomi
Christopher Funk
Thomas Funkhouser
Antonino Furnari
Ryo Furukawa
Erik Gärtner
Raghudeep Gadde
Matheus Gadelha
Vandit Gajjar
Trevor Gale
Juergen Gall
Mathias Gallardo
Guillermo Gallego
Orazio Gallo
Chuang Gan
Zhe Gan
Madan Ravi Ganesh
Aditya Ganeshan
Siddha Ganju
Bin-Bin Gao
Changxin Gao
Feng Gao
Hongchang Gao

Jin Gao
Jiyang Gao
Junbin Gao
Katelyn Gao
Lin Gao
Mingfei Gao
Ruiqi Gao
Ruohan Gao
Shenghua Gao
Yuan Gao
Yue Gao
Noa Garcia
Alberto Garcia-Garcia
Guillermo
    Garcia-Hernando
Jacob R. Gardner
Animesh Garg
Kshitiz Garg
Rahul Garg
Ravi Garg
Philip N. Garner
Kirill Gavrilyuk
Paul Gay
Shiming Ge
Weifeng Ge
Baris Gecer
Xin Geng
Kyle Genova
Stamatios Georgoulis
Bernard Ghanem
Michael Gharbi
Kamran Ghasedi
Golnaz Ghiasi
Arnab Ghosh
Partha Ghosh
Silvio Giancola
Andrew Gilbert
Rohit Girdhar
Xavier Giro-i-Nieto
Thomas Gittings
Ioannis Gkioulekas
Clement Godard
Vaibhava Goel
Bastian Goldluecke
Lluis Gomez
Nuno Gonçalves

Dong Gong
Ke Gong
Mingming Gong
Abel Gonzalez-Garcia
Ariel Gordon
Daniel Gordon
Paulo Gotardo
Venu Madhav Govindu
Ankit Goyal
Priya Goyal
Raghav Goyal
Benjamin Graham
Douglas Gray
Brent A. Griffin
Etienne Grossmann
David Gu
Jiayuan Gu
Jiuxiang Gu
Lin Gu
Qiao Gu
Shuhang Gu
Jose J. Guerrero
Paul Guerrero
Jie Gui
Jean-Yves Guillemaut
Riza Alp Guler
Erhan Gundogdu
Fatma Guney
Guodong Guo
Kaiwen Guo
Qi Guo
Sheng Guo
Shi Guo
Tiantong Guo
Xiaojie Guo
Yijie Guo
Yiluan Guo
Yuanfang Guo
Yulan Guo
Agrim Gupta
Ankush Gupta
Mohit Gupta
Saurabh Gupta
Tanmay Gupta
Danna Gurari
Abner Guzman-Rivera

JunYoung Gwak
Michael Gygli
Jung-Woo Ha
Simon Hadfield
Isma Hadji
Bjoern Haefner
Taeyoung Hahn
Levente Hajder
Peter Hall
Emanuela Haller
Stefan Haller
Bumsub Ham
Abdullah Hamdi
Dongyoon Han
Hu Han
Jungong Han
Junwei Han
Kai Han
Tian Han
Xiaoguang Han
Xintong Han
Yahong Han
Ankur Handa
Zekun Hao
Albert Haque
Tatsuya Harada
Mehrtash Harandi
Adam W. Harley
Mahmudul Hasan
Atsushi Hashimoto
Ali Hatamizadeh
Munawar Hayat
Dongliang He
Jingrui He
Junfeng He
Kaiming He
Kun He
Lei He
Pan He
Ran He
Shengfeng He
Tong He
Weipeng He
Xuming He
Yang He
Yihui He

Zhihai He
Chinmay Hegde
Janne Heikkila
Mattias P. Heinrich
Stéphane Herbin
Alexander Hermans
Luis Herranz
John R. Hershey
Aaron Hertzmann
Roei Herzig
Anders Heyden
Steven Hickson
Otmar Hilliges
Tomas Hodan
Judy Hoffman
Michael Hofmann
Yannick Hold-Geoffroy
Namdar Homayounfar
Sina Honari
Richang Hong
Seunghoon Hong
Xiaopeng Hong
Yi Hong
Hidekata Hontani
Anthony Hoogs
Yedid Hoshen
Mir Rayat Imtiaz Hossain
Junhui Hou
Le Hou
Lu Hou
Tingbo Hou
Wei-Lin Hsiao
Cheng-Chun Hsu
Gee-Sern Jison Hsu
Kuang-jui Hsu
Changbo Hu
Di Hu
Guosheng Hu
Han Hu
Hao Hu
Hexiang Hu
Hou-Ning Hu
Jie Hu
Junlin Hu
Nan Hu
Ping Hu

Ronghang Hu
Xiaowei Hu
Yinlin Hu
Yuan-Ting Hu
Zhe Hu
Binh-Son Hua
Yang Hua
Bingyao Huang
Di Huang
Dong Huang
Fay Huang
Haibin Huang
Haozhi Huang
Heng Huang
Huaibo Huang
Jia-Bin Huang
Jing Huang
Jingwei Huang
Kaizhu Huang
Lei Huang
Qiangui Huang
Qiaoying Huang
Qingqiu Huang
Qixing Huang
Shaoli Huang
Sheng Huang
Siyuan Huang
Weilin Huang
Wenbing Huang
Xiangru Huang
Xun Huang
Yan Huang
Yifei Huang
Yue Huang
Zhiwu Huang
Zilong Huang
Minyoung Huh
Zhuo Hui
Matthias B. Hullin
Martin Humenberger
Wei-Chih Hung
Zhouyuan Huo
Junhwa Hur
Noureldien Hussein
Jyh-Jing Hwang
Seong Jae Hwang

Sung Ju Hwang
Ichiro Ide
Ivo Ihrke
Daiki Ikami
Satoshi Ikehata
Nazli Ikizler-Cinbis
Sunghoon Im
Yani Ioannou
Radu Tudor Ionescu
Umar Iqbal
Go Irie
Ahmet Iscen
Md Amirul Islam
Vamsi Ithapu
Nathan Jacobs
Arpit Jain
Himalaya Jain
Suyog Jain
Stuart James
Won-Dong Jang
Yunseok Jang
Ronnachai Jaroensri
Dinesh Jayaraman
Sadeep Jayasumana
Suren Jayasuriya
Herve Jegou
Simon Jenni
Hae-Gon Jeon
Yunho Jeon
Koteswar R. Jerripothula
Hueihan Jhuang
I-hong Jhuo
Dinghuang Ji
Hui Ji
Jingwei Ji
Pan Ji
Yanli Ji
Baoxiong Jia
Kui Jia
Xu Jia
Chiyu Max Jiang
Haiyong Jiang
Hao Jiang
Huaizu Jiang
Huajie Jiang
Ke Jiang

Lai Jiang
Li Jiang
Lu Jiang
Ming Jiang
Peng Jiang
Shuqiang Jiang
Wei Jiang
Xudong Jiang
Zhuolin Jiang
Jianbo Jiao
Zequn Jie
Dakai Jin
Kyong Hwan Jin
Lianwen Jin
SouYoung Jin
Xiaojie Jin
Xin Jin
Nebojsa Jojic
Alexis Joly
Michael Jeffrey Jones
Hanbyul Joo
Jungseock Joo
Kyungdon Joo
Ajjen Joshi
Shantanu H. Joshi
Da-Cheng Juan
Marco Körner
Kevin Köser
Asim Kadav
Christine Kaeser-Chen
Kushal Kafle
Dagmar Kainmueller
Ioannis A. Kakadiaris
Zdenek Kalal
Nima Kalantari
Yannis Kalantidis
Mahdi M. Kalayeh
Anmol Kalia
Sinan Kalkan
Vicky Kalogeiton
Ashwin Kalyan
Joni-kristian Kamarainen
Gerda Kamberova
Chandra Kambhamettu
Martin Kampel
Meina Kan

Christopher Kanan
Kenichi Kanatani
Angjoo Kanazawa
Atsushi Kanehira
Takuhiro Kaneko
Asako Kanezaki
Bingyi Kang
Di Kang
Sunghun Kang
Zhao Kang
Vadim Kantorov
Abhishek Kar
Amlan Kar
Theofanis Karaletsos
Leonid Karlinsky
Kevin Karsch
Angelos Katharopoulos
Isinsu Katircioglu
Hiroharu Kato
Zoltan Kato
Dotan Kaufman
Jan Kautz
Rei Kawakami
Qiuhong Ke
Wadim Kehl
Petr Kellnhofer
Aniruddha Kembhavi
Cem Keskin
Margret Keuper
Daniel Keysers
Ashkan Khakzar
Fahad Khan
Naeemullah Khan
Salman Khan
Siddhesh Khandelwal
Rawal Khirodkar
Anna Khoreva
Tejas Khot
Parmeshwar Khurd
Hadi Kiapour
Joe Kileel
Chanho Kim
Dahun Kim
Edward Kim
Eunwoo Kim
Han-ul Kim

Gil Levi
Evgeny Levinkov
Aviad Levis
Jose Lezama
Ang Li
Bin Li
Bing Li
Boyi Li
Changsheng Li
Chao Li
Chen Li
Cheng Li
Chenglong Li
Chi Li
Chun-Guang Li
Chun-Liang Li
Chunyuan Li
Dong Li
Guanbin Li
Hao Li
Haoxiang Li
Hongsheng Li
Hongyang Li
Houqiang Li
Huibin Li
Jia Li
Jianan Li
Jianguo Li
Junnan Li
Junxuan Li
Kai Li
Ke Li
Kejie Li
Kunpeng Li
Lerenhan Li
Li Erran Li
Mengtian Li
Mu Li
Peihua Li
Peiyi Li
Ping Li
Qi Li
Qing Li
Ruiyu Li
Ruoteng Li
Shaozi Li

Sheng Li
Shiwei Li
Shuang Li
Siyang Li
Stan Z. Li
Tianye Li
Wei Li
Weixin Li
Wen Li
Wenbo Li
Xiaomeng Li
Xin Li
Xiu Li
Xuelong Li
Xueting Li
Yan Li
Yandong Li
Yanghao Li
Yehao Li
Yi Li
Yijun Li
Yikang LI
Yining Li
Yongjie Li
Yu Li
Yu-Jhe Li
Yunpeng Li
Yunsheng Li
Yunzhu Li
Zhe Li
Zhen Li
Zhengqi Li
Zhenyang Li
Zhuwen Li
Dongze Lian
Xiaochen Lian
Zhouhui Lian
Chen Liang
Jie Liang
Ming Liang
Paul Pu Liang
Pengpeng Liang
Shu Liang
Wei Liang
Jing Liao
Minghui Liao

Renjie Liao
Shengcai Liao
Shuai Liao
Yiyi Liao
Ser-Nam Lim
Chen-Hsuan Lin
Chung-Ching Lin
Dahua Lin
Ji Lin
Kevin Lin
Tianwei Lin
Tsung-Yi Lin
Tsung-Yu Lin
Wei-An Lin
Weiyao Lin
Yen-Chen Lin
Yuewei Lin
David B. Lindell
Drew Linsley
Krzysztof Lis
Roee Litman
Jim Little
An-An Liu
Bo Liu
Buyu Liu
Chao Liu
Chen Liu
Cheng-lin Liu
Chenxi Liu
Dong Liu
Feng Liu
Guilin Liu
Haomiao Liu
Heshan Liu
Hong Liu
Ji Liu
Jingen Liu
Jun Liu
Lanlan Liu
Li Liu
Liu Liu
Mengyuan Liu
Miaomiao Liu
Nian Liu
Ping Liu
Risheng Liu

Sheng Liu
Shu Liu
Shuaicheng Liu
Sifei Liu
Siqi Liu
Siying Liu
Songtao Liu
Ting Liu
Tongliang Liu
Tyng-Luh Liu
Wanquan Liu
Wei Liu
Weiyang Liu
Weizhe Liu
Wenyu Liu
Wu Liu
Xialei Liu
Xianglong Liu
Xiaodong Liu
Xiaofeng Liu
Xihui Liu
Xingyu Liu
Xinwang Liu
Xuanqing Liu
Xuebo Liu
Yang Liu
Yaojie Liu
Yebin Liu
Yen-Cheng Liu
Yiming Liu
Yu Liu
Yu-Shen Liu
Yufan Liu
Yun Liu
Zheng Liu
Zhijian Liu
Zhuang Liu
Zichuan Liu
Ziwei Liu
Zongyi Liu
Stephan Liwicki
Liliana Lo Presti
Chengjiang Long
Fuchen Long
Mingsheng Long
Xiang Long

Yang Long
Charles T. Loop
Antonio Lopez
Roberto J. Lopez-Sastre
Javier Lorenzo-Navarro
Manolis Lourakis
Boyu Lu
Canyi Lu
Feng Lu
Guoyu Lu
Hongtao Lu
Jiajun Lu
Jiasen Lu
Jiwen Lu
Kaiyue Lu
Le Lu
Shao-Ping Lu
Shijian Lu
Xiankai Lu
Xin Lu
Yao Lu
Yiping Lu
Yongxi Lu
Yongyi Lu
Zhiwu Lu
Fujun Luan
Benjamin E. Lundell
Hao Luo
Jian-Hao Luo
Ruotian Luo
Weixin Luo
Wenhan Luo
Wenjie Luo
Yan Luo
Zelun Luo
Zixin Luo
Khoa Luu
Zhaoyang Lv
Pengyuan Lyu
Thomas Möllenhoff
Matthias Müller
Bingpeng Ma
Chih-Yao Ma
Chongyang Ma
Huimin Ma
Jiayi Ma

K. T. Ma
Ke Ma
Lin Ma
Liqian Ma
Shugao Ma
Wei-Chiu Ma
Xiaojian Ma
Xingjun Ma
Zhanyu Ma
Zheng Ma
Radek Jakob Mackowiak
Ludovic Magerand
Shweta Mahajan
Siddharth Mahendran
Long Mai
Ameesh Makadia
Oscar Mendez Maldonado
Mateusz Malinowski
Yury Malkov
Arun Mallya
Dipu Manandhar
Massimiliano Mancini
Fabian Manhardt
Kevis-kokitsi Maninis
Varun Manjunatha
Junhua Mao
Xudong Mao
Alina Marcu
Edgar Margffoy-Tuay
Dmitrii Marin
Manuel J. Marin-Jimenez
Kenneth Marino
Niki Martinel
Julieta Martinez
Jonathan Masci
Tomohiro Mashita
Iacopo Masi
David Masip
Daniela Massiceti
Stefan Mathe
Yusuke Matsui
Tetsu Matsukawa
Iain A. Matthews
Kevin James Matzen
Bruce Allen Maxwell
Stephen Maybank

Björn Ommer
Mohamed Omran
Elisabeta Oneata
Michael Opitz
Jose Oramas
Tribhuvanesh Orekondy
Shaul Oron
Sergio Orts-Escolano
Ivan Oseledets
Aljosa Osep
Magnus Oskarsson
Anton Osokin
Martin R. Oswald
Wanli Ouyang
Andrew Owens
Mete Ozay
Mustafa Ozuysal
Eduardo Pérez-Pellitero
Gautam Pai
Dipan Kumar Pal
P. H. Pamplona Savarese
Jinshan Pan
Junting Pan
Xingang Pan
Yingwei Pan
Yannis Panagakis
Rameswar Panda
Guan Pang
Jiahao Pang
Jiangmiao Pang
Tianyu Pang
Sharath Pankanti
Nicolas Papadakis
Dim Papadopoulos
George Papandreou
Toufiq Parag
Shaifali Parashar
Sarah Parisot
Eunhyeok Park
Hyun Soo Park
Jaesik Park
Min-Gyu Park
Taesung Park
Alvaro Parra
C. Alejandro Parraga
Despoina Paschalidou

Nikolaos Passalis
Vishal Patel
Viorica Patraucean
Badri Narayana Patro
Danda Pani Paudel
Sujoy Paul
Georgios Pavlakos
Ioannis Pavlidis
Vladimir Pavlovic
Nick Pears
Kim Steenstrup Pedersen
Selen Pehlivan
Shmuel Peleg
Chao Peng
Houwen Peng
Wen-Hsiao Peng
Xi Peng
Xiaojiang Peng
Xingchao Peng
Yuxin Peng
Federico Perazzi
Juan Camilo Perez
Vishwanath Peri
Federico Pernici
Luca Del Pero
Florent Perronnin
Stavros Petridis
Henning Petzka
Patrick Peursum
Michael Pfeiffer
Hanspeter Pfister
Roman Pflugfelder
Minh Tri Pham
Yongri Piao
David Picard
Tomasz Pieciak
A. J. Piergiovanni
Andrea Pilzer
Pedro O. Pinheiro
Silvia Laura Pintea
Lerrel Pinto
Axel Pinz
Robinson Piramuthu
Fiora Pirri
Leonid Pishchulin
Francesco Pittaluga

Daniel Pizarro
Tobias Plötz
Mirco Planamente
Matteo Poggi
Moacir A. Ponti
Parita Pooj
Fatih Porikli
Horst Possegger
Omid Poursaeed
Ameya Prabhu
Viraj Uday Prabhu
Dilip Prasad
Brian L. Price
True Price
Maria Priisalu
Veronique Prinet
Victor Adrian Prisacariu
Jan Prokaj
Sergey Prokudin
Nicolas Pugeault
Xavier Puig
Albert Pumarola
Pulak Purkait
Senthil Purushwalkam
Charles R. Qi
Hang Qi
Haozhi Qi
Lu Qi
Mengshi Qi
Siyuan Qi
Xiaojuan Qi
Yuankai Qi
Shengju Qian
Xuelin Qian
Siyuan Qiao
Yu Qiao
Jie Qin
Qiang Qiu
Weichao Qiu
Zhaofan Qiu
Kha Gia Quach
Yuhui Quan
Yvain Queau
Julian Quiroga
Faisal Qureshi
Mahdi Rad

Filip Radenovic
Petia Radeva
Venkatesh
  B. Radhakrishnan
Ilija Radosavovic
Noha Radwan
Rahul Raguram
Tanzila Rahman
Amit Raj
Ajit Rajwade
Kandan Ramakrishnan
Santhosh
  K. Ramakrishnan
Srikumar Ramalingam
Ravi Ramamoorthi
Vasili Ramanishka
Ramprasaath R. Selvaraju
Francois Rameau
Visvanathan Ramesh
Santu Rana
Rene Ranftl
Anand Rangarajan
Anurag Ranjan
Viresh Ranjan
Yongming Rao
Carolina Raposo
Vivek Rathod
Sathya N. Ravi
Avinash Ravichandran
Tammy Riklin Raviv
Daniel Rebain
Sylvestre-Alvise Rebuffi
N. Dinesh Reddy
Timo Rehfeld
Paolo Remagnino
Konstantinos Rematas
Edoardo Remelli
Dongwei Ren
Haibing Ren
Jian Ren
Jimmy Ren
Mengye Ren
Weihong Ren
Wenqi Ren
Zhile Ren
Zhongzheng Ren

Zhou Ren
Vijay Rengarajan
Md A. Reza
Farzaneh Rezaeianaran
Hamed R. Tavakoli
Nicholas Rhinehart
Helge Rhodin
Elisa Ricci
Alexander Richard
Eitan Richardson
Elad Richardson
Christian Richardt
Stephan Richter
Gernot Riegler
Daniel Ritchie
Tobias Ritschel
Samuel Rivera
Yong Man Ro
Richard Roberts
Joseph Robinson
Ignacio Rocco
Mrigank Rochan
Emanuele Rodolà
Mikel D. Rodriguez
Giorgio Roffo
Grégory Rogez
Gemma Roig
Javier Romero
Xuejian Rong
Yu Rong
Amir Rosenfeld
Bodo Rosenhahn
Guy Rosman
Arun Ross
Paolo Rota
Peter M. Roth
Anastasios Roussos
Anirban Roy
Sebastien Roy
Aruni RoyChowdhury
Artem Rozantsev
Ognjen Rudovic
Daniel Rueckert
Adria Ruiz
Javier Ruiz-del-solar
Christian Rupprecht

Chris Russell
Dan Ruta
Jongbin Ryu
Ömer Sümer
Alexandre Sablayrolles
Faraz Saeedan
Ryusuke Sagawa
Christos Sagonas
Tonmoy Saikia
Hideo Saito
Kuniaki Saito
Shunsuke Saito
Shunta Saito
Ken Sakurada
Joaquin Salas
Fatemeh Sadat Saleh
Mahdi Saleh
Pouya Samangouei
Leo Sampaio
  Ferraz Ribeiro
Artsiom Olegovich
  Sanakoyeu
Enrique Sanchez
Patsorn Sangkloy
Anush Sankaran
Aswin Sankaranarayanan
Swami Sankaranarayanan
Rodrigo Santa Cruz
Amartya Sanyal
Archana Sapkota
Nikolaos Sarafianos
Jun Sato
Shin'ichi Satoh
Hosnieh Sattar
Arman Savran
Manolis Savva
Alexander Sax
Hanno Scharr
Simone Schaub-Meyer
Konrad Schindler
Dmitrij Schlesinger
Uwe Schmidt
Dirk Schnieders
Björn Schuller
Samuel Schulter
Idan Schwartz

William Robson Schwartz
Alex Schwing
Sinisa Segvic
Lorenzo Seidenari
Pradeep Sen
Ozan Sener
Soumyadip Sengupta
Arda Senocak
Mojtaba Seyedhosseini
Shishir Shah
Shital Shah
Sohil Atul Shah
Tamar Rott Shaham
Huasong Shan
Qi Shan
Shiguang Shan
Jing Shao
Roman Shapovalov
Gaurav Sharma
Vivek Sharma
Viktoriia Sharmanska
Dongyu She
Sumit Shekhar
Evan Shelhamer
Chengyao Shen
Chunhua Shen
Falong Shen
Jie Shen
Li Shen
Liyue Shen
Shuhan Shen
Tianwei Shen
Wei Shen
William B. Shen
Yantao Shen
Ying Shen
Yiru Shen
Yujun Shen
Yuming Shen
Zhiqiang Shen
Ziyi Shen
Lu Sheng
Yu Sheng
Rakshith Shetty
Baoguang Shi
Guangming Shi

Hailin Shi
Miaojing Shi
Yemin Shi
Zhenmei Shi
Zhiyuan Shi
Kevin Jonathan Shih
Shiliang Shiliang
Hyunjung Shim
Atsushi Shimada
Nobutaka Shimada
Daeyun Shin
Young Min Shin
Koichi Shinoda
Konstantin Shmelkov
Michael Zheng Shou
Abhinav Shrivastava
Tianmin Shu
Zhixin Shu
Hong-Han Shuai
Pushkar Shukla
Christian Siagian
Mennatullah M. Siam
Kaleem Siddiqi
Karan Sikka
Jae-Young Sim
Christian Simon
Martin Simonovsky
Dheeraj Singaraju
Bharat Singh
Gurkirt Singh
Krishna Kumar Singh
Maneesh Kumar Singh
Richa Singh
Saurabh Singh
Suriya Singh
Vikas Singh
Sudipta N. Sinha
Vincent Sitzmann
Josef Sivic
Gregory Slabaugh
Miroslava Slavcheva
Ron Slossberg
Brandon Smith
Kevin Smith
Vladimir Smutny
Noah Snavely

Roger
    D. Soberanis-Mukul
Kihyuk Sohn
Francesco Solera
Eric Sommerlade
Sanghyun Son
Byung Cheol Song
Chunfeng Song
Dongjin Song
Jiaming Song
Jie Song
Jifei Song
Jingkuan Song
Mingli Song
Shiyu Song
Shuran Song
Xiao Song
Yafei Song
Yale Song
Yang Song
Yi-Zhe Song
Yibing Song
Humberto Sossa
Cesar de Souza
Adrian Spurr
Srinath Sridhar
Suraj Srinivas
Pratul P. Srinivasan
Anuj Srivastava
Tania Stathaki
Christopher Stauffer
Simon Stent
Rainer Stiefelhagen
Pierre Stock
Julian Straub
Jonathan C. Stroud
Joerg Stueckler
Jan Stuehmer
David Stutz
Chi Su
Hang Su
Jong-Chyi Su
Shuochen Su
Yu-Chuan Su
Ramanathan Subramanian
Yusuke Sugano

Masanori Suganuma	Xiaoyang Tan	Andrea Torsello
Yumin Suh	Kenichiro Tanaka	Fabio Tosi
Mohammed Suhail	Masayuki Tanaka	Du Tran
Yao Sui	Chang Tang	Luan Tran
Heung-Il Suk	Chengzhou Tang	Ngoc-Trung Tran
Josephine Sullivan	Danhang Tang	Quan Hung Tran
Baochen Sun	Ming Tang	Truyen Tran
Chen Sun	Peng Tang	Rudolph Triebel
Chong Sun	Qingming Tang	Martin Trimmel
Deqing Sun	Wei Tang	Shashank Tripathi
Jin Sun	Xu Tang	Subarna Tripathi
Liang Sun	Yansong Tang	Leonardo Trujillo
Lin Sun	Youbao Tang	Eduard Trulls
Qianru Sun	Yuxing Tang	Tomasz Trzcinski
Shao-Hua Sun	Zhiqiang Tang	Sam Tsai
Shuyang Sun	Tatsunori Taniai	Yi-Hsuan Tsai
Weiwei Sun	Junli Tao	Hung-Yu Tseng
Wenxiu Sun	Xin Tao	Stavros Tsogkas
Xiaoshuai Sun	Makarand Tapaswi	Aggeliki Tsoli
Xiaoxiao Sun	Jean-Philippe Tarel	Devis Tuia
Xingyuan Sun	Lyne Tchapmi	Shubham Tulsiani
Yifan Sun	Zachary Teed	Sergey Tulyakov
Zhun Sun	Bugra Tekin	Frederick Tung
Sabine Susstrunk	Damien Teney	Tony Tung
David Suter	Ayush Tewari	Daniyar Turmukhambetov
Supasorn Suwajanakorn	Christian Theobalt	Ambrish Tyagi
Tomas Svoboda	Christopher Thomas	Radim Tylecek
Eran Swears	Diego Thomas	Christos Tzelepis
Paul Swoboda	Jim Thomas	Georgios Tzimiropoulos
Attila Szabo	Rajat Mani Thomas	Dimitrios Tzionas
Richard Szeliski	Xinmei Tian	Seiichi Uchida
Duy-Nguyen Ta	Yapeng Tian	Norimichi Ukita
Andrea Tagliasacchi	Yingli Tian	Dmitry Ulyanov
Yuichi Taguchi	Yonglong Tian	Martin Urschler
Ying Tai	Zhi Tian	Yoshitaka Ushiku
Keita Takahashi	Zhuotao Tian	Ben Usman
Kouske Takahashi	Kinh Tieu	Alexander Vakhitov
Jun Takamatsu	Joseph Tighe	Julien P. C. Valentin
Hugues Talbot	Massimo Tistarelli	Jack Valmadre
Toru Tamaki	Matthew Toews	Ernest Valveny
Chaowei Tan	Carl Toft	Joost van de Weijer
Fuwen Tan	Pavel Tokmakov	Jan van Gemert
Mingkui Tan	Federico Tombari	Koen Van Leemput
Mingxing Tan	Chetan Tonde	Gul Varol
Qingyang Tan	Yan Tong	Sebastiano Vascon
Robby T. Tan	Alessio Tonioni	M. Alex O. Vasilescu

Subeesh Vasu
Mayank Vatsa
David Vazquez
Javier Vazquez-Corral
Ashok Veeraraghavan
Erik Velasco-Salido
Raviteja Vemulapalli
Jonathan Ventura
Manisha Verma
Roberto Vezzani
Ruben Villegas
Minh Vo
MinhDuc Vo
Nam Vo
Michele Volpi
Riccardo Volpi
Carl Vondrick
Konstantinos Vougioukas
Tuan-Hung Vu
Sven Wachsmuth
Neal Wadhwa
Catherine Wah
Jacob C. Walker
Thomas S. A. Wallis
Chengde Wan
Jun Wan
Liang Wan
Renjie Wan
Baoyuan Wang
Boyu Wang
Cheng Wang
Chu Wang
Chuan Wang
Chunyu Wang
Dequan Wang
Di Wang
Dilin Wang
Dong Wang
Fang Wang
Guanzhi Wang
Guoyin Wang
Hanzi Wang
Hao Wang
He Wang
Heng Wang
Hongcheng Wang

Hongxing Wang
Hua Wang
Jian Wang
Jingbo Wang
Jinglu Wang
Jingya Wang
Jinjun Wang
Jinqiao Wang
Jue Wang
Ke Wang
Keze Wang
Le Wang
Lei Wang
Lezi Wang
Li Wang
Liang Wang
Lijun Wang
Limin Wang
Linwei Wang
Lizhi Wang
Mengjiao Wang
Mingzhe Wang
Minsi Wang
Naiyan Wang
Nannan Wang
Ning Wang
Oliver Wang
Pei Wang
Peng Wang
Pichao Wang
Qi Wang
Qian Wang
Qiaosong Wang
Qifei Wang
Qilong Wang
Qing Wang
Qingzhong Wang
Quan Wang
Rui Wang
Ruiping Wang
Ruixing Wang
Shangfei Wang
Shenlong Wang
Shiyao Wang
Shuhui Wang
Song Wang

Tao Wang
Tianlu Wang
Tiantian Wang
Ting-chun Wang
Tingwu Wang
Wei Wang
Weiyue Wang
Wenguan Wang
Wenlin Wang
Wenqi Wang
Xiang Wang
Xiaobo Wang
Xiaofang Wang
Xiaoling Wang
Xiaolong Wang
Xiaosong Wang
Xiaoyu Wang
Xin Eric Wang
Xinchao Wang
Xinggang Wang
Xintao Wang
Yali Wang
Yan Wang
Yang Wang
Yangang Wang
Yaxing Wang
Yi Wang
Yida Wang
Yilin Wang
Yiming Wang
Yisen Wang
Yongtao Wang
Yu-Xiong Wang
Yue Wang
Yujiang Wang
Yunbo Wang
Yunhe Wang
Zengmao Wang
Zhangyang Wang
Zhaowen Wang
Zhe Wang
Zhecan Wang
Zheng Wang
Zhixiang Wang
Zilei Wang
Jianqiao Wangni

Anne S. Wannenwetsch
Jan Dirk Wegner
Scott Wehrwein
Donglai Wei
Kaixuan Wei
Longhui Wei
Pengxu Wei
Ping Wei
Qi Wei
Shih-En Wei
Xing Wei
Yunchao Wei
Zijun Wei
Jerod Weinman
Michael Weinmann
Philippe Weinzaepfel
Yair Weiss
Bihan Wen
Longyin Wen
Wei Wen
Junwu Weng
Tsui-Wei Weng
Xinshuo Weng
Eric Wengrowski
Tomas Werner
Gordon Wetzstein
Tobias Weyand
Patrick Wieschollek
Maggie Wigness
Erik Wijmans
Richard Wildes
Olivia Wiles
Chris Williams
Williem Williem
Kyle Wilson
Calden Wloka
Nicolai Wojke
Christian Wolf
Yongkang Wong
Sanghyun Woo
Scott Workman
Baoyuan Wu
Bichen Wu
Chao-Yuan Wu
Huikai Wu
Jiajun Wu

Jialin Wu
Jiaxiang Wu
Jiqing Wu
Jonathan Wu
Lifang Wu
Qi Wu
Qiang Wu
Ruizheng Wu
Shangzhe Wu
Shun-Cheng Wu
Tianfu Wu
Wayne Wu
Wenxuan Wu
Xiao Wu
Xiaohe Wu
Xinxiao Wu
Yang Wu
Yi Wu
Yiming Wu
Ying Nian Wu
Yue Wu
Zheng Wu
Zhenyu Wu
Zhirong Wu
Zuxuan Wu
Stefanie Wuhrer
Jonas Wulff
Changqun Xia
Fangting Xia
Fei Xia
Gui-Song Xia
Lu Xia
Xide Xia
Yin Xia
Yingce Xia
Yongqin Xian
Lei Xiang
Shiming Xiang
Bin Xiao
Fanyi Xiao
Guobao Xiao
Huaxin Xiao
Taihong Xiao
Tete Xiao
Tong Xiao
Wang Xiao

Yang Xiao
Cihang Xie
Guosen Xie
Jianwen Xie
Lingxi Xie
Sirui Xie
Weidi Xie
Wenxuan Xie
Xiaohua Xie
Fuyong Xing
Jun Xing
Junliang Xing
Bo Xiong
Peixi Xiong
Yu Xiong
Yuanjun Xiong
Zhiwei Xiong
Chang Xu
Chenliang Xu
Dan Xu
Danfei Xu
Hang Xu
Hongteng Xu
Huijuan Xu
Jingwei Xu
Jun Xu
Kai Xu
Mengmeng Xu
Mingze Xu
Qianqian Xu
Ran Xu
Weijian Xu
Xiangyu Xu
Xiaogang Xu
Xing Xu
Xun Xu
Yanyu Xu
Yichao Xu
Yong Xu
Yongchao Xu
Yuanlu Xu
Zenglin Xu
Zheng Xu
Chuhui Xue
Jia Xue
Nan Xue

Tianfan Xue
Xiangyang Xue
Abhay Yadav
Yasushi Yagi
I. Zeki Yalniz
Kota Yamaguchi
Toshihiko Yamasaki
Takayoshi Yamashita
Junchi Yan
Ke Yan
Qingan Yan
Sijie Yan
Xinchen Yan
Yan Yan
Yichao Yan
Zhicheng Yan
Keiji Yanai
Bin Yang
Ceyuan Yang
Dawei Yang
Dong Yang
Fan Yang
Guandao Yang
Guorun Yang
Haichuan Yang
Hao Yang
Jianwei Yang
Jiaolong Yang
Jie Yang
Jing Yang
Kaiyu Yang
Linjie Yang
Meng Yang
Michael Ying Yang
Nan Yang
Shuai Yang
Shuo Yang
Tianyu Yang
Tien-Ju Yang
Tsun-Yi Yang
Wei Yang
Wenhan Yang
Xiao Yang
Xiaodong Yang
Xin Yang
Yan Yang

Yanchao Yang
Yee Hong Yang
Yezhou Yang
Zhenheng Yang
Anbang Yao
Angela Yao
Cong Yao
Jian Yao
Li Yao
Ting Yao
Yao Yao
Zhewei Yao
Chengxi Ye
Jianbo Ye
Keren Ye
Linwei Ye
Mang Ye
Mao Ye
Qi Ye
Qixiang Ye
Mei-Chen Yeh
Raymond Yeh
Yu-Ying Yeh
Sai-Kit Yeung
Serena Yeung
Kwang Moo Yi
Li Yi
Renjiao Yi
Alper Yilmaz
Junho Yim
Lijun Yin
Weidong Yin
Xi Yin
Zhichao Yin
Tatsuya Yokota
Ryo Yonetani
Donggeun Yoo
Jae Shin Yoon
Ju Hong Yoon
Sung-eui Yoon
Laurent Younes
Changqian Yu
Fisher Yu
Gang Yu
Jiahui Yu
Kaicheng Yu

Ke Yu
Lequan Yu
Ning Yu
Qian Yu
Ronald Yu
Ruichi Yu
Shoou-I Yu
Tao Yu
Tianshu Yu
Xiang Yu
Xin Yu
Xiyu Yu
Youngjae Yu
Yu Yu
Zhiding Yu
Chunfeng Yuan
Ganzhao Yuan
Jinwei Yuan
Lu Yuan
Quan Yuan
Shanxin Yuan
Tongtong Yuan
Wenjia Yuan
Ye Yuan
Yuan Yuan
Yuhui Yuan
Huanjing Yue
Xiangyu Yue
Ersin Yumer
Sergey Zagoruyko
Egor Zakharov
Amir Zamir
Andrei Zanfir
Mihai Zanfir
Pablo Zegers
Bernhard Zeisl
John S. Zelek
Niclas Zeller
Huayi Zeng
Jiabei Zeng
Wenjun Zeng
Yu Zeng
Xiaohua Zhai
Fangneng Zhan
Huangying Zhan
Kun Zhan

Xiaohang Zhan
Baochang Zhang
Bowen Zhang
Cecilia Zhang
Changqing Zhang
Chao Zhang
Chengquan Zhang
Chi Zhang
Chongyang Zhang
Dingwen Zhang
Dong Zhang
Feihu Zhang
Hang Zhang
Hanwang Zhang
Hao Zhang
He Zhang
Hongguang Zhang
Hua Zhang
Ji Zhang
Jianguo Zhang
Jianming Zhang
Jiawei Zhang
Jie Zhang
Jing Zhang
Juyong Zhang
Kai Zhang
Kaipeng Zhang
Ke Zhang
Le Zhang
Lei Zhang
Li Zhang
Lihe Zhang
Linguang Zhang
Lu Zhang
Mi Zhang
Mingda Zhang
Peng Zhang
Pingping Zhang
Qian Zhang
Qilin Zhang
Quanshi Zhang
Richard Zhang
Rui Zhang
Runze Zhang
Shengping Zhang
Shifeng Zhang

Shuai Zhang
Songyang Zhang
Tao Zhang
Ting Zhang
Tong Zhang
Wayne Zhang
Wei Zhang
Weizhong Zhang
Wenwei Zhang
Xiangyu Zhang
Xiaolin Zhang
Xiaopeng Zhang
Xiaoqin Zhang
Xiuming Zhang
Ya Zhang
Yang Zhang
Yimin Zhang
Yinda Zhang
Ying Zhang
Yongfei Zhang
Yu Zhang
Yulun Zhang
Yunhua Zhang
Yuting Zhang
Zhanpeng Zhang
Zhao Zhang
Zhaoxiang Zhang
Zhen Zhang
Zheng Zhang
Zhifei Zhang
Zhijin Zhang
Zhishuai Zhang
Ziming Zhang
Bo Zhao
Chen Zhao
Fang Zhao
Haiyu Zhao
Han Zhao
Hang Zhao
Hengshuang Zhao
Jian Zhao
Kai Zhao
Liang Zhao
Long Zhao
Qian Zhao
Qibin Zhao

Qijun Zhao
Rui Zhao
Shenglin Zhao
Sicheng Zhao
Tianyi Zhao
Wenda Zhao
Xiangyun Zhao
Xin Zhao
Yang Zhao
Yue Zhao
Zhichen Zhao
Zijing Zhao
Xiantong Zhen
Chuanxia Zheng
Feng Zheng
Haiyong Zheng
Jia Zheng
Kang Zheng
Shuai Kyle Zheng
Wei-Shi Zheng
Yinqiang Zheng
Zerong Zheng
Zhedong Zheng
Zilong Zheng
Bineng Zhong
Fangwei Zhong
Guangyu Zhong
Yiran Zhong
Yujie Zhong
Zhun Zhong
Chunluan Zhou
Huiyu Zhou
Jiahuan Zhou
Jun Zhou
Lei Zhou
Luowei Zhou
Luping Zhou
Mo Zhou
Ning Zhou
Pan Zhou
Peng Zhou
Qianyi Zhou
S. Kevin Zhou
Sanping Zhou
Wengang Zhou
Xingyi Zhou

Yanzhao Zhou	Wei Zhu	Christian Zimmermann
Yi Zhou	Xiangyu Zhu	Karel Zimmermann
Yin Zhou	Xinge Zhu	Larry Zitnick
Yipin Zhou	Xizhou Zhu	Mohammadreza
Yuyin Zhou	Yanjun Zhu	Zolfaghari
Zihan Zhou	Yi Zhu	Maria Zontak
Alex Zihao Zhu	Yixin Zhu	Daniel Zoran
Chenchen Zhu	Yizhe Zhu	Changqing Zou
Feng Zhu	Yousong Zhu	Chuhang Zou
Guangming Zhu	Zhe Zhu	Danping Zou
Ji Zhu	Zhen Zhu	Qi Zou
Jun-Yan Zhu	Zheng Zhu	Yang Zou
Lei Zhu	Zhenyao Zhu	Yuliang Zou
Linchao Zhu	Zhihui Zhu	Georgios Zoumpourlis
Rui Zhu	Zhuotun Zhu	Wangmeng Zuo
Shizhan Zhu	Bingbing Zhuang	Xinxin Zuo
Tyler Lixuan Zhu	Wei Zhuo	

Additional Reviewers

Victoria Fernandez Abrevaya	Jonathan P. Crall	Jaedong Hwang
Maya Aghaei	Kenan Dai	Andrey Ignatov
Allam Allam	Lucas Deecke	Muhammad
Christine Allen-Blanchette	Karan Desai	Abdullah Jamal
Nicolas Aziere	Prithviraj Dhar	Saumya Jetley
Assia Benbihi	Jing Dong	Meiguang Jin
Neha Bhargava	Wei Dong	Jeff Johnson
Bharat Lal Bhatnagar	Turan Kaan Elgin	Minsoo Kang
Joanna Bitton	Francis Engelmann	Saeed Khorram
Judy Borowski	Erik Englesson	Mohammad Rami Koujan
Amine Bourki	Fartash Faghri	Nilesh Kulkarni
Romain Brégier	Zicong Fan	Sudhakar Kumawat
Tali Brayer	Yang Fu	Abdelhak Lemkhenter
Sebastian Bujwid	Risheek Garrepalli	Alexander Levine
Andrea Burns	Yifan Ge	Jiachen Li
Yun-Hao Cao	Marco Godi	Jing Li
Yuning Chai	Helmut Grabner	Jun Li
Xiaojun Chang	Shuxuan Guo	Yi Li
Bo Chen	Jianfeng He	Liang Liao
Shuo Chen	Zhezhi He	Ruochen Liao
Zhixiang Chen	Samitha Herath	Tzu-Heng Lin
Junsuk Choe	Chih-Hui Ho	Phillip Lippe
Hung-Kuo Chu	Yicong Hong	Bao-di Liu
	Vincent Tao Hu	Bo Liu
	Julio Hurtado	Fangchen Liu

Hanxiao Liu	Ketul Shah	Yunyang Xiong
Hongyu Liu	Rajvi Shah	An Xu
Huidong Liu	Hengcan Shi	Chi Xu
Miao Liu	Xiangxi Shi	Yinghao Xu
Xinxin Liu	Yujiao Shi	Fei Xue
Yongfei Liu	William A. P. Smith	Tingyun Yan
Yu-Lun Liu	Guoxian Song	Zike Yan
Amir Livne	Robin Strudel	Chao Yang
Tiange Luo	Abby Stylianou	Heran Yang
Wei Ma	Xinwei Sun	Ren Yang
Xiaoxuan Ma	Reuben Tan	Wenfei Yang
Ioannis Marras	Qingyi Tao	Xu Yang
Georg Martius	Kedar S. Tatwawadi	Rajeev Yasarla
Effrosyni Mavroudi	Anh Tuan Tran	Shaokai Ye
Tim Meinhardt	Son Dinh Tran	Yufei Ye
Givi Meishvili	Eleni Triantafillou	Kun Yi
Meng Meng	Aristeidis Tsitiridis	Haichao Yu
Zihang Meng	Md Zasim Uddin	Hanchao Yu
Zhongqi Miao	Andrea Vedaldi	Ruixuan Yu
Gyeongsik Moon	Evangelos Ververas	Liangzhe Yuan
Khoi Nguyen	Vidit Vidit	Chen-Lin Zhang
Yung-Kyun Noh	Paul Voigtlaender	Fandong Zhang
Antonio Norelli	Bo Wan	Tianyi Zhang
Jaeyoo Park	Huanyu Wang	Yang Zhang
Alexander Pashevich	Huiyu Wang	Yiyi Zhang
Mandela Patrick	Junqiu Wang	Yongshun Zhang
Mary Phuong	Pengxiao Wang	Yu Zhang
Bingqiao Qian	Tai Wang	Zhiwei Zhang
Yu Qiao	Xinyao Wang	Jiaojiao Zhao
Zhen Qiao	Tomoki Watanabe	Yipu Zhao
Sai Saketh Rambhatla	Mark Weber	Xingjian Zhen
Aniket Roy	Xi Wei	Haizhong Zheng
Amelie Royer	Botong Wu	Tiancheng Zhi
Parikshit Vishwas	James Wu	Chengju Zhou
Sakurikar	Jiamin Wu	Hao Zhou
Mark Sandler	Rujie Wu	Hao Zhu
Mert Bülent Sarıyıldız	Yu Wu	Alexander Zimin
Tanner Schmidt	Rongchang Xie	
Anshul B. Shah	Wei Xiong	

Contents – Part XXV

Faster AutoAugment: Learning Augmentation Strategies Using Backpropagation

Ryuichiro Hataya[1,2]([✉]), Jan Zdenek[1], Kazuki Yoshizoe[2],
and Hideki Nakayama[1]

[1] Graduate School of Information Science and Technology,
The University of Tokyo, Tokyo, Japan
{hataya,jan,nakayama}@nlab.ci.i.u-tokyo.ac.jp
[2] RIKEN Center for Advanced Intelligence Project, Tokyo, Japan
kazuki.yoshizoe@riken.jp

Abstract. Data augmentation methods are indispensable heuristics to boost the performance of deep neural networks, especially in image recognition tasks. Recently, several studies have shown that augmentation strategies found by search algorithms outperform hand-made strategies. Such methods employ black-box search algorithms over image transformations with continuous or discrete parameters and require a long time to obtain better strategies. In this paper, we propose a differentiable policy search pipeline for data augmentation, which is much faster than previous methods. We introduce approximate gradients for several transformation operations with discrete parameters as well as a differentiable mechanism for selecting operations. As the objective of training, we minimize the distance between the distributions of augmented and original data, which can be differentiated. We show that our method, Faster AutoAugment, achieves significantly faster searching than prior methods without a performance drop.

1 Introduction

Data augmentation is a powerful technique for machine learning to virtually increase the amount and diversity of data, which improves performance especially in image recognition tasks. Conventional data augmentation methods include geometric transformations such as rotation and color enhancement such as autocontrast. Similarly to selecting other hyperparameters, the designers of data augmentation strategies usually select transformation operations based on their prior knowledge (e.g., required invariance). For example, horizontal flipping is expected to be effective for general object recognition but probably not for digit recognition. In addition to the selection, the designers need to combine several operations and set their magnitudes (e.g., degree of rotation). Therefore, designing of data augmentation strategies is a complex combinatorial problem.

When designing data augmentation strategies in a data-driven manner, one can regard the problem as searching for optimal hyperparameters in a

© Springer Nature Switzerland AG 2020
A. Vedaldi et al. (Eds.): ECCV 2020, LNCS 12370, pp. 1–16, 2020.
https://doi.org/10.1007/978-3-030-58595-2_1

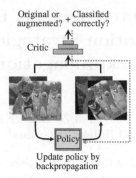

Fig. 1. Overview of our proposed model. We propose to use a **differentiable data augmentation pipeline** to achieve a faster policy search by using adversarial learning.

Table 1. Faster AutoAugment (Faster AA) is much faster than the other methods without a significant performance drop (see Sect. 5). GPU hours comparison of Faster AA, AutoAugment (AA) [5], PBA [12] and Fast AutoAugment (Fast AA) [18].

Dataset	AA	PBA	Fast AA	Faster AA (ours)
CIFAR-10	5,000	5.0	3.5	**0.23**
SVHN	1,000	1.0	1.5	**0.061**
ImageNet	15,000	–	450	**2.3**

search space, which becomes prohibitively large as the number of combinations increases. Therefore, efficient methods are required to find optimal strategies. If gradient information of these hyperparameters is available, they can be efficiently optimized by gradient descent [20]. However, the gradient information is usually difficult to obtain because some magnitude parameters are discrete and the selection of operations is non-differentiable. Therefore, previous research on automatically designing data augmentation policies has used black-box optimization methods that require no gradient information. For example, AutoAugment [5] used reinforcement learning.

In this paper, we propose to solve the problem by approximating gradient information and thus enabling gradient-based optimization for data augmentation policies. To this end, we approximate the gradients of discrete image operations using a straight-through estimator [3] and make the selection of operations differentiable by incorporating a recent differentiable neural architecture search method [19]. As the objective, we minimize the distance between the distributions of the original and augmented images, because we want the data augmentation pipeline to transform images so that it fills sparsely populated data points in the training data [18] (see Fig. 2). To make the transformed images match the distribution of original images, we use adversarial learning (see Fig. 1). As a result, the search process becomes end-to-end differentiable and significantly

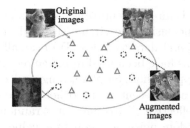

Fig. 2. We regard data augmentation as a process that **fills missing data points of the original training data**; therefore, our objective is to minimize the distance between the distributions of augmented and original data using adversarial learning.

faster than prior methods such as AutoAugment, PBA and Fast AutoAugment (see Table 1[1]).

We empirically show that our method, which we call Faster AutoAugment, enables a much faster policy search while achieving performance comparable to that of prior methods on the standard benchmarks of CIFAR-10, CIFAR-100 [16], SVHN [21] and ImageNet [27].

In summary, our contributions are threefold:

1. We introduce gradient approximations for several non-differentiable data augmentation operations.
2. We make the searching of data augmentation policies end-to-end differentiable by gradient approximations, a differentiable selection of operations and a differentiable objective that measures the distance between the original and augmented image distributions.
3. We show that our proposed method, Faster AutoAugment, significantly reduces the search time compared with prior methods without a crucial performance drop.

2 Related Work

Neural Architecture Search (NAS). NAS aims to automatically design architectures of neural networks to achieve a higher performance than manually designed ones. To this end, NAS algorithms are required to select better combinations of components (e.g., convolution with a 3×3 kernel) from discrete search spaces using search algorithms such as reinforcement learning [38] and evolution strategy [25]. Recently, DARTS [19] achieved a faster search by relaxing the discrete search space to a continuous one which allowed the use of gradient-based optimization. While AutoAugment [5] was inspired by [38], our method is influenced by DARTS [19].

---

[1] Note that [18] and our study estimated the GPU hours with an NVIDIA V100 GPU while [5] did with an NVIDIA P100 GPU.

Data Augmentation. Data augmentation methods improve the performance of learnable models by increasing the virtual size and diversity of training data without collecting additional data samples. Traditionally, geometric and color-enhancing transformations have been used in image recognition tasks. For example, [11,17] randomly applied horizontal flipping and cropping as well as the alternation of image hues. In recent years, other image manipulation methods have been shown to be effective. [6,37] cut out a random patch from an image and replaced it with random noise or a constant value. Another strategy is to mix multiple images of different classes either by convex combinations [30,36] or by creating a patchwork from them [34]. In these studies, the selection of operations, their magnitudes and the probabilities to be applied were carefully manually designed.

Automating Data Augmentation. Similar to NAS, it is a natural direction to aim to automate data augmentation. One direction is to search for better combinations of symbolic operations using black-box optimization techniques such as reinforcement learning [5,24], evolution strategy [32], Bayesian optimization [18] and population-based training [12]. As the objective, [5,12,32] directly aimed to minimize the error rate, or equivalently to maximize accuracy, while [18,24] attempted to match the densities of augmented and original images. Another direction is to use generative adversarial networks (GANs) [9]. [1,31] used conditional GANs to generate images that promote the performance of image classifiers. [28,29] used GANs to modify the outputs of simulators to look like real objects. Automating data augmentation can also be applied to representation learning such as semi-supervised learning [4,33] and domain generalization [32].

3 Preliminaries

In this section, we describe the common basis of AutoAugment [5], PBA [12] and Fast AutoAugment [18] (see also Fig. 3). Faster AutoAugment also follows this problem setting.

In these methods, input images are augmented by a policy that consists of L different subpolicies $S^{(l)}$ ($l = 1, 2, \ldots, L$). A randomly selected subpolicy transforms each image X. A single subpolicy consists of K consecutive image processing operations $O_1^{(l)}, \ldots, O_K^{(l)}$, which are applied to the image one by one. We refer to the number of consecutive operations K as the operation count. In the rest of this paper, we focus on subpolicies; therefore, we omit the superscript l. Each method first searches for better policies. After the search phase, the obtained policy is used as a data augmentation pipeline to train neural networks.

3.1 Operations

Operations used in each subpolicy include affine transformations such as `shear_x` and color-enhancing operations such as `solarize`. Additionaly, we

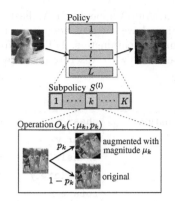

Fig. 3. Schematic view of the problem setting. Each image is augmented by a **subpolicy** randomly selected from the **policy**. A single subpolicy is composed of K consecutive **operations** $(O_1, \ldots, O_K)$, such as `shear_x` and `solarize`. An operation O_k operates a given image with the probability p_k and magnitude μ_k.

use `cutout` [6] and `sample_pairing` [13] following [5,12,18]. We show all 16 operations used in these methods in Table 2. Let the set of operations be $\mathcal{O} = \{\text{shear\_x}, \text{solarize}, \ldots\}$.

Some operations have magnitude parameters that are free variables, e.g., the angle in `rotate`. On the other hand, some operations, such as `invert`, have no magnitude parameters. For simplicity, we use the following expressions as if every operation has a magnitude parameter $\mu_O (\in [0, 1])$. Each operation is applied with the probability $p_O (\in [0, 1])$. Therefore, each image $\boldsymbol{X}$ is augmented as

$$\boldsymbol{X} \rightarrow \begin{cases} O(\boldsymbol{X}; \mu_O) & \text{(with probability } p_O) \\ \boldsymbol{X} & \text{(with probability } 1 - p_O). \end{cases} \tag{1}$$

Rewriting this mapping as $O(\cdot; \mu_O, p_O)$, each subpolicy S consisting of operations $O_1, O_2, \ldots, O_K$ can be written as

$$S(\boldsymbol{X}; \boldsymbol{\mu}_S, \boldsymbol{p}_S) = (O_K \circ \cdots \circ O_1)(\boldsymbol{X}; \boldsymbol{\mu}_S, \boldsymbol{p}_S), \tag{2}$$

where $\boldsymbol{\mu}_S = (\mu_{O_1}, \ldots, \mu_{O_K})$ and $\boldsymbol{p}_S = (p_{O_1}, \ldots, p_{O_K})$. In the rest of this paper, we represent an image operation as O, $O(\cdot; \mu)$ and $O(\cdot; \mu, p)$ interchangeably according to the context.

3.2 Search Space

The goal of searching is to find the best operation combination $O_1, \ldots, O_K$ and parameter sets $(\boldsymbol{\mu}_S, \boldsymbol{p}_S)$ for L subpolicies. Therefore, the size of the total search space is roughly $(\#\mathcal{O} \times [0, 1] \times [0, 1])^{KL}$. Using multiple subpolicies results in a prohibitively large search space for brute-force searching. [18] used Bayesian optimization in this search space. [5,12] discretized the continuous part $[0, 1]$ into 10 or 11 values and searched the space using reinforcement learning and

Table 2. Operations used in AutoAugment, PBA, Fast AutoAugment and Faster AutoAugment. Some operations have discrete magnitude parameters μ, while others have no or continuous magnitude parameters. Different from previous methods, we approximate gradients of operations w.r.t. discrete magnitude μ, which we describe in Sect. 4.1.

	Operation	Magnitude μ
Affine transformation	shear_x	continuous
	shear_y	continuous
	translate_x	continuous
	translate_y	continuous
	rotate	continuous
	flip	none
Color enhancing operations	solarize	discrete
	posterize	discrete
	invert	none
	contrast	continuous
	color	continuous
	brightness	continuous
	sharpness	none
	auto_contrast	none
	equalize	none
Other operations	cutout	discrete
	sample_pairing	continuous

population-based training. Nevertheless, the problem is still difficult to solve naively even after discretizing the search space. For instance, if the number of subpolicies L is 10 with $K = 2$ consecutive operations, the discretized space size becomes $(16 \times 10 \times 11)^{2 \times 10} \approx 8.1 \times 10^{64}$.

Previous methods [5,12,18] used black-box optimization. Therefore, they needed to train CNNs with candidate policies and obtain their validation accuracy. The repetition of this process requires a long time. In contrast, Faster AutoAugment achieves a faster search with gradient-based optimization to avoid repetitive evaluations, even though the search space is the same as that in Fast AutoAugment. We describe the details of Faster AutoAugment in the next section.

4   Faster AutoAugment

Faster AutoAugment explores the search space to find better policies in a gradient-based manner, which distinguishes our method. In Sect. 4.1, we describe the details of the gradient approximation for policy searching. To accomplish gradient-based training, we adopt distance minimization between the distributions of the augmented and original images as the learning objective, which we present in Sect. 4.2.

4.1 Differentiable Data Augmentation Pipeline

Previous search methods [5,12,18] have used image processing libraries (e.g., Pillow) that do not support backpropagation through the operations in Table 2. Contrary to previous methods, we modify these operations to be differentiable with respect to the probability p and magnitude μ. Thanks to this modification, the search problem becomes an optimization problem. The sequence of operations in each subpolicy also needs to be optimized in the same manner.

Probability Parameter p. First, we regard (1) as $bO(\boldsymbol{X};\mu)+(1-b)\boldsymbol{X}$, where $b \in \{0,1\}$ is sampled from the Bernoulli distribution $\mathrm{Bern}(b;p)$, i.e., $b = 1$ with the probability p. Since this distribution is non-differentiable, we instead use the relaxed Bernoulli distribution [14]

$$\mathrm{ReBern}(b;p,\lambda) = \varsigma(\frac{1}{\lambda}\{\log\frac{p}{1-p} + \log\frac{u}{1-u}\}). \tag{3}$$

Here, $\varsigma(x) = \dfrac{1}{1+\exp(-x)}$ is a sigmoid function that keeps the range of the function in $(0,1)$ and u is a value sampled from a uniform distribution on $[0,1]$. At a low temperature λ, this relaxed distribution behaves similarly to a Bernoulli distribution. Using this reparameterization, each operation $O(\cdot;\mu_O,p_O)$ can be differentiable w.r.t. its probability parameter p.

Magnitude Parameter μ. For some operations, such as `rotate` or `translate_x`, their gradients w.r.t. their magnitude parameter μ can be obtained easily. However, some operations such as `posterize` and `solarize` discretize magnitude values. In such cases, gradients w.r.t. μ cannot backpropagate through these operations. Thus, we approximate their gradient in a similar manner to the straight-through estimator [3,22]. More precisely, we approximate the (i,j)th element of an augmented image by an operator O as

$$\tilde{O}(\boldsymbol{X};\mu)_{i,j} = \mathrm{StopGrad}(O(\boldsymbol{X};\mu)_{i,j} - \mu) + \mu, \tag{4}$$

where StopGrad is a stop gradient operation, which treats its operand as a constant. During the forward computation, the augmentation is exactly operated: $\tilde{O}(\boldsymbol{X};\mu)_{i,j} = O(\boldsymbol{X};\mu)_{i,j}$. However, during the backward computation, the first term of the right-hand side of Eq. 4 is ignored because it is constant, and then we obtain an approximated gradient:

$$\frac{\partial O(\boldsymbol{X})_{i,j}}{\partial \mu} \approx \frac{\partial \tilde{O}(\boldsymbol{X})_{i,j}}{\partial \mu} = 1. \tag{5}$$

Despite its simplicity, we find that this method works well in our experiments. Using this approximation, each operation $O(\cdot; \mu_O, p_O)$ can be differentiable w.r.t. its magnitude parameter μ.

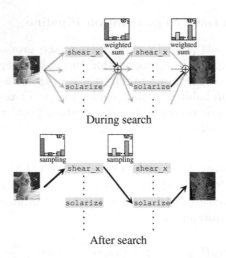

Fig. 4. Schematic view of the selection of operations in a single subpolicy when $K = 2$. During the search, we apply all operations to an image and take the weighted sum of the results as an augmented image. The weights $\boldsymbol{w}_1$ and $\boldsymbol{w}_2$ are also updated as other parameters. After the search, we sample operations according to the trained weights.

Selecting Operations in Subpolicies. Each subpolicy S consists of K consecutive operations. To select the appropriate operation O_k where $k \in \{1, 2, \ldots, K\}$, we use a strategy similar to the one used in NAS [19] (see also Algorithm 1 and Fig. 4 for details). To be specific, selecting the nth operation in $\mathcal{O}$ is equal to applying all operations $O_k^{(1)}, O_k^{(2)}, \ldots, O_k^{(\#\mathcal{O})}$ and selecting a result by multiplying a one-hot vector whose nth element is 1. We approximate this onehot vector by weighted sum of the outputs of all operations:

$$O_k(\boldsymbol{X}; \mu_k, p_k) \approx \sum_{m=1}^{\#\mathcal{O}} [\sigma_\eta(\boldsymbol{w}_k)]_m O_k^{(m)}(\boldsymbol{X}; \mu_k^{(m)}, p_k^{(m)}). \tag{6}$$

Here, $O_k^{(m)}$ is an operation in $\mathcal{O}$, and $O_k^{(m)}$ and $O_k^{(m')}$ are different operations if $m \neq m'$. $\boldsymbol{w}_k$ is a learnable parameter and σ_η is the softmax function $\sigma_\eta(\boldsymbol{z}) = \dfrac{\exp(\boldsymbol{z}/\eta)}{\sum_j \exp(z_i/\eta)}$ with a temperature parameter $\eta > 0$. At a low temperature η, $\sigma_\eta(\boldsymbol{w}_k)$ becomes a onehot-like vector. During inference, we sample the kth operation according to the categorical distribution $\text{Cat}(\sigma_k(\boldsymbol{w}_k))$.

Algorithm 1. Selection of operations in a single subpolicy during a search. Refer to Figure 4 for the case of $K = 2$.

X: input image, $\{w_1, \ldots, w_K\}$: learnable weights,
σ_η: softmax function with temperature η
for k in $\{1, 2, \ldots, K\}$:

Augment X by the kth stage operations: $X \leftarrow \sum_{n=1}^{\#\mathcal{O}} [\sigma_\eta(w_k)]_n O_k^{(n)}(X; \mu_k^{(n)}, p_k^{(n)})$

return X

4.2 Data Augmentation as Density Matching

Using the techniques described above, we can backpropagate through the data augmentation process. In this section, we describe the objective of policy learning.

One possible objective is the minimization of the validation loss as in DARTS [19]. Such formulation requires a nested optimization with an inner loop for parameter optimization and an outer loop for hyperparameter or architecture optimization. Unfortunately, this optimization takes a long time and requires a large memory footprint [7], which makes it impossible to apply it to training on large-scale datasets such as ImageNet. Moreover, data augmentation is not applied during the outer loop, i.e., validation, which differs from NAS that uses a searched architecture during the outer loop. Thus, we adopt a different of adversarial learning to avoid the nested loop.

Data augmentation can be seen as a process that fills missing data points in training data [18,24,31]. Therefore, we minimize the distance between distributions of the original and augmented images. This goal can be achieved by minimizing the Wasserstein distance between these distributions d_θ using a stable Wasserstein GAN with a gradient penalty [2,10]. Here, θ is the parameters of its critic. Unlike typical GANs for image modification, our model does not have a typical generator that learns to transform images using conventional neural network layers. Instead, a policy—explained in previous sections—is trained and transforms images using predefined operations. Following prior work [5,12,18], we use WideResNet-40-2 [35] (for CIFAR-10, CIFAR-100 and SVHN) or ResNet-50 [11] (for ImageNet) and add a two-layer perceptron that serves as a critic alongside the original classifier. The classification loss is used to prevent images of a certain class from being transformed into images of another class. Algorithm 2 depicts the detailed procedure. Importantly, we match different minibatches $\mathcal{B}$ and $\mathcal{B}'$ and randomly initialize M, P, W, which are expected to prevent policies from being trapped into "no-op" solutions, as shown in Fig. 5.

5 Experiments and Results

In this section, we show the empirical results of our approach on CIFAR-10, CIFAR-100 [16], SVHN [21] and ImageNet [27] datasets and compare the results

---

Algorithm 2. Training of Faster AutoAugment

M, P, W: learnable parameters of a subpolicy corresponding to μ, p, w, respectively
$d_\theta(\cdot, \cdot)$: distance between two densities with learnable parameters θ, f: image classifier, $\mathcal{L}$: cross entropy loss, ϵ: coefficient of classification loss, $\mathcal{D}$: training set
while not converge :
    Sample a pair of batches $\mathcal{B}, \mathcal{B}'$ from $\mathcal{D}$
    Augment data $\mathcal{A} = \{S(\boldsymbol{X}; M, P, W); (\boldsymbol{X}, \cdot) \in \mathcal{B}\}$
    Measure distance $d = d_\theta(\mathcal{A}, \mathcal{B}')$
    Obtain classification loss $l = \mathbb{E}_{(\boldsymbol{X}, y) \sim \mathcal{A}} \mathcal{L}(f(\boldsymbol{X}), y) + \mathbb{E}_{(\boldsymbol{X}', y') \sim \mathcal{B}'} \mathcal{L}(f(\boldsymbol{X}'), y')$
    Update parameters M, P, W, θ to minimize $d + \epsilon l$ using SGD (e.g., Adam)

---

with those of AutoAugment [5], PBA [12] and Fast AutoAugment [18]. Except for ImageNet, we run all experiments three times and report the average results. Details of the datasets are presented in Table 3.

5.1 Experimental Details

Implementation Details. Prior methods [5,12,18] employed Python's Pillow[2] as the image processing library. We transplant the operations described in Sect. 3.1 to PyTorch [23], a tensor computation library with automatic differentiation. For geometric operations, we extend functions in kornia [26]. We implement color-enhancing operations, sample pairing [13] and cutout [6] using PyTorch. Operations with discrete magnitude parameters are implemented as described in Sect. 4.1 with additional CUDA kernels.

We use CNN models and baseline preprocessing procedures available from Fast AutoAugment's repository[3] and follow their settings and hyperparameters for CNN training such as the initial learning rate and learning rate scheduling.

Experimental Settings. To compare our results with those of previous studies [5,12,18], we follow their experimental settings on each dataset. We train the policy on randomly selected subsets of each dataset presented in Table 3. In the evaluation phase, we train CNN models from scratch on each dataset with learned Faster AutoAugment policies. For SVHN, we use both training and additional datasets.

Similar to Fast AutoAugment [18], our policies are composed of 10 subpolicies, each of which has operation count $K = 2$ as described in Sect. 3.2. We train the policies for 20 epochs using ResNet-50 for ImageNet and WideResNet-40-2 for other datasets. In all experiments, we set the temperature parameters λ and η to 0.05. We use Adam optimizer [15] with a learning rate of 1.0^{-3}, coefficients for running averages (betas) of $(0, 0.999)$, the coefficient for the classification loss ϵ of 0.1 and the coefficient for the gradient penalty of 10. Because GPUs

---

[2] https://python-pillow.org/.
[3] https://github.com/kakaobrain/fast-autoaugment/tree/master/FastAutoAugment/networks.

are optimized for batched tensor computation, we apply subpolicies to chunks of images. The number of chunks determines the balance between speed and diversity. We set the chunk size to 16 for ImageNet and 8 for the other datasets during search. For evaluation, we use chunk sizes of 32 for ImageNet and 16 for other datasets.

Table 3. Summary of datasets used in the experiments. For the policy training on ImageNet, we use only 6,000 images from the 120 selected classes following [5,18].

Dataset	Training set size	Subset size for policy training
CIFAR-10 [16]	50,000	4,000
CIFAR-100 [16]	50,000	4,000
SVHN [21]	603,000	1,000
ImageNet [27]	1,200,000	6,000

5.2 Results

CIFAR-10 and CIFAR-100. In Table 4, we show test error rates on CIFAR-10 and CIFAR-100 with various CNN models: WideResNet-40-2, WideResNet-28-10 [35] and Shake-Shake (26 $2\times\{32, 96, 112\}$d) [8]. We train WideResNets for 200 epochs and Shake-Shakes for 1,800 epochs as in [5], and report averaged values over three runs for Faster AutoAugment. The results of the baseline and Cutout are from [5,18]. Faster AutoAugment not only shows competitive results with prior methods, but is also significantly faster to train (see Table 1). For CIFAR-100, we report results with policies trained on reduced CIFAR-10 following [5] as well as policies trained on reduced CIFAR-100. The latter results are better than the former ones, which suggests the importance of training policy on the target dataset.

We also show several examples of augmented images in Fig. 5. The policy seems often to use color-enhancing operations as reported in AutoAugment [5].

In Table 5[4], we report error rates on reduced CIFAR-10 to show the effect of Faster AutoAugment in the low-resource scenario. In this experiment, we randomly sample 4,000 images from the training dataset. We train the policy using the subset and evaluate the policy with WideResNet-28-10 on the same subset for 200 epochs. As can be seen, Faster AutoAugment improves the performance 7.7% over Cutout and achieves a similar error rate to AutoAugment. This result implies that data augmentation can moderately reduce the difficulty in learning from small data.

---

[4] [5] reported better baseline and Cutout performance than us (18.8% and 16.5% respectively), but we could not reproduce the results in [5].

original images   augmented images   subpolicies used

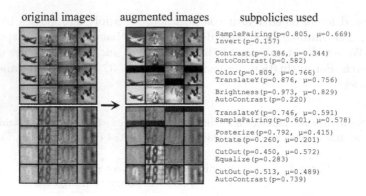

SamplePairing(p=0.805, μ=0.669)
Invert(p=0.157)

Contrast(p=0.386, μ=0.344)
AutoContrast(p=0.582)

Color(p=0.809, μ=0.766)
TranslateY(p=0.876, μ=0.756)

Brightness(p=0.973, μ=0.829)
AutoContrast(p=0.220)

TranslateY(p=0.746, μ=0.591)
SamplePairing(p=0.601, μ=0.578)

Posterize(p=0.792, μ=0.415)
Rotate(p=0.260, μ=0.201)

CutOut(p=0.450, μ=0.572)
Equalize(p=0.283)

CutOut(p=0.513, μ=0.489)
AutoContrast(p=0.739)

Fig. 5. Original and augmented images of CIFAR-10 (upper) and SVHN (lower). As can been seen, Faster AutoAugment can transform original images into diverse augmented images with subpolicies as shown on the right-hand side.

Table 4. Faster AutoAugment yields performance comparable to prior methods. Test error rates on CIFAR-10, CIFAR-100 and SVHN. We report average rates over three runs. For CIFAR-100, we report results obtained with policies trained on CIFAR-10/CIFAR-100.

Dataset	Model	Baseline	Cutout [6]	AA [5]	PBA [12]	Fast AA [18]	Faster AA (ours)
CIFAR-10	WideResNet-40-2 [35]	5.3	4.1	3.7	–	3.6	3.7
	WideResNet-28-10 [35]	3.9	3.1	2.6	2.6	2.7	2.6
	Shake-Shake (26 2 × 32d) [8]	3.6	3.0	2.5	2.5	2.7	2.7
	Shake-Shake (26 2 × 96d) [8]	2.9	2.6	1.9	2.0	2.0	2.0
	Shake-Shake (26 2 × 112d) [8]	2.8	2.6	1.9	2.0	2.0	2.0
CIFAR-100	WideResNet-40-2 [35]	26.0	25.2	20.7	–	20.7	22.1/21.4
	WideResNet-28-10 [35]	18.8	18.4	17.1	16.7	17.3	17.8/17.3
	Shake-Shake (26 2 × 96d) [8]	17.1	16.0	14.3	15.3	14.9	15.6/15.0
SVHN	WideResNet-28-10 [35]	1.5	1.3	1.1	1.2	1.1	1.2

SVHN. In Table 4, we show test error rates on SVHN with WideResNet-28-10 trained for 200 epochs. For Faster AutoAugment, we report the average value of three runs. Faster AutoAugment achieves an error rate of 1.2%, which is a 0.1% improvement over Cutout and on a par with PBA. The augmented images are shown in Fig. 5. We also show the augmented images in Fig. 5 with the obtained subpolicies, which seem to select more geometric transformations than CIFAR-10's policy as reported in [5].

ImageNet. In Table 6, we compare the top-1 and top-5 validation error rates on ImageNet with those of [5,18]. To align our results with [5], we also train ResNet-50 for 200 epochs. [5,18] reported top-1/top-5 error rates of 23.1%/6.5%. Faster AutoAugment achieves a 0.6% improvement over the baseline for top-1 error rate. This gain verifies that Faster AutoAugment has an effect comparable to prior methods on a large and complex dataset. The performance is slightly worse than AutoAugment and Fast AutoAugment, which may be attributed to

Table 5. Test error rates with models trained on reduced CIFAR-10, which consists of 4,000 images randomly sampled from the training set. We show that the policy obtained by Faster AutoAugment is useful for a low-resource scenario.

Baseline	Cutout [6]	AA [5]	Faster AA (ours)
24.3	22.5	14.1	14.8

Table 6. Top-1/Top-5 validation error rates on ImageNet [27] with ResNet-50 [11]. Faster AutoAugment achieves comparable performance to AA and Fast AA.

Baseline	AA [5]	Fast AA [18]	Faster AA (ours)
23.7/6.9	22.4/6.2	22.4/6.3	23.1/6.5

the limited number of different subpolicies for each minibatch because of the number of chunks, which we describe in Sect. 5.1.

6   Analysis

Changing the Number of Subpolicies. The number of subpolicies L is arbitrary. Figure 6 shows the relationship between the number of subpolicies and the final test error on CIFAR-10 dataset with WideResNet-40-2. As can be seen, the more subpolicies we have, the lower the error rate is. This phenomenon is straightforward because the number of subpolicies determines the diversity of augmented images. Importantly, an increase in the number of subpolicies results in the exponential growth of the search space, which is prohibitive for standard search methods.

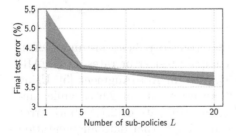

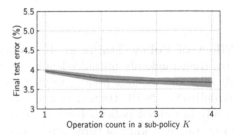

Fig. 6. The performance increases with the number of sub-policies. Relationship between the number of subpolicies and the test error rate (CIFAR-10 with WideResNet-40-2). We plot test error rates and their standard deviations averaged over three runs.

Fig. 7. The performance increases with the operation count. Relationship between the operation count of each subpolicy and the average test error rate of three runs (CIFAR-10 with WideResNet-40-2).

Changing the Operation Count. The operation count K of each subpolicy is also arbitrary. Similarly to the number of subpolicies L, increasing the operation count of a subpolicy K also exponentially increases the search space. We change K from 1 to 4 on CIFAR-10 dataset with WideResNet-40-2. We present the resulting error rates in Fig. 7. As can be seen, as the operation count in each subpolicy grows, the performance increases, i.e., the error rate decreases. These results show that Faster AutoAugment is scalable to a large search space.

Changing the Data Size. In the main experiments in Sect. 5, we used a subset of CIFAR-10 of 4,000 images for policy training. To validate the effect of this sampling, we train a policy on the full CIFAR-10 of 50,000 images as in [18] and evaluate the obtained policy with WideResNet-40-2. We find that the increase of data size causes a significant performance drop (from 3.7% to 4.1%) with subpolicies of $L = 10$. We hypothesize that this drop is because of lower capability of the policy when $L = 10$. Therefore, we train a policy with $L = 80$ subpolicies and randomly sample 10 subpolicies to evaluate the policy, which results in comparable error rates (3.8% and 3.7%). We present the results in comparison with those of Fast AutoAugment [18] in Table 7, which shows the effectiveness of using subsets for Fast AutoAugment and Faster AutoAugment.

Table 7. Test error rates on CIFAR-10 using policies trained on reduced CIFAR-10 (4,000 images) and full CIFAR-10 (50,000 images) with WideResNet-40-2.

Data size	Fast AA [18]	Faster AA (ours)
4,000	3.6	3.7
50,000	3.7	3.8

Effect of Policy Training. To confirm that trained policies are more effective than randomly initialized policies, we compare test error rates on CIFAR-10 with and without policy training, as performed in AutoAugment [5]. Using WideResNet-28-10, trained policies achieve an error rate of 2.6%, while randomly initialized policies have a slightly higher error rate of 2.7% (both error rates are an average of three runs). These results imply that data augmentation policy searching is a meaningful research direction, but still has much room to improve.

7   Conclusion

In this paper, we proposed Faster AutoAugment, which achieves faster policy searching for data augmentation than previous methods [5,12,18]. To achieve this, we introduced gradient approximation for several non-differentiable image operations and made the policy search process end-to-end differentiable. We verified our method on several standard benchmarks and showed that Faster AutoAugment could achieve competitive performance with other methods for automatic data augmentation. Moreover, our additional experiments suggest that gradient-based policy optimization can be scaled to more complex scenarios.

We believe that faster policy searching will be beneficial for research on representation learning such as semi-supervised learning [4,33] and domain generalization [32]. Additionally, learning from limited data using learnable policies might be an interesting future direction.

Acknowledgement. The research results were achieved as a part of the "Research and Development of Deep Learning Technology for Advanced Multilingual Speech Translation", the Commissioned Research of the National Institute of Information and Communications Technology, JAPAN. This work was also supported by JSPS KAKENHI Grant Numbers JP19H04166, JP19K22861 and JP20H04251. We used the RAIDEN system for the experiments.

References

1. Antoniou, A., Storkey, A., Edwards, H.: Data augmentation generative adversarial networks. In: ICLR (2018)
2. Arjovsky, M., Chintala, S., Bottou, L.: Wasserstein GAN. In: ICML (2017)
3. Bengio, Y., Léonard, N., Courville, A.: Estimating or propagating gradients through stochastic neurons for conditional computation. arXiv (2013)
4. Berthelot, D., Carlini, N., Goodfellow, I., Papernot, N., Oliver, A., Raffel, C.: MixMatch: a holistic approach to semi-supervised learning. In: NeurIPS (2019)
5. Cubuk, E.D., Zoph, B., Mane, D., Vasudevan, V., Le, Q.V.: AutoAugment: learning augmentation policies from data. In: CVPR (2019)
6. DeVries, T., Taylor, G.W.: Improved regularization of convolutional neural networks with cutout. arXiv (2017)
7. Finn, C., Abbeel, P., Levine, S.: Model-agnostic meta-learning for fast adaptation of deep networks. In: ICML (2017)
8. Gastaldi, X.: Shake-shake regularization of 3-branch residual networks. In: ICLR (2017)
9. Goodfellow, I., et al.: Generative adversarial networks. In: NIPS (2014)
10. Gulrajani, I., Ahmed, F., Arjovsky, M., Dumoulin, V., Courville, A.: Improved training of wasserstein GANs. In: NIPS (2017)
11. He, K., Zhang, X., Ren, S., Sun, J.: Deep residual learning for image recognition. In: CVPR (2016)
12. Ho, D., Liang, E., Stoica, I., Abbeel, P., Chen, X.: Population based augmentation: efficient learning of augmentation policy schedules. In: ICML (2019)
13. Inoue, H.: Data augmentation by pairing samples for images classification. arXiv (2018)
14. Jang, E., Gu, S., Poole, B.: Categorical reparameterization with gumbel-softmax. In: ICLR (2017)
15. Kingma, D.P., Ba, J.L.: Adam: a method for stochastic optimization. In: ICLR (2015)
16. Krizhevsky, A.: Learning multiple layers of features from tiny images. Technical report (2009)

17. Krizhevsky, A., Sutskever, I., Hinton, G.E.: ImageNet classification with deep convolutional neural networks. In: NIPS (2012)
18. Lim, S., Kim, I., Kim, T., Kim, C., Kim, S.: Fast autoaugment. In: NeurIPS (2019)
19. Liu, H., Simonyan, K., Yang, Y.: DARTS: differentiable architecture search. In: ICLR (2018)
20. Maclaurin, D., Duvenaud, D., Adams, R.: Gradient-based hyperparameter optimization through reversible learning. In: Bach, F., Blei, D. (eds.) ICML (2015)
21. Netzer, Y., Wang, T., Coates, A., Bissacco, A., Wu, B., Ng, A.Y.: Reading digits in natural images with unsupervised feature learning. In: NIPS Workshop on Deep Learning and Unsupervised Feature Learning (2011)
22. van den Oord, A., Vinyals, O., Kavukcuoglu, K.: Neural discrete representation learning. In: NIPS (2017)
23. Paszke, A., et al.: Pytorch: an imperative style, high-performance deep learning library. In: NeurIPS (2019)
24. Ratner, A.J., Ehrenberg, H.R., Hussain, Z., Dunnmon, J., Ré, C.: Learning to compose domain-specific transformations for data augmentation. In: NIPS (2017)
25. Real, E., Aggarwal, A., Huang, Y., Le, Q.V.: Regularized evolution for image classifier architecture search. In: AAAI (2019)
26. Riba, E., Mishkin, D., Ponsa, D., Rublee, E., Bradski, G.: Kornia: an open source differentiable computer vision library for PyTorch. In: WACV (2019)
27. Russakovsky, O., et al.: ImageNet large scale visual recognition challenge. Int. J. Comput. Vis. **115**(3), 211–252 (2015). https://doi.org/10.1007/s11263-015-0816-y
28. Shrivastava, A., Pfister, T., Tuzel, O., Susskind, J., Wang, W., Webb, R.: Learning from simulated and unsupervised images through adversarial training. In: CVPR (2017)
29. Sixt, L., Wild, B., Landgraf, T.: RenderGAN: generating realistic labeled data. In: Frontiers Robotics AI (2018)
30. Tokozume, Y., Ushiku, Y., Harada, T.: Between-class Learning for image classification. In: CVPR (2018)
31. Tran, T., Pham, T., Carneiro, G., Palmer, L., Reid, I.: A bayesian data augmentation approach for learning deep models. In: NIPS (2017)
32. Volpi, R., Murino, V.: Addressing model vulnerability to distributional shifts over image transformation sets. In: ICCV (2019)
33. Xie, Q., Dai, Z., Hovy, E., Luong, M.T., Le, Q.V.: Unsupervised data augmentation. arXiv (2019)
34. Yun, S., Han, D., Oh, S.J., Chun, S., Choe, J., Yoo, Y.: CutMIx: regularization strategy to train strong classifiers with localizable features. In: ICCV (2019)
35. Zagoruyko, S., Komodakis, N.: Wide residual networks. In: BMVC (2016)
36. Zhang, H., Cisse, M., Dauphin, Y.N., Lopez-Paz, D.: mixup: beyond empirical risk minimization. In: ICLR (2018)
37. Zhong, Z., Zheng, L., Kang, G., Li, S., Yang, Y.: Random erasing data augmentation. arXiv (2017)
38. Zoph, B., Le, Q.V.: Neural architecture search with reinforcement learning. In: ICLR (2017)

Hand-Transformer: Non-Autoregressive Structured Modeling for 3D Hand Pose Estimation

Lin Huang[1]([⊠]), Jianchao Tan[2], Ji Liu[2], and Junsong Yuan[1]

[1] State University of New York, Buffalo, USA
{lhuang27,jsyuan}@buffalo.edu
[2] Y-tech, Kwai Inc., Beijing, China
{jianchaotan,jiliu}@kuaishou.com

Abstract. 3D hand pose estimation is still far from a well-solved problem mainly due to the highly nonlinear dynamics of hand pose and the difficulties of modeling its inherent structural dependencies. To address this issue, we connect this structured output learning problem with the structured modeling framework in sequence transduction field. Standard transduction models like Transformer adopt an autoregressive connection to capture dependencies from previously generated tokens and further correlate this information with the input sequence in order to prioritize the set of relevant input tokens for current token generation. To borrow wisdom from this structured learning framework while avoiding the sequential modeling for hand pose, taking a 3D point set as input, we propose to leverage the Transformer architecture with a novel non-autoregressive structured decoding mechanism. Specifically, instead of using previously generated results, our decoder utilizes a reference hand pose to provide equivalent dependencies among hand joints for each output joint generation. By imposing the reference structural dependencies, we can correlate the information with the input 3D points through a multi-head attention mechanism, aiming to discover informative points from different perspectives, towards each hand joint localization. We demonstrate our model's effectiveness over multiple challenging hand pose datasets, comparing with several state-of-the-art methods.

Keywords: 3D hand pose estimation · Structured learning · Attention · Non-autoregressive transformer

1 Introduction

Articulated 3D hand pose estimation has been one of the most essential topics in computer vision because of its significant role in human behavior analysis and

Electronic supplementary material The online version of this chapter (https:// doi.org/10.1007/978-3-030-58595-2_2) contains supplementary material, which is available to authorized users.

understanding, leading to enormous practical applications in human-computer interactions, robotics, and virtual/augmented reality, etc. With the advances of deep learning algorithms as well as the emergence of consumer level depth sensors, notable progress has been brought to 3D hand pose estimation field [14–16,18,26,28,30,32,36,39,40,43,44,47,50,51,54].

Despite significant success achieved in recent years, it is still challenging to obtain precise and robust hand pose due to complex pose variations, large variability in global orientation, self-similarity between fingers, and severe self-occlusion, etc. To tackle this structured output learning problem, we argue it is vital for learning algorithms to not only explore the intrinsic dependencies from input data, but also fully exploit the structural correlations among hand joints as well as its dependencies with input data, both of which has been fewly discussed. In our work, we focus on 3D point cloud as input, a simple yet effective representation converted from depth data, aiming to take advantage of these vital information from it.

To make use of above mentioned information towards hand pose estimation, we connect the articulated pose estimation problem with the sequence transduction tasks in Natural Language Processing (NLP) field. As another type of structured output prediction problem, state-of-the-art sequence transduction algorithms [1,41,48] fully exploit these correlations, following a classic encoder-decoder framework. They utilize an autoregressive decoding strategy to model sequential correlations among output tokens while also capturing global dependencies between the input and output sequence through attention mechanism. These modeling techniques have led to drastic performance improvements in generating syntactically and semantically valid sentences, such as language translations and image captions. Thus, to borrow wisdom from these strategies, we propose to leverage the Transformer model as our fundamental building block to take advantage of all these missing pieces for robust 3D hand pose estimation.

As a structured learning task, we should first pay attention to the inherent dependencies among hand joints since human hands are highly articulated and inherently structured. For instance, pinky finger cannot be bend without bending the ring finger or all fingers cannot bend backward too much [27]. Most current works simply treat pose as a set of independent 3D joints [14,16,30,32] while a few studies have enforced pose-related constraints in the form of either pre-trained kinematic models [22,30,31,53,54] or hand-crafted priors [42]. However, due to the large variations in hand motions, there are more correlations that cannot be captured via such pre-defined constraints. Thus, learning a model that can adaptively model the structural patterns is necessary for these cases. Inspired by the autoregressive decoding mechanism used in sequence transduction tasks, we can enforce pose patterns by conditioning each joint generation on previously generated joints. However, the autoregressive factorization nature results in heavy inference latency. In addition, given a specific order of hand joints, the sequential modeling assumes each joint is mainly correlated with "previous" joints in the order. However, hand joints should be inter-correlated with both "previous" and "future" ones. Thus, if we only consider sequential

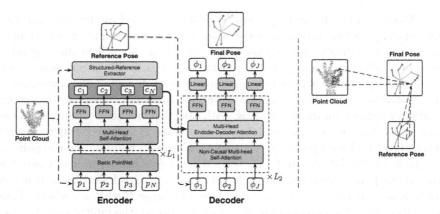

Fig. 1. Left: Overview of our proposed NARHT model composed of 3 components. The encoder computes point-wise features c_i for each input point p_i. The structured-reference extractor will feed a reference pose $\tilde{\phi}_j$ into decoder. Then decoder further models the dependencies among reference joints and correlate this information with point-wise features c_i for each joint generation ϕ_j. Right: An illustration of our non-autoregressive structured decoding strategy. Each joint generation is conditioned on the reference pose dependencies and relevant input points. N, J, L_1, and L_2 is the number of input points, hand joints, encoder layers, and decoder layers, respectively.

correlations, this might cause inferior and physically invalid poses due to biased modeling.

Motivated by recently proposed Non-AutoRegressive Transformer (NART) models [19,21,37,46], we propose to replace the autoregressive factorization of the Transformer with a novel non-autoregressive structured learning mechanism designed for 3D hand pose estimation. Instead of using previously generated tokens as decoder input, representative NART models directly feed a modified copy of input tokens to decoder, aiming to generate all output tokens simultaneously. Obviously, it provides drastic inference speedup but comes at the cost of performance degradation due to the removal of information from output tokens. To preserve the parallelism while feeding necessary pose-related information to the decoder, we design a structured-reference extractor, aiming to provide a reference hand pose in the form of joint-wise features and use its inherent correlations to approximate that of output pose. Thus, given the reference pose to the decoder, we adopt a non-causal self-attention layer [19] to capture its inherent dependencies towards each output joint generation. By exposing the extracted reference pose to the decoder, our model is able to generate all joints in parallel, conditioned on pose-related information.

Beyond drawing the dependencies from structured input and output data, respectively, the Transformer network further models the correlations between the input and output to explore the relevant input information. By modeling the correlations, what each output token generation can access is not only its relation with previously generated tokens but also the informative input features. Motivated by this strategy, our Transformer-based model also correlates each output joint generation with the input points via an multi-head attention mechanism. Specifically, for certain joint estimation, we utilize the dependencies among reference hand joints as queries to attend over input points. The goal is to adaptively discover informative points that contribute towards each joint generation, from different representation subspaces. Then, we merge the attention-weighted information along with the dependencies among reference joints to localize certain output joint. This scheme is similar to current state-of-the-art voting-based techniques [18,26,44,47] which mainly take the pairwise point to point Euclidean offsets as vote scores. Nevertheless, we can easily find cases where points with small Euclidean but large Geodesic offsets can contribute less than those with small Geodesic but large Euclidean offsets. Thus, this strategy might lead to sub-optimal results. Instead, the multi-head attention generalizes the offsets-based techniques by letting the model decide itself regarding which aspects to look at towards certain joint generation. Thus, we argue our method also extends this line of work to a more adaptive version with more various aspects being examined, based on the multi-head attention mechanism.

In summary, our main contributions are shown as follows:

- We propose a novel Non-AutoRegressive Hand Transformer (NARHT) for 3D hand pose estimation from unordered point sets. To the best of our knowledge, it is the very first attempt to connect the structured hand pose estimation with the Transformer-based transduction frameworks in NLP field.
- We design a non-autoregressive structured decoding strategy specifically for articulated pose estimation to replace the autoregressive factorization of traditional Transformer, aiming to break the sequential inference bottleneck and provide necessary pose information during the decoding process.
- Using pose dependencies as queries, we further implement a fully adaptive point-wise voting scheme through a multi-head attention mechanism. This scheme correlates the captured pose dependencies for each output joint with input points from different aspects, contributing to precise joint localization.

2   Related Work

3D Hand Pose Estimation. 3D hand pose estimation has received much attention in computer vision over the last decade. The developed approaches can be categorized into three types: generative approaches, discriminative approaches, and hybrid approaches. Our method is more related with the discriminative line of works. Most discriminative approaches [6,12,32,36,40,43,44,44,47] directly feed 2D depth maps as images into 2D CNNs. Nevertheless, the mismatch between the 2.5D depth data and the 2D learning algorithms cannot guarantee a full exploration of the input 3D geometric information. Subsequent methods [15] project depth maps into multi-views and feed them into multi-view CNNs. However, the separate pipelines with multi-view fusion is non-trivial to deal with. To further address the problem, 3D voxels [11,16,28] comes into play

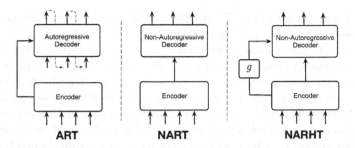

Fig. 2. Left: Classic encoder-decoder framework in sequence transduction tasks, such as AutoRegressive Transformer (ART) [41]. Middle: Recently proposed encoder-decoder framework without autoregressive connection, such as Non-AutoRegressive Transformer (NART) [19,21,37,46]. Right: Our proposed encoder-decoder framework with additional function g as the structured-reference extractor (NARHT).

for direct 3D geometric modeling. Moon et al. [28], which is still one of the state-of-the-art methods, exploits voxel-to-voxel predictions to estimate the per-voxel likelihood for each joint. But the volumteric pipeline causes high computation burden due to the need of large memory. Recent years, there is an obvious trend shifting towards RGB-based solutions [3,4,17,23,29,49,52,57] because of the convenience of data acquisition. However, the ambiguities in single RGB camera and the lack of texture features make current techniques still far more ubiquitous than depth-based methods. A lot of attentions have also been paid to the 3D point-based techniques [7,8,14,18,26]. Ge et al. [14] proposes a hand PointNet for directly mapping the unordered point sets to 3D hand poses. But as an irregular data format, more efforts can be applied in order to fully explore its geometric information. In this paper, motivated by several sequence transduction algorithms [1,19,21,37,41,46,48], we propose a novel mechanism for directly operating on input points while injecting the pose-related dependencies for robust pose estimation.

3   Methodology

Our proposed NARHT model is illustrated in Fig. 1. Given a set of unordered 3D points converted from hand depth image, our target is to infer a corresponding 3D hand pose, which is parameterized as a set of 3D joint coordinates $\Phi^{cam} = \{\phi_1^{cam}, ..., \phi_J^{cam}\}$ in the camera Coordinate System (C.S.), where J is the number of hand joints. To obtain robust hand poses, we propose to leverage a Transformer-based architecture with a non-autoregressive structured decoding strategy. The model follows the typical encoder-decoder frameworks [2,9,38,41], with an additional structured-reference extractor for non-autoregressive decoding. Specifically, following [14,18] to make our model more robust to hand orientations, we first downsample and normalize the input point set to N points in OBB C.S., represented as $\mathcal{P} = \{p_1, ..., p_N\}$. The hand joints Φ^{cam} is also transformed into OBB C.S., denoted as $\Phi = \{\phi_1, ..., \phi_J\}$. Then, we feed the normalized points $\mathcal{P}$ into the encoder to generate enhanced point-wise representations $\mathcal{C} = \{c_1, ..., c_N\}$. We utilize a basic PointNet [33], followed by a permutation-invariant self-attention layer to better capture the long-range dependencies among input points. During decoding, to impose structured pose patterns for each joint generation, we first adopt a structured-reference extractor to take the input points and generate a reference hand pose in the form of joint-wise features $\tilde{\Phi} = \{\tilde{\phi}_1, ..., \tilde{\phi}_J\}$. The reference pose is further exposed to the decoder and a non-causal self-attention layer [19] is used to capture the structural dependencies among its joints, which serves as an approximation to that of the target hand pose. Then, we correlate the captured pose dependencies with the point-wise features $\mathcal{C}$ to discover the relevant points from different representation subspaces towards certain joint generation, using the encoder-decoder attention module. Finally, we merge all the attention-weighted point-wise features along with the captured dependencies to infer each joint location in parallel. Based on this decoding strategy, our model is able to simultaneously generate all joints conditioned on pose-related information.

3.1 Tranformer Revisited

For structured output learning problems, besides extracting features from input data, we should always investigate the inherent dependencies of structured output as well as its correlations with the input data in order to generate precise and valid results, such as 3D articulated poses, language translations, and image captions. Transformer [41], established as state-of-the-art transduction model, exactly takes advantage of all these information with a solely attention-based mechanism to generate syntactically and semantically correct sentences. In particular, AutoRegressive Transformer (ART), following the classic encoder-decoder frameworks, adopts self-attention layer to first capture long-range dependencies from input structured data and previously generated output tokens, respectively. Then it further utilizes encoder-decoder attention to model dependencies between input and previously generated output. Finally, Transformer can sequentially generate token conditioned on the captured information.

The superior performance achieved by Transformer mainly comes down to the combination of autoregressive decoding with the attention mechanism for modeling the structural dependencies from data. Therefore, to translate this framework into our case, we keep the attention mechanism while extending the autoregressive decoding to a more suited strategy for 3D hand pose estimation. In the following sections, we continue revisiting both key concepts.

Multi-Head Attention. Attention mechanism [1,24] is used to adaptively aggregate the set of input values without regard to their distance, according to the attention weights that measure the compatibility of given query with a set of keys. Formally, we first assume the dimension of each query and key is d_k and dimension of value is d_v, then a scaled dot-product attention mapping [41] can be computed as:

$$Attention\,(\boldsymbol{Q}, \boldsymbol{K}, \boldsymbol{V}) = softmax\left(\frac{\boldsymbol{Q}\boldsymbol{K}^T}{\sqrt{d_k}}\right)\boldsymbol{V}, \tag{1}$$

where matrices $\boldsymbol{Q}$, $\boldsymbol{K}$, and $\boldsymbol{V}$ denote a set of queries, keys, and values, respectively. Moreover, to extend the capacity of exploring different subspaces, the attention can be extended to cases with multi-head [41]:

$$\begin{cases} MultiHead\,(\boldsymbol{Q}, \boldsymbol{K}, \boldsymbol{V}) = Concat\,(head_1, ..., head_h)\,\boldsymbol{W}^O, \\ head_i = Attention\left(\boldsymbol{Q}\boldsymbol{W}_i^Q, \boldsymbol{K}\boldsymbol{W}_i^K, \boldsymbol{V}\boldsymbol{W}_i^V\right); \end{cases} \tag{2}$$

where linear transformations $\boldsymbol{W}_i^Q \in \mathbb{R}^{d_{model} \times d_k}$, $\boldsymbol{W}_i^K \in \mathbb{R}^{d_{model} \times d_k}$, $\boldsymbol{W}_i^V \in \mathbb{R}^{d_{model} \times d_v}$, and $\boldsymbol{W}^O \in \mathbb{R}^{hd_v \times d_{model}}$ are parameter matrices. h is the number of subspaces and $d_k = d_v = d_{model}/h = 32$ in our implementation. We mainly rely on two variants of attention in our model. The first one is self-attention for capturing long-range dependencies from input and reference hand pose, respectively. The keys and queries are from same set of elements. The second one is encoder-decoder attention to prioritize the subset of input points where relevant information is present for certain joint generation. The keys and queries are from two sets of elements.

Autoregressive Decoding. As mentioned previously, Transformer generates each token in an autoregressive manner. Thus, the decoding mechanism conditions the generation of each token on the inherent dependencies among previously generated tokens, as shown in Fig. 2. Formally, given a source sentence $\boldsymbol{X} = \{\boldsymbol{x}_1, ..., \boldsymbol{x}_{T'}\}$ with length T', the autoregressive decoding factors the distribution of output sequence $\boldsymbol{Y} = \{\boldsymbol{y}_1, ..., \boldsymbol{y}_T\}$ with length T into a chain of conditional probabilities with a left-to-right sequential structure [19,41]:

$$p_{art}\,(\boldsymbol{Y}|\boldsymbol{X}; \boldsymbol{\theta}) - \prod_{t=1}^{T} p\,(\boldsymbol{y}_t|\boldsymbol{y}_{1:t-1}, \boldsymbol{x}_{1:T'}; \boldsymbol{\theta}), \tag{3}$$

where $\boldsymbol{\theta}$ is the model parameters. As shown in Eq. 3, despite its ability to capture inherent dependencies from output sequence, the autoregressive decoding suffers from high inference latency since the generation of tth token $\boldsymbol{y}_t$ depends on previously generated tokens $\boldsymbol{y}_{1:t-1}$. In addition, the sequential modeling might not work well towards hand motion, leading to sub-optimal results, since hand joints are inter-correlated with each other rather than constrained only in a sequential manner. Thus, we propose a non-autoregressive structured decoding mechanism to replace the slow sequential modeling process and enforce more reasonable pose dependencies into decoding process.

3.2   Non-Autoregressive Structured Decoding

Recently proposed Non-AutoRegressive Transformer (NART) models [19,21,37] remove the sequential dependence on previously generated tokens and directly feed a modified copy of input sequence $\boldsymbol{X}' = \{\boldsymbol{x}'_1, ..., \boldsymbol{x}'_{T'}\}$ to decoder, as shown in Fig. 2. It can achieve significant inference speedup, however, at the cost of inferior accuracy compared to ART models due to the lack of information from output sequence. The decoding process can be formulated as:

$$p_{nart}(\boldsymbol{Y}|\boldsymbol{X}; \boldsymbol{\theta}) = \prod_{t=1}^{T} p(\boldsymbol{y}_t|\boldsymbol{x}'_{1:T'}, \boldsymbol{x}_{1:T'}; \boldsymbol{\theta}). \tag{4}$$

This motivates us to come up with a similar architecture with the ability to explore the structured output patterns and run in parallel. We propose a novel non-autoregressive structured learning mechanism designed for 3D hand pose estimation. Instead of feeding previously generated results or modified copy of input, we let the decoder take a reference pose in the form of joint-wise features $\tilde{\boldsymbol{\Phi}} = \{\tilde{\boldsymbol{\phi}}_1, ..., \tilde{\boldsymbol{\phi}}_J\}$, generated by a structured-reference extractor. Exposing the reference pose to the decoder, we further employ a non-causal self-attention layer [19] for drawing the correlations among reference joints. Guided by the captured reference pose dependencies, we then adopt the encoder-decoder attention mechanism used in the Transformer to discover the informative input points from different representation subspaces. This presents a fully adaptive point-wise voting scheme, aiming to better capture correlations between output joints and input points. We aggregate the weighted point-wise features along with the pose dependencies and pass it through a Position-wise Feed-Forward Network (FFN) [41] to obtain the decoder output. Finally, the decoder output will go through a Fully Connected (FC) layer to obtain each joint coordinates. The decoding process can be formulated as:

$$p_{narht}(\boldsymbol{\Phi}|\mathcal{P}; \boldsymbol{\theta}) = \prod_{j=1}^{J} p\left(\boldsymbol{\phi}_j|\tilde{\boldsymbol{\phi}}_{1:J}, \boldsymbol{p}_{1:N}; \boldsymbol{\theta}\right), \tag{5}$$

where $\boldsymbol{\theta}$ is the model parameters. In this manner, our model can simultaneously generate all hand joints conditioned on the necessary pose patterns. For training, we adopt maximum likelihood estimation method with a squared L2 loss between the ground truth $\hat{\boldsymbol{\Phi}} = \{\hat{\boldsymbol{\phi}}_1, ..., \hat{\boldsymbol{\phi}}_J\}$ and the estimated joint coordinates. The loss for each training sample is defined as:

$$\mathcal{L}_1 = \sum_{j=1}^{J} \|\boldsymbol{\phi}_j - \hat{\boldsymbol{\phi}}_j\|_2^2. \tag{6}$$

Structured-Reference Extractor. In order to expose more reasonable pose-related information to the decoder, we replace the inefficient autoregressive factorization nature of Transformer model with a novel non-autoregressive structured learning mechanism. As shown in Fig. 1, we feed the normalized 3D points into a structured-reference extractor in the goal to generate a reference hand pose in the form of joint-wise features $\tilde{\boldsymbol{\Phi}} = \{\tilde{\boldsymbol{\phi}}_1, ..., \tilde{\boldsymbol{\phi}}_J\}$. By exposing the reference pose to the decoder, the decoder can capture the correlations among reference joints as an approximation to that of the target pose and use this information to better constrain the output space, leading to more precise and physically valid hand joints.

Specifically, we adopt a PointNet++-based network [34] to map the input points $\mathcal{P}$ to a latent feature vector and transform it into J points with 64-dim features. We then pass it through a MLP network to obtain J points with d_{model}-dim features, which gives us reference pose in the form of joint-wise features.

We also apply an intermediate supervision to encourage the reference pose to include more information regarding the ground truth. Thus, we add a FC layer for regressing a hand pose $\Phi' = \{\phi'_1, ..., \phi'_J\}$ from the joint-wise features. The second loss term is given below:

$$\mathcal{L}_2 = \sum_{j=1}^{J} \|\phi'_j - \hat{\phi}_j\|_2^2. \tag{7}$$

Non-Causal Self-Attention. Conventional Transformer conditions each output token generation on previously generated results without the access for the information from the future decoding steps. Given the reference pose output from the sturcutred-reference extractor, the decoder in our model could avoid this autoregressive factorization and explore the dependencies among all J reference hand joints. Therefore, we can avoid the causal mask used in the masked self-attention module of the traditional Transformer decoder. Moreover, similar to [19], we mask out each reference joint's position only from attending to itself, aiming to model the dependencies among reference joints without seeing itself.

Point-Wise Voting. Another key benefit of using the Transformer model is that it can model the global dependencies between the input and output tokens via a encoder-decoder attention mechanism. This strategy can be extended to a fully adaptive point-wise voting scheme for hand joint localization. Specifically, in our model, we utilize the captured dependencies among reference joints as queries to attend over all input points for each output joint generation. It will put strong focus on parts of the input points and help the decoding process select the informative points that can contribute to certain joint generation. Compared with the popular Euclidean offsets-based voting-scheme [18,26,44,47], the attention-based mechanism is more adaptive and comprehensive. Moreover, the multi-head self-attention mechanism enables the voting-scheme to be performed from different representation subspaces, adding more perspectives to the relevant point searching. The per-point votes will be merged with the captured dependencies to decide each 3D joint location.

3.3   Encoder

The goal for our encoder is similar to that in the Transformer, which is to draw long-range dependencies from the input data and compute point-wise representation. Various methods have been proposed for direct operation on point cloud.

Table 1. Comparison with state-of-the-art methods on ICVL [39] (Left), MSRA [36] (Middle), and NYU [40] (Right). "Error" indicates the mean joint distance error in (mm).

Methods	Error	Methods	Error	Methods	Error
DeepModel [53]	11.56	Feedback [32]	15.97	DeepPrior [31]	20.75
DeepPrior [31]	10.40	CrossingNets [43]	12.20	DeepModel [53]	17.04
CrossingNets [43]	10.20	REN (9x6x6) [20]	9.79	Feedback [32]	15.97
HBE [55]	8.62	3D CNN [16]	9.58	CrossingNets [43]	15.50
DeepPrior++ [30]	8.10	DeepPrior++ [30]	9.50	3D CNN [16]	14.11
REN ($9 \times 6 \times 6$) [20]	7.31	Pose-REN [6]	8.65	REN (9x6x6) [20]	12.69
DenseReg [44]	7.24	Hand PointNet [14]	8.51	DeepPrior++ [30]	12.24
SHPR-Net [7]	7.22	CrossInfoNet [12]	7.86	Pose-REN [6]	11.81
Hand PointNet [14]	6.94	SHPR-Net [7]	7.76	SHPR-Net [7]	10.78
Pose-REN [6]	6.79	Point-to-Point [18]	7.71	Hand PointNet [14]	10.54
CrossInfoNet [12]	6.73	V2V-PoseNet [28]	7.59	DenseReg [44]	10.21
A2J [47]	6.46	DenseReg [44]	7.23	CrossInfoNet [12]	10.08
Point-to-Point [18]	6.33	NARHT (Ours)	7.55	Point-to-Point [18]	9.05
V2V-PoseNet [28]	6.28			Point-to-Pose [26]	8.99
NARHT (Ours)	6.47			A2J [47]	8.61
				V2V-PoseNet [28]	8.42
				NARHT (Ours)	9.80

The classic PointNet [33] operates on each point independently without consideration of the inherent geometric correlations. Subsequent methods mainly rely on convolution-based multi-resolution hierarchy to resolve this issue. However, many recent studies [5,10,35,45,56] have shown convolution-based design is inefficient to capture long-range dependencies while also causing optimization difficulties. In addition, the transformation invariance caused by the widely used pooling operation tends to cause loss of precise localization information which is vital for articulated pose estimation. Thus, in our work, we first feed the input points into a basic PointNet-based network [33] to extract basic point-wise features and further adopt self-attention layer to enhance the representation by modeling the inherent dependencies among different points.

3.4 End-to-End Training

We utilize loss functions $\mathcal{L}_1$ and $\mathcal{L}_2$ mentioned above to jointly supervise the end-to-end learning procedure of our NARHT model, which is formulated as:

$$\mathcal{L} = \lambda\mathcal{L}_1 + \mathcal{L}_2, \tag{8}$$

where $\lambda = 10$ is the weight coefficient to balance $\mathcal{L}_1$ and $\mathcal{L}_2$.

4 Experiments

4.1 Datasets

ICVL Dataset [39]. It contains 22k frames for training and 1.5k frames for testing. The dataset also includes an additional 300k augmented frames with in-

Table 2. Left: Ablation study for several components of our Non-AutoRegressive Hand Transformer (NARHT) on ICVL [39]. Right: Comparison of inference time on single GPU.

Dataset	Compoent	Error	Methods	FPS (single GPU)
ICVL	Autoregressive transformer	8.57	V2V-PoseNet[28]	3.5
	P2P as encoder	6.70	DenseReg [14]	27.8
	Coordinate-based reference pose	6.67	Point-to-Point [18]	41.8
	NARHT (Ours)	6.47	NARHT (Ours)	43.2

plane rotations. The dataset provides 16 annotated joints. **MSRA Dataset** [36]. It consists of 76.5k depth images captured from 9 subjects. Each subject contains 17 hand gestures and each hand gesture has about 500 frames with segmented hand depth image. The ground truth annotations contains 21 joints. We adopt the common leave-one-subject-out cross-validation strategy for evaluation on this dataset. **NYU Dataset** [40]. It 72K training 8.2K testing frames. For each frame, the RGBD data from three Kinects is provided. Following the common protocol, we only use the frontal view with a subset of 14 ground truth joints. **HANDS 2017 Dataset** [50]. It consists of 957k training and 295k testing frames, which are sampled from BigHand2.2M [51] and FHAD [13] datasets. The testing set has seen subjects in training set and unseen subjects. The dataset provides 21 annotated 3D joints.

4.2   Evaluation Metrics

We adopt two most commonly used metrics in literature to evaluate the performance of 3D hand pose estimation. The first metric is the 3D per-joint Euclidean distance mean error (in mm) on all test frames as well as the overall 3D Euclidean distance mean error (in mm) of each frames' total joints across all test frames. This metric demonstrates the overall performance of each estimated joint and hand pose. The second metric is the fraction of good frames that have all joints within a specified distance to ground truth. This metric is considered more strict, which better indicates the performance of a given estimation technique.

4.3   Implementation Details

Input. We set the number of sampled points as $N = 1024$ and also concatenate each input 3D coordinate with estimated 3D surface normal. **Encoder.** We adopt a basic PointNet-based Network [33] followed by a standard Transformer encoder. The PointNet structure consists of 1 MaxPool layer and 2 MLP networks. Each MLP is composed of 3 FC layers. We use the Transformer encoder with headers h as 8, d_{model} as 256, layer number L_1 as 3 and do not use Position Encoding module. **Decoder.** We adopt PointNet++-based Network [34] as Structured-Reference Extractor and a modified standard Transformer decoder. The PointNet++ structure consists of 3 set abstraction layers followed by 1 MaxPool layer and 1 MLP for extracting joint-wise features. For the modified

Transformer decoder, we replace the Masked Multi-Head Attention layer with a Non-Causal Multi-Head Attention layer [19]. We set headers h as 8, d_{model} as 256, layer number L_2 as 6. Position Encoding module is not used. We only have 1 FC layer as the final layer to convert the decoder output to joint coordinates. **Training.** For training NARHT, we use Adam [25] optimizer with initial learning rate as 1e–3, λ as 10. The learning rate is divided by 10 after 40 epochs. Following [14,18], we adopt similar strategies for data augmentation with random arm lengths and random stretch factors. All experiments were conducted on single NVIDIA TITAN Xp GPU using PyTorch framework, with the batch size of 16 for training and evaluation.

4.4   Ablation Study

We choose ICVL dataset to conduct ablation study and evaluate the results using mean joint distance error in (mm) metric. The results are shown in Table 2.

Effectiveness of Non-Autoregressive Structured Decoding. To verify the effectiveness of our proposed non-autoregressive stuctured decoding, we compare our NARHT model with Autoregressive Transformer-based (ART) model, which is to use the original Transformer [41] for 3D hand pose estimation. We implement with scheduled sampling [2] as the training strategy for ART model. With the autoregressive decoding, we can see a obvious performance drop. More importantly, the ART model runs much slower than our NARHT model due to the sequential modeling. These help demonstrate that hand joints should not be modeled only in a sequential manner and our non-autoregressive decoding process can use the reference pose dependencies for better joint localization.

Impact of the Representation of Reference Pose. We examine the impact of the representation used for reference pose. The reference pose is generated by the structured-reference extractor and fed into our decoder. Thus we could use either joint-wise coordinates or joint-wise features as decoder input. According to the results, the coordinates-based representation is inferior to the feature-based representation, which might be caused by the lack of flexibility for the coordinates-based format.

Effectiveness of Self-Attention Layer. To demonstrate the effectiveness of self-attention layer for drawing long-range dependencies from input points, we also implement a model using the Point-to-Point [18] architecture as encoder without any self-attention layers. Besides the mean distance error, the runtimes for both encoders per frame on average are compared. Although the improvement (0.23 mm) shown in Table 2 is small, our attention-based encoder (3.80 ms) has much higher running efficiency than point-to-point-based encoder (35.90 ms). This verifies our point that self-attention layer can better capture long-range dependencies in a much more efficient manner.

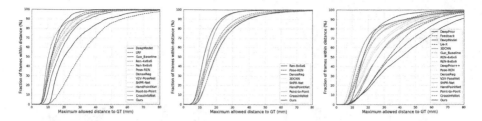

Fig. 3. Comparison with state-of-the-art methods on ICVL [39] (Left), MSRA [36] (Middle), and NYU [40] (Right) datasets. The proportions of good frames is used for comparison.

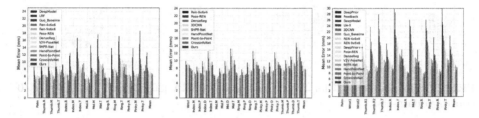

Fig. 4. Comparison with state-of-the-art methods on ICVL [39] (Left), MSRA [36] (Middle), and NYU [40] (Right) datasets. The per-joint mean error distances is used for comparison (R: root, T: tip).

4.5 Comparisons with the State-of-the-Arts

We compare the performance of the proposed NARHT on multiple public 3D hand pose datasets with most of state-of-the-art methods, including 2D and 3D-based approaches [6,7,12,14,16,18,20,28,30–32,43,44,47,53,55]. The comprehensive experimental results are given in Fig. 3 on fraction of good frames over different thresholds, Fig. 4 on per-joint mean error (mm), Table 1 on mean joint distance error (mm), and Table 2 on inference speed.

Before we perform specific analysis for each dataset. We want to point out, in terms of the percentage of good frames, when the error threshold is larger 20 mm for ICVL, 5 mm for MSRA, 30 mm for NYU, our method is superior to previous state-of-the-art methods by a certain margin. This reveals, compared with other methods, our model has the most number of good frames with all estimated joints within a certain range deviated from the ground truth joint. This also verifies the robustness of our model and meets our expectation since we explicitly enforce necessary structured pose patterns into the decoding process. Some qualitative results for three datasets are also presented in Fig. 5.

ICVL. Our method can outperform other methods except for the A2J [47], Point-to-Point [18], and V2V-PoseNet [28] on overall mean distance error shown in Table 1. However, as shown in Table 2, while our mean error is slightly infe-

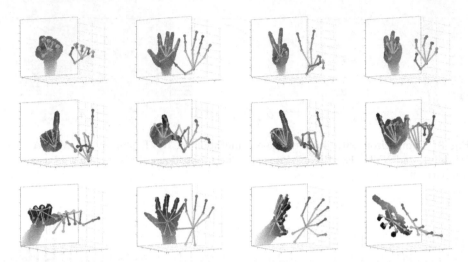

Fig. 5. Qualitative results for ICVL [39] (Top), MSRA [36] (Middle) and NYU [40] (Bottom) datasets.

rior to V2V-PoseNet, Point-to-Point, our method has higher inference efficiency, especially compared with V2V-PoseNet.

MSRA. Our method is superior to the current methods except for DenseReg [44] on the overall mean distance error. However, as mentioned above, our method has the best fraction of good frames when the threshold is larger 5 mm on MSRA and better results over almost all thresholds than DenseReg. More importantly, although our method is 3D-oriented, our model still runs much faster than DenseReg according to Table 2.

NYU. In terms of the overall mean error distances, our method in most cases outperforms current state-of-the-art models, except for A2J, Point-to-Pose [26], V2V-PoseNet, and Point-to-Point. However, our model is superior to Point-to-Point and V2V-PoseNet on fraction of good frames when the threshold is larger 30 mm by a large margin. Since we do not have the curve for A2J and Point-to-Pose, we cannot compare on this aspect.

HANDS 2017. We also compare with A2J, Point-to-Pose, V2V-PoseNet, and Hand PointNet [14] on HANDS 2017. While our mean distance error is inferior to A2J, Point-to-Pose, and V2V-PoseNet on seen cases, our model outperforms other methods except for A2J on unseen data.

5   Conclusion

In this paper, we propose to connect structured hand pose estimation problem with the sequence transduction tasks in NLP field in the goal to fully investigate related structural information for precise pose prediction. Following the Transformer framework and proposed non-autoregressive decoding strategy, we can condition each joint generation on necessary pose dependencies as well as selective input features. Experimental results on multiple challenging datasets verify the effectiveness of our model, comparing to state-of-the-art methods in real-time performance. In the future, we plan to explore more possibilities regarding bridging the gap between the structured output learning problems in pose estimation and NLP fields, such as pose estimation from RGB images and image captioning.

References

1. Bahdanau, D., Cho, K., Bengio, Y.: Neural machine translation by jointly learning to align and translate. arXiv preprint arXiv:1409.0473 (2014)
2. Bengio, S., Vinyals, O., Jaitly, N., Shazeer, N.: Scheduled sampling for sequence prediction with recurrent neural networks. In: NIPS (2015)
3. Cai, Y., Ge, L., Cai, J., Yuan, J.: Weakly-supervised 3D hand pose estimation from monocular RGB images. In: ECCV (2018)
4. Cai, Y., et al.: Exploiting spatial-temporal relationships for 3D pose estimation via graph convolutional networks. In: ICCV (2019)
5. Chaudhari, S., Polatkan, G., Ramanath, R., Mithal, V.: An attentive survey of attention models. arXiv preprint arXiv:1904.02874 (2019)
6. Chen, X., Wang, G., Guo, H., Zhang, C.: Pose guided structured region ensemble network for cascaded hand pose estimation. Neurocomputing **395**, 138–149 (2019)
7. Chen, X., Wang, G., Zhang, C., Kim, T.K., Ji, X.: Shpr-net: deep semantic hand pose regression from point clouds. IEEE Access **6**, 43425–43439 (2018)
8. Chen, Y., Tu, Z., Ge, L., Zhang, D., Chen, R., Yuan, J.: SO-HandNet: self-organizing network for 3D hand pose estimation with semi-supervised learning. In: ICCV (2019)
9. Cho, K., et al.: Learning phrase representations using RNN encoder-decoder for statistical machine translation. arXiv preprint arXiv:1406.1078 (2014)
10. Cordonnier, J.B., Loukas, A., Jaggi, M.: On the relationship between self-attention and convolutional layers. In: ICLR (2019)
11. Deng, X., Yang, S., Zhang, Y., Tan, P., Chang, L., Wang, H.: Hand3D: hand pose estimation using 3D neural network. arXiv preprint arXiv:1704.02224 (2017)
12. Du, K., Lin, X., Sun, Y., Ma, X.: Crossinfonet: multi-task information sharing based hand pose estimation. In: CVPR (2019)
13. Garcia-Hernando, G., Yuan, S., Baek, S., Kim, T.K.: First-person hand action benchmark with RGB-d videos and 3D hand pose annotations. In: CVPR (2018)
14. Ge, L., Cai, Y., Weng, J., Yuan, J.: Hand pointnet: 3D hand pose estimation using point sets. In: CVPR (2018)
15. Ge, L., Liang, H., Yuan, J., Thalmann, D.: Robust 3D hand pose estimation in single depth images: from single-view CNN to multi-view CNNs. In: CVPR (2016)
16. Ge, L., Liang, H., Yuan, J., Thalmann, D.: 3D convolutional neural networks for efficient and robust hand pose estimation from single depth images. In: CVPR (2017)
17. Ge, L., et al.: 3D hand shape and pose estimation from a single RGB image. In: CVPR (2019)

18. Ge, L., Ren, Z., Yuan, J.: Point-to-point regression pointnet for 3D hand pose estimation. In: ECCV (2018)
19. Gu, J., Bradbury, J., Xiong, C., Li, V.O., Socher, R.: Non-autoregressive neural machine translation. arXiv preprint arXiv:1711.02281 (2017)
20. Guo, H., Wang, G., Chen, X., Zhang, C., Qiao, F., Yang, H.: Region ensemble network: improving convolutional network for hand pose estimation. In: ICIP (2017)
21. Guo, J., Tan, X., He, D., Qin, T., Xu, L., Liu, T.Y.: Non-autoregressive neural machine translation with enhanced decoder input. In: AAAI (2019)
22. Hasson, Y., et al.: Learning joint reconstruction of hands and manipulated objects. In: CVPR (2019)
23. Iqbal, U., Molchanov, P., Breuel Juergen Gall, T., Kautz, J.: Hand pose estimation via latent 2.5 d heatmap regression. In: ECCV (2018)
24. Kim, Y., Denton, C., Hoang, L., Rush, A.M.: Structured attention networks. arXiv preprint arXiv:1702.00887 (2017)
25. Kingma, D.P., Ba, J.: Adam: a method for stochastic optimization. arXiv preprint arXiv:1412.6980 (2014)
26. Li, S., Lee, D.: Point-to-pose voting based hand pose estimation using residual permutation equivariant layer. In: CVPR (2019)
27. Lin, J., Wu, Y., Huang, T.S.: Modeling the constraints of human hand motion. In: Proceedings Workshop on Human Motion (2000)
28. Moon, G., Chang, J., Lee, K.M.: V2V-PoseNet: voxel-to-voxel prediction network for accurate 3D hand and human pose estimation from a single depth map. In: CVPR (2018)
29. Mueller, F., et al.: Ganerated hands for real-time 3D hand tracking from monocular RGB. In: CVPR (2018)
30. Oberweger, M., Lepetit, V.: DeepPrior++: improving fast and accurate 3D hand pose estimation. In: ICCV Workshop (2017)
31. Oberweger, M., Wohlhart, P., Lepetit, V.: Hands deep in deep learning for hand pose estimation. In: CVWW (2015)
32. Oberweger, M., Wohlhart, P., Lepetit, V.: Training a feedback loop for hand pose estimation. In: ICCV (2015)
33. Qi, C.R., Su, H., Mo, K., Guibas, L.J.: PointNet: deep learning on point sets for 3D classification and segmentation. In: CVPR (2017)
34. Qi, C.R., Yi, L., Su, H., Guibas, L.J.: PointNet++: deep hierarchical feature learning on point sets in a metric space. In: NIPS (2017)
35. Ramachandran, P., Parmar, N., Vaswani, A., Bello, I., Levskaya, A., Shlens, J.: Stand-alone self-attention in vision models. In: NIPS (2019)
36. Sun, X., Wei, Y., Liang, S., Tang, X., Sun, J.: Cascaded hand pose regression. In: CVPR (2015)
37. Sun, Z., Li, Z., Wang, H., He, D., Lin, Z., Deng, Z.: Fast structured decoding for sequence models. In: NIPS (2019)
38. Sutskever, I., Vinyals, O., Le, Q.V.: Sequence to sequence learning with neural networks. In: NIPS (2014)
39. Tang, D., Jin Chang, H., Tejani, A., Kim, T.K.: Latent regression forest: structured estimation of 3D articulated hand posture. In: CVPR (2014)
40. Tompson, J., Stein, M., Lecun, Y., Perlin, K.: Real-time continuous pose recovery of human hands using convolutional networks. ACM Trans. Graph. (TOG) **33**(5), 169 (2014)
41. Vaswani, A., et al.: Attention is all you need. In: NIPS (2017)
42. Wan, C., Probst, T., Gool, L.V., Yao, A.: Self-supervised 3D hand pose estimation through training by fitting. In: CVPR (2019)

43. Wan, C., Probst, T., Van Gool, L., Yao, A.: Crossing nets: dual generative models with a shared latent space for hand pose estimation. In: CVPR (2017)
44. Wan, C., Probst, T., Van Gool, L., Yao, A.: Dense 3D regression for hand pose estimation. In: CVPR (2018)
45. Wang, X., Girshick, R., Gupta, A., He, K.: Non-local neural networks. In: CVPR (2018)
46. Wang, Y., Tian, F., He, D., Qin, T., Zhai, C., Liu, T.Y.: Non-autoregressive machine translation with auxiliary regularization. In: AAAI (2019)
47. Xiong, F., et al.: A2J: anchor-to-joint regression network for 3D articulated pose estimation from a single depth image. In: ICCV (2019)
48. Xu, K., et al.: Show, attend and tell: neural image caption generation with visual attention. In: ICML (2015)
49. Yang, L., Li, S., Lee, D., Yao, A.: Aligning latent spaces for 3D hand pose estimation. In: ICCV (2019)
50. Yuan, S., Ye, Q., Garcia-Hernando, G., Kim, T.K.: The 2017 hands in the million challenge on 3D hand pose estimation. arXiv preprint arXiv:1707.02237 (2017)
51. Yuan, S., Ye, Q., Stenger, B., Jain, S., Kim, T.K.: BigHand2.2M benchmark: hand pose dataset and state of the art analysis. In: CVPR (2017)
52. Zhang, X., Li, Q., Mo, H., Zhang, W., Zheng, W.: End-to-end hand mesh recovery from a monocular RGB image. In: ICCV (2019)
53. Zhou, X., Sun, X., Zhang, W., Liang, S., Wei, Y.: Deep kinematic pose regression. In: Hua, G., Jégou, H. (eds.) ECCV 2016. LNCS, vol. 9915, pp. 186–201. Springer, Cham (2016). https://doi.org/10.1007/978-3-319-49409-8_17
54. Zhou, X., Wan, Q., Zhang, W., Xue, X., Wei, Y.: Model-based deep hand pose estimation. In: IJCAI (2016)
55. Zhou, Y., Lu, J., Du, K., Lin, X., Sun, Y., Ma, X.: HBE: hand branch ensemble network for real-time 3D hand pose estimation. In: ECCV (2018)
56. Zhu, X., Cheng, D., Zhang, Z., Lin, S., Dai, J.: An empirical study of spatial attention mechanisms in deep networks. In: ICCV (2019)
57. Zimmermann, C., Brox, T.: Learning to estimate 3D hand pose from single RGB images. In: ICCV (2017)

Boundary-Aware Cascade Networks
for Temporal Action Segmentation

Zhenzhi Wang[1], Ziteng Gao[1], Limin Wang[1(✉)] (iD), Zhifeng Li[2],
and Gangshan Wu[1]

[1] State Key Laboratory for Novel Software Technology,
Nanjing University, Nanjing, China
`zhenzhiwang@outlook.com,gzt@outlook.com,{lmwang,gswu}@nju.edu.cn`
[2] Tencent AI Lab, Shenzhen, China
`michaelzfli@tencent.com`

Abstract. Identifying human action segments in an untrimmed video is still challenging due to boundary ambiguity and over-segmentation issues. To address these problems, we present a new boundary-aware cascade network by introducing two novel components. First, we devise a new cascading paradigm, called Stage Cascade, to enable our model to have adaptive receptive fields and more confident predictions for ambiguous frames. Second, we design a general and principled smoothing operation, termed as local barrier pooling, to aggregate local predictions by leveraging semantic boundary information. Moreover, these two components can be jointly fine-tuned in an end-to-end manner. We perform experiments on three challenging datasets: 50Salads, GTEA and Breakfast dataset, demonstrating that our framework significantly outperforms the current state-of-the-art methods. The code is available at https://github.com/MCG-NJU/BCN.

Keywords: Temporal action segmentation · Cascade strategy · Smoothing operator · Untrimmed video

1 Introduction

Understanding human actions in videos is of great importance for many real-life applications such as surveillance and interactive robotics. Recognizing actions from short trimmed videos has achieved great performance [1,24,28–31]. However, densely labeling all the frames in a long untrimmed video is still challenging compared with action recognition. Recent works on temporal action segmentation mainly focus on capturing complex temporal structure with enriched temporal modeling. Typical methods include bi-directional LSTM networks [9,25]

Electronic supplementary material The online version of this chapter (https://doi.org/10.1007/978-3-030-58595-2_3) contains supplementary material, which is available to authorized users.

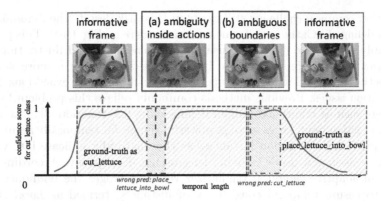

Fig. 1. Illustration of challenges: (a) the woman taking new lettuce in a long 'cut lettuce' action leads to a short misclassified 'place lettuce into bowl' result; (b) visual similarity between cutting lettuce and holding lettuce with a knife and a hand makes action boundary ambiguous. Our motivation is to tackle (b) by our stage cascade (SC) which greatly improves accuracy near boundaries, while (a) may exacerbate over-segmentation errors for the enhanced discrimination ability of SC, which will be alleviated by our proposed boundary-aware temporal regularizer: local barrier pooling.

and temporal convolution with encoder-decoder structure [13, 16] or dilated convolution [13]. The recent state-of-the-art MS-TCN [3] stacks multiple dilated convolutions to enlarge temporal modeling capacity and achieve extremely large receptive field in order to operate on the full temporal resolution.

Although modeling complex temporal structures is vital for segmenting hard-to-recoginze frames, simply increasing modeling capacity incurs overfitting problems for simple frames aside from more computation cost. Moreover, some frames are ambiguous other than difficult such as action boundaries (e.g., Fig. 1(b)) due to sudden label changes but gradual transitions of visual features. Training a single model on these inconsistent samples tend to output low confident or even wrong predictions for ambiguous frames. Given the concurrent existence of informative and ambiguous frames in a video, a more dynamic temporal modeling method is desired to cope with these problems.

To tackle the challenge above, we design a new temporal action segmentation method, termed as *Stage Cascade* (SC), which leverages cascade strategy on stage level and enable networks to predict frames through different and adaptive stages based on their complexities. Different from previous works on the enlarged modeling capacity but fixed receptive field [3, 13, 16], SC provides a new perspective for modeling adaptive temporal structure. Stages are allocated for each frame on the criterion of accuracy to modulate the stage-wise effective receptive fields. The unique design of SC enables to dynamically model sudden label changes and progressively produce better and more confident predictions in a simple-to-hard manner, where early stages focus on recognizing simple frames and late stages pay more attention to ambiguous and difficult frames.

Another common challenge still exists in this task despite the dynamic temporal modeling of SC: the over-segmentation errors (e.g., Fig. 1(a)). This problem is probably even worse in SC because of noise sensitivity and fluctuating stage assignment during inference. Thus, it is expected to devise a more adaptive and effective temporal smoothing operation to suppress the exacerbated over-segmentation issues. Previous methods commonly relieve this problem by prior knowledge such as additional temporal smoothing loss function [3]. Instead, we argue that action boundaries serve as powerful signals for temporally regularizing smooth predictions of action instances, as they naturally indicate intervals for semantic consistency inside and border-crossing discrepancy. Accordingly, we present an adaptive temporal regularizer which leverages the boundary information to ensure temporal consistency of instances, termed as *Local Barrier Pooling* (LBP). LBP predicts action boundaries from a binary classification network, whose supervision signals are derived from the segmentation ground truth. Then, LBP performs local aggregation of frame-level action predictions, where the aggregating weights are video-specific and boundary-aware. In this sense, LBP is able to greatly reduce unexpected over-segmentations by smoothing noisy predictions with confident ones.

We evaluate our framework on three challenging datasets for action segmentation: 50Salads [26], GTEA [5] and Breakfast dataset [11]. Experimental results demonstrate that the combination of our SC and LBP yields a notable performance gain against with the strong baseline [3], which is the current state-of-the-art method. In particular, our method achieves about 4% gain in frame-wise accuracy for all datasets and a consistent improvement about 4% for GTEA, 6% for 50salads and 10% for Breakfast in F1 score as the scale of datasets increases. In summary, our paper makes two main contributions:

- Our cascade design is the first attempt in the task of temporal action segmentation by enabling temporal models to have dynamic temporal modeling and achieve more confident results. This new cascade design provides a general solution to improve frame-level recognition accuracy over the existing multi-stage action segmentation methods.
- We explicitly improve the smoothness of frame-wise predictions by cooperating action boundary information with them for the first time in action segmentation task. To achieve this, we propose a novel temporal regularizer *Local Barrier Pooling* (LBP) which alleviates over-segmentation problem and meanwhile avoids reducing segmentation accuracy. Our LBP is differentiable which enables end-to-end training of our framework.

2   Related Work

Temporal Action Segmentation. Segmentation methods typically use temporal models for frame labeling upon extracted frame-level features. For example, Fathi *et al.* [4] modeled actions by the change of objects' states. Lea *et al.* [13] presented a temporal convolutional network for action segmentation and detection using an encoder-decoder architecture to capture long-range dependencies.

Lei *et al.* [16] introduced deformable convolutions into [13] and added a residual stream with high temporal resolution. Farha *et al.* [3] extended dilated temporal convolution in speech synthesis [20] to action segmentation for capturing long-term dependencies and operated it on the full temporal resolution. Gammulle *et al.* [6] proposed a conditional GAN model to utilize multiple modalities for better extraction of salient details from environmental context. These works mainly focused on improving receptive field for modeling long-term dependency with encoder-decoder structure [13,16], dilated convolution [3] or deformable convolution [16]. Different from these methods, our framework tackles the problems of inaccurate boundaries and misclassified short actions caused by existing long-term temporal modeling methods via adaptive receptive field, and provides a general improvement on existing multi-stage temporal model. Our method also provides a general smoothing operator to solve over-segmentation problem inside long actions.

Temporal Action Detection. Many of action detection methods share similar temporal modeling with our task. Singh *et al.* [25] used a multi-stream bi-directional recurrent neural network for fine-grained action detection. Yeung *et al.* [32] used reinforcement learning and RNNs to predict temporal intervals of actions based on glimpses of a small portion of the video. Zhao *et al.* [33] modeled temporal structure of actions by structured temporal pyramid. Gao *et al.* [7] extended Faster R-CNN [21] to action detection by iteratively regressing boundaries. Lin *et al.* [19] employed binary classification to predict boundaries of action instances in a sequence of temporal locations and evaluate proposals combined by these classified boundaries. Although two tasks are similar, their methods can not be directly applied to the other task for both different goal of output and different metrics.

Deep Learning Cascade. Cascade networks have been studied in detection [17], pose estimation [27] and semantic segmentation [18]. Li *et al.* [17] adopted CNN cascade for face detection, which quickly rejects false detections in early stages and refines detections in later stages. DeepPose [27] employed a divide-and-conquer strategy and designed a deep regression cascade framework for pose estimation. Li *et al.* [18] reduced computational cost and improved accuracy of semantic segmentation by distinguishing easy pixels from the hard ones and only propagate pixels with low confidence to subsequent networks. Our cascade framework differs from previous ones in adjusting weights of loss functions and combining stages' predictions for parts of a sample (i.e., frames of a video) similar to attention mechanism, but not accept or reject the whole sample [17] or a part of the sample [18] in each step.

3   Boundary-Aware Cascade Networks

As analyzed in Sect. 1, we observe that temporal action segmentation is challenging mainly in two situations: (1) ambiguous frames near action boundary

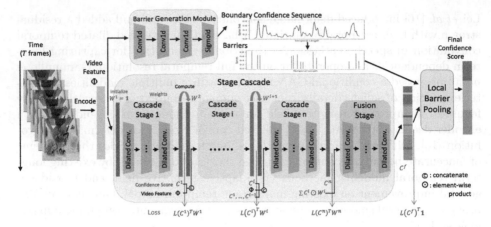

Fig. 2. Overview of our framework. Given an untrimmed video, we first encode it into a feature sequence Φ. *Stage Cascade* handles the video feature in cascade manner: cascade stages receive Φ and all previous stages' outputs, then predict frame-wise confidence scores, which will determine the weights of loss functions over frames and aggregation of cascade stages' outputs for fusion stage; *Barrier Generation Module* evaluates the boundary probabilities of each temporal location and selects barriers for our novel temporal regularizer: local barrier pooling.

or sudden actions; (2) ambiguous frames inside a long action. To address these issues, as shown in Fig. 2, we present a unified framework by designing a new stage cascade architecture and a novel local barrier pooling. The stage cascade architecture focuses on learning a progressively weak-to-strong frame-level classifier, where early stage recognize informative frames with weak capacity and later stage pay more attention to ambiguous frames with stronger capacity. The local barrier pooling presents a new smoothing technique by leveraging explicit action instance boundary with a attentive aggregation operation. These two new modules are unified in our *Boundary-aware Cascade Network* (BCN) framework with a two-branch architecture and the whole pipeline can be easily optimized in an end-to-end manner.

Our BCN provides a general and adaptive framework to boost temporal action segmentation performance in videos for any multi-stage models. To demonstrate the effectiveness of BCN, we use the state-of-the-art MS-TCN [3] as the backbone, and aim to improve action segmentation performance over a very strong baseline. Sect. 3.2 illustrates how to adapt the existing action segmentation approach into our *stage cascade*. Sect. 3.3 shows how our proposed novel *Local Barrier Pooling* is applied to action segmentation task using boundary information. Sect. 3.4 introduces the training procedure of our framework.

3.1   Video Encoding

To save the memory consumption, we first extract visual features with an off-the-shelf pre-trained video network. Given an untrimmed video with T frames

$X_{1:T} = \{x_t\}_{t=1}^{T}$ as the input, our goal is to predict the class label for frames $C_{1:T} = \{c_t\}_{t=1}^{T}$. Video encoding aims to obtain a condensed video representation capturing appearance and motion patterns of video clips. In particular, following the baseline [3] for fair comparison, we use I3D [1] without fine-tune as our video encoder ϕ to generate a sequence of feature vectors $\Phi = \{\phi(x_1), \phi(x_2), ..., \phi(x_T)\} \in \mathbb{R}^{T \times D}$ where $D = 2048$ is feature dimension. Then extracted video features are fed into BCN for temporal action segmentation.

3.2 Stage Cascade

The goal of stage cascade is to generally boost the performance of frame-level classification network by treating video frames with modules of different complexities. Specifically, for informative frames in long action segments, we can use a weak model of low capacity yet still able to capture long-term temporal dependency in order to prevent over-fitting; and for ambiguous frames near action boundaries or in sudden actions, we should devise a stronger model of high capacity with adaptive receptive field and focus on ambiguous frames for a more precise prediction. Our stage cascade adaptively process different frames with different stages and obtain the frame-level prediction that mainly rely on the corresponding stage. In practice, cascade strategy will automatically assign a weight distribution to all the cascade stages for each frame. We initialize the weights of first stage w_t^1 with 1 for all frames and update the ith $(i \geq 1)$ cascade stage's weight w_t^i for t^{th} frame as follows:

$$
w_t^i = \begin{cases}
e^{-c_t^{i-1}} w_t^{i-1} & \text{if } c_t^{i-1} \geq \rho, \\
e^{c_t^{i-1}} w_t^{i-1} & \text{if } \forall j \leq i-1, c_t^j < \rho \\
w_t^{i-1} & \text{if } c_t^{i-1} < \rho \text{ and } \exists j < i-1, c_t^j \geq \rho
\end{cases}
\tag{1}
$$

where ρ is a parameter and c_t^i is confidence score of tth frame for i^{th} cascade stage. In Eq. (1), we mainly adjust the weights for the next stage by the factor $e^{c_t^{i-1}}$: increasing weights by $e^{c_t^{i-1}}$ for less confident frames, and decreasing weights by $e^{-c_t^{i-1}}$ for very confident frames. In addition, we enforce that exactly one stage should dominate the weight among n stages for each frame, so we will stop increasing weights again once any earlier stage shows enough confidence for it. The prediction of all cascade stages will be aggregated as the input of *fusion stage* according to the weight matrix $\mathbf{w}_{i,t}$ as follows:

$$
c_t^f = \frac{\sum_i w_t^i c_t^i}{\sum_i w_t^i},
\tag{2}
$$

The fused classification score c_t^f combine the outputs of different stages adaptively for each frame and it will be passed to the fusion stage to yield final prediction of stage cascade. The fusion stage aims to smooth frame-wise classification results and generate more reasonable temporal segmentation result.

Following the common practice in action segmentation [3], we add loss functions for all cascade stages and fusion stage to make training converge stably, which are composed of a classification loss and a smoothing loss in [3]. For smoothing loss, we use the same form as baseline for all cascade stages and the fusion stage. For classification loss, we keep fusion stage's loss the same with baseline (Eq. (3), left) and adjust the distribution of loss for each cascade stage over frames (Eq. (3), right) according to weight matrix $\mathbf{w}_{i,t}$ get in Eq. (1). Note that the weight matrix is aggregated in the direction of i for fusing classification score and t for adjusting distribution of loss, respectively.

$$\mathcal{L}_{baseline} = \frac{1}{T} \sum_t -\log(y_{t,c}), \quad \mathcal{L}_i^{SC} = -\frac{\sum_t w_t^i \cdot \log(y_{t,c})}{\sum_t w_t^i} \tag{3}$$

Based on the analysis above, over-segmentations are more likely to arise for SC being more flexible than baseline and there are many stage switches, which leads to the input of fusion stage being less smooth. Moreover, when encountering the situation analyzed above (Fig. 1(a)), all methods, even with additional smoothing loss function in [3], can lead to over-segmentation errors, which is a common challenge to this task. To generally improve smoothness of action segmentation methods adaptively, we propose the following local barrier pooling.

Implementation Details. Our stage cascade is composed of several cascade stages and a fusion stage, where each stage is a SS-TCN in [3]. In MS-TCN [3], each stage only receives confidence score of the last stage as input except that the first stage receives video feature. Different from MS-TCN, our cascade stages take concatenation of video feature and all previous stages' outputs (similar to the structure of DenseNet [10]) as input and evaluates current frame-wise classification score. For the weight adjustment strategy, we use confidence score of ground truth class to update weights in training and the maximum confidence score among classes in testing. The confidence-score-selection gap between training and testing may also lead to more over-segmentation problems.

3.3   Local Barrier Pooling

To avoid over-segmentation risk with more powerful discriminative ability of the proposed Stage Cascade, we need to ensure the temporal consistency of predictions inside an action. Previous work has shown that auxiliary losses of temporal consistency [3] might be beneficial for good segmentation result. However, we find the help of auxiliary losses is limited and implicit, and temporal models including recent state-of-the-art model [3] still tend to over-segment actions.

We resort to a more explicit approach, i.e., the smoothing operator inside networks for consistent frame-wise predictions within the same action instance. Heuristic smoothing operators like gaussian smoothing and average pooling with fixed window sizes may be effective only when the action duration is much longer

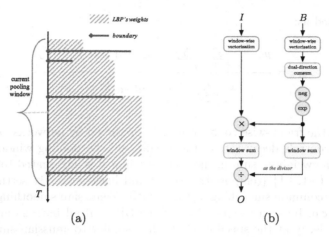

Fig. 3. (a) Visualization of our proposed Local Barrier Pooling in "hard" version. Given barriers (denoted as purple bar), for frame located in dash line, the unnormalized weights of LBP in a local window is shown as shadow region. (b) Architecture of LBP, in which I is frame-wise confidence scores, B is barriers and O is output of LBP.

than window sizes or there happens to be only one action instance in a video, which is a tight restriction. Instead, we expect the smoothing operator to be separative between different action instances and consistent inside one action instance, meanwhile have adaptive smoothing window size with regard to different action duration.

The action boundary gives us a good point to achieve both separative and adaptive properties for expected smoothing procedure since a action boundary naturally indicates a start or end of an action. Motivated by adaptive pooling operator aware of spatial importance [8], we design the local barrier pooling (LBP), a smoothing operator aware of action boundaries to ensure the consistency of predictions within action instances. At a macro level, LBP regards action boundaries as barriers in the diffusion of each class's actionness. LBP can be simply decomposed into two steps after the prediction of existing models: *First*, train a classification network to predict boundaries and then select temporal locations with high confidence to be boundaries. *Second*, compute the weighted sum of predictions in a local pooling window where weights are aware of and adaptive on barriers across from the pooling center.

Local Barrier Pooling. LBP generates smoother predictions from the output of temporal model by averaging predictions among neighborhood with adaptive weights aware of action boundaries. For each frame, LBP utilizes a local pooling window centering in current frame and from center calculates weights in two directions. As shown in Fig. 3, LBP decreases the weight by an adaptive ratio when it meets a barrier. The output of LBP $y'_{t,c}$ in temporal location t and class

c is formulated as:

$$y'_{t,c} = \frac{y_{t,c} + \sum\limits_{s\in\{-1,+1\}} \sum\limits_{\beta=1}^{L} y_{t+s\cdot\beta,c} \exp(-\alpha \sum\limits_{j=1}^{\beta} b_{t+s\cdot j})}{1 + \sum\limits_{s\in\{-1,+1\}} \sum\limits_{\beta=1}^{L} \exp(-\alpha \sum\limits_{j=1}^{\beta} b_{t+s\cdot j})} \tag{4}$$

where $y_{t,c}$ is the frame-wise confidence score predicted by networks, b_t is barrier strength, α controls decay rate of the weight and the pooling window's length is $2L + 1$. The weighted sum in the pooling window is aggregated to two directions as $s \in \{-1, +1\}$ (temporally forward and backward). By setting barriers heuristically, common smoothing methods such as gaussian smoothing and average pooling can be seen as special cases of LBP: i) if all barriers are set to 1, weights will decay at the speed of $e^{-\alpha x}$, thus similar to gaussian smoothing at $e^{-\frac{x^2}{2\sigma}}$; ii) if there are no barriers, weights will be uniform distribution which is identical to average pooling. Different from heuristic smoothing methods, our LBP introduce the boundary information b_t to parameterize its weights, which is sample-dependent. Evaluation on LBP and two heuristic smoothing methods shows that our boundary-aware smoothing operator LBP achieves better performance than its two special cases.

Barrier Generation Module. To provide input-dependent boundary information for LBP, we use temporal evaluation module (TEM) of BSN [19] as Barrier Generation Module (BGM) upon the extracted video feature sequence $\Phi = \{\phi(x_t)\}_{t=1}^{T}$, which is a binary classification model for boundaries. The original form of TEM operates on a fixed-length feature sequence, yet it makes joint training of SC and BGM unstable. So we adjust two version of BGM (1) 'resized' version: we resize input scale to fixed-length l_w by linear interpolation and use identical network to TEM. We select temporal location t according to confidence score p_t outputted by BGM where $p_t > 0.5$ and is a local maximal ($p_t > p_{t-1}$ and $p_t > p_{t+1}$) as barriers, then resize back to original scale T by nearest neighbor interpolation. (2) 'full-length' version: we use original scale T and replace convolution layers of TEM with dilated convolution (dilation of 2^l, $l \in \{2,3,4\}$) to be BGM, then we keep all the p_t as barriers.

We keep all hyper-parameters the same as [19] except '$p_t > 0.5$' (0.9 in [19]) for the following reason: unlike TEM, BGM doesn't seek for best precision of detecting boundaries, but it hopes to provide complete barrier information for LBP to smooth predictions inside action instances and meanwhile do not harm accuracy among boundary regions. So we choose common practice as '$p_t > 0.5$' since our LBP is insensitive to few false positives. Selecting local maximal is used for removing repeated barriers near one boundary. We keep all the p_t in 'full-length' version because of training stability and the same reason above.

3.4 Training BCN

Training our BCN has two parts: pre-training Barrier Generation Module (BGM) and joint training Stage Cascade (SC) and BGM. We first construct action boundary ground-truths on segmentation annotations following [19] and pre-train our BGM by binary classification loss. The purpose of pre-training BGM is to provide accurate boundary predictions at the start of joint training, and to fully optimize BGM's parameters because of different convergence rates of SC and BGM. Then we train SC and BGM jointly on original ground-truths only using frame-wise classification loss, where parameters of BGM can also be fine-tuned by backward gradients because our LBP is differentiable.

Stage Cascade. Follow the baseline [3], our loss functions are (1) cross-entropy loss for classification, which will be adaptively adjusted for each frame following Eq. (3); (2) truncated mean squared error over the frame-wise log-probabilities for smoothing. Please refer to [3] or our appendix for details.

Barrier Generation Module. Given a ground truth sequence Ψ with temporal length l, we accumulate frame-wise annotations as segments $\varphi_g = (t_s, t_e)$ (in which $d_g = t_e - t_s$) and use the starting region $r_g^s = [t_s - d_g/10, t_s + d_g/10]$ and ending region $r_g^e = [t_e - d_g/10, t_e + d_g/10]$ as boundary regions. We assign a duration of $\frac{1}{l}$ to each frame and calculate the temporal intersection over union (tIOU) between each frame and boundary regions as the annotation. We use a binary logistic regression loss for classifying boundaries following [19].

Training Details. For LBP, we use a pooling window of 39, 99 and 159 in GTEA, 50Salads and Breakfast dataset respectively. We set $\alpha = 1$ in 'resized' version and $\alpha = 0.2$ for 'full-length' version. Our experiment shows that α has little influence on predictions because BGM will adaptively adjust the value of barriers in joint training. We use threshold $\rho = 0.8$ to train SC and 4 stages in MS-TCN [3] as the backbone of SC for fair comparison. We set the number of channels to 256, and then keep all other hyper-parameters the same with [3]. For joint training, we use Adam optimizer with a learning rate 10^{-3} and multiply it by 0.3 every 20 epoch for 50Salads and GTEA dataset and a learning rate $5 \cdot 10^{-4}$ and multiply it by 0.3 every 30 epochs for Breakfast dataset. For pre-training BGM, we use learning rate 10^{-3} for 50Salads and GTEA, and $5 \cdot 10^{-4}$ for Breakfast, then multiply them by 0.3 every 100 epochs. Despite larger epochs for training, the computational cost of BGM is much smaller compared to the main network SC.

4 Experiments

Dataset. We evaluate our proposed BCN on three challenging action segmentation datasets: 50Salads [26], GTEA [5] and the Breakfast dataset [11].

The **50Salads** contains 50 videos of 25 people preparing salads in kitchen environment with 17 action classes in the mid-level. Each video contains 9000 to 18000 frames and 20 action instances on average such as `cut tomato`. Although this is a multi-modal dataset, we only use RGB data in videos. We perform 5-fold cross-validation and report the average results for evaluation.

The **GTEA** is composed of 28 egocentric and dynamic-view videos and includes four subjects performing seven daily activities. We utilize 11 action classes including background class and perform 4-fold cross-validation for evaluation.

The **Breakfast** dataset is among the largest dataset for action segmentation task, which has 1,712 videos of cooking breakfast in the kitchen environment with a overall duration of 66.7 h. Overall, there are 48 different actions where each video contains 6 action instances on average. We use the standard 4-fold cross-validation for evaluation.

Evaluation Metrics. For all the datasets, we report the following evaluation metrics as in [13]: frame-wise **accuracy**, segmental **edit score** and the segmental **F1 score** at temporal intersection over union (tIoU) thresholds 0.10, 0.25 and 0.5, denoted by $F1@\{10, 25, 50\}$. The commonly used accuracy fails to take the temporal structure of the prediction into account and does not reflect over-segmentation errors, so results with large amount of action segments against temporal continuity in human actions can still score high. So we also adopt edit score proposed by [13] which penalizes over-segmentation errors and F1 score proposed by [15] which is similar to mean average precision (mAP) widely used in detection task.

4.1   Study on SC and LBP

In this section, we demonstrate the ability of our proposed SC and LBP by comparing to their variants and other counterparts. To justify our framework's ability, we specify the following baselines and BCN variants: (1) MS-TCN: backbone with 4 stages and 10 layers per stage; (2) MS-TCN w/ feature: video feature passing into each stage, which provides the same information with BCN. Another two more stronger form of MS-TCN: (3) MS-TCN w/ 5 stages; (4) MS-TCN w/ 12 layers per stage; (5) Stage Cascade: our SC with 3 cascade stage and 1 fusion stage; (6) MS-TCN w/ LBP: (2) with LBP as post-processing; (7) MS-TCN w/ attention&LBP: (6) with traditional attention mechanism where weights are predicted from each stage itself (i.e., additional 1-dim of output).

Comparison between BCN and its important counterparts are summarized in Table 1. Baselines and variants (1) - (7) are placed in the first seven rows and BCN is placed in the last row. In our experiment, BCN has SC, 1 embedding 'full-length' LBP in joint training and testing, and 4 times of 'resized' LBP as post-processing as default based on our ablation study. We have some observation here from Table 1. Firstly, MS-TCN with more information (i.e., video feature) passing to higher stages will not lead to performance gain while our

Table 1. Comparison with baseline and BCN's variants on 50Salads (mid). The 1st and 2nd of each criterion are boldfaced and underlined respectively. (* reported in [3])

Methods	F1@{10,25,50}			Edit	Acc
MS-TCN*	76.3	74.0	64.5	67.9	80.7
MS-TCN w/ feature*	56.2	53.7	45.8	47.6	76.8
MS-TCN (5 stages)*	76.4	73.4	63.6	69.2	79.5
MS-TCN (12 layers)*	77.8	75.2	66.9	69.6	80.5
Stage Cascade	56.4	54.3	48.9	52.6	<u>83.4</u>
MS-TCN w/ LBP	78.3	75.9	66.1	68.1	81.5
MS-TCN w/ attention& LBP	<u>78.9</u>	<u>77.2</u>	<u>68.5</u>	<u>71.3</u>	82.7
BCN (SC w/ LBP)	**82.3**	**81.3**	**74.0**	**74.3**	**84.4**

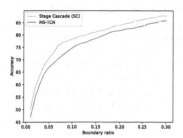

Fig. 4. Stage Cascade's accuracy gain over baseline.

Table 2. LBP and two heuristic smoothing operators on 50Salads (mid).

Smoothing operators	F1@{10,25,50}			Edit	Acc
Average (all barriers set as '0')	80.1	77.3	69.1	72.7	82.4
Gaussian-like (all barriers set as '1')	77.0	74.6	64.9	68.7	82.5
LBP (barriers from BGM)	**82.3**	**81.3**	**74.0**	**74.3**	**84.4**

SC will. Secondly, SC increases segmentation accuracy and damages F1 score in the same time, implying that it tends to predict over-segment predictions without LBP for challenges shown in Fig. 1(a) because of enhanced discriminative ability. Thirdly, LBP itself can improve both F1 score and accuracy without SC by correcting over-segmentation errors, which is consistent with our analysis. Furthermore, LBP can compensate the exacerbated over-segmentation problem caused by SC. With the help of LBP, our cascade strategy is superior to commonly used attention mechanism which does not consider the relations between stages and outputs weights by each stage separately.

To reveal the reason behind SC's improvement, we collect the accuracy gain over baseline about distances from boundaries. Similar to the construction of groundtruth in BGM, we represent regions by the incremental part when the boundary ratio increases. Comparison between accuracy of SC and the baseline in Fig. 4 show that SC mainly improves accuracy near boundary regions, which is consistent to our analysis in Sect. 3.2.

Comparison between LBP and two heuristic temporal regularizer in Table 2 illustrates that our proposed boundary-aware and input-dependent temporal regularizer LBP is more effective than its special cases which are unable to utilize boundary information thus unsuitable for temporal action segmentation task.

Table 3. Study on probability thresholds for stage cascade on 50Salads (mid).

Threshold	F1@{10,25,50}			Edit	Acc
0.5	81.6	79.7	71.5	74.2	83.0
0.6	82.1	80.9	71.9	74.1	83.3
0.7	81.9	80.5	72.4	74.0	83.9
0.8	**82.3**	**81.3**	**74.0**	**74.3**	**84.4**
0.9	80.6	79.1	69.7	73.3	82.9

Table 4. Study on the number of Cascade Stages on 50Salads dataset.

50Salads (mid)	F1@{10,25,50}			Edit	Acc
MS-TCN (3 stages)	71.5	68.6	61.1	64.0	78.6
MS-TCN (4 stages)	76.3	74.0	64.5	67.9	80.7
BCN (2 cascade stages)	81.2	79.2	71.3	73.5	83.6
BCN (3 cascade stages)	**82.3**	**81.3**	**74.0**	**74.3**	**84.4**
BCN (4 cascade stages)	80.7	78.9	71.5	72.9	83.5

4.2   Ablation Study on Hyper-parameters

We also investigate the effects of threshold ρ, number of stages in SC and LBP's pooling window size. Our ablation studies strictly follows existing works and all the comparisons are *fair*. Experiments show that both SC and LBP are insensitive to most of the hyper-parameters, which proves our framework's robustness. Please refer to appendix for other less important hyper-parameters.

Study on Probability Thresholds. Based on frame-wise confidence score of the previous cascade, SC can update weights adaptively, where threshold ρ controls the frame distribution in SC: smaller ρ encourages more frames to be handled in early stage while larger ρ tends to progressively classify most of frames by the later stages. In extreme cases, weights in SC will monotonically increase when $\rho = 1$ and decrease when $\rho = 0$. As shown in Table 3, BCN achieves the best performance with $\rho = 0.8$, which lead to the distribution about 26:21:53 for 3 cascade stages of SC. Although the value of ρ is dataset-dependent which can be chosen empirically using a validation set, our experiment shows that ρ has little influence on our methods in Table 3 and our methods achieve good results in GTEA and Breakfast datasets with the $\rho = 0.8$ obtained in 50Salads.

Study on the Number of Cascade Stages. Commonly we use 3 cascade stages and 1 fusion stage in our experiments for *fair* comparison with baseline, yet we construct a 2-stage BCN to justify that our performance gain is not obtained from more computational cost or parameters. SC only updates the weights for stage 2 w_t^2 and keep all w_t^1 to be 1 for 2-stage BCN. Table 4 shows our framework with less capacity not only surpasses its baseline by large margin, but also outperforms MS-TCN's best result, which proves the effectiveness of our method. Comparison between BCN with different stages shows that our method's behavior is similar to the backbone: the performance will not be better if we add more stages, just like the result of Table 1 in [3].

Study on LBP's Pooling Window Size. As Fig. 5 shows, larger pooling window size generally benefits all the metrics, which demonstrates that small windows can not provide enough confident temporal neighborhood to correct

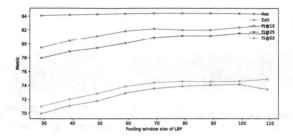

Fig. 5. Metrics as functions of LBP's pooling window size on 50Salads (mid).

Table 5. Comparison with the state-of-the-art on 50Salads, GTEA and Breakfast dataset. (* uses multi-modal data, † obtained from [2])

50Salads (mid)	F1@{10,25,50}			Edit	Acc	GTEA	F1@{10,25,50}			Edit	Acc
Spatial CNN [14]	32.3	27.1	18.9	24.8	54.9	Bi-LSTM [25]	66.5	59.0	43.6	–	55.5
IDT+LM [22]	44.4	38.9	27.8	45.8	48.7	ED-TCN [13]	72.2	69.3	56.0	–	64.0
Dilated TCN [13]	52.2	47.6	37.4	43.1	59.3	TDRN [16]	79.2	74.4	62.7	74.1	70.1
ST-CNN [14]	55.9	49.6	37.1	45.9	59.4	MS-TCN [3]	85.8	83.4	69.8	79.0	76.3
Bi-LSTM [25]	62.6	58.3	47.0	55.6	55.7	Coupled GAN [6]*	80.1	77.9	69.1	72.8	78.5
ED-TCN [13]	68.0	63.9	52.6	59.8	64.7	BCN	**88.5**	**87.1**	**77.3**	**84.4**	**79.8**
TDRN [16]	72.9	68.5	57.2	66.0	68.1	**Breakfast**	F1@{10,25,50}			Edit	Acc
MS-TCN [3]	76.3	74.0	64.5	67.9	80.7	ED-TCN [13]†	–	–	–	–	43.3
Coupled GAN [6]*	80.1	78.7	71.1	76.9	74.5	TCFPN [2]	–	–	–	–	52.0
BCN	**82.3**	**81.3**	**74.0**	**74.3**	**84.4**	HTK (64) [12]	–	–	–	–	56.3
						GRU [23]†	–	–	–	–	60.6
						MS-TCN (I3D) [3]	52.6	48.1	37.9	61.7	66.3
						BCN	**68.7**	**65.5**	**55.0**	**66.2**	**70.4**

misclassified frames and a large window is necessary for smoothing predictions due to the existence of long duration actions. We also observe that the performance drops a little when we stretch the window too large. This may be because pooling weights are lowered rather than being zeros across barriers in LBP and then there might be unexpected long-term interactions between action instances.

4.3   Comparison with the State of the Art

In Table 5, we compare our BCN to the state-of-the-art methods on three challenging benchmarks: 50Salads, GTEA and Breakfast datasets with I3D features (without fine-tune). Our model leads to notable gains compared to previous competitive methods in all datasets, especially in the larger Breakfast dataset. Qualitative results on two datasets are shown in Fig. 6 (please refer to appendix for GTEA dataset), visualizing that our predictions have high accuracy and the weight assignment is consist to our analysis of BCN where hard frames near boundaries are handled by later stages with higher capacity. Our model's frame-wise confidence score's entropy is far below the baseline's, indicating more confident predictions. It's worth noting that there is only a minor extra computational burden in our models compared to the baseline.

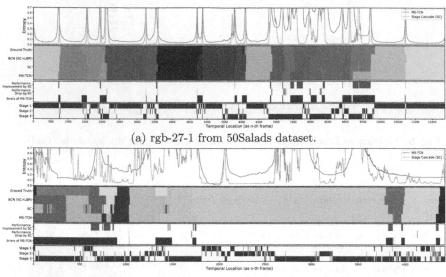

(a) rgb-27-1 from 50Salads dataset.

(b) P13 cam01 P13 pancake from Breakfast dataset.

Fig. 6. Qualitative results on 50Salads and Breakfast datasets. There are several rows: (1) Frame-wise entropy of SC vs. baseline [3]; (2) Action segmentation results of groundtruth, BCN, SC and baseline; (3) SC's improvement (red) and performance drop (green) over baseline, and baseline's error (purple); (4) The cascade stage among stage 1,2 or 3 which dominates the weight is in blue. (Color figure online)

5   Conclusion

We have presented a new framework called boundary-aware cascade network (BCN) for temporal action segmentation, which consists of two components: a stage cascade module that adaptively adjusts weights to enable later stages to focus on harder frames, and a local barrier pooling to improve the smoothness of predictions by explicitly utilizing semantic boundary information. Our empirical evaluation on the benchmark 50Salads, GTEA and Breakfast demonstrated that BCN outperforms the state-of-the-art models by a large margin. The superior performance of BCN is owe to the fact that it is able to predict more precise action segments and greatly reduce over-segmentation artifacts. It implies merits of our end-to-end learning of stage cascade and local barrier pooling over simply stacking deeper layers of temporal convolutions.

Acknowledgements. This work is supported by Tencent AI Lab Rhino-Bird Focused Research Program (No. JR202025), the National Science Foundation of China (No. 61921006), Program for Innovative Talents and Entrepreneur in Jiangsu Province, and Collaborative Innovation Center of Novel Software Technology and Industrialization.

References

1. Carreira, J., Zisserman, A.: Quo vadis, action recognition? A new model and the kinetics dataset. In: 2017 IEEE Conference on Computer Vision and Pattern Recognition, CVPR 2017, Honolulu, HI, USA, 21–26 July 2017, pp. 4724–4733 (2017)
2. Ding, L., Xu, C.: Weakly-supervised action segmentation with iterative soft boundary assignment. In: 2018 IEEE Conference on Computer Vision and Pattern Recognition, CVPR 2018, Salt Lake City, UT, USA, 18–22 June 2018, pp. 6508–6516 (2018)
3. Farha, Y.A., Gall, J.: MS-TCN: multi-stage temporal convolutional network for action segmentation. In: IEEE Conference on Computer Vision and Pattern Recognition, CVPR 2019, Long Beach, CA, USA, 16–20 June 2019, pp. 3575–3584 (2019)
4. Fathi, A., Rehg, J.M.: Modeling actions through state changes. In: 2013 IEEE Conference on Computer Vision and Pattern Recognition, Portland, OR, USA, 23–28 June 2013, pp. 2579–2586 (2013)
5. Fathi, A., Ren, X., Rehg, J.M.: Learning to recognize objects in egocentric activities. In: The 24th IEEE Conference on Computer Vision and Pattern Recognition, CVPR 2011, Colorado Springs, CO, USA, 20–25 June 2011, pp. 3281–3288 (2011)
6. Gammulle, H., Fernando, T., Denman, S., Sridharan, S., Fookes, C.: Coupled generative adversarial network for continuous fine-grained action segmentation. In: IEEE Winter Conference on Applications of Computer Vision, WACV 2019, Waikoloa Village, HI, USA, 7–11 January 2019, pp. 200–209 (2019)
7. Gao, J., Yang, Z., Nevatia, R.: Cascaded boundary regression for temporal action detection. In: British Machine Vision Conference 2017, BMVC 2017, London, UK, 4–7 September 2017 (2017)
8. Gao, Z., Wang, L., Wu, G.: LIP: local importance-based pooling. In: 2019 IEEE/CVF International Conference on Computer Vision, ICCV 2019, Seoul, Korea (South), 27 October–2 November 2019, pp. 3354–3363 (2019)
9. Huang, D.-A., Fei-Fei, L., Niebles, J.C.: Connectionist temporal modeling for weakly supervised action labeling. In: Leibe, B., Matas, J., Sebe, N., Welling, M. (eds.) ECCV 2016. LNCS, vol. 9908, pp. 137–153. Springer, Cham (2016). https://doi.org/10.1007/978-3-319-46493-0_9
10. Huang, G., Liu, Z., van der Maaten, L., Weinberger, K.Q.: Densely connected convolutional networks. In: 2017 IEEE Conference on Computer Vision and Pattern Recognition, CVPR 2017, Honolulu, HI, USA, 21–26 July 2017, pp. 2261–2269. IEEE Computer Society (2017)
11. Kuehne, H., Arslan, A.B., Serre, T.: The language of actions: recovering the syntax and semantics of goal-directed human activities. In: 2014 IEEE Conference on Computer Vision and Pattern Recognition, CVPR 2014, Columbus, OH, USA, 23–28 June 2014, pp. 780–787 (2014)
12. Kuehne, H., Gall, J., Serre, T.: An end-to-end generative framework for video segmentation and recognition. In: 2016 IEEE Winter Conference on Applications of Computer Vision, WACV 2016, Lake Placid, NY, USA, 7–10 March 2016, pp. 1–8 (2016)
13. Lea, C., Flynn, M.D., Vidal, R., Reiter, A., Hager, G.D.: Temporal convolutional networks for action segmentation and detection. In: 2017 IEEE Conference on Computer Vision and Pattern Recognition, CVPR 2017, Honolulu, HI, USA, 21–26 July 2017, pp. 1003–1012 (2017)

14. Lea, C., Reiter, A., Vidal, R., Hager, G.D.: Segmental spatiotemporal CNNs for fine-grained action segmentation. In: Leibe, B., Matas, J., Sebe, N., Welling, M. (eds.) ECCV 2016. LNCS, vol. 9907, pp. 36–52. Springer, Cham (2016). https://doi.org/10.1007/978-3-319-46487-9_3

15. Lea, C., Vidal, R., Hager, G.D.: Learning convolutional action primitives for fine-grained action recognition. In: 2016 IEEE International Conference on Robotics and Automation, ICRA 2016, Stockholm, Sweden, 16–21 May 2016, pp. 1642–1649 (2016)

16. Lei, P., Todorovic, S.: Temporal deformable residual networks for action segmentation in videos. In: 2018 IEEE Conference on Computer Vision and Pattern Recognition, CVPR 2018, Salt Lake City, UT, USA, 18–22 June 2018, pp. 6742–6751 (2018)

17. Li, H., Lin, Z., Shen, X., Brandt, J., Hua, G.: A convolutional neural network cascade for face detection. In: IEEE Conference on Computer Vision and Pattern Recognition, CVPR 2015, Boston, MA, USA, 7–12 June 2015, pp. 5325–5334 (2015)

18. Li, X., Liu, Z., Luo, P., Loy, C.C., Tang, X.: Not all pixels are equal: difficulty-aware semantic segmentation via deep layer cascade. In: 2017 IEEE Conference on Computer Vision and Pattern Recognition, CVPR 2017, Honolulu, HI, USA, 21–26 July 2017, pp. 6459–6468 (2017)

19. Lin, T., Zhao, X., Su, H., Wang, C., Yang, M.: BSN: boundary sensitive network for temporal action proposal generation. In: Ferrari, V., Hebert, M., Sminchisescu, C., Weiss, Y. (eds.) ECCV 2018. LNCS, vol. 11208, pp. 3–21. Springer, Cham (2018). https://doi.org/10.1007/978-3-030-01225-0_1

20. van den Oord, A., et al.: Wavenet: a generative model for raw audio. In: The 9th ISCA Speech Synthesis Workshop, Sunnyvale, CA, USA, 13–15 September 2016, p. 125 (2016)

21. Ren, S., He, K., Girshick, R.B., Sun, J.: Faster R-CNN: towards real-time object detection with region proposal networks. In: Advances in Neural Information Processing Systems 28: Annual Conference on Neural Information Processing Systems 2015, Montreal, Quebec, Canada, 7–12 December 2015, pp. 91–99 (2015)

22. Richard, A., Gall, J.: Temporal action detection using a statistical language model. In: 2016 IEEE Conference on Computer Vision and Pattern Recognition, CVPR 2016, Las Vegas, NV, USA, 27–30 June 2016, pp. 3131–3140 (2016)

23. Richard, A., Kuehne, H., Gall, J.: Weakly supervised action learning with RNN based fine-to-coarse modeling. In: 2017 IEEE Conference on Computer Vision and Pattern Recognition, CVPR 2017, Honolulu, HI, USA, 21–26 July 2017, pp. 1273–1282 (2017)

24. Simonyan, K., Zisserman, A.: Two-stream convolutional networks for action recognition in videos. In: Ghahramani, Z., Welling, M., Cortes, C., Lawrence, N.D., Weinberger, K.Q. (eds.) Advances in Neural Information Processing Systems, vol. 27, pp. 568–576. Curran Associates, Inc. (2014)

25. Singh, B., Marks, T.K., Jones, M.J., Tuzel, O., Shao, M.: A multi-stream bi-directional recurrent neural network for fine-grained action detection. In: 2016 IEEE Conference on Computer Vision and Pattern Recognition, CVPR 2016, Las Vegas, NV, USA, 27–30 June 2016, pp. 1961–1970 (2016)

26. Stein, S., McKenna, S.J.: Combining embedded accelerometers with computer vision for recognizing food preparation activities. In: The 2013 ACM International Joint Conference on Pervasive and Ubiquitous Computing, UbiComp 2013, Zurich, Switzerland, 8–12 September 2013, pp. 729–738 (2013)

27. Toshev, A., Szegedy, C.: DeepPose: human pose estimation via deep neural networks. In: 2014 IEEE Conference on Computer Vision and Pattern Recognition, CVPR 2014, Columbus, OH, USA, 23–28 June 2014, pp. 1653–1660 (2014)
28. Tran, D., Bourdev, L., Fergus, R., Torresani, L., Paluri, M.: Learning spatiotemporal features with 3D convolutional networks. In: Proceedings of the 2015 IEEE International Conference on Computer Vision (ICCV), ICCV 2015, pp. 4489–4497 (2015)
29. Wang, L., Li, W., Li, W., Gool, L.V.: Appearance-and-relation networks for video classification. In: 2018 IEEE Conference on Computer Vision and Pattern Recognition, CVPR 2018, Salt Lake City, UT, USA, 18–22 June 2018, pp. 1430–1439. IEEE Computer Society (2018)
30. Wang, L., Qiao, Y., Tang, X.: Action recognition with trajectory-pooled deep-convolutional descriptors. In: IEEE Conference on Computer Vision and Pattern Recognition, CVPR 2015, Boston, MA, USA, 7–12 June 2015, pp. 4305–4314. IEEE Computer Society (2015)
31. Wang, L., et al.: Temporal segment networks: towards good practices for deep action recognition. In: Leibe, B., Matas, J., Sebe, N., Welling, M. (eds.) ECCV 2016. LNCS, vol. 9912, pp. 20–36. Springer, Cham (2016). https://doi.org/10.1007/978-3-319-46484-8_2
32. Yeung, S., Russakovsky, O., Mori, G., Fei-Fei, L.: End-to-end learning of action detection from frame glimpses in videos. In: 2016 IEEE Conference on Computer Vision and Pattern Recognition, CVPR 2016, Las Vegas, NV, USA, 27–30 June 2016, pp. 2678–2687 (2016)
33. Zhao, Y., Xiong, Y., Wang, L., Wu, Z., Tang, X., Lin, D.: Temporal action detection with structured segment networks. In: IEEE International Conference on Computer Vision, ICCV 2017, Venice, Italy, 22–29 October 2017, pp. 2933–2942 (2017)

Towards Content-Independent Multi-Reference Super-Resolution: Adaptive Pattern Matching and Feature Aggregation

Xu Yan[1], Weibing Zhao[1], Kun Yuan[1,2], Ruimao Zhang[3], Zhen Li[1(✉)], and Shuguang Cui[1]

[1] Shenzhen Research Institute of Big Data,
The Chinese University of Hong Kong, Shenzhen, China
{xuyan1,weibingzhao}@link.cuhk.edu.cn, lizhen@cuhk.edu.cn
[2] University of Ottawa, Ottawa, Canada
[3] SenseTime Research, Shenzhen, China

Abstract. Recovering realistic textures from a largely down-sampled low resolution (LR) image with complicated patterns is a challenging problem in image super-resolution. This work investigates a novel multi-reference based super-resolution problem by proposing a Content Independent Multi-Reference Super-Resolution (CIMR-SR) model, which is able to adaptively match the visual pattern between references and target image in the low resolution and enhance the feature representation of the target image in the higher resolution. CIMR-SR significantly improves the flexibility of the recently proposed reference-based super-resolution (RefSR), which needs to select the specific high-resolution reference (e.g., content similarity, camera view and relative scale) for each target image. In practice, a universal reference pool (RP) is built up for recovering all LR targets by searching the local matched patterns. By exploiting feature-based patch searching and attentive reference feature aggregation, the proposed CIMR-SR generates realistic images with much better perceptual quality and richer fine-details. Extensive experiments demonstrate the proposed CIMR-SR outperforms state-of-the-art methods in both qualitative and quantitative reconstructions.

Keywords: Super-resolution · Content-independent multi-reference · Universal reference pool · Local feature enhancement

---

X. Yan and W. Zhao—Equal first authorship.

Electronic supplementary material The online version of this chapter (https://doi.org/10.1007/978-3-030-58595-2_4) contains supplementary material, which is available to authorized users.

A. Vedaldi et al. (Eds.): ECCV 2020, LNCS 12370, pp. 52–68, 2020.
https://doi.org/10.1007/978-3-030-58595-2_4

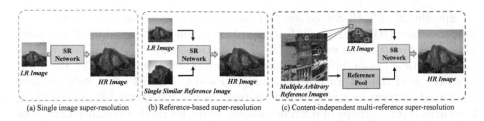

(a) Single image super-resolution   (b) Reference-based super-resolution   (c) Content-independent multi-reference super-resolution

Fig. 1. Comparison between single image super-resolution (SISR), reference-based super-resolution (RefSR) and our proposed content-independent multi-reference super-resolution (CIMR-SR). Within (c), the patches marked in the same color stand for the similar patterns in feature space.

1 Introduction

As one of the fundamental low-level vision problems, image super-resolution [4], which aims to reconstruct the high-resolution (HR) image from its low-resolution (LR) observation, has attracted increasing attention in both academic and industry. As shown in Fig. 1, the previous methods can be roughly divided into two categories, termed single image super-resolution (SISR) [3,27,31,34], and reference-based super-resolution (RefSR) [20,21,35,36]. For SISR, since the fine texture presented in original HR is usually lost in the LR, it becomes extremely difficult to recover fine textures when handling large up-scaling factors tasks. Therefore, RefSR [33,36] is meticulously proposed to address such issues by feature transferring between the HR reference images and the LR image. Although state-of-the-art RefSR significantly improves the quality of the reconstructed HR image, it is still suffering from the following problems to further improve the perceptual quality and generate richer fine-details.

- To get similar content or homogeneous patterns for LR images, most of the previous RefSR methods impose strict restrictions on the correlation between HR references and LR images, e.g., content similarity, camera view, and relative scale. However, such constraints are usually impractical in a lot of real applications.
- Different local regions within the LR image usually exhibit different reconstruction proprieties. The existing deep architectures lack the ability to adaptively enhance the feature representation from various patterns.

To address the above issues, in this work, we investigate a novel reference-based SR problem, that is, a universal multi-reference oriented image super-resolution, by proposing a Content-Independent Multi-Reference Super Resolution (CIMR-SR) model. As shown in Fig. 1, CIMR-SR breaks the restrictions of the previous RefSR methods on HR reference images by applying multiple arbitrary reference images. It could adaptively match local patterns from these content-independent reference images and aggregate them in the feature space to remarkably promote an ultimate representation ability of LR image.

Specifically, CIMR-SR consists of two major components, i.e., a universal reference pool (RP) and a local feature enhancement (LFE) module. The former is used to store various local patches (i.e., represented by the high-level feature representations) from the reference image to adaptively compensate for the information loss of the LR. In practice, the proposed CIMR-SR adaptively matches the visual patterns between the local patches in RP and target LR image. Then, it returns several groups of reference feature maps for further enhancement. The later is designed to aggregate the above-assembled feature maps and original feature representation of LR images. Unlike directly swapping the closest feature point on one single image [35], the LFE module achieves to aggregate similar feature points from multiple reference patches, making the network suitable for generating complex local details.

The **contributions** of this work are three folds. (1) To our best knowledge, this is the first work to address the multi-reference based image super-resolution by using deep learning with an end-to-end training mechanism. A novel CIMR-SR scheme is proposed to adaptively search the similar local visual patterns to enhance the feature representation of the target LR image. (2) A universal Reference Pool (RP) is constructed as a container for general local feature patterns and its memory burden is alleviated in conjunction with the diversity-insurance sampling strategy. In addition, an effective LFE module is firstly proposed to deal with feature aggregation for various patterns. (3) Extensive quantitative and qualitative experiments have demonstrated that the proposed CIMR-SR can generate realistic images with much better perceptual quality and richer fine-details, outperforming state-of-the-art methods.

2   Related Work

Deep Learning in SISR. Dong et al. [5] firstly attempted to learn an end-to-end mapping from HR-LR pairs by convolutional networks, various subsequent works tend to design the network deeper or wider to enhance the model representation capacity and computational efficiency. For example, a VGG style network VDSR [11] is proposed with a multi-scale training strategy to meet tasks at different scales. Furthermore, EDSR [12] is proposed by stacking modified residual blocks [8] to significantly improve the performance. As the depth of network plays a vital role in SISR, RCAN [33] improves the inferior performance with a very deep model by adopting attention mechanism and shared-source skip connections to bypass redundant information. SAN [3] further use the second-order attention mechanism, and implement a non-locally enhanced residual group for long-distance dependency learning.

In general, the approaches mentioned above aim at minimizing reconstructed loss with no prior included. In addition, some other works incorporate the prior in perceptual-related constraints to recover more visually plausible SR images. For instance, SRGAN [14] adds perceptual loss and generative adversarial strategy to address the issue of over-smoothing in SISR. SFTGAN [23] incorporates segmentation maps to induce categorical priors to generate offline transformation parameters for spatial-wise feature modulation. In this way, perceptual-related priors were implicitly incorporated to achieve better visual quality. However, although using adversarial strategies increases plausible visual quality, it results in the quantitative criteria (i.e., PSNR) reduction and fake textures generation.

Besides, there are some previous works focus on the LR images with a more realistic degradation (called blind SR). Specifically, blind SR introduces the complex blur kernels (e.g., motion blur in [27]) or DSLR camera's degradation process (e.g., zooming in [32], ISP pipeline in [28]) to produce the LR-HR paired training set instead of the fixed bicubic kernel. Thus, the assumption about the degradation process limits it into specific scenarios (e.g., specific camera). On the contrary, this paper focuses on how to transfer features between LR and multiple external references with normal SISR training strategies.

Reference-Based Super-Resolution. In contrast to SISR taking only a single LR image as the input, recent works use additional images from different views or scenes to assist the SR process, called RefSR. Traditional methods use sparse signal representation and linear combination [29] or example-based method [7] for reference utilization without data-driven training process. According to where the additional images come from, RefSR could be divided into two categories: internal and external RefSR. Compared with internal RefSR [6,9,20,21] utilizes the self-similarity of images to refer patches from itself, references in external RefSR could be acquired in multiple ways, such as from adjacent frames in a video [16], from web retrieval and external database [30]. As for external RefSR methods, a typical work is CrossNet [36], which learns the alignment parameters from optical flow to warp the feature between input LR and the reference image. However, this model highly depends on the assumption that the references need to be well aligned with the LR images. To address the alignment issue, SRNTT [35] refers to the work in style transfer and swap the most similar feature in the neural space during the SR process, which enables the learning of long-distance dependency and complicated feature transferring process. However, patch swap strategy limits itself to the closest feature with a narrow field of view in feature space, thus hampering the feature transferring process.

3 Methods

Given the specified down-scale factor s, the proposed CIMR-SR aims to estimate the SR image I^{SR} with the size $H \times W \times 3$ from its LR counterpart I^{LR} with the size $H/s \times W/s \times 3$ and the given M arbitrary content-independent reference images $\boldsymbol{I}^{Ref} = \{I_i^{Ref}\}_{i=1}^M$. To achieve the above goal, we firstly construct a reference pool (RP) in Sect. 3.1, which contains feature points converted from the features of reference patches. It provides additional information for detailed texture generation. And then we propose the local feature enhancement (LFE) module in Sect. 3.2, which selects reference features and aggregates group features by the effective feature searching and the feature aggregation mechanisms.

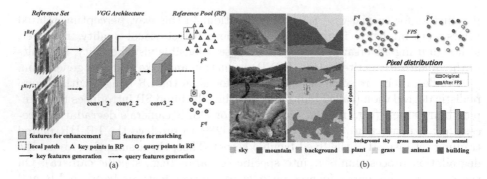

Fig. 2. (a) **RP generation.** Multiple HR-Refs (I^{Ref}) and LR-Refs ($I^{Ref\downarrow\uparrow}$) images are transferred from the RGB space to the feature space through a pre-trained CNN. Within the RP, each 3×3 local patch on feature map `conv3_2` is reshaped to a feature point and acts as a query feature, which can be mapped to larger patches on `conv2_2` or `conv1_2` stored as key features. (b) **Farthest Point Sampling (FPS).** The left feature point set indicates the original feature distribution, while the right is uniformly distributed over categories after FPS. Here different colors indicate different semantics.

3.1   Reference Pool

Reference Pool (RP) is constructed for storing all reference information from multiple HR-Refs. Therefore, it needs to satisfy the following criteria:

- C1: Universal content-independent references should be collected and there is no restriction on pixel alignment with LR image;
- C2: Efficient and accurate feature searching and aggregation should be supported while exploiting such RP as external information.

C1. To satisfy condition C1, we map multiple reference images to a high-dimensional feature space offline without any pixel alignment restriction. As shown in Fig. 2(a), for each reference image HR-Ref I_i^{Ref}, the j-th patch $I_{i,j}^{Ref}$ is transferred to a feature point through a pre-trained CNN, where i and j denote the index of reference image and patches. Concretely, there are two different kinds of features: which termed to the feature points generated from patches of HR-Refs and blurred LR-Refs as *key features* and *query features*, respectively. The *key features* are beneficial to restore high-resolution information and will be saved for feature aggregation, while *query features* will be used in feature matching with the LR image. Note that each LR-Ref is obtained by down-sampling and up-sampling corresponding HR-Ref to match the frequency band of the I^{LR} through bicubic interpolation. Therefore, the key features F_i^k and query features F_i^q for the i-th HR-Ref are obtained by,

$$F_i^k = \mathcal{F}(I_i^{Ref})_{l_k}, \ F_i^q = \mathcal{F}(I_i^{Ref\downarrow\uparrow})_{l_q}, F_i^k \in \mathbb{R}^{N^k \times D^k}, \ F_i^q \in \mathbb{R}^{N^q \times D^q}, \quad (1)$$

where l_k and l_q are specified layers from a feature extractor $\mathcal{F}$ (e.g., `conv3_2`), sign $\downarrow$ and $\uparrow$ denotes down-sample and up-sample operations. Besides, output F_i^k

and F_i^q can also be seen as feature space point sets, which have point numbers N^k and N^q with dimensions D^k and D^q. Here D^k and D^q are the product of feature dimension of specified layers and the size of local patches on feature maps. Therefore, we break the restriction of pixel alignment and transfer image information into feature space. Furthermore, the constrains about the reference images in previous methods can be solved by building a universal reference pool (RP). Once arbitrary HR-Refs are offered, the RP would provide diverse patterns with various semantics and textures for LR reconstruction.

C2. It is non-trivial to build a universal RP not only considering the memory limitation and time efficiency but also satisfying the constrain C2. Concretely, the distribution in RP tends to be locally dense and uneven, easily dominated by monotonous textures, which increases the computational cost and difficulty for conventional feature searching and aggregation. To solve the issues, we exploit Farthest Point Sampling (FPS) algorithm [18] on query features for RP construction.

Firstly, we collect multiple HR-Refs as $\boldsymbol{I}^{Ref} = \{I_i^{Ref}\}_{i=1}^M$ and transfer them into feature space point set $\boldsymbol{F}^q \in \mathbb{R}^{N \times D^q}$ by Eq. (1). Here N is the total point number of all query features, which will increase as the number of HR-Ref images increases. After that, we sample a subset of N' points ($N' < N$) as $\hat{\boldsymbol{F}}^q$ through FPS sampling. In each iteration FPS selects a new feature point from original features, it will choose the feature that has the farthest distance between all existing sampled features. It can achieve an approximate uniform sampling in feature space and has better coverage of the entire point set. Therefore, it is a good manner to reduce redundancy in a certain space. As illustrated in Fig. 2(b), before the FPS, most of the pixels in the image belong to the sky and grass, which share similar features without complex texture. It leads the SR network dominated by monotonous textures and prone to a sub-optimal reconstruction. With the assistance of FPS, we can keep the diversity of features while reducing local redundancy, i.e., the distribution of feature points for each semantic and texture remains appropriately uniform. This resolves the efficiency and accuracy problems of RP, which benefits the subsequent LFE module.

3.2 Local Feature Enhancement Module

Be equipped with various features provided in RP, it is non-trivial to aggregate the high-dimensional features for each local region of LR effectively and efficiently. Especially, non-parametric operation, i.e., patch swapping [35], only considering the most similar features, which undoubtedly damages the diversity of features enhancement. To address the problems mentioned above, the Local Feature Enhancement (LFE) module is introduced to effectively search usable features and aggregate them for local regions of the LR image, thus producing enhanced features for reconstruction. Specifically, LFE contains two parts:

- *Feature Searching* retrieves K most similar feature points from query features $\hat{\boldsymbol{F}}^q$ for each local patch of input LR (see Fig. 3);

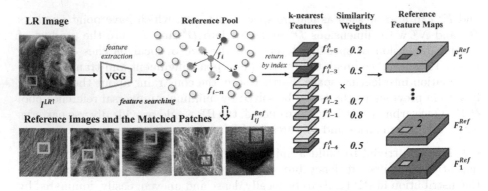

Fig. 3. Feature searching and realignment with $K = 5$. It shows features of i-th LR local patch (blue) corresponds to 5 points in query features (e.g., none-white points), which will generate 5 selected reference feature maps by assembling the key features. Besides, i-th position on reference feature maps can be obtained by multiplying the selected key features with their corresponding similarity weights. (Color figure online)

- *Feature Aggregation* aligns and fuses the searched key features and generates enhanced feature maps for HR reconstruction (see Fig. 4).

Feature Searching. Before matching most similar features, we firstly apply bicubic up-sampling on the LR image I^{LR} to get an up-scaled one $I^{LR\uparrow}$ with the same spatial size as I^{HR}. Then, we use the same feature extractor $\mathcal{F}$ to generate LR features $F = \mathcal{F}(I^{LR\uparrow})_{l_q}$ with size $N^l \times D^q$, where each feature point $f_i \in F$ represents a 3×3 patch on the LR feature map. Then, $\forall f_i \in F$, we find indices $\mathcal{N}(f_i)$ of K most similar features in $\hat{F}^q$ by ranking their normalized inner product similarities [35]. After feature searching, index vectors $\{\mathcal{N}(f_i)\}_{i=1}^{N^l}$ are stacked by rows into a global index matrix $\mathcal{N}(F)$.

Feature Aggregation. After feature searching, we use global index matrix $\mathcal{N}(F)$ to choose key features according to their corresponding query features (see the mapping in Fig. 2(a)). The overlaps of adjacent key features on the rearranged feature map will be divided by their overlap number. Then, we obtain K aligned reference feature maps $\boldsymbol{F}^A = \{F_k^A\}_{k=1}^K$. Besides, the normalized similarity score of each query feature between LR features is also rearranged to K aligned similarity matrix $\boldsymbol{S}^A = \{S_k^A\}_{k=1}^K$. The i-th element of the k-th matrix S_k^A records the inner product between the k-th query feature patch and the i-th LR feature patch, which is corresponding to the i-th patch in $\boldsymbol{F}_k^A$. Finally, we generate reference feature maps by multiplying aligned reference feature maps with corresponding element-wise similarity. Concretely, the i-th patch of the k-th reference feature map is obtained by

$$f_{i-k}^{Ref} = f_{i-k}^A \cdot S_{i-k}^A, \ k = 1, ..., K \tag{2}$$

Therefore, the LFE module can be constructed as a general component for any SR backbone (collectively called SRNet). Figure 4 shows that conducting a

LFE module after the last pixel shuffle layer of SRNet (the feature map with original scale). For input LR image I^{LR}, it obtains K reference feature maps $\boldsymbol{F}^{Ref}$ through feature searching. After that, to obtain enhanced features, it aggregate features by using hidden output of the SRNet (F^H) and K reference feature maps,

$$F^P = \mathcal{P}_{k=1}^K \{\mathcal{R}(F^H \| F_k^{Ref})\}, \tag{3}$$

where $(\cdot \| \cdot)$ denotes concatenate operation and $\mathcal{P}, \mathcal{R}$ denotes element-wise addition and passing through share-weighted residual blocks.

As shown in Fig. 4 and Eq. (3), the feature aggregation firstly concatenates the hidden features of SRNet with each reference feature map respectively. Then a set of share-weighted residual blocks is used for each combined feature map. Finally, a fusion function aggregates information of all reference features to a single fused feature map, which retains the most informative texture feature in all reference feature maps and greatly facilitates the reconstruction of HR. Besides, a skip-connection will be used between hidden features and fused features, generating an enhanced feature map F^E by conducting element-wise addition between F^P and F^H. After a convolution layer changes the channel dimension, the output I^{SR} can be obtained. It should be noted that here we just give a simple case of the LFE module, which is a plug-and-play component and can be used in other positions of SRNet (i.e., all of three scales in 4× upscaling).

3.3   Loss Function

To recover the mapping from LR to HR and leverage the natural texture from references, l_1-norm content loss $\mathcal{L}_c$ is adopted to optimize weights of our model,

$$\mathcal{L}_c = \| I^{SR} - I^{HR} \|_1, \tag{4}$$

where I^{SR} and I^{HR} denotes output and ground truth of single sample.

Furthermore, we modify texture matching loss [19] to multi-reference scenario and take into account the texture difference between I^{SR} and F^{Ref}. We require the texture of neural feature space $\mathcal{F}(I^{SR})$ to be close to each aligned reference feature maps, where $\mathcal{F}(\cdot)_{l_k}$ denotes the same feature extractor in key features generation. Specifically, we define a texture loss $\mathcal{L}_{tex}$ as

$$\mathcal{L}_{tex} = \frac{1}{K} \sum_{k=1}^K \| Gr(\mathcal{F}(I^{SR})_{l_k} \cdot S_k^A) - Gr(F_k^A \cdot S_k^A) \|_F, \tag{5}$$

where $Gr(\cdot)$ computes the Gram matrix, and K normalized similarity matrix defined in Eq. (2) are used to determine the effect of each position. Intuitively, textures dissimilar to I^{SR} will have lower weight, and thus receiving lower penalty in texture learning.

Apart from content loss and texture loss, generative adversarial loss [10] $\mathcal{L}_{adv}$ will also be utilized upon the WGAN [1] with gradient penalty. This helps stabilize the training process and improve the visual quality of synthesised images.

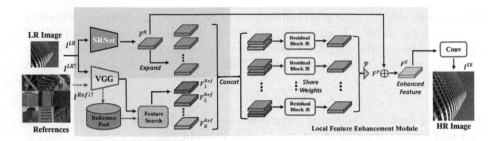

Fig. 4. Inner structure of LFE module. Blue and grey part illustrate the SISR network and the procedure of feature searching from RP detailed in Fig. 2 and 3. Yellow part depicts the Local Feature Enhancement (LFE) module. LFE module can be a general component embedded in any SRNet, which aggregates hidden output of SRNet with reference feature maps to an enhanced feature map. (Color figure online)

Furthermore, we adopt the perceptual loss [2] to motivate our model inclined to the solutions in the manifold of natural images. The perceptual loss $\mathcal{L}_p$ measures the distance in the feature space and enforce the feature alignment. Combining all together, the overall loss function of our model is finally designed as

$$\mathcal{L} = \mathcal{L}_c + \gamma_{tex}\mathcal{L}_{tex} + \gamma_{adv}\mathcal{L}_{adv} + \gamma_p\mathcal{L}_p, \qquad (6)$$

where weights γ_p, γ_{adv} and γ_{tex} are $1e-4$, $1e-6$ and $1e-4$, respectively.

3.4 Network Architecture

During the experiment, we use MDSR [15] as our SRNet. We set the residual block number equal to 80 and hidden layer channel number equal to 64. Considering the efficiency and effeteness, we use $K = 3$ for feature searching. The feature extractor VGG-19 is pre-trained on ImageNet, whose conv3_2 is used for query feature while all of conv1_2, conv2_2 and conv3_2 are responsible for key feature representations. Therefore, for the 4× upscaling SR, we conduct three LFE modules on different scales. On each scale feature map (i.e., 4× down-scale, 2× down-scale or original scale), we generate K reference feature maps according to search results of query features. The architecture of share-weighted residue blocks is the same as the neural texture transfer in [35].

For RP generation, we directly select 300 HR-Refs from Outdoor Scene (OST) [23] as our reference, which is a dataset for scene images reconstruction. It contains seven categories, sky, mountain, plant, grass, water, animal, and building. For each category, there are 1k to 2k images that only cover that category. The total amount of the training set is 10,324. Here, we adopt a training set with explicit semantic prior for our RP construction. We firstly randomly crop 1,000 HR candidates with size 128 × 128 in each category, then we use the FPS algorithm to sample final 300 of them as our initial reference pool.

4   Experiment Results

4.1   Dataset

Following the setting in [35,36], we trained our model on CUFED5 dataset and test with down-scale factor 4× on three standard benchmark datasets: Urban100 [9], Sun80 [22] and CUFED5 test set. Noted that CUFED5 only contains 13,761 160 × 160 input-reference pairs as the training set and 126 images with different sizes as the test set. In CUFED5, most images have relatively low resolution, and there are many moving people and complicated objects in each image, which makes the training and testing on CUFED5 extremely challenging.

4.2   Implementation Details

To further verify the rationality of our model, we test our model on both content-independent and content-similar references. For the former, we use our RP as extra information, which will be used in both training and evaluation processes. As for content-similar references, we conduct a similar training strategy in [35] and use reference images with different similarity levels during evaluation.

Content-Independent References. Before the training, we use the pre-trained VGG to collect key features and query features offline from the initial RP. Then we use Farthest Point Sampling with the sample ratio factor $r = 16$ on both query and key features to generate final RP and save key features for further usage. After that, we conduct feature searching and save the global indices $\mathcal{N}(F)$ for each LR image. We adopt strategy mentioned in [35] to match K query features with the largest inner product for each LR patch, which can be implemented by a convolution operator using the LR patch as the kernel. During the training, we feed input images and corresponding global indices into our model, and the model selects features from preserved key features and synthesizes the aligned reference feature maps. Unlike [35] uses offline storage for feature maps of the entire training set, we only save entire key features and the mapping index of each local region. This strategy greatly reduces memory consumption and achieves efficiency in data augmentation at the same time. Besides, calculating indices offline will notably accelerate training speed and require almost no extra time in data feeding. More detailed training protocol will be described in the supplementary material.

Content-Similar References. The overall strategy is consistent with the process mentioned above, but here we use given reference images to generate and save aligned reference feature maps offline rather than global indices. At the same time, specific data augmentation (the "warp" in the caption of Table 2) is conducted on each reference image.

4.3   Quantitative Evaluation

Content-Independent References. Following standard protocols, we obtain all LR images by bicubic down-scaling (4×) from the HR images. For fair

Table 1. PSNR/SSIM comparison among different SR methods on four datasets: methods are grouped by SISR (top) and RefSR (bottom), and the best result is in bold. All the SR results are evaluated by PSNR and SSIM metrics on the Y channel of transformed YCbCr space.

Algorithm	CUFED5	Urban100	Sun80
Bicubic	24.18/0.684	23.14/0.674	27.24/0.739
SRCNN [4]	25.33/0.745	24.41/0.738	28.26/0.781
SCN [26]	25.45/0.743	24.52/0.741	27.93/0.786
DRCN [12]	25.26/0.734	25.14/0.760	27.84/0.785
LapSRN [13]	24.92/0.730	24.26/0.735	27.70/0.783
MDSR [15]	25.93/0.777	25.51/0.783	28.52/0.792
EDSR [15]	25.90/0.776	25.50/0.783	28.49/0.789
SRGAN [14]	24.40/0.702	24.07/0.729	26.76/0.725
RCAN [33]	**26.32/0.789**	**25.65/0.785**	**28.67/0.795**
SAN [3]	26.29/0.789	25.63/0.783	28.66/0.795
LandMark [30]	24.91/0.718	-	27.68/0.776
CrossNet [36]	25.48/0.764	25.11/0.764	28.52/0.793
SRNTT [35]	25.61/0.764	25.09/0.774	27.59/0.756
CIMR	26.16/0.781	25.24/0.778	29.67/0.806
SRNTT*-ℓ_2 [35]	25.98/0.776	25.54/0.784	28.49/0.791
SRNTT-ℓ_2 [35]	26.24/0.784	25.50/0.783	28.54/0.793
CIMR-ℓ_2	**26.35/0.789**	**25.77/0.792**	**30.07/0.813**

comparison on PSNR/SSIM with those methods mainly minimizing MSE, e.g., MDSR [15] and SRNTT-ℓ_2 [35], we first train a PSNR-oriented model emphasizing on the ℓ_2 minimization, called CIMR-ℓ_2. Next, we train a GAN-based model named CIMR, focusing on the aspect of visual quality compared with other methods with GAN fine-tuning. Since [35] uses content-similar references in their paper, we implement SRNTT*-ℓ_2 by using reference patches in initial RP to compare their model in content-independent references scenario. Specifically, we use FPS to sample 80 patches from initial RP as their references (i.e., the maximum amount of references SRNTT could hold). At the same time, we compare the result reported in their paper.

As shown in Table 1, it is obvious that our model gains higher scores on all the benchmark datasets. We achieve better performance than SRNTT-ℓ_2 on CUFED5 even if they use references with high similarity of input, which is usually invalid and impractical in the real world. Despite the nonexistence of references with high similarity, it is surprising to notice our performance is much higher than previous methods on Sun80. This success may owe to that many outdoor-related textures like the wave, sky and vegetation are adaptively covered in our constructed RP, strengthening the applicability for outdoor sce-

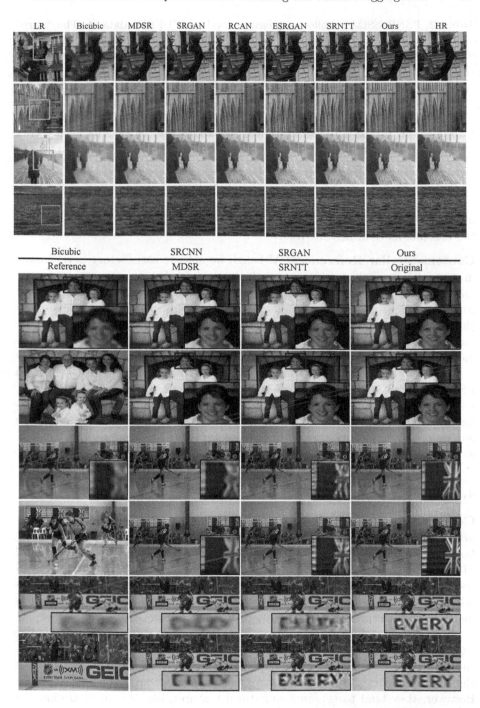

Fig. 5. Upper part (content-independent references): visualization of 003, 032 and 065 in Urban100 and N00_17_0_34matches29 in CUFED [25]. **Lower part** (content-similar references): visualization of 047_0, 044_0, 002_0 in CUFED5, where our CIMR-SR and SRNTT both use content-similar references (i.e., 047_3, 044_3, 002_1).

Table 2. PSNR/SSIM at different reference levels on CUFED5 dataset. The "warp" denotes the data augmentation with random translation (quarter to half width/height), rotation (10–30°), and scaling (1.2–2.0× upscaling) from the original HR image.

Algorithm	HR (warp)	L1	L2	L3	L4	All
CrossNet	25.49/.764	25.48/.764	25.48/.764	25.47/.763	25.46/.763	-
SRNTT-ℓ_2	29.29/.889	26.15/.781	26.04/.776	25.98/.775	25.95/.774	26.24/.784
CIMR-ℓ_2	29.82/.903	**27.32/.805**	**27.05/.799**	**26.92/.796**	**26.86/.794**	**27.44/.810**
SRNTT	**33.87/.959**	25.42/.758	25.32/.752	25.24/.751	25.23/.750	25.61/.764
CIMR	30.73/.918	26.50/.786	26.47/.784	26.45/.784	26.44/.784	26.63/.790

narios. Furthermore, our method achieves a large improvement compared with the baseline method MDSR [15].

Content-Similar References. Although we achieve satisfactory performance in content-independent references evaluation, to further investigate our performance when meeting content-similar references, we designed the experiment using reference images with different similarity levels. Specifically, there are four similar level HR-Refs in the CUFED5 test set, ranked by SIFT [17] feature matching, which decline from L1 to L4. We also compare results using augmented HR and all the four HR-Refs in Table 2.

As shown in Table 2, we compare CIMR, CrossNet, and SRNTT in both PSNR-oriented and GAN implementation, where our results are much higher. For the HR (warp) column in Table 2, the ability of our model for directly transferring information on HR itself is slightly worse than SRNTT. This is because our model finds multiple reference patches for each LR local region, but it is worthy note that there is no practical value in using HR itself for SR.

4.4 Qualitative Evaluation

Content-Independent References. For the fair comparison, the state-of-the-art SISR and RefSR methods we choose are MDSR [15], SRGAN [14], ESRGAN [24] and RCAN [33], among which RCAN and MDSR are the most powerful SISR methods with the highest PSNR/SSIM scores. The SRGAN and ESRGAN could achieve a satisfactory performance on visual quality because of adversarial learning. SRNTT* with the same setting in the quantitative experiment is included as the representative of state-of-the-art RefSR.

As shown in the upper part of Fig. 5, although PSNR-oriented methods like RCAN and MDSR could present higher criteria, they tend to produce blurry textures while preserving sharp edges. SRGAN and ESRGAN could largely improve the high-frequency details since the generative adversarial learning strategy. However, they tend to generate unnatural textures, like the noise around the sculpture. SRNTT [35] is a powerful technique that could produce an extremely visually pleasing result and high criteria when the HR-Ref images and the LR image share the same scene. However, due to the fact that our sampled patches

Table 3. Comparison of adopting different `conv` layers for CIMR. Left part shows PSNR at different reference levels on CUFED5 test set. Right part describes running time, including offline feature searching and forward inference time.

Method-ℓ_2	HR(warp)	L1	L2	L3	L4	FS	Forward
SRNTT	29.29	26.15	26.04	25.98	25.95	2.726	**0.351**
conv1	28.24	26.97	26.89	26.84	26.79	2.045	0.783
conv2	28.77	27.06	26.93	26.92	26.85	1.551	0.535
conv3	27.31	26.26	26.06	26.02	26.03	**1.020**	0.361
conv2/3	27.87	27.27	27.01	26.89	26.82	2.571	1.077
conv1/2/3	**29.82**	**27.32**	**27.05**	**26.92**	**26.86**	4.616	1.551

for SRNTT include some water wave patterns from the swimming pool, the generated water waves in SRNTT are a little bit brighter and tend to present monotonous blue, which indicates the inferior feature transferring capability of patch swapping in SRNTT. In contrast, our method employed with RP and LFE module could lead to more natural and realistic textures when reconstructing the head of the sculpture and boardwalk.

Content-Similar References. We further compare qualitative evaluation with similar references. We selected three samples from CUFED5 and compared SRCNN [4], SRGAN [14], SRNTT [35], and our baseline MDSR [15] in the lower part of Fig. 5. We achieve better results in texture details and a huge improvement over baseline. More visualization results will be provided in the supplementary material.

4.5   Ablation Study

In this section, we investigate the effectiveness of utilizing multiple scales key features as compared to using a single scale. We use the feature maps extracted from `conv1_2`, `conv2_2` and `conv3_2` to generate key features and feed them into corresponding LFE modules. In addition to quantitative metrics, comparison in the speed of feature searching (FS, also represents patch swap in SRNTT) (s/sample), model forwarding (s/batch) during the training process with batch size 8 are applied to measure the efficiency of our model.

In Table 3, it shows that adding key features in 2× scale hidden layer of SRNet obtains the best improvement while using key features from `conv3_2` perform the worst. Furthermore, in our proposed CIMR-SR model, we also provide users with more flexible options to achieve further improvement according to specific requirements, at the cost of importing more LFE modules and more computations. It should be noted that even if we only use the key features from `conv3_2`, we can achieve comparable results with SRNTT while increase the speed by twice. These results fully demonstrate the effectiveness of our model to enhance LR from multiple similar patches in feature space.

5   Conclusion

To our best knowledge, this is the first work to deal with arbitrary multiple references oriented image super-resolution problem with deep learning. To achieve this goal, we proposed a Content-Independent Multi-Reference Super-Resolution (CIMR-SR) model. It can adaptively match local patterns from a universal reference pool and aggregate them in the feature space by the LFE module to strengthen the discriminative learning ability on representing the LR image. Extensive experiments demonstrate that our proposed CIMR-SR model can achieve better quantitative results and generate realistic images with more details as well, outperforming the state-of-the-art methods.

Acknowledgements. The work was supported in part by the Key Area R&D Program of Guangdong Province with grant No. 2018B030338001, by the National Key R&D Program of China with grant No. 2018YFB1800800, by Natural Science Foundation of China with grant NSFC-61629101, by Guangdong Zhujiang Project No. 2017ZT07X152, by Shenzhen Key Lab Fund No. ZDSYS201707 251409055, by NSFC-Youth 61902335, Guangdong Province Basic and Applied Basic Research Fund Project Regional Joint Fund-Key Project No. 2019B1515120039 and CCF-Tencent Open Fund.

References

1. Arjovsky, M., Chintala, S., Bottou, L.: Wasserstein GAN. arXiv preprint arXiv:1701.07875 (2017)
2. Bruna, J., Sprechmann, P., LeCun, Y.: Super-resolution with deep convolutional sufficient statistics. arXiv preprint arXiv:1511.05666 (2015)
3. Dai, T., Cai, J., Zhang, Y., Xia, S.T., Zhang, L.: Second-order attention network for single image super-resolution. In: Proceedings of the IEEE Conference on Computer Vision and Pattern Recognition, pp. 11065–11074 (2019)
4. Dong, C., Loy, C.C., He, K., Tang, X.: Learning a deep convolutional network for image super-resolution. In: Fleet, D., Pajdla, T., Schiele, B., Tuytelaars, T. (eds.) ECCV 2014. LNCS, vol. 8692, pp. 184–199. Springer, Cham (2014). https://doi.org/10.1007/978-3-319-10593-2_13
5. Dong, C., Loy, C.C., He, K., Tang, X.: Image super-resolution using deep convolutional networks. IEEE Trans. Pattern Anal. Mach. Intell. **38**(2), 295–307 (2015)
6. Freedman, G., Fattal, R.: Image and video upscaling from local self-examples. ACM Trans. Graph. (TOG) **30**(2), 12 (2011)
7. Freeman, W.T., Jones, T.R., Pasztor, E.C.: Example-based super-resolution. IEEE Comput. Graphics Appl. **22**(2), 56–65 (2002)
8. He, K., Zhang, X., Ren, S., Sun, J.: Deep residual learning for image recognition. In: Proceedings of the IEEE Conference on Computer Vision and Pattern Recognition, pp. 770–778 (2016)
9. Huang, J.B., Singh, A., Ahuja, N.: Single image super-resolution from transformed self-exemplars. In: Proceedings of the IEEE Conference on Computer Vision and Pattern Recognition, pp. 5197–5206 (2015)
10. Isola, P., Zhu, J.Y., Zhou, T., Efros, A.A.: Image-to-image translation with conditional adversarial networks. In: Proceedings of the IEEE Conference on Computer Vision and Pattern Recognition, pp. 1125–1134 (2017)

11. Kim, J., Kwon Lee, J., Mu Lee, K.: Accurate image super-resolution using very deep convolutional networks. In: Proceedings of the IEEE Conference on Computer Vision and Pattern Recognition, pp. 1646–1654 (2016)
12. Kim, J., Kwon Lee, J., Mu Lee, K.: Deeply-recursive convolutional network for image super-resolution. In: Proceedings of the IEEE Conference on Computer Vision and Pattern Recognition, pp. 1637–1645 (2016)
13. Lai, W.S., Huang, J.B., Ahuja, N., Yang, M.H.: Deep Laplacian pyramid networks for fast and accurate super-resolution. In: Proceedings of the IEEE Conference on Computer Vision and Pattern Recognition, pp. 624–632 (2017)
14. Ledig, C., et al.: Photo-realistic single image super-resolution using a generative adversarial network. In: Proceedings of the IEEE Conference on Computer Vision and Pattern Recognition, pp. 4681–4690 (2017)
15. Lim, B., Son, S., Kim, H., Nah, S., Mu Lee, K.: Enhanced deep residual networks for single image super-resolution. In: Proceedings of the IEEE Conference on Computer Vision and Pattern Recognition Workshops, pp. 136–144 (2017)
16. Liu, C., Sun, D.: A Bayesian approach to adaptive video super resolution. In: CVPR 2011, pp. 209–216. IEEE (2011)
17. Lowe, D.G.: Object recognition from local scale-invariant features. In: Proceedings of the Seventh IEEE International Conference on Computer Vision, vol. 2, pp. 1150–1157. IEEE (1999)
18. Qi, C.R., Su, H., Mo, K., Guibas, L.J.: PointNet: deep learning on point sets for 3D classification and segmentation. In: Proceedings of the IEEE Conference on Computer Vision and Pattern Recognition, pp. 652–660 (2017)
19. Sajjadi, M.S., Scholkopf, B., Hirsch, M.: EnhanceNet: single image super-resolution through automated texture synthesis. In: Proceedings of the IEEE International Conference on Computer Vision, pp. 4491–4500 (2017)
20. Shaham, T.R., Dekel, T., Michaeli, T.: SinGAN: learning a generative model from a single natural image. In: Proceedings of the IEEE International Conference on Computer Vision, pp. 4570–4580 (2019)
21. Shocher, A., Cohen, N., Irani, M.: "Zero-shot" super-resolution using deep internal learning. In: Proceedings of the IEEE Conference on Computer Vision and Pattern Recognition, pp. 3118–3126 (2018)
22. Sun, L., Hays, J.: Super-resolution from internet-scale scene matching. In: 2012 IEEE International Conference on Computational Photography (ICCP), pp. 1–12. IEEE (2012)
23. Wang, X., Yu, K., Dong, C., Change Loy, C.: Recovering realistic texture in image super-resolution by deep spatial feature transform. In: Proceedings of the IEEE Conference on Computer Vision and Pattern Recognition, pp. 606–615 (2018)
24. Wang, X., et al.: ESRGAN: enhanced super-resolution generative adversarial networks. In: Leal-Taixé, L., Roth, S. (eds.) ECCV 2018. LNCS, vol. 11133, pp. 63–79. Springer, Cham (2019). https://doi.org/10.1007/978-3-030-11021-5_5
25. Wang, Y., Lin, Z., Shen, X., Mech, R., Miller, G., Cottrell, G.W.: Event-specific image importance. In: The IEEE Conference on Computer Vision and Pattern Recognition (CVPR) (2016)
26. Wang, Z., Liu, D., Yang, J., Han, W., Huang, T.: Deep networks for image super-resolution with sparse prior. In: Proceedings of the IEEE International Conference on Computer Vision, pp. 370–378 (2015)
27. Xu, X., Ma, Y., Sun, W.: Towards real scene super-resolution with raw images. In: Proceedings of the IEEE Conference on Computer Vision and Pattern Recognition, pp. 1723–1731 (2019)

28. Xu, X., Sun, D., Pan, J., Zhang, Y., Pfister, H., Yang, M.H.: Learning to super-resolve blurry face and text images. In: Proceedings of the IEEE International Conference on Computer Vision, pp. 251–260 (2017)
29. Yang, J., Wright, J., Huang, T.S., Ma, Y.: Image super-resolution via sparse representation. IEEE Trans. Image Process. **19**(11), 2861–2873 (2010)
30. Yue, H., Sun, X., Yang, J., Wu, F.: Landmark image super-resolution by retrieving web images. IEEE Trans. Image Process. **22**(12), 4865–4878 (2013)
31. Zhang, K., Zuo, W., Zhang, L.: Learning a single convolutional super-resolution network for multiple degradations. In: Proceedings of the IEEE Conference on Computer Vision and Pattern Recognition, pp. 3262–3271 (2018)
32. Zhang, X., Chen, Q., Ng, R., Koltun, V.: Zoom to learn, learn to zoom. In: Proceedings of the IEEE Conference on Computer Vision and Pattern Recognition, pp. 3762–3770 (2019)
33. Zhang, Y., Li, K., Li, K., Wang, L., Zhong, B., Fu, Y.: Image super-resolution using very deep residual channel attention networks. In: Ferrari, V., Hebert, M., Sminchisescu, C., Weiss, Y. (eds.) ECCV 2018. LNCS, vol. 11211, pp. 294–310. Springer, Cham (2018). https://doi.org/10.1007/978-3-030-01234-2_18
34. Zhang, Y., Tian, Y., Kong, Y., Zhong, B., Fu, Y.: Residual dense network for image super-resolution. In: Proceedings of the IEEE Conference on Computer Vision and Pattern Recognition, pp. 2472–2481 (2018)
35. Zhang, Z., Wang, Z., Lin, Z., Qi, H.: Image super-resolution by neural texture transfer. In: Proceedings of the IEEE Conference on Computer Vision and Pattern Recognition, pp. 7982–7991 (2019)
36. Zheng, H., Ji, M., Wang, H., Liu, Y., Fang, L.: CrossNet: an end-to-end reference-based super resolution network using cross-scale warping. In: Ferrari, V., Hebert, M., Sminchisescu, C., Weiss, Y. (eds.) ECCV 2018. LNCS, vol. 11210, pp. 87–104. Springer, Cham (2018). https://doi.org/10.1007/978-3-030-01231-1_6

Inference Graphs for CNN Interpretation

Yael Konforti$^{(\boxtimes)}$, Alon Shpigler$^{(\boxtimes)}$, Boaz Lerner$^{(\boxtimes)}$, and Aharon Bar-Hillel$^{(\boxtimes)}$

Ben-Gurion University of the Negev, Beer Sheva, Israel
{yaelkonf,alonshp}@post.bgu.ac.il, {boaz,barhille}@bgu.ac.il

Abstract. Convolutional neural networks (CNNs) have achieved superior accuracy in many visual related tasks. However, the inference process through intermediate layers is opaque, making it difficult to interpret such networks or develop trust in their operation. We propose to model the network hidden layers activity using probabilistic models. The activity patterns in layers of interest are modeled as Gaussian mixture models, and transition probabilities between clusters in consecutive modeled layers are estimated. Based on maximum-likelihood considerations, nodes and paths relevant for network prediction are chosen, connected, and visualized as an inference graph. We show that such graphs are useful for understanding the general inference process of a class, as well as explaining decisions the network makes regarding specific images.

1 Introduction

Thanks to their impressive performance, convolutional neural networks (CNNs) are the leading architecture for tasks in computer vision [1–3]. However, due to their complex end-to-end training and architecture, understanding of their decision-making process and task assignment across hidden layers is lacking. This turns network interpretability into a difficult problem, and undermines usage of deep networks when high reliability and inference transparency are required. Understanding CNN reasoning by decomposing it into layer-wise stages can provide insights about cases of failure, and reveal weak spots in the network architecture, training scheme, or data-collection mechanism. In turn, these insights can lead to more robust networks and develop more trust in CNN decisions.

As we see it, enabling human understanding of the deep network inference process requires facing a main challenge of transforming CNN activities into discrete representations amendable to human reasoning. Deep networks operate through a series of distributed layer representations. Human language, however, is made up of discrete symbols, i.e., words, having meaning grounded by their

---

Y. Konforti and A. Shpigler—Equal contribution.
Code for inference graphs algorithm released at github.com/yaelkon/GMM-CNN.

Electronic supplementary material The online version of this chapter (https://doi.org/10.1007/978-3-030-58595-2_5) contains supplementary material, which is available to authorized users.

© Springer Nature Switzerland AG 2020
A. Vedaldi et al. (Eds.): ECCV 2020, LNCS 12370, pp. 69–84, 2020.
https://doi.org/10.1007/978-3-030-58595-2_5

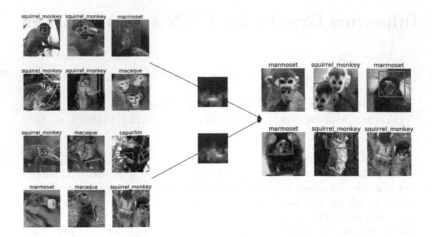

Fig. 1. Visual words connected to form an inference path. Two visual words in a lower network layer (left) (each is represented by six most typical images), representing the monkey eye (top) and face (bottom), explain a visual word in an upper network layer (right) that represents the monkey face. The heatmaps show spatial densities of lower-layer visual words in the receptive field of the higher-level word (see Sect. 4.3).

reference in the world of objects, predicates, and their interrelations. The question of interest in this respect is: *Can we convert distributed representations into a human-oriented language?* More technically, can we learn a dictionary of visual words and model their interrelationships, leading to an interpretable inference graph?

To address this, we suggest to describe the inference process of a network with probabilistic models. We model activity vectors in each layer as arising from a multivariate Gaussian mixture model (GMM). Layer activity in fully connected (FC) layers, or spatial location activity in convolutional layers, is associated with one of K clusters (GMM components), each representing a visual word. Connections between visual words of consecutive layers are modeled using conditional probabilities. For a multilayer perceptron (MLP) network, a full model with efficient inference can be obtained using a hidden Markov model (HMM). For the convolutional layers, each spatial location has its own hidden variable and dependencies among visual words in consecutive layers are described using conditional probability tables. Given a selected subset of images to be explained (either a specific image or images of an entire class), we describe the decision process of the network using an inference graph, representing the visual words used in different hidden layers and their probabilistic connections. As the full graph may contain thousands of visual words, a useful explanation has to find informative subgraphs, containing the most explanatory words w.r.t the network decision, and the likely paths connecting them. We suggest an algorithm for finding such graphs based on maximum-likelihood considerations.

Our contributions are: (i) a new approach for network interpretation, providing a formalism for probabilistic reasoning about inference processes in deep networks, and (ii) a graph-mining algorithm and visual tools enabling inference understanding. Our suggested inference graph provides a succinct summary of the inference process performed on a specific class of images or a single image, as inference progresses through the network layers. An example of visual nodes and the inferred connection between them is shown in Fig. 1.

2 Related Work

Network Visualization. Several techniques have been suggested to visualize network behavior. In activation maximization [4], the input that maximizes the score of a given hidden unit is visualized by carrying out regularized gradient ascent optimization in the image space, as was applied to output class neurons [5] and intermediate layer neurons [6]. Another technique [5] visualizes the gradient strength in the original image space for a specific example, providing a "saliency map" showing class score sensitivity to image pixels. The idea was extended to an entire class of interest in [7]. In [8], the role of neurons in intermediate layers was visualized by an inverse de-convolution network.

Simplifying Network Representation. Similar to our work, several works looked for categorizing features through clustering [9,10]. Liao et al. [9] added a regularization term encouraging the network representation to form three kinds of clusters governed by examples, spatial locations, and channels. A similar approach was introduced for learning class discriminative clusters of spatial columns [10]. However, these approaches influence the trained network and trade accuracy for explainability, whereas ours finds meaningful inference explanations without interfering with the network learning process.

Modeling Relationships Between Consecutive Layer Representations. In CNNVis [11], neurons in each layer are clustered to form groups having similar activity patterns. For the clustering, a neuron was described using a C-dimensional vector of its average activity on each class $1, .., C$. A graph between clusters of subsequent layers was then formed based on the average weight strengths between cluster neurons. Note that this method clusters neurons, while we cluster activity vectors (of neuronal columns) across examples. Olah et al. [12] proposed a tool for visualizing the network path for a single image. They decomposed each layer's activations into groups using matrix factorization, and connected groups from consecutive layers into a graph structure similar to [11].

3 Method

Inference graphs for an MLP, for which a full graphical model can be suggested, are presented in Sect. 3.1. The more general case of a CNN is discussed in Sect. 3.2, and its related graph-mining algorithm in Sect. 3.3. Models can be trained on the full set of network layers or on a subset, indexed by $l \in \{1, \ldots, L\}$.

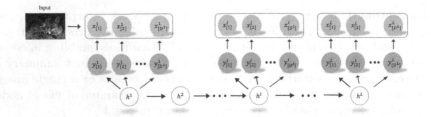

Fig. 2. HMM for MLP networks. Orange rectangles represent post-ReLU layer activity. Activation $x^l[d]$ of neuron d in layer l is generated from a rectified Gaussian density, where $x^l[d]$'s parent, $y^l[d]$, is a Gaussian density before rectification, and h^l is a hidden variable generating the hidden vector of multivariate Gaussians. (Color figure online)

3.1 Inference Graphs for MLPs

The hidden layer activity of an MLP network composed of FC layers can be modeled by a single probabilistic graphical model with an HMM structure, enabling closed-form inference. The model structure is shown in Fig. 2.

The activation vector of the lth FC layer with D^l neurons, $x^l = (x^l[1], .., x^l[D^l]) \in \mathbb{R}^{D^l}$, results from a mixture of K^l components with a discrete hidden variable $h^l \in \{1, ..., K^l\}$ denoting the component index a sample is assigned to, i.e. its cluster. To model the ReLU operation, each activation $x^l[d]$ is generated from a rectified Gaussian distribution [13]. The conditional probability $P(x^l|h^l)$ is hence assumed to be a rectified multivariate Gaussian distribution with a diagonal covariance matrix. Connections between hidden variables in consecutive layers are modeled by a conditional probability table (CPT) $P(h^l|h^{l-1})$.

Using this generative model, an activity pattern for the network is sampled by three steps. First, a path $(h^1, \ldots, h^L)$ of hidden states is generated according to the transition probabilities $P(h^l = k|h^{l-1} = k') = t^l_{k,k'}$, where $t^l \in \mathbb{R}^{K^l \times K^{l-1}}$ is a learned CPT. For notation simplicity, we define $h^0 = \{\}$, so $P(h^1|h^0)$ is actually $P(h^1)$ parametrized by $P(h^1 = k) = t^1_k$. After path generation, "pre-ReLU" Gaussian vectors $(y^1, \ldots, y^L)$, with $y^l \in \mathbb{R}^{D^l}$, are generated based on the chosen hidden variables. A single variable $y^l[d]$ is formed according to

$$P(y^l[d]|h^l = k) \sim \mathcal{N}(y^l[d]|\mu^l_{d,k}, \sigma^l_{d,k}), \tag{1}$$

where $\mu^l_{d,k}$ and $\sigma^l_{d,k}$ are the mean and standard deviation of the dth element in the kth component of layer l. Since the observed activity $x^l[d]$, generated as $x^l[d] = max(y^l[d], 0)$, is a deterministic function of $y^l[d]$, its conditional probability $P(x^l[d]|y^l[d])$ can be written as

$$P(x^l[d]|y^l[d]) = \begin{cases} \delta_{x^l[d]=y^l[d]} & , y^l[d] > 0 \\ \delta_{x^l[d]=0} & , y^l[d] \leq 0 \end{cases}, \tag{2}$$

with $\delta_{(x=c)}$ as the Dirac delta function concentrating the distribution mass at c.

The full likelihood of the model is given by

$$P(X, Y, H | \Theta) = \prod_{l=1}^{L} P(h^l | h^{l-1}) P(y^l | h^l) P(x^l | y^l), \quad (3)$$

where Y, H, X are tuples representing their respective variables across all layers (e.g., $H = \{h_l\}_{l=1}^{L}$), and the equation's components are stated above.

Training Algorithm: In [14], the EM formulation was suggested for training a mixture of rectified Gaussians. We extended this idea to the HMM formulation in an online setting. Following [15], the online EM algorithm tracks the sufficient statistics using running averages, and updates the model parameters using these statistics.

Explicit update formulas in terms of the tracked sufficient statistics are presented in the Supplementary Material.

3.2 Inference Graphs for CNNs

Layer Dictionaries: In a CNN, the activation output of the lth convolutional layer is a tensor $X^l \in R^{H^l \times W^l \times D^l}$, where H^l, W^l, and D^l correspond to the height, width, and number of maps, respectively. We consider the activation tensor as consisting of $H^l \times W^l$ spatial column examples, $x_p^l \in R^{D^l}$, located at $p = (i, j) \in \{\{1, \ldots, H^l\} \times \{1, \ldots W^l\}\}$, and wish to model each such location as containing a separate visual word from a dictionary shared by all locations.

The number of hidden variables (one per location) is much larger than that in an FC layer (where a single hidden variable per layer was used), and their connectivity pattern across layers is dense, leading to a graphical model with high induced width, but with infeasible exact inference. Hence, we turn to simpler model and training techniques that are scalable to the size and complexity of CNNs. In this model, spatial column x_p^l is described as arising from a GMM of K^l clusters, regarded as visual words forming the layer dictionary. Using a training image set $S_T = \{(I_n, y_n)\}_{n=1}^{N_T}$, the GMM is trained independently for each layer of interest. While each location p in layer l has a separate hidden random variable, h_p^l, the GMM parameters are shared across all the spatial locations of that layer. After model training, the activity tensor of layer l for an example I can be mapped into a tensor $P \in R^{H^l \times W^l \times K^l}$, holding $P(h_p^l(I) = k)$. With slight abuse of notation, we say that $h_p^l(I) = k^*$ (an activation column of image I in position p is assigned to cluster k^*) iff $k^* = \operatorname{argmax}_k P(h_p^l(I) = k)$. Accordingly, visual word k in layer l is the cluster $C_k^l = \{(I, p), I \in S_T : h_p^l(I) = k\}$ containing activations over all positions for all images in the training set S_T, where cluster k has the highest $P(h_p^l(I) = k)$.

When the CNN also contains global layers, these can be modeled using a GMM trained on the layer's activity vectors. This can be regarded as a degenerate case of convolutional layer modeling, where the number of spatial locations is one. Specifically, the output layer of the network, X^L, containing the M class of predicted probabilities, is modeled using a GMM of M components. This GMM is not trained, and instead is fixed such that $\mu_{d,m} = 1$ for $d = m$ and 0 otherwise, with a constant standard deviation of $\sigma_{d,m} = 0.1$. In this setting, cluster m of the output layer contains images that the network predicts to be of class m.

Probabilistic Connections Between Layer Dictionaries: Transition probabilities between visual words in consecutive layers are modeled a-posteriori. For two consecutive modeled layers l' and l ($l' < l$), the receptive field $R(p)$ of location p in layer l is defined as the set of locations $\{q = p + o : o \in O\}$ in layer l' used in the computation of x_p^l. O is a set of $\{(\Delta x, \Delta y)\}$ integer offsets. Using a validation sample $S_V = \{I_n\}_{n=1}^{N_V}$, we compute the co-occurrence matrix $N \in M^{K^l \times K^{l'}}$ between the visual words contained in the dictionaries of layers l and l',

$$N(k, k') = \left| \{(I_n, p, q) : h_p^l(I_n) = k, h_q^{l'}(I_n) = k', q \in R(p)\} \right|. \tag{4}$$

Using N, we can obtain the following first and second order statistics:

$$\hat{P}(h^l = k) = \frac{\sum_j N(k, j)}{\sum_{i,j} N(i, j)} \tag{5}$$

$$\hat{P}\left(h_q^{l'} = k' | h_p^l = k, q \in R(p)\right) = \frac{N(k, k')}{\sum_j N(k, j)} \tag{6}$$

$$= \frac{\left| \{(I_n, p, q) : h_p^l(I_n) = k, h_q^{l'}(I_n) = k', q \in R(p)\} \right|}{|O| \cdot \left| \{(I_n, p) : h_p^l(I_n) = k\} \right|} = \frac{1}{|O|} \sum_{o \in O} \hat{P}(h_{p+o}^{l'} = k' | h_p^l = k).$$

The transition probabilities as defined above are abbreviated in the following discussion to $\hat{P}(h^{l'} = k' | h^l = k)$. These probabilities are averaged over specific positions in the receptive field, since modeling of position-specific transition probabilities separately would lead to proliferation in the parameters number.

Training Algorithm: The GMM parameters Θ^l of layer l are trained by associating a GMM layer to each modeled layer of the network. Since we do not wish to alter the network's behavior, the GMM gradients do not propagate towards lower layers of the network. We considered two optimization approaches for training Θ^l:

(1) *Generative loss*—The optimization objective is to minimize the negative log-likelihood function:

$$\mathcal{L}_G(X^l(I_n), \Theta^l) = - \sum_{p \in \{1,...,H^l\} \times \{1,...,W^l\}} \log \sum_{k=1}^{K^l} \pi_k^l G(x_p^l(I_n) | \mu_k^l, \Sigma_k^l) \tag{7}$$

where G is the Gaussian distribution function, and π_k^l is the mixture probability of the k'th component in layer l.

(2) *Discriminative loss*—The probability tensor P is summarized into a histogram of visual words $Hist^l(X^l(I_n)) \in R^{K^l}$ using a global pooling operation. A linear classifier $\mathcal{W} \cdot Hist^l(X^l(I_n))$ is formed and optimized by minimizing a cross entropy loss, where $\mathcal{W}$ is the classifier weights vector,

$$\mathcal{L}_D(X^l(I_n), \Theta^l, y_n) = -\log P(\hat{y}_n = y_n | \mathcal{W} \cdot Hist^l(X^l(I_n), \Theta^l)) \qquad (8)$$

and $\hat{y}_n$ is the predicted output after a softmax transformation. Empirical comparison between these two approaches is given in Sect. 4.3.

For ImageNet-scale networks, full modeling of the entire network at once may require thousands of visual words per layer. Training such large dictionaries is not feasible with current GPU memory limitations (12 GB for a TitanX). Our solution is to train a class-specific model, explaining network behavior for a specific class m and its "neighboring" classes, i.e., all classes erroneously predicted by the network for images of class m. The set of neighboring classes is chosen based on the network's confusion matrix computed on the validation set. The model is trained on all training images of class m and its neighbors.

3.3 Graph Node Selection Algorithm

Consider a graph in which column activity clusters (i.e., visual words) $\{C^l_k\}^{L,K^l}_{l=1,k=1}$ are the nodes, and transition probabilities between clusters of consecutive layers quantify edges between the nodes. Typically, this graph contains thousands of nodes and, thus, is not feasible for human interpretation. However, specific subgraphs may have high explanatory value. Specifically, nodes (clusters) of the final layer C^L_k in this graph represent images for which the network predicted a class k. To understand this decision, we evaluate clusters in the previous layer $C^{L-1}_{k'}$ using a score based on the transition probabilities $P(h^L = k | h^{L-1} = k')$. The step of finding such a set of "explanatory" clusters in layer $L-1$ is repeated to lower layers. Below, we develop an iterative algorithm that using a validation subset of images $\Omega = \{I_n\}^N_{n=1}$ outputs a subgraph of the nodes that most "explain" the network decisions on Ω, where "explanation" is defined in the maximum-likelihood sense. We first explain node selection for a single visual word in a single image, and then extend this notion to a full algorithm operating on multiple visual words and images.

Explaining a Single Visual Word: Consider an instance of a single visual word $h^l_p(I) = s$, derived from a column activity location p in layer l for image I. Given this visual word, we look for the visual words in $R(p)$ most contributing to its likelihood, given by (omitting the image notation I in $h^l_p(I)$ for brevity):

$$P\left(h^l_p = s \big| \{h^{l'}_q : q \in R(p)\}\right) = \frac{P\left(\{h^{l'}_q : q \in R(p)\} \big| h^l_p = s\right) \cdot P(h^l_p = s)}{P\left(\{h^{l'}_q : q \in R(p)\}\right)}$$

$$\approx \frac{\prod_{q \in R(p)} P(h^{l'}_q | h^l_p = s) \cdot P(h^l_p = s)}{\prod_{q \in R(p)} P(h^{l'}_q)}. \qquad (9)$$

Algorithm 1. Inference graph building

Input: CNN CN, a set Ω of images predicted by CN to class m, network model $\{\Theta^l, \hat{P}(h^l = k), \hat{P}(h^l = k|h^{l'} = k')\}_{l=1,k=1,k'=1}^{L,K^l,K^{l'}}$, Z - number of allowed nodes per layer.
Output: An inference graph $G = (N, E)$, where N and E hold clusters (nodes) and their weighted connections (edges) in the graph, respectively
Initialization: Push Ω through the network model to get $\{Q_{t,s}^l(\Omega)\}_{l=1}^{L-1}$ (Eq. 15) and clusters $\{C_i^l\}_{l=1,i=1}^{L,K^l}$. Set $S = m$, $N = C_m^L$, and $E = \emptyset$
For $l = L - 1, \ldots, 1$
    For $t = 1, \ldots, K^l$, compute $S^l(\Omega, S, t)$ (Eq. 16)
    Choose $(z_1^l, \ldots, z_Z^l)$ to be the Z clusters indices with the largest scores $S^l(\Omega, S, t)$
    Set $S = (z_1^l, \ldots, z_Z^l)$ and $e_{i,j}^l = S^l(\Omega, z_i^{l+1}, z_j^l)$, $\forall i, j = 1, \ldots Z$
    Set $N = N \cup \{C_{z_i^l}^l\}_{i=1}^{Z}$ and $E = E \cup \{e_{i,j}^l\}_{i=1,j=1}^{Z,Z}$ // nodes and edges update

---

In the last step, two simplifying assumptions were made: conditional independence over locations in the receptive field (nominator) and independence of locations (denominator). Taking the logarithm, we decompose the expression:

$$\underbrace{\log P(h_p^l = s)}_{\text{constant } A} + \sum_{q \in R(p)} \log \frac{P(h_q^{l'} | h_p^l = s)}{P(h_q^{l'})}$$

$$= A + \sum_{t=1,\ldots,K^{l'}} \left| \{q : h_q^{l'} = t, q \in R(p)\} \right| \log \frac{P(h_q^{l'} = t | h_p^l = s, q \in R(p))}{P(h_q^{l'} = t)}. \tag{10}$$

Denote by $Q_t^{l'}(I, p) = \left| \{q : h_q^{l'} = t, q \in R(p)\} \right|$ the number of times visual word t appears in the receptive field of location p. We look for a subset of words $T \subset \{1, \ldots, K^{l'}\}$, which contribute the most to the likelihood of $h_p^l = s$. Thus, the problem we solve is

$$\max_{|T|=Z} \left\{ \sum_{t \in T} Q_t^{l'}(I, p) \log \frac{P(h_q^{l'} = t | h_p^l = s, q \in R(p))}{P(h_q^{l'} = t)} \right\}. \tag{11}$$

The solution is obtained by choosing the first Z words for which the score

$$S^{l'}(I, s, t) = Q_t^{l'}(I, p) \log \frac{P(h_q^{l'} = t | h_p^l = s, q \in R(p))}{P(h_q^{l'} = t)} \tag{12}$$

is the highest. Intuitively, the score of the tth visual word is the product of two terms, $Q_t^{l'}(I, p)$, which measures the word frequency in the receptive field, and $\log \frac{P(h_q^{l'} = t | h_p^l = s, q \in R(p))}{P(h_q^{l'} = t)}$, which measures how likely it is to see word t in the receptive field compared to seeing it in general. To compute the probabilities in the log term of the score, we use the estimations $\hat{P}(h^l = k)$ and $\hat{P}(h^{l'} = k'|h^l = k)$ made using Eqs. 5 and 6, respectively.

Explaining Multiple Words and Images: The optimization problem presented in Eq. 11 can be extended to multiple visual words in multiple images using column position and image independence assumptions. Assume a set of validation images Ω is being analyzed, and a set of words $S \subset \{1, \ldots, K^l\}$ from layer l has to be explained by lower layer words for these images. We would like to maximize the likelihood of the set of all column activities $\{h_p^l(I_n) : h_p^l \in S, I_n \in \Omega\}$, in which a word from S appears. Assuming column position independence, this likelihood decomposes into terms similar to Eq. 9:

$$
\log P\Big(\{h_p^l(I_n) : h_p^l(I_n) \in S, I_n \in \Omega\} \big| \{h_q^{l'}(I_n) : I_n \in \Omega\}\Big)
$$
$$
= \sum_{n=1}^{N} \sum_{s \in S} \sum_{\{p : h_p^l(I_n) = s\}} \log P\big(h_p^l(I_n) \big| h_q^{l'}(I_n), q \in R(p)\big). \tag{13}
$$

Repeating the derivation also given in Eqs. 9, 10, and 11 for this expression, we get a similar optimization problem,

$$
\max_{\substack{T \\ |T| = Z}} \left\{ \sum_{t \in T} \sum_{s \in S} Q_{t,s}^{l'}(\Omega) \log \frac{P\big(h_q^{l'} = t | h_p^l = s, q \in R(p)\big)}{P\big(h_q^{l'} = t\big)} \right\}, \tag{14}
$$

where $Q_{t,s}^{l'}(\Omega)$ is the aggregation of $Q_t^{l'}(I,p)$ over multiple positions and images

$$
Q_{t,s}^{l'}(\Omega) = \sum_{n=1}^{N} \sum_{\{p : h_p^l(I_n) = s\}} Q_t^{l'}(I_n, p). \tag{15}
$$

That is, $Q_{t,s}^{l'}(\Omega)$ is the number of occurrences of word s with word t in its receptive field in all the images in Ω. The solution is given by choosing the Z words in layer l' for which the score

$$
S^{l'}(\Omega, S, t) = \sum_{s \in S} Q_{t,s}^{l'}(\Omega) \log \frac{P\big(h_q^{l'} = t | h_p^l = s, q \in R(p)\big)}{P\big(h_q^{l'} = t\big)} \tag{16}
$$

is maximized. The inference graph is generated by going over the layers backwards, from the top layer, for which the decision has to be explained, and downwards towards the input layer, selecting the explaining nodes using the score of Eq. 16. See Algorithm 1 for details.

4   Results

The HMM for MLP formalism was tested by training a fully connected network on the CIFAR10 [16] dataset, containing 10 classes. The network included six layers with the first five containing $1,000$ neurons each. Based on a preliminary evaluation, the number of visual words K^l was set at 40 for all layers.

CNN models included ResNet20 [2] trained on CIFAR10, and VGG-16 [17] and ResNet50 [2] trained on the ILSVRC 2012 dataset [18]. For ResNet20, the

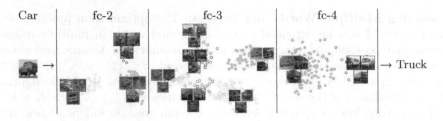

Fig. 3. MLP inference path. Three main decision junctions of a misclassified example in a 6-layer network. Subclusters are visualized by the three most representative examples. Points from the subcluster chosen by this example are marked by full circles.

output of all add-layers after each skip connection were modeled, as these outputs are expected to contain aggregated information. For ResNet50 there are 16 add layers and the output of add-layers 3, 7, 13, and 16 were modeled. For VGG-16, the first convolutional layers at each block were modeled (four layers in total). The numbers of visual words were set at $100, 200, 450$, and $1,500$ for Layers 1–4, respectively, according to the GPU memory limitation.

In all experiments and modeled layers, the GMM's mean parameters were initialized using K^l randomly selected examples. The variance parameters were initialized as K variances computed from $1,000$ random examples. Prior probabilities were uniformly initialized to be $\frac{1}{K^l}$.

4.1   MLP Inference Path

In MLP networks, the entire layer activity is assigned to a single cluster. To visualize such a cluster, we consider it as a "decision junction", where a decision regarding the consecutive layer cluster is made. For this visualization, the activity vectors in the C_k^l cluster are labeled according to their consecutive layer clusters, forming subclusters for this cluster. We use linear discriminant analysis (LDA) [19] to find a 2D projection of the activity vectors that maximize the separation of the examples with respect to their subcluster labels. Each subcluster is visualized using the three examples with the minimal l_2 distance to the subcluster center.

The inference path for an example I is defined to be the maximum a-posteriori (MAP) cluster sequence, i.e., $H = (h^1, ..., h^L)$, satisfying

$$\max_{h^1,...,h^L} \log P(h^1, ..., h^L | X(I)), \tag{17}$$

where H can be found using the Viterbi algorithm [20].

Such inference paths are useful for error diagnosis. In Fig. 3, a partial path containing three decision junctions of an erroneous "car" example in the CIFAR10 network is presented. It can be seen that the example's likely "decisions" in layer fc-3 leads to car and truck clusters in the consecutive layer. At this point, due to its unconventional rear appearance, resembling a truck front, this

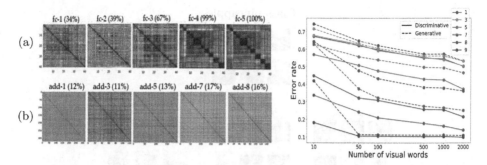

Fig. 4. Left: Cluster similarity matrices for increasing layer indices in a 6-layer MLP (a) and ResNet20 (b) both trained on CIFAR10. The average percentage of dominant class examples (across clusters) is stated above each matrix. **Right:** Error rates of a linear classifier trained over word histograms taken from six ResNet20 conv-layers (1, 3, 5, 7, 8, and 9) trained with either a generative or discriminative loss (Sect. 3.2).

car example was wrongly associated with a "truck" subcluster, an association that remained until the classification layer.

4.2 Cluster Similarity Across Layers

A plausible assumption about network layer representations is that early layers are input dominated, while representations in late layers are more class-related. This phenomenon can be observed in our framework by considering how distance between clusters changes as a function of layer index. In Fig. 4 (left), similarity matrices are presented. Each matrix shows Euclidean distances between centers of the clusters from a single layer. Clusters are ordered by their dominant class index, defined as the class whose examples are the most frequent in the cluster. For an MLP network, presented in Fig. 4 (top left), the progression toward class-related representation is evident from the emerging block structure in Layers 3–5, indicating increasing similarity between clusters representing the same class.

In contrast, as seen in Fig. 4 (bottom left), CNN clusters (representing column activities) stay local and diverse, even at the uppermost layers where their receptive fields cover the entire input space. This phenomenon is demonstrated by the lack of block structure, as well as the relatively low frequency of the dominant class in a cluster. This indicates that the final CNN classification is based on several class-oriented words, which are not similar, and appear simultaneously in different image regions.

4.3 CNN Inference Graphs

Loss and Dictionary Size. Figure 4 (right) shows the errors obtained for linear classification using dictionary histograms (Eq. 8), as a function of dictionary size. Graphs are shown for dictionaries obtained using losses $\mathcal{L}_G$ (7) and $\mathcal{L}_D$ (8), for several intermediate convolutional layers of the CIFAR10 network. For all layers,

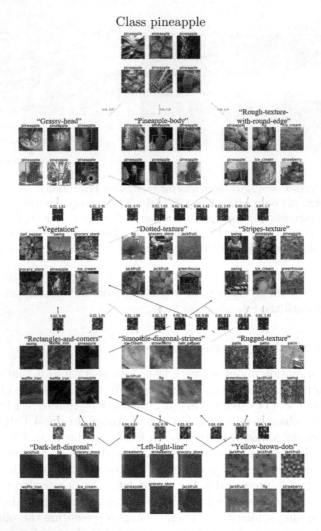

Fig. 5. Pineapple inference graph. The graph is generated by training a model on "pineapple" class and its neighboring classes. The top node is a visual word of the output layer, representing the predicted class "pineapple". The lower levels in the graph show the three most influential words in preceding modeled layers. Visual words are manifested by the six representative examples for which $P(h^l = k|x_p^l)$ is the highest. For the two highest layers, examples are presented by showing the example image with a rectangle highlighting the receptive field of the word's location. For lower layers, the receptive field patches themselves are shown. Images are annotated by their true label. Arrows are shown when the log-ratio term is positive, colored green for significant connections in which the term is higher than 1. They are annotated by the frequency of the lower word in the receptive field (left) and the log ratio (right) (the two components of the score in Eq. 16). In addition, for each arrow, a heatmap is shown indicating the frequent locations of the lower-level visual words in the receptive field of the higher-level word. A tag above each visual word was added by the authors for figure explanation convenience. The figure is best inspected by zooming in on clusters of interest.

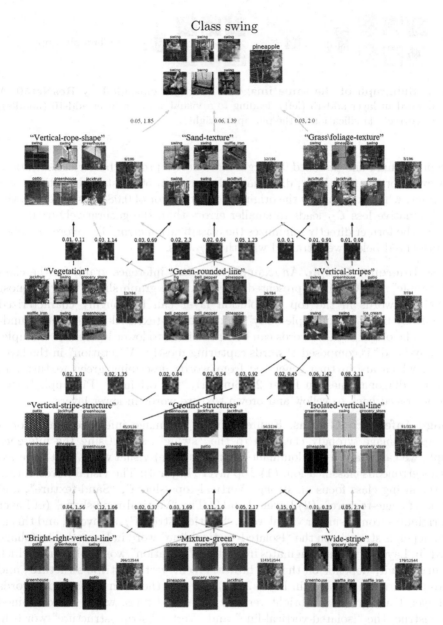

Fig. 6. An image inference graph of an erroneous image. An image inference graph for a pineapple image wrongly classified to the class "swing". The model is generated using "pineapple" and its neighboring classes (same as in Fig. 5), where the neighbor class "swing" is included. The graph is generated by applying the node selection algorithm (Sect. 3.3) to a set Ω containing this single erroneous image. The analyzed image is shown on the right side of each cluster node, with red dots marking spatial locations assigned to the cluster. The fraction of spatial examples belonging to the cluster (in this image) appears in the title. (Color figure online)

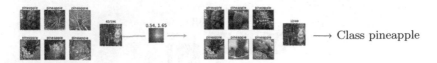

Fig. 7. Subgraph of the same image as in Fig. 6 classified by ResNet50. A visual word in layer add-13 (left), leading to a visual word in layer add-16 (middle), and to correct classification of the pineapple (right).

except the final one (indexed 9), larger dictionaries provide better classification. However, for the final layer, dictionaries larger than 50 clusters do not increase accuracy, which approaches the original network error of 0.088. As expected, the discriminative loss $\mathcal{L}_D$ leads to smaller errors than the generatively-optimized loss, as the former directly minimizes the classification error. Therefore, all models presented below were trained with the $\mathcal{L}_D$ loss.

Class Inference Graph. An example of a class inference graph for the class "pineapple" in VGG-16 is presented in Fig. 5. The graph shows that the most influential words in the top convolution layer can be roughly characterized as "Grassy-head", "Pineapple-body", and "Rough-textured-with(lower)-round-edge". The origin of these words can be traced back to lower layers. For example, "Grassy-head" is composed of words capturing mostly "Vegetation" in the layer below, which are in turn generated from words describing green texture and multiple diagonal lines (in Layer 2). Similarly, the origin of "Pineapple-body" can be traced back to yellow and brown texture words in lower layers.

Image Inference Graphs. Figure 6 shows an image inference graph for a pineapple image wrongly classified to the "swing" class. Using the inference graph, we can analyze the dominant (representative) visual words that have led to this erroneous classification: **(1)** Top layer (Layer 4): The visual words voting for the swing class focus on strong "Vertical-rope-shape", "Sand-texture", and "Grass/foliage-texture". **(2)** Layers 3 and 2: The "Vertical-rope-shape" (of Layer 4) originates from a similar visual word, "Vertical-stripes", of Layer 3, and this in turn depends strongly on the "Isolated-vertical-line" word in Layer 2. The foliage word (in Layer 4) mainly originates from the "Vegetation" word in Layer 3, which in turn heavily depends on the two brown/green "vertical-stripe-structure" and "Ground-structure" words in Layer 2. **(3)** Layer 1: the main explanatory words in Layer 1 are green and bright vertical edges and lines, which are combined to construct the "Isolated-vertical-line" and "Vertical-stripe-structure" words in Layer 2.

In Fig. 7, we show a partial inference graph of the same "pineapple" image wrongly classified to class "swing" by VGG-16 (Fig. 6), which is successfully classified by ResNet50. As can be seen in the top layer of the graph (add-16, middle), Resnet50 successfully detects the pineapple location in the image, where both visual words presented contain strong "pineapple" features. Additional examples of class and image inference graphs are given in the Supplementary Material.

5 Conclusions

We introduced a new approach for interpreting hidden layers activity of deep neural networks by learning dictionaries of activity clusters and transition probabilities between clusters of consecutive modeled layers. We formalized a maximum-likelihood criterion for mining clusters relevant for network prediction, which enable building explanatory inference graphs of manageable size. Inference graphs can be constructed for an entire class, to understand the general network reasoning for this class, or for specific images, for which error analysis may specifically be sought. The tools developed can be used to verify the soundness of the network reasoning and to understand its hidden inference mechanisms, or conversely to reveal network weaknesses.

Acknowledgments. This work was supported by the Israeli Ministry of Science and Technology and Israel Innovation Authority through the Phenomics consortium.

References

1. Krizhevsky, A., Sutskever, I., Hinton, G.E.: ImageNet classification with deep convolutional neural networks. In: Advances in Neural Information Processing Systems, pp. 1097–1105 (2012)
2. He, K., Zhang, X., Ren, S., Sun, J.: Deep residual learning for image recognition. In: Proceedings of the IEEE Conference on Computer Vision and Pattern Recognition, pp. 770–778 (2016)
3. Huang, G., Liu, Z., Van Der Maaten, L., Weinberger, K.Q.: Densely connected convolutional networks. In: Proceedings of the IEEE Conference on Computer Vision and Pattern Recognition, pp. 4700–4708 (2017)
4. Erhan, D., Bengio, Y., Courville, A., Vincent, P.: Visualizing higher-layer features of a deep network. University of Montreal, vol. 1341, no. 3, p. 1 (2009)
5. Simonyan, K., Vedaldi, A., Zisserman, A.: Deep inside convolutional networks: visualising image classification models and saliency maps. arXiv preprint arXiv:1312.6034 (2013)
6. Yosinski, J., Clune, J., Nguyen, A.M., Fuchs, T., Lipson, H.: Understanding neural networks through deep visualization. CoRR abs/1506.06579 (2015)
7. Zhou, B., Khosla, A., Lapedriza, A., Oliva, A., Torralba, A.: Learning deep features for discriminative localization. In: Proceedings of the IEEE Conference on Computer Vision and Pattern Recognition, pp. 2921–2929 (2016)
8. Zeiler, M.D., Fergus, R.: Visualizing and understanding convolutional networks. In: Fleet, D., Pajdla, T., Schiele, B., Tuytelaars, T. (eds.) ECCV 2014. LNCS, vol. 8689, pp. 818–833. Springer, Cham (2014). https://doi.org/10.1007/978-3-319-10590-1_53
9. Liao, R., Schwing, A., Zemel, R., Urtasun, R.: Learning deep parsimonious representations. In: Advances in Neural Information Processing Systems, pp. 5076–5084 (2016)
10. Chen, C., Li, O., Tao, D., Barnett, A., Rudin, C., Su, J.K.: This looks like that: deep learning for interpretable image recognition. In: Advances in Neural Information Processing Systems, pp. 8928–8939 (2019)

11. Liu, M., Shi, J., Li, Z., Li, C., Zhu, J., Liu, S.: Towards better analysis of deep convolutional neural networks. IEEE Trans. Visual Comput. Graphics **23**(1), 91–100 (2016)
12. Olah, C., et al.: The building blocks of interpretability. Distill **3**(3), e10 (2018)
13. Socci, N.D., Lee, D.D., Seung, H.S.: The rectified Gaussian distribution. In: Advances in Neural Information Processing Systems, pp. 350–356 (1998)
14. Lee, G., Scott, C.: EM algorithms for multivariate Gaussian mixture models with truncated and censored data. Comput. Stat. Data Anal. **56**(9), 2816–2829 (2012)
15. Cappé, O., Moulines, E.: On-line expectation-maximization algorithm for latent data models. J. R. Stat. Soc. Ser. B (Stat. Methodol.) **71**(3), 593–613 (2009)
16. Krizhevsky, A., Hinton, G., et al.: Learning multiple layers of features from tiny images. Technical report, University of Toronto (2009)
17. Simonyan, K., Zisserman, A.: Very deep convolutional networks for large-scale image recognition. arXiv preprint arXiv:1409.1556 (2014)
18. Russakovsky, O., et al.: ImageNet large scale visual recognition challenge. Int. J. Comput. Vision **115**(3), 211–252 (2015). https://doi.org/10.1007/s11263-015-0816-y
19. Fukunaga, K.: Introduction to Statistical Pattern Recognition. Academic Press, New York (1990)
20. Forney, G.D.: The Viterbi algorithm. Proc. IEEE **61**(3), 268–278 (1973)

An End-to-End OCR Text Re-organization Sequence Learning for Rich-Text Detail Image Comprehension

Liangcheng Li[1,2,3], Feiyu Gao[2], Jiajun Bu[1,3,4]($\boxtimes$), Yongpan Wang[1,2,3], Zhi Yu[1,3,4], and Qi Zheng[2]

[1] Zhejiang Provincial Key Laboratory of Service Robot, College of Computer Science, Zhejiang University, Hangzhou, China
{liangcheng_li,bjj,yuzhirenzhe}@zju.edu.cn
[2] Alibaba Group, Hangzhou, China
feiyu.gfy@alibaba-inc.com, {yongpan,yongqi.zq}@taobao.com
[3] Alibaba-Zhejiang University Joint Institute of Frontier Technologies, Hangzhou, China
[4] Ningbo Research Institute, Zhejiang University, Ningbo, China

Abstract. Nowadays the description of detailed images helps users know more about the commodities. With the help of OCR technology, the description text can be detected and recognized as auxiliary information to remove the visually impaired users' comprehension barriers. However, for lack of proper logical structure among these OCR text blocks, it is challenging to comprehend the detailed images accurately. To tackle the above problems, we propose a novel end-to-end OCR text reorganizing model. Specifically, we create a Graph Neural Network with an attention map to encode the text blocks with visual layout features, with which an attention-based sequence decoder inspired by the Pointer Network and a Sinkhorn global optimization will reorder the OCR text into a proper sequence. Experimental results illustrate that our model outperforms the other baselines, and the real experiment of the blind users' experience shows that our model improves their comprehension.

Keywords: OCR text re-organization · Graph neural network · Pointer network

1 Introduction

The internet era has given rise to the development of E-commerce and a large number of relevant platforms are springing up, such as Taobao, Jingdong and Amazon. Nowadays people are apt to participate in these websites for communications with online sellers and transactions on diverse commodities. To attract

© Springer Nature Switzerland AG 2020
A. Vedaldi et al. (Eds.): ECCV 2020, LNCS 12370, pp. 85–100, 2020.
https://doi.org/10.1007/978-3-030-58595-2_6

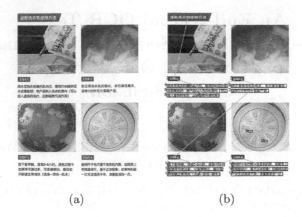

(a)   (b)

Fig. 1. Example of a detail image (a) and the right reading order in (b). The blue boxes are the text blocks provided by OCR technology, the top-left red corner marks are the indexes of the text blocks. The green arrow lines in (b) show the proper reading route instead of reading from left to right and top to bottom simply. (Color figure online)

more consumers, these sellers take advantage of rich description text and commodity pictures to synthesize stylistic detail images, which help the consumers know their products as intuitive as possible.

Nevertheless, most detailed images are designed for healthy people who can comprehend both the image and text information directly. They ignore the demand of the visually impaired people who account for more than 27% of the world's population, such as the blind or the elderly. Since most existing screen readers cannot recognize the image format information, an interaction barrier between the visually impaired people and the e-commerce world has emerged. As the text is an essential tool for humankind's communication, it is an alternative to choose the description text in these detailed images for comprehension. Optical Character Recognition (OCR) technology devotes to mining the text information from several images, with its full application in scene text understanding [34], such as PhotoOCR [4], DocumentOCR [16]. Most classical and prevalent works on OCR concentrate on text detection [8,13,32] and recognition [1,5,14,20]. They extract the characters in images and organize them into several text blocks according to semantic information, which performs well on many scene-text images, and detailed images are no exception.

However, the text in detail images has a flexible layout. It uses diverse typography structures to convey the product information, which causes the comprehending problem as the text blocks from OCR technology are discrete and lacking in **context order** without image structure. So it is often confusing for the visually impaired consumers when the screen reader reads the text blocks at an arbitrary order. Figure 1(a) shows an example of a detailed image, the blue boxes are the text blocks provided by OCR technology and the top-left red corner marks are the indexes of the text blocks. If the screen reader reads these text blocks from left to right and top to bottom, the visually impaired consumers are doomed to misinterpret even hardly comprehend the detailed images. Only the reading order in Fig. 1(b) shows the same information that the raw detail image is expressed.

In this paper, we propose a novel end-to-end OCR text re-organization model for detailed image comprehension to tackle the problem as mentioned above. Based on the text detection feature extracted by a fully convolutional network (FCN), we use the text blocks to construct a graph structure and cast the problem to a graph to sequence model. Specifically, under the assumption that all the detailed images are probably be laid out regularly [15], we apply a graph convolution network (GCN) model with an attention mask to encode the logical layout information of the text blocks. A sequence decoder based on Pointer Network (PN) is proposed to obtain the text blocks' final order. We also introduce the Sinkhorn layer to make optimal global normalization by transforming the decoder predictions into doubly-stochastic matrices. Experiments on real-world detail image datasets have been conducted and show our method outperforms other sequence-oriented baselines both on local and global sequence evaluations. A real user experience test on blind people is also launched and shows the improvement of their comprehension.

Our contributions are threefold. First, to our best knowledge, it is the first time to propose the reading order problem for a rich-text detailed image based on OCR text blocks. Second, we propose an end-to-end graph to sequence model to solve the text blocks' re-organization problem using graph convolution network and pointer attention mechanism. Last, we design both quantitative sequence evaluation and real user experience tests among the blind people to convince our model's rationality and feasibility.

2 Related Work

Since the reading order re-organization problem is rarely mentioned and similar to the fields on sequence modeling, in this section, we briefly discuss related works on it. We also discuss traditional research on document analysis to show the similarities and differences with our work.

2.1 Sequence Modeling

Sequence modeling has been widely researched in many fields. In computer vision, it aims to learn a proper order for a set of images according to some predefined rules [22]. A typical variation of this task is the jigsaw puzzle problem [18,24], which needs to recover an image from a tile of puzzle segments. Jigsaw puzzle problems can be abstracted as ordering the image segments based on their shape or texture, especially on the boundaries [11,19]. It is similar when regarding the OCR text blocks as sub-image regions and reconstructs their order. However, these methods are not suitable because OCR text blocks are discrete and isolated, with no joint boundary and continuous texture information.

Meanwhile, in natural language processing, RNN-based [21] Sequence-to-Sequence model (Seq2Seq) [27] and Neural Turing Machines [12] can solve most generative sequence tasks. However, they cannot solve the permutation problem where the outputs' size depends on the inputs directly. Vinyal et al. propose Pointer Network [29] which uses an attention mechanism to find the proper units from the input sequence and permute these as output. One of its application, text summarization, show the similarities of our work as they select some key information from the original text for summarization [7,10]. Recently they are prevalent with the dynamic decision whether generating new words or permuting words from the original text inspired by the pointer mechanism [23,33]. However, it is not suitable to generate the summarization of complete text information because the description text is carefully selected by the sellers to show the selling points [6], let alone the word deletion in extractive summarization. Meanwhile, as there remain some mistakes during the OCR text detection and recognition process, it is hard to guarantee the accuracy of the summarization under NLP features. Finally, sellers may tend to use concise and isolated phrases or words to describe their product, which has no grammar or syntax structure so that the summarization will fail to get whole sentences.

Furthermore, another line of research for sequence modeling has been devoted to converting other complex structures into sequences. Xu et al. [31] propose a graph to sequence model (Graph2Seq) with a GCN encoder and an attention Seq2Seq decoder to solve the bAbI artificial intelligence tasks [30]; Vinyals et al. [28] apply the attention mechanisms on input sets and propose the set to sequence model (Set2Seq) for language modeling and parsing tasks; Eriguchi et al. [9] design a tree to sequence (Tree2Seq) structure for extracting syntactic information for sentences. The commonality of these models is that their sequence decoders are all based on the Seq2Seq model, causing the limitation of output dictionary dependence.

2.2 Document Analysis

Document analysis mainly includes two steps: document layout analysis and document understanding. The former process detects and annotates the physical structure of documents, and the latter process has several comprehension applications such as document retrieval, content categorization, text recognition [3]. However, most layout structure extraction and comprehension tasks on traditional documents are cast to a classification problem, which is different from text ordering tasks on scene-text images. It is hard to find homogeneous text regions and define semantic categories of the OCR text blocks with diverse layouts and open designs. Furthermore, scene texts with unique layouts and designs imply the visual cues and orders for comprehending the whole image, while document content analysis scheme is not suited for obtaining the order context.

3 Re-organization Model Architecture

Since the traditional sequence modeling methods cannot directly apply to the detailed image comprehension problem. This section sheds light on an end-to-end model to re-organize the OCR text block image regions for comprehension based on layout analysis. Specifically, we first define the re-organization task and then introduce the graph-based encoding method with an attention mask to get the layout embedding, finally we introduce a pointer-based attention decoder to solve the ordering problem.

3.1 Task Definition

Given a set of text block images generated by OCR text detection and recognition from an original detail image, we need to generate a proper permutation of these blocks under which its text sequence can be comprehend. Formally, let us define an detail image with its OCR text block set $\mathcal{T} = \{t_1, t_2, \cdots, t_n\}$ where t_i refers to the ith text block. Meanwhile, we also define an target permutation $\mathcal{P}^{\mathcal{T}} = <\mathcal{P}_1, \mathcal{P}_2, \cdots, \mathcal{P}_{m(\mathcal{T})}>$ where $m(\mathcal{T})$ is the indices of each unit in the text block set $\mathcal{T}$ between 1 and n. We are suggested to train an ordering model with the parameters w by maximizing the conditional probabilities for the training set as follows:

$$w^* = \arg\max_w \sum_{\mathcal{T},\mathcal{P}^{\mathcal{T}}} \log p\left(\mathcal{P}^{\mathcal{T}} | \mathcal{T}; w\right) \tag{1}$$

where the sum operation means the sum of the total training examples. Actually, we cast the discrete image block re-organization process to a supervised sequence ordering problem.

3.2 Graph Construction

We model each detail image as a graph of text blocks in which each independent text block are regarded as nodes with the image feature comprised for their attributes. We also take advantage of the geometric information (e.g. position) of the text blocks and construct edges to represent the original relations among them. Mathematically, we cast a detail image to a directed weighted graph structure $\mathcal{G} = (\mathcal{N}, \mathcal{E})$, where $\mathcal{N} = \{f(t_1), f(t_2), \cdots, f(t_n)\}$ is the set of n text blocks (i.e. nodes) and $f(t_i)$ stands for the attributes of the ith text block, while $\mathcal{E} = \{r(e_{i,1}), r(e_{i,2}), \cdots, r(e_{i,n-1})\}$ is the set of edges and $e_{i,j}$ is the direct edge from node i to node j and $r(e_{i,j})$ stands for the attributes of the $e_{i,j}$ direct edge. In fact, we construct the fully connected graph for text blocks in a detail image primarily.

In order to obtain the attribute $f(t_i)$ for the ith node, we consider the image feature which is related to the layout and image semantic feature instead of the text feature because the detail images do not have strict morphology and syntax structures. Given a detail image, we apply the Fully Convolutional Network (FCN) [17] model on detecting the text regions, then we extract its backbone and use the pretrained parameters from text detection to get the feature map of the total image. Combined with the text region bounding box, we get the text block feature as the node attributes with bi-linear interpolation technique.

As for the directed edge attributes, we consider the geometric information and take advantage of the position coordinates of the text blocks. Since the rectangle text regions are in difference size, we apply the relative position inspired by [16] to represent the edge attribute between node t_i and t_j as follows:

$$r\left(e_{i,j}\right) = \left[\Delta_{i,j}X, \Delta_{i,j}Y, \frac{l_i}{h_i}, \frac{l_j}{h_i}, \frac{h_j}{h_i}, \frac{h_j}{l_i}, \frac{l_j}{l_i}\right] \tag{2}$$

where $\Delta_{i,j}X$ and $\Delta_{i,j}Y$ stand for the horizontal and vertical euclidean distance of two text blocks based on their top-left coordinates, while l_i and h_i stand for the width and height of the ith text block respectively. The third to eighth values of the attributes are the shape ratio of the node t^i, with four relative height and width of node t^j. Because the text blocks are not single points and have different region shapes, it is necessary to consider the impact of the shape instead of only using the euclidean distance of vertexes.

To summarize, we construct the graph of text blocks in a detail image with its node embedded the image textual features and its edge embedded the geometric features primarily, as Fig. 2 depicts.

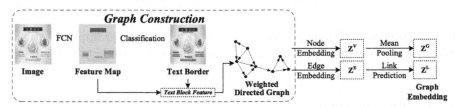

Fig. 2. The framework of graph construction and graph convolutional encoder module

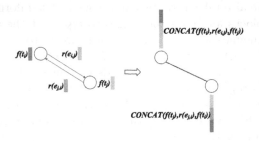

Fig. 3. The transformation of the directed weighted graph. The new feature contains the concatenation of two node feature vectors with the edge feature vector of their directed link.

3.3 Graph Convolutional Encoder

Compared to the traditional convolutional network, graph convolution is applied to the discrete data structure and learn the embeddings of nodes through the aggregation of their local neighbors. In this paper, we simultaneously perform the convolution operation on both nodes and edges. Because two directed edges link every two nodes, we deal with the node feature vector with the concatenation of two-node feature vectors and an edge feature vector that links them, as Fig. 3 depicts. That is, for two text blocks' nodes t_i and t_j with two edges e_i and e_j between them, we define a new compound node $c_{i,j}$ with its feature vector $\boldsymbol{h}_{i,j}^0$ at 0th layer as follows:

$$\boldsymbol{h}_{i,j}^0 = \text{CONCAT}\left(f^0\left(t_i\right), r^0\left(e_{i,j}\right), f^0\left(t_j\right)\right) \tag{3}$$

then we can iteratively compute the l_{th} layer feature $h_{i,j}^l$ as follows:

$$\boldsymbol{h}_{i,j}^l = \sigma\left(\left(\boldsymbol{W}_v^l\right)^T \cdot \boldsymbol{h}_{i,j}^{l-1}\right) \tag{4}$$

where σ refers to the nonlinear activation function, and W_v^l refers to the node weight parameters of the lth layer. However, to get the hidden representation of node t_i instead of compound node $c_{i,j}$, we also need to analyze and aggregate the proper local neighbors of the node t_i. Instead of using the traditional aggregator architectures like mean or LSTM aggregators, we use the self-attention mechanism on different hidden layers. Mathematically, the attention output embedding $f^l\left(t_i\right)$ for the node t_i at l^{th} layer can be calculated as follows:

$$f^l\left(t_i\right) = \sigma\left(\sum_{j \in \{k | \forall k \in NB(i)\}} \alpha_{i,j}^l \boldsymbol{h}_{i,j}^l\right) \tag{5}$$

where σ is a nonlinear activation function. Since we will mask the node with very low attention value and do not regard them as a proper local neighbor, $NB(i)$ refers to the local neighbors of the node t_i. Likewise, $\alpha_{i,j}^l$ refers to the attention coefficient between node t_i and t_j. Based on the [2], the attention coefficient can be defined as follows:

$$\alpha_{i,j}^l = \frac{\exp\left(\sigma\left(\left(\boldsymbol{w}_a^l\right)^T \boldsymbol{h}_{i,j}\right)\right)}{\sum_{u \in \{k | \forall k \in NB(i)\}} \exp\left(\sigma\left(\left(\boldsymbol{w}_a^l\right)^T \boldsymbol{h}_{i,u}\right)\right)} \tag{6}$$

where the σ refers to the LeakyReLU activation function, w_a^l is a attention weight vector of the lth layer.

Meanwhile, we perform the edge embedding with more easier operation as we find that the compound node $c_{i,j}$ represents the edge link information of two nodes, so we define the convolution output embedding $r^l(e_{i,j})$ for the edge $e_{i,j}$ at l^{th} layer as follows:

$$r^l(e_{i,j}) = \sigma\left(\left(\boldsymbol{W}_e^l\right)^T \cdot \boldsymbol{h}_{i,j}^{l-1}\right) \tag{7}$$

where σ is a nonlinear activation function, and $\boldsymbol{W}_e^l$ refers to the edge weight parameters of the lth layer.

The intermediate output $f^l(t_i)$, $r^l(e_{i,j})$ and $f^l(t_j)$ can be send to the next graph convolution layer as inputs according to Eq. 3. After K graph convolution operations, we can obtain the final node embedding feature matrix $\boldsymbol{Z}^V$ which combined by $f^K(t_i), \forall t_i \in \mathcal{N}$ and edge embedding feature matrix $\boldsymbol{Z}^E$ which combined by $r^K(e_{i,j}), \forall e_{i,j} \in \mathcal{E}$. Finally, we perform mean pooling operation on the node embedding to obtain the final graph representation $\boldsymbol{Z}^G$ as sequence, which is fed to the downstream pointer-based sequence decoder for the result order. Meanwhile, we use a fully-connected neural network to perform link prediction task for obtaining the relation features $\boldsymbol{Z}^L$ of the text blocks, which implies the layout constraints for the downstream decoder task. In Sect. 3.5 we will illustrate more about the layout constraints. The right blocks of Fig. 2 shows the process of the encoder.

3.4 Pointer-Based Attention Decoder

As for a sequence problem, the decoder of the text block re-organization task happens sequentially. That is, at each time step s, the decoder will output the node t_s according to the embeddings of the encoder and the previous output $t_{s'}$ which $s' < s$. In this task, we have no output vocabulary and the nodes in the output sequence are just from the inputs. Therefore we apply a pointer-based decoder with a single-head attention mechanism. Figure 4 depicts the decoding process.

The information considered by the decoder at each time step s includes three embeddings, the graph embeddings from the encoder including node embeddings and layout constraints, and the previous (last) node embedding. Hence that at the first step we will use a special start label and learn the first node v^{input} as input placeholder. Formally, we define this information as a concatenating context vector $\boldsymbol{h}_c$ and compute as follows:

$$\boldsymbol{h}_c = \begin{cases} [\boldsymbol{Z}^G, \boldsymbol{Z}^L, \boldsymbol{h}_{t_{s-1}}], s > 1 \\ [\boldsymbol{Z}^G, \boldsymbol{Z}^L, \boldsymbol{v}^{input}], s = 1 \end{cases} \tag{8}$$

where $[\cdot, \cdot, \cdot]$ is the horizontal concatenation. With the context vector, we will decode the corresponding node and use the result to update itself for the next prediction. Under the attention mechanism, we can compute a single query q_c from the context vector as follows:

$$\boldsymbol{q}_c = W^Q \boldsymbol{h}_c, \boldsymbol{k}_i = W^K \boldsymbol{h}_i, \boldsymbol{v}_i = W^V \boldsymbol{h}_i \tag{9}$$

where W^Q, W^K, W^V are the learning parameters and $\boldsymbol{h}_i$ is the node embedding, from which we get its key $\boldsymbol{k}_i$ and value $\boldsymbol{v}_i$. After that, we can compute the relation score of the query with all nodes, and mask the already visited nodes. the score $a_{c,i}$ is defined as follows:

$$
a_{c,i} = \begin{cases} \dfrac{\boldsymbol{q}_c^T \boldsymbol{k}_i}{\sqrt{d_h}}, & if \; i \neq s', \forall s' < s \\ -\inf, & otherwise \end{cases}
\tag{10}
$$

where d_h is the node embedding dimentionality. Then we can compute the output softmax probability p_i of node t_i as follows:

$$
p_i = \frac{\exp(a_{c,i})}{\sum_j \exp(a_{c,j})}
\tag{11}
$$

the decoder will choose the node with max probability as the output of each time step.

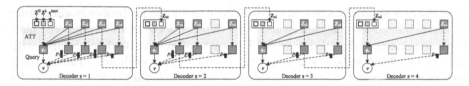

Fig. 4. The framework of pointer-based attention decoder. The decoder takes the graph embeddings including node embeddings and layout constraints. At each time step s, the decoder takes advantage of the graph embeddings and the last output node embedding where the learned placeholder is used at the first step. Once a node has been output, it will be masked and cannot be considered anymore. The example depicts that the output sequence $< t_3, t_1, t_2, t_4 >$ is decoded sequentially.

3.5 Sinkhorn Global Optimization

To improve the efficiency and make the max probability more significant, Sinkhorn normalization algorithm can be applied in the attention matrix. Because each text block has unique link to the next one, we can cast the attention matrix into a double-stochastic matrix with rows and columns summing to one. In Sinkhorn theory, any non-negative square matrix can be transformed into a double-stochastic matrix via iteratively scaling its rows and columns to one alternatively [25,26]. Consider the attention matrix $\boldsymbol{A}^{n \times n}$ before the final prediction, and it can be transformed to a double-stochastic matrix by alternatively performing row and column normalization until its rows and columns summing to one. the row R and column C normalizing operations are defined as follows:

$$
R_{i,j}(A) = \frac{A_{i,j}}{\sum_{k=1}^{n} A_{i,k}}; C_{i,j}(A) = \frac{A_{i,j}}{\sum_{k=1}^{n} A_{k,j}}.
\tag{12}
$$

And the Sinkhorn normalization SH for the l-th iteration is operated recursively by the following rules:

$$SH^n(\boldsymbol{A}) = \begin{cases} \boldsymbol{A}, & \text{if } n = 0 \\ C\left(R\left(SH^{n-1}(\boldsymbol{A})\right)\right), & \text{otherwise} \end{cases} \tag{13}$$

Then we can add Sinkhorn normalization for global optimal max probability of the output text block at each time step.

4 Experiments

In this section, we apply our model on real Detailed Image (DI) datasets with several types of products and use both global and local sequence evaluation methods to compare our model with other baselines. Furthermore, we launch a real user experience test on blind people and analyze their feedbacks.

4.1 Dataset

Since there is no work on re-organizing OCR text blocks for proper reading order on detail image, we first collect and label detail images from e-commerce platforms to construct the DI datasets. DI consists of about 10k detail images with more than 130k text blocks from several product types such as cosmetics, daily necessities, detergents, and the number of text block ranges from 5 to 50 for each detailed image. Due to some bad OCR results, redundant information, and irrelevant descriptions, we ignore these text blocks during the reordering process to guarantee that each text block's content is valid and necessary for comprehension. The layout of text blocks in DI includes horizontally text, multi-column text, ring, star and single key-value structural text, which implies different logical reading order. We communicate with real users including the visually impaired and the designers of the text images to understand how to comprehend the image only by the texts contained, then we induct and define the proper text order as all the text blocks from OCR are in the order of visual information acquisition, and keep the semantically related text blocks as close as possible in the ordering sequence. For our model, we assign 80% of the dataset for training, 15% for validation and 15% for the test.

4.2 Baselines

We compare the performance of our model with the following designed baselines.

Position-Greedy (POS-Greedy). This method considers the position of the text blocks and under the row-major order to scan the OCR text blocks. It will select the nearest text block of the current one as its next linked one. Under the statistics, more than 98% detail images satisfy the rule that its first text block is relatively close to the top or left region, so we use it to decide the first block of the sequence.

Position-hierarchy (POS-Hier). This method considers the global minimum distance among all the pairs of OCR text blocks, then merge the pair into a new block iteratively and row-major order rules order the two text blocks.

Position-MLP (POS-MLP). This model only considers the geometrical feature with an MLP to predict the partial order of each pair. It solves the text block re-organization task according to the partial order pairs.

4.3   Evaluation Metrics

Since it is a sequence order problem, we first use the **total order accuracy** of the detail image as the global sequence evaluation metric. We compare the ground truth sequence with our model's predict sequence by single block position matching, if there exist two blocks mismatching, the prediction of the detail image fails. The total order accuracy can be computed as the ratio of the number of detail images whose OCR text blocks are perfectly matched.

Other than the global sequence evaluation, we are inspired by the evaluation for discrete words in machine translation and apply the **BLEU** score for evaluating the local continuous coverage rate of the discrete OCR text blocks. Hence that we re-organize the text blocks from the input, it is meaningless to compute one block coverage (BLEU-1) as they always show the same value.

4.4   Results and Analysis

We first resize all the detailed images for 768×768 resolution as normalized input for feature extraction from the pretrained backbone, then we feed them into a two-layer graph convolution encoder for obtaining the graph embeddings, then the attention decoder will predict the sequence of the text blocks. We perform the last three models ten times within 300 epochs on NVIDIA Tesla P100 until convergence and choose the best one on the validation set. The main results are depicts in Table 1. As we can see, our proposed model GCN-PN and GCN-PN-Sinkhorn outperform among the baselines on global sequence prediction, which seems that the image feature from FCN is beneficial to predict more accurate re-organized sequence, because it is reasonable that the layout is related to the image feature and can help to infer the reading order. Meanwhile, the GCN encoder and PN decoder provide a more powerful order relation analysis than the rule-based method. Besides, adding Sinkhorn normalizing operation into the decoder is beneficial for total order prediction. It considers the total links among the text blocks and can weaken some potential wrong links that maybe only locally optimal.

Furthermore, we make a deep analysis on the local sub-sequence coverage. Intuitively, we use the BLEU score which is usually evaluated for machine translation tasks. Since we can consider each of the text blocks in the result sequence as a separate unit like word, we can compute the BLEU-2 and BLEU-4 for evaluating the coverage rate on 2 and 4 subsequent text blocks. Table 2 depicts the

Table 1. Total order accuracy of these models on DI test data

Method	Total order Acc
POS-Greedy	0.41 ± 0.008
POS-Hier	0.70 ± 0.010
POS-MLP	0.75 ± 0.010
GCN-PN	0.79 ± 0.009
GCN-PN-Sinkhorn	**0.86 ± 0.005**

results. Hence, we use the NLTK package to compute the BLEU score, which adds a normalization to it and maps it into a value at $[0, 1]$ intervals. When the perfect matching happens, the value goes to 1, otherwise it goes to zero, and the large the value is, the higher the coverage rate is. From the table we can find that our GCN-PN-Sinkhorn model gets the highest coverage rate both on 2 and 4 subsequent text blocks, which implies the global order optimization also benefits the local order optimization. Hence that we also find the POS-Hier methods get high BLEU-2 score but low BLEU-4 score because this method merges two nearest blocks at each ordering step, it pays more attention to the 2-neighboring text blocks or text block groups. Furthermore, normal MLP may be more easily confused by some wrong sub links than attention-based GCN-PN models and are inferior to them on local evaluation. The greedy method shows the worst results on global and local evaluation because reading order on many complex layouts does not simply depend on position, such as multi-column, which has the rule that is reading the total column context one by one.

Table 2. The BLEU scores of these models on DI test data

Method	BLEU-2	BLEU-4
POS-Greedy	0.76	0.40
POS-Hier	0.89	0.66
POS-MLP	0.82	0.62
GCN-PN	0.90	0.71
GCN-PN-Sinkhorn	**0.92**	**0.74**

Figure 5 and Fig. 6 show more details of the visual results. Figure 5 shows a multi-column structure example and we can find the POS-Hier (5(b)) and our GCN-PN-Sinkhorn model (5(f)) perform well as the ground truth, which also implies their ability for ordering local text blocks. Sinkhorn based model performs well than GCN-PN (5(e)) and POS-MLP because of the global optimizing to reduce the probability of some wrong links. Meanwhile, the Greedy method is easy to make a mistake and causes many inverse reading order links because it is highly sensitive to a variation on the text blocks' coordinates. Figure 6 shows a

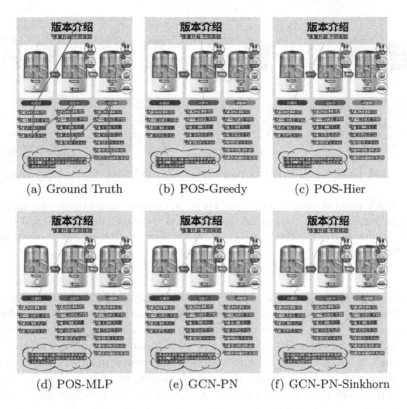

(a) Ground Truth   (b) POS-Greedy   (c) POS-Hier

(d) POS-MLP   (e) GCN-PN   (f) GCN-PN-Sinkhorn

Fig. 5. An example of visualized reading order results. (a) is the ground truth order with orange arrow lines and (b)–(f) are the results of the methods with green arrow lines indicating the reading order. (Color figure online)

KV-table structure example and we find that POS-Hier (6(b)) cannot deal with this structure well because some keys in the table are more closed than keys to their values, resulting in a wrong merge operation. POS-MLP (6(c)) can order part of the former text blocks but failed at the latter ones, which implies the shortage of long order sequences. Our two model shows the same good results (6(d)) because the encoder-decoder structure can keep and use more global layout information to order the sequence.

4.5   Real User Experience

We also design a real user experience in which the real blind people will participate in our test and check the predicted text block sequence that can be comprehended fluently. In this test, we use our model to generate the text block sequence from 113 detail images as a test group and use the untreated text block sequence (ordered by the reading scheme from top to bottom and left to right) as a control group. Meanwhile, three blind people who all receive compulsory

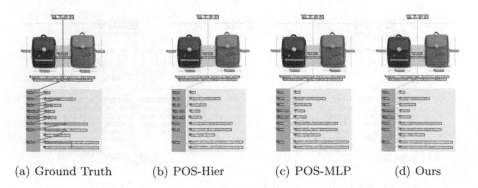

(a) Ground Truth   (b) POS-Hier   (c) POS-MLP   (d) Ours

Fig. 6. A KV-table structure example of visualized reading order results for analyzing row-major locality. (a) is the ground truth order with orange arrow lines and (b)–(d) are the results of the methods with green arrow lines indicating the reading order. (Color figure online)

education and often participate in online shopping are invited to our experiment. Their task is to hear both of the sequences and decide which one is better to comprehend. There is no other comprehension assistance during the experiment, and three of them do not know the corresponding model of the sequence beforehand. It takes them a week to complete the task and submit their choices and feedbacks. The result shows that all the subjects believe that our model outperforms more than 70% detailed images to help them comprehend well.

5   Conclusion

In this paper, we focus on the OCR text reordering problems. An end-to-end re-organization sequence learning structure is first proposed in the e-commerce scene. With a pretrained text detection network FCN, we extract the image feature and incorporate it with the geometric feature to build a weighted directed graph structure. Then a graph convolution encoder with a self-attention mechanism is considered to obtain the graph embeddings. Then a pointer-based attention decoder with a Sinkhorn global normalization is applied to predict the permutation. Our model outperforms the baselines both on global and local evaluations and will help get a more accurate and thorough comprehension of detailed images, especially for the visually impaired.

Acknowledgement. This work is supported by Alibaba-Zhejiang University Joint Institute of Frontier Technologies, The National Key R&D Program of China (No. 2018YFC2002603, 2018YFB1403202), Zhejiang Provincial Natural Science Foundation of China (No. LZ13F020001), the National Natural Science Foundation of China (No. 61972349, 61173185, 61173186) and the National Key Technology R&D Program of China (No. 2012BAI34B01, 2014BAK15B02).

References

1. Baek, Y., Lee, B., Han, D., Yun, S., Lee, H.: Character region awareness for text detection. In: Proceedings of the IEEE Conference on Computer Vision and Pattern Recognition, pp. 9365–9374 (2019)
2. Bahdanau, D., Cho, K., Bengio, Y.: Neural machine translation by jointly learning to align and translate. arXiv preprint arXiv:1409.0473 (2014)
3. Binmakhashen, G.M., Mahmoud, S.A.: Document layout analysis: a comprehensive survey. ACM Comput. Surveys (CSUR) **52**(6), 1–36 (2019)
4. Bissacco, A., Cummins, M., Netzer, Y., Neven, H.: PhotoOCR: reading text in uncontrolled conditions. In: Proceedings of the IEEE International Conference on Computer Vision, pp. 785–792 (2013)
5. Busta, M., Neumann, L., Matas, J.: Deep TextSpotter: an end-to-end trainable scene text localization and recognition framework. In: Proceedings of the IEEE International Conference on Computer Vision, pp. 2204–2212 (2017)
6. Chakraborty, A., Paranjape, B., Kakarla, S., Ganguly, N.: Stop clickbait: detecting and preventing clickbaits in online news media. In: 2016 IEEE/ACM International Conference on Advances in Social Networks Analysis and Mining (ASONAM), pp. 9–16. IEEE (2016)
7. Cheng, J., Lapata, M.: Neural summarization by extracting sentences and words. arXiv preprint arXiv:1603.07252 (2016)
8. Dai, Y., et al.: Fused text segmentation networks for multi-oriented scene text detection. In: 2018 24th International Conference on Pattern Recognition (ICPR), pp. 3604–3609. IEEE (2018)
9. Eriguchi, A., Hashimoto, K., Tsuruoka, Y.: Tree-to-sequence attentional neural machine translation. arXiv preprint arXiv:1603.06075 (2016)
10. Filippova, K., Alfonseca, E., Colmenares, C.A., Kaiser, L., Vinyals, O.: Sentence compression by deletion with LSTMs. In: Proceedings of the 2015 Conference on Empirical Methods in Natural Language Processing, pp. 360–368 (2015)
11. Freeman, H., Garder, L.: Apictorial Jigsaw puzzles: the computer solution of a problem in pattern recognition. IEEE Trans. Electron. Comput. **2**, 118–127 (1964)
12. Graves, A., Wayne, G., Danihelka, I.: Neural turing machines. arXiv preprint arXiv:1410.5401 (2014)
13. Jaderberg, M., Simonyan, K., Vedaldi, A., Zisserman, A.: Reading text in the wild with convolutional neural networks. Int. J. Comput. Vis. **116**(1), 1–20 (2016)
14. Khare, V., Shivakumara, P., Raveendran, P., Blumenstein, M.: A blind deconvolution model for scene text detection and recognition in video. Pattern Recogn. **54**, 128–148 (2016)
15. Kool, W., van Hoof, H., Welling, M.: Attention, learn to solve routing problems! arXiv preprint arXiv:1803.08475 (2018)
16. Liu, X., Gao, F., Zhang, Q., Zhao, H.: Graph convolution for multimodal information extraction from visually rich documents. arXiv preprint arXiv:1903.11279 (2019)
17. Long, J., Shelhamer, E., Darrell, T.: Fully convolutional networks for semantic segmentation. In: Proceedings of the IEEE Conference on Computer Vision and Pattern Recognition, pp. 3431–3440 (2015)
18. Noroozi, M., Favaro, P.: Unsupervised learning of visual representations by solving Jigsaw puzzles. In: Leibe, B., Matas, J., Sebe, N., Welling, M. (eds.) ECCV 2016. LNCS, vol. 9910, pp. 69–84. Springer, Cham (2016). https://doi.org/10.1007/978-3-319-46466-4_5

19. Pomeranz, D., Shemesh, M., Ben-Shahar, O.: A fully automated greedy square jigsaw puzzle solver. In: CVPR 2011, pp. 9–16. IEEE (2011)
20. Rong, X., Yi, C., Tian, Y.: Unambiguous text localization and retrieval for cluttered scenes. In: Proceedings of the IEEE Conference on Computer Vision and Pattern Recognition, pp. 5494–5502 (2017)
21. Rumelhart, D.E., Hinton, G.E., Williams, R.J.: Learning internal representations by error propagation. California Univ San Diego La Jolla Inst for Cognitive Science, Tech. rep. (1985)
22. Cruz, R.S., Fernando, B., Cherian, A., Gould, S.: DeepPermNet: visual permutation learning. In: Proceedings of the IEEE Conference on Computer Vision and Pattern Recognition, pp. 3949–3957 (2017)
23. See, A., Liu, P.J., Manning, C.D.: Get to the point: summarization with pointer-generator networks. arXiv preprint arXiv:1704.04368 (2017)
24. Sholomon, D., David, O., Netanyahu, N.S.: A genetic algorithm-based solver for very large Jigsaw puzzles. In: Proceedings of the IEEE Conference on Computer Vision and Pattern Recognition, pp. 1767–1774 (2013)
25. Sinkhorn, R.: A relationship between arbitrary positive matrices and doubly stochastic matrices. Ann. Math. Stat. **35**(2), 876–879 (1964)
26. Sinkhorn, R., Knopp, P.: Concerning nonnegative matrices and doubly stochastic matrices. Pac. J. Math. **21**(2), 343–348 (1967)
27. Sutskever, I., Vinyals, O., Le, Q.V.: Sequence to sequence learning with neural networks. In: Advances in Neural Information Processing Systems, pp. 3104–3112 (2014)
28. Vinyals, O., Bengio, S., Kudlur, M.: Order matters: sequence to sequence for sets. arXiv preprint arXiv:1511.06391 (2015)
29. Vinyals, O., Fortunato, M., Jaitly, N.: Pointer networks. In: Advances in Neural Information Processing Systems, pp. 2692–2700 (2015)
30. Weston, J., et al.: Towards AI-complete question answering: a set of prerequisite toy tasks. arXiv preprint arXiv:1502.05698 (2015)
31. Xu, K., Wu, L., Wang, Z., Feng, Y., Witbrock, M., Sheinin, V.: Graph2Seq: graph to sequence learning with attention-based neural networks. arXiv preprint arXiv:1804.00823 (2018)
32. Yin, F., Wu, Y.C., Zhang, X.Y., Liu, C.L.: Scene text recognition with sliding convolutional character models. arXiv preprint arXiv:1709.01727 (2017)
33. You, Y., Jia, W., Liu, T., Yang, W.: Improving abstractive document summarization with salient information modeling. In: Proceedings of the 57th Annual Meeting of the Association for Computational Linguistics, pp. 2132–2141 (2019)
34. Zhu, Y., Yao, C., Bai, X.: Scene text detection and recognition: recent advances and future trends. Front. Comput. Sci. **10**(1), 19–36 (2016)

Improving Query Efficiency of Black-Box Adversarial Attack

Yang Bai[1,4], Yuyuan Zeng[2,4], Yong Jiang[1,2,4(✉)], Yisen Wang[3(✉)],
Shu-Tao Xia[2,4], and Weiwei Guo[5]

[1] Tsinghua Berkeley Shenzhen Institute, Tsinghua University, Beijing, China
{y-bai17,zengyy19}@mails.tsinghua.edu.cn, jiangy@sz.tsinghua.edu.cn
[2] Tsinghua Shenzhen International Graduate School, Tsinghua University,
Beijing, China
[3] Shanghai Jiao Tong University, Shanghai, China
eewangyisen@gmail.com
[4] PCL Research Center of Networks and Communications, Peng Cheng Laboratory,
Shenzhen, China
[5] vivo AI Lab, Shenzhen, China

Abstract. Deep neural networks (DNNs) have demonstrated excellent performance on various tasks, however they are under the risk of adversarial examples that can be easily generated when the target model is accessible to an attacker (white-box setting). As plenty of machine learning models have been deployed via online services that only provide query outputs from inaccessible models (*e.g.*, Google Cloud Vision API2), black-box adversarial attacks (inaccessible target model) are of critical security concerns in practice rather than white-box ones. However, existing query-based black-box adversarial attacks often require excessive model queries to maintain a high attack success rate. Therefore, in order to improve query efficiency, we explore the distribution of adversarial examples around benign inputs with the help of image structure information characterized by a Neural Process, and propose a Neural Process based black-box adversarial attack (NP-Attack) in this paper. Extensive experiments show that NP-Attack could greatly decrease the query counts under the black-box setting. Code is available at https://github.com/Sandy-Zeng/NPAttack.

Keywords: Black-box adversarial attack · Adversarial distribution · Query efficiency · Neural Process

---

Y. Bai and Y. Zeng—Equal contribution.

Electronic supplementary material The online version of this chapter (https://doi.org/10.1007/978-3-030-58595-2_7) contains supplementary material, which is available to authorized users.

A. Vedaldi et al. (Eds.): ECCV 2020, LNCS 12370, pp. 101–116, 2020.
https://doi.org/10.1007/978-3-030-58595-2_7

1   Introduction

Deep neural networks (DNNs) have been deployed on many real-world complex tasks and demonstrated excellent performance, such as computer vision [12], speech recognition [28], and natural language processing [7]. However, DNNs are found vulnerable to adversarial examples, *i.e.*, DNNs will make incorrect predictions confidently when inputs are added with some well designed imperceptible perturbations [11], thus various adversarial defense methods are proposed [2,29,30]. Adversarial examples can be crafted following either a white-box setting (the adversary has full access to the target model) or a black-box setting (the adversary has no information of the target model). White-box methods such as Fast Gradient Sign Method (FGSM) [11], Projected Gradient Decent (PGD) [21], Carlini & Wagner (CW) [3] and other universal attacks [19,23] only pose limited threats to DNN models which are usually kept secret in practice. Meanwhile transferability-based black-box attacks, *e.g.*, momentum boosting [8] and skip gradient [33], need to train a surrogate model separately and only obtain a moderate attack success rate.

As modern machine learning systems, *e.g.*, Google Cloud Vision API2 (https://cloud.google.com/vision/) and Google Photos3 (https://photos.google.com/), are often provided as a kind of service, one common scenario is that we can query the system in a number of times and get the output results [1]. Based on this, *query*-based black-box attacks that directly generate adversarial examples on the target model are proposed such as ZOO [4]. These query-based methods could bring almost 100% attack success rates while their query complexity is quite high (not acceptable). Therefore, how to significantly reduce the query complexity while maintaining the attack success rate simultaneously is still an open problem. There are several existing work to reduce the query complexity. For examples, AutoZOOM [26] compresses the attack dimension while QL [13] adopts an efficient gradient estimation strategy. Different from the above example-wise adversarial example generation, $\mathcal{N}$Attack [18] proposes to model the adversarial distribution and sample from it to generate adversarial examples, which indeed reduces the query counts. However, the distribution is based on the simple pixel-wise mapping functions (*e.g.*, $tanh$), which is the bottleneck of its query complexity.

Inspired by the above observations, in this paper, we introduce the structure information of the image into consideration to further reduce the required query counts when modeling the distribution of adversarial examples. To be specific, the structure is characterized by a Neural Process (NP) [10], an efficient auto-encoder method to model a distribution over regression functions with a deterministic variable focusing on local information and a latent variable focusing on global information. Based on NP, we then propose a Neural Process based black-box attack, named NP-Attack. NP can be pre-trained on benign examples, and then used to reconstruct adversarial examples through optimizing above mentioned variables, which is definitely efficient than previous pixel-wise operations in $\mathcal{N}$Attack. As a proof-of-concept, we conduct an experiment to compare these two distribution-based attacks: $\mathcal{N}$Attack and NP-Attack. Both attacks are

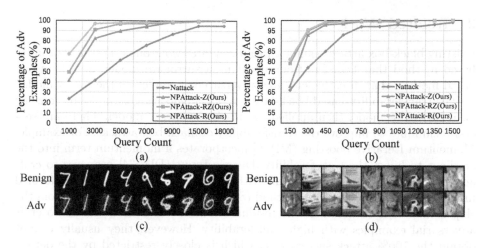

Fig. 1. Comparison of two distribution-based black-box attacks: $\mathcal{N}$Attack and our proposed NP-Attack. Percentage of adversarial examples with different query counts generated by $\mathcal{N}$Attack and NP-Attack on MNIST (a) and CIFAR10 (b), and the corresponding NP-Attack generated adversarial examples and benign examples of MNIST (c) and CIFAR10 (d). It is demonstrated that NP-Attack is more query efficient compared to $\mathcal{N}$Attack when generating adversarial examples.

conducted by limiting the same maximal query count, and the maximal distortion of L_∞ is set to 0.05 for CIFAR10 and 0.2 for MNIST. The percentage of adversarial examples returned at the maximal query count is plotted in Fig. 1. We can see that the adversarial distribution optimized in NP-Attack (three variants) contains a higher percentage of adversarial examples under the same query counts compared to $\mathcal{N}$Attack, which illustrates NP-Attack is more efficient in optimizing and modeling the adversarial distributions. Figure 1 also gives some examples of adversarial examples generated in our NP-Attack, which are also visual integrity. Our main contributions could be summarized as follows:

- We propose a distribution based black-box attack, Neural Process based black-box attack (NP-Attack), which uses the image structure information for modeling adversarial distributions and reduces the required query counts.
- NP-Attack has several optimization variants due to the variables in NP. The optimization on deterministic variable focuses more on the local information, while optimization on latent variable focuses more on the global information. The different optimization variants have different effects on the location of adversarial perturbations, which brings more flexibility for NP-Attack.
- Extensive experiments demonstrate the superiority of our proposed NP-Attack. On both untargeted and targeted attacks, NP-Attack greatly reduces the needed query counts under the same attack success rate and distortion, compared with the state-of-the-art query-based black-box attacks.

2   Related Work

Existing black-box attacks can be categorized into two groups: 1) transferability-based method that transfers from attacking a surrogate model; and 2) query-based method that directly generates adversarial examples on the target model.

For transferability-based black-box attacks, adversarial examples are crafted on a surrogate model then applied to attack the target model. There are several techniques to improve the transferability of black-box attacks. For example, Momentum Iterative boosting (MI) [8] incorporates a momentum term into the gradient to boost the transferability. Diverse Input (DI) [34] proposes to craft adversarial examples using gradient with respect to the randomly-transformed input example. Skip Gradient Method (SGM) [33] uses more gradients from the skip connections rather than the residual modules via a decay factor to craft adversarial examples with high transferability. However, they usually cannot obtain the 100% attack success rate, which is closely restricted by the dependency between the surrogate model and the target model.

For query-based black-box attacks, they could be further classified as decision-based (query results are one-hot labels) [5] or score-based ones (query results are scores). The score-based attacks are investigated in this paper. This kind of method estimates the gradient of the target model via a large number of queries, which is then used to generate adversarial examples. ZOO [4] explores gradient estimation methods by querying the target model as an oracle. They use zeroth-order stochastic coordinate descent along with dimension reduction, hierarchical attack and importance sampling techniques, to directly estimate the gradients of the targeted model for generating adversarial examples. However, ZOO requires numerous queries to estimate the gradients with respect to all pixels. Further, AutoZOOM [26] operates the gradient estimation in latent space, using an offline pre-trained auto-encoder or a bilinear mapping function to compress the attack dimension. It then applies an adaptive random gradient estimation strategy to balance query counts and distortion, which improves the query efficiency by a great deal. Meta Attack [9] pre-trains a meta attacker model to estimate the black-box gradient, which efficiently reduces the query counts. Beyond zeroth-order optimization-based approaches, QL [13] proposes to use a Natural Evolution Strategy (NES) [31] to enhance query efficiency. Bandits [14] further introduces time and data priors under NES. $\mathcal{N}$Attack [18] is another kind of black-box attack that explicitly models the adversarial distribution with a Gaussian distribution. The adversarial attack is hence formalized as an optimization problem, which searches the Gaussian distribution under the guidance of increasing the attack success rate of target models.

Following the general NES structure, we explore the adversarial distribution in a more efficient way using some high-level information of images in this paper.

3   Proposed Neural Process-Based Black-Box Attack

In this section, we propose a Neural Process-based Black-box Attack (NP-Attack) with significantly reduced query counts. NP-Attack models the

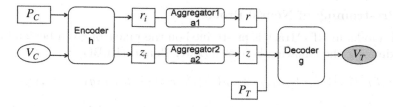

Fig. 2. The structure of NP model trained on pixels of one image. Here, V_C and V_T are the context and target pixel values, then P_C and P_T are the corresponding pixel positions. z_i and r_i are pixel-wise latent variables and deterministic variables.

distribution of adversarial examples efficiently by a Neural Process that utilizes the high-level structure information of images rather than the pixel-level information.

3.1 Preliminaries of Neural Process

Neural Process (NP) [10] is a combination of the best from neural networks and Gaussian Process [22,32], which could efficiently estimate the uncertainty in the predictions. It could be expanded into an attentive version, called Attentive Neural Process (ANP) [15,27], which is applied in our NP-Attack.[1]

As pixel values in one image subject to a Gaussian Process, NP is applied to reconstruct images by predicting their pixel values. As shown in Fig. 2, the structure of NP consists of the following three parts: 1) *Encoder h*, whose inputs are context pixel pairs concatenating pixel positions and values; 2) *Aggregator a*, which summarizes the outputs of the encoder as latent variable z from a Gaussian distribution $\mathcal{N}(\mu, \sigma^2)$ and deterministic variable r; 3) *Decoder g*, which takes the sampled latent variable z, deterministic variable r and target pixel position P_T as inputs and predicts the target pixel value V_T. Overall, NP models the distributions as:

$$p\left(V_T \middle| P_C, P_T, V_C\right) = \int p(V_T | P_T, r, z) q(z | s_C) dz, \qquad (1)$$

Here P, V represents pixel position and value, and C, T are random subsets of context and target, s_C is the distribution modeled over (P_C, V_C). In Eq. 1, Latent variable z accounts for uncertainty in the predictions of V_T for observed (P_C, V_C), while r is calculated by a deterministic function which aggregates (P_C, V_C) into a finite dimensional representation with permutation invariance in C. The interpretation of the latent path is that z gives rise to correlations in the marginal distribution of the target predictions V_T, modeling the global structure of the stochastic process realization, whereas the deterministic path r models the fine-grained local structure.

---

[1] We still use NP in the following without ambiguity.

3.2   Pre-training of Neural Process

The NP model in NP-Attack is pre-trained on the pixels of given benign images by maximizing the following Evidence Lower Bound (ELBO)[2]:

$$\log p\left(V_T | P_T, P_C, V_C\right) \geq \mathrm{E}_{q(z | s_T)}\left[\log p\left(V_T | P_T, r, z\right)\right] - D_{KL}\left(q\left(z | s_T\right) \| q\left(z | s_C\right)\right). \tag{2}$$

Like s_C defined above, s_T represents the distribution modeled over (P_T, V_T). To be specific, the s_C and s_T are both the whole pixels in one image during the pre-training process in NP-Attack. Once trained, NP shares the same encoder and decoder on the same image set even on different selected images, varying on latent variables and deterministic variables corresponding to different images. Note that such pre-training process is independent from the main attack part on the benign examples, which means the encoder and decoder are fixed after pre-training and could keep some structure information of images.

The pre-trained NP models a distribution by variables z and r, where z is sampled from a Gaussian distribution $\mathcal{N}(\mu, \sigma^2)$, thus the latent variables and deterministic variable are in fact (μ, σ) and r. As NP models the pixel-wise distribution in one image, its structure information is kept in such NP. Adversarial examples and benign examples are imperceptible to human eyes, sharing a similar visual structure. Thus we utilize the pre-trained NP and find that adversarial examples could be reconstructed successfully by optimizing the above mentioned variables for a new distribution and sampling from this optimized distribution.

3.3   Overview of the Proposed NP-Attack

Equipped with the pre-trained NP, we can propose the distribution-based NP-Attack. The key idea of distribution-based attack is to model the adversarial distribution around the small region of one natural example x, such that a sample drawn from this distribution is likely an adversarial example. Compared to previous distribution-based $\mathcal{N}$Attack, the difference lies on the method of modeling the adversarial distribution. $\mathcal{N}$Attack models such adversarial distribution just on pixel level with a Gaussian distribution focusing on pixels independently, not considering any other information on the structure of pixel values in one image. However, our proposed NP-Attack utilizes the decoder of a pre-trained NP model and only optimizes latent variables or deterministic variables, in which case the fixed decoder could hold some structure information of pixels in one image, improving the optimization efficiency in modeling adversarial distributions.

Specifically, the objective function L in our NP-Attack is defined on S, an intersection of a latent region modeled by NP and a L_p-ball centered around the benign example x, i.e., $S = S_p(x) \bigcap \mathrm{NP}(x)$. Given l as the loss defined on a given example point, the objective L with regard to adversarial distribution in our optimization criterion is:

$$L((\mu, \sigma), r | x) := \int_{x-\epsilon}^{x+\epsilon} l(x_{rec}) g(x_{rec} | (\mu, \sigma), r) h((\mu, \sigma), r | x) dx_{rec} \tag{3}$$

---

[2] The implementation details of ANP are shown in the Appendix A.

where g and h are the decoder and encoder of pre-trained NP, μ, σ, r denote for the variables to be optimized in NP-Attack, x_{rec} denotes the image reconstructed by NP, ϵ denotes the L_p ball restriction. By optimizing on such objective L, we could achieve our aim to model the latent manifold of adversarial examples.

As the target model could return scores in each query, the original loss function is defined as:

$$
l(x) := \begin{cases} \max(0, \max_{c \neq y} \log F(x)_c - \log F(x)_y), & \text{targeted,} \\ \max(0, \log F(x)_y - \max_{c \neq y} \log F(x)_c), & \text{untargeted.} \end{cases} \tag{4}
$$

where $F(x)$ denotes the softmax outputs, y is the true label in untargeted attack or the target label in targeted attack, and c is other labels except y.

In summary, the procedures on modeling and sampling from distribution in NP-Attack are shown in Algorithm 1: 1) Feed a benign example x, and compute r and (μ, σ) from the *Encoder* h of NP; 2) Sample z from $\mathcal{N}(\mu, \sigma^2)$; and 3) Reconstruct x_{rec} with the optimized (r, z) from the *Decoder* g of NP (shown in the following Sect. 3.4), then project x_{rec} back into the L_p-ball centered at x.

3.4   Optimization of NP-Attack

As the reconstructed image x_{rec} is mainly dependent on the sampled r, z and pre-trained *Decoder* g of NP, there are three optimization options: NP-Attack-R/Z/RZ corresponding to the optimized variables r, z or both. As the three branches share the similar optimization function, we take **NP-Attack-R** as an example here, and other optimization options are shown in the Appendix B.

In this case, r is a variable in NP, cooperating with z to reconstruct an image. The difference of r from z is that r is a deterministic variable. That is, z shares the same distribution in one image for all pixels, while r is independent for different pixels thus with better freedom. As adversarial perturbations are computed and added on pixels, the optimization on r might be more reasonable. The benefit of optimizing r than $\mathcal{N}$Attack is that r is in the latent space with a larger latent dimension (128 dimension in our NP-Attack) for each pixel, which owns more capacity to perturb.

We define the loss L on some search distribution $\Pi(R \mid r)$. Omitting z while inheriting *Decoder* g from the pre-trained NP, the estimated loss function in our NP-Attack could be considered as: $L = \mathbb{E}_{\Pi(R \mid r)} l(g(R))$. To simplify the optimization, we give $R \sim \mathcal{N}(r, \sigma'^2)$, where σ' is a hyper-parameter. Then the optimization of r could be implemented by adding some random Gaussian noises and using NES. The optimization function could be computed as:

$$
r_{t+1} \leftarrow r_t - \frac{\eta}{b} \sum_{i=1}^{b} l(g(R_i)) \nabla_{r_t} \log \mathcal{N}(R_i \mid r_t, \sigma'^2), \tag{5}
$$

where b is the batch size. Given that $R_i = r_t + p_i \sigma'$, where p_i is sampled from the standard Gaussian distribution $\mathcal{N}(0, I)$, and σ' is a hyper-parameter, not essentially equal to σ in z, $\nabla_{r_t} \log \mathcal{N}(R_i \mid r_t, \sigma'^2) \propto \sigma'^{-1} p_i$.

Algorithm 1. NP-Attack

Input: natural image x, label y, target neural network F, pre-trained NP model
    (*Encoder h, Decoder g, Aggregator a*), maximal optimization iteration T, sample
    size b, projecting function P, learning rate η
1: Compute the variables from *Encoder h* on image x: $\mathcal{N}(\mu, \sigma^2), r \leftarrow h(x)$
2: **for** $t = 0$ **to** $T - 1$ **do**
3:    **if** F(x) $\neq$ y (untargeted) or F(x) = y (targeted) **then**
4:      attack success.
5:    **else**
6:      Sample perturbations from Gaussian distribution: $p_i \sim \mathcal{N}(0, I), i = 1, 2, ..., b$.
7:      Add the perturbation p_i in NP-Attack-R/Z/RZ, specifically on μ or r or both,

$$\begin{cases} z_i \sim \mathcal{N}(\mu, \sigma^2), r_i = r + p_i\sigma, & \text{NP-Attack-R,} \\ z_i \sim \mathcal{N}(\mu + p_i\sigma, \sigma^2), r_i = r, & \text{NP-Attack-Z,} \\ z_i \sim \mathcal{N}(\mu + p_i\sigma, \sigma^2), r_i = r + p_i\sigma, & \text{NP-Attack-RZ.} \end{cases}$$

8:      Reconstruct the image from *Decoder g*, and use project function P to restrict
      its maximal distortion: $x_i = P(g(z_i, r_i))$.
9:      Compute the losses of these reconstructed image series x_i under targeted or
      untargeted setting,

$$l_i = \begin{cases} \max(0, \max_{c \neq y} \log F(x_i)_c - \log F(x_i)_y), & \text{targeted,} \\ \max(0, \log F(x_i)_y - \max_{c \neq y} \log F(x_i)_c), & \text{untargeted.} \end{cases}$$

      The corresponding loss $l_i = l_i - mean(l)$.
10:     Update μ or r or both as optimization:

$$\begin{cases} r_{t+1} \leftarrow r_t - \dfrac{\eta}{b\sigma} \sum_{i=1}^{b} l_i p_i, & \text{NP-Attack-R,} \\[2mm] \mu_{t+1} \leftarrow \mu_t - \dfrac{\eta}{b\sigma} \sum_{i=1}^{b} l_i p_i, & \text{NP-Attack-Z,} \\[2mm] \mu_{t+1} \leftarrow \mu_t - \dfrac{\eta}{b\sigma} \sum_{i=1}^{b} l_i p_i, r_{t+1} \leftarrow r_t - \dfrac{\eta}{b\sigma} \sum_{i=1}^{b} l_i p_i, & \text{NP-Attack-RZ.} \end{cases}$$

11:    **end if**
12: **end for**

3.5 Discussion

As the adversarial examples in our NP-Attack is sampled and reconstructed through the decoder of the benign pre-trained NP, we study on the examples reconstructed by NP. Figure 3 shows that the adversarial examples and benign ones could both be reconstructed by benign pre-trained NP, sharing the same decoder, optimized with different latent variables. However, noised examples (added with slight Gaussian noises) could absolutely not be reconstructed by such NP. This phenomenon contributes to the query efficiency of NP-Attack compared to $\mathcal{N}$Attack, as the appliance of NP filters the noised examples away, the distributions modeled by NP are with higher percentages of adversarial examples, which keep consistency with the Fig. 1.

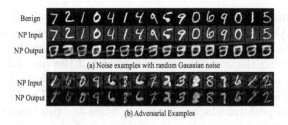

(a) Noise examples with random Gaussian noise

(b) Adversarial Examples

Fig. 3. The reconstruction of pre-trained NP. Given noise examples with random Gaussian noises (a) and adversarial examples generated by PGD attack (b) under $L_\infty = 0.2$ as the input of the benign pre-trained NP model, the adversarial examples could be reconstructed while noised examples could not.

Moreover, we discuss the difference between NP and other auto-encoder models, like VAE [16]. Note that the variables in NP are different from VAE. In VAE, the latent variable z is on the whole image set, which means a different sample would refer to the reconstruction of a different image. In NP, the distribution of z is modeled independently on one image. So the optimization of z in VAE to model adversarial distribution could lead to a collapse on distributions with high possibility. On the contrary, the Gaussian distribution of z in NP could be optimized independently on different images towards adversarial distribution. Moreover, NP has another variable r, which is also modeled on one image and different from z, bringing more flexibility.

4   Experiment

In this section, we evaluate our method on three benchmark image classification datasets MNIST [20], CIFAR10 [17] and ImageNet [6]. We compare our proposed NP-Attack with several score-based black-box attack techniques with regard to distortion (ϵ), average query count (i.e. the number of evaluations on black-box model) and attack success rate (ASR). We firstly provide a comprehensive understanding of NP-Attack where we test the performance of our NP-Attack under different experimental settings. After that, we conduct untargeted and targeted attacks on benchmark datasets MNIST, CIFAR10 and ImageNet to show the superiority of our method in reducing query counts.

Experimental Setups. For MNIST, a MLP model is trained with three fully connected layers, achieving 98.50% accuracy. For CIFAR10, the WideResNet [35] is adopted, achieving 94.10% accuracy. For ImageNet, we use the pre-trained Inception-V3 model [25], achieving 78% accuracy. The baseline query based black-box techniques are ZOO [4], AutoZOOM [26], QL [13] and $\mathcal{N}$Attack [18]. The results of those compared methods are reproduced by the code released in the original paper with default settings.

NP Pre-training. For NP-Attack, NP models are pre-trained on the train set of MNIST, CIFAR10 and ImageNet respectively which takes around 5, 45 and 72 hours on a single NVIDIA GTX 1080 TI GPU. The dimensions of r and z are both 128. Regarding the computational overhead of the pre-training, we would like to point out that the pre-training of NP is over the whole dataset while the black-box attack is performed on a single image per time. The pre-trained model is used for free to perform black-box attack, when the pre-training is complete. Thus, the pre-training is a off-line operation, which is totally separated from the on-line black-box attack. The overhead of pre-training will not affect the black-box attack phase.

4.1 Empirical Understanding of NP-Attack

We evaluate the performance of NP-Attack under different experimental settings, including various sample sizes, maximum distortion, and optimization methods (optimizing r, z or both). Experiments are conducted on MNIST with 200 correctly classified images selected from the test set.

Optimization Method. We first investigate the performance of our NP-Attack with different optimization methods, *i.e.*, optimizing over the variable r, z or both. The experimental results are summarized in Table 1. The L_∞ distortion is set to 0.2 for MNIST and 0.05 for CIFAR10. Optimizing r is more query efficient, for the reason that r is modeled independent for different pixels in NP while z is modeled as a same Gaussian distribution over all pixels in one image. NP-Attack-R and NP-Attack-Z show the upper and lower bound of our NP based attack. The adversarial examples generated by different optimization methods are shown in Appendix C.

Table 1. Evaluation of NP-Attack under untargeted setting by optimizing the variables r, z or both on 200 correctly classified images from MNIST and CIFAR-10.

Attack method	MNIST			CIFAR10		
	ASR	L_2 Dist	Query count	ASR	L_2 Dist	Query count
NP-Attack-R	100%	3.07	**1,190**	100%	1.75	**96**
NP-Attack-Z	100%	3.55	1,665	100%	1.68	150
NP-Attack-RZ	100%	3.65	1,460	100%	1.80	98

Sample Size. We test the sample size $b \in \{10, 20, 30, 40, 50\}$ and set the L_∞ distortion to 0.2. Noted that query count is linearly related to sample size, as $Q = T \times b$, where T represents iteration count and Q represents query count. The changes of ASR with the maximal query count are plotted in Fig. 4(a). It

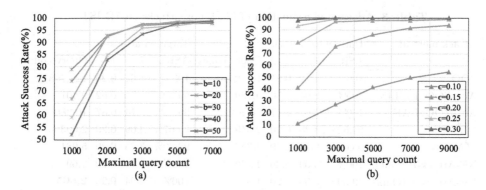

Fig. 4. Change of ASRs when limiting the query counts on MNIST with NP-Attack-R. (a) Different curves represent performance under different sample sizes. (b) Different curves represent restricting different maximal distortion.

Table 2. Evaluation of NP-Attack-R under untargeted setting on MNIST with different sample sizes. The maximal query count is 7000 and L_∞ distortion is restricted to 0.2.

Sample size (b)	Iteration nums (T)	ASR	L_2 Dist	Avg query count
10	700	98.01%	4.3707	**723**
20	350	98.51%	3.9478	786
30	233	**99.00%**	3.6675	940
40	175	**99.00%**	3.4675	1,074
50	140	**99.00%**	**3.3277**	1,203

shows that our NP-Attack could achieve over 90% ASR with different sample sizes when the maximal query count is larger than 7000. The ASR, L_2 distortion and average query count when the maximal query count is 7000 are reported in Table 2. We can see that, with a larger sample size, the iteration T is reduced along with larger average query counts. However, we can get higher ASRs and smaller L_2 distortion by increasing the sample size, illustrating a more accurate estimation of the perturbation direction.

Maximal Distortion. It is a trade-off between the distortion and query counts in black-box attack. We set the sample size $b = 10$ and test the L_∞ distortion $\epsilon \in \{0.10, 0.15, 0.20, 0.25, 0.30\}$. The change of ASRs with various maximal query counts is shown in Fig. 4(b). When $\epsilon = 0.3$, our NP-Attack achieves 98% ASR with only 1000 maximal query counts. With the 5000 query counts, NP-Attack can achieve nearly 100% ASR when L_∞ is larger than 0.2.

4.2   Evaluation on MNIST and CIFAR10

For both MNIST and CIFAR10, we randomly select 1000 correctly classified images from the test set for untargeted attack. For targeted attack, 100 correctly

Table 3. Adversarial evaluation of black-box attacks on MNIST.

Attack method	Untargeted attack				Targeted attack			
	ASR	L_2	L_∞	Query count	ASR	L_2	L_∞	Query count
ZOO	100%	1.12	0.21	107,264	100%	1.64	0.29	128,768
AutoZOOM-BiLIN	100%	2.01	0.50	9,129	99.89%	2.78	0.62	9,401
AutoZOOM-AE	100%	2.62	0.67	10,202	99.89%	3.74	0.87	10,380
QL	96.62%	3.38	0.20	2,549	99.67%	3.09	0.20	2,693
$\mathcal{N}$Attack	95.09%	2.14	0.20	4,357	98.22%	3.33	0.20	5,981
NP-Attack-R (Ours)	100%	3.09	0.20	**1,226**	100%	3.72	0.20	2,693
NP-Attack-Z (Ours)	99.90%	3.55	0.20	1,680	100%	3.94	0.20	**2,605**

Table 4. Adversarial evaluation of black-box attacks on CIFAR10.

Attack method	Untargeted attack				Targeted attack			
	ASR	L_2	L_∞	Query count	ASR	L_2	L_∞	Query count
ZOO	100%	0.12	0.02	208,384	99.52%	0.19	0.02	230,912
AutoZOOM-BiLIN	100%	1.56	0.15	8,113	100%	2.13	0.21	8,266
AutoZOOM-AE	100%	1.88	0.16	7,113	100%	2.78	0.24	8,217
QL	98.40%	1.91	0.05	857	99.55%	2.11	0.05	616
$\mathcal{N}$Attack	99.89%	2.61	0.05	183	100%	2.61	0.05	1,151
NP-Attack-R (Ours)	100%	1.74	0.05	**94**	100%	1.85	0.05	**589**
NP-Attack-Z (Ours)	100%	1.67	0.05	144	100%	1.78	0.05	936

classified images are selected from test set, for each image the target labels are set to the other 9 classes and a total 900 attacks are performed. In our experiments, the L_∞ distortion is restricted to 0.2 for MNIST and 0.05 for CIFAR10 following the setting of [14]. For untargeted attack, the maximal iteration is $T = 900$ and sample size is $b = 30$ while for targeted attack $T = 2000$, $b = 50$. The learning rate is $\eta = 0.01$ in default setting. A total query count is obtained by multiplying the number of iterations and the query count per iteration.

Note that the query count per iteration varies in different black-box attack techniques. ZOO uses the parallel coordinate-wise estimation with a batch of 128 pixels, resulting in 256 query counts per iteration. In AutoZOOM, the attack stages could be divided into initial attack success and post-success fine-tuning. In each iteration, the number of random vector is set to 1 at the first stage to find the initial attack success examples and then set to q at the second stage to reduce the distortion at the same level with other techniques. Thus the query count for AutoZOOM is $q + 1$ per iteration. For QL, $\mathcal{N}$Attack and our NP-Attack, query count in each iteration is the sample size b. For a fair comparison, we set the same sample size for these three NES algorithm based methods. Besides, both ZOO and AutoZOOM are optimization-based methods which quickly attack the model successfully and generate adversarial examples with quite large distortion and continuously perform post-success fine-tuning to reduce the distortion. We report the final fine-tuning query count and the distortion after fine-tuning for ZOO and AutoZOOM.

The experimental results are shown in Tables 3 and 4. We report the ASRs, L_2 distortion, L_∞ distortion and average query counts. As mentioned in Sect. 4.1, performance of NP-Attack-RZ is between NP-Attack-R and NP-Attack-Z. Thus, in the following experiments, we only show the results of NP-Attack-R and NP-Attack-Z to benchmark the upper and lower bound of our NP based attack. Compared to ZOO, our NP-Attack-R can reduce the query count by 98.86% and 99.95% on MNIST and CIFAR10 respectively under untargeted attack setting, while for targeted attack, NP-Attack-R reduces the query count by 96.91% and 99.74% on MNIST and CIFAR10. The comparison shows that though ZOO achieves 100% ASR, it is far from query efficient, requiring over 100,000 queries to generate considerable adversarial examples, implying high costs in computation and time. When it comes to AutoZOOM, it could significantly reduce the query count by proposing an adaptive random gradient estimation strategy. AutoZOOM-BiLIN and AutoZOOM-AE leverage a simple bilinear resizer or auto-encoder as the decoder respectively to reduce the dimension of adversarial perturbations. AutoZOOM based method can attack the model successfully with quite fewer initial success query counts, but the distortion is unacceptable at initial success. It still requires much more queries to fine-tuning. Compared to AutoZOOM, our NP-Attack methods outperform not only in query counts but also in the L_∞ distortion. QL utilizes NES algorithm to estimate the gradient, thus the performance of such technique hinges on the quality of the estimated gradient. QL shows its superiority in targeted attack for the reason that gradient-based methods are easier to find the targeted direction. In contrast, $\mathcal{N}$Attack and our NP-Attack both utilize NES to estimate the adversarial distribution. Compared to QL, our NP-Attack-R could achieve much better results in untargeted attack and comparable results in targeted attack. Compared to $\mathcal{N}$Attack, our NP-Attack could achieve higher ASRs and fewer query counts under both targeted or untargeted settings, due to the outstanding distribution modeling capacity of the NP model. In general, NP-Attack obtains the best trade-off between query counts and distortion. More experimental results on various architectures such as ResNet18 [12] and VGG16 [24] are reported in Appendix D.

4.3 Evaluation on ImageNet

The dimension of the images in ImageNet is relatively larger, which requires more queries to generate adversarial examples. We randomly select 100 correctly classified images from the test set to perform untargeted and targeted black-box attacks on ImageNet. For each image in targeted attack, a random label except the true one out of 1000 classes is selected to serve as the target. The L_∞ distortion is restricted to 0.05 following the setting of [13,14], $T = 600$, $b = 100$ and the learning rate $\eta = 0.005$. To improve the query efficiency on images with large sizes, ZOO and AutoZOOM utilize the techniques such as hierarchical attack and compressing dimension of attack space. For our NP-Attack, we also perform such compression. To be specific, we resize the images to $32 \times 32 \times 3$ to train the NP model, then we add perturbations on each $32 \times 32 \times 3$ patch, which is cut independently from the original images. Although using the attack dimension reduction, our NP-Attack method still outperforms.

The experimental results are summarized in Table 5. Due to the large image sizes, ZOO suffers from low ASRs and tremendous model evaluations especially for targeted attack. For other three compared attacks, they achieve 100% ASRs at the cost of over 10,000 queries in targeted attack and over 1,000 queries in untargeted attack. While for our NP-Attack, NP-Attack-R can achieve 100% ASR with only 867 queries, yielding a 94.45% query reduction ratio compared to ZOO in untargeted attack. In targeted attack, NP-Attack-R and NP-Attack-Z get over 98% ASRs and reduce the query counts to 8,001 and 11,383 respectively, which exceed all the compared methods. This demonstrates that our NP-Attack can scale to ImageNet set. The generated adversarial examples by NP-Attack-R are shown in Appendix E.

Table 5. Adversarial evaluation of black-box attacks on ImageNet.

Attack method	Untargeted attack			Targeted attack		
	ASR	L_2 Dist	Query count	ASR	L_2 Dist	Query count
ZOO	90%	1.20	15,631	78%	3.43	2.11×10^6
AutoZOOM-BiLIN	100%	9.34	3,024	100%	11.26	14,228
QL	100%	17.72	3,985	100%	17.39	33,360
$\mathcal{N}$Attack	100%	24.01	2,075	100%	24.14	14,229
Bandits	100%	–	1,165	100%	–	25,341
NP-Attack-R (Ours)	100%	10.96	**867**	98.02%	14.38	**8,001**
NP-Attack-Z (Ours)	96.04%	12.37	1,236	98.02%	14.60	11,383

5   Conclusions

In this paper, we focus on improving the query efficiency in black-box attack by modeling the high-level distribution of adversarial examples. By considering the structure information of pixels in one image rather than individual pixels, which is realized by a decoder of benign pre-trained Neural Process model, we propose the Neural Process-based black-box attack (NP-Attack) to greatly reduce the required query complexity. Evaluated on MNIST, CIFAR10 and ImageNet with regard to query count and attack success rate, our proposed NP-Attack achieves the state-of-the-art results, showing its efficiency and superiority under the black-box adversarial attack setting. Moreover, when pre-training the NP model on adversarial image examples instead of benign examples, we believe the query efficiency could be further improved, which is left for our future work.

Acknowledgement. This work is supported in part by the National Key Research and Development Program of China under Grant 2018YFB1800204, the National Natural Science Foundation of China under Grant 61771273, the R&D Program of Shenzhen under Grant JCYJ20180508152204044, and the project 'PCL Future Greater-Bay Area Network Facilities for Large-scale Experiments and Applications (LZC0019)'. We also thanks for the GPUs supported by vivo and Rejoice Sport Tech. co., LTD.

References

1. Bai, J., et al.: Targeted attack for deep hashing based retrieval. In: ECCV (2020)
2. Bai, Y., Feng, Y., Wang, Y., Dai, T., Xia, S.T., Jiang, Y.: Hilbert-based generative defense for adversarial examples. In: ICCV (2019)
3. Carlini, N., Wagner, D.: Towards evaluating the robustness of neural networks. In: S and P (2017)
4. Chen, P.Y., Zhang, H., Sharma, Y., Yi, J., Hsieh, C.J.: ZOO: zeroth order optimization based black-box attacks to deep neural networks without training substitute models. arXiv preprint arXiv:1708.03999 (2017)
5. Chen, W., Zhang, Z., Hu, X., Wu, B.: Boosting decision-based black-box adversarial attacks with random sign flip. In: ECCV (2020)
6. Deng, J., Dong, W., Socher, R., Li, L.J., Li, K., Fei-Fei, L.: ImageNet: a large-scale hierarchical image database. In: CVPR (2009)
7. Devlin, J., Chang, M.W., Lee, K., Toutanova, K.: BERT: pre-training of deep bidirectional transformers for language understanding. In: NAACL (2019)
8. Dong, Y., et al.: Boosting adversarial attacks with momentum. In: CVPR (2018)
9. Du, J., Zhang, H., Zhou, J.T., Yang, Y., Feng, J.: Query-efficient meta attack to deep neural networks. In: ICLR (2020)
10. Garnelo, M., Schwarz, J., Dan, R., Viola, F., Teh, Y.W.: Neural processes. In: ICLR (2018)
11. Goodfellow, I.J., Shlens, J., Szegedy, C.: Explaining and harnessing adversarial examples. In: ICLR (2015)
12. He, K., Zhang, X., Ren, S., Sun, J.: Deep residual learning for image recognition. In: CVPR (2016)
13. Ilyas, A., Engstrom, L., Athalye, A., Lin, J.: Black-box adversarial attacks with limited queries and information. In: ICML (2018)
14. Ilyas, A., Engstrom, L., Madry, A.: Prior convictions: black-box adversarial attacks with bandits and priors. arXiv preprint arXiv:1807.07978 (2018)
15. Kim, H., et al.: Attentive neural processes. In: ICLR (2019)
16. Kingma, D.P., Welling, M.: Auto-encoding variational Bayes. In: ICLR (2014)
17. Krizhevsky, A., Hinton, G.: Learning multiple layers of features from tiny images. Technical report, University of Toronto (2009)
18. Li, Y., Li, L., Wang, L., Zhang, T., Gong, B.: NATTACK: learning the distributions of adversarial examples for an improved black-box attack on deep neural networks. In: ICML (2019)
19. Liu, X., Bai, Y., Xia, S.T., Jiang, Y.: Self-adaptive feature fool. In: ICASSP (2020)
20. Lécun, Y., Bottou, L., Bengio, Y., Haffner, P.: Gradient-based learning applied to document recognition. Proc. IEEE **86**(11), 2278–2324 (1998)
21. Madry, A., Makelov, A., Schmidt, L., Tsipras, D., Vladu, A.: Towards deep learning models resistant to adversarial attacks. In: ICLR (2018)
22. Matthews, A., Rowland, M., Hron, J., Turner, R., Ghahramani, Z.: Gaussian process behaviour in wide deep neural networks. In: ICLR (2018)

23. Moosavi-Dezfooli, S.M., Fawzi, A., Fawzi, O., Frossard, P.: Universal adversarial perturbations. In: CVPR (2017)
24. Simonyan, K., Zisserman, A.: Very deep convolutional networks for large-scale image recognition. Comput. Sci. (2014)
25. Szegedy, C., Vanhoucke, V., Ioffe, S., Shlens, J., Wojna, Z.: Rethinking the inception architecture for computer vision. In: CVPR (2016)
26. Tu, C.C., et al.: AutoZOOM: autoencoder-based zeroth order optimization method for attacking black-box neural networks. In: AAAI (2019)
27. Vaswani, A., et al.: Attention is all you need. In: NeurIPS (2017)
28. Wang, Y., Deng, X., Pu, S., Huang, Z.: Residual convolutional CTC networks for automatic speech recognition. arXiv preprint arXiv:1702.07793 (2017)
29. Wang, Y., Ma, X., Bailey, J., Yi, J., Zhou, B., Gu, Q.: On the convergence and robustness of adversarial training. In: ICML (2019)
30. Wang, Y., Zou, D., Yi, J., Bailey, J., Ma, X., Gu, Q.: Improving adversarial robustness requires revisiting misclassified examples. In: ICLR (2020)
31. Wierstra, D., Schaul, T., Peters, J., Schmidhuber, J.: Natural evolution strategies. In: CEC (2008)
32. Wistuba, M., Schilling, N., Schmidt-Thieme, L.: Scalable Gaussian process-based transfer surrogates for hyperparameter optimization. Mach. Learn. 107(1), 43–78 (2018)
33. Wu, D., Wang, Y., Xia, S.T., Bailey, J., Ma, X.: Skip connections matter: on the transferability of adversarial examples generated with ResNets. In: ICLR (2020)
34. Xie, C., et al.: Improving transferability of adversarial examples with input diversity. In: CVPR (2019)
35. Zagoruyko, S., Komodakis, N.: Wide residual networks. arXiv preprint arXiv:1605.07146 (2016)

Self-similarity Student for Partial Label Histopathology Image Segmentation

Hsien-Tzu Cheng[1]([✉]), Chun-Fu Yeh[1], Po-Chen Kuo[1,3], Andy Wei[1],
Keng-Chi Liu[1], Mong-Chi Ko[1], Kuan-Hua Chao[1], Yu-Ching Peng[2],
and Tyng-Luh Liu[1,4]

[1] Taiwan AI Labs, Taipei, Taiwan
hstzcheng@ailabs.tw
[2] Taipei Veterans General Hospital, Taipei, Taiwan
[3] National Taiwan University College of Medicine, Taipei, Taiwan
[4] Institute of Information Science, Academia Sinica, Taipei, Taiwan

Abstract. Delineation of cancerous regions in gigapixel whole slide images (WSIs) is a crucial diagnostic procedure in digital pathology. This process is time-consuming because of the large search space in the gigapixel WSIs, causing chances of omission and misinterpretation at indistinct tumor lesions. To tackle this, the development of an automated cancerous region segmentation method is imperative. We frame this issue as a modeling problem with partial label WSIs, where some cancerous regions may be misclassified as benign and vice versa, producing patches with noisy labels. To learn from these patches, we propose Self-similarity Student, combining teacher-student model paradigm with similarity learning. Specifically, for each patch, we first sample its similar and dissimilar patches according to spatial distance. A teacher-student model is then introduced, featuring the exponential moving average on both student model weights and teacher predictions ensemble. While our student model takes patches, teacher model takes all their corresponding similar and dissimilar patches for learning robust representation against noisy label patches. Following this similarity learning, our similarity ensemble merges similar patches' ensembled predictions as the pseudo-label of a given patch to counteract its noisy label. On the CAMELYON16 dataset, our method substantially outperforms state-of-the-art noise-aware learning methods by 5% and the supervised-trained baseline by 10% in various degrees of noise. Moreover, our method is superior to the baseline on our TVGH TURP dataset with 2% improvement, demonstrating the generalizability to more clinical histopathology segmentation tasks.

Keywords: Whole slide image · Histopathology · Noisy label

H.-T. Cheng and C.-F. Yeh—Contributed equally to this work.

Electronic supplementary material The online version of this chapter (https://doi.org/10.1007/978-3-030-58595-2_8) contains supplementary material, which is available to authorized users.

© Springer Nature Switzerland AG 2020
A. Vedaldi et al. (Eds.): ECCV 2020, LNCS 12370, pp. 117–132, 2020.
https://doi.org/10.1007/978-3-030-58595-2_8

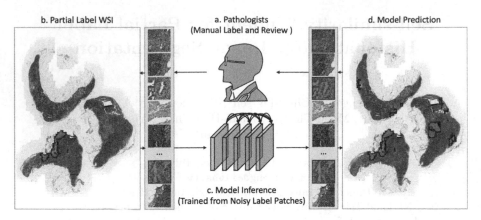

Fig. 1. Overview of our application scenario. The cancerous regions and patches are masked by the cyan color. a. Pathologists manually annotate partial cancer regions in WSIs because of time constraints or misinterpretation. b. A partial label WSI with some lesions omission c. Our model inference with patches. d. The model output of patches combines to WSI for lesions prediction. This prediction can be used as a pseudo ground truth label for model training or for pathologists to review. (Color figure online)

1 Introduction

Digital pathology and deep learning (DL) techniques possess the potential to transform the clinical practice of pathology diagnosis. Conventionally, the gold standard for pathology diagnosis is the process of pathologists inspecting hematoxylin and eosin (H$E) stained tissue specimens on glass slides using optical microscopes. This is time-consuming and error-prone. With the rising adoption of digital pathology, the digitized slide, namely whole slide image (WSI), mitigates the aforementioned issue. However, making diagnosis via manual inspection in gigapixel WSI is still labor intensive. The DL algorithms, particularly tailored to analyze WSI [10], would empower digital pathology and subsequently automate pathology diagnosis.

Identification of cancer regions in gigapixel WSI is considered the bottleneck of pathology diagnosis. Breaking this bottleneck, the CAMELYON16 challenge [2] serves as a milestone toward the automated segmentation of lymph node metastases in WSI. With detailed pixel-level annotation provided in this CAMELYON16 dataset, several fully-supervised DL algorithms have demonstrated the segmentation performance on par with pathologists [2,10]. Still, amassing large scale WSI datasets for other diseases with the annotation comparable to CAMELYON16 requires a team of skilled pathologists and brings another bottleneck for the automation of digital pathology in clinical practice. To be scalable in clinics, DL algorithms, which leverage semi-supervised and weakly-supervised learning frameworks, may be effective.

To relieve the need of fine-grained annotations in WSI, semi-supervised and weakly-supervised learning frameworks deserve careful consideration. Recent work has successfully applied multiple instance learning (MIL) framework to detect cancer regions in WSI with weak labels (patient-level diagnosis) [3,26]. Nevertheless, research of the kind heavily depends on large datasets (more than 40,000 WSIs) to learn useful feature representations. This limits its applicability to the automation of digital pathology. Semi-supervised learning framework, on the other hand, demonstrates its potential to learn from datasets with part of them being completely or partially labeled [3,20]. Such application scenario resembles the common clinical context, where pathologists miss small cancer regions and fail to identify the distinct boundary of tumor cells out of benign ones in WSI. Therefore, our paper aims to solve this issue with the technique originated from semi-supervised learning.

Inherent noises in partial label WSI may impede the learning ability of DL models. To alleviate the negative influence of noisy labels, teacher-student learning paradigm [22], common in semi-supervised learning, tends to be helpful. Different from most of the semi-supervised works applying this paradigm to generate pseudo ground truths for unlabeled samples, those pseudo ground truths can also be used to eliminate or counteract noisy samples [17]. Motivated by such paradigm, we further propose an approach to tackle the inherent noises originated from the modeling process with partial label WSI. Figure 1 illustrates the application scenario of our proposed method and the inherent noises our method attempts to mitigate.

To accelerate the automation of digital pathology and deal with the subsequent modeling issue from partial label WSI, our proposed teacher-student model features the following strategies and contributions:

1. We propose Self-similarity Student, a teacher-student based model embedded with self-similarity learning and similarity predictions ensemble, to recognize cancer lesions from noisy label patches in partial label WSIs.
2. Our self-similarity learning approach is motivated by the nature of tissue morphology, learning representation with a similarity loss that enforces nearby patches in a WSI to be closer in feature space.
3. Our similarity ensemble approach generates pseudo label of a given patch in the partial label WSI. The similarity ensembled pseudo label is updated based on the consensus between predictions ensemble of the patch and its nearby patches, making the pseudo label more robust.
4. The result on the CAMELYON16 dataset shows that our Self-similarity Student method achieves more than 10% performance boost compared to the supervised-trained baseline and more than 5% to the best previous art.
5. The result of our method shows 2% improvement over the baseline on our TVGH TURP cancer dataset, demonstrating the generalizability to more clinical histopathology segmentation tasks.

2   Related Work

We discuss the relevant literature in two aspects, namely, recent research efforts on designing automatic analysis techniques for digital histopathology, and deep learning methods dealing with the semi-supervised scenario or noisy data, each of which is closely related to the problem setting of our method.

Digital Histopathology. Concerning the extremely large sizes of WSIs (around $100k \times 50k$ pixels), designing automatic and effective machine learning techniques for histopathological image analysis is much needed in clinical practice [10]. Introduced by [8], a CNN-based model has been proposed for patch-wise WSI classification, following a count-based aggregation for WSI-level classification. Lee and Paeng [13] further adopt CNNs, comprising a patch-level detector and a slide-level classifier, for WSI metastasis detection and pN-stage classification of breast cancer. In [21], Takahama et al. propose to explore the global information from semantic segmentation to enhance the local classification performance on WSIs. To achieve this goal, they establish a DNN model that combines a patch-based classification module and a whole slide segmentation module. Campanella et al. [3] develop a clinical-grade computational pathology framework that utilizes multiple instance learning (MIL) based deep learning techniques to carry out a thorough study over a cancer dataset of 44, 732 WSIs from 15, 187 patients. The MIL setting allows the convenience of skipping annotating WSIs at the pixel level and also yields good classification performance. For automated segmentation of cancer regions in gigapixel WSIs, several works have addressed the challenging problem with deep learning in either fully supervised [23], or weakly supervised setting [26]. By assuming the correlation between image features of cancer subtypes and image magnifications, Tokunaga et al. [23] propose the adaptive weighting multi-field-of-view CNN to carry out semantic segmentation for pathological WSIs. More recently, Xu et al. [26] introduce the CAMEL framework to address histopathology image segmentation in a weakly-supervised manner. Driven by MIL-based label enrichment, their method requires only image-level labels of training data, and progressively predicts instance-level labels and then pixel-level labels. For the post-process to combine patches, [14,15] proposed to combine patches in multiple level of overlapping for smoother and less noisy WSI lesion segmentation. To clearly demonstrate the robustness of our method on dealing with noisy labeled data, we only conduct basic post-process, combining non-overlapped patches to WSIs, in all of our experiments.

Noisy Label and Semi-supervised Learning. The issue of noisy labeling in histopathological imaging is a major concern. In practice, the unreliable labeling is unavoidable in that manually annotating huge-size WSIs beyond image-level is inherently a daunting task. In addition, noisy labeling could also result from partially annotating WSIs as we aim to address in this work. Le et al. [12] develop a *noisy label classification* (NLC) to predict regions of pancreatic cancer in WSIs.

Their method leverages a small set of clean samples to yield a weighting scheme for alleviating the effect of noisy training data. The *self-ensemble label filtering* (SELF) introduced in [17] first uses the training dataset-wise running averages of the network predictions to filter noisy labels and then applies semi-supervised learning to achieve model training. SELF is shown to outperform other noise-aware techniques across different datasets and architectures. On semi-supervised learning, the temporal ensembling framework introduced in [11] is a pioneering effort on proposing self-ensembling mechanism that uses ensemble predictions to improve the quality of predictions on unknown labels. Their method is demonstrated to achieve significant improvements on standard benchmark datasets such as CIFAR-10 and CIFAR-100. Xie et al. [25] develop a self-training method that a teacher model is learned from the labeled ImageNet images and is used to annotate pseudo labels from extra unlabeled data. Then the augmented training data of labeled and pseudo labeled images are used to learn the student model, where noise is injected to achieve generalization. The roles of teacher and student are then switched and the learning process is repeatedly carried out to obtain the final model. Our work differs from these previous arts in the following: (a) pseudo-labels from teacher-student model are used to counteract noisy labels instead of assigning them to unlabeled samples. (b) our pseudo-label of each patch is generated from the consensus of predictions ensemble of its similar patches.

3 Methodology

In this section, we elaborate our Self-similarity Student method for cancerous region segmentation in partial label WSIs. The preliminaries and notations are firstly shown in Sect. 3.1. Next, we provide an overview of our proposed algorithm in Sect. 3.2. After that, the method to construct similarity embedding is introduced in Sect. 3.3. At last, we describe the details of Self-similarity Student for noisy label learning in Sect. 3.4.

3.1 Preliminaries and Notations

Given a complete label WSI dataset $\{\mathring{D}_{train}, \mathring{D}_{val}, \mathring{D}_{test}\} = \mathring{D}$, we generate our partial label dataset $\{D_{train}, D_{val}\} = D$ for modeling and hold out clean test set $\mathring{D}_{test}$ for final evaluation. In partial label dataset D, k cancer lesions $(k_{top}$ or $k_{rand})$ per WSI are kept and the remaining ones are relabeled as non-cancerous regions. The k_{top} and k_{rand} stand for the top k largest and random k cancer lesions respectively. Moreover, patches $\{P_{train}, P_{val}\} = P$, which represent patch-label pairs (p, y), are sampled from D. Since D is partially annotated, label y of each patch p may be noisy. For each (p, y) of a given WSI, we further sample its similar and dissimilar patches according to distance l, producing its similar (p^+, y^+) and dissimilar (p^-, y^-) bag of patches. The details of how we generate D and (p, y) are illustrated in Fig. 3 and described in Sect. 3.3.

As to the teacher-student model, we consider f to be a model with corresponding weights θ and augmentation η. Thus, we write the teacher model as

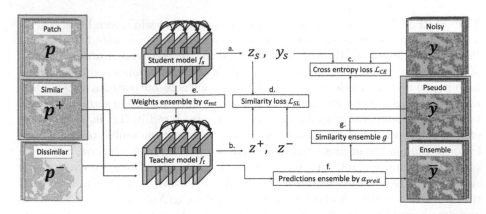

Fig. 2. Overview of our model training pipeline refers to Algorithm 1. For each epoch, we first train our student-teacher model (colored in blue) by means of p, p^+, p^-, with noisy label y and pseudo label $\hat{y}$. $\mathcal{L}_{CE}$, $\mathcal{L}_{SL}$, and student weights EMA are calculated in every batch for the update. After f_s and f_t updated, we loop all patches again (colored in green), conducting EMA predictions ensemble then similarity ensemble to update our ensembled predictions $\bar{y}$ and pseudo label $\hat{y}$ which will be used in the next epoch. (Color figure online)

$f_t(\theta_t, \eta_t)$ and student model as $f_s(\theta_s, \eta_s)$. Additionally, we denote the feature embedding of a given patch from teacher model and student model by z_t and z_s. Similarly, the feature embeddings of similar and dissimilar pair (p^+ and p^-) for a given patch (p) from teacher model are expressed as z_t^+ and z_t^- respectively.

3.2 Overview of Self-similarity Student

Figure 2 illustrates an overview of our proposed approach. To deal with the noisy label patches (p, y), our Self-similarity Student method builds upon two core concepts: teacher-student learning and similarity embedding. We build up our teacher and student models similar to the previous works [11,22]. That is, the teacher model f_t is the exponential moving average (EMA) of the student model f_s, which makes the intermediate representations more stable and facilitate student to learn robust representations against noisy samples. Besides the EMA of model weights for teacher model, we further leverage the ensemble of teacher model predictions for each patch to make the pseudo-label of each patch more consistent [1,17]. Different from [17] using predictions ensemble to filter noisy samples, the predictions ensemble $\bar{y}$ of each patch p in our approach serves as the basis of its pseudo-labels $\hat{y}$ for complementary supervision, both counteracting noisy patches and making the most of original labels y from (p, y).

In addition to the predictions ensemble, we introduce a similarity learning method to make the pseudo-labels of each patch more robust. This proposed method is motivated by the intrinsic property of tissue morphology in WSIs and the unsupervised visual representation learning work [7]. Because nearby

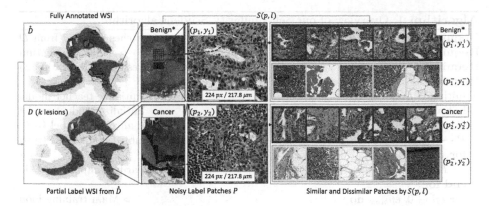

Fig. 3. Similarity sampling. To simulate the scenario of training our model by only partial label WSIs, each k-lesion-remained D is sampled from the $\mathring{D}$. From D we sample noisy label patches P, illustrating 2 example patches (p_1, y_1) and (p_2, y_2). By the $\mathcal{S}(p, l)$ with distance threshold l denoted in the orange grid, we can further sample the similar patches (p^+, y^+) in orange box and dissimilar (p^-, y^-) patches in gray box of each patch p. The noisy label case occurs here because of the false benign (Benign*) label of p_1 which should be revised as Cancer by our model. (Color figure online)

patches, which share similar morphological characteristics, tend to have the same labels, the generation of the pseudo-label $\hat{y}$ of a given patch p could refer to its neighboring ones, namely p^+. Here, the pseudo-label $\hat{y}$ of a given patch p is defined as a function $g(\bar{y}, \bar{y}^+)$. The $\bar{y}$ and $\bar{y}^+$ are the teacher predictions ensemble of a given patch p and that of its similar pairs p^+ respectively. In this paper, we implement function g as the average of $\bar{y}$ and $\bar{y}^+$. Following this intuition, we further apply similarity loss, which is a unique version of contrastive loss, to encourage the feature embeddings z of nearby patches (z and its z^+) to become closer and those of dissimilar ones (z and its z^-) to be distinct in feature space. Details of the construction of similarity embedding by applying similarity loss are described in Sect. 3.3 and in pseudo code provided in Algorithm 3.2.

3.3 Construction of Similarity Embedding

Inspired by pathologists' empirical knowledge and the work [6], we formulate a similarity sampling strategy with respect to the distance l between patches on a WSI, detailed in Fig. 3. For each patch (p, y), we sample multiple patches p^+ and p^- by distance-based similarity sampling strategy $\mathcal{S}$ within a WSI:

$$\mathcal{S}(p, l) = \begin{cases} p_i^+ \in p^+, i \in \{1, ..., N^+\}, & \text{if } \|coord(p) - coord(p_i)\| \le l, \\ p_j^- \in p^-, j \in \{1, ..., N^-\}, & \text{otherwise.} \end{cases} \tag{1}$$

where $coord$ denotes the coordinates of a patch on its original WSI and N stands for the total number of patches in a WSI. Hence, there are $N^+(< N)$ similar patches p^+ having Euclidean length to p within distance l and $N^-(= N - N^+)$ dissimilar patches p^- outside of that threshold.

Algorithm 1. Overview of our Self-similarity Student algorithm

---

Require: $\{P_{train}, P_{val}\} = P$ ▷ Noisy set of patches sampled from D
Require: $\alpha_{mt}, \alpha_{pred} \in (0,1) \subset \mathbb{R}$ ▷ EMA momentum
Require: $l, ep_{max} \in \mathbb{N}$ ▷ Distance threshold and max epoch
Require: $\mathcal{O} =$ model weights gradient optimizer, e.g. Adam
    Initialize $f_t(\theta_t, \eta_t)$ ▷ Initialize teacher model
    Initialize $f_s(\theta_s, \eta_s)$ ▷ Initialize student model
    $\hat{P} \leftarrow P_{train}$ ▷ Initialize all pseudo label $(p, \hat{y})$
    $\bar{P} \leftarrow P_{train}$ ▷ Initialize all ensembled predictions $(p, \bar{y})$
    for all $(p, y) \in P_{train}$ **do**
       $P_{train} \ni ((p^+, y^+), (p^-, y^-)) \leftarrow \mathcal{S}(p, l)$ ▷ Similarity sampling (Eq. 1)
    end for
    for $ep \leftarrow 0, ep_{max}$ **do**   ▷ Main training loop
       for all $(p, y) \in P_{train}, (p, \hat{y}) \in \hat{P}$ **do**
          $y_s, z_s \leftarrow f_s(p)$ ▷ **a.** Student forward
          $z_t^+ \leftarrow f_t(p^+)$ ▷ **b.** Teacher forward (Ignore y_t^+ and y_t^-)
          $z_t^- \leftarrow f_t(p^-)$
          $loss_{ce} \leftarrow \mathcal{L}_{CE}(y, y_s) + \mathcal{L}_{CE}(\hat{y}, y_s)$ ▷ **c.** Cross entropy loss (Eq. 3)
          $loss_{sl} \leftarrow \mathcal{L}_{SL}(z_s, z_t^+, z_t^-)$ ▷ **d.** Similarity embedding (Eq. 2)
          $\theta_s \leftarrow \mathcal{O}(\theta_s, loss_{ce} + loss_{sl})$ ▷ Update student's weights
          $\theta_t \leftarrow \alpha_{mt}\theta_t + (1 - \alpha_{mt})\theta_s$ ▷ **e.** Update teacher's weights
       end for
       for all $(p, \bar{y}) \in \bar{P}$ **do**   ▷ **f.** Predictions ensemble
          $\bar{y} \leftarrow \alpha_{pred}\bar{y} + (1 - \alpha_{pred})f_t(p)$ ▷ Update ensembled predictions per patch
       end for
       for all $(p, \bar{y}) \in \bar{P}, (p, \hat{y}) \in \hat{P}$ **do**   ▷ **g.** Similarity ensemble as pseudo label
          $\hat{y} \leftarrow g(\bar{y}, \bar{y}^+)$ ▷ Consensus of nearby predictions
       end for
    end for

To learn similarity embeddings in teacher-student models, a unique form of InfoNCE [18] is considered in this paper. The formulation for similarity loss $\mathcal{L}_{SL}$ is as follows:

$$\mathcal{L}_{SL}(z_s, z_t^+, z_t^-) = -\log \frac{\sum_{i=1}^{N^+} \exp(z_s \cdot z_{t_i}^+/\tau)}{\sum_{i=1}^{N^+} \exp(z_s \cdot z_{t_i}^+/\tau) + \sum_{j=1}^{N^-} \exp(z_s \cdot z_{t_j}^-/\tau)} \quad (2)$$

where τ [24] is a temperature hyper-parameter, z_s is the student feature embedding for p, and z_t^+ and z_t^- respectively are the teacher feature embeddings of its similar patches p^+ and dissimilar patches p^- corresponding to p.

For time and memory efficiency to calculate $\mathcal{L}_{SL}$ in each iteration, we simplify Eq. (2) by randomly sampling one patch from p^+ and that from p^- for a given patch p and further deriving $\mathcal{L}_{SL}$. This could be regarded as the log loss of a two-class softmax-based classifier, attempting to classify z_s as z_t. The dot products between the student feature embedding z_s and the teacher feature embeddings, z_t^+ and z_t^-, can be viewed as the local similarity measurements.

3.4   Self-similarity Student for Noisy Label Learning

In our proposed approach, the Self-similarity Student learns to both cluster local similar patches and classify each patch with the supervision from original labels y and pseudo-labels $\hat{y}$. Unlike semi-supervised learning methods treating pseudo-labels from teacher-student paradigm as ground truths for unlabeled samples, the pseudo-labels $\hat{y}$ in our method are used to counteract noisy labels y in (p, y). With the similarity constraint mentioned in Sect. 3.3, a pseudo-label $\hat{y}$ of a given patch p, which is derived from the consensus between its predictions ensemble $\bar{y}$ and that $\bar{y}^{+}$ of its similar patches p^{+}, is guaranteed to be more stable and robust to noises.

Overall, we apply two categories of losses to encourage our Self-similarity Student to learn from noisy patch-label pairs (p, y): $\mathcal{L}_{SL}$ and $\mathcal{L}_{CE}$. Specifically, $\mathcal{L}_{CE}$ includes the cross entropy loss between student predictions and original labels y, shown in Eq. (3), and the cross entropy loss between student predictions and pseudo-labels $\hat{y}$.

$$\mathcal{L}_{CE}(y, f_s(p)) = -\log \sum_{k=0}^{N} y_k \log(f_s(p_k)). \tag{3}$$

The overall lose function of our method can be written as

$$\mathcal{L}_{overall} = \mathcal{L}_{CE}(y, f_s(p)) + \mathcal{L}_{CE}(\hat{y}, f_s(p)) + \mathcal{L}_{SL}(z_s, z_t^+, z_t^-). \tag{4}$$

4   Experimental Result

In this section, we first elaborate our experimental details about the implementation and dataset settings in Sect. 4.1 and Sect. 4.2. Next, the performance comparisons between our method and other variants are reported in Sect. 4.3, Sect. 4.4 are Sect. 4.5. Lastly, Sect. 4.6 shows the performance on the TVGH TURP datasct, suggesting the generalization potential of our method to other clinical WSI data. For performance evaluation, we use the dice similarity coefficient (DSC) as our patch-level metric and the free-response receiver operating characteristic (FROC) curve as our lesion-level metric. The FROC curve is defined as the plot of sensitivity versus the average number of false-positives per slide and the final FROC score is the average sensitivity at 6 predefined false positive rates, including 1/4, 1/2, 1, 2, 4, 8 false positives per slide [2].

4.1   Implementation Details

We implement all baseline methods and our variants based on DenseNet121 [9] baseline with its official ImageNet [5] pretrained weight from PyTorch [19] model zoo. For optimizer $\mathcal{O}$ settings, we use Adam optimizer with learning rate 1e−4 and weight decay 4e−5, dividing learning rate by 2 per 50 epochs. The default random seed is set to 2020, dropout rate to 0.2, and batch size to 48 in all our experiments for fair comparison. Referred to common stain augmentations for WSIs [13] and those used in robust mean-teacher based methods [4,25], we choose several augmentations to train all our models, as augmentations are proven crucial to the mean-teacher based model performance. For similarity sampling, we choose $l = 1$ mm considering empirical cancer lesion diameter from pathologists' view. We also set $\alpha_{mt} = 0.999$, $\alpha_{pred} = 0.9$, $N^+ = 1$, $N^- = 1$, and $\tau = 0.07$ in all our experiments. All our models are trained and tested for inference using one Nvidia RTX 2080 Ti GPU.

Here, we describe implementation details about the state-of-the-art baselines, as in Sect. 4.3. We conduct similarity sampling on our method and ablation study only. For student network in Noisy Student [25], we scale up the default dropout 2.5 times and all default augmentation functions 1.5 times. The teacher networks in both Mean Teacher [22] are updated every batch by EMA of student's weights, while Predictions Ensemble [17] and Noisy Student are updated every epoch. We also change label filtering [17] to our relabel mechanism for balancing positive and negative samples. To the best of our knowledge, Mean Teacher, Predictions Ensemble, Noisy Student, and other relevant teacher-student methods are not designed for and experimented on noisy labeled histopathology WSIs yet.

4.2   Dataset

The CAMELYON16 dataset consists of 270 WSIs for training and 130 WSIs for testing. We randomly sample 243 WSIs as $\mathring{D}_{train}$ and 27 WSIs as $\mathring{D}_{val}$ from 270 WSIs. The 130 WSIs ($\mathring{D}_{test}$) are used for final evaluation. To simulate the clinical context of having unidentified cancer regions in WSI, we create partial label dataset D_{train} and D_{val} out of $\mathring{D}_{train}$ and $\mathring{D}_{val}$ by retaining k_{top} and k_{rand} cancer regions in each WSI. As shown in Table 1, we choose the number of k to be 1, 2, and 3. For example, $k_{top} = 1$ means that only the largest caner lesion in each WSI is kept and the rest is regarded as benign tissue. It could be recognized that k_{rand} tasks are more challenging than k_{top} tasks due to the injected noises.

To further sample patches p from WSIs in D_{train} and D_{val}, we run OTSU thresholding [27] and set a 50% foreground-background ratio to extract foreground tissues. Following [12], cancerous patches $(p, y = 1)$ are defined to have more than 50% intersection of their areas with either k_{top} or k_{rand} cancerous regions, and benign patches $(p, y = 0)$ are the ones fully from the area outside of those cancerous regions. The resulting patch-label pairs $(p, y) \in P$ with resolution 224 px × 224 px are sampled from 10× magnification WSIs (0.972 μm/px), i.e. the receptive field of a patch covers 217.8 μm × 217.8 μm.

4.3   Comparison with Previous Arts

To benchmark our Self-similarity Student, we further implement several state-of-the-art methods, including Mean Teacher [22], Noisy Student [25], and Predictions Ensemble [17]. Demonstrated in Table 3, the results of our method outperform previous arts evaluated on $k_{top} = 1$ and $k_{rand} = 1$ tasks. Our method achieves 93.76 DSC & 36.9 FROC on the $k_{top} = 1$ task, and 85.56 DSC & 31.88

Table 1. Number of patches in training set and statistics for various k_{top} and k_{rand} tasks. "Complete" denotes the task using the original $\mathring{D}$ with clean ground truth. We sample P from D for k_{top} and k_{rand} tasks. The ratio of noisiness declines as more lesions per WSI are correctly labeled.

Label	Complete	k_{top}			k_{rand}		
		1	2	3	1	2	3
Benign	588286	597500	592454	590482	606342	604331	600122
Cancer	21730	12516	17562	19534	2819	5188	8358
Ratio of correct cancer patches		57.60%	80.82%	89.89%	12.97%	23.87%	38.46%
Ratio of noisiness		42.40%	19.18%	10.11%	87.03%	76.13%	61.54%
Number of cancer lesions		91	150	193	91	150	193
Average size of lesions (mm^2)		6.7814	5.7527	4.9959	2.0587	1.8747	2.5277

FROC on the more challenging $k_{rand} = 1$ task, which achieves more than 10% performance boost compared to the supervised-trained baseline and more than 5% performance boost compared to the best previous art.

Moreover, Fig. 5 shows the $k_{top} = 1$ qualitative comparison between our method and the baselines. Inferred from these results, our Self-similarity Student could both correctly identify more cancer regions and cancer cells (patches) with only a few false positives. For the implementation details of baseline methods, see Supp. Sect. 2. For the illustration of effectiveness of our self-similarity embedding method, see Supp. Sect. 3. For more qualitative results, see Supp. Sect. 4 (Table 2).

Table 2. Comparison with Previous Arts. All results are trained with single cancer lesion per WSI and evaluated on the clean testing set $\mathring{D}_{test}$. Our method outperforms other techniques in $k_{top} = 1$ task (only one largest cancer region is annotated per WSI) and the more challenging $k_{rand} = 1$ task (only one random cancer region is annotated per WSI)

Method	$k_{top} = 1$		$k_{rand} = 1$	
	DSC	FROC	DSC	FROC
Baseline DenseNet121 [9]	83.08	29.99	63.08	28.09
Mean Teacher [22]	86.83	34.13	74.45	28.45
Noisy Student [25]	84.90	34.21	77.46	30.06
Prediction Ensemble [17]	88.60	33.41	75.59	30.20
Self-sim Student (**Ours**)	**93.76**	**36.90**	**85.56**	**31.88**

4.4   Comparison with Various Label Ratio

In this section, we compare the performances of the models trained from partially labeled training set described in Sect. 4.2. The results in Table 3 indicate that our method achieves comparable or better performance than DenseNet121 baseline in all experimental settings. These further suggest that our Self-similarity Student can still learn to discriminate most of the cancer regions from benign parts even in the situation, where there are 50% cancer regions unidentified in training set.

4.5   Ablation Study

To demonstrate the contributions by each part of our Self-similarity Student method, we conduct a set of experiments in $k_{rand} = 1$ task. Baseline indicates the DenseNet121 network trained with $\mathcal{L}_{CE}(y, \hat{y})$ whereas Sim-embedding shows the performance of Baseline plus $\mathcal{L}_{SL}$. Furthermore, Pred-ensemble uses the teacher predictions ensemble of each patch as its pseudo label while Sim-ensemble derives pseudo-labels by averaging the predictions ensemble from patches and their corresponding similar pairs (Fig. 4).

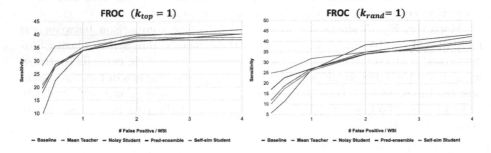

Fig. 4. FROC result. Our method, colored in red, yields the highest FROC score compared to baselines. Moreover, at the relatively low false positive rate, our method outperforms all the baselines with higher sensitivity. (Color figure online)

Shown in Table 4, each component in Self-similarity Student contributes to its overall performance. Most importantly, this justifies the effectiveness of our method, which makes pseudo-labels more robust against noisy labels by using predictions ensemble from similar pairs.

4.6   Generalizability of Our Method

To evaluate the potential generalizability of our method, we conduct experiments on the transurethral resection of prostate (TURP) data from the Department of Pathology, Taipei Veterans General Hospital (TVGH). The TVGH TURP dataset consists of 71 WSIs with annotated cancerous lesions, defined as regions with Gleason score greater than 3+3. The training set consists of 58 WSIs within 13 WSIs for validation. The actual size of each WSI is about 45.7 mm × 24.7 mm with 0.25 μm/px pixel spacing. We follow the same patch extraction strategy in CAMELYON16 dataset, producing totally 459273 patches from 4× zoomed

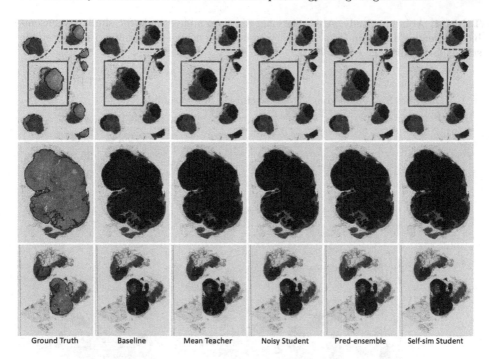

Ground Truth Baseline Mean Teacher Noisy Student Pred-ensemble Self-sim Student

Fig. 5. Qualitative comparison with previous arts. Red boxes indicate zoomed-in region-of-interest. The regions in green color indicate true positives and yellow indicate false positives. The cyan color denotes ground truth (false negatives if no prediction overlapped). The top row demonstrates our method with lower false positives, especially compared to Mean Teacher. The lower two rows show that our method achieves higher sensitivity compared to all other baselines. (Color figure online)

Table 3. Performance of models trained in various noisy label ratios. Complete denotes the results trained from original ground truths. All results are from the clean testing set, demonstrating that our model is capable of learning from limited noisy ground truth while still having competent performance.

Method	Metrics	Complete	k_{top}			k_{rand}		
			1	2	3	1	2	3
Baseline	DSC	92.68	83.08	87.40	90.41	63.08	70.02	78.39
DenseNet121 [9]	FROC	41.12	29.99	38.37	**40.18**	28.09	35.90	33.22
Self-sim Student	DSC	90.49	**93.76**	**93.98**	**91.29**	**85.56**	**87.57**	**90.20**
(Ours)	FROC	39.52	**36.90**	**38.94**	39.16	**31.88**	**36.54**	**35.08**

TURP WSIs with receptive field $224 \times 224\,\mu m$. Our method achieves 77.24 DSC on the 13 WSIs testing set, which is better than the supervise-trained baseline with 75.36 DSC. The qualitative result is shown in Fig. 6 and Supp. Sect. 4.

Table 4. Ablation Study. Abbreviations: Sim-ensemble stands for similarity ensemble; Sim-embedding stands for similarity embedding using loss learning; Pred-ensemble stands for predictions ensemble.

Ablation study				DSC	FROC
Baseline	Sim-embedding	Pred-ensemble	Sim-ensemble		
✓				63.08	28.09
✓	✓			68.42	28.24
✓		✓		75.59	30.20
✓	✓	✓	✓	**85.56**	**31.88**

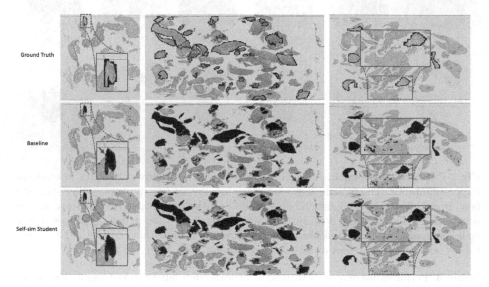

Fig. 6. Qualitative result on the testing set of TVGH TURP dataset. The color code is the same as Fig. 5. Our Self-similarity Student is able to predict cancer regions more precisely than the baseline with better grouped patterns. (Color figure online)

5   Conclusion

Computer vision technique is the key to accelerate the automation of digital pathology in clinical practice, particularly the identification of cancer regions in WSI. In this research, we propose a teacher-student framework, Self-similarity Student, to address partial label WSI, which relieves the burden on pathologists. The result shows that our method outperforms previous arts at least 5% in terms of DSC, suggesting that Self-similarity Student possesses more robust representations against noisy labels. Following these meticulous experiments, the advantage of similarity ensemble for modeling with partial label WSI is verified. More importantly, our approach is capable of generalizing to TURP dataset, which identifies cancer regions out of benign ones with fewer false positives.

To sum, Self-similarity Student can be a potent method to tackle the problems originated from partial label WSI dataset. In future work, we aim to pursue the potential of Self-similarity Student for semi-supervised learning in small-sized WSI datasets, truly contributing to the automation of cancer region delineation.

Acknowledgment. We thank Yi-Chin Tu, the chairman of Taiwan AI Labs, for the generous support of this project. We also thank the intensive assistance made by the Department of Pathology and Laboratory Medicine, Taipei Veterans General Hospital. Lastly, we appreciate Tsun-Hsiao Wang at National Yang-Ming University for his contribution on delineating cancerous regions in WSIs of TVGH TURP dataset.

References

1. Bachman, P., Alsharif, O., Precup, D.: Learning with pseudo-ensembles. In: Advances in Neural Information Processing Systems, pp. 3365–3373 (2014)
2. Bejnordi, B.E., et al.: Diagnostic assessment of deep learning algorithms for detection of lymph node metastases in women with breast cancer. JAMA **318**(22), 2199–2210 (2017)
3. Campanella, G., et al.: Clinical-grade computational pathology using weakly supervised deep learning on whole slide images. Nat. Med. **25**(8), 1301–1309 (2019)
4. Cubuk, E.D., Zoph, B., Shlens, J., Le, Q.V.: RandAugment: practical automated data augmentation with a reduced search space. arXiv preprint arXiv:1909.13719 (2019)
5. Deng, J., Dong, W., Socher, R., Li, L.J., Li, K., Fei-Fei, L.: ImageNet: a large-scale hierarchical image database. In: 2009 IEEE Conference on Computer Vision and Pattern Recognition, pp. 248–255. IEEE (2009)
6. Gildenblat, J., Klaiman, E.: Self-supervised similarity learning for digital pathology. arXiv preprint arXiv:1905.08139 (2019)
7. He, K., Fan, H., Wu, Y., Xie, S., Girshick, R.: Momentum contrast for unsupervised visual representation learning. arXiv preprint arXiv:1911.05722 (2019)
8. Hou, L., Samaras, D., Kurc, T.M., Gao, Y., Davis, J.E., Saltz, J.H.: Patch-based convolutional neural network for whole slide tissue image classification. In: Proceedings of the IEEE Conference on Computer Vision and Pattern Recognition, pp. 2424–2433 (2016)
9. Huang, G., Liu, Z., Van Der Maaten, L., Weinberger, K.Q.: Densely connected convolutional networks. In: Proceedings of the IEEE Conference on Computer Vision and Pattern Recognition, pp. 4700–4708 (2017)
10. Komura, D., Ishikawa, S.: Machine learning methods for histopathological image analysis. Comput. Struct. Biotechnol. J. **16**, 34–42 (2018)
11. Laine, S., Aila, T.: Temporal ensembling for semi-supervised learning. arXiv preprint arXiv:1610.02242 (2016)
12. Le, H., Samaras, D., Kurc, T., Gupta, R., Shroyer, K., Saltz, J.: Pancreatic cancer detection in whole slide images using noisy label annotations. In: Shen, D., et al. (eds.) MICCAI 2019. LNCS, vol. 11764, pp. 541–549. Springer, Cham (2019). https://doi.org/10.1007/978-3-030-32239-7_60
13. Lee, B., Paeng, K.: A robust and effective approach towards accurate metastasis detection and pN-stage classification in breast cancer. In: Frangi, A.F., Schnabel, J.A., Davatzikos, C., Alberola-López, C., Fichtinger, G. (eds.) MICCAI 2018. LNCS, vol. 11071, pp. 841–850. Springer, Cham (2018). https://doi.org/10.1007/978-3-030-00934-2_93

14. Lin, H., Chen, H., Dou, Q., Wang, L., Qin, J., Heng, P.A.: ScanNet: a fast and dense scanning framework for metastastic breast cancer detection from whole-slide image. In: 2018 IEEE Winter Conference on Applications of Computer Vision (WACV), pp. 539–546. IEEE (2018)
15. Lin, H., Chen, H., Graham, S., Dou, Q., Rajpoot, N., Heng, P.A.: Fast ScanNet: fast and dense analysis of multi-gigapixel whole-slide images for cancer metastasis detection. IEEE Trans. Med. Imaging **38**(8), 1948–1958 (2019)
16. McInnes, L., Healy, J., Melville, J.: UMAP: uniform manifold approximation and projection for dimension reduction. arXiv e-prints, February 2018
17. Nguyen, D.T., Mummadi, C.K., Ngo, T.P.N., Nguyen, T.H.P., Beggel, L., Brox, T.: Self: learning to filter noisy labels with self-ensembling. arXiv preprint arXiv:1910.01842 (2019)
18. Oord, A.v.d., Li, Y., Vinyals, O.: Representation learning with contrastive predictive coding. arXiv preprint arXiv:1807.03748 (2018)
19. Paszke, A., et al.: PyTorch: an imperative style, high-performance deep learning library. In: Advances in Neural Information Processing Systems, pp. 8024–8035 (2019)
20. Peikari, M., Salama, S., Nofech-Mozes, S., Martel, A.L.: A cluster-then-label semi-supervised learning approach for pathology image classification. Sci. Rep. **8**(1), 1–13 (2018)
21. Takahama, S., et al.: Multi-stage pathological image classification using semantic segmentation. In: Proceedings of the IEEE International Conference on Computer Vision, pp. 10702–10711 (2019)
22. Tarvainen, A., Valpola, H.: Mean teachers are better role models: Weight-averaged consistency targets improve semi-supervised deep learning results. In: Advances in Neural Information Processing Systems, pp. 1195–1204 (2017)
23. Tokunaga, H., Teramoto, Y., Yoshizawa, A., Bise, R.: Adaptive weighting multi-field-of-view CNN for semantic segmentation in pathology. In: Proceedings of the IEEE Conference on Computer Vision and Pattern Recognition, pp. 12597–12606 (2019)
24. Wu, Z., Xiong, Y., Yu, S.X., Lin, D.: Unsupervised feature learning via non-parametric instance discrimination. In: Proceedings of the IEEE Conference on Computer Vision and Pattern Recognition, pp. 3733–3742 (2018)
25. Xie, Q., Hovy, E., Luong, M.T., Le, Q.V.: Self-training with noisy student improves ImageNet classification. arXiv preprint arXiv:1911.04252 (2019)
26. Xu, G., et al.: CAMEL: a weakly supervised learning framework for histopathology image segmentation. In: Proceedings of the IEEE International Conference on Computer Vision, pp. 10682–10691 (2019)
27. Zhang, J., Hu, J.: Image segmentation based on 2D Otsu method with histogram analysis. In: 2008 International Conference on Computer Science and Software Engineering, vol. 6, pp. 105–108. IEEE (2008)

BioMetricNet: Deep Unconstrained Face Verification Through Learning of Metrics Regularized onto Gaussian Distributions

Arslan Ali$^{(\boxtimes)}$, Matteo Testa , Tiziano Bianchi , and Enrico Magli

Department of Electronics and Telecommunications,
Politecnico di Torino, Turin, Italy
{arslan.ali,matteo.testa,tiziano.bianchi,enrico.magli}@polito.it

Abstract. We present BioMetricNet: a novel framework for deep unconstrained face verification which learns a regularized metric to compare
facial features. Differently from popular methods such as FaceNet, the
proposed approach does not impose any specific metric on facial features;
instead, it shapes the decision space by learning a latent representation
in which matching and non-matching pairs are mapped onto clearly separated and well-behaved target distributions. In particular, the network
jointly learns the best feature representation, and the best metric that
follows the target distributions, to be used to discriminate face images.
In this paper we present this general framework, first of its kind for facial
verification, and tailor it to Gaussian distributions. This choice enables
the use of a simple linear decision boundary that can be tuned to achieve
the desired trade-off between false alarm and genuine acceptance rate,
and leads to a loss function that can be written in closed form. Extensive analysis and experimentation on publicly available datasets such as
Labeled Faces in the wild (LFW), Youtube faces (YTF), Celebrities in
Frontal-Profile in the Wild (CFP), and challenging datasets like cross-age
LFW (CALFW), cross-pose LFW (CPLFW), In-the-wild Age Dataset
(AgeDB) show a significant performance improvement and confirms the
effectiveness and supcriority of BioMetricNet over existing state-of-the-
art methods.

Keywords: Biometrics · Face verification · Biometric authentication

1 Introduction

Over the last few years, huge progress has been made in the deep learning community. Advances in convolutional neural networks (CNN) have led to unprecedented accuracy in many computer vision tasks. One of those that have attracted
computer vision researchers since its inception is being able to recognize a person from a picture of their face. This task, which has countless applications, is
still far to be marked as a solved problem. Given a pair of (properly aligned)
face images, the goal is to make a decision on whether they represent the same
person or not.

© Springer Nature Switzerland AG 2020
A. Vedaldi et al. (Eds.): ECCV 2020, LNCS 12370, pp. 133–149, 2020.
https://doi.org/10.1007/978-3-030-58595-2_9

Early attempts in the field required the design of handcrafted features that could capture the most significant traits that are unique to each person. Furthermore, they had to be computed from a precisely aligned and illumination normalized picture. The complexity of handling the non-linear variations that may occur in face images later became evident, and explained the fact that those methods tend to fail in non-ideal conditions.

A breakthrough was then made possible by employing features learned through CNN-based networks, e.g. DeepFace [1] and DeepID [2]. As in previous methods, once the features of two test faces have been computed, a distance measure (typically ℓ_2 norm) is employed for the verification task: if the distance is below a certain threshold the two test faces are classified as belonging to the same person, otherwise not. The loss employed to compute such features is the softmax cross-entropy. Indeed, it was found that the generalization ability could be improved by maximizing inter-class variance and minimizing intra-class variance. Works such as [3, 4] adopted this strategy by accounting for a large margin, in the Euclidean space, between "contrastive" embeddings. A further advance was then brought by FaceNet [5] which introduced the triplet-loss, whereby the distance between the embeddings is evaluated in relative rather than absolute terms. The introduction of the anchor samples in the training process allows to learn embeddings for which the anchor-positive distance is minimized while the anchor-negative distance is maximized. Even though this latter work has led to better embeddings, it has been shown that it is oftentimes complex to train [6]. The focus eventually shifted to the design of new architectures employing metrics other than ℓ_2 norm to provide more strict margins. In [7] and [8] the authors propose to use angular distance metrics to enforce a large margin between negative examples and thus reduce the number of false positives.

In all of the above-mentioned methods, a pre-determined analytical metric is used to compute the distance between two embeddings, and the loss function is designed in order to ensure a large margin (in terms of the employed metric) among the features of negative pairs while compacting the distance among the positive ones. It is important to underline that the chosen metric is a critical aspect in the design of such neural networks. Indeed, a large performance increase has been achieved with the shift from Euclidean to angular distance metrics [9, 10].

In this work we propose a different approach: not only we aim to learn the most discriminative features, but also to jointly learn the best (possibly highly non-linear) metric to compare such features. The only requirement we impose determines how the metric should behave depending on whether the features are coming from matching or non-matching pairs. Specifically, we regularize the metric output such that its values follow two different statistical distributions: one for matching pairs, and the other for non-matching pairs (see Fig. 1).

The idea of relying on the (empirical) distributions of the feature distances in order to improve their discriminative ability was discussed in [11]. In the above work, the authors introduce the histogram loss in order to minimize the overlap between the histograms of the distances of matching and non-matching feature

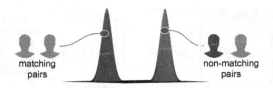

Fig. 1. The goal of BioMetricNet is to map the input pairs onto target distributions in the latent space. Matching pairs (same user - blue) are mapped to a target distribution whose mean value is far from that of the non-matching pairs (different users - red). (Color figure online)

pairs, so as to obtain more regularized features. However, while this approach fits well clustering tasks in which one is only interested in relative distances between pairs, it is not suited for the verification problem we are considering in this paper: the decision boundary between the two histograms is highly dependent on the employed dataset and does not generalize across different data distributions. The approach we follow is rather different: by regularizing a latent space by means of target distributions we *impose* the desired shape (based on a possibly highly non-linear metric) and thus have a known and fixed decision boundary which generalizes across different datasets. This seminal idea of employing target distributions was first introduced in [12] and [13]. However, it is important to underline that in [12] and [13] it was used to solve a one-against-all classification problem, regularizing a latent space such that the biometric traits of *a single user* would be mapped onto a distribution, and those of every other possible user onto another distribution, so that a thresholding decision could be used to identify biometric traits belonging to that specific user. The above methods also required a user-specific training of the neural network.

Conversely, besides learning features, the neural network proposed in this paper, which we name BioMetricNet, shapes the decision *metric* such that pairs of similar faces are mapped to a distribution, whereas pair of dissimilar faces are mapped to a different distribution, thereby avoiding user-specific training. This approach has several advantages: i) Since the distributions are known, and generally simple, the decision boundaries are simple, too. This is in contrast with the typical behavior of neural networks, which tend to yield very complex boundaries; ii) If the distributions are taken as Gaussian with the same variance, then a hyperplane is the optimal decision boundary. This leads to a very simple classifier, which learns a complex mapping to a high-dimensional latent space, in a way that mimics kernel-based methods. Moreover, Gaussian distributions are amenable to writing the loss function in closed form; iii) Mapping to known distributions easily enables to obtain confidences for each test sample, as more difficult pairs are mapped to the tails of the distributions. Since in BioMetricNet the distribution of the metric output values is known, the decision threshold can be tuned to achieve the desired level of false alarm rate or genuine acceptance rate.

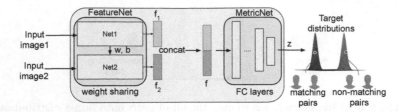

Fig. 2. BioMetricNet architecture during the training phase. After face detection and alignment, matching and non-matching face pairs are given as an input to the FeatureNet to extract the discriminative face features from the image space $\mathbf{x}$ into feature vector space $\mathbf{f}_i \in \mathbb{R}^d$. The feature vectors are concatenated $\mathbf{f} = [\mathbf{f}_1 \mathbf{f}_2] \in \mathbb{R}^{2d}$ and passed to the MetricNet which maps $\mathbf{f}$ onto well-behaved target distributions $\mathbf{z} \in \mathbb{R}^p$ in the latent space.

The resulting design, employing the best learned metric for the task at hand, allows us to improve over the state-of-the-art also in the case of very challenging datasets, as will be shown in Sect. 3.7. We stress that, although in this paper BioMetricNet is applied to faces, the method is general and can be applied to other biometric traits or data types; this is left as future work.

2   Proposed Method

BioMetricNet strives to learn meaningful features of the input faces along with a discriminative metric to be used to compare two sets of facial features. More specifically, as depicted in Fig. 2, BioMetricNet is made of two sub-networks: FeatureNet and MetricNet. The former is a siamese network which processes pairs of input faces $\mathbf{x} = [\mathbf{x}_1, \mathbf{x}_2]$ and outputs a pair of facial features $\mathbf{f} = [\mathbf{f}_1, \mathbf{f}_2]$ for both matching and non-matching input pairs. MetricNet is then employed to map these feature pairs onto a point $\mathbf{z}$ in a p-dimensional space in which a decision is made. These two networks are trained as a single entity to match the desired behavior. Their architecture is described more in detail in Sect. 2.1.

The novelty of our approach is that we do not impose any predetermined metric between $\mathbf{f}_1$ and $\mathbf{f}_2$: the metric is rather learned by MetricNet shaping the decision space according to two target distributions through the loss function, as described in the following. The loss function forces the value of the learned metric to follow different statistical distributions when applied to matching and non-matching pairs, respectively. Although arbitrary target distributions can be employed, a natural choice is to use distributions that have far-enough mass centers, lead to simple decision boundaries, and lend themselves to writing the loss function in a closed form.

For BioMetricNet, let us denote as $\mathbb{P}_m$ and $\mathbb{P}_n$ the desired target distributions for matching and non-matching pairs, respectively. We choose $\mathbb{P}_m$ and $\mathbb{P}_n$ to be multivariate Gaussian distributions over a p-dimensional space:

$$\mathbb{P}_m = \mathcal{N}(\boldsymbol{\mu}_m, \boldsymbol{\Sigma}_m), \ \mathbb{P}_n = \mathcal{N}(\boldsymbol{\mu}_n, \boldsymbol{\Sigma}_n), \tag{1}$$

where $\boldsymbol{\Sigma}_m = \sigma_m^2 \mathbb{I}_p$ and $\boldsymbol{\Sigma}_n = \sigma_n^2 \mathbb{I}_p$ are diagonal covariance matrices and $\boldsymbol{\mu}_m = \mu_m \mathbf{1}_p^T$, $\boldsymbol{\mu}_n = \mu_n \mathbf{1}_p^T$ are the expected values. The choice of using Gaussian distributions is a very natural one in this context. Because of the central limit theorem [14], the output of fully connected layers tends to be Gaussian distributed. Moreover, if $\boldsymbol{\Sigma}_m = \boldsymbol{\Sigma}_n$, then a linear decision boundary (hyperplane) is optimal for this Gaussian discrimination problem. Therefore, while in general BioMetricNet can be trained to match arbitrary distributions, in the following we will describe this specific case. It can also be noted that using different variance for the two distributions would complicate the choice of the parameters, since the optimal variance will be specific to the considered dataset in order to match its intra and inter-class variances.

As said above, in the Gaussian case the loss function can be written in closed form. Let us define $\mathbf{x}_m$ and $\mathbf{x}_n$ as the pairs of matching and non matching face images, respectively. In the same way we define $\mathbf{f}_m$ and $\mathbf{f}_n$ as the corresponding features output by FeatureNet. MetricNet can be seen as a generic encoding function $H(\cdot)$ of the input feature pairs $\mathbf{z} = H(\mathbf{f})$, where $\mathbf{z} \in \mathbb{R}^p$, such that $\mathbf{z}_m \sim \mathbb{P}_m$ if $\mathbf{f} = \mathbf{f}_m$ and $\mathbf{z}_n \sim \mathbb{P}_n$ if $\mathbf{f} = \mathbf{f}_n$. As previously described, we want to regularize the metric space where the latent representations $\mathbf{z}$ lie in order to constrain the metric behavior. Since the distributions we want to impose are Gaussian, the Kullback-Leibler (KL) divergence between the sample and target distributions can be obtained in closed-form as a function of only first and second order statistics and can be easily minimized. More specifically, the KL divergence for multivariate Gaussian distributions can be written as:

$$\mathcal{L}_m = \frac{1}{2}\left[\log \frac{|\boldsymbol{\Sigma}_m|}{|\boldsymbol{\Sigma}_{Sm}|} - p + \mathrm{tr}(\boldsymbol{\Sigma}_m^{-1}\boldsymbol{\Sigma}_{Sm}) + (\boldsymbol{\mu}_m - \boldsymbol{\mu}_{Sm})^{\mathsf{T}}\boldsymbol{\Sigma}_m^{-1}(\boldsymbol{\mu}_m - \boldsymbol{\mu}_{Sm})\right].$$

(2)

where the subscript S indicates the sample statistics.

Interestingly, since we only need the first and second order statistics of $\mathbf{z}$, we can capture this information batch-wise. As will be explained in detail in Sect. 2.2, during the training the network is given as input a set of face pairs from which a subset of $b/2$ difficult matching and $b/2$ difficult non-matching face pairs are extracted, being b the batch size. Letting $\mathbf{X} \in \mathbb{R}^{b \times r}$ with r the size of a face pair, this results in a collection of latent space points $\mathbf{Z} \in \mathbb{R}^{b \times p}$ after the encoding. We thus compute first and second order statistics of the encoded representations $\mathbf{Z}_m, \mathbf{Z}_n$ related to matching ($\boldsymbol{\mu}_{Sm}$, $\boldsymbol{\Sigma}_{Sm}$) and non-matching ($\boldsymbol{\mu}_{Sn}$, $\boldsymbol{\Sigma}_{Sn}$) input faces respectively. More in detail, let us denote as $\boldsymbol{\Sigma}_{Sm}^{(ii)}$ the i-th diagonal entry of the sample covariance matrix of $\mathbf{Z}_m$. The diagonal covariance assumption allows us to further simplify (2) as:

$$\mathcal{L}_m = \frac{1}{2}\left[\log \frac{\sigma_m^{2p}}{\prod_i \boldsymbol{\Sigma}_{Sm}^{(ii)}} - p + \frac{\sum_i \boldsymbol{\Sigma}_{Sm}^{(ii)}}{\sigma_m^2} + \frac{\|\boldsymbol{\mu}_m - \boldsymbol{\mu}_{Sm}\|_2}{\sigma_m^2}\right].$$

(3)

This loss captures the statistics of the matching pairs and enforces the target distribution $\mathbb{P}_m$. For brevity we omit the derivation of $\mathcal{L}_n$ which is obtained similarly.

Then, the overall loss function which will be minimized end-to-end across the whole network (FeatureNet and MetricNet) is given by $\mathcal{L} = \mathcal{L}_m + \mathcal{L}_n$.

2.1   Architecture

In the following we discuss the architecture and implementation strategy of FeatureNet and MetricNet.

FeatureNet. The goal of FeatureNet is to extract the most distinctive facial features from the input pairs. The architectural design of FeatureNet is crucial. In general, one may employ any state-of-the-art neural network architecture able to learn good features. Due to its fast convergence, in our tests we employ a siamese Inception-ResNet-V1 [15]. The output size of the stem block in Inception-ResNet is $35 \times 35 \times 256$, followed by 5 blocks of Inception-ResNet-A, 10 blocks of Inception-ResNet-B and 5 blocks of Inception-ResNet-C. At the bottom of the network we employ a fully connected layer with output size equal to the feature vector dimensionality d. The employed dropout rate is 0.8. The pairs of feature vectors $\mathbf{f}_1$ and $\mathbf{f}_2$ in output of FeatureNet are concatenated resulting in $\mathbf{f} = [\mathbf{f}_1 \mathbf{f}_2] \in \mathbb{R}^{2d}$ and given as input to MetricNet.

MetricNet. The goal of MetricNet is to learn the best metric based on feature vector $\mathbf{f}$ and to map it onto the target distributions in the latent space. MetricNet consists of 7 fully connected layers with ReLU activation functions at the output of each layer. At the last layer, no activation function is employed. The input size of MetricNet is $2d$, the first fully connected layer has an output size equal to $2d$, the output size keeps decreasing gradually by a factor of 2 with the final layer having an output size equal to the latent space dimensionality p.

We also highlight that MetricNet, by taking as input $\mathbf{f} = [\mathbf{f}_1, \mathbf{f}_2]$, allows us to model any arbitrary nonlinear correlations between the feature vectors. Indeed, the use of an arbitrary combination of the input features entries has been proven to be highly effective, see e.g. [16,17].

2.2   Pairs Selection During Training

For improved convergence, BioMetricNet selects the most difficult matching and non-matching pairs during training, i.e., those far from the mean values of the target distributions and close to the threshold. For each mini-batch, at the end of the forward pass we select the subset of matching pairs whose output $\mathbf{z}_m$ is sufficiently distant from the mass center of $\mathbb{P}_m$, i.e. $||\mathbf{z}_m - \boldsymbol{\mu}_m||_\infty \geq 2\sigma_m$. Similarly, for the non-matching pairs we select those which result in a $\mathbf{z}_n$ such that $||\mathbf{z}_n - \boldsymbol{\mu}_n||_\infty \geq 2\sigma_n$. Then, in the backward pass we minimize the loss over a subset of $b/2$ difficult matching and $b/2$ difficult non-matching pairs with b

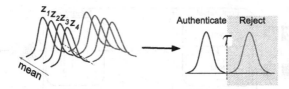

Fig. 3. During the testing phase, we obtain the latent vectors of the input image pair and its three horizontal flips. For all experiments, the final latent space vector is calculated as $\bar{\mathbf{z}} = \frac{1}{4}\left(\sum_{i=1}^{4}\mathbf{z}_i\right)$. Pairs are classified as matching and non-matching by comparing $\bar{\mathbf{z}}$ with a threshold τ.

being the mini-batch size of the selected difficult pairs. In order to have a stable training, the backward pass is executed only when we are able to collect $b/2$ difficult matching and $b/2$ difficult non-matching pairs, else the mini-batch is discarded.

The rationale behind this choice comes from the result of the latent space regularization. Indeed, as one traverses the latent space from $\boldsymbol{\mu}_m$ towards $\boldsymbol{\mu}_n$, one moves from very similar face pairs to very dissimilar ones. Points close to the threshold can be thought of as representing pairs for which the matching/non-matching uncertainty is high. As the training proceeds, at every new epoch the network improves the mapping of the "difficult" pairs as it is trained on pairs for which it is more difficult to determine whether they represent a match or not.

2.3 Authentication

In the testing phase, a pair of images are passed through the whole network in order to compute the related metric value $\mathbf{z}$. Then, a decision is made according to this value. As said, for our choice of target distributions a hyperplane can be used for the optimal decision, i.e., we can use the test

$$(\boldsymbol{\mu}_m - \boldsymbol{\mu}_n)^T\mathbf{z} \lessgtr (\boldsymbol{\mu}_m - \boldsymbol{\mu}_n)^T(\boldsymbol{\mu}_m + \boldsymbol{\mu}_n)/2. \qquad (4)$$

For $p = 1$, this boils down to comparing the scalar $\mathbf{z}$ with a threshold $\tau = (\mu_m + \mu_n)/2$.

However, we consider an improved approach which is able to capture additional information: we use flipped images to compute supplementary features as done in the recent literature [8,10]. Namely, given an image pair, we compute the metric output $\mathbf{z}$ for the original image pair as well as the 3 pairs resulting from the possible combinations of horizontally flipped and non-flipped images. We employ a horizontal flip defined as $(x, y) \rightarrow (width - x - 1, y)$. We thus obtain 4 metric values. Then, the decision is performed on a value $\bar{\mathbf{z}} = \frac{1}{4}\left(\sum_{i=1}^{4}\mathbf{z}_i\right)$, where $\mathbf{z}_i$ is the metric output corresponding to the i-th image flip combination, see Fig. 3. The expected value of $\bar{\mathbf{z}}$ in case of matching and non-matching pairs is still equal to $\boldsymbol{\mu}_m$ and $\boldsymbol{\mu}_n$, respectively. Therefore, the test (4) will still be valid on $\bar{\mathbf{z}}$. Figure 4 depicts BioMetricNet during the authentication phase. P1 represents the input image pair, and P2, P3, and P4 represent the three horizontal flips.

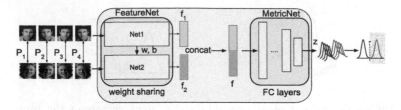

Fig. 4. BioMetricNet architecture during the testing phase. Given a pair of images to be tested, after face detection and alignment, by accounting for all the possible horizontal flip combinations, we obtain 4 image pairs, i.e. P_1, P_2, P_3 and P_4. The latent vectors of the corresponding pairs are computed and aggregated to $\bar{z}$ and compared with a threshold τ.

3   Experiments

3.1   Experimental Settings

The network is trained with Adam optimizer [18] using stochastic gradient descent [19,20]. Each epoch consists of 720 people with each person having a minimum of 5 images to ensure enough matching and non-matching pairs. We set the batch size b to 220 difficult pairs to obtain statistically significant first and second order statistics. Each batch is balanced, i.e. it contains half matching and half non-matching pairs. The initial learning rate is set to 0.01 with an exponential decay factor of 0.98 after every 5 epochs. In total, the network is trained for 500000 iterations. Weight decay is set to 2×10^{-4}. We further employ dropout with a keep probability value equal to 0.8. All experiments are implemented in TensorFlow [21]. For the augmentation horizontal flips of the images are taken.

3.2   Preprocessing

For preprocessing we follow the strategies adopted by most recent papers in the field [8–10]. For both the training and testing datasets, we employ MTCNN [22] to generate normalized facial crops of size 160×160 with face alignment based on five facial points. As a final step, the images are mean normalized and constrained in the range $[-1, 1]$ as done in [8–10].

3.3   Datasets

Training. The training datasets are those commonly used in recent works in the field. More in detail, we use different datasets for training and testing phases. The datasets we employ during training are Casia [23] (0.49M images having 10k identities) and MS1M-DeepGlint (3.9M images having 87k identities) [24].

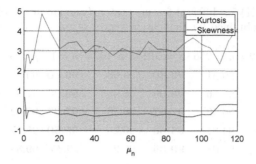

Fig. 5. Kurtosis and skewness of the latent space metric on LFW when $\mathbb{P}_n = \mathcal{N}(w, 1)$ where $w = [0.5, 120]$, and $\mathbb{P}_m = \mathcal{N}(0, 1)$. If the means of the two distribution are too far apart the training process becomes unstable, hence it affects the kurtosis and skewness of the imposed distributions.

Testing. BioMetricNet, in the current setting, has been developed for 1:1 verification in a face authentication scenario, particularly, when there is a single image template per subject. Therefore, BioMetricNet has been validated on 6 popular unconstrained face datasets for 1:1 verification, excluding large scale datasets like MegaFace [25] and IJB [26] used for set-based face recognition, i.e., deciding whether two *sets* of images of a face belong to the same person or not.

Labeled Faces in the Wild (LFW) [27] and YouTube Faces (YTF) [28] are the most commonly used datasets for unconstrained face verification on images and videos. LFW consists of 13233 face images collected from 5749 people. YTF consists of 3425 videos of 1595 people. Latest deep learning models for face verification are powerful enough to achieve almost perfect accuracy on LFW and YTF, making the related results not very informative. For detailed insights we further test BioMetricNet on more challenging datasets such as Cross-Age LFW (CALFW) [29] which is constructed by selecting 3000 positive face pairs with age gap from LFW to add the aging process to intraclass variance, and Cross-Pose LFW (CPLFW) [30] which is constructed from 3000 face pairs of LFW with pose difference to add pose variation to intra-class variance. Finally, we evaluate our method on Celebrity dataset in frontal and profile views (CFP) [31] having 500 identities with 7000 images, and in-the-wild age database (AgeDB) [32] containing 16488 images of 568 identities. For all the datasets, we report the results for 6000 pairs of testing images and videos having 3000 matching and 3000 non-matching pairs. For reporting the performance we follow the standard protocol of *unrestricted with labeled outside data* as done in [5,9,10].

3.4 Effect of Feature Vector Dimensionality

We explored the effect of different dimensionality of the feature vector by fixing $p = 1$, and varying d, see Table 1. It can be observed that small values of d are not sufficient to capture the most discriminative facial features. On the other hand, a too large feature space (1024) causes overfitting and thus a performance

Table 1. Accuracy (%) for different feature vector d and latent vector p dimensionality. Highest accuracy is obtained for the feature vector of size $d = 512$ and for $p = 1$

Dataset	$d = 128$	$d = 256$	$d = 512$	$d = 1024$	$p = 1$	$p = 3$	$p = 8$	$p = 16$
LFW	99.47	99.51	**99.80**	99.63	**99.80**	99.75	99.74	99.72
YTF	97.57	97.76	**98.06**	98.0	**98.06**	97.85	97.73	97.76
CALFW	96.48	96.59	**97.07**	96.78	**97.07**	97.02	96.92	96.93
CPLFW	94.89	94.81	**95.60**	95.25	**95.60**	95.57	95.13	95.43
CFP-FP	99.01	99.08	**99.35**	99.25	99.35	99.33	99.33	**99.47**

drop. We picked the best value, i.e. $d = 512$, since in our experiments this choice leads to the highest accuracy.

3.5   Effect of Latent Space Dimensionality

In order to select the optimal latent space size we explored different dimensionalities by fixing $d = 512$. The results are shown in Table 1. In this case, as a general behavior it can be observed that an increase in p leads to a performance drop.

Since p affects the number of parameters at the very bottom of MetricNet (an FC network), its choice strongly affects the overall performance. We conjecture that large values of p might be beneficial for very complex dataset, for which the amount of training data is typically large. Indeed, samples in a higher dimensional latent space are generally more linearly separable. This is even more important when the number of data points is very large. On the other hand, too large values of p might lead to a performance drop as it becomes difficult to learn a mapping onto large latent space. From Table 1 it can be seen that for most of the datasets, $p = 1$ is sufficient. On the other hand, for CFP-FP it can be seen that the highest accuracy (even though by a small amount) is reached for $p = 16$. In this case, a higher latent space dimensionality provides room to achieve a better separation. Since $p = 1$ provides optimal or close to optimal results in all cases, we choose this value for the experiments.

3.6   Parameters of Target Distributions

In this section, we perform an experiment to explore the behavior of different parameters of the target distributions. At first, let us recall that we set the two distributions to have the same variance $\sigma_m = \sigma_n = \sigma$. This allows us to have only a single free parameter, i.e. the ratio $(\mu_m - \mu_n)/\sigma$, affecting our design, in terms of how far apart we place the distributions compared to the chosen variance. Without loss of generality, this can be tested by setting the distributions to be $\mathbb{P}_m = \mathcal{N}(0, 1)$ and $\mathbb{P}_n = \mathcal{N}(w, 1)$, where $w = [0.5, 120]$. From now on if not differently specified we will consider $p = 1$ and $d = 512$.

Table 2. Verification accuracy % of different methods on LFW, YTF, CALFW, CPLFW, CFP-FP and AgeDB. BioMetricNet achieves state-of-the-art results for YTF, CALFW, CPLFW, CFP-FP, and AgeDB and obtains similar accuracy to the state-of-the-art for LFW

Method	# Image	LFW	YTF	CALFW	CPLFW	CFP-FP	AgeDB
SphereFace [8]	0.5M	99.42	95.0	90.30	81.40	94.38	91.70
SphereFace+ [33]	0.5M	99.47	–	–	–	–	–
FaceNet [5]	200M	99.63	95.10	–	–	–	89.98
VGGFace [1]	2.6M	98.95	97.30	90.57	84.00	–	–
DeepID [2]	0.2M	99.47	93.20	–	–	–	–
ArcFace [9]	5.8M	**99.82**	98.02	95.45	92.08	98.37	95.15
CenterLoss [34]	0.7M	99.28	94.9	85.48	77.48	–	–
DeepFace [35]	4.4M	97.35	91.4	–	–	–	–
Baidu [36]	1.3M	99.13	–	–	–	–	–
RangeLoss [37]	5M	99.52	93.7	–	–	–	–
MarginalLoss [38]	3.8M	99.48	95.98	–	–	–	–
CosFace [10]	5M	99.73	97.6	–	–	95.44	–
BioMetricNet	3.8M	**99.80**	**98.06**	**97.07**	**95.60**	**99.35**	**96.12**

In more detail, in Fig. 5 we show the skewness and kurtosis of the latent representation as a function of w for LFW dataset. It can be seen that in the region corresponding to $20 \leq w \leq 90$ the skewness and kurtosis are close to 0 and 3, respectively, and the accuracy is high, showing that the training indeed converges to Gaussian distributions. We eventually choose $\mu_m = 0$ and $\mu_n = 40$ to keep the distributions sufficiently far apart from each other. Further, if the difference between μ_m and μ_n is too large (e.g. $\mu_n > 90$), the training process becomes unstable and the distributions become far from Gaussian.

3.7   Performance Comparison

Table 2 reports the maximum verification accuracy obtained for different methods on several datasets. For YTF and LFW as reported in Table 2, it can be observed that BioMetricNet achieves higher accuracy with respect to other methods. In particular, it achieves an accuracy of 98.06% and 99.80% for YTF and LFW datasets respectively. On these two datasets, ArcFace obtains a comparable accuracy.

For a more in-depth comparison we further test BioMetricNet on more challenging datasets, i.e. CALFW, CPLFW, CFP-FP and AgeDB. State-of-the-art results on these datasets are far from the "almost perfect" accuracy we previously observed. In Table 2 we compare the verification performance for these datasets. As can be observed, BioMetricNet significantly outperforms the baseline methods (CosFace, ArcFace, and SphereFace). For CPLFW, BioMetricNet

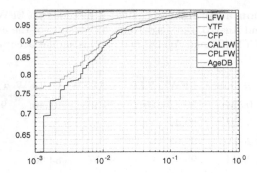

Fig. 6. ROC curve of BioMetricNet on LFW, YTF, CFP, CALFW, CPLFW and AgeDB.

Table 3. GAR obtained for LFW, YTF, CFP, CALFW, CPLFW and AgeDB at FAR $= \{10^{-2}, 10^{-3}\}$

Dataset	GAR@10^{-2}FAR%	GAR@10^{-3}FAR%
LFW	99.87	99.20
YTF	96.93	90.87
CALFW	94.63	88.13
CPLFW	87.73	61.27
CFP-FP	99.43	97.57
AgeDB-30	89.23	74.70

achieves an accuracy of 95.60% obtaining an error rate that is 3.52% lower than previous state-of-the-art results, outperforming ArcFace by a significant margin. For CALFW, BioMetricNet achieves an accuracy of 97.07% which is 1.62% lower than previous state-of-the-art results. For CFP dataset BioMetricNet achieves an accuracy of 99.35% lowering the error rate by about 1% with respect to Arc-Face. Finally, for AgeDB BioMetricNet achieves an accuracy of 96.12% lowering the error rate by about 1% compared to ArcFace.

To summarise, when compared to state-of-art approaches BioMetricNet consistently achieves higher accuracy, proving that, by learning the metric to be used to compare facial features in a regularized space, the discrimination ability of the network is increased. This becomes more evident on more challenging datasets where the gap from perfect accuracy is larger.

3.8   ROC Analysis

The Receiver Operating Characteristic (ROC) analysis of BioMetricNet is illustrated in Fig. 6. This curve depicts the Genuine Acceptance Rate (GAR), namely the relative number of correctly accepted matching pairs as function of the False Acceptance Rate (FAR), the relative number of incorrectly accepted

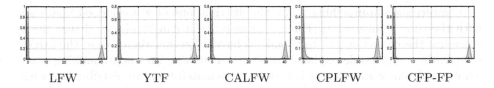

Fig. 7. Histogram of **z** decision statistics of BioMetricNet matching and non-matching pairs from (a) LFW; (b) YTF; (c) CALFW; (d) CPLFW; (e) CFP-FP. Blue area indicates matching pairs while red indicates non-matching pairs.

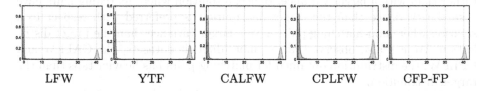

Fig. 8. Histogram of **z̄** decision statistics of BioMetricNet matching and non-matching pairs from (a) LFW; (b) YTF; (c) CALFW; (d) CPLFW; (e) CFP-FP. Blue area indicates matching pairs while red indicates non-matching pairs.

non-matching pairs. Furthermore, we report the GAR at different FAR values, namely FAR = $\{10^{-2}, 10^{-3}\}$ in Table 3. By means of the ROC, we can analyze how the verification task solved by BioMetricNet generalizes across different datasets. It is immediate to notice that, as a result of clear separation and low contamination of the area between the matching and non-matching distributions, high GARs are obtained at low FARs. This is generally true at different "complexity" levels as exposed by the considered datasets. More in detail, for LFW at FAR = 10^{-2} and FAR = 10^{-3} high GARs of 99.87% and 99.20% are obtained, see Table 3. For YTF at FAR = 10^{-2} and FAR = 10^{-3}, GARs of 96.93% and 90.87% are obtained. The same behavior can be observed for CFP. For challenging datasets of CALFW CPLFW and AgeDB it can be observed that the ROC curves obtained are comparatively lower compared to LFW, YTF, and CFP. The GARs at FAR = 10^{-2} and FAR = 10^{-3} comes to be 94.63% and 88.13% for CALFW, 87.73% and 61.27% for CPLFW and 89.23% and 74.70% for AgeDB respectively.

3.9   Analysis of Metrics Distribution

BioMetricNet closely maps the metrics for matching and non-matching pairs onto the imposed target Gaussian distributions. To analyze more in depth the effects of the latent space regularization, we depict the histograms of **z** and **z̄** computed over different test datasets, in Fig. 7 and Fig. 8 respectively. At first, it can be noticed that for both **z** and **z̄** the proposed regularisation is able to shape the latent space as intended by providing Gaussian-shaped distributions. Observing the histograms of **z** and **z̄**, it can be noticed that for all the datasets BioMetricNet very effectively separates matching and non-matching pairs.

Concerning non-matching pairs, the distributions of $\mathbf{z}$ are indeed Gaussian with the chosen parameters. For matching pairs, it can be observed that the $\mathbf{z}$ score has the correct mean, but tends to have a lower variance than the target distribution. A possible explanation is that matching and non-matching pairs exhibit different variability, so it is difficult to match them to distributions with the same variance. Indeed, for a fixed number of persons, the number of possible non-matching pairs is much larger than the number of possible matching pairs. Moreover, the KL divergence is not symmetric and the chosen loss tends to promote sample distributions with a smaller variance than the target one, rather than with a larger variance. Hence, a solution where matching pairs have a smaller variance than the target distribution is preferred with respect to a solution where non-matching pairs have a larger variance than the target distribution. We can also observe that for more difficult datasets, like CALFW and CPLFW, the distribution obtained for matching pairs has heavier tails than the target distribution.

The histogram for $\bar{\mathbf{z}}$ scores in Fig. 8 shows that the variance of both matching and non-matching pairs is slightly reduced with respect to that of $\mathbf{z}$. Since reduced variance means increased verification accuracy, this justifies using $\bar{\mathbf{z}}$ over $\mathbf{z}$. Furthermore, the decision boundary we are using depends only on mean values, which are preserved, and thus it is not affected by the slight decrease in variance.

4   Conclusions

We have presented a novel and innovative approach for unconstrained face verification mapping learned discriminative facial features onto a regularized metric space, in which matching and non-matching pairs follow specific and well-behaved distributions. The proposed solution, which does not impose a specific metric, but allows the network to learn the best metric given the target distributions, leads to improved accuracy compared to the state of the art. In BioMetricNet distances between input pairs behave more regularly, and instead of learning a complex partition of the input space, we learn a complex metric over it which further enables the use of much simpler boundaries in the decision phase. With extensive experiments, on multiple datasets with several state-of-the-art benchmark methods, we showed that BioMetricNet consistently outperforms other existing techniques. Future work will consider BioMetricNet in the context of 3D face verification and adversarial attacks. Moreover, considering the slight mismatch between metric distributions and target distributions, it is worth investigating if alternative parameter choices for the target distributions can lead to improved results.

Acknowledgment. This work results from the research cooperation with Sony R&D Center Europe Stuttgart Laboratory 1.

References

1. Parkhi, O.M., Vedaldi, A., Zisserman, A., et al.: Deep Face Recognition. In: British Machine Vision Conference, vol. 1, p. 6 (2015)
2. Sun, Y., Chen, Y., Wang, X., Tang, X.: Deep learning face representation by joint identification-verification. In: Advances in Neural Information Processing Systems, pp. 1988–1996 (2014)
3. Sun, Y., Liang, D., Wang, X., Tang, X.: DeepID3: face recognition with very deep neural networks. arXiv preprint arXiv:1502.00873 (2015)
4. Sun, Y., Wang, X., Tang, X.: Deeply learned face representations are sparse, selective, and robust. In: Proceedings of the IEEE Conference on Computer Vision and Pattern Recognition, pp. 2892–2900 (2015)
5. Schroff, F., Kalenichenko, D., Philbin, J.: FaceNet: a unified embedding for face recognition and clustering. In: Proceedings of the IEEE Conference on Computer Vision and Pattern Recognition, pp. 815–823 (2015)
6. Wang, J., Zhou, F., Wen, S., Liu, X., Lin, Y.: Deep metric learning with angular loss. In: Proceedings of the IEEE International Conference on Computer Vision, pp. 2593–2601 (2017)
7. Liu, W., Wen, Y., Yu, Z., Yang, M.: Large-margin softmax loss for convolutional neural networks. In: International Conference on Machine Learning, vol. 2, p. 7 (2016)
8. Liu, W., Wen, Y., Yu, Z., Li, M., Raj, B., Song, L.: SphereFace: deep hypersphere embedding for face recognition. In: Proceedings of the IEEE Conference on Computer Vision and Pattern Recognition, pp. 212–220 (2017)
9. Deng, J., Guo, J., Xue, N., Zafeiriou, S.: ArcFace: additive angular margin loss for deep face recognition. In: Proceedings of the IEEE Conference on Computer Vision and Pattern Recognition, pp. 4690–4699 (2019)
10. Wang, H., et al.: CosFace: large margin cosine loss for deep face recognition. In: Proceedings of the IEEE Conference on Computer Vision and Pattern Recognition, pp. 5265–5274 (2018)
11. Ustinova, E., Lempitsky, V.: Learning deep embeddings with histogram loss. In: Advances in Neural Information Processing Systems, pp. 4170–4178 (2016)
12. Testa, M., Ali, A., Bianchi, T., Magli, E.: Learning mappings onto regularized latent spaces for biometric authentication. In: Proceedings of the IEEE International Workshop on Multimedia Signal Processing (2019)
13. Ali, A., Testa, M., Bianchi, T., Magli, E.: Authnet: biometric authentication through adversarial learning. In, : IEEE 29th International Workshop on Machine Learning for Signal Processing (MLSP), vol. 2019, pp. 1–6. IEEE (2019)
14. Neal, R.M.: Bayesian Learning for Neural Networks, vol. 118. Springer, Heidelberg (2012)
15. Szegedy, C., Ioffe, S., Vanhoucke, V., Alemi, A.A.: Inception-v4, Inception-ResNet and the impact of residual connections on learning. In: Thirty-First AAAI Conference on Artificial Intelligence (2017)
16. Chen, K., Tao, W.: Once for all: a two-flow convolutional neural network for visual tracking. IEEE Trans. Circuits Syst. Video Technol. **28**(12), 3377–3386 (2017)
17. Held, D., Thrun, S., Savarese, S.: Learning to track at 100 FPS with deep regression networks. In: Leibe, B., Matas, J., Sebe, N., Welling, M. (eds.) ECCV 2016. LNCS, vol. 9905, pp. 749–765. Springer, Cham (2016). https://doi.org/10.1007/978-3-319-46448-0_45

18. Kingma, D.P., Ba, J.: Adam: a Method for Stochastic Optimization. arXiv preprint arXiv:1412.6980 (2014)
19. LeCun, Y., et al.: Backpropagation applied to handwritten zip code recognition. Neural Comput. 1(4), 541–551 (1989)
20. Rumelhart, D.E., Hinton, G.E., Williams, R.J., et al.: Learning representations by back-propagating errors. Cogn. Model. 5(3), 1 (1988)
21. Abadi, M., et al.: TensorFlow: a system for large-scale machine learning. In: 12th {USENIX} Symposium on Operating Systems Design and Implementation, pp. 265–283 (2016)
22. Zhang, K., Zhang, Z., Li, Z., Qiao, Y.: Joint face detection and alignment using multitask cascaded convolutional networks. IEEE Signal Process. Lett. 23(10), 1499–1503 (2016)
23. Yi, D., Lei, Z., Liao, S., Li, S.Z.: Learning face representation from scratch. arXiv preprint arXiv:1411.7923 (2014)
24. http://trillionpairs.deepglint.com/overview
25. Kemelmacher-Shlizerman, I., Seitz, S.M., Miller, D., Brossard, E.: The MegaFace benchmark: 1 million faces for recognition at scale. In: Proceedings of the IEEE Conference on Computer Vision and Pattern Recognition, pp. 4873–4882 (2016)
26. Maze, B., et al.: IARPA Janus benchmark-C: face dataset and protocol. In: 2018 International Conference on Biometrics (ICB), pp. 158–165. IEEE (2018)
27. Huang, G.B., Mattar, M., Berg, T., Learned-Miller, E.: Labeled Faces in the Wild: A Database for Studying Face Recognition in Unconstrained Environments (2008)
28. Wolf, L., Hassner, T., Maoz, I.: Face recognition in unconstrained videos with matched background similarity. IEEE (2011)
29. Zheng, T., Deng, W., Hu, J.: Cross-Age LFW: a database for studying cross-age face recognition in unconstrained environments. arXiv preprint arXiv:1708.08197 (2017)
30. Zheng, T., Deng, W.: Cross-Pose LFW: a database for studying crosspose face recognition in unconstrained environments. Technical report, Beijing University of Posts and Telecommunications (2018). 18–01
31. Sengupta, S., Chen, J.C., Castillo, C., Patel, V.M., Chellappa, R., Jacobs, D.W.: Frontal to profile face verification in the wild. In: 2016 IEEE Winter Conference on Applications of Computer Vision, pp. 1–9. IEEE (2016)
32. Moschoglou, S., Papaioannou, A., Sagonas, C., Deng, J., Kotsia, I., Zafeiriou, S.: AgeDB: the first manually collected, in-the-wild age database. In: Proceedings of the IEEE Conference on Computer Vision and Pattern Recognition Workshops, pp. 51–59 (2017)
33. Liu, W., et al.: Learning towards minimum hyperspherical energy. In: Advances in Neural Information Processing Systems, pp. 6222–6233 (2018)
34. Wen, Y., Zhang, K., Li, Z., Qiao, Yu.: A discriminative feature learning approach for deep face recognition. In: Leibe, B., Matas, J., Sebe, N., Welling, M. (eds.) ECCV 2016. LNCS, vol. 9911, pp. 499–515. Springer, Cham (2016). https://doi.org/10.1007/978-3-319-46478-7_31
35. Taigman, Y., Yang, M., Ranzato, M., Wolf, L.: DeepFace: closing the gap to human-level performance in face verification. In: Proceedings of the IEEE Conference on Computer Vision and Pattern Recognition, pp. 1701–1708 (2014)

36. Liu, J., Deng, Y., Bai, T., Wei, Z., Huang, C.: Targeting ultimate accuracy: face recognition via deep embedding. arXiv preprint arXiv:1506.07310 (2015)

37. Zhang, X., Fang, Z., Wen, Y., Li, Z., Qiao, Y.: Range loss for deep face recognition with long-tailed training data. In: Proceedings of the IEEE International Conference on Computer Vision, pp. 5409–5418 (2017)

38. Deng, J., Zhou, Y., Zafeiriou, S.: Marginal loss for deep face recognition. In: Proceedings of the IEEE Conference on Computer Vision and Pattern Recognition Workshops, pp. 60–68 (2017)

A Decoupled Learning Scheme
for Real-World Burst Denoising
from Raw Images

Zhetong Liang[1,2], Shi Guo[1,2], Hong Gu[3], Huaqi Zhang[3], and Lei Zhang[1,2(✉)]

[1] Department of Computing, The Hong Kong Polytechnic University, Kowloon, Hong Kong
{csztliang,csshiguo,cslzhang}@comp.polyu.edu.hk
[2] DAMO Academy, Alibaba Group, Hangzhou, China
[3] vivo Mobile Communication Co., Ltd, Dongguan, China
{guhong,zhanghuaqi}@vivo.com

Abstract. The recently developed burst denoising approach, which reduces noise by using multiple frames captured in a short time, has demonstrated much better denoising performance than its single-frame counterparts. However, existing learning based burst denoising methods are limited by two factors. On one hand, most of the models are trained on video sequences with synthetic noise. When applied to real-world raw image sequences, visual artifacts often appear due to the different noise statistics. On the other hand, there lacks a real-world burst denoising benchmark of dynamic scenes because the generation of clean ground-truth is very difficult due to the presence of object motions. In this paper, a novel multi-frame CNN model is carefully designed, which decouples the learning of motion from the learning of noise statistics. Consequently, an alternating learning algorithm is developed to learn how to align adjacent frames from a synthetic noisy video dataset, and learn to adapt to the raw noise statistics from real-world noisy datasets of static scenes. Finally, the trained model can be applied to real-world dynamic sequences for burst denoising. Extensive experiments on both synthetic video datasets and real-world dynamic sequences demonstrate the leading burst denoising performance of our proposed method.

Keywords: Burst denoising · Real-world image denoising · Convolutional neural networks · Decoupled learning

1 Introduction

The imaging quality of smartphone cameras is much affected by the small aperture and small CMOS sensor, which limit the amount of collected light and

L. Zhang—This work is supported by the Hong Kong RGC RIF grant (R5001-18).

Electronic supplementary material The online version of this chapter (https://doi.org/10.1007/978-3-030-58595-2_10) contains supplementary material, which is available to authorized users.

A. Vedaldi et al. (Eds.): ECCV 2020, LNCS 12370, pp. 150–166, 2020.
https://doi.org/10.1007/978-3-030-58595-2_10

result in heavy noise in the raw images. Denoising is a crucial step in the camera image processing pipeline (ISP) to remove the noise and reveal the latent image details. The denoising algorithms can be divided into single-frame denoising methods [3,12,17,38] and burst denoising methods [15,18,27,42]. While the former ones take a single-frame image as input for processing and are easier to implement, their denoising performance is limited, especially under the low-light environment. The recently developed burst denoising methods capture multiple frames in a short time as input, and thus they can leverage more redundant information for noise removal, leading to much better denoising quality.

The burst denoising problem can be addressed by hand-crafted methods [11,12,18,25,42] or learning-based methods [15,27,35]. The traditional hand-crafted algorithms are often manually designed to exploit the spatio-temporal similarities. For example, the well-known VBM3D method [11] denoises an image patch by finding and fusing its similar patches in the adjacent frames. In contrast, the learning-based methods train a denoising model by using pairwise datasets with a noisy image sequence as input and a clean image as ground-truth. In particular, the rapid development of deep convolutional neural networks (CNNs) [15,27,35] largely facilitate the research of learning based burst denoising. The CNN model is powerful to learn a set of nonlinear transformations from the noisy input to the clean output, including frame alignment, fusion and post processing, achieving superior performance to traditional burst denoising methods.

Despite the great progress, the learning-based burst denoising methods are limited by two factors. On one hand, the current multi-frame CNN models are mostly trained on video datasets with synthetic noise, e.g., Gaussian or Poisson-Gaussian noises. When the learned models are applied to real-world raw image sequences, whose noise distribution and statistics are more complex, unpleasant visual artifacts such as color shift and residual noise will appear. One the other hand, there lacks a real-world dataset for learning burst denoising models of dynamic sequence. This is mainly because in the presence of scene motion (e.g., hand shake motion and object motion), it is difficult to craft a clean ground-truth frame by using existing ground-truth generation techniques, such as using low ISO setting [9] or averaging multiple frames [1]. Misalignment problem will occur, which significantly degrades the quality of ground-truth. It is highly desirable to develop a burst denoising CNN model that can adapt to the real-world noise statistics without the need of a real-world pairwise burst image dataset.

There are two key issues in designing such a burst denoising CNN model. Firstly, to enable multi-frame processing, the CNN model should be able to align input frames to compensate the scene motion caused by hand shake and object movement in real scenarios. Second, the CNN model should be able to adapt to real-world noise for better generalization to real-world burst images. Based on the above considerations, in this paper we propose a decoupled learning framework for real-world burst denoising. First, a novel multi-frame CNN model is carefully designed with modular architecture which decouples the learning of motion from the learning of noise adaption. Second, an alternative learning algorithm is developed to leverage the complementary information from two datasets we prepared. One is a video dataset with synthetic noise, where the model learns to perform frame alignment, while the other is a real-world burst image dataset of static scenes, from which the model learns to adapt to raw noise statistics. With the designed CNN model and our decoupled learning algorithm, the learned CNN model achieves leading performance in real-world burst denoising without the need of a pairwise real-world burst dataset for training.

The rest of the paper is organized as follows. Section 2 reviews some related work. Section 3 describes in detail the proposed decoupled learning method. Section 4 presents the experimental results and Sect. 5 concludes the paper.

2   Related Work

2.1   Synthetic Image Denoising

Many image denoising algorithms are developed and evaluated on the images corrupted by synthetic noise. At early stage, prior knowledge of natural images is exploited for denoising, including statistical prior [29,31], sparsity prior [2,14,26] and non-local self-similarity [7,12,16,25,34]. The performance of these traditional methods is limited because the hand-crafted priors are not strong enough to characterize the complex structures of natural images. Recently, deep learning-based approaches have been developed for denoising tasks with substantial progress [3,21,24,32,36,38,39]. The DnCNN model showed that a CNN-based method can outperform non-CNN denoising methods by a large margin [38]. Recently, Anwar *et al.* introduced the feature attention operation into the denoising CNN model, achieving state-of-the-art image quality [3]. Other representative works include FFDNet [39], MemNet [32], MWCNN [24], etc.

2.2   Real-World Image Denoising

The research on real-world image restoration has not been fully conducted until recently owe to the several real-world datasets constructed for this purpose [1,8,9,28,40]. For the task of real-world denoising, Plotz *et al.* established a benchmark [28], where a pairwise dataset is collected by taking high/low ISO images. Abdelhamed *et al.* built a dataset of static scenes collected by smartphone cameras [1]. Each data pair is composed of a sequence of noisy raw images and the corresponding clean ground-truth image created by frame averaging. Chen *et al.* collected an image dataset [9] and a video dataset [10] by using high/low ISO settings to capture static noisy/clean raw images in low-light environment.

In addition to these real-world datasets, several works have been reported to synthesize realistic data for denoising [5,13,17,27]. Tim *et al.* [5] and Guo *et al.* [17] proposed to reverse the ISP pipeline on the sRGB images and generate noisy training images that are close to the camera raw data. However, these methods are compromised schemes which cannot cope with the real-world scenes with heavy noise corruption and object motion.

2.3 Burst Denoising

Burst denoising methods, an advantage over single-frame ones, take a noisy image sequence as input, and perform a series of operations, including frame alignment, temporal fusion and post-processing, to reproduce the underlying scene [6,11,18,23,25,42]. The frame alignment operation aims to build the correspondence between the dynamic contents of the target and reference frames. Some works adopt block matching for alignment [11,12,18,25,42], while others use optical flow methods [6,23]. The fusion operation aims to merge the outputs from multiple frames, which should be robust to alignment error. Representative approaches include collaborative filtering [12], non-local means [6] and frequency domain fusion [18].

Recently, a few works have been proposed to learn frame alignment and fusion from the input sequences for burst denoising. The KPN model [27] predicts the convolutional kernels to selectively fuse a burst of images with object motion. Xue et al. [35] designed a CNN model that explicitly consists of frame alignment, fusion and post-processing modules. Godard et al. [15] proposed a recurrent architecture for burst denoising, which can increase the image quality by accumulating noisy images. These learning-based methods achieve better image quality than their non-learning counterparts.

3 Decoupled Learning Network for Burst Denoising

3.1 Problem Statement

Given a sequence of N noisy raw images (e.g., in the Bayer color filter array (CFA) pattern [4]) captured by a handheld camera, denoted by $I = \{I_1, I_2, ..., I_N\}$, our goal is to estimate a clean RGB image O from I, i.e., $O = f(I; \theta)$, where $f(\cdot; \theta)$ denotes the denoising model (e.g., a CNN model in our work) parameterized by θ. We consider one frame from I as the reference frame, denoted by I_r, and denoise it by aligning and fusing it with other frames $I_i, i \neq r$.

To denoise real-world burst image sequences of dynamic scenes, the CNN model should learn to simultaneously align frames and adapt to real-world noise from some training dataset. Considering the fact that there lacks a real-world burst image dataset of dynamic scenes with ground-truth clean images, we propose to use two types of datasets for training, which can be generated by using the publically accessible data. One is a synthetic noisy video dataset of dynamic scenes, denoted by $\mathcal{D}_d$ (subscript "d" for dynamic). Each data pair (I_d, G_d) in $\mathcal{D}_d$ consists of a noisy video sequence I_d and a clean ground-truth frame G_d. The other is a real-world burst image dataset of static scenes, denoted by $\mathcal{D}_s$ (subscript "s" for static). Each data pair (I_s, G_s) in $\mathcal{D}_s$ consists of a noisy raw image sequence I_s and a ground-truth clean RGB image G_s.

$\mathcal{D}_d$ can be easily built by using the many high quality video sequences [35], while $\mathcal{D}_s$ can be built by the existing frame averaging method [1]. These two datasets have complementary information. The video dataset $\mathcal{D}_d$ contains rich dynamic scene motions, but the noise is synthetic and not real. In contrast, the static burst dataset $\mathcal{D}_s$ does not contain scene motion, but can provide information of real noise statistics. In this paper, we investigate how to learn a CNN model $f(\cdot; \theta)$ from $\mathcal{D}_d$ and $\mathcal{D}_s$, and present a decoupled learning scheme to achieve this goal.

3.2   Datasets Preparation

Before we present the CNN model architecture and the decoupled learning scheme, the two required datasets, $\mathcal{D}_d$ and $\mathcal{D}_s$, must be prepared. We present how to use the existing data to build these two datasets in this section.

Preparation of $\mathcal{D}_d$. We collect high quality video sequences from some video dataset (e.g., Vimeo-90k dataset [35]) to prepare $\mathcal{D}_d$. Specifically, every N consecutive frames are extracted as a burst sequence from the videos. However, directly adding noise to those sequences will make $\mathcal{D}_d$ deviate too much from the real-world dynamic noisy image sequences. Inspired by the work of [5], we propose to reverse the ISP pipeline and add noise to the reversed raw images so that the synthesized noisy sequences can be more realistic.

Specifically, we reverse four key ISP operations, including gamma correction, color space conversion, white balance and demosaicking, together with realistic noise synthesis, for building $\mathcal{D}_d$. A reverse gamma conversion with parameter γ is applied on a video frame L, where γ is sampled from a uniform distribution within range [2.0, 2.6]. Then, a reverse color space conversion C is applied, with the color matrix randomly interpolated by the color matrices given in static real-world dataset $\mathcal{D}_s$. Next, a reverse white balance gain of $W = 1/(r_g, 1, b_g)$ is applied with r_g and b_g matched to the statistics in $\mathcal{D}_s$. Finally, we obtain the synthetic clean RGB image of a frame as $G = WCL^\gamma$.

To synthesize the noisy input, a mosaicking mask M is applied to G, yielding a Bayer CFA pattern image, denoted by G_M. Then Poisson-Gaussian noise which is approximated by heteroscedastic Gaussian [27] is added to the CFA image to synthesize noisy raw image I:

$$I = G_M + n(G_M) \tag{1}$$

where noise n is dependent on the signal intensity g at each location:

$$n(g) \sim \mathcal{N}(\mu = g, \sigma^2 = \lambda_{shot} g + \lambda_{read}^2) \tag{2}$$

where $\mathcal{N}(\mu, \sigma^2)$ is Gaussian distribution. λ_{shot} and λ_{read} are the shot noise and readout noise, which are uniformly sampled in the range (0.00001, 0.01) and (0, 0.058), respectively.

By the above described process, we can synthesize a sequence of noisy raw images I and take them as $\boldsymbol{I}_d$. The clean RGB image G of the center frame is taken as the ground-truth G_d. A data pair $(\boldsymbol{I}_d, G_d)$ is then constructed for $\mathcal{D}_d$.

Preparation of $\mathcal{D}_s$. We use the static burst image datasets in [1,9] to prepare dataset $\mathcal{D}_s$. We extract 140 and 162 groups of data pairs in [9] and [1],

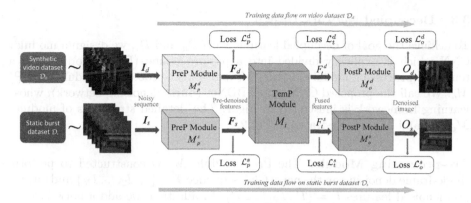

Fig. 1. The decoupled learning framework for our burst denoising network (BDNet).

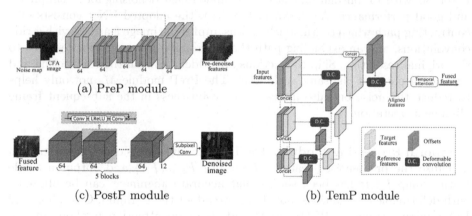

Fig. 2. The structure of the PreP module M_p, TemP module M_t and PostP module M_o of the proposed BDNet.

respectively. Each group contains a static noisy sequence of 5 raw images and a clean RGB ground-truth. We propose to add simple motions to the static burst sequences to facilitate the learning of frame alignment. Specifically, for a raw noisy image sequence, we add vertical and horizontal global shifts to its frames (except for its reference frame I_r):

$$\hat{I}_i = I_i(x + x_i, y + y_i), \quad for \quad i \neq r \tag{3}$$

where the shift x_i and y_i are uniformly sampled from the range $[-4, 4]$.

The ground-truth image G_s is already available in the static noisy image datasets [1,9]. After adding simple motions to its adjacent noisy frames and taking them as I_s, a data pair (I_s, G_s) for the dataset D_s can be generated.

3.3 Decoupled Network Design

To achieve the goal of decoupled learning with $\mathcal{D}_d$ and $\mathcal{D}_s$, we design a modular CNN which is explicitly divided into a pre-processing (PreP) module M_p, a temporal processing module (TemP) M_t and a post-processing module (PostP) M_o. We call the proposed CNN model BDNet (burst denoising network), whose learning framework is illustrated in Fig. 1. The detailed structures of modules M_p, M_t and M_o are illustrated in Fig. 2.

Pre-processing Module. The PreP module M_p is constructed to perform single-frame denoising on the noisy CFA sequence $I = \{I_1, I_2, ..., I_N\}$ and output pre-denoised features $F = \{F_1, F_2, ..., F_N\}$. In addition, we add a noise level as input, which is obtained by $\sqrt{\lambda_{shot} + \lambda_{read}^2}$. We adopt a multi-scale (three scales) UNet [30] with 15 convolutional layers for single image denoising for its simplicity and good performance. As shown in Fig. 2(a), the adopted UNet consists of a contracting path which continuously downsamples the image features with stride convolutions, and an expanding path that gradually upsamples the features to the original resolution. Skip connections are added between the contracting and expanding paths at the same scale level. The PreP module M_p not only helps to reduce the noise but also increases the robustness in the subsequent frame alignment operation.

Temporal Processing Module. The TemP module M_t is constructed to align and fuse the pre-denoised features $F = \{F_1, F_2, ..., F_N\}$ and output a single feature map F_t. It has been shown that accurate alignment can be obtained with deformable convolutions [33]. Thus, we adopt the Pyramid, Cascading and Deformable alignment (PCD) model and temporal attention methods in [33] as the alignment and fusion components in our TemP module, respectively. As shown in Fig. 1(b), the PCD takes a pair of reference and target features as input, and progressively warps the target feature to the reference feature in a multi-scale and cascading manner. The temporal attention component fuses all the aligned features according to their similarities to the reference feature.

Post-processing Module. The PostP module M_o takes the fused feature F_t as input and conducts some refinement operations to reconstruct a clean image. As shown in Fig. 1(c), we deploy 5 residual blocks to build M_o, each containing two convolutional layers. Then a 1×1 convolutional and a sub-pixel convolutional layer are applied to output the denoised RGB image O.

3.4 Decoupled Learning Process

Given the BDNet model in Sect. 3.3 and the two prepared datasets $\mathcal{D}_d$ and $\mathcal{D}_s$ in Sect. 3.2, the remaining question is how to effectively learn frame alignment and real-world noise adaptation for burst denoising. We propose a decoupled learning method to this end, which is illustrated in Fig. 1.

First, considering that the noise statistics in the dynamic video dataset $\mathcal{D}_d$ (synthetic noise) and static burst dataset $\mathcal{D}_s$ (real-world noise) are different, different CNN modules should be deployed for each case to avoid mixed learning. Therefore, we train and deploy two instances of the PreP module M_p with the same architecture but different parameters. These two module instances, denoted by M_p^d and M_p^s, transform the synthetic noisy sequences $\boldsymbol{I}_d$ (from $\mathcal{D}_d$) and real-world noisy sequences $\boldsymbol{I}_s$ (from $\mathcal{D}_s$) to pre-denoised feature sequences $\boldsymbol{F}_d$ and $\boldsymbol{F}_s$, respectively. We assign a pair of sub-losses, denoted by $\mathcal{L}_p^d$ and $\mathcal{L}_p^s$, for the pre-denoising modules

$$\begin{cases} \min \mathcal{L}_p^d(G_d, Recon_1(F_{d,r})) \\ \min \mathcal{L}_p^s(G_s, Recon_1(F_{s,r})) \end{cases} \tag{4}$$

where $F_{d,r}$ and $F_{s,r}$ are the reference feature maps in the pre-denoised feature sequences $\boldsymbol{F}_d$ and $\boldsymbol{F}_s$, respectively. This pair of sub-losses $\mathcal{L}_p^d$ and $\mathcal{L}_p^s$ (e.g., ℓ_1 loss) calculate the errors between the ground-truths G_d, G_s from the two datasets and the images reconstructed from the pre-denoised reference features $F_{d,r}$, $F_{s,r}$, respectively. The reconstruction operation $Recon_1$ is performed by a shared 1×1 convolution that reduces the channel size, followed by a sub-pixel convolution to expand to the original resolution. Since the features are initially denoised, they are in a relatively clean signal space, which facilitate the subsequent frame alignment learning.

Second, we deploy one TemP module M_t to receive the feature sequences $\boldsymbol{F}_d$ and $\boldsymbol{F}_s$, perform frame alignment and fusion, and output the fused features F_t^d and F_t^s, respectively. Since both $\boldsymbol{F}_d$ and $\boldsymbol{F}_s$ are in a relatively clean latent space, the learned frame alignment capability of $\boldsymbol{F}_d$ can be transferred to $\boldsymbol{F}_s$. A pair of sub-losses, denoted by $\mathcal{L}_t^d$ and $\mathcal{L}_t^s$, are deployed on M_t:

$$\begin{cases} \min \mathcal{L}_t^d(G_d, Recon_2(F_t^d)) \\ \min \mathcal{L}_t^s(G_s, Recon_2(F_t^s)) \end{cases} \tag{5}$$

The sub-losses compare the ground-truths G_d and G_s with the images reconstructed from the fused features F_t^d and F_t^s, respectively. The reconstruction operation $Recon_2$ consists of a shared 1×1 convolution followed by a sub-pixel convolution.

Third, considering that the dataset $\mathcal{D}_d$ is generated by reversing the ISP, while the images in dataset $\mathcal{D}_s$ are collected in the real raw image domain, the ground-truth images of the two datasets may have some appearance differences. In particular, the ground-truth images in $\mathcal{D}_s$ have genuine image structures, whereas the ones in $\mathcal{D}_d$ may have artifacts caused by reversing ISP. Therefore, different CNN modules should be deployed to learn different types of ground-truths. We assign two instances of PostP module M_o, denoted by M_o^d and M_o^s, to transform the fused features F_t^d and F_t^s to the final denoised images O_d and O_s, respectively. A pair of sub-losses, denoted by $\mathcal{L}_o^d$ and $\mathcal{L}_o^s$, are deployed to compare G_d and G_s with the denoised images O_d and O_s, respectively:

$$\begin{cases} \min \mathcal{L}_o^d(G_d, O_d) \\ \min \mathcal{L}_o^s(G_s, O_s) \end{cases} \tag{6}$$

Finally, in the training process, we have two sets of loss functions $\mathcal{L}^d$ and $\mathcal{L}^s$ to update the BDNet on $\mathcal{D}_d$ and $\mathcal{D}_s$, respectively, which are as follows:

$$\begin{cases} \mathcal{L}^d = w_p(k) \cdot \mathcal{L}_p^d + w_t(k) \cdot \mathcal{L}_t^d + w_o(k) \cdot \mathcal{L}_o^d \\ \mathcal{L}^s = w_p(k) \cdot \mathcal{L}_p^s + w_t(k) \cdot \mathcal{L}_t^s + w_o(k) \cdot \mathcal{L}_o^s \end{cases} \tag{7}$$

where $w_p(k)$, $w_t(k)$ and $w_o(k)$ are the weights assigned on the sub-losses, which are variables dependent on the global epochs k in the training. We adopt an adaptive weighting scheme to train the modules progressively by setting:

$$\begin{cases} w_p(k) = 0.1^{\frac{k}{K}}, & 1 \leq k \leq K, \quad else \quad 0.1 \\ w_t(k) = 0.1 \cdot 10^{\frac{k-K}{K}}, & K \leq k \leq 2K, \quad else \quad 0.1 \\ w_o(k) = 0.1 \cdot 10^{\frac{k-2K}{K}}, & 2K \leq k \leq 3K, \quad else \quad 0.1 \end{cases} \tag{8}$$

Under this weighting scheme, the three pairs of sub-losses in Eq. (7) dominate the training process in turn. In the first K epochs, $w_p(k)$ gradually decreases from 1 to 0.1, while the others remain at 0.1. This setting emphasizes the sub-losses $\mathcal{L}_p^d$ and $\mathcal{L}_p^s$ that optimize the PreP module. Then, during the epochs from K to $2K$, the weight $w_t(k)$ gradually ascends from 0.1 to 1, with the others remain at 0.1. At this stage, the sub-loss $\mathcal{L}_t^d$ and $\mathcal{L}_t^s$ dominate the training, focusing on the TemP module. Lastly, during the epoch from $2K$ to $3K$, the weight $w_o(k)$ on sub-losses $\mathcal{L}_o^d$ and $\mathcal{L}_o^s$ ascends from 0.1 to 1, with the other weights remaining at 0.1. This stage focuses on the training of the PostP module.

We adopt ℓ_1 loss for all the sub-losses involved in Eq. (7). An alternative training scheme is adopted to assign J_1 iterations for loss $\mathcal{L}^d$ and J_2 iterations for loss $\mathcal{L}^s$ in one cycle. In the testing stage, the modules M_p^d and M_o^d are removed, and only the M_p^s, M_t and M_o^s modules are used to form the final BDNet model.

4   Experiments

In this section, we conduct experiments to verify the effectiveness of proposed decoupled learning approach for burst denoising. We evaluate our BDNet on both synthetic noisy video dataset and real-world noisy sequences quantitatively and qualitatively. The peak signal-to-noise ratio (PSNR) and structural similarity (SSIM) [41] are used as the quantitative metrics.

The kernel size of the convolutional layers of our BDNet is set to 3×3. Leaky ReLU is used as the activation function. The number of input frames N of a burst sequence is set to 5 for all multi-frame methods in the comparison. In all experiments, we use the Adam optimizer ($\beta_1 = 0.9, \beta_2 = 0.99$) [19] to train BDNet and other competing CNN models. The initial learning rate is set to 10^{-4}, and it exponentially decays by 0.1 at 3/4 of the total epochs. The parameter K in Eq. (8) is set to 30. In the decoupled training, we update the model for $J_1 = 3$ iterations on $\mathcal{D}_d$ and $J_2 = 1$ on $\mathcal{D}_s$ in one cycle. In all training, the batch size is set to 2 and the patch size is set to 128×128. Random rotations, vertical and horizontal flippings are applied for data augmentation.

Table 1. Quantitative results (PSNR/SSIM) on the synthetic test sets. G25, G50 and PG indicates Gaussian $\sigma = 25$, Gaussian $\sigma = 50$ and Poisson-Gaussian noise, respectively.

	VBM4D	DNCNN	RIDNet	KPN	TOFlow	BDNet
G25	28.30/0.735	32.60/0.870	34.74/0.908	34.84/0.907	34.99/0.902	36.78/0.937
G50	25.92/0.621	29.32/0.776	31.47/0.821	32.44/0.862	31.95/0.829	34.03/0.900
PG	30.48/0.845	35.79/0.934	38.34/0.954	37.77/0.940	37.90/0.951	39.45/0.965

4.1 Datasets

Training Set. For dynamic video dataset $\mathcal{D}_d$, we extract 20,000 image sequences from the Vimeo-90K video dataset [35], each containing 5 consecutive frames. As for $\mathcal{D}_s$, we leverage the SIDD [1] and SID datasets [9] to build it for multi-camera training since none of the two datasets has enough training data for a single camera. Specifically, we combine the Sony training set of SID (162 image sequences) and 140 image sequences selected from SIDD training set as our static burst dataset $\mathcal{D}_s$.

Testing Set. Our testing set consists of a synthetic test set and a real-world test set. For the synthetic test set, we extract another 200 image sequences (different from the training sequences in scene and content) from the Vimeo-90k dataset [35], denoted by Vimeo-200. For the real-world test set, we build a static test set, denoted by Real-static, for quantitative evaluation, as well as a dynamic test set, denoted by Real-dynamic, for qualitative perceptual evaluation because the ground-truths are hard to generate for dynamic scenes. The Real-static set is composed of the Sony test set (50 image sequences) in SID dataset [9] and 20 image sequences selected from the SIDD dataset [1]. For the Real-dynamic test set, we use iPhone 7 to capture 20 dynamic noisy image sequences in low-light environment. All the images are stored in raw format.

4.2 Results on Synthetic Noisy Sequences

We firstly evaluate the burst denoising performance of our BDNet on synthetic noisy data. We compare BDNet with several representative and state-of-the-art methods which are popularly used for synthetic noisy video denoising, including VBM4D [25], DnCNN [38], RIDNet [3], KPN [27] and TOFlow [35]. Among them, VBM4D is a classical patch based video denoising method; DnCNN and RIDNet are single-frame denoising CNN models; and KPN and TOFlow are CNN based multi-frame denoising models. We train all the CNN based models, including BDNet, until convergence on the dataset $\mathcal{D}_d$. We add three types of noises, including Gaussian noise with $\sigma = 25$ (G25), Gaussian noise with $\sigma = 50$ (G50) and Poisson-Gaussian noise (PG) defined in Eq. (2), to the Vimeo-200 test set, and apply the competing models to these synthetic noisy sequences.

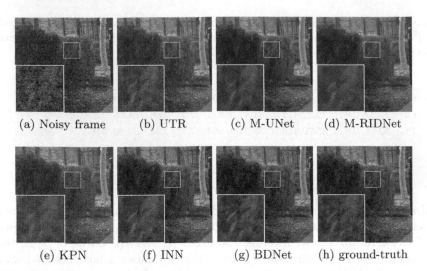

(a) Noisy frame   (b) UTR   (c) M-UNet   (d) M-RIDNet

(e) KPN   (f) INN   (g) BDNet   (h) ground-truth

Fig. 3. Denoising Results of the compared methods on Real-static test set. White balance gain and a gamma conversion with parameter 2.2 are applied for better visualization.

Table 2. Quantitative evaluation on the real-static test set.

	VBM4D	UTR	UNet	M-UNet	RIDNet	M-RIDNet	KPN	INN	BDNet
PSNR	40.49	42.02	43.85	44.23	44.17	44.54	39.68	43.95	45.31
SSIM	0.901	0.897	0.954	0.964	0.960	0.968	0.867	0.964	0.971

Table 1 shows the PSNR/SSIM results of the compared methods. We can see that the proposed BDNet achieves the highest PSNR and SSIM scores in all cases. While TOFlow performs well in the cases of low noise levels, i.e., G25 and PG, its performance heavily degrades in the case of higher noise level, i.e., G50. This is because it performs frame alignment in the image domain, but the alignment accuracy is affected by the heavy image noise. While the single-frame models, DnCNN and RIDNet, have relatively lower PSNR/SSIM scores, RIDNet performs well on PG noise, which may be attributed to its robust feature attention modules. For the visual comparison of the denoising results, the reader can refer to the **supplementary file** for details.

4.3   Results on Real-World Noisy Sequences

We use the "Real-static" (for quantitative evaluation) and "Real-dynamic" (for qualitative evaluation) test sets to evaluate the performance of BDNet on real-world burst noisy sequences. We compare BDNet with those methods popularly used for real-world image denoising in literature, including VBM4D [25], UNet [9], RIDNet [3], Unprocess-to-raw (UTR) [5], KPN [27] and INN [20]. Both UTR and KPN methods learn real-world denoising by synthesizing data that resemble

(a)   (b)   (c)   (d)   (e)   (f)

Fig. 4. Denoising results of the compared methods on Real-dynamic test set. (a) Noisy reference frame. (b) Noisy patches. (c) M-RIDNet. (d) KPN. (e) INN. (f) BDNet. White balance gain and a gamma conversion with parameter 2.2 are applied for better visualization. Best viewed on screen with zoom-in.

raw noisy images. In particular, UTR reverses the ISP pipeline, while KPN adds motion and noise to clean images to synthesize a burst of noisy images. In addition, the INN method use global affine transformation to align frames and performs burst denoising by learning a trainable proximal operation. For fair comparison, we make the following configurations.

1) First, for the single-frame denoising methods UNet and RIDNet, we build a multi-frame version for them, denoted by M-UNet and M-RIDNet, respectively. M-UNet and M-RIDNet first denoise each frame in the noisy sequence, and then apply optical flow alignment [37] to fuse the denoised frames by average fusion, resulting in the finally denoised sequences.
2) Second, the UTR method learns a single-frame CNN. For fair comparison with UTR, we replace its single-frame CNN by our multi-frame BDNet structure and re-train it on $\mathcal{D}_d$.
3) Third, we re-train KPN on dataset $\mathcal{D}_d$ using the same data synthesis setting as the original paper [27], including ISP pipeline reversing and noise generation.
4) At last, we train UNet, RIDNet and INN models on dataset $\mathcal{D}_s$ until convergence, and use the models with the best testing performance.

Table 2 shows the quantitative evaluation results on the "Real-static" test set. It is clear that the proposed BDNet obtains the highest PSNR and SSIM scores. UTR and KPN have low objective scores since they are not able to adapt to the real-world static test data. The two multi-frame models, M-UNet

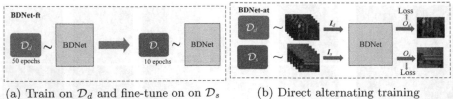

(a) Train on $\mathcal{D}_d$ and fine-tune on on $\mathcal{D}_s$　　　　(b) Direct alternating training

Fig. 5. Illustration of different learning schemes for real-world burst denoising with dynamic scenes. Please refer to the text for detailed descriptions.

Table 3. Quantitative results (PSNR/SSIM) of different learning schemes on the Real-static test set.

BDNet-ft	BDNet-at	Default setting
45.17/0.968	44.67/0.967	**45.31/0.971**

and M-RIDNet, obtain higher scores than their single-frame counterparts, which proves that the multi-frame fusion helps for realistic noise removal. However, their PSNR/SSIM results are still lower than the proposed BDNet. Figure 3 compares visually the denoising results of the compared methods on one image in the Real-static test set. One can see that the proposed BDNet is able to remove the noise without blurring the details, whereas the other methods tend to over-smooth the image details. In addition, the UTR method leaves residual noise in the image (Fig. 3(b)) because it is not adapted to the real-world dataset.

We then compare the competing models on the Real-dynamic test set. Since no ground-truths are available, we can only make qualitative comparisons on them. Figure 4 shows the results, where we can see that those competing methods have residual noise or artifacts caused by scene motion. In particular, the KPN method has severe color shift on image with large noise (the plant area in Fig. 4(d)). The M-RIDNet and INN methods encounter motion artifacts in the car area in Fig. 4(c)(e)). This is because optical flow and global affine alignment cannot effectively count for the local object motion. In contrast, the proposed BDNet is able to compensate for scene motion and restore the clean details. More visual comparison results can be found in the **supplementary file**.

4.4   Ablation Study

To better validate the effectiveness of our decoupled learning strategy, we make some ablation studies here by comparing it with two other intuitive training strategies using $\mathcal{D}_d$ and $\mathcal{D}_s$, which are illustrated in Fig. 5. The first scheme, denoted by BDNet-ft, trains BDNet on dataset $\mathcal{D}_d$ and fine-tunes it on $\mathcal{D}_s$ till convergence. The second scheme, denoted by BDNet-at, directly alternates the training on $\mathcal{D}_d$ and $\mathcal{D}_s$ without deploying two instances of the PreP module M_p and the PostP module M_o.

(a)   (b)   (c)   (d)   (e)

Fig. 6. The results on a raw image sequence with large noise in Real-static test set by different learning schemes. (a) Noisy patch. (b) BDNet-ft. (c) BDN-at. (d) Default BDNet. (e) Ground-truth.

(a)   (b)   (c)   (d)   (e)

Fig. 7. The results on an raw image sequence in Real-dynamic test set by different learning schemes. (a) Noisy reference frame. (b) Noisy patch. (c) BDNet-ft. (d) BDN-at. (e) Default BDNet. Best viewed on screen with zoom-in.

Table 3 shows the quantitative results of the compared schemes on the Real-static test set. It can be seen that BDNet-at has much lower PSNR/SSIM scores than BDNet, which validates the importance of using two instances for M_p and M_o. BDNet-ft achieves similar PSNR/SSIM scores to BDNet. This is mainly because it utilizes $\mathcal{D}_s$ in the training while this quantitative test is also on static scenes. However, the perceptual quality of BDNet-ft and BDNet-na is much worse than BDNet for both Real-static and Real-dynamic scenarios. Figure 6 shows the denoising results of three schemes on a static low-light sequence. One can see that BDNet-ft and BDNet-na generate visual artifacts in the street lamp area due to insufficient adaption to real-world noise. Figure 7 shows the denoising results on dynamic scenes. It can be seen that BDNet-ft causes ghost artifacts in the car area with large motion, because its fine-tuning on static dataset corrupts the learned alignment ability. In contrast, the decoupled learning scheme can achieve both merits of aligning dynamic sequences and revealing fine details in real-world scenes. More visual comparison results can be found in the **supplementary file**.

5   Conclusion

It is a challenging problem to learn a burst denoising network for real-world dynamic noisy sequences because of the lack of a pairwise training dataset. In this paper, we proposed to leverage two types of existing datasets, a synthetic noisy video dataset and a static real-world burst dataset, to address this issue. We designed a modular CNN model, and proposed a decoupled learning approach, which learns to align adjacent frames from the synthetic video dataset and learns to adapt to raw noise statistics from the static burst dataset. The trained CNN model, namely BDNet, can be well applied to real-world dynamic noisy sequences and it obtains compelling detail reconstruction quality with little motion blur. BDNet achieves leading performance, both quantitatively and qualitatively, on the task of burst image sequence denoising in real-world scenes.

References

1. Abdelhamed, A., Lin, S., Brown, M.S.: A high-quality denoising dataset for smartphone cameras. In: IEEE Conference on Computer Vision and Pattern Recognition (CVPR), June 2018
2. Aharon, M., Elad, M., Bruckstein, A.: K-SVD: an algorithm for designing overcomplete dictionaries for sparse representation. IEEE Trans. Signal Process. $54(11)$, 4311–4322 (2006). https://doi.org/10.1109/TSP.2006.881199
3. Anwar, S., Barnes, N.: Real image denoising with feature attention. In: The IEEE International Conference on Computer Vision (ICCV), October 2019
4. Bayer, B.E.: Color imaging array. US Patent 3,971,065, 20 July 1976
5. Brooks, T., Mildenhall, B., Xue, T., Chen, J., Sharlet, D., Barron, J.T.: Unprocessing images for learned raw denoising. In: IEEE Conference on Computer Vision and Pattern Recognition (CVPR) (2019)
6. Buades, A., Lisani, J., Miladinović, M.: Patch-based video denoising with optical flow estimation. IEEE Trans. Image Process. $25(6)$, 2573–2586 (2016). https://doi. org/10.1109/TIP.2016.2551639
7. Buades, A., Coll, B., Morel, J.M.: A non-local algorithm for image denoising. In: 2005 IEEE Computer Society Conference on Computer Vision and Pattern Recognition (CVPR 2005), vol. 2, pp. 60–65. IEEE (2005)
8. Cai, J., Zeng, H., Yong, H., Cao, Z., Zhang, L.: Toward real-world single image super-resolution: a new benchmark and a new model. In: Proceedings of the IEEE International Conference on Computer Vision (2019)
9. Chen, C., Chen, Q., Xu, J., Koltun, V.: Learning to see in the dark. In: Proceedings of the IEEE/CVF Conference on Computer Vision and Pattern Recognition, pp. 3291–3300, June 2018. https://doi.org/10.1109/CVPR.2018.00347
10. Chen, C., Chen, Q., Do, M.N., Koltun, V.: Seeing motion in the dark. In: The IEEE International Conference on Computer Vision (ICCV), October 2019
11. Dabov, K., Foi, A., Egiazarian, K.: Video denoising by sparse 3D transform-domain collaborative filtering. In: Proceedings of the 15th European Signal Processing Conference, pp. 145–149, September 2007
12. Dabov, K., Foi, A., Katkovnik, V., Egiazarian, K.: Image denoising by sparse 3-D transform-domain collaborative filtering. IEEE Trans. Image Process. $16(8)$, 2080–2095 (2007). https://doi.org/10.1109/TIP.2007.901238
13. Ehret, T., Davy, A., Arias, P., Facciolo, G.: Joint demosaicking and denoising by fine-tuning of bursts of raw images. In: Proceedings of the IEEE International Conference on Computer Vision, pp. 8868–8877 (2019)
14. Elad, M., Aharon, M.: Image denoising via sparse and redundant representations over learned dictionaries. IEEE Trans. Image Process. $15(12)$, 3736–3745 (2006). https://doi.org/10.1109/TIP.2006.881969

15. Godard, C., Matzen, K., Uyttendaele, M.: Deep burst denoising. In: Ferrari, V., Hebert, M., Sminchisescu, C., Weiss, Y. (eds.) ECCV 2018. LNCS, vol. 11219, pp. 560–577. Springer, Cham (2018). https://doi.org/10.1007/978-3-030-01267-0_33

16. Gu, S., Zhang, L., Zuo, W., Feng, X.: Weighted nuclear norm minimization with application to image denoising. In: Proceedings of the IEEE Conference on Computer Vision and Pattern Recognition, pp. 2862–2869, June 2014. https://doi.org/10.1109/CVPR.2014.366

17. Guo, S., Yan, Z., Zhang, K., Zuo, W., Zhang, L.: Toward convolutional blind denoising of real photographs. In: 2019 IEEE Conference on Computer Vision and Pattern Recognition (CVPR) (2019)

18. Hasinoff, S.W., et al.: Burst photography for high dynamic range and low-light imaging on mobile cameras. ACM Trans. Graph. 35(6), 192:1–192:12 (2016)

19. Kingma, D.P., Ba, J.: Adam: a method for stochastic optimization. arXiv preprint arXiv:1412.6980 (2014)

20. Kokkinos, F., Lefkimmiatis, S.: Iterative residual CNNs for burst photography applications. In: IEEE Conference on Computer Vision and Pattern Recognition, CVPR 2019, Long Beach, CA, USA, 16–20 June 2019, pp. 5929–5938. Computer Vision Foundation/IEEE (2019)

21. Lefkimmiatis, S.: Non-local color image denoising with convolutional neural networks. In: Proceedings of the IEEE Conference on Computer Vision and Pattern Recognition (CVPR), pp. 5882–5891, July 2017. https://doi.org/10.1109/CVPR.2017.623

22. Lehtinen, J., et al.: Noise2Noise: learning image restoration without clean data. In: Dy, J.G., Krause, A. (eds.) Proceedings of the 35th International Conference on Machine Learning, ICML 2018, Stockholmsmässan, Stockholm, Sweden, 10–15 July 2018. PMLR (2018). Proceedings of Machine Learning Research, vol. 80, pp. 2971–2980

23. Liu, C., Freeman, W.T.: A high-quality video denoising algorithm based on reliable motion estimation. In: Daniilidis, K., Maragos, P., Paragios, N. (eds.) ECCV 2010. LNCS, vol. 6313, pp. 706–719. Springer, Heidelberg (2010). https://doi.org/10.1007/978-3-642-15558-1_51

24. Liu, P., Zhang, H., Zhang, K., Lin, L., Zuo, W.: Multi-level wavelet-CNN for image restoration. In: Proceedings of the IEEE/CVF Conference on Computer Vision and Pattern Recognition Workshops (CVPRW), pp. 886–88609, June 2018. https://doi.org/10.1109/CVPRW.2018.00121

25. Maggioni, M., Boracchi, G., Foi, A., Egiazarian, K.: Video denoising, deblocking, and enhancement through separable 4-D nonlocal spatiotemporal transforms. IEEE Trans. Image Process. 21(9), 3952–3966 (2012). https://doi.org/10.1109/TIP.2012.2199324

26. Mairal, J., Bach, F.R., Ponce, J., Sapiro, G., Zisserman, A.: Non-local sparse models for image restoration. In: IEEE 12th International Conference on Computer Vision, ICCV 2009, Kyoto, Japan, 27 September–4 October 2009, pp. 2272–2279. IEEE Computer Society (2009). https://doi.org/10.1109/ICCV.2009.5459452

27. Mildenhall, B., Barron, J.T., Chen, J., Sharlet, D., Ng, R., Carroll, R.: Burst denoising with kernel prediction networks. In: Proceedings of the IEEE/CVF Conference on Computer Vision and Pattern Recognition, pp. 2502–2510, June 2018. https://doi.org/10.1109/CVPR.2018.00265

28. Plötz, T., Roth, S.: Benchmarking denoising algorithms with real photographs. In: Proceedings of the IEEE Conference on Computer Vision and Pattern Recognition (CVPR), pp. 2750–2759, July 2017. https://doi.org/10.1109/CVPR.2017.294

29. Portilla, J., Strela, V., Wainwright, M.J., Simoncelli, E.P.: Image denoising using scale mixtures of Gaussians in the wavelet domain. IEEE Trans. Image Process. **12**(11), 1338–1351 (2003). https://doi.org/10.1109/TIP.2003.818640

30. Ronneberger, O., Fischer, P., Brox, T.: U-Net: convolutional networks for biomedical image segmentation. In: Navab, N., Hornegger, J., Wells, W.M., Frangi, A.F. (eds.) MICCAI 2015. LNCS, vol. 9351, pp. 234–241. Springer, Cham (2015). https://doi.org/10.1007/978-3-319-24574-4_28

31. Roth, S., Black, M.J.: Fields of experts: a framework for learning image priors. In: Proceedings of the IEEE Computer Society Conference on Computer Vision and Pattern Recognition (CVPR 2005), vol. 2, pp. 860–867, June 2005. https://doi.org/10.1109/CVPR.2005.160

32. Tai, Y., Yang, J., Liu, X., Xu, C.: MemNet: a persistent memory network for image restoration. In: Proceedings of the IEEE International Conference on Computer Vision (ICCV), pp. 4549–4557, October 2017. https://doi.org/10.1109/ICCV.2017.486

33. Wang, X., Chan, K.C., Yu, K., Dong, C., Loy, C.C.: EDVR: video restoration with enhanced deformable convolutional networks. In: The IEEE Conference on Computer Vision and Pattern Recognition Workshops (CVPRW), June 2019

34. Xu, J., Zhang, L., Zhang, D., Feng, X.: Multi-channel weighted nuclear norm minimization for real color image denoising. In: Proceedings of the IEEE International Conference on Computer Vision (ICCV), pp. 1105–1113, October 2017. https://doi.org/10.1109/ICCV.2017.125

35. Xue, T., Chen, B., Wu, J., Wei, D., Freeman, W.T.: Video enhancement with task-oriented flow. Int. J. Comput. Vision (IJCV) **127**(8), 1106–1125 (2019)

36. Yang, D., Sun, J.: BM3D-Net: a convolutional neural network for transform-domain collaborative filtering. IEEE Signal Process. Lett. **25**(1), 55–59 (2018). https://doi.org/10.1109/LSP.2017.2768660

37. Zach, C., Pock, T., Bischof, H.: A duality based approach for realtime TV-L^1 optical flow. In: Hamprecht, F.A., Schnörr, C., Jähne, B. (eds.) DAGM 2007. LNCS, vol. 4713, pp. 214–223. Springer, Heidelberg (2007). https://doi.org/10.1007/978-3-540-74936-3_22

38. Zhang, K., Zuo, W., Chen, Y., Meng, D., Zhang, L.: Beyond a Gaussian denoiser: residual learning of deep CNN for image denoising. IEEE Trans. Image Process. **26**(7), 3142–3155 (2017). https://doi.org/10.1109/TIP.2017.2662206

39. Zhang, K., Zuo, W., Zhang, L.: FFDNet: toward a fast and flexible solution for CNN-based image denoising. IEEE Trans. Image Process. **27**(9), 4608–4622 (2018). https://doi.org/10.1109/TIP.2018.2839891

40. Zhang, X., Chen, Q., Ng, R., Koltun, V.: Zoom to learn, learn to zoom. In: Proceedings of the IEEE Conference on Computer Vision and Pattern Recognition (2019)

41. Wang, Z., Bovik, A.C., Sheikh, H.R., Simoncelli, E.P.: Image quality assessment: from error visibility to structural similarity. IEEE Trans. Image Process. **13**(4), 600–612 (2004). https://doi.org/10.1109/TIP.2003.819861

42. Liu, Z., Yuan, L., Tang, X., Uyttendaele, M., Sun, J.: Fast burst images denoising. ACM Trans. Graph. (TOG) **33**(6), 1–9 (2014)

Global-and-Local Relative Position Embedding for Unsupervised Video Summarization

Yunjae Jung[1], Donghyeon Cho[2], Sanghyun Woo[1], and In So Kweon[1(✉)]

[1] Korea Advanced Institute of Science and Technology, Daejeon, Korea
yun9298a@gmail.com, {shwoo93,iskweon77}@kaist.ac.kr
[2] Chungnam National University, Daejeon, Korea
cdh12242@gmail.com

Abstract. In order to summarize a content video properly, it is important to grasp the sequential structure of video as well as the long-term dependency between frames. The necessity of them is more obvious, especially for unsupervised learning. One possible solution is to utilize a well-known technique in the field of natural language processing for long-term dependency and sequential property: self-attention with relative position embedding (RPE). However, compared to natural language processing, video summarization requires capturing a much longer length of the global context. In this paper, we therefore present a novel input decomposition strategy, which samples the input both globally and locally. This provides an effective temporal window for RPE to operate and improves overall computational efficiency significantly. By combining both **G**lobal-and-**L**ocal input decomposition and **RPE** together, we come up with **GL-RPE**. Our approach allows the network to capture both local and global interdependencies between video frames effectively. Since GL-RPE can be easily integrated into the existing methods, we apply it to two different unsupervised backbones. We provide extensive ablation studies and visual analysis to verify the effectiveness of the proposals. We demonstrate our approach achieves new state-of-the-art performance using the recently proposed rank order-based metrics: Kendall's τ and Spearman's ρ. Furthermore, despite our method is unsupervised, we show ours perform on par with the fully-supervised method.

Keywords: Video summarization · Relative position embedding · Unsupervised Learning

1 Introduction

Video summarization is a task selecting keyframes from the untrimmed whole video, and those selected keyframes should represent entire input video frames.

Electronic supplementary material The online version of this chapter (https://doi.org/10.1007/978-3-030-58595-2_11) contains supplementary material, which is available to authorized users.

A. Vedaldi et al. (Eds.): ECCV 2020, LNCS 12370, pp. 167–183, 2020.
https://doi.org/10.1007/978-3-030-58595-2_11

As content videos have recently begun to flood through various video platforms such as Youtube, there is a growing demand for video summarization techniques. In line with this demand, there have been a lot of video summarization-related researches: conventional methods [6,8,10,12,13,15–18,20,23–25,31], supervised learning based methods [5,7,27,28,39,40,42,43], and recent unsupervised methods [9,19,26,27,35,36,44].

As the content video becomes longer, it is difficult to generate a video summary that takes into account the entire story of the video, without considering the long-term dependency on the time axis. Therefore, previous methods that focus mainly on semantic objects, action, motion, and diversity show clear limitations. Even the latest LSTM-based methods [19,42,43] are vulnerable to long-term-term dependency. Inspired by self-attention [33], one of the most widely used technologies in the natural language processing (NLP) field [1,4,37], we try to solve the long-term dependency problem for the content video summarization in this paper. Furthermore, we incorporate relative position information [29] with self-attention (RPE) to overcome shortcomings of self-attention not dealing with the sequential properties in the video.

However, directly applying the self-attention to the entire video brings two unfavorable issues in practice. First, the large dimension of the feature for each frame inhibits an efficient relation computation. Second, due to the lengthy content video, long-term relation modeling becomes very challenging. A natural solution to overcome these intractabilities is the decomposition of input video using sampling. One may attempt to sample a certain amount of input video frames sequentially. Though, in this case, the difference between the relative positions of the last frame in the previous batch set and the first frame in the current batch set could be large even though they are actually very close. Therefore, we instead sample the input video frames, both locally and globally. The standard sequential sampling is the local sampling, whereas the stridden sampling corresponds to global sampling. We see the local and global sampling methods compensate each other and cancel out the errors caused by the previous naive solution. Combining input decomposition with RPE, our method can successfully consider not only the long-term dependency but also the sequential properties of content video effectively. We call the proposed method **G**lobal and **L**ocal-**R**elative **P**osition **E**mbedding (GL-RPE).

As far as we know, this work is the first attempt to apply self-attention with relative position representation for unsupervised video summarization. Our GL-RPE not only shows the state-of-the-art performance in the recently introduced rank order statistics-based evaluation metric [21], but it can also be combined with various backbone networks [9,19] for video summarization. Moreover, we show that GL-RPE with an unsupervised method achieves better performance than conventional supervised method [40]. Our contributions can be summarized as follows:

1. To our best knowledge, it is the first time that self-attention with relative position embedding is explored in the video summarization task.

2. We present a novel method called **GL-RPE** to handle both long-term dependency and sequential properties of the content video effectively. Our proposed method is general, thus can be easily integrated into the existing unsupervised video summarization approaches.
3. We conduct extensive ablation studies and provide intuitive visual analysis to validate the effectiveness of the proposed method.
4. With the GL-RPE, we achieve new state-of-the-art performance in the recently proposed rank order statistics-based metrics: Kendall's τ and Spearman's ρ. Notably, unsupervised learning approaches combined with GL-RPE outperform existing supervised based approach.

2 Related Work

In this section, we review the most relevant works, including recent deep learning-based video summarization approaches, and self-attention.

Supervised. With the progress of deep neural network, supervised learning-based video summarization approaches [40,42] emerged as a promising solution and outperformed the previous hand-crafted feature-based methods [12,13,18, 20,30]. Zhang *et al.* [40] firstly proposed a deep network for supervised video summarization, using the datasets containing human-made annotations such as TVSum [30], OVP [2] and SumMe [6]. Also, the LSTM-based models were introduced to handle a diverse range of temporal information. The follow-up studies [42,43] proposed a hierarchical recurrent neural network that is more powerful in exploiting long-term temporal dependency among frames.

Unsupervised. Recently, unsupervised methods are receiving renewed attention because video summaries are highly subjective and significantly lack human animations in practice. Based on the assumption that features of good summary can reconstruct the features of the full original video, Mahasseni *et al.* [19] proposed a GAN-based method to supervise LSTM networks without human annotations. In [44], Zhou *et al.*considered unsupervised video summarization task as a sequential decision-making process. The authors then proposed an end-to-end deep summarization network (DSN) using reinforcement learning. Jung *et al.* [9] extend the work of [19] by introducing a two-stream network to handle both local and global frames. Besides, the variance loss is designed to avoid a trivial solution (i.e., identity mapping).

Self-attention. Vaswani *et al.* [33] first introduced the concept of self-attention. It captures long-range relations by explicitly attending to all the features in the word sequence, which allows the model to build a direct relationship with other long-distance representations. Due mainly to its powerful distant relation modeling ability, it replaces commonly used recurrent architectures and is

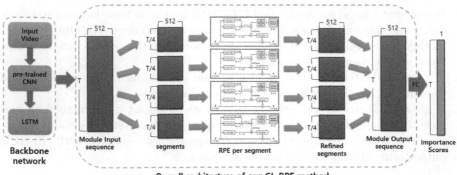

Overall architecture of our GL-RPE method

Fig. 1. The overview of our approach, including both the backbone summarization model [9,19], and the proposed GL-RPE. First, the backbone network embeds the T video frames to $T \times 512$ features. We then divide the input sequence into a total of 4 segments globally and locally (we set to 4 for the illustration) (Sect. 3.3). Each feature segment is refined with RPE (Sect. 3.1 and Sect. 3.2). The enhanced features segments are merged back in the original order for the final prediction.

widely adopted in various natural language processing tasks [1,4,37]. The proposed formulation has been applied to other fields as well: object/action recognition [34], image generation [38], and image restoration [41]. We also attempt to utilize the self-attention for the unsupervised video summarization. However, we empirically observe that directly applying self-attention does not give meaningful improvement due to lengthy video frames. We thus propose to sample the video frames globally and locally to make input compatible with self-attention and improve the computational efficiency at the same time.

Position Encoding. Unlike RNN and LSTM, the self-attention cannot capture position information by design. This is critical, considering that the model is otherwise is entirely invariant to the sequence order, which is harmful for video summarization. To overcome this issue, we adopt relative position embedding [29], which ensures translation-equivariance property and allows the model to generalize unseen sequence length during training. We empirically confirm that relative position indeed helps to capture the sequential properties of video content, improving the video summarization performance further.

3   Proposed Method

In this section, we describe our key solution of the global-and-local relative position embedding module. The module is designed to aggregate the global context non-locally [33], and to be aware of the relative position between frames [29]. An apparent distinction with previous works [4,29,33] is that our target task deals with videos that are relatively longer than the word sequences. In fact, we

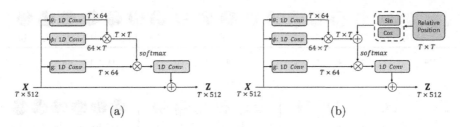

Fig. 2. (a) Self-attention embedding (SAE). The input X is refined by self-attention layers. (b) Relative position embedding (RPE). The input X is reinforced by considering relative positions. The $\oplus$ and $\otimes$ represent addition and matrix multiplication respectively.

observe that the direct application of the module to the video brings marginal improvement. To make input compatible, we thus propose to decompose the input video sequences into two scales, i.e., global and local. We then associate the frames with the proposed module. We evaluate our method by integrating the proposed module into the recent state-of-the-art unsupervised video summarization models; VAE-GAN [19] and CSNet [9]. The overview is shown in Fig. 1. We show our approach can successfully extract global and local inter-frame dependencies, and thus it boosts the baseline performance significantly. We detail our proposals below.

3.1   Video Self-attention Embedding (SAE)

To capture and utilize the inter-frame relations, we design a module that is based on the scaled dot-product attention [33, 34]. The attention layer first transforms an input feature into queries (Q), keys (K), and values (V) using linear embedding matrices. The affinity matrix is then obtained through the matrix multiplication of queries and keys. We then normalize the computed affinity matrix and fetch the values based on it (see Fig. 2-(a)). Note that we squeeze the spatial axis to only focus on extracting the temporal relations. The self-attention embedding module can be expressed as:

$$y = \text{softmax}((W_\theta\, x)^T W_\phi\, x)\, W_g\, x,$$

$$Z = x + W_z\, y,$$

(1)

where W_θ, W_ϕ, W_g, and W_z denote linear embedding layers. We apply SAE to the outputs of LSTM in the base architectures. Since the past memories of LSTM are diluted as time-step accumulates, we employ SAE to complement this by its long-range temporal relation encoding ability.

3.2   Video Relative Position Embedding (RPE)

The original scaled dot-product attention does not explicitly model relative or absolute position information in its structure. To alleviate the lack of position

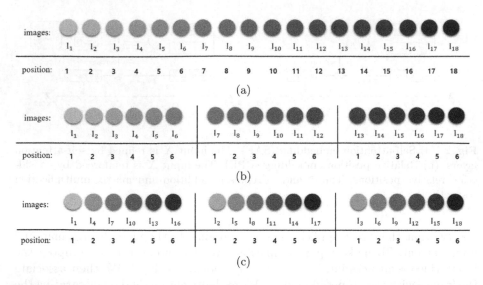

Fig. 3. The concept of proposed global-and-local decomposition. (a) Original video frames with the according indices, (b) Local sampling of video frames, and (c) Global sampling by skipping.

information, we extend the SPE with relative position representation [29]. The relative position representation satisfies the translation-equivariance property, which is helpful when dealing with the sequence of frames, and also encourages the model to generalize well on the unseen sequence length during training. By incorporating the relative position, the module knows by how far two positions are apart in a sequence. This involves learning a relative position embedding for each possible pairwise distance between query and key. We describe our method below. First, the differences in frame indices between query and key are computed. Then, the different wavelengths of sinusoid functions are utilized to embed the relative distances. Finally, the encoded relative positions are embedded into $T \times T$ matrix as illustrated in Fig. 2-(b). Our relative position embedding (RPE) can be formulated as follow:

$$RP_{(rpos,i+j)} = \sin(\frac{rpos}{freq^{((i+j)/d)}}),$$

$$RP_{(rpos,i+j+1)} = \cos(\frac{rpos}{freq^{((i+j)/d)}}),$$

$$a = (W_\theta\, x)^T\, W_\phi\, x + RP,$$

$$y = \text{softmax}(a)\, W_g\, x,$$

$$Z = x + W_z\, y,$$

(2)

where $rpos$ denotes relative positions between frames and is calculated as $j - i$. d is set to $2T$, and $freq$ is set to 10000. W_θ, W_ϕ, W_g, and W_z are 1-D convolutions.

3.3   Global-and-Local Input Decomposition

To handle very long videos, we present a novel global-and-local input decomposition technique. We begin by illustrating the basic case. Please refer the Fig. 3. Consider the general case of Fig. 3-(a). As the length T of a sequence increases (e.g., long-duration videos), the position embedding matrix of $T \times T$ becomes proportionally large. This makes the model difficult to capture the fine-grained relational features between the distant frames. In other words, the embedding matrix becomes less discriminative. Moreover, in terms of model learning, only the small subset of frames might dominate the learning process when a softmax is used in a large matrix. Thus, we see it suffices to perform the computation over a small fraction of frames. Motivated by our observation, we explore a new approach to tackle these challenges; our key idea is to sample the frames globally and locally and compute the relative position embedding for each separately. More specifically, for the global sampling, we skip the frames given the fixed stride rate as shown in Fig. 3-(c). For the local sampling, we set sampling stride to 1 as described in Fig. 3-(b). Then, we compute the relative position embedding in parallel (i.e., both global and local), and finally, merge them back to obtain the relative position embedding matrix. When the temporal size of an input x is T, the global and local segments can be described as:

$$x = x_1 \oplus x_2 \oplus x_3 \oplus \cdots \oplus x_{T-1} \oplus x_T,$$

$$x^G_{(n,k)} = x_k \oplus x_{n+k} \oplus x_{2n+k} \oplus \cdots \oplus x_{T-n+k}, \tag{3}$$

$$x^L_{(n,k)} = x_{\lfloor \frac{T}{n}(k-1) \rfloor + 1} \oplus x_{\lfloor \frac{T}{n}(k-1) \rfloor + 2} \oplus \cdots \oplus x_{\lfloor \frac{T}{n}k \rfloor},$$

where $\oplus$ indicates the operation of concatenation along the temporal dimension, and n is the total number of segments, and k is a k-th feature in the n-th segment. The global and local segments are denoted to $x^G_{(n,k)}$ and $x^L_{(n,k)}$ respectively. We see the proposed input decomposition not only enhances the computation efficiency but also facilitates the exploitation of global and local inter-frame dependencies effectively.

3.4   Complexity Analysis

We combine **Global-and-Local** input decomposition with **RPE**, and come up with our final model, **GL-RPE**. The global-and-local input decomposition not only provides effective window size for the RPE operation but also improves the computational efficiency. Given a $T \times C$ input feature sequences, where T and C denote the total number of frames and channel dimensions of the feature, respectively, the total computational complexity of RPE is $O(CT^2)$. With the input decomposition of N segments, the complexity significantly reduces to $O(\frac{CT^2}{N})$. In this paper, we set the number of segments to 8 after conducting thorough parameter analysis in the experiment section (see Table 1).

4   Experiments

The implementation details are explained in Sect. 4.1. The benchmark datasets and evaluation metrics are in Sect. 4.2 and Sect. 4.3. Both the F-score [40] and the recently proposed rank-order correlation coefficients: Kendall's τ [11] and Spearman's ρ [45] are detailed. In Sect. 4.4, extensive ablation studies are carried out. In particular, we evaluate the impact of our major proposals: input decomposition, self-attention, and relative position. Since our approach is general, we can easily apply it to the existing methods. Thus, in Sect. 4.5, we show that our approach consistently boosts the state-of-the-art baselines with large margins, demonstrating its efficacy. Combined with CSNet [9], we achieve new state-of-the-art performance on TVSum [30] benchmark.

4.1   Implementation Details

We develop the proposed method in our Pytorch platform [22]. The ADAM [14] optimizer is used with the learning rate of 1e-4. It is decreased by 0.1 for every step size 10. The input video is sampled with 2 frames per second, and its spatial resolution is resized to 224×224. Every T frames in the video are forwarded to GoogLeNet [32], which is pre-trained on ImageNet [3]. This results in $T \times 1024$ features. Finally, the 1024 channel dimension is reduced to 512 using bidirectional LSTM. We apply our GL-RPE method on these features (see Fig. 1).

In our relative position embedding (RPE), the internal $T \times T$ matrix is expensive in terms of memory and computation. This induces an inefficient feature learning. The proposed global-and-local concept alleviates these problems effectively by decomposing the input sequence into n segments. As a result, the matrix becomes a size of $(T/n) \times (T/n)$ for each segment. We then apply the proposed self-attention modules to each segment. The enhanced feature segments after the refinement are merged back in the original order. Since our approach is more like a module, experiments are mostly conducted combined with the recent state-of-the-art backbone models [9,19].

4.2   Datasets

We use TVSum [30] and SumMe [6] datasets for the experiments. The TVSum dataset contains 50 videos up to 10 min, and 20 users annotate the importance score for each frame. Since each user has a different opinion on how important the frames are, evaluation of the individual user-label is conducted separately. Then, the results are averaged to measure overall performance. The SumMe dataset provides 25 videos up to 6 min and is also labeled on a per-frame importance score by a maximum of 18 users. Both TVSum and SumMe provide suitable forms of labels to measure F-score, which measures the intersection of selected frames based on importance scores. On the contrary, the recently suggested Kendall's τ and the Spearman's ρ are directly computed on importance scores, and only TVSum has a proper form of labels for the metrics [21].

4.3 Evaluation Metric

F-Score. Video F-score is formulated in [40]. They suggest three experimental settings: 'Canonical', 'Augmented', and 'Transfer'. First, the 'Canonical' is a plain mode of dividing one dataset into the training and test set. Second, the 'Augmented' setting includes additional data in the training set. Lastly, the 'Transfer' setting excludes the test data, which is used in training in the 'Canonical' setting. After then, lots of follow-up studies [9,19,26,27,40,43,44] benchmarked their approaches using F-score. We detail the F-score formula below.

The kernel temporal segmentation (KTS) [24] is used to produce scene change boundaries. The key-shot is then selected based on the kernel-wise importance scores. For a given video, we consider the predicted key-shot (A) and the ground truth key-shot (B). The precision (P) and the recall (R) are accordingly computed as:

$$P = \frac{\text{overlap of } A \text{ and } B}{\text{duration of } A},$$
$$R = \frac{\text{overlap of } A \text{ and } B}{\text{duration of } B}. \tag{4}$$

Finally, the F-score is then obtained as follows:

$$\text{F-score} = \frac{2 * P * R}{P + R}. \tag{5}$$

Rank Correlation Coefficients. While KTS-based F-score is known to be effective, recent study [21] points out that a randomly generated summary can, in fact, achieve similar F-score as the state-of-the-art methods. Therefore, as an alternative to the F-score, the rank correlation coefficients are presented. By exploiting well-established statistics that compare the ordinal association, the similarity between ground truth and predicted importance scores are much well evaluated than the F-score. In particular, Kendall's τ [11] and Spearman's ρ [45] correlation coefficients are adopted. With the recently presented metrics [21], the randomized summary now produces 0 scores while the human summary achieves the best. We thus consider rank-based metrics are more reliable than the F-score for the accurate video summary evaluation.

In this work, we benchmark our method using both F-score and rank-based metrics. We show our method achieves new state-of-the-art performance on rank-based metrics.

Table 1. (a) Ablation study for global-and-local self-attention embedding (GL-SAE). (b) Ablation study for global-and-local relative position embedding (GL-RPE). The TVSum [30] dataset is used in both tables. The CSNet [9] is used as a backbone model.

Method	Kendall's τ	Spearman's ρ	Method	Kendall's τ	Spearman's ρ
Baseline	0.025	0.034	Baseline	0.025	0.034
SAE	0.034	0.045	RPE	0.033	0.044
SAE+Global$_2$	0.038	0.050	RPE+Global$_2$	0.033	0.044
SAE+Local$_2$	0.040	0.053	RPE+Local$_2$	0.037	0.049
SAE+GL$_2$	0.037	0.048	RPE+GL$_2$	0.039	0.051
SAE+Global$_4$	0.058	0.076	RPE+Global$_4$	0.056	0.074
SAE+Local$_4$	0.057	0.075	RPE+Local$_4$	0.057	0.075
SAE+GL$_4$	0.059	0.078	RPE+GL$_4$	0.058	0.076
SAE+Global$_6$	0.061	0.079	RPE+Glocal$_6$	0.060	0.078
SAE+Local$_6$	0.063	0.082	RPE+Local$_6$	0.060	0.079
SAE+GL$_6$	0.060	0.079	RPE+GL$_6$	0.062	0.081
SAE+Global$_8$	0.065	0.085	RPE+Local$_8$	0.064	0.084
SAE+Local$_8$	0.065	0.085	RPE+GL$_8$	0.067	0.088
SAE+GL$_8$	**0.066**	**0.087**	RPE+GL$_8$	**0.070**	**0.091**
SAE+Global$_{10}$	0.061	0.080	RPE+Global$_{10}$	0.063	0.082
SAE+Local$_{10}$	0.064	0.083	RPE+Local$_{10}$	0.065	0.085
SAE+GL$_{10}$	0.064	0.084	RPE+GL$_{10}$	0.066	0.086
(a) SAE			(b) RPE		

4.4   Ablation Study

We conduct ablation studies to verify the effectiveness of our major proposals empirically. We first show the impact of adopting self-attention embedding. We then combine it with the global-and-local input decomposition. While adopting self-attention brings positive effect, we observe the marginal improvement without the input decomposition. Combining both the global-and-local input decomposition and the self-attention, we come up with the GL-RPE method. We show that the proposed GL-RPE dramatically improves the baseline scores. The ablation results are summarized in Table 1.

Baseline. We adopt the state-of-the-art unsupervised video summarization method, CSNet [9], as a backbone model for the experiment. It produces scores of 0.025 and 0.034 for Kendall's τ and Spearman's ρ, respectively. We set these scores as a baseline.

Impact of Self-attention Embedding. We begin by introducing the self-attention embedding (SAE). We see the positive effect of SAE. Specifically, the SAE increases the baseline scores from 0.025 and 0.034 to 0.034 and 0.045. The

Table 2. F-score (%) of existing methods including recent state-of-the-art approach.

Method	SumMe			TVSum		
	Can.	Aug.	Tr.	Can.	Aug.	Tr.
DPP-LSTM [40]	38.6	42.9	41.8	54.7	59.6	58.7
DR-DSN [44]	41.4	42.8	42.4	57.6	58.4	57.8
HSA-RNN [43]	–	44.1	–	–	59.8	–
SUM-FCN [27]	47.5	51.1	44.1	56.8	59.2	58.2
UnpairedVSN [26]	–	47.5	41.6	–	55.6	55.7
GAN [19]	39.1	43.4	–	51.7	59.5	–
CSNet [9]	**51.3**	52.1	45.1	58.8	59.0	59.2
CSNet+GL+RPE	50.2	–	–	**59.1**	–	–

results show that the long-term, global dependency modeling is crucial for the video summarization task. In the meantime, the relative position embedding (RPE) increases the baseline scores from 0.025 and 0.033 to 0.034 and 0.044. While RPE outperforms the baseline, we do not observe meaningful improvement over the SAE, despite the incorporation of relative position information. We see this is because the embedding matrix of $T \times T$ is inefficiently large for the effective position embedding, and thus it brings no remarkable enhancement.

Impact of Input Decomposition. We now investigate the impact of input decomposition. In this experiment, we attempt to confirm two main arguments empirically. 1) Input decomposition is essential for the self-attention embedding. 2) Using both the global and local decomposition produces finer representation. We experiment with 5 different numbers of input segments: 2, 4, 6, 8, and 10. We also report 3 different input decomposition methods: global-only ($Global_n$), local-only ($Local_n$), global-and-local (GL_n). Regardless of the input segment numbers, in Table 1, we can observe the general tendency of performance improvement with the input decomposition. One interesting point to note is that, as the number of segments increases, the performance improvement becomes large. The performance eventually saturates at 8. This shows that the input decomposition is indeed effective for capturing the inter-frame relations, and there exists an effective processing window size (i.e., $\frac{T}{8} \times \frac{T}{8}$) when using self-attention modules. Meanwhile, we explore the effect of using both the global and local input segments. We observe that the impact of global and local decomposition becomes apparent when using relative position information, and the number of segments increases. The relative position allows the module to be aware of the distance, and this information becomes crucial when dealing with both the global and local segments. The RPE + GL_8 shows the best results of 0.070 and 0.091 for Kendall's τ and Spearman's ρ. We use this configuration for the following experiments.

Table 3. Comparison with the state-of-the-art methods. The TVSum dataset is used in this table.

Method	Kendall's τ	Spearman's ρ
Random	0.000	0.000
dppLSTM [40]	0.042	0.055
DR-DSN [44]	0.020	0.026
GAN [19]	0.024	0.032
GAN+RPE	0.033	0.044
GAN+GL+RPE	0.064	0.084
CSNet [9]	0.025	0.034
CSNet+RPE	0.033	0.044
CSNet+GL+RPE	**0.070**	**0.091**
Human	0.177	0.204

As a brief summary, we use self-attention with relative position information (RPE). Moreover, to effectively process the video content, we decompose the input globally and locally (Global-and-local input decomposition). We combine both proposals (GL-RPE) and successfully exploit global dependency and the sequential properties of video content effectively.

4.5   Comparison with the State-of-the-Art Methods

We compare our results with the existing state-of-the-arts using both F-score and rank-based metrics (*i.e.*, Kendall's τ and Spearman's ρ). The results are summarized in Table 2 and Table 3.

F-Score. As the most existing methods only provide F-scores in their work, we also follow the standard evaluation protocol to benchmark our method. Our CSNet+GL+RPE are measured on both SumMe [6] and TVSum [30] datasets on the 'Canonical' experimental setting. We achieve state-of-the-art performance in the TVSum dataset. In the case of SumMe, our result is comparable to the existing method.

Rank Correlation Coefficients. We now use a more reliable evaluation metric, Kendall's τ and Spearman's ρ, which are recently proposed in [21]. Since the proposed GL-RPE is general, we see it can be easily integrated into the existing networks. Here, we use two different unsupervised models [9, 19] to evaluate the impact of GL-RPE. As can be shown in Table 3, RPE improves the baseline performances. With the additional global-and-local input decomposition (GL), the improvement becomes much significant. The tendency holds for both backbones. This again shows that capturing both the global and local inter-frame relations is crucial (RPE), and the impact increases when the input is decomposed into

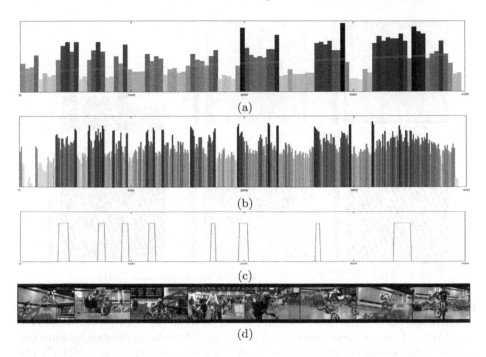

Fig. 4. The qualitative results of importance scores and selected frames. (a) Ground truth importance scores. (b) Predicted importance scores. (c) Post-processed prediction scores with the KTS algorithm. (d) Selected frames. The 42nd video of TVSum dataset is used in this figure.

an adequate size (GL). Note that we achieve state-of-the-art results of 0.070 and 0.091 when the GL-RPE is combined with CSNet [9]. Moreover, we outperform the supervised model dppLSTM [40] with a large margin.

4.6   Visualization

Here, 1) the frame-level importance scores (Fig. 4) and 2) the embedding matrix in the self-attention (Fig. 5) are visualized for better understanding of our approach. In Fig. 4, we provide (a) the ground truth scores, (b) predicted scores, (c) post-processed scores with KTS algorithm, and (d) the selected frames for summary. The frame-level scores are colored by their importance (i.e., the darker, the more important). Despite using unsupervised backbone [9], we can clearly see that our prediction scores well aligns with the ground-truth scores.

To see the actual effect of the proposed relative position embedding (RPE), we visualize the internal embedding matrix, $T \times T$, in the module. In Fig. 5, we show (a) self-attention embedding matrix without relative position, (b) row-wise softmax of (a) (i.e., SAE), (c) predicted importance scores, (d) relative position matrix, (e) self-attention embedding with relative position, and (f) row-wise softmax of (e) (i.e., RPE). As shown in (a) and (b), we see that the self-attention

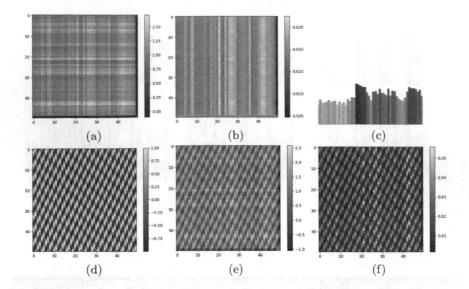

Fig. 5. The visualization of the embedding matrix in the self-attention module. (a) The self-attention embedding matrix without relative position. (b) The row-wise softmax of (a) (SAE). (c) The predicted importance scores. (d) The relative position information. (e) The self-attention embedding matrix with relative position (i.e., (a) + (d)). (f) The row-wise softmax of (e) (RPE).

captures key-frames globally. Though, compared to (e) and (f), the difference between the informative and non-informative frames is small. This implies that the relative position information, (d), makes the embedding to be discriminative across different time steps. The effect of relative position becomes significant after the row-wise softmax operation ((b) v.s. (f)). Note that the embedding matrix (f) well aligns with the final prediction scores, which means the model attempt to reflect the captured inter-frame relations in their predictions.

5   Conclusion

In this paper, we have explored the self-attention mechanism with relative position embedding for unsupervised video summarization. Self-attention makes handling long-term dependency among frames possible while relative position embedding provides sequential properties of the input video. We also use a global-and-local strategy to efficiently get the self-attention of a video that has a large and high dimensionality. We demonstrated the effectiveness of the proposed method through extensive ablation experiments. In terms of recently introduced rank order statistics-based evaluation metrics, our method obtains superior results over previous methods, even including supervised learning-based approaches. Also, we provide qualitative visualizations to illustrate that our method well highlights proper key segments in the video without any supervision. We hope many follow-up studies come up with our findings and results.

References

1. Dai, Z., Yang, Z., Yang, Y., Carbonell, J., Le, Q.V., Salakhutdinov, R.: Transformer-XL: attentive language models beyond a fixed-length context. arXiv preprint arXiv:1901.02860 (2019)
2. De Avila, S.E.F., Lopes, A.P.B., da Luz Jr, A., de Albuquerque Araújo, A.: VSUMM: a mechanism designed to produce static video summaries and a novel evaluation method. Pattern Recogn. Lett. **32**(1), 56–68 (2011)
3. Deng, J., Dong, W., Socher, R., Li, L.J., Li, K., Fei-Fei, L.: ImageNet: a large-scale hierarchical image database. In: Proceedings of Computer Vision and Pattern Recognition (CVPR), pp. 248–255. IEEE (2009)
4. Devlin, J., Chang, M.W., Lee, K., Toutanova, K.: BERT: pre-training of deep bidirectional transformers for language understanding. arXiv preprint arXiv:1810.04805 (2018)
5. Gong, B., Chao, W.L., Grauman, K., Sha, F.: Diverse sequential subset selection for supervised video summarization. In: Proceedings of Neural Information Processing Systems (NeurIPS), pp. 2069–2077 (2014)
6. Gygli, M., Grabner, H., Riemenschneider, H., Van Gool, L.: Creating summaries from user videos. In: Fleet, D., Pajdla, T., Schiele, B., Tuytelaars, T. (eds.) ECCV 2014. LNCS, vol. 8695, pp. 505–520. Springer, Cham (2014). https://doi.org/10.1007/978-3-319-10584-0_33
7. Gygli, M., Grabner, H., Van Gool, L.: Video summarization by learning submodular mixtures of objectives. In: Proceedings of Computer Vision and Pattern Recognition (CVPR), pp. 3090–3098 (2015)
8. Joshi, N., Kienzle, W., Toelle, M., Uyttendaele, M., Cohen, M.F.: Real-time hyperlapse creation via optimal frame selection. ACM Trans. Graph. (TOG) **34**(4), 63 (2015)
9. Jung, Y., Cho, D., Kim, D., Woo, S., Kweon, I.S.: Discriminative feature learning for unsupervised video summarization. In: Proceedings of Association for the Advancement of Artificial Intelligence (AAAI), vol. 33, pp. 8537–8544 (2019)
10. Kang, H.W., Matsushita, Y., Tang, X., Chen, X.Q.: Space-time video montage. In: Proceedings of Computer Vision and Pattern Recognition (CVPR), vol. 2, pp. 1331–1338. IEEE (2006)
11. Kendall, M.G.: The treatment of ties in ranking problems. Biometrika **33**(3), 239–251 (1945)
12. Khosla, A., Hamid, R., Lin, C.J., Sundaresan, N.: Large-scale video summarization using web-image priors. In: Proceedings of Computer Vision and Pattern Recognition (CVPR), pp. 2698–2705 (2013)
13. Kim, G., Xing, E.P.: Reconstructing storyline graphs for image recommendation from web community photos. In: Proceedings of Computer Vision and Pattern Recognition (CVPR), pp. 3882–3889 (2014)
14. Kingma, D.P., Ba, J.: Adam: a method for stochastic optimization. In: Proceedings of International Conference on Learning Representations (ICLR) (2015)
15. Kopf, J., Cohen, M.F., Szeliski, R.: First-person hyper-lapse videos. ACM Trans. Graph. (TOG) **33**(4), 78 (2014)
16. Lee, Y.J., Ghosh, J., Grauman, K.: Discovering important people and objects for egocentric video summarization. In: Proceedings of Computer Vision and Pattern Recognition (CVPR), pp. 1346–1353. IEEE (2012)
17. Liu, D., Hua, G., Chen, T.: A hierarchical visual model for video object summarization. IEEE Trans. Pattern Anal. Mach. Intell. (TPAMI) **32**(12), 2178–2190 (2010)

18. Lu, Z., Grauman, K.: Story-driven summarization for egocentric video. In: Proceedings of Computer Vision and Pattern Recognition (CVPR), pp. 2714–2721 (2013)
19. Mahasseni, B., Lam, M., Todorovic, S.: Unsupervised video summarization with adversarial LSTM networks. In: Proceedings of Computer Vision and Pattern Recognition (CVPR), vol. 1 (2017)
20. Ngo, C.W., Ma, Y.F., Zhang, H.J.: Automatic video summarization by graph modeling. In: Ninth IEEE International Conference on Computer Vision 2003, Proceedings, pp. 104–109. IEEE (2003)
21. Otani, M., Nakashima, Y., Rahtu, E., Heikkila, J.: Rethinking the evaluation of video summaries. In: Proceedings of Computer Vision and Pattern Recognition (CVPR), pp. 7596–7604 (2019)
22. Paszke, A., et al.: Automatic differentiation in PyTorch. In: Proceedings of Neural Information Processing Systems Workshop (NIPS-W) (2017)
23. Poleg, Y., Halperin, T., Arora, C., Peleg, S.: EgoSampling: fast-forward and stereo for egocentric videos. In: Proceedings of Computer Vision and Pattern Recognition (CVPR), pp. 4768–4776 (2015)
24. Potapov, D., Douze, M., Harchaoui, Z., Schmid, C.: Category-specific video summarization. In: Fleet, D., Pajdla, T., Schiele, B., Tuytelaars, T. (eds.) ECCV 2014. LNCS, vol. 8694, pp. 540–555. Springer, Cham (2014). https://doi.org/10.1007/978-3-319-10599-4_35
25. Pritch, Y., Rav-Acha, A., Peleg, S.: Nonchronological video synopsis and indexing. IEEE Trans. Pattern Anal. Mach. Intell. (TPAMI) 30(11), 1971–1984 (2008)
26. Rochan, M., Wang, Y.: Video summarization by learning from unpaired data. In: Proceedings of Computer Vision and Pattern Recognition (CVPR), pp. 7902–7911 (2019)
27. Rochan, M., Ye, L., Wang, Y.: Video summarization using fully convolutional sequence networks. In: Ferrari, V., Hebert, M., Sminchisescu, C., Weiss, Y. (eds.) ECCV 2018. LNCS, vol. 11216, pp. 358–374. Springer, Cham (2018). https://doi.org/10.1007/978-3-030-01258-8_22
28. Sharghi, A., Laurel, J.S., Gong, B.: Query-focused video summarization: dataset, evaluation, and a memory network based approach. In: Proceedings of Computer Vision and Pattern Recognition (CVPR), pp. 2127–2136 (2017)
29. Shaw, P., Uszkoreit, J., Vaswani, A.: Self-attention with relative position representations. Proceedings of North American Chapter of the Association for Computational Linguistics (2018)
30. Song, Y., Vallmitjana, J., Stent, A., Jaimes, A.: TVSum: summarizing web videos using titles. In: Proceedings of Computer Vision and Pattern Recognition (CVPR), pp. 5179–5187 (2015)
31. Sun, M., Farhadi, A., Taskar, B., Seitz, S.: Salient montages from unconstrained videos. In: Fleet, D., Pajdla, T., Schiele, B., Tuytelaars, T. (eds.) ECCV 2014. LNCS, vol. 8695, pp. 472–488. Springer, Cham (2014). https://doi.org/10.1007/978-3-319-10584-0_31
32. Szegedy, C., et al.: Going deeper with convolutions. In: Proceedings of Computer Vision and Pattern Recognition (CVPR), pp. 1–9 (2015)
33. Vaswani, A., et al.: Attention is all you need. In: Proceedings of Neural Information Processing Systems (NeurIPS), pp. 5998–6008 (2017)
34. Wang, X., Girshick, R., Gupta, A., He, K.: Non-local neural networks. In: Proceedings of Computer Vision and Pattern Recognition (CVPR), pp. 7794–7803 (2018)

35. Wei, H., Ni, B., Yan, Y., Yu, H., Yang, X., Yao, C.: Video summarization via semantic attended networks. In: Proceedings of Association for the Advancement of Artificial Intelligence (AAAI) (2018)
36. Yang, H., Wang, B., Lin, S., Wipf, D., Guo, M., Guo, B.: Unsupervised extraction of video highlights via robust recurrent auto-encoders. In: Proceedings of International Conference on Computer Vision (ICCV), pp. 4633–4641 (2015)
37. Yang, Z., Dai, Z., Yang, Y., Carbonell, J., Salakhutdinov, R.R., Le, Q.V.: XLNet: generalized autoregressive pretraining for language understanding. In: Advances in Neural Information Processing Systems, pp. 5754–5764 (2019)
38. Zhang, H., Goodfellow, I., Metaxas, D., Odena, A.: Self-attention generative adversarial networks. arXiv preprint arXiv:1805.08318 (2018)
39. Zhang, K., Chao, W.L., Sha, F., Grauman, K.: Summary transfer: exemplar-based subset selection for video summarization. In: Proceedings of Computer Vision and Pattern Recognition (CVPR), pp. 1059–1067 (2016)
40. Zhang, K., Chao, W.-L., Sha, F., Grauman, K.: Video summarization with long short-term memory. In: Leibe, B., Matas, J., Sebe, N., Welling, M. (eds.) ECCV 2016. LNCS, vol. 9911, pp. 766–782. Springer, Cham (2016). https://doi.org/10. 1007/978-3-319-46478-7_47
41. Zhang, Y., Li, K., Li, K., Zhong, B., Fu, Y.: Residual non-local attention networks for image restoration. In: Proceedings of International Conference on Learning Representations (ICLR) (2019)
42. Zhao, B., Li, X., Lu, X.: Hierarchical recurrent neural network for video summarization. In: Proceedings of Multimedia Conference (MM), pp. 863–871. ACM (2017)
43. Zhao, B., Li, X., Lu, X.: HSA-RNN: hierarchical structure-adaptive RNN for video summarization. In: Proceedings of Computer Vision and Pattern Recognition (CVPR), pp. 7405–7414 (2018)
44. Zhou, K., Qiao, Y.: Deep reinforcement learning for unsupervised video summarization with diversity-representativeness reward. In: Proceedings of Association for the Advancement of Artificial Intelligence (AAAI) (2018)
45. Zwillinger, D., Kokoska, S.: CRC Standard Probability and Statistics Tables and Formulae. CRC Press, Boca Raton (1999)

Real-World Blur Dataset for Learning and Benchmarking Deblurring Algorithms

Jaesung Rim[1], Haeyun Lee[1], Jucheol Won[2], and Sunghyun Cho[2(✉)]

[1] DGIST, Daegu, Korea
{jsrim,haeyun}@dgist.ac.kr
[2] POSTECH, Pohang, Korea
{jcwon,s.cho}@postech.ac.kr

Abstract. Numerous learning-based approaches to single image deblurring for camera and object motion blurs have recently been proposed. To generalize such approaches to real-world blurs, large datasets of real blurred images and their ground truth sharp images are essential. However, there are still no such datasets, thus all the existing approaches resort to synthetic ones, which leads to the failure of deblurring real-world images. In this work, we present a large-scale dataset of real-world blurred images and ground truth sharp images for learning and benchmarking single image deblurring methods. To collect our dataset, we build an image acquisition system to simultaneously capture geometrically aligned pairs of blurred and sharp images, and develop a postprocessing method to produce high-quality ground truth images. We analyze the effect of our postprocessing method and the performance of existing deblurring methods. Our analysis shows that our dataset significantly improves deblurring quality for real-world blurred images.

1   Introduction

Images captured in low-light environments such as at night or in a dark room often suffer from motion blur caused by camera shakes or object motions as the camera requires a long exposure time. Such motion blur severely degrades the image quality, and the performance of other computer vision tasks such as object recognition. Thus, image deblurring, a problem to restore a sharp image from a blurred one, has been extensively studied for decades [6,7,12,33,38,40,45,46].

Recently, several deep learning-based approaches [21,22,31,42] have been proposed and shown a significant improvement. To learn deblurring of real-world blurred images, they require a large-scale dataset of real-world blurred images and their corresponding ground truth sharp images. However, there exist no such datasets so far due to difficulties involved with acquisition of real-world data, which forces the existing approaches to resort to synthetic datasets, e.g., the

Electronic supplementary material The online version of this chapter (https://doi.org/10.1007/978-3-030-58595-2_12) contains supplementary material, which is available to authorized users.

© Springer Nature Switzerland AG 2020
A. Vedaldi et al. (Eds.): ECCV 2020, LNCS 12370, pp. 184–201, 2020.
https://doi.org/10.1007/978-3-030-58595-2_12

GoPro dataset [31]. As a result, they do not generalize well to real-world blurred images as will be shown in our experiments.

The main challenge in developing a real-world blur dataset is that the contents of a blurred image and its ground truth sharp image should be geometrically aligned under the presence of blur. This means that the two images should be taken at the same camera position, which is difficult as the camera must be shaken to take a blurred image. Besides, a real-world blur dataset for image deblurring should satisfy the following requirements. First, the dataset should cover the most common scenarios for camera shakes, i.e., low-light environments where motion blurs most frequently occur. Second, the ground truth sharp images should have as little noise as possible. Lastly, the blurred and ground truth sharp images should be photometrically aligned.

In this paper, we present the first large-scale dataset of real-world blurred images for learning and benchmarking single image deblurring methods, which is dubbed *RealBlur*. Our dataset consists of two subsets sharing the same image contents, one of which is generated from camera raw images, and the other from JPEG images processed by the camera ISP. Each subset provides 4,556 pairs of blurred and ground truth sharp images of 232 low-light static scenes. The blurred images in the dataset are blurred by camera shakes, and captured in low-light environments such as streets at night, and indoor rooms to cover the most common scenarios for motion blurs. To tackle the challenge of geometric alignment, we build an image acquisition system that can simultaneously capture a pair of blurred and sharp images that are geometrically aligned. We also develop a postprocessing method to produce high-quality ground truth images.

With the *RealBlur* dataset, we provide various analyses. We analyze the accuracy of our geometric alignment and its effect on learning of image deblurring. We evaluate existing synthetic datasets as well as ours and seek for the best strategy for training. We also benchmark existing deblurring methods and analyze their performance. Our analysis shows that the *RealBlur* dataset greatly improves the performance of deep learning-based deblurring methods on real-world blurred images. The analysis also shows that networks trained with our dataset can generalize well to dynamic scenes with moving objects.

2   Related Work

Single-Image Deblurring. Traditional deblurring approaches [6,7,12,24,25, 33,38,40,45,46] often model image blur using a convolution operation as:

$$b = k * l + n \tag{1}$$

where b, l, and n denote a blurry image, a latent image, and additive noise, respectively. $*$ is a convolution operator, and k is a blur kernel. Based on this model, previous approaches solve an inverse problem to find k and l from b. Unfortunately, they often fail to handle real-world blurred images because of their restrictive blur model and the ill-posedness of the inverse problem. To deal with more realistic blur, several approaches with extended blur models have been

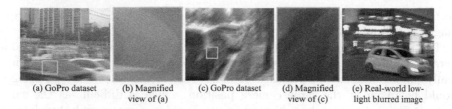

| (a) GoPro dataset | (b) Magnified view of (a) | (c) GoPro dataset | (d) Magnified view of (c) | (e) Real-world low-light blurred image |

Fig. 1. The synthetically blurred images in (a) and (c) in the GoPro dataset [31] are captured in well-lit environments and have unrealistic discontinuous blurs. Blending sharp images cannot mimic saturated light streaks often observed in real-world blurred images like (e) due to the limited dynamic range of sharp images.

proposed, but their performance is still limited due to the inherent ill-posedness of the inverse problem [8,14,17–19,44].

Recent deep learning-based approaches [21,22,31,42] overcome such limitations by learning a mapping from a blurry image to its corresponding sharp image from a large collection of data. However, their performance is limited due to the lack of real-world blur datasets. Recently, a few unsupervised learning-based approaches have been proposed, which do not require geometrically-aligned blurred and sharp images for learning [27,28]. However, they are limited to specific domains, e.g., faces and texts, as they rely on generative adversarial networks [13] (Fig. 1).

Deblurring Datasets. Several datasets have been proposed along with deblurring methods. However, most of them are designed not for learning but for evaluation of deblurring algorithms. Levin *et al.* [24] proposed a dataset of 32 images blurred by real camera shakes. Sun *et al.* [40] introduced a synthetic dataset generated from 80 natural images and the eight blur kernels. Köhler *et al.* [20] introduced a dataset of 48 blurred images with spatially-varying blur caused by real camera shakes. All these datasets are too small to train neural networks, and unrealistic as they are either synthetically generated or captured in controlled lab environments. Lai *et al.* [23] introduced a dataset of 100 real blurred images for benchmarking deblurring methods. However, their dataset does not provide ground truth sharp images, which are essential for learning image deblurring.

Recently, several synthetic datasets for learning image deblurring have been proposed [30–32,39,51]. To synthetically generate blurred images, they capture sharp video frames using a high-speed camera, and blend them. The resulting images have blurs caused by both spatially-varying camera shakes and object motions. However, due to the extremely short exposure times of the high-speed camera, all the sharp frames were captured in well-lit environments, which are unrealistic for motion blurs to occur. Also, blending sharp frames cannot perfectly mimic the long exposure time of real blurry images because of temporal gaps between adjacent video frames and the limited dynamic range. Thus,

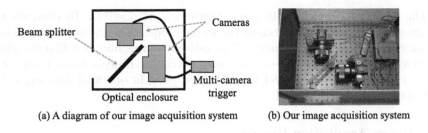

(a) A diagram of our image acquisition system   (b) Our image acquisition system

Fig. 2. Our image acquisition system and its diagram.

networks trained with them do not generalize well to real-world blurry images captured in low-light environments as will be shown in Sect. 5.

Hybrid Imaging. Our image acquisition system is inspired by previous hybrid imaging approaches. Ben-Ezra and Nayar [2] proposed an hybrid camera system equipped with an additional high-speed low-resolution camera to capture the camera motion. Tai *et al.* [41] extended the approach for spatially-varying blur. Li *et al.* [26] proposed a hybrid camera system for motion deblurring and depth map super-resolution. Yuan *et al.* [47] and Šorel *et al.* [52] capture a pair of noisy and blurred images using exposure bracketing for accurate blur kernel estimation. However, all these approaches are designed for blur kernel estimation, and provide neither high-quality ground-truth images nor sophisticated postprocessing methods like ours.

3 Image Acquisition System and Process

3.1 Image Acquisition System

To capture blurred and sharp images simultaneously, we built a dual camera system (Fig. 2). Our system consists of a beam splitter and two cameras so that the cameras can capture the same scene. The cameras and beam splitter are installed in an optical enclosure to protect them from light coming from outside the viewing direction. One camera captures a blurry image with a low shutter speed, while the other captures a sharp image with a high shutter speed. The two cameras and their lenses are of the same models (Sony A7RM3, Samyang 14mm F2.8 MF). The cameras are synchronized by a multi-camera trigger to capture images simultaneously. Our system is designed to use high-end mirrorless cameras with full-frame sensors and wide-angle lenses based on the following reasons. First, we want to reflect the in-camera processing of conventional cameras into our dataset because blurry JPEG images processed by camera ISPs are more common than raw images. Second, full-frame sensors and wide-angle lenses can gather a larger amount of light than small sensors and narrow-angle lenses so they can more effectively suppress noise. Wide-angle lenses also help avoid defocus blur that may adversely affect learning of motion deblurring.

The cameras are physically aligned as much as possible. To evaluate the alignment of the cameras, we conducted stereo calibration [15,50] and estimated the baseline between the cameras. The estimated baseline is 8.22 mm, which corresponds to disparity of less than four pixels for objects more than 7.8 m away in the full resolution, and less than one pixel in our final dataset, which contains images downsampled by 1/4.

3.2 Image Acquisition Process

Using our image acquisition system, we captured blurred images of various indoor and outdoor scenes. For each scene, we first captured a pair of two sharp images, referred to as a reference pair, which will be used for geometric and photometric alignment of sharp and blurred images in the postprocessing step. We then captured 20 pairs of blurred and sharp images of the same scene to increase the amount of images and the diversity of camera shakes. For reference pairs, we set the shutter speed to 1/80 s and adjusted ISO and the aperture size to avoid blur caused by camera shakes. Then, we used the same camera setting for one camera to capture sharp images, while we set the shutter speed of the other camera to 1/2 s and the ISO value 40 times lower than the reference ISO value to capture blurred images of the same brightness. To capture diverse camera shakes, we simply held our system still for some images, and randomly moved the system for the others. In both cases, blurred images are obtained due to the long exposure time. We captured 4,738 pairs of images of 232 different scenes including reference pairs. We captured all images both in the camera raw and JPEG formats, and generated two datasets: *RealBlur-R* from the raw images, and *RealBlur-J* from the JPEG images. Figure 3 shows samples of the blurred images in the *RealBlur* dataset.

Fig. 3. Blurred images in the *RealBlur* dataset. Our dataset consists of both dim-lit indoor and outdoor scenes where motion blur commonly occurs.

4   Postprocessing

The captured image pairs are postprocessed for noise reduction, and geometric and photometric alignment. Figure 4 shows an overview of our postprocessing.

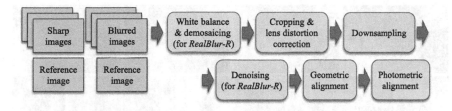

Fig. 4. Overall procedure of our postprocessing.

We first briefly explain the postprocessing procedure for *RealBlur-R*. For each pair of sharp and blurred images, we first apply white balance and demosaicing. For white balance, we use the white balance parameters obtained from the cameras. For demosaicing, we use the adaptive homogeneity-directed demosaicing [16][1]. As we use a beam splitter and an optical enclosure as well as wide-angle lenses, images have invalid areas along the boundaries that capture outside the beam splitter or inside the optical enclosure. Thus, we crop out such regions. We then correct lens distortions in the cropped images using distortion parameters estimated in a separate calibration step [15]. Then, we downsample the images, and perform denoising to the downsampled sharp image. Finally, we perform geometric and photometric alignment. The sizes of the images from the cameras, after cropping, and after downsampling are 7952 × 5304, 2721 × 3094, and 680 × 773, respectively. For *RealBlur-J*, we follow the same procedure except for white balance, demosaicing, and denoising, as they are performed by camera ISPs. In the following, we explain the downsampling, denoising, and geometric and photometric alignment steps in more detail.

4.1   Downsampling and Denoising

In the downsampling step, we downsample images by 1/4 for each axis. The downsampling has three purposes. First, while the image resolutions of recent cameras are very high, even the latest deep learning-based deblurring methods cannot handle such high-resolution images. Second, as we use high ISO values to capture sharp images, they have amplified noise, which can adversely affect training and evaluation of deblurring methods using the sharp images. Downsampling can reduce such noise as it averages nearby pixel intensities. Third, as the alignment of the cameras in our image acquisition system is not perfect, there can exist a small amount of parallax between sharp and blurred images, which can also be effectively reduced by downsampling.

   While we reduce noise by downsampling, the downsampled images may still have remaining noise. To further reduce noise, we apply denoising to the sharp images in the denoising step. For each sharp image, we estimate the amount of noise using Chen *et al.*'s method [5]. We then apply the BM3D denoising method [10] setting the noise level parameter to 1.5 times the estimated noise

---

[1] We used the *libraw* library for decoding and demosaicing raw images.

| (a) Before geometric alignment | (b) After alignment using a reference homography | (c) After phase-correlation based alignment | (d) After blur kernel-based alignment |

Fig. 5. Geometric alignment. Each alignment result is shown as a stereo-anaglyph image, where the sharp and blurred images are visualized in red and cyan, respectively, and overlaid to each other. The blurred image has slightly non-uniform blur due to camera shakes so the shapes of cyan light streaks differ across different regions. (Color figure online)

level. We denoise only sharp images. Regarding blurred images, noise is not an issue because it is natural for them to have noise as they are supposed to be captured in low-light conditions, and also because networks trained with noisy blurred images will simply learn both denoising and deblurring.

4.2 Geometric Alignment

Although our image acquisition system has physically well-aligned cameras, there still exists some amount of geometric misalignment (Fig. 5(a)). Furthermore, the positions of the cameras may slightly change over time due to camera shakes. To address this issue, we conduct a carefully designed geometric alignment process consisting of three steps.

In the first step, we roughly align each blurred and sharp image pair using a homography. As estimating a homography from a blurred and sharp image pair is difficult due to blur, we use a homography estimated from the reference pair corresponding to the target blurred and sharp image pair. For homography estimation, we use the enhanced correlation coefficients method [11] as it is robust to photometric misalignment. Note that geometric alignment using a single homography is possible thanks to the short baseline of our system and the downsampling step, which makes parallax between two images mostly negligible.

Even after alignment using a homography, there can still exist minuscule misalignment between blurred and sharp images due to their different shutter speeds. Specifically, while the multi-camera trigger in our system synchronizes the shutters to open at the same time, they still close at different moments due to their different shutter speeds. Thus, after the shutter of one camera is closed, the other camera still captures incoming lights while moving, causing misalignment between blurred and sharp images. As a result, simply applying the homography of a reference pair results in objects in the sharp image aligned to corners of their corresponding blurry objects in the blurred image, not the centers (Fig. 5(b)).

Thus, in the second step, we estimate the remaining misalignment between each pair of blurred and sharp images, and align them. To this end, we use a phase correlation-based approach [35] that can robustly estimate a similarity transform under the presence of blur (see our supplementary material for the analysis about its robustness to camera shakes). Figure 5(c) shows an example of the phase correlation-based alignment, where the red and cyan light reflections are better aligned so that they appear brighter.

The phase correlation-based alignment, however, cannot align the contents in the blurred and sharp images with respect to their centers. Thus, in the third step, we align the blurred and sharp images to match their centers. Our third step is inspired by traditional blur model-based deblurring approaches. Traditional blur model-based approaches such as [4,9,37] often align images or blur kernels with respect to the centers of mass, or centroids, of blur kernels to align their deblurring results with blurry input images. Following such approaches, we align images to match the center of an object in a sharp image with the center of its corresponding object in a blurred image in an additional alignment step for each pair of blurry and sharp images. To this end, we estimate a blur kernel of the blurred image using its corresponding sharp image assuming that the scene is static and camera shake is nearly spatially-invariant. Following conventional blur kernel estimation methods [6,7,46], we estimate a blur kernel k by minimizing the following energy function:

$$E(k) = \|k * \nabla s - \nabla b\|^2 + \lambda \|\nabla k\|^2 \tag{2}$$

where s and b are sharp and blurred images, respectively, and ∇ is a gradient operator. λ is the regularization weight, which we set $\lambda = 10^3$ in our experiment. Then, we compute the centroid of the estimated blur kernel k, and align the sharp image by shifting it according to the centroid (Fig. 5(d)). As will be shown in Sect. 5.1, the centroid-based alignment effectively reduces the receptive field size required for deblurring, and enables effective learning of deblurring.

Note that each step in our geometric alignment is essential for accurate alignment as they provide different characteristics. The first step based on the reference pair can align images using a homography but is less accurate. The second step improves the accuracy of alignment in the presence of blur, but is restricted to a similarity transform. The third step can accurately align images based on the centroid while being restricted to translation. The effect of each step will be analyzed in Sect. 5.1.

4.3 Photometric Alignment

Although we use cameras and lenses of the same models, their images may have slight intensity difference. To resolve this, we perform photometric alignment based on a linear model following [1,3,34]. Specifically, for geometrically aligned sharp and blurred images s and b, we photometrically align s to b by applying a linear transform $\alpha s + \beta$ so that $\alpha s + \beta \approx b$. The coefficients α and β are difficult to estimate from s and b due to the blur in b. Thus, we estimate them from the reference pair corresponding to s and b. Specifically, α and β are estimated as $\alpha = \sigma_1/\sigma_2$ and $\beta = \mu_1 - \alpha\mu_2$ where σ_1 and σ_2 are the standard deviations of the reference images, and μ_1 and μ_2 are their means. To process color images, we apply the photometric alignment to each color channel independently.

5   Experiments

In this section, we analyze our dataset and verify its effect on image deblurring. We also benchmark existing deblurring algorithms on real-world blurry images, and study the effect of our dataset. Additional examples and analyses, e.g., the distribution of blur sizes in our dataset, and the generalization ability to images captured by other cameras, can be found in the supplementary material. All data including the dataset is available on our project webpage[2].

Datasets and Evaluation Measure. For the benchmark, we randomly select 182 scenes from *RealBlur-R* and *RealBlur-J* as our training sets and the remaining 50 scenes as our test sets. Each training set consists of 3,758 image pairs including 182 reference pairs, while each test set consists of 980 image pairs without reference pairs. We include reference pairs in our training sets so that networks can learn the identity mapping for sharp images. Besides *Real-Blur*, we also consider two existing deblurring datasets: GoPro [31], and Köhler *et al.*'s [20]. The GoPro dataset, which is the most widely used by recent deep learning-based approaches, is a synthetic dataset generated by blending sharp video frames captured by a high-speed camera. The GoPro dataset provides 2,103 and 1,111 pairs of blurred and sharp images for its training and test sets. Köhler *et al.*'s dataset is a small-scale set of images with real camera shakes, which are captured in a controlled lab environment. We also consider another purely synthetic dataset, which is generated from the BSD500 segmentation dataset [29] as follows. For each image in BSD500, we randomly generate 40 synthetic uniform motion blur kernels using Schmidt *et al.*'s method [36] and convolve the image with them to obtain 20,000 blurred images. The sharp images and the blurred images are then aligned with respect to the centroid of the blur kernels. We refer to this dataset as BSD-B in the remainder of this section.

Deblurring may produce misaligned results even when blur is successfully removed. To deal with such misalignment when measuring the quality of deblurring results against ground truth images, we adopt a similar approach to Köhler *et al.* [20] in all the experiments. We first aligns a deblurring result to its ground truth sharp image using a homography estimated by the enhanced correlation coefficients method [11], and computes PSNRs or SSIMs [43].

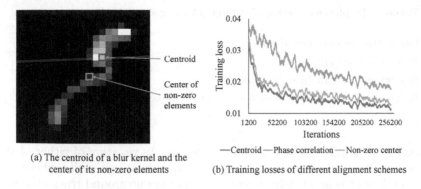

(a) The centroid of a blur kernel and the center of its non-zero elements

(b) Training losses of different alignment schemes

Fig. 6. Training losses of different alignment methods.

5.1 Analysis on Geometric Alignment

Effect of Geometric Alignment. We analyze the effect of geometric alignment with respect to the centroids of blur kernels on the learning of deblurring. Restoring a sharp pixel requires information from nearby pixels in a blurred image, which sets a lower bound for the receptive field size required for deblurring. Alignment using the centroid of a blur kernel can effectively reduce the required receptive field size and ease the training of networks while visually matching the centers of blurry image contents and their corresponding sharp contents. Another possibly more optimal approach to reducing the required receptive field size is to align an image to the center of the non-zero elements of its blur kernel as it is the closest point to all non-zero kernel elements (Fig. 6(a)). We refer to the center of non-zero elements as the non-zero center for brevity. However, we found that this approach is less effective than using the centroids as discussed below. While it is unclear why, we conjecture that it is because the centroid is the most central position in terms of information amount where we can utilize information of nearby pixels most effectively.

To verify the effectiveness of the centroid-based alignment, we conduct a simple experiment. We generate three differently aligned sets from BSD-B: aligned using translation estimated by the phase correlation [35], aligned to the non-zero centers, and aligned to the centroids. We train SRN-DeblurNet [42], which is a state-of-the-art deep learning-based approach, with the three sets separately, and compare their performance on Köhler et al.'s dataset [20]. The average PSNR values of the phase correlation-, non-zero center-, and centroid-based datasets are 26.48, 27.80, and 28.07 dBs, respectively. Moreover, the centroid-based alignment also results in the most efficient training as shown in Fig. 6(b). This result proves that the alignment based on the centroids of blur kernels in our postprocesing is essential for effective learning of image deblurring.

Geometric Alignment Accuracy. Our geometric alignment assumes a couple of assumptions. First, a pair of blurred and sharp images can be aligned with a single homography. Second, blurred images have nearly uniform blur so that

Table 1. Displacement error of variants of our geometric alignment process.

Geometric alignment methods	Error (pixels)
Reference homography	4.9454
Reference homography+blur kernel	0.8701
Reference homography+phase correlation+blur kernel (ours)	0.8058

images can be aligned using a single blur kernel. As violation of either of them can degrade the accuracy of our geometric alignment, we verify whether the resulting dataset is accurately aligned. As there are no ground truth alignment, we indirectly compute the average displacement error for each image pair as follows. For each pair of blurred and sharp images that are aligned, we first divide them into a 2×2 regular grid. For each grid cell, we estimate a local blur kernel solving Eq. (2). Then, we compute the centroid of the estimated blur kernel. If the blurred and sharp images cannot be aligned using a single homography, or the blurred image has spatially-varying blur, the centroid will be off center of the blur kernel. Thus, we compute the displacement between the centroid and the image center of the local blur kernel as displacement error.

Table 1 shows that the average displacement error of our dataset after our geometric alignment is only less than 1 pixel. The table also shows the average displacement error of other variants of our geometric alignment process to verify the effect of each component. As shown in the table, image pairs aligned using homographies from reference pairs have large displacement error due to the different shutter speeds (1st row). It also shows that the blur kernel-based alignment significantly reduces error (2nd row), and that phase correlation-based alignment further improves the accuracy (3rd row).

As we can estimate local blur kernels, we may directly use them for geometric alignment. For example, we can compute the centroids of local blur kernels estimated from a 2×2 grid, then derive a homography from them instead of global translation to align images. However, we found that this approach is less reliable for our dataset and causes larger error because blur kernel estimation is unreliable on textureless image regions or image regions with saturated pixels. Thus, we designed our geometric alignment process to estimate a single global blur kernel that can be more reliably estimated.

5.2   Benchmark

Dataset Comparison and Training Strategy. Before benchmarking existing deblurring approaches, we first compare the performance of our datasets with other datasets, and seek for the best strategy for training deblurring networks. Specifically, we prepare differently trained models of a deblurring network using several possible combinations of different training sets including ours. Then, we investigate their performance on different test sets. For evaluation, we use SRN-DeblurNet [42]. As a pre-trained version of SRN-DeblurNet trained with the

Table 2. Performance comparison of different datasets. We trained a deblurring network of Tao *et al.* [42] using different training sets and measured its performance.

Training sets				Test sets (PSNR/SSIM)		
RealBlur-R	GoPro	BSD-B	Pre-trained	*RealBlur-R*	Köhler	GoPro
	✓			35.66/0.9472	26.79/0.7963	30.72/0.9074
		✓		34.96/0.9132	28.07/0.8259	29.01/0.8768
✓				36.47/0.9515	24.72/0.7422	23.99/0.7675
✓	✓			38.47/0.9632	26.96/0.7991	30.02/0.8946
✓		✓		38.62/0.9649	27.99/0.8249	29.02/0.8774
✓	✓	✓		38.58/0.9646	28.00/0.8241	29.93/0.8931
✓			✓	38.73/0.9646	26.38/0.7942	26.56/0.8422
✓	✓		✓	38.65/0.9646	27.04/0.8017	30.53/0.9045
✓		✓	✓	38.71/0.9657	28.18/0.8294	29.22/0.8824
✓	✓	✓	✓	38.65/0.9652	28.14/0.8311	30.30/0.9006

Table 3. Performance comparison of different datasets. We trained a deblurring network of Tao *et al.* [42] using different training sets and measured its performance.

Training sets				Test sets (PSNR/SSIM)		
RealBlur-J	GoPro	BSD-B	Pre-trained	*RealBlur-J*	Köhler	GoPro
	✓			28.56/0.8674	26.79/0.7963	30.72/0.9074
		✓		28.68/0.8675	28.07/0.8259	29.01/0.8768
✓				31.02/0.8987	26.57/0.7986	26.68/0.8403
✓	✓			31.21/0.9018	26.94/0.8044	29.91/0.8923
✓		✓		31.30/0.9058	27.88/0.8249	28.97/0.8785
✓	✓	✓		31.37/0.9063	27.74/0.8229	29.90/0.8926
✓			✓	31.32/0.9070	26.77/0.8044	27.18/0.8603
✓	✓		✓	31.40/0.9078	27.13/0.8113	30.46/0.9034
✓		✓	✓	31.44/0.9105	28.06/0.8319	29.21/0.8842
✓	✓	✓	✓	31.38/0.9091	27.82/0.8260	30.30/0.9004

GoPro dataset is already available, we also include it in our experiment. We refer the readers to the supplementary material for details about training.

Tables 2 and 3 show the performance of different combinations of the training sets on different test sets. The column 'Pre-trained' indicates whether the network is trained from the pre-trained weights using the GoPro dataset or from scratch. The tables show that the GoPro dataset (1st rows in Tables 2 and 3) achieves lower performance on the *RealBlur* test sets compared to the other combinations in general, which proves that the GoPro dataset is not realistic enough to cover real-world blurred images. The BSD-B dataset (2nd rows in Tables 2 and 3) also achieves low performance on the *RealBlur* test sets, but high performance on Köhler *et al.*'s test set, which is possibly because Köhler *et al.*'s dataset is close to synthetic as its images are captured in a controlled lab environment. On the other hand, our training sets (3rd rows in Tables 2 and 3) achieve higher performance on the *RealBlur* test sets, which validates the necessity of real-world blur training data.

The tables also show that using multiple training sets together tends to achieve higher performance on multiple test sets, as it increases the amount of training data and the range of image contents. Among different combinations, we found that training with all datasets and pre-trained weights achieves relatively good performance on all test sets. Thus, we use it as our default training strategy in the rest of this section.

Table 4. Benchmark of state-of-the-art deblurring methods on real-world blurred images. Purple: traditional optimization-based methods. Black: deep learning-based methods. Blue*: models trained with our dataset. Methods are sorted in the descending order with respect to PSNR.

RealBlur-J		RealBlur-R	
Methods	PSNR/SSIM	Methods	PSNR/SSIM
SRN-DeblurNet* [42]	31.38/0.9091	SRN-DeblurNet* [42]	38.65/0.9652
DeblurGAN-v2* [22]	29.69/0.8703	DeblurGAN-v2* [22]	36.44/0.9347
DeblurGAN-v2 [22]	28.70/0.8662	Zhang *et al.* [49]	35.70/0.9481
SRN-DeblurNet [42]	28.56/0.8674	SRN-DeblurNet [42]	35.66/0.9472
Zhang *et al.* [49]	28.42/0.8596	Zhang *et al.* [48]	35.48/0.9466
DeblurGAN [21]	27.97/0.8343	DeblurGAN-v2 [22]	35.26/0.9440
Nah *et al.* [31]	27.87/0.8274	Xu *et al.* [46]	34.46/0.9368
Zhang *et al.* [48]	27.80/0.8472	Pan *et al.* [33]	34.01/0.9162
Pan *et al.* [33]	27.22/0.7901	DeblurGAN [21]	33.79/0.9034
Xu *et al.* [46]	27.14/0.8303	Hu *et al.* [18]	33.67/0.9158
Hu *et al.* [18]	26.41/0.8028	Nah *et al.* [31]	32.51/0.8406

Benchmarking Deblurring Methods. We then benchmark state-of-the-art deblurring methods including both traditional optimization-based [18,33,46] and recent deep learning-based approaches [21,22,31,42,48,49] using our test sets. For all the deep learning-based approaches, we use pre-trained models provided by the authors. For DeblurGAN-v2 [22] and SRN-DeblurNet [42], we also include models trained with our training strategy.

Table 4 shows a summary of the benchmark. In the benchmark, the traditional methods achieve relatively low PSNR and SSIM values both for the *RealBlur-R* and *RealBlur-J* test sets, often failing to estimate correct blur kernels. Such traditional approaches are known to vulnerable to noise, saturated pixels, and non-uniform blur, which are common in real low-light images. On the other hand, the deep learning-based methods are more successful in terms of

Fig. 7. Qualitative comparison of different deblurring methods on the *RealBlur-J* and *RealBlur-R* test sets. (a)-(j) Deblurring results using *RealBlur-J*. (k)-(t) Deblurring results using *RealBlur-R*. For visualization, the examples of *RealBlur-R* are gamma-corrected. Methods marked with '*' in blue are trained with our datasets. (Color figure online)

both PSNR and SSIM, as they are more robust to noise and non-uniform blur. The deep learning-based approaches trained with our training sets show the best performance proving the benefits of training with real low-light blurred images.

Figure 7 shows a qualitative comparison of the deep learning-based methods in Table 4. All the models trained without real-world blurred images fail to restore light streaks as well as other image details. On the other hand, the models trained with our datasets show better restored results. The results of SRN-DeblurNet [42] trained with our dataset in Fig. 7(i) and (s) show accurately restored image details. The results of DeblurGAN-v2 [22] trained with our dataset in Fig. 7(g) and (q) also show better restored details than the others, while slightly worse than those of SRN-DeblurNet trained with our datasets.

Dynamic Scenes. Our dataset consists of static scenes without moving objects. Thus, one natural question that follows is whether networks trained with our dataset can handle dynamic scenes with moving objects. To answer the question,

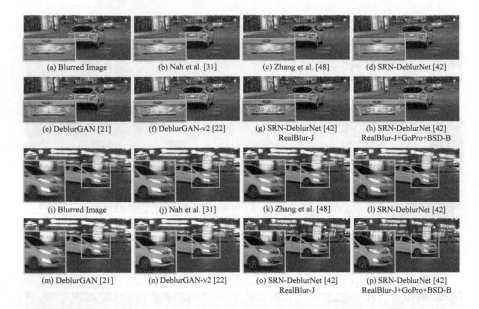

Fig. 8. Qualitative comparison of different methods on images of dynamic scenes.

we investigate the performance of our dataset on dynamic scenes. To this end, we collected a set of real blurred images with moving objects without ground truth sharp images. We used a camera of a different model (Sony A7M2) and different lenses (SEL85F18, SEL1635Z) instead of our image acquisition system to collect images. Then, we perform qualitative evaluation of the performance of deep learning-based methods trained with different training sets.

Figure 8 shows results of deep learning-based methods with different training sets. The blurred images in Fig. 8 have spatially-varying blurs caused by object motions. For all the methods in this experiment, we use pre-trained models provided by the authors unless specified. While *RealBlur-J* does not have any moving objects, the results in Fig. 8(g) and (o) show that the networks trained only with *RealBlur-J* can successfully restore sharp images. Moreover, the networks trained with *RealBlur-J* can produce better results than the networks trained only with the GoPro dataset, even though the GoPro dataset includes a large number of dynamic scenes. We refer the readers to the supplementary material for more examples.

6   Conclusion

In this paper, we presented the *RealBlur* dataset, which is the first large-scale real-world blur dataset for learning image deblurring. To collect dataset, we built an image acquisition system that can simultaneously capture a pair of blurred and sharp images. We developed a postprocessing method to produce high-quality ground truth images, and analyzed the effect and accuracy of its geometric alignment. Our experiments showed that the *RealBlur* dataset can greatly improve the performance of deep learning-based deblurring approaches on real-world blurred images by camera shakes and moving objects.

Limitations and Future Work. Our *RealBlur* dataset consists of static scenes without moving objects. While we demonstrated that neural networks trained with *RealBlur* can deal with dynamic scenes qualitatively, a dataset of dynamic scenes is essential for quantitative evaluation of dynamic scene deblurring. Although we used high-end mirrorless cameras to collect real-world blurred images, a much larger number of users use smartphone cameras. Thus, collecting a dataset for such low-end cameras would be an interesting future work. Our work can provide a basis for developing deblurring methods for real-world blurred images. It would also be interesting future work to develop a more realistic generative model for synthesizing blurry images, which can be used for learning image deblurring, and the *RealBlur* dataset can be used as a basis for it.

Acknowledgement. This work was supported by Samsung Research Funding & Incubation Center of Samsung Electronics under Project Number SRFC-IT1801-05.

References

1. Abdelhamed, A., Lin, S., Brown, M.S.: A high-quality denoising dataset for smartphone cameras. In: CVPR, June 2018
2. Ben-Ezra, M., Nayar, S.: Motion deblurring using hybrid imaging. In: CVPR, pp. 657–664 (2003)
3. Cai, J., Zeng, H., Yong, H., Cao, Z., Zhang, L.: Toward real-world single image super-resolution: a new benchmark and a new model. In: ICCV, October 2019
4. Chakrabarti, A.: A neural approach to blind motion deblurring. In: Leibe, B., Matas, J., Sebe, N., Welling, M. (eds.) ECCV 2016. LNCS, vol. 9907, pp. 221–235. Springer, Cham (2016). https://doi.org/10.1007/978-3-319-46487-9_14
5. Chen, G., Zhu, F., Ann Heng, P.: An efficient statistical method for image noise level estimation. In: ICCV, December 2015
6. Cho, S., Lee, S.: Convergence analysis of map based blur kernel estimation. In: ICCV, pp. 4818–4826, October 2017
7. Cho, S., Lee, S.: Fast motion deblurring. ACM Trans. Graph. **28**(5), 145:1–145:8 (2009)
8. Cho, S., Wang, J., Lee, S.: Handling outliers in non-blind image deconvolution. In: ICCV (2011)
9. Cho, T.S., Paris, S., Horn, B.K.P., Freeman, W.T.: Blur kernel estimation using the radon transform. In: CVPR (2011)
10. Dabov, K., Foi, A., Katkovnik, V., Egiazarian, K.: Image denoising by sparse 3-D transform-domain collaborative filtering. TIP **16**(8), 2080–2095 (2007)
11. Evangelidis, G.D., Psarakis, E.Z.: Parametric image alignment using enhanced correlation coefficient maximization. TPAMI **30**(10), 1858–1865 (2008)
12. Fergus, R., Singh, B., Hertzmann, A., Roweis, S.T., Freeman, W.T.: Removing camera shake from a single photograph. ACM Trans. Graph. **25**(3), 787–794 (2006)

13. Goodfellow, I., et al.: Generative adversarial nets. In: Ghahramani, Z., Welling, M., Cortes, C., Lawrence, N.D., Weinberger, K.Q. (eds.) Advances in Neural Information Processing Systems 27, pp. 2672–2680. Curran Associates, Inc. (2014). http:// papers.nips.cc/paper/5423-generative-adversarial-nets.pdf
14. Gupta, A., Joshi, N., Lawrence Zitnick, C., Cohen, M., Curless, B.: Single image deblurring using motion density functions. In: Daniilidis, K., Maragos, P., Paragios, N. (eds.) ECCV 2010. LNCS, vol. 6311, pp. 171–184. Springer, Heidelberg (2010). https://doi.org/10.1007/978-3-642-15549-9_13
15. Heikkila, J., Silven, O.: A four-step camera calibration procedure with implicit image correction. In: CVPR, CVPR 1997, p. 1106. IEEE Computer Society, USA (1997)
16. Hirakawa, K., Parks, T.W.: Adaptive homogeneity-directed demosaicing algorithm. TIP **14**(3), 360–369 (2005)
17. Hirsch, M., Schuler, C.J., Harmeling, S., Schölkopf, B.: Fast removal of non-uniform camera shake. In: ICCV, pp. 463–470 (2011)
18. Hu, Z., Cho, S., Wang, J., Yang, M.: Deblurring low-light images with light streaks. IEEE Trans. Pattern Anal. Mach. Intell. **40**(10), 2329–2341 (2018)
19. Kim, T.H., Lee, K.M.: Segmentation-free dynamic scene deblurring. In: CVPR, pp. 2766–2773, June 2014
20. Köhler, R., Hirsch, M., Mohler, B., Schölkopf, B., Harmeling, S.: Recording and playback of camera shake: benchmarking blind deconvolution with a real-world database. In: Fitzgibbon, A., Lazebnik, S., Perona, P., Sato, Y., Schmid, C. (eds.) ECCV 2012. LNCS, vol. 7578, pp. 27–40. Springer, Heidelberg (2012). https://doi. org/10.1007/978-3-642-33786-4_3
21. Kupyn, O., Budzan, V., Mykhailych, M., Mishkin, D., Matas, J.: DeblurGAN: blind motion deblurring using conditional adversarial networks. In: CVPR, June 2018
22. Kupyn, O., Martyniuk, T., Wu, J., Wang, Z.: DeblurGAN-v2: deblurring (orders-of-magnitude) faster and better. In: ICCV, October 2019
23. Lai, W.S., Huang, J.B., Hu, Z., Ahuja, N., Yang, M.H.: A comparative study for single image blind deblurring. In: CVPR, June 2016
24. Levin, A., Weiss, Y., Durand, F., Freeman, W.T.: Understanding and evaluating blind deconvolution algorithms. In: CVPR, pp. 1964–1971 (2009)
25. Levin, A., Weiss, Y., Durand, F., Freeman, W.T.: Efficient marginal likelihood optimization in blind deconvolution. In: CVPR, pp. 2657–2664 (2011)
26. Li, F., Yu, J., Chai, J.: A hybrid camera for motion deblurring and depth map super-resolution. In: CVPR (2008)
27. Lu, B., Chen, J.C., Chellappa, R.: Unsupervised domain-specific deblurring via disentangled representations. In: Proceedings of the IEEE/CVF Conference on Computer Vision and Pattern Recognition (CVPR), June 2019
28. Madam, N.T., Kumar, S., Rajagopalan, A.N.: Unsupervised class-specific deblurring. In: Ferrari, V., Hebert, M., Sminchisescu, C., Weiss, Y. (eds.) ECCV 2018. LNCS, vol. 11214, pp. 358–374. Springer, Cham (2018). https://doi.org/10.1007/978-3-030-01249-6_22
29. Martin, D., Fowlkes, C., Tal, D., Malik, J.: A database of human segmented natural images and its application to evaluating segmentation algorithms and measuring ecological statistics. In: ICCV, vol. 2, pp. 416–423 (2001)
30. Nah, S., et al.: NTIRE 2019 challenge on video deblurring and super-resolution: dataset and study. In: The IEEE Conference on Computer Vision and Pattern Recognition (CVPR) Workshops, June 2019

31. Nah, S., Hyun Kim, T., Mu Lee, K.: Deep multi-scale convolutional neural network for dynamic scene deblurring. In: CVPR, July 2017

32. Noroozi, M., Chandramouli, P., Favaro, P.: Motion deblurring in the wild. In: Roth, V., Vetter, T. (eds.) GCPR 2017. LNCS, vol. 10496, pp. 65–77. Springer, Cham (2017). https://doi.org/10.1007/978-3-319-66709-6_6

33. Pan, J., Sun, D., Pfister, H., Yang, M.H.: Blind image deblurring using dark channel prior. In: CVPR, pp. 1628–1636 (2016)

34. Plotz, T., Roth, S.: Benchmarking denoising algorithms with real photographs. In: CVPR, July 2017

35. Reddy, B.S., Chatterji, B.N.: An FFT-based technique for translation, rotation, and scale-invariant image registration. TIP **5**(8), 1266–1271 (1996)

36. Schmidt, U., Jancsary, J., Nowozin, S., Roth, S., Rother, C.: Cascades of regression tree fields for image restoration. TPAMI **38**(4), 677–689 (2016). https://doi.org/10.1109/TPAMI.2015.2441053

37. Schuler, C.J., Hirsch, M., Harmeling, S., Schölkopf, B.: Learning to deblur. TPAMI **38**(7), 1439–1451 (2016)

38. Shan, Q., Jia, J., Agarwala, A.: High-quality motion deblurring from a single image. ACM Trans. Graph. **27**(3), 73:1–73:10 (2008)

39. Su, S., Delbracio, M., Wang, J., Sapiro, G., Heidrich, W., Wang, O.: Deep video deblurring for hand-held cameras. In: CVPR, pp. 237–246, July 2017

40. Sun, L., Cho, S., Wang, J., Hays, J.: Edge-based blur kernel estimation using patch priors. In: ICCP (2013)

41. Tai, Y.W., Du, H., Brown, M.S., Lin, S.: Image/video deblurring using a hybrid camera. In: CVPR (2008)

42. Tao, X., Gao, H., Shen, X., Wang, J., Jia, J.: Scale-recurrent network for deep image deblurring. In: CVPR, June 2018

43. Wang, Z., Bovik, A.C., Sheikh, H.R., Simoncelli, E.P.: Image quality assessment: from error visibility to structural similarity. TIP **13**(4), 600–612 (2004). https://doi.org/10.1109/TIP.2003.819861

44. Whyte, O., Sivic, J., Zisserman, A., Ponce, J.: Non-uniform deblurring for shaken images. In: CVPR, pp. 491–498 (2010)

45. Xu, L., Jia, J.: Two-phase kernel estimation for robust motion deblurring. In: Daniilidis, K., Maragos, P., Paragios, N. (eds.) ECCV 2010. LNCS, vol. 6311, pp. 157–170. Springer, Heidelberg (2010). https://doi.org/10.1007/978-3-642-15549-9_12

46. Xu, L., Zheng, S., Jia, J.: Unnatural L0 sparse representation for natural image deblurring. In: CVPR (2013)

47. Yuan, L., Sun, J., Quan, L., Shum, H.: Image deblurring with blurred/noisy image pairs. In: SIGGRAPH (2007)

48. Zhang, H., Dai, Y., Li, H., Koniusz, P.: Deep stacked hierarchical multi-patch network for image deblurring. In: CVPR, June 2019

49. Zhang, J., et al.: Dynamic scene deblurring using spatially variant recurrent neural networks. In: CVPR, June 2018

50. Zhang, Z.: A flexible new technique for camera calibration. TPAMI **22**(11), 1330–1334 (2000)

51. Zhou, S., Zhang, J., Zuo, W., Xie, H., Pan, J., Ren, J.S.: DAVANet: stereo deblurring with view aggregation. In: CVPR, pp. 10988–10997, June 2019

52. Šorel, M., Šroubek, F.: Space-variant deblurring using one blurred and one under-exposed image. In: ICIP, pp. 157–160 (2009)

SPARK: Spatial-Aware Online Incremental Attack Against Visual Tracking

Qing Guo[1,2], Xiaofei Xie[2], Felix Juefei-Xu[3], Lei Ma[4], Zhongguo Li[1], Wanli Xue[5], Wei Feng[1(✉)], and Yang Liu[2]

[1] College of Intelligence and Computing, Tianjin University, Tianjin, China
tsingqguo@gmail.com, wfeng@tju.edu.cn
[2] Nanyang Technological University, Singapore, Singapore
[3] Alibaba Group, San Mateo, USA
[4] Kyushu University, Fukuoka, Japan
[5] Tianjin University of Technology, Tianjin, China

Abstract. Adversarial attacks of deep neural networks have been intensively studied on image, audio, and natural language classification tasks. Nevertheless, as a typical while important real-world application, the adversarial attacks of online video tracking that traces an object's moving trajectory instead of its category are rarely explored. In this paper, we identify a new task for the adversarial attack to visual tracking: online generating imperceptible perturbations that mislead trackers along with an incorrect (Untargeted Attack, UA) or specified trajectory (Targeted Attack, TA). To this end, we first propose a *spatial-aware* basic attack by adapting existing attack methods, *i.e.*, FGSM, BIM, and C&W, and comprehensively analyze the attacking performance. We identify that online object tracking poses two new challenges: 1) it is difficult to generate imperceptible perturbations that can transfer across frames, and 2) realtime trackers require the attack to satisfy a certain level of efficiency. To address these challenges, we further propose the **spatial-aware online incremental attack** (a.k.a. SPARK) that performs spatial-temporal sparse incremental perturbations online and makes the adversarial attack less perceptible. In addition, as an optimization-based method, SPARK quickly converges to very small losses within several iterations by considering historical incremental perturbations, making it much more efficient than basic attacks. The in-depth evaluation of the state-of-the-art trackers (*i.e.*, SiamRPN++ with AlexNet, MobileNetv2, and ResNet-50, and SiamDW) on OTB100, VOT2018, UAV123, and LaSOT demonstrates the effectiveness and transferability of SPARK in misleading the trackers under both UA and TA with minor perturbations.

Q. Guo and X. Xie—Contributed equally to this work.

Electronic supplementary material The online version of this chapter (https://doi.org/10.1007/978-3-030-58595-2_13) contains supplementary material, which is available to authorized users.

Keywords: Online incremental attack · Visual object tracking · Adversarial attack

1   Introduction

While deep learning achieves tremendous success over the past decade, the recently intensive investigation on various tasks *e.g.*, image classification [15, 38,48], object detection [55], and semantic segmentation [36], reveal that the state-of-the-art deep neural networks (DNNs) are still vulnerable from adversarial examples. The minor perturbations on an image, although often imperceptible by human beings, can easily fool a DNN model resulting in incorrect decisions. This leads to great concerns especially when a DNN is applied in the safety- and security-critical scenarios. For a particular task, the domain-specific study and the understanding of how adversarial attacks influence a DNN would be a key to reduce such impacts towards further robustness enhancement [52].

Besides image processing tasks, recent studies also emerge to investigate the adversarial attacks to other diverse types of tasks, *e.g.*, speech recognition [3,5,43], natural language processing [23,44,57], continuous states in reinforcement learning [46], action recognition and object detection [51,52]. Visual object tracking (VOT), which performs online object localization and moving trajectory identification, is a typical while important component in many safety- and security-critical applications, with urgent industrial demands, *e.g.*, autonomous driving, video surveillance, general-purpose cyber-physical systems. For example, a VOT is often embedded into a self-driving car or unmanned aerial vehicle (UAV) as a key perception component, that drives the system to follow a target object (see Fig. 1). Adversarial examples could mislead the car or UAV with incorrect perceptions, causing navigation into dangerous environments and even resulting in severe accidents. Therefore, it is of great importance to perform a comprehensive study of adversarial attacks on visual object tracking. To this date, however, there exist limited studies on the influence of the adversarial attack on VOT relevant tasks, without which the deployed real-world systems would be exposed to high potential safety risks.

Different from image, speech and natural language processing tasks, online object tracking poses several new challenges to the adversarial attack techniques. *First*, compared with existing sequential-input-relevant tasks, *e.g.*, audios [3], natural languages [23] or videos [52] for classification that have access to the complete sequential data, object tracking processes incoming frames one by one in order. When a current frame t is under attack, all the previous frames (*i.e.*, $\{1, 2 \ldots t - 1\}$) are already analyzed and cannot be changed. At the same time, the future frames (*i.e.*, $\{t + 1, \ldots\}$) are still unavailable and cannot be immediately attacked as well. With limited temporal data segments and the dynamic scene changes, it is even more difficult to generate imperceptible yet effective adversarial perturbations that can transfer over time (*i.e.*, multiple consecutive frames). *In addition*, the object tracking often depends on a target designated object template cropped from the first frame of a video [1,29] for further analysis.

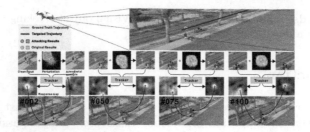

Fig. 1. An example of our adversarial attack to online VOT that drives an UAV [40] to move along the targeted trajectory (the blue line), which causes divergence from the object moving path (the green line). The perturbations are enlarged by ×255 for better visualization. (Color figure online)

The different initially designated object might lead to different tracking analysis, which renders the universal adversarial perturbation [38] often ineffective.

Furthermore, object tracking usually functions at real-time speed. Thus, it requires the attacks to be efficient enough so that the adversarial perturbation of the current frame can be completed before the next frame arrives. Although the gradient descent-based methods (*e.g.*, FGSM [15], BIM [27]) are demonstrated to be effective in attacking the image classifier, they still encounter efficiency issues in fooling the state-of-the-art trackers when multiple frames quickly arrive.

To better understand the challenges and uniqueness in attacking the VOT, we first propose a *spatial-aware* basic attack method by adapting the existing state-of-the-art attacking techniques (*i.e.*, FGSM, BIM, C&W) that are used to attack each frame individually. Our empirical study confirms that the basic attack is indeed ineffective for attacking the VOT, due to the consecutive temporal frames in real-time. Based on this, we further propose the *spatial-aware online incremental attack* (SPARK) method that can generate more imperceptible perturbations online in terms of both effectiveness and efficiency. The main contributions of this paper are as follows:

- We formalize the adversarial attack problem for the VOT, *i.e.*, generating imperceptible perturbations online to mislead visual trackers that traces an object, into an incorrect (Untargeted Attack, UA) or specified (Targeted Attack, TA) trajectory.
- We propose several *basic attacks* by adapting existing attacks (*i.e.*, FGSM, BIM, C&W) and further perform an empirical study for better understanding challenges of adversarial attacks on real-time object tracking.
- We propose a new *spatial-aware online incremental attack* (SPARK) method that can efficiently generate imperceptible perturbations for real-time VOT.
- Our in-depth evaluation demonstrates the effectiveness and efficiency of SPARK in attacking the state-of-the-art SiamRPN++ trackers with AlexNet, MobileNetv2, and ResNet-50 models [28,29] and SiamDW trackers [60] under UA and TA. The generated attacks also exhibit strong transferability to the online updating variants of SiamRPN trackers.

2   Related Work

Adversarial Examples. Extensive studies have shown the vulnerability of DNNs from adversarial attacks [32]. [48] initially shown the existence of adversarial examples, and [15] proposed the efficient FGSM that was later improved via iterative method [27] and momentum term [9]. Similarly, [42] proposed the Jacobian-based saliency map attack with high success rate, while [2] realized effective attack by optimization methods (C&W) under different norms. Further adversarial attacks were extended to tasks like object detection [30,55,61], semantic segmentation [37,55], and testing techniques for DNNs [10,35,56].

Recent works also confirmed the existence of adversarial examples in sequential data processing, *e.g.*, speech recognition [3,5,43], natural language [14,23], and video processing [52]. Different from these works, our attack aims at misleading trackers with limited online data access, *i.e.*, the future frames are unavailable, the past frames cannot be attacked either. Among the most relevant work to ours, [52] proposed the $L_{2,1}$ norm-based attack to generate sparse perturbations for action recognition, under the condition that the whole video data is available and the perturbations of multiple frames can be jointly tuned. [30] attacked the region proposal network (RPN) that is also used in the SiamRPN trackers [29]. However, this attack is to fool object detectors to predict inaccurate bounding boxes, thus cannot be directly used to attack trackers aiming to mislead to an incorrect trajectory. [51] proposed the video object detection attack by addressing each frame independently, which is not suitable for online tracking where the tracker often runs at real-time speed. Another related work [31] studied when to attack an agent in the reinforcement learning context. In contrast, this work mainly explores how to use temporal constraints to online generate imperceptible and effective perturbations to mislead real-time trackers.

Visual Object Tracking. Visual tracking is a fundamental computer vision problem, estimating positions of an object (specified at the first frame) over frames [54]. Existing trackers can be roughly summarized to three categories, including correlation filter (CF)-based [4,7,13,18,34,58], classification & updating-based [17,41,45] and Siamese network-based trackers [1,12,16,49, 50,62]. Among these works, Siamese network-based methods learn the matching models offline and track objects without updating parameters, which well balances the efficiency and accuracy. In particular, the SiamRPN can adapt objects' aspect ratio changing and run beyond real time [29]. In this paper, we choose SiamRPN++ [28] with AlexNet, MobileNetv2, and ResNet50 as subject models due to following reasons: 1) SiamRPN++ trackers are widely adopted with high potential to real-world applications [24,28]. The study of attacking to improve their robustness is crucial for industrial deployment with safety concerns. 2) Compared with other frameworks (*e.g.*, CF), SiamRPN is a near end-to-end deep architecture with fewer hyper-parameters, making it more suitable to investigate the attacks. In addition to SiamRPN++, we attack another state-of-the-art tracker, *i.e.*, SiamDW [60], to show the generalization of our method.

Difference to PAT [53]. To the best of our knowledge, until now, there has been a limited study on attacking online object tracking. [53] generated physical adversarial textures (PAT) via white-box attack to fool the GOTURN tracker [21]. The main differences between our method and PAT are: (**1**) Their attack objectives are distinctly and totally different. As shown in Fig. 2, PAT is to generate *perceptible texture* and let the GOTURN tracker lock on it while our method is to online produce *imperceptible perturbations* that mislead state-of-the-art trackers, *e.g.*, SiamRPN++ [28], along an incorrect or specified trajectory. (**2**) Different theoretical novelties. PAT is to improve an existing Expectation Over Transformation (EOT)-based attack by studying the need to randomize over different transformation variables. Our work reveals the new challenges in attacking visual tracking and proposes a novel method, *i.e.*, spatial-aware online incremental attack, which can address these challenges properly. (**3**) Different subject models. PAT validates its method by attacking a light deep regression tracker, *i.e.*, GOTURN that has low tracking accuracy on modern benchmarks [11,24,54]. We use our method to attack the state-of-the-art trackers, *e.g.*, SiamRPN++ [28] and SiamDW [60].

Fig. 2. PAT [53] vs. SPARK.

3   Spatial-Aware Online Adversarial Attack

3.1   Problem Definition

Let $\mathcal{V} = \{\mathbf{X}_t\}_1^T$ be an online video with T frames, where $\mathbf{X}_t$ is the tth frame. Given a tracker $\phi_\theta(\cdot)$ with parameters θ, we crop an object template $\mathbf{T}$ (*i.e.*, the target object) from the first frame. The tracker is tasked to predict bounding boxes that tightly wrap the object in further incoming frames.

To locate the object at frame t, the tracker calculates $\{(y_t^i, \mathbf{b}_t^i)\}_{i=1}^N = \phi_\theta(\mathbf{X}_t, \mathbf{T})$, where $\{\mathbf{b}_t^i \in \Re^{4\times1}\}_{i=1}^N$ are N object candidates in $\mathbf{X}_t$ and y_t^i indicates the positive activation of the ith candidate (*i.e.*, $\mathbf{b}_t^i$). We denote the tracker's predictive bounding box of the target object at the clean tth frame by $\mathbf{b}_t^{\text{gt}} \in \Re^{4\times1}$ and the object tracker assigns the predictive result $OT(\mathbf{X}_t, \mathbf{T}) = \mathbf{b}_t^{\text{gt}} = \mathbf{b}_t^k$, where $k = \arg\max_{1\le i\le N}(y_t^i)$, *i.e.*, the bounding box with highest activate value is selected as the *predictive object* at frame t. The above tracking process covers most of the state-of-the-art trackers, *e.g.*, Siamese network-based trackers [1,8,12,19,28,59,60] and correlation filter-based trackers [6,16,47]. We define the adversarial attacks on tracking as follows:

Untargeted Attack (UA). UA is to generate adversarial examples $\{\mathbf{X}_t^{\text{a}}\}_1^T$ such that $\forall 1 \le t \le T$, $\text{IoU}(OT(\mathbf{X}_t^{\text{a}}, \mathbf{T}), \mathbf{b}_t^{\text{gt}}) = 0$, where $\text{IoU}(\cdot)$ is the Intersection over Union between two bounding boxes.

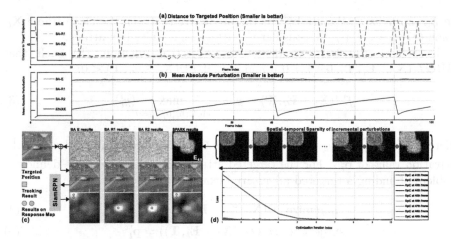

Fig. 3. Analysis of our basic attack (BA) and spatial-aware online incremental attack (SPARK). (a) shows the distance between the targeted position and predicted object position after attacking. A smaller distance means the attack is more effective. (b) shows the mean absolute perturbation of each frame. A smaller MAP leads to less imperceptible perturbation. (c) presents the adversarial perturbations of 4 attack methods at frame 49, corresponding adversarial examples, and response maps from SiamRPN-AlexNet. (d) includes the incremental perturbations from frame 41 to 49 and the loss values at each frame. The perturbations are enlarged by ×255 for better visualization.

Targeted Attack (TA). Suppose a *targeted trajectory* $\{\mathbf{p}_t^{tr}\}_1^T$ desires the trajectory we hope the attacked tracker to output, *e.g.*, the blue line in Fig. 1. TA is to generate adversarial examples $\{\mathbf{X}_t^a\}_1^T$ such that $\forall 1 \leq t \leq T$, $ce(OT(\mathbf{X}_t^a, \mathbf{T})) = \mathbf{p}_t^{tr}$, where $ce(\cdot)$ shows the center position of the bounding box and $\mathbf{p}_t^{tr}$ depicts the targeted position at the tth frame.

Intuitively, UA is to make the trackers predict incorrect bounding boxes of a target object at all frames by adding small distortions to online captured frames while TA aims to intentionally drive trackers to output desired object positions specified by the *targeted trajectory*.

3.2   Basic Attack

We first propose the basic attacks by adapting existing adversarial methods at each frame. To attack a tracker $OT(\cdot)$, we can use another tracker $OT'(\cdot)$ to generate adversarial examples. For untargeted attack (UA), at frame t, we formally define the problem of finding an adversarial example as follows:

$$\text{minimize}\ \ \mathcal{D}(\mathbf{X}_t, \mathbf{X}_t + \mathbf{E}_t) \tag{1}$$

$$\text{subject to}\ \ \text{IoU}(OT'(\mathbf{X}_t + \mathbf{E}_t, \mathbf{T}), \mathbf{b}_t^{gt'}) = 0 \tag{2}$$

where $\mathbf{X}_t^a = \mathbf{X}_t + \mathbf{E}_t$ and $\mathbf{E}_t$ is the desired distortion that changes the result of the tracker and $\mathcal{D}$ is a distance metric. We follow the setup of FGSM and use the L_∞ norm as $\mathcal{D}$. We use $\mathbf{b}_t^{\text{gt}'}$ as the predictive result on the clean frame $\mathbf{X}_t$. When $OT(\cdot) = OT'(\cdot)$, we consider the attack as a white-box attack.

To achieve the UA, we define the objective function f^{ua} such that $\text{IoU}(OT'(\mathbf{X}_t + \mathbf{E}_t, \mathbf{T}), \mathbf{b}^{\text{gt}'}) = 0$ if and only if $f^{\text{ua}}(\mathbf{X}_t + \mathbf{E}_t, \mathbf{T}) < 0$:

$$f^{\text{ua}}(\mathbf{X}_t + \mathbf{E}_t, \mathbf{T}) = y_t^{\text{gt}'} - \max_{\text{IoU}(\mathbf{b}_t^i, \mathbf{b}_t^{gt'})=0} (y_t^i) \tag{3}$$

where $\{(y_t^i, \mathbf{b}_t^i)\}_{i=1}^N = \phi_{\theta'}(\mathbf{X}_t + \mathbf{E}_t, \mathbf{T})$, θ' is $OT'(\cdot)$'s parameters, and $y_t^{\text{gt}'}$ is the activation value of $\mathbf{b}_t^{gt'}$. For the targeted attack (TA), at frame t, we define the problem of finding a targeted adversarial example as follows:

$$\text{minimize}\ \ \mathcal{D}(\mathbf{X}_t, \mathbf{X}_t + \mathbf{E}_t) \tag{4}$$

$$\text{subject to}\ \ ce(OT'(\mathbf{X}_t + \mathbf{E}_t, \mathbf{T})) = \mathbf{p}_t^{\text{tr}} \tag{5}$$

where $\mathbf{p}_t^{\text{tr}}$ is the targeted position at frame t and $ce(\cdot)$ outputs the center position of a bounding box. To achieve the goal, we define the objective function f^{ta} such that $ce(OT'(\mathbf{X}_t + \mathbf{E}_t, \mathbf{T})) = \mathbf{p}_t^{\text{tr}}$ if and only if $f^{\text{ta}}(\mathbf{X}_t + \mathbf{E}_t, \mathbf{T}) < 0$:

$$f^{\text{ta}}(\mathbf{X}_t + \mathbf{E}_t, \mathbf{T}) = y_t^{\text{gt}'} - \max_{ce(\mathbf{b}_t^i)=\mathbf{p}_t^{\text{tr}}} (y_t^i) \tag{6}$$

To perform the basic attack, FGSM [15], BIM [27] and C&W [2] are adapted to optimize the objective functions (i.e., Eq. (3) and (6)). In this paper, we mainly focus on the white-box attack on visual object tracking by setting $OT(\cdot) = OT'(\cdot)$ while studying the transferability of different trackers in the experiments.

3.3 Empirical Study

In the following, we perform an empirical study on evaluating the effectiveness of the basic attack. In particular, we perform two kinds of basic targeted attacks on a state-of-the-art tracker, i.e., SiamRPN-AlexNet[1] to answer two research questions: 1) how effective is the attack by applying basic attack on each frame? 2) how is its impact of the temporal frames in the video?:

BA-E: Online attacking each frame by using FGSM, BIM, and C&W to optimize Eq. (6), respectively.

BA-R: Randomly select some frames and perform the basic attack on these frames using FGSM, BIM, and C&W. For frames between two selected frames, we use the perturbation from the first selected one to distort frames in the interval and see if basic attacks could transfer across time. For example, we attack 1st and 10th frames with basic attacks while distorting the 2th to 9th frames with the perturbation of 1st frame.

---

[1] We select SiamRPN-AlexNet, since it is a representative Siamese network tracker and achieves high accuracy on modern benchmarks with beyond real-time speed.

Table 1. Comparing basic attacks, *i.e.*, BA-E, BA-R1, and BA-R2 with our SPARK under TA on the OTB100 dataset.

	BA-E			BA-R1			BA-R2			SPARK
	FGSM	BIM	C& W	FGSM	BIM	C&W	FGSM	BIM	C&W	
Succ. Rate (%)	8.0	69.6	57.7	6.6	17.8	17.5	6.7	53.7	23.5	78.9
Mean Absolute Perturbation	1.24	5.88	1.31	1.23	5.96	0.26	1.23	3.36	1.27	1.04
Aver. Iter. Num per frame	1	10	10	0.10	0.95	0.94	0.10	4.6	4.6	2.25
Aver. Cost per frame (ms)	56.2	326.0	264.0	5.50	39.1	24.8	5.68	189.5	121.4	62.1

Note that BA-E and BA-R can answer the two questions, respectively. To be specific, we have configured two BA-R attacks. First, each frame is to be attacked with a probability 0.1 (denoted as **BA-R1**). Second, we perform the basic attack with an interval 10, *i.e.*, attack at the 1th, 11th, 21th, ... frame (denoted as **BA-R2**). Table 1 shows the success rate, mean absolute perturbation, and average iteration per frame of BA-E, BA-R1, and BA-R2 for attacking SiamRPN-AlexNet tracker on OTB100 under TA. We see that: 1) BA-E methods via BIM and C&W get high success rate by attacking each frame. Nevertheless, their perturbations are large and attacking each frame with 10 iterations is time-consuming and beyond real-time tracker. Although FGSM is efficient, its success rate is much lower. 2) Randomly attacking 10% frames, *i.e.*, BA-R1, is about 10 times faster than BA-E. However, the success rate drops significantly. 3) BA-R2 method attacking at every 10 frames is efficient while sacrificing the success rate. Compared with BA-R1, with the same attacking rate, *i.e.*, 10% frames, BA-R2 has higher success rate than BA-R1. For example, base on BIM, BA-R2 has over two times larger success rate. It infers that perturbations of neighbor 10 frames have some transferability due to the temporal smoothness.

A case study based on BIM is shown in Fig. 3, where we use the three BA attacks to mislead the SiamRPN-AlexNet to locate an interested object at the top left of the scene (targeted position in Fig. 3(c)). Instead of following the standard tracking pipeline, we crop the frame according to the ground truth and get a region where the object are always at the center. We show the distance between the targeted position (Fig. 3(a)) and tracking results, and the mean absolute perturbation (MAP) (Fig. 3(b)) at frame level. We reach consistent conclusion with Table 1. As the simplest solution, BA-E attacks the tracker successfully at some time (distance to the targeted position is less than 20) with the MAP around 5. However, the attack is inefficient and not suitable for real-time tracking. In addition, according to Fig. 3(c), the perturbations are large and perceptible. The results answer the first question: attacking on each frame is not effective, *i.e.*, time-consuming and bigger MAP.

Consider the temporal property among frames, if the attack can be transferred between the adjacent frames, we could only attack some frames while reducing the overhead, *e.g.*, BA-R1 and BA-R2. Unfortunately, the results in Table 1 and Fig. 3 show that BA-R1 and BA-R2 only work at the specific frames on which the attacks are performed. The results answer the second question: the perturbations generated by BA is difficult to transfer to the next frames directly due to the dynamic scene in the video (see the results from BA-R1 and BA-R2).

3.4   Online Incremental Attack

Base on the empirical study results from basic attacks, we identify that attacking on each frame directly is not effective. As the frames are sequential and the nearby frames are very similar, our deep analysis found that transferability exists between nearby frames. However, how to effectively use the perturbations from previous frames while being imperceptible when we attack a new coming frame is questionable. A straightforward way is to add previous perturbations to a new calculated one, which will increase the success rate of attacking but lead to significant distortions. To solve this problem, we propose *spatial-aware online incremental attack (SPARK)* that generates more imperceptible adversarial examples more efficiently for tracking. The intuition of SPARK is that we still attack each frame, but apply previous perturbations on the new frame combined with small but effective *incremental perturbation* via optimization.

At frame t, the UA with SPARK is formally defined as:

$$\text{minimize}\quad \mathcal{D}(\mathbf{X}_t, \mathbf{X}_t + \mathbf{E}_{t-1} + \epsilon_t) \tag{7}$$

$$\text{subject to}\quad \text{IoU}(OT'(\mathbf{X}_t + \mathbf{E}_{t-1} + \epsilon_t, \mathbf{T}), \mathbf{b}_t^{\text{gt}'}) = 0 \tag{8}$$

where $\mathbf{E}_{t-1}$ is the perturbation of the previous frame (*i.e.*, $t-1$th fame) and ϵ_t is the incremental perturbation. Here, the 'incremental' means $\epsilon_t = \mathbf{E}_t - \mathbf{E}_{t-1}$, and we further have $\mathbf{E}_t = \epsilon_t + \sum_{t_0}^{t-1} \epsilon_\tau$, where $t_0 = t - L$ and $\{\epsilon_\tau\}_{t-L}^{t-1}$ are $L-1$ previous incremental perturbations, and $\epsilon_{t_0} = E_{t_0}$. We denote $t_0 = t - L$ as the start of an attack along the timeline. Based on Eq. 3, we introduce a new objective function by using $L_{2,1}$ norm to regularize $\{\epsilon_\tau\}_{t_0}^{t}$ that leads to small and spatial-temporal sparse ϵ_t.

$$f^{\text{ua}}(\mathbf{X}_t + \epsilon_t + \sum_{t-L}^{t-1} \epsilon_\tau, \mathbf{T}) + \lambda \|\Gamma\|_{2,1}, \tag{9}$$

where $\Gamma = [\epsilon_{t-L}, ..., \epsilon_{t-1}, \epsilon_t]$ is a matrix that concatenates all incremental values. Similarly, the TA with SPARK is formally defined as:

$$\text{minimize}\quad \mathcal{D}(\mathbf{X}_t, \mathbf{X}_t + \mathbf{E}_{t-1} + \epsilon_t) \tag{10}$$

$$\text{subject to}\quad ce(OT'(\mathbf{X}_t + \mathbf{E}_{t-1} + \epsilon_t, \mathbf{T})) = \mathbf{p}_t^{\text{tr}}. \tag{11}$$

We also modify the objective function Eq. 6 by adding the $L_{2,1}$ norm and obtain

$$f^{\text{ta}}(\mathbf{X}_t + \epsilon_t + \sum_{t-L}^{t-1} \epsilon_\tau, \mathbf{T}) + \lambda \|\Gamma\|_{2,1}. \tag{12}$$

We use the sign gradient descent to minimize the two objective functions, *i.e.*, Eq. 9 and 12, with the step size of 0.3, followed by a clip operation. In Eq. 9

and 12, λ controls the regularization degree and we set it to a constant 0.00001. Online minimizing Eq. 9 and 12 can be effective and efficient. First, optimizing the incremental perturbation is equivalent to optimizing $\mathbf{E}_t$ by regarding $\mathbf{E}_{t-1}$ as the start point. Since neighboring frames of a video is usually similar, such start point helps get an effective perturbation within very few iterations. Second, the $L_{2,1}$ norm make incremental perturbations to be spatial-temporal sparse and let $\mathbf{E}_t$ to be more imperceptible. For example, when applying SPARK on the SiamRPN-AlexNet-based trackers, we find following observations:

Spatial-Temporal Sparsity of Incremental Perturbations: The incremental perturbations become gradually sparse along the space and time (see Fig. 3(d)). This facilitates generating more imperceptible perturbations than BA methods. In addition, SPARK gets the smallest MAP across all frames with higher success rate than BA-E on OTB100 (see Fig. 3(b)).

Efficient Optimization: Figure 3(d) depicts the loss values during optimization from frame 41 to 49. At frame 41, it takes about 7 iterations to converge. However, at other frames, we obtain minimum loss in only two iterations. It enables more efficient attack than BA methods. As presented in Table 1, SPARK only uses 2.25 iterations at average to achieve 78.9% success rate.

The sparsity and efficiency of SPARK potentially avoid high-cost iterations at each frame. In practice, we perform SPARK at every 30 frames[2] and calculate $\mathbf{E}_{t_0}$ by optimizing Eq. 9 or Eq. 12 with 10 iterations. In addition, instead of the whole frame to accelerate the attacking speed. The search region of the tth frame is cropped from $\mathbf{X}_t$ at the center of predictive result of frame $t - 1$, i.e., $\mathbf{b}_{t-1}^{a}$, and the trackers can be reformulated as $\phi_{\theta'}(\mathbf{X}_t, \mathbf{T}, \mathbf{b}_{t-1}^{a})$ and $\phi_{\theta}(\mathbf{X}_t, \mathbf{T}, \mathbf{b}_{t-1}^{a})$. We will discuss the attack results without $\mathbf{b}_{t-1}^{a}$ in the experiments. We perform both UA and TA against visual tracking and summarize the attack process of SPARK for TA in Algorithm 1. At frame t, we first load a clean frame $\mathbf{X}_t$. If t cannot be evenly divisible by 30, we optimize the objective function, i.e., Eq. 12, with 2 iterations and get ϵ_t. Then, we add ϵ_t into $\mathcal{E}$ that stores previous incremental perturbations, i.e., $\{\epsilon_\tau\}_{t_0}^{t-1}$, and obtain $\mathbf{E}_t = \sum \mathcal{E}$. If t can be evenly divisible by 30, we clear $\mathcal{E}$ and start a new round attack.

Algorithm 1: Online adversarial perturbations for TA

Input: A video $\mathcal{V} = \{\mathbf{X}_t\}_1^T$; the object template $\mathbf{T}$;
    targeted trajectory $\{\mathbf{p}_t^{tr}\}$; the attacked tracker
    $\phi_\theta(\cdot)$; the tracker to perform attack: $\phi_{\theta'}(\cdot)$.
Output: Adversarial Perturbations $\{\mathbf{E}_t\}_1^T$.
Initialize the incremental perturbation set $\mathcal{E}$ as empty;
for $t = 2$ to T **do**
    Loading frame $\mathbf{X}_t$;
    if $\mod(t, 30) = 0$ **then**
        max_iter = 10;
        Empty $\mathcal{E}$;
        $t_0 = t$;
    else
        max_iter = 2;
    $\epsilon_t = \text{SPARK}(\phi_{\theta'}(\mathbf{X}_t + \mathcal{E}, \mathbf{T}, \mathbf{b}_{t-1}^{a}), \mathbf{p}_t^{tr}, \text{max\_iter})$;
    Add ϵ_t to $\mathcal{E} = \{\epsilon_\tau\}_{t_0}^{t-1}$;
    $\mathbf{E}_t = \sum \mathcal{E}$;
    $(y_t^a, \mathbf{b}_t^a) = \arg\max_{y_t} \phi_\theta(\mathbf{X}_t + \mathbf{E}_t, \mathbf{T}, \mathbf{b}_{t-1}^{a})$;
    $t = t + 1$;

---

4 Experimental Results

4.1 Setting

Datasets. We select 4 widely used datasets, *i.e.*, **OTB100** [54], **VOT2018** [24], **UAV123** [39], and **LaSOT** [11] as subject datasets.

Models. Siamese network [1, 12, 16, 28, 29, 62] is a dominant tracking scheme that achieves top accuracy with beyond real-time speed. We select SiamRPN-based trackers [28, 29] that use AlexNet [26], MobileNetv2 [22], and ResNet-50 [20] as backbones, since they are built on the same pipeline and achieve the state-of-the-art performance on various benchmarks. We also study the attacks on online updating variants of SiamRPN-based trackers and the SiamDW tracker [60].

Metrics. We evaluate the effectiveness of adversarial perturbations on the basis of center location error (CLE) between predicted bounding boxes and the ground truth or targeted positions. In particular, given the bounding box annotation at frame t, *i.e.*, $\mathbf{b}_t^{\mathrm{an}}$, we say that a tracker locates an object successfully, if we have $\mathrm{CLE}(\mathbf{b}_t, \mathbf{b}_t^{\mathrm{an}}) = \|ce(\mathbf{b}_t) - ce(\mathbf{b}_t^{\mathrm{an}})\|_2 < 20$ where $\mathbf{b}_t$ is the predicted box [54]. Similarly, we say an attacker succeeds at frame t when $\|ce(\mathbf{b}_t) - \mathbf{p}_t^{\mathrm{tr}}\|_2 < 20$ where $\mathbf{p}_t^{\mathrm{tr}}$ is the tth position on a given targeted trajectory. With above notations, we define precision drop for UA, success rate for TA, and MAP for both UA and TA: (1) **Prec. Drop:** Following [51] and [55], for UA, we use precision drop of a tracker (after attacking) to evaluate the generated adversarial perturbations. The precision of a tracker is the rate of frames where the tracker can locate the object successfully. (2) **Succ. Rate:** For TA, Succ. Rate denotes the rate of frames where an attack method fools a tracker successfully. (3) **MAP:** Following [52], we use the mean absolute perturbation (MAP) to measure the distortion of adversarial perturbations. For a video dataset containing D videos, we have $\mathrm{MAP} = \frac{1}{D*K} \sum_d \sum_k \frac{1}{M*C} \sum_i \sum_c |\mathbf{E}_{k,d}(i, c)|$, where K, M and C refer to the number of frames, pixels and channels, respectively.

Configuration. For TA, the targeted trajectory, *i.e.*, $\{\mathbf{p}_t^{\mathrm{tr}}\}_1^T$, is constructed by adding random offset values to the targeted position of previous frame, *i.e.*, $\mathbf{p}_t^{\mathrm{tr}} = \mathbf{p}_{t-1}^{\mathrm{tr}} + \Delta\mathbf{p}$, where $\Delta\mathbf{p}$ is in the range of 1 to 10. The generated trajectories are often more challenging than manual ones due to their irregular shapes.

4.2 Comparison Results

Baselines. Up to present, there still lacks research about adversarial attack on online object tracking. Therefore, we compare with baselines by constructing basic attacks and extending the existing video attack technique. To further demonstrate the advantages of SPARK over existing methods, we extend the BA-E in Table 1 such that it has the same configuration with SPARK for a more fair comparison.

To be specific, original BA-E attacks each frame with 10 iterations. However, in Algorithm 1, SPARK attacks every 30 frames with 10 iterations while the frame in interval are attacked with only 2 iterations. We configure the new BA-E with the similar iteration strategy and adopt different optimization methods (*i.e.*, FGSM, BIM [27], MI-FGSM [9], and C&W). In addition, we tried our best to compare with the existing method, *i.e.*, [52] designed for action recogni-

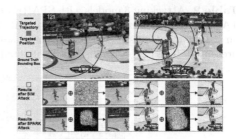

Fig. 4. BIM vs. SPARK under TA. We use a spiral line as the targeted trajectory that embraces the object at most of the time and makes the TA challenge.

tion. However, it uses all frames of a video to predict the category and cannot directly be used for attacking online tracking. We made an extension of it, *i.e.*, when attacking at frame t, the previous 30 frames are used to generate the adversarial.

Results. Table 2 shows the TA/UA results on the four datasets. Column *Org. Prec.* gives the precision of the original tracker. We observe that: 1) Compared with the existing attacks, SPARK achieves the highest Prec. Drop for UA and Succ. Rate for TA on most of datasets and models. For the results of attacking SiamRPN-Res50 on OTB100, SPARK gets slightly smaller Proc. Drop than MI-FGSM but generates more imperceptible perturbations. 2) SPARK generates imperceptible perturbations. When attacking SiamRPN-AlexNet on all datasets, SPARK always gets more imperceptible perturbations than FGSM, BIM, MI-FGSM, and C&W. [52] produces the smallest perturbations but the attacking is not effective. Similar results can be also found on other three datasets. 3) In general, it is more difficult to attack deeper models for all attacks, since the Prec. Drop and Succ. Rate of almost all attacks gradually become smaller as the models become more complex. In summary, the results indicate the effectiveness of SPARK in attacking the tracking models with small distortions. In addition to the quantitative results, we give a concrete example base on BIM and SPARK (see Fig. 4). Compared with BIM, SPARK lets the SiamRPN-AlexNet tracker always produces bounding boxes on the targeted trajectory with a sparse perturbation, indicating the effectiveness of SPARK.

Table 2. Attacking 3 models with SPARK on OTB100 and VOT2018 for both UA and TA. The comparison results of 5 existing attack methods are also reported. The results on 2 larger datasets, *i.e.*, UAV123 and LaSOT, for attacking SiamRPN-AlexNet are presented. The best 3 results are highlighted by red, green, and **blue**, respectively.

SiamRPN	Attacks	Untargeted Attack (UA)						Targeted Attack (TA)				
		OTB100			VOT2018			OTB100		VOT2018		
		Org. Prec. (%)	Prec. Drop (%)	MAP	Org. Prec. (%)	Prec. Drop (%)	MAP	Succ. Rate (%)	MAP	Succ. Rate (%)	MAP	
AlexNet	PGSM	85.3	8.0	1.24	65.8	13.6	1.24	7.9	1.24	4.3	1.24	
	BIM	85.3	72.1	2.17	65.8	57.4	2.28	38.8	2.14	48.5	2.10	
	MI-PGSM	85.3	68.4	3.70	65.8	58.2	4.31	41.8	3.18	47.0	3.17	
	C&W	85.3	54.2	1.31	65.8	50.6	1.26	25.7	1.27	25.7	1.23	
	Wei	85.3	25.9	0.21	65.8	33.6	0.30	16.0	0.27	20.9	0.24	
	SPARK	85.3	78.9	1.04	65.8	61.6	1.03	74.6	1.36	78.9	1.38	
Mob.	PGSM	86.4	6.7	1.00	69.3	14.1	0.99	7.9	1.00	3.4	0.99	
	BIM	86.4	37.8	1.07	69.3	46.2	1.06	30.3	1.06	32.9	1.05	
	MI-PGSM	86.4	43.5	1.71	69.3	46.0	1.73	33.5	1.70	32.7	1.71	
	C&W	86.4	23.6	1.04	69.3	28.2	1.02	13.7	1.05	8.9	1.01	
	Wei	86.4	39.4	0.84	69.3	27.8	0.54	11.3	0.51	7.0	0.53	
	SPARK	86.4	54.1	1.66	69.3	55.5	1.25	51.4	1.65	45.5	1.21	
ResSO	PGSM	87.8	4.5	0.99	72.8	8.1	0.99	7.7	0.92	2.9	0.99	
	BIM	87.8	27.0	1.10	72.8	39.1	1.10	17.1	1.09	17.0	1.08	
	MI-PGSM	87.8	31.9	1.72	72.8	41.8	1.75	18.8	1.71	19.5	1.72	
	C&W	87.8	14.6	1.03	72.8	20.4	1.01	10.0	1.04	5.3	1.01	
	Wei	87.8	9.7	0.65	72.8	15.7	0.68	9.7	0.78	4.8	0.69	
	SPARK	87.8	29.8	1.67	72.8	54.3	1.26	23.8	1.70	39.5	1.26	

SiamRPN	Attacks	Untargeted Attack (UA)						Targeted Attack (TA)				
		UAV123			LaSOT			UAV123		LaSOT		
		Org. Prec.	Prec. Drop	MAP	Org. Prec.	Prec. Drop	MAP	Succ. Rate	MAP	Succ. Rate	MAP	
AlexNet	PGSM	76.9	3.7	1.25	43.5	4.0	1.22	3.7	1.25	4.0	1.22	
	BIM	76.9	36.4	1.70	43.5	32.0	1.64	28.7	1.75	17.4	1.73	
	MI-PGSM	76.9	31.5	2.54	43.5	31.6	2.50	28.3	2.53	17.8	2.46	
	C&W	76.9	17.0	1.37	43.5	19.9	1.29	11.0	1.36	8.7	1.28	
	Wei	76.9	5.6	0.31	43.5	9.3	0.29	6.8	0.37	5.9	0.31	
	SPARK	76.9	43.6	1.13	43.5	38.2	0.93	54.8	1.06	48.9	1.09	

Table 3. Left sub-table shows the results of attacking DSiamRPN trackers on OTB100 for UA and TA while the right one presents the results of attacking SiamDW trackers.

	UA Attack		TA Attack		UA Attack		TA Attack
	Org. Prec. (%)	Prec. Drop (%)	Succ. Rate (%)		Org. Prec. (%)	Prec. Drop (%)	Succ. Rate (%)
DSiam-AlexNet	86.6	78.5	65.9	SiamDW-CIResNet	83.0	58.1	21.5
DSiam-Mob	87.8	56.8	44.4	SiamDW-CIResNext	81.7	74.2	29.4
DSiam-Res50	90.3	37.1	20.4	SiamDW-CIResIncep	82.3	70.2	30.8

4.3   Analysis of SPARK

Results Under Challenging Attributes. OTB dataset contains 11 subsets corresponding to 11 interference attributes[3]. Figure 5 shows results of six methods for SiamRPN-AlexNet on 11 subsets. We observe that: 1) SPARK has much larger Prec. Drop and Succ. Rate than baselines on all subsets except the LR one for both UA and TA. 2) The advantages of SPARK over baselines for TA is more significant than that for UA. 3) BIM, Wei, MIFGSM, and C&W are much more effective under the LR attribute than others. This may be caused by the limited effective information in LR frames, which leads to less discriminative deep representation and lets the attacking more easier.

Transferability Across Models. We discuss the transferability across models, which is to apply perturbations generated from one model to another. In Table 4, the values in the UA and TA parts are the *Prec. Drop* and *Succ. Rate*, respectively. We see that the transferability across models also exists in attacking object tracking. All attack methods lead to the precision drop to some extent.

---

[3] The 11 attributes are illumination variation (IV), scale variation (SV), in-plane rotation (IPR), outplane rotation (OPR), deformation (DEF), occlusion (OCC), motion blur (MB), fast motion (FM), background clutter (BC), out-of-view (OV), and low resolution (LR).

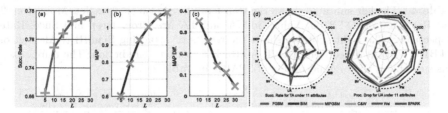

Fig. 5. (a) and (b) are the Succ. Rate and MAP of 6 variants of SPARK under TA for SiamRPN-AlexNet. The 6 variants are built by using different number of previous perturbations for Eq. (12) and (c) shows the MAP difference between neighboring variants.(d) Attacking SiamRPN-AlexNet with the 6 compared methods on the 11 subsets of OTB100 for both TA and UA.

The limited transferability may be caused by the insufficient iterations during online process and can be further studied in the future.

Validation of the Online Incremental Attack. We implement six variants of SPARK by setting $L \in \{5, 10, 15, 20, 25, 30\}$ in Eq. 12 to analyze how historical incremental perturbations affect attacking results. For example, when attacking the frame t with $L = 5$, we use previous 5 incremental perturbations to generate $\mathbf{E}_t$. We use these SPARKs to attack SiamRPN-AlexNet under TA on OTB100 and report the Succ. Rate, MAP, and MAP difference (MAP Diff.(L)) in Fig. 3, where MAP Diff.(L)=MAP(SPARK(L))-MAP(SPARK$(L-1)$). We see that: 1) the Succ. Rate increases with the growing of L. It demonstrates that historical incremental perturbations do help achieve more effective attack. 2) Although MAP also gets larger as the L increases, the MAP Diff. gradually decrease. This validates the advantages of SPARK, that is, it can not only leverage temporal transferability effectively but also maintaining the imperceptible perturbations.

SPARK without Object Template T and the Attacked Tracker's Predictions. As discussed in Sect. 3.4 and Algorithm 1, the tracked object, *i.e.*, the template $\mathbf{T}$, should be given during attack. Besides, our method is performed on the search region of $\phi_\theta(\cdot)$ and require the attacked tracker's prediction, *i.e.*, $\mathbf{b}^a_{t-1}$, as an additional input. These two factors might limit the application of our method. Here, we demonstrate that we can realize effective attack without these two factors. For the template $\mathbf{T}$, given the first frame of an online video, we use SSD [33] to detect all possible objects in the frame and select the object nearest to the frame center as the template. As presented in Table 4, without the $\mathbf{T}$, SPARK-no$\mathbf{T}$ achieves 71.0% Prec. Drop under UA and is slightly lower than the original SPARK. For the attacked tracker's prediction, we replace the $\mathbf{b}^a_{t-1}$ in the Algorithm 1 with $\mathbf{b}^{a'}_{t-1}$. Then, we can perform attack on the search region of $\phi_{\theta'}(\cdot)$ and propagate the perturbations to the whole frame. Without the attacked tracker's predictions, SPARK-no$\mathbf{b}^a_t$ gets 67.7% Prec. Drops under UA which is slightly lower than the original SPARK.

Transferability to Online Updating Trackers. We build three online updating trackers via dynamic Siamese tracking (DSiam) [16], and get: DSiamRPN-

Table 4. The left subtable shows the transferability between AlexNet, MobileNetv2, and ResNet50 on OTB100. Values in UA and TA are Proc. Drop and Succ. Rate, respectively. The right subtable shows the results of attacking SiamRPN-AlexNet on OTB100 without object template **T** or attacked tracker's prediction. The third row of this subtable is the original results of SPARK in Table 2.

	Proc. Drop of UA from			Succ. Rate of TA from				Untargeted Attack (UA)		Targeted Attack (TA)
	AlexNet	Mob.Net	Res50	AlexNet	Mob.Net	Res50		Org. Prec	Prec. Drop	Succ. Rate
SiamRPN-AlexNet	78.9	6.7	2.0	74.6	6.2	6.7	SPARK-no**T**	85.3	71.0	50.6
SiamRPN-Mob	3.5	54.1	2.7	6.3	51.4	6.6	SPARK-nob$_i^p$	85.3	67.7	46.2
SiamRPN-Res50	7.5	16.1	29.8	6.2	6.5	23.8	SPARK	85.3	78.9	74.6

AlexNet, MobileNetv2, and ResNet-50. We then use the adversarial perturbations from SiamRPN to attack the DSiamRPN trackers. In Table 3, we see that: 1) DSiam indeed improves the precision of three SiamRPN trackers. 2) The adversarial perturbations from SiamRPNs are still effective for DSaim versions with 78.5%, 56.8%, and 37.1% precision drops which are larger than the results in Table 2 due to the corrupted tracking models updated by adversarial examples.

Attacking SiamDW [60]. We validate the generality of SPARK by attacking another tracker, *i.e.*, SiamDW [60] that is the winner of [25]. As shown in the Table 3, without changing any attack parameters, SPARK significantly reduces the precision of SiamDW trackers under the UA, demonstrating its generality.

5   Conclusion

In this paper, we explored adversarial perturbations for misleading the online visual object tracking along an incorrect (untarged attack, UA) or specified (targeted attack, TA) trajectory. An optimization-based method, namely *spatial-aware online incremental attack* (SPARK), was proposed to overcome the challenges introduced in this new task. SPARK optimizes perturbations with a $L_{2,1}$ regularization norm and considers the influence of historical attacking results, thus is more effective. Experimental results on OTB100, VOT2018, UAV123, and LaSOT showed that SPARK successfully fool the state-of-the-art trackers.

Acknowledgements. This work was supported by the National Natural Science Foundation of China (NSFC) under Grant 61671325, Grant 61572354, Grant 61672376, Grant U1803264, and Grant 61906135, the Singapore National Research Foundation under the National Cybersecurity R&D Program No. NRF2018NCR-NCR005-0001 and the NRF Investigatorship No. NRFI06-2020-0022, and the National Satellite of Excellence in Trustworthy Software System No. NRF2018NCR-NSOE003-0001. It was also supported by JSPS KAKENHI Grant No. 20H04168, 19K24348, 19H04086, and JST-Mirai Program Grant No. JPMJMI18BB, Japan. We also gratefully acknowledge the support of NVIDIA AI Tech Center (NVAITC) to our research.

References

1. Bertinetto, L., Valmadre, J., Henriques, J.F., Vedaldi, A., Torr, P.H.S.: Fully-convolutional siamese networks for object tracking. arXiv preprint arXiv:1606.09549 (2016)
2. Carlini, N., Wagner, D.: Towards evaluating the robustness of neural networks. In: 2017 IEEE Symposium on Security and Privacy (SP), pp. 39–57 (2017)
3. Carlini, N., Wagner, D.: Audio adversarial examples: targeted attacks on speech-to-text. arXiv:1801.01944 (2018)
4. Chen, Z., Guo, Q., Wan, L., Feng, W.: Background-suppressed correlation filters for visual tracking. In: ICME, pp. 1–6 (2018)
5. Cisse, M., Adi, Y., Neverova, N., Keshet, J.: Houdini: Fooling deep structured prediction models. arXiv:1707.05373 (2017)
6. Dai, K., Dong Wang, H.L., Sun, C., Li, J.: Visual tracking via adaptive spatially-regularized correlation filters. In: CVPR, pp. 4665–4674 (2019)
7. Danelljan, M., Bhat, G., Khan, F.S., Felsberg, M.: ECO: efficient convolution operators for tracking. In: CVPR, pp. 6931–6939 (2017)
8. Dong, X., Shen, J.: Triplet loss in siamese network for object tracking. In: Ferrari, V., Hebert, M., Sminchisescu, C., Weiss, Y. (eds.) ECCV 2018. LNCS, vol. 11217, pp. 472–488. Springer, Cham (2018). https://doi.org/10.1007/978-3-030-01261-8_28
9. Dong, Y., et al.: Boosting adversarial attacks with momentum. In: CVPR, pp. 9185–9193 (2018)
10. Du, X., Xie, X., Li, Y., Ma, L., Liu, Y., Zhao, J.: DeepStellar: model-based quantitative analysis of stateful deep learning systems. In: ESEC/FSE, pp. 477–487 (2019)
11. Fan, H., et al.: LaSOT: a high-quality benchmark for large-scale single object tracking. In: CVPR, pp. 5369–5378 (2019)
12. Fan, H., Ling, H.: Siamese cascaded region proposal networks for real-time visual tracking. In: CVPR, pp. 7944–7953 (2019)
13. Feng, W., Han, R., Guo, Q., Zhu, J., Wang, S.: Dynamic saliency-aware regularization for correlation filter-based object tracking. IEEE TIP **28**(7), 3232–3245 (2019)
14. Gao, J., Lanchantin, J., Soffa, M.L., Qi, Y.: Black-box generation of adversarial text sequences to evade deep learning classifiers. In: SPW, pp. 50–56 (2018)
15. Goodfellow, I.J., Shlens, J., Szegedy, C.: Explaining and harnessing adversarial examples. arXiv:1412.6572 (2014)
16. Guo, Q., Feng, W., Zhou, C., Huang, R., Wan, L., Wang, S.: Learning dynamic Siamese network for visual object tracking. In: ICCV, pp. 1781–1789 (2017)
17. Guo, Q., Feng, W., Zhou, C., Pun, C., Wu, B.: Structure-regularized compressive tracking with online data-driven sampling. IEEE TIP **26**(12), 5692–5705 (2017)
18. Guo, Q., Han, R., Feng, W., Chen, Z., Wan, L.: Selective spatial regularization by reinforcement learned decision making for object tracking. IEEE TIP **29**, 2999–3013 (2020)
19. He, A., Luo, C., Tian, X., Zeng, W.: A twofold Siamese network for real-time object tracking. In: CVPR, pp. 4834–4843 (2018)
20. He, K., Zhang, X., Ren, S., Sun, J.: Deep residual learning for image recognition. In: CVPR, pp. 770–778 (2016)

21. Held, D., Thrun, S., Savarese, S.: Learning to track at 100 FPS with deep regression networks. In: Leibe, B., Matas, J., Sebe, N., Welling, M. (eds.) ECCV 2016. LNCS, vol. 9905, pp. 749–765. Springer, Cham (2016). https://doi.org/10.1007/978-3-319-46448-0_45

22. Howard, A.G., et al.: MobileNets: efficient convolutional neural networks for mobile vision applications. arXiv preprint arXiv:1704.04861 (2017)

23. Jin, D., Jin, Z., Zhou, J.T., Szolovits, P.: Is bert really robust? natural language attack on text classification and entailment. arXiv:1907.11932 (2019)

24. Kristan, M., et al.: The sixth visual object tracking VOT2018 challenge results. In: Leal-Taixé, L., Roth, S. (eds.) ECCV 2018. LNCS, vol. 11129, pp. 3–53. Springer, Cham (2019). https://doi.org/10.1007/978-3-030-11009-3_1

25. Kristan, M., et al.: The seventh visual object tracking vot2019 challenge results. In: ICCVW, pp. 2206–2241 (2019)

26. Krizhevsky, A., Sutskever, I., Hinton, G.E.: ImageNet classification with deep convolutional neural networks. In: NIPS, pp. 1097–1105 (2012)

27. Kurakin, A., Goodfellow, I., Bengio, S.: Adversarial examples in the physical world. ICLR (Workshop) (2017)

28. Li, B., Wu, W., Wang, Q., Zhang, F., Xing, J., Yan, J.: SiamRPN++: evolution of Siamese visual tracking with very deep networks. In: CVPR, pp. 4282–4291 (2019)

29. Li, B., Wu, W., Zhu, Z., Yan, J., Hu, X.: High performance visual tracking with Siamese region proposal network. In: CVPR, pp. 8971–8980 (2018)

30. Li, Y., Tian, D., Chang, M.C., Bian, X., Lyu, S.: Robust adversarial perturbation on deep proposal-based models. In: BMVC, pp. 1–11 (2018)

31. Lin, Y.C., Hong, Z.W., Liao, Y.H., Shi, M.L., Liu, M.Y., Sun, M.: Tactics of adversarial attack on deep reinforcement learning agents. In: IJCAI, pp. 3756–3762 (2017)

32. Ling, X., et al.: DEEPSEC: a uniform platform for security analysis of deep learning model. In: IEEE Symposium on Security and Privacy (SP), pp. 673–690 (2019)

33. Liu, W., et al.: SSD: single shot multibox detector. In: Leibe, B., Matas, J., Sebe, N., Welling, M. (eds.) ECCV 2016. LNCS, vol. 9905, pp. 21–37. Springer, Cham (2016). https://doi.org/10.1007/978-3-319-46448-0_2

34. Lukežič, A., Vojíř, T., Čehovin, L., Matas, J., Kristan, M.: Discriminative correlation filter with channel and spatial reliability. In: CVPR, pp. 4847–4856 (2017)

35. Ma, L., et al.: DeepGauge: multi-granularity testing criteria for deep learning systems. In: ASE, pp. 120–131 (2018)

36. Metzen, J.H., Kumar, M.C., Brox, T., Fischer, V.: Universal adversarial perturbations against semantic image segmentation. In: ICCV, pp. 2774–2783 (2017)

37. Moosavi-Dezfooli, S.M., Fawzi, A., Fawzi, O., Frossard, P.: Universal adversarial perturbations. In: CVPR, pp. 86–94 (2017)

38. Moosavi-Dezfooli, S.M., Fawzi, A., Frossard, P.: DeepFool: a simple and accurate method to fool deep neural networks. In: CVPR, pp. 2574–2582 (2016)

39. Mueller, M., Smith, N., Ghanem, B.: A benchmark and simulator for UAV tracking. In: Leibe, B., Matas, J., Sebe, N., Welling, M. (eds.) ECCV 2016. LNCS, vol. 9905, pp. 445–461. Springer, Cham (2016). https://doi.org/10.1007/978-3-319-46448-0_27

40. Müller, M., Bibi, A., Giancola, S., Alsubaihi, S., Ghanem, B.: TrackingNet: a large-scale dataset and benchmark for object tracking in the wild. In: Ferrari, V., Hebert, M., Sminchisescu, C., Weiss, Y. (eds.) ECCV 2018. LNCS, vol. 11205, pp. 310–327. Springer, Cham (2018). https://doi.org/10.1007/978-3-030-01246-5_19

41. Nam, H., Han, B.: Learning multi-domain convolutional neural networks for visual tracking. In: CVPR, pp. 4293–4302 (2016)

42. Papernot, N., McDaniel, P.D., Jha, S., Fredrikson, M., Celik, Z.B., Swami, A.: The limitations of deep learning in adversarial settings. In: IEEE European Symposium on Security and Privacy (EuroS P), pp. 372–387 (2016)

43. Qin, Y., Carlini, N., Goodfellow, I., Cottrell, G., Raffel, C.: Imperceptible, robust, and targeted adversarial examples for automatic speech recognition. arXiv:1903.10346 (2019)

44. Ren, S., Deng, Y., He, K., Che, W.: Generating natural language adversarial examples through probability weighted word saliency. In: ACL, pp. 1085–1097 (2019)

45. Song, Y., et al.: Vital: visual tracking via adversarial learning. In: CVPR, pp. 8990–8999 (2018)

46. Sun, J., et al.: Stealthy and efficient adversarial attacks against deep reinforcement learning. In: AAAI, pp. 5883–5891 (2020)

47. Sun, Y., Sun, C., Wang, D., Lu, H., He, Y.: Roi pooled correlation filters for visual tracking. In: CVPR, pp. 5776–5784 (2019)

48. Szegedy, C., et al.: Intriguing properties of neural networks. arXiv:1312.6199 (2013)

49. Wang, Q., Zhang, L., Bertinetto, L., Hu, W., Torr, P.H.: Fast online object tracking and segmentation: a unifying approach. In: CVPR, pp. 1328–1338 (2019)

50. Wang, X., Li, C., Luo, B., Tang, J.: SINT++: robust visual tracking via adversarial positive instance generation. In: CVPR, pp. 4864–4873 (2018)

51. Wei, X., Liang, S., Chen, N., Cao, X.: Transferable adversarial attacks for image and video object detection. In: IJCAI, pp. 954–960 (2019)

52. Wei, X., Zhu, J., Yuan, S., Su, H.: Sparse adversarial perturbations for videos. In: AAAI, pp. 8973–8980 (2019)

53. Wiyatno, R.R., Xu, A.: Physical adversarial textures that fool visual object tracking. arXiv:1904.11042 (2019)

54. Wu, Y., Lim, J., Yang, M.H.: Object tracking benchmark. IEEE TPAMI **37**(9), 1834–1848 (2015)

55. Xie, C., Wang, J., Zhang, Z., Zhou, Y., Xie, L., Yuille, A.L.: Adversarial examples for semantic segmentation and object detection. In: ICCV, pp. 1378–1387 (2017)

56. Xie, X., et al.: DeepHunter: a coverage-guided fuzz testing framework for deep neural networks. In: ISSTA, pp. 146–157 (2019)

57. Zhang, H., Zhou, H., Miao, N., Li, L.: Generating fluent adversarial examples for natural languages. In: ACL, pp. 5564–5569 (2019)

58. Zhang, P., Guo, Q., Feng, W.: Fast and object-adaptive spatial regularization for correlation filters based tracking. Neurocomputing **337**, 129–143 (2019)

59. Zhang, Y., Wang, L., Qi, J., Wang, D., Feng, M., Lu, H.: Structured Siamese network for real-time visual tracking. In: Ferrari, V., Hebert, M., Sminchisescu, C., Weiss, Y. (eds.) ECCV 2018. LNCS, vol. 11213, pp. 355–370. Springer, Cham (2018). https://doi.org/10.1007/978-3-030-01240-3_22

60. Zhang, Z., Peng, H.: Deeper and wider Siamese networks for real-time visual tracking. In: CVPR, pp. 4586–4595 (2019)

61. Zhao, Y., Zhu, H., Liang, R., Shen, Q., Zhang, S., Chen, K.: Seeing isn't believing: practical adversarial attack against object detectors. In: CCS, pp. 1989–2004 (2019)

62. Zhu, Z., Wang, Q., Li, B., Wu, W., Yan, J., Hu, W.: Distractor-aware Siamese networks for visual object tracking. In: Ferrari, V., Hebert, M., Sminchisescu, C., Weiss, Y. (eds.) ECCV 2018. LNCS, vol. 11213, pp. 103–119. Springer, Cham (2018). https://doi.org/10.1007/978-3-030-01240-3_7

CenterNet Heatmap Propagation for Real-Time Video Object Detection

Zhujun Xu$^{(\boxtimes)}$, Emir Hrustic, and Damien Vivet

ISAE-SUPAERO, Université de Toulouse, Toulouse, France
{zhujun.xu,emir.hrustic,damien.vivet}@isae.fr

Abstract. The existing methods for video object detection mainly depend on two-stage image object detectors. The fact that two-stage detectors are generally slow makes it difficult to apply in real-time scenarios. Moreover, adapting directly existing methods to a one-stage detector is inefficient or infeasible. In this work, we introduce a method based on a one-stage detector called CenterNet. We propagate the previous reliable long-term detection in the form of heatmap to boost results of upcoming image. Our method achieves the online real-time performance on ImageNet VID dataset with 76.7% mAP at 37 FPS and the offline performance 78.4% mAP at 34 FPS.

Keywords: Video object detection · Real-time · Heatmap propagation · One-stage detector

1 Introduction

Image object detection benefits a lot from the development of Convolutional Neural Networks (CNNs) over the last years. As a fundamental element of many vision tasks, such as visual surveillance, autonomous driving, etc., many CNN based structures [5,8,9,13,17,19] have been proposed, which achieve excellent performance in still images. However, many real world applications require video object detection. When directly applying these still image detectors to a video stream, the accuracy suffers from sampled image quality problem caused by motion blur or incomplete object appearance.

Previous works [3,7,18,20] have been conducted to compensate the loss by using temporal information naturally provided by videos. Most of them are developed on the base of two-stage detectors like Region-based CNN (R-CNN). On one hand, it's well known that most two-stage detectors are too slow to achieve real-time performance. On the other hand, adapting existing temporal information merging methods to one-stage detectors is challenging or even infeasible. Indeed, the representation of object bounding boxes differs a lot between these

Electronic supplementary material The online version of this chapter (https://doi.org/10.1007/978-3-030-58595-2_14) contains supplementary material, which is available to authorized users.

A. Vedaldi et al. (Eds.): ECCV 2020, LNCS 12370, pp. 220–234, 2020.
https://doi.org/10.1007/978-3-030-58595-2_14

two categories of detectors and, moreover, some methods manipulate on Region of Interests (RoIs) pooled features which do not exist in one-stage structures.

In this paper, we propose a heatmap propagation method as an effective solution for video object detection. We implement our method on a one-stage detector called CenterNet [19] which outputs a heatmap to detect the center of all objects in an image of different classes. For one frame of a video clip, we transform the stable detected objects to a propagation heatmap. In the obtained heatmap, we highlight potential positions of each object's center with its confidence score of corresponding class. For the next frame, a balanced heatmap is generated considering both the propagation heatmap and the network output heatmap. This is similar to generate an online tracklet of each object and we update the confidence score by each frame detection result. The rest of this paper is structured as follows. Section 2 presents the object detection state of the art. Section 3 details our contribution and Sect. 4 presents the implementation details. Finally, Sect. 5 presents the results of our approach.

2   Related Work

2.1   Image Object Detection

One-Stage and Two-Stage Detectors. Generally speaking, there are two types of state-of-the-art image object detectors, the two-stage detectors and the one-stage detectors. Two-stage detectors first use a Region Proposal Network (RPN) to detect RoIs which potentially contain an object. Then, based on pooled features inside RoIs, separated detection heads of network identify the class of object and regress the bounding box. In contrast, one stage detectors directly achieve the classification and regression on the entire feature map. Usually, sophisticated two-stage detectors are more accurate, but slower compared to one-stage detectors. However, several works [13,14,19] have proven that the accuracy of one-stage detectors can be competitive with even real-time speed.

Anchor Based and Heatmap Based Detectors. From the perspectives of object bounding box representation, the detectors can be divided into two groups: anchor based and heatmap based. Anchor based detectors like R-CNN [8,9,15], R-FCN [5] have prefixed bounding boxes at every output spatial position which are called anchor boxes. The regression values estimated by the network are the differences between anchor boxes and object real bounding boxes, typically a scale-invariant translation of the centers and a log-space translation of the width and height. [9] Heatmap based detectors like CornerNet [13], CenterNet [19], detect keypoints of object bounding box, like the vertices or the center. The network outputs heatmaps of keypoints and several regression values for offset or raw bounding box size depending on different structures. To cover as much object shapes as possible, anchor based methods will prefix different size and height/width ratio for anchor boxes. This will obviously increase output dimension which turns out to be a computational burden. Thus the compromise between robustness and speed remains hard to solve. However, the heatmap based detectors avoid such dilemma, as all regression values are raw pixel coordinate values without the need of any preset.

2.2 Video Object Detection

Considering video object detection, a trivial solution is to apply directly an image object detector on the video. However, videos usually contain moving objects or represent a motion as the camera is moving. This results in low image quality, which has undesirable influence on the detection performance. Nevertheless, videos contain temporal information, such as the consistency of the same object in consecutive frames. Using such information to compensate image quality defect is worth considering. D&T method [7] uses feature map correlation to regress bounding boxes variances of the same object across consecutive frames. A viterbi algorithm is applied to do box level association. FGFA [20] uses optical flow information predicted by a pretrained flow network [6,12] to align and aggregate relevant features from consecutive frames. However, the pretrained optical flow network does not always generalize to new datasets. Spatiotemporal Sampling Networks (STSN) [1] uses deformable convolutions to aggregate relevant features which is more generalized. AdaScale [3] reshapes the image size to an adaptive resolution which produces better accuracy and speed. The fact that most of these works use a two-stage anchor based detector makes it hard to achieve real-time detection. Scale-Time Lattice method [2] proposes a framework of temporal propagation and spatial refinement to extend the detection results on sparse key frames to dense video frames. Our method can also be integrated into this framework. Our approach is inspired by [18], where the author proposed a method of re-scoring tracklet to improve single frame detection. Still it is implemented with R-CNN detectors.

3 Proposed Method

3.1 Background: CenterNet

CenterNet [19] is a one-stage heatmap based object detector. The principle of this method is to predict the position of the center and the size of objects in images. Given an input RGB image of width w and height h, $I \in R^{w \times h \times 3}$, the network outputs a downsampled heatmap $\hat{Y} \in [0,1]^{\frac{w}{R} \times \frac{h}{R} \times C}$, where R is output stride and C is the number of classes. We note $W = \frac{w}{R}, H = \frac{h}{R}$ as the output spatial size. A prediction $\hat{Y}_{x,y,c} = 1$ corresponds to the center of an object of class c at position (x, y), while $\hat{Y}_{x,y,c} = 0$ corresponds to background. In addition, the network predicts a local offset $\hat{O} \in R^{W \times H \times 2}$ to recover the discretization error by the output stride and a regression $\hat{S} \in R^{W \times H \times 2}$ for object size.

As shown in Fig. 1, the entire network contains 3 components. A general convolutional network, N_{feat}, like ResNet [11] extracts feature maps from input

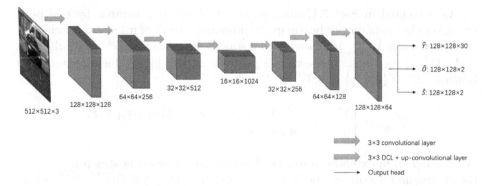

Fig. 1. CenterNet with ResNet-101 backbones. Orange arrows represent N_{feat}. Green arrows represent N_{decv}. Black line arrows represent 3 separate heads N_{head}.

image. A deconvolutional network, N_{decv}, is built of 3×3 deformable convolutional layers (DCLs) [4] and up-convolutional layers. It refines the feature maps into output spatial scale. Finally, 3 separate heads, N_{head}, share the same backbone feature maps and output $\hat{Y}$, $\hat{O}$ and $\hat{S}$. Due to computational cost, all classes share the same prediction of offset and object size. So, the final output size of network is $W \times H \times (C + 4)$.

At inference time, by applying a 3×3 max pooling operation, all peaks whose value is greater or equal to its 8 neighbors in the heatmap of each class will be extracted from $\hat{Y}$. Only the top 100 peaks will be kept. For a peak at position $(\hat{x}_i, \hat{y}_i)$, we use offset prediction $\hat{O}_{x_i,y_i} = (\delta\hat{x}_i, \delta\hat{y}_i)$ and size prediction $\hat{S}_{x_i,y_i} = (\hat{w}_i, \hat{h}_i)$ to produce the bounding box of object as:

$$\begin{aligned}
&(\hat{x}_i + \delta\hat{x}_i - \hat{w}_i/2, \quad \hat{y}_i + \delta\hat{y}_i - \hat{h}_i/2, \\
&\hat{x}_i + \delta\hat{x}_i + \hat{w}_i/2, \quad \hat{y}_i + \delta\hat{y}_i + \hat{h}_i/2).
\end{aligned} \tag{1}$$

We refer the reader to the original work of CenterNet [19] for further detail.

3.2   Heatmap Propagation

Still-image object detectors like CenterNet are very effective to process static images. However, due to quality problems of sampled images like blurring or object occlusion, such detectors may produce unstable results when directly applied to consecutive images of video clips. We propose an online real-time method heatmap propagation (HP) for video object detection by propagating previous long-term stable detection results to upcoming image.

Let $D^t = \{d_i^t\}_{i=1}^m$ be the set of **m** predicted objects in frame t of a video. For each object d_i^t detected at time t, we count the number of consecutive frames up to frame t where the object appears and define the number as tracklet length l_i^t. For a new object detected in frame t, $l_i^t = 1$. We also have the predicted bounding box size $s_i^t = (w_i^t, h_i^t)$ for each object.

As presented in Sect. 3.1, each predicted object is generated by one peak $(\hat{x}_i, \hat{y}_i)$ of class c_i in output heatmap. To propagate result of frame t to frame $t+1$, each peak value $\hat{Y}^t_{\hat{x}_i\hat{y}_ic_i}$ is dilated with a square kernel of size $2P+1$ resulting in $(2P+1)^2 - 1$ positions. As shown in Fig. 2(a) and (b), this produces an extended heatmap $H^t_i = \{h^t_{i,xyc}\} \in [0,1]^{W \times H \times C}$ where:

$$h^t_{i,xyc} = \begin{cases} \hat{Y}_{\hat{x}_i\hat{y}_ic_i} & if \quad c = c_i, |x - \hat{x}_i| \leq P, |y - \hat{y}_i| \leq P, \\ 0 & otherwise. \end{cases} \tag{2}$$

We overlap all $\mathbf{m}$ extended heatmaps into one propagation heatmap by keeping the maximum value in each position and class: $\overline{H} = \{\overline{h}_{xyc}\} \in [0,1]^{W \times H \times C}$ where $\overline{h}_{xyc} = \max\limits_{i \in [1,m]} (h^t_{i,xyc})$ (See Fig. 2(b) and (c)). Although occlusion of objects may exist, the centers of objects are rarely located at the same point. Thus keeping the maximum value remains an effective way to collect all detection results. The propagation heatmap will inherit tracklet length from frame t, $\overline{L} = \{\overline{l}_{xyc}\}$ where:

$$\overline{l}_{xyc} = \begin{cases} l^t_i & where \quad i = \arg\max\limits_{i \in [1,m]}(h^t_{i,xyc}) \quad if \quad \overline{h}_{xyc} > 0 \\ 0 & if \quad \overline{h}_{xyc} = 0 \end{cases} \tag{3}$$

Similarly, the bounding box size information will also be inherited, $\overline{S} = \{\overline{s}_{xyc}\} \in R^{W \times H \times C \times 2}$ where:

$$\overline{s}_{xyc} = \begin{cases} s^t_i & where \quad i = \arg\max\limits_{i \in [1,m]}(h^t_{i,xyc}) \quad if \quad \overline{h}_{xyc} > 0 \\ 0 & if \quad \overline{h}_{xyc} = 0 \end{cases} \tag{4}$$

We combine the network output heatmap of frame $t+1$: $\hat{Y}^{t+1} = \{\hat{Y}^{t+1}_{xyc}\} \in [0,1]^{W \times H \times C}$ and propagation heatmap from frame t: $\overline{H} = \{\overline{h}_{xyc}\}$ to a long-term heatmap in the following way:

$$\overline{Y}^{t+1}_{xyc} = \frac{\hat{Y}^{t+1}_{xyc} + \beta\overline{h}_{xyc}\overline{l}_{xyc}}{1 + \beta\overline{l}_{xyc}}, \tag{5}$$

where β is a confidence parameter for long-term detection ($\beta = 2$ by default). Equation 5 serves as a temporal average with update prediction $\hat{Y}^{t+1}_{xyc}$. To be robust to large variance in image, we set the final heatmap as a balance between the long-term heatmap and instant detection heatmap of network:

$$\tilde{Y}^{t+1}_{xyc} = (1 - \alpha)\hat{Y}^{t+1}_{xyc} + \alpha\overline{Y}^{t+1}_{xyc} \tag{6}$$

where α is a balance parameter ($\alpha = 0.98$ by default). The necessity of this balance equation will be analysed in Sect. 5.3. These 2 steps are shown in Fig. 2(c), (d) and (e).

For bounding box prediction, we calculate a weighted size by combining propagated size information $\overline{S}$ and network output size $\hat{S} = \{\hat{S}_{xy}\} \in R^{W \times H \times 2}$ based on $\overline{H}$ and $\hat{H}^{t+1}$:

$$\tilde{S}_{xyc}^{t+1} = \frac{\hat{Y}_{xyc}^{t+1} \hat{S}_{xy}^{t+1} + \overline{h}_{xyc} \overline{s}_{xyc}}{\hat{Y}_{xyc}^{t+1} + \overline{h}_{xyc}}. \tag{7}$$

To be clear, we use class-agnostic box size prediction in network. To propagate the size information with class-specific heatmap, we broadcast the same size prediction in all class channel for Eq. 7. Unlike Eq. 5, we don't involve tracklet length here, because the size of object projection in image may change during time due to the relative movement between camera and object. Thus we only use the previous and the current estimation.

Finally, we apply the same procedure as CenterNet on the balanced heatmap to produce detection in frame $t+1$, $D^{t+1} = \{d_j^{t+1}\}_{j=1}^n$. We update the tracklet length in the following way: $l_j^{t+1} = \overline{l}_{\hat{x}_j \hat{y}_j c_j} + 1$, where $(\hat{x}_j, \hat{y}_j)$ is the center position of d_j^{t+1} and c_j is its class.

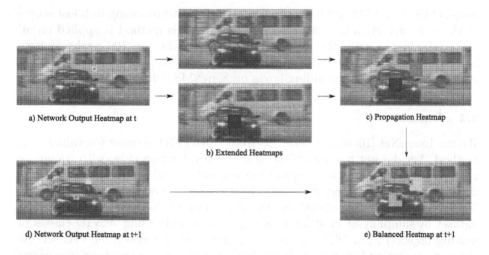

a) Network Output Heatmap at t

b) Extended Heatmaps

c) Propagation Heatmap

d) Network Output Heatmap at t+1

e) Balanced Heatmap at t+1

Fig. 2. Illustration of HP (Heatmap Propagation). In a), two cars are detected with high scores at frame t. In d), the detection scores become lower due to image quality at frame $t + 1$. In e), after the HP operation, response at relative positions of heatmap has been enhanced. Detection with higher scores can be extracted.

4   Implementation Details

4.1   Architecture

CenterNet. In this work, we use ResNet-101 as feature extraction network, N_{feat}, for the purpose of fair comparison with other methods. Following the same structure as original paper, the N_{decv} is built by 3 upsampling layers with 256, 128, 64 channel, respectively. One 3×3 deformable convolutional layer is added before each up-convolution with channel 256, 128, 64, respectively. Each output head is built by a 3×3 convolutional layer with 64 channel followed by a 1×1 convolution with corresponding channel (C for $\hat{Y}$ or 2 for $\hat{O}$ and $\hat{Y}$) to generate desired output.

Heatmap Propagation. A peak point extraction is proposed in [19] to take the place of Non-Maximum Suppression (NMS). However, we still observe a slight performance improvement when applying NMS after the extraction. The dilatation of heatmap is efficiently implemented by a $(2P+1) \times (2P+1)$ max pooling layer. The peak extraction operation in CenterNet is implemented by a 3×3 max pooling layer. We notice that this may produce false detection at the edge of dilated square as the extraction is too local. A bigger kernel of size $(2P+1) \times (2P+1)$ is used in our case and provides better performances than the original one.

Seq-NMS. Seq-NMS [10] is an effective off-line post-processing to boost scores of the weak detection in video. In original work, this method is applied on all proposals. In our case, the CenterNet only keeps the top 100 peaks and we ignore all bounding boxes with a score under 0.05. For each frame, we apply a very limited number of bounding boxes on Seq-NMS, which makes it faster.

4.2 Dataset

We use ImageNet [16] object detection from video (VID) dataset to evaluate our method. The dataset has 3862 training and 550 validation video with framerate at 25–30 fps. There are 30 classes of moving objects, which are a subset of 200 classes in ImageNet object detection (DET) dataset. Following the protocol in [7,18,20], we train the network on an intersection of ImageNet DET and VID dataset by sampling at most 2K images per class (only using 30 VID classes of moving objects) from DET set and 10 frames of each video from VID set. As the test annotation is not publicly available, we measure the performance of our method by calculating the mean average precision (mAP) on the validation set.

4.3 Training and Inference

For both training and inference, we resize all input image to 512×512 with zero padding for non-square shape images. With the output stride $R = 4$, the output resolution is 128×128. Most two-stage detectors resize input image to a shorter side of 600 pixels. We don't use this configuration in our work for two reasons. Firstly, the output heatmap size of our CenterNet is proportional to input resolution. A larger input resolution will increase the runtime throughout the entire network. This is different from two-stage detectors, where the increase of resolution only brings extra burden to the part before the Region Proposal

Network. The runtime after RoIPooling is only affected by the number of RoIs. Actually, if we use the larger input size, our method's runtime will be about 27 FPS, which is slightly below 30 FPS real-time criteria. Secondly, when using larger resolution, we noticed a slight decrease in AP_{50} with dataset ImageNet VID. This is also analyzed in original CenterNet paper, where they marked 0.3 decrease in AP_{50} with dataset MS coco. Even though they marked a 0.9 increase in AP_{75}, and a 0.1 increase in comprehensive AP, the official evaluation of ImageNet VID is AP_{50}.

During training for CenterNet, random flip, random scaling from 0.6 to 1.4 are used as data augmentation and SGD is used as optimizer. We train the whole network with a batch-size of 32 (on 2 GPUs) and a learning rate of 10^{-4} for 50 epochs followed by a learning rate of 10^{-5} for 30 epochs.

For inference, no augmentation is applied. We use the full validation set for experiments. We apply NMS with IoU threshold of 0.3.

5   Experiments

5.1   Quantitative Result

We show the results for our methods and state-of-the-art in Table 1. All results are conducted with ResNet-101 as backbones. First, we compare our method with the baseline CenterNet. Our method improves 3.1% mAP with an extra 6ms runtime. We also compare results after Seq-NMS to prove the effectiveness of our method and a 2.5% mAP improvement is observed. In both two case, our method maintains a real-time performance. Even combined with Seq-NMS, our method works at 34 FPS. Next, we compare with the state-of-the-art and our method achieves competitive accuracy. However, most of the two-stage based detectors can not achieve the 25–30 FPS standard of ImageNet VID dataset. The AdaScale works at 21 FPS. Our method achieves better accuracy with 1.7 times faster runtime. The Scale-Time Lattice framework reaches the real-time performance by doing sparse key frame detection. Their base detector is still a Faster R-CNN. Our method can be integrated into this frame for a better tradeoff.

We also conduct experiments with DLA-34 as backbones. Unlike original work of CenterNet, the DLA-34 baseline only achieves a mAP of 69.1% in our test. Nevertheless, our method raises the mAP to 71.3%. We believe this is relative to the dataset, as MS coco has more classes and images are clearer.

In purpose of fair comparison, we conduct a simple interpolation between CenterNet's detection outputs of consecutive frames. However, we don't see a remarkable improvement in performance. Actually, this is also a special case of our method. We set $P = 0$. This makes the extended heatmap for one object become one point. So the overlap of all extended heatmaps becomes a simple superposition. If there is a detected object at position (x,y,c) in frame t, we have:

$$\overline{h}_{xyc} = \max_{i \in [1,m]} (h_{i,xyc}^t) = \hat{Y}_{xyc}^t \tag{8}$$

Set $\beta \to \infty$, Eq. 5 becomes:

$$\overline{Y}_{xyc}^{t+1} = \overline{h}_{xyc} \tag{9}$$

Set $\alpha = 0.5$, Eq. 6 becomes:

$$\tilde{Y}_{xyc}^{t+1} = 0.5(\hat{Y}_{xyc}^{t+1} + \overline{Y}_{xyc}^{t+1}) \tag{10}$$

Finally, we have:

$$\tilde{Y}_{xyc}^{t+1} = 0.5(\hat{Y}_{xyc}^{t+1} + \hat{Y}_{xyc}^{t}) \tag{11}$$

Table 1. Performance comparison on the ImageNet VID validation set. For methods marked with -, the runtime is not provided in the original papers. With the fact that these methods add computational components on two-stage detectors baseline, the runtime shall be longer than that of R-FCN.

Methods	$mAP_{50}(\%)$	Runtime (ms)	FPS
R-FCN [3]	74.2	75	13
AdaScale [3]	75.6	47	21
FGFA/+Seq-NMS [20]	76.3/78.4	733/873	1.2/1.1
D& T/+Viterbi [7]	75.8/79.8	141/187	6.8/5.5
STSN/+Seq-NMS [1]	78.9/80.4	–	–
Tracklet-Conditioned/+FGFA [18]	79.4/83.5	–	–
Scale-Time Lattice [2]	79/79.8	16.1/200	62/5
CenterNet/+Seq-NMS	73.6/75.9	21/23	47/43
CenterNet+interpolation/+Seq-NMS	73.6/75.9	22/24	45/42
CenterNet+HP/+Seq-NMS	76.7/78.4	27/29	37/34

5.2 Qualitative Result

We also conduct qualitative experiments to better explain the mechanism of our method. Figure 3 shows some typical examples where our HP method improves detection result compared to baseline CenterNet. One typical case is that the still image detector can miss some detection in certain sample images of a video clip. This usually happens to non consecutive images. The HP can easily boost the score at missing position if the previous image includes a long-term stable detection. This largely solves the problem of transient object lost in long video. Another typical case is that the still image detector can generate inferior bounding boxes when the object blends into background. This happens frequently with motion blur which makes it difficult to distinguish between the textures of the object and the background. Our method assumes small displacement of the object's center and maintain a smooth variation of bounding box size along the time as we calculate the weighted size with the previous bounding box of the

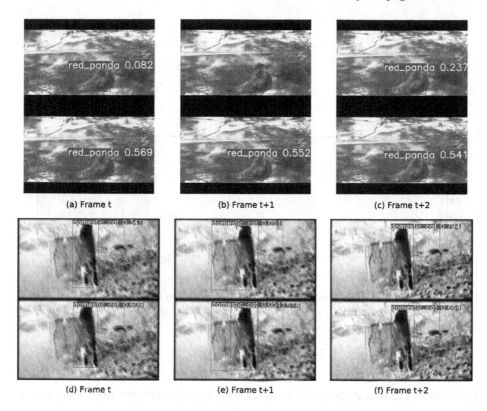

Fig. 3. Examples of qualitative result. For each of the 6 images, the upper part is CenterNet result, the lower part is result after HP method. Images (a), (b), (c) is a scenario where the target object is transiently lost. In frame t+1, the network output score is below the detection threshold 0.05. In frame t+2, the object is detect again. With HP, we can keep detecting the object with better confidence. Images (d), (e), (f) is a scenario where the object blends into background. In frame t+1, the detected center is totally biased. After HP, we maintain the correct center with detection in frame t. Although the score drops from 0.609 to 0.518, it rises back to 0.664 as frame t+2 has a clear detection. Different from a tremendous score variance (0.341 - 0.051 - 0.794), we keep a stable detection with better bounding boxes.

same object. This helps to correct the mentioned problem and maintain stable detection in the aspect of bounding box size.

In Fig. 4, we compare the evolution of detection scores by baseline and our method. In both video clips, our method recovers cliff drops in several frames (e.g. frame 60, 80–100, 120–140 in video 1. frame 110–160, 240–300 in video 2) and the result is much smoother. This means our method gives less false positives than vanilla baseline. Thus when we apply off-line process like Seq-NMS, the average of detection scores turns out to be more reliable. More stable detection is also preferred in many further vision applications like visual object tracking.

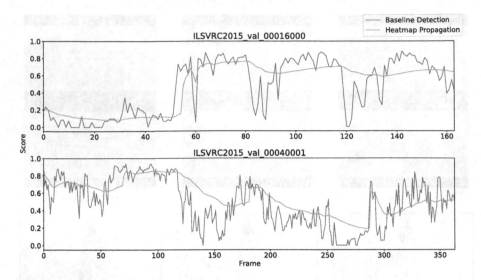

Fig. 4. Evolution of detection scores of 2 video clips. Green lines are CenterNet results. Red lines are results with HP. In both video, our method produces the smoother line, which means the more stable detection.

5.3 Ablation Study

Extended Heatmap Size P. In our method, each detected object in output heatmap will be extended into a square with side length 2P+1. As we increase P, one tracklet will boost a boarder space in final heatmap, which turns out to be more robust to fast movement. However, this may create some false positives (FP). A typical example: due to image quality, the baseline detector makes a correct detection with a high score and a parasitic detection (biased center) with low score for the same object. Usually, this weak FP will disappear rapidly. If P is too large, the precise detection in previous frame will boost both the correct detection and the parasitic detection in the current frame. So that the FP will last for longer. We calculate the maximum displacement of the center in output resolution $\Delta_i = \max(|x_i^{t+1} - x_i^t|, |y_i^{t+1} - y_i^t|)$ for each object pair in ImageNet VID validation set. One object pair means that the same object appears in two consecutive frames. There are 272038 ground-truth (GT) pairs in the whole set. 1220 pairs among them have a Δ_i greater than 5, which represent 0.45% cases. Thus we test P from 0 to 5, and results are shown in Table 2.

For more detail of our method's performance concerning this parameter, we break down the results into 3 motion speeds, based on whether the ground-truth object pair's motion is slow ($\Delta_i < 2$), median ($2 \leq \Delta_i < 4$), or fast ($\Delta_i \geq 4$). Some classes usually have fast motion, while others have the opposite, so we use the class-agnostic precision ($\frac{TP}{TP+FP}$) vs recall ($\frac{TP}{TP+FN}$) to better display the results. As shown in Fig. 5, small value of P has better performance in slow motion and vice versa. This is consistent with our previous explanation. The default value of P in this paper is adapted to general scenes. For applications

Table 2. Ablation study of extended heatmap size P. Uncovered GT pairs stands for the proportion of GT pairs with $\Delta_i > P$.

P (default marked by *)	0	1	2*	3	4	5
Uncovered GT pairs (%)	60.4	11.3	3.7	1.6	0.79	0.45
$mAP_{50}(\%)$	75	76.5	76.7	76.4	75.8	75.5

with high-speed scenes, a greater value of P is favorable. Besides, our method surpasses the baseline (and the simple interpolation version) in all 3 subsets. Table 3 presents a direct number comparison between baseline and our method.

Parameter α and β. We also investigate the influence of the parameter α and β in Eq. 6 and Eq. 5, respectively. The results are shown in Table 4 and Table 5.

If we only use Eq. 5 in our design ($\alpha = 1$), we observe a remarkable decrease of accuracy. This is the case where we are completely confident with long-term heatmap. This can produce catastrophic results when an object with long length tracklet has one large spatial variance. The HP may create a false detection near previous center and it will last for a long time. Another typical example is when a long tracked object quits the camera's field of view. In that case, the HP will keep boosting the last position for a long time. For the above reasons, the balance operation with parameter α is necessary.

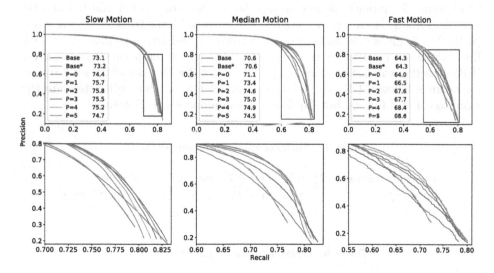

Fig. 5. Precision vs recall of different object pair motions. We add a zoom-in version below each figure which provides a better view of content in the black square. Each legend is followed by the corresponding average precision. Base stands for CenterNet and Base* stands for the simple interpolation version.

Table 3. Numerical comparison of 75% recall and 65% recall. Compared values are shown in the form of "baseline/our method in default setting". Our method outperforms the baseline with both recall configurations in all 3 subsets and the whole valid set.

		GT	FN	FP	Precision (%)
75% Recall	Slow	254190	63548	114741/67930	62.4/73.7
	Median	14820	3705	14499/5219	43.4/68.0
	Fast	3028	757	5473/3734	29.3/37.8
	Overall	272038	68010	131973/75648	60.7/73.0
65% Recall	Slow	254190	88967	22199/17797	88.2/90.3
	Median	14820	5187	1891/1504	83.6/86.5
	Fast	3028	1060	1264/911	60.9/68.4
	Overall	272038	95214	24560/19814	87.8/89.9

Different from α which has a linear effect on the heatmap, β imports a nonlinear effect with the tracklet length. With greater value of β, we put more confidence on the long-term part in update score. If we only use Eq. 6 in our design ($\beta \to \infty$), we face a contradiction in the choice of α. If α is not large enough, we can hardly recover the cliff fall of score, which is a typical case due to image quality problem. For example, $\alpha = 0.5$, we track an object with score of 0.9 for 20 frames, and the baseline output score drops to 0.1 at 21st and 22nd frame. Equation 6 alone can only boost the score to 0.5 and 0.3 at 21st and 22nd frame. However, by weighing the average by the tracklet length, Eq. 5 (with $\beta = 2$) gives 0.88 and 0.86, respectively. To achieve a similar effect with Eq. 6 alone, we need to set $\alpha \geq 0.97$. In that case, a temporary false positive (FP) detection will last too long. E.g. we have a FP with score of 0.8 for 1 frame, the score is below 0.1 for the following frames. Our method will attenuate the score to 0.4 in 3 frames, but Eq. 6 ($\alpha = 0.97$) alone needs 27 frames.

Table 4. Ablation study of parameters α

α (default marked by *)	0.5	0.6	0.7	0.8	0.9	0.95	0.98*	1
mAP_{50}(%)	74.6	74.9	75.1	75.3	76.1	76.3	76.7	75.3

Table 5. Ablation study of parameters β

β (default marked by *)	0.5	1	2*	5	10	100	1000
mAP_{50}(%)	75.7	76.4	76.7	76.4	76	75.1	75

6   Conclusion

In this paper, we introduce a real-time video object detection method Heatmap Propagation based on CenterNet. Compared with state-of-the-art methods which are mainly based on two-stage detectors and far from real-time performance, our method achieves competitive results with real-time speed. Compared with our baseline CenterNet, our method achieves better accuracy with only 6ms extra runtime per frame and produces smoother and more stable results for further applications. Our future work will include experiments of Heatmap Propagation on other object detection approaches or semantic segmentation for video.

Acknowledgements. This work was supported by the Agence Nationale de la Recherche (ANR-the French national research agency) (ANR-17-CE22-0001-01) and by the French FUI (FUI STAR: DOS0075476 00).

References

1. Bertasius, G., Torresani, L., Shi, J.: Object detection in video with spatiotemporal sampling networks. In: Ferrari, V., Hebert, M., Sminchisescu, C., Weiss, Y. (eds.) ECCV 2018. LNCS, vol. 11216, pp. 342–357. Springer, Cham (2018). https://doi.org/10.1007/978-3-030-01258-8_21

2. Chen, K., et al.: Optimizing video object detection via a scale-time lattice. In: 2018 IEEE/CVF Conference on Computer Vision and Pattern Recognition, pp. 7814–7823 (2018)

3. Chin, T.W., Ding, R., Marculescu, D.: AdaScale: towards real-time video object detection using adaptive scaling. arXiv preprint arXiv:1902.02910, February 2019

4. Dai, J., et al.: Deformable convolutional networks. In: 2017 IEEE International Conference on Computer Vision (ICCV), pp. 764–773 (2017)

5. Dai, J., Li, Y., He, K., Sun, J.: R-FCN: object detection via region-based fully convolutional networks. In: Lee, D.D., Sugiyama, M., Luxburg, U.V., Guyon, I., Garnett, R. (eds.) Advances in Neural Information Processing Systems, vol. 29, pp. 379–387. Curran Associates, Inc. (2016). http://papers.nips.cc/paper/6465-r-fcn-object-detection-via-region-based-fully-convolutional-networks.pdf

6. Dosovitskiy, A., et al.: FlowNet: learning optical flow with convolutional networks. In: 2015 IEEE International Conference on Computer Vision (ICCV), pp. 2758–2766 (2015)

7. Feichtenhofer, C., Pinz, A., Zisserman, A.: Detect to track and track to detect. In: 2017 IEEE International Conference on Computer Vision (ICCV), pp. 3057–3065 (2017)

8. Girshick, R.: Fast R-CNN. In: 2015 IEEE International Conference on Computer Vision (ICCV), pp. 1440–1448 (2015)

9. Girshick, R., Donahue, J., Darrell, T., Malik, J.: Rich feature hierarchies for accurate object detection and semantic segmentation. In: 2014 IEEE Conference on Computer Vision and Pattern Recognition, pp. 580–587 (2014)

10. Han, W., et al.: Seq-NMS for video object detection. arXiv preprint arXiv:1602.08465, February 2016

11. He, K., Zhang, X., Ren, S., Sun, J.: Deep residual learning for image recognition. In: 2016 IEEE Conference on Computer Vision and Pattern Recognition (CVPR), pp. 770–778 (2016)

12. Ilg, E., Mayer, N., Saikia, T., Keuper, M., Dosovitskiy, A., Brox, T.: FlowNet 2.0: evolution of optical flow estimation with deep networks. In: 2017 IEEE Conference on Computer Vision and Pattern Recognition (CVPR), pp. 1647–1655 (2017)
13. Law, H., Deng, J.: CornerNet: detecting objects as paired keypoints. In: Ferrari, V., Hebert, M., Sminchisescu, C., Weiss, Y. (eds.) Computer Vision – ECCV 2018. LNCS, vol. 11218, pp. 765–781. Springer, Cham (2018). https://doi.org/10.1007/978-3-030-01264-9_45
14. Lin, T., Goyal, P., Girshick, R., He, K., Dollár, P.: Focal loss for dense object detection. In: 2017 IEEE International Conference on Computer Vision (ICCV), pp. 2999–3007 (2017)
15. Ren, S., He, K., Girshick, R., Sun, J.: Faster R-CNN: towards real-time object detection with region proposal networks. IEEE Trans. Pattern Anal. Mach. Intell. **39**(6), 1137–1149 (2017)
16. Russakovsky, O., et al.: ImageNet large scale visual recognition challenge. Int. J. Comput. Vis. **115**, 211–252 (2014)
17. Tian, Z., Shen, C., Chen, H., He, T.: FCOS: fully convolutional one-stage object detection. In: 2019 IEEE/CVF International Conference on Computer Vision (ICCV), pp. 9626–9635 (2019)
18. Zhang, Z., Cheng, D., Zhu, X., Lin, S., Dai, J.: Integrated object detection and tracking with tracklet-conditioned detection. arXiv preprint arXiv:1811.11167, November 2018
19. Zhou, X., Wang, D., Krähenbühl, P.: Objects as points. arXiv preprint arXiv:1904.07850, April 2019
20. Zhu, X., Wang, Y., Dai, J., Yuan, L., Wei, Y.: Flow-guided feature aggregation for video object detection. In: 2017 IEEE International Conference on Computer Vision (ICCV), pp. 408–417 (2017)

Hierarchical Dynamic Filtering Network for RGB-D Salient Object Detection

Youwei Pang[1], Lihe Zhang[1(✉)], Xiaoqi Zhao[1], and Huchuan Lu[1,2]

[1] Dalian University of Technology, Dalian, China
{lartpang,zxq}@mail.dlut.edu.cn
[2] Peng Cheng Laboratory, Shenzhen, China
{zhanglihe,lhchuan}@dlut.edu.cn

Abstract. The main purpose of RGB-D salient object detection (SOD) is how to better integrate and utilize cross-modal fusion information. In this paper, we explore these issues from a new perspective. We integrate the features of different modalities through densely connected structures and use their mixed features to generate dynamic filters with receptive fields of different sizes. In the end, we implement a kind of more flexible and efficient multi-scale cross-modal feature processing, i.e. dynamic dilated pyramid module. In order to make the predictions have sharper edges and consistent saliency regions, we design a hybrid enhanced loss function to further optimize the results. This loss function is also validated to be effective in the single-modal RGB SOD task. In terms of six metrics, the proposed method outperforms the existing twelve methods on eight challenging benchmark datasets. A large number of experiments verify the effectiveness of the proposed module and loss function. Our code, model and results are available at https://github.com/lartpang/HDFNet.

Keywords: RGB-D Salient Object Detection · Cross-modal fusion · Dynamic dilated pyramid module · Hybrid enhanced loss

1 Introduction

Salient object detection (SOD) aims to model the mechanism of human visual attention and mine the most salient objects or regions in data such as images or videos. SOD has been widely applied in many computer vision tasks, such as scene classification [38], video segmentation [13], semantic segmentation [44], foreground map evaluation [10,11] visual tracking [30], person re-identification [39], light field image segmentation [43] and so on.

With the advent of the fully convolutional network [29], deep learning-based SOD models [17,27] have made great progress. Some methods [22,33,50,51]

Electronic supplementary material The online version of this chapter (https://doi.org/10.1007/978-3-030-58595-2_15) contains supplementary material, which is available to authorized users.

A. Vedaldi et al. (Eds.): ECCV 2020, LNCS 12370, pp. 235–252, 2020.
https://doi.org/10.1007/978-3-030-58595-2_15

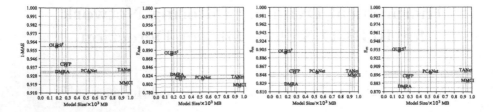

Fig. 1. Comparisons in model size and accuracy.

have achieved very good performance on the existing benchmark datasets. However, these works are mainly based on RGB data. They still face severe challenges when handling the cluttered or low-contrast scenes. Recently, some works [2,4,6,8,14,37,53] introduce the depth data as an aid to further improve the detection performance. The depth information can more intuitively express spatial structures of the objects in a scene and provide a powerful supplement for the detection and recognition of salient objects. Using complementary modal cues, the scene can be further deeply and intelligently understood. However, limited by the way of using the depth information, RGB-D salient object detection is still great challenging.

It is well known that RGB images contain rich appearance and detail information while depth images contain more spatial structure information. They complement each other for many vision tasks. RGB-D SOD approaches aim to formulate cross-modal fusion in different manners. Most of them integrate depth and RGB features by element-wise addition [4,36], concatenation [3,12] and convolution operations [2,42]. Some methods compute attention map [49] or saliency map [42] via a shallow or deep CNN network from pure depth images. Because of using the fixed parameters for different samples during the testing phase, the generalization capability of these models is weakened. Moreover, for dense prediction task, the loss in each spatial position is usually different. Thus, the actual optimization direction of gradients in different positions may be varying. The weight-sharing convolution operation across different positions, which is used in the existing methods, causes that the training process of each parameter relies on the global gradient. This forces the network to learn trade-off and suboptimal parameters. To address these problems, we propose a dynamic dilated pyramid module (DDPM), which uses RGB-depth mixed features to adaptively adjust convolution kernels for different input samples and processing locations. These kernels can capture rich semantic cues at multiple scales with the help of the pyramid structure and the dilated convolution. This design is capable of making more efficient convolution operations for current RGB features and promotes the network to obtain more flexible and targeted features for saliency prediction.

Early deep learning-based SOD models [14], which use fully connected layers, destroy the spatial structure of the data. This issue is alleviated to some extent by using the fully convolutional network. But the intrinsic gridding operation and the repeated down-sampling lead to the loss of numerous details in the predicted results. Although many methods frequently combine shallower features to restore feature resolution, the improvement is still limited. While some approaches [9, 17] leverage CRF post-processing to refine subtle structures, which has a large computational cost. In this work, we design a new hybrid enhanced loss function (HEL). The HEL encourages the consistency between the area around edges and the interior of objects, thereby achieving sharper boundaries and a solid saliency area.

Our main contributions are summarized as follows:

- We propose a simple yet effective hierarchical dynamic filtering network (HDFNet) for RGB-D SOD. Especially, we provide a new perspective to utilize depth information. The depth and RGB features are combined to generate region-aware dynamic filters to guide the decoding in RGB stream.
- We propose a hybrid enhanced loss and verify its effectiveness in both RGB and RGB-D SOD tasks. It can effectively optimize the details of predictions and enhance the consistency of salient regions without additional parameters.
- We compare the proposed method with twelve state-of-the-art methods on eight datasets. It achieves the best performance under six evaluation metrics. Meanwhile, we implement a forward reasoning speed of 52 FPS on an NVIDIA GTX 1080 Ti GPU. The size of our VGG16-based model is about 170 MB (Fig. 1).

2   Related Word

RGB-D Salient Object Detection. The early methods are mainly based on hand-crafted features, such as contrast [6] and shape [7]. Limited by the representation ability of the features, they can not cope with complex scenes. Please refer to [12] for more details about traditional methods. In recent years, FCN-based methods have shown great potential and some of them achieve very good performance in the RGB-D SOD task [12,36,49]. Chen and Li [2] progressively combine the current depth/RGB features and the preceding fused feature by a series of convolution and element-wise addition operations to build the cross fusion modules. Recently, they concatenate depth and RGB features and feed them into an additional CNN stream to achieve multi-level cross-modal fusion [3]. Wang and Gong [42] respectively build a saliency prediction stream for RGB and depth inputs and then fuse their predictions and their preceding features to obtain final prediction via several convolutional layers. Zhao et al [49] insert a lightweight net between adjacent encoding blocks to compute a contrast map from the depth input and use it to enhance the features from the RGB stream. Piao et al [36] combine multi-level paired complementary features from RGB and depth streams by convolution and nonlinear operations. Fan et al [12] design a depth depurator to remove the low-quality depth input, and for high-quality one they feed the concatenated 4-channel input into a convolutional neural network to achieve cross-modal fusion. Different from these methods, we use the RGB-depth mixed features to generate "adaptive" multi-scale convolution kernels to filter and enhance the decoding features from the RGB stream.

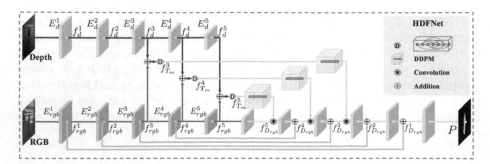

Fig. 2. The overall architecture of HDFNet. The network is based on two-stream structure. The two encoders use the same network (such as VGG-16 [40], VGG-19 [40], or ResNet-50 [16]), and are fed RGB and depth images, respectively. The details of HDFNet are introduced in Sect. 3.

Dynamic Filters. The works closely related to ours are [20] and [15]. The conception of the dynamic filter is firstly proposed in video and stereo prediction task [20]. The filter is utilized to enhance the representation of its corresponding input in a self-learning manner. While we use multi-modal information to generate multi-scale filters to dynamically strengthen the cross-modal complementarity and suppress the inter-modality incompatibility. Besides, the kernel computation in [20] introduces a large number of parameters and is difficultly extended at multiple scales, which significantly increases parameters and causes optimization difficulties. To efficiently achieve hierarchical dynamic filters, we introduce the idea of depth-wise separable convolution [18] and dilated convolution [48]. In [15], the filters are computed by pooling the input feature. They share kernel parameters across different positions, which is only an image-specific filter generator. In contrast, we design position-specific and image-specific filters to provide cross-modal contextual guidance for the decoder. The parameter update of dynamic filters is determined by the gradients of local neighborhoods to achieve more targeted adjustments and guarantee the overall performance of optimization.

3   Proposed Method

In this section, we first introduce the overall structure of the proposed method and then detail two main components, including the dynamic dilated pyramid module (DDPM) and the hybrid enhanced loss (HEL).

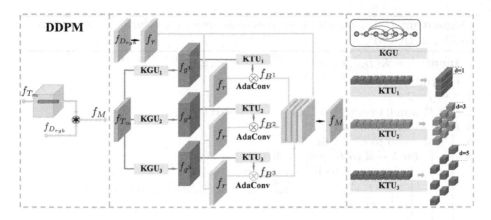

Fig. 3. The structure of the dynamic dilated pyramid module. The DDPM contains two submodules: kernel generation units (KGUs) and kernel transformation units (KTUs). KGUs generate adaptive kernel tensors and KTUs transform these tensors to the regular form of convolution kernels with different dilation rates.

3.1 Two Stream Structure

We build a two-stream network, which structure is shown in Fig. 2. It has two inputs: one is an RGB image and the other is a depth image, which corresponds to the RGB and depth streams, respectively. Through convolution blocks $\{E_{rgb}^i\}_{i=1}^5$ and $\{E_d^i\}_{i=1}^5$ in two encoding networks, we can obtain the intermediate features with different resolutions, which are recorded as f^1, f^2, f^3, f^4, f^5 from large to small. The third-level features still retain enough valid information. Besides, the shallower features contain more noise and also cause higher computational cost due to the larger resolution. To balance efficiency and effectiveness, we only utilize the features f_d^3, f_d^4, f_d^5 from the deepest three blocks in the depth stream. These features are respectively combined with the features f_{rgb}^3, f_{rgb}^4, f_{rgb}^5 from the RGB stream. Then, we use a dense block [19] to build the transport layer, which combines rich and various receptive fields and generates powerful mixed features f_{T_m} with both spatial structures and appearance details. These features are fed into the DDPM to produce multi-scale convolution kernels that are used to filter the features $f_{D_{rgb}}$ from the decoder. The resulted features f_M are merged in the top-down pathway by element-wise addition. After recovering the resolution layer by layer, we obtain the final prediction P, which is supervised by the ground truth G.

3.2 Dynamic Dilated Pyramid Module

In order to make more reasonable and effective use of the mixed features f_{T_m} from the dense transport layer, we employ DDPMs to generate the adaptive kernel for decoding RGB features. The DDPMs contain two inputs: the mixed feature f_{T_m} and the feature $f_{D_{rgb}}$ from the decoder. On one hand, for specific

---

Algorithm 1: The operation process of adaptive convolution $\otimes$ related to KTU_j in DDPM^i.

Input: $f_r^i = \mathcal{R}(f_{D_{rgb}}^i) \in \mathbb{R}^{N \times C' \times H' \times W'}$, $f_{g^j}^i \in \mathbb{R}^{N \times (9 \times C') \times H' \times W'}$

Output: $f_{B^j}^i \in \mathbb{R}^{N \times C' \times H' \times W'}$.

1   $d \leftarrow j \times 2 - 1$;

2   pad f_r^i with 0 from (H', W') to $(H' + 2 \times d, W' + 2 \times d)$;

3   **for** $n \leftarrow 0$ **to** $N - 1$ **do**

4   **for** $c \leftarrow 0$ **to** $C' - 1$ **do**

5   **for** $h \leftarrow d$ **to** $H' + d - 1$ **do**

6   **for** $w \leftarrow d$ **to** $W' + d - 1$ **do**

7                  $(f_{B^j}^i)_{[n,c,h,w]} \leftarrow \sum_{l=-1}^{1} \sum_{m=-1}^{1} \{(f_{g^j}^i)_{[n,(l+1)\times 3+(m+1),h,w]}$

                        $\times (f_r^i)_{[n,c,h+l\times d,w+m\times d]}\}$;

---

position in feature maps $f_{D_{rgb}}$, we use kernel generation units (KGUs) to yield independent weight tensors, i.e. f_g, that can cover a 3×3, 7×7 or 11×11 square neighborhood. KGUs are also a kind of dense structure [19]. The module contains 4 densely connected layers and each layer is connected to all the others in a feed-forward fashion, which can further strengthen feature propagation and expression capabilities, encourage feature reuse and greatly improve parameter efficiency. Then, by recombining kernel tensors and inserting different numbers of zeros, kernel transformation units (KTUs) construct regular convolution kernels with different dilation rates. Please see "KTU" shown in Fig. 3 and introduced in Algorithm 1 for a more intuitive presentation. On the other hand, after preliminary dimension reduction, the other input $f_{D_{rgb}}$ is re-weighted and integrated into three parallel branches to obtain the enhanced features $\{f_{B^j}\}_{j=1}^3$. Note that this is actually a channel-wise adjustment and the operation of each channel is independent. Finally, after concating and merging $\{f_{B^j}\}_{j=1}^3$ and the reduced $f_{D_{rgb}}$, the resulted features $\{f_M^i\}_{i=3}^5$ become more discriminative.

The entire process can be formulated as follows:

$$
\begin{aligned}
f_M^i &= \mathcal{DDPM}^i(f_{D_{rgb}}^i, f_{T_m}^i) \\
&= \mathcal{F}(\mathcal{C}(\mathcal{R}(f_{D_{rgb}}^i), f_{B^1}^i, f_{B^2}^i, f_{B^3}^i) \\
&= \mathcal{F}(\mathcal{C}(\mathcal{R}(f_{D_{rgb}}^i), \mathcal{KTU}_1^i(\mathcal{KGU}_1^i(f_{T_m}^i)) \otimes \mathcal{R}(f_{D_{rgb}}^i), \\
&\quad \mathcal{KTU}_2^i(\mathcal{KGU}_2^i(f_{T_m}^i)) \otimes \mathcal{R}(f_{D_{rgb}}^i), \\
&\quad \mathcal{KTU}_3^i(\mathcal{KGU}_3^i(f_{T_m}^i)) \otimes \mathcal{R}(f_{D_{rgb}}^i))),
\end{aligned} \tag{1}
$$

where f_M^i represents the feature from the DDPM^i related to the $f_{D_{rgb}}^i$. $\mathcal{DDPM}(\cdot)$, $\mathcal{KGU}(\cdot)$ and $\mathcal{KTU}(\cdot)$ denote the operation of the corresponding module. $\mathcal{R}(\cdot)$ is a 1×1 convolution operation, which is used to reduce the number of channels from 64 to 16. $\otimes$ is an adaptive convolution operation as shown in Algorithm 1. $\mathcal{C}(\cdot)$ is a concatenation operation and $\mathcal{F}(\cdot)$ is a 3×3 convolution to fuse the concatenated features from different branches. More details is as shown in Fig. 3.

3.3   Hybrid Enhanced Loss

No matter for RGB or RGB-D based SOD tasks, good prediction requires the salient area to be clearly and completely highlighted. This contains two aspects: one is the sharpness of boundaries and the other is the consistency of intra-class. We start with the loss function and design a new loss to constrain the edges and the fore-/background regions to separately achieve high-contrast predictions.

The common loss function in the SOD task is binary cross entropy (BCE). It is a pixel-level loss, which independently performs error calculation and supervision at different positions. The main form is as follows:

$$L_{bce} = \frac{1}{N \times H \times W} \sum_{n}^{N} \sum_{h}^{H} \sum_{w}^{W} \left[g \log p + (1-g) \log(1-p) \right], \tag{2}$$

where $P = \{p | 0 < p < 1\} \in \mathbb{R}^{N \times 1 \times H \times W}$ and $G = \{g | 0 < g < 1\} \in \mathbb{R}^{N \times 1 \times H \times W}$ respectively represent the prediction and the corresponding ground truch. N, H and W are the batchsize, height and width of the input data, respectively. It calculates the error between the ground truth g and the prediction p at each position, and the loss L_{bce} accumulates and averages the errors of all positions.

In order to further enhance the strength of supervision at higher levels such as edges and regions, we specially constrain and optimize the regions near the edges. In particular, the loss is formulated as follows:

$$L_e = \frac{\sum_h^H \sum_w^W (e * |p - g|)}{\sum_h^H \sum_w^W e},$$
$$e = \begin{cases} 0 & \text{if } (G - \mathcal{P}(G))_{[h,w]} = 0, \\ 1 & \text{if } (G - \mathcal{P}(G))_{[h,w]} \neq 0, \end{cases} \tag{3}$$

where L_e represents the edge enhanced loss (EEL), and $\mathcal{P}(\cdot)$ denotes the average pooling operation with a 5×5 slide window. In Eq. 3, we can obtain the local region near the contour of the ground truth by calculating e. In this region, the difference L_e between the prediction p and the ground truth g can be calculated. Through this loss, the optimization process can target the contours of salient objects.

In addition, we also design a region enhanced loss (REL) to constrain the prediction of intra-class. By respectively calculating the prediction errors within the foreground class and the background class, fore-/background predictions can be independently optimized. Specifically, the REL L_r is written as:

$$L_r = \frac{\sum_n^N (L_f + L_b)}{N},$$

$$L_f = \frac{\sum_h^H \sum_w^W (g - g * p)}{\sum_h^H \sum_w^W g}, \tag{4}$$

$$L_b = \frac{\sum_h^H \sum_w^W (1 - g) * p}{\sum_h^H \sum_w^W (1 - g)},$$

where L_f and L_b denote the fore-/background losses, respectively. The losses compute the normalized prediction errors in the intra-class regions. They depict the region-level supervision. Finally, we integrate these three losses (L_{bce}, L_e and L_r) to obtain the hybrid enhanced loss (HEL), which can optimize the prediction at two different levels. The total loss is expressed as follows:

$$L = L_{bce} + L_e + L_r. \tag{5}$$

4   Experiments

4.1   Datasets

To fully verify the effectiveness of the proposed method, we evaluated the results on eight benchmark datasets. **LFSD** [24] is a small dataset that contains 100 images with depth information and human-labeled ground truths and is built for saliency detection on the light filed. **NJUD** [21] contains 1,985 groups of RGB, depth, and label images, which are collected from the Internet, 3D movies, and photographs taken by a Fuji W3 stereo camera. **NLPR** [34] is also called **RGBD1000**, which contains 1,000 natural RGBD images captured by Microsoft Kinect together with the human-marked ground truth. **RGBD135** [6] is also named **DES**, which consists of 135 images about indoor scenes collected by Microsoft Kinect. **SIP** [12] includes 1,000 images with many challenging situations from various outdoor scenarios and these images emphasize salient persons in real-world scenes. **SSD** [52] contains 80 images picked up from three stereo movies. **STEREO** [32] is also called **SSB**, which contains 1,000 stereoscopic images downloaded from the Internet. **DUTRGBD** [36] is a new and large dataset and contains 800 indoor and 400 outdoor scenes paired with the depth maps and ground truths.

For comprehensively and fairly evaluating different methods, we follow the setting of [36]. On the DUTRGBD, we use 800 images for training and 400 images for testing. For the other seven datasets, we follow the data partition of [2, 4, 14, 36] to use 1,485 samples from the NJUD and 700 samples from the NLPR as the training set and the remaining samples in these datasets are used for testing.

4.2   Evaluation Metrics

There are six widely used metrics for evaluating RGB and RGB-D SOD models: Precision-Recall (PR) curve, F-measure [1], weighted F-measure [31], MAE [35],

Table 1. Results (↑: F_{max}, F_{ada} [1], F_β^ω [31], S_m [10] and E_m [11]; ↓: MAE [35]) of different RGB-D SOD methods across eight datasets. The best results are highlight in red. ♮: Traditional methods. †: VGG-16 [40] as backbone. ‡: VGG-19 [40] as backbone. ♯: ResNet-50 [16] as backbone. -: No data available.

	Metric	DES♮[6]	DCMC♮[8]	CDCP♮[53]	DF†[37]	CTMF†[14]	PCANet†[2]	MMCI†[4]	TANet†[3]	APNet†[42]	CPFP†[49]	OURS†	DMRA‡[36]	OURS‡	D3Net‡[12]	OURS♯
LFSD [24]	F_{max}	0.377	0.850	0.680	0.854	0.815	0.829	0.813	0.827	0.780	0.850	0.860	0.872	0.858	0.849	0.883
	F_{ada}	0.227	0.815	0.634	0.810	0.781	0.793	0.779	0.794	0.742	0.813	0.831	0.849	0.833	0.801	0.843
	F_β^ω	0.274	0.601	0.518	0.642	0.696	0.716	0.663	0.719	0.671	0.775	0.792	0.811	0.793	0.756	0.806
	MAE	0.416	0.155	0.199	0.142	0.120	0.112	0.132	0.111	0.133	0.088	0.085	0.076	0.083	0.099	0.076
	S_m	0.440	0.754	0.658	0.786	0.796	0.800	0.787	0.801	0.738	0.828	0.847	0.847	0.844	0.832	0.854
	E_m	0.492	0.842	0.737	0.841	0.851	0.856	0.840	0.851	0.810	0.867	0.883	0.899	0.886	0.860	0.891
NJUD [21]	F_{max}	0.328	0.769	0.661	0.789	0.857	0.887	0.868	0.888	0.804	0.890	0.924	0.906	0.922	0.903	0.922
	F_{ada}	0.165	0.715	0.618	0.744	0.788	0.844	0.813	0.844	0.768	0.837	0.894	0.872	0.887	0.840	0.889
	F_β^ω	0.234	0.497	0.510	0.545	0.720	0.803	0.739	0.805	0.696	0.828	0.881	0.847	0.877	0.833	0.877
	MAE	0.448	0.167	0.182	0.151	0.085	0.059	0.079	0.061	0.100	0.053	0.037	0.051	0.038	0.051	0.038
	S_m	0.413	0.703	0.672	0.735	0.849	0.877	0.859	0.878	0.772	0.878	0.911	0.885	0.911	0.895	0.908
	E_m	0.491	0.796	0.751	0.818	0.866	0.909	0.882	0.909	0.847	0.900	0.934	0.920	0.932	0.901	0.932
NLPR [34]	F_{max}	0.695	0.413	0.687	0.752	0.841	0.864	0.841	0.876	0.816	0.883	0.917	0.888	0.919	0.904	0.927
	F_{ada}	0.583	0.328	0.591	0.683	0.724	0.795	0.730	0.796	0.747	0.818	0.878	0.855	0.883	0.834	0.889
	F_β^ω	0.254	0.259	0.501	0.516	0.679	0.762	0.676	0.780	0.693	0.807	0.869	0.839	0.871	0.826	0.882
	MAE	0.300	0.196	0.114	0.100	0.056	0.044	0.059	0.041	0.058	0.038	0.027	0.031	0.027	0.034	0.023
	S_m	0.582	0.550	0.724	0.769	0.860	0.873	0.856	0.886	0.799	0.884	0.916	0.898	0.915	0.906	0.923
	E_m	0.760	0.685	0.786	0.840	0.869	0.916	0.872	0.916	0.884	0.920	0.948	0.942	0.951	0.934	0.957
RGBD135 [6]	F_{max}	0.800	0.311	0.681	0.625	0.865	0.842	0.839	0.853	0.775	0.882	0.934	0.906	0.941	0.917	0.932
	F_{ada}	0.695	0.234	0.594	0.573	0.778	0.774	0.762	0.795	0.730	0.829	0.919	0.867	0.918	0.876	0.912
	F_β^ω	0.301	0.169	0.478	0.392	0.686	0.711	0.650	0.740	0.641	0.787	0.902	0.843	0.913	0.831	0.895
	MAE	0.288	0.196	0.120	0.131	0.055	0.050	0.065	0.046	0.068	0.038	0.020	0.030	0.017	0.030	0.021
	S_m	0.632	0.469	0.709	0.685	0.863	0.843	0.848	0.858	0.770	0.872	0.932	0.899	0.937	0.904	0.926
	E_m	0.678	0.676	0.810	0.806	0.911	0.912	0.904	0.919	0.874	0.927	0.973	0.944	0.976	0.956	0.971
SIP [12]	F_{max}	0.720	0.680	0.544	0.704	0.720	0.860	0.840	0.851	0.756	0.870	0.904	0.847	0.907	0.882	0.910
	F_{ada}	0.644	0.645	0.495	0.673	0.684	0.825	0.795	0.809	0.705	0.819	0.863	0.815	0.870	0.793	0.875
	F_β^ω	0.342	0.413	0.397	0.406	0.535	0.768	0.711	0.748	0.617	0.788	0.835	0.734	0.844	0.793	0.848
	MAE	0.298	0.186	0.224	0.185	0.139	0.071	0.086	0.075	0.118	0.064	0.050	0.088	0.047	0.063	0.047
	S_m	0.616	0.683	0.595	0.653	0.716	0.842	0.833	0.835	0.720	0.850	0.878	0.800	0.885	0.864	0.886
	E_m	0.751	0.786	0.722	0.794	0.824	0.900	0.886	0.894	0.815	0.899	0.920	0.858	0.924	0.903	0.924
SSD [52]	F_{max}	0.260	0.750	0.576	0.763	0.755	0.844	0.823	0.834	0.735	0.801	0.872	0.858	0.883	0.872	0.885
	F_{ada}	0.073	0.684	0.524	0.709	0.709	0.786	0.748	0.766	0.694	0.726	0.844	0.821	0.847	0.793	0.842
	F_β^ω	0.172	0.480	0.429	0.536	0.622	0.733	0.662	0.727	0.589	0.708	0.808	0.787	0.819	0.780	0.821
	MAE	0.500	0.168	0.219	0.151	0.100	0.063	0.082	0.063	0.118	0.082	0.058	0.058	0.046	0.058	0.045
	S_m	0.341	0.706	0.603	0.741	0.776	0.842	0.813	0.839	0.714	0.807	0.866	0.856	0.875	0.866	0.879
	E_m	0.475	0.790	0.714	0.801	0.838	0.890	0.860	0.886	0.803	0.832	0.913	0.898	0.911	0.892	0.911
STEREO [32]	F_{max}	0.738	0.789	0.704	0.789	0.848	0.875	0.877	0.878	0.848	0.889	0.918	0.802	0.916	0.897	0.910
	F_{ada}	0.594	0.742	0.666	0.742	0.771	0.826	0.829	0.835	0.807	0.830	0.879	0.762	0.875	0.833	0.867
	F_β^ω	0.375	0.520	0.558	0.549	0.698	0.778	0.760	0.787	0.752	0.817	0.863	0.647	0.859	0.815	0.853
	MAE	0.295	0.148	0.149	0.141	0.086	0.064	0.068	0.060	0.075	0.051	0.039	0.087	0.040	0.054	0.041
	S_m	0.642	0.731	0.713	0.757	0.848	0.875	0.813	0.871	0.825	0.879	0.906	0.752	0.903	0.891	0.900
	E_m	0.086	0.831	0.796	0.836	0.870	0.907	0.905	0.916	0.887	0.907	0.937	0.816	0.934	0.911	0.931
DUTRGBD [36]	F_{max}	0.770	0.444	0.658	0.774	0.842	0.809	0.804	0.823	-	0.787	0.926	0.908	0.934	-	0.930
	F_{ada}	0.667	0.405	0.633	0.747	0.792	0.760	0.753	0.778	-	0.735	0.892	0.883	0.894	-	0.885
	F_β^ω	0.380	0.284	0.521	0.536	0.682	0.688	0.628	0.705	-	0.638	0.865	0.852	0.871	-	0.864
	MAE	0.280	0.243	0.159	0.145	0.097	0.100	0.112	0.093	-	0.100	0.040	0.048	0.039	-	0.041
	S_m	0.659	0.499	0.687	0.729	0.831	0.801	0.791	0.808	-	0.749	0.905	0.887	0.911	-	0.907
	E_m	0.751	0.712	0.794	0.842	0.882	0.863	0.856	0.871	-	0.815	0.938	0.887	0.941	-	0.938
AveMetric	F_{max}	0.654	0.666	0.642	0.756	0.811	0.861	0.850	0.862	0.801	0.868	0.914	0.855	0.915	0.893	0.915
	F_{ada}	0.534	0.618	0.595	0.714	0.747	0.814	0.794	0.815	0.755	0.813	0.878	0.822	0.878	0.834	0.877
	F_β^ω	0.325	0.425	0.491	0.502	0.652	0.761	0.712	0.764	0.684	0.784	0.857	0.756	0.859	0.810	0.858
	MAE	0.325	0.179	0.174	0.151	0.099	0.068	0.081	0.067	0.093	0.061	0.041	0.069	0.041	0.055	0.041
	S_m	0.585	0.661	0.669	0.721	0.809	0.853	0.844	0.853	0.773	0.853	0.898	0.824	0.900	0.883	0.899
	E_m	0.686	0.781	0.765	0.822	0.859	0.899	0.885	0.901	0.853	0.892	0.933	0.876	0.933	0.909	0.932

S-measure [10] and E-measure [11]. **PR Curve.** We use a series of fixed thresholds from 0 to 255 to binarize the gray prediction map, and then calculate several groups of precision (Pre) and recall (Rec) with ground truth by $Pre = \frac{TP}{TP+FP}$ and $Rec = \frac{TP}{TP+FN}$. Based on them, we can plot a precision-recall curve to describe the performance of the model. **F-measure** [1]. It is a region-based similarity metric and is formulated as the weighted harmonic mean (the weight is set to 0.3) of Pre and Rec. In this paper, we employ the threshold changing from 0 to 255 to get F_{max}, and use twice the mean value of the prediction P as the threshold to obtain F_{ada}. In addition, since F-measure reflects the performance of the binary predictions under different thresholds, we evaluate the consistency and uniformity at the regional level according to F-measure threshold curves. **weighted F-measure** (F_β^ω) [31]. It is proposed to improve the existing metric F-measure. It defines a weighted precision, which is a measure of exactness, and a weighted recall, which is a measure of completeness and follows the

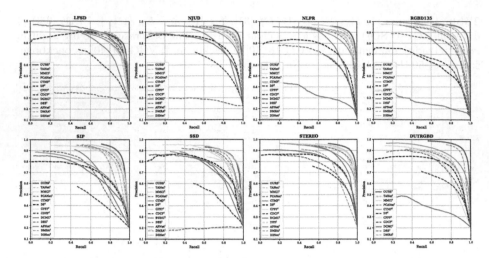

Fig. 4. Precision (vertical axis) recall (horizontal axis) curves on eight RGB-D salient object detection datasets.

form of F-measure. **MAE** [35]. This metric estimates the approximation degree between the saliency map and ground-truth map, and it is normalized to $[0, 1]$. It focuses on pixel-level performance. **S-measure** (S_m) [10]. It calculates the object-/region-aware structure similarities S_o/S_r between prediction and ground truth by the equation: $S_m = \alpha \cdot S_o + (1 - \alpha) \cdot S_r$, $\alpha = 0.5$. **E-measure** (E_m) [11]. This measure utilizes the mean-removed predictions and ground truths to compute the similarity, which characterizes both image-level statistics and local pixel matching.

4.3 Implementation Details

Parameter Setting. Two encoders of the proposed model are based on the same model, such as VGG-16 [40], VGG-19 [40], and ResNet-50 [16]. In both encoders, only the convolutional layers in corresponding classification networks are retained, and the last pooling layer of VGG-16 and VGG-19 is removed at the same time. During the training phase, we use the weight parameters pretrained on the ImageNet to initialize the encoders. Also, since the depth image is a single channel data, we change the channel number of its corresponding input layer from 3 to 1, and its parameters are initialized randomly by PyTorch. The parameters of the remaining structures are all initialized randomly.

Training Setting. During the training stage, we apply random horizontal flipping, random rotating as data augmentation for RGB images and depth images. In addition, we employ random color jittering and normalization for RGB images. We use the momentum SGD optimizer with a weight decay of $5e-4$, an initial learning rate of $5e-3$, and a momentum of 0.9. Besides, we apply a "poly" strategy [28] with a factor of 0.9. The input images are resized

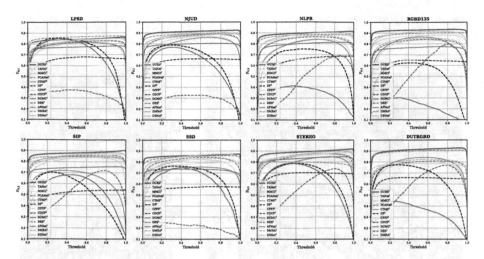

Fig. 5. F-measure (vertical axis) threshold (horizontal axis) curves on eight RGB-D salient object detection datasets.

to 320 × 320. We train the model for 30 epochs on an NVIDIA GTX 1080 Ti GPU with a batch size of 4 to obtain the final model.

Testing Details. During the testing stage, we resize RGB and depth images to 320 × 320 and normalize RGB images. Besides, the final prediction is rescaled to the original size for evaluation.

4.4 Comparisons

In order to fully demonstrate the effectiveness of the proposed method, we compared it with the existing twelve RGB-D based SOD models, including DES [6], DCMC [8], CDCP [53], DF [37], CTMF [14], PCANet [2], MMCI [4], TANet [3], AFNet [42], CPFP [49], DMRA [36] and D3Net [12]. For fair comparisons, all saliency maps of these methods are directly provided by authors or computed by their released codes. Besides, the codes and results of AFNet [42] and D3Net [12] on the DUTRGBD [36] dataset are not publicly available. Therefore, their results on this dataset are not listed.

Quantitative Evaluation. In Table 1, we list the results of all competitors on eight datasets and six metrics. It can be seen that the proposed method performs best on most datasets and achieve significant performance improvement. On the DUTRGBD [36], our models based on VGG-16, VGG-19 and ResNet-50 have surpassed the second-best model DMRA [36] by 2.02%, 2.85% and 2.45% on F_{max}, and 16.09%, 17.88% and 13.56% on MAE. At the same time, on the recent dataset SIP [12], they have increased by 3.83%, 4.65% and 5.23% on F_{ada}, 5.22%, 6.37% and 6.84% on F_{β}^{ω}, and 20.94%, 24.65% and 24.91% on MAE, over the D3Net [12]. Because the existing RGB-D SOD datasets are relatively small, we propose a new calculation method to measure the performance of

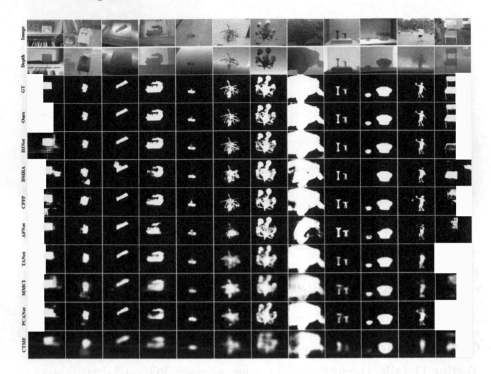

Fig. 6. The visualization results of some recent methods and ours.

models. According to the proportion of each testing set in all testing datasets, the results on all datasets are weighted and summed to obtain an overall performance evaluation, which is listed in the row "AveMetric" in Table 1. It can be seen that our structure achieves similar and excellent results on different backbones, which shows that our structure has less dependence on the performance of the backbone. In addition, we show a scatter plot based on the average performance of each model on all datasets and the model size in Fig. 1. Our model has the smallest size while achieving the best result. We demonstrate the PR curves and the F-measure curves in Fig. 4 and Fig. 5. Our approach (red solid line) achieves very good results on these datasets. As shown in Fig. 5, our results are much flatter at most thresholds, which reflects that our prediction results are more uniform and consistent.

Qualitative Evaluation. In Fig. 6, we list some representative results. These examples include scenarios with varying complexity, as well as different types of objects, including cluttered background (Column 1 and 2), simple scene (Column 3 and 4), small objects (Column 5), complex objects (Column 6 and 7), large objects (Column 8), multiple objects (Column 9 and 10) and low contrast between foreground and background (Column 11 and 12). It can be seen that the proposed method can consistently produce more accurate and complete saliency maps with higher contrast.

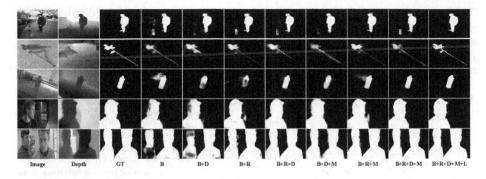

Image   Depth   GT   B   B+D   B+R   B+R+D   B+D+M   B+R+M   B+R+D+M   B+R+D+M+L

Fig. 7. Visual comparisons for showing the benefits of the proposed components. GT: Ground truth; B: Baseline; D: Dense transport layer for depth features; R: Dense transport layer for RGB features; M: DDPM; L: HEL.

4.5   Ablation Study

In this section, we perform ablation analysis over the main components of the HDFNet and further investigate their importance and contributions. Our baseline model, i.e. Model 1, uses the commonly used encoder-decoder structure, and all ablation experiments are based on the VGG-16 backbone. In the baseline model, the output features of the last three stages in the depth stream are added to the decoder after compressing the channel to 64 through an independent 1×1 convolution. In order to evaluate the benefits of cross-modal fusion at the dense transport layer (i.e. Model 6), we feed single-modal features into this layer to build Model 2 (i.e. "$+\mathbf{T}_d$") and Model 4 (i.e. "$+\mathbf{T}_{rgb}$"). Thus, the followed dynamic filters in the DDPM will be determined only by depth features or RGB features, respectively.

Dynamic Dilated Pyramid Module. Based on Model 2, Model 4, and Model 6, we add the dynamic dilated pyramid module to obtain Model 3, Model 5, and Model 7, respectively. In Table 2, we show the performance improvement contributed by different structures in terms of the weighted average metrics "AveMetric". It can be seen that the DDPM significantly improves performance. Specifically, by comparing Model 3, 5 and 7 with Model 2, 4 and 6, we achieve a relative improvement of 1.47%, 3.11% and 2.11% in terms of F_β^ω and 5.01%, 10.29% and 6.77% in terms of MAE, respectively. We can see that even without the HEL, the average performance of Model 7 already exceeds these existing models. More comparisons can be found in the supplementary material.

In addition, we compare the design of the dynamic filter in DCM [15] with ours. It can be seen that the proposed DDPM (Model 7) has obvious advantages over the DCM (Model 8), and it respectively increases by 3.91%, 5.60%, and 18.07% in terms of F_{ada}, F_β^ω and MAE. In Fig. 7, we can see that the noise in depth images interferes with the final predictions. By the cross-modal guidance from the DDPMs, the interference is effectively suppressed.

Table 2. Ablation experiments. $+\mathbf{T}_d$: Using a dense transport layer for depth features. $+\mathbf{T}_{rgb}$: Using a dense transport layer for RGB features. $+\mathbf{DDPM}$: Using a DDPM after the transport layer. $+\mathbf{DCM}$: Using the DCM [15] after the transport layer. $+\mathbf{L}_e$: Using the edge loss as the auxiliary loss. $+\mathbf{L}_f$: Using the foreground loss as the auxiliary loss. $+\mathbf{L}_b$: Using the background loss as the auxiliary loss.

Model	No.	Baseline	$+T_d$	$+T_{rgb}$	$+DDPM$	$+DCM$	$+L_e$	$+L_f$	$+L_b$	F_{max}	F_{ada}	F_β^ω	MAE	S_m	E_m
Ours†	1	✔								0.875	0.819	0.768	0.067	0.865	0.898
	2	✔	✔							0.879	0.820	0.768	0.066	0.868	0.899
	3	✔	✔		✔					0.882	0.820	0.780	0.063	0.873	0.900
	4	✔		✔						0.884	0.839	0.787	0.060	0.874	0.909
	5	✔		✔	✔					0.896	0.852	0.811	0.054	0.886	0.916
	6	✔	✔	✔						0.898	0.846	0.803	0.056	0.884	0.913
	7	✔	✔	✔	✔					0.904	0.856	0.820	0.052	0.893	0.918
	8	✔	✔	✔		✔				0.878	0.823	0.777	0.064	0.871	0.903
	9	✔	✔	✔	✔		✔			0.909	0.878	0.849	0.044	0.898	0.929
	10	✔	✔	✔	✔			✔		0.909	0.845	0.827	0.050	0.887	0.916
	11	✔	✔	✔	✔				✔	0.907	0.874	0.836	0.048	0.895	0.926
	12	✔	✔	✔	✔		✔	✔	✔	0.914	0.878	0.857	0.041	0.898	0.933
R3Net18 [9]	13									0.828	0.714	0.716	0.072	0.831	0.830
	14						✔	✔	✔	0.832	0.731	0.740	0.069	0.835	0.844
CPD19 [45]	15									0.848	0.790	0.769	0.052	0.856	0.889
	16						✔	✔	✔	0.849	0.804	0.792	0.049	0.857	0.898
PoolNet19 [26]	15									0.832	0.755	0.728	0.060	0.841	0.865
	16						✔	✔	✔	0.861	0.811	0.799	0.046	0.862	0.902
GCPANet20 [5]	17									0.847	0.766	0.744	0.061	0.854	0.869
	18						✔	✔	✔	0.854	0.779	0.773	0.055	0.856	0.880

Hybrid Enhanced Loss. As shown in Table 2, the proposed hybrid enhanced loss brings huge performance improvements by comparing Model 7 with Model 12. We evaluate each component in the HEL (Model 9, 10, and 11) and all of them contribute to the final performance. In addition, the benefits of this loss are also clearly reflected in Fig. 5 where the curves of the proposed model are more straight, and Fig. 7 where the predictions of the model "B+R+D+M+L" have higher contrast than ones of the model "B+D+R+M". Since the design goal of the HEL is to solve the general requirements of SOD tasks, we evaluate its effectiveness on several recent RGB SOD models [5,9,26,45]. For a fair comparison, we retrain these models using the released code. Most of hyper-parameters are the same as the default values given by their corresponding code. The average performance "AveMetric" on five main RGB SOD datasets (DUTS [41], ECSSD [46], HKU-IS [23], PASCAL-S [25] and DUT-OMRON [47]) is shown in Table 2. More experimental details and results can be found in supplementary materials.

5   Conclusions

In this paper, we revisit the role that depth information should play in the RGB-D based SOD task. We consider the characteristics of spatial structures contained in depth information and combine it with RGB information with rich appearance details. After that, the model generates adaptive filters with different receptive field sizes through the dynamic dilated pyramid module. It can make full use of semantic cues from multi-modal mixed features to achieve multi-scale cross-modal guidance, thereby enhancing the representation capabilities of the decoder. At the same time, we can obtain clearer predictions with the aid of additional region-level supervision to the regions around the edges and fore-/background regions. Expensive experiments on eight datasets and six metrics demonstrate the effectiveness of the designed components. The proposed approach achieves state-of-the-art performance with small model size and high running speed.

Acknowledgements. This work was supported in part by the National Key R&D Program of China #2018AAA0102003, National Natural Science Foundation of China #61876202, #61725202, #61751212 and #61829102, the Dalian Science and Technology Innovation Foundation #2019J12GX039, and the Fundamental Research Funds for the Central Universities #DUT20ZD212.

References

1. Achanta, R., Hemami, S., Estrada, F., Süsstrunk, S.: Frequency-tuned salient region detection. In: Proceedings of IEEE Conference on Computer Vision and Pattern Recognition, pp. 1597–1604 (2009)
2. Chen, H., Li, Y.: Progressively complementarity-aware fusion network for RGB-D salient object detection. In: Proceedings of IEEE Conference on Computer Vision and Pattern Recognition, pp. 3051–3060 (2018)
3. Chen, H., Li, Y.: Three-stream attention-aware network for RGB-D salient object detection. IEEE Trans. Image Process. **28**(6), 2825–2835 (2019)
4. Chen, H., Li, Y., Su, D.: Multi-modal fusion network with multi-scale multi-path and cross-modal interactions for RGB-D salient object detection. Pattern Recogn. **86**, 376–385 (2019)
5. Chen, Z., Xu, Q., Cong, R., Huang, Q.: Global context-aware progressive aggregation network for salient object detection. In: AAAI Conference on Artificial Intelligence (2020)
6. Cheng, Y., Fu, H., Wei, X., Xiao, J., Cao, X.: Depth enhanced saliency detection method. In: Proceedings of the International Conference on Internet Multimedia Computing and Service, pp. 23–27 (2014)
7. Ciptadi, A., Hermans, T., Rehg, J.M.: An in depth view of saliency (2013)
8. Cong, R., Lei, J., Zhang, C., Huang, Q., Cao, X., Hou, C.: Saliency detection for stereoscopic images based on depth confidence analysis and multiple cues fusion. IEEE Signal Process. Lett. **23**(6), 819–823 (2016)
9. Deng, Z., et al.: R3Net: recurrent residual refinement network for saliency detection. In: International Joint Conference on Artificial Intelligence, pp. 684–690 (2018)
10. Fan, D.P., Cheng, M.M., Liu, Y., Li, T., Borji, A.: Structure-measure: a new way to evaluate foreground maps. In: Proceedings of the IEEE International Conference on Computer Vision, pp. 4548–4557 (2017)
11. Fan, D.P., Gong, C., Cao, Y., Ren, B., Cheng, M.M., Borji, A.: Enhanced-alignment measure for binary foreground map evaluation. In: International Joint Conference on Artificial Intelligence, pp. 698–704 (2018)

12. Fan, D.P., et al.: Rethinking RGB-D salient object detection: models, datasets, and large-scale benchmarks. arXiv preprint arXiv:1907.06781 (2019)
13. Fan, D.P., Wang, W., Cheng, M.M., Shen, J.: Shifting more attention to video salient object detection. In: Proceedings of IEEE Conference on Computer Vision and Pattern Recognition, pp. 8554–8564 (2019)
14. Han, J., Chen, H., Liu, N., Yan, C., Li, X.: CNNs-based RGB-D saliency detection via cross-view transfer and multiview fusion. IEEE Trans. Cybern. **48**(11), 3171–3183 (2017)
15. He, J., Deng, Z., Qiao, Y.: Dynamic multi-scale filters for semantic segmentation. In: Proceedings of the IEEE International Conference on Computer Vision, pp. 3562–3572 (2019)
16. He, K., Zhang, X., Ren, S., Sun, J.: Deep residual learning for image recognition. In: Proceedings of IEEE Conference on Computer Vision and Pattern Recognition, pp. 770–778 (2016)
17. Hou, Q., Cheng, M.M., Hu, X., Borji, A., Tu, Z., Torr, P.H.: Deeply supervised salient object detection with short connections. In: Proceedings of IEEE Conference on Computer Vision and Pattern Recognition, pp. 3203–3212 (2017)
18. Howard, A.G., et al.: MobileNets: efficient convolutional neural networks for mobile vision applications. arXiv preprint arXiv:1704.04861 (2017)
19. Huang, G., Liu, Z., Van Der Maaten, L., Weinberger, K.Q.: Densely connected convolutional networks. In: Proceedings of IEEE Conference on Computer Vision and Pattern Recognition, pp. 4700–4708 (2017)
20. Jia, X., De Brabandere, B., Tuytelaars, T., Gool, L.V.: Dynamic filter networks. In: Conference and Workshop on Neural Information Processing Systems, pp. 667–675 (2016)
21. Ju, R., Liu, Y., Ren, T., Ge, L., Wu, G.: Depth-aware salient object detection using anisotropic center-surround difference. Signal Process. Image Commun. **38**, 115–126 (2015)
22. Wei, J., Wang, S., Huang, Q.: F3Net: fusion, feedback and focus for salient object detection. In: AAAI Conference on Artificial Intelligence (2020)
23. Li, G., Yu, Y.: Visual saliency based on multiscale deep features. In: Proceedings of IEEE Conference on Computer Vision and Pattern Recognition, pp. 5455–5463 (2015)
24. Li, N., et al.: Saliency detection on light field. In: Proceedings of IEEE Conference on Computer Vision and Pattern Recognition, pp. 2806–2813 (2014)
25. Li, Y., Hou, X., Koch, C., Rehg, J.M., Yuille, A.L.: The secrets of salient object segmentation. In: Proceedings of IEEE Conference on Computer Vision and Pattern Recognition, pp. 280–287 (2014)
26. Liu, J.J., Hou, Q., Cheng, M.M., Feng, J., Jiang, J.: A simple pooling-based design for real-time salient object detection. In: Proceedings of IEEE Conference on Computer Vision and Pattern Recognition (2019)
27. Liu, N., Han, J., Yang, M.H.: PicaNet: learning pixel-wise contextual attention for saliency detection. In: Proceedings of IEEE Conference on Computer Vision and Pattern Recognition, pp. 3089–3098 (2018)
28. Liu, W., Rabinovich, A., Berg, A.C.: ParseNet: looking wider to see better. arXiv preprint arXiv:1506.04579 (2015)
29. Long, J., Shelhamer, E., Darrell, T.: Fully convolutional networks for semantic segmentation. In: Proceedings of IEEE Conference on Computer Vision and Pattern Recognition, pp. 3431–3440 (2015)
30. Mahadevan, V., Vasconcelos, N.: Saliency-based discriminant tracking. In: Proceedings of IEEE Conference on Computer Vision and Pattern Recognition (2009)

31. Margolin, R., Zelnik-Manor, L., Tal, A.: How to evaluate foreground maps? In: Proceedings of IEEE Conference on Computer Vision and Pattern Recognition, pp. 248–255 (2014)
32. Niu, Y., Geng, Y., Li, X., Liu, F.: Leveraging stereopsis for saliency analysis. In: Proceedings of IEEE Conference on Computer Vision and Pattern Recognition, pp. 454–461 (2012)
33. Pang, Y., Zhao, X., Zhang, L., Lu, H.: Multi-scale interactive network for salient object detection. In: Proceedings of IEEE Conference on Computer Vision and Pattern Recognition (2020)
34. Peng, H., Li, B., Xiong, W., Hu, W., Ji, R.: RGBD salient object detection: a benchmark and algorithms. In: Fleet, D., Pajdla, T., Schiele, B., Tuytelaars, T. (eds.) ECCV 2014. LNCS, vol. 8691, pp. 92–109. Springer, Cham (2014). https://doi.org/10.1007/978-3-319-10578-9_7
35. Perazzi, F., Krähenbühl, P., Pritch, Y., Hornung, A.: Saliency filters: contrast based filtering for salient region detection. In: Proceedings of IEEE Conference on Computer Vision and Pattern Recognition, pp. 733–740 (2012)
36. Piao, Y., Ji, W., Li, J., Zhang, M., Lu, H.: Depth-induced multi-scale recurrent attention network for saliency detection. In: Proceedings of the IEEE International Conference on Computer Vision, pp. 7254–7263 (2019)
37. Qu, L., He, S., Zhang, J., Tian, J., Tang, Y., Yang, Q.: RGBD salient object detection via deep fusion. IEEE Trans. Image Process. 26(5), 2274–2285 (2017)
38. Ren, Z., Gao, S., Chia, L.T., Tsang, I.W.H.: Region-based saliency detection and its application in object recognition. IEEE Trans. Circuits Syst. Video Technol. 24(5), 769–779 (2013)
39. Rui, Z., Ouyang, W., Wang, X.: Unsupervised salience learning for person re-identification. In: Proceedings of IEEE Conference on Computer Vision and Pattern Recognition (2013)
40. Simonyan, K., Zisserman, A.: Very deep convolutional networks for large-scale image recognition. arXiv preprint arXiv:1409.1556 (2014)
41. Wang, L., et al.: Learning to detect salient objects with image-level supervision. In: Proceedings of IEEE Conference on Computer Vision and Pattern Recognition, pp. 136–145 (2017)
42. Wang, N., Gong, X.: Adaptive fusion for RGB-D salient object detection. IEEE Access 7, 55277–55284 (2019)
43. Wang, T., Piao, Y., Li, X., Zhang, L., Lu, H.: Deep learning for light field saliency detection. In: Proceedings of the IEEE International Conference on Computer Vision, October 2019
44. Wei, Y., et al.: STC: a simple to complex framework for weakly-supervised semantic segmentation. IEEE Trans. Pattern Anal. Mach. Intell. 39(11), 2314–2320 (2016)
45. Wu, Z., Su, L., Huang, Q.: Cascaded partial decoder for fast and accurate salient object detection. In: Proceedings of IEEE Conference on Computer Vision and Pattern Recognition, pp. 3907–3916 (2019)
46. Yan, Q., Xu, L., Shi, J., Jia, J.: Hierarchical saliency detection. In: Proceedings of IEEE Conference on Computer Vision and Pattern Recognition, pp. 1155–1162 (2013)
47. Yang, C., Zhang, L., Lu, H., Ruan, X., Yang, M.H.: Saliency detection via graph-based manifold ranking. In: Proceedings of IEEE Conference on Computer Vision and Pattern Recognition, pp. 3166–3173 (2013)
48. Yu, F., Koltun, V.: Multi-scale context aggregation by dilated convolutions. In: Bengio, Y., LeCun, Y. (eds.) International Conference on Learning Representations (2016). http://arxiv.org/abs/1511.07122

49. Zhao, J.X., Cao, Y., Fan, D.P., Cheng, M.M., Li, X.Y., Zhang, L.: Contrast prior and fluid pyramid integration for RGBD salient object detection. In: Proceedings of IEEE Conference on Computer Vision and Pattern Recognition, pp. 3927–3936 (2019)
50. Zhao, J.X., Liu, J.J., Fan, D.P., Cao, Y., Yang, J., Cheng, M.M.: EGNet: edge guidance network for salient object detection. In: Proceedings of the IEEE International Conference on Computer Vision, October 2019
51. Zhao, X., Pang, Y., Zhang, L., Lu, H., Zhang, L.: Suppress and balance: A simple gated network for salient object detection. In: Proceedings of European Conference on Computer Vision (2020)
52. Zhu, C., Li, G.: A three-pathway psychobiological framework of salient object detection using stereoscopic technology. In: International Conference on Computer Vision Workshops, pp. 3008–3014 (2017)
53. Zhu, C., Li, G., Wang, W., Wang, R.: An innovative salient object detection using center-dark channel prior. In: International Conference on Computer Vision Workshops, pp. 1509–1515 (2017)

SOLAR: Second-Order Loss and Attention for Image Retrieval

Tony Ng[1]([⊠]), Vassileios Balntas[2], Yurun Tian[1], and Krystian Mikolajczyk[1]

[1] MatchLab, Imperial College London, London, UK
{tony.ng14,y.tian,k.mikolajczyk}@imperial.ac.uk
[2] Facebook Reality Labs, Pittsburgh, USA
vassileios@fb.com

Abstract. Recent works in deep-learning have shown that second-order information is beneficial in many computer-vision tasks. Second-order information can be enforced both in the spatial context and the abstract feature dimensions. In this work, we explore two second-order components. One is focused on second-order spatial information to increase the performance of image descriptors, both local and global. It is used to re-weight feature maps, and thus emphasise salient image locations that are subsequently used for description. The second component is concerned with a second-order similarity (SOS) loss, that we extend to global descriptors for image retrieval, and is used to enhance the triplet loss with hard-negative mining. We validate our approach on two different tasks and datasets for image retrieval and image matching. The results show that our two second-order components complement each other, bringing significant performance improvements in both tasks and lead to state-of-the-art results across the public benchmarks. Code available at: http://github.com/tonyngjichun/SOLAR.

Keywords: Image retrieval · Descriptors · Features

1 Introduction

Second-order information is receiving increasing attention in computer-vision. It can be exploited in image retrieval in form of spatial auto-correlation of features, or by second-order similarities in a metric space. Bilinear features [10,13,24] compute second-order correlation, but significantly expand feature dimensions, requiring subsequent dimensionality reduction. Second-order (self) attention, successful in natural-language processing (NLP) [52], tackles the dimensionality problem with a multi-headed approach and is hence studied extensively in various vision areas [53,55,58,59]. Although recent deep-learning based global descriptors provide effective ways to aggregate features into a compact global

Electronic supplementary material The online version of this chapter (https://doi.org/10.1007/978-3-030-58595-2_16) contains supplementary material, which is available to authorized users.

A. Vedaldi et al. (Eds.): ECCV 2020, LNCS 12370, pp. 253–270, 2020.
https://doi.org/10.1007/978-3-030-58595-2_16

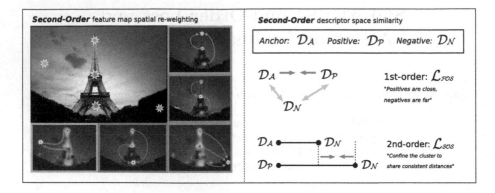

Fig. 1. Illustration of our SOLAR (**S**econd-**O**rder **L**oss and **A**ttention for image **R**etrieval) descriptor. **Left.** We exploit second-order spatial relations, re-weighting the feature maps to give a better global representation of the image. **Right.** We also apply second-order similarity of learning descriptor distances during training of SOLAR.

vector, they have not explored the correlations between features within a feature map. Meanwhile, second-order similarity [47] has recently been shown to improve patch descriptors for image matching, and has been widely adopted in different vision tasks. In this work, we exploit the second-order relations between features at different spatial locations and combine with second-order descriptor similarity to improve feature descriptors for image retrieval and matching. This is illustrated in Fig. 1. On the left, we learn optimal relative feature contribution spatially (colours of the stars correspond to the frame borders showing the attention for that location). On the right, we use second-order similarity in the descriptor space to make the distance between clusters consistent.

Our main contributions are the following:

a) We combine the second-order spatial attention and the second-order descriptor loss to improve image features for retrieval and matching.
b) We show how to combine second-order attention for consecutive feature maps at different resolution to improve the descriptors and we perform a thorough ablation study on its effects.
c) We demonstrate that the combination of second-order spatial information and similarity loss generalises well in the context of local and global descriptor learning.
d) We validate our method with extensive evaluation on two public benchmarks for image retrieval and matching, showing significant improvements compared to the state-of-the-art.

2   Related Work

Methods for image retrieval [2,18,35–37] and place recognition [3,11,31] can be divided into two broad categories: *local aggregation* and *global single-pass*. Most methods prior to deep-learning were based on *local aggregation*, e.g. Bag-of-Words (BoW) [43] which aggregates a set of handcrafted, SIFT-like [9,25] local features into a single global vector [17–20,35,36,43,48,50]. While many of the *local aggregation* methods carried-over into the deep-learning era [31,44,45], the CNNs [16,23,42] with highly expressive feature maps [12] provided an effective approach for global descriptor encoding. Early attempts were mostly hybrid methods, exploring CNN features as direct analogies to local descriptors and aggregating them with similar techniques [1,4,44]. Later works showed that CNN feature maps can be embedded into a descriptor with a *single-pass* of a pooling operation [15,38,39,51], while matching the level of performance from *local aggregation* methods. We group these methods into *global single-pass*.

Local Aggregation methods generally consist of two steps. First, local features are detected and described by hand-crafted operators such as SIFT [25] and SURF [9], or CNN-based local descriptors [4,31]. Second, the descriptors are combined into a compact vector. Early works on BoW assigned local descriptors to visual words through various size codebooks [43]. They were then encoded with matching techniques e.g. Hamming Embedding [18], Fisher Kernels [33,34] and Selective Match Kernels [48]; or with aggregation techniques e.g. k-means [30, 35] and VLAD [19,20]. With the advent of CNN descriptors [46,47,57], learnt features [4,14,29,31] led to substantial improvements in challenging, large-scale retrieval benchmarks [31,37]. Some hybrid methods also learn local-to-global encoding [1,5]. A recent state-of-the-art *local aggregation* system [45] considers features only from regions-of-interest [40], filtering out the irrelevant ones such as the sky, background and moving objects.

Global Single-Pass methods, in contrast, do not separate the extraction and aggregation steps. Instead, the global descriptor is generated by a single forward-pass through a CNN. Notice that even though hybrid methods use CNN features as local descriptors followed by *local aggregations* [1,29], thus generating the global descriptor through a forward-pass of a CNN, we do not consider them to be strictly *global single-pass*, as an individual local representation is still required and aggregated with a handcrafted encoding technique. In order to aggregate a feature map from a CNN, either a general [12] one or fine-tuned on retrieval-specific datasets [39], a global pooling operation must be applied. Various *global single-pass* methods differ mostly by the pooling operations, which include Max-pooling [51], SPoC [4], CroW [21], R-MAC [51] and GeM [39]. GeM pooling has been shown to give excellent results in a recent work that optimises a differentiable approximation of the average-precision metric [41].

Second-Order Attention mechanisms proved successful in NLP [52]. It has since gained popularity in various computer-vision tasks, including video classification [53], GANs [58], semantics segmentation [53,59] and person reID [55].

However, it has not been employed for visual representation and descriptor learning, in particular for image retrieval and matching tasks. On the other hand, **Second-Order Similarity** has only recently been introduced to representation learning [47] on local patches by confining the second-order distance in clusters to be similar and distributing them in the area of the unit hypersphere of the descriptor space. Our work is the first to exploit the second-order spatial attention in descriptor learning and to combine it with second-order descriptor loss for learning global image representation for retrieval.

3   Method

In this section, we first present the state-of-the-art Generalised-Mean (GeM) pooling [39] which we then extend with our second-order spatial pooling, followed by second-order similarity loss, whitening and descriptor normalisation.

3.1   Preliminaries

From an input image $I \in \mathbb{R}^{H,W,3}$ processed through a Fully-Convolutional Network (FCN) denoted by θ, we obtain a feature map $\mathbf{f} = \theta(I) \in \mathbb{R}^{h,w,d}$ where h, w and d are height, width and feature dimensionality, respectively. For $h, w > 1$, Generalised-Mean (GeM) pooling was proposed in [39] as a flexible way to aggregate the feature map into a single descriptor vector $\mathbf{D} = \text{GeM}(\mathbf{f}, p)$. The GeM pooling with learnable parameter p is defined as

$$\text{GeM}\,(\mathbf{f},\ p) = \left(\frac{1}{N} \sum_{i=0}^{N} f_i^p \right)^{\frac{1}{p}}. \tag{1}$$

3.2   Second-Order Spatial Pooling

Motivation. There are two main motivations for using spatial second-order attention specifically for image retrieval. First, p in Eq. 1 is able to adjust each local contribution from $\mathbf{f}$ to the global descriptor $\mathbf{D}$ according the their corresponding feature activation, *i.e. absolute* magnitude of a feature vector, which is considered a first-order measurement. Thus, it assumes the independence of various locations in the map and does not include any *relative* contribution of each spatial feature with respect to the other features.

This is followed closely by the second motivation, where in the case of FCNs such as VGG [42] and ResNet [16], each local feature that contributes to the global descriptor $\mathbf{D}$ has a limited receptive field covering pixels from the input image. Thus, in Eq. 1, for a specific f_i, GeM pooling lacks information on its relation to other features $\{f_k : k \neq i\}$ in $\mathbf{f}$.

Therefore we propose to generate a map $\mathbf{f}^{so}$ with local features $f_{i,j}^{so}$ that reflect the correlations between all spatial locations from within $\mathbf{f}^{so}$, hence the 'second-order'. Ideally, this will allow the model to learn the optimal *relative* contribution of each spatial feature to the final descriptor $\mathbf{D}$.

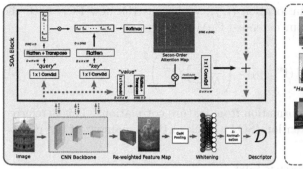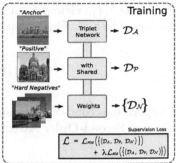

Fig. 2. Pipeline for our proposed global descriptor, SOLAR. We insert a number of Second-Order Attention (SOA) blocks at different levels of a CNN backbone, followed by GeM [39] pooling, whitening and ℓ_2 normalisation. We train SOLAR using a triplet network combining first and second-order descriptor loss.

Formulation. Let each location (i, j) in map $\mathbf{f}$ correspond to (i_I, j_I) when projected onto the input image I. Assuming a rectangular receptive field $R = [R_x, R_y]$ each vector $f_{i,j} \in \mathbf{f}$ is a function of the input pixels $I_{\mathcal{R}}$ included in the receptive field R.

To incorporate second-order spatial information into the feature pooling, we adopt the non-local block [53]. A visualisation of the concept is shown in the top left of Fig. 2. First, we generate two projections of feature map $\mathbf{f}$ termed *query* $\mathbf{q}$ head, and *key* $\mathbf{k}$ head, each obtained through 1×1 convolutions[1]. Then, by flattening both tensors, we obtain $\mathbf{q}$ and $\mathbf{k}$ with shape $d \times hw$. The second-order attention map $\mathbf{z}$ is then computed through

$$\mathbf{z} = \text{softmax}(\alpha \cdot \mathbf{q}^\mathsf{T}\mathbf{k}), \tag{2}$$

where α is a scaling factor and $\mathbf{z}$ has shape $hw \times hw$, enabling each $f_{i,j}$ to correlate with features from the whole map $\mathbf{f}$. A third projection of $\mathbf{f}$ is then obtained by *value* head $\mathbf{v}$, in a similar way to $\mathbf{q}$ and $\mathbf{k}$, but resulting in shape $hw \times d$. Finally, $\mathbf{f}^{so}$ map is obtained from the first-order features $\mathbf{f}$ by the second-order attention

$$\mathbf{f}^{so} = \mathbf{f} + \psi\left(\mathbf{z} \times \mathbf{v}\right), \tag{3}$$

where ψ is another 1×1 convolution (see footnote 1) to control the influence of the attention. Thus, a new feature $f_{i,j}^{so}$ in the second-order map $\mathbf{f}^{so}$ (reshaped to $h \times w \times d$), is a function of features from all locations in $\mathbf{f}$

$$f_{i,j}^{so} = g(\mathbf{z}_{ij} \odot \mathbf{f}), \tag{4}$$

where g denotes the combination of all convolutional operations within the non-local block. We can express each feature $f_{i,j}^{so}$ as a function of the full input image

---

[1] We omit Batch-Norm, ReLU and channel reduction for simplicity. Please refer to our code for the exact model details: http://github.com/tonyngjichun/SOLAR.

$f^{so}_{i,j} = \phi(i, j, I)$, viewed from location (i, j), with ϕ as the new FCN with the non-local block(s). Finally, our extended GeM-pooling

$$\text{GeM}(\mathbf{f}^{so}, \ p) = \left(\frac{1}{N} \sum_{i=0}^{N} f_i^{so^p}\right)^{\frac{1}{p}} \tag{5}$$

incorporates second-order information from feature correlations. This is referred to as the **Second-Order Attention (SOA)** block in the remainder of the paper.

3.3 Second-Order Similarity Loss

First-Order Similarity. The triplet loss is a standard formulation for learning first-order descriptors [8,27,46]. Given a set of triplets formed by anchor, positive and negative images, their corresponding global descriptors are denoted as $\{(\mathbf{D}_a, \mathbf{D}_p, \mathbf{D}_n)\}$. The triplet loss with margin m can be considered as first-order in the descriptor space

$$\mathcal{L}_{FOS} = \frac{1}{|\{(\mathbf{D}_a, \mathbf{D}_p, \mathbf{D}_n)\}|} \sum_{\{(\mathbf{D}_a, \mathbf{D}_p, \mathbf{D}_n)\}} \max\left(0, \|\mathbf{D}_a - \mathbf{D}_p\|^2 - \|\mathbf{D}_a - \mathbf{D}_n\|^2 + m\right) \tag{6}$$

Second-Order Similarity. Following SOSNet [47] in local features, a second-order similarity loss can also be applied to global descriptors. We hard-mine negative pairs as in [39] and calculate the SOS loss for our descriptors

$$\mathcal{L}_{SOS} = \frac{1}{|\{(\mathbf{D}_a, \mathbf{D}_p, \mathbf{D}_n)\}|} \sum_{\{(\mathbf{D}_a, \mathbf{D}_p, \mathbf{D}_n)\}} \left(\|\mathbf{D}_a - \mathbf{D}_n\|^2 - \|\mathbf{D}_p - \mathbf{D}_n\|^2\right)^{\frac{1}{2}}. \tag{7}$$

The final objective function is a combination of first and second-order loss for global descriptors obtained with second-order spatial attention balanced by λ

$$\mathcal{L} = \mathcal{L}_{FOS} + \lambda \mathcal{L}_{SOS}. \tag{8}$$

3.4 Descriptor Whitening

Whitening operation is crucial for obtaining well performing descriptors. While the original work in GeM [39] used a linear projection for descriptor whitening [26], recent experiments[2] show superior results from whitening operation learnt end-to-end. We follow this new approach, by inserting a bias-enabled fully-connected layer after GeM pooling with ℓ_2-norm, and train it end-to-end.

3.5 Network Architecture and Training

The pipeline of our proposed method is shown in Fig. 2. The SOA blocks are insert-able at any feature maps (including intermediate ones), as they serve

---

[2] http://github.com/filipradenovic/cnnimageretrieval-pytorch.

as learnt feature attention mechanisms. During training all triplets are passed through shared weight networks. Hard-negative mining is also performed at the start of every epoch from a random pool of negatives and it is assured that no negatives from each triplet are from the same scene/landmark class. This is to provide high sample variability from within the mini-batch. Details are described in Sect. 6.

4   Results on Large-Scale Image Retrieval

In this section, we present results of SOLAR on large-scale image retrieval tasks and compare to the existing methods, both *local aggregation* and *global single-pass*.

4.1   Datasets

Google Landmarks 18 (GL18). [45] is an extension to the original Kaggle challenge [31] dataset. It contains over 1.2 million photos from $15k$ landmarks around the world. These landmarks cover a wide-range of classes from historic cities to modern metropolitan areas to nature scenery. GL18 also contains over $80k$ bounding boxes singling out the most prominent landmark in each image. In this work it serves as a semi-automatically labelled training dataset.

Revisited Oxford and Paris. [37] is the commonly used dataset for evaluating the performance of global descriptors on large-scale image retrieval tasks. Oxford [35] and Paris [36] datasets were recently revisited by removing annotation errors and adding new images. The Revisted-Oxford ($\mathcal{R}$Oxf) and Revisited-Paris ($\mathcal{R}$Par) datasets contain 4,993 and 6,322 images respectively, and each with 70 queries by a bounding box depicting the most prominent landmark in that query. The evaluation protocol is divided into three difficulty levels – *Easy*, *Medium* and *Hard*. The mean average precision (mAP) and mean precision at rank 10 (mP@10) are usually reported as performance metrics. The supplementary 1M-distractors ($\mathcal{R}$1M) database contains 1-million extra images to test the robustness of descriptors, using the same protocols and metrics as in $\mathcal{R}$Oxf-$\mathcal{R}$Par.

4.2   Comparison to the State-of-the-Art on Image Retrieval

SOTA. Recent works on large-scale image retrieval [41,45,56] select GeM [39] trained on the SfM120k dataset with the contrastive loss as the baseline for *global single-pass* methods. However, an update on the GitHub repo by GeM's authors (see footnote 2) sets the new state-of-the-art results from GeM trained on the GL18 [45] dataset, with the triplet loss as in Eq. 6. This setting outperforms the recent method that proposed the AP-loss [41] trained on GL18, when evaluated on $\mathcal{R}$Oxf-$\mathcal{R}$Par [37]. Therefore, unlike other recent papers, we select GeM [39] trained on GL18 with the triplet loss as our baseline, and we denote it ResNet101-GeM [SOTA] in Table 1. We also advocate the use of GL18 training dataset

Table 1. Large-scale image retrieval results of our proposed second-order method against the state-of-the-art on $\mathcal{R}$Oxf-$\mathcal{R}$Par [37] and their respective $\mathcal{R}$1M-distractors sets. We evaluate against the *Medium* and *Hard* protocols with the mAP and mP@10 metrics. For *global single-pass* methods, the first term refers to the backbone CNN. [O] denotes results from off-the-shelf networks pretrained on Imagenet. Our method uses ResNet101 with SOA† denoting the best configuration described in Table 2. SOLAR† is the full proposed method including the **S**econd-**O**rder similarity **L**oss

Method	Medium								Hard							
	$\mathcal{R}$Oxf		$\mathcal{R}$Oxf+$\mathcal{R}$1M		$\mathcal{R}$Par		$\mathcal{R}$Par+$\mathcal{R}$1M		$\mathcal{R}$Oxf		$\mathcal{R}$Oxf+$\mathcal{R}$1M		$\mathcal{R}$Par		$\mathcal{R}$Par+$\mathcal{R}$1M	
	mAP	mP@10	mAP	mP@10	mAP	mP@10	mAP	mP@10	mAP	mP@10	mAP	mP@10	mAP	mP@10	mAP	mP@10
Local Agg.																
HesAff-rSIFT-ASMK* [49]	60.4	85.6	45.0	76.0	61.2	97.9	42.0	95.3	36.4	56.7	25.7	42.1	34.5	80.6	16.5	63.4
DELF-ASMK* [45]	65.7	87.9	–	–	77.1	98.7	–	–	41.0	57.9	–	–	54.6	90.9	–	–
DELF-D2R-R-ASMK* [45]	69.9	89.0	–	–	78.7	99.0	–	–	45.6	61.9	–	–	57.7	93.0	–	–
— DELF [GL18] [45]	73.3	90.0	61.0	84.6	80.7	99.1	60.2	97.9	47.6	64.3	33.6	53.7	61.3	93.4	29.9	82.4
Global Single-Pass																
AlexNet-GeM [39]	43.3	62.1	24.2	42.8	58.0	91.6	29.9	84.6	17.1	26.2	9.4	11.9	29.7	67.6	8.4	39.6
VGG16-GeM [39]	61.9	82.7	42.6	68.1	69.3	97.9	45.4	94.1	33.7	51.0	19.0	29.4	44.3	83.7	19.1	64.9
ResNet101-R-MAC [15]	60.9	78.1	39.3	62.1	78.9	96.9	54.8	93.9	32.4	50.0	12.5	24.9	59.4	86.1	28.0	70.0
ResNet101-SPoC [4] [O]	39.8	61.0	21.5	40.4	69.2	96.7	41.6	92.0	12.4	23.8	2.8	5.6	44.7	78.0	15.3	54.4
ResNet101-CroW [21]	41.4	58.8	22.5	40.5	62.9	94.4	34.1	87.1	13.9	25.7	3.0	6.6	36.9	77.9	10.3	45.1
ResNet101-GeM [39] [O]	45.8	66.2	25.6	45.1	69.7	97.6	46.2	94.0	18.1	31.3	4.7	13.4	47.0	84.9	20.3	70.4
ResNet101-GeM [39]	64.7	84.7	45.2	71.7	77.2	98.1	52.3	95.3	38.5	53.0	19.9	34.9	56.3	89.1	24.7	73.3
ResNet101-GeM+DAME [56]	65.3	85.0	44.7	70.1	77.1	98.4	50.3	94.6	40.4	56.3	22.8	35.6	56.0	88.0	22.0	69.0
ResNet101-GeM+AP [41]	67.5	–	47.5	–	80.1	–	52.5	–	42.8	–	23.2	–	60.5	–	25.1	–
ResNet101-GeM [SOTA] [39]	67.3	84.7	49.5	–	80.6	96.7	57.3	–	44.3	59.7	25.7	–	61.5	90.7	29.8	–
Ours																
ResNet101-GeM+SOS	67.6	84.7	50.0	73.1	80.9	96.6	57.6	94.4	44.9	60.1	26.2	42.9	61.9	91.0	30.3	78.9
ResNet101+SOA†	68.6	85.7	51.3	74.7	81.4	96.6	58.8	94.6	46.9	62.7	28.3	46.0	63.7	91.9	32.4	80.9
ResNet101+SOLAR†	69.9	86.7	53.5	76.7	81.6	97.1	59.2	94.9	47.9	63.0	29.9	48.9	64.5	93.0	33.4	81.6

as the new standard protocol for large-scale image retrieval. The inconsistency of training sets that can be observed across different works makes it difficult to assess what performance gains can be attributed to the proposed methods, rather than the training sets.

Comparison of SOLAR against other state-of-the-art image retrieval methods on $\mathcal{R}$Oxf-$\mathcal{R}$Par [37] data is presented in Table 1. By adding SOA blocks, we achieve state-of-the-art mAP and mP@10 performance, and improve by a large margin all other *global single-pass* methods, for both *Medium* and *Hard* protocols. Adding the Second-Order Loss (denoted by SOLAR†), the results are further improved by 1%. SOLAR outperforms mAP of the baseline in the most challenging *Hard* protocol for $\mathcal{R}$Oxf and $\mathcal{R}$Par by significant 3.6% and 3.0% gains respectively, as well as 3.3% and 2.7% in mP@10. Our method also outperforms the state-of-the-art *local aggregation* method of DELF-D2R-R-ASMK* in mAP on $\mathcal{R}$Oxf-*Hard* by 0.3%, $\mathcal{R}$Par-*Medium* by 0.9% and $\mathcal{R}$Par-*Hard* by 3.2%.

For $\mathcal{R}$-1M, SOLAR also achieves the state-of-the-art performance across *global single-pass* methods, outperforming in mAP the SOTA by 4.0% on $\mathcal{R}$Oxf-*Medium*, 4.2% on $\mathcal{R}$Oxf-*Hard*; and by 1.9% on $\mathcal{R}$Par-*Medium*, 3.6% on $\mathcal{R}$Par-*Hard*. Compared to ResNet101-GeM+AP [41] the improvements are even higher (6.0%, 6.7%, 6.7% and 8.3%). As for *local aggregation*, SOLAR still achieves comparable results in the $\mathcal{R}$-1M set and even outperforms DELF-D2R-R-ASMK* by 3.5% in mAP for $\mathcal{R}$Par-*Hard*.

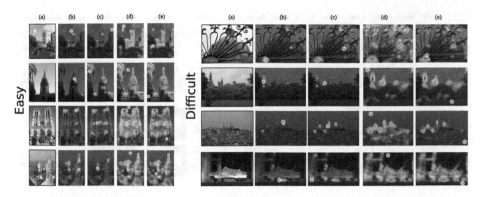

Fig. 3. Qualitative examples of second-order attention maps on the $\mathcal{R}$Oxf-$\mathcal{R}$Par dataset [37]. Each row depicts (a): the source image and four corresponding second-order attention maps obtained for specific spatial locations (marked by pink stars). For each example, four spatial pixel locations are selected – (b): on the dominant landmark, (c): on a secondary landmark, (d): on the sky and (e): on another background part other than the sky. **Left:** easy examples. **Right:** difficult examples.

Speed & Memory Costs. It should be noted that the memory requirement for *local aggregation* descriptors is much higher than for *global single-pass* e.g. 27.6 GB as reported in DELF-D2R-R-ASMK* [45] *vs.* 7.7GB for GeM [39] & SOLAR descriptors in the $\mathcal{R}$1M-distractors set. SOLAR also runs with a significantly faster speed compared to DELF-D2R-R-ASMK*, *i.e.* 0.15 s processing time per image *vs.* >1.5 s on a Titan Xp GPU. The SOAs in SOLAR only cause an extra 7.4% cost in inference time compared to GeM. For the $\mathcal{R}$-1M distractors set, the extraction time difference is a significant 1.5 days *vs.* weeks required for DELF-D2R-R-ASMK*. Hence, SOLAR is much more suitable for large-scale retrieval tasks given its scalability when compared to *local aggregation* methods, as well as the performance when compared to *global single-pass* methods.

Moreover, we observe that during training the network converges faster and leads to higher performance on the benchmarks when training **only** the SOAs and the whitening layer, *i.e.* freezing backbone weights. Not only does this greatly reduce the training time, it also indicates that the SOAs are optimised for *re-weighting* the features, as will be described in the following section.

4.3 Qualitative Retrieval Results

We visualise the effects of second-order feature map re-weighting in Fig. 3. For locations in the background ((d) & (e)), the attention from that feature is sparsely distributed within the main landmark(s). On the other hand, when the feature is located within a landmark ((b) & (c)), the attention is then on highly distinctive regions including informative features from outside of its receptive field.

This is visible on both, easy examples (**left** in Fig. 3), where there is a clear landmark with distinctive features at similar scales located in the centre

Fig. 4. Qualitative comparison between the baseline GeM (top) and SOLAR (bottom). (Color figure online)

and occupies a significant portion of the image, as well as challenging examples (**right** in Fig. 3). For example, the top right example has significant occlusion; in the second and third row the landmark is far-away and a large portion of the image is background; and in the bottom row with night-time image. We can see that even for these hard examples, the second-order attention maps are consistent. This provides qualitative evidence that the spatial re-weighting of feature maps, through second-order attentions, is able to assist the network in learning relative contributions from various features into the final descriptor.

We also compare the results from image retrieval in Fig. 4 on very challenging examples in $\mathcal{R}$Oxf-*Hard* [37]. The rows for each example show the query bounding box in yellow, and the Top-7 ranked retrieved images by the baseline ResNet101+GeM [SOTA] [39] and our ResNet101+SOLAR†, with green and red borders denoting correct and incorrect retrievals. While GeM performs reasonably well on these examples, it has a tendency to rank high the images containing some similar features, resulting in more false positives. On the other hand, SOLAR is able to leverage the global correlation from the second-order attentions to increase, in the top few ranks, the number of correct (green) retrievals.

5   Ablation Study

In this section we evaluate the impact of SOLAR on descriptor performance. We first show how SOLAR leads to learning the optimal feature contribution for pooling a global descriptor from the feature map. Next, we break it down into the two second-order components. Lastly, we extend SOLAR to patch datasets to show that it generalises well to local descriptors for image matching task.

5.1   Optimal Feature Contribution

In Sect. 4.3, we have shown in Fig. 3, that SOAs are effectively *re-weighting* individual feature contributions into the global descriptor based on their uniqueness within the image. Figure 4 shows examples of improved retrieval results by

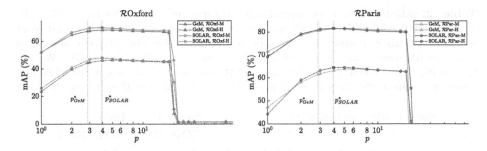

Fig. 5. Comparison of mAP against p on $\mathcal{R}$Oxf-$\mathcal{R}$Par between SOLAR $vs.$ GeM.

SOLAR compared to GeM. In this section, we conduct a detailed quantitative assessment on the advantages over GeM in optimal feature contributions.

In Fig. 5 we compare the performance of the baseline (ResNet101-GeM [SOTA]) $vs.$ SOLAR for different values of p-norm in Eq. 1. We show the mAP of both methods on the *Hard* and *Medium* protocols of $\mathcal{R}$Oxf-$\mathcal{R}$Par [37] for p ranging from $p = 1$ (*i.e.* equal contribution) to $p = 100$ (*i.e.* focused on the strongest features). Note that p is a learnable parameter, we therefore mark the p learnt by each method with dotted-lines on the graphs. The mAP is clearly increasing as p is raised from 1 to the learnt value, then drops gradually up to $p \approx 20$, after which mAP rapidly decreases to a very weak performance. For high values of p, GeM-pooling approaches Max-pooling [51]. However, $\lim_{p \to \infty} f_i^p = 0 \; \forall \; |f_i| \leq 1$, causing numerical instabilities in Eq. 1. Hence, in the implementation, feature magnitudes are clipped to a minimum of 10^{-6}, explaining why mAPs fall after a threshold of p and differ from Max-pooling [51].

We observe that SOLAR outperforms GeM across most values of p, especially in *Hard* examples of both $\mathcal{R}$Oxf and $\mathcal{R}$Par. More importantly, when comparing the values of p learnt by GeM (p^*_{GeM}) and SOLAR (p^*_{SOLAR}), p^*_{SOLAR} corresponds to the peak of each of SOLAR's mAP curve, while p^*_{GeM} is sub-optimal to the best mAPs. This further supports that our SOAs facilitate learning the optimal relative contributions of each feature to the global descriptor.

5.2 Impact of Second-Order Components on Image Retrieval

The results in Sect. 4.2 show that by simultaneously exploiting second-order spatial information through the SOA blocks and second-order descriptor similarity through the SOS loss, we greatly improve image retrieval performance. In this section, we perform an ablation study by gradually incorporating separate second-order components in SOLAR, and discuss the results on image retrieval.

In Table 2 we present the impact of adding the second-order loss (SOS) and spatial (SOAs) components, with ResNet101+GeM [SOTA] [39] as the baseline. Firstly, by adding SOS in training, the mAPs improved slightly for < 1%. Then, we look at the effects of adding SOAs into ResNet101 [16], which contains 5 fully-convolutional blocks conv1 to conv5_x. In retrieval, the input image typically

Table 2. Ablation study of second-order components on $\mathcal{R}$Oxf-$\mathcal{R}$Par [37]. We use ResNet101-GeM [SOTA] [39] as baseline and incrementally add second-order loss and attention components. Results are in mAP for the *Medium* and *Hard* protocols.Ablation study of second-order components on $\mathcal{R}$Oxf-$\mathcal{R}$Par [37]. We use ResNet101-GeM [SOTA] [39] as baseline and incrementally add second-order loss and attention components. Results are in mAP for the *Medium* and *Hard* protocols.

Second-order component(s)		Medium		Hard	
		$\mathcal{R}$Oxf	$\mathcal{R}$Par	$\mathcal{R}$Oxf	$\mathcal{R}$Par
None (Baseline)	ResNet101-GeM [SOTA]	67.3	80.6	44.3	61.5
Loss (SOS)	ResNet101-GeM+SOS	67.6	80.9	44.9	61.9
Spatial (SOA)	ResNet101+SOA$_4$	68.2	81.0	45.7	62.3
	ResNet101+SOA$_5$	68.3	81.3	45.9	62.8
	ResNet101+SOA$_{4,5}$	68.6	81.4	46.9	63.7
Both (SOLAR)	ResNet101+SOLAR	**69.9**	**81.6**	**47.9**	**64.5**

has high resolution (1000+ pixels on longer side), inserting SOA blocks before `conv4_x` is computationally too expensive given the $\mathcal{O}(n^2)$ complexity of Eq. 2. Table 2 shows that our proposed SOA insertions improve retrieval mAP for 0.93% with SOA$_4$, 1.15% with SOA$_5$ and 1.78% with SOA$_{4,5}$. This shows that fine-tuning SOAs alone are more effective than retraining the backbone with SOS. More importantly, we observe that addition of consecutive SOAs is beneficial and that the improvement brought by fine-tuning on SOA$_5$ is higher than SOA$_4$. We believe that this is due to for large images, where the spatial second-order information is still rich and fine-grained even at the last feature map. As SOA$_5$ re-weights the last feature map before GeM pooling, it adds second-order spatial information directly into the global descriptor, resulting in a better performance.

Lastly, combining SOS and SOA (*i.e.* SOLAR) gives the best mAPs, and the gain by SOS on SOA ($> 1\%$) is more than that of SOS on baseline ($< 1\%$). This further supports that the two second-order components complement each other.

5.3   Generalisation to Image Matching with Local Descriptors

To validate the generalisation ability of SOLAR besides retrieval with global descriptors, we further test it on local descriptor learning. Local patches have different statistics than images, containing less semantic information. However, some degree of structure is still present in patches, thus spatial correlation is still informative [28]. Therefore, we train a local descriptor network with the proposed spatial SOAs. With the second-order similarity included in local SOSNet [47], it is straightforward to directly insert SOAs into SOSNet.

Datasets. In contrast to image retrieval, there are several tasks in different benchmarks to evaluate the performance of local descriptors. Most frequently used are the UBC Patches [54] and HPatches [7], as well as other localisation benchmarks that test both feature detectors and descriptors simultaneously.

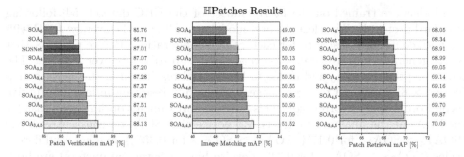

Fig. 6. Patch description performance on HPatches. Each of the configurations is denoted as SOA followed by the numbers indicating layers in SOSNet [47] backbone after which the blocks are inserted. We train all models with the *liberty* subset of UBC and select the model with the lowest average FPR@95. Patches are resized to 32×32.

UBC Patches [54], consists of three scenes (*liberty, notredame*, and *yosemite*) from which corresponding patches are extracted. Models are trained on one scene and tested on the other two for evaluation. Previous works [8, 27, 28, 46, 47] report the false positive rate at 95% recall (**FPR@95**) on the 100K test pairs. However, the performance on this dataset has saturated, and the limitations of the **FPR@95** metric have also been pointed out [6]. Moreover, the evaluation task for UBC is different in nature from retrieval. Therefore, we leave the results for UBC in the supplementary material and use UBC data only for training, which is a standard protocol for the HPatches benchmark.

HPatches [7] contains over 1.5 million patches extracted from 116 scenes with varying viewpoint and illumination. There are three evaluation tasks: *Patch Verification, Image Matching* and *Patch Retrieval*.

Impact of SOA at Different Layers. SOSNet [47] uses the L2-Net [46] architecture as the backbone. There are 7 convolutional layers in L2-Net which takes a 32×32 grayscale input patch and outputs a local descriptor with dimensionality of 128. The L2-Net architecture is presented in the supplementary material. The SOA block can be inserted at each intermediate feature map except for Layer-7, as the spatial dimension is reduced to 1×1 only. The earlier the SOA block(s) is inserted, the higher the resolution and more second-order information can be exploited. However, this comes at two costs. First, the complexity of Eq. 2 is $\mathcal{O}(n^2)$, where n is the product of the two spatial dimensions. Second, the channel depth is shallower at early layers (32 in the first two *vs.* 128 in the final three layers), *i.e.* each spatial feature in the early layers is less informative.

The results on HPatches with our SOLAR patch descriptors are presented in Fig. 6. To investigate how second-order spatial information changes in patch description, we insert 1 to 3 SOA blocks from between Layers-3 to 7 of L2-Net (Layers-1 & 2 add too much computational cost), giving the set of results {SOA_3, SOA_4, SOA_5, SOA_6, $SOA_{3,4}$, $SOA_{3,5}$, $SOA_{4,5}$, $SOA_{4,6}$, $SOA_{3,4,5}$, $SOA_{4,5,6}$}.

Models are trained on the *liberty* subset of the UBC dataset [54] following standard protocols. We select the best model according to the average **FPR@95** on *notredame* and *yosemite* for each SOA configuration. Figure 6 shows that SOAs generally improve *Patch Retrieval* mAP, up to 1.75% over SOSNet. The only exception is SOA_6 and is due to low spatial resolution of this feature map (only 8×8) compared to large images in Sect. 5.2, resulting in less informative second-order spatial correlation. This poses a more difficult optimisation task for the SOAs at the final feature levels. We notice that SOAs on consecutive levels ($SOA_{3,4} > SOA_{3,5}$ for 0.17%, $SOA_{4,5} > SOA_{4,6}$ for 0.45%), and across different scales ($SOA_{3,5} > SOA_{4,5}$ for 0.34% despite having fewer parameters) are both beneficial to retrieval, further validating the results from Sect. 5.2. The results on *Patch Verification* and *Image Matching* are consistent with *Patch Retrieval*, especially with the ordering *w.r.t.* different SOA configurations. This shows that our SOLAR descriptor also extends well to describing local patches, generalising well between tasks of image retrieval and matching.

6   Implementation Details

GeM+SOLAR. We start with ResNet101-GeM [39] pre-trained on GL18[3] and fine-tune the SOAs and the whitening layer with Eq. 8. We train for a maximum of 50 epochs on the same GL18 [45] dataset using Adam [22] with an initial learning rate of $1e^{-6}$ ($1e^{-4}$ for p) and exponential decay rate of 0.01. For each epoch 2000 anchors are randomly selected. The triplets are formed, for every anchor, with 1 positive and 5 hard-negatives mined from 20,000 negative samples, each from a separate landmark, yielding 5 triplets $\{(\mathbf{D}_a, \mathbf{D}_p, \mathbf{D}_n)\}$ for Eqs. 6 and 7. The batch-size is 8. We use margin $m = 1.25$ for the triplet loss and $\lambda = 10$ for SOS loss. At test time, we follow [39] by passing 3 scales $[1, \sqrt{2}, \frac{1}{\sqrt{2}}]$ to the network and taking the average of the output descriptors.

SOSNet+SOAs. We re-implemented SOSNet [47] with the details in the original paper to serve as a baseline (100 epochs max). SOAs are inserted and trained with identical settings. All experiments are implemented in PyTorch [32]. For GeM+SOLAR†, fine-tuning takes roughly 12 h across 4 1080Ti GPUs. For SOS-NET+SOAs, each training takes roughly 5 h on a single 1080Ti GPU.

7   Conclusion

In this work, we propose SOLAR, a global descriptor that utilises second-order information through both spatial attention and descriptor similarity for large-scale image retrieval. We conduct detailed quantitative and qualitative studies on the impact of incorporating second-order attention that learns to effectively re-weight feature maps, and combine with the second-order information from descriptors similarity to produce better representation for retrieval. We extend

---

[3] http://cmp.felk.cvut.cz/cnnimageretrieval/data/networks/gl18/.

the SOLAR approach to local patch descriptors and show that it improves upon the current state-of-the-art without extra supervision, proving that such second-order combination generalises to different type of data. SOLAR achieves state-of-the-art image retrieval performance on the challenging $\mathcal{R}$Paris+1M benchmark compared to similar *global single-pass* methods by a large margin of 3.6% as well as outperforms *local aggregation* methods by 3.5%, while running at a fraction of both time and memory costs. Our approach also improves state-of-the-art for local descriptors in HPatches benchmark by 1.75%.

Acknowledgement. This work was supported by UK EPSRC EP/S032398/1 & EP/N007743/1 grants. We also thank Giorgos Tolias for providing $\mathcal{R}$-1M results of ResNet101-GeM [SOTA] in Table 1.

References

1. Arandjelović, R., Gronat, P., Torii, A., Pajdla, T., Sivic, J.: NetVLAD: CNN architecture for weakly supervised place recognition. In: CVPR (2016)
2. Arandjelović, R., Zisserman, A.: Three things everyone should know to improve object retrieval. In: CVPR (2012)
3. Arandjelović, R., Zisserman, A.: DisLocation: scalable descriptor distinctiveness for location recognition. In: Cremers, D., Reid, I., Saito, H., Yang, M.-H. (eds.) ACCV 2014. LNCS, vol. 9006, pp. 188–204. Springer, Cham (2015). https://doi.org/10.1007/978-3-319-16817-3_13
4. Babenko, A., Lempitsky, V.: Aggregating deep convolutional features for image retrieval. In: ICCV (2015)
5. Babenko, A., Slesarev, A., Chigorin, A., Lempitsky, V.: Neural codes for image retrieval. In: Fleet, D., Pajdla, T., Schiele, B., Tuytelaars, T. (eds.) ECCV 2014. LNCS, vol. 8689, pp. 584–599. Springer, Cham (2014). https://doi.org/10.1007/978-3-319-10590-1_38
6. Balntas, V., Lenc, K., Vedaldi, A., Tuytelaars, T., Matas, J., Mikolajczyk, K.: Hpatches: a benchmark and evaluation of handcrafted and learned local descriptors. TPAMI (2019)
7. Balntas, V., Lenc, K., Vedaldi, A., Mikolajczyk, K.: Hpatches: a benchmark and evaluation of handcrafted and learned local descriptors. In: CVPR (2017)
8. Balntas, V., Riba, E., Ponsa, D., Mikolajczyk, K.: Learning local feature descriptors with triplets and shallow convolutional neural networks. In: BMVC (2016)
9. Bay, H., Tuytelaars, T., Van Gool, L.: SURF: speeded up robust features. In: Leonardis, A., Bischof, H., Pinz, A. (eds.) ECCV 2006. LNCS, vol. 3951, pp. 404–417. Springer, Heidelberg (2006). https://doi.org/10.1007/11744023_32
10. Carreira, J., Caseiro, R., Batista, J., Sminchisescu, C.: Semantic segmentation with second-order pooling. In: Fitzgibbon, A., Lazebnik, S., Perona, P., Sato, Y., Schmid, C. (eds.) ECCV 2012. LNCS, vol. 7578, pp. 430–443. Springer, Heidelberg (2012). https://doi.org/10.1007/978-3-642-33786-4_32
11. Chen, D.M., et al.: City-scale landmark identification on mobile devices. In: CVPR (2011)
12. Deng, J., Dong, W., Socher, R., Li, L.J., Li, K., Li, F.F.: ImageNet: a large-scale hierarchical image database. In: CVPR (2009)
13. Gao, Y., Beijbom, O., Zhang, N., Darrell, T.: Compact bilinear pooling. In: CVPR (2016)

14. Gong, Y., Wang, L., Guo, R., Lazebnik, S.: Multi-scale orderless pooling of deep convolutional activation features. In: Fleet, D., Pajdla, T., Schiele, B., Tuytelaars, T. (eds.) ECCV 2014. LNCS, vol. 8695, pp. 392–407. Springer, Cham (2014). https://doi.org/10.1007/978-3-319-10584-0_26

15. Gordo, A., Almazán, J., Revaud, J., Larlus, D.: Deep image retrieval: learning global representations for image search. In: Leibe, B., Matas, J., Sebe, N., Welling, M. (eds.) ECCV 2016. LNCS, vol. 9910, pp. 241–257. Springer, Cham (2016). https://doi.org/10.1007/978-3-319-46466-4_15

16. He, K., Zhang, X., Ren, S., Sun, J.: Deep residual learning for image recognition. In: CVPR (2016)

17. Jégou, H., Chum, O.: Negative evidences and co-occurences in image retrieval: the benefit of PCA and whitening. In: Fitzgibbon, A., Lazebnik, S., Perona, P., Sato, Y., Schmid, C. (eds.) ECCV 2012. LNCS, vol. 7573, pp. 774–787. Springer, Heidelberg (2012). https://doi.org/10.1007/978-3-642-33709-3_55

18. Jegou, H., Douze, M., Schmid, C.: Hamming embedding and weak geometric consistency for large scale image search. In: Forsyth, D., Torr, P., Zisserman, A. (eds.) ECCV 2008. LNCS, vol. 5302, pp. 304–317. Springer, Heidelberg (2008). https://doi.org/10.1007/978-3-540-88682-2_24

19. Jégou, H., Douze, M., Schmid, C., Pérez, P.: Aggregating local descriptors into a compact image representation. In: CVPR (2010)

20. Jégou, H., Perronnin, F., Douze, M., Sánchez, J., Pérez, P., Schmid, C.: Aggregating local images descriptors into compact codes. TPAMI **34**, 1704–1716 (2012)

21. Kalantidis, Y., Mellina, C., Osindero, S.: Cross-dimensional weighting for aggregated deep convolutional features. In: Hua, G., Jégou, H. (eds.) ECCV 2016. LNCS, vol. 9913, pp. 685–701. Springer, Cham (2016). https://doi.org/10.1007/978-3-319-46604-0_48

22. Kingma, D.P., Ba, J.: Adam: a method for stochastic optimization. In: ICLR (2015)

23. Krizhevsky, A., Sutskever, I., Hinton, G.E.: ImageNet classification with deep convolutional neural networks. In: NeurIPS (2012)

24. Lin, T., RoyChowdhury, A., Maji, S.: Bilinear CNN models for fine-grained visual recognition. In: ICCV (2015)

25. Lowe, D.G.: Distinctive image features from scale-invariant keypoints. In: IJCV (2004)

26. Mikolajczyk, K., Matas, J.: Improving descriptors for fast tree matching by optimal linear projection. In: ICCV (2007)

27. Mishchuk, A., Mishkin, D., Radenović, F., Matas, J.: Working hard to know your neighbor's margins: Local descriptor learning loss. In: NeurIPS (2017)

28. Mukundan, A., Tolias, G., Chum, O.: Explicit spatial encoding for deep local descriptors. In: CVPR (2019)

29. Ng, J.Y.H., Yang, F., Davis, L.S.: Exploiting local features from deep networks for image retrieval. In: CVPR Workshops (2015)

30. Nistér, D., Stewénius, H.: Scalable recognition with a vocabulary tree. In: CVPR (2006)

31. Noh, H., Araujo, A., Sim, J., Weyand, T., Han, B.: Image retrieval with deep local features and attention-based keypoints. In: ICCV (2017)

32. Paszke, A., et al.: PyTorch: an imperative style, high-performance deep learning library. In: NeurIPS (2019)

33. Perronnin, F., Liu, Y., Sánchez, J., Poirier, H.: Large-scale image retrieval with compressed fisher vectors. In: CVPR (2010)

34. Perronnin, F., Sánchez, J., Mensink, T.: Improving the fisher kernel for large-scale image classification. In: Daniilidis, K., Maragos, P., Paragios, N. (eds.) ECCV 2010. LNCS, vol. 6314, pp. 143–156. Springer, Heidelberg (2010). https://doi.org/10.1007/978-3-642-15561-1_11

35. Philbin, J., Chum, O., Isard, M., Sivic, J., Zisserman, A.: Object retrieval with large vocabularies and fast spatial matching. In: CVPR (2007)

36. Philbin, J., Chum, O., Isard, M., Sivic, J., Zisserman, A.: Lost in quantization: Improving particular object retrieval in large scale image databases. In: CVPR (2008)

37. Radenović, F., Iscen, A., Tolias, G., Avrithis, Y., Chum, O.: Revisiting Oxford and Paris: large-scale image retrieval benchmarking. In: CVPR (2018)

38. Radenović, F., Tolias, G., Chum, O.: CNN image retrieval learns from BoW: unsupervised fine-tuning with hard examples. In: Leibe, B., Matas, J., Sebe, N., Welling, M. (eds.) ECCV 2016. LNCS, vol. 9905, pp. 3–20. Springer, Cham (2016). https://doi.org/10.1007/978-3-319-46448-0_1

39. Radenović, F., Tolias, G., Chum, O.: Fine-tuning CNN image retrieval with no human annotation. TPAMI **41**, 1655–1668 (2018)

40. Ren, S., He, K., Girshick, R., Sun, J.: Faster R-CNN: towards real-time object detection with region proposal networks. In: NeurIPS (2015)

41. Revaud, J., Almazán, J., Sampaio de Rezende, R., Roberto de Souza, C.: Learning with average precision: Training image retrieval with a listwise loss. In: ICCV (2019)

42. Simonyan, K., Zisserman, A.: Very deep convolutional networks for large-scale image recognition. In: ICLR (2015)

43. Sivic, J., Zisserman, A.: Video Google: a text retrieval approach to object matching in videos. In: ICCV (2003)

44. Sydorov, V., Sakurada, M., Lampert, C.H.: Deep fisher kernels - end to end learning of the fisher kernel GMM parameters. In: CVPR (2014)

45. Teichmann, M., Araujo, A., Zhu, M., Sim, J.: Detect-to-retrieve: efficient regional aggregation for image search. In: CVPR (2019)

46. Tian, Y., Fan, B., Wu, F.: L2-Net: deep learning of discriminative patch descriptor in Euclidean space. In: CVPR (2017)

47. Tian, Y., Yu, X., Fan, B., Fuchao, W., Heijnen, H., Balntas, V.: SOSNet: second order similarity regularization for local descriptor learning. In: CVPR (2019)

48. Tolias, G., Avrithis, Y., Jégou, H.: To aggregate or not to aggregate: selective match kernels for image search. In: ICCV (2013)

49. Tolias, G., Avrithis, Y., Jégou, H.: Image search with selective match kernels: aggregation across single and multiple images. In: IJCV (2015)

50. Tolias, G., Furon, T., Jégou, H.: Orientation covariant aggregation of local descriptors with embeddings. In: Fleet, D., Pajdla, T., Schiele, B., Tuytelaars, T. (eds.) ECCV 2014. LNCS, vol. 8694, pp. 382–397. Springer, Cham (2014). https://doi.org/10.1007/978-3-319-10599-4_25

51. Tolias, G., Sicre, R., Jégou, H.: Particular object retrieval with integral max-pooling of CNN activations. In: ICLR (2016)

52. Vaswani, A., et al.: Attention is all you need. In: NeurIPS (2017)

53. Wang, X., Girshick, R., Gupta, A., He, K.: Non-local neural networks. In: CVPR (2018)

54. Winder, S.A., Brown, M.: Learning local image descriptors. In: CVPR (2007)

55. Xia, B.N., Gong, Y., Zhang, Y., Poellabauer, C.: Second-order non-local attention networks for person re-identification. In: ICCV (2019)

56. Yang, T.Y., Nguyen, D.K., Heijnen, H., Balntas, V.: DAME WEB: DynAmic MEan with whitening ensemble binarization for landmark retrieval without human annotation. In: ICCV Workshops (2019)
57. Yi, K.M., Trulls, E., Lepetit, V., Fua, P.: LIFT: learned invariant feature transform. In: Leibe, B., Matas, J., Sebe, N., Welling, M. (eds.) ECCV 2016. LNCS, vol. 9910, pp. 467–483. Springer, Cham (2016). https://doi.org/10.1007/978-3-319-46466-4_28
58. Zhang, H., Goodfellow, I., Metaxas, D., Odena, A.: Self-attention generative adversarial networks. In: ICML (2019)
59. Zhu, Z., Xu, M., Bai, S., Huang, T., Bain, X.: Asymmetric non-local neural networks for semantic segmentation. In: ICCV (2019)

Fixing Localization Errors to Improve Image Classification

Guolei Sun[1]([✉]), Salman Khan[2], Wen Li[3], Hisham Cholakkal[2],
Fahad Shahbaz Khan[2], and Luc Van Gool[1]

[1] ETH Zurich, Zürich, Switzerland
`guolei.sun@vision.ee.ethz.ch`
[2] Mohamed Bin Zayed University of Artificial Intelligence, Abu Dhabi, UAE
[3] University of Electronic Science and Technology of China, Chengdu, China

Abstract. Deep neural networks are generally considered black-box
models that offer less interpretability for their decision process. To
address this limitation, Class Activation Map (CAM) provides an attractive solution that visualizes class-specific discriminative regions in an
input image. The remarkable ability of CAMs to locate class discriminating regions has been exploited in weakly-supervised segmentation and
localization tasks. In this work, we explore a new direction towards the
possible use of CAM in deep network learning process. We note that
such visualizations lend insights into the workings of deep CNNs and
could be leveraged to introduce additional constraints during the learning stage. Specifically, the CAMs for negative classes (negative CAMs)
often have false activations even though those classes are absent from
an image. Thereby, we propose a loss function that seeks to minimize
peaks within the negative CAMs, called '*Homogeneous Negative CAM*'
loss. This way, in an effort to fix localization errors, our loss provides
an extra supervisory signal that helps the model to better discriminate
between similar classes. Our designed loss function is easy to implement
and can be readily integrated into existing DNNs. We evaluate it on
a number of classification tasks including large-scale recognition, multi-
label classification and fine-grained recognition. Our loss provides better
performance compared to other loss functions across the studied tasks.
Additionally, we show that the proposed loss function provides higher
robustness against adversarial attacks and noisy labels.

1 Introduction

The conventional training strategy for deep neural networks (DNNs) involves
loss functions that operate on the logit space [19,30]. Given an input, a DNN
model learns a function that maps it to the output label space, where the loss
is computed. The network thus learned is considered a 'black-box' model whose
prediction process lacks transparency for human understanding and interpretation. To resolve this limitation of DNNs, a number of approaches have been

---

G. Sun and S. Khan—Equal contribution.

© Springer Nature Switzerland AG 2020
A. Vedaldi et al. (Eds.): ECCV 2020, LNCS 12370, pp. 271–287, 2020.
https://doi.org/10.1007/978-3-030-58595-2_17

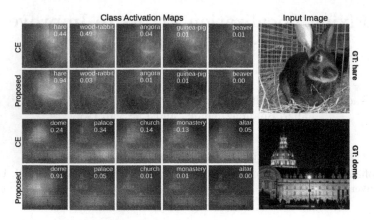

Fig. 1. Comparison of the class activation maps (CAMs) between the baseline (CE loss) and our proposed loss, for sample images from ImageNet [6]. Positive CAMs are shown on the far left, followed by top four negative CAMs, which are ranked based on classification probability. For each CAM, the corresponding class name and predicted probability are shown in the upper right region. For the baseline, there are many false activations in the negative CAMs (see *first* and *third* row). In contrast, our method produces clearer negative CAMs, thus avoiding localization errors and leading to a higher classification accuracy.

proposed to visualize the decision process within deep networks [31,32,42]. These approaches provide interpretable and intuitive explanations for DNN decisions, making them more transparent and explainable. One popular way to visualize the internal mechanics of DNNs is using the attention visualization corresponding to each category.

Zhou *et al.* [46] proposed class activation mapping (CAM), which illustrates the discriminative spatial regions in an image that are relevant to a specific class. Due to their remarkable ability to locate class-specific discriminative regions, CAMs have been shown to provide cost-free localizations for objects using just the image-level labels. In this work, we show that the interpretation provided by CAMs, into the internal mechanics of DNNs, can be exploited to add additional constraints and provide an extra supervisory signal during network optimization. Concretely, since a CAM provides coarse object location for a class, if the class is *absent*, the corresponding CAM should be *relatively* clear and have *no* or *less* attentive regions (peaks), compared with the CAM for the *positive* class. Hence, our novel loss function, called *Homogeneous Negative CAM* (HNC) loss, is proposed to suppress the peaks in the activation maps corresponding to the negative classes.

Despite the simplicity of our approach, it provides clear gains in problems such as image recognition, multi-label classification and fine-grained recognition. For example, compared to the Cross Entropy (CE) loss baseline, HNC loss delivers *absolute* top-1 accuracy gains of 1.2% and 1.1% on CIFAR-100 and ImageNet datasets, respectively. The suppression of negative CAMs provides an additional supervision to the deep network, which helps resolve confusions regarding the final prediction, thereby helps improve the overall classification performance. As shown in Fig. 1, removing false peaks from negative CAMs also results in visualizations that are more consistent and faithful to given class labels for an image. Furthermore, we demonstrate that the HNC loss improves robustness of the learned model towards adversarial attacks and noisy labels.

2   Related Works

In this section, we first introduce popular network visualization approaches, and then review the recent advances in loss functions for optimizing the DNNs.

Network Visualization. Patterns that can maximally activate particular units within a deep network were synthesized using gradient information in [11,27,32]. Deep feature representations have also been inverted to reconstruct the corresponding input image [9,27]. Another category of visualization methods including DeConvNet [42] and Guided Back-propagation [33] amplify the salient patterns in an image by modifying the raw gradients. As such, the above-mentioned visualization methods are either non-discriminative for different classes or illustrate model behavior as a whole, instead of providing an image-specific visualization. To address this requisite, [46] proposed an activation visualization mechanism (i.e. CAM) that sheds light on the implicit attention of a DNN on an image. While [46] is applicable to a specific class of architectures (e.g., without fully connected layers), [31] extended the concept to work with a broader range of DNN architectures. Due to the class-discriminative nature and simplistic design of [46], we base our loss formulation on class activation maps.

Loss Functions. A major factor in deep neural network's design is the choice of a correct objective function. Cross-entropy loss is hitherto the most popular loss function for computer vision problems such as classification, retrieval, detection and segmentation [13]. For special cases, alternative loss functions have been proposed in the literature, which can be grouped into two main classes, (a) max-margin loss functions and (b) data-imbalance losses. The margin maximizing loss functions put relative constraints with respect to other class boundaries such that each class is well-separated in the output space [7,12,26]. These constraints are generally posed as an angular margin [7,25,26,37], a spatial distance measure [16] or as a ranking penalty for multi-label classification problems [12,44]. In the second category, cost-sensitive objectives [8,17,18] are designed to re-weight the loss such that all classes in a long-tail data distribution are adequately modeled. From another perspective, a set of loss functions seek to re-balance back-propagated gradients by focusing on difficult examples and putting less emphasis on easy cases [23,29].

The closest to our approach are [2,10,15]. Among these, [10] seeks to minimize the peaks in the output 'logit' space to improve generalization on fine-grained tasks. Guo *et al.* [15] work on CAMs, but impose a consistency constraint that tries to obtain similar CAMs for original and transformed images. Finally, [2] flattens out the negative class scores in the logit-space to achieve adversarial robustness. In contrast to these loss functions, we seek to remove peaks with in the CAMs for negative classes, thus ensuring that implicit CNN attention conforms with the information available from ground-truth labels. We extensively compare our approach with the above mentioned loss functions and demonstrate significant improvements.

3   Method

In this section, we first introduce class activation maps, and then give a detailed description of our loss, followed by gradients analysis. Finally, we show the comparative analysis between two proposed variants of HNC loss.

3.1   Class Activation Maps

Consider the multi-class image classification task with n classes. Let I be a training image with ground-truth label $l \in J$, where $J = \{1, 2, ..., n\}$ is the label set. Let $F \in \mathbb{R}^{c \times h \times w}$ denotes the high-level feature maps, output from network's last convolution layer, where c, h, w denote number of channels, height and width of the feature maps, respectively. After passing F through a global average pooling (GAP) layer and a fully connected (FC) layer with weight matrix $W \in \mathbb{R}^{c \times n}$, class confidence scores $s = \{s_i : i \in J\} \in \mathbb{R}^n$ are obtained to make the final predictions.

Class activation mapping [46] is a simple visualization approach that has shown great potential in localizing discriminative regions corresponding to a class. As a result, it has been used in both weakly supervised and fully supervised settings for a variety of tasks, such as classification [46], object localization [3,49], segmentation [34,47] and counting [4]. As shown in [46], we can simply convolve the feature maps F and W to obtain class activation maps $M \in \mathbb{R}^{n \times h \times w}$,

$$M_o = \sum_k w_{k,o} F_k, \tag{1}$$

where $M_o \in \mathbb{R}^{h \times w}$ is the class activation map (CAM) corresponding to an output class 'o', $w_{k,o}$ is the element in the kth row and o^{th} column of matrix W, and $F_k \in \mathbb{R}^{h \times w}$ is the feature map corresponding to the kth channel. For simplicity, the bias term is omitted in Eq. 1.

Most previous works use the CAM of the positive class, e.g., as a clue for coarse object localization [1,4], and ignore the CAMs for negative classes. However, we find that there are many false peaks in negative CAMs as showed in Fig. 1, which in turn negatively affect the classification performance resulting in false positives. Following this intuition, we propose a novel loss to suppress the highly activated regions in the negative CAMs.

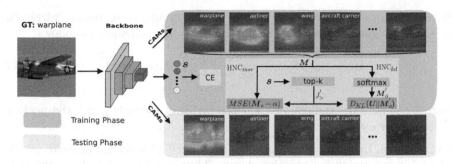

Fig. 2. Overview of our proposed *Homogeneous Negative CAM* loss. From *left* to *right*, a positive class activation map (CAM) followed by a group of negative CAMs is shown. Negative CAMs are ranked based on their classification scores. Our proposed loss (two variants: HNC_{mse} and HNC_{kd}) is designed to suppress the false activations in the negative CAMs. As shown on top, during the early training phase, there are several false peaks in the negative CAMs. After training with our loss, the negative CAMs generated during the inference stage are flattened out, which leads to a correct prediction.

3.2 Our Proposed Loss

Our Idea. The basic idea of our '*Homogeneous Negative CAM*' (HNC) loss is to suppress the false activations on the class activation maps for negative classes (see Fig. 2). When the positive class and the negative class are very different (*e.g.*, plane vs. tree), it is understandable that the CAM for a negative class should not be focused on any particular region. For the situation where the positive and negative classes are similar (*e.g.*, warplane vs. airliner), our loss remains relevant. By using our proposed loss, the CAM for the negative class is forced to be *relatively* clearer (less peaks), helping the network to resolve the confusions between similar classes and leading to correct prediction. Suppressing the false activations in the CAMs thus provides additional supervision to the network, compared to the normal CE loss which only suppresses the class confidence scores for negative classes (average of negative CAMs).

We develop two alternatives for enforcing homogeneity in negative CAMs. The first approach simply uses the Mean Square Error (MSE) loss to suppress the peak responses, while the second approach minimizes the KL-divergence between negative CAMs and a uniform map. We refer to these two approaches as the HNC_{mse} loss and HNC_{kd} loss, respectively.

HNC_{mse} Loss. The general idea is to suppress the CAMs for the top-k negative classes (with k highest confidence scores) using the MSE loss.

We define J' as the set of all negative classes: $J' = \{i : i \in J \wedge i \neq l\}$. Let $s' = \{s_i : i \in J'\}$ be the set containing the confidence scores of all negative classes. We compute the kth highest values of s' and denote it as t_k. Next, we obtain $J'_>$ by thresholding s using t_k, defined as follows:

$$J'_> = \{i : i \in J' \wedge s_i \geq t_k\}$$

where, $J'_>$ contains the negative classes whose confidence scores are within the top-k of all negative classes. Then, our HNC_{mse} loss is defined as follows:

$$\text{HNC}_{mse}(\boldsymbol{M}, l) = \frac{1}{hw} \sum_{o \in J'_>} \sum_{i,j} \left(\boldsymbol{M}_o(i,j) - \alpha \right)^2, \tag{2}$$

where i, j denote the indices and α is the constant towards which the peaks in $\boldsymbol{M}_o$ are suppressed and we set it as 0 for all $o \in J'_>$.

HNC_{kd} **Loss.** In an ideal situation, the negative CAMs should be clear, providing no focused region for negative classes. Thus, we propose to force the top-k negative CAMs to have a uniform spatial distribution. Let $\boldsymbol{U} \in \mathbb{R}^{h \times w}$ be a uniform probability matrix with all elements equal to $1/(hw)$. Our HNC_{kd} loss minimizes the KL-divergence between the negative CAMs and $\boldsymbol{U}$:

$$\text{HNC}_{kd}(\boldsymbol{M}, l) = \sum_{o \in J'_>} D_{KL}\left(\boldsymbol{U} \| \boldsymbol{M}'_o\right), \tag{3}$$

where $\boldsymbol{M}'_o = \sigma(\boldsymbol{M}_o)$ and σ is the softmax activation function to convert $\boldsymbol{M}_o$ to a probability map. We denote,

$$D_{KL}(\boldsymbol{U} \| \boldsymbol{M}'_o) = \sum_{i,j} \boldsymbol{U}(i,j) \log \frac{\boldsymbol{U}(i,j)}{\boldsymbol{M}'_o(i,j)} = const - \frac{1}{hw} \sum_{i,j} \log \left(\boldsymbol{M}'_o(i,j) \right), \tag{4}$$

where $const$ is a constant. After removing the constant and combining Eq. 3 and Eq. 4, we get the HNC_{kd} loss as:

$$\text{HNC}_{kd}(\boldsymbol{M}, l) = -\frac{1}{hw} \sum_{o \in J'_>} \sum_{i,j} \log \left(\boldsymbol{M}'_o(i,j) \right). \tag{5}$$

Overall Loss. The overall loss is the weighted combination of cross entropy and HNC losses. We note that our proposed loss can also be used together with other image classification losses, e.g., Focal loss [23] and LGM loss [36]. In this work, we stick with combining our loss function with the basic cross entropy loss to demonstrate the *concept (idea)* and clearly show its benefit. Hence, cross entropy loss is the fair baseline and used frequently in our experiments (Sect. 4). As shown by our results (Sect. 4), this combination works well on various tasks and datasets. The cross entropy (CE) loss is defined on class confidence scores $\boldsymbol{s}$ as:

$$\text{CE}(\boldsymbol{s}, l) = -\log \frac{\exp\left(s_l\right)}{\sum_{i \in J} \exp(s_i)}, \tag{6}$$

where s_i is the ith element of $\boldsymbol{s}$. The overall loss is defined as follows:

$$\mathcal{L}_{cl}(\boldsymbol{s}, \boldsymbol{M}, l) = \text{CE}(\boldsymbol{s}, l) + \lambda \, \text{HNC}(\boldsymbol{M}, l). \tag{7}$$

Here, λ is the hyper-parameter controlling the weight of the HNC loss, which can be implemented according to Eq. 2 or Eq. 5.

Multi-label Classification. For multi-label classification, we adopt the *weighted sigmoid cross-entropy* (SCE) loss, as in [22]. For an image I, let $l = \{l_i \in J\}$ denotes the set containing all ground-truth classes. Then, the loss function is,

$$\text{SCE}(\boldsymbol{s}, \boldsymbol{l}) = -\frac{1}{n}\Big(\sum_{o\in l} u_o \log \frac{1}{1+\exp(-s_o)} + \sum_{o\notin l} u_o \log \frac{\exp(-s_o)}{1+\exp(-s_o)}\Big),$$

$$u_o = \exp(1-p_o)[o \in l] + \exp(p_o)[o \notin l], \tag{8}$$

where p_o is the probability of positive samples for class 'o' in the training set. Despite the SCE loss being used, we can generate class activation maps and $J'_>$ in the same way as multi-class classification. The overall loss for multi-label classification ($\mathcal{L}_{mlc}$) is as follows:

$$\mathcal{L}_{mlc}(\boldsymbol{s}, \boldsymbol{M}, \boldsymbol{l}) = \text{SCE}(\boldsymbol{s}, \boldsymbol{l}) + \lambda\, \text{HNC}(\boldsymbol{M}, \boldsymbol{l}). \tag{9}$$

Here, the HNC loss can be implemented according to Eq. 2 or Eq. 5.

3.3 Gradient Analysis

We consider the overall loss given by Eq. 7. Since, $s_o = \frac{1}{hw}\sum_{i,j} M_o(i,j)$, we can compute the derivative of the overall loss with respect to $M_o(i,j)$ to obtain the gradient formulae denoting the effect of change in class-activation maps on the net loss. For simplicity, we write $M_o(i,j)$ as $M_o^{i,j}$ here. First, for the cross entropy loss, by chain rule:

$$\frac{\partial \text{CE}(\boldsymbol{s}, \boldsymbol{l})}{\partial M_o^{i,j}} = \frac{\partial \text{CE}}{\partial s_o} \cdot \frac{\partial s_o}{\partial M_o^{i,j}}, \quad \text{where } \frac{\partial \text{CE}}{\partial s_o} = \frac{\exp(s_o)}{\sum_k \exp(s_k)} - y_o, \frac{\partial s_o}{\partial M_o^{i,j}} = \frac{1}{hw},$$

$$\frac{\partial \text{CE}(\boldsymbol{s}, \boldsymbol{l})}{\partial M_o^{i,j}} = \beta \frac{\exp(\beta \sum_{i,j} M_o^{i,j})}{\sum_k \exp(\beta \sum_{i,j} M_k^{i,j})} - \beta y_o, \tag{10}$$

where $\boldsymbol{y}$ is a one-hot encoded vector and $\beta = \frac{1}{hw}$. Similarly for HNC_{mse},

$$\frac{\partial \text{HNC}_{mse}}{\partial M_o^{i,j}} = 2\beta(M_o^{i,j} - \alpha). \tag{11}$$

For the KL divergence, the derivative is given by:

$$\frac{\partial \text{HNC}_{kl}}{\partial M_o^{i,j}} = \frac{\exp(M_o^{i,j})}{\sum_{i',j'} \exp(M_o^{i',j'})} - \beta. \tag{12}$$

Discussion. For cross entropy loss, we observe that the gradient for every location of the class activation map M_o, is always the *same* regardless of the pixel intensities, as seen from Eq. 10. It is expected, since the CE works directly on the class confidence scores, which is the average of M_o. However, for our

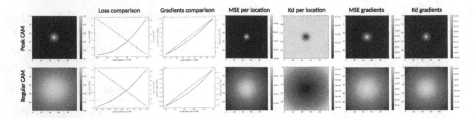

Fig. 3. Comparison between HNC_{mse} and HNC_{kd}. Peak and Regular CAM cases are shown as toy examples to illustrate the behavior of both losses. Both pixel maps (columns 4–7) and line plots (columns 2–3) are shown. (*best viewed with zoom*)

loss, the gradients (Eq. 11 and Eq. 12) for different locations of the M_o can be *different*. Specifically, a false peak region of the top-k negative CAMs has higher gradients than non-peaked regions. As a result, those regions would be suppressed more, helping network to better differentiate the positive class and those top-k negative classes (the most confusing ones).

One may argue that when using a normal CE loss, some regions of the negative CAMs can be very negative and our loss can have the effect of further increasing those negative values. Note that this scenario is unlikely because our loss is used together with CE loss. CE loss pushes the overall scores of negative CAMs to be small while our loss pushes the negative CAMs to be homogeneous (without peaks). The overall effect is that peaks will be suppressed.

3.4 Comparison: HNC_{mse} vs. HNC_{kd}

In order to study the comparative nature of both proposed loss functions, we consider two typical cases for CAM. (a) A highly-focused CAM with a single peak region (*peak CAM*). (b) A normal case where the CAM is neither too focused nor too spread out (*regular CAM*). These two example cases are shown from top to bottom in Fig. 3. For each case, we illustrate a comparison between loss and gradient values for HNC_{mse} and HNC_{kd} loss functions. From the gradients maps (last two columns in Fig. 3), we clearly observe that for our loss, different locations of the CAMs can have different gradients, which is consistent with our analysis in Sect. 3.3. Below, we derive an alternate form for HNC_{kd} that will help us better understand the comparison between the two variants.

Proposition 1. *The minimization of HNC_{kd} is equivalent to minimizing the maximum (peak) value in M_o, while simultaneously maximizing the average CAM response $\bar{M}_o$ (mean of M_o) : $o \in J'_>$ to obtain a homogeneous CAM.*

Proof. Consider the loss defined in Eq. 5. By putting $M'_o = \sigma(M_o)$ and simplifying, we get:

$$HNC_{kd}(M, l) = \sum_{o \in J'_>} \left[\log \sum_{i',j'} \exp(M_o^{i',j'}) - \bar{M}_o \right],$$

where, the first term on the right is the Log-Sum-Exp (LSE) function, which is a smooth approximation of the max operation. Then, since $\text{LSE}(\boldsymbol{M}_o) > \max(\boldsymbol{M}_o)$, HNC_{kd} acts as an upper bound for the following expression:

$$\text{HNC}_{kd}(\boldsymbol{M}, l) > \sum_{o \in J'_>} \left[\max(\boldsymbol{M}_o) - \bar{M}_o \right].$$

As a result, when minimizing HNC_{kd}, we are effectively reducing the peak values in negative CAMs, while simultaneously maximizing the average CAM response.
□

The above proposition shows that the loss values for HNC_{kd} follow a linear relation with the local values in the input CAM. On the other hand, HNC_{mse} imposes a quadratic penalty that focuses more on the extreme values. Thereby, HNC_{mse} is relatively more sensitive to outliers in the CAM, while HNC_{kd} applies a relatively smoother penalty. In our experiments, we notice nearly similar performance from both HNC_{kd} and HNC_{mse}.

4   Experiments

In this section, we conduct extensive experiments to demonstrate the effectiveness of our proposed loss function. Specifically, we evaluate our loss on general image recognition (see Sect. 4.1), multi-label classification (see Sect. 4.2), fine-grained classification (see Sect. 4.3), adversarial robustness (see Sect. 4.4), and noisy label learning (see Sect. 4.5). Then, ablation studies are performed in Sect. 4.6. All experiments are carried out using the Pytorch framework on NVIDIA Tesla V100 GPUs.

4.1   General Image Classification

For the task of general image classification, we evaluate our loss on the CIFAR-100 [20] and ImageNet (ILSVRC 2012) [6]. Below, we summarize our results.

CIFAR-100 Classification: CIFAR-100 consists of 60,000 images in total. Among these images, 50,000 are used for training while the remaining 10,000 are used for testing. CIFAR-100 has a total of 100 classes, each with 600 images. The results are averaged over 5 runs.

We train two backbone networks, ResNet-56 and ResNet-110, from scratch with our loss. We use input images with the original resolution after standard data augmentation, i.e., random flipping and cropping with a padding of 4 pixels on each side. The learning rate is initially set to 0.1, and dropped by a factor of 0.1 at 84 and 122 epochs. We train our model for 164 epochs in total.

Table 1 shows the comparisons between our loss and other recent or top-performing loss functions including Center loss [39], Large-margin Gaussian Mixture (LGM) loss [36], Focal loss [23], Class-balanced (CB) Focal loss [5], Angular softmax (A-Softmax) loss [25], Large-margin cosine (LMC) loss [38], Additive

Table 1. Performance comparisons between different loss functions on CIFAR-100. *: the number is taken from the corresponding paper. Results show that our loss outperforms other losses by a clear margin.

Loss functions	Publication	ResNet-56		ResNet-110	
		Top-1	Top-5	Top-1	Top-5
Cross entropy	–	72.40	92.68	73.79	93.11
Center loss [39]	ECCV16	72.72	93.06	74.27	93.20
LGM loss [36]	CVPR18	73.08	93.10	74.34	93.06
Focal loss [23]	ICCV17	73.09	93.07	74.34	93.34
CB focal loss [5]	CVPR19	73.09	93.07	74.34	93.34
A-Softmax loss [25]	CVPR17	72.20	91.28	72.72	90.41
LMC loss [38]	CVPR17	71.52	91.64	73.15	91.88
AAM loss [7]	CVPR19	71.41	91.66	73.72	91.86
Anchor loss* [29]	ICCV19	–	–	74.38	92.45
Ours (HNC_{mse})	–	73.35	93.11	**75.00**	93.58
Ours (HNC_{kd})	–	**73.47**	**93.29**	74.76	**93.65**

Table 2. Error rates of different losses on ImageNet. For ResNet-101, our loss outperforms the baseline by 1.1% in terms of Top-1 error.

Loss functions	ResNet-101		ResNet-152	
	Top-1	Top-5	Top-1	Top-5
CE (reproduced)	23.2	6.7	22.9	6.6
LGM* [36]	22.7	7.1	–	–
Ours (HNC_{mse})	22.3	**6.4**	21.9	6.1
Ours (HNC_{kd})	**22.1**	**6.4**	**21.8**	**6.0**

Table 3. Accuracy of different losses with ResNet-50 on CUB-200-2011. Ours surpasses CE by 1.1%.

Loss functions	Top-1
CE	86.0
Center loss [39]	86.5
Focal loss [23]	85.8
Ours (HNC_{mse})	**87.1**
Ours (HNC_{kd})	86.9

Angular Margin (AAM) loss [7], and Anchor loss [29]. Among these loss functions, [2,7,25,36,38] focus on margin maximization between classes to enhance the performance, [39] performs clustering and [5,23,29] focus on discriminating hard examples. In contrast, our approach develops a simple constraint for intermediate CAMs of negative classes.

The results show that our loss clearly outperforms other methods. Remarkably, compared to the CE loss, our loss achieves 1.07% and 1.21% improvements (top-1 accuracy) on ResNet-56 and ResNet-110, respectively. The fact that our loss has a larger margin over CE using ResNet-110 than ResNet-56 is possibly due to the higher redundancy in a larger network, which can lead to more serious over-fitting. Among other loss functions, both the LGM loss [36] and Focal loss

Table 4. Comparisons between methods w/ and w/o our loss on MS-COCO using different metrics. 'ResNet-101†' represents the baseline implemented with complex data augmentations in [48] and * means the number is taken from [15]. Our loss provides a gain over both basic and strong baselines.

Method		All						
		mAP	F1-C	P-C	R-C	F1-O	P-O	R-O
ResNet-101† [48]		75.2	69.5	80.8	63.4	74.4	82.1	68.0
ResNet-101-SRN* [48]		77.1	71.2	81.6	65.4	75.8	82.7	69.9
Baseline	ResNet-101*	74.9	69.7	70.1	69.7	73.7	73.6	73.7
Ours	ResNet-101+HNC$_{mse}$	**77.8**	**72.3**	**78.9**	67.4	**76.5**	**81.9**	71.9
	ResNet-101+HNC$_{kd}$	77.6	**72.3**	75.8	**69.7**	76.1	78.2	**74.1**
Baseline	AC* [15]	77.5	72.2	77.4	68.3	76.3	79.8	73.1
Ours	AC+HNC$_{mse}$	**78.5**	72.8	**79.6**	67.9	**76.9**	**82.3**	72.1
	AC+HNC$_{kd}$	78.2	**72.9**	76.8	**70.0**	76.6	78.6	**74.7**

[23] perform well, but are inferior to our loss for both ResNet-56 and ResNet-110. Note that CB Focal [5] was designed for targeting class-imbalance in the training set. For CIFAR-100, since all classes have the same number of images, CB Focal performs as well as the Focal loss. The loss functions that operate on the hyper-sphere manifold [7,25,38] perform a bit lower which demonstrates the manifold assumption does not hold true for CIFAR-100.

ImageNet Classification: ImageNet [6] is a large-scale dataset for visual recognition. It contains ∼1.2 million training and 50,000 validation images.

We train ResNet-101 and ResNet-152 with the proposed loss. Basically, input image is random cropped to size of 224×224 by scale and aspect ratio. Following [40], an initial learning rate of 0.1 is used and dropped by a factor of 0.1 after every 30 epochs. We use a weight decay of 0.0001 and a momentum of 0.9. The training is terminated at 120 epochs. Training is conducted on 8 Tesla V100 GPUs, using a total batch size of 256. To make fair comparison, all models are trained under the same strategy, unless specifically stated.

Table 2 shows results of our loss on ImageNet. Though our loss is simple, it proves very effective for large-scale recognition task. By simply replacing the CE with HNC loss, the error rate is reduced by a margin of 1.1% on both ResNet-101 and ResNet-152. Our loss also outperforms the recently proposed LGM loss [36], which is based on the assumption that deep features follow a Gaussian Mixture distribution. Note that, similar to CIFAR-100, both variants of our loss give comparable results.

4.2 Multi-label Classification

We conduct multi-label classification experiments on MS-COCO dataset [24]. It contains 82,783 training and 40,504 validation images, annotated with 80 labels.

Since ground-truth labels are not available for the test set, we train our network on the training set and evaluate it on the validation set, following [15]. Our loss is tested on the official implementation of [15].

We follow the same training strategy as in [15]. Namely, an input size of 288 × 288 is used, and we fine-tune ResNet-101, pretrained on the ImageNet dataset. The initial learning rate is 0.001, and dropped with a factor 0.1 after 6 and 8 epochs. Following other works in multi-label classification [15,43], the evaluation metrics we choose are: mean Average Precision (mAP), as well as macro and micro precision/recall/F1-score (denoted as P-C, R-C, F1-C, P-O, R-O, F1-O, respectively). For details of these metrics, we refer to [43].

The performance comparisons between HNC and baselines are shown in Table 4. In terms of mAP, both HNC_{mse} and HNC_{kd} outperform the baselines. Specifically, for the baseline ResNet-101, HNC_{mse} achieves a gain of 2.9% in mAP. For the stronger baseline method named Attention Consistency (AC) [15], HNC_{mse} is also superior and achieves a 1.0% increment. Notably, the AC approach is also a loss working on the CAMs. It forces the transformed CAMs of original images to be consistent with the CAMs of the transformed images. Our loss is related to AC since both can reduce the over-fitting (due to redundancy) in the network. But AC does not explicitly consider the negative CAMs, which have many false activations and need to be suppressed.

Table 5. Performance comparison of our loss against FGSM attack with different perturbations (ϵ) on CIFAR-100 using ResNet-110 architecture.

ϵ	CE	Center loss [39]	**Ours** (HNC_{mse})	**Ours** (HNC_{kd})
0.05	14.55	14.76	23.92	**29.80**
0.1	9.89	10.42	17.20	**21.80**
0.2	6.15	7.17	11.01	**12.96**
0.3	3.79	5.54	6.90	**7.06**

Table 6. CIFAR-100 results with symmetric (a) and asymmetric (b) noise.

Noise type	r	0.2	0.4	0.6	0.8	Noise type	r	0.1	0.2	0.3	0.4
Symmetric	CE	51.98	38.76	22.48	9.16	Asymmetric	CE	63.10	56.60	49.33	40.89
	HNC_{mse}	**58.98**	**48.03**	**32.86**	**14.73**		HNC_{mse}	**67.18**	**62.91**	**56.12**	**46.51**
	HNC_{kd}	56.59	44.86	29.15	12.20		HNC_{kd}	65.33	59.72	51.98	43.04
(a)						(b)					

4.3 Fine-Grained Classification

For fine-grained classification, we evaluate our loss on the CUB-200-2011 dataset [35], which is widely used for this task. It contains 5,994 training and 5,794 test images, each of which belongs to one of 200 bird classes.

We fine-tune ResNet-50, which is pretrained on the ImageNet dataset. The initial learning rate is set to 0.001 and reduced by 0.1 after 50 epochs. A total batch size of 16 is used and the model is trained using 2 GPUs.

Table 3 shows the results of different losses with ResNet-50 on CUB-200-2011. Both HNC_{mse} and HNC_{kd} outperform the baseline (ResNet-50 with CE loss), by a margin of 1.1% and 0.9%, respectively. Remarkably, our proposed loss also outperforms other losses, including Center loss [39], and Focal loss [23].

4.4 Adversarial Robustness

Since our proposed loss suppresses negative CAMs, we anticipate this strategy to be helpful against adversarial attacks. Adversarial examples are generated by intentionally adding small but imperceptible perturbations to the inputs, which cause the model to make wrong predictions with high confidence [14]. We consider the most challenging attack case, i.e., the white-box attack, where all the model parameters and training details are known to the adversary. Specifically, we use the fast gradient sign method (FGSM) [14], which adopts the gradient back-propagated from the training loss to determine the direction of the perturbation. An adversarial example I^* is generated by: $I^* = I + \epsilon \cdot sign(\nabla_I L(I,l))$, where ϵ is the magnitude of perturbation, I is the input image, l is the ground-truth label for the input, and $L(I,l)$ is the classification loss function. We select $\epsilon \in \{0.05, 0.1, 0.2, 0.3\}$ for our experiments.

Table 5 shows performance of different losses under FGSM attack on CIFAR-100 with ResNet-110. We compare with Center loss and CE loss. For all considered ϵ, our loss is more robust than the others.

The higher robustness of HNC loss is potentially because it constraints the intermediate activations that have been shown to provide better deterrence against perturbations [28,41]. Interestingly, we found HNC_{kd} to be considerably better than HNC_{mse} in this task. This is primarily due to the reason that HNC_{mse} focuses on the outliers, thus adversarial noise that is generally low in strength can sneak in easily. In contrast, HNC_{kd} gives an equal penalty to all deviated negative CAM values, thus blocking away the maliciously crafted perturbations.

4.5 Learning from Noisy Labels

Here, we show the effectiveness of our loss for learning from noisy labels. This area has recently attracted lots of research attention. We test on CIFAR-100 using ResNet-110 following the training strategy described in Sect. 4.1. We use both the symmetric noise setting, where label noise is uniformly distributed among all categories with probability r, and asymmetric noise setting, where each ground-truth class is flipped to the next class circularly with probability r. Thus, $r \in [0,1]$ denotes the noise rate. Following [21], we choose r of 0.2, 0.4, 0.6, and 0.8 for symmetric noise, and r of 0.1, 0.2, 0.3, 0.4 for asymmetric noise. Following [45], we retain 10% of training data as validation set.

Table 7. Comparison between HNC and CE on various networks. Our loss outperforms baseline for all considered architectures.

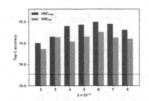

	Setting	CE	**Ours (HNC)**
ResNet-110	–	73.79	**75.00**
DenseNet-BC	$k = 12$, $d = 100$	77.32	**78.78**
ResNeXt-29	$c = 8$, $d = 64$	81.77	**82.32**
ResNeXt-29	$c = 16$, $d = 64$	81.98	**82.81**

Fig. 4. Top-1 accuracy of HNC for different λ. Dotted line shows the CE loss.

The results are shown in Table 6 where we report test accuracy of the last epoch. Our HNC loss outperforms the baseline (CE) with a large margin. Remarkably, for symmetric noise with noise rate 0.6, our loss obtains a absolute improvement of 10.38%, compared with the baseline.

4.6 Ablation Study

We conduct ablation studies on the CIFAR-100. Firstly, we show how λ, the factor balancing the CE and HNC, affects the accuracy. Figure 4 shows the change in performance with respect to λ. For both HNC_{mse} and HNC_{kd}, the effect of λ follows a similar trend. In the beginning, classification accuracy increases when λ is increased. This is potentially because the negative CAMs are more suppressed and thus become smoother when λ increases. However, after a certain threshold, the performance drops as λ is further increased. This is because with very large λ, the relative weight of the CE loss is lower and the network loses focus on classification task. For all considered values of λ, our loss outperforms the baseline (CE loss), which again validates the soundness of our proposal.

We also compare HNC performance across various architectures. Since HNC_{mse} and HNC_{kd} performs similarly, we compare HNC_{mse} with CE in Table 7. Our loss outperforms CE for different architectures, which shows its effectiveness.

4.7 Qualitative Results and Analysis

We show the qualitative results in Fig. 5. The main effect of our loss on CAMs can be summarized into two cases: (i) clearing the negative CAMs and locating a similar discriminative region as the baseline (top samples in Fig. 5); (ii) clearing the negative CAMs but locating a totally different and more discriminative region (below samples in Fig. 5). We conjecture that if our constraints can be satisfied when locating a similar region, the first case happens. However, if the positive class and negative classes are very difficult to separate, i.e. the relevant region located by the baseline is not discriminative enough, then the network is forced to find a different and more informative region to classify objects.

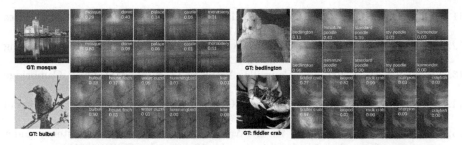

Fig. 5. Qualitative comparisons of CAMs between our method and baseline (CE), for images from ImageNet [6]. For each sample, we first show original image (left), followed by the CAMs of the baseline (top) and our loss (below). The CAMs follow the sequence: the positive CAM on left and then top-4 negative CAMs (ranked by the score). For each CAM, the class name and probability are shown in white. For all considered cases, our loss clears the negative CAMs, thus leading to the correct prediction.

5   Conclusion

In this paper, we propose a novel loss (HNC) to suppress false activations in the negative CAMs. Its effectiveness is demonstrated by extensive experiments on various tasks: generic image recognition, multi-label classification, fine-grained classification, adversarial robustness, and learning from noisy labels. We observe that our loss successfully clears the negative CAMs and leads to consistent visualizations and improved performance across all studied tasks.

References

1. Ahn, J., Cho, S., Kwak, S.: Weakly supervised learning of instance segmentation with inter-pixel relations. In: CVPR (2019)
2. Chen, H.Y., et al.: Improving adversarial robustness via guided complement entropy. In: ICCV (2019)
3. Choe, J., Oh, S.J., Lee, S., Chun, S., Akata, Z., Shim, H.: Evaluating weakly supervised object localization methods right. In: CVPR (2020)
4. Cholakkal, H., Sun, G., Khan, F.S., Shao, L.: Object counting and instance segmentation with image-level supervision. In: CVPR (2019)
5. Cui, Y., Jia, M., Lin, T.Y., Song, Y., Belongie, S.: Class-balanced loss based on effective number of samples. In: CVPR (2019)
6. Deng, J., Dong, W., Socher, R., Li, L.J., Li, K., Fei-Fei, L.: Imagenet: a large-scale hierarchical image database. In: CVPR (2009)
7. Deng, J., Guo, J., Xue, N., Zafeiriou, S.: Arcface: additive angular margin loss for deep face recognition. In: CVPR (2019)
8. Dong, Q., Gong, S., Zhu, X.: Class rectification hard mining for imbalanced deep learning. In: ICCV (2017)
9. Dosovitskiy, A., Brox, T.: Inverting visual representations with convolutional networks. In: CVPR (2016)
10. Dubey, A., Gupta, O., Raskar, R., Naik, N.: Maximum-entropy fine grained classification. In: NeurIPS (2018)

11. Erhan, D., Bengio, Y., Courville, A., Vincent, P.: Visualizing higher-layer features of a deep network. Univ. Montreal **1341**(3), 1 (2009)
12. Gong, Y., Jia, Y., Leung, T.K., Toshev, A., Ioffe, S.: Deep convolutional ranking for multi label image annotation. In: ICLR (2014)
13. Goodfellow, I., Bengio, Y., Courville, A.: Deep Learning. MIT press, Cambridge (2016)
14. Goodfellow, I.J., Shlens, J., Szegedy, C.: Explaining and harnessing adversarial examples. In: ICLR (2015)
15. Guo, H., Zheng, K., Fan, X., Yu, H., Wang, S.: Visual attention consistency under image transforms for multi-label image classification. In: CVPR (2019)
16. Hayat, M., Khan, S., Zamir, S.W., Shen, J., Shao, L.: Gaussian affinity for max-margin class imbalanced learning. In: ICCV (2019)
17. Huang, C., Li, Y., Change Loy, C., Tang, X.: Learning deep representation for imbalanced classification. In: CVPR (2016)
18. Khan, S.H., Hayat, M., Bennamoun, M., Sohel, F.A., Togneri, R.: Cost-sensitive learning of deep feature representations from imbalanced data. IEEE Trans. Neural Netw. Learn. Syst. **29**(8), 3573–3587 (2018)
19. Khan, S., Rahmani, H., Shah, S.A.A., Bennamoun, M.: A guide to convolutional neural networks for computer vision. Synth. Lect. Comput. Vis. **8**(1), 1–207 (2018)
20. Krizhevsky, A., Hinton, G., et al.: Learning multiple layers of features from tiny images. Technical report, Citeseer (2009)
21. Kun, Y., Jianxin, W.: Probabilistic end-to-end noise correction for learning with noisy labels. In: CVPR (2019)
22. Li, D., Chen, X., Huang, K.: Multi-attribute learning for pedestrian attribute recognition in surveillance scenarios. In: ACPR (2015)
23. Lin, T.Y., Goyal, P., Girshick, R., He, K., Dollár, P.: Focal loss for dense object detection. In: ICCV (2017)
24. Lin, T.Y., et al.: Microsoft COCO: common objects in context. In: Fleet, D., Pajdla, T., Schiele, B., Tuytelaars, T. (eds.) ECCV 2014. LNCS, vol. 8693, pp. 740–755. Springer, Cham (2014). https://doi.org/10.1007/978-3-319-10602-1_48
25. Liu, W., Wen, Y., Yu, Z., Li, M., Raj, B., Song, L.: Sphereface: deep hypersphere embedding for face recognition. In: CVPR (2017)
26. Liu, W., Wen, Y., Yu, Z., Yang, M.: Large-margin softmax loss for convolutional neural networks. In: ICML (2016)
27. Mahendran, A., Vedaldi, A.: Visualizing deep convolutional neural networks using natural pre-images. IJCV **120**(3), 233–255 (2016)
28. Mustafa, A., Khan, S., Hayat, M., Goecke, R., Shen, J., Shao, L.: Adversarial defense by restricting the hidden space of deep neural networks. In: ICCV (2019)
29. Ryou, S., Jeong, S.G., Perona, P.: Anchor loss: modulating loss scale based on prediction difficulty. In: ICCV (2019)
30. Schmidhuber, J.: Deep learning in neural networks: an overview. Neural Netw. **61**, 85–117 (2015)
31. Selvaraju, R.R., Cogswell, M., Das, A., Vedantam, R., Parikh, D., Batra, D.: Gradcam: visual explanations from deep networks via gradient-based localization. In: ICCV (2017)
32. Simonyan, K., Vedaldi, A., Zisserman, A.: Deep inside convolutional networks: Visualising image classification models and saliency maps. arXiv preprint arXiv:1312.6034 (2013)
33. Springenberg, J.T., Dosovitskiy, A., Brox, T., Riedmiller, M.: Striving for simplicity: The all convolutional net. arXiv preprint arXiv:1412.6806 (2014)

34. Sun, G., Wang, W., Dai, J., Van Gool, L.: Mining cross-image semantics for weakly supervised semantic segmentation. arXiv preprint (2020)
35. Wah, C., Branson, S., Welinder, P., Perona, P., Belongie, S.: The caltech-ucsd birds-200-2011 dataset (2011)
36. Wan, W., Zhong, Y., Li, T., Chen, J.: Rethinking feature distribution for loss functions in image classification. In: CVPR (2018)
37. Wang, F., Cheng, J., Liu, W., Liu, H.: Additive margin softmax for face verification. IEEE Signal Process. Lett. 25(7), 926–930 (2018)
38. Wang, H., et al.: Cosface: Large margin cosine loss for deep face recognition. In: CVPR (2018)
39. Wen, Y., Zhang, K., Li, Z., Qiao, Yu.: A discriminative feature learning approach for deep face recognition. In: Leibe, B., Matas, J., Sebe, N., Welling, M. (eds.) ECCV 2016. LNCS, vol. 9911, pp. 499–515. Springer, Cham (2016). https://doi.org/10.1007/978-3-319-46478-7_31
40. Woo, S., Park, J., Lee, J.Y., So Kweon, I.: Cbam: convolutional block attention module. In: ECCV (2018)
41. Xie, C., Wu, Y., Maaten, L.V.d., Yuille, A.L., He, K.: Feature denoising for improving adversarial robustness. In: CVPR (2019)
42. Zeiler, M.D., Fergus, R.: Visualizing and understanding convolutional networks. In: Fleet, D., Pajdla, T., Schiele, B., Tuytelaars, T. (eds.) ECCV 2014. LNCS, vol. 8689, pp. 818–833. Springer, Cham (2014). https://doi.org/10.1007/978-3-319-10590-1_53
43. Zhang, M.L., Zhou, Z.H.: A review on multi-label learning algorithms. TKDE 26(8), 1819–1837 (2013)
44. Zhang, Y., Gong, B., Shah, M.: Fast zero-shot image tagging. In: CVPR (2016)
45. Zhang, Z., Sabuncu, M.: Generalized cross entropy loss for training deep neural networks with noisy labels. In: NeurIPS (2018)
46. Zhou, B., Khosla, A.A.L., Oliva, A., Torralba, A.: Learning deep features for discriminative localization. In: CVPR (2016)
47. Zhou, Y., Zhu, Y., Ye, Q., Qiu, Q., Jiao, J.: Weakly supervised instance segmentation using class peak response. In: CVPR (2018)
48. Zhu, F., Li, H., Ouyang, W., Yu, N., Wang, X.: Learning spatial regularization with image-level supervisions for multi-label image classification. In: CVPR (2017)
49. Zhu, Y., Zhou, Y., Ye, Q., Qiu, Q., Jiao, J.: Soft proposal networks for weakly supervised object localization. In: ICCV (2017)

PatchPerPix for Instance Segmentation

Lisa Mais⑩, Peter Hirsch⑩, and Dagmar Kainmueller(✉)⑩

Berlin Institute of Health/Max-Delbrueck-Center for Molecular Medicine
in the Helmholtz Association, Berlin, Germany
{lisa.mais,peter.hirsch,dagmar.kainmueller}@mdc-berlin.de

Abstract. We present a novel method for proposal free instance segmentation that can handle sophisticated object shapes which span large parts of an image and form dense object clusters with crossovers. Our method is based on predicting dense local shape descriptors, which we assemble to form instances. All instances are assembled simultaneously in one go. To our knowledge, our method is the first non-iterative method that yields instances that are composed of learnt shape patches. We evaluate our method on a diverse range of data domains, where it defines the new state of the art on four benchmarks, namely the ISBI 2012 EM segmentation benchmark, the BBBC010 C. elegans dataset, and 2d as well as 3d fluorescence microscopy data of cell nuclei. We show furthermore that our method also applies to 3d light microscopy data of Drosophila neurons, which exhibit extreme cases of complex shape clusters.

1 Introduction

The task of instance segmentation has a wide range of applications in natural images as well as microscopy images from the biomedical domain. A prevalent class of instance segmentation methods, namely proposal-based methods based on RCNN [10,11], has proven successful in cases where instance location and size can be well-approximated by bounding boxes. However, in many cases, especially in the biomedical domain, this does not hold: Instances may span widely across the image, and hence multiple instances may have very similar, large bounding boxes. To complicate things, instances may be densely clustered, in some cases overlapping, including crossovers. Proposal-free methods are applicable in such cases, where popular choices include metric learning/instance coloring [4,7,17, 18], affinity-based methods [8,9,20,30], and learnt watershed [3,31]. However, respective pixel-wise predictions do not explicitly capture instance shape, nor are they suitable for disentangling overlapping instances.

L. Mais and P. Hirsch—Contributed equally, listed in random order.
Code available: https://github.com/Kainmueller-Lab/PatchPerPix.

Electronic supplementary material The online version of this chapter (https:// doi.org/10.1007/978-3-030-58595-2_18) contains supplementary material, which is available to authorized users.

© Springer Nature Switzerland AG 2020
A. Vedaldi et al. (Eds.): ECCV 2020, LNCS 12370, pp. 288–304, 2020.
https://doi.org/10.1007/978-3-030-58595-2_18

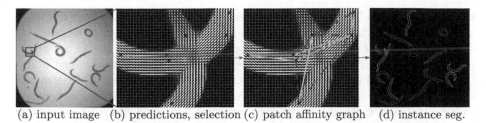

(a) input image   (b) predictions, selection (c) patch affinity graph   (d) instance seg.

Fig. 1. PatchPerPix overview. Given the raw input image (a), a CNN predicts dense patches for each pixel (b, best seen with zoom) which are then used to find a consensus for each pair of pixels within the patch size. The patches that best agree with this consensus are selected (shown in red in b) and connected to form a patch affinity graph. (c) Edges of the patch affinity graph are assigned scores derived from the agreement of the *merged* shape patches with the consensus. The final instance segmentation (d) is obtained by signed graph partitioning. Shown in (c,d) is the result of connected component analysis on the positive subgraph, where edges with negative scores are depicted in red. (Color figure online)

To overcome these limitations, we propose to (1) densely predict representations of the shapes of instance patches, (2) cover the image foreground with the most plausible shape patches, and (3) puzzle together complete instance shapes from these patches by means of partitioning a patch affinity graph. The approach of covering the image by selecting from a redundant set of instance patch predictions allows for naturally handling overlap (including crossovers), as overlapping instance patches can be selected, potentially resulting in pixels covered by multiple instances.

Our general idea is closely related to Singling Out Networks [32]. However, they are different in that they rely on a dictionary of known instances, thereby limiting the variability of objects they can handle, and they only consider predicting whole instances and not patches of instances, thereby limiting the size of feasible object categories.

Our shape prediction network predicts, for each pixel of the input image, a representation of the local shape of the instance this pixel belongs to, namely a *shape patch* of the pixel's instance. The architecture we propose is derived from the U-Net [26], thus allowing for efficient dense prediction. As representations of instance patch shapes, we explore local binary masks, as well as encodings (i.e. compressed versions) of these. The idea of predicting instance shape masks per pixel of an image has been pursued before [5,6,15]. However, all these approaches work on the assumption that a shape mask can capture a complete instance shape. Thus they are designed for object categories common to natural images rather than for disentangling clusters of complex shapes that occupy similar bounding boxes, as relevant in the biomedical domain. Predicting shape encodings instead of binary masks is also not new [15]. However, besides only considering complete instance shapes as opposed to our patches of instances, in [15], shape encoding and respective decoder are trained separately, where we show in our work that end-to-end training yields considerable improvement.

The variant of our method that predicts local binary masks as shape representations is closely related to methods that employ long-range affinities [9,16,20,30]. In essence, our predicted binary patches can be interpreted as dense affinities in a neighborhood around each pixel. However, in contrast to affinity-based methods, we instead interpret our predictions as patches of instances, from which we puzzle together complete instances. This way, our yielded global instance shapes are assembled from *learned shape patches*, a property that does not hold for affinity-based methods. Note that in this respect, our method is related to CELIS [23], which learns to agglomerate super-pixels to form instances with plausible shapes, yet their initial pixel-wise predictions do not capture object shape. Furthermore, our method is related to Flood Filling Networks [13], an iterative method that learns to expand instances one-by-one. In contrast, our method segments all instances simultaneously in one pass.

We show in a quantitative evaluation that our method is the new state of the art on the ISBI 2012 challenge on segmentation of neuronal structures in EM stacks [1], outperforms the previous state of the art [17,25,32] on the BBBC010 benchmark dataset of worm images [28] by a large margin, and also outperforms the state of the art [12,27,29] on 2d and 3d light microscopy images of densely packed cell nuclei. Last but not least, we demonstrate that our method also applies to the complex tree-like shapes of neurons in 3d light microscopy images.

In summary, our contributions are:

- A novel method for segmenting instances of complex shapes that spread widely across an image in crowded scenarios, with overlaps and crossovers.
- Instance segmentations are assembled from learnt shape pieces. Our method is, to our knowledge, the first such method that is not iterative, i.e. we compute all instances in one pass.
- Our method defines the new state of the art on the competitive ISBI 2012 EM segmentation challenge, considerably outperforms the state of the art on the challenging BBBC010 C. elegans dataset, and also defines the new state of the art on 2d and 3d benchmark data of cell nuclei.

2   PatchPerPix for Instance Segmentation

We train a CNN to predict dense local shape patches, from which we assemble all instances in an image simultaneously in a one-pass pipeline. Figure 1 and Suppl. Fig. 5 provide an overview of our proposed method, which we term *PatchPerPix*.

Formally, our CNN yields an estimate $p \colon \mathrm{Dom}(I) \times \mathcal{P} \to [0, 1]$ of the function

$$p^* \colon \mathrm{Dom}(I) \times \mathcal{P} \to \{0, 1\}$$

$$(\mathbf{x}, \mathbf{dx}) \mapsto \begin{cases} 1 \text{ if Instance}(\mathbf{x}) = \text{Instance}(\mathbf{x} + \mathbf{dx}) \text{ and } \mathbf{x}, \mathbf{x} + \mathbf{dx} \in \mathrm{fg}(I) \\ 0 \text{ otherwise} \end{cases}$$

that captures, for each pixel $\mathbf{x} \in \mathcal{R}^d$ in the foreground fg(I) of a d-dimensional image I, and each pixel $\mathbf{x} + \mathbf{dx}$ at a fixed, dense set of offsets $\mathcal{P} \subset \mathcal{R}^d$, whether $\mathbf{x}$ and $\mathbf{x} + \mathbf{dx}$ belong to the same instance.

Section 2.1 describes our proposed instance assembly pipeline given the estimated function p. Section 2.2 describes the CNN architectures we explore to yield p.

2.1   Instance Assembly

We denote a restriction of the estimated function p to a single pixel as

$$p_{\mathbf{x}} \colon \mathbf{x} + \mathcal{P} \to [0, 1], \ \mathbf{y} \mapsto p(\mathbf{x}, \mathbf{y} - \mathbf{x})$$

We denote the domain of $p_{\mathbf{x}}$ as patch$(p_{\mathbf{x}}) := \mathbf{x} + \mathcal{P}$. For each patch, the pixels that are predicted to belong to the same instance as $\mathbf{x}$ by means of a probability threshold t, i.e. the pixels classified as foreground w.r.t. the instance at $\mathbf{x}$, are denoted as

$$\mathrm{fg}(p_{\mathbf{x}}) := \{\mathbf{y} \in \mathrm{patch}(p_{\mathbf{x}}) : p_{\mathbf{x}}(\mathbf{y}) > t\}, \tag{1}$$

and, accordingly, the respective background pixels as

$$\mathrm{bg}(p_{\mathbf{x}}) := \{\mathbf{y} \in \mathrm{patch}(p_{\mathbf{x}}) : p_{\mathbf{x}}(\mathbf{y}) < 1 - t\}. \tag{2}$$

For each pixel pair $(\mathbf{y}, \mathbf{z})$ covered by at least one informative patch, i.e. $\exists \mathbf{x} \in \mathrm{Dom}(I) : \{\mathbf{y}, \mathbf{z}\} \subset \mathrm{patch}(p_{\mathbf{x}}) \wedge \{\mathbf{y}, \mathbf{z}\} \cap \mathrm{fg}(p_{\mathbf{x}}) \neq \emptyset$, summing up observations from all patches yields a consensus that $\mathbf{y}$ and $\mathbf{z}$ belong to the same instance, i.e. a consensus affinity

$$\mathrm{aff}(\mathbf{y}, \mathbf{z}) := \frac{1}{Z_{\mathrm{aff}}(\mathbf{y}, \mathbf{z})} \cdot \Big(\sum_{\substack{\mathbf{x} \in \mathrm{Dom}(I): \\ \{\mathbf{y}, \mathbf{z}\} \subset \mathrm{fg}(p_{\mathbf{x}})}} p_{\mathbf{x}}(\mathbf{y}) \cdot p_{\mathbf{x}}(\mathbf{z})$$

$$- \sum_{\substack{\mathbf{x} \in \mathrm{Dom}(I): \\ \mathbf{y} \in \mathrm{fg}(p_{\mathbf{x}}), \mathbf{z} \in \mathrm{bg}(p_{\mathbf{x}})}} p_{\mathbf{x}}(\mathbf{y}) \cdot (1 - p_{\mathbf{x}}(\mathbf{z})) - \sum_{\substack{\mathbf{x} \in \mathrm{Dom}(I): \\ \mathbf{y} \in \mathrm{bg}(p_{\mathbf{x}}), \mathbf{z} \in \mathrm{fg}(p_{\mathbf{x}})}} (1 - p_{\mathbf{x}}(\mathbf{y})) \cdot p_{\mathbf{x}}(\mathbf{z}) \Big)$$

$$\tag{3}$$

with normalization factor

$$Z_{\mathrm{aff}}(\mathbf{y}, \mathbf{z}) := |\{\mathbf{x} \in \mathrm{Dom}(I) : \{\mathbf{y}, \mathbf{z}\} \subset \mathrm{patch}(p_{\mathbf{x}}) \wedge \{\mathbf{y}, \mathbf{z}\} \cap \mathrm{fg}(p_{\mathbf{x}}) \neq \emptyset\}|. \tag{4}$$

Given these consensus affinities, we define a score for each patch with non-empty foreground by assessing how well it agrees with the consensus:

$$\mathrm{score}(p_{\mathbf{x}}) := \frac{1}{Z_{\mathrm{score}}(p_{\mathbf{x}})} \cdot \Big(\sum_{\{\mathbf{y}, \mathbf{z}\} \subset \mathrm{fg}(p_{\mathbf{x}})} \mathrm{aff}(\mathbf{y}, \mathbf{z}) - \sum_{\substack{\mathbf{y} \in \mathrm{fg}(p_{\mathbf{x}}), \\ \mathbf{z} \in \mathrm{bg}(p_{\mathbf{x}})}} \mathrm{aff}(\mathbf{y}, \mathbf{z}) \Big) \tag{5}$$

with normalization factor

$$Z_{\mathrm{score}}(p_{\mathbf{x}}) := |\{\{\mathbf{y}, \mathbf{z}\} \subset \mathrm{patch}(p_{\mathbf{x}}) : \{\mathbf{y}, \mathbf{z}\} \cap \mathrm{fg}(p_{\mathbf{x}}) \neq \emptyset\}|.$$

We rank all patches w.r.t. their score (Eq. 5). We employ a greedy set cover algorithm to select high-ranking patches whose patch foregrounds $\mathrm{fg}(p_\mathbf{x})$ fully cover the image foreground $\mathrm{fg}(I)$. Section 2.2 describes how we obtain the image foreground. In more detail, the set cover algorithm proceeds as follows: Iterating from high to low score over the ranked list of patches, we pre-select patches if they cover previously uncovered image foreground, until the image foreground is fully covered. We further thin out this pre-selection as follows: We iteratively select as next patch from the pre-selection the patch that covers the most remaining foreground, until the whole foreground is covered.

Given this selection of high-ranking patches, the consensus affinities (Eq. 3) allow us to define a score that measures for a *pair of patches* whether they belong to the same instance, i.e. a consensus affinity between $p_\mathbf{x}$ and $p_\mathbf{y}$:

$$\mathrm{paff}(p_\mathbf{x}, p_\mathbf{y}) := \frac{1}{Z_{\mathrm{paff}}(p_\mathbf{x}, p_\mathbf{y})} \cdot \sum_{\substack{\mathbf{v} \in \mathrm{fg}(p_\mathbf{x}), \\ \mathbf{w} \in \mathrm{fg}(p_\mathbf{y})}} \mathrm{aff}(\mathbf{v}, \mathbf{w}) \tag{6}$$

with normalization factor

$$Z_{\mathrm{paff}}(p_\mathbf{x}, p_\mathbf{y}) := |\{\mathbf{v} \in \mathrm{fg}(p_\mathbf{x}), \mathbf{w} \in \mathrm{fg}(p_\mathbf{y}) :$$
$$\exists \mathbf{z} : \{\mathbf{v}, \mathbf{w}\} \subset \mathrm{patch}(p_\mathbf{z}) \wedge \{\mathbf{v}, \mathbf{w}\} \cap \mathrm{fg}(p_\mathbf{z}) \neq \emptyset\}|.$$

We compute patch pair affinities (Eq. 6) between selected high-ranking patches iff the respective $Z_{\mathrm{paff}}(\cdot, \cdot) > 0$, yielding a patch affinity graph. We partition this graph via connected component analysis on the positive subgraph, or alternatively by means of the mutex watershed algorithm [30], depending on the application domain. We obtain the final instance segmentation by assigning, per connected component, a unique instance ID to all pixels contained in the union of the respective patch foregrounds. Note that in general, this may assign multiple instance IDs to some pixels, which is desired in some, but not all, applications. In case overlapping instances are not desired, we assign the ID of the patch prediction with highest probability at the respective pixel.

We implemented the computationally expensive parts of our instance assembly pipeline in CUDA for efficient execution. In applications with sparse image foreground, we further improve computational efficiency by restricting $\mathrm{patch}(p_\mathbf{x})$ to the image foreground, i.e. $\mathrm{patch}_{\mathrm{sparse}}(p_\mathbf{x}) := \mathrm{patch}(p_\mathbf{x}) \cap \mathrm{fg}(I)$.

2.2   CNN Architecture

We train a deep convolutional neural network to predict the function p. It does so by predicting $p_\mathbf{x}(\mathbf{x} + \mathcal{P})$ for each pixel of the input image. Thus the cardinality of the set $\mathcal{P}$ determines the number of output channels of the network. We train the network w.r.t. standard cross-entropy loss averaged over all outputs. We use a U-Net [26] as backbone architecture. To facilitate predictions of shape representations with hundreds of dimensions, we keep the number of feature maps fixed (instead of reducing) in the upward path of the U-Net. Thus we

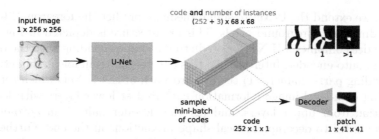

Fig. 2. ppp+dec architecture: A U-Net predicts shape patch encodings, which are fed into the decoding path of an auto-encoder. Additional outputs of the U-Net predict the number of instances at each pixel. U-Net and decoder are trained jointly end-to-end. Categorical cross-entropy is used for the number of instances, and binary cross-entropy for the patch predictions. Both losses are summed up without weighting. The batch of codes that is run through the decoder is sampled from pixels for which the number of instances is predicted to be 1.

avoid having to predict high-dimensional pixel-wise outputs from only tens of feature maps as present in the penultimate layer of a standard U-Net.

Our baseline PatchPerPix architecture, termed **ppp**, is a U-Net that directly outputs $p_\mathbf{x}$ at each pixel $\mathbf{x}$ of the input image I. To estimate the image foreground $fg(I)$, we include offset $\mathbf{0}$ in $\mathcal{P}$. A practical issue with ppp is that the size of the predicted patches, i.e. the number of outputs of the U-Net, is limited by GPU memory. Furthermore, in most application domains, the variety of possible patch predictions, and hence the amount of information contained in each, is limited. Therefore, in addition to our baseline model, we explore two variants that learn compressed representations of $p_\mathbf{x}$ and decode these via (1) the decoder part of a separately trained autoencoder (ppp+ae), and (2) a decoder that is trained end-to-end with the backbone U-Net (ppp+dec), as described in the following.

ppp+ae. In a separate first step, we train a fully convolutional autoencoder on patches of ground truth binary masks to learn a patch latent space. The backbone U-Net is then trained to regress a respective learnt latent vector (a.k.a. "encoding" or "code") for each pixel of the input image w.r.t. sum of squared differences loss. To de-compress patch predictions for our instance assembly pipeline, the decoder part of the pre-trained autoencoder is employed. We add an extra output channel to the U-Net to predict a foreground mask, trained w.r.t. cross-entropy loss and added to the code loss without any weighting. Codes are decoded for all foreground pixels obtained by thresholding the foreground mask.

ppp+dec. Here, we attach the decoder part of the autoencoder used in ppp+ae to the end of the U-Net and train the resulting joint network end-to-end from scratch w.r.t. cross-entropy. As before, the U-Net part of the network outputs the code. However, there is no loss employed directly on the code. To fit end-to-end training onto GPU memory, we sample codes from ground truth foreground pixels at training time, which are then fed to the decoder network. Similarly to ppp+ae, we extend the U-Net to simultaneously predict the foreground to allow for decoding only foreground pixels. This architecture is depicted in Fig. 2.

ppp+dec combines a U-Net for predicting a shape encoding with the decoder part of an auto-encoder. Interestingly, this end-to-end trainable architecture has two decoding parts, namely (1) the upward path of the U-Net, which serves for combining high-level image information captured at lower layers with low-level information from upper layers, and (2) the decoder half of an auto-encoder, which is needed to decompress local shape predictions in the end. Furthermore, especially when dealing with sparse data, the U-Net performs many dispensable computations, namely on background pixels. Hence we investigated whether our proposed architecture could be replaced by a standard encoder-decoder architecture alone, with one encoding and one decoding path, like e.g. [2], as follows:

ed-ppp. Our architecture takes an image patch the size of our shape patches plus some surrounding receptive field as input, and generates a shape patch for the respective central pixel's instance as output. It is applied in a sliding window fashion on all pixels in the image foreground. We use 3×3 down- and upsampling to facilitate the singling out of the center pixel's instance from its neighboring instances. To determine for which pixels to run the encoder-decoder network, we train a separate U-Net to generate a foreground mask in a preceding step.

2.3   Overlapping Regions

The case of multiple objects sharing pixels can be found in many biomedical applications, e.g. in 2d images of model organisms such as worms that crawl on top of each other, or neurons in light microscopy data that share pixels due to the partial volume effect. As pixels located in areas of overlap belong to multiple instances, their respective shape patch is not well-defined. Hence we exclude these pixels from the entire pipeline. During training, we achieve this by masking out these areas in the loss computation. To detect overlap at test time, we predict the number of instances per pixel by extending the foreground classification task by an "overlap" class, which, as before, is trained jointly with the patch predictions by means of added cross-entropy loss. This information is then used in the instance assembly: Pixels in overlapping regions are discarded, i.e. their respective shape patches do not contribute to the consensus and cannot be selected. This constitutes a limitation of our method in that (i) only overlapping regions with a maximum diameter of smaller than the size of the patches can be covered completely by patch shapes, and (ii) only occlusions within the range of the neighborhood used in the patch graph generation can be bridged.

3   Results

We evaluate our method on four benchmark datasets, which comprise overlapping objects, sophisticated object shapes, and, to show the generic applicability of our method, also simple object shapes. The first dataset, the BBBC010 C.

elegans dataset [21], exhibits clusters of overlapping objects with large, coinciding bounding boxes. The second dataset, the ISBI 2012 Challenge on segmenting neuronal structures in electron microscopy [1], exhibits densely clustered objects with sophisticated shapes that span the whole image, albeit without overlaps. The third and fourth dataset exhibit densely clustered objects of simple, approximately ellipsoidal shapes, namely 2d and 3d fluorescence light microscopy datasets of cell nuclei [27,29]. Our results define the new state of the art in all cases, as detailed in Sects. 3.1, 3.2, and 3.3. Furthermore, we study the impact of individual steps of our instance assembly pipeline as well as our proposed network architecture designs on BBBC010. Last, we show promising qualitative results on 3d light microscopy data of neurons, which exhibit extreme cases of sophisticated object shapes that form dense clusters with overlaps (Sect. 3.4).

3.1 BBBC010 C. Elegans Worm Disentanglement

The **BBBC010** dataset from the Broad Bioimage Benchmark Collection [21][1] consists of 100 brightfield microscopy images showing multiple C. elegans worms per image, which may overlap and cluster. As ground truth, to capture overlaps correctly, BBBC010 provides an individual binary mask for each worm.

In this Section, we report a quantitative evaluation of our method in comparison with related work [17,25,32]. Furthermore, we report a comparison of the neural network architecture designs we explored, as well as an ablation study that assesses the impact of individual steps of our instance assembly pipeline. Patch- and code-size hyperparameters are studied in the Supplement. We report results in terms of the AP_{dsb} metric used in the kaggle 2018 data science bowl, which takes both missing and spurious instances into account[2]. We also report a range of additional metrics that have been reported for competing approaches, including the slightly different AP_{COCO}, thus enabling direct comparability.

As backbone CNN architecture we employ a 4-level U-Net [26] starting with 40 feature maps, with two-fold down- and upsampling operations, and constant number of feature maps during upsampling. Our network takes raw brightfield images as sole input, while [17,25,32] additionally exploit ground truth segmentations of the image foreground as input. In the ppp architecture, we employ a patch size of 25×25, yielding a U-Net with 625 outputs. In the ppp+ae and ppp+dec architectures, we employ a code of size 252 as intermediate output of the U-Net, which is then fed into a decoder network to yield a patch of size 41×41. The ed-ppp architecture takes 81×81 patches of the raw image as input and predicts 41×41 shape patches. It applies 3×3 max-pooling three times, and has two convolutional layers on each level. At the bottleneck, the code has an extent of $3 \times 3 \times 256$ and uses 1×1 convolutions. The network is symmetric and uses same padding. The output is cropped to obtain the desired patch shape.

As in related work [17,25,32], we divide the BBBC010 dataset into training- and test set with 50 images each. We apply 2-fold cross-validation on the test set

---

[1] BBBC010v1: C.elegans infection live/dead image set version 1 provided by Fred Ausubel.

[2] https://www.kaggle.com/c/data-science-bowl-2018.

Table 1. Quantitative results on the BBBC010 dataset. Top: We compare to competing approaches in various metrics due to a missing standard: [17,25] report COCO metrics [19], [32] plot the recall for different thresholds, [28] evaluate the percentage of ground truth worms which are matched with pixelwise F1 score above 0.8. Bottom: Results for the architecture setups we explored.

BBBC010						
AP_{COCO}	$avAP_{[0.5:0.05:0.95]}$	$AP_{0.5}$	$AP_{0.75}$	$Recall_{0.5}$	$Recall_{0.8}$	$F1_{0.8}$
Semi-conv Ops [25]	0.569	0.885	0.661	–	–	–
SON [32]	–	–	–	~ 0.97	~ 0.7	–
WormToolbox [28]	–	–	–	–	–	0.81
Harmonic Emb. [17]	0.724	0.900	0.723	–	–	–
PatchPerPix (ppp+dec)	**0.775**	**0.939**	**0.891**	**0.987**	**0.895**	**0.978**
AP_{dsb}	$avAP_{[0.5:0.05:0.95]}$	$AP_{0.5}$	$AP_{0.6}$	$AP_{0.7}$	$AP_{0.8}$	$AP_{0.9}$
ppp	0.689	0.890	0.872	0.840	0.710	0.372
ppp+ae	0.617	0.878	0.831	0.783	0.610	0.199
ppp+dec	**0.727**	**0.930**	**0.905**	**0.879**	**0.792**	**0.386**
ed-ppp	0.675	0.891	0.853	0.820	0.734	0.309

to determine the number of training steps and the patch foreground threshold t (Eq. 1), individually in all experiments. For training, we use standard augmentation including elastic deformations in all experiments. Contrary to [32], we do not augment the number of worms synthetically, but focus on crowded regions during training. For patch graph partitioning, we explore connected component analysis on the positive subgraph (CC) as well as the mutex watershed (MWS) [30]. In our result tables, MWS is the default if not noted otherwise.

Table 1 compares state-of-the-art methods [17,25,32] and PatchPerPix variants. Table 2 lists results of our ablation study. Figure 3 shows exemplary Patch-PerPix results for different CNN architectures. Suppl. Fig. 1 compares Patch-PerPix with Singling Out Networks [32] on an exemplary image.

PatchPerPix improves over competing methods by a considerable margin (cf. Table 1, top). Singling Out Networks (SON [32]) are of limited pixel accuracy by design, hence superior performance of PatchPerPix at high IoU thresholds is no surprise. However, PatchPerPix is not just more pixel accurate, but outperforms SON across the IoU threshold range. PatchPerPix also outperforms Harmonic Embeddings [17], a metric learning variant that amends the restricted pixel accuracy of SON, yet struggles at disentangling dense clusters of worms.

Interestingly, ppp+dec does not just outperform the separately trained ppp+ae, but also outperforms ed+ppp. I.e., *using a full U-Net as an encoder,* followed by a standard decoder, considerably outperforms a standard encoder-decoder architecture applied in a sliding-window fashion (cf. Table 1, bottom).

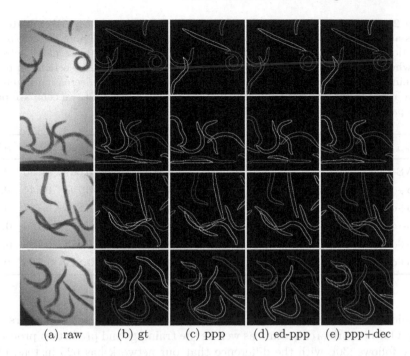

(a) raw   (b) gt   (c) ppp   (d) ed-ppp   (e) ppp+dec

Fig. 3. Qualitative results for exemplary challenging regions of the BBBC010 dataset. All architectures are able to handle crowded and overlapping regions, where ppp+dec yields fewest errors. However, rare shapes such as very bent worms are segmented with slightly higher accuracy by ppp.

Our ablation study (Table 2) shows the significant impact of two core ideas of our instance assembly pipeline, namely consensus affinity computation (absent in MWS-Dense, avAP -0.176) and selecting a sparse set of high-ranking patch predictions while weeding out low-ranking ones by means of consensus agreement scores (absent in ppp+dec w/o selection, avAP - 0.131). These scores correlate significantly with true patch quality (cf. Suppl. Fig. 4). Thinning out a pre-selection of high ranking patches has a small impact on accuracy (ppp+dec w/o thinout, avAP - 0.004), yet also positively affects run-time. Patch graph partitioning via CC vs. MWS are on a par on the BBBC010 data.

Suppl. Fig. 2 shows exemplary failure cases of ppp+dec. Interestingly, strongly bent worms are captured with inferior pixel accuracy by our encoding-based model ppp+dec as opposed to ppp (see Suppl. Fig. 2 right and Fig. 3 top row).

3.2 ISBI 2012 Neuron EM Segmentation

We evaluate our method on the ISBI 2012 Challenge on segmenting neuronal structures in electron microscopy (EM) data [1]. The data consists of 30 slices of 512×512 pixels with known ground truth (training data), and another 30

Table 2. Ablation study for PatchPerPix on the BBBC010 dataset. We ablate consensus affinity computation as a whole by running graph partitioning directly on the predictions p interpreted as dense affinities (MWS-Dense). We ablate patch selection as a whole (ppp+dec w/o selection), and thinning of the patch selection (ppp+dec w/o thinout). We run ppp+dec with a standard U-Net, i.e. with decreasing number of feature maps in the up-sampling path (ppp+dec std U-Net). Last, we compare patch graph partitioning with CC vs. MWS.

AP_{dsb}	$avAP_{[0.5:0.05:0.95]}$	$AP_{0.5}$	$AP_{0.6}$	$AP_{0.7}$	$AP_{0.8}$	$AP_{0.9}$
MWS-Dense	0.551	0.687	0.676	0.661	0.586	0.326
ppp+dec w/o selection	0.596	0.878	0.853	0.798	0.544	0.157
ppp+dec w/o thinout	0.723	0.924	0.898	0.871	0.788	0.393
ppp+dec std U-Net	0.719	0.916	0.891	0.873	0.766	**0.406**
ppp+dec, CC	0.723	0.922	0.894	0.873	0.780	**0.406**
ppp+dec, MWS	**0.727**	**0.930**	**0.905**	**0.879**	**0.792**	0.386

such slices for which ground truth is kept secret by the Challenge organizers (test data). Our network architecture as well as the training- and prediction procedure closely follows [30], with the difference that our network has 625 instead of 17 outputs, namely patches of size $1 \times 25 \times 25$, and we do not reduce the number of filters in the upward path of the U-Net. For partitioning the patch graph, we use the mutex watershed algorithm [30], which has proven powerful in avoiding false mergers in case of missing neuron membrane signal in the image data.

Our method is the leading entry on the Challenge's leaderboard[3] at present among thousands of submissions by more than 200 teams. Table 3 lists results obtained with PatchPerPix in terms of the Challenge error metrics, robust Rand score (rRAND) and robust information theoretic measure (rINF), evaluated on the test data. For comparison, the table also lists the previous state of the art as obtained via sparse affinity predictions processed with the mutex watershed algorithm [30] (MWS). Furthermore, as an additional baseline, we interpreted our patch predictions as dense affinities which we processed with the mutex watershed algorithm as in [30] (MWS-Dense). PatchPerPix slightly outperforms MWS in terms of the leaderboard-defining rRAND score. This can be attributed to fewer mistakes on large neuronal bodies which have respective large impact on the rRAND score. However, the number of such large mistakes we were able to identify by eye on the test set is very small in both approaches.

Interestingly, MWS-Dense performs considerably worse than both PatchPer-Pix and MWS. The difference between MWS-Dense and PatchPerPix can be attributed to individual erroneous predictions causing errors in MWS-Dense, which are amended in PatchPerPix by our proposed consensus voting and patch selection scheme. As for the difference between MWS-Dense and MWS, we hypothesize that this is due to MWS smartly distinguishing between purely

---

[3] http://brainiac2.mit.edu/isbi_challenge/leaders-board-new.

Table 3. Quantitative results for the ISBI 2012 Challenge on segmenting neuronal structures in electron microscopy data [1]. PatchPerPix defines the current state-of-the-art in terms of the leaderboard-defining rRAND score.

ISBI2012	rRAND	rINF
PatchPerPix	**0.988290**	0.991544
MWS [30]	0.987922	**0.991833**
MWS-Dense	0.979112	0.989625

attractive short-range- and purely repulsive long-range affinities. Instead, MWS-Dense treats all affinities as both attractive and repulsive.

3.3 Nuclei Segmentation in 2d and 3d

We evaluate our method on 2d and 3d fluorescence microscopy images of cell nuclei. The 2d dataset is a subset of the kaggle 2018 data science bowl[4] as defined in [27]. It consists of 380 training, 67 validation and 50 test images. We refer to this dataset as **dsb2018**. The 3d dataset consists of 28 confocal microscopy images collected and annotated by [22]. Image size is approximately $140 \times 140 \times 1100$ pixels. Each image shows hundreds of nuclei, with multiple dense clusters. An example is shown in Suppl. Fig. 3. We partition the data as in [12,29], with 18 images for training, 3 for validation, and 7 for testing. We refer to this dataset as **nuclei3d**.

For dsb2018, our CNN architecture is a 4-level U-Net, with 40 initial feature maps, that predicts foreground/background labels as well as codes of size 256, decoded into patches of size 25×25. We determine the number of training steps as well as the patch threshold on the validation set. For nuclei3d, we employ a 3-level 3d U-Net with 20 initial feature maps, tripled after each downsampling step. We predict patches of size $9 \times 9 \times 9$. We filter out instances smaller than a threshold. We determine the number of training steps, the patch threshold, and the instance size threshold on the validation set.

Table 4 lists our results in comparison to the previous state of the art on this data [12,27,29]. We furthermore compare to MALA [8], an affinity-based instance segmentation method trained with a structured loss, which is an established baseline for a different kind of 3d data, namely 3d electron microscopy of neuronal structures, but does not explicitly capture instance shape. For MALA, we employ the same backbone U-Net as for PatchPerPix for a fair comparison.

Superior avAP of PatchPerPix compared to [27,29] can be attributed to superior performance at high IoU thresholds, where StarDist's pixel accuracy is limited due to its coarse polyhedral shape representation, especially in 3d. We list IoU thresholds down to 0.1 as in [29], indicating that PatchPerPix is on a par with StarDist in terms of topological segmentation errors like false splits and

---

[4] BBBC038v1: available from the Broad Bioimage Benchmark Collection [21].

Table 4. Quantitative results for the nuclei datasets dsb2018 and nuclei3d. We report average precision (AP_{dsb}) for multiple IoU thresholds.

AP_{dsb}	avAP [0.5:0.1:0.9]	$AP_{0.1}$	$AP_{0.2}$	$AP_{0.3}$	$AP_{0.4}$	$AP_{0.5}$	$AP_{0.6}$	$AP_{0.7}$	$AP_{0.8}$	$AP_{0.9}$
				dsb2018						
Mask R-CNN[27]	0.594	-	-	-	-	0.832	0.773	0.684	0.489	0.189
StarDist[27]	0.584	-	-	-	-	0.864	0.804	0.685	0.450	0.119
PatchPerPix	**0.693**	**0.919**	**0.919**	**0.915**	**0.898**	**0.868**	**0.827**	**0.755**	**0.635**	**0.379**
				nuclei3d						
MALA [8]	0.381	0.895	0.887	0.859	0.803	0.699	0.605	0.424	0.166	0.012
StarDist 3D[29]	0.406	0.936	0.926	0.905	**0.855**	0.765	0.647	0.460	0.154	0.004
3-label+cpv[12]	0.425	**0.937**	**0.930**	**0.907**	0.848	0.750	0.641	0.473	0.224	**0.035**
PatchPerPix	**0.436**	0.926	0.918	0.900	0.853	**0.766**	**0.668**	**0.493**	**0.228**	0.027

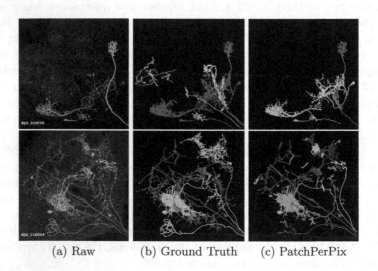

(a) Raw   (b) Ground Truth   (c) PatchPerPix

Fig. 4. Qualitative results on 3d neuron light microscopy examples. (a) Maximum intensity projection of raw images. Orange circles indicate overlapping areas in 3d. Ground truth data (b) were generated by manual segmentation using VVD Viewer. PatchPerPix (c) shows promising results on this challenging dataset. (Color figure online)

false mergers of nuclei. Compared to a recently proposed 3-label U-Net trained with an auxiliary task [12], again, the high pixel accuracy of PatchPerPix leads to slightly higher avAP, while [12] is slightly superior at low IoU thresholds.

On dsb2018, we observed a similar improvement of ppp+dec over ppp as on BBBC010. However, this does not hold for nuclei3d, where ppp+dec did not improve over ppp. We hypothesize that encodings are less able to capture the ellipsoidal shape of nuclei at the very small 3d patch size of $9 \times 9 \times 9$ we're bound to achieve manageable computational performance of instance assembly in 3d (see Suppl. Table 4 for run-times). This performance bottleneck constitutes a current limitation of our method on 3d data, and is subject to future work.

3.4   Neuron Separation in 3d Light Microscopy Data

We aim to identify and segment neurons of the fruit fly brain (GAL4 lines [14]) in an unpublished dataset of 3d multicolor confocal microscopy images. The imaging is done by stochastic labeling able to express different densities of neurons [24] (cf. Fig. 4a). This instance segmentation task is very challenging as the number of neurons can be high and image quality is bounded by the necessity to perform large-scale imaging. Moreover, the neurons are very thin, tree-like structures which are intertwined and may overlap due to partial volume effects.

As this dataset is still in the process of being curated and extended, and no competing approach has yet been reported, we do not perform a quantitative evaluation of PatchPerPix, but show the quality of exemplary results on a test set of two images in Fig. 4. We use a 3-level 3d U-Net with $2\times$ down- and upsampling and 12 initial feature maps, tripled at each downsampling. The predicted patches are of size $7 \times 7 \times 7$ pixels. Our results serve as proof-of-concept that our method is applicable and yields reasonable results for thin, complex tree-like structures in large 3d image volumes.

4   Conclusion

In this work we present a novel generic method for instance segmentation that comprises a CNN to predict dense local shape descriptors and a one-pass instance assembly pipeline. The method is able to handle objects of sophisticated shapes that appear in dense clusters with overlaps, including crossovers. It is the first to assemble all instances from learnt shape patches, simultaneously in one pass. We successfully applied our method to a range of domains, showing that it (1) outperforms the state of the art on the heavily contested ISBI 2012 challenge on neuron segmentation in electron microscopy, (2) outperforms the state of the art on the challenging BBBC010 C. elegans worm data by a large margin, (3) outperforms the state of the art on 2d and 3d fluorescence microscopy data of densely clustered cell nuclei (on par in terms of cell detection performance, better in terms of pixel accuracy), showing that our method performs well also for simple (blob-like) instance shapes, and (4) can be applied to extreme cases of instance shapes, like neurons in 3d fluorescence microscopy. Future work will tackle a performance bottleneck that becomes relevant on 3d data, where we're currently restricted to patch sizes that are most probably sub-optimally small.

Acknowledgments. We wish to thank Constantin Pape for his invaluable help in reproducing the training- and prediction setup from [30], Carolina Waehlby for help with the BBBC010 data, Stephan Saalfeld and Carsten Rother for inspiring discussions, the FlyLight Project Team (https://www.janelia.org/project-team/flylight) at Janelia Research Campus for providing unpublished data, and Claire Managan and Ramya Kappagantula (Janelia Project Technical Resources) for their conscientious manual neuron segmentations. P.H., L.M. and D.K. were funded by the Berlin Institute of Health and the Max Delbrueck Center for Molecular Medicine. P.H. was funded by HFSP grant RGP0021/2018-102. P.H., L.M. and D.K. were supported by the HHMI Janelia Visiting Scientist Program. VVD Viewer (https://github.com/takashi310/VVD_Viewer) is an open-source software funded by NIH grant R01-GM098151-01.

References

1. Arganda-Carreras, I., et al.: Crowdsourcing the creation of image segmentation algorithms for connectomics. Front. Neuroanat. **9**, 142 (2015)
2. Badrinarayanan, V., Kendall, A., Cipolla, R.: SegNet: a deep convolutional encoder-decoder architecture for image segmentation. IEEE Trans. Pattern Anal. Mach. Intell. **39**(12), 2481–2495 (2017)
3. Bai, M., Urtasun, R.: Deep watershed transform for instance segmentation. CoRR abs/1611.08303 (2016)
4. Chen, L., Strauch, M., Merhof, D.: Instance segmentation of biomedical images with an object-aware embedding learned with local constraints. In: Shen, D., et al. (eds.) MICCAI 2019. LNCS, vol. 11764, pp. 451–459. Springer, Cham (2019). https://doi.org/10.1007/978-3-030-32239-7_50
5. Chen, X., Girshick, R.B., He, K., Dollár, P.: TensorMask: a foundation for dense object segmentation. CoRR abs/1903.12174 (2019). http://arxiv.org/abs/1903.12174
6. Dai, J., He, K., Li, Y., Ren, S., Sun, J.: Instance-sensitive fully convolutional networks. CoRR abs/1603.08678 (2016), http://arxiv.org/abs/1603.08678
7. De Brabandere, B., Neven, D., Van Gool, L.: Semantic instance segmentation with a discriminative loss function. arXiv preprint arXiv:1708.02551 (2017)
8. Funke, J., et al.: Large scale image segmentation with structured loss based deep learning for connectome reconstruction. IEEE Trans. Pattern Anal. Mach. Intell. (2018). https://doi.org/10.1109/TPAMI.2018.2835450
9. Gao, N., et al.: SSAP: single-shot instance segmentation with affinity pyramid. In: Proceedings of the IEEE International Conference on Computer Vision, pp. 642–651 (2019)
10. Girshick, R., Donahue, J., Darrell, T., Malik, J.: Rich feature hierarchies for accurate object detection and semantic segmentation. In: Proceedings of the 2014 IEEE Conference on Computer Vision and Pattern Recognition. CVPR 2014, pp. 580–587. IEEE Computer Society, Washington, DC (2014). https://doi.org/10.1109/CVPR.2014.81
11. He, K., Gkioxari, G., Dollár, P., Girshick, R.: Mask R-CNN (2017). http://arxiv.org/abs/1703.06870. Comment: open source; appendix on more results
12. Hirsch, P., Kainmueller, D.: An auxiliary task for learning nuclei segmentation in 3d microscopy images. In: Medical Imaging with Deep Learning (MIDL), July 2020
13. Januszewski, M., Maitin-Shepard, J., Li, P., Kornfeld, J., Denk, W., Jain, V.: Flood-filling networks. CoRR abs/1611.00421 (2016). http://arxiv.org/abs/1611.00421
14. Jenett, A., et al.: A gal4-driver line resource for drosophila neurobiology. Cell reports **2**(4), 991–1001 (2012). https://doi.org/10.1016/j.celrep.2012.09.011, https://www.ncbi.nlm.nih.gov/pubmed/23063364, 23063364[pmid]

15. Jetley, S., Sapienza, M., Golodetz, S., Torr, P.H.S.: Straight to shapes: real-time detection of encoded shapes. CoRR abs/1611.07932 (2016), http://arxiv.org/abs/1611.07932

16. Keuper, M., Levinkov, E., Bonneel, N., Lavoué, G., Brox, T., Andres, B.: Efficient decomposition of image and mesh graphs by lifted multicuts. In: Proceedings of the IEEE International Conference on Computer Vision, pp. 1751–1759 (2015)

17. Kulikov, V., Lempitsky, V.: Instance segmentation of biological images using harmonic embeddings. In: Proceedings of the IEEE/CVF Conference on Computer Vision and Pattern Recognition (CVPR), June 2020

18. Lee, K., Lu, R., Luther, K., Seung, H.S.: Learning dense voxel embeddings for 3D neuron reconstruction (2019)

19. Lin, T.-Y., et al.: Microsoft COCO: common objects in context. In: Fleet, D., Pajdla, T., Schiele, B., Tuytelaars, T. (eds.) ECCV 2014. LNCS, vol. 8693, pp. 740–755. Springer, Cham (2014). https://doi.org/10.1007/978-3-319-10602-1_48

20. Liu, Y., et al.: Affinity derivation and graph merge for instance segmentation. CoRR abs/1811.10870 (2018). http://arxiv.org/abs/1811.10870

21. Ljosa, V., Sokolnicki, K.L., Carpenter, A.E.: Annotated high-throughput microscopy image sets for validation. Nat. Methods **9**, 637 EP (2012). https://doi.org/10.1038/nmeth.2083

22. Long, F., Peng, H., Liu, X., Kim, S.K., Myers, E.: A 3D digital atlas of C. elegans and its application to single-cell analyses. Nat. Methods **6**(9), 667–672 (2009). https://doi.org/10.1038/nmeth.1366

23. Maitin-Shepard, J.B., Jain, V., Januszewski, M., Li, P., Abbeel, P.: Combinatorial energy learning for image segmentation. In: Lee, D.D., Sugiyama, M., Luxburg, U.V., Guyon, I., Garnett, R. (eds.) Advances in Neural Information Processing Systems 29, pp. 1966–1974. Curran Associates, Inc. (2016). http://papers.nips.cc/paper/6595-combinatorial-energy-learning-for-image-segmentation.pdf

24. Nern, A., Pfeiffer, B.D., Rubin, G.M.: Optimized tools for multicolor stochastic labeling reveal diverse stereotyped cell arrangements in the fly visual system. Proc. Natl. Acad. Sci. **112**(22), E2967–E2976 (2015). https://doi.org/10.1073/pnas.1506763112, https://www.pnas.org/content/112/22/E2967

25. Novotny, D., Albanie, S., Larlus, D., Vedaldi, A.: Semi-convolutional operators for instance segmentation. In: Ferrari, V., Hebert, M., Sminchisescu, C., Weiss, Y. (eds.) ECCV 2018. LNCS, vol. 11205, pp. 89–105. Springer, Cham (2018). https://doi.org/10.1007/978-3-030-01246-5_6

26. Ronneberger, O., Fischer, P., Brox, T.: U-Net: convolutional networks for biomedical image segmentation. In: Navab, N., Hornegger, J., Wells, W.M., Frangi, A.F. (eds.) MICCAI 2015. LNCS, vol. 9351, pp. 234–241. Springer, Cham (2015). https://doi.org/10.1007/978-3-319-24574-4_28

27. Schmidt, U., Weigert, M., Broaddus, C., Myers, G.: Cell detection with star-convex polygons. CoRR abs/1806.03535 (2018)

28. Wählby, C., et al.: An image analysis toolbox for high-throughput c. elegans assays. Nat. Methods **9**(7), 714–716 (2012). https://doi.org/10.1038/nmeth.1984

29. Weigert, M., Schmidt, U., Haase, R., Sugawara, K., Myers, G.: Star-convex polyhedra for 3D object detection and segmentation in microscopy. arXiv:1908.03636 (2019)

30. Wolf, S., et al.: The mutex watershed: efficient, parameter-free image partitioning. In: Ferrari, V., Hebert, M., Sminchisescu, C., Weiss, Y. (eds.) ECCV 2018. LNCS, vol. 11208, pp. 571–587. Springer, Cham (2018). https://doi.org/10.1007/978-3-030-01225-0_34

31. Wolf, S., Schott, L., Kothe, U., Hamprecht, F.: Learned watershed: end-to-end learning of seeded segmentation. In: Proceedings of the IEEE International Conference on Computer Vision, pp. 2011–2019 (2017)
32. Yurchenko, V., Lempitsky, V.S.: Parsing images of overlapping organisms with deep singling-out networks. In: 2017 IEEE Conference on Computer Vision and Pattern Recognition. CVPR 2017, Honolulu, HI, USA, 21–26 July 2017, pp. 4752–4760 (2017). https://doi.org/10.1109/CVPR.2017.505

Attend and Segment: Attention Guided Active Semantic Segmentation

Soroush Seifi[✉][iD] and Tinne Tuytelaars[iD]

KU Leuven, Kasteelpark Arenberg 10, 3001 Leuven, Belgium
{soroush.seifi,tinne.tuytelaars}@esat.kuleuven.be

Abstract. In a dynamic environment, an agent with a limited field of view/resource cannot fully observe the scene before attempting to parse it. The deployment of common semantic segmentation architectures is not feasible in such settings. In this paper we propose a method to gradually segment a scene given a sequence of partial observations. The main idea is to refine an agent's understanding of the environment by attending the areas it is most uncertain about. Our method includes a self-supervised attention mechanism and a specialized architecture to maintain and exploit spatial memory maps for filling-in the unseen areas in the environment. The agent can select and attend an area while relying on the cues coming from the visited areas to hallucinate the other parts. We reach a mean pixel-wise accuracy of 78.1%, 80.9% and 76.5% on CityScapes, CamVid, and Kitti datasets by processing only 18% of the image pixels (10 retina-like glimpses). We perform an ablation study on the number of glimpses, input image size and effectiveness of retina-like glimpses. We compare our method to several baselines and show that the optimal results are achieved by having access to a very low resolution view of the scene at the first timestep.

Keywords: Visual attention · Active exploration · Partial observability · Semantic segmentation

1 Introduction

Semantic segmentation has been extensively studied in the recent years due to its crucial role in many tasks such as autonomous driving, medical imaging, augmented reality etc. [1–4]. Architectures such as FCN, U-Net, DeepLab etc. [5–8] have pushed its accuracy further and further each year. All these architectures assume that the input is fully observable. They deploy deep layers of convolutional kernels on all input pixels to generate a segmentation mask.

In contrast, in this paper we study the problem of parsing an environment with very low observability. We define an active agent with a highly limited

---

Electronic supplementary material The online version of this chapter (https://doi.org/10.1007/978-3-030-58595-2_19) contains supplementary material, which is available to authorized users.

© Springer Nature Switzerland AG 2020
A. Vedaldi et al. (Eds.): ECCV 2020, LNCS 12370, pp. 305–321, 2020.
https://doi.org/10.1007/978-3-030-58595-2_19

Fig. 1. Our model predicts a segmentation map for the full environment (last row) by attending 8 downscaled glimpses containing only 18% of the pixels (third row).

camera bandwidth (less than 2% of all input pixels) which cannot see the whole scene (input image) at once. Instead it can choose a very small part of it, called a 'glimpse', to focus its attention on. The agent has the freedom to change its viewing direction at each time step and take a new glimpse of the scene. However, depending on a pixel budget, it is limited in the number of glimpses it can see. After reaching this limit, the agent should output a segmentation map for the whole scene including the unvisited areas.

This setting is in line with previous works on 'active visual exploration' such as [9–11] where an agent tries to explore, reconstruct and classify its environment after taking a series of glimpses. Inspired by those works, we take a step forward to solve an 'active semantic segmentation' problem which: 1) is more practical compared to image reconstruction and 2) is more challenging compared to scene classification as there is a need to classify all visited and unvisited pixels. Furthermore we introduce a novel self-supervised attention mechanism which tells the agent where to look next without the need for reinforcement learning [9,10] or supervision coming from the image reconstruction loss [11].

Our agent is trained end-to-end, segments the visited glimpses and uses their extracted features to extrapolate and segment areas of the environment it has never seen before. We use specialized modules to segment the local neighbourhood of the glimpses and to exploit long-range dependencies between the visited pixels to segment the other unseen parts.

Our proposed method can be applied in scenarios where processing the whole scene in full resolution is not an option. This could be because 1) the agent's field of view is restricted and cannot capture the whole scene at once, 2) there is a limited bandwidth for data transmission between the agent and the processing unit, 3) processing all pixels from the scene in a sliding window fashion is redundant or impossible due to resource limitations, or 4) there is a need to process at least some parts in higher resolution.

We propose two solutions for such an agent: 1) Start from a random glimpse and intelligently choose the next few glimpses to segment the whole scene or 2) Start from a (very) low resolution view of the whole scene and refine the segmentation by attending the areas with highest uncertainties. We show that the first method outperforms various baselines where the agent selects the next location based on a given heuristic while the second method can yield results comparable to processing the whole input at full resolution, for a fraction of the pixel budget.

Similar to the arguments in [9–11], autonomous systems relying on high resolution 360° cameras could benefit the most from our architecture. However, due to lack of annotated segmentation datasets with 360° images we adapted standard benchmark datasets for semantic segmentation, namely CityScapes, Kitti and CamVid [1,2,12], to our setting. Figure 1 illustrates the segmentations produced by our method after taking 8 retina-like glimpses on these datasets. We provide several baselines for our work along with an ablation study on the number of glimpses for each dataset. To the best of our knowledge, we are the first to tackle the problem of 'active semantic segmentation' with very low observability.

The remainder of this paper is organized as follows. Section 2 provides a literature review. Section 3 defines our method. In Sect. 4 we provide our experimental results and we conclude the paper in Sect. 5.

2 Related Work

Semantic Segmentation. Semantic segmentation is one of the key challenges towards understanding a scene for an autonomous agent [13]. Different methods and tricks have been proposed to solve this task relying on deep Convolutional Neural Networks (CNNs) [5–8,13,14]. In this paper, we tackle the problem where an agent dynamically changes its viewing direction and receives partial observations from its environment. This agent is required to intelligently explore and segment its environment. Therefore, this study deviates from the common semantic segmentation architectures where the input is static and fully observable. Our work is close to [15] where an agent tries to segment an object in a video stream by looking at a specific part of each frame. However, in this work we produce a segmentation map for all input pixels for a static image.

Active Vision. Active vision gives the freedom to an autonomous agent to manipulate its sensors and choose the input data which it finds most useful for learning a task [16]. Such an agent might manipulate objects, move in an environment, change its viewing direction etc. [17–20]. In this paper, we study the active setting as [9–11] where an agent can decide where to look next in the scene (i.e. selecting a glimpse) with a goal of exploration. These studies evaluate their work on image reconstruction and scene classification. Such tasks demonstrate that the agent can potentially learn an attention policy and build a good representation of the environment with few glimpses. However, the practical use case for such an agent is not clear. Besides, the results from those works imply that the extrapolation beyond the seen glimpses in the image reconstruction case is mostly limited to filling in the unseen areas with uniform colors. Therefore, instead in this paper we tackle the active exploration problem for semantic segmentation where the agent needs to reason about the unseen areas and assign a semantic label to every pixel in the image. This allows focusing on the semantics, rather than the precise color or texture, which is difficult to predict. We believe such an agent is fundamentally more useful than the one solving an image reconstruction task.

Memory in Partially Observable Environments. A critical challenge for an active agent in a partially observable environment is to understand the correlations and the spatial organization of the observations it receives. Many architectures combine LSTM layers with deep reinforcement learning to update their representation of the environment at each timestep [9, 10, 21–24]. However, studies such as [11, 25–27] show that maintaining a spatial memory of the environment is more effective albeit being more expensive in terms of memory usage. In this study we use similar architectures to those proposed in [11, 15] and maintain the extracted features in spatial memory maps. These partially filled memory maps are exploited at each time step to segment the whole scene.

Visual Attention. We use the word 'attention' to denote a mechanism for choosing the best possible location in the environment to attend next. This is different from those works in the literature where the attention mechanism weights the extracted features from the whole input according to their importance/relevance (a.k.a self-attention [28,29], soft attention [21,30,31] or 'global' attention [32]). Instead, this work is close to the hard attention mechanism defined in [15,21,22] where the information about the input is gathered sequentially by attending only a specific part of the input at each timestep. However, unlike the studies on hard attention, our attention mechanism does not rely on reinforcement learning, is differentiable and is trained with self-supervision. We take inspiration from [33] to derive an uncertainty value for each pixel in the predicted segmentation map. Consequently, the area with the highest uncertainty is attended to next.

Image Generation and Out-Painting. Unlike various inpainting methods which reconstruct missing image regions based on their surrounding pixels [34–36], image outpainting's purpose is to restore an image given only a part of it [37–39]. The active agent defined in [9–11] implicitly solves an outpainting problem. Such an agent should be able to exploit the spatial relationship of the visible areas to extrapolate and reconstruct the missing parts. Studies such as [9,10,40] incorporate the spatial information using explicit coordinates while [11,15] maintain spatial memory maps for this purpose. In this study, we follow the later approach to extrapolate beyond the seen glimpses and assign a semantic label to each pixel in those regions.

Retina Camera Technology. Taking inspiration from the human's retina setting, our method benefits from the retina-like glimpses where the resolution changes spatially based on the distance to a point of interest [41]. This way the agent can use its pixel budget more efficiently. In this work we use common downscaling techniques to construct a retina-like glimpse. However, in practice,

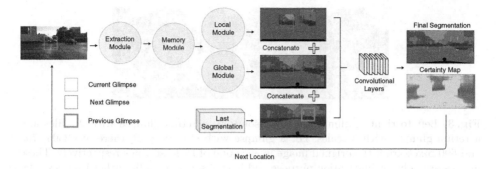

Fig. 2. Architecture Overview

our method can be implemented on top of retina sensors introduced in [41–43] to visit the parts of the environment suggested by our attention mechanism without seeing and processing the other parts.

3 Method

Our architecture consists of four main components. Figure 2 shows an overview of our architecture. The 'Extraction Module' extracts features for each attended glimpse. The 'Memory Module' gathers the features for all visited glimpses in spatial memory maps. The 'Local Module' segments the attended regions and their neighborhood while the 'Global Module' predicts a general layout of the whole scene. The final segmentation and uncertainty maps at each step are derived based on the outputs of the local and global modules and the final segmentation map from the previous step. The area with the highest uncertainty is selected as the next location for attendance. Figure 2 provides an overview of our architecture. In the following subsections we describe each module in more detail.

3.1 Extraction Module

Retina Glimpses. The extraction module receives a glimpse which is scaled down on the areas that are located further from its center ('Retina-like glimpses' [11,22]). This way the agent can use its pixel budget more efficiently. Figure 3 shows 3 different retina setting used in our experiments.

Architecture. This module uses a shallow stack of convolutional layers to extract features F_t from the visited glimpse at time step t. Its architecture resembles the encoder part of U-net with only 32 channels for its bottleneck activations. Figure 4 shows the architecture for this module.

Fig. 3. Left to right: a glimpse in full-resolution, a retina glimpse with 2 scales and a retina glimpse with 3 scales. For a glimpse with size 48 × 48, there are 2304, 768 and 590 pixels from the original image in each one of these settings respectively. These images are only for illustration purpose and have a size of 96 × 96 rather than 48 × 48.

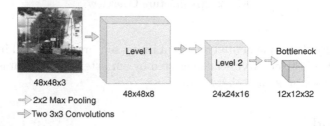

Fig. 4. Extraction module: The extracted features in each level of this encoder are stored for all glimpses by memory module.

3.2 Memory Module

The memory module maintains 3 different matrices, one for each encoder level in Fig. 4. We denote these matrices as 'Level 1', 'Level 2' ('intermediate' memories) and 'Bottleneck' memory. In case that the agent visits all possible non-overlapping glimpses in the image, these matrices would contain the extracted features for the whole input image. Otherwise they are only partially filled with the information from the visited glimpses. In our setting, where the number of glimpses is limited, one can think of these memories as the representation for the whole input image after applying a dropout layer on top. This implicit drop out mechanism prevents the agent from overfitting to the data. Figure 5 illustrates the memory module for the 'Bottleneck memory'; since bottleneck features are derived after two 2 × 2 pooling layers, their position in the feature memory is equal to glimpse's position in the image divided by 4. In case of overlap between two glimpses, these memories are updated with the features of the newest glimpse in the overlapping area.

3.3 Local Module

This module exploits the local correlations of the features in the memory to expand the segmentations for the visited glimpses. Since the convolutional kernels have a limited receptive field, these expansions remain local to each glimpse. At the same time, for two glimpses which are located close to each other it can

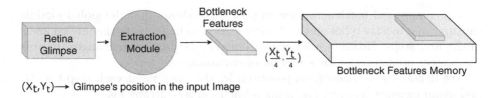

Fig. 5. Memory Module: Bottleneck features are stored in their corresponding spatial position in the memory.

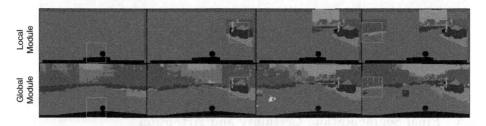

Fig. 6. Local module segments and expands the predictions for each glimpse while the global module predicts the general structure of the whole scene.

benefit from the features from both glimpses to expand a larger area. Figure 6 (top) illustrates this for 4 time-steps.

The features in the 'Bottleneck memory' are extracted using the encoder represented in Fig. 4. Consequently, we define a decoder architecture symmetrical with this encoder to generate the segmentations. The features in the 'intermediate' memories are used as skip connections while decoding. The extraction and local module together define an architecture similar to U-net. However, the encoder extracts the features for each glimpse separately from the others while the decoder operates on a partially filled memory which contains the features for all glimpses visited until the current timestep. Figure 7 illustrates the architecture of the local module. We denote the segmentation produced by this module at each step t as L_t and measure its error e_{L_t} using a binary cross-entropy loss.

3.4 Global Module

To complement the task of the local module, the global module exploits the long-range dependencies of the features in the memory and predicts the general structure of the scene.

To achieve this, it compresses the 'Bottleneck memory' with strided convolutions to 4 times smaller in each dimension (height, width and depth). Next, it deploys convolutional layers with a kernel size equal to the size of the compressed memory, thus taking into account all the features in the memory at once to predict a downscaled segmentation of the environment. This segmentation gets upscaled to the input's resolution with the help of 'intermediate' memories and with a similar architecture to the one depicted in Fig. 7 (though starting from a compressed bottleneck memory). Figure 6 shows that the global module captures and mostly relies on the dataset's prior to hallucinate the unseen areas in the first steps. However, with more glimpses, its prediction changes towards the correct prediction of the structure of environment.

We denote the segmentation produced by this module at each step t as G_t and again measure its error e_{G_t} using a binary cross-entropy loss.

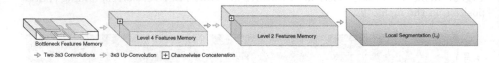

Fig. 7. Local Module's Architecture.

3.5   Final Segmentation, Certainty and Attention

At each step our architecture produces a segmentation map S_t along with an extra channel C_t as our certainty map. These maps are derived by concatenating the previous segmentation map S_{t-1}, the local segmentation L_t and the global segmentation G_t and using a series of convolution layers to combine them into a refined segmentation and a new certainty map.

Inspired by the proposed method in [33] for learning the aleatoric and epistemic uncertainty measures while optimizing the loss function, we define the loss for each module at step t according to the Eqs. 1, 2 and 3:

$$L_{L_t} = L_{L_{t-1}} + C_t \times e_{L_t} + U_t \tag{1}$$

$$L_{G_t} = L_{G_{t-1}} + C_t \times e_{G_t} + U_t \tag{2}$$

$$L_{S_t} = L_{S_{t-1}} + C_t \times e_{S_t} + U_t \tag{3}$$

L_{L_0}, L_{G_0} and L_{S_0} are initialized to zero. C_t denotes the predicted certainty map at step t while U_t is a regularizer term to prevent minimizing the loss by setting C_t to zero. We define U_t as:

$$U_t = \exp^{-C_t} \tag{4}$$

U_t measures the uncertainty for each pixel. The agent learns to minimize L_{L_t}, L_{G_t} and L_{S_t} by assigning low values to C_t (high values to U_t) in the areas where the loss is high (i.e. uncertain areas). Similarly, it assigns high values to C_t (low values to U_t) for the areas with high certainty where the loss is low.

At step t, the optimizer minimizes the sum of the loss functions defined above. We denote this sum as L_t:

$$L_t = L_{L_t} + L_{G_t} + L_{S_t} \tag{5}$$

At the final stage of each step, the certainty map C_t is divided into 16×16 non-overlapping patches and the patch with lowest sum (lowest certainty) is selected as the next location for attendance.

4   Experiments

We evaluate our method on the CityScapes, Kitti and CamVid datasets [1,2,12]. For the CityScapes dataset we report our results on the provided validation set while for the Kitti and CamVid datasets we set a random 20% split of the data to validate our method.

4.1   Retina Setting

In a first experiment, we show our results for the 3 different retina settings depicted in Fig. 3. In this figure, although all glimpses cover the same area, they differ in the number of pixels they process from the input image. Table 1 compares the ratio of processed pixels to the input image size for different retina settings. Each glimpse covers a 48×48 patch of a 128×256 input image (or 96×96 patch of a 256×512 image). As is clear from this table, retina glimpses allow the agent to cover larger areas of the environment while efficiently using its pixel budget.

Table 1. Ratio of pixels in a glimpse to the image size for different retina settings.

# Glimpses	Full resolution	2 Scales	3 Scales
1	7.0 %	2.3%	1.8%
2	14.0%	4.6%	3.6%
3	21.0%	7.0%	5.4%
4	28.1%	9.3%	7.2%
5	35.1%	11.7%	9.0%
6	42.1%	14.0%	10.8%
7	49.2%	16.4%	12.6%
8	56.2%	18.7%	14.4%
9	63.2%	21.0%	16.2%
10	70.3%	23.4%	18.0%

Figure 8 (Left) demonstrates the performance of our model for each retina setting. In these experiments we set the input image size to 128×256 and each glimpse covers a 48×48 patch of the input. Similarly, the right part of this figure summarises the experiments where the input image size is 256×512 and each glimpse covers a 96×96 area of the input (ratios remain consistent with Table 1).

Table 1 and Fig. 8 imply that the agent can use its pixel budget most efficiently using the 3-scales retina setting. An agent with a pixel budget of 18% can achieve an accuracy of 78.1% with 3 scales. With the same pixel budget, the 2-scales glimpse and full resolution glimpse cover a smaller area of the input image and thus their accuracy decreases to less than 77.2% and 71.9% respectively.

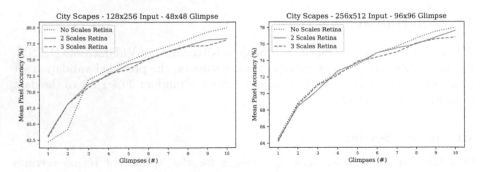

Fig. 8. Comparison of different retina settings' performance. 3-scales retina can perform equally well while using a much lower pixel budget.

Furthermore, a comparison of the left and the right part of Fig. 8 implies that if we maintain the ratio for the glimpse's coverage according to the input size, our method achieves similar results. Therefore, we evaluate the rest of our experiments in this paper using the 128×256 input size and a 3-scales retina with a coverage of 48×48 pixels. Table 2 reports the results for Cityscapes, Camvid and Kitti datasets in such settings.

Table 2. Mean Pixel Accuracy for each dataset for different number of glimpses.

Glimpses	CityScapes	Camvid	Kitti
1	63%	68.2%	64.3%
2	68.1%	73.0%	69.6%
3	70.7%	75.3%	72.1%
4	72.8%	77.8%	72.4%
5	73.5%	78.5%	73.2%
6	75.2%	78.9%	74.9%
7	76.2%	79.8%	75.1%
8	77.1%	80.4%	75.3%
9	77.2%	80.6%	76.0%
10	78.1%	80.9%	76.1%

4.2 Baselines

In this section we evaluate our attention mechanism using different baselines. We compare against a 'random agent' which selects the next glimpse's location by randomly sampling from the input locations. Next, we consider the fact that the images in the datasets with road scenes are captured through a dashboard camera. In this case, salient parts of the image typically lie somewhere near the horizon. Consequently, we compare our method against a 'Horizon agent' where it can only look at the uncertain areas in the middle rows of the image. Finally, we compare our method against a 'Restricted Movement agent' that looks at positions nearby to the current glimpse in the next step. This baseline is in line with the setting in previous literature on image reconstruction [9, 10]. It evaluates our attention mechanism's exploratory performance and our method's ability to correlate glimpses coming from far spatial locations.

Figure 9 summarises our results on CityScapes dataset (See supplementary material for Camvid and Kitti.)   Results presented in Fig. 9 suggest that remain-

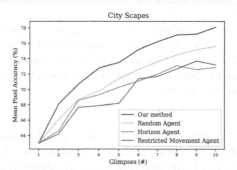

Fig. 9. Comparison against baselines.

ing local to the horizon or the visited regions of the image forces the agent to hallucinate larger parts of the environment thus making the task more difficult. Furthermore, overlapping glimpses which are more likely to occur for the horizon and restricted movement agents can potentially waste a part of the agent's pixel budget without adding much information for the segmentation. Therefore, solving this task requires a more sophisticated strategy for exploration of the input rather than scan of the nearby locations. Finally, the comparison between our method and the random agent shows the effectiveness of our proposed attention/uncertainty prediction. Figure 10 confirms this by illustrating the output of the glimpse-only agent's modules for 6 time-steps. While remaining uncertain about most parts of the environment after the first glimpse, the agent imagines itself to be in a road with cars to its side. By taking the next glimpse above the horizon it predicts the general structure of the buildings and trees surrounding the road. In the few next steps it attends the areas along the horizon which contain more details that the agent is uncertain about.

4.3   Glimpse-Only, Hybrid and Scale-Only Agents

In this section, we propose an extension of our proposed method which can achieve higher accuracy with smaller number of glimpses in case it is allowed to capture the whole scene at once at a low resolution. To evaluate this, we define

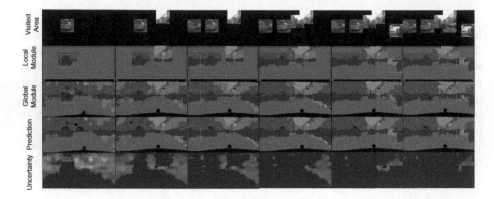

Fig. 10. The glimpse-only agent refines its predictions by attending the most uncertain areas. The local module expands the segmentations for the visited areas. The global module predicts the general layout of the environment. The final segmentation is derived by combining the last step's segmentation (initialized to zero) and the local and global modules' segmentations.

three agents for the experiments in this section: 1) Glimpse-only agent: Similar to the previous experiments, the agent cannot capture the whole scene at once. It takes the first glimpse randomly and relies on the attention mechanism to select the attended areas in the next steps. 2) Hybrid agent: The agent can capture the whole scene but cannot process all pixels. It dedicates a part of its pixel budget to see the whole scene in low resolution. This helps the agent to capture the general structure of the environment and use its remaining pixel budget to refine its segmentation by attending the uncertain areas. For this setting we experimented with an agent which scales down the input to 32×32 (see supplementary materials for 16×8), which corresponds to almost 2 retina glimpses with 3 scales. 3) Scale-only agent: The agent 'must' scale down the whole scene to its pixel budget. In this case, it does not take any glimpses and only relies on the scaled down view of the input. We define this agent as a baseline for the hybrid agent. The hybrid and scale-only agents use an architecture similar to the extraction module to encode the downscaled input. These features are decoded to a segmentation map using a symmetrical architecture to the extraction module. This would resemble a shallow U-net architecture. The scale-only agent upscales its segmentation to the input's resolution with bilinear interpolation.

Figure 11 and Table 3 summarise our results for the agents defined above. As is clear from Fig. 11, the hybrid agent outperforms the glimpse-only one. However, the performance gap between these two agents decreases with the number of glimpses. For smaller number of glimpses the glimpse-only agent needs to hallucinate larger parts of the environment while the hybrid agent can rely on the downscaled input to fill-in the missing parts. Another interesting property for the hybrid agent is that it can achieve optimal results in much smaller number of steps (e.g. 2 glimpses in case of Kitti.)

Finally, a comparison between Table 3 and Fig. 11 suggests that the glimpse-only agent performs favorably compared to the scale-only agent given the same pixel budget. However, in most cases the hybrid agent performs the best. This is due to the fact that such agent can decide which areas to attend in full resolution while its scaled down view of the scene is sufficient for parsing the other areas.

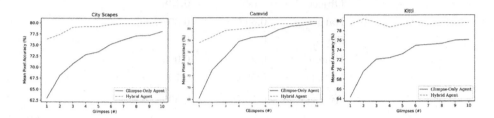

Fig. 11. Our method's performance for different number of glimpses. The gap between the glimpse-only and the hybrid agent decreases for higher number of glimpses.

Table 3. Scale-only agent; segmentation results by scaling down the input. Second column denotes the number of possible retina-like glimpses given the pixel budget for each experiment.

Scales	Glimpse Budget	CityScapes	Camvid	Kitti
1 (128×256) (Full)	≈ 56	80.7	81.3	81.7
1/4 (64×128)	≈ 14	80.4	80.9	80.4
1/16 (32×64)	≈ 4	78.9	79.4	75.5

4.4   IOU Evaluation

In this section we compare the Mean IOU accuracy of the glimpse-only agent with 10 glimpses to the accuracy of an architecture similar to U-net (with 256 channels at its bottleneck) working on full 128×256 images from the CityScapes dataset. Table 4 compares our results for different categories in this dataset. For this evaluation all segmentations are bilinearly upscaled to the raw input image size of (1024×2048).

Our method compares well to an architecture working on the full image taking into account that our approach only processes 18% of the input pixels. The most difficult category for our method is 'Object'. In a partial view of an environment it is easy to miss small objects such as traffic signs and poles. Therefore it would be a difficult task for our method to hallucinate such objects lying in the unseen regions of the environment.

Table 4. Mean IOU comparison on CityScapes dataset. Our method using only 18% of the pixels in the image comes relatively close to U-net which observes the full image.

Category	Our Method	U-net
Flat	0.907	0.938
Construction	0.641	0.746
Object	0.046	0.138
Nature	0.647	0.808
Sky	0.503	0.809
Human	0.216	0.006
Vehicle	0.599	0.798
Average	0.508	0.590

5   Conclusion

By taking inspiration from the recent works on active visual exploration [9–11], in this study we tackled the problem of semantic segmentation with partial observability. In this scenario an agent with limited field of view and computational resources needs to understand the scene. Given a limited budget in terms of the number of pixels that can be processed, such an agent should look at the most informative parts of an environment to segment it in whole. We proposed a self-supervised attention mechanism to guide the agent on deciding where to attend next. The agent uses spatial memory maps and exploits the correlations among the visited areas in the memory in order to hallucinate the unseen parts of the environment. Moreover, we introduced a two-stream architecture, with one stream specialized on the local information and the other working on the global cues. We demonstrated that our model performs favorably in comparison to a solution obtained by scaling down the input to the pixel budget. Finally, our experiments indicated that an agent which combines a scaled down segmentation of the whole environment with the proposed attention mechanism performs the best.

In the future, we would investigate datasets with less prior knowledge consisting of various scene categories such as ADE20k [44]. Next, having in mind that consecutive frames in a video stream share most of their content, we would look into a video segmentation problem with partial observability.

Acknowledgment. This work was supported by the FWO SBO project Omnidrone (https://www.omnidrone720.com/).

References

1. Cordts, M., et al.: The cityscapes dataset for semantic urban scene understanding. In: Proceedings of the IEEE Conference on Computer Vision and Pattern Recognition, pp. 3213–3223 (2016)

2. Geiger, A., Lenz, P., Urtasun, R.: Are we ready for autonomous driving? the KITTI vision benchmark suite. In: 2012 IEEE Conference on Computer Vision and Pattern Recognition, pp. 3354–3361. IEEE (2012)

3. Havaei, M., et al.: Brain tumor segmentation with deep neural networks. Med. Image Anal. **35**, 18–31 (2017)

4. Yu, L., Yang, X., Chen, H., Qin, J., Heng, P.A.: Volumetric convnets with mixed residual connections for automated prostate segmentation from 3D MR images. In: Thirty-First AAAI Conference on Artificial Intelligence (2017)

5. Long, J., Shelhamer, E., Darrell, T.: Fully convolutional networks for semantic segmentation. In: Proceedings of the IEEE Conference on Computer Vision and Pattern Recognition, pp. 3431–3440 (2015)

6. Ronneberger, O., Fischer, P., Brox, T.: U-Net: convolutional networks for biomedical image segmentation. In: Navab, N., Hornegger, J., Wells, W.M., Frangi, A.F. (eds.) MICCAI 2015. LNCS, vol. 9351, pp. 234–241. Springer, Cham (2015). https://doi.org/10.1007/978-3-319-24574-4_28

7. Li, H., Xiong, P., An, J., Wang, L.: Pyramid attention network for semantic segmentation. In: The British Machine Vision Conference (2018)

8. Chen, L.-C., Papandreou, G., Kokkinos, I., Murphy, K., Yuille, A.L.: DeepLab: semantic image segmentation with deep convolutional nets, atrous convolution, and fully connected CRFs. IEEE Trans. Pattern Anal. Mach. Intell. **40**(4), 834–848 (2017)

9. Ramakrishnan, S.K., Grauman, K.: Sidekick policy learning for active visual exploration. In: Ferrari, V., Hebert, M., Sminchisescu, C., Weiss, Y. (eds.) ECCV 2018. LNCS, vol. 11216, pp. 424–442. Springer, Cham (2018). https://doi.org/10.1007/978-3-030-01258-8_26

10. Jayaraman, D., Grauman, K.: Learning to look around: intelligently exploring unseen environments for unknown tasks. In: Proceedings of the IEEE Conference on Computer Vision and Pattern Recognition, pp. 1238–1247 (2018)

11. Seifi, S., Tuytelaars, T.: Where to look next: unsupervised active visual exploration on 360° input. arXiv preprint arXiv:1909.10304 (2019)

12. Brostow, G.J., Shotton, J., Fauqueur, J., Cipolla, R.: Segmentation and recognition using structure from motion point clouds. In: Forsyth, D., Torr, P., Zisserman, A. (eds.) ECCV 2008. LNCS, vol. 5302, pp. 44–57. Springer, Heidelberg (2008). https://doi.org/10.1007/978-3-540-88682-2_5

13. Garcia-Garcia, A., Orts-Escolano, S., Oprea, S., Villena-Martinez, V., Garcia-Rodriguez, J.: A review on deep learning techniques applied to semantic segmentation. arXiv preprint arXiv:1704.06857 (2017)

14. Chen, L.-C., Papandreou, G., Kokkinos, I., Murphy, K., Yuille, A.L.: Semantic image segmentation with deep convolutional nets and fully connected CRFs. arXiv preprint arXiv:1412.7062 (2014)

15. Chai, Y.: Patchwork: a patch-wise attention network for efficient object detection and segmentation in video streams. In: Proceedings of the IEEE International Conference on Computer Vision, pp. 3415–3424 (2019)

16. Aloimonos, J., Weiss, I., Bandyopadhyay, A.: Active vision. Int. J. Comput. Vis. **1**(4), 333–356 (1988). https://doi.org/10.1007/BF00133571

17. Navarro-Alarcon, D., et al.: Automatic 3-D manipulation of soft objects by robotic arms with an adaptive deformation model. IEEE Trans. Robot. **32**(2), 429–441 (2016)

18. Caicedo, J.C., Lazebnik, S.: Active object localization with deep reinforcement learning. In: Proceedings of the IEEE International Conference on Computer Vision, pp. 2488–2496 (2015)

19. Aydemir, A., Pronobis, A., Göbelbecker, M., Jensfelt, P.: Active visual object search in unknown environments using uncertain semantics. IEEE Trans. Rob. **29**(4), 986–1002 (2013)
20. Gupta, S., Davidson, J., Levine, S., Sukthankar, R., Malik, J.: Cognitive mapping and planning for visual navigation. In: Proceedings of the IEEE Conference on Computer Vision and Pattern Recognition, pp. 2616–2625 (2017)
21. Xu, K., et al.: Show, attend and tell: neural image caption generation with visual attention. In: International conference on machine learning, pp. 2048–2057 (2015)
22. Mnih, V., Heess, N., Graves, A., et al.: Recurrent models of visual attention. In: Advances in Neural Information Processing Systems, pp. 2204–2212 (2014)
23. Hausknecht, M., Stone, P.: Deep recurrent Q-learning for partially observable MDPs. In: 2015 AAAI Fall Symposium Series (2015)
24. Mnih, V., et al.: Asynchronous methods for deep reinforcement learning. In: International Conference on Machine Learning, pp. 1928–1937 (2016)
25. Parisotto, E., Salakhutdinov, R.: Neural map: structured memory for deep reinforcement learning. arXiv preprint arXiv:1702.08360 (2017)
26. Henriques, J.F., Vedaldi, A.: MapNet: an allocentric spatial memory for mapping environments. In: Proceedings of the IEEE Conference on Computer Vision and Pattern Recognition, pp. 8476–8484 (2018)
27. Oh, J., Chockalingam, V., Singh, S., Lee, H.: Control of memory, active perception, and action in minecraft. arXiv preprint arXiv:1605.09128 (2016)
28. Cheng, J., Dong, L., Lapata, M.: Long short-term memory-networks for machine reading. In: Proceedings of the Conference on Empirical Methods in Natural Language Processing (2016)
29. Zhang, H., Goodfellow, I., Metaxas, D., Odena, A.: Self-attention generative adversarial networks. In: International Conference on Machine Learning, pp. 7354–7363 (2019)
30. Vaswani, A., et al.: Attention is all you need. In: Advances in Neural Information Processing Systems, pp. 5998–6008 (2017)
31. Bahdanau, D., Cho, K., Bengio, Y.: Neural machine translation by jointly learning to align and translate. arXiv preprint arXiv:1409.0473 (2014)
32. Luong, M.-T., Pham, H., Manning, C.D.: Effective approaches to attention-based neural machine translation. In: Proceedings of the Conference on Empirical Methods in Natural Language Processing (2015)
33. Kendall, A., Gal, Y.: What uncertainties do we need in Bayesian deep learning for computer vision? In: Advances in Neural Information Processing Systems, pp. 5574–5584 (2017)
34. Pathak, D., Krahenbuhl, P., Donahue, J., Darrell, T., Efros, A.A.: Context encoders: feature learning by inpainting. In: Proceedings of the IEEE Conference on Computer Vision and Pattern Recognition, pp. 2536–2544 (2016)
35. Liu, G., Reda, F.A., Shih, K.J., Wang, T.-C., Tao, A., Catanzaro, B.: Image inpainting for irregular holes using partial convolutions. In: Ferrari, V., Hebert, M., Sminchisescu, C., Weiss, Y. (eds.) ECCV 2018. LNCS, vol. 11215, pp. 89–105. Springer, Cham (2018). https://doi.org/10.1007/978-3-030-01252-6_6
36. Yu, J., Lin, Z., Yang, J., Shen, X., Lu, X., Huang, T.S.: Generative image inpainting with contextual attention. In: Proceedings of the IEEE Conference on Computer Vision and Pattern Recognition, pp. 5505–5514 (2018)
37. Wang, M., Lai, Y., Liang, Y., Martin, R.R., Hu, S.-M.: BiggerPicture: data-driven image extrapolation using graph matching. ACM Trans. Graph. **33**(6), 173 (2014)

38. Wang, Y., Tao, X., Shen, X., Jia, J.: Wide-context semantic image extrapolation. In: Proceedings of the IEEE Conference on Computer Vision and Pattern Recognition, pp. 1399–1408 (2019)
39. Sabini, M., Rusak, G.: Painting outside the box: image outpainting with GANs. arXiv preprint arXiv:1808.08483 (2018)
40. Lin, C.H., Chang, C.-C., Chen, Y.-S., Juan, D.-C., Wei, W., Chen, H.-T.: COCO-GAN: generation by parts via conditional coordinating. In: Proceedings of the IEEE International Conference on Computer Vision, pp. 4512–4521 (2019)
41. Sandini, G., Metta, G.: Retina-like sensors: motivations, technology and applications. In: Barth, F.G., Humphrey, J.A.C., Secomb, T.W. (eds.) Sensors and Sensing in Biology and Engineering, pp. 251–262. Springer, Vienna (2003). https://doi.org/10.1007/978-3-7091-6025-1_18
42. Graydon, O.: Retina-like single-pixel camera. Nat. Photonics 11(6), 335–335 (2017)
43. Ude, A.: Foveal vision for humanoid robots. In: Humanoid Robotics and Neuroscience: Science, Engineering and Society. CRC Press/Taylor& Francis, Boca Raton (2015)
44. Zhou, B., Zhao, H., Puig, X., Fidler, S., Barriuso, A., Torralba, A.: Scene parsing through ADE20K dataset. In: Proceedings of the IEEE Conference on Computer Vision and Pattern Recognition, pp. 633–641 (2017)

Accelerating CNN Training by Pruning Activation Gradients

Xucheng Ye[1], Pengcheng Dai[2], Junyu Luo[1], Xin Guo[1], Yingjie Qi[1], Jianlei Yang[1(✉)], and Yiran Chen[3]

[1] SCSE, BDBC, Beihang University, Beijing, China
`jianlei@buaa.edu.cn`
[2] SME, BDBC, Beihang University, Beijing, China
[3] ECE, Duke University, Durham, NC, USA

Abstract. Sparsification is an efficient approach to accelerate CNN inference, but it is challenging to take advantage of sparsity in training procedure because the involved gradients are dynamically changed. Actually, an important observation shows that most of the activation gradients in back-propagation are very close to zero and only have a tiny impact on weight-updating. Hence, we consider pruning these very small gradients randomly to accelerate CNN training according to the statistical distribution of activation gradients. Meanwhile, we theoretically analyze the impact of pruning algorithm on the convergence. The proposed approach is evaluated on AlexNet and ResNet-{18, 34, 50, 101, 152} with CIFAR-{10, 100} and ImageNet datasets. Experimental results show that our training approach could substantially achieve up to 5.92× speedups at back-propagation stage with negligible accuracy loss.

Keywords: CNN training · Acceleration · Gradients pruning

1 Introduction

Convolutional Neural Networks (CNNs) have been widely applied to many tasks and various devices in recent years. However, the network structures are becoming more and more complex, making the training of CNN on large scale datasets very time consuming, especially with limited hardware resources. Some previous researches have shown that CNN training could be finished within minutes on high performance computation platforms [1–3], but thousands of GPUs have to be utilized, which is not feasible for many scenarios. Even though there are many existing works on network compressing, most of them are focused on inference [4]. Our work aims to reduce the training workloads efficiently, enabling large scale training on budgeted computation platforms.

This work is supported in part by the National Natural Science Foundation of China (61602022), State Key Laboratory of Software Development Environment (SKLSDE-2018ZX-07), CCF-Tencent IAGR20180101 and the 111 Talent Program B16001.

ⓒ Springer Nature Switzerland AG 2020
A. Vedaldi et al. (Eds.): ECCV 2020, LNCS 12370, pp. 322–338, 2020.
https://doi.org/10.1007/978-3-030-58595-2_20

The essential optimization step of CNN training is to perform Stochastic Gradient Descent (SGD) algorithm in back-propagation procedure. There are several data types involved in training dataflow: weights, weight gradients, activations, activation gradients. Back-propagation starts from computing the weight gradients with the activations and then performs weights update [5]. Among these steps, *activation gradients back-propagation* and *weight gradients computation* require intensive convolution operations thus dominate the total training cost. It is well known that computation cost can be reduced by skipping over zero-values. Since these two convolution steps require the activation gradients as input, improving the sparsity of activation gradients should significantly reduce the computation cost and memory footprint during back-propagation procedure.

Without loss of generality, we assume that the numerical values of activation gradient satisfy normal distributions, and a threshold τ can be calculated based on this hypothesis. And then *stochastic pruning* is applied on the activation gradients with the threshold τ while the gradients are set to zero or $\pm\tau$ randomly. Since the ReLU layers usually make the gradients distributed irregularly, we divide common networks into two categories, one is networks using Conv-ReLU as basic blocks such as AlexNet [6] and VGGNet [7], another is those using Conv-BN-ReLU structure such as ResNet [8]. Experiments show that our pruning method works for both Conv-ReLU structure and Conv-BN-ReLU structure in modern networks. A mathematical analysis is provided to demonstrate that stochastic pruning can maintain the convergence properties of CNN training. Additionally, our proposed training scheme is evaluated both on Intel CPU and ARM CPU platforms, which could achieve $1.71\times \sim 3.99\times$ and $1.79\times \sim 5.92\times$ speedups, respectively, when compared with no pruning utilized at back-propagation stage.

2   Related Works

Weight pruning is a well-known acceleration technique for CNN inference phase which has been widely researched and achieved outstanding advances. Pruning of weights can be divided into five categories [4]: element-level [9], vector-level [10], kernel-level [11], group-level [12] and filter-level pruning [13–17]. Weight pruning focuses on raising parameters sparsity of convolutional layers.

Weight gradients pruning is proposed for training acceleration by reducing communication cost of weight gradients exchanging in distributed learning system. Aji [18] prunes 99% weight gradients with the smallest absolute value by a heuristic algorithm. According to filters' correlationship, Prakash [19] prunes 30% filters temporarily to improve training efficiency.

Activation gradients pruning is another approach to reduce training cost but is rarely researched because activation gradients are generated dynamically during back-propagation. Most previous works adopt *top-k* as the base algorithm for sparsification. For MLP training, Sun [20] adopts *min-heap* algorithm to find and retain the k elements with the largest absolute value in the activation gradients for each layer, and discards the remaining elements to improve sparsity. Wei

[21] further applies this scheme to CNN's training, but only evaluated on LeNet. In the case of larger networks and more complex datasets, directly dropping redundant gradients will cause significant loss of learnt information. To alleviate this problem, Zhang [22] stores the un-propagated gradients at the last learning step in memory and adds them to the gradients before *top-k* sparsification in the current iteration. Our work can be categorized into this scope. We propose two novel algorithms to determine the pruning threshold and preserve the valuable information, respectively.

Quantization is another common way to reduce the computational complexity and memory consumption of training. Gupta's work [23] maintains the accuracy by training the model in the precision of 16-bit fixed-point number with stochastic rounding. DoReFaNet [24] derived from AlexNet [6] utilizes 1-bit, 2-bit and 6-bit fixed-point number to represent weights, activations and gradients respectively, but brings visible accuracy drop. Park [25] proposed a value-aware quantization method by using low-precision on small values, which can significantly reduce memory consumption when training ResNet-152 [8] and Inception-V3 [26] with 98% activations quantified to 3-bit. Micikevicius [5] keeps an FP32 copy for weight update and adopts FP16 for computation, which is efficient for training acceleration. Our approach can be regarded as gradients sparsification, and can be also integrated with gradients quantization methods.

3   Methodologies

3.1   General Dataflow

The convolution (Conv) layer involved in each training iteration usually includes four stages: *Forward, Activation Gradients Back-propagation, Weight Gradients Computation* and *Weight Update*. To present the calculation of these stages, some definitions and notations are introduced and adopted throughout this paper:

- $\mathbf{I}$ denotes the input of each layer at *Forward* stage.
- $\mathbf{O}$ denotes the output of each layer at *Forward* stage.
- $\mathbf{W}$ denotes the weights of Conv layer.
- $\mathrm{d}\mathbf{I}$ denotes the gradients of I.
- $\mathrm{d}\mathbf{O}$ denotes the gradients of O.
- $\mathrm{d}\mathbf{W}$ denotes the gradients of W.
- $*$ denotes the 2-D convolution.
- η denotes the learning rate.
- $\mathbf{W}^+$ denotes the sequentially reversed of $\mathbf{W}$.

And the four training stages of Conv layer can be summarized as:

- *Forward* $\mathbf{O} = \mathbf{I} * \mathbf{W}$ (notice that we leave out bias here)
- *Activation Gradients Back-Propagation(AGBP)*: $\mathrm{d}\mathbf{I} = \mathbf{W}^+ * \mathrm{d}\mathbf{O}$
- *Weight Gradients Computation(WGC)*: $\mathrm{d}\mathbf{W} = \mathrm{d}\mathbf{O} * \mathbf{I}$
- *Weight Update*: $\mathbf{W} \leftarrow \mathbf{W} - \eta \cdot \mathrm{d}\mathbf{W}$

We found that activation gradients involved in back-propagation stage are almost full of *very small values* that are extremely close to zero. It is reasonable to assume that pruning those extremely small values has little effect on weight update stage. Meanwhile, existing works show that pruning redundant elements in convolution calculations can effectively reduce arithmetic complexity. Therefore, we make a hypothesis that the involved `Conv` layers computations in training can be accelerated substantially by pruning activation gradients.

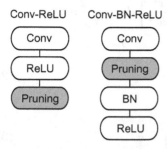

Fig. 1. Pruning stages involved for two typical structures: `Conv-ReLU` and `Conv-BN-ReLU`.

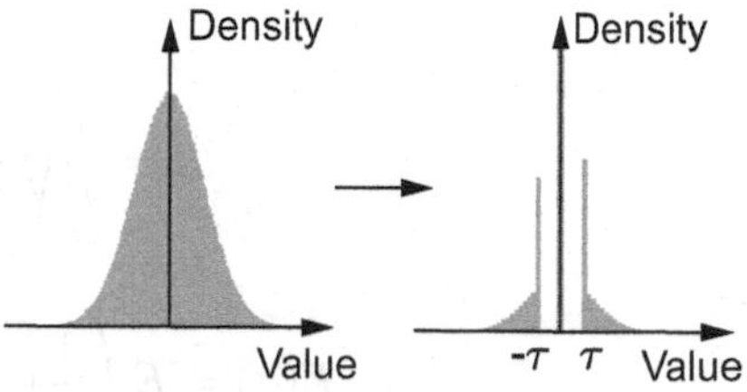

Fig. 2. Effect of *stochastic pruning*, where τ is the pruning threshold.

3.2   Sparsification Algorithms

Distribution Based Threshold Determination (DBTD). The most important concern of pruning is to determine which elements should be selected for discarding. Previous works [20] use min-heap algorithm to select which elements going to be pruned. However, they will introduce inevitable overhead significantly when implemented on heterogeneous platforms such as FPGA or ASIC. Hence, we propose a new threshold determination method with less time complexity and more hardware compatibility.

Firstly, we analyze the distribution of activation gradients for two typical structures of modern CNN models, as shown in Fig. 1. For `Conv-ReLU` structure, where a `Conv` layer is followed by a `ReLU` layer, output activation gradients d$\mathbf{O}$ are sparse, but subject to an irregular distribution. On the other hand, the input activation gradients d$\mathbf{I}$, which will be propagated to the previous layer, is almost full of non-zero values. Statistics show that the probability distribution of d$\mathbf{I}$ is symmetrical around zero and its probability density function decreases with the increment of absolute value $|\mathbf{dI}(\cdot)|$. For `Conv-BN-ReLU` structure, a BN layer is located between `Conv` and `ReLU` layer, and d$\mathbf{O}$ subjects to the similar distribution of d$\mathbf{I}$. With the same hypothesis [27], these gradients are assumed to subject to a normal distribution with mean value 0 and variance σ^2.

For `Conv-ReLU` structure, dO can inherit the sparsity from dI of last `Conv` layer because `ReLU` layer will not reduce the sparsity. Thus dI can be treated as pruning target g in `Conv-ReLU` structure. For `Conv-BN-ReLU` structure, dO is considered as pruning target g. In this way, the distribution of g in both situations could be unified to normal distribution. Supposing that the scale of g is n, we calculate the mean value of the absolute values from gradient data g, and the expectation of it is:

$$E\left(\frac{1}{n}\sum_{i=1}^{n}|g_i|\right) = \frac{n}{\sqrt{2\pi\sigma^2}}\int |x|\exp\left\{-\frac{x^2}{2\sigma^2}\right\}dx = \sqrt{\frac{2}{\pi}}n\sigma. \tag{1}$$

Let

$$\hat{\sigma} = \frac{1}{n}\sqrt{\frac{2}{\pi}}\sum_{i=1}^{n}|g_i|, \tag{2}$$

then

$$E(\hat{\sigma}) = E\left(\frac{1}{n}\sqrt{\frac{2}{\pi}}\sum_{i=1}^{n}|g_i|\right) = \sigma. \tag{3}$$

Clearly, $\hat{\sigma}$ is an unbiased estimator of parameter σ.

Here we adopt the mean value of the absolute values because the computational overhead is acceptable. Base on the assumption, we can compute the threshold τ with the cumulative distribution function of the standard normal distribution Φ, target pruning rate p and $\hat{\sigma}$ by:

$$\tau = \Phi^{-1}\left(\frac{1-p}{2}\right)\hat{\sigma}. \tag{4}$$

Stochastic Pruning. Pruning a few gradients with small values has little impact on weights update. However, once all of these small gradients are set to 0, the distribution of activation gradients will be affected significantly, which will influence the weights update and cause severe accuracy loss. Inspired by *Stochastic Rounding* in [23], we adopt stochastic pruning to solve this problem.

Stochastic pruning treats gradients as an one-dimensional vector g with length n, and all the components whose absolute value is smaller than the threshold τ will be pruned. The algorithm details are demonstrated in Algorithm 1. The effect of stochastic pruning on gradient distribution is illustrated in Fig. 2.

Algorithm 1: Stochastic Pruning

Input: original activation gradients g, threshold τ
Output: sparse activation gradients $\hat{g}$
for $i = 1; i \leq n; i = i + 1$ **do**
　if $|g_i| < \tau$ **then**
　　Generate a random number $r \in [0, 1]$;
　　if $|g_i| > r\tau$ **then**
　　　| $\hat{g}_i = (g_i > 0) ? \tau : (-\tau)$;
　　else
　　　| $\hat{g}_i = 0$;
　　end
　end
end

Stochastic pruning could maintain the mathematical expectation of the gradients distribution while completing the pruning. Mathematical analysis in Sect. 4 will show that such a gradients sparsification method for CNN training does not affect its convergence.

In summary, compared with existing works, our scheme has two advantages:

(1) *Lower runtime cost*: the arithmetic complexity of *DBTD* is $\mathcal{O}(n)$, less than top-k which is at least $\mathcal{O}(n \log k)$, where k stands for the number of reversed elements. Meanwhile, *DBTD* is more hardware friendly and easier to be implemented on heterogeneous platform because it does not require frequent comparison operations.
(2) *Lower memory footprint*: our *Stochastic Pruning* approach could preserve the convergence rate and does not require any extra memory consumption. In contrast, [22] needs to store the un-propagated gradients of the last training steps, which is more memory consuming.

4   Convergence Analysis

The convergence rate of our proposed stochastic pruning is analyzed in this section. *Please note that it is not a rigorous mathematical proof, but just provide some intuition on why the gradients pruning method works.* We expect that our training method with stochastic pruning has similar convergence rate with origin training process under the GOGA (General Online Gradient Algorithm) framework [28].

In [28], L. Bottou considers a learning problem as follows: suppose that there is an unknown distribution $P(z)$ and can only get a batch of samples z_t each iteration, where t denotes iteration times. The goal of training is to find the optimal parameters w which minimize the loss function $Q(z, w)$. For convenience, we define the cost function as:

$$C(w) \triangleq \mathbf{E_z}Q(z, w) \triangleq \int Q(z, w) \, dP(z). \tag{5}$$

And the involved update rule for the online learning system is formulated as:

$$w_{t+1} = w_t - \gamma_t H\left(z_t, w_t\right), \tag{6}$$

where γ_t is the learning rate, $H\left(\cdot\right)$ is the update function. It will finally converge as long as the following assumptions are satisfied.

Assumption 1. *The cost function* $C(w_t)$ *has a single global minimum* w^* *and satisfies the condition that*

$$\forall \varepsilon, \quad \inf_{(w-w^*)^2 > \varepsilon} (w - w^*)\nabla_w C(w) > 0. \tag{7}$$

Assumption 2. *Learning rate* γ_t *fulfills that*

$$\sum_{t=1}^{\infty} \gamma_t = \infty, \qquad and \qquad \sum_{t=1}^{\infty} \gamma_t^2 < \infty. \tag{8}$$

Assumption 3. *For each iteration, the update function* $H(z_t, w_t)$ *meets that*

$$\mathbf{E}\left[H(z, w)\right] = \nabla_w C(w), \tag{9}$$

and

$$\mathbf{E}\left[H(z, w)^2\right] \leq \alpha + \beta(w - w^*)^2, \tag{10}$$

where α *and* β *are finite constants, the update function* $H(z, w)$ *consists of the calculated gradients by back-propagation algorithm.*

The only difference between our proposed algorithm and [28] is the update function $H(z, w)$. For original algorithm, the update function $H(z_t, w_t)$ satisfies:

$$\mathbf{E}\left[H(z, w)\right] = \nabla_w C(w). \tag{11}$$

In proposed algorithm, a gradients pruning method is applied on the update function, denoted as $\hat{H}(z, w)$. In this case, if we assume original back-propagation algorithm meets all the assumptions, the proposed algorithm also satisfies *Assumption 1* and 2. If *Assumption 3* can be also held by the proposed algorithm, we can say that both algorithms have similar convergence. For convenience, their corresponding gradients are denoted as $G \triangleq H(z, w)$ and $\hat{G} \triangleq \hat{H}(z, w)$.

In the following we will first prove that though $\hat{G} \neq G$, the expectations of them are the same. What's more, we expect the extra noise introduced by gradient pruning is not significant enough to violate *Assumption* 3. More precisely, the following equations should be held:

$$\mathbf{E}\left[\hat{G}\right] = \mathbf{E}\left[G\right], \tag{12}$$

$$\mathbf{E}\left[\hat{G}^2\right] \leq \alpha + \beta \mathbf{E}\left[G^2\right]. \tag{13}$$

To discuss *Assumption* 3, we first give a lemma:

Lemma 1. *For a stochastic variable x, we get another stochastic variable y by applying Algorithm 1 to x with threshold τ, which means*

$$y = \text{Prune}(x) = \begin{cases} x & \text{i.f.f. } |x| \geq \tau \\ 0 & \text{with probability } p = \dfrac{\tau - x}{\tau} \quad \text{i.f.f. } |x| < \tau \\ \tau & \text{with probability } p = \dfrac{x}{\tau} \quad \text{i.f.f. } |x| < \tau \end{cases} \qquad (14)$$

Then y satisfies

$$\text{E}[y] = \text{E}\left[\text{Prune}(x)\right] = \text{E}[x], \qquad (15)$$

$$\text{E}[y^2] = \text{E}\left[\text{Prune}(x)^2\right] \leq \tau^2 + \text{E}[x^2]. \qquad (16)$$

Then we can discuss the expectation and variance of gradients $\hat{G}$.

4.1   Expectation of Gradients

Lemma 1 means that gradients pruning will not affect the expectation of activation gradients, which can be utilized to prove Eq. (12). Let G represent the gradients of the whole network parameters with N layers. Thus we can split it into layer-wise gradients:

$$G = (G_1, G_2, \cdots, G_l, \cdots, G_N) \qquad (17)$$

where G_l represents the gradients of l-th layer weights. Let GO_l represents the activation gradients for l-th layer, we have:

$$GO_l = F_1(GO_{l+1}, \omega), \qquad and \qquad G_l = F_2(GO_l) \qquad (18)$$

where F_1 and F_2 represents the back-propagation operation for l-th layer.
  The same thing can be done for $\hat{G}$ which means:

$$\hat{G} = (\hat{G}_1, \hat{G}_2, \cdots, \hat{G}_l, \cdots, \hat{G}_N), \qquad (19)$$

$$\hat{GO}_l = \text{Prune}\left[F_1(\hat{GO}_{l+1}, \omega)\right], \qquad (20)$$

$$\hat{G}_l = F_2\left(\hat{GO}_l\right). \qquad (21)$$

To prove Eq. (12), we only need to prove that for each l,

$$\mathbf{E}\left[\hat{G}_l\right] = \mathbf{E}\left[G_l\right], \qquad (22)$$

$$\mathbf{E}\left[\hat{GO}_l\right] = \mathbf{E}\left[GO_l\right]. \qquad (23)$$

Note that Eq. (23) is already held for the last layer. Because the last layer is the start of back-propagation and the proposed algorithm is the same with original algorithm before the last layer's gradients G are calculated, we only need to prove that:

$$\mathbf{E}[G_l] = F_1(\mathbf{E}[GO_l]) \tag{24}$$

$$\mathbf{E}[GO_l] = F_2(\mathbf{E}[GO_{l+1}]) \tag{25}$$

Because if Eq. (24) and Eq. (25) are held, we can prove Eq. (9) by using *Lemma* 1.

Proof. Assume Eq. (23) is satisfied for $(l + 1)$-th layer. Then for l-th layer

$$\mathrm{E}[\hat{G}_l] = F_1\left(\mathbf{E}\left[\hat{GO_l}\right]\right) \tag{26}$$

$$= F_1\left(F_2\left(\mathbf{E}\left[\mathrm{Prune}\left(\hat{GO}_{l+1}\right)\right]\right)\right) \tag{27}$$

$$= F_1\left(F_2\left(\mathbf{E}\left[\hat{GO}_{l+1}\right]\right)\right) \tag{28}$$

$$= F_1\left(F_2\left(\mathbf{E}[GO_{l+1}]\right)\right) \tag{29}$$

$$= F_1\left(\mathbf{E}[GO_l]\right) \tag{30}$$

$$= \mathrm{E}[G_l] \tag{31}$$

The equality of Eq. (26) and Eq. (31) could be guaranteed by Eq. (24). Equation (27) and Eq. (30) is true because of Eq. (25). Equation (28) is right due to *Lemma* 1. Since the assumption Eq. (23) is true for the last layer, then for all l, Eq. (9) is right.

As for Eq. (24) and Eq. (25) is true because they are linear operation except ReLU in the case of CNN and the back-propagation of ReLU can exchange with expectation. Here we denote the back-propagation of ReLU as ReLU'. ReLU' will set the operand to zero or hold its value. For the former one,

$$\mathbf{E}[\mathrm{ReLU'}(x)] = 0 = \mathrm{ReLU'}(\mathbf{E}[x]).$$

For the latter one,

$$\mathbf{E}[\mathrm{ReLU'}(x)] = \mathbf{E}[x] = \mathrm{ReLU'}(\mathbf{E}[x]).$$

Thus we prove that the expectation of gradients in the proposed algorithm is the same with the original algorithm.

4.2 Variance of Gradients

It is difficult to prove that Eq. (10) can be also satisfied in the proposed gradient pruning algorithm. However, we can give some intuition that this may be right if original training method meets this condition. Equation (10) tell us that, to guarantee the convergence during stochastic gradient descend, variance of gradients in each step should not be too large. The proposed gradient pruning method will indeed bring extra noise to the gradients. But we believe the extra noise is not significant enough to violate Eq. (10). The extra gradients noise is determined by two factors. First is the noise generated by pruning method. Second is the propagation of the pruning noise in the following back-propagation process.

From Eq. (16) we can tell that the variance of the pruned gradients will only increase by a constant number relating to threshold τ. This will certainly obey the condition in Eq. (10). What's more, the noise is then propagating through Conv and ReLU layers, whose operation is either linear or sublinear. Thus we can expect that the increase of variance will still be quadratic, which satisfies Eq. (10). In this way, we can say that the proposed pruning algorithm has almost the same convergence with the original algorithm under the GOGA framework.

5 Implementation

5.1 Accuracy Evaluation

PyTorch [29] framework is utilized to estimate the impact on accuracy for our gradient pruning method. The straight-through estimator (STE) is adopted in our implementation. We introduce an extra Pruning layer for different Conv block as shown in Fig. 1. As mentioned above, the input and output of this layer can be denoted as $\mathbf{I}$ and $\mathbf{O}$. The essence of this Pruning layer is a STE which can be defined as below:

$$\text{Forward: } \mathbf{O} = \mathbf{I}$$

$$\text{Backward: } \mathbf{dI} = Stochastic\_Pruning\,(\mathbf{dO}, DBTD(\mathbf{dO}, p))$$

5.2 Speedup Evaluation

To estimate the acceleration effect of our algorithm, we modify the backward Conv layers in Caffe [30] framework, which is widely used in deep learning deployment. As mentioned in Sect. 3.1, two main steps of training stage: $AGBP$, WGC are all based on convolution. Most modern deep learning frameworks including Caffe convert convolution into matrix multiplication by applying the combination of im2col and col2im functions, where im2col turns a 3-D feature map tensor into a 2-D matrix for exploiting data reuse, and col2im is the inverse function of im2col. Hence, our training acceleration with sparse activation gradients can be accomplished by replacing the original matrix multiplication with sparse matrix multiplication.

With our proposed algorithm, the activation gradients $\mathbf{dO}$ can be fairly sparse. However, weight $\mathbf{W}$ and activation $\mathbf{O}$ are completely dense. We found that dense $\times$ sparse matrix multiplication is required for $AGBP$ step. However, the existing BLAS library such as Intel MKL only supports sparse $\times$ dense multiplication. To solve this problem, we turn to compute the transpose of $\mathbf{dI}$ according to the basic property of matrix multiplication $(AB)^T = B^T A^T$, where both A and B are matrices.

To reduce the computation cost, we modify the original im2col and col2im functions to im2col_trans and col2im_trans so that we can get transposed matrix directly after calling these functions. Since plenty of runtime can be saved by using **sparse** × **dense** multiplication, we can also achieve relatively high speedup in the overall back-propagation process, though transpose functions will cost extra runtime. The modified procedure can be summarized as:

$$AGBP: \mathrm{d}\mathbf{I} = \texttt{col2im\_trans}\left(\texttt{sdmm}\left(\texttt{im2col\_trans}\left(\mathrm{d}\mathbf{O}\right), \texttt{transpose}\left(\mathbf{W}\right)\right)\right)$$

$$WGC: \mathrm{d}\mathbf{W} = \texttt{sdmm}\left(\mathrm{d}\mathbf{O}, \texttt{im2col}\left(\mathbf{I}\right)\right)$$

Here **sdmm** denotes the general **sparse** × **dense** matrix multiplication.

6   Experimental Results

In this section, experiments are conducted to demonstrate that the proposed approach could reduce the training cost significantly with a negligible model accuracy loss.

6.1   Datasets and Models

Three datasets are utilized including CIFAR-10, CIFAR-100 [31] and ImageNet [32]. AlexNet [6] and ResNet [8] are evaluated while ResNet include Res-{18, 34, 50, 101, 152}. The last layer size of each model is changed in order to adapt them on CIFAR datasets. Additionally for AlexNet, the kernels in first two convolution layers are set as 3×3 with padding $= 2$ and stride $= 1$. For FC-1 and FC-2 layers in AlexNet, they are also resized to 4096×2048 and 2048×2048, respectively. For ResNet, kernels in first layer are replaced by 3×3 kernels with padding $= 1$ and stride $= 1$. Meanwhile, the pooling layer before FC-1 in ResNet is set to Average-Pooling with the size of 4×4.

6.2   Training Settings

All the 6 models mentioned above are trained for 300 epochs on CIFAR-{10, 100} datasets. While for ImageNet, AlexNet, ResNet-{18, 34, 50} are only trained for 180 epochs due to our limited computing resources.

The Momentum SGD is adopted for all training with momentum $= 0.9$ and weight decay $= 5 \times 10^{-4}$. Learning rate lr is set to 0.05 for AlexNet and 0.1 for the others. lr-decay is set to 0.1/100 for CIFAR-{10, 100} and 0.1/45 for ImageNet.

6.3   Results and Discussions

We set the target pruning rate p defined in Sect. 3.2 varying from 70%, 80%, 90% to 99% for comparison with the baseline. All the training are run directly without any fine-tuning.

Table 1. Evaluation results on CIFAR-10, where acc% means the training accuracy and ρ_{nnz} means the average density of non-zeros.

Model	Baseline		$p = 70\%$		$p = 80\%$		$p = 90\%$		$p = 99\%$	
	acc%	ρ_{nnz}	acc%	ρ_{nnz}	acc%	ρ_{nnz}	acc%	ρ_{nnz}	acc%	ρ_{nnz}
AlexNet	90.50	0.09	90.34	0.01	**90.55**	0.01	90.31	0.01	89.66	0.01
ResNet-18	95.04	1	**95.23**	0.24	95.04	0.22	94.91	0.20	95.18	0.16
ResNet-34	94.90	1	95.13	0.24	95.09	0.21	**95.16**	0.19	95.02	0.15
ResNet-50	94.94	1	**95.36**	0.22	95.13	0.20	95.01	0.17	95.28	0.14
ResNet-101	95.60	1	**95.61**	0.24	95.48	0.22	95.60	0.19	94.77	0.12
ResNet-152	**95.70**	1	95.13	0.18	95.58	0.18	95.45	0.16	93.84	0.08

Table 2. Evaluation results on CIFAR-100, where acc% means the training accuracy and ρ_{nnz} means the average density of non-zeros.

Model	Baseline		$p = 70\%$		$p = 80\%$		$p = 90\%$		$p = 99\%$	
	acc%	ρ_{nnz}	acc%	ρ_{nnz}	acc%	ρ_{nnz}	acc%	ρ_{nnz}	acc%	ρ_{nnz}
AlexNet	67.61	0.10	67.49	0.03	**68.13**	0.03	67.99	0.03	67.93	0.02
ResNet-18	76.47	1	76.89	0.27	**77.16**	0.25	76.44	0.23	76.66	0.19
ResNet-34	77.51	1	77.72	0.24	**78.04**	0.22	77.84	0.20	77.40	0.17
ResNet-50	77.74	1	78.83	0.25	78.27	0.22	**78.92**	0.20	78.52	0.16
ResNet-101	**79.70**	1	78.22	0.23	79.10	0.21	79.08	0.19	77.13	0.13
ResNet-152	79.25	1	**80.51**	0.22	79.42	0.19	79.76	0.18	76.40	0.10

Accuracy Analysis. From Table 1, Table 2 and Table 3 we find that there is no obvious accuracy lost for most situations. And even for ResNet-50 on CIFAR-100, there is 1% accuracy improvement. But for AlexNet on ImageNet, there is a significant accuracy loss when using very aggressive pruning policy like $p = 99\%$. In summary, the accuracy loss is almost negligible when a non-aggressive policy is adopted for gradients pruning.

Gradients Sparsity. The gradients density illustrated in Table 1, Table 2, Table 3 has shown the ratio of non-zero gradients over all gradients, which is related to the amount of calculations. Notice that the output of *DBTD* is the estimation of pruning threshold, so the actual sparsity of each Conv layer's activation gradients will be different, and ρ_{nnz} is calculated by dividing the number of non-zero activation gradients by the number of all gradients for all Conv layers.

Although the basic block of AlexNet is Conv-ReLU whose activation gradients are relatively sparse, our method could still reduce the gradients density for about $5\times \sim 10\times$ on CIFAR-{10, 100} and $3\times \sim 5\times$ on ImageNet. While it comes to ResNet, whose basic block is Conv-BN-ReLU and activation gradients are naturally fully dense, our method could reduce the gradients density to

Table 3. Evaluation results on ImageNet, where acc% means the training accuracy and ρ_{nnz} means the average density of non-zeros.

Model	Baseline		$p = 70\%$		$p = 80\%$		$p = 90\%$		$p = 99\%$	
	acc%	ρ_{nnz}	acc%	ρ_{nnz}	acc%	ρ_{nnz}	acc%	ρ_{nnz}	acc%	ρ_{nnz}
AlexNet	56.38	0.07	**57.10**	0.05	56.84	0.04	55.38	0.04	39.58	0.02
ResNet-18	68.73	1	**69.02**	0.34	68.85	0.33	68.66	0.31	68.74	0.28
ResNet-34	**72.93**	1	72.92	0.35	72.86	0.33	72.74	0.30	72.42	0.30

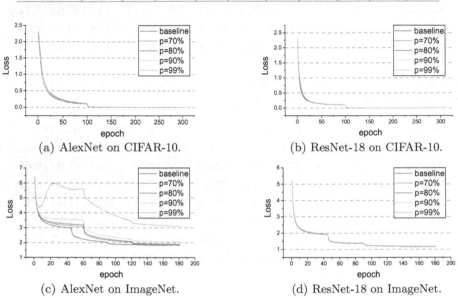

(a) AlexNet on CIFAR-10.　　　　　(b) ResNet-18 on CIFAR-10.

(c) AlexNet on ImageNet.　　　　　(d) ResNet-18 on ImageNet.

Fig. 3. Training loss of AlexNet/ResNet on CIFAR-10 and ImageNet.

$10\% \sim 30\%$. In addition, the deeper networks could obtain a relative lower gradients density, which means that it works better for complicated networks.

Convergence Rate. The training loss is also displayed Fig. 3 for AlexNet, ResNet-18 on CIFAR-10 and ImageNet datasets. Figure 3b and Fig. 3d show that ResNet-18 is very robust for gradients pruning. For AlexNet, the gradients pruning could be still robust on CIFAR-10. However, Fig. 3d confirms that sparsification with a larger p will impact the convergence rate. In conclusion, our pruning method doesn't have significant effect on the convergence rate in most cases. This conclusion accords with the our convergence analysis on Sect. 4.

Acceleration on Desktop CPU. To examine the performance of our proposed approach in practical applications, we implement experiments on low computation power scenarios, where there exists an urgent need for acceleration in the training process. We use 1 core Intel CPU (Intel Xeon E5–2680 v4 2.4 GHz) as computation platform and Intel MKL as BLAS library for evaluation. We set

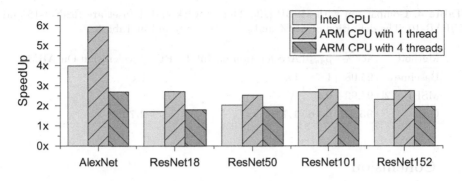

Fig. 4. Speedup evaluation results on CPU. The height of the bar denotes the average acceleration rate of all selected epochs.

$p = 99\%$ for ResNet-{18,50,101,152} and AlexNet on CIFAR-10 dataset and export the d$\mathbf{O}$/$\mathbf{I}$/$\mathbf{W}$ from the training process of accuracy evaluation experiment every 50 epochs, and use those data to collect the latency of *AFBP* and *WGC* in our framework. The baseline of this experiment is the original back-propagation implementation of Caffe. According to the results in Fig. 4, our algorithm can achieve $1.71\times \sim 3.99\times$ speedup on average. These speedups refer to the acceleration of back-propagation while the forward stage is not included.

Acceleration on ARM CPU. We further evaluate our approach on ARM platform which is wildly used in edge computing. We choose Raspberry Pi 4B (with ARMv7 1500 Hz) as experimental device and Eigen3 [33] as BLAS library in this experiment because Intel MKL can't be deployed on ARM. In ARM experiment, we use the same setting as the desktop CPU experiment in Sect. 6.3. Besides, we evaluate our approach with both single thread and four threads. According to Fig. 4, in single thread experiments, the speedup of `Conv` Layer's back-propagation stage on ARM platform can be up to $5.92\times$ with AlexNet. As for those networks that use `Conv-BN-RELU` as the basic module such as ResNet-{18,50,101,152}, our approach can also achieve $2.52\times \sim 2.79\times$ acceleration. On the other hand, the acceleration rate decrease in four thread experiment but can still reach $1.79\times \sim 2.78\times$ speedup. The results illustrate that our algorithm still performs well on embedded device which is more urgent in reducing calculation time.

Comparison with Existing Works. Meprop [20] has only experiments on MLP. [21] supplements the CNN evaluation on the basis of Meprop [20]. However, their chosen networks are unrepresentative because they are too naive to be adopted in practical applications. Based on [21], MSBP [22] makes further improvements, which is comparing with our method as illustrated in Table. 4. Our proposed algorithm can achieve higher sparsity than MSBP while keeping a better accuracy than baseline and MSBP on CIFAR-10. More importantly, the experiment result also shows that our work is also well performed on ImageNet which is more challenging but has not been evaluated in existing works.

Table 4. Comparison with MSBP [22]. The network and dataset are ResNet-18 and CIFAR-10. The definition of acc% and ρ_{nnz} can be found in Table 3.

Method	acc%	ρ_{nnz}	Acceleration on Intel CPU	Acceleration On ARM
Baseline	95.08	1	1×	1×
MSBP [22]	94.92	0.4	\	\
Ours	**95.18**	**0.16**	**1.71×**	**2.70×**

7   Conclusion

In this paper, we propose a new dynamically gradients pruning algorithm for CNN training. Different from the existing works, we assume the activation gradients of CNN satisfy normal distribution and then estimate their variance according to their average absolute value. After that, we calculate the pruning threshold according to the variance and a preset parameter p. The gradients are pruned randomly if they are under the threshold. Evaluations on state-of-the-art models have confirmed that our gradients pruning approach could accelerate the back-propagation up to 3.99× on desktop CPU and 5.92× on ARM CPU with a negligible accuracy loss.

References

1. Goyal, P., et al.: Accurate, large minibatch sgd: training imagenet in 1 hour. arXiv preprint arXiv:1706.02677 (2017)
2. You, Y., Zhang, Z., Hsieh, C.J., Demmel, J., Keutzer, K.: Imagenet training in minutes. In: Proceedings of the 47th International Conference on Parallel Processing, p. 1. ACM (2018)
3. Jia, X., et al.: Highly scalable deep learning training system with mixed-precision: training imagenet in four minutes. arXiv preprint arXiv:1807.11205 (2018)
4. Cheng, J., Wang, P.S., Li, G., Hu, Q.H., Lu, H.Q.: Recent advances in efficient computation of deep convolutional neural networks. Front. Inform. Technol. Electron. Eng. **19**(1), 64–77 (2018)
5. Micikevicius, P., et al.: Mixed precision training. arXiv preprint arXiv:1710.03740 (2017)
6. Krizhevsky, A., Sutskever, I., Hinton, G.E.: ImageNet classification with deep convolutional neural networks. In: Proceedings of the Advances in Neural Information Processing Systems, pp. 1097–1105 (2012)
7. Simonyan, K., Zisserman, A.: Very deep convolutional networks for large-scale image recognition. arXiv preprint arXiv:1409.1556 (2014)
8. He, K., Zhang, X., Ren, S., Sun, J.: Deep residual learning for image recognition. In: Proceedings of the IEEE Conference on Computer Vision and Pattern Recognition, pp. 770–778 (2016)
9. Han, S., Mao, H., Dally, W.J.: Deep compression: compressing deep neural networks with pruning, trained quantization and huffman coding. arXiv preprint arXiv:1510.00149 (2015)

10. Mao, H., et al.: Exploring the regularity of sparse structure in convolutional neural networks. arXiv preprint arXiv:1705.08922 (2017)
11. Anwar, S., Hwang, K., Sung, W.: Structured pruning of deep convolutional neural networks. ACM J. Emerg. Technol. Comput. Syst. **13**(3), 32 (2017)
12. Lebedev, V., Lempitsky, V.: Fast convnets using group-wise brain damage. In: Proceedings of the IEEE Conference on Computer Vision and Pattern Recognition, pp. 2554–2564 (2016)
13. Luo, J.H., Wu, J., Lin, W.: Thinet: a filter level pruning method for deep neural network compression. In: Proceedings of the IEEE International Conference on Computer Vision, pp. 5058–5066 (2017)
14. He, Y., Zhang, X., Sun, J.: Channel pruning for accelerating very deep neural networks. In: Proceedings of the IEEE International Conference on Computer Vision, pp. 1389–1397 (2017)
15. Liu, Z., Li, J., Shen, Z., Huang, G., Yan, S., Zhang, C.: Learning efficient convolutional networks through network slimming. In: Proceedings of the IEEE International Conference on Computer Vision, pp. 2736–2744 (2017)
16. Wen, W., Xu, C., Wu, C., Wang, Y., Chen, Y., Li, H.: Coordinating filters for faster deep neural networks. In: Proceedings of the IEEE International Conference on Computer Vision, pp. 658–666 (2017)
17. Wen, W., et al.: Learning intrinsic sparse structures within long short-term memory. arXiv preprint arXiv:1709.05027 (2017)
18. Aji, A.F., Heafield, K.: Sparse communication for distributed gradient descent. arXiv preprint arXiv:1704.05021 (2017)
19. Prakash, A., Storer, J., Florencio, D., Zhang, C.: Repr: improved training of convolutional filters. arXiv preprint arXiv:1811.07275 (2018)
20. Sun, X., Ren, X., Ma, S., Wang, H.: meprop: sparsified back propagation for accelerated deep learning with reduced overfitting. In: Proceedings of the 34th International Conference on Machine Learning, vol. 70, pp. 3299–3308 (2017)
21. Wei, B., Sun, X., Ren, X., Xu, J.: Minimal effort back propagation for convolutional neural networks. arXiv preprint arXiv:1709.05804 (2017)
22. Zhang, Z., Yang, P., Ren, X., Sun, X.: Memorized sparse backpropagation. arXiv preprint arXiv:1905.10194 (2019)
23. Gupta, S., Agrawal, A., Gopalakrishnan, K., Narayanan, P.: Deep learning with limited numerical precision. In: Proceedings of the International Conference on Machine Learning, pp. 1737–1746 (2015)
24. Zhou, S., Wu, Y., Ni, Z., Zhou, X., Wen, H., Zou, Y.: DoReFa-Net: training low bitwidth convolutional neural networks with low bitwidth gradients. arXiv preprint arXiv:1606.06160 (2016)
25. Park, E., Yoo, S., Vajda, P.: Value-aware quantization for training and inference of neural networks. In: Proceedings of the European Conference on Computer Vision, pp. 580–595 (2018)
26. Szegedy, C., Vanhoucke, V., Ioffe, S., Shlens, J., Wojna, Z.: Rethinking the inception architecture for computer vision. In: Proceedings of the IEEE Conference on Computer Vision and Pattern Recognition, pp. 2818–2826 (2016)
27. Wen, W., et al.: TernGrad: ternary gradients to reduce communication in distributed deep learning. In: Proceedings of the Advances in Neural Information Processing Systems, pp. 1509–1519 (2017)
28. Bottou, L.: Online learning and stochastic approximations. On-Line Learn. Neural Netw. **17**(9), 142 (1998)
29. Paszke, A., et al.: Automatic differentiation in PyTorch. In: NIPS Workshop (2017)

30. Jia, Y., et al.: Caffe: convolutional architecture for fast feature embedding. arXiv preprint arXiv:1408.5093 (2014)
31. Krizhevsky, A., Hinton, G.: Learning multiple layers of features from tiny images. Technical report, Citeseer (2009)
32. Deng, J., Dong, W., Socher, R., Li, L.J., Li, K., Li, F.F.: ImageNet: a large-scale hierarchical image database. In: Proceedings of the IEEE Conference on Computer Vision and Pattern Recognition, pp. 248–255 (2009)
33. Guennebaud, G., Jacob, B., et al.: Eigen v3. http://eigen.tuxfamily.org (2010)

Global and Local Enhancement Networks for Paired and Unpaired Image Enhancement

Han-Ul Kim[1], Young Jun Koh[2]([✉]), and Chang-Su Kim[1]

[1] Korea University, Seoul, Korea
hanulkim@mcl.korea.ac.kr, changsukim@korea.ac.kr
[2] Chungnam National University, Daejeon, Korea
yjkoh@cnu.ac.kr

Abstract. A novel approach for paired and unpaired image enhancement is proposed in this work. First, we develop global enhancement network (GEN) and local enhancement network (LEN), which can faithfully enhance images. The proposed GEN performs the channel-wise intensity transforms that can be trained easier than the pixel-wise prediction. The proposed LEN refines GEN results based on spatial filtering. Second, we propose different training schemes for paired learning and unpaired learning to train GEN and LEN. Especially, we propose a two-stage training scheme based on generative adversarial networks for unpaired learning. Experimental results demonstrate that the proposed algorithm outperforms the state-of-the-arts in paired and unpaired image enhancement. Notably, the proposed unpaired image enhancement algorithm provides better results than recent state-of-the-art paired image enhancement algorithms. The source codes and trained models are available at https://github.com/hukim1124/GleNet.

Keywords: Image enhancement · Unpaired learning · Generative adversarial network

1 Introduction

Nowadays, many people take photographs to record everyday life as well as important events. However, uncontrolled environments often make photographs have low dynamic ranges or distorted color tones. Therefore, image enhancement becomes more popular that edits photographs to improve their aesthetic quality. Image enhancement methods can be categorized into global and local approaches. The former derives a transformation function that maps input color to output color. On the other hand, the latter performs spatial filtering to determine a pixel color according to local neighborhood information. Professional software

Electronic supplementary material The online version of this chapter (https:// doi.org/10.1007/978-3-030-58595-2_21) contains supplementary material, which is available to authorized users.

© Springer Nature Switzerland AG 2020
A. Vedaldi et al. (Eds.): ECCV 2020, LNCS 12370, pp. 339–354, 2020.
https://doi.org/10.1007/978-3-030-58595-2_21

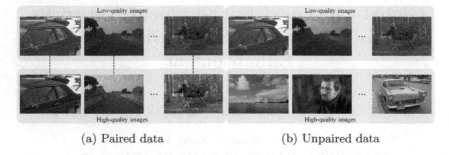

(a) Paired data   (b) Unpaired data

Fig. 1. Examples of paired and unpaired data

applications such as Photoshop provide various global and local enhancement tools to support manual image enhancement. However, the manual process is time-consuming. Moreover, its results highly depend on users' skills and experience.

For automatic image enhancement, many studies have been proposed. Most early studies focus on the global approach since it is more stable and requires less computational complexity than the local approach. However, using only a single transformation function may be insufficient to produce satisfying enhanced images. In contrast, recent studies [8,25,30,33] based on deep learning mainly take the local approach. These methods learn a robust pixel-wise mapping from lots of paired data, which consists of inputs and ground-truth enhanced images, and provide promising enhanced images. However, they require many image pairs of low-quality and high-quality images as in Fig. 1(a). To overcome this problem, unpaired image enhancement, which does not require the image pairs, has drawn much attention to many researches [4,5,12,19,26,34]. Especially, generative adversarial networks (GANs) [4,5,19] or reinforcement learning [12,26,34] are employed to achieve unpaired image enhancement using unpaired data in Fig. 1(b). However, despite some progress by existing studies, their results are not satisfying when compared with existing paired image enhancement methods.

In this paper, we propose two networks, global enhancement network (GEN) and local enhancement network (LEN), to achieve both paired and unpaired image enhancement. GEN performs the channel-wise intensity transform, which can be trained much easier than the pixel-wise prediction based on U-Net architecture [27]. LEN conducts spatial filtering to refine GEN results. We then develop two training schemes for paired learning and unpaired learning. Especially, we propose a two-stage training scheme for unpaired learning based on generative adversarial networks. Experiments on the MIT-Adobe 5 K dataset [2] demonstrate that the proposed method outperforms the state-of-the-arts in both paired and unpaired image enhancement. Moreover, it is shown that the proposed unpaired method yields better enhanced results than conventional paired methods.

To summarize, this work has three main contributions:

- We propose GEN and LEN for both paired and unpaired image enhancement.
- We propose the two-stage training scheme for unpaired image enhancement.
- The proposed method shows outstanding performance on the MIT-Adobe 5 K dataset.

2 Related Work

Early studies on image enhancement mainly focus on improving the global contrast of an input image [16,24]. They often derive a transformation function that maps input pixel values to output pixel values. The global contrast technique uses a single mapping function for all pixels in an entire image. For instance, power-law (gamma) and log transformations [9] are well-known global methods. Histogram equalization [9] and its variants [1,17,21–23,29,32] modify the histogram of an image to stretch its limited dynamic range. Retinex methods [3,6,7,11,13,14,31,35] decompose an image into reflectance and illumination [20], and modify the illumination to enhance a poorly lit image. However, these methods may not emulate the complex mapping function between an image and its professionally enhanced version.

Recent studies on image enhancement take data-driven approaches that learn the mapping between input and enhanced images using a large dataset. For this purpose, Bychkovsky *et al.* [2] introduced the MIT-Adobe 5 K dataset, which contains 5,000 input images and enhanced images retouched by 5 different photographers. This dataset is widely adopted to train deep neural networks. Yan *et al.* [33] predicts a pixel-wise color mapping using image descriptors from a deep neural network. Lore *et al.* [25] first adopt an autoencoder approach to enhance low-light images. Gharbi *et al.* [8] achieved real-time image enhancement by developing deep bilateral learning, which predicts local affine transforms. Based on the retinex theory, Wang *et al.* [30] proposed a deep network to estimate an image-to-illumination mapping function. These deep learning methods [8,25,30,33] yield promising enhancement performances, but they are limited in that they demand many pairs of input and enhanced images to train their networks.

Collecting pairs of input and manually enhanced images is a labor-intensive task. To overcome this problem, unpaired learning methods [4,5,12,19,26,34], which do not require paired data, have been proposed. Park *et al.* [26] adopted deep reinforcement learning to mimic step-by-step human retouching processes. Also, they proposed a distort-and-recover training scheme, which distorts a high-quality image to generate a pseudo input and trains networks to enhance the generated pseudo input to be similar to the corresponding high-quality image. Deng *et al.* [5] employed a generative adversarial network (GAN) to develop an aesthetic-driven image enhancement method. Chen *et al.* [4] proposed an adaptive weighting scheme for stable training of two-way GANs. Hu *et al.* [12] integrated an adversarial loss into reinforcement learning to generate a sequence of enhancement operations. Yu *et al.* [34] trained local exposures with deep reinforcement adversarial learning, which divides an image into sub-images and

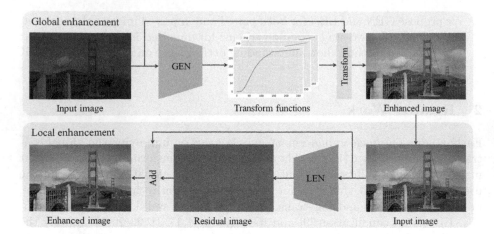

Fig. 2. Overview of the proposed global enhancement network (GEN) and local enhancement network (LEN).

enhances them with different policies. Recently, Kosugi and Toshihiko [19] combined reinforcement learning and adversarial learning to control tools in professional image editing software. However, these unpaired learning methods provide relatively poor results than paired learning methods.

3   Proposed Algorithm

3.1   Model

Figure 2 shows an overview of the proposed image enhancement framework. First, we develop GEN that produce channel-wise intensity transform functions to achieve global image enhancement. Second, we learn LEN, which performs spatial filtering, to refine global enhanced images. Let us describe each network subsequently.

Global Enhancement Network: Let $\mathbf{I}(p) = (I_r(p), I_g(p), I_b(p))^T$ denote 8-bit intensity for red, greed, and blue channels at pixel position p. Also, let $\mathbf{w}_c = [w_{c,0}, \ldots, w_{c,255}]^T$ denote the transformation function for the channel $c \in \{r, g, b\}$, whose kth element $w_{c,k}$ maps intensity k in I_c to intensity $w_{c,k}$ in the output intensity $\tilde{I}_c$. Thus, the transformed intensity for the channel c at pixel p is defined as

$$\tilde{I}_c(p) = \mathbf{v}_p^T \mathbf{w}_c \tag{1}$$

where $\mathbf{v}_p^T$ denotes a 256-dimensional one-hot vector, whose $I_c(p)$th element is 1 and the others are 0.

Given an RGB image of size 256×256, GEN produces a 768-dimensional vector $\mathbf{w} = \mathbf{w}_r \| \mathbf{w}_g \| \mathbf{w}_b$, which is a concatenated vector of three transformation functions $\mathbf{w}_r, \mathbf{w}_g, \mathbf{w}_b$. Table 1 specifies the detailed architecture of GEN.

Table 1. Specification for global enhancement network.

Stage	Operator	Output resolution	Channels
1	Conv5x5	128×128	16
2	Inverted Residual, 5x5	64×64	24
3	Inverted Residual, 5x5	32×32	40
4	Inverted Residual, 5x5	16×16	80
5	Inverted Residual, 5x5	8×8	112
6	Conv1x1 & Pool 8x8	1×1	768
7	Conv1x1	1×1	768

We employ the inverted residual block in MobileNetV3 [4] to reduces the number of network parameters. All "Conv" operations except the last one include convolution filters, batch normalization, and swish activation. The last "Conv" only contains convolution filters. Finally, we perform the channel-wise intensity transformation to obtain global enhanced images by sequentially applying output functions $\mathbf{w}_r$, $\mathbf{w}_g$, and $\mathbf{w}_b$ to (1). Note that GEN can be trained in an end-to-end manner, since the intensity transformation is differentiable operation.

The proposed GEN has advantages when compared with the conventional image enhancement network in [4], which contains a decoder to produce pixel-wise color predictions. First, GEN can enhance an image regardless of its resolution scale by performing the channel-wise intensity transformation unlike the pixel-wise color prediction [4]. In other words, the channel-wise intensity transformation can produce enhanced images without any image resize process, while the pixel-wise color prediction often requires the resize process according to the spatial size of input images. Second, GEN can save the memory for network parameters, since it does not require a decoder part to restore the spatial resolution of enhanced images. Third, training GEN is much easier than the networks that have the encoder-decoder architecture. In Sect. 4.1, we will clarify that GEN requires less training steps for the convergence than the encoder-decoder architecture does.

Different from early global enhancement methods, we do not suppose that the three color intensity transformation functions should be a monotonic function. Most existing global methods focus on enhancing the gray intensity instead of color intensities and suppose the monotonic constraint to prevent annoying artifacts due to the reservation of the gray intensity ordering. However, the monotonic constraint does not work in the channel-wise intensity transformation. Figure 3 shows examples of pairs of input and retouched images and their channel-wise intensity transformation functions. In these example, we see that there are many non-monotonic functions between low-quality and high-quality images.

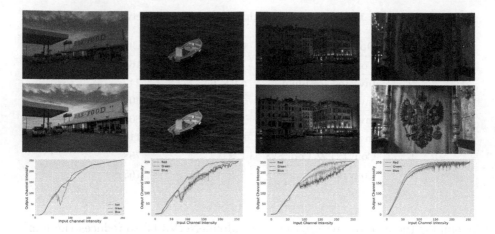

Fig. 3. From top to bottom, input images, retouched images, and channel-wise intensity transformation functions.

Local Enhancement Network. Despite many strengths in GEN, it is limited in that GEN considers only one-to-one mapping. However, as in Fig. 3, there are many one-to-many mappings, which are delineated by shading in the channel-wise transformation functions, between low-quality and high-quality images. Moreover, GEN may experience difficulty on removing noises and blur in an input image through the channel-wise intensity transformation. Therefore, we develop LEN, which performs spatial filtering for local enhancement, to overcome these limitations of GEN.

Table 2 provides the specification of the LEN architecture. LEN has an encoder-decoder structure. The encoder takes an enhanced images $\tilde{I}_{global}$ of GEN. The encoder reduces the spatial resolution of I_{global} to exploit larger receptive fields for spatial filtering, while the decoder performs up-sampling to restore the spatial resolution. LEN uses the inverted residual block to decrease the number of network parameters. In Table 2, "Upsample" denotes the bilinear interpolation to increase the size of the feature map with scale factor 2. "Concat" layers in the 6th, 8th, and 10th stages concatenates the previous stage results with the outputs of the 3rd, 2nd, and 1st stages, respectively. The last convolution layer yields the residual image $\Delta\tilde{I}_{local}$ for enhancing local regions of $\tilde{I}_{global}$. Finally, the enhanced image $\tilde{I}$ is obtained by

$$\tilde{I} = \tilde{I}_{global} + \Delta\tilde{I}_{local}. \tag{2}$$

3.2 Learning

We describe training schemes for unpaired learning and paired learning. First, we train GEN and LEN using pairs of low-quality and high-quality images for paired learning. Second, we propose the two-stage training scheme to learn GEN and LEN in unpaired learning. Let us explain each training scheme subsequently.

Table 2. Specification for local enhancement network.

Stage	Operator	Output resolution	Channels
1	Conv5x5	H × W	16
2	Inverted Residual, 5x5	H/2 × W/2	24
3	Inverted Residual, 5x5	H/4 × W/4	40
4	Inverted Residual, 5x5	H/8 × W/8	80
5	Inverted Residual, 5x5	H/8 × W/8	40
6	Upsample & Concat	H/4 × W/4	80
7	Inverted Residual, 5x5	H/4 × W/4	24
8	Upsample & Concat	H/2 × W/2	48
9	Inverted Residual, 5x5	H/2 × W/2	16
10	Upsample & Concat	H × W	32
11	Conv5x5 & Add	H × W	3

Paired Learning: Suppose the set of image pairs $\{(I_i^{\mathrm{LQ}}, I_i^{\mathrm{HQ}})\}_{i=1}^N$ are available, where I_i^{LQ} and I_i^{HQ} are the low-quality image and its high-quality image, respectively. We train GEN and LEN simultaneously to minimize the color loss and the perceptual loss between the estimated image $\tilde{I}_i^{\mathrm{HQ}}$ and the ground-truth high-quality image I_i^{HQ}. The total loss is defined as

$$\mathcal{L}_{\mathrm{p}} = \|\tilde{I}_i^{\mathrm{HQ}} - I_i^{\mathrm{HQ}}\|_1 + \lambda_{\mathrm{p}} \sum_{k=2,4,6} \|\phi^k(\tilde{I}_i^{\mathrm{HQ}}) - \phi^k(I_i^{\mathrm{HQ}})\|_1. \qquad (3)$$

The color loss in the first term penalizes the mean absolute error between the predicted and ground-truth high-quality images. On the other hand, the second term is the perceptual loss [15] to encourage the enhanced image and the ground-truth image to have similar features on the pre-trained embedding space. Thus, we employ VGG-16 [28] pre-trained on ImageNet to extract features. In (3), $\phi^k(\cdot)$ denotes the feature, which is extracted from the kth VGG-16 layer. The hyper parameter λ_{p} balances two loss components.

Unpaired Learning: Let $\{I_i^{\mathrm{LQ}}\}_{i=1}^M \in \mathbf{I}^{\mathrm{LQ}}$ and $\{I_j^{\mathrm{HQ}}\}_{j=1}^N \in \mathbf{I}^{\mathrm{HQ}}$ be the sets of low-quality images and high-quality images, respectively. Our goal in unpaired learning is to learn GEN and LEN using unpaired training samples $\mathbf{I}^{\mathrm{LQ}}$ and $\mathbf{I}^{\mathrm{HQ}}$. First, we adopt the adversarial learning framework to train GEN. We regard GEN as a generator. Also, the architecture of a discriminator is the same as the generator except the last convolution layer to produce a scalar output that discriminates between generated samples and real samples. Then, we design two types of GANs, where the one enhances low-quality to high-quality images (Fig. 4(a)), and the other degrades high-quality to low-quality images (Fig. 4(b)). Let $G_{\mathrm{e}} : \mathbf{I}^{\mathrm{LQ}} \rightarrow \mathbf{I}^{\mathrm{HQ}}$ and $G_{\mathrm{d}} : \mathbf{I}^{\mathrm{HQ}} \rightarrow \mathbf{I}^{\mathrm{LQ}}$ denote mapping functions for generators to enhance and degrade input images, respectively. Also, let

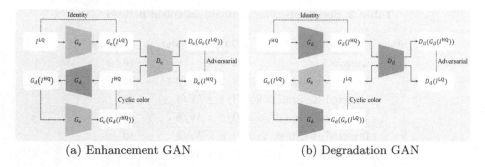

(a) Enhancement GAN   (b) Degradation GAN

Fig. 4. The network architectures of (a) enhancement GAN and (b) degradation GAN.

D_e and D_d denote discriminators to discriminate between high-quality images $\{I^{HQ}\}$ and enhanced images $\{G_e(I^{LQ})\}$ and between low-quality images $\{I^{LQ}\}$ and degraded images $\{G_d(I^{HQ})\}$, respectively.

We employ the Wasserstein GAN with gradient penalty (WGAN-GP) [10] to define objective functions of generators and discriminators. The discriminator losses $\mathcal{L}_{D_e}$ and $\mathcal{L}_{D_d}$ for D_e and D_d are defined as

$$\mathcal{L}_{D_e} = D_e(G_e(I^{LQ})) - D_e(I^{HQ}) + \lambda_{gp}(\|\nabla_{\bar{I}^{HQ}} D_e(\bar{I}^{HQ})\|_2 - 1)^2$$
$$\mathcal{L}_{D_d} = D_d(G_d(I^{HQ})) - D_d(I^{LQ}) + \lambda_{gp}(\|\nabla_{\bar{I}^{LQ}} D_B(\bar{I}^{LQ})\|_2 - 1)^2. \tag{4}$$

In both discriminator losses $\mathcal{L}_{D_e}$ and $\mathcal{L}_{D_d}$, the first two terms are adversarial losses. The last terms are gradient penalty to satisfy the Lipschitz constraint in WGAN-GP. The image $\bar{I}^{HQ}$ is obtained by interpolating $G_e(I^{LQ})$ and I^{HQ} with random weights. Similarly, $\bar{I}^{LQ}$ is computed using $G_d(I^{HQ})$ and I^{LQ}. The hyper-parameter λ_{gp} is a weight for the gradient penalty.

Also, for training generators G_e and G_d, we define the loss functions as

$$\mathcal{L}_{G_e} = -D_e(G_e(I^{LQ})) + \lambda_i\|G_e(I^{LQ}) - I^{LQ}\|_1 + \lambda_c\|G_e(G_d(I^{HQ})) - I^{HQ}\|_1$$
$$\mathcal{L}_{G_d} = -D_d(G_d(I^{HQ})) + \lambda_i\|G_d(I^{HQ}) - I^{HQ}\|_1 + \lambda_c\|G_d(G_e(I^{LQ})) - I^{LQ}\|_1 \tag{5}$$

which is composed of adversarial, identity, and cyclic color losses. The adversarial loss (first term) penalizes the Wasserstein distance between generated images and real images. The identity loss (second term) prevents generated images from becoming too different from input images. Note that the identity supports stable training by reducing the space of possible mapping functions. Also, we design the cyclic color loss (third term), which enforces that the reconstructed image should be similar to its origin. For instance, the cyclic color loss minimizes the mean absolute error between $G_e(G_d(I^{HQ}))$ and I^{HQ} to train the enhancement GAN in Fig. 4(a). To this end, we can learn the generator G_e to yield enhanced images that are similar to the high-quality images in $\mathbf{I}^{HQ}$. Note that the cyclic color loss is different from the cyclic consistency loss in [36], which argues that I^{LQ} and $G_d(G_e(I^{LQ}))$ should be similar for training G_e. In Sect. 4.2, we will verify the effectiveness of the proposed cyclic color loss as compared with the cyclic consistency loss in [36].

Next, we train LEN using the trained GEN. Notice that training LEN is more difficult than training GEN since LEN is designed to produce the pixel-wise prediction, which requires the more complicated mapping function than the channel-wise intensity transform in GEN. Therefore, we take a different approach to train LEN. More specifically, we degrade a high-quality image I^{HQ} in the training samples using the generator G_d to obtain a pseudo pair of low-quality and high-quality images, $(G_d(I^{HQ}), I^{HQ})$. Then, we enhance the degraded image using the generator G_e. To this end, we can obtain a pseudo pair of global enhanced image and high-quality images, $(G_e(G_d(I^{HQ})), I^{HQ})$. Finally, we train LEN using this paired data by minimizing the loss in (3).

4   Experiments

Experiments are organized as follows. In Sect. 4.1, we verify the effectiveness of GEN and LEN when pairs of low-quality and high-quality images are available. We compare the performance of the proposed GEN and LEN with state-of-the-art algorithms based on paired learning. In Sect. 4.2, we train GEN and LEN using the proposed unpaired learning and perform the comparison with state-of-the-art methods in unpaired image enhancement.

For all experiments, we use the MIT-Adobe 5 K dataset [2] that contains 5,000 input images, each of which was manually retouched by five different photographers (A/B/C/D/E). Thus, there are five sets of 5,000 pairs of input and retouched images, one set for each photographer. Among these sets, we use high-quality images retouched by photographer C only for training and test as done in most existing image enhancement algorithms. We split the 5,000 images into 500 and 4,500 images, which are used for the training and test sets, respectively. We use all 4,500 image pairs in training set for paired learning. In contrast, for unpaired learning, the 4,500 image pairs divided into two groups, each of which has 2,250 image pairs. Then, 2,250 input images in the first group are included in the low-quality image set, while 2,250 retouched images in the second group are used for the high-quality image set. Notice that images in the low-quality set and the high-quality set are not overlapped.

For quantitative assessment, we employ PSNR and SSIM, which measure, respectively, color and structural similarity between predicted and ground-truth high-quality images.

4.1   Paired Learning

For paired learning, we use 4,500 training image pairs to train GEN and LEN. We minimize the loss in (3) using the Adam optimizer [18] with an learning rate of 1.0×10^{-4}. The training is iterated for 25,000 mini-batches. The mini-batch size is 16. For data augmentation, we randomly rotate images by multiples of 90 degrees. The parameter λ_p in (3) is fixed to 0.04.

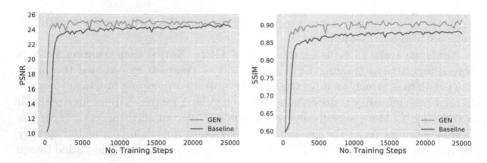

Fig. 5. PSNR and SSIM scores of GEN and the baseline network according to the number of training iterations.

Table 3. Quantitative comparison of the proposed algorithm with state-of-the-art methods based on paired learning. The best results are boldfaced.

Method	HDRNet [8]	DPE [4]	DUPE [30]	GEN	GEN & LEN
PSNR	23.44	22.34	23.61	25.47	**25.88**
SSIM	0.882	0.873	0.887	0.917	**0.925**

First, we verify the effectiveness of the proposed GEN by comparing the channel-wise intensity transform in GEN with the pixel-wise color prediction. For this comparison, we design a baseline network, which produces pixel-wise enhanced results. More specifically, the baseline network has the encoder-decoder architecture, where the encoder has the same structure as the encoder in GEN, and the decoder consists of 6 up-sample blocks to perform bilinear interpolation, concatenation, and convolution filtering, subsequently. The detailed architecture of the baseline network can be found in the supplementary material. Figure 5 shows PSNR and SSIM scores of GEN and the baseline network according to training steps. We observe that GEN achieves faster training than the baseline through the channel-wise intensity transform. This is because the space of possible functions for the intensity transform is much smaller than that of the pixel-wise color transform. Notably, the proposed GEN surpasses the best performance of the baseline networks within 5,000 iterations in both metrics.

Next, we compare the proposed GEN and LEN with recent state-of-the-art algorithms [4,8,30]. For comparison, we obtain the results of conventional algorithms using the source codes and settings provided by respective authors. Table 3 reports PSNR and SSIM scores. The proposed GEN significantly outperforms all conventional algorithms. For instance, it convinces margins of 1.86dB and 0.030 against DUPE [30] in terms of PSNR and SSIM. Also, LEN overcomes the one-to-many mapping problems of GEN by exploiting local neighbor information. Note that LEN further improves results of GEN, and thus joint GEN and LEN (GEN & LEN) achieves the best performance in both metrics.

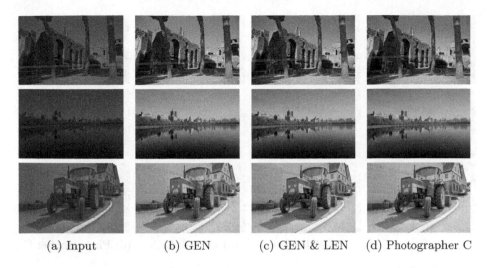

| (a) Input | (b) GEN | (c) GEN & LEN | (d) Photographer C |

Fig. 6. Qualitative comparison between GEN and GEN & LEN methods.

Figure 6 illustrates the efficacy of the proposed LEN. In Fig. 6(b), GEN yields slightly different color tones in the sky, water, and a tractor compared to photographer C's retouched images in Fig. 6(d). This is because GEN fails to deal with one-to-many transformation. For instance, since sky and ground regions in the first row in Fig. 6(a) have similar intensities in the blue channel. Then, GEN produces similar blue intensities between the sky and ground regions. Therefore, as in Fig. 6(b), blue intensities in the sky region are not sufficiently enhanced since GEN is tailored to enhance the ground region. LEN overcomes this problem through effective spatial filtering, as in Fig. 6(c). Compare to GEN, GEN & LEN yields more visually pleasing results, which have similar color tones to the manually retouched images in Fig. 6(d).

Figure 7 compares the proposed algorithm with DUPE [30] qualitatively. In Fig. 7(h), DUPE [30] fails to express similar color tones and brightness to photographer C's retouched images in Fig. 7(d). Also, the results of DUPE have limited contrast. On the other hand, the proposed algorithm successfully yields high-quality images with vivid color tones, which are similar to photographer C's retouched images.

4.2   Unpaired Learning

We perform the two-stage training for unpaired image enhancement. Specifically, we train GEN and LEN for 5,000 and 25,000 mini-batches, respectively, where the size of mini-batch is fixed to 8. The Adam optimizer [18] is employed again. We set the initial learning rate to 1.0×10^{-4}, and reduce it by a factor of 0.5 every 10,000 mini-batches. Hyper parameters λ_{gp}, λ_i, λ_c, and λ_p are set to 10, 5, 50, and 0.04, respectively. For data augmentation, we randomly rotate images by multiples of 90 degrees.

(a) Input   (b) DUPE [30]   (c) GEN & LEN   (d) Photographer C

Fig. 7. Qualitative comparison of the proposed algorithm with DUPE [30].

Table 4. Quantitative comparison of the proposed algorithm with state-of-the-art methods based on unpaired learning. The best results are boldfaced.

Method	D& R [26]	DPE [4]	FRL [19]	GEN	GEN & LEN
PSNR	21.60	21.86	22.27	23.74	**23.82**
SSIM	0.875	0.880	0.881	0.885	**0.889**

In Table 4, we compare the proposed algorithm with the conventional unpaired image enhancement algorithms [4,19,26] using the MIT-Adobe 5 K dataset. The proposed GEN outperforms all conventional algorithms since it can be easily trained with unpaired data. This indicates that the channel-wise intensity transform in GEN is suitable for unpaired learning. Also, we see that GEN & LEN improves both PSNR and SSIM scores, as compared with GEN, and yields the best results in all metrics. It is worth pointing that GEN & LEN outperforms all conventional paired image enhancement algorithms in Table 3, even though only unpaired data is used for training.

Figure 8 qualitatively compares the proposed algorithm with FRL [19]. The proposed GEN & LEN model provides more faithful images than FRL. For instance, FRL fails to increase brightness sufficiently, as in images in Fig. 8(b). In contrast, the proposed algorithm successfully enhances low-quality images to be similar to high-quality images retouched by Photographer C.

The proposed training scheme in unpaired learning generates pseudo paired data to train LEN. For the generation of pseudo paired data, each high-quality image is first degraded ($I^{HQ} \rightarrow G_d(I^{HQ})$) and then the degraded image is enhanced to mimic global image enhancement ($G_d(I^{HQ}) \rightarrow G_e(G_d(I^{HQ}))$). We qualitatively analyze the accuracy of the pseudo pair generation. Figure 9(a) and

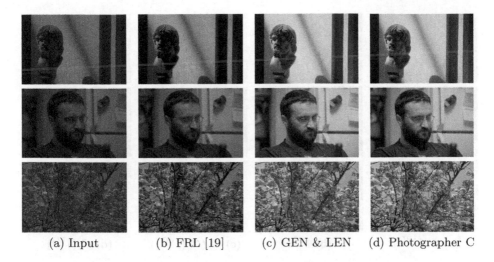

(a) Input   (b) FRL [19]   (c) GEN & LEN   (d) Photographer C

Fig. 8. Qualitative comparison of the proposed algorithm with FRL [19].

Table 5. PSNR and SSIM scores in different training schemes.

Model	Training	PSNR	SSIM
GEN	WGAN-GP	23.05	0.868
GEN & LEN*	WGAN-GP	21.78	0.847
GEN	CWGAN-GP	23.11	0.869
GEN & LEN	CWGAN-GP	23.18	0.874
GEN	Proposed	23.74	0.885
GEN & LEN	Proposed	23.82	0.889

(b) show degraded images and real low-quality images, respectively. We observe that the degraded images $G_d(I^{HQ})$ are well imitated with real images I^{LQ}. Also, it is worth pointing out that global enhanced images from the degraded images and low-quality images are similar to each other, as in Fig.(c) and (d).

In Table 5, we analyze the efficacy of the proposed training schemes. "WGAN-GP" denotes the training scheme that only adopts the adversarial loss in (4) and (5). In other words, it does not utilize the degradation GAN. Notice that pseudo paired data cannot be obtained without the degradation GAN. Therefore, joint GEN and LEN (GEN & LEN*) in "WGAN-GP" training scheme is learned using the adversarial loss only. Low PSNR and SSIM scores in GEN & LEN* indicate that pseudo paired data is essential to train LEN. On the other hand, GEN in "WGAN-GP" yields reasonable performance as compared with GEN & LEN*. Because GEN based on the intensity transform is more suitable for unpaired learning than LEN. "CWGAN-GP" training scheme substitutes the cyclic color loss in (5) with the cyclic consistency loss in [36]. We can see that the cyclic color loss is more effective than the cyclic consistency loss in [36].

(a) $G_d(I^{HQ})$ (b) I^{LQ} (c) $G_e(G_d(I^{HQ}))$ (d) $G_e(I^{LQ})$

Fig. 9. Examples of (a) degraded images (b) real low-quality images (c) global enhancement results from degraded images, and (d) global enhancement results from low-quality images.

5 Conclusions

In this paper, we proposed a novel algorithm to achieve both paired and unpaired image enhancement. The proposed GEN performs the channel-wise intensity transformations and LEN improves the global enhanced images from GEN. For training GEN and LEN, we developed paired learning and unpaired learning methods. For unpaired learning, we proposed the two-stage training scheme based on GANs to exploit the strengths of GEN that can be trained easily. Experimental results demonstrated that the proposed algorithm outperforms the state-of-the-art algorithms on the MIT-Adobe 5 K dataset. Remarkably, GEN and LEN, which are trained by the proposed unpaired learning, outperforms the conventional paired image enhancement algorithms.

Acknowledgements. This work was supported in part by the MSIT (Ministry of Science and ICT), Korea, under the ITRC (Information Technology Research Center) support program (IITP-2020-2016-0-00464) supervised by the IITP (Institute for Information & communications Technology Promotion), in part by the National Research Foundation of Korea (NRF) through the Korea Government (MSIP) under Grant NRF-2018R1A2B3003896, and in part by the research fund of Chungnam National University.

References

1. Arici, T., Dikbas, S., Altunbasak, Y.: A histogram modification framework and its application for image contrast enhancement. IEEE Trans. Image Process. **18**(9), 1921–1935 (2009)

2. Bychkovsky, V., Paris, S., Chan, E., Durand, F.: Learning photographic global tonal adjustment with a database of input/output image pairs. In: CVPR (2011)
3. Cai, B., Xu, X., Guo, K., Jia, K., Hu, B., Tao, D.: A joint intrinsic-extrinsic prior model for retinex. In: ICCV (2017)
4. Chen, Y.S., Wang, Y.C., Kao, M.H., Chuang, Y.Y.: Deep photo enhancer: unpaired learning for image enhancement from photographs with GANs. In: CVPR (2018)
5. Deng, Y., Loy, C.C., Tang, X.: Aesthetic-driven image enhancement by adversarial learning. In: ACM MM (2018)
6. Fu, X., Liao, Y., Zeng, D., Huang, Y., Zhang, X.P., Ding, X.: A probabilistic method for image enhancement with simultaneous illumination and reflectance estimation. IEEE Trans. Image Process. **24**(12), 4965–4977 (2015)
7. Fu, X., Zeng, D., Huang, Y., Zhang, X.P., Ding, X.: A weighted variational model for simultaneous reflectance and illumination estimation. In: CVPR (2016)
8. Gharbi, M., Chen, J., Barron, J.T., Hasinoff, S.W., Durand, F.: Deep bilateral learning for real-time image enhancement. ACM Trans. Graph. **36**(4), 1–12 (2017)
9. Gonzalez, R.C., Woods, R.E.: Digital Image Processing. 4th edn. Pearson (2018)
10. Gulrajani, I., Ahmed, F., Arjovsky, M., Dumoulin, V., Courville, A.C.: Improved training of wasserstein gans. In: NeurIPS, pp. 5767–5777 (2017)
11. Guo, X., Li, Y., Ling, H.: Lime: low-light image enhancement via illumination map estimation. IEEE Trans. Image Process. **26**(2), 982–993 (2016)
12. Hu, Y., He, H., Xu, C., Wang, B., Lin, S.: Exposure: a white-box photo post-processing framework. ACM Trans. Graph. **37**(2), 1–17 (2018)
13. Jobson, D.J., Rahman, Z.U., Woodell, G.A.: A multiscale retinex for bridging the gap between color images and the human observation of scenes. IEEE Trans. Image Process. **6**(7), 965–976 (1997)
14. Jobson, D.J., Rahman, Z.U., Woodell, G.A.: Properties and performance of a center/surround retinex. IEEE Trans. Image Process. **6**(3), 451–462 (1997)
15. Johnson, J., Alahi, A., Fei-Fei, L.: Perceptual losses for real-time style transfer and super-resolution. In: Leibe, B., Matas, J., Sebe, N., Welling, M. (eds.) ECCV 2016. LNCS, vol. 9906, pp. 694–711. Springer, Cham (2016). https://doi.org/10.1007/978-3-319-46475-6_43
16. Kim, J.H., Jang, W.D., Sim, J.Y., Kim, C.S.: Optimized contrast enhancement for real-time image and video dehazing. J. Vis. Commun. Image Represent. **24**(3), 410–425 (2013)
17. Kim, Y.T.: Contrast enhancement using brightness preserving bi-histogram equalization. IEEE Trans. Consum. Electro. **43**(1), 1–8 (1997)
18. Kingma, D.P., Ba, J.: Adam: a method for stochastic optimization. In: ICLR (2014)
19. Kosugi, S., Yamasaki, T.: Unpaired image enhancement featuring reinforcement-learning-controlled image editing software. In: AAAI (2020)
20. Land, E.H.: The retinex theory of color vision. Sci. Am. **237**(6), 108–129 (1977)
21. Lee, C., Kim, J.H., Lee, C., Kim, C.S.: Optimized brightness compensation and contrast enhancement for transmissive liquid crystal displays. IEEE Trans. Circ. Syst. Video Technol. **24**(4), 576–590 (2014)
22. Lee, C., Lee, C., Kim, C.S.: Contrast enhancement based on layered difference representation of 2D histograms. IEEE Trans. Image Process. **22**(12), 5372–5384 (2013)
23. Lee, C., Lee, C., Lee, Y.Y., Kim, C.S.: Power-constrained contrast enhancement for emissive displays based on histogram equalization. IEEE Trans. Image Process. **21**(1), 80–93 (2011)

24. Lim, J., Heo, M., Lee, C., Kim, C.S.: Contrast enhancement of noisy low-light images based on structure-texture-noise decomposition. J. Vis. Commun. Image. Represent. **45**, 107–121 (2017)

25. Lore, K.G., Akintayo, A., Sarkar, S.: LLNet: a deep autoencoder approach to natural low-light image enhancement. Pattern Recognit. **61**, 650–662 (2017)

26. Park, J., Lee, J.Y., Yoo, D., Kweon, I.S.: Distort-and-recover: color enhancement using deep reinforcement learning. In: CVPR (2018)

27. Ronneberger, O., Fischer, P., Brox, T.: U-Net: convolutional networks for biomedical image segmentation. In: Navab, N., Hornegger, J., Wells, W.M., Frangi, A.F. (eds.) MICCAI 2015. LNCS, vol. 9351, pp. 234–241. Springer, Cham (2015). https://doi.org/10.1007/978-3-319-24574-4_28

28. Simonyan, K., Zisserman, A.: Very deep convolutional networks for large-scale image recognition. In: ICLR (2015)

29. Stark, J.A.: Adaptive image contrast enhancement using generalizations of histogram equalization. IEEE Trans. Image Process. **9**(5), 889–896 (2000)

30. Wang, R., Zhang, Q., Fu, C.W., Shen, X., Zheng, W.S., Jia, J.: Underexposed photo enhancement using deep illumination estimation. In: CVPR (2019)

31. Wang, S., Zheng, J., Hu, H.M., Li, B.: Naturalness preserved enhancement algorithm for non-uniform illumination images. IEEE Trans. Image Process. **22**(9), 3538–3548 (2013)

32. Wang, Y., Chen, Q., Zhang, B.: Image enhancement based on equal area dualistic sub-image histogram equalization method. IEEE Trans. Consum. Electro. **45**(1), 68–75 (1999)

33. Yan, Z., Zhang, H., Wang, B., Paris, S., Yu, Y.: Automatic photo adjustment using deep neural networks. ACM Trans. Graph. **35**(2), 1–15 (2016)

34. Yu, R., Liu, W., Zhang, Y., Qu, Z., Zhao, D., Zhang, B.: Deepexposure: learning to expose photos with asynchronously reinforced adversarial learning. In: NeurIPS (2018)

35. Yue, H., Yang, J., Sun, X., Wu, F., Hou, C.: Contrast enhancement based on intrinsic image decomposition. IEEE Trans. Image Process. **26**(8), 3981–3994 (2017)

36. Zhu, J.Y., Park, T., Isola, P., Efros, A.A.: Unpaired image-to-image translation using cycle-consistent adversarial networks. In: ICCV (2017)

Probabilistic Anchor Assignment with IoU Prediction for Object Detection

Kang Kim[1(✉)] and Hee Seok Lee[2]

[1] XL8 Inc., San Jose, USA
kai@xl8.ai
[2] Qualcomm Korea YH, Seoul, South Korea
heeseokl@qti.qualcomm.com

Abstract. In object detection, determining which anchors to assign as positive or negative samples, known as *anchor assignment*, has been revealed as a core procedure that can significantly affect a model's performance. In this paper we propose a novel anchor assignment strategy that adaptively separates anchors into positive and negative samples for a ground truth bounding box according to the model's learning status such that it is able to reason about the separation in a probabilistic manner. To do so we first calculate the scores of anchors conditioned on the model and fit a probability distribution to these scores. The model is then trained with anchors separated into positive and negative samples according to their probabilities. Moreover, we investigate the gap between the training and testing objectives and propose to predict the Intersection-over-Unions of detected boxes as a measure of localization quality to reduce the discrepancy. The combined score of classification and localization qualities serving as a box selection metric in non-maximum suppression well aligns with the proposed anchor assignment strategy and leads significant performance improvements. The proposed methods only add a single convolutional layer to RetinaNet baseline and does not require multiple anchors per location, so are efficient. Experimental results verify the effectiveness of the proposed methods. Especially, our models set new records for single-stage detectors on MS COCO test-dev dataset with various backbones. Code is available at https://github.com/kkhoot/PAA.

1 Introduction

Object detection in which objects in a given image are classified and localized, is considered as one of the fundamental problems in Computer Vision. Since the seminal work of R-CNN [8], recent advances in object detection have shown rapid

---

K. Kim—Work done while at Qualcomm Korea YH.

Electronic supplementary material The online version of this chapter (https://doi.org/10.1007/978-3-030-58595-2_22) contains supplementary material, which is available to authorized users.

© Springer Nature Switzerland AG 2020
A. Vedaldi et al. (Eds.): ECCV 2020, LNCS 12370, pp. 355–371, 2020.
https://doi.org/10.1007/978-3-030-58595-2_22

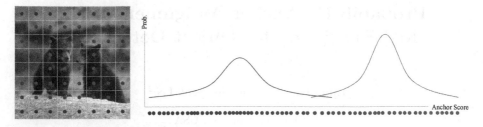

Fig. 1. An examplary case of anchor scores calculated by a detector model and their distribution. The scores are based on the loss objectives of classification and localization to reflect how each anchor contains meaningful cues identifiable by the model to detect a target object. We model the scores as samples from a probability distribution using Gaussian Mixture Model of two modalities (one for positive and the other for negative samples). Anchors are assigned as positive or negative samples according to their probabilities. Image source: [1]

improvements with many innovative architectural designs [21, 28, 41, 43], training objectives [3, 7, 22, 29] and post-processing schemes [2, 13, 15] with strong CNN backbones [5, 11, 17, 19, 31, 32, 36]. For most of CNN-based detectors, a dominant paradigm of representing objects of various sizes and shapes is to enumerate anchor boxes of multiple scales and aspect ratios at every spatial location. In this paradigm, *anchor assignment* procedure in which anchors are assigned as positive or negative samples needs to be performed. The most common strategy to determine positive samples is to use Intersection-over-Union (IoU) between an anchor and a ground truth (GT) bounding box. For each GT box, one or more anchors are assigned as positive samples if its IoU with the GT box exceeds a certain threshold. Target values for both classification and localization (i.e. regression offsets) of these anchors are determined by the object category and the spatial coordinate of the GT box.

Although the simplicity and intuitiveness of this heuristic make it a popular choice, it has a clear limitation in that it ignores the actual *content* of the intersecting region, which may contain noisy background, nearby objects or few meaningful parts of the target object to be detected. Several recent studies [16, 20, 34, 40, 42] have identified this limitation and suggested various new anchor assignment strategies. These works include selecting positive samples based on the detection-specific likelihood [42], the statistics of anchor IoUs [40] or the cleanness score of anchors [16, 20]. All these methods show improvements compared to the baseline, and verify the importance of anchor assignment in object detection.

In this paper we would like to extend some of these ideas further and propose a novel anchor assignment strategy. In order for an anchor assignment strategy to be effective, a flexible number of anchors should be assigned as positives (or negatives) not only on IoUs between anchors and a GT box but also on how probable it is that a model can reason about the assignment. In this respect, the model needs to take part in the assignment procedure, and positive samples need to vary depending on the model. When no anchor has a high IoU for a GT box, some of the anchors need to be assigned as positive samples to reduce the impact of the improper anchor design. In this case, anchors in which the model finds the most meaningful cues about the target object (that may not necessarily be anchors of the highest IoU) can be assigned as positives. On the other side, when there are many anchors that the model finds equally of high quality and competitive, all of these anchors need to be treated as positives not to confuse the training process. Most importantly, to satisfy all these conditions, the quality of anchors as a positive sample needs to be evaluated reflecting the *model's current learning status*, i.e. its parameter values.

With this motivation, we propose a probabilistic anchor assignment (PAA) strategy that adaptively separates a set of anchors into positive and negative samples for a GT box according to the learning status of the model associated with it. To do so we first define a score of a detected bounding box that reflects both the classification and localization qualities. We then identify the connection between this score and the training objectives and represent the score as the combination of two loss objectives. Based on this scoring scheme, we calculate the scores of individual anchors that reflect how the model finds useful cues to detect a target object in each anchor. With these anchor scores, we aim to find a probability distribution of two modalities that best represents the scores as positive or negative samples as in Fig. 1. Under the found probability distribution, anchors with probabilities from the positive component are high are selected as positive samples. This transforms the anchor assignment problem to a maximum likelihood estimation for a probability distribution where the parameters of the distribution is determined by anchor scores. Based on the assumption that anchor scores calculated by the model are samples drawn from a probability distribution, it is expected that the model can infer the sample separation in a probabilistic way, leading to easier training of the model compared to other non-probabilistic assignments. Moreover, since positive samples are adaptively selected based on the anchor score distribution, it does not require a pre-defined number of positive samples nor an IoU threshold.

On top of that, we identify that in most modern object detectors, there is inconsistency between the testing scheme (selecting boxes according to the classification score only during NMS) and the training scheme (minimizing both classification and localization losses). Ideally, the quality of detected boxes should be measured based not only on classification but also on localization. To improve this incomplete scoring scheme and at the same time to reduce the discrepancy of objectives between the training and testing procedures, we propose to predict the IoU of a detected box as a localization quality, and multiply the classification score by the IoU score as a metric to rank detected boxes. This scoring is intuitive, and allows the box scoring scheme in the testing procedure to share the same ground not only with the objectives used during training, but also with the proposed anchor assignment strategy that brings both classification and localization into account, as depicted in Fig. 2. Combined with the proposed PAA, this simple extension significantly contributes to detection performance. We also

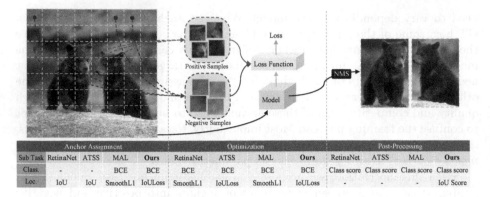

Fig. 2. Illustration of three key procedures of object detectors and comparison between RetinaNet [22], ATSS [40], MAL [16] and ours about in which form classification and localization tasks are concerned in each procedure. Unlike others, we bring both tasks into account for all three procedures. For the localization task, we use IoU-based metrics to align the objectives of each procedure.

compare the IoU prediction with the centerness prediction [33, 40] and show the superiority of the proposed method.

With an additional improvement in post-processing named score voting, each of our methods shows clear improvements as revealed in the ablation studies. In particular, on COCO test-dev set [23] all our models achieve new state-of-the-art performance with significant margins. Our model only requires to add a single convolutional layer, and uses a single anchor per spatial locations similar to [40], resulting in a smaller number of parameters compared to RetinaNet [22]. The proposed anchor assignment can be parallelized using GPUs and does not require extra computes in testing time. All this evidence verifies the efficacy of our proposed methods. The contributions of this paper are summarized as below:

1. We model the anchor assignment as a probabilistic procedure by calculating anchor scores from a detector model and maximizing the likelihood of these scores for a probability distribution. This allows the model to infer the assignment in a probabilistic way and adaptively determines positive samples.
2. To align the objectives of anchor assignment, optimization and post-processing procedures, we propose to predict the IoU of detected boxes and use the unified score of classification and localization as a ranking metric for NMS. On top of that, we propose the score voting method as an additional post-processing using the unified score to further boost the performance.
3. We perform extensive ablation studies and verify the effectiveness of the proposed methods. Our experiments on MS COCO dataset with five backbones set up new AP records for all tested settings.

2   Related Work

2.1   Recent Advances in Object Detection

Since Region-CNN [8] and its improvements [7,28], the concept of anchors and offset regression between anchors and ground truth (GT) boxes along with object category classification has been widely adopted. In many cases, multiple anchors of different scales and aspect ratios are assigned to each spatial location to cover various object sizes and shapes. Anchors that have IoU values greater than a threshold with one of GT boxes are considered as positive samples. Some systems use two-stage detectors [7,8,21,28], which apply the anchor mechanism in a region proposal network (RPN) for class-agnostic object proposals. A second-stage detection head is run on aligned features [10,28] of each proposal. Some systems use single-stage detectors [22,24–26,41,43], which does not have RPN and directly predict object categories and regression offsets at each spatial location. More recently, anchor-free models that do not rely on anchors to define positive and negative samples and regression offsets have been introduced. These models predict various key points such as corners [18], extreme points [44], center points [6,33] or arbitrary feature points [38] induced from deformable convolution [5,45] combines anchor-based detectors with anchor-free detection by adding additional anchor-free regression branches. It has been found in [40] that anchor-based and anchor-free models show similar performance when they use the same anchor assignment strategy.

2.2   Anchor Assignment in Object Detection

The task of selecting which anchors (or locations for anchor-free models) are to be designated as positive or negative samples has recently been identified as a crucial factor that greatly affects a model's performance [37,40,42]. In this regard, several methods have been proposed to overcome the limitation of the IoU-based hard anchor assignment. MetaAnchor [37] predicts the parameters of the anchor functions (the last convolutional layers of detection heads) dynamically and takes anchor shapes as an argument, which provides the ability to change anchors in training and testing. Rather than enumerating pre-defined anchors across spatial locations, GuidedAnchoring [34] defines the locations of anchors near the center of GTs as positives and predicts their shapes. FreeAnchor [42] proposes a detection-customized likelihood that considers both the recall and precision of samples into account and determines positive anchors based on the estimated likelihood. ATSS [40] suggests an adaptive anchor assignment that calculates the mean and standard deviation of IoU values from a set of close anchors for each GT. It assigns anchors whose IoU values are higher than the sum of the mean and the standard deviation as positives. Although these works show some improvements, they either require additional layers and complicated structures [34,37], or force only one anchor to have a full classification score which is not desirable in cases where multiple anchors are of high quality and competitive [42], or rely on IoUs between pre-defined anchors and GTs and consider neither the actual content of the intersecting regions nor the model's learning status [40].

Similar to our work, MultipleAnchorLearning (MAL) [16] and NoisyAnchor [20] define anchor score functions based on classification and localization losses. However, they do not model the anchor selection procedure as a likelihood maximization for a probability distribution; rather, they choose a fixed number of best scoring anchors. Such a mechanism prevents these models from selecting a flexible number of positive samples according to the model's learning status and input. MAL uses a linear scheduling that reduces the number of positives as training proceeds and requires a heuristic feature perturbation to mitigate it. NoisyAnchor fixes the number of positive samples throughout training. Also, they either miss the relation between the anchor scoring scheme and the box selection objective in NMS [16] or only indirectly relate them using soft-labels [20].

2.3 Predicting Localization Quality in Object Detection

Predicting IoUs as a localization quality of detected bounding boxes is not new. YOLO and YOLOv2 [25,26] predict "objectness score", which is the IoU of a detected box with its corresponding GT box, and multiply it with the classification score during inference. However, they do not investigate its effectiveness compared to the method that uses classification scores only, and their latest version [27] removes this prediction. IoU-Net [15] also predicts the IoUs of predicted boxes and proposed "IoU-guided NMS" that uses predicted IoUs instead of classification scores as the ranking keyword, and adjusts the selected box's score as the maximum score of overlapping boxes. Although this approach can be effective, they do not correlate the classification score with the IoU as a unified score, nor do they relate the NMS procedure and the anchor assignment process. In contrast to predicting IoUs, some works [4,12] add an additional head to predict the variance of localization to regularize training [12] or penalize the classification score in testing [4].

3   Proposed Methods

3.1   Probabilistic Anchor Assignment Algorithm

Our goal here is to devise an anchor assignment strategy that takes three key considerations into account: Firstly, it should measure the quality of a given anchor based on how likely the model associated with it finds evidence to identify the target object with that anchor. Secondly, the separation of anchors into positive and negative samples should be adaptive so that it does not require a hyperparameter such as an IoU threshold. Lastly, the assignment strategy should be formulated as a likelihood maximization for a probability distribution in order for the model to be able to reason about the assignment in a probabilistic way. In this respect, we design an anchor scoring scheme and propose an anchor assignment that brings the scoring scheme into account.

Specifically, let us define the score of an anchor that reflects the quality of its bounding box prediction for the closest ground truth (GT) g. One intuitive way is to calculate a classification score (compatibility with the GT class) and a localization score (compatibility with the GT box) and multiply them:

$$S(f_\theta(a, x), g) = S_{cls}(f_\theta(a, x), g) \times S_{loc}(f_\theta(a, x), g)^\lambda \tag{1}$$

where S_{cls}, S_{loc}, and λ are the score of classification and localization of anchor a given g and a scalar to control the relative weight of two scores, respectively. x and f_θ are an input image and a model with parameters θ. Note that this scoring function is dependent on the model parameters θ. We can define and get S_{cls} from the output of the classification head. How to define S_{loc} is less obvious, since the output of the localization head is encoded offset values rather than a score. Here we use the Intersection-over-Union (IoU) of a predicted box with its GT box as S_{loc}, as its range matches that of the classification score and its values naturally correspond to the quality of localization:

$$S_{loc}(f_\theta(a, x), g) = \text{IoU}(f_\theta(a, x), g) \tag{2}$$

Taking the negative logarithm of score function S, we get the following:

$$\begin{aligned} -\log S(f_\theta(a, x), g) &= -\log S_{cls}(f_\theta(a, x), g) - \lambda \log S_{loc}(f_\theta(a, x), g) \\ &= \mathcal{L}_{cls}(f_\theta(a, x), g) + \lambda \mathcal{L}_{IoU}(f_\theta(a, x), g) \end{aligned} \tag{3}$$

where $\mathcal{L}_{cls}$ and $\mathcal{L}_{IoU}$ denote binary cross entropy loss[1] and IoU loss [39] respectively. One can also replace any of the losses with a more advanced objective such as Focal Loss [22] or GIoU Loss [29]. It is then legitimate that the negative sum of the two losses can act as a scoring function of an anchor given a GT box.

To allow a model to be able to reason about whether it should predict an anchor as a positive sample in a probabilistic way, we model anchor scores for a certain GT as samples drawn from a probability distribution and maximize the likelihood of the anchor scores w.r.t the parameters of the distribution. The anchors are then separated into positive and negative samples according to the probability of each being a positive or a negative. Since our goal is to distinguish a set of anchors into two groups (positives and negatives), any probability distribution that can model the multi-modality of samples can be used. Here we choose Gaussian Mixture Model (GMM) of two modalities to model the anchor score distribution.

$$P(a|x, g, \theta) = w_1 \mathcal{N}_1(a; m_1, p_1) + w_2 \mathcal{N}_2(a; m_2, p_2) \tag{4}$$

where w_1, m_1, p_1 and w_2, m_2, p_2 represent the weight, mean and precision of two Gaussians, respectively. Given a set of anchor scores, the likelihood of this GMM can be optimized using Expectation-Maximization (EM) algorithm.

---

[1] We assume a binary classification task. Extending it to a multi-class case is straightforward.

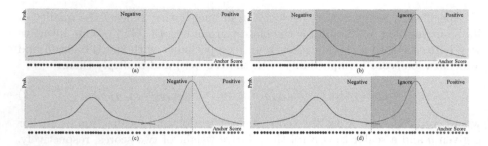

Fig. 3. Different boundary schemes to separate anchors using their probabilities.

With the parameters of GMM estimated by EM, the probability of each anchor being a positive or a negative sample can be determined. With these probability values, various techniques can be used to separate the anchors into two groups. Figure 3 illustrates different examples of separation boundaries based on anchor probabilities. The proposed algorithm using one of these boundary schemes is described in Procedure 1. To calculate anchor scores, anchors are first allocated to the GT of the highest IoU (Line 3). To make EM efficient, we collect top K anchors from each pyramid level (Line 5–11) and perform EM (Line 12). Non-top K anchors are assigned as negative samples (Line 16).

Note that the number of positive samples is adaptively determined depending on the estimated probability distribution conditioned on the model's parameters. This is in contrast to previous approaches that ignore the model [40] or heuristically determine the number of samples as a hyperparameter [16,20] without modeling the anchor assignment as a likelihood maximization for a probability distribution. FreeAnchor [42] defines a detection-customized likelihood and models the product of the recall and the precision as the training objective. But their approach is significantly different than ours in that we do not separately design likelihoods for recall and precision, nor do we restrict the number of anchors that have a full classification score to one. In contrast, our likelihood is based on a simple one-dimensional GMM of two modalities conditioned on the model's parameters, allowing the anchor assignment strategy to be easily identified by the model. This results in easier learning compared to other anchor assignment methods that require complicated sub-routines (e.g. the mean-max function to stabilize training [42] or the anchor depression procedure to avoid local minima [16]) and thus leads to better performance as shown in the experiments.

To summarize our method and plug it into the training process of an object detector, we formulate the final training objective for an input image x (we omit x for brevity):

$$\text{argmax}_\theta \prod_g \prod_{a \in \mathcal{A}_g} P_{pos}(a, \theta, g) S_{pos}(a, \theta, g) + P_{neg}(a, \theta, g) S_{neg}(a, \theta) \quad (5)$$

$$S_{pos}(a, \theta, g) = S(f_\theta(a), g)$$
$$= \exp(-\mathcal{L}_{cls}(f_\theta(a), g) - \lambda \mathcal{L}_{IoU}(f_\theta(a)), g) \tag{6}$$

$$S_{neg}(a, \theta) = \exp(-\mathcal{L}_{cls}(f_\theta(a), \varnothing)) \tag{7}$$

where $P_{pos}(a, \theta, g)$ and $P_{neg}(a, \theta, g)$ indicate the probability of an anchor being a positive or a negative and can be obtained by the proposed PAA. $\varnothing$ means the background class. Our PAA algorithm can be viewed as a procedure to compute P_{pos} and P_{neg} and approximate them as binary values (i.e. separate anchors into two groups) to ease optimization. In each training iteration, after estimating P_{pos} and P_{neg}, the gradients of the loss objectives w.r.t. θ can be calculated and stochastic gradient descent can be performed.

Procedure 1. Probabilistic anchor assignment algorithm.

Input: $\mathcal{G}, \mathcal{A}, \mathcal{A}_i, \mathcal{L}, \mathcal{K}$
 $\mathcal{G}$ is a set of ground-truth boxes
 $\mathcal{A}$ is a set of all anchor boxes
 $\mathcal{A}_i$ is a set of anchor boxes from i_{th} pyramid level
 $\mathcal{L}$ is the number of pyramid levels
 $\mathcal{K}$ is the number of candidate anchors for each pyramid
Output: $\mathcal{P}, \mathcal{N}, \mathcal{I}$
 $\mathcal{P}$ is a set of positive samples
 $\mathcal{N}$ is a set of negative samples
 $\mathcal{I}$ is a set of ignoring samples
1: $\mathcal{P} \leftarrow \varnothing, \mathcal{N} \leftarrow \varnothing$
2: **for** $g \in \mathcal{G}$ **do**
3: $\mathcal{A}_g \leftarrow$ GetAnchors($\mathcal{A}, g, \mathcal{G}$) {Get all anchors that has g as best GT w.r.t. IoU.}
4: $\mathcal{C}_g \leftarrow \varnothing$
5: **for** $i = 1$ **to** $\mathcal{L}$ **do**
6:   $\mathcal{A}_i^g \leftarrow \mathcal{A}_i \cap \mathcal{A}_g$
7:   $\mathcal{S}_i \leftarrow$ ComputeAnchorScores($\mathcal{A}_i^g, g$) {Negative of Eq.3}
8:   $t_i \leftarrow$ FindKthLargest($s_i, \mathcal{K}$)
9:   $\mathcal{C}_g^i \leftarrow \{a_j \in \mathcal{A}_i^g \mid t_i \leq s_j \in \mathcal{S}_i\}$
10:   $\mathcal{C}_g \leftarrow \mathcal{C}_g \cup \mathcal{C}_g^i$
11: **end for**
12: $B, F \leftarrow$ FitGMM($\mathcal{C}_g, 2$) {B, F: Probabilties of two Gaussians for $\mathcal{C}_g$}
13: $\mathcal{N}_g, \mathcal{P}_g \leftarrow$ SeparateAnchors($\mathcal{C}_g, B, F$) {Separate anchors using one of Fig.3.}
14: $\mathcal{P} \leftarrow \mathcal{P} \cup \mathcal{P}_g, \mathcal{N} \leftarrow \mathcal{N} \cup \mathcal{N}_g, \mathcal{I} \leftarrow \mathcal{I} \cup (\mathcal{C}_g - \mathcal{P}_g - \mathcal{N}_g)$
15: **end for**
16: $\mathcal{N} \leftarrow \mathcal{N} \cup (\mathcal{A} - \mathcal{P} - \mathcal{N} - \mathcal{I})$
17: **return** $\mathcal{P}, \mathcal{N}, \mathcal{I}$

3.2 IoU Prediction as Localization Quality

The anchor scoring function in the proposed anchor assignment is derived from the training objective (i.e. the combined loss of two tasks), so the anchor assignment procedure is well aligned with the loss optimization. However, this is not the case for the testing procedure where the non-maximum suppression (NMS) is performed solely on the classification score. To remedy this, the localization quality can be incorporated into NMS procedure so that the same scoring function (Eq. 1) can be used. However, GT information is only available during training, and so IoU between a detected box and its corresponding GT box cannot be computed at test time.

Here we propose a simple solution to this: we extend our model to predict the IoU of a predicted box with its corresponding GT box. This extension is straightforward as it requires a single convolutional layer as an additional prediction head that outputs a scalar value per anchor. We use Sigmoid activation on the output to obtain valid IoU values. The training objective then becomes (we omit input x for brevity):

$$\mathcal{L}(f_\theta(a), g) = \mathcal{L}_{cls}(f_\theta(a), g) + \lambda_1 \mathcal{L}_{IoU}(f_\theta(a), g) + \lambda_2 \mathcal{L}_{IoUP}(f_\theta(a), g) \quad (8)$$

where L_{IoUP} is IoU prediction loss defined as binary cross entropy between predicted IoUs and true IoUs. With the predicted IoU, we compute the unified score of the detected box using Eq. 1 and use it as a ranking metric for NMS procedure. As shown in the experiments, bringing IoU prediction into NMS significantly improves performance, especially when coupled with the proposed probabilistic anchor assignment. The overall network architecture is exactly the same as the one in FCOS [33] and ATSS [40], which is RetinaNet with modified feature towers and an auxiliary prediction head. Note that this structure uses only a single anchor per spatial location and so has a smaller number of parameters and FLOPs compared to RetinaNet-based models using nine anchors.

3.3 Score Voting

As an additional improvement method here we propose a simple yet effective post-processing scheme. The proposed score voting method works on each box b of remaining boxes after NMS procedure as follows:

$$p_i = e^{-(1-\text{IoU}(b,b_i))^2/\sigma_t} \quad (9)$$

$$\hat{b} = \frac{\sum_i p_i s_i b_i}{\sum_i p_i s_i} \text{ subject to IoU}(b, b_i) > 0 \quad (10)$$

where $\hat{b}$, s_i and σ_t is the updated box, the score computed by Eq. 1 and a hyperparameter to adjust the weights of adjacent boxes b_i respectively. It is noted that this voting algorithm is inspired by "variance voting" described in [12] and p_i is defined in the same way. However, we do not use the variance prediction to calculate the weight of each neighboring box. Instead we use the unified score of classification and localization s_i as a weight along with p_i.

We found that using p_i alone as a box weight leads to a performance improvement, and multiplying it by s_i further boost the performance. In contrast to the variance voting, detectors without the variance prediction are capable of using the score voting by just weighting boxes with p_i. Detectors with IoU prediction

Table 1. Ablation studies on COCO minival set with Res50 backbone. **Left:** Comparison of anchor separation boundaries in Fig. 3, fixed numbers of positives (FNP) and fixed positive score ranges (FSR). **Right:** Effects of individual methods.

Anchor Sep.	AP	AP50	AP75
Fig.3. (a)	40.5	58.8	43.4
Fig.3. (b)	40.8	59.1	44.0
Fig.3. (c)	40.6	58.8	43.7
Fig.3. (d)	40.7	59.1	44.0
FNP (5)	39.5	58.0	42.7
FNP (10)	40.1	58.5	43.3
FNP (20)	40.0	58.5	43.1
FSR (> 0.1)	23.8	38.5	25.2
FSR (> 0.2)	19.3	33.2	19.8
FSR (> 0.3)	training failed		

Method	Aux. task	Voting	AP	AP50	AP75
IoU			34.6	53.0	36.7
IoU	IoU pred.		36.0	54.0	38.9
PAA			39.9	59.1	42.8
PAA	Center pred.		39.8	58.3	43.2
PAA	IoU pred.		40.8	59.1	44.0
PAA	IoU pred.	✓	**41.0**	**59.1**	**44.4**
ATSS	Center pred.		39.4	57.4	42.4
ATSS	IoU pred.		39.8	57.9	43.2

head, like ours, can multiply it by s_i for better accuracy. Unlike the classification score only, s_i can act as a reliable weight since it does not assign large weights to boxes that have a high classification score and a poor localization quality.

4 Experiments

In this section we conduct extensive experiments to verify the effectiveness of the proposed methods on MS COCO benchmark [23]. We follow the common practice of using 'trainval35k' as training data (about 118k images) for all experiments. For ablation studies we measure accuracy on 'minival' of 5k images and comparisons with previous methods are done on 'test-dev' of about 20k images. All accuracy numbers are computed using the official COCO evaluation code.

4.1 Training Details

We use a COCO training setting which is the same as [40] in the batch size, frozen Batch Normalization, learning rate, etc. The exact setting can be found in the supplementary material. For ablation studies we use Res50 backbone and run 135k iterations of training. For comparisons with previous methods we run 180k iterations with various backbones. Similar to recent works [33,40], we use GroupNorm [35] in detection feature towers, Focal Loss [22] as the classification loss, GIoU Loss [29] as the localization loss, and add trainable scalars to the regression head. λ_1 is set to 1 to compute anchor scores and 1.3 when calculating Eq. 3. λ_2 is set to 0.5 to balance the scales of each loss term. σ_t is set to 0.025 if the score voting is used. Note that we do *not* use "centerness" prediction or "center sampling" [33,40] in our models. We set $\mathcal{K}$ to 9 although our method is not sensitive to its value similar to [40]. For GMM optimization, we set the minimum and maximum score of the candidate anchors as the mean of two Gaussians and set the precision values to one as an initialization of EM.

Table 2. Left: Performance comparison on COCO minival dataset with Res50 backbone. All models were trained with 135 K iterations. **Right**: Average errors of IoU prediction on COCO minival set for various backbones.

Method	AP	AP50	AP75	APs	APm	APl		Backbone	IoU Pred. Err.
RetinaNet	36.7	55.8	39.0	19.7	40.1	49.1		Res50	0.093
MAL [16]	38.4	56.8	41.1	-	-	-		Res101	0.092
ATSS [40]	39.4	57.4	42.4	23.0	42.9	51.9		ResNext101	0.09
Ours	**41.0**	**59.1**	**44.4**	**24.2**	**45.2**	**54.2**		Res101-DCN	0.086

4.2   Ablation Studies

Comparison Between Different Anchor Separation Points. Here we compare the anchor separation boundaries depicted in Fig. 3. The left table in Table 1 shows that choosing any of the separation scheme works well. This shows the stability of the proposed anchor assignment method as it is not sensitive to small boundary changes. We also compare our method with two simpler methods, namely fixed numbers of positives (FNP) and fixed positive score ranges (FSR). FNP defines a pre-defined number of top-scoring samples as positives while FSR treats all anchors whose scores exceed a certain threshold as positives. As the results in the right of Table 1 show, both methods show worse performance than PAA. FSR (>0.3) fails because the model cannot find anchors whose scores are within the range at early iterations. This shows an advantage of PAA that adaptively determines the separation boundaries without hyperparameters that require careful hand-tuning and so are hard to be adaptive per data.

Effects of Individual Modules. In this section we verify the effectiveness of individual modules of the proposed methods. Accuracy numbers for various combinations are in Table 1. Changing anchor assignment from the IoU-based hard assignment to the proposed PAA shows improvements of 5.3% in AP score. Adding IoU prediction head and applying the unified score function in NMS procedure further boosts the performance to 40.8%. To further verify the impact of IoU prediction, we compare it with centerness prediction used in [33,40]. As can be seen in the results, centerness does not bring improvements to PAA. This is expected as weighting scores of detected boxes according to its centerness can hinder the detection of acentric or slanted objects. This shows that centerness-based scoring does not generalize well and the proposed IoU-based scoring can overcome this limitation. We also verify that IoU prediction is more effective than centerness prediction for ATSS [40] (39.8% vs. 39.4%). Finally, applying the score voting improves the performance to 41.0%, surpassing previous methods with Res50 backbone in Table 2.Left with significant margins.

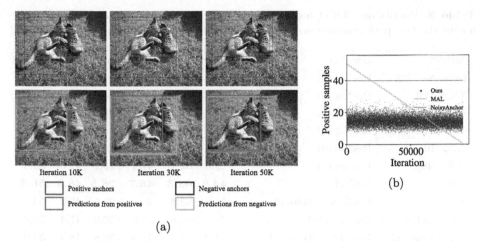

Fig. 4. (a) Evolution of anchor assignment and predicted boxes during training. (b) Plot of the number of positive samples per single GT box throughout training iterations. For our method, the numbers are averaged over a GPU for better visualization (individual values vary between 1 and 40).

Accuracy of IoU Prediction. We calculate the average error of IoU prediction for various backbones in Table 2.Right. All backbones show less than 0.1 errors, showing that IoU prediction is plausible with an additional convolutional head.

Visualization of Anchor Assignment. We visualize positive and negative samples separated by PAA in Fig. 4a. As training proceeds, the distinction between positive and negative samples becomes clearer. Note that the positive anchors do not necessarily have larger IoU values with the target bounding box than the negative ones. Also, many negative anchors in the iteration 30k and 50k have high IoU values. Methods with a fixed number of positive samples [16,20] can assign these anchors as positives, and the model might predict these anchors with high scores during inference. Finally, many positive anchors have more accurate localization as training proceeds. In contrast to ours, methods like FreeAnchor [42] penalize all these anchors except the single best one, which can confuse training.

Statistics of Positive Samples. To compare our method and recent works that also select positive samples by scoring anchors, we plot the number of positive samples according to training iterations in Fig. 4b. Unlike methods that either fix the number of samples [20] or use a linear decay [16], ours choose a different number of samples per iteration, showing the adaptability of the method.

Table 3. Results on COCO test-dev set. * indicates multi-scale testing. Bold text means the best performance among models with the same or a similar backbone.

Method	Backbone	AP	AP50	AP75	APs	APm	APl
RetinaNet [22]	ResNet101	39.1	59.1	42.3	21.8	42.7	50.2
FCOS [33]	ResNet101	41.5	60.7	45.0	24.4	44.8	51.6
NoisyAnchor [20]	ResNet101	41.8	61.1	44.9	23.4	44.9	52.9
FreeAnchor [42]	ResNet101	43.1	62.2	46.4	24.5	46.1	54.8
MAL [16]	ResNet101	43.6	61.8	47.1	25.0	46.9	55.8
ATSS [40]	ResNet101	43.6	62.1	47.4	26.1	47.0	53.6
Ours	ResNet101	**44.8**	**63.3**	**48.7**	**26.5**	**48.8**	**56.3**
FCOS [33]	ResNeXt-64x4d-101	43.2	62.8	46.6	26.5	46.2	53.3
NoisyAnchor [20]	ResNeXt101	44.1	63.8	47.5	26.0	47.4	55.0
FreeAnchor [42]	ResNeXt-64x4d-101	44.9	64.3	48.5	26.8	48.3	55.9
ATSS [40]	ResNeXt-64x4d-101	45.6	64.6	49.7	28.5	48.9	55.6
MAL [16]	ResNeXt101	45.9	65.4	49.7	27.8	49.1	57.8
Ours	ResNeXt-64x4d-101	**46.6**	**65.6**	**50.8**	**28.8**	**50.4**	**57.9**
MAL [16]*	ResNeXt101	47.0	66.1	51.2	30.2	50.1	58.9
Ours*	ResNeXt-64x4d-101	**49.4**	**67.7**	**54.9**	**32.7**	**51.9**	**60.9**
RepPoints [38]	ResNet101-DCN	45.0	**66.1**	49.0	26.6	48.6	57.5
ATSS [40]	ResNet101-DCN	46.3	64.7	50.4	27.7	49.8	58.4
Ours	ResNet101-DCN	**47.4**	65.7	**51.6**	**27.9**	**51.3**	**60.6**
ATSS [40]	ResNeXt-64x4d-101-DCN	47.7	66.5	51.9	29.7	50.8	59.4
Ours	ResNeXt-64x4d-101-DCN	**49.0**	**67.8**	**53.3**	**30.2**	**52.8**	**62.2**
ATSS [40]*	ResNeXt-64x4d-101-DCN	50.7	68.9	56.3	33.2	52.9	62.2
Ours*	ResNeXt-64x4d-101-DCN	**51.4**	**69.7**	**57.0**	**34.0**	**53.8**	**64.0**
Ours	ResNeXt-32x8d-152-DCN	50.8	69.7	55.1	31.4	54.7	65.2
Ours*	ResNeXt-32x8d-152-DCN	53.5	71.6	59.1	36.0	56.3	66.9

4.3   Comparison with State-of-the-Art Methods

To verify our methods with previous state-of-the-art ones, we conduct experiments with five backbones as in Table 3. We first compare our models trained with Res10 and previous models trained with the same backbone. Our Res101 model achieves 44.8% accuracy, surpassing previous best models [16,40] of 43.6 %. With ResNext101 our model improves to 46.6% (single-scale testing) and 49.4% (multi-scale testing) which also beats the previous best model of 45.9% and 47.0% [16]. Then we extend our models by applying the deformable convolution to the backbones and the last layer of feature towers same as [40]. These models also outperform the counterparts of ATSS, showing 1.1% and 1.3% improvements. Finally, with the deformable ResNext152 backbone, our models set new records for both the single scale testing (50.8%) and the multi-scale testing (53.5%).

5   Conclusions

In this paper we proposed a probabilistic anchor assignment (PAA) algorithm in which the anchor assignment is performed as a likelihood optimization for a probability distribution given anchor scores computed by the model associated with it. The core of PAA is in determining positive and negative samples in favor of the model so that it can infer the separation in a probabilistically reasonable way, leading to easier training compared to the heuristic IoU hard assignment or non-probabilistic assignment strategies. In addition to PAA, we identified the discrepancy of objectives in key procedures of object detection and proposed IoU prediction as a measure of localization quality to apply a unified score of classification and localization to NMS procedure. We also provided the score voting method which is a simple yet effective post-processing scheme that is applicable to most dense object detectors. Experiments showed that the proposed methods significantly boosted the detection performance, and surpassed all previous methods on COCO test-dev set.

References

1. NPS Photo. https://www.nps.gov/features/yell/slidefile/mammals/grizzlybear/Images/00110.jpg
2. Bodla, N., Singh, B., Chellappa, R., Davis, L.S.: Soft-nms-improving object detection with one line of code. In: Proceedings of the IEEE International Conference on Computer Vision, pp. 5561–5569 (2017)
3. Chen, K., et al.: Towards accurate one-stage object detection with ap-loss. In: Proceedings of the IEEE Conference on Computer Vision and Pattern Recognition, pp. 5119–5127 (2019)
4. Choi, J., Chun, D., Kim, H., Lee, H.J.: Gaussian yolov3: an accurate and fast object detector using localization uncertainty for autonomous driving. In: Proceedings of the IEEE International Conference on Computer Vision, pp. 502–511 (2019)
5. Dai, J., et al.: Deformable convolutional networks. In: Proceedings of the IEEE International Conference on Computer Vision, pp. 764–773 (2017)
6. Duan, K., Bai, S., Xie, L., Qi, H., Huang, Q., Tian, Q.: Centernet: keypoint triplets for object detection. In: Proceedings of the IEEE International Conference on Computer Vision, pp. 6569–6578 (2019)
7. Girshick, R.: Fast r-cnn. In: Proceedings of the IEEE International Conference on Computer Vision, pp. 1440–1448 (2015)
8. Girshick, R., Donahue, J., Darrell, T., Malik, J.: Rich feature hierarchies for accurate object detection and semantic segmentation. In: Proceedings of the IEEE Conference on Computer Vision and Pattern Recognition, pp. 580–587 (2014)
9. Goyal, P., et al.: Accurate, large minibatch sgd: training imagenet in 1 hour. arXiv preprint arXiv:1706.02677 (2017)
10. He, K., Gkioxari, G., Dollár, P., Girshick, R.: Mask r-cnn. In: Proceedings of the IEEE International Conference on Computer Vision, pp. 2961–2969 (2017)
11. He, K., Zhang, X., Ren, S., Sun, J.: Deep residual learning for image recognition. In: Proceedings of the IEEE Conference on Computer Vision and Pattern Recognition, pp. 770–778 (2016)

12. He, Y., Zhu, C., Wang, J., Savvides, M., Zhang, X.: Bounding box regression with uncertainty for accurate object detection. In: Proceedings of the IEEE Conference on Computer Vision and Pattern Recognition, pp. 2888–2897 (2019)
13. Hosang, J., Benenson, R., Schiele, B.: Learning non-maximum suppression. In: Proceedings of the IEEE Conference on Computer Vision and Pattern Recognition, pp. 4507–4515 (2017)
14. Ioffe, S., Szegedy, C.: Batch normalization: accelerating deep network training by reducing internal covariate shift. arXiv preprint arXiv:1502.03167 (2015)
15. Jiang, B., Luo, R., Mao, J., Xiao, T., Jiang, Y.: Acquisition of localization confidence for accurate object detection. In: Proceedings of the European Conference on Computer Vision (ECCV), pp. 784–799 (2018)
16. Ke, W., Zhang, T., Huang, Z., Ye, Q., Liu, J., Huang, D.: Multiple anchor learning for visual object detection. arXiv preprint arXiv:1912.02252 (2019)
17. Krizhevsky, A., Sutskever, I., Hinton, G.E.: Imagenet classification with deep convolutional neural networks. In: Advances in Neural Information Processing Systems, pp. 1097–1105 (2012)
18. Law, H., Deng, J.: Cornernet: detecting objects as paired keypoints. In: Proceedings of the European Conference on Computer Vision (ECCV), pp. 734–750 (2018)
19. LeCun, Y., et al.: Backpropagation applied to handwritten zip code recognition. Neural Comput. 1(4), 541–551 (1989)
20. Li, H., Wu, Z., Zhu, C., Xiong, C., Socher, R., Davis, L.S.: Learning from noisy anchors for one-stage object detection. arXiv preprint arXiv:1912.05086 (2019)
21. Lin, T.Y., Dollár, P., Girshick, R., He, K., Hariharan, B., Belongie, S.: Feature pyramid networks for object detection. In: Proceedings of the IEEE Conference on Computer Vision and Pattern Recognition, pp. 2117–2125 (2017)
22. Lin, T.Y., Goyal, P., Girshick, R., He, K., Dollár, P.: Focal loss for dense object detection. In: Proceedings of the IEEE International Conference on Computer Vision, pp. 2980–2988 (2017)
23. Lin, T., et al.: Microsoft COCO: common objects in context. In: Fleet, D., Pajdla, T., Schiele, B., Tuytelaars, T. (eds.) ECCV 2014. LNCS, vol. 8693, pp. 740–755. Springer, Cham (2014). https://doi.org/10.1007/978-3-319-10602-1_48
24. Liu, W., et al.: SSD: single shot multibox detector. In: Leibe, B., Matas, J., Sebe, N., Welling, M. (eds.) ECCV 2016. LNCS, vol. 9905, pp. 21–37. Springer, Cham (2016). https://doi.org/10.1007/978-3-319-46448-0_2
25. Redmon, J., Divvala, S., Girshick, R., Farhadi, A.: You only look once: unified, real-time object detection. In: Proceedings of the IEEE Conference on Computer Vision and Pattern Recognition, pp. 779–788 (2016)
26. Redmon, J., Farhadi, A.: Yolo9000: better, faster, stronger. In: Proceedings of the IEEE Conference on Computer Vision and Pattern Recognition, pp. 7263–7271 (2017)
27. Redmon, J., Farhadi, A.: Yolov3: an incremental improvement. arXiv preprint arXiv:1804.02767 (2018)
28. Ren, S., He, K., Girshick, R., Sun, J.: Faster r-cnn: towards real-time object detection with region proposal networks. In: Advances in Neural Information Processing Systems, pp. 91–99 (2015)
29. Rezatofighi, H., Tsoi, N., Gwak, J., Sadeghian, A., Reid, I., Savarese, S.: Generalized intersection over union: a metric and a loss for bounding box regression. In: Proceedings of the IEEE Conference on Computer Vision and Pattern Recognition, pp. 658–666 (2019)
30. Russakovsky, O., et al.: Imagenet large scale visual recognition challenge. Int. J. Comput. Vis. 115(3), 211–252 (2015)

31. Simonyan, K., Zisserman, A.: Very deep convolutional networks for large-scale image recognition. arXiv preprint arXiv:1409.1556 (2014)

32. Szegedy, C., et al.: Going deeper with convolutions. In: Proceedings of the IEEE Conference on Computer Vision and Pattern Recognition, pp. 1–9 (2015)

33. Tian, Z., Shen, C., Chen, H., He, T.: Fcos: fully convolutional one-stage object detection. In: Proceedings of the IEEE International Conference on Computer Vision, pp. 9627–9636 (2019)

34. Wang, J., Chen, K., Yang, S., Loy, C.C., Lin, D.: Region proposal by guided anchoring. In: Proceedings of the IEEE Conference on Computer Vision and Pattern Recognition, pp. 2965–2974 (2019)

35. Wu, Y., He, K.: Group normalization. In: Proceedings of the European Conference on Computer Vision (ECCV), pp. 3–19 (2018)

36. Xie, S., Girshick, R., Dollár, P., Tu, Z., He, K.: Aggregated residual transformations for deep neural networks. In: Proceedings of the IEEE Conference on Computer Vision and Pattern Recognition, pp. 1492–1500 (2017)

37. Yang, T., Zhang, X., Li, Z., Zhang, W., Sun, J.: Metaanchor: learning to detect objects with customized anchors. In: Advances in Neural Information Processing Systems, pp. 320–330 (2018)

38. Yang, Z., Liu, S., Hu, H., Wang, L., Lin, S.: Reppoints: point set representation for object detection. In: Proceedings of the IEEE International Conference on Computer Vision, pp. 9657–9666 (2019)

39. Yu, J., Jiang, Y., Wang, Z., Cao, Z., Huang, T.: Unitbox: an advanced object detection network. In: Proceedings of the 24th ACM International Conference on Multimedia, pp. 516–520 (2016)

40. Zhang, S., Chi, C., Yao, Y., Lei, Z., Li, S.Z.: Bridging the gap between anchor-based and anchor-free detection via adaptive training sample selection. arXiv preprint arXiv:1912.02424 (2019)

41. Zhang, S., Wen, L., Bian, X., Lei, Z., Li, S.Z.: Single-shot refinement neural network for object detection. In: Proceedings of the IEEE Conference on Computer Vision and Pattern Recognition, pp. 4203–4212 (2018)

42. Zhang, X., Wan, F., Liu, C., Ji, R., Ye, Q.: Freeanchor: learning to match anchors for visual object detection. In: Advances in Neural Information Processing Systems, pp. 147–155 (2019)

43. Zhao, Q., et al.: M2det: a single-shot object detector based on multi-level feature pyramid network. Proc. AAAI Conf. Artif. Intell. **33**, 9259–9266 (2019)

44. Zhou, X., Zhuo, J., Krahenbuhl, P.: Bottom-up object detection by grouping extreme and center points. In: Proceedings of the IEEE Conference on Computer Vision and Pattern Recognition, pp. 850–859 (2019)

45. Zhu, C., He, Y., Savvides, M.: Feature selective anchor-free module for single-shot object detection. In: Proceedings of the IEEE Conference on Computer Vision and Pattern Recognition, pp. 840–849 (2019)

Eyeglasses 3D Shape Reconstruction from a Single Face Image

Yating Wang[1], Quan Wang[2], and Feng Xu[1(✉)]

[1] BNRist and School of Software, Tsinghua University, Beijing, China
feng-xu@tsinghua.edu.cn
[2] SenseTime Group Limited, Beijing, China

Abstract. A complete 3D face reconstruction requires to explicitly model the eyeglasses on the face, which is less investigated in the literature. In this paper, we present an automatic system that recovers the 3D shape of eyeglasses from a single face image with an arbitrary head pose. To achieve this goal, we first trains a neural network to jointly perform glasses landmark detection and segmentation, which carry the sparse and dense glasses shape information respectively for 3D glasses pose estimation and shape recovery. To solve the ambiguity in 2D to 3D reconstruction, our system fully explores the prior knowledge including the relative motion constraint between face and glasses and the planar and symmetric shape prior feature of glasses. From the qualitative and quantitative experiments, we see that our system reconstructs promising 3D shapes of eyeglasses for various poses.

1 Introduction

Eyeglasses exist in many facial images. They can somehow be considered as extending components for human face, which influence face appearance dramatically. Reconstructing glasses explicitly is beneficial for many applications. For example, reconstructing 3D face as well as glasses on the face obviously achieves a more complete face modeling. With known glasses shape and pose, the interference caused by glasses occlusion can be eliminated in many face-related tasks such as face shape/appearance reconstruction and face authentication. Moreover, applications related to glasses can also be realized based on the glasses reconstruction, like glasses design, removal, and virtual try-on.

Reconstructing 3D glasses from a single face image is challenging, which suffers the following difficulties. First, features for reconstructing glasses are less investigated in the literature, neither the handcraft features nor the learning-based features. Second, glasses in images may vary a lot due to the large head pose changes, which increases the ambiguity in reconstructing 3D glasses from a single 2D image.

Electronic supplementary material The online version of this chapter (https://doi.org/10.1007/978-3-030-58595-2_23) contains supplementary material, which is available to authorized users.

Fig. 1. Our system reconstructs eyeglasses from single input face image with an arbitrary head pose. More results can be found in the result section and supplementary materials.

Some previous techniques have worked on this topic and tried to overcome some of the aforementioned difficulties. [13] distinguishes the face and glasses depth estimated from multi-view RGB images and reconstructs coarse 3D glasses. They propose a generic model representing the outer contour of glasses based on the glasses geometry commonality, and they optimize the contour by the symmetry shape prior feature of glasses. [28] realizes glasses segmentation from frontal face image also by the symmetry constraints, and reconstructs glasses frame by deforming the prior shape. However, these eyeglasses reconstruction techniques require either multi-view images or frontal face images. To the best of our knowledge, no previous work could reconstruct 3D glasses from a single face image with various head poses.

This paper proposes the first fully automatic system to recover glasses 3D shape from a single face image with an arbitrary head pose. Figure 1 shows some results of our system. To guide the reconstruction of glasses, we extract two kinds of glasses features from images, i.e. the glasses landmarks and segmentation mask. We define glasses landmarks which represent the overall sparse shape of glasses as well as its pose in 3D space, which are never defined before. While the segmentation mask gives dense information describing the shape details of glasses, we observe that these two kinds of features are highly correlated and thus we propose a joint learning framework which trains one single network to perform the two tasks together.

To solve the large ambiguity in 2D to 3D estimation of glasses reconstruction, we involve various prior knowledge in our method. We leverage the well-studied face reconstruction techniques to construct motion direction constraints and contact constraints to solve the ambiguity in glasses pose estimation. Observing the planar shape of glasses (arms excluded), we frontalize the glasses so that the task of 3D shape retrieval and 3D shape deformation could be performed by 2D cues. The left-right symmetrical prior is also involved to further constrain the reconstructed 3D shape. With a technique fully exploring these priors, we successfully achieve 3D glasses reconstruction from a single face image.

2   Related Works

2.1   3D Face Reconstruction

Faces occupy a central place in conveying human identity, expression and emotion. As a consequence, face 3D reconstruction is required in a wide range of applications. Multi-view registration [1] and shape from shading [8,9,18,19] are the most common ways to achieve face reconstruction. Recently, deep learning is also applied in this task and achieves promising results [5–7,16,22,24,29]. As glasses influence human face appearance significantly, simultaneously reconstructing face and glasses will achieve better completeness, which is not fully investigated yet. Besides, glasses cause the most common occlusions on the face, distracting face reconstruction frequently. Some methods are proposed to solve the occlusion of glasses [13] or other objects [3,4,23] in face reconstruction. In this paper, we explicitly reconstruct detailed glasses shape as well as the face shape, which will improve the realism and quality of face reconstruction.

2.2   Glasses Reconstruction

Few works focus on glasses 3D reconstruction. [28] presents a method to reconstruct 3D glasses shape from a single frontal face image by extracting glasses frame contour and deforming existing glasses 3D template. Then the authors use the reconstructed glasses 3D model to achieve virtual glasses try-on. In [13], an approach operating on multi-view RGB images was proposed to automatically reconstruct face by ignoring the segmented depth of glasses and then use the segmented glasses depth to reconstruct glasses. But to the best of our knowledge, no previous works focus on recovering 3D glasses from a single face image of an arbitrary head pose.

2.3   Glasses Manipulation

Most works related to eyeglasses focus on glasses detection, removal and virtual try-on. As glasses cover large portions of the face, many human face applications are visibly affected by glasses. Consequently, glasses removal is of much concern in the literature. In [25], a method was proposed to automatically locate eyeglasses and fill the glasses region to synthesize a face image without glasses. [15] proposes an algorithm for glasses removal by recursive error compensation using PCA reconstruction. Notice that both these two methods operate on frontal face images. Besides, some works exploit glasses virtual try-on, by which users choose desired glasses from images or glasses database, and the chosen glasses will be blended onto the users' photos [12,14,21,27,28]. We believe that by reconstructing glasses from limited inputs, applications related to glasses could perform better. So it is interesting and also our possible future work to investigate how to utilize the 3D glasses reconstruction techniques to perform the tasks discussed in this subsection.

3   Overview

The whole pipeline is shown in Fig. 2. Our system takes a face image with glasses as input. Firstly, to guide the reconstruction, we extract image features including detecting the face and glasses landmarks and segmenting out pixels representing

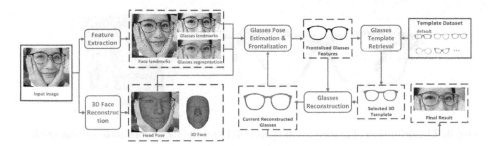

Fig. 2. Pipeline of the proposed system.

glasses. Then we recover the 3D face and estimate the head pose using the face landmarks. To reconstruct the 3D shape of glasses, we iterate the following three steps until convergence.

1. Using the glasses landmarks and the current 3D glasses (initialized by a default template), we estimate the glasses pose and frontalize the glasses features (i.e. the glasses landmarks and glasses mask).
2. We select the best glasses template from a small dataset by the frontalized glasses mask.
3. After building the correspondences between the frontalized mask contour and the contour vertices of the chosen template, we deform the template to fit the shape of the input glasses.

The rest of this paper is organized as follows. Sect. 4 reviews our feature extraction including landmark detection and glasses segmentation. Sect. 5 introduces glasses pose estimation and glasses feature frontalization. Then Sect. 6 illustrates our glasses retrieval method and Sect. 7 introduces correspondences searching and glasses deformation method. Finally, Sect. 8 demonstrates the experiments to evaluate our technique.

4   Feature Extraction

For the following face and glasses reconstruction steps, we extract three types of features which are face landmarks, glasses landmarks, and glasses segmentation mask. For face landmark detection, as this is a well-investigated task, we directly use the method proposed by [26] which detects 98 face landmarks for each face in images. As there are no previous works which define and detect landmarks for glasses, we propose our technique to handle this based on our goal of glasses reconstruction. The definitions of the 21 glasses landmarks are shown in the left of Fig. 3. The glasses frame can be expressed by one outer closed curve and two inner closed curves. To reduce the semantic ambiguity of landmarks, we define the landmarks on these curves. Meanwhile, glasses segmentation in our paper is defined to segment the glasses frame (except the two arms) from images.

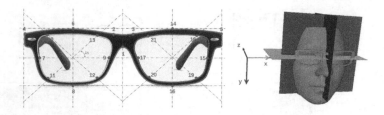

Fig. 3. The definition of glasses landmarks (left) and the face coordinate system (right).

We use U-Net proposed in [17] to simultaneously predict the glasses landmarks and the segmentation mask. The face area, cropped by face landmarks and resized to 256*256 resolution, serves as the input of the network. The network outputs 21+1 256*256 maps. The first 21 are the heatmaps for the 21 landmarks and the last one is the segmentation feature map. As there is no available dataset for glasses segmentation or landmark prediction, we first collect 5300 face images half from the Internet and half recorded by ourselves. The internet images cover various glasses styles while our recorded data contains large pose differences. After excluding the images with rimless or half rim or incomplete glasses which are unable to be labeled, we get 3300 images to construct our dataset. Finally, we manually label landmarks and segmentation masks for images in the dataset. We would like to release our dataset for future research. Notice that the ground truth heatmaps used to supervise landmark prediction are established by applying 2D Gaussian filtering at the labeled landmarks. And the ground truth probability maps are just the labeled binary segmentation masks.

To train the network, we use the weighted sum of the standard MSE loss for landmark heatmaps and the cross-entropy loss for the glasses segmentation probability map:

$$loss = \lambda_{balance} * loss_{landmark} + loss_{segment} \tag{1}$$

$$loss_{landmark} = \sum_{i=1}^{n=21} (x_i - y_i)^2 \tag{2}$$

$$loss_{segment} = -[y * log\sigma(x) + (1 - y) * log(1 - \sigma(x))] \tag{3}$$

where x_i and y_i refer to the output and the ground truth heatmaps of landmark i, x and y refers to the output segmentation feature map and the ground truth segmentation mask respectively, and $\sigma(x)$ refers to the output segmentation probability map where $\sigma(.)$ refers to the sigmoid function.

In the testing, we extract pixels of the highest value in the landmark heatmaps as landmarks and pixels whose probabilities are larger than 0.5 in the segmentation probability map as the glasses segmentation mask.

5 Glasses Pose Estimation and Frontalization

This part introduces how to estimate the glasses pose and frontalize all the aforementioned glasses features for the following glasses shape reconstruction. Besides the features, this step also requires a 3D mesh model of the glasses. The mesh model is initialized by a template and is updated according to the image information in an iterative manner as described in Sect. 3.

Our key idea here is to combine the face pose estimation with the glasses pose estimation. There are two major reasons for this. First, combining faces with glasses can give a more complete reconstruction of face region, which is usually not considered by previous face reconstruction techniques. Second, as the face and glasses have a strong relationship in position and rotation, the well-studied face reconstruction techniques can be used to benefit glasses reconstruction, especially in determining the glasses poses.

5.1 Face Reconstruction

In practice, we first solve the image-based face reconstruction problem following the method in [2]. This method takes a parametric face model, predefined 3D landmarks on the model and the 2D facial landmarks in the image space as the input. To be more specific, we assume a zero-skew perspective camera with square pixels and the principal point at the image center. Then the 3D-to-2D projection can be formulated as:

$$
\begin{bmatrix} u \\ v \\ 1 \end{bmatrix} = \begin{bmatrix} f & 0 & u_0 \\ 0 & f & v_0 \\ 0 & 0 & 1 \end{bmatrix} * [\mathbf{R}|\mathbf{t}] * \begin{bmatrix} x \\ y \\ z \\ 1 \end{bmatrix} \tag{4}
$$

where (x, y, z) refers to a 3D vertex in the face coordinate system as shown in the right of Fig. 3, (u, v) refers to its 2D projection, and (u_0, v_0) refers to the image coordinate of the image center. $\mathbf{R} \in \mathbb{R}^{3\times 3}$ and $\mathbf{t} \in \mathbb{R}^3$ define the coordinate transformation of a point from the face coordinate system to the camera coordinate system. f refers to the focal length. Notice that here $=$ means equal for two homogeneous coordinates which may have a scale difference. Then we apply the 3D-to-2D projection to the face landmarks and thus estimate the parameters θ_{face}, which includes camera parameter f, the head pose and the shape and expression parameters of the parametric face model, by minimizing the L2 distance between the projected 3D face landmarks and the detected 2D landmarks:

$$
\arg\min_{\theta_{face}} \sum_{i=0}^{m-1} \left\| \mathbf{p}_i^p - \mathbf{p}_i^l \right\|_2^2 \tag{5}
$$

Here m indicates the number of the face landmarks. $\mathbf{p}_i^p$ and $\mathbf{p}_i^l$ indicate the projected and the detected 2D position of the landmark i. In our experiments, we guess some values for focal length f, based on which we use ePnP algorithm

[11] to calculate the closed-form solution of the head pose, and then we choose the best one (with minimum error) to be the initial value. Then we iteratively estimate all parameters in θ_{face}. Notice that as the used face model is trained with real human face data and thus already gets the scale information, we do not need to consider the face scale in the optimization. More details including some other regularization terms can be found in [2].

5.2 Glasses Pose Estimation

Then we solve for pose of the glasses. As we have also predefined the glasses landmarks on the glasses mesh model and detected the 2D glasses landmarks in the image, we could solve the glasses pose using similar optimization as Eq. 5. However, as glasses of similar shapes may vary in size, the scale of glasses needs to be solved, which is impossible for pure glasses reconstruction as the 3D-to-2D projection has an inherent scale ambiguity. Furthermore, the planarity of glasses (the arms are excluded) also aggravates the instability of pose estimation. As a consequence, we use the solved head pose to constrain the glasses pose estimation.

We first manually pose the template glasses on the template face. Then we could represent the glasses in the face coordinate system and the global motion of the glasses could be expressed as:

$$[\mathbf{R}|\mathbf{t}] = \left[\mathbf{R}^f|\mathbf{t}^f\right] * [\mathbf{R}^g|\mathbf{t}^g] * s^g \tag{6}$$

where $[\mathbf{R}^g|\mathbf{t}^g]$ is the relative motion between the glasses and the face and s^g is the scale factor of the glasses. In most cases, the initial pose of the glasses on the face is almost correct and thus $\mathbf{R}^g$ should be close to $\mathbf{I}$ and $\mathbf{t}^g$ should be $\mathbf{0}$. Thus given the new projection formulation of the points on the glasses, we have the new energy to be minimized:

$$\arg\min_{\mathbf{R}^g, \mathbf{t}^g, s^g} \sum_{j=0}^{n-1} \left\|\mathbf{p}_j^p - \mathbf{p}_j^l\right\|_2^2 + \lambda \left\|\mathbf{R}^g - \mathbf{I}\right\|_2^2 + \lambda \left\|\mathbf{t}^g - \mathbf{0}\right\|_2^2 \tag{7}$$

where n is the number of glasses landmarks, λ controls the weights of different terms. The parameters like f, $\mathbf{R}^f$, and $\mathbf{t}^f$ have already been estimated in the face reconstruction step.

However, glasses may not always be in the pose as shown in the right of Fig. 3. Sometimes, glasses could be on the forehead or on the nose tip as shown in Fig. 1. To handle these cases, we does not directly constrain $\mathbf{R}^g$ and $\mathbf{t}^g$, but transfer them into 7 motion parameters $\theta_{glasses} = \{r_x^g, r_y^g, r_z^g, t_x^g, t_y^g, t_z^g, s^g\}$ after adding s^g and constrain $\theta_{glasses}^{sub} = \{r_y^g, r_z^g, t_x^g\}$ to be $\mathbf{0}$. This constraint is based on the observation that even for the uncommon cases in Fig. 1, the glasses will still not have the rotation around the y and z-axis or the translation on the x-axis.

However, even with the constraint on $\theta_{glasses}^{sub}$, the scale ambiguity in the 3D-to-2D projection still exists. To further solve this ambiguity, we propose a physical constraint that the two nose pads should be constrained on the face. So the final optimization for glasses pose estimation is:

$$\arg\min_{\theta_{glasses}} \sum_{j=0}^{n-1} \left\| \mathbf{P}_j^p - \mathbf{P}_j^l \right\|_2^2 + \lambda \left\| \theta_{glasses}^{sub} - \mathbf{0} \right\|_2^2 + \gamma \sum_{k=0}^{1} \left\| \mathbf{P}_k^g - \mathbf{P}_k^f \right\|_2^2 \qquad (8)$$

where $\mathbf{P}_k^g$ denotes a manually defined 3D point representing one nose pad and $\mathbf{P}_k^f$ is its contacting point on the face. In practice, Eq. 8 is optimized in an iterative manner and for each iteration, $\mathbf{P}_k^f$ is the closest point of $\mathbf{P}_k^g$ on the face. λ and γ are chosen to be very large to make the constraints firmly satisfied. Notice that as our template glasses models may not have nose pads, we manually label two virtual points as the contact points on nose pads, which have fixed orientations to the geometry center of the glasses.

5.3   Frontalization

After obtaining θ_{face}, $\theta_{glasses}$ and the face and glasses mesh models, we get the 3D reconstruction of the face and glasses, which will be the final outputs when they are obtained by the last iteration. For the earlier iterations, we need to frontalize the glasses features (only the segmentation mask) by the following steps. For a pixel (u, v) on the glasses, we calculate its corresponding (x, y, z) in the camera coordinate system by θ_{face} and $\theta_{glasses}$. Notice that in the early iterations, the shape of the reconstructed glasses is not accurate that a pixel may not be able to back-projected onto the 3D glasses model. Since the glasses frame is almost on a plane, we fit a plane to get the 3D positions of the glasses pixels. The projected 3D points form our proxy glasses M_{pry}. Then by setting a proper θ_{face}^{frt} and $\theta_{glasses}^{frt}$, we can make the proxy glasses face the camera center along the camera's z-axis (denoted as M_{pry}^{frt}) and get the frontalized 2D glasses m_{pry}^{frt} by image projection.

6   Glasses Template Retrieval

In this section, we will use the frontalized glasses mask m_{pry}^{frt} (Fig. 4(a)) to find the best glasses mesh model in our glasses dataset. Actually, our dataset only contains 9 glasses mesh models with large shape differences. We do not require too many glasses models because we also have a shape deformation step that can deform a glasses mesh to the specific glasses shape in the input image. In practice, we find that these 9 models are almost enough to handle most daily glasses. If there is a new pair of glasses with a very unique shape, we just need to ask an artist to make one model with a similar shape and add it to our dataset.

The reason that we frontalize the glasses features is that most glasses models are plane-like. Notice that we do not consider glasses arms in this work. In this situation, the frontalized 2D shape contains the major information of the glasses and some 3D tasks could be simplified to 2D. Here, the 3D shape retrieval is performed in the 2D space.

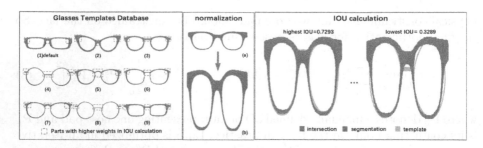

Fig. 4. An illustration for shape retrieval. From left to right: masks of all glasses in the dataset; a frontalized input glasses mask before and after the normalization; IOU calculation. In IOU calculation, we show the highest and lowest IOU between the input and the templates (3) and (4) in the dataset, respectively. We got the highest IOU between the input and (3), so (3) is the "best" template for the input. It is clear that (3) is much closer to the input than (4) and is much easier to be deformed to the shape of the input.

To be specific, the frontalized glasses mask m_{pry}^{frt} is first normalized to be an N*N square image (Fig. 4(b)). At the same time, the 9 glasses in the dataset are also transformed and projected to be frontalized (Fig. 4:Left) and then normalized similarly. After extracting the segmentation masks of the 9 glasses in the normalized images, we calculate IOU between the query mask and each of the 9 masks in dataset to represent the similarity. Notice that different parts of the glasses have different difficulties to deform to another shape. Based on this observation, different parts should have different weights in calculating similarity. So before IOU calculation, we manually assign higher weights on parts that are hard to deform for every candidate model, like glasses bridge or hinges. In this manner, these regions will contribute more to the similarity. Notice that the weight map for each template will be normalized to make sure the retrieval is fair for all the templates. Finally, the glasses with the highest IOU are chosen from the dataset for the next step which will deform this glasses to fit the input image.

The retrieval is performed in all the iterations of the glasses reconstruction method as shown on the right side of Fig. 2. Except for the early iterations, we add the current deformed glasses model as the 10th model for retrieval. Not surprisingly, in most cases, the 10th model will be chosen as the retrieval result as it becomes more and more similar to the real shape of the input. However, for some input, if the glasses shape is too different from the initial template, the pose estimation may be wrong in the beginning, leading to a wrong retrieval result in the first iteration. In the following iterations, as the pose becomes better, the wrong retrieval could be corrected in this retrieval step and the system could recover from the errors. This is the reason we perform retrieval in every iteration.

7   Glasses Reconstruction

In this section, we will deform the retrieved glasses mesh model to fit the glasses in the input image. Remember that the glasses features and the glasses mesh have both been frontalized by the method in Sect. 5. We again use the frontalized 2D information to guide the deformation. We first extract contours from the segmentation mask m_{pry}^{frt} using OpenCV. And then build dense correspondences between the contour vertices on the model and pixels of the contours. Next, a Laplacian-based deformation is performed on the model guided by the correspondences. With the last two steps iterating, a better and better glasses shape is obtained.

7.1   Correspondence Search

In the previous section, we use the normalized images to calculate similarity. Here, we again use the normalized images to find correspondences between the predefined contour vertexes on the retrieved mesh model and the contours of m_{pry}^{frt}. In the normalized images, we find that the closet points are good approximation of the correspondences as the large scale shape differences between glasses are dramatically compensated in the normalized images. With the iterations in the glasses deformation, the glasses shape becomes better and better, and thus the closest points also become better and better in finding the real correspondences. So we use this ICP method on the normalized images to find correspondences. Notice that the errors caused by inner and outer contour mismatching are very likely to happen. To eliminate this, for each point, we calculate the direction from this point to the average position of its 2D neighbors in a small circle, and then use a threshold to filter out the candidates whose direction is quite different, as the inner and outer contour points have very different directions.

7.2   Glasses Deformation

This part elaborates on how to deform the retrieved glasses mesh driven by the correspondences. We follow the Laplacian deformation approach presented in [20], using the correspondences searched in the previous step as constraints and enforcing the deformed model to keep horizontally symmetrical. In Sect. 5, the glasses mesh is placed to be symmetrical about plane $x = 0$. We define V and V' denoting the sets of vertices of the original and deformed 3D mesh, and $\mathbf{v} = (x, y, z)$ and $\mathbf{v}' = (x', y', z')$ denoting a particular vertex, respectively. We denote the set of correspondences by C, and $\mathbf{v}_j$ in C has a corresponding 3D point $\mathbf{p}_j = (u_j, v_j, w_j)$ in M_{pry}^{frt}. Notice that we have fitted a plane to the glasses model to perform the frontalization, which may bring some errors in the value of w_j. So we keep z-coordinates of $\mathbf{v}_j$ unchanged through the deformation, and $\mathbf{p}_j$ in C is replaced by $\mathbf{c}_j = (u_j, v_j, z_j)$.

Then the deformation can be formulated as the optimization of the following object function:

$$E(V') = \lambda_C E_C(V') + \lambda_L E_L(V, V') + \lambda_S E_S(V') \qquad (9)$$

where E_C calculates the euclidean distance between the corresponding points pair:

$$E_C = \sum_{j \in C} \left\| \mathbf{v}_j' - \mathbf{c}_j \right\|_2^2. \tag{10}$$

E_L strives to preserve the Laplacian coordinates, resulting in detail-preserving and smooth deformation:

$$E_L = \left\| L(V) - L(V') \right\|_2^2, \tag{11}$$

where $L(.)$ is the transformation from Cartesian coordinates to Laplacian coordinates. E_S enforces that the deformed model to be horizontally symmetrical:

$$E_S = \sum_{i=1}^{N} |x_i' + x_{k(i)}'|^2 + |y_i' - y_{k(i)}'|^2 + |z_i' - z_{k(i)}'|^2. \tag{12}$$

Here, before the deformation, for each vertex v_i of each glasses model in dataset, we find a vertex $v_{k(i)}$ that is the nearest vertex to the point $(-x_i, y_i, z_i)$ as the symmetric vertex of v_i. Notice that this step only needs to be performed once. Finally, $\mathbf{x}', \mathbf{y}', \mathbf{z}'$ can be solved though linear optimization.

8   Experimental Results

In this section, we first introduce implementation details of our method. Then we evaluate two key components, the joint trained feature extraction network and the glasses pose estimation aided by head pose. Next, we evaluate whole system by analyzing the final results. Finally, we discuss limitations of our work.

8.1   Implementation Details

The network for joint landmark detection and segmentation is implemented in PyTorch. We set the sigma of Gaussian filtering used in heatmaps generation to be 5. The network is trained for 25 epochs on a GTX2080 using Adam [10] as the optimizer. In our experiments, the landmark prediction task reaches convergence faster than segmentation. Firstly, we set $\lambda_{balance}$ to be 200 and the learning rate to be 0.001. When the landmark loss no longer declines (12 epochs), we set $\lambda_{balance}$ to be 50 and the learning rate to be 0.0005 to achieve better segmentation. We randomly split our dataset to 3000 images for training and 300 for testing. For the rest of our technique, we set $\lambda = 400$, $\gamma = 1500$, $\lambda_C = 25$, $\lambda_L = 1$, and $\lambda_S = 100$, which are tuned for the best performance.

8.2   Feature Extraction Network

Firstly, we demonstrate effectiveness of the joint training network. We compare it with training the two tasks separately with the same network structure. We train

Fig. 5. Feature extraction of our joint training network. **Top**: landmark prediction. **Bottom**: segmentation.

a U-Net to predict landmark heatmaps using Adam with learning rate $= 0.001$, which converges in 16 epochs. Meanwhile, we train another U-Net to predict segmentation, which converges in 20 epochs. In Table. 1, we show the quantitative results of the three networks on 300 testing images of 256*256 resolution. We use dice coefficient $2 \times (|X \bigcap Y|)/(|X| + |Y|)$ to measure the performance of the segmentation and the average L2 distance to measure landmark prediction. Here X and Y denote the output and the ground truth masks. It can be seen our joint training method achieves better feature extraction results. Another benefit is that only one network is needed for the two tasks. Figure 5 shows some qualitative results. We can see that our method handles various head and glasses poses, glasses styles, illuminations, and occlusions. Notice that the dice coefficient is not high in our task. This is because the frame of glasses is very thin, thus a litter mismatch may cause a very low dice coefficient. But in this situation, the final result may not look bad, which is the common case in our experiments.

Table 1. Quantitative evaluation of joint training for glasses landmark detection and segmentation.

–	Landmark L2 error	Segmentation dice coeff
Joint training	0.8378	0.8183
Landmark only	0.8701	–
Segmentation only	–	0.7801

8.3 Glasses Pose Estimation

Here, we evaluate our glasses pose estimation method. In Fig. 6, we show the glasses pose estimation results of different solutions: our proposed method, ours without physical constraint and ours without physical and $\theta_{glasses}^{sub}$ constraints. We render template glasses and face from two perspectives for better visualization. As Fig. 6 shows, without physical constraint, the solved glasses may float on face (d, top) or interact with face (d, bottom). Without both two kinds of constraints, the glasses may have wrong z-direction rotations (e, top) or x-direction translations(e, bottom). The wrong estimation is due to the inherent ambiguity in 2D to 3D estimation and will lead to the failure of the whole system.

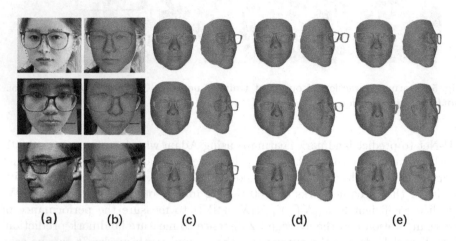

Fig. 6. Comparison of glasses pose estimation among different constraining methods. (a): face/glasses landmarks and glasses segmentation. (b): face reconstruction. (c): glasses pose of our proposed method. (d): glasses pose without physical constraints. (e): glasses pose without physical and $\theta_{glasses}^{sub}$ constraints. (c–e) are rendered under two perspectives while reserving the relative motion between the glasses and the face.

8.4   Final Results

Figure 7 and Fig. 1 show our 3D reconstruction results for different glasses styles with different glasses poses. With the correctly extracted glasses features and reconstructed faces, our method achieves promising results in both glasses shape and pose estimation. More results can be found in our supplementary material.

As we do not have the ground truth 3D glasses models, quantitative evaluation is performed by using the standard dice coefficient metric between the ground truth segmentation masks and the projected masks of the reconstructed glasses. Here we first compare our method with the only single image based glasses reconstruction method [28]. The comparison is performed on their test images as they have published their results. From Table 2, we can see our method and [28] are comparable and we believe the difference is majorly due to the used templates. Please notice that this comparison is performed on frontal face images as [28] does not handle other head poses by design.

The focus of our method is to handle extreme head poses so we also report the quantitative results on our 300 test images in Table 2, where extreme head poses and various glasses styles are included. Though the dice coefficient is worse as the test set is much more challenging, visual reconstruction results are still very promising, which are shown in Fig. 7, Fig. 1 and the supplementary material.

Table 2. Dice coefficient between the ground truth segmentation mask and the projection of the reconstructed glasses.

	[28] on [28]'s test set	ours on [28]'s test set	Ours on our test set
Dice coeff	0.7306	0.6885	0.5552

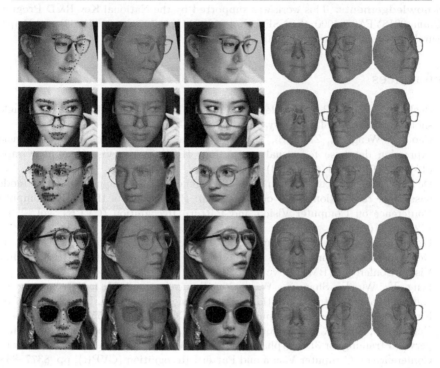

Fig. 7. Results of our method. From left to right, we show glasses/face landmarks and glasses segmentation, face reconstruction, glasses reconstruction, full reconstruction under different perspectives.

8.5 Limitations

Our method relies on glasses features extraction, so it cannot handle cases where the two tasks fail, like rimless or half rim glasses, and will fail if glasses is heavily occluded or outside the image. Besides, our results do not contain glasses arms as our glasses models do not contain them. More complete reconstruction will be achieved if glasses arms are considered.

9   Conclusions

We propose a system that reconstructs eyeglasses 3D shape from a single portrait image. The system is capable to handle extreme head and glasses poses. The trained neural network jointly predicts glasses landmark and segmentation from images. The iterative reconstruction method leverages face reconstruction and utilizes shape commonality of glasses to achieve glasses reconstruction of extreme poses. Our method promotes the technique of full face reconstruction with glasses 3D shape and pose estimation.

Acknowledgements. This work was supported by the National Key R&D Program of China 2018YFA0704000, the NSFC (No. 61822111, 61727808, 61671268) and Beijing Natural Science Foundation (JQ19015, L182052).

References

1. Beeler, T., Bickel, B., Beardsley, P., Sumner, B., Gross, M.: High-quality single-shot capture of facial geometry. ACM Trans. Graph. (ToG), 1–9 (2010)
2. Cao, C., Weng, Y., Zhou, S., Tong, Y., Zhou, K.: FaceWarehouse: a 3D facial expression database for visual computing. IEEE Trans. Vis. Comput. Graph. (TVCG) **20**(3), 413–425 (2013)
3. De Smet, M., Fransens, R., Van Gool, L.: A generalized EM approach for 3D model based face recognition under occlusions. In: Proceedings of the IEEE Computer Conference on Computer Vision and Pattern Recognition (CVPR), vol. 2, pp. 1423–1430 (2006)
4. Egger, B., Schneider, A., Blumer, C., Forster, A., Schönborn, S., Vetter, T.: Occlusion-aware 3D morphable face models. In: Proceedings of the British Machine Vision Conference (BMVC), vol. 2, p. 4 (2016)
5. Feng, Y., Wu, F., Shao, X., Wang, Y., Zhou, X.: Joint 3D face reconstruction and dense alignment with position map regression network. In: Proceedings of the European Conference on Computer Vision (ECCV), pp. 534–551 (2018)
6. Genova, K., Cole, F., Maschinot, A., Sarna, A., Vlasic, D., Freeman, W.T.: Unsupervised training for 3D morphable model regression. In: Proceedings of the IEEE Conference on Computer Vision and Pattern Recognition (CVPR), pp. 8377–8386 (2018)
7. Huynh, L., et al.: Mesoscopic facial geometry inference using deep neural networks. In: Proceedings of the IEEE Conference on Computer Vision and Pattern Recognition (CVPR), pp. 8407–8416 (2018)
8. Jiang, L., Zhang, J., Deng, B., Li, H., Liu, L.: 3D face reconstruction with geometry details from a single image. IEEE Trans. Image Process. (TIP) **27**(10), 4756–4770 (2018)
9. Kemelmacher-Shlizerman, I., Basri, R.: 3D face reconstruction from a single image using a single reference face shape. IEEE Trans. Pattern Anal. Mach. Intell. (TPAMI) **33**(2), 394–405 (2010)
10. Kingma, D., Ba, J.: Adam: a method for stochastic optimization. arXiv preprint arXiv:1412.6980 (2014)
11. Lepetit, V., Moreno-Noguer, F., Fua, P.: EPnP: an accurate O(n) solution to the PnP problem. Int. J. Comput. Vis. (IJCV) **81**(2), 155–166 (2009)
12. Li, J., Yang, J.: Eyeglasses try-on based on improved Poisson equations. In: Proceedings of the International Conference on Multimedia Technology (ICMT), pp. 3058–3061 (2011)
13. Maninchedda, F., Oswald, M.R., Pollefeys, M.: Fast 3D reconstruction of faces with glasses. In: Proceedings of the IEEE Conference on Computer Vision and Pattern Recognition (CVPR), pp. 6599–6608 (2017)

14. Niswar, A., Khan, I.R., Farbiz, F.: Virtual try-on of eyeglasses using 3D model of the head. In: Proceedings of the International Conference on Virtual Reality Continuum and its Applications in Industry (VRCAI), pp. 435–438 (2011)
15. Park, J.S., Oh, Y.H., Ahn, S.C., Lee, S.W.: Glasses removal from facial image using recursive error compensation. IEEE Trans. Pattern Anal. Mach. Intell. (TPAMI) **27**(5), 805–811 (2005)
16. Richardson, E., Sela, M., Or-El, R., Kimmel, R.: Learning detailed face reconstruction from a single image. In: Proceedings of the IEEE Conference on Computer Vision and Pattern Recognition (CVPR), pp. 1259–1268 (2017)
17. Ronneberger, O., Fischer, P., Brox, T.: U-Net: convolutional networks for biomedical image segmentation. In: Proceedings of the International Conference on Medical Image Computing and Computer-Assisted Intervention (MICCAI) (2015)
18. Roth, J., Tong, Y., Liu, X.: Unconstrained 3D face reconstruction. In: Proceedings of the IEEE Conference on Computer Vision and Pattern Recognition (CVPR), pp. 2606–2615 (2015)
19. Smith, W.A., Hancock, E.R.: Recovering facial shape using a statistical model of surface normal direction. IEEE Trans. Patt. Anal. Mach. Intell. (TPAMI) **28**(12), 1914–1930 (2006)
20. Sorkine, O.: Differential representations for mesh processing. Comput. Graph. Forum **4**, 789–807 (2006)
21. Tang, D., Zhang, J., Tang, K., Xu, L., Fang, L.: Making 3D eyeglasses try-on practical. In: Proceedings of the IEEE International Conference on Multimedia and Expo Workshops (ICMEW), pp. 1–6 (2014)
22. Tewari, A., et al.: Self-supervised multi-level face model learning for monocular reconstruction at over 250 hz. In: Proceedings of the IEEE Conference on Computer Vision and Pattern Recognition (CVPR), pp. 2549–2559 (2018)
23. Tran, A.T., Hassner, T., Masi, I., Paz, E., Nirkin, Y., Medioni, G.G.: Extreme 3D face reconstruction: seeing through occlusions. In: Proceedings of the IEEE Conference on Computer Vision and Pattern Recognition (CVPR), pp. 3935–3944 (2018)
24. Tran, L., Liu, X.: Nonlinear 3D face morphable model. In: Proceedings of the IEEE Conference on Computer Vision and Pattern Recognition (CVPR), pp. 7346–7355 (2018)
25. Wu, C., Liu, C., Shum, H.Y., Xy, Y.Q., Zhang, Z.: Automatic eyeglasses removal from face images. IEEE Trans. Pattern Anal. Mach. Intell. (TPAMI) **26**(3), 322–336 (2004)
26. Wu, W., Qian, C., Yang, S., Wang, Q., Cai, Y., Zhou, Q.: Look at boundary: a boundary-aware face alignment algorithm. In: Proceedings of the IEEE Conference on Computer Vision and Pattern Recognition (CVPR) (2018)
27. Yuan, M., Khan, I., Farbiz, F., Niswar, A., Huang, Z.: A mixed reality system for virtual glasses try-on. In: Proceedings of the International Conference on Virtual Reality Continuum and Its Applications in Industry (VRCAI), December 2011
28. Yuan, X., Tang, D., Liu, Y., Ling, Q., Fang, L.: Magic glasses: from 2D to 3D. IEEE Trans. Circ. Syst. Video Technol. (TCSVT) **27**(4), 843–854 (2016)
29. Zeng, X., Peng, X., Qiao, Y.: DF2Net: a dense-fine-finer network for detailed 3D face reconstruction. In: Proceedings of the IEEE International Conference on Computer Vision (ICCV), pp. 2315–2324 (2019)

Temporal Complementary Learning for Video Person Re-identification

Ruibing Hou[1,2], Hong Chang[1,2(✉)], Bingpeng Ma[2], Shiguang Shan[1,2,3], and Xilin Chen[1,2]

[1] Key Laboratory of Intelligent Information Processing of Chinese Academy of Sciences (CAS), Institute of Computing Technology, CAS, Beijing 100190, China
ruibing.hou@vipl.ict.ac.cn, {changhong,sgshan,xlchen}@ict.ac.cn
[2] University of Chinese Academy of Sciences, Beijing 100049, China
bpma@ucas.ac.cn
[3] CAS Center for Excellence in Brain Science and Intelligence Technology, Beijing, China

Abstract. This paper proposes a *Temporal Complementary Learning Network* that extracts complementary features of consecutive video frames for video person re-identification. Firstly, we introduce a *Temporal Saliency Erasing* (TSE) module including a saliency erasing operation and a series of ordered learners. Specifically, for a specific frame of a video, the saliency erasing operation drives the specific learner to mine new and complementary parts by erasing the parts activated by previous frames. Such that the diverse visual features can be discovered for consecutive frames and finally form an integral characteristic of the target identity. Furthermore, a *Temporal Saliency Boosting* (TSB) module is designed to propagate the salient information among video frames to enhance the salient feature. It is complementary to TSE by effectively alleviating the information loss caused by the erasing operation of TSE. Extensive experiments show our method performs favorably against state-of-the-arts. The source code is available at https://github.com/blue-blue272/VideoReID-TCLNet.

Keywords: Video person re-identification · Complementary learning · Feature Enhancing

1 Introduction

Person re-identification (reID) aims at retrieving particular persons from non-overlapping camera views. It plays a significant role in video surveillance analysis. Image person reID has achieved great progress in term of the methods [12,35,45] and large benchmarks construction [39,48,50]. Recently, with the emergence of large video benchmarks [40,47] and the growth of computational resource, video person reID has been attracting a significant amount of attention. The video data contain richer spatial appearance information and temporal cues, which can be exploited for more robust reID.

© Springer Nature Switzerland AG 2020
A. Vedaldi et al. (Eds.): ECCV 2020, LNCS 12370, pp. 388–405, 2020.
https://doi.org/10.1007/978-3-030-58595-2_24

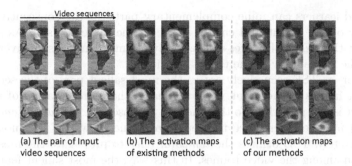

(a) The pair of Input   (b) The activation maps   (c) The activation maps
video sequences   of existing methods   of our methods

Fig. 1. An example of class activation maps [52] of a pair of input video sequences of existing method [26] and our method. Warmer color with higher value (Color figure online)

Current state-of-the-art approaches for video person reID are based on deep neural networks. The mainstream approaches usually consider a sequence of frames as input, and utilize convolutional neural networks (CNNs) to extract the feature for each frame independently, followed by temporal feature aggregation, e.g., through recurrent layer [28,41,53] or temporal attention layer [26,32,41]. With the powerful deep networks and large-scale labeled benchmarks, these methods achieve favorable performance and efficiency.

Despite the significant progress in video person reID, most existing methods do not take full advantage of the rich spatial-temporal clues in the video. To be specific, since the pedestrian frames of a video are highly similar and the existing methods perform the same operation on each frame, these methods typically produce highly redundant features for the frames of a video. The redundant features typically attend to the same local salient parts [11], which are difficult to distinguish the persons with similar appearance. For example, as illustrated in Fig. 1(b), the upper clothes of the sequence pair attract the most attention, but are difficult to distinguish the two pedestrians. Therefore, it is appealing to explore a way of fully mining the spatial-temporal clues in the video, which can discover diverse visual cues for different frames of a video to form a full characteristic of each identify.

In this paper, we propose a *Temporal Complementary Learning Network* (TCLNet) for fully exploiting the spatial-temporal information of the video data. Firstly, we introduce a *Temporal Saliency Erasing* (TSE) module consisting of a saliency erasing operation and a series of ordered adversary learners. The key idea is to extract complementary features for consecutive frames of a video by the adversary learners. In particular, the first learner is firstly leveraged to extract the most salient feature for the first frame of a video sequence. Then, for the feature map of the second frame, the *saliency erasing operation* utilizes the *temporal cues* to erase the region attended by the first learner. Then we feed the feature excluding the erased region into the second learner for discovering new and complementary parts. By recursively erasing all previous discovered parts, the ordered learners can mine complementary parts for the consecutive frames and finally obtain an integral characteristic of the target person. As shown in Fig. 1(c), with TSE, the features of consecutive frames can focus on diverse parts, covering the whole body of the target identity.

However, as TSE recursively erases the most salient part of the second and subsequent frames of the input video sequence, the representation of the most salient part is less powerful. To this end, we propose a *Temporal Saliency Boosting* (TSB) module to enhance the representational power of the most salient part. Concretely, TSB utilizes the *temporal cues* to propagate the most salient information among the video frames. In this way, the most salient features can capture the visual cues across all frames of video, hence exhibit stronger representational capability.

The proposed two modules can be inserted in any deep CNNs to extract complementary features for video frames. To the best of our knowledge, it is the first attempt to extract complementary features for the consecutive frames of a video. We demonstrate the effectiveness of the proposed method on three challenging video reID benchmarks, and our method outperforms the state-of-the-art methods under multiple evaluation metrics.

2   Related Work

Person Re-identification. Person reID for still images has been extensively studied [2,5,7,12,23,35,45,49]. Recently, researchers start to pay attention to video reID [8,13,21,26,41]. The existing methods can be divided into two categories, *i.e.*, image-set based methods and temporal-sequence based methods.

Image-set based methods consider a video as a set of disordered images. These methods usually extract the features of each frame independently, then use a specific temporal pooling strategy to aggregate the frame-level features. For example, Zheng *et al.* [47] apply an average pooling across all frames to obtain the video feature. The works [21,26,32,46] further use a temporal attention mechanism that assigns a quality score to each frame for weighted average pooling. These methods exhibit promising efficiency, but totally ignore the temporal cues of the video data.

Temporal-sequence based methods exploit the temporal cues for video representation learning. The early works [28,41,53] use the optical flows to encode the short-term motion information among adjacent frames. Mclaughlin *et al.* [38] propose a recurrent architecture [14] to aggregate the frame-level representations and yield a sequence-level feature representations. Zhang *et al.* [44] argue that the recurrent structure may not be optimal to learn temporal dependencies and propose to learn orderless ensemble ranking. Liao *et al.* [22] propose to use 3D convolution for spatial-temporal feature learning. Recently, some works [13,19,22] apply non-local blocks [37] to capture long-term temporal cues.

Nevertheless, these methods perform the same operation on each frame, leading to that the features of different frames are highly redundant. Therefore in this work, we propose a temporal complementary learning mechanism to extract complementary features for consecutive frames of a video, which is able to obtain an integral characteristic of the target identity for better reID.

Erasing Pixels or Activations. *Image based erasing* has been widely applied as a data augmentation technique. For instance, the works [4,51] randomly erase a rectangle region of the input images during training. Singh *et al.* [31] propose to divide the image into a grid with fixed patch size and randomly mask each patch. *Feature based erasing* typically drops the feature activations. Dropout [33] drops the feature units randomly, which is a widely used regularization technique to prevent overfitting. DropBlock [6] randomly drops a contiguous region of the convolutional features for CNNs. In the work [3], all feature maps in the same batch are dropped in a consistent way for better metric learning.

Our work is fundamentally different from the existing erasing methods in two folds. Firstly, **the basic idea is different.** The above methods typically use the erasing strategy to regularize the *training* of networks to prevents overfitting. Differently, our method uses the erasing operation to extract complementary features for video frames during both training and testing phases. Secondly, **the erasing mechanism is different.** The existing methods usually randomly erase the pixels or activations without any high-level guidance. Our method erases the regions for each frame guided by the activated parts of previous frames, which guarantees the frame pays attention to new person parts thus is more efficient.

Recently, Liu *et al.* [24,25] also propose to use saliency to guide erasing to learn complementary features. However, the purpose and implementation of these methods are different from ours. Specifically, these methods perform *image erasing* on *a singe image input*. On the contrary, our method performs *feature erasing* on *a video sequence* that allows for extracting complementary features for consecutive video frames.

3 Temporal Complementary Learning Network

The proposed Temporal Complementary Learning Network for video person reID includes two novel components, *i.e.* TSE for complementary feature mining and TSB for enhancing the most salient feature.

3.1 Temporal Saliency Erasing Module

Compared to images, video data contain richer spatial-temporal information, which should be fully exploited for more robust feature representation. However, most existing methods perform the same operation on each frame, resulting in highly redundant features of different frames that only highlight a local part [42, 49], as shown in Fig. 1(b). To this end, we design a *temporal saliency erasing module* to mine complementary parts from consecutive frames of a video to form an integral characteristic of the target person.

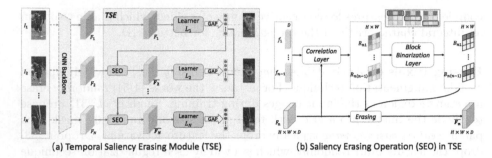

(a) Temporal Saliency Erasing Module (TSE) 　　　(b) Saliency Erasing Operation (SEO) in TSE

Fig. 2. (a) The architecture of TSE. (b) *Saliency erasing operation* in TSE for feature map F_n $(n > 1)$

TSE Overview. As shown in Fig. 2(a), TSE iteratively performs two operations on each frame: adversarially erasing the parts discovered by previous frames with a *saliency erasing operation* (SEO) and learning a specific *learner* for discovering new part to extract complementary feature. Concretely, the input of TSE is the set of frame-level feature maps $\{F_n\}_{n=1}^{N}(F_n \in \mathbb{R}^{H \times W \times D})$ of a video segment $\{I_n\}_{n=1}^{N}$ after a CNN Backbone, where the video segment contains N consecutive frames and n is the index of the video frame, and H, W and D denote the height, width and channel number of the feature map respectively. Firstly, TSE uses the learner L_1 followed by a GAP (global average pooling) layer to extract the most salient feature $f_1 \in \mathbb{R}^{D_1}$ for I_1, which is denoted as:

$$f_1 = \text{GAP}(L_1(F_1)). \tag{1}$$

Then, SEO erases the feature map F_2 of frame I_2 guided by the mined discriminative part of f_1. The erased feature map is then fed into learner L_2. As the part attended by learner L_1 has been removed, the learner L_2 is naturally driven to discover new discriminative parts for identifying the target person. Recursively, for the frame feature map F_n $(n > 1)$, TSE firstly applies SEO to erases all parts discovered by previous frames to form the erased feature map $\overline{F_n}$, and then uses its specific learner L_n to mine new parts and obtain the feature vector f_n, which can be formulated as:

$$\overline{F_n} = \text{SEO}(F_n; f_1, \ldots, f_{n-1}), \quad f_n = \text{GAP}(L_n(\overline{F_n})) \ (1 < n \leq N). \tag{2}$$

The *saliency erasing operation* and *learners* repeatedly perform on the N consecutive frames of the input segment. Finally, the integral characteristic of target person can be obtained by combining the features produced by these frames.

Correlation Layer of SEO. The implementation of SEO (Eq. 2) is illustrated in Fig. 2(b). For the feature map F_n of frame I_n to be erased, a *correlation layer* is firstly designed to obtain the correlation maps between previous-frame feature vectors $f_k(k < n)$ and F_n. In particular, we firstly consider the feature vector at every spatial location (i, j) of F_n as a D dimensional local descriptor $F_n^{(i,j)}$. Then the *correlation layer* computes the semantic relevance between f_k and all the local descriptors of F_n with dot-produce similarity [37] to get the corresponding correlation map $R_{nk} \in \mathbb{R}^{H \times W}$ as:

$$R_{nk}^{(i,j)} = (F_n^{(i,j)})^T \left(w^T f_k \right) \quad (1 \le i \le H, 1 \le j \le W, 1 \le k \le n - 1). \quad (3)$$

Here $w \in \mathbb{R}^{D_1 \times D}$ projects f_k to the feature space of F_n, matching the number of channels to that of F_n. Equation 3 shows that the local descriptors that describe the part activated by f_k tend to present higher relevance values in R_{nk}. Thus R_{nk} can localize the regions in F_n of the parts activated by the previous-frame feature vector f_k.

Block Binarization Layer of SEO. The correlation maps are then used to generate the binary masks to identify the regions to be erased. A valiant approach is to conduct a threshold on the correlation maps. However, it usually produces noncontinuous regions. As pointed by [6], since the convolutional feature units are correlated spatially, when erasing the feature units discontinuously, information about the erased units can still be transmitted to the next layer. To this end, we design a *block binarization layer* to generate the binary mask which can erase a contiguous region of a feature map. As shown in Fig. 2(b), we search the most highlighted continuous area in the correlation map using a *sliding block*. Formally, for a correlation map of size $H \times W$ and the sliding block of size $h_e \times w_e$, when we move the block with horizontal and vertical strides s_w and s_h respectively, the total number of block position can be computed as $N_{pos} = \left(\lfloor \frac{H - h_e}{s_h} \rfloor + 1 \right) \times \left(\lfloor \frac{W - w_e}{s_w} \rfloor + 1 \right)$. Thus N_{pos} candidate blocks can be obtained for each correlation map. We then define the correlation value of a block as the sum of the correlation values of the items in the block. Finally, we select the candidate block with the highest correlation value as the block to be erased, i.e., the binary mask $B_{nk} \in \mathbb{R}^{H \times W}$ of correlation map R_{nk} is generated by setting the values of the units in the selected block to 0 and others to 1. We then merge the masks $\{B_{nk}\}_{k=1}^{n-1}$ to a fused mask B_n for the feature map F_n, which is calculated as:

$$B_n = B_{n1} \odot B_{n2} \odot \cdots \odot B_{n(n-1)}, \quad (4)$$

where $\odot$ is element-wise product operation.

Erasing Operation in SEO. In order to make TSE end-to-end trainable, we employ a gate mechanism to erase the feature map F_n. In particular, we apply a softmax layer to the fused correlation map, from which we erase the selected block using B_n to obtain a gate map $G_n \in \mathbb{R}^{H \times W}$:

$$G_n = \text{softmax} \left(R_{n1} \odot R_{n2} \odot \cdots \odot R_{n(n-1)} \right) \odot B_n. \quad (5)$$

F_n is erased based on B_n and G_n to generate the erased feature map $\overline{F_n}$. For consistency, we also apply the erasing operation on F_1 with a binary mask filling

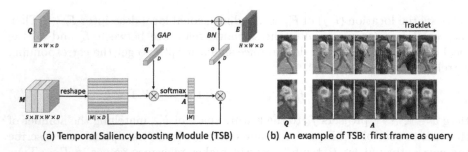

(a) Temporal Saliency boosting Module (TSB)   (b) An example of TSB: first frame as query

Fig. 3. (a) The architecture of TSB. (b) Visualization of probability map A computed on a video sequence, where we take the first frame as the query

with 1. In this way, the gradients can propagate to the parameter w of SEO and TSE can be trained by back-propagation.

3.2 Temporal Saliency Boosting Module

Although TSE can extract complementary features for input segment frames, the *saliency erasing operation* inevitably leads to information loss of the most salient part. To address this problem, we propose a *temporal saliency boosting module*. Since before the erasing operation, the intermediate feature maps of all high quality frames usually focus on the most salient parts. TSB is proposed to propagate the most salient information among the intermediate frame-level feature maps. In this way, the most salient feature can fully capture the visual cues in all frames thus presents strong discriminative power.

The structure of TSB is illustrated in Fig. 3(a), which takes a set of frame-level feature maps of a video as the input. TSB is based on a *query-memory* attention mechanism, where we respectively consider the feature map of each frame as the query $Q \in \mathbb{R}^{H \times W \times D}$, and the memory $M \in \mathbb{R}^{S \times H \times W \times D}$ containing a collection of feature maps from the remaining S frames of the video is used to enhance the representational power of the query. Specifically, we firstly squeeze Q to a descriptor which can describe the query statistics. This is achieved by using GAP (global average pooling) to generate the channel-wise statistics $q \in \mathbb{R}^D$. Then we reshape M to $\mathbb{R}^{|M| \times D}$ ($|M| = S \times H \times W$) which can be viewed as a set of D-dimensional local descriptors. Corresponding, a probability map $A \in \mathbb{R}^{|M|}$ can be obtained regarding how well the query vector matches each descriptor of the memory through cosine similarity:

$$A_i = \frac{\exp(\tau \bar{q}^T \bar{M}_i)}{\sum_{j=1}^{|M|} \exp(\tau \bar{q}^T \bar{M}_j)}, \tag{6}$$

where $M_i \in \mathbb{R}^D$ denotes the ith local descriptor of M, $\bar{q}$ and $\bar{M}_i$ is the normalized q and M_i with L_2 norm, and τ is the temperature hyperparameter. The output $o \in \mathbb{R}^D$ is then calculated as the sum of all the items in the memory weighted by their probabilities as $o = M^T A$. In this way, the descriptors of M that are

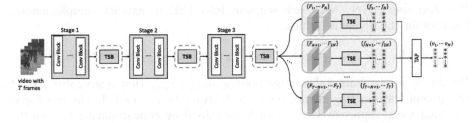

Fig. 4. The architecture of TCLNet. TAP denotes temporal average pooling layer

similar to the query present higher weights, which can avoid the corruption of low quality frames, *e.g.*, the occluded frames shown in Fig. 3(b).

At last, we propagate the weighted descriptor o to the query Q with a residual learning scheme, which is defined as $E = \mathrm{BN}(o) + Q$. Here, BN is a batch normalization [15] layer to adjust the scale of o to the query Q. Notably, before entering the BN layer, $o \in \mathbb{R}^D$ is duplicated along the spatial dimensions to $\mathbb{R}^{H \times W \times D}$ to be compatible with the size of Q.

Taking the first frame of a video sequence as the query example, Fig. 3(b) visualizes its initial feature map Q and corresponding probability map A. We can observe that Q roughly focuses on the most salient part (*i.e.*, shirts), and the probability map A can localize this part in other frames. Notably, through the *query-memory* matching, the corrupted frames presents lower weights in A, which indicates their features are suppressed during propagation and the output feature is robust to corruption. With the information propagation, the output feature fully captures the most salient visual cues in all frames of the video thus presents stronger representational power.

3.3   Overall Architecture

The architecture of Temporal Complementary Learning Network (TCLNct) that integrates TSE and TSB modules is illustrated in Fig. 4. Our network is built on ResNet-50 [9] pretrained on ImageNet [17]. ResNet-50 consists of four consecutive stages, *i.e.*, *stage*1–4, which respectively contains 3, 4, 6 and 3 residual blocks. We adopt the first three stages (*stage*1–3) as the backbone and the last stage (*stage*4) as the learners of TSE. TSB can be inserted into the backbone to any stage and TSE is added to the end of the backbone. In order to reduce the network complexity, the N learners of TSE share the same parameters for the first two residual blocks and have their own parameters in the last block.

Formally, given an video consisting of T consecutive frames, the backbone with inserted TSB firstly extracts features for each frame, which is denoted as $\mathcal{F} = \{F_1, F_2, \ldots, F_T\}$. Since the number of discriminative visual cues is usually finite, we only extract complementary features for N ($N < T$) consecutive frames. In particular, we equally divide $\mathcal{F}$ into L segments $\{C_k\}_{k=1}^L$ where each segment contains N consecutive feature maps, *i.e.*, $C_k = \{F_{(k-1)N+1}, \ldots, F_{kN}\}$.

We then respectively feed each segment into TSE to extract complementary features for the segment frames:

$$c_k = \{f_{(k-1)N+1}, \ldots, f_{kN}\} = \text{TSE}(F_{(k-1)N+1}, \ldots, F_{kN}) = \text{TSE}(C_k). \quad (7)$$

We finally apply temporal average pooling on $\{c_k\}_{k=1}^{L}$ that aggregates the set of segment features to generate the video features $\{v_1, \ldots v_N\}$. In the test stage, the final video representation v can be obtained by concatenating the feature vectors extracted by all learners, $i.e.$, $v = [\hat{v}_1, \ldots, \hat{v}_N]$, where $\hat{v}_i$ denotes the L2-normalization of v_i.

Objective Function. Following the standard identity classification paradigm [12,35], we add a classification layer to each video vector v_i. Cross entropy loss is then used for every v_i to guide the training of the corresponding learner. Recently, some works [22,34] use the combination of cross entropy loss and batch triplet loss [10] to train the network. To fairly compare with this methods, we also explore a batch triplet loss during training.

4   Experiments

4.1   Dataset and Settings

Datasets. MARS [47], DukeMTMC-VideoReID [40] and iLIDS-VID [36] datasets are used for evaluation.

Implementation Details. Our method is implemented using the PyTorch framework [29]. During training, we sample four frames from each video sequence as input and each frame is resized to 256×128. We only adopt random flipping for data augmentation. The initial learning rate is set to 0.0003 with a decay factor 0.1 at every 40 epochs. Adam optimizer [18] is used with a mini-batch size of 32 for 150 epochs training. TSB is added to stage2 of the backbone. In TSE, the number of learners, $i.e$, the number of frames in each divided segment (N in Eq. 7), is set to 2, the height of erased block h_e is set to 3 and the width w_e is set to 8, and the strides s_h and s_w of sliding block are both set to 1. During testing, given an input of entire video, the video feature is extracted using the trained TCLNet for retrieval under cosine distance. Notably, $we\ use\ all\ the\ frames\ of\ a$ $video\ to\ obtain\ the\ video\ feature\ in\ the\ testing\ phase.$

4.2   Comparison with State-of-the-Art Methods

In Table 1, we compare our method with state-of-the-arts on MARS, DukeMTMC-VideoReID and iLIDS-VID datasets. Our method outperforms the best existing methods. It is noted that: **(1)** The gaps between our results and those that consider the video as a set of unordered images [10,21,26,40,43,46,47] are significant: about 5% mAP improvement on MARS. The significant improvements demonstrate that it is effective to employ the temporal cues for video

Table 1. Comparison with related methods on MARS, DukeMTMC-VideoReID and iLIDS-VID datasets. The methods are separated into two groups: image-set based methods (**IS**) and temporal-sequence based methods (**TS**). * denotes those trained with the combination of cross entropy loss and triplet loss

Methods		MARS		Duke-Video		iLIDS-VID
		mAP	top-1	mAP	top-1	top-1
IS	Mars [47]	49.3	68.3	–	–	53.0
	SeqDecision* [43]	–	71.2	–	–	60.2
	QAN* [26]	51.7	73.7	–	–	68.0
	DRSA [21]	65.8	82.3	–	–	80.2
	EUG [40]	67.4	80.8	78.3	83.6	–
	AttDriven [46]	78.2	87.0	–	–	86.3
TS	ASTPN [41]	–	44.0	–	–	62.0
	SeeForest* [53]	50.7	70.6	–	–	55.2
	DuATM* [30]	67.7	81.2	–	–	–
	M3D [20]	84.4	74.1			84.4
	Snipped [1]	76.1	86.3	–	–	85.4
	V3D* [22]	77.0	84.3	–	–	81.3
	GLTP [19]	78.5	87.0	93.7	**96.3**	86.0
	COSAM* [34]	79.9	84.9	94.1	95.4	–
	VRSTC [13]	82.3	88.5	93.5	95.0	83.4
	TCLNet	**83.0**	**88.8**	95.2	**96.3**	84.3
	TCLNet-tri*	**85.1**	**89.8**	**96.2**	**96.9**	**86.6**

reID. (**2**) Recent works [13,20,22] uses 3D CNN or non-local blocks to learn the temporal cues, which require high computational complexity. Our TCLNet puts much less overheads with a better performance on MARS: about 1% mAP improvement. We attribute this improvement to the complementary features learned from video frames which enhance the discriminative capability of reID models. (**3**) The works [22,26,30,34,43,53] use the triplet loss to promote the performance. To fairly compare with them, we also adopt a triplet loss which further increases our performance by about 1%. It still outperforms the best performing work [34] by a large margin.

4.3 Ablation Study

We investigate the effectiveness of TSE and TSB modules by conducting a series of ablation studies on MARS dataset. We adopt ResNet-50 [9] with temporal average pooling as baseline (denoted as base.). In this part, all models are trained with only cross entropy loss.

Table 2. Component analysis of the proposed network on MARS. We also report the number of floating-point operations (GFLOPs) for a four-frames sequence, and the parameter number (Params) of the models

Models	GFLOPs	Params	mAP	top-1
Base	16.246	23.5M	79.6	86.8
Base.+TSE-wo-SEO	16.246	27.9M	80.9	87.2
Base.+TSE	16.251	29.9M	**82.5**	**88.2**
Base.+TSB	16.254	23.5M	82.3	87.6
TCLNet (TSE+TSB)	16.259	29.9M	**83.0**	**88.8**
TCLNet (TSE+TSB-stage1)	16.267	29.9M	82.2	87.4
TCLNet (TSE+TSB-stage2)	16.259	29.9M	**83.0**	**88.8**
TCLNet (TSE+TSB-stage3)	16.255	29.9M	82.6	88.2
TCLNet (TSE+TSB-stage23)	16.263	29.9M	82.7	88.2

Effectiveness of TSE. We firstly evaluate the effect of TSE by replacing the stage4 layer of baseline with TSE (**base.+TSE**). As shown in Table 2, TSE module improves the performance remarkably. Compared with the baseline, employing TSE brings 2.9% mAP and 1.4% top-1 accuracy gains respectively with negligible computational overhead. We argue that the learners of TSE work collaboratively to mine complementary parts so as to generate integral characteristic of the target identity, which helps to distinguish different identities with seemingly similar local parts. An example is shown in Fig. 5.

Effectiveness of *Saliency Erasing Operation* in TSE. It is noteworthy that the improvement of TSE dose not just come from the increased parameters by its learners. To see this, we introduce a variant of TSE, *i.e.*, **TSE-wo-SEO**, which adopts a series of ordered learners for consecutive frames without the *saliency erasing operation*. As shown in Table 2, TSE-wo-SEO brings only a small improvement over the baseline, indicating that the visual features captured by different learners are almost the same without the *saliency erasing operation*. While TSE performs significantly better than TSE-wo-SEO, which validates the powerful capability of the *saliency erasing operation* to force different learners to focus on diverse image parts so as to discover integral visual features. Overall, we can see that the improvement of TSE mainly comes from the *saliency erasing operation* rather than the increased parameters.

TSE *w.r.t* Number of Ordered Learners. As shown in Fig. 2(a), TSE contains N ordered learners that mine complementary parts for N consecutive frames. Table 3(a) studies the impact of the number of learners N on the model base.+TSE. We can observe that the performance increases as more learners are considered to mine complementary parts. However, the performance drops largely when N reaches to 4. In this case, most discriminative parts have been

Table 3. Impact of TSE hyper-parameters on MARS

| (a) The number of ordered learners | | | | | (b) Erased block height h_e | | |
N	GFLOPs	Params	mAP	top-1	h_e	mAP	top-1
1 (base.)	16.246	23.5M	79.6	86.8	2	81.8	87.2
2	16.251	29.9M	**82.5**	88.2	3	**82.5**	**88.2**
3	16.252	34.5M	82.4	**88.4**	4	82.0	87.4
4	16.253	38.9M	81.0	87.0	5	81.7	87.2

erased in the last frame of the input segment, the fourth learner has to activate non-discriminative regions, *e.g.*, the background, which corrupts the final video representation. Considering the model complexity, we set N to 2 in our work.

TSE *w.r.t* Erased Block Size. In our network, TSE is applied for the frame-level feature map with size 16×8. Because of the spatial structure of the pedestrian images, we fix the erased width to the width of the feature map to erase entire rows of the feature map. Table 3(b) studies the impact of the erased height h_e on the performance of TSE. We observe the best performance when $h_e = 3$, and it becomes worse when the erased height is larger or smaller. We can conclude: 1) too small erased size cannot effectively encourage the current learner to discover the complementary parts; 2) too large erased size force the current learner to activate non-discriminative image parts, *e.g.*, background.

Effectiveness of TSB. We further assess the effectiveness of TSB module by adding it to the stage2 of baseline (**base.+TSB**) in Table 2. TSB individually brings 2.7% mAP and 0.8% top-1 accuracy gains with an extremely small increase in computational complexity. The improvements indicate that it is effective to enhance the feature representation power by propagating the salient features among the video frames. When we integrate TSE and TSB modules together to TCLNet, the performance can be further improved by about 1% on mAP and top-1 accuracy.

Efficient Positions to Place TSB. Table 2 compares a single TSB module added to different stages of ResNet50 in our TCLNet. The improvements of an TSB module in stage2 and stage3 are similar, but smaller in stage1. One possible explanation is that stage1 has a big spatial size 64×32 that is not very expressive and sufficient to provide precise semantic information. We also present the results of more TSB modules. In particular, we add a TSB module to stage2 and stage3 of the backbone respectively. However, we observe that adding more TSB modules does not bring improvement, indicating that one TSB module is enough for enhancing the salient features.

Complexity Comparisons. As shown in Table 2. We can observe that TSE and TSB introduce negligible computational overhead. In particular, TCLNet requires 16.259 GFLOPs, corresponding to only 0.08% relative increase over original model (base.). The increased computation cost mainly comes from the correlation map of TSE and probability map of TSB, which can be worked out by matrix multiplications thus occupy little time in GPU libraries. TCLNet introduces 6.4M parameters to baseline, which mainly come from the learners of TSE. Noting that only extending the baseline with a series of learners (base.+TES-wo-SEO) brings marginal improvement, showing the improvement of TCLNet is not just because of the added parameters.

Single Shot reID. TSE is easy to generalize to single shot reID, where different learners discover diverse visual cues for the input image. We compare ResNet50 and ResNet50+TSE on Market1501 dataset [48]. ResNet50+TSE outperforms ResNet50 by 3.2% mAP (85.3%/80.3%), which indicates the good generality of our method.

4.4   Comparison with Related Approaches

Comparison TSE with Other Erasing Strategies. Table 4(a) compares various erasing methods that are applied to baseline. DropBlock [6] *randomly* drops a contiguous regions of the convolution features during *training* to *prevent overfitting*. As shown in Table 4(a), DropBlock brings marginal improvements while TSE significantly outperforms DropBlock by 2.7% mAP and 1.3% top-1 accuracy. The significant improvements show that it is more efficient to use our erasing strategy to extract complementary features for consecutive frames in video reID tasks. Random Erasing (RE) [51] randomly erases a rectangle region of the *input images* during training, which is a widely used data augmentation technique. As shown in Table 4(a), TSE still outperforms RE. Furthermore, as a data augmentation technique, RE is compatible with our method, in which the performance can be furthered lifted 0.4% mAP when combining with RE.

Comparison TSB with Other Feature Propagation Strategies. Table 4(b) compares TSB with other feature propagation strategies. We can see that our TSB significantly outperforms 3D convolution. We argue that 3D convolution is prone to the corruption of low quality frames and hard to optimize because of the large parameter overhead. Compared with non-local (NL) [37] method, our TSB can achieve comparable performance under less computation budge and model size. More importantly, TSB is more effective to combine with TSE, where TCLNet (TSE+TSB) outperforms base.+TSE+NL by 1.2% top-1 accuracy. We argue that TSB only propagates the *salient information* among video frames which is more complementary to TSE module.

Table 4. Compare TSB and TSE modules with related approaches on MARS

(a) TSE *vs.* other erasing methods			(b) TSB *vs.* other feature propagation methods				
Models	mAP	top-1	Models	GFLOPs	Params	mAP	top-1
base.	79.6	86.8	base.+3D [16]	22.756	33.7M	80.0	86.1
base.+DropBlock [6]	79.8	86.9	base.+NL [37]	21.615	25.6M	**82.4**	**87.6**
base.+RE [51]	81.5	86.6	base.+TSB	16.254	23.5M	82.3	**87.6**
base.+TSE	**82.5**	**88.2**	base.+TSE+NL	21.619	32.1M	82.6	87.6
base.+TSE+RE	**82.9**	88.1	TCLNet	16.259	29.9M	**83.0**	**88.8**

4.5   Visualization Analysis

Visualization of Feature Maps. For qualitative analysis, we compare the visualization results of feature maps extracted by baseline and TCLNet for some input video segments. As shown in Fig. 5(b), the features of baseline only pay attention to some local regions, *i.e.*, the red T shirts, which are difficult to distinguish the different pedestrians in Fig. 5(a). Instead, TCLNet is able to mine complementary parts for consecutive frames. As shown in Fig. 5(c), for a video segment consisting of two consecutive frames, the feature of the first frame learned by the learner L_1 is most related to the red T shirts, while the learner L_2 activates the lower body for the second frame. With the complementary parts mined by learner L_2, different persons with similar local appearances become distinguishable. So the final ranking results can be improved significantly.

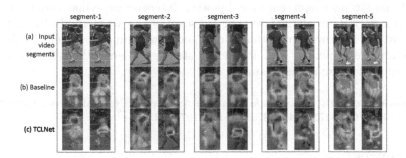

Fig. 5. Feature map visualization of baseline and TCLNet

Visualization of Feature Distribution. Furthermore, we choose a number of person IDs with similar appearances from the test set of MARS to visualize the feature distribution by t-SNE [27]. These pedestrians wear blue shirts with small inter-person variation as shown in Fig. 6(c). For the baseline that only focuses on local parts, the features belonging to these different identities are staggered. With TSE extracting complementary features and TSB enhancing salient features, the features of different identities extracted by TCLNet become

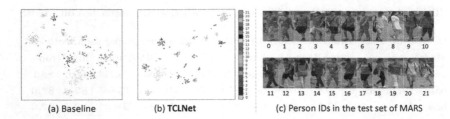

(a) Baseline   (b) **TCLNet**   (c) Person IDs in the test set of MARS

Fig. 6. tSNE visualization of feature distribution of baseline and TCLNe on MARS test set. Different colors indicate different identities (Color figure online)

more separable. Specifically, by comparing Fig. 6(a) and (b), we can observe that for some identities that are hard to be distinguished by baseline, the proposed model can better distinguish them, $e.g.$, the 1st, 3rd and 4th identities.

5   Conclusions

In this work, we propose a novel Temporal Complementary Learning Network for video person reID. Firstly, we introduce the Temporal Saliency Erasing module for complementary feature learning of video frames. TSE employs a saliency erasing strategy to progressively discover diverse and complementary visual cues for consecutive frames of a video. Furthermore, we propose the Temporal Saliency Boosting module to propagate the salient information among video frames. After propagation, the salient features capture the visual cues of all frames in a video and obtain stronger representational power. Extensive experiments demonstrate the superiority of our method over current state-of-the-art methods. In the future work, we will improve our method for longer-term temporal modeling. Also, we will combine our method with an efficient strategy to erase the noisy frames for more robust feature representation.

Acknowledgement. This work is partially supported by Natural Science Foundation of China (NSFC): 61732004, 61876171 and 61976203.

References

1. Chen, D., Li, H., Xiao, T., Yi, S., Wang, X.: Video person re-identification with competitive snippet-similarity aggregation and co-attentive snippet embedding. In: CVPR, pp. 1169–1178 (2018)
2. Chen, D., Xu, D., Li, H., Sebe, N., Wang, X.: Group consistent similarity learning via deep CRF for person re-identification. In: CVPR, pp. 8649–8658 (2018)
3. Dai, Z., Chen, M., Zhu, S., Tan, P.: Batch feature erasing for person re-identification and beyond. arXiv preprint arXiv:1811.07130 1(2), 3 (2018)
4. DeVries, T., Taylor, G.W.: Improved regularization of convolutional neural networks with cutout. arXiv preprint arXiv:1708.04552 (2017)
5. Ge, Y., Gu, X., Chen, M., Wang, H., Yang, D.: Deep multi-metric learning for person re-identification. In: ICME, pp. 1–6 (2018)

6. Ghiasi, G., Lin, T.Y., Le, Q.V.: DropBlock: a regularization method for convolutional networks. In: NeurIPS, pp. 10727–10737 (2018)
7. Gu, X., Ma, B., Chang, H., Shan, S., Chen, X.: Temporal knowledge propagation for image-to-video person re-identification. In: ICCV, pp. 9647–9656 (2019)
8. Gu, X., Ma, B., Chang, H., Zhang, H., Chen, X.: Appearance-preserving 3d convolution for video-based person re-identification. In: ECCV (2020)
9. He, K., Zhang, X., Ren, S., Sun, J.: Deep residual learning for image recognition. In: CVPR, pp. 770–778 (2016)
10. Hermans, A., Beyer, L., Leibe, B.: In defense of the triplet loss for person reidentification. arXiv preprint arXiv: 1703.07737 (2017)
11. Hou, R., Chang, H., Ma, B., Shan, S., Chen, X.: Cross attention network for few-shot classification. In: NeurIPS, pp. 4003–4014 (2019)
12. Hou, R., Ma, B., Chang, H., Gu, X., Shan, S., Chen, X.: Interaction-and-aggregation network for person re-identification. In: CVPR, pp. 9317–9326 (2019)
13. Hou, R., Ma, B., Chang, H., Gu, X., Shan, S., Chen, X.: VRSTC: occlusion-free video person re-identification. In: CVPR, pp. 7183–7192 (2019)
14. Hou, R., Chang, H., Ma, B., Chen, X.: Video prediction with bidirectional constraint network. In: FG, pp. 1–8 (2019)
15. Ioffe, S., Szegedy, C.: Batch normalization: accelerating deep network training by reducing internal covariate shift. arXiv preprint arXiv:1502.03167 (2015)
16. Ji, S., Xu, W., Yang, M., Yu, K.: 3D convolutional neural networks for human action recognition. IEEE Trans. Pattern Anal. Mach. Intell. $35(1)$, 221–231 (2012)
17. Karpathy, A., Toderici, G., Shetty, S., Leung, T., Sukthankar, R., Fei-Fei, L.: Large-scale video classification with convolutional neural networks. In: CVPR, pp. 1725–1732 (2014)
18. Kingma, D.P., Ba, J.: Adam: a method for stochastic optimization. arXiv preprint arXiv:1412.6980 (2014)
19. Li, J., Wang, J., Tian, Q., Gao, W., Zhang, S.: Global-local temporal representations for video person re-identification. In: ICCV (2019)
20. Li, J., Zhang, S., Huang, T.: Multi-scale 3D convolution network for video based person re-identification. In: AAAI (2019)
21. Li, S., Bak, S., Carr, P., Hetang, C., Wang., X.: Diversity regularized spatiotemporal attention for video-based person re-identification. In: CVPR, pp. 369–378 (2018)
22. Liao, X., He, L., Yang, Z.: Video-based person re-identification via 3D convolutional networks and non-local attention. In: ACCV (2018)
23. Liu, F., Zhang, L.: View confusion feature learning for person re-identification. In: CVPR, pp. 6639–6648 (2019)
24. Liu, N., Zhao, Q., Zhang, N., Cheng, X., Zhu, J.: Pose-guided complementary features learning for Amur tiger re-identification. In: ICCV Workshops (2019)
25. Liu, S., Hao, X., Zhang, R., Zhang, Z., Durrani, T.S.: Adversarial erasing attention for person re-identification in camera networks under complex environments. IEEE Access 8, 56469–56479 (2020)
26. Liu, Y., Yan, J., Ouyang, W.: Quality aware network for set to set recognition. In: CVPR, pp. 4694–4703 (2017)
27. Maaten, L.V.D., Hinton, G.: Visualizing data using t-SNE. J. Mach. Learn. Res. 9, 2579–2605 (2008)
28. McLaughlin, N., del Rincon, J.M., Miller, P.C.: Recurrent convolutional network for video-based person re-identification. In: CVPR, pp. 1325–1334 (2016)
29. Paszke, A., et al.: Automatic differentiation in PyTorch. In: NeurIPS Workshop (2017)

30. Si, J., et al.: Dual attention matching network for context-aware feature sequence based person re-identification. In: CVPR (2018)
31. Singh, K.K., Lee, Y.J.: Hide-and-seek: forcing a network to be meticulous for weakly-supervised object and action localization. In: ICCV (2017)
32. Song, G., Leng, B., Liu, Y., Hetang, C., Cai, S.: Region-based quality estimation network for large-scale person re-identification. arXiv preprint arXiv:1711.08766 (2017)
33. Srivastava, N., Hinton, G., Krizhevsky, A., Sutskever, I., Salakhutdinov, R.: Dropout: a simple way to prevent neural networks from overfitting. J. Mach. Learn. Res. **15**(1), 1929–1958 (2014)
34. Subramaniam, A., Nambiar, A., Mittal, A.: Co-segmentation inspired attention networks for video-based person re-identification. In: ICCV (2019)
35. Sun, Y., Zheng, L., Yang, Y., Tian, Q., Wang, S.: Beyond part models: person retrieval with refined part pooling (and a strong convolutional baseline). In: ECCV, pp. 480–496 (2018)
36. Wang, T., Gong, S., Zhu, X., Wang, S.: Person re-identification by video ranking. In: ECCV, pp. 688–703 (2014)
37. Wang, X., Girshick, R., Gupta, A., He, K.: Non-local neural networks. In: CVPR, pp. 7794–7803 (2018)
38. Wang, X., Shrivastava, A., Gupta, A.: A-Fast-RCNN: hard positive generation via adversary for object detection. In: CVPR, pp. 2606–2615 (2017)
39. Wei, L., Zhang, S., Gao, W., Tian, Q.: Person trasfer GAN to bridge domain gap for person re-identification. In: CVPR, pp. 79–88 (2018)
40. Wu, Y., Lin, Y., Dong, X., Yan, Y., Quyang, W., Yang, Y.: Exploit the unknown gradually: one-shot video-based person re-identification by stepwise learning. In: CVPR, pp. 5177–5186 (2018)
41. Xu, S., Cheng, Y., Gu, K., Yang, Y., Chang, S., Zhou, P.: Jointly attentive spatial-temporal pooling networks for video-based person re-identification. In: ICCV, pp. 4743–4752 (2017)
42. Yang, W., Huang, H., Zhang, Z., Chen, X., Huang, K., Zhang., S.: Towards rich feature discovery with class activation maps augmentation for person re-identification. In: CVPR (2019)
43. Zhang, J., Wang, N., Zhang, L.: Multi-shot pedestrian re-identification via sequential decision making. In: CVPR (2018)
44. Zhang, L., et al.: Ordered or orderless: a revisit for video based person re-identification. IEEE Trans. Pattern Anal. Mach. Intell. (2020)
45. Zhang, Z., Lan, C., Zeng, W., Chen, Z.: Densely semantically aligned person re-identification. In: CVPR, pp. 667–676 (2019)
46. Zhao, Y., Shen, X., Jin, Z., Lu, H., Hua, X.: Attribute-driven feature disentangling and temporal aggregation for video person re-identification. In: CVPR (2019)
47. Zheng, L., et al.: MARS: a video benchmark for large-scale person re-identification. In: ECCV, pp. 868–884 (2016)
48. Zheng, L., Shen, L., Tian, L., Wang, S., Wang, J., Tian, Q.: Scalable person re-identification: a benchmark. In: ICCV, pp. 1116–1124 (2015)
49. Zheng, M., Karanam, S., Wu, Z., Radke, R.J.: Re-identification with consistent attentive Siamese networks. In: CVPR, pp. 5735–5744 (2019)
50. Zheng, Z., Zheng, L., Yang, Y.: Unlabeled samples generated by GAN improve the person re-identification baseline in vitro. In: ICCV, pp. 3754–3762 (2017)
51. Zhong, Z., Zheng, L., Kang, G., Li, S., Yang, Y.: Random erasing data augmentation. arXiv preprint arXiv:1708.04896 (2017)

52. Zhou, B., Khosla, A., Lapedriza, A., Oliva, A., Torralba, A.: Learning deep features for discriminative localization. In: CVPR, pp. 2921–2929 (2016)
53. Zhou, Z., Huang, Y., Wang, W., Wang, L., Tan., T.: See the forest for the trees: joint spatial and temporal recurrent neural networks for video-based person re-identification. In: CVPR, pp. 6776–6785 (2017)

HoughNet: Integrating Near and Long-Range Evidence for Bottom-Up Object Detection

Nermin Samet[1]([⊠]), Samet Hicsonmez[2], and Emre Akbas[1]

[1] Department of Computer Engineering, Middle East Technical University,
Ankara, Turkey
{nermin,emre}@ceng.metu.edu.tr
[2] Department of Computer Engineering, Hacettepe University, Ankara, Turkey
samethicsonmez@hacettepe.edu.tr

Abstract. This paper presents HoughNet, a one-stage, anchor-free, voting-based, bottom-up object detection method. Inspired by the Generalized Hough Transform, HoughNet determines the presence of an object at a certain location by the sum of the votes cast on that location. Votes are collected from both near and long-distance locations based on a log-polar vote field. Thanks to this voting mechanism, HoughNet is able to integrate both near and long-range, class-conditional evidence for visual recognition, thereby generalizing and enhancing current object detection methodology, which typically relies on only local evidence. On the COCO dataset, HoughNet's best model achieves 46.4 *AP* (and 65.1 *AP*$_{50}$), performing on par with the state-of-the-art in bottom-up object detection and outperforming most major one-stage and two-stage methods. We further validate the effectiveness of our proposal in another task, namely, "labels to photo" image generation by integrating the voting module of HoughNet to two different GAN models and showing that the accuracy is significantly improved in both cases. Code is available at https://github.com/nerminsamet/houghnet.

Keywords: Object detection · Voting · Bottom-up recognition · Hough transform · Image-to-image translation

1 Introduction

Deep learning has brought on remarkable improvements in object detection. Performance on widely used benchmark datasets, as measured by mean average-precision (mAP), has at least doubled (from 0.33 mAP [15] [11] to 0.80 mAP on PASCAL VOC [17]; and from 0.2 mAP [28] to around 0.5 mAP on COCO [27])

Electronic supplementary material The online version of this chapter (https://doi.org/10.1007/978-3-030-58595-2_25) contains supplementary material, which is available to authorized users.

© Springer Nature Switzerland AG 2020
A. Vedaldi et al. (Eds.): ECCV 2020, LNCS 12370, pp. 406–423, 2020.
https://doi.org/10.1007/978-3-030-58595-2_25

in comparison to the previous generation (pre-deep-learning, shallow) methods. Current state-of-the-art, deep learning based object detectors [27,30,38,41] predominantly follow a top-down approach where objects are detected holistically via rectangular region classification. This was not the case with the pre-deep-learning methods. The bottom-up approach was a major research focus as exemplified by the prominent voting-based (the Implicit Shape Model [24]) and part-based (the Deformable Parts Model [10]) methods. However, today, among deep learning based object detectors, the bottom-up approach has not been sufficiently explored with a few exceptions (e.g. CornerNet [23], ExtremeNet [52]).

In this paper, we propose Hough-Net, a one-stage, anchor-free, voting-based, bottom-up object detection method. HoughNet is based on the idea of voting, inspired by the Generalized Hough Transform [2,18]. In its most generic form, the goal of GHT is to detect a whole shape based on its parts. Each part produces a hypothesis, i.e. casts its vote, regarding the location of the whole shape. Then, the location with the most votes is selected as the result. Similarly, in HoughNet, the presence of an object belonging to a certain class at a particular location is determined by the sum of the class-conditional votes cast on that location (Fig. 1). HoughNet

Fig. 1. (Left) A sample "mouse" detection, shown with yellow bounding box, by HoughNet. (Right) The locations that vote for this detection. Colors indicate vote strength. In addition to the local votes originating from the mouse itself, there are strong votes from nearby "keyboard" objects, which shows that HoughNet is able to utilize both short and long-range evidence for detection. More examples can be seen in Fig. 4

processes the input image using a convolutional neural network to produce an intermediate score map per class. Scores in these maps indicate the presence of visual structures that would support the detection of an object instance. These structures could be object parts, partial objects or patterns belonging to the same or other classes. We name these score maps as "visual evidence" maps. Each spatial location in a visual evidence map votes for target areas that are likely to contain objects. Target areas are determined by placing a log-polar grid, which we call the "vote field," centered at the voter location. The purpose of using a log-polar vote field is to reduce the spatial precision of the vote as the distance between voter location and target area increases. This is inspired by foveated vision systems found in nature, where the spatial resolution rapidly decreases from the fovea towards the periphery [22]. Once all visual evidence is processed through voting, the accumulated votes are recorded in object presence maps, where the peaks indicate the presence of object instances.

Current state-of-the-art object detectors rely on local (or short-range) visual evidence to decide whether there is an object at that location (as in top-down methods) or an important keypoint such as a corner (as in bottom-up methods). On the other hand, HoughNet is able to integrate both short and long-range visual evidence through voting. An example is illustrated in Fig. 1, where the detected mouse gets strong votes from two keyboards, one of which is literally at the other side of the image. In another example (Fig. 4, row 2, col 1), a ball on the right-edge of the image is voting for the baseball bat on the left-edge. On the COCO dataset, HoughNet achieves comparable results with the state-of-the-art bottom-up detector CenterNet [9], while being the fastest object detector among bottom-up detectors. It outperforms prominent one-stage (RetinaNet [27]) and two-stage detectors (Faster RCNN [41], Mask RCNN [16]). To further show the effectiveness of our approach, we used the voting module of HoughNet in another task, namely, "labels to photo" image generation. Specifically, we integrated the voting module to two different GAN models (CycleGAN [54] and Pix2Pix [20]) and showed that the performance is improved in both cases.

Our main contribution in this work is HoughNet, a voting-based bottom-up object detection method that is able to integrate near and long-range evidence for object detection. As a minor contribution, we created a mini training set called "COCO minitrain", a curated subset of COCO train2017 set, to reduce the computational cost of ablation experiments. We validated COCO minitrain in two ways by (i) showing that the COCO val2017 performance of a model trained on COCO minitrain is strongly positively correlated with the performance of the same model trained on COCO train2017, and (ii) showing that COCO minitrain set preserves the object instance statistics.

2   Related Work

Methods Using Log-Polar Fields/Representations. Many biological systems have foveated vision where the spatial resolution decreases from the fovea (point of fixation) towards the periphery. Inspired by this phenomenon, computer vision researchers have used log-polar fields for many different purposes including shape description [4], feature extraction [1] and foveated sampling/imaging [44].

Non-Deep, Voting-Based Object Detection Methods. In the pre-deep learning era, generalized Hough Transform (GHT) based voting methods have been used for object detection. The most influential work was the Implicit Shape Model (ISM) [24]. In ISM, Leibe et al. [24] applied GHT for object detection/recognition and segmentation. During the training of the ISM, first, interest points are extracted and then a visual codebook (i.e. dictionary) is created using an unsupervised clustering algorithm applied on the patches extracted around interest points. Next, the algorithm matches the patches around each interest point to the visual word with the smallest distance. In the last step, the positions of the patches relative to the center of the object are associated with the corresponding visual words and stored in a table. During inference, patches extracted around interest points are matched to closest visual words. Each matched visual word casts votes for the object center. In the last stage, the location that has the most votes is identified, and object detection is performed using the patches that vote for this location. Later, ISM was further extended with discriminative frameworks [3,14,32,33,37]. Okada [33] ensembled randomized trees using image patches as voting elements. Similarly, Gall and Lempitsky [14] proposed to learn a mapping between image patches and votes using random forest framework. In order to fix the accumulation of inconsistent votes of ISM, Razavi et al. [37] augmented the Hough space with latent variables to enforce consistency between votes. In Max-margin Hough Transform [32], Maji and Malik showed the importance of learning visual words in a discriminative max-margin framework. Barinova et al. [3] detected multiple objects using energy optimization instead of non-maxima suppression peak selection of ISM.

HoughNet is similar to ISM and its variants described above only at the idea level as all are voting based methods. There are two major differences: (i) HoughNet uses deep neural networks for part/feature (i.e. visual evidence) estimation, whereas ISM uses hand-crafted features; (ii) ISM uses a discrete set of visual words (obtained by unsupervised clustering) and each word's vote is exactly known (stored in a table) after training. In HoughNet, however, there is not a discrete set of words and vote is carried through a log-polar vote field which takes into account the location precision as a function of target area.

Bottom-Up Object Detection Methods. Apart from the classical one-stage [12,27,30,39,40] vs. two-stage [16,41] categorization of object detectors, we can also categorize the current approaches into two: top-down and bottom-up. In the top-down approach [27,30,39,41], a near-exhaustive list of object hypotheses in the form of rectangular boxes are generated and objects are predicted in a holistic manner based on these boxes. Designing the hypotheses space (e.g. parameters of anchor boxes) is a problem by itself [45]. Typically, a single template is responsible for the detection of the whole object. In this sense, recent anchor-free methods [43,51] are also top-down. On the other hand, in the bottom-up approach, objects *emerge* from the detection of parts (or sub-object structures). For example, in CornerNet [23], top-left and bottom-right corners of objects are detected first, and then, they are paired to form whole objects. Following CornerNet, ExtremeNet [52] groups extreme points (e.g. left-most, etc.) and center points to form objects. Together with corner pairs of CornerNet [23], CenterNet [9] adds center point to model each object as a triplet. HoughNet follows the bottom-up approach based on a voting strategy: object presence score is voted (aggregated) from a wide area covering short and long-range evidence.

Deep, Voting-Based Object Detection Methods. Qi et al. [36] apply Hough voting for 3D object detection in point clouds. Sheshkus et al. [42] utilize Hough transform for vanishing points detection in the documents. For automatic pedestrian and car detection, Gabriel et al. [13] proposed using discriminative generalized Hough transform for proposal generation in edge images, later to further refine the boxes, they fed these proposals to deep networks. In the deep learning era, we are not the first to use a log-polar vote field in a voting-based model. Lifshitz et al. [25] used a log-polar map to estimate keypoints for single person human pose estimation. Apart from the fact that [25] is tackling the human pose estimation task, there are several subtle differences. First, they prepare ground

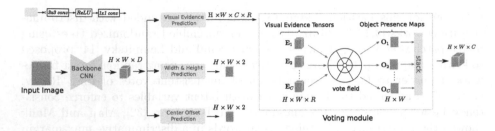

Fig. 2. Overall processing pipeline of HoughNet

truth voting maps for each keypoint such that keypoints vote for every other one depending on its relative position in the log polar map. This requires manually creating static voting maps. Specifically, their model learns $H \times W \times R \times C$ voting map, where R is the number of bins and C is the augmented keypoints. In order to produce keypoint heatmaps they perform vote aggregation at test phase. Second, this design restricts the model to learn only the keypoint locations as voters. When we consider the object detection task and its complexity, it is not trivial to decide the voters of the objects and prepare supervised static voting maps as in human pose estimation. Moreover, this design limits the voters to reside only inside of the object (e.g. person) unlike our approach where an object could get votes from far away regions. To overcome these issues, unlike their model we apply vote aggregation during training (they perform vote aggregation only at test phase). This allows us to expose the latent patterns between objects and voters for each class. In this way, our voting module is able to get votes from non-labeled objects (see the last row of Fig. 4). To the best of our knowledge, we are the first to use a log-polar vote field in a voting-based deep learning model to integrate the **long range interactions** for object detection.

Similar to HoughNet, Non-local neural networks (NLNN) [46] and Relation networks (RN) [19] integrate long-range features. As a fundamental difference, in NLNN, the relative displacement between interacting features is not taken into account. However, HoughNet uses this information encoded through the regions of the log-polar vote field. RN models object-object relations explicitly for proposal-based two-stage detectors.

3   HoughNet: The Method and The Models

The overall processing pipeline of our method is illustrated in Fig. 2. To give a brief overview, the input image first passes through a backbone CNN, the output of which is connected to three different branches carrying out the predictions of (i) visual evidence scores, (ii) objects' bounding box dimensions (width and height), and (iii) objects' center location offsets. The first branch is where the voting occurs. Before we describe our voting mechanism in detail, we first introduce the log-polar vote field.

3.1   The Log-Polar "Vote Field"

We use the set of regions in a standard log-polar coordinate system to define the regions through which votes are collected. A log-polar coordinate system is defined by the number and radii of eccentricity bins (or rings) and the number of angle bins. We call the set of cells or regions formed in such a coordinate system as the "vote field" (Fig. 3). In our experiments, we used different vote fields with different parameters (number of angle bins, etc.) as explained in the Experiments section. In the following, R denotes the number of regions in the vote field and K_r is the number of pixels in a particular region r. $\Delta_r(i)$ denotes the relative spatial coordinates of the ith pixel in the rth region, with respect to the center of the field. We implement the vote field as a fixed-weight (non-learnable) transposed-convolution filter as further explained below.

3.2   Voting Module

After the input image is passed through the backbone network and the "visual evidence" branch, the voting module of Hough-Net receives C tensors $\mathbf{E}_1, \mathbf{E}_2, \ldots, \mathbf{E}_C$, each of size $H \times W \times R$, where C is the number of classes, H and W are spatial dimensions and R is the number of regions in the vote field. Each of these tensors contains class-conditional (i.e. for a specific class) "visual evidence" scores. The job of the voting module is to produce C "object presence" maps $\mathbf{O}_1, \mathbf{O}_2, \ldots, \mathbf{O}_C$, each of size $H \times W$. Then, peaks in these maps will indicate the presence of object instances. The voting process, which converts the visual evidence tensors (e.g. $\mathbf{E}_c$) to object presence maps (e.g. $\mathbf{O}_c$), works as described below.

Suppose we wanted to process the visual evidence at the ith row, j^{th} column and the rth channel of an evidence tensor $\mathbf{E}$. When we place our vote field on a 2D map, centered

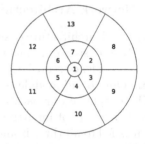

Fig. 3. A log-polar "vote field" used in the voting module of HoughNet. Numbers indicate region ids. A vote field is parametrized by the number of angle bins, and the number and radii of eccentricity bins, or rings. In this particular vote field, there are a total of 13 regions, 6 angle bins and 3 rings. The radii of the rings are 2, 8 and 16, respectively

at location (i, j), the region r marks the target area to be voted on, whose coordinates can be computed by adding the coordinate offsets $\Delta_r(\cdot)$ to (i, j). Then, we add the visual evidence score $\mathbf{E}(i, j, r)$ to the target area of the object presence map. Note that this operation can be efficiently implemented using the "transposed convolution" (or "deconvolution") operation. Visual evidence scores from locations other than (i, j) are processed in the same way and the scores are accumulated in the object presence map. We formally define this procedure in

---

Algorithm 1. Vote aggregation algorithm

Input: Visual evidence tensor $\mathbf{E}_c$, Vote field relative coordinates Δ
Output: Object presence map $\mathbf{O}_c$
  Initialize $\mathbf{O}_c$ with all zeros
  for each pixel (i, j, r) in $\mathbf{E}_c$ **do**
    /* K_r: number of pixels in the vote field region r */
    for $k = 1$ to K_r **do**
      $(y, x) \leftarrow (i, j) + \Delta_r(k)$
      $\mathbf{O}_c(y, x) \leftarrow \mathbf{O}_c(y, x) + \frac{1}{K_r}\mathbf{E}_c(i, j, r)$
    end for
  end for

Algorithm 1, which takes in a visual evidence tensor as input and produces an object presence map.[1]

3.3 Network Architecture

Our network architecture design follows that of "Objects as Points" (OAP) [51]. HoughNet consists of a backbone and three subsequent branches which predict (i) visual evidence scores, (ii) bounding box widths and heights, and (iii) center offsets. Our voting module is attached to the visual evidence branch (Fig. 2).

The output of our backbone network is a feature map of size $H \times W \times D$, which is a result of inputting an image of size $4H \times 4W \times 3$. The backbone's output is fed to all three branches. Each branch has one convolutional layer with 3×3 filters followed by a ReLU layer and another convolutional layer with 1×1 filters. The visual evidence branch outputs $H \times W \times C \times R$ sized output where C and R correspond to the number of classes and vote field regions, respectively. The width/height prediction branch outputs $H \times W \times 2$ sized output which predicts heights and widths for each possible object center. Finally, center offset branch predicts relative displacement of center locations across the spatial axes.

Objective Functions. For the optimization of the visual evidence branch, we use the modified focal loss [27] introduced in CornerNet [23] (also used in [51,52]). In order to recover the lost precision of the center points due to down-sampling operations through the network, center offset prediction branch outputs class-agnostic local offsets of object centers. We optimize this branch using the L_1 loss as the other bottom-up detectors [23,51,52] do. Finally, our width & height prediction branch outputs class-agnostic width and height values of objects. For the optimization of this branch, we use L_1 loss by scaling the loss by 0.1 as proposed in OAP [51]. The overall loss is the sum of the losses from all branches.

---

[1] We provide a step-by-step animation of the voting process at https://shorturl.at/ilOP2.

4 Experiments

This section presents the experiments we conducted to show the effectiveness of our proposed method. First, we studied how different parameters of the vote field affect the final object detection performance. Next, we present several performance comparisons between HoughNet and the current state-of-the-art methods, on the COCO dataset. After presenting sample visual results for qualitative inspection, we describe our experiments on the "labels to photo" task. We used PyTorch [35] to implement HoughNet.

Training and Inference Details. We ran our experiments on 4 V100 GPUs. For training, we used 512 × 512 images unless stated otherwise. The training setup is not uniform across different experiments, mainly due to different backbones.

The inference pipeline is common for all HoughNet models. We extract center locations by applying a 3 × 3 max pooling operation on object presence heatmaps and pick the highest scoring 100 points as detections. Then, we adjust these points using the predicted center offset values. Final bounding boxes are generated using the predicted width & height values on these detections. For testing, we follow the other bottom-up methods [23,51,52] and use two modes: (i) single-scale, horizontal-flip testing (SS testing mode), and (ii) multi-scale, horizontal-flip testing (MS testing mode). In MS, we use the following scale values, $0.6, 1.0, 1.2, 1.5, 1.8$. To merge augmented test results, we use Soft-NMS [5], and keep the top 100 detections. All tests are performed on a single V100 GPU.

4.1 Mini COCO

For faster analysis in our ablation experiments, we created "COCO minitrain" as a statistically validated mini training set. It is a subset of the COCO train2017 dataset, containing $25K$ images (about 20% of train2017) and around $184K$ objects across 80 object categories. We randomly sampled these images from the full set while preserving the following three quantities as much as possible: (i) proportion of object instances from each class, (ii) overall ratios of small, medium and large objects, (iii) per class ratios of small, medium and large objects.

To validate COCO minitrain, we computed the correlation between the val2017 performance of a model when it is trained on minitrain with the same of when it is trained on train2017. Over six different object detectors (Faster R-CNN, Mask R-CNN, RetinaNet, CornerNet, ExtremeNet and HoughNet), the Pearson correlation coefficients turned out to be 0.74 and 0.92 for AP and AP_{50}, respectively. These values indicate strong positive correlation. Further details on minitrain can be found at https://github.com/giddyyupp/coco-minitrain.

4.2 Ablation Experiments

Here we analyze the effects of the number of angle and ring bins of the vote field on performance. Models are trained on COCO minitrain and evaluated on `val2017` set with SS testing mode. The backbone is Resnet-101 [17]. In order to get higher resolution feature maps, we add three deconvolution layers on top of the default Resnet-101 network, similar to [47]. We add 3×3 convolution filters before each 4×4 deconvolution layer, and put batchnorm and ReLU layers after convolution and deconvolution filters. We trained the network with a batch size of 44 for 140 epochs with Adam optimizer [21]. Initial learning rate 1.75×10^{-4} was divided by 10 at epochs 90 and 120.

Angle Bins. We started with a large, 65 by 65, vote field with 5 rings. We set the radius of these rings from the most inner one to the most outer one as 2, 8, 16, 32 and 64 pixels, respectively. We experimented with $60°$, $90°$, $180°$ and $360°$ bins. We do not split the center ring (i.e. region with id 1 in Fig. 3) into further regions. Results are presented in Table 1a. For the $180°$ experiment, we divide the vote field horizontally. $90°$ yields the best performance considering both AP and AP_{50}. We used this setting in the rest of the experiments.

Effects of Center and Periphery. We conducted experiments to analyze the importance of votes coming from different rings of the vote field. Results are presented in Table 1b. In the *Only Center* case, we only keep the center ring and disable the rest. In this way, we only aggregate votes from features of the object center directly. This case corresponds to a traditional object detection paradigm where only local (short-range) evidence is used. This experiment shows that votes from outer rings help improve performance. For the *No Center* case, we only disable the center ring. We observe that there is only 0.2 decrease in AP. This suggests that the evidence for successful detection is embedded mostly around the object center not directly inside the object center. In order to observe the power of long-range votes, we con-

Table 1. Ablation experiments for the vote field. (a) Effect of angle bins on performance. Vote field with $90°$ has the best performance (considering AP and AP_{50}). (b) Effect of central and peripheral regions. Here, the angle bin is $90°$ and the ring count is four. Disabling any of center or periphery hurts performance, cf. (a). (c) Effect of number of rings. Angle is $90°$ and vote field size is updated according to the radius of the last ring. Using 3 rings yields the best result. It is also the fastest model

Model	AP	AP_{50}	AP_{75}	AP_S	AP_M	AP_L	FPS
60°	**24.6**	41.3	25.0	**8.2**	27.7	36.2	3.4
90°	**24.6**	**41.5**	25.0	**8.2**	27.7	36.2	**3.5**
180°	24.5	41.1	24.8	8.1	27.7	**36.3**	**3.5**
360°	**24.6**	41.1	**25.1**	8.0	**27.8**	**36.3**	**3.5**
(a) Varying the number of angle bins							
Only Center	23.8	39.5	24.5	**7.9**	26.8	34.7	**3.5**
No Center	**24.4**	**40.9**	**24.9**	7.4	**27.6**	**37.1**	3.3
Only Context	23.6	39.7	24.2	7.4	26.4	35.9	3.4
(b) Effectiveness of votes from center or periphery							
5 Rings	24.6	**41.5**	25.0	**8.2**	27.7	36.2	3.5
4 Rings	24.5	41.1	25.3	**8.2**	**27.8**	36.1	7.8
3 Rings	**24.8**	41.3	**25.6**	**8.4**	27.6	**37.5**	**15.6**
(c) Varying ring counts							

ducted another experiment called "Only Context," where we disabled the two most inner rings and used only the three outer rings for vote aggregation. This model reduced AP by 1.0 point compared to the full model.

Ring Count. To find out how far an object should get votes from, we discard outer ring layers one by one as presented in Table 1c. The models with 5 rings, 4 rings and 3 rings have 17, 13 and 9 voting regions and 65, 33 and 17 vote field sizes, respectively. The model with 3 rings yields the best performance on AP metric and is the fastest one at the same time. On the other hand, the model with 5 rings yields 0.2 AP_{50} improvement over the model with 3 rings.

From all these ablation experiments, we decided to use the model with 5 rings and 90° as our *Base Model*. Considering both speed and accuracy, we decided to use the model with 3 rings and 90° as our *Light Model*.

Voting Module vs. Dilated Convolution Dilated convolution [48], which can include long-range features, could be considered as an alternative to our voting module. To compare performance, we trained models on `train2017` and evaluated them on `val2017` using the SS testing mode.

Baseline: We consider OAP with ResNet-101-DCN backbone as baseline. The last 1×1 convolution layer of center prediction branch in OAP, receives $H \times W \times D$ tensor and outputs object center heatmaps with a tensor of size $H \times W \times C$.

Table 2. Comparing our voting module to an equivalent (in terms of number of parameters and the spatial filter size) dilated convolution filter on COCO `val2017` set. Models are trained on COCO `train2017` and results are presented on SS testing mode

Method	AP	AP_{50}	AP_{75}	AP_S	AP_M	AP_L
Baseline	36.2	54.8	38.7	16.3	41.6	52.3
+ Dilated conv	36.6	56.1	39.2	16.7	42.0	53.6
+ Voting module	**37.3**	**56.6**	**39.9**	**16.8**	**42.6**	**55.2**

Baseline + Voting Module: We first adapt the last layer of center prediction branch in baseline to output $H \times W \times C \times R$ tensor, then attach our voting module on top of the center prediction branch. Adding the voting module increases parameters of the layer by R times. The log-polar vote field is 65×65, and has 5 rings (90°). With 5 rings and 90° we end up with $R = 17$ regions.

Baseline + Dilated Convolution: We use dilated convolution with kernel size 4×4 and dilation rate 22 for the last layer of the center prediction branch in baseline. Using 4×4 kernel increases parameters 16 times which is approximately equal to R in the *Baseline + Voting Module*. Using dilation rate 22, the filter size becomes 67×67 which is close to 65×65 log-polar vote field.

Table 3. HoughNet results on COCO `val2017` set for different training setups. † indicates initialization with CornerNet weights, * indicates initialization with ExtremeNet weights. Results are given for SS and MS testing modes, respectively

Models	Backbone	AP	AP_{50}	AP_{75}	AP_S	AP_M	AP_L	FPS
Base	R-101	36.0 / 40.7	55.2 / 60.6	38.4 / 43.9	16.2 / 22.5	41.7 / 44.2	52.0 / 55.7	3.5 / 0.5
Base	R-101-DCN	37.3 / 41.6	56.6 / 61.2	39.9 / 44.9	16.8 / 22.6	42.6 / 44.8	55.2 / 58.8	3.3 / 0.4
Light	R-101-DCN	37.2 / 41.5	56.5 / 61.5	39.6 / 44.5	16.8 / 22.5	42.5 / 44.8	54.9 / 58.4	**14.3** / 2.1
Light	HG-104	40.9 / 43.7	59.2 / 61.9	44.1 / 47.3	23.8 / 27.5	45.3 / 45.9	52.6 / 56.2	6.1 / 0.8
Light	HG-104*	41.7 / 44.7	60.5 / 63.2	45.6 / 48.9	23.9 / 28.0	45.7 / 47.0	54.6 / 58.1	5.9 / 0.8
Light	HG-104*	43.0 / **46.1**	62.2 / **64.6**	46.9 / **50.3**	25.5 / **30.0**	47.6 / **48.8**	55.8 / **59.7**	5.7 / 0.8

Table 4. Comparison with baseline (OAP) on val2017. Results are given for single scale and multi scale test modes, respectively

Method	AP	AP_{50}	AP_{75}	AP_S	AP_M	AP_L	$moLRP \downarrow$
Baseline w R-101-DCN	36.2 / 39.2	54.8 / 58.6	38.7 / 41.9	16.3 / 20.5	41.6 / 42.6	52.3 / 56.2	71.1 / 68.3
+ Voting module	**37.2 / 41.5**	**56.5 / 61.5**	**39.6 / 44.5**	**16.8 / 22.5**	**42.5 / 44.8**	**54.9 / 58.4**	**69.9 / 66.6**
Baseline w HG-104	42.2 / 45.1	61.1 / 63.5	46.0 / 49.3	25.2 / 27.8	46.4 / 47.7	55.2 / **60.3**	66.1 / 63.9
+ Voting module	**43.0 / 46.1**	**62.2 / 64.6**	**46.9 / 50.3**	**25.5 / 30.0**	**47.6 / 48.8**	**55.8** / 59.7	**65.6 / 63.1**

Table 5. Comparison with the state-of-the-art on COCO test-dev. The methods are divided into three groups: two-stage, one-stage top-down and one-st age bottom-up. The best results are boldfaced separately for each group. Backbone names are shortened: R is ResNet, X is ResNeXt, F is FPN and HG is HourGlass. * indicates that the FPS values were obtained on the same AWS machine with a V100 GPU using the official repos in SS setup. The rest of the FPS are from their corresponding papers. F. R-CNN is Faster R-CNN

Method	Backbone	Initialize	Train size	Test size	AP	AP_{50}	AP_{75}	AP_S	AP_M	AP_L	FPS
Two-stage detectors:											
R-FCN [8]	R-101	ImageNet	800×800	600×600	29.9	51.9	–	10.8	32.8	45.0	5.9
CoupleNet [55]	R-101	ImageNet	ori	ori	34.4	54.8	37.2	13.4	38.1	50.8	–
F. R-CNN+++ [17]	R-101	ImageNet	1000×600	1000×600	34.9	55.7	37.4	15.6	38.7	50.9	–
F. R-CNN [26]	R-101-F	ImageNet	1000×600	1000×600	36.2	59.1	39.0	18.2	39.0	48.2	5.0
Mask R-CNN [16]	X-101-F	ImageNet	1300×800	1300×800	39.8	62.3	43.4	22.1	43.2	51.2	11.0
Cascade R-CNN [6]	R-101	ImageNet	–	–	42.8	62.1	46.3	23.7	45.5	55.2	**12.0**
PANet [29]	X-101	ImageNet	1400×840	1400×840	**47.4**	**67.2**	**51.8**	**30.1**	**51.7**	**60.0**	–
One-stage detectors:											
Top Down:											
SSD [30]	VGG-16	ImageNet	512×512	512×512	28.8	48.5	30.3	10.9	31.8	43.5	–
YOLOv3 [39]	Darknet	ImageNet	608×608	608×608	33.0	57.9	34.4	18.3	35.4	41.9	**20.0**
DSSD513 [12]	R-101	ImageNet	513×513	513×513	33.2	53.3	35.2	13.0	35.4	51.1	–
RefineDet (SS) [49]	R-101	ImageNet	512×512	512×512	36.4	57.5	39.5	16.6	39.9	51.4	–
RetinaNet [27]	X-101-F	ImageNet	1300×800	1300×800	40.8	61.1	44.1	24.1	44.2	51.2	5.4
RefineDet (MS) [49]	R-101	ImageNet	512×512	≤2.25×	41.8	62.9	45.7	25.6	45.1	54.1	–
OAP (SS) [51]	HG-104	ExtremeNet	512×512	ori	42.1	61.1	45.9	24.1	45.5	52.8	9.6*
FSAF (SS) [53]	X-101	ImageNet	1300×800	1300×800	42.9	63.8	46.3	26.6	46.2	52.7	2.7
FSAF (MS) [53]	X-101	ImageNet	1300×800	~≤2.0×	44.6	65.2	48.6	29.7	47.1	54.6	–
FCOS [43]	X-101-F	ImageNet	1300×800	1300×800	44.7	64.1	48.4	27.6	47.5	55.6	7.0*
FreeAnchor (SS) [50]	X-101-F	ImageNet	1300×960	1300×960	44.9	64.3	48.5	26.8	48.3	55.9	–
OAP (MS) [51]	HG-104	ExtremeNet	512×512	≤1.5×	45.1	63.9	49.3	26.6	47.1	57.7	–
FreeAnchor (MS) [50]	X-101-F	ImageNet	1300×960	~≤2.0×	**47.3**	**66.3**	**51.5**	**30.6**	**50.4**	**59.0**	–
Bottom Up:											
ExtremeNet (SS) [52]	HG-104	–	511×511	ori	40.2	55.5	43.2	20.4	43.2	53.1	3.0*
CornerNet (SS) [23]	HG-104	–	511×511	ori	40.5	56.5	43.1	19.4	42.7	53.9	5.2*
CornerNet (MS) [23]	HG-104	–	511×511	≤1.5×	42.1	57.8	45.3	20.8	44.8	56.7	–
ExtremeNet (MS) [52]	HG-104	–	511×511	≤1.5×	43.7	60.5	47.0	24.1	46.9	57.6	–
CenterNet (SS) [9]	HG-104	–	511×511	ori	44.9	62.4	48.1	25.6	47.4	57.4	4.8*
CenterNet (MS) [9]	HG-104	–	511×511	≤1.8×	**47.0**	64.5	**50.7**	28.9	**49.9**	**58.9**	–
HoughNet (SS)	HG-104	–	512×512	ori	40.8	59.1	44.2	22.9	44.4	51.1	**6.4***
HoughNet (MS)	HG-104	–	512×512	≤1.8×	44.0	62.4	47.7	26.4	45.4	55.2	–
HoughNet (SS)	HG-104	ExtremeNet	512×512	ori	43.1	62.2	46.8	24.6	47.0	54.4	**6.4***
HoughNet (MS)	HG-104	ExtremeNet	512×512	≤1.8×	46.4	**65.1**	**50.7**	**29.1**	48.5	58.1	–

For a fair comparison with *Baseline*, both *Baseline + Voting Module* and the *Baseline + Dilated Convolution* use Resnet-101-DCN backbone. Our voting module outperforms dilated convolution in all cases (Table 2).

4.3   Performance of HoughNet and Comparison with Baseline

In Table 3, we present the performance of HoughNet for different backbone networks, initializations and our base-vs-light model, on the val2017 set. There is a significant speed difference between Base and Light models. Our light model with R-101-DCN backbone is the fastest one (14.3 FPS) achieving 37.2 AP and 56.5 AP_{50}. We observe that initializing the backbone with a pretrained model improves the detection performance. In Table 4, we compare HoughNet's performance with its baseline OAP [51] for two different backbones. HoughNet is especially effective for small objects, it improves the baseline by 2.1 and 2.2 AP points for R-101-DCN and HG-104 backbones, respectively. We also provide results for the recently introduced *moLRP* [34] metric, which combines localization, precision and recall in a single metric. Lower values are better.

4.4   Comparison with the State-of-the-Art

For comparison with the state-of-the-art, we use Hourglass-104 [23] backbone. We train Hourglass model with a batch size of 36 for 100 epochs using the Adam optimizer [21]. We set the initial learning rate to 2.5×10^{-4} and divided it by 10 at epoch 90. Table 5 presents performances of HoughNet and several established state-of-the-art detectors. First, we compare HoughNet with OAP [51] since it is the model on which we built HoughNet. In OAP, they did not present any results for "from scratch" training. Instead they fine-tuned their model from ExtremeNet weights. When we do the same (i.e. initialize HoughNet with ExtremeNet weights), we obtain better results than OAP. However as expected, HoughNet is slower than OAP. Among the one-stage bottom-up object detectors, HoughNet performs on-par with the best bottom-up object detector by achieving 46.4 AP against 47.0 AP of CenterNet [9]. HoughNet outperforms CenterNet on AP_{50} (65.1 AP_{50} vs. 64.5 AP_{50}). Note that, since our model is initialized with ExtremeNet weights, which makes use of the segmentation masks in its own training, our model effectively uses more data compared to CenterNet. HoughNet is the fastest among one-stage bottom-up detectors. It is faster than CenterNet, CornerNet and more than twice as fast as ExtremeNet.

We provide visualization of votes for sample detections of HoughNet for qualitative visual inspection (Fig. 4). These detections clearly show that HoughNet is able to make use of long-range visual evidence.

4.5   Using Our Voting Module in Another Task

One task where long-range interactions could be useful is the task of image generation from a given label map. There are two main approaches to solve this task; using unpaired and paired data for training. We take CycleGAN [54] and Pix2Pix [20] as our baselines for

Table 6. Comparison of FCN scores for the "labels to photo" task on the Cityscapes [7] dataset

Method	Per-pixel acc.	Per-class acc.	Class IOU
CycleGAN	0.43	0.14	0.09
+ Voting	**0.52**	**0.17**	**0.13**
pix2pix	0.71	**0.25**	0.18
+ Voting	**0.76**	**0.25**	**0.20**

unpaired and paired approaches, respectively. We attach our voting module at the end of CycleGAN [54] and Pix2Pix [20] models.

Detection	Voters	Detection	Voters	Detection	Voters

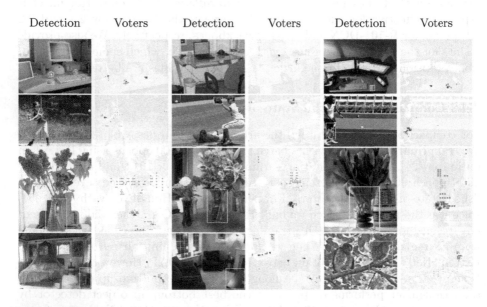

Fig. 4. Sample detections of HoughNet and their vote maps. In the "detection" columns, we show a correctly detected object, marked with a yellow bounding box. In the "voters" columns, the locations that vote for the detection are shown. Colors indicate vote strength based on the standard "jet" colormap (red is high, blue is low; Fig. 1). In the **top row**, there are three "mouse" detections. In all cases, in addition to the local votes (that are on the mouse itself), there are strong votes coming from nearby "keyboard" objects. This voting pattern is justified given that mouse and keyboard objects frequently co-appear. A similar behavior is observed in the detections of "baseball bat", "baseball glove" and "tennis racket" in the **second row**, where they get strong votes from "ball" objects that are far-away. Similarly, in the **third row**, "vase" detections get strong votes from the flowers. In the first example of the **bottom row**, "dining table" detection gets strong votes from the candle object, probably because they co-occur frequently. Candle is not among the 80 classes of COCO dataset. Similarly, in the second example in the **bottom row**, "dining table" has strong votes from objects and parts of a standard living room. In the last example, partially occluded bird gets strong votes (stronger than the local votes on the bird itself) from the tree branch (Color figure online)

Input   CycleGAN   + Voting   Input   Pix2Pix   + Voting

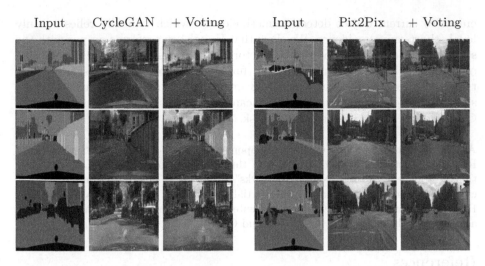

Fig. 5. Sample qualitative results for the "labels to photo" task. When integrated with CycleGAN, our voting module helps generate better images in the sense that the image conforms to the input label map better. In all three images, CycleGAN fails to generate sky, buildings and falsely generates vegetation in the last image. When used with Pix2Pix, it helps generate more detailed images. In the first row, cars and buildings can be barely seen for Pix2Pix. Similarly, a bus is generated as a car and a bicycle is silhouetted in the second and third images, respectively. Our voting module fixes these errors

For quantitative comparison, we use the Cityscapes [7] dataset. In Table 6, we present FCN scores [31] (which is used as the measure of success in this task) of CycleGAN and Pix2Pix with and without our voting module. To obtain the "without" result, we used the already trained model shared by the authors. We obtained the "with" result using the official training code from their repositories. In both cases evaluation was done using the official test and evaluation scripts from their repos. Results show that using the voting module improves FCN scores by large margins. Qualitative inspection also shows that when our voting module is attached, the generated images conform to the given input segmentation maps better (Fig. 5). This is the main reason for the quantitative improvement. Since Pix2Pix is trained with paired data, generated images follow input segmentation maps, however, Pix2Pix fails to generate small details.

5   Conclusion

In this paper, we presented HoughNet, a new, one-stage, anchor-free, voting-based, bottom-up object detection method. HoughNet determines the presence of an object at a specific location by the sum of the votes cast on that location. Voting module of HoughNet is able to use both short and long-range evidence through its log-polar vote field. Thanks to this ability, HoughNet generalizes and enhances current object detection methodology, which typically relies on only local (short-range) evidence. We show that HoughNet performs on-par with the state-of-the-art bottom-up object detector, and obtains comparable results with one-stage and two-stage methods. To further validate our proposal, we used the voting module of HoughNet in an image generation task. Specifically, we showed that our voting module significantly improves the performance of two GAN models in a "labels to photo" task.

Acknowledgments. This work was supported by the Scientific and Technological Research Council of Turkey (TÜBİTAK) through the project titled "Object Detection in Videos with Deep Neural Networks" (grant #117E054). The numerical calculations reported in this paper were partially performed at TÜBİTAK ULAKBİM, High Performance and Grid Computing Center (TRUBA resources). We also gratefully acknowledge the support of the AWS Cloud Credits for Research program.

References

1. Akbas, E., Eckstein, M.P.: Object detection through search with a foveated visual system. PLoS Comput. Biol. **13**(10), e1005743 (2017)
2. Ballard, D.H., et al.: Generalizing the Hough transform to detect arbitrary shapes. Pattern Recogn. **13**, 111–122 (1981)
3. Barinova, O., Lempitsky, V., Kholi, P.: On detection of multiple object instances using hough transforms. IEEE Trans. Patt. Anal. Mach. Intell. **34**(9), 1773–1784 (2012)
4. Belongie, S., Malik, J., Puzicha, J.: Shape matching and object recognition using shape contexts. IEEE Trans. Pattern Anal. Mach. Intell. **24**(4), 509–522 (2002). https://doi.org/10.1109/34.993558
5. Bodla, N., Singh, B., Chellappa, R., Davis, L.S.: Soft-NMS-improving object detection with one line of code. In: IEEE International Conference on Computer Vision, pp. 5561–5569 (2017)
6. Cai, Z., Vasconcelos, N.: Cascade R-CNN: delving into high quality object detection. In: IEEE Conference on Computer Vision and Pattern Recognition, pp. 6154–6162 (2018)
7. Cordts, M., et al.: The cityscapes dataset for semantic urban scene understanding. In: IEEE Conference on Computer Vision and Pattern Recognition, pp. 3213–3223 (2016)
8. Dai, J., Li, Y., He, K., Sun, J.: R-FCN: object detection via region-based fully convolutional networks. In: Advances in Neural Information Processing Systems, pp. 379–387 (2016)
9. Duan, K., Bai, S., Xie, L., Qi, H., Huang, Q., Tian, Q.: CenterNet: keypoint triplets for object detection. In: IEEE International Conference on Computer Vision (2019)
10. Felzenszwalb, P.F., Girshick, R.B., McAllester, D., Ramanan, D.: Object detection with discriminatively trained part based models. IEEE Trans. Pattern Anal. Mach. Intell. **32**, 1627–1645 (2010)
11. Felzenszwalb, P.F., Girshick, R.B., McAllester, D., Ramanan, D.: Object detection with discriminatively trained part-based models. IEEE Trans. Pattern Anal. Mach. Intell. **32**(9), 1627–1645 (2009)
12. Fu, C.Y., Liu, W., Ranga, A., Tyagi, A., Berg, A.C.: DSSD: deconvolutional single shot detector. arXiv preprint arXiv:1701.06659 (2017)

13. Gabriel, E., Schleiss, M., Schramm, H., Meyer, C.: Analysis of the discriminative generalized hough transform as a proposal generator for a deep network in automatic pedestrian and car detection. J. Electron. Imaging **27**(5), 051228 (2018)

14. Gall, J., Lempitsky, V.: Class-specific Hough forests for object detection. In: IEEE Conference on Computer Vision and Pattern Recognition (2009)

15. Girshick, R.B., Felzenszwalb, P.F., McAllester, D.: Discriminatively trained deformable part models, release 5. http://people.cs.uchicago.edu/rbg/latent-release5/

16. He, K., Gkioxari, G., Dollár, P., Girshick, R.B.: Mask R-CNN. In: IEEE International Conference on Computer Vision, pp. 2980–2988 (2017)

17. He, K., Zhang, X., Ren, S., Sun, J.: Deep residual learning for image recognition. In: IEEE Conference on Computer Vision and Pattern Recognition, pp. 770–778 (2016)

18. Hough, P.V.C.: Machine analysis of bubble chamber pictures, vol. C 590914, pp. 554–558 (1959)

19. Hu, H., Gu, J., Zhang, Z., Dai, J., Wei, Y.: Relation networks for object detection. In: IEEE Conference on Computer Vision and Pattern Recognition, pp. 3588–3597 (2018)

20. Isola, P., Zhu, J.Y., Zhou, T., Efros, A.A.: Image-to-image translation with conditional adversarial networks. In: IEEE Conference on Computer Vision and Pattern Recognition, pp. 1125–1134 (2017)

21. Kingma, D.P., Ba, J.: Adam: a method for stochastic optimization. arXiv preprint arXiv:1412.6980 (2014)

22. Land, M., Tatler, B.: Looking and Acting: Vision and Eye Movements in Natural Behaviour. Oxford University Press, Oxford (2009)

23. Law, H., Deng, J.: CornerNet: detecting objects as paired keypoints. In: European Conference on Computer Vision, pp. 734–750 (2018)

24. Leibe, B., Leonardis, A., Schiele, B.: Robust object detection with interleaved categorization and segmentation. Int. J. Comput. Vis. **77**(1), 259–289 (2008)

25. Lifshitz, I., Fetaya, E., Ullman, S.: Human pose estimation using deep consensus voting. In: European Conference on Computer Vision (2016)

26. Lin, T., Dollár, P., Girshick, R.B., He, K., Hariharan, B., Belongie, S.J.: Feature pyramid networks for object detection. In: IEEE Conference on Computer Vision and Pattern Recognition, pp. 936–944 (2017)

27. Lin, T., Goyal, P., Girshick, R.B., He, K., Dollár, P.: Focal loss for dense object detection. In: IEEE International Conference on Computer Vision (2017)

28. Lin, T.-Y., et al.: Microsoft COCO: common objects in context. In: Fleet, D., Pajdla, T., Schiele, B., Tuytelaars, T. (eds.) ECCV 2014. LNCS, vol. 8693, pp. 740–755. Springer, Cham (2014). https://doi.org/10.1007/978-3-319-10602-1_48

29. Liu, S., Qi, L., Qin, H., Shi, J., Jia, J.: Path aggregation network for instance segmentation. In: IEEE Conference on Computer Vision and Pattern Recognition, pp. 8759–8768 (2018)

30. Liu, W., et al.: SSD: single shot multibox detector. In: European Conference on Computer Vision (2016)

31. Long, J., Shelhamer, E., Darrell, T.: Fully convolutional networks for semantic segmentation. In: IEEE Conference on Computer Vision and Pattern Recognition, pp. 3431–3440 (2015)

32. Maji, S., Malik, J.: Object detection using a max-margin Hough transform. In: IEEE Conference on Computer Vision and Pattern Recognition (2009)

33. Okada, R.: Discriminative generalized Hough transform for object detection. In: IEEE International Conference on Computer Vision (2009)

34. Oksuz, K., Cam, B., Akbas, E., Kalkan, S.: Localization recall precision (LRP): a new performance metric for object detection. In: European Conference on Computer Vision (ECCV) (2018)
35. Paszke, A., et al.: PyTorch: an imperative style, high-performance deep learning library. In: Advances in Neural Information Processing Systems, pp. 8024–8035. Curran Associates, Inc. (2019). http://papers.neurips.cc/paper/9015-pytorch-an-imperative-style-high-performance-deep-learning-library.pdf
36. Qi, C.R., Litany, O., He, K., Guibas, L.J.: Deep Hough voting for 3D object detection in point clouds. In: IEEE International Conference on Computer Vision (2019)
37. Razavi, N., Gall, J., Kohli, P., Van Gool, L.: Latent Hough transform for object detection. In: European Conference on Computer Vision (2012)
38. Redmon, J., Farhadi, A.: YOLO9000: better, faster, stronger. In: IEEE Conference on Computer Vision and Pattern Recognition (2017)
39. Redmon, J., Farhadi, A.: Yolov3: an incremental improvement. arXiv preprint arXiv:1804.02767 (2018)
40. Ren, J., et al.: Accurate single stage detector using recurrent rolling convolution. In: IEEE Conference on Computer Vision and Pattern Recognition (2017)
41. Ren, S., He, K., Girshick, R., Sun, J.: Faster R-CNN: towards real-time object detection with region proposal networks. In: Advances in Neural Information Processing Systems, pp. 91–99 (2015)
42. Sheshkus, A., Ingacheva, A., Arlazarov, V., Nikolaev, D.: HoughNet: neural network architecture for vanishing points detection (2019)
43. Tian, Z., Shen, C., Chen, H., He, T.: FCOS: fully convolutional one-stage object detection. In: IEEE International Conference on Computer Vision (2019)
44. Traver, V.J., Bernardino, A.: A review of log-polar imaging for visual perception in robotics. Rob. Auton. Syst. **58**(4), 378–398 (2010)
45. Wang, J., Chen, K., Yang, S., Loy, C.C., Lin, D.: Region proposal by guided anchoring. In: IEEE Conference on Computer Vision and Pattern Recognition (2019)
46. Wang, X., Girshick, R., Gupta, A., He, K.: Non-local neural networks. In: IEEE Conference on Computer Vision and Pattern Recognition, pp. 7794–7803 (2018)
47. Xiao, B., Wu, H., Wei, Y.: Simple baselines for human pose estimation and tracking. In: European Conference on Computer Vision, pp. 466–481 (2018)
48. Yu, F., Koltun, V.: Multi-scale context aggregation by dilated convolutions. CoRR (2015)
49. Zhang, S., Wen, L., Bian, X., Lei, Z., Li, S.Z.: Single-shot refinement neural network for object detection. In: IEEE Conference on Computer Vision and Pattern Recognition, pp. 4203–4212 (2018)
50. Zhang, X., Wan, F., Liu, C., Ji, R., Ye, Q.: FreeAnchor: learning to match anchors for visual object detection. In: Advances in Neural Information Processing Systems (2019)
51. Zhou, X., Wang, D., Krähenbühl, P.: Objects as points. arXiv preprint arXiv:1904.07850 (2019)
52. Zhou, X., Zhuo, J., Krähenbühl, P.: Bottom-up object detection by grouping extreme and center points. In: IEEE Conference on Computer Vision and Pattern Recognition (2019)

53. Zhu, C., He, Y., Savvides, M.: Feature selective anchor-free module for single-shot object detection. In: IEEE Conference on Computer Vision and Pattern Recognition (2019)

54. Zhu, J.Y., Park, T., Isola, P., Efros, A.A.: Unpaired image-to-image translation using cycle-consistent adversarial networks. In: IEEE International Conference on Computer Vision, pp. 2223–2232 (2017)

55. Zhu, Y., Zhao, C., Wang, J., Zhao, X., Wu, Y., Lu, H.: CoupleNet: coupling global structure with local parts for object detection. In: IEEE International Conference on Computer Vision, pp. 4126–4134 (2017)

Graph Wasserstein Correlation Analysis for Movie Retrieval

Xueya Zhang, Tong Zhang, Xiaobin Hong, Zhen Cui[(✉)], and Jian Yang

Key Lab of Intelligent Perception and Systems for High-Dimensional Information of Ministry of Education, School of Computer Science and Engineering, Nanjing University of Science and Technology, Nanjing, China
{zhangxueya,tong.zhang,xbhong,zhen.cui,csjyang}@njust.edu.cn

Abstract. Movie graphs play an important role to bridge heterogenous modalities of videos and texts in human-centric retrieval. In this work, we propose Graph Wasserstein Correlation Analysis (GWCA) to deal with the core issue therein, i.e, cross heterogeneous graph comparison. Spectral graph filtering is introduced to encode graph signals, which are then embedded as probability distributions in a Wasserstein space, called graph Wasserstein metric learning. Such a seamless integration of graph signal filtering together with metric learning results in a surprise consistency on both learning processes, in which the goal of metric learning is just to optimize signal filters or vice versa. Further, we derive the solution of the graph comparison model as a classic generalized eigenvalue decomposition problem, which has an exactly closed-form solution. Finally, GWCA together with movie/text graphs generation are unified into the framework of movie retrieval to evaluate our proposed method. Extensive experiments on MovieGrpahs dataset demonstrate the effectiveness of our GWCA as well as the entire framework.

Keywords: Graph Wasserstein metric · Graph correlation analysis · Movie retrieval

1 Introduction

Nowadays, people show growing enthusiasm in searching desired movie clips, which contain either attractive plots or funny dialogue with vivid performance of actors, for multiple purposes including materials accumulation for presentation and entertainment. However, in many cases, they can just describe their understanding/impression of plots or dialogue content of those target clips, but are hardly accessible to the exact movie names or frame locations. This makes

---

X. Zhang and T. Zhang – Equal contributions.

Electronic supplementary material The online version of this chapter (https://doi.org/10.1007/978-3-030-58595-2_26) contains supplementary material, which is available to authorized users.

A. Vedaldi et al. (Eds.): ECCV 2020, LNCS 12370, pp. 424–439, 2020.
https://doi.org/10.1007/978-3-030-58595-2_26

it time/energy-consuming and tedious to search the desired clips by manually browsing those movies one by one. Consequently, automatic movie-text retrieval become quite necessary and meaningful.

Among movie retrieval, the elements mainly consist of visual videos and descriptive texts, which have been investigated in some cross tasks such as video description [6] and video/image query and answer (Q & A) [28]. Most methods take some sophisticated dynamic models, e.g.,gated recurrent unit (GRU) [8] and long-short term memory (LSTM) [32], to capture the dynamics within both videos and texts, and then bridge them based on those obtained representation. However, these do not cater to flexible movie contour search, where some actors might be only posed by one searcher. Just to address this case, recently MovieGraphs dataset [30] is successfully initiated with annotated graphs to describe the interactions of entities in movie clips, and provides rather appropriate evaluations on more flexible movie-description retrieval for boosting machine understanding on movie clips.

Motivated by this case, in this work, we follow the technique line of graph modeling, which is more versatile to describe structured information in human-centric situation of movie graph retrieval. As a universal tool, graph can represent various data in the real world by defining nodes and edges that reveal multiple relationships between objects. For one given movie clip, those actors or other entities could be understood as nodes, their interactions may be defined as the edge connections. Accordingly, the text description can also be modeled with graph structure. Hence, the task of movie retrieval can be converted into the problem of graph searching, whose core issue is the comparisons between graph structured data. The inter-graph comparison contains two crucial problems: graph signal processing and graph distance metric. The former focuses on how to mine useful information from graph structure data, while the latter concerns the measurement of two graphs. On one hand, the obstacle to encode graph signals is not only to process graph signals as discrete time signal but also need model dependencies arising from irregular data. On the other hand, for graph structured data, Euclidean metrics fundamentally limit the ability to capture latent semantic structures, which however need not conform to Euclidean spatial assumptions. Further, could graph signal processing be seamlessly integrated with graph distance metric learning for more effective comparisons between graph data?

In this paper, we propose a Graph Wasserstein Correlation Analysis (GWCA) method to deal with the comparisons of pairwise movie graphs. The proposed GWCA elegantly formulates graph signal encoding together with graph distance metric learning into a unified model. Inspired by the recent spectral graph theory, we encode graph structure data with spectral graph filtering, which generalizes the previous classic signal processing. Instead of direct frequency domain, we take an approximation strategy, i.e., the polynomial of graph Laplacian, to efficiently encode graph data. The encoded signals of graph are embedded as probability distributions in a Wasserstein space, which is much larger and more flexible than Euclidean space. Accordingly, the distance between graph data is defined in Wasserstein space, which is called Wasserstein metric. Such a metric can not only captures the similarity of the distributions of graph signals, but also be able to preserve the transitivity in embedding space. In this way, graph signal filtering and Wasserstein metric learning are jointly encapsulated into a unified mathematic model, which efficiently preserves the first-order and second-order proximity of the nodes of graph, empowering the learned node representations to reflect both graph topology structure. Surprisingly, we derive this model as a classic eigenvalue decomposition problem with closed-form solution, where the solution is just associated with graph encoding. Finally, our GWCA is used to movie graph retrieval, where multiple heterogeneous graphs are built and crossly-compared, e.g., annotation graph versus description graph, video graph versus annotation graph, etc. Extensive experiments on MovieGraphs dataset demonstrate the effectiveness of our proposed method, and new state-of-the-art results are also achieved.

In summary, our contribution are three folds:

- We propose an elegant inter-graph comparison model by seamlessly integrating graph signals filtering together with graph Wasserstein metric learning, where the latter is just the optimization of the former.
- We derive the solution of model as a classic generalized eigenvalue decomposition problem, which has an exact closed-form solution.
- We design an entire framework for movie retrieval including graph generation and GWCA, and finally validate the effectiveness of our proposed method.

2   Related Work

Most relevant works are proposed to inference across vision and text, where multiple tasks are tackled including image-text modeling [13,21,33], video/image query and answer (Q & A) [28] and video-text retrieval [9,26]. For image-text understanding, a majority of work generate descriptive sentences for vision, and especially, [6] including sentence generation and image retrieval to find the bi-directional mapping between images and their textual descriptions. For video based works,[3] focus on understanding action of characters with scripts and [11] learn the relations among actors. [18] proposed the method using the retrieved action samples for visual learning and achieving action classification based on texts. In [22], authors propose an LSTM with visual semantic embedding method. Recently, Vicol *et al.* [30] proposed a new dataset MovieGraphs for retrieving videos and text with graphs, which also shows graphs containing sufficient information help us to understand the video and text better.

Graph Signal Processing. Graphs are generic data representation forms, which describe the geometric structures of data domains effectively. From the perspective of graph signal processing, the data on these graphs can be regarded as a finite collection of samples, and the sample at each vertex in the graph is graph signal. [27] concluded that spectral graph theory is regarded as the tool for defining the frequency spectra , and as an extension of the Fourier

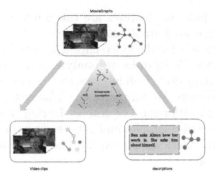

Fig. 1. Our proposed GWCA is used in two retrieval tasks. It jointly encapsulates graph signal filtering and Wasserstein metric learning into a unified mathematic model and W1 and W2 are learned in this process. Section 3 shows more details.

transform of the graph. It benefits the construction of expander graphs [14], spectral clustering [31] and so on, including definitions and notations such as the Non-Normalized Graph Laplacian and Graph Fourier Transform. References [2,12,25,29] generate low dimensional representations for high-dimensional data through spectral graph theory and the graph Laplacian [7], projecting the data on a low-dimensional subspace generated by a small subset of the Laplacian eigenbasis [2].

Generalized operators like filtering and translation then become the basis of developing the localized, multi-scale transforms. In [5], the basic graph spectral filtering enable discrete versions of continuous filtering, known as Gaussian smoothing, bilateral filtering, anisotropic diffusion, and non-local means filtering. Especially, Bruna *et al.* [4] consider possible generalizations of CNNs, which extends convolution networks to graph domains. Then Defferrard *et al.* [10] proposed a fast spectral filter, which use the Chebyshev polynomial approximation so that they are of the same linear computation complexity. Kipf *et al.* [16] motivate the convolutional architecture with a localized first-order approximation of spectral graph convolutions. In particular, [17,20,24] propose the literature of graph coarsening, downsampling and reduction. These graph modeling methods have also been applied to many tasks, such as node classification [15,35], action recognition [19] and user recommendation [34].

3   Overview

In our task, we need to retrieval video clips and their descriptions using manually annotated graphs in [30] as queries. To better analyze the correspondence between annotated graphs, descriptions and video clips, we transform them into graph structured data and the task is converted into the problem of graph searching. For each pair of samples, we let $\mathbf{X}_1 \in \mathbb{R}^{n_1 \times d_1}, \mathbf{X}_2 \in \mathbb{R}^{n_2 \times d_2}$ denote the graph of samples in each pair respectively. To represent the annotated graph and constructed ourselves, following features are taken into consideration : 1) word embeddings for the annotated graph and the description; 2) features extracted by different neural networks for the video clip. The detail of the graph construction can be found in Sect. 5. In order to analyze graph correlation of different magnitudes features, we project them into the same space and maximize the correlation between projections. We minimize the Wasserstein distance, that is, to learn weight parameters with regard of graphs. During training, we perform the metric training with pairwise samples and get weight parameters. In the process of testing, we search the most similar clip for the query over all the other clips with learned information.

4   Graph Correlation Analysis

Given a pair of (heterogeneous) graphs, e.g., annotation graph versus description graph, we denote them as $\mathcal{G}_1 = (\mathcal{V}_1, \mathbf{A}_1, \mathbf{X}_1)$ and $\mathcal{G}_2 = (\mathcal{V}_2, \mathbf{A}_2, \mathbf{X}_2)$, where $\mathcal{V}_1, \mathcal{V}_2$ are the node sets with the node numbers $|\mathcal{V}_1| = n_1$ and $|\mathcal{V}_2| = n_2$. The adjacent matrices $\mathbf{A}_1 \in \mathbb{R}^{n_1 \times n_1}, \mathbf{A}_2 \in \mathbb{R}^{n_2 \times n_2}$ record connections of edges, graph signals $\mathbf{X}_1 \in \mathbb{R}^{n_1 \times d_1}, \mathbf{X}_2 \in \mathbb{R}^{n_2 \times d_2}$ describe attributes of all nodes, where each row corresponds to the signal vector of one node therein and d_1, d_2 are the dimensions of signals. Our ultimate aim is to measure the distance of these two graphs $\mathcal{G}_1, \mathcal{G}_2$. Formally, we define the distance metric learning on these two graphs as

$$\mathcal{D}(\mathcal{G}_1, \mathcal{G}_2) = \mathcal{M}(\mathcal{F}(\mathcal{G}_1), \mathcal{F}(\mathcal{G}_2)), \tag{1}$$

where $\mathcal{F}(\cdot)$ is a function of graph signal processing, $\mathcal{M}(\cdot)$ is a distance metric function between two graphs.

4.1   Graph Filtering Versus Graph Metric

Below we detailedly introduce the graph signal filtering function $\mathcal{F}$ and the graph metric learning function $\mathcal{M}$, and derive the consistency of their learning process that the metric learning could be viewed as signal filtering and vice versa.

Graph Signal Filtering. In spectral graph theory, one main operator is the graph Laplacian operator, defined as $\mathbf{L} = \mathbf{D} - \mathbf{A}$, where $\mathbf{D} \in \mathbb{R}^{n \times n}$ is the diagonal degree matrix with $D_{ii} = \sum_j A_{ij}$. The popular option is to normalize graph Laplacian, i.e.,

$$\mathbf{L}^{\text{norm}} = \mathbf{D}^{-\frac{1}{2}} \mathbf{L} \mathbf{D}^{-\frac{1}{2}} = \mathbf{I} - \mathbf{D}^{-\frac{1}{2}} \mathbf{A} \mathbf{D}^{-\frac{1}{2}}, \tag{2}$$

where each edge A_{ij} is multiplied by a factor $\frac{1}{\sqrt{D_{ii}D_{jj}}}$, and $\mathbf{I}$ is an identity matrix. Unless otherwise specified, below we use the normalized version. Due to the symmetric and positive definite (SPD) property, the graph Laplacian $\mathbf{L}$ is with a complete set of orthonormal eigenvectors. Formally, we can decompose the Laplacian matrix into

$$\mathbf{L} = \mathbf{U} \Lambda \mathbf{U}^{\top}, \tag{3}$$

where $\Lambda = diag([\lambda_1, \lambda_2, \cdots, \lambda_n])$ with the spectrum $\lambda_i \geq 0$. In analogy to the classic Fourier transform, the graph Fourier transform and its inverse transform are defined as [27]

$$\hat{\mathbf{x}} = \mathbf{U}^\top \mathbf{x}, \quad \mathbf{x} = \mathbf{U}\hat{\mathbf{x}}, \tag{4}$$

where $\mathbf{x} \in \mathbb{R}^n$ is a graph signal of spatial domain, and $\hat{\mathbf{x}}$ is the corresponding frequency signal.

Let $\mathcal{F}(\cdot)$ denote the filter function on graph $\mathcal{G}$, we can define the frequency response on an input signal $\mathbf{x}$ as $\hat{z}(\lambda_l) = \hat{x}(\lambda_l)\hat{\mathcal{F}}(\lambda_l)$, and the inverse graph Fourier transform [27] as $z(i) = \sum_{l=1}^{N} \hat{x}(\lambda_l)\hat{\mathcal{F}}(\lambda_l)u_l(i)$, where $\hat{z}(\lambda_l), \hat{x}(\lambda_l), \hat{\mathcal{F}}(\lambda_l)$ are the Fourier coefficients w.r.t the spectrum λ_l. In matrix form, the filtering process can be rewritten as

$$\mathbf{z} = \hat{\mathcal{F}}(\mathbf{L})\mathbf{x} = \mathbf{U}diag[\hat{\mathcal{F}}(\lambda_1), \cdots, \hat{\mathcal{F}}(\lambda_n)]\mathbf{U}^\top \mathbf{x}. \tag{5}$$

Given the input signal $\mathbf{x}$ and the output response $\mathbf{z}$, our aim is to learn the filter function $\hat{\mathcal{F}}(\cdot)$ in frequency domain, which suffers high-burden eigenvalue decomposition. To bypass it, we use a low order polynomial to approximate $\hat{\mathcal{F}}(\cdot)$, formally, $\hat{\mathcal{F}}(\lambda_l) = \sum_{k=0}^{K-1} \theta_k \lambda_l^k$, where $\theta = [\theta_0, \theta_1, \cdots, \theta_{K-1}]^\top \in \mathbb{R}^K$ is a vector of parameters w.r.t the polynomial coefficients, and K is the order number. By plug it into Eq. (5), we can have

$$\mathbf{z} = \mathbf{U}diag[\sum_{k=0}^{K-1} \theta_k \lambda_1^k, \cdots, \sum_{k=0}^{K-1} \theta_k \lambda_n^k]\mathbf{U}^\top \mathbf{x}$$

$$= \sum_{k=0}^{K-1} \theta_k \mathbf{U}diag[\lambda_1^k, \cdots, \lambda_n^k]\mathbf{U}^\top \mathbf{x} = \sum_{k=0}^{K-1} \theta_k \mathbf{L}^k \mathbf{x}.$$

Further, we may extend it to multi-dimensional signals $\mathbf{X}$, each of which is with different parameter, formally,

$$\mathbf{z} = \sum_{k=0}^{K-1} \sum_{j=1}^{d} \Theta_{kj} \mathbf{L}^k \mathbf{X}_{*j} = \sum_{k=0}^{K-1} \mathbf{L}^k \mathbf{X} \mathbf{w}^{(k)}, \tag{6}$$

$$\text{s.t. }, \quad \mathbf{w}^{(k)} = [\Theta_{k1}, \Theta_{k2}, \cdots, \Theta_{kd}]^\top, \tag{7}$$

where $\mathbf{X}_{*j}$ takes the j-th column of the matrix $\mathbf{X}$, Θ is the parameter to be learnt, and $\mathbf{w}^{(k)}$ is associated to the k-order term of the polynomial of graph Laplacian.

Graph Wasserstein Metric Learning. Below we derive that $\mathbf{w}^{(k)}$ is also the parameters to be learnt in metric learning. To simply the derivation, we consider the k-order case and meantime omit the superscript of $\mathbf{w}^{(k)}$. For a pair of graphs $\mathcal{G}_1, \mathcal{G}_2$, the filtering response in the k-order case may be written as

$$\tilde{\mathbf{x}}_1 = \mathbf{L}_1^k \mathbf{X}_1 \mathbf{w}_1, \quad \tilde{\mathbf{x}}_2 = \mathbf{L}_2^k \mathbf{X}_2 \mathbf{w}_2, \tag{8}$$

where $\widetilde{\mathbf{x}}_1 \in \mathbb{R}^{n_1}, \widetilde{\mathbf{x}}_2 \in \mathbb{R}^{n_2}$ are one-dimensional signal of all nodes, and $\mathbf{w}_1 \in \mathbb{R}^{d_1}, \mathbf{w}_2 \in \mathbb{R}^{d_2}$ are the graph filtering parameters for the k-th polynomial term case.

We use the 2th Wasserstein distance (abbreviated as W_2) for the output signals $\widetilde{\mathbf{x}}_1, \widetilde{\mathbf{x}}_2$. Note that each node only carries with one signal, and multi-channel signals could be easily extended. Formally, when all nodes of one graph is viewed a set of signals, we define second-order statistic distance as follows

$$\mathcal{D} = \|\mu_1 - \mu_2\|_2^2 + tr(\Sigma_1 + \Sigma_2 - 2(\Sigma_1^{1/2} \Sigma_2 \Sigma_1^{1/2})^{1/2}), \tag{9}$$

$$\text{s.t. ,} \quad \mu_1 = \frac{1}{n_1} \mathbf{1}_{n_1}^\top \widetilde{\mathbf{x}}_1, \quad \mu_2 = \frac{1}{n_2} \mathbf{1}_{n_2}^\top \widetilde{\mathbf{x}}_2, \tag{10}$$

$$\Sigma_1 = \frac{1}{n_1} (\widetilde{\mathbf{x}}_1 - \mu_1)^\top (\widetilde{\mathbf{x}}_1 - \mu_1), \tag{11}$$

$$\Sigma_2 = \frac{1}{n_2} (\widetilde{\mathbf{x}}_2 - \mu_2)^\top (\widetilde{\mathbf{x}}_2 - \mu_2). \tag{12}$$

By integrating Eq. (8), Eq. (10), Eq. (11) and Eq. (12) into the distance metic in Eq. (9), we can derive out the following formulas

$$\mu_1^\top \mu_1 = \mathbf{w}_1^\top \mathbf{X}_1 \mathcal{K}_{\mu_1} \mathbf{X}_1 \mathbf{w}_1, \tag{13}$$

$$\mu_2^\top \mu_2 = \mathbf{w}_2^\top \mathbf{X}_2 \mathcal{K}_{\mu_2} \mathbf{X}_2 \mathbf{w}_2, \tag{14}$$

$$\mu_1^\top \mu_2 = \mathbf{w}_1^\top \mathbf{X}_1 \mathcal{K}_{\mu_1 \mu_2} \mathbf{X}_2 \mathbf{w}_2, \tag{15}$$

$$\Sigma_1 = \mathbf{w}_1^\top \mathbf{X}_1 \mathcal{K}_{\Sigma_1} \mathbf{X}_1 \mathbf{w}_1, \tag{16}$$

$$\Sigma_2 = \mathbf{w}_2^\top \mathbf{X}_2 \mathcal{K}_{\Sigma_2} \mathbf{X}_2 \mathbf{w}_2, \tag{17}$$

$$(\Sigma_1 \Sigma_2)^{1/2} \geq \mathbf{w}_1^\top \mathbf{X}_1^\top \mathcal{K}_{\Sigma_1 \Sigma_2} \mathbf{X}_2 \mathbf{w}_2 \tag{18}$$

where each kernel term $\mathcal{K}$ is defined as

$$\mathcal{K}_{\mu_1} = \frac{1}{n_1^2} (\mathbf{L}_1^k)^\top \mathbf{1}_{n_1} \mathbf{1}_{n_1}^\top \mathbf{L}_1^k, \tag{19}$$

$$\mathcal{K}_{\mu_2} = \frac{1}{n_2^2} (\mathbf{L}_2^k)^\top \mathbf{1}_{n_2} \mathbf{1}_{n_2}^\top \mathbf{L}_2^k, \tag{20}$$

$$\mathcal{K}_{\mu_1 \mu_2} = \frac{1}{n_1 n_2} (\mathbf{L}_1^k)^\top \mathbf{1}_{n_1} \mathbf{1}_{n_2}^\top \mathbf{L}_2^k, \tag{21}$$

$$\mathcal{K}_{\Sigma_1} = \frac{1}{n_1} (\mathbf{L}_1^k - \frac{1}{n_1} \mathbf{1}\mathbf{1}^\top \mathbf{L}_1^k)^\top (\mathbf{L}_1^k - \frac{1}{n_1} \mathbf{1}\mathbf{1}^\top \mathbf{L}_1^k), \tag{22}$$

$$\mathcal{K}_{\Sigma_2} = \frac{1}{n_2} (\mathbf{L}_2^k - \frac{1}{n_2} \mathbf{1}\mathbf{1}^\top \mathbf{L}_2^k)^\top (\mathbf{L}_2^k - \frac{1}{n_2} \mathbf{1}\mathbf{1}^\top \mathbf{L}_2^k), \tag{23}$$

$$\mathcal{K}_{\Sigma_1 \Sigma_2} = \frac{1}{\sqrt{n_1 n_2}} (\mathbf{L}_1^k - \frac{1}{n_1} \mathbf{1}\mathbf{1}\mathbf{L}_1^k)^\top (\mathbf{L}_2^k - \frac{1}{n_2} \mathbf{1}\mathbf{1}\mathbf{L}_2^k). \tag{24}$$

In the above formulas, we can easily derive them except Eq. (18). Next we give the derivation process of $(\Sigma_1 \Sigma_2)^{1/2}$. We denote $\widetilde{\mathbf{x}}_1' = \widetilde{\mathbf{x}}_1 - \mu_1$ and $\widetilde{\mathbf{x}}_2' = \widetilde{\mathbf{x}}_2 - \mu_2$, and suppose the same dimensions (i.e., $n_1 = n_2$)[1], and then can have

$$(\Sigma_1 \Sigma_2)^{1/2} = (\frac{1}{n_1 n_2} (\widetilde{\mathbf{x}}_1')^\top \widetilde{\mathbf{x}}_1' (\widetilde{\mathbf{x}}_2')^\top \widetilde{\mathbf{x}}_2')^{1/2} \tag{25}$$

$$\geq \frac{1}{\sqrt{n_1 n_2}} (\widetilde{\mathbf{x}}_1')^\top \widetilde{\mathbf{x}}_2', \tag{26}$$

where this inequation employs Cauchy inequality: $\sum_{i=1}^{n} a_i^2 \sum_{i=1}^{n} b_i^2 \geq (\sum_{i=1}^{n} a_i b_i)^2$. Next we plug Eq. (8) and Eq. (10) into the above equation and define the kernel term in Eq. (24). After a series of derivation, we can reach the final Eq. (18).

Now we can obtain the upper bound of Wasserstein distance metric, i.e.,

$$\begin{aligned}
\mathcal{D} \leq \ & \mathbf{w}_1^\top \mathbf{X}_1^\top (\mathcal{K}_{\mu_1} + \mathcal{K}_{\Sigma_1}) \mathbf{X}_1 \mathbf{w}_1 \\
& + \mathbf{w}_2^\top \mathbf{X}_2^\top (\mathcal{K}_{\mu_2} + \mathcal{K}_{\Sigma_2}) \mathbf{X}_2 \mathbf{w}_2 \\
& - 2\mathbf{w}_1^\top \mathbf{X}_1^\top (\mathcal{K}_{\mu_1 \mu_2} + \mathcal{K}_{\Sigma_1 \Sigma_2}) \mathbf{X}_2 \mathbf{w}_2.
\end{aligned} \tag{27}$$

The above bound is obviously the metric learning in Wasserstein space if we extend $\mathbf{w}_1, \mathbf{w}_2$ to multi-channel responses. Therefore, the Wasserstein metric learning is consistent with graph signal filtering. In other words, the aim of metric learning is to learn graph filters, and vice verse.

Wasserstein Correlation Analysis. Given M pairs of matching graphs, $\{(\mathcal{G}_1^{(m)}, \mathcal{G}_2^{(m)})\}|_{m=1}^{M}$, we expect to learn the projection to make their as closer as possible, formally,

$$\arg \min_{\mathbf{w}_1, \mathbf{w}_2} \sum_{m=1}^{M} \mathcal{D}(\mathcal{G}_1^{(m)}, \mathcal{G}_2^{(m)}). \tag{28}$$

We replace $\mathcal{D}$ with Eq. (27), and then the objective function can be rewritten as

$$\arg \min_{\mathbf{w}_1, \mathbf{w}_2} \ \mathbf{w}_1^\top \mathcal{C}_1 \mathbf{w}_1 + \mathbf{w}_2^\top \mathcal{C}_2 \mathbf{w}_2 - 2\mathbf{w}_1^\top \mathcal{C}_{12} \mathbf{w}_2, \tag{29}$$

where

$$\mathcal{C}_1 = \sum_{m=1}^{M} (\mathbf{X}_1^{(m)})^\top (\mathcal{K}_{\mu_1} + \mathcal{K}_{\Sigma_1}) \mathbf{X}_1^{(m)}, \tag{30}$$

$$\mathcal{C}_2 = \sum_{m=1}^{M} (\mathbf{X}_2^{(m)})^\top (\mathcal{K}_{\mu_2} + \mathcal{K}_{\Sigma_2}) \mathbf{X}_2^{(m)}, \tag{31}$$

$$\mathcal{C}_{12} = \sum_{m=1}^{M} (\mathbf{X}_1^{(m)})^\top (\mathcal{K}_{\mu_1 \mu_2} + \mathcal{K}_{\Sigma_1 \Sigma_2}) \mathbf{X}_2^{(m)}. \tag{32}$$

---

[1] We can pad zero values to one of them to produce the same dimensions for them.

An elegant alternative of the solution is to maximize the following objective function

$$\arg \max_{\mathbf{w}_1, \mathbf{w}_2} \frac{\mathbf{w}_1^\top \mathcal{C}_{12} \mathbf{w}_2}{\sqrt{\mathbf{w}_1^\top \mathcal{C}_1 \mathbf{w}_1} \sqrt{\mathbf{w}_2^\top \mathcal{C}_2 \mathbf{w}_2}}. \tag{33}$$

which finally falls into the category of canonical correlation analysis. Hence, this maximum optimization has a closed-form solution, which can be derived as the eigenvalue decomposition from

$$\mathcal{C}_1^{-1} \mathcal{C}_{12} \mathcal{C}_2^{-1} \mathcal{C}_{21} \mathbf{w}_1 = \rho^2 \mathbf{w}_1 \tag{34}$$

$$\mathcal{C}_2^{-1} \mathcal{C}_{21} \mathcal{C}_1^{-1} \mathcal{C}_{12} \mathbf{w}_2 = \rho^2 \mathbf{w}_2 \tag{35}$$

where $\mathbf{w}_1, \mathbf{w}_2$ are eigenvectors and ρ is the correlation coefficient.

Consequently, those eigenvectors with large correlation coefficients may be chosen as multi-channel projection functions. Further, with the change of the order k, we can learn the corresponding filtering functions also metrics.

5   Graph Generation

In this section, we introduce how we generate graphs on the MovieGraphs dataset. As structural difference exists between videos and descriptions of movies, different graphs are constructed accordingly.

5.1   Graph Construction on Videos

Formally, a graph can be denoted as $\mathcal{G} = (\mathcal{V}, \mathcal{E})$, where $\mathcal{V}$ and $\mathcal{E}$ are the sets of nodes and edges, respectively. Following the configuration of the Moviegraphs dataset, four types of nodes, which correspond to the nodes in the manually annotated graph of the dataset, are taken into account for video clips denoted as M. Nodes of character and attribute are denoted with the notations v^{ch} and v^{att} respectively. Another two independent nodes named scene and situation are specifically denoted as v^{sc} and v^{si}. Below, we introduce how we learn embeddings of these nodes, and set up connections between them.

Scene and Situation. Scene and situation provide the context of the video. For each video clip, the Resnet is used to extract features from those frames, and features of every ten frames are averaged as the representation of scene and situation denoted as $\mathbf{x}_{sc} \in \mathbb{R}^{2048}$ and $\mathbf{x}_{si} \in \mathbb{R}^{2048}$, which is similar with the previous work [30].

Character. In the graph retrieval video task, in order to obtain the features of different types of nodes, e.g. facial expression and age, we first perform face detection on each frame [1], and then construct multiple clusters where each cluster is formed by those faces belonging to the same person. Moreover, we assign each cluster with one name according to the actor list in IMDB by comparing the features between the cluster and the actor picture (also provided in IMDB). Specifically, in the process of constructing face clusters, facial features are first extracted, and accordingly the Euclidean distances are calculated between faces for comparison. Also, a threshold is set to determine whether they are the same person. For each face cluster not aligned with an actor name, we randomly choose an unassigned name in the actor list for it.

Attribute. For each face cluster, its attribute node include age, gender, emotion, etc. Each attribute node is represented by the extracted feature of the predicted attribute value [23] (e.g. "male" for gender), which is formally denoted as $\mathbf{x}_{att} \in \mathbb{R}^{300}$. These nodes form a graph where nodes with similar embeddings are connected.

5.2   Graph Construction on Descriptions

In moviegraphs dataset, each video clip has a natural language description. To construct one graph for each description of the movie clip, after splitting the sentence and removing stopwords and notations, we statistics the total words while keep previous order to obtain a small corpus. Here we regard each word as graph node v^{des}, and each node in the textual graph has the representation of a fixed length by using GloVe embeddings [23]. Moreover, the intense of the edge between nodes is defined as the similarity between their embeddings.

6   Experiments

We conduct experiments on the MovieGraphs dataset with our proposed GWCA. The performance of GWCA is also compared with the results of those retrieval tasks in MovieGraphs [30]. Moreover, we conduct an ablation study to discuss the influence of different distance metrics and different orders of receptive fields.

6.1   Dataset and Settings

MovieGraphs dataset consists of 51 movies with annotated textual description and graphs. Each movie is split into multiple rough scenes and then manually refined. As a result, the dataset contains 7637 clips in total and each clip has an annotated description and graph. There are 35 words on average in the description, and the average number of nodes per graph is also about 35. In the experiment, following the protocol in [30], the dataset is split into 5050 clips for training, 1060 clips for validation and 1527 clips for testing.

Two retrieval tasks are evaluated to test the performance: (1) descriptions retrieval using annotated graphs as queries, and (2) video clips retrieval using annotated graphs as queries. In the test stage, for each query graph, we search all the descriptions/video clips to find the most similar one. Following the previous work [30], we use "Recall" as the evaluation metric, and calculate the Recall@1(R@1), Recall@5(R@5) and Recall10(R@10) to explore the effectiveness of our GWCA. There R@K stands for the fraction of correct predicted results in the top K predictions.

6.2   The Comparison Results

We compare our proposed GWCA with those state-of-the-art methods, and the results are shown in Table 1.

Table 1. The comparison results of two different retrieval tasks.

Method	Description			Method	Video		
	R@1	R@5	R@10		R@1	R@5	R@10
GloVe,idf·max-sum	61.3	81.6	86.9	sc	1.1	4.3	7.7
GloVe,max-sum	62.1	81.3	87.2	sc,si	1.0	5.4	8.7
TF·IDF	61.6	83.8	89.7	sc,si,a	2.2	9.4	15.5
GWCA	**67.6**	**87.8**	**91.9**	sc,si,a (ours)	**2.4**	**10.1**	**16.2**

Description Retrieval Using Graphs as Queries. The results of description retrieval with query graphs are shown in Table 1, from the first row to third row in the second column. For the compared methods, GloVe means that the GloVe word embedding is employed; max-sum and idf·max-sum are pooling strategies with word embedding. Specifically, idf·max-sum weights words with rarity. The previous method [30] finds the best matching word in description for each word in the manually annotated graph, and sum up them to compute the similarity. Then this processed score is fed into the loss function. According to Table 1, GloVe with the pooling strategy of max-sum achieves limited performance gain comparing with GloVe. TF·IDF, which uses an identity sparse matrix to initialize features, performs better than GloVe. Among these compared methods, our GWCA shows the best performance, where the score of Recall@1 is about 5.5% higher than GloVe with max-sum pooling. Besides, for those words with similar meaning/embedding which are sometimes confusing, our GWCA is still effective enough to compute the correlation and fulfill the retrieval task well. This observation demonstrates that GWCA successfully formulates graph signal encoding together with graph distance metric learning into a unified model. Besides, we show some retrieval examples in Fig. 2.

Video Retrieval Using Graphs as Queries. This experiment aims to measure the performance of our method to retrieve videos based on the given annotated graphs. The result is shown in the third and fourth columns in Table 1. The characters 'si', 'sc' and 'a' indicate that we start with the scene, situation, attributes, and characters as part of graphs, while their corresponding methods all compute the cosine similarity to measure the distances between nodes. The reported result of our GWCA employs all the four kinds of nodes, and achieves the best performance. According to the shown result, we have the following observations: (1) the four different nodes, i.e. situation, scene, attribute and

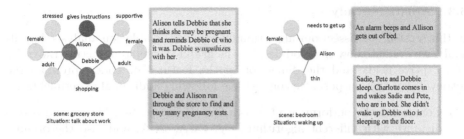

Fig. 2. The results for retrieved descriptions with graphs. We show the top-2 retrieved clips. The sub-graphs indicate the query graphs. The green boxes indicate the ground-truth and the red boxes indicate the quite similar one. (Color figure online)

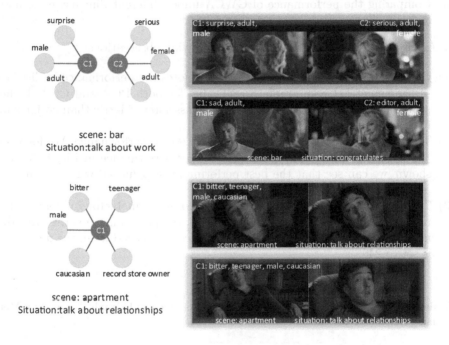

Fig. 3. The results for retrieved video clips with graphs. We show the top-2 retrieved clips. The red boxes indicate results that are quite similar in meaning to the query, and the green boxes indicate ground-truth. (Color figure online)

characters, all contribute to the video retrieval; (2) compared with other methods, our GWCA is advantageous in understanding the graph structure as it jointly encapsulates graph signal filtering and Wasserstein metric learning into a unified mathematic model helps to enhance the node representation ability. Some examples of the retrieved videos are visualized in Fig. 3 for the intuitive impression of our GWCA.

6.3   Ablation Study

In this section, we dissect our algorithm by conducting ablation analysis. Specifically, we evaluate how the modules, i.e. the graph Wasserstein metric, the order of receptive fields, and the dimension of the features of nodes, promote the retrieval. For this purpose, we conduct the following additional experiments:

(1) Comparing the performance between Graph Wasserstein Metric and cosine distance with different algorithms, e.g. PCA, CCA, and also the original feature without learning. The result is shown in Table 2.
(2) Comparing the performance of GWCA under different values of the order of receptive field k. Please see the result in Fig. 4. Fusion means the features of those orders that are lower than k are fused together as the feature.
(3) Comparing the performance of GWCA under different dimensions of node features. The result is shown in Fig. 5.

According to the results, we have the following observations:

(1) Graph Wasserstein Metric effectively promotes the performance in distance measurement between graph. Specifically, for both PCA and CCA, higher performances are achieved with Graph Wasserstein Metric than cosine similarity.
(2) The order of receptive field k also influences the performance. We focus on the situation of fusion as it achieves higher performance in Fig. 4. As it is shown, we can see that the best performance is achieved when k equals 2, otherwise the performance drops.
(3) The dimension of node feature is also an important factor influencing the retrieval performance. According to Fig. 5, the performance varies with different dimensions, and the best performance is achieved when the dimension is set to 240.

Table 2. The comparison results between cosine distance and Graph Wasserstein Metric using different algorithms.

Method		R@1	R@5	R@10
Ori feature	cos	4.07	12.4	19.6
PCA	cos	35.9	55.5	64.8
	w-2	62.1	77.7	86.7
CCA	cos	61.9	78.3	85.3
	w-2	66.4	82.7	88.3
GWCA		**67.6**	**87.8**	**91.9**

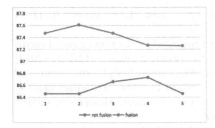

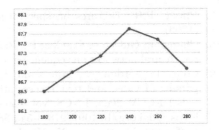

Fig. 4. Test Recall@5 with different orders, using GWCA in the description retrieval task.

Fig. 5. Test Recall@5 with different dimensions, using GWCA in the description retrieval task.

7 Conclusion

In this paper, a Graph Wasserstein Correlation Analysis (GWCA) method was proposed to deal with the comparisons of pairwise movie graphs and show the effectiveness. We relabel some content ourselves after downloading the existing data, and then use GWCA to formulate graph signal encoding together with graph distance metric learning on this dataset. In this way, graph signal filtering and Wasserstein metric learning are jointly encapsulated into a unified model, which efficiently preserves the proximity of the nodes of graph and empowering the learned node representations. Extensive experiments and our visualizations analyze our method and we believe that our contribution can be applied to many domains.

Acknowledgments. This work was supported by the National Natural Science Foundation of China (Grants Nos. 61906094, 61972204), the Natural Science Foundation of Jiangsu Province (Grant Nos. BK20190019, BK20190452), and the fundamental research funds for the central universities (No. 30919011232).

References

1. https://github.com/ageitgey/face_recognition/blob/master/README_Simplified_Chinese.md/
2. Belkin, M., Niyogi, P.: Laplacian Eigenmaps for dimensionality reduction and data representation. Neural Comput. **15**(6), 1373–1396 (2003)
3. Bojanowski, P., Bach, F., Laptev, I., Ponce, J., Schmid, C., Sivic, J.: Finding actors and actions in movies. In: Proceedings of the IEEE International Conference on Computer Vision, pp. 2280–2287 (2013)
4. Bruna, J., Zaremba, W., Szlam, A., Lecun, Y.: Spectral networks and locally connected networks on graphs. Comput. Sci. (2014)
5. Buades, A., Coll, B., Morel, J.M.: A review of image denoising algorithms, with a new one. Multiscale Model. Simul. **4**(2), 490–530 (2005)
6. Chen, X., Zitnick, C.L.: Learning a recurrent visual representation for image caption generation. arXiv preprint arXiv:1411.5654 (2014)

7. Chung, F.R.: Lectures on spectral graph theory. CBMS Lect. Fresno **6**, 17–21 (1996)
8. Chung, J., Gulcehre, C., Cho, K., Bengio, Y.: Empirical evaluation of gated recurrent neural networks on sequence modeling. arXiv preprint arXiv:1412.3555 (2014)
9. Cour, T., Jordan, C., Miltsakaki, E., Taskar, B.: Movie/Script: alignment and parsing of video and text transcription. In: Forsyth, D., Torr, P., Zisserman, A. (eds.) ECCV 2008. LNCS, vol. 5305, pp. 158–171. Springer, Heidelberg (2008). https://doi.org/10.1007/978-3-540-88693-8_12
10. Defferrard, M., Bresson, X., Vandergheynst, P.: Convolutional neural networks on graphs with fast localized spectral filtering. In: Advances in neural information processing systems, pp. 3844–3852 (2016)
11. Ding, L., Yilmaz, A.: Learning relations among movie characters: a social network perspective. In: Daniilidis, K., Maragos, P., Paragios, N. (eds.) ECCV 2010. LNCS, vol. 6314, pp. 410–423. Springer, Heidelberg (2010). https://doi.org/10.1007/978-3-642-15561-1_30
12. Donoho, D.L., Grimes, C.: Hessian eigenmaps: locally linear embedding techniques for high-dimensional data. Proc. Natl. Acad. Sci. **100**(10), 5591–5596 (2003)
13. Farhadi, A., et al.: Every picture tells a story: generating sentences from images. In: Daniilidis, K., Maragos, P., Paragios, N. (eds.) ECCV 2010. LNCS, vol. 6314, pp. 15–29. Springer, Heidelberg (2010). https://doi.org/10.1007/978-3-642-15561-1_2
14. Hoory, S., Linial, N., Wigderson, A.: Expander graphs and their applications. Bull. Am. Math. Soc. **43**(4), 439–561 (2006)
15. Jiang, J., Cui, Z., Xu, C., Yang, J.: Gaussian-induced convolution for graphs. In: Proceedings of the AAAI Conference on Artificial Intelligence, vol. 33, pp. 4007–4014 (2019)
16. Kipf, T.N., Welling, M.: Semi-supervised classification with graph convolutional networks. arXiv preprint arXiv:1609.02907 (2016)
17. Lafon, S., Lee, A.B.: Diffusion maps and coarse-graining: a unified framework for dimensionality reduction, graph partitioning, and data set parameterization. IEEE Trans. Pattern Anal. Mach. Intell. **28**(9), 1393–1403 (2006)
18. Laptev, I., Marszalek, M., Schmid, C., Rozenfeld, B.: Learning realistic human actions from movies. In: 2008 IEEE Conference on Computer Vision and Pattern Recognition, pp. 1–8. IEEE (2008)
19. Li, B., Li, X., Zhang, Z., Wu, F.: Spatio-temporal graph routing for skeleton-based action recognition. In: Proceedings of the AAAI Conference on Artificial Intelligence, vol. 33, pp. 8561–8568 (2019)
20. Narang, S.K., Ortega, A.: Lifting based wavelet transforms on graphs. In: Proceedings: APSIPA ASC 2009: Asia-Pacific Signal and Information Processing Association, 2009 Annual Summit and Conference, Asia-Pacific Signal and Information Processing Association, 2009 Annual ..., pp. 441–444 (2009)
21. Ordonez, V., Kulkarni, G., Berg, T.L.: Im2Text: describing images using 1 million captioned photographs. In: Advances in Neural Information Processing Systems, pp. 1143–1151 (2011)
22. Pan, Y., Mei, T., Yao, T., Li, H., Rui, Y.: Jointly modeling embedding and translation to bridge video and language. In: Proceedings of the IEEE Conference on Computer Vision and Pattern Recognition, pp. 4594–4602 (2016)
23. Pennington, J., Socher, R., Manning, C.: GloVe: global vectors for word representation. In: Proceedings of the 2014 Conference on Empirical Methods in Natural Language Processing (EMNLP), pp. 1532–1543 (2014)

24. Ron, D., Safro, I., Brandt, A.: Relaxation-based coarsening and multiscale graph organization. Multiscale Model. Simul. **9**(1), 407–423 (2011)
25. Roweis, S.T., Saul, L.K.: Nonlinear dimensionality reduction by locally linear embedding. Sci. **290**(5500), 2323–2326 (2000)
26. Sankar, P., Jawahar, C., Zisserman, A.: Subtitle-free movie to script alignment. In: Proceedings of the British Machine Vision Conference, pp. 121:1–121:11 (2009)
27. Shuman, D.I., Narang, S.K., Frossard, P., Ortega, A., Vandergheynst, P.: The emerging field of signal processing on graphs: extending high-dimensional data analysis to networks and other irregular domains. IEEE Signal Process. Mag. **30**(3), 83–98 (2013)
28. Tapaswi, M., Zhu, Y., Stiefelhagen, R., Torralba, A., Urtasun, R., Fidler, S.: MovieQA: understanding stories in movies through question-answering. In: Proceedings of the IEEE Conference on Computer Vision and Pattern Recognition, pp. 4631–4640 (2016)
29. Tenenbaum, J.B., De Silva, V., Langford, J.C.: A global geometric framework for nonlinear dimensionality reduction. Sci. **290**(5500), 2319–2323 (2000)
30. Vicol, P., Tapaswi, M., Castrejon, L., Fidler, S.: MovieGraphs: towards understanding human-centric situations from videos. In: Proceedings of the IEEE Conference on Computer Vision and Pattern Recognition, pp. 8581–8590 (2018)
31. Von Luxburg, U.: A tutorial on spectral clustering. Stat. Comput. **17**(4), 395–416 (2007)
32. Xingjian, S., Chen, Z., Wang, H., Yeung, D.Y., Wong, W.K., Woo, W.C.: Convolutional LSTM network: a machine learning approach for precipitation nowcasting. In: Advances in neural information processing systems, pp. 802–810 (2015)
33. Yang, Y., Teo, C.L., Daumé III, H., Aloimonos, Y.: Corpus-guided sentence generation of natural images. In: Proceedings of the Conference on Empirical Methods in Natural Language Processing, pp. 444–454. Association for Computational Linguistics (2011)
34. Zhang, T., et al.: Cross-graph convolution learning for large-scale text-picture shopping guide in e-commerce search. In: 2020 IEEE 36th International Conference on Data Engineering (ICDE), pp. 1657–1666. IEEE (2020)
35. Zhao, W., Cui, Z., Xu, C., Li, C., Zhang, T., Yang, J.: Hashing graph convolution for node classification. In: Proceedings of the 28th ACM International Conference on Information and Knowledge Management, pp. 519–528 (2019)

Context-Aware RCNN: A Baseline for Action Detection in Videos

Jianchao Wu[1], Zhanghui Kuang[2](ID), Limin Wang[1](✉)(ID), Wayne Zhang[2](ID), and Gangshan Wu[1]

[1] State Key Laboratory for Novel Software Technology, Nanjing University,
Nanjing, China
lmwang@nju.edu.cn
[2] SenseTime Research, Hong Kong, China

Abstract. Video action detection approaches usually conduct actor-centric action recognition over RoI-pooled features following the standard pipeline of Faster-RCNN. In this work, we first empirically find the recognition accuracy is highly correlated with the bounding box size of an actor, and thus higher resolution of actors contributes to better performance. However, video models require dense sampling in time to achieve accurate recognition. To fit in GPU memory, the frames to backbone network must be kept low-resolution, resulting in a coarse feature map in RoI-Pooling layer. Thus, we revisit RCNN for actor-centric action recognition via cropping and resizing image patches around actors before feature extraction with I3D deep network. Moreover, we found that expanding actor bounding boxes slightly and fusing the context features can further boost the performance. Consequently, we develop a surprisingly effective baseline (Context-Aware RCNN) and it achieves new state-of-the-art results on two challenging action detection benchmarks of AVA and JHMDB. Our observations challenge the conventional wisdom of RoI-Pooling based pipeline and encourage researchers rethink the importance of resolution in actor-centric action recognition. Our approach can serve as a strong baseline for video action detection and is expected to inspire new ideas for this filed. The code is available at https://github.com/MCG-NJU/CRCNN-Action.

Keywords: Action detection · Context-Aware RCNN · Baseline

1 Introduction

This paper focuses on recognizing actor-centric actions for spatio-temporal action detection, including person pose actions, person-object interaction actions, and person-person interaction actions, which have wide applications across robotics, security, and health. The mainstream approaches [5,7,10,31,41] of action detection follow the Faster-RCNN [27] style pipeline: classifying 3D convolutional

---

J. Wu—Part of the work is done during an internship at SenseTime EIG Research.

A. Vedaldi et al. (Eds.): ECCV 2020, LNCS 12370, pp. 440–456, 2020.
https://doi.org/10.1007/978-3-030-58595-2_27

Fig. 1. Actor-centric action recognition heavily relies on local details (indicated by red rectangles) to distinguish between fine-grained actions. The top row shows the discriminative local region between "eat" and "smoke" while the bottom row shows that between "write" and "read"

features RoI-pooled over actor proposals into action categories. Although they achieve significant progress, the action detection performance remains relatively low [10].

RoI-Pooling based pipeline is the de facto standard for object recognition, which has been validated to be more efficient while without any accuracy degradation in Fast RCNN [8] and Faster RCNN [27]. Different from object recognition, actor-centric action recognition heavily depends on discriminative local regions to distinguish between fine-grained actions as shown in Fig. 1. *e.g.*, one differentiates "eat" from "smoke" via mouth regions of actors only. Therefore, actor-centric action recognition requires representations preserve more spatial details. However, video backbone networks are memory-consuming and have to take low-resolution images as inputs. This analysis prompts two questions:

– Can RoI-Pooling based pipeline, which is widely used in the mainstream approaches of actor-centric action recognition, preserve the discriminative spatial details?
– If not, how to preserve adequate discriminative spatial details?

To answer the first question, we conduct experiments with the representative RoI-Pooling based pipeline on AVA dataset [10], and evaluate action detection performance with different actor box sizes. We empirically found that RoI-Pooling based pipeline performs poorly when the bounding box size of actor is small, and action detection performance is highly correlated with actor size as shown in Fig. 2. We believe that the RoI-Pooling based pipeline losses many discriminative spatial details from bottom to top during network inference when actor sizes are small.

To answer the second question, we revisit RCNN-like method [9] in actor-centric action recognition. Given actor bounding boxes predicted by an off-the-

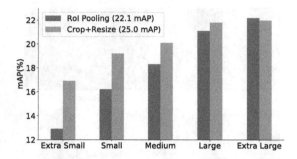

Fig. 2. We revisit RCNN-like method for action detection where actor boxes are cropped directly from original video and resized to a fixed resolution. Comparison of frame-level mAP performance at different bounding box sizes on AVA [10]

shelf person detector, we crop and then resize each actor to a fixed resolution, which is fed into an 3D CNN network to extract actor-centric features with full resolution for action classification. In this way, our approach can enlarge the input resolution of small actors and preserve their discriminative spatial details, which suppresses the performance degradation due to small sizes of actors as shown in Fig. 2.

Contextual information plays an important role in actor-centric action recognition, especially for actions related to person-person interactions or person-object interactions, such as "talk to a person" and "ride a bicycle". To this end, we fuse the scene feature from the whole video clip and long-term feature from long-range temporal context, which further boosts the final performance. This makes RCNN context-aware.

Although simple, proposed Context-Aware RCNN is remarkably effective. We extensively evaluate it on two popular action detection datasets, *i.e.*, AVA [10] and JHMDB [15]. It achieves new state-of-the-art results. Specifically, it with I3D ResNet-50 pushes the mAP of AVA to 28.0%, improving that of the best ever reported method Long-Term Feature Bank (LFB) [41] by 2.2% and even outperforming LFB with a much bigger backbone I3D ResNet-101.

Our main **contributions** are summarized in two aspects:

- We empirically investigate the drawback of current de facto standard pipeline of action detection and find that it losses many discriminative spatial details due to small resolutions of actors.
- We revisit RCNN-like method and propose a simple yet effective Context-Aware RCNN for action detection, which achieves a new state-of-the-art performance on two popular datasets. *i.e.*, AVA [10] and JHMDB [15]. Thanks to its simplicity, it is easy to implement and can serve as a strong baseline and start point for further research in the field of action detection.

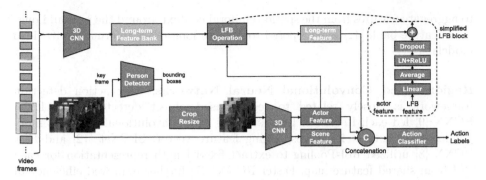

Fig. 3. An overview of proposed Context-Aware RCNN. We first localize actors at key frames using one person detector. Then, actors are cropped from the video clip, resized to one fixed resolution, and fed into one 3D CNN to extract actor features. Scene features and long-term features are also extracted as context information. Finally, these three features are aggregated and fed into one action classifier to predict action labels

2   Related Work

Action Recognition. Thanks to the breakthrough of Convolutional Neural Networks (CNN) [13,19,21,29,32], video action recognition has evolved rapidly in recent years [5,6,16,28,36,39,40]. Many datasets [1,18,20,30] have been proposed to foster research in video classification. Simonyan *et al.* [28] designed a two-stream architecture to capture appearance and motion information with different network streams. The two-stream CNNs achieved superior performance, but need to perform time-consuming optical flow calculation in advance. 3D CNNs [16,33] extended 2D convolution to model static appearance and temporal motion directly from stacked RGB inputs. Recent methods decomposed the 3D convolutions into separate 2D spatial and 1D temporal convolutions [26,34,42]. There were also efforts that explore long-range temporal modeling in videos [24,39,43]. Wang *et al.* [39] utilized a temporal segment network (TSN) to perform sparse sampling and temporal aggregation. These works mainly focused on action recognition on well-trimmed videos, where the models only need to classify short video clips to action labels. However, most videos are untrimmed and long in the practical applications. Some recent works explored temporal action detection [3,23,38,45] and spatio-temporal action localization [7,10,14,17,31,41] on untrimmed videos.

Spatio-Temporal Action Localization. Most action detection models [7, 10,14,17,22,31,37,41] extended object detection frameworks to handle videos. Actor boxes were first computed by person detector and then classified to action labels. Many of recent works focused on incorporating context information to improve recognizing human action [7,31,41]. ACRN [31] computed pair-wise relation information from actor and global scene features, and generated relation features for action classification. In [7], a transformer architecture [35] was used to aggregate features from the spatio-temporal context around the person. Long-term feature bank [41] was proposed to provide long-range information to video models.

Region-Based Convolutional Neural Networks. Our action detection framework is closely related to region-based object detectors [8,9,11,27]. RCNN [9] fed each Region of Interest (RoI) into convolutional networks independently to extract its corresponding feature vector. SPPNet [12] and Fast RCNN [8] utilized RoI-Pooling to extract fixed length representation for each RoI from shared feature map. Faster RCNN [27] further improved efficiency of RCNN by using Region Proposal Network (RPN) to generate proposals. Most recently, Cheng *et al.* [4] found that redundant context information could lead to inferior classification capacity of Faster RCNN. They used RCNN as a complement to improve the classification performance of Faster RCNN. In this work, we adopt a RCNN-like network to extract actor features for actor-centric action classification.

3   Approach

For the task of spatio-temporal action localization, we need to localize every person at each key frame, and recognize their actions. In this section, we will give a detailed description of our action detection approach. First, we present an overview of proposed Context-Aware RCNN. Then, we introduce how to extract discriminative features of each person using RCNN-like network [9]. Finally, we take into account scene context and long-range context in our model.

3.1   Method Overview

The overall framework of our proposed network for action detection is illustrated in Fig. 3. Our action detection framework follows the popular paradigm of frame-based action detection [5,31,41], which contains two key stages: actor localization and action classification. Given a key frame from the original video, a person detector is first used to localize actors at the key frame, obtaining a set of 2D bounding boxes. Then for each actor bounding box, the local appearance features around actor are extracted for the classification of human activities.

Motivated by the success of 2D object detection algorithms, recent action detection methods [5,31,41] typically follow Faster-RCNN [27] architecture to use 3D RoI-Pooling to extract actor features from the clip feature map based on actor boxes. In this work, we analyze that RoI-Pooling is sub-optimal to get discriminative features for action recognition because it losses many spatial details for small actors. We use RCNN-like method to extract actor-centric features with full resolution. Actor bounding boxes are used to crop actor tubes from the original video. Then the cropped images are fed into non-local I3D network [40] to extract deep representations of actors.

Moreover, we notice that context information is important to accurately recognize human activities. Apart from using local actor features, we utilize a parameters shared network to extract global scene features of the whole video clip. Besides that, a simplified non-local operation is used to capture long-range temporal context information from long-term feature bank [41]. Finally, actor features, global scene features and long-term features are aggregated by concatenation for action classification.

3.2 Extracting Actor Features

Person Detector. For accurate actor localization, we follow previous works [5, 41] that use an off-the-shelf person detector to pre-compute person proposals. The person detector takes the key frame as input, and outputs a set of act bounding boxes. We use the proposals provided by [41] on the AVA dataset to perform a fair comparison with state-of-the-art methods [5,41]. The proposals are detected by a Faster RCNN with a ResNeXt-101-FPN. For JHMDB dataset, we train a Faster RCNN with a ResNet-50-FPN on its training set.

Backbone. We use the I3D ResNet-50 network with non-local blocks as the backbone model for action classification. The backbone model is pre-trained on ImageNet and 'inflated' into a 3D network using the I3D [2] method. Then the model is pre-trained for video classification on Kinetics-400 [2] equipped with non-local blocks [40]. Following the recommendation from [41], we set the stride of res_5 to 1 and use a dilation of 2 in res_5. The resulting network downsamples the temporal dimension by a factor of 2, and downsamples the spatial dimension by a factor of 16. Given an input of shape $T \times H \times W \times 3$, the backbone network outputs one feature map with a shape $T/2 \times H/16 \times W/16 \times 2048$.

Extracting Actor Features by RCNN. RoI-Pooling [8] is introduced to extract Region of Interest (RoI) features from convolutional feature maps to a fixed size representation for the object classification. RoIAlign [11] fixes the misalignments between the RoI and the extracted features by removing the harsh quantization of RoI-Pooling. However, the RoI-Pooling (or RoIAlign) may not be optimal to extract discriminative features for fine-grained action classification. To correctly distinguish fine-grained action classes (*e.g.* "smoking" and "eating"), one has to focus on the local representative patterns (*e.g.* "cigarette" and "food"). CNNs typically have a large downsample stride and receptive field at last layers of the network. And state-of-the-art video models require dense sampling in time to achieve high recognition performance. Therefore, to fit in GPU memory the video inputs to action detection framework must keep low-resolution (*e.g.* 224 × 224 in [5,41] and 400 × 400 in [7]). For small actors, their sizes are very small at the last feature map of the backbone CNN network and local detail information is lost. In such case, the current action detection architectures have poor sensitivity to finer details for fine-grained action recognition.

Given the above analysis, we can conclude that using coarse representations from RoI-Pooling could not utilize the full potential of the classification power of deep video models. In this work, we propose to use RCNN-like network in the action detection framework. That is to say, actors are cropped directly from original video clip and resized to one fixed resolution. In this way, the network can only see visual contents in their bounding boxes. Moreover, the image inputs of small actors are enlarged to capture fine-grained details.

Our model takes the short video clip of T frames as the network input, sparsely sampled from 64 neighboring frames of the key frame with a temporal stride τ. For an actor bounding box at key frame, we replicate the box along the temporal axis. We conduct cropping according to the replicated box at each frame and resize the resulted image patches to a fixed resolution $H \times W$. Then the actor clip with shape $T \times H \times W \times 3$ is fed to the backbone, followed by a global average pooling, resulting in a 2048-dimensional feature vector as the actor feature. For incorporating visual information around actor, we expand the actor bounding boxes slightly during training and inference.

3.3   Context Modeling

Context information plays an important role for understanding human activities, Using only local actor features, the model could have poor performance due to the lack of context information. We take into account two kinds of context information in our model to make RCNN context-aware: scene context in the short video clip and long-term context over the entire span of long video.

Scene Context Features. We feed the entire video clip to a 3D convolutional network, followed by global average pooling, to yield a 2048-dimensional scene feature vector. A parameters shared backbone network is used to compute actor features and scene features. We have tried to use independent backbone networks. However, it resulted in a poor performance.

Long-Term Context Features. We adapt offline memory network architecture: long-term feature bank (LFB) [41] to capture long-range temporal information. We compute LFB as all actor features centered at the current clip within window size of 61 s. As illustrated in Fig. 3, LFB operation, which consists of simplified LFB blocks, is used to extract long-term features by taking LFB and actor features as inputs. We pre-process these two kinds of input using dimension reduction and dropout following [41]. Different from [41], we replace the softmax attention weighted sum with average pooling and remove the last linear layer in the original LFB NL block, Empirically, we found that this simplified version has a similar performance to original LFB NL block. Three simplified LFB blocks are used as LFB operation in our experiments. The output of LFB operation is a 512-dimensional long-term feature vector.

Finally, actor features, scene features and long-term features are aggregated by concatenation and fed into the action classifier. For AVA dataset, which is a multi-label classification task, we use the per-class sigmoid loss. For JHMDB dataset, we use the softmax loss.

4 Experiments

In this section, we first introduce two widely-adopted datasets for spatio-temporal action localization and the implementation details of our approach. Then, we perform a number of ablation studies to understand the effects of proposed components in our model. We also compare the performance with the state-of-the-art methods to show the effectiveness and generality of our model.

4.1 Datasets and Implementation Details

Datasets. We conduct experiments on two publicly available spatio-temporal action localization datasets, i.e., the AVA [10] and the JHMDB [15] dataset.

AVA [10] is a recently released large-scale action detection dataset. We use the AVA version 2.1 benchmark, which is composed of 211k training and 57k validation video segments. Annotations are provided for key frames sparsely sampled at 1 FPS. Each person at key frame is labeled with one bounding box together with multi-label action labels from 80 atomic action classes. Following the standard protocol [10], we evaluate over 60 classes. We report mean Average Precision (mAP) performance on frame level using an IoU threshold of 0.5.

JHMDB [15] dataset contains 928 temporally trimmed short video clips with 21 action classes. Every frame in JHMDB is annotated with one actor bounding box and a single action label. As is standard practice, we conduct experiments on three training/validation splits, and report the average frame-level mAP with IoU threshold of 0.5 over three splits.

Implementation Details. We adopt the synchronous SGD with a mini-batch size of 16 on 8 GPUs. We keep batch normalization layers frozen during training. For the AVA dataset, we train the network for 140k iterations with a learning rate of 0.04 which is decreased by a factor of 10 at iteration 100k and 120k. We use linear warmup for the first 1000 iteration. Dropout of 0.3 is used before the final classifier layer and weight decay is set as 10^{-6}. For the JHMDB dataset, we adopt the same learning rate schedule except for using an initial learning rate of 0.001. Dropout of 0.5 and weight decay of 10^{-7} are used.

Data augmentation is used to improve generalization. We randomly extend boxes in height and width with scale $\in [1, s]$ during training and use a fixed scale s during inference. The default s is 1.5. It is then cropped from the image and resized to 224×224 for training and 256×256 for testing. If a box crosses the image boundary, we crop the region within the image. For the entire video frame inputs, we perform random scaling such that the short side $\in [256, 320]$, and random cropping of 224×224 for training. At test time, we rescale the short side to 256 pixels and use a single center crop of 256×256. Moreover, random flipping is used during training.

Table 1. AVA validation results using only actor features. We show the mAP performance on frame level using IoU threshold of 0.5

(a) RoI Pooling vs. RCNN-like method. RCNN-like method is consistently better than the RoI Pooling with different input sampling $T \times \tau$. T denotes the number of input frames, and τ denotes temporal sample stride

Method	$T \times \tau$	mAP
RoI Pooling	8×8	20.1
	16×4	21.9
	32×2	22.1
Crop+Resize	8×8	23.1
	16×4	24.7
	32×2	25.0

(b) Performance comparison with different actor box sizes. Extracting actor features via cropping and resizing is helpful to improve the performance on small actor boxes

Size / Method	Extra small	Small	Medium	Large	Extra large
RoI Pooling	12.9	16.2	18.3	21.1	22.2
Crop+Resize	16.9	19.2	20.1	21.8	22.0
Improvement	+4.0	+3.0	+1.8	+0.7	−0.2

(c) Performance of different input resolutions using the cropping with resizing method. Input resolution is crucial for actor-centric action recognition

Resolution	224×224	192×192	160×160	112×112
mAP	25.0	24.3	23.7	21.4

(d) Performance comparison with different actor numbers in the frame. The performance decreases as more people appear in the key frame

Count / Method	$[1, 1]$	$[2, 3]$	$[4, 5]$	$[6, 7]$	$[8, 9]$	$[9, 37]$
RoI Pooling	29.2	23.7	25.3	25.1	22.4	17.2
Crop+Resize	35.2	25.9	27.1	27.6	26.3	22.9
Improvement	+6.0	+2.2	+1.8	+2.5	+3.9	+5.7

(e) Performance comparison when expanding actor bounding boxes by different scales. Here "*" indicates using RoI Pooling. The others use cropping with resizing

Max scale	1.2	1.5	1.8	2.0	2.5	1.5^{*}
mAP	24.1	25.0	24.8	25.0	24.3	21.6

We initialize the 3D ResNet-50 backbone network with non-local blocks by pre-training on action classification dataset Kinetics-400 [18]. The model using only actor feature and scene feature can be trained end-to-end. We follow [41] to train the model with long-term feature bank in two stages: we first fine-tune the 3D CNN to compute features for long-term feature bank. Then we fine-tune the whole model which aggregates long-term features and short-term features.

4.2 Ablation Study

In this subsection, we perform detailed ablation studies on the AVA dataset to investigate effects of different components in our model. This dataset provides a challenging benchmark for our analysis as it consists of a large set of examples.

RoI-Pooling v.s Crop+Resize. We begin our experiments by comparing RCNN-like method for extracting actor features with RoI-Pooling based method. To this end, we train the model only using actor features for action classification without using scene feature or long term feature. For RoI-Pooling baseline, following state-of-the-art methods [5,41], we first average pool the last feature map of res$_5$ over the time axis. Then RoIAlign [11] is used, followed by spatial max pooling, to yield a 2048-dimensional vector as actor features. The results are listed in Table 1a at different input frames. We first observe that taking more frames as inputs gives steady performance improvement, due to incorporating more temporal information. Moreover, using cropped and resized images as inputs brings a significant performance boost over the RoI-Pooling method across all temporal lengths. In particular, it achieves mAP of 25.0% only using non-local 3D ResNet-50 to extract actor features for action classification without context modeling. It outperforms RoI-Pooling method by 2.9%. We further perform a number of ablation experiments to better understand where does the gain come from. By default, $T \times \tau = 32 \times 2$ (sample 32-frame clip with temporal stride 2 as inputs) and cropping with resizing are used .

Impact of Box Size. Table 1b compares the performance with respect to the size of the actor bounding box. Following [7], we break down the performance of model into 5 bins according to the size of actor bounding box: "extra small", "small", "medium", "large" and "extra large". Each bin is defined by the thresholds of percentage image area covered by the box: $(0, 8.11\%)$ for "extra small", $(8.11\%, 17.11\%)$ for "small", $(17.11\%, 29.24\%)$ for "medium", $(29.24\%, 47.2\%)$ for "large", and $(47.2\%, 100.0\%)$ for "extra large". And every bin has similar ground truth box count on validation set. We split the prediction and ground truth boxes on validation set into bins, and evaluate mAP at each bin. We can see that bigger actor bounding boxes obtain better performance. The models perform poorly when actor boxes are small due to the lost of local detail information. Moreover, we find extracting actor features via cropping and resizing is helpful to improve the performance on small actor boxes, and offers similar performance on big actor boxes. This demonstrates that RoI-Pooling method losses discriminative spatial details of actors due to small resolution of actors in the RoI-Pooling layer. And RCNN-like method enlarges the actor input size which can help better preserve finer detail information. We believe this suggests a promising future research direction that extracts high-resolution representations for action recognition in action detection systems.

Impact of Input Resolution. We further investigate the effect of the actor input resolution. The actor boxes are cropped from the images and resized to different resolutions as network inputs for actor feature extraction. The results are reported in Table 1c. As expected, it shows that using low resolution images as inputs results in the performance drops dramatically. This confirms that input resolution is crucial for actor-centric action recognition.

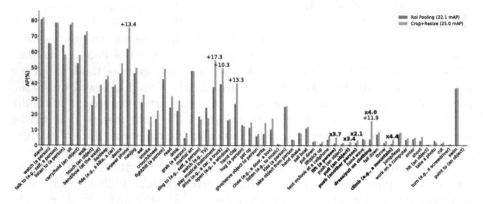

Fig. 4. Per-category AP on the AVA dataset. RoI-Pooling based method v.s RCNN-like method using cropping with resizing. Categories are sorted by the number of examples. (Green: 5 categories with largest absolute performance increase. **Bold**: 5 categories with largest relative performance increase. Orange: categories with decreased performance). (Color figure online)

Impact of Actor Count in the Scene. In Table 1d, we compare the performance with respect to the number of GT boxes in the key frame. The performance generally decreases as more people appear in the key frame. The RCNN-like method achieves significant improvements when there is only one person in the frame. We conjecture that single person scene relies more on local details for activity recognition. Moreover the performance improvement is also large when the scene has very many people where the actor boxes are often small.

How Does Performance Change Across Actions. Next, we compare the AP performance of RoI-Pooling baseline and RCNN-like method for each action class in Fig. 4. The action classes are sorted by the number of the examples. The RCNN-like method improves performance in 50 out of 60 classes. We highlight the 5 highest absolute performance increase categories and 5 largest relative increase categories. Recognizing these action labels correctly needs to focus on the local representative patterns around the actor (*e.g.* "musical instrument" for "play musical instrument"). RCNN-like method enlarges the resolution of small box and is able to focus on the local discriminative regions of the videos. The RCNN-like method yields slightly worse performance on 10 classes: "watch (*e.g.* TV)" (-6.8 AP), "listen to" (-6.1 AP), "sing to" (-1.9 AP) and so on. These are categories where modeling context information is critical. We conjecture that RoI-Pooling can incorporate scene information due to bigger receptive field. But RCNN-like method can only extract actor feature within the box. Such issues motivate us to explicitly compute context features in our framework.

Impact of the Scale to Expand Bounding Box. We experiment with different scales to expand the actor box. The results are shown in Table 1e. Expanding the bounding box slightly is helpful to improve performance of our model. However, too large scale hurts the performance due to incorporate redundant context information. We also conduct experiment based on RoI-Pooling, which shows it doesn't help to improve RoI-Pooling method ($22.1\% \rightarrow 21.6\%$). By default, the scale 1.5 is used in the experiments.

Table 2. AVA validation results using scene features and long-term features. We compare the performance of different methods to fuse context features. NL denotes Non-Local. Simple fusion methods (Concat, NL average) offer similar performance to complicated fusion methods

Scene feature	Long-term feature	mAP
–	–	24.7
Concat	–	25.7
Transformer+concat	-	25.8
Concat	NL attention	27.6
Concat	NL average	27.8
Concat	NL average w/o last linear	28.0

Trade-Off Between Performance and Time Efficiency. We measured the inference wall-clock time of RoI-Pooling based method and RCNN-like method on the validation set of the AVA dataset. The result is as follows: RoI-Pooling based method achieves mAP 22.1% using 4548 s. And RCNN-like method achieves mAP 25.0% using 7500 s. RCNN-like pipeline uses around $1.65\times$ more inference-time than RoI-Pooling based pipeline. RCNN-like pipeline achieves better recognition performance at the cost of more inference-time.

Impact of Context Modeling. We now extend our model to use scene features and long-term features as context information. The results are shown in

Table 3. Comparison with the state-of-the-art methods on the AVA and JHMDB datasets

(a) Comparison with state-of-the-art on the AVA v2.1

Method	Flow	Video pretrain	Backbone	mAP
AVA baseline [10]	✓	Kinetics-400	I3D	15.6
ACRN [31]	✓	Kinetics-400	S3D	17.4
Relation graph [44]		Kinetics-400	R50-NL	22.2
VAT [7]		Kinetics-400	I3D	25.0
SlowFast [5]		Kinetics-400	R50	24.2
SlowFast [5]		Kinetics-400	R101	26.3
SlowFast [5]		Kinetics-600	R101-NL	28.2
LFB [41]		Kinetics-400	R50-NL	25.8
LFB [41]		Kinetics-400	R101-NL	27.1
Context-Aware RCNN		Kinetics-400	R50-NL	28.0

(b) Comparison with state-of-the-art on the JHMDB dataset

Method	Flow	Video pretrain	Backbone	mAP
Two-stream RCNN [25]	✓		VGG	58.5
T-CNN [14]			C3D	61.3
ACT [17]	✓		VGG	65.7
AVA baseline [10]	✓	Kinetics-400	I3D	73.3
ACRN [31]	✓	Kinetics-400	S3D	77.9
Context-Aware RCNN		Kinetics-400	R50-NL	79.2

Table 2. We first study the effect of scene features which are extracted from the entire video clip. To reduce computational cost, we set $T \times \tau = 16 \times 4$ when scene features are used. We concatenate the scene features and actor features for action classification. We observe that the usage of scene features bring significant performance improvement ($24.7\% \rightarrow 25.7\%$). We also try to use actor features to attend to scene features in global feature map by Transformer-styled blocks [7], but fail to find they offer obvious performance improvement. We further add long-term features to our model, which are extracted by non-local function from long-term feature bank. Different from [41], we use a simplified non-local version as described in Sect. 3.3. We can see that incorporating long-term features leads to large performance gain ($25.7\% \rightarrow 28.0\%$). Moreover, our simplified non-local version can achieve slightly better results. Interestingly, using simple average pooling offers similar performance to using attention weighted sum.

4.3 Comparison with the State of the Art

We compare our model with the state-of-the-art methods in Table 3. For fair comparison, we consider methods that only use single model and single crop for testing. We also list other important factors such as backbone architectures.

Fig. 5. Visualization on the AVA dataset. For each example, we show the key frame with ground-truth boxes (Red) and predicted boxes (Green), together with surrounding 4 frames. The ground-truth and predicted labels are presented under the pictures. Multiple labels of one actor are marked with same text color, and actors are labeled from left to right. Our best model with mAP 28.0 is used. (Color figure online)

Table 3a shows the comparison with previous results on the AVA dataset. Under the similar settings, which use Kinetics-400 to pre-train and ResNet-50 as backbone, our method outperforms LFB [41] by 2.2% (28.0% versus 25.8%). Our ResNet-50 model even yields better performance than LFB using deeper ResNet-101 (28.0% versus 27.1%). Meanwhile, our model achieves comparable performance (28.0% versus 28.2%) to SlowFastNet [5] which use stronger backbone (SlowFast-ResNet-101) and more pre-training data (Kinetics-600).

We further evaluate our model on the JHMDB dataset. The results and comparison with previous methods are listed in Table 3b. We only use actor features and scene features for action classification, because the videos of JHMDB dataset are short. And $T \times \tau = 16 \times 4$ is used. Our method achieves the state-of-the-art performance of 79.2% by using only RGB frames. This outstanding performance shows the effectiveness and generality of our model.

4.4 Qualitative Results

Finally, we qualitatively visualize several example predictions on the AVA dataset in Fig. 5. As we can see, the difficulty in the AVA lies in actor-centric action recognition, and the actor localization is less challenging [10]. Overall, our model offers good action detection results, but still has difficulty to recognize action requiring fine grained discrimination. For the example in the bottom right corner, the model fails to predict the right person's answering phone action.

5 Conclusion

In this paper, we have revisited RCNN-like method to extract actor features via cropping and resizing in action detection framework. This approach provides a simple way to enlarge the input resolution of small actor boxes and preserve their discriminative spatial details. Moreover, we present a simple and effective Context-Aware RCNN for action detection which aggregates actor features, scene features and long-term features. It achieves state-of-the-art performance on challenging benchmarks. We conduct comprehensive ablation studies to validate the effectiveness of different components in our model. Our approach can serve as a simple and strong baseline for action detection. In the future, we plan to further study how to improve the sensitivity of action detection model to fine-grained details of human activities. Moreover, effective context reasoning method is also a promising research direction.

Acknowledgements. This work is supported by SenseTime Research Fund for Young Scholars, the National Science Foundation of China (No. 61921006), Program for Innovative Talents and Entrepreneur in Jiangsu Province, and Collaborative Innovation Center of Novel Software Technology and Industrialization.

References

1. Abu-El-Haija, S., et al.: Youtube-8M: A large-scale video classification benchmark. CoRR abs/1609.08675 (2016)
2. Carreira, J., Zisserman, A.: Quo vadis, action recognition? A new model and the kinetics dataset. In: CVPR, pp. 4724–4733 (2017)
3. Chao, Y., Vijayanarasimhan, S., Seybold, B., Ross, D.A., Deng, J., Sukthankar, R.: Rethinking the faster R-CNN architecture for temporal action localization. In: CVPR, pp. 1130–1139 (2018)
4. Cheng, B., Wei, Y., Shi, H., Feris, R., Xiong, J., Huang, T.: Revisiting RCNN: on awakening the classification power of faster RCNN. In: Ferrari, V., Hebert, M., Sminchisescu, C., Weiss, Y. (eds.) ECCV 2018. LNCS, vol. 11219, pp. 473–490. Springer, Cham (2018). https://doi.org/10.1007/978-3-030-01267-0_28
5. Feichtenhofer, C., Fan, H., Malik, J., He, K.: Slowfast networks for video recognition. CoRR abs/1812.03982 (2018)
6. Gan, C., Wang, N., Yang, Y., Yeung, D., Hauptmann, A.G.: DevNet: a deep event network for multimedia event detection and evidence recounting. In: CVPR, pp. 2568–2577 (2015)
7. Girdhar, R., Carreira, J., Doersch, C., Zisserman, A.: Video action transformer network. In: CVPR, pp. 244–253 (2019)
8. Girshick, R.B.: Fast R-CNN. In: ICCV, pp. 1440–1448 (2015)
9. Girshick, R.B., Donahue, J., Darrell, T., Malik, J.: Rich feature hierarchies for accurate object detection and semantic segmentation. In: CVPR, pp. 580–587 (2014)
10. Gu, C., et al.: AVA: a video dataset of spatio-temporally localized atomic visual actions. In: CVPR, pp. 6047–6056 (2018)
11. He, K., Gkioxari, G., Dollár, P., Girshick, R.B.: Mask R-CNN. In: ICCV, pp. 2980–2988 (2017)
12. He, K., Zhang, X., Ren, S., Sun, J.: Spatial pyramid pooling in deep convolutional networks for visual recognition. In: Fleet, D., Pajdla, T., Schiele, B., Tuytelaars, T. (eds.) ECCV 2014. LNCS, vol. 8691, pp. 346–361. Springer, Cham (2014). https://doi.org/10.1007/978-3-319-10578-9_23
13. He, K., Zhang, X., Ren, S., Sun, J.: Deep residual learning for image recognition. In: CVPR, pp. 770–778 (2016)

14. Hou, R., Chen, C., Shah, M.: Tube convolutional neural network (T-CNN) for action detection in videos. In: ICCV, pp. 5823–5832 (2017)
15. Jhuang, H., Gall, J., Zuffi, S., Schmid, C., Black, M.J.: Towards understanding action recognition. In: ICCV, pp. 3192–3199 (2013)
16. Ji, S., Xu, W., Yang, M., Yu, K.: 3D convolutional neural networks for human action recognition. In: ICML, pp. 495–502 (2010)
17. Kalogeiton, V., Weinzaepfel, P., Ferrari, V., Schmid, C.: Action tubelet detector for spatio-temporal action localization. In: ICCV, pp. 4415–4423 (2017)
18. Kay, W., et al.: The kinetics human action video dataset. CoRR abs/1705.06950 (2017)
19. Krizhevsky, A., Sutskever, I., Hinton, G.E.: ImageNet classification with deep convolutional neural networks. In: NIPS, pp. 1106–1114 (2012)
20. Kuehne, H., Jhuang, H., Garrote, E., Poggio, T.A., Serre, T.: HMDB: a large video database for human motion recognition. In: ICCV, pp. 2556–2563 (2011)
21. LeCun, Y., Bottou, L., Bengio, Y., Haffner, P.: Gradient-based learning applied to document recognition. Proc. IEEE **86**(11), 2278–2324 (1998)
22. Li, Y., Wang, Z., Wang, L., Wu, G.: Actions as moving points. CoRR abs/2001.04608 (2020)
23. Lin, T., Zhao, X., Su, H., Wang, C., Yang, M.: BSN: boundary sensitive network for temporal action proposal generation. In: Ferrari, V., Hebert, M., Sminchisescu, C., Weiss, Y. (eds.) ECCV 2018. LNCS, vol. 11208, pp. 3–21. Springer, Cham (2018). https://doi.org/10.1007/978-3-030-01225-0_1
24. Ng, J.Y., Hausknecht, M.J., Vijayanarasimhan, S., Vinyals, O., Monga, R., Toderici, G.: Beyond short snippets: deep networks for video classification. In: CVPR, pp. 4694–4702 (2015)
25. Peng, X., Schmid, C.: Multi-region two-stream R-CNN for action detection. In: Leibe, B., Matas, J., Sebe, N., Welling, M. (eds.) ECCV 2016. LNCS, vol. 9908, pp. 744–759. Springer, Cham (2016). https://doi.org/10.1007/978-3-319-46493-0_45
26. Qiu, Z., Yao, T., Mei, T.: Learning spatio-temporal representation with pseudo-3D residual networks. In: ICCV, pp. 5534–5542 (2017)
27. Ren, S., He, K., Girshick, R.B., Sun, J.: Faster R-CNN: towards real-time object detection with region proposal networks. In: NIPS, pp. 91–99 (2015)
28. Simonyan, K., Zisserman, A.: Two-stream convolutional networks for action recognition in videos. In: NIPS, pp. 568–576 (2014)
29. Simonyan, K., Zisserman, A.: Very deep convolutional networks for large-scale image recognition. In: ICLR (2015)
30. Soomro, K., Zamir, A.R., Shah, M.: UCF101: a dataset of 101 human actions classes from videos in the wild. CoRR abs/1212.0402 (2012)
31. Sun, C., Shrivastava, A., Vondrick, C., Murphy, K., Sukthankar, R., Schmid, C.: Actor-centric relation network. In: Ferrari, V., Hebert, M., Sminchisescu, C., Weiss, Y. (eds.) ECCV 2018. LNCS, vol. 11215, pp. 335–351. Springer, Cham (2018). https://doi.org/10.1007/978-3-030-01252-6_20
32. Szegedy, C., et al.: Going deeper with convolutions. In: CVPR, pp. 1–9 (2015)
33. Tran, D., Bourdev, L.D., Fergus, R., Torresani, L., Paluri, M.: Learning spatiotemporal features with 3D convolutional networks. In: ICCV, pp. 4489–4497 (2015)
34. Tran, D., Wang, H., Torresani, L., Ray, J., LeCun, Y., Paluri, M.: A closer look at spatiotemporal convolutions for action recognition. In: CVPR, pp. 6450–6459 (2018)
35. Vaswani, A., et al.: Attention is all you need. In: NIPS, pp. 5998–6008 (2017)
36. Wang, L., Qiao, Y., Tang, X.: Action recognition with trajectory-pooled deep-convolutional descriptors. In: CVPR, pp. 4305–4314 (2015)

37. Wang, L., Qiao, Y., Tang, X., Van Gool, L.: Actionness estimation using hybrid fully convolutional networks. In: CVPR, pp. 2708–2717 (2016)
38. Wang, L., Xiong, Y., Lin, D., Van Gool, L.: UntrimmedNets for weakly supervised action recognition and detection. In: CVPR, pp. 6402–6411 (2017)
39. Wang, L., et al.: Temporal segment networks: towards good practices for deep action recognition. In: Leibe, B., Matas, J., Sebe, N., Welling, M. (eds.) ECCV 2016. LNCS, vol. 9912, pp. 20–36. Springer, Cham (2016). https://doi.org/10.1007/978-3-319-46484-8_2
40. Wang, X., Girshick, R.B., Gupta, A., He, K.: Non-local neural networks. In: CVPR, pp. 7794–7803 (2018)
41. Wu, C., Feichtenhofer, C., Fan, H., He, K., Krähenbühl, P., Girshick, R.B.: Long-term feature banks for detailed video understanding. In: CVPR, pp. 284–293 (2019)
42. Xie, S., Sun, C., Huang, J., Tu, Z., Murphy, K.: Rethinking spatiotemporal feature learning for video understanding. CoRR abs/1712.04851 (2017)
43. Zhang, S., Guo, S., Huang, W., Scott, M.R., Wang, L.: V4D: 4D convolutional neural networks for video-level representation learning. In: ICLR (2020)
44. Zhang, Y., Tokmakov, P., Hebert, M., Schmid, C.: A structured model for action detection. In: CVPR, pp. 9975–9984 (2019)
45. Zhao, Y., Xiong, Y., Wang, L., Wu, Z., Tang, X., Lin, D.: Temporal action detection with structured segment networks. Int. J. Comput. Vis. 128(1), 74–95 (2020)

Full-Time Monocular Road Detection Using Zero-Distribution Prior of Angle of Polarization

Ning Li[1], Yongqiang Zhao[1](✉), Quan Pan[1], Seong G. Kong[2],
and Jonathan Cheung-Wai Chan[3]

[1] Northwestern Polytechnical University, Xi'an 710072, China
ln_neo@mail.nwpu.edu.cn, {zhaoyq,quanpan}@nwpu.edu.cn
[2] Sejong University, Seoul 05006, South Korea
skong@sejong.edu
[3] Vrije Universiteit Brussel, 1050 Brussel, Belgium
jcheungw@etrovub.be

Abstract. This paper presents a road detection technique based on long-wave infrared (LWIR) polarization imaging for autonomous navigation regardless of illumination conditions, day and night. Division of Focal Plane (DoFP) imaging technology enables acquisition of infrared polarization images in real time using a monocular camera. Zero-distribution prior embodies the zero-distribution of Angle of Polarization (AoP) of a road scene image, which provides a significant contrast between the road and the background. This paper combines zero-distribution of AoP, the difference of Degree of linear Polarization (DoP), and the edge information to segment the road region in the scene. We developed a LWIR DoFP Dataset of Road Scene (LDDRS) consisting of 2,113 annotated images. Experiment results on the LDDRS dataset demonstrate the merits of the proposed road detection method based on the zero-distribution prior. The LDDRS dataset is available at https://github.com/polwork/LDDRS.

Keywords: Road detection · Polarization prior · Angle of Polarization · LWIR DoFP sensor

1 Introduction

Road detection is a crucial task for traffic safety and intelligent transportation systems such as Advanced Driver Assistant System (ADAS) [17]. Various sensing modalities such as vision [21,32,42,49] and LiDAR [26,29] have been used for this purpose. Vision-based methods include passive monocular [21,32] and the stereo imaging [42,49], which provides high resolution color, texture and

Electronic supplementary material The online version of this chapter (https://doi.org/10.1007/978-3-030-58595-2_28) contains supplementary material, which is available to authorized users.

© Springer Nature Switzerland AG 2020
A. Vedaldi et al. (Eds.): ECCV 2020, LNCS 12370, pp. 457–473, 2020.
https://doi.org/10.1007/978-3-030-58595-2_28

lane marking information for road detection. Stereo imaging can obtain depth information, but still less information than 3D LiDAR. Vision-based methods, however, are unable to perform properly in low illumination conditions, darkness, and strong illumination variations such as headlight of incoming cars at night. LiDAR is an active modality for lane and road detection, measuring 3D structure of a vehicle nearby using an active light source enabling LiDAR to be employed all the time, day and night. A major drawback of LiDAR is relatively high cost and bulkiness. While thermal infrared cameras are often used for pedestrian/animal detection [5,23], but not for road detection since radiation difference between road and the background is too small especially at night when thermal equilibrium is reached.

Polarization has a physical property of light that provides characteristic information of an object such as three-dimensional (3D) normal [38], surface smoothness [43], and material composition [18]. Polarization imaging has been widely applied in 3D reconstruction [9], anti-interference object detection [24], visual navigation [40], image dehazing [41], and biomedical imaging [13]. To our best knowledge, no published literatures have investigated the use of polarization for road detection. Division of Focal Plane (DoFP) imaging technology [12,44] enables acquisition of infrared polarization images in real time with a monocular camera. A DoFP infrared polarization camera consists of traditional infrared focal plane and a micro polarizer array which captures polarization information in real time. DoFP cameras have similar dimensions, weight, and power consumption as traditional uncooled thermal cameras, suitable for installing on vehicles in real situations. We use a long-wave infrared (LWIR) DoFP polarimeter as sensing modality to obtain polarization characteristics of the road.

This paper presents a road detection method based on zero-distribution prior of the road. Zero-distribution prior embodies the zero-distribution of Angle of Polarization (AoP) of the road region, which provides a significant contrast between the road and the background. Using this prior, a coarse mask for the road region is obtained. Then we propose a statistical method with road vanishing assumption to locate the horizon. The road area is located usually in the lower part of the horizon to significantly reduce computational burden. This paper combines zero-distribution of AoP, the difference of Degree of linear Polarization (DoP), and the edge information to segment the road region in the scene. Then we refine the detection result by removing fragmented parts using a confidence map. The definitions of AoP and DoP can be found in the Supplementary Material. To evaluate the proposed method, we captured thousands of LWIR DoFP images of various road scenes, including urban roads and highways during day and night times. A total of 2,113 annotated LWIR DoFP images forms a benchmark database named LWIR DoFP Dataset of Road Scenes (LDDRS).

As contributions, this paper proposes: (1) A zero-distribution prior to represent distinctive characteristics of the road; (2) A statistical method to detect the horizon; (3) A joint road detection approach to segment the road; (4) A database of LWIR DoFP images for benchmarking road detection algorithms.

2   Related Works

Thermal Sensor: As the most related work, LWIR imagers are mainly used in ADAS [5] to detect pedestrians or animals at night since emitted radiation of human is greater than the environment. Several methods have been developed to detect the pedestrian, including enhanced thresholding segmentation technique [36], adaptive fuzzy C-means clustering, and CNN based approach [19]. LWIR imagers are also used to improve the road detection in low light conditions by thermal-RGB fusion [48], stereo thermal cameras [34], or multi-frames information [47]. Yet thermal characteristics between road and the background may reach equilibrium at night.

Monocular Vision: Many road detection methods have been developed for conventional RGB cameras based on high-resolution intensity, color, and texture information. Some constrain the road region by detecting lane markings. Wang *et al.* [46] use a straight-curve model to detect curvy road in highways. Some road models are based on the statistics or shape information to segment the road. Lu [30] proposed a self-learned statistical model to re-label each pixel in the input image based on a likelihood ratio classifier. Other road segmentation methods use vanishing point to constrain road boundary. For example, a Gabor filter [21] and a gLoG filter [22] are used to locate the vanishing point of road with a voting-based scheme. Inspired by the Fully Convolutional Network (FCN) [28] designed for semantic segmentation task, several road detection methods are proposed based on deep learning including Up-Conv-Poly [32], FCN-LC [31] and DLT-Net [37]. Utilizing the pixel-wise classification of FCN, these methods have enhanced road detection performances. However, the inherent drawback of visible camera in low light condition limits the performance of a monocular vision system at night or in low illumination conditions.

Stereo Imaging and LiDAR: A disparity map [14] generated by stereo matching of two captured visible images can provide depth information to play a key role in road detection. The traditional vanishing-point-constraint methods [33,49] and deep learning method [39] based on a disparity map are developed in stereo vision system. Unfortunately, this approach also suffers from the same limitation with the monocular vision system in low light environments. LiDAR, on the other hand, uses an active light source to reconstruct 3D representation of an object. As an active perception modality, LiDAR provides a strong cue to detect road as used in several works [16,26,29,50]. However, the detection accuracy is easily affected by dust, haze or rain [35].

3   Zero-Distribution Prior

The zero-distribution prior is based on the theory that thermal emissions are partially linearly polarized parallel to the plane of incidence [9]. For a road region, most values of AoP are near zero,

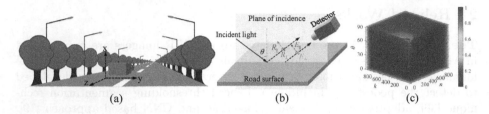

Fig. 1. (a) The image coordinate system of LWIR DoFP camera. (b) Mode of how the thermal radiation captured by detector is formed in LWIR. (c) $\varepsilon_\|(\theta, n')^2 - \varepsilon_\perp(\theta, n')^2$ vary with respect to θ, n and k

$$A(x) \approx 0, x \in \Omega \tag{1}$$

where A denotes an AoP image and Ω denotes a set of pixels in the road region. This characteristic of AoP in the road region is called *zero-distribution prior of AoP*. In Fig. 1(a), we assume that the road plane is parallel with the y axis in the image coordinate system, so zero-distribution of AoP means that the thermal radiations of road are partially linearly polarized parallel to x-z plane of an incident light in Fig. 1(b). Therefore, the Stokes parameter S_1 of road should be positive and S_2 should near zero (see Supplementary Materials for definition of S_1 and S_2). Figure 1(b) shows that the thermal radiation reaches the DoFP LWIR detector contains reflected radiation R and emitted radiation E, and both are expressed as the sum of two orthogonal polarized components, i.e. $R = R_\| + R_\perp$ and $E = E_\| + E_\perp$. For the road scene, the emitted thermal radiation dominates the energies that reach the camera. In [4], S_2 of thermal emissions have been demonstrated to be zero for objects that are large compared to the emitted wavelength [20], so here we only focus on the sign of S_1. Based on Kirchoff's law [45] and Fresnel's equations [15], we have (See Supplementary Material for derivation)

$$S_1 = n \cos\theta \cdot P(T_1)^2 \cdot \left(\varepsilon_\|(\theta, n')^2 - \varepsilon_\perp(\theta, n')^2\right) \tag{2}$$

where $P(T_1)$ denotes the Planck Blackbody radiance curve at temperature T_1 of road, ε is the emissivity and the special subscripts $\|$ and $\perp$ are added to ε that correspond to respectively the polarized components parallel and perpendicular to the plane of incidence, and ε is decided by incident angle θ and complex index of refraction $n' = n + ki$ of road. So the sign of S_1 is decided by the sign of $\varepsilon_\|(\theta, n')^2 - \varepsilon_\perp(\theta, n')^2$ because $n > 0$ and $\cos\theta > 0$ ($\theta \in (0, 90°)$). Since the exact refraction of the road is unknown, the intervals are set to $n \in (0, 1000]$ and $k \in (0, 1000]$. We calculate the value of $\varepsilon_\|(\theta, n')^2 - \varepsilon_\perp(\theta, n')^2$ and plot the result with θ, n and k in Fig. 1(c). The quantity $\varepsilon_\|(\theta, n')^2 - \varepsilon_\perp(\theta, n')^2$ is positive in a sufficiently large interval, so S_1 is also positive. We further make a statistical analysis of the distribution of S_1 and S_2 in road region of 2,113 images in Fig. 3(a) where basically all the values of S_1 in road region are positive and most values of S_2 are around zero. Since the S_1 in road region is positive and S_2 is close to zero, the AoP of road is zero distributed. Figure 2 shows several road scene images

Fig. 2. Top: example images in our DoFP road scene database. Bottom: the corresponding AoP images

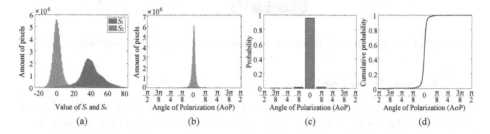

Fig. 3. (a) The distribution of S_1 and S_2 in road region of the 2,113 road images. (b) Histogram of the AoP of the pixels in road region of all the 2,113 road images, and (c) Corresponding probability distribution and (d) Cumulative distribution

and the corresponding AoP images in false color. A statistical analysis of the distribution of AoP A in road region of the 2,113 images produces the results in Fig. 3(b)–(d). Approximately 96% of the pixels of road in the AoP images have values in $\left(-\frac{\pi}{16}, \frac{\pi}{16}\right)$, so most AoP values in road region are near zero. Using this property, more generally, the AoP of each position in a plane is the same. Intuitively, the proposed prior can also be effective for other applications such as plane detection or defect detection in roads (e.g. potholes or obstacles). In Sect. 4, this prior is used to detect the horizon and segment the road.

4   Road Detection with Zero-Distribution Prior

The proposed zero-distribution prior poses a strong constraint on road detection. Figure 4 shows the proposed road detection method based on the zero-distribution prior. An input DoFP image is denoised [1] and demosaicked [25] to generate four high resolution polarization images and then the Stokes parameters, AoP and DoP are computed (See Eqs. (1) and (2) in Supplementary Material). We use the zero-distribution prior for horizon detection, and the road region is restricted under the horizon in the image. Then we propose a joint road detection method that combines AoP, DoP, and the edge information to segment the road. The final road detection result is obtained by refining a road confidence map.

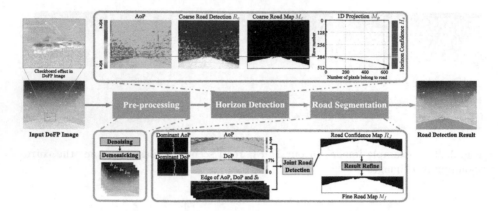

Fig. 4. The proposed road detection method based on the zero-distribution prior

4.1 Horizon Detection

A coarse road map is obtained based on the strong constraint of zero-distribution prior. Since the value of AoP in road region is near zero, we find a coarse road estimation using

$$R_c(x) = \exp(-\gamma |A(x) - \sigma|) \tag{3}$$

where x is pixel position, γ was set to 0.01 and σ was set to 0 in the experiment based on the zero-distribution prior. Then, we threshold $t = 0.75$ as the road, followed by a morphological open operation to remove the small noise regions:

$$M_c = \Im(R_c, t) \odot X \ , \ \ \Im(R_c, t) = \begin{cases} 1, R_c \geq t \\ 0, R_c < t \end{cases} \tag{4}$$

where $\odot$ is the morphological open operation and X is the structural element. M_c provides a coarse road detection result, and a horizon locates where the road vanishes. As the road vanishes in Fig. 4, the number of pixels belonging to road in each row decreases from bottom to top. We make a one-dimensional (1D) projection of the coarse road map M_c by

$$M_p(r) = \sum_{j=1}^{w} M_c(r, j) \tag{5}$$

where w is the width of the image, r is the row number and M_p represents the number of pixels that belong to road in each row in M_c. In Fig. 4, the horizon corresponds to the intersection of the green line and the x-axis in M_p. Horizon can be obtained by locating where they intersect. Rather than fitting the straight line in M_p directly, we propose to find the position in x-axis where the lines (determined by every two points that have fixed rows apart in M_p) intersect with x-axis most. To realize this, a horizon confidence map is generated by

$$H(r) = \sum_{l=1}^{h-s} [\wp((l, M_p(l)), (l+s, M_p(l+s))) = r] \tag{6}$$

where h is the height of the image, l is the row number and $\wp(\mathbf{x}, \mathbf{y})$ indicates the row where the straight line (determined by $\mathbf{x}$ and $\mathbf{y}$) intersects with the x-axis in M_p, and here we choose every two points that have two rows apart, that is $s = 3$. $[\cdot]$ equals 1 if the value inside the bracket is true and 0 otherwise. One may notice that the biggest value or the dominant values in H may lie several pixels away from the ground-truth horizon. To overcome this problem, we propose a simple post-processing of H by

$$H_e(r) = \sum_{i=r-\rho}^{r+\rho} H(i) \tag{7}$$

where H_e is the piecewise cumulative energy of H, and we set $\rho = 3$. With this simple step, we improve the robustness of horizon detection and we can locate the horizon by finding the biggest energy in H_e, as shown by the red line in Fig. 4. The proposed horizon detection method is efficient and robust, and the road is restricted in the lower part of the image.

4.2   Road Segmentation

In Sect. 4.1, we generate a coarse road detection result with the strong constraint of zero-distribution prior, and the horizon restrict the road in a small part of the image which reduces the computation load. The AoP for car surface are similar to that of the road as in Fig. 2 and Fig. 6(c). Therefore, cars can be misclassified as the road if we only use the zero-distribution prior. There exist some differences in DoP between the road and cars. The DoP of the hood and windshield of a car is usually higher than the DoP of the road, while the other surfaces of a car are always lower than that of the road as shown in Fig. 6(b). This observation agrees with previous research for vehicle detection [10,11]. We selected 200 images that contain various vehicles and computed the DoP distribution of the road and cars. Figure 5 shows that clear differences of DoP exist between road and vehicle (See Supplementary Material for details). This characteristic helps separate the vehicle and road. This paper combines the AoP, DoP and the edge information for road detection. Inspired by [27], the road confidence map is obtained by the proposed joint road detection as:

$$R_J(x) = \frac{2}{1 + \exp\left[\eta\left(1 + \eta_1 C_E(x)\right)\left(C_A(x) + C_D(x)\right)\right]} \tag{8}$$

where

$$C_A(x) = \begin{cases} \exp\left[\eta_2\left(|A(x) - A_d| - \alpha_1\right)\right], A(x) \geq A_d \\ \exp\left[\eta_2\left(|A(x) - A_d| - \alpha_2\right)\right], A(x) < A_d \end{cases} \tag{9}$$

$$C_D(x) = \begin{cases} \exp\left[\eta_3\left(|D(x) - D_d| - \beta_1\right)\right], D(x) \geq D_d \\ \exp\left[\eta_3\left(|D(x) - D_d| - \beta_2\right)\right], D(x) < D_d \end{cases} \tag{10}$$

$$C_E(x) = \omega_1 E_D(x) + \omega_2 E_A(x) + \omega_3 E_I(x) \tag{11}$$

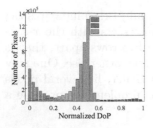

Fig. 5. Histogram of range normalized DoP in road and different part of vehicle regions of 200 road scenes

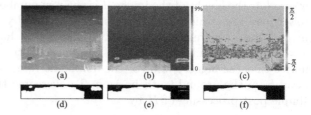

Fig. 6. (a) Intensity image. (b) DoP image in false color. (c) AoP image in false color. (d) Coarse road map. (e) Road confidence map. (f) Refined road detection result. (d)–(f) only shows the region below the horizon

where C_A is the constraint of AoP image A, C_D is the constraint of DoP image D, and C_E is the edge constraint. In Eq. (11), E_D, E_A and E_I are edge information of DoP image, AoP image and the intensity image (S_0), respectively, and ω_1, ω_2 and ω_3 are corresponding weights ($\omega_1 = 0.3$, $\omega_2 = 0.5$ and $\omega_3 = 0.2$). η, η_1, η_2 and η_3 are weights of above three constraints ($\eta = 10^{-7}$, $\eta_1 = 1.9$, $\eta_2 = 0.2$ and $\eta_3 = 0.2$ in our experiment). A_d and D_d are dominate values of AoP and DoP in road region respectively obtained by the statistics of A and D of the road region in coarse road map M_c. The bias terms $\alpha_1 = \frac{\pi}{50}$, $\alpha_2 = \frac{\pi}{16}$, $\beta_1 = \beta_0 + 0.02$, $\beta_2 = \beta_0 + 0.12$ and β_0 is set as the half of the distribution range of the most DoP in road region. With Eq. (8), a pixel belongs to road will get a higher value near 1, and near 0 if otherwise. One can notice that for the constraint of AoP and DoP images in Eqs. (9) and (10), we punish the values greater than A_d and D_d more, because the shadow or wet areas of road usually have lower AoP and DoP values. The edges of DoP image, AoP image and the intensity image provide the road boundary information, so C_E is used to separate the road with other region by giving more punishment on strong edge.

With the road confidence map R_J, we can get a refined road map. First, the pixels in R_J are binarized by $\Im(R_J, \tau)$ and $\tau = 0.95$, and we assume that m separated regions $K(i), i = 1...m$ are obtained. Then remove all the small pieces whose areas $N_{K(i)}$ (defined as the number of pixels belong to $K(i)$) are smaller than 2% of the total detected area $N_t = \sum_{i=1}^{m} N_{K(i)}$. We take the biggest one in $K(i)$ as road and we can compute the mean DoP D_m and mean intensity I_m of road region. The remaining small pieces whose mean DoP or intensity value are different from D_m or I_m more than the preset threshold will be simply removed ($\tau_I = 40$ in 8 bit image and $\tau_D = \beta_0$). Finally, the refined road map M_f is obtained by applying the background region growing to fill the holes in road region.

For the road scene in Fig. 6, the front and back windshields are detected as road in the coarse road map (Fig. 6(d)). But these false detections are mostly removed with the proposed joint road detection method (Fig. 6(e)). And the refined detection result is obtained after removing small speckles in the road

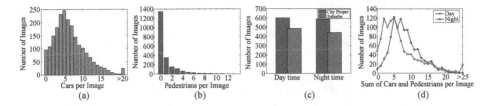

Fig. 7. Object geometry statistics of LDDRS. Histograms for the two most predominant categories (a) 'cars' and (b) 'pedestrians'. (c) Data distribution from day to night in city proper and suburbs. (d) Histograms for sum of cars and pedestrians at day and night

confidence map (Fig. 6(f)). The proposed joint road detection is applied only in the part under the horizon detected in the last section. The proposed road detection method is simple yet efficient and robust with the constraint of the zero-distribution prior. The performance of the proposed method will be demonstrated in Sect. 5.

5   Experiment Results

Dataset. The proposed method is based on LWIR polarization imaging. To our best knowledge, there is no existing dataset with this specific information/feature available for the work. The only related LWIR dataset is described in KAIST [8]; its images of road are with only intensity information, no polarization. To test the proposed method, we build a LWIR DoFP dataset of road scene (LDDRS) with 2,113 images which provides both IR intensity (S_0) and polarization information. The DoFP images are captured with a self-developed uncooled infrared DoFP camera with 512×640 resolution in 14 bits. The dataset includes urban road and highway both day and night. The road regions of all 2,113 images are manually annotated. Statistics of our LDDRS are shown in Fig. 7. LDDRS contains different traffic situations that there are different number of cars and pedestrians in road scene. For the input DoFP images, a BM3D method [1] is used to reduce the noise and then a polarization demosaicking method [25] with a polarization difference model is applied to generate four high resolution images in four orientations. Based on these four images, the AoP, DoP and intensity images can be obtained by using the Stokes equations [15].

Evaluation on Horizon Detection. First, we evaluate the performance of our proposed horizon detection method. The error between the estimation and the ground-truth horizon is defined as the absolute difference in their vertical coordinates. Figure 8 shows quantitative assessment of the proposed method. The horizontal axis of Fig. 8 represents the distance errors, where about 80% of horizon detection results have distance error smaller than 15 pixels. The horizon detection is used to improve the road detection robustness and effectiveness.

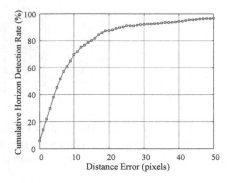

Fig. 8. Statistics of the horizon estimation accuracy of the proposed method

Table 1. Results of road detection with and without horizon constraint

Methods	PRE (%)	REC (%)	IoU (%)	Running time (ms)
w/o horizon constraint	72.65	71.87	67.52	194
with horizon constraint	93.48	94.50	88.69	67

To further test the necessity of horizon detection, we evaluate the road detection performance with and without horizon constraint. And three evaluation criteria are used including precision (PRE), recall (REC), and Intersection over Union (IoU) to assess the performance of road detection. Table 1 shows that the road detection performance is improved by over 20% and execution efficiency increased by about three times when with horizon constraint, which demonstrates the necessity of horizon detection.

Evaluation on Road Segmentation. To evaluate the performance of different road detection methods, PRE, REC and IoU are used as assessment criteria. For comparison, three kinds of single image road detection methods are chosen. First kind of road detection method is designed especially for thermal infrared sensors such as the region-growing based method [47] which applies temporal information of sequential frames to refine the drivable region detection. The second kind of road detection method uses a predefined road mask to build a statistical model for road and background such as SSRD [30] which applies a self-learned statistical model to re-label each pixel in the input image base on a likelihood ratio classifier. The third kind is the deep-learning based semantic segmentation methods such as DeepLab series [6,7], encoder-decoder network [3], FCN [28] and so on, are most powerful methods for pixelwise classification. Here we use the DeepLabv3+ [7] in our dataset to test the performance of road segmentation.

The region-growing based method [47] is applied to the intensity image, as denoted as RG. The SSRD method is applied on the HSV fusion [2] image (Fig. 10(b)) of intensity image, AoP image and DoP image. The DeepLabv3+ is test on the intensity image, RGB fusion image (fusion of intensity image,

Fig. 9. Comparison of the road detection accuracy. Green region corresponds to true positive. Red region represents false negative. Blue region denotes false positive. (Color figure online)

Table 2. Results comparison of different road detection methods, the best results are shown in bold

Methods	PRE (%)	REC (%)	IoU (%)
RG [47]	74.68	87.40	67.69
SSRD [30]	82.45	83.76	71.60
DeepLabv3+ [7] with intensity image	79.65	**99.35**	79.28
DeepLabv3+ [7] with RGB fusion image	87.88	98.65	86.90
DeepLabv3+ [7] with HSV fusion image	89.34	99.19	88.73
Proposed method on test set	93.19	94.84	**88.74**
Proposed method on whole set	**93.48**	94.50	88.69

AoP image and DoP image in R, G, B channels respectively) and the HSV fusion image and are denoted as DL3p_I (DeepLabv3+ with the intensity image), DL3p_RGB (DeepLabv3+ with the RGB fusion image) and DL3p_HSV (DeepLabv3+ with the HSV fusion image) respectively. For DeepLabv3+, ResNet-101 is used as network backbone. And for dataset split, 1690 images are randomly selected for training, 211 images are used for validation and the rest 212 images are used for test. Considering the limited size of our LDDRS dataset, the DeepLabv3+ is initially trained with KAIST thermal infrared road scene dataset [47], and then the final model is fine-tuned using our training images. The quantitative assessments for these methods are shown in Table 2. Figure 9 shows some visual comparison results of road region detection by the above methods, and for all the visual results, green region corresponds to true positive, red region represents false negative and blue region denotes false positive.

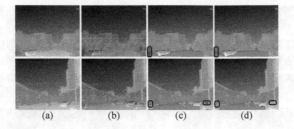

(a)   (b)   (c)   (d)

Fig. 10. (a) Intensity image. (b) HSV fusion image. (c) Results based on DeepLabv3+ with the HSV image. (d) Ours results

Table 3. Comparison of AoP-DoP-edge constraint and AoP constraint only

Constraints	PRE (%)	REC (%)	IoU (%)
AoP only	90.21	94.12	85.41
AoP+DoP+Edge	93.48	94.50	88.69

Table 2 and Fig. 9 show that the proposed method outperforms conventional techniques, and achieve comparable results with the state-of-the-art deep learning method DeepLabv3+. The recall of our method is not as high as other methods because our scheme tends to detect the road as accurate as possible and the low confidence pixels and small pieces that belong to road are discarded in the refinement process, which leads to a lower recall. Besides, the proposed method achieves highest precision especially for the separation between car and road. For example, as shown in the regions delineated in black rectangles in Fig. 10, the windshield of car and road are similar in the HSV fusion image and low occurrence of vehicle hoods compared with the road surface, making this particularity difficult to learn, so the DL3p_HSV method may wrongly detect this car part as road while our method performs well. Methods using intensity image, including RG and DeepLabv3+, have good recall performance but poor precision, because it is difficult to separate road and cars or the background when they have similar thermal radiation. In contrast, methods apply polarization information such as SSRD, DeepLabv3+ and our method perform well both on precision and recall and have higher IoU, which demonstrates the power of the infrared polarization imaging in augmenting the full-time road detection. On the other hand, DeepLabv3+ road detection methods trained with the HSV fusion image outperform that trained with RGB fusion image, because HSV fusion of polarization images can reveal polarization characteristics better than the RGB fusion.

To evaluate how different traffic situations affect the road detection performance of different methods, we test the above road detection methods when the scenes contain different number of cars and pedestrians. Figure 11(a) shows that most methods cannot detect road well under a complex road condition except for the DL3p_HSV and our method. The performance of the methods using inten-

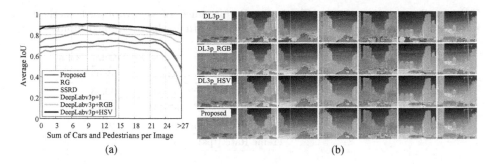

(a)   (b)

Fig. 11. (a) Average IoU performance when there are different number of cars and pedestrians in scene. (b) Comparison of DeepLabv3+ methods and our method under several difficult traffic situations

sity image and SSRD decline after there are more than 22 cars and pedestrians in scene while our method and the DeepLabv3+ methods trained with HSV fusion image still work well. Figure 11(b) shows the comparison of DeepLabv3+ methods and our method under several difficult traffic situations. When there are many cars in image, DL3p_I may wrongly detect parts of car as road because these parts may have similar thermal radiation with road. DL3p_HSV and DL3p_RGB benefit from the polarization information and obtain more compelling performance under these difficult situations. The proposed method separates most of cars from road with the strong constraint of the proposed zero-distribution prior and the difference of DoP.

To demonstrate the power of the proposed zero-distribution prior, we test the performance of our road detection method with the AoP constraint only and with the AoP-DoP-edge constraint, the results are shown in Table 3. Note that the result of AoP constraint only is obtained by simply removing all the small pieces whose areas are smaller than 2% of the total detected area in M_c under the detected horizon. The road detection performance of our proposed method with only AoP constraint is still better than most of other methods except the DeepLabv3+ with the HSV and RGB fusion images. The AoP constraint have low precision performance due to the similar AoP between road and vehicle, where the DoP-and-edge constraint is used to solve this problem. More results of road detection videos, horizon detection and different traffic situations can be found in the Supplementary Material.

Evaluation on Execution Efficiency. The computational time is also an important factor for ADAS to evaluate road detection method. Our method is implemented in Matlab and tested on a general PC with 64 GB memory and Intel Xeon E3-1225 CPU. The DeepLabv3+ method is tested on a GTX 1080Ti GPU, and other methods are tested in a same PC which runs our method. The average running time of a 512×640 input image is shown in Table 4, and the time of denoising and demosaicking is discarded here. On the average, it takes 0.067 s for the proposed method to process an image and it is 5 times faster than the

Table 4. Running time comparison of different methods

Methods	Time (s/frame)
RG	2.761
SSRD	17.32
DeepLabv3+	0.351
Proposed	**0.067**

Table 5. Performance of the proposed method under 2 times and 4 times down-sampled inputs

Criteria	Ours-2×d_s	Ours-4×d_s
PRE (%)	93.03	92.95
REC (%)	93.53	90.98
IoU (%)	87.43	85.76
Running Time (ms)	30	16
Frame Rate (fps)	33	62

DeepLabv3+ method, it is benefited from the powerful zero-distribution prior and the horizon detection.

The resolution of LWIR camera is usually low. To test the robustness and the effectiveness of the proposed method, we down-sample the input image by 2 times (2×d_s) and 4 times (4×d_s), and apply our road detection method on these two low resolution inputs. As shown in Table 5, the results under 2 times down-sampled input still outperform the DeepLabv3+ method trained with RGB fusion image and achieve a real-time performance with 33 fps cause the 2 times down-sampling barely damage the overall polarization information of scene. With 4 times down-sampled input, the proposed method achieves compelling results even with a higher speed.

It should be noted that the proposed method may fail when the road is wet or the polarization characteristic of car is quite similar with road. When the road is covered with water, the dominant energy reaches the camera is reflected radiation rather than the emitted radiation as assumed in Sect. 3. And the DoP of car is affected by the temperature and the viewing angle, so the precision of the proposed method may be influenced when the DoP of car is similar with the road. Our future work aims to solve these limitations.

6   Conclusion

This paper presents a road detection technique based on LWIR polarization imaging for autonomous navigation regardless of illumination conditions. We use DoFP infrared imaging technology to acquire infrared polarization information in real time with a monocular camera. The proposed zero-distribution prior of AoP provides a powerful constraint for road detection. Based on this prior, we propose a statistical method with a road vanishing assumption to locate the horizon to reduce computation. We combine zero-distribution of AoP, the difference of DoP, and the edge information to segment the road region in the scene. We developed a LWIR DoFP dataset consisting of 2,113 annotated images. Experiment results on the dataset demonstrate that the proposed method successfully detects the road regardless of illumination conditions, day and night.

Acknowledgment. This work was supported in part by the National Natural Science Foundation of China (NSFC) under Grant 61771391, in part by the Science, Technology and Innovation Commission of Shenzhen Municipality under Grants JCYJ20170815162956949 and JCYJ20180306171146740, Key R & D plan of Shaanxi Province 2020ZDLGY07-11, and by Institute of Information & Communications Technology Planning & Evaluation (IITP) grant funded by Korean government (MSIT) (No. 2019-0-00231, Development of artificial intelligence based video security technology and systems for public infrastructure safety).

References

1. Abubakar, A., Zhao, X., Li, S., Takruri, M., Bastaki, E., Bermak, A.: A block-matching and 3-D filtering algorithm for Gaussian noise in DoFP polarization images. IEEE Sens. J. **18**(18), 7429–7435 (2018)

2. Aïnouz, S., Zallat, J., de Martino, A., Collet, C.: Physical interpretation of polarization-encoded images by color preview. Opt. Express (OE) **14**(13), 5916–5927 (2006)

3. Badrinarayanan, V., Kendall, A., Cipolla, R.: SegNet: a deep convolutional encoder-decoder architecture for image segmentation. IEEE Trans. Pattern Anal. Mach. Intell. (TPAMI) **39**(12), 2481–2495 (2017)

4. Bertilone, D.: Stokes parameters and partial polarization of far-field radiation emitted by hot bodies. JOSA A **11**(8), 2298–2304 (1994)

5. Bertozzi, M., et al.: IR pedestrian detection for advanced driver assistance systems. In: Michaelis, B., Krell, G. (eds.) DAGM 2003. LNCS, vol. 2781, pp. 582–590. Springer, Heidelberg (2003). https://doi.org/10.1007/978-3-540-45243-0_74

6. Chen, L.C., Papandreou, G., Kokkinos, I., Murphy, K., Yuille, A.L.: DeepLab: semantic image segmentation with deep convolutional nets, atrous convolution, and fully connected CRFs. IEEE Trans. Pattern Anal. Mach. Intell. (TPAMI) **40**(4), 834–848 (2017)

7. Chen, L.-C., Zhu, Y., Papandreou, G., Schroff, F., Adam, H.: Encoder-decoder with atrous separable convolution for semantic image segmentation. In: Ferrari, V., Hebert, M., Sminchisescu, C., Weiss, Y. (eds.) ECCV 2018. LNCS, vol. 11211, pp. 833–851. Springer, Cham (2018). https://doi.org/10.1007/978-3-030-01234-2_49

8. Choi, Y., et al.: KAIST multi-spectral day/night data set for autonomous and assisted driving. IEEE Trans. Intell. Transp. Syst. (TITS) **19**(3), 934–948 (2018)

9. Coniglio, N., Mathieu, A., Aubreton, O., Stolz, C.: Characterizing weld pool surfaces from polarization state of thermal emissions. Opt. Letters (OL) **38**(12), 2086–2088 (2013)

10. Dickson, C.N., Wallace, A.M., Kitchin, M., Connor, B.: Long-wave infrared polarimetric cluster-based vehicle detection. JOSA A **32**(12), 2307–2315 (2015)

11. Dickson, C., Wallace, A.M., Kitchin, M., Connor, B.: Improving infrared vehicle detection with polarisation (2013)

12. Garcia, M., Edmiston, C., Marinov, R., Vail, A., Gruev, V.: Bio-inspired color-polarization imager for real-time in situ imaging. Optica **4**(10), 1263–1271 (2017)

13. Garcia, M., et al.: Bio-inspired imager improves sensitivity in near-infrared fluorescence image-guided surgery. Optica **5**(4), 413–422 (2018)

14. Geiger, A., Roser, M., Urtasun, R.: Efficient large-scale stereo matching. In: Kimmel, R., Klette, R., Sugimoto, A. (eds.) ACCV 2010. LNCS, vol. 6492, pp. 25–38. Springer, Heidelberg (2011). https://doi.org/10.1007/978-3-642-19315-6_3

15. Goldstein, D.H.: Polarized Light. CRC Press, Boca Raton (2016)
16. Gu, S., Zhang, Y., Tang, J., Yang, J., Kong, H.: Road detection through CRF based LiDAR-camera fusion. In: 2019 International Conference on Robotics and Automation (ICRA), pp. 3832–3838. IEEE (2019)
17. Hillel, A.B., Lerner, R., Levi, D., Raz, G.: Recent progress in road and lane detection: a survey. Mach. Vis. Appl. **25**(3), 727–745 (2014)
18. Hyde, M.W., Cain, S.C., Schmidt, J.D., Havrilla, M.J.: Material classification of an unknown object using turbulence-degraded polarimetric imagery. IEEE Trans. Geosci. Remote Sens. (TGRS) **49**(1), 264–276 (2010)
19. John, V., Mita, S., Liu, Z., Qi, B.: Pedestrian detection in thermal images using adaptive fuzzy C-means clustering and convolutional neural networks. In: 2015 14th IAPR International Conference on Machine Vision Applications (MVA), pp. 246–249. IEEE (2015)
20. Klein, L.J., Ingvarsson, S., Hamann, H.F.: Changing the emission of polarized thermal radiation from metallic nanoheaters. Opt. Express (OE) **17**(20), 17963–17969 (2009)
21. Kong, H., Audibert, J.Y., Ponce, J.: Vanishing point detection for road detection. In: 2009 IEEE Conference on Computer Vision and Pattern Recognition (CVPR), pp. 96–103. IEEE (2009)
22. Kong, H., Sarma, S.E., Tang, F.: Generalizing Laplacian of Gaussian filters for vanishing-point detection. IEEE Trans. Intell. Transp. Syst. (TITS) **14**(1), 408–418 (2012)
23. Kwak, J.Y., Ko, B.C., Nam, J.Y.: Pedestrian tracking using online boosted random ferns learning in far-infrared imagery for safe driving at night. IEEE Trans. Intell. Transp. Syst. (TITS) **18**(1), 69–81 (2016)
24. Li, N., Zhao, Y., Pan, Q., Kong, S.G.: Removal of reflections in LWIR image with polarization characteristics. Opt. Express (OE) **26**(13), 16488–16504 (2018)
25. Li, N., Zhao, Y., Pan, Q., Kong, S.G.: Demosaicking DoFP images using Newton's polynomial interpolation and polarization difference model. Opt. Express (OE) **27**(2), 1376–1391 (2019)
26. Li, Q., et al.: LO-Net: deep real-time LiDAR odometry. In: Proceedings of the IEEE Conference on Computer Vision and Pattern Recognition (CVPR), pp. 8473–8482 (2019)
27. Li, S., Seybold, B., Vorobyov, A., Fathi, A., Huang, Q., Jay Kuo, C.C.: Instance embedding transfer to unsupervised video object segmentation. In: Proceedings of the IEEE Conference on Computer Vision and Pattern Recognition (CVPR), pp. 6526–6535 (2018)
28. Long, J., Shelhamer, E., Darrell, T.: Fully convolutional networks for semantic segmentation. In: Proceedings of the IEEE Conference on Computer Vision and Pattern Recognition (CVPR), pp. 3431–3440 (2015)
29. Lu, W., Zhou, Y., Wan, G., Hou, S., Song, S.: L3-Net: towards learning based LiDAR localization for autonomous driving. In: Proceedings of the IEEE Conference on Computer Vision and Pattern Recognition (CVPR), pp. 6389–6398 (2019)
30. Lu, X.: Self-supervised road detection from a single image. In: 2015 IEEE International Conference on Image Processing (ICIP), pp. 2989–2993. IEEE (2015)
31. Mendes, C.C.T., Frémont, V., Wolf, D.F.: Exploiting fully convolutional neural networks for fast road detection. In: 2016 IEEE International Conference on Robotics and Automation (ICRA), pp. 3174–3179. IEEE (2016)
32. Oliveira, G.L., Burgard, W., Brox, T.: Efficient deep models for monocular road segmentation. In: 2016 IEEE/RSJ International Conference on Intelligent Robots and Systems (IROS), pp. 4885–4891. IEEE (2016)

33. Ozgunalp, U., Fan, R., Ai, X., Dahnoun, N.: Multiple lane detection algorithm based on novel dense vanishing point estimation. IEEE Trans. Intell. Transp. Syst. (TITS) **18**(3), 621–632 (2016)
34. Peláez, G., Bacara, D., de la Escalera, A., García, F., Olaverri-Monreal, C.: Road detection with thermal cameras through 3D information. In: 2015 IEEE Intelligent Vehicles Symposium (IV), pp. 255–260. IEEE (2015)
35. Peynot, T., Underwood, J., Scheding, S.: Towards reliable perception for unmanned ground vehicles in challenging conditions. In: 2009 IEEE/RSJ International Conference on Intelligent Robots and Systems (IROS), pp. 1170–1176. IEEE (2009)
36. Piniarski, K., Pawłowski, P.: Efficient pedestrian detection with enhanced object segmentation in far IR night vision. In: 2017 Signal Processing: Algorithms, Architectures, Arrangements, and Applications (SPA), pp. 160–165. IEEE (2017)
37. Qian, Y., Dolan, J.M., Yang, M.: DLT-Net: Joint detection of drivable areas, lane lines, and traffic objects. IEEE Trans. Intell. Transp. Syst. (TITS) **99**, 1–10 (2019)
38. Rahmann, S., Canterakis, N.: Reconstruction of specular surfaces using polarization imaging. In: Proceedings of the IEEE Conference on Computer Vision and Pattern Recognition (CVPR), vol. 1, p. I. IEEE (2001)
39. Rashed, H., El Sallab, A., Yogamani, S., ElHelw, M.: Motion and depth augmented semantic segmentation for autonomous navigation. In: Proceedings of the IEEE Conference on Computer Vision and Pattern Recognition Workshops (CVPRW) (2019)
40. Reda, M., Zhao, Y., Chan, J.C.W.: Polarization guided autoregressive model for depth recovery. IEEE Photonics J. **9**(3), 1–16 (2017)
41. Shen, L., Zhao, Y., Peng, Q., Chan, J.C.W., Kong, S.G.: An iterative image dehazing method with polarization. IEEE Trans. Multimedia (TMM) **21**(5), 1093–1107 (2018)
42. Su, Y., Zhang, Y., Lu, T., Yang, J., Kong, H.: Vanishing point constrained lane detection with a stereo camera. IEEE Trans. Intell. Transp. Syst. (TITS) **19**(8), 2739–2744 (2017)
43. Terrier, P., Devlaminck, V., Charbois, J.M.: Segmentation of rough surfaces using a polarization imaging system. JOSA A **25**(2), 423–430 (2008)
44. Tyo, J.S., Goldstein, D.L., Chenault, D.B., Shaw, J.A.: Review of passive imaging polarimetry for remote sensing applications. Appl. Opt. (AO) **45**(22), 5453–5469 (2006)
45. Born, M., Wolf, E.: Principles of Optics. Cambridge University Press, Cambridge (1999)
46. Wang, H., Wang, Y., Zhao, X., Wang, G., Huang, H., Zhang, J.: Lane detection of curving road for structural highway with straight-curve model on vision. IEEE Trans. Veh. Technol. (TVT) **68**(6), 5321–5330 (2019)
47. Yoon, J.S., et al.: Thermal-infrared based drivable region detection. In: 2016 IEEE Intelligent Vehicles Symposium (IV), pp. 978–985. IEEE (2016)
48. Zhang, W., Cai, X., Huang, K., Zhang, Z.: A novel RGB-T based real-time road detection on low cost embedded devices. In: Bi, Y., Chen, G., Deng, Q., Wang, Y. (eds.) ESTC 2017. CCIS, vol. 857, pp. 17–26. Springer, Singapore (2018). https://doi.org/10.1007/978-981-13-1026-3_2
49. Zhang, Y., Su, Y., Yang, J., Ponce, J., Kong, H.: When Dijkstra meets vanishing point: a stereo vision approach for road detection. IEEE Trans. Image Process. (TIP) **27**(5), 2176–2188 (2018)
50. Zhang, Y., Wang, J., Wang, X., Dolan, J.M.: Road-segmentation-based curb detection method for self-driving via a 3D-LiDAR sensor. IEEE Trans. Intell. Transp. Syst. (TITS) **19**(12), 3981–3991 (2018)

A Flexible Recurrent Residual Pyramid Network for Video Frame Interpolation

Haoxian Zhang[1,3], Yang Zhao[2,3], and Ronggang Wang[1,3]([✉])

[1] School of Electronic and Computer Engineering,
Peking University Shenzhen Graduate School, Shenzhen, China
haoxianz@pku.edu.cn, rgwang@pkusz.edu.cn
[2] School of Computer and Information, Hefei University of Technology, Hefei, China
yzhao@hfut.edu.cn
[3] Peng Cheng Laboratory, Shenzhen, China

Abstract. Video frame interpolation (VFI) aims at synthesizing new video frames in-between existing frames to generate smoother high frame rate videos. Current methods usually use the fixed pre-trained networks to generate interpolated-frames for different resolutions and scenes. However, the fixed pre-trained networks are difficult to be tailored for a variety of cases. Inspired by classical pyramid energy minimization optical flow algorithms, this paper proposes a recurrent residual pyramid network (RRPN) for video frame interpolation. In the proposed network, different pyramid levels share the same weights and base-network, named recurrent residual layer (RRL). In RRL, residual displacements between warped images are detected to gradually refine optical flows rather than directly predict the flows or frames. Owing to the flexible recurrent residual pyramid architecture, we can customize the number of pyramid levels, and make trade-offs between calculations and quality based on the application scenarios. Moreover, occlusion masks are also generated in this recurrent residual way to solve occlusion better. Finally, a refinement network is added to enhance the details for final output with contextual and edge information. Experimental results demonstrate that the RRPN is more flexible and efficient than current VFI networks but has fewer parameters. In particular, the RRPN, which avoid over-reliance on datasets and network structures, shows superior performance for large motion cases.

Keywords: Video frame interpolation · Customizable pyramid network · Arbitrary resolution and scenes · Adjustable calculation

1 Introduction

Video frame interpolation (VFI) is a classic computer vision task with a wide range of applications, such as novel view interpolation synthesis [9], frame rate

Electronic supplementary material The online version of this chapter (https://doi.org/10.1007/978-3-030-58595-2_29) contains supplementary material, which is available to authorized users.

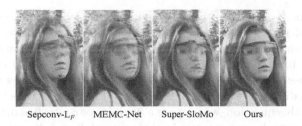

Sepconv-L_F MEMC-Net   Super-SloMo   Ours

Fig. 1. A challenging **4K** (**3840 × 2160**) example from DAVIS [28]. As the resolution increases, the pixel displacements increase, which makes fixed pre-trained models difficult to estimate motion. Our method can handle arbitrary resolution cases with flexibility and adjustable calculation.

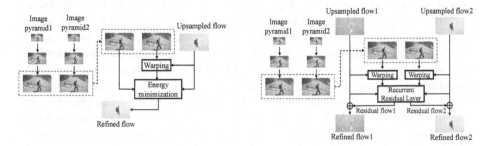

Fig. 2. *Left*: The traditional pyramid energy minimization optical flow architecture [6, 11] with flexibility. *Right*: The proposed recurrent residual pyramid architecture inherits the flexible structure from traditional method, which estimates residual flows between two warped images at each pyramid level by a reusable CNN.

conversion [24], slow motion [15]. As deep learning has achieved significant success in many computer vision tasks, increasingly more deep-learning-based methods are proposed to obtain high quality interpolated frames. Long *et al.* [22] regard VFI as an image generation task, and use CNNs to directly generate intermediate frames without an intermediate motion estimation step, which may cause blurry results. To avoid blurring artifacts and produce high quality intermediate frames, many CNN-based methods utilize an effective intermediate motion estimation step before frame interpolation [3,15,21,26,42]. However, large motion and occlusions are still challenging for these CNN-based approaches.

To handle large motion in VFI, current methods rely on improving model architecture, increasing the number of parameters, and enlarging the training set that contains enough large motion cases. For example, Van *et al.* [1], Bao *et al.* [3] and Niklaus *et al.* [25] adopt coarse-to-fine flow estimation architecture to estimate more accurate optical flow. Niklaus *et al.* [27] train a big enough spatially-adaptive convolution kernel for each pixel to cover large motion. But these fixed pre-trained models face two problems. First, as shown in Fig. 1, when encountering cases with larger resolutions or motion scales that were not considered in training data, the performance of these methods tends to be significantly degraded. Second, a model originally trained for high resolution videos leads to an increased number of parameters. When applied for smaller resolution or motion scale videos, the oversized network has significant computational redundancy. Hence, fixed pre-trained model is not very effective to handle a wide variety of scenes in the wild. Is it possible to train a flexible network that can be tailored for different scenarios, instead of training separate networks?

To address this question, we propose a flexible coarse-to-fine network inspired by classical pyramid energy minimization optical flow estimation algorithms. This architecture can customize the number of pyramid layers and make trade-offs between calculations and quality based on the application scenario. As shown in Fig. 2 (*Left*), classical pyramid optical flow algorithm usually utilizes energy minimization operation to detect residual flow between first image and the warped second image at each pyramid level, which is warped by upsampled flow from last pyramid level. These algorithms can design different numbers of layers for various cases of different difficulties. Meanwhile, high quality optical flow can be accurately estimated by means of the coarse-to-fine refinement. In VFI tasks, we mainly solve optimal optical flow from the target time position to adjacent two frames, and then pre-warp frames guided by flow and blend them to final output. Therefore, the similar structure can naturally be applied to solve motion estimation for VFI with flexibility, as in Fig. 2 (*Right*). This structure can arbitrarily divide a difficult large task into multiple simple small tasks, and a CNN-based module is utilized to solve the sub-problem in each pyramid layer. In this way, the optical flows would be iteratively refined by residual flows with the same network, which avoid over-reliance on datasets and network complexity.

Therefore, a flexible Recurrent Residual Pyramid Network (RRPN) is proposed in this paper. In the training phase, we design a multi-layers recurrent pyramid network, in which each pyramid layer shares same structure and weights. As mentioned before, the residual learning strategy is used in the pyramid network to gradually refine the flow. Hence, each pyramid layer is named as recurrent residual layer (RRL). Occlusion maps, which are also generated in this recurrent and residual way, are applied to the warped images before fusion to solve occlusion better. In the testing phase, the RRL can be easily applied more times than that in training phase. Moreover, in order to improve the details and sharpness of the output frame, a refinement network is presented after the pyramid, which simultaneously takes the warped frames, warped contextual feature, warped edge maps and occlusion maps as input. The contextual feature and the edge maps are extracted via pre-trained VGG19 [33] and HED [40].

The entire network is trained end-to-end using more than 80K collected frame groups. Experimental results demonstrate that the recurrent residual approach can achieve state-of-the-art performance on several datasets, including Middlebury [2], UCF101 [34], Thumos15 [16] (720P videos), ActivityNet [8] (1080P videos) and H.266 4K test sequences [5,35], with higher flexibility and lower complexity. In particular, the proposed method shows superior performance when facing with large motion cases that not contained in the training data.

2   Related Work

Common frame interpolation approaches usually generate intermediate frames with an intermediate motion estimation step [21], which usually is optical flow [12,29,36]. In this section, we mainly discuss recent learning-based VFI and optical flow estimation algorithms.

Video Frame Interpolation. Deep voxel flow [21] estimates a 3D optical flow across space and time, to samples pixels from adjacent frames. However, inaccuracies in voxel flow estimation lead to unsatisfactory results sometimes. Van et al. [1] combine DVF with coarse-to-fine architecture to achieve better results, while its performance is still limited by the number of the pyramid levels. Niklaus et al. [27] utilize a CNN to combine motion estimation and pixel synthesis into a single convolution step. They estimate spatially-adaptive convolution kernels for each pixel to synthesize a intermediate frame. While their prediction are limited by the size of adaptive kernels when faced with large motion. Bao et al. [4] first warp input frames by optical flow and then estimate kernels to sample pixels, which inherits the benefits from both flow-based and kernel-based approaches. Jiang et al. [15] estimate bidirectional flow between two frames, and then synthesize intermediate flow fields to generate the intermediate frame at the arbitrary time step. Liu et al. [20] propose a cycle consistency loss to make synthesized frames more reliable by reconstructing input frames with synthesized frames. Recently, Zhang et al. [43] effectively uses spatio-temporal information contained in multiple frames to generate high-quality intermediate frames.

Optical Flow Estimation. As a pioneer of CNN-based methods, Dosovitskiy et al. [7] develop two network architectures of FlowNetS and FlowNetC, which proved that a U-Net [32] architecture can be used to predict optical flow effectively. Ilg et al. [13] design a much larger FlowNet2 based on FlowNetS and FlowNetC to achieve better performance. In addition to the supervised learning, learning optical flow using CNNs in an unsupervised way has also been explored [19,23,30,37]. Recently, many deep networks are designed by considering classical principles of optical flow, such as coarse-to-fine strategy and iterative residual refinement, and have achieved better results with less computation [12,29,36].

3   Proposed Approach

Given consecutive two input frames $I = \{I_0, I_1\}$, the goal of VFI is to predict the intermediate frame I_t at the temporal location t in between I_0 and I_1, $t \in (0, 1)$. Let us assume $F = \{F_{t \to 0}, F_{t \to 1}\}$ to represent the predicted optical flow from I_t to I_0 and I_1. The intermediate frame I_t can be synthesized through warping two frames guided by these flow and then fusing them as follows:

$$I_t = M_{t \leftarrow 0} \otimes w(I_0, F_{t \to 0}) + M_{t \leftarrow 1} \otimes w(I_1, F_{t \to 1}), \qquad (1)$$

where $w(\cdot, \cdot)$ denotes a backward warping function, which can be implemented using bilinear interpolation [21] and is differentiable. $M = \{M_{t \leftarrow 0}, M_{t \leftarrow 1}\}$

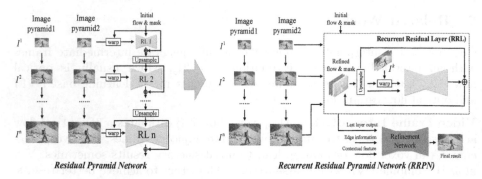

Fig. 3. *Left*: A Residual Pyramid Network with several residual layers (RL) to detect residual flows between warped images at each pyramid level. *Right*: Overview of the Recurrent Residual Pyramid Network (RRPN), which utilizes the single recurrent residual layer (RRL) with shared weights at each pyramid level to iteratively update optical flows. Moreover, a refinement network that combines edge information and contexture feature are used to enhance the final output.

denote occlusion maps of the two warped frames, where $\sum_{i=0}^{1} M_{t\leftarrow i}(i,j) = 1$, $M_{t\leftarrow i}(i,j) \in [0,1]$. (i,j) denote the pixel coordinate and $\otimes$ denotes element-wise multiplication. Occlusion areas often results in artifacts in the warped frames. Therefore, occlusion masks [15,42] are estimated and only pixels that are not occluded are used in interpolation.

3.1   Recurrent Residual Pyramid Network (RRPN)

Pyramid framework is commonly used in traditional computer vision and pattern recognition tasks, which can effectively divide a difficult task into multiple simple tasks, especially for motion estimation. Residual learning strategy is also useful in many CNN-based image restoration methods that utilize a global residual connection to improve the convergency and force the networks to learn the high-frequency details. To inherit the benefits of these effective strategies, we first present a residual pyramid network similar to FIGAN [1], in which a series of base-networks are composed in coarse-to-fine manner to refine VFI results, as shown in Fig. 3 (*Left*). In each pyramid layer, residual displacement are predicted from warped images, and then propagate to higher resolution layers of the pyramid to update optical flows. Hence, the optical flows are gradually improved until high-quality optical flows are obtained at full resolution. In order to avoid error propagation in the iterative process, all warped images are resampled by updated optical flows from original input at each pyramid level, rather than being resampled by residual flows from warped images. Therefore, the unsupervised motion information are kept track of, composed, and passed through the network instead of being absorbed into warped images. By refining optical flows and occlusion masks with residual flows and residual masks at each pyramid level, the estimation accuracy of motion and occlusion can also be increased. Note that the values of initial flows and masks are 0 and 0.5, respectively.

However, this fixed residual pyramid network still cannot well handle a wide variety of VFI scenes in the wild, because different numbers of pyramid layers should be set for videos with different resolutions. Moreover, increasing the layers of residual pyramid network also lead to larger amount of parameters. Hence, design of numbers of pyramid layers becomes another difficult question. One common way is to carefully select the number of layers to make a balance between performance and computational complexity. However, a pyramid with fixed layers either is insufficient to deal with complex larger motion cases, or increases computational redundancy for easy smaller motion cases. In order to address this problem in a flexible and efficient way, we propose a Recurrent Residual Pyramid Network (RRPN) based on weight sharing strategy. Each layer of the pyramid uses the same network with shared weights to detect the residual displacement of warped images. Therefore, the number of pyramid layers can be customized according to the application scenario to achieve a trade-off between calculations and quality.

The structure of proposed RRPN is shown in Fig. 3 (*Right*), which adopts similar architecture as the residual pyramid network. However, each pyramid layer adopts the same base-network with shared weights in recurrent way, named Recurrent Residual Layer (RRL). Finally, a refinement network is presented to further enhance the details of final output with contextual and edge information. Let $u(\cdot)$ be the upsampling function using bilinear interpolation. I^k denotes the image from k-th layer of the image pyramid. β^k denotes the ratio of the resolution between I^k and I^{k-1}. M^k, m^k, F^k and f^k denote occlusion mask M, residual mask m, optical flow F and residual flow f, respectively. At the k-th level of the pyramid, F^k and M^k can be described as follows,

$$f^k, m^k = RRL(w(I^k, u(\beta^k F^{k-1})), u(\beta^k F^{k-1}), u(M^{k-1})) \qquad (2)$$

$$F^k = u(\beta^k F^{k-1}) + f^k \qquad (3)$$

$$M^k = u(M^{k-1}) + m^k \qquad (4)$$

3.2   Recurrent Residual Layer (RRL)

As shown in Fig. 4, RRL estimates the residual displacements between warped images to gradually refine optical flows rather than directly predicts the flows or frames. The backbone of RRL is a U-Net architecture. (The configuration details are provided in the supplementary material.) Moreover, the feature extractor consists of 3 convolutional layers and the context network is design based on dilated convolutions, which has 4 convolutional layers with dilation constants of [2, 4, 8, 1]. The spatial kernel for all convolutional layers above is 3×3 except the first hierarchy of U-Net encoder, which adopts 7×7 kernels.

In this paper, we train a 3-level RRPN with the same RRL at each pyramid level to enforce the RRL to learn residual displacement detection. This results in a single effective unsupervised optical flow predictor RRL that can be applied

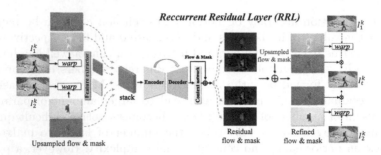

Fig. 4. Illustration of the RRL and only the target frame at each pyramid level is used as supervisory signal. The RRL uses the same siamese convolutional layer as feature extractor to provide good features to establish correspondence, particularly in the presence of shadows and lighting changes. Moreover, context network is also used to post-process the residual flow and mask[36].

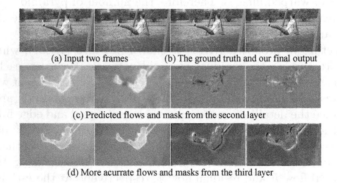

Fig. 5. Samples of predicted flows and masks from a 3-level Recurrent Residual Pyramid Network that indicates the single RRL can gradually refine the result.

multiple times across pyramid structure. The predicted flows are visualized in Fig. 5. We can observe that residual flows and residual masks can be effectively predicted to refined the optical flow and occlusion masks in coarse-to-fine way, in spite of using the same RRL at each pyramid layer. Note that the RRL can be easily applied more times in testing phase than that in training stage, and the performance continues to increase until saturation. This implies that RRL can help to achieve better performance with flexibility. In addition, this compact and flexible method also sheds the reliance on large motion datasets. By inheriting the merits of traditional pyramid framework, the RRPN can arbitrarily decompose large prediction task into multiple simple small prediction tasks. Therefore, the RRL can be only trained to learn small increment motion estimation and does not require a dataset which covers a wide range of motion.

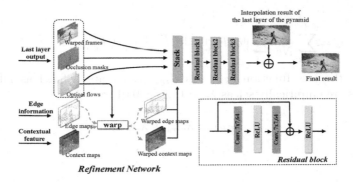

Fig. 6. Illustration of the refinement network.

3.3 Refinement Network

To further enhance the visual quality of output frame, a refinement network, which consists of 3 residual blocks, is added after the last layer of the recurrent residual pyramid to predict the residuals between the ground-truth frame and the blended frame. Generating the final output via blending two warped frames with occlusion maps usually leads to the loss of rich contextual information [25]. Meanwhile pixels with larger gradients tend to have large errors [20]. Therefore, we use *conv1* layer of a pre-trained VGG19 [33] and *side-output1* of HED [40] to extract the contextual feature and the edge map of original frames. Then we concatenate the warped input frames, occlusion maps, output flows, warped contextual feature, and warped edge maps as input, as shown in Fig. 6.

3.4 Loss Function

For each pyramid layer of d-level RRPN, we denote the interpolated frame by $\widehat{I}_t^k$ and its ground truth by I_t^k. Moreover, $\widehat{I}_t$ and I_t denote the output of refinement network and the target frame, respectively. We mainly use *Reconstruction loss* and *Edge-aware smoothness loss* in this paper.

Reconstruction loss l_{r1} and l_{r2} [3,15,21] are traditional MAE loss functions, where pixel values are normalized into the range $[-1, 1]$.

$$l_{r1} = \sum_{k=1}^{d} \left\| I_t^k - \hat{I}_t^k \right\|_1 \qquad (5)$$

$$l_{r2} = \left\| I_t - \hat{I}_t \right\|_1 \qquad (6)$$

Edge-aware smoothness loss l_s [10], which is a spatial coherence regularization, is added to encourage neighboring pixels to have similar flow values. As flow discontinuities often occur at image gradients, we weight this cost with an edge-aware term by means of image gradients, where N^k is the number of pixels at each pyramid level and (i, j) denote the pixel coordinate.

$$l_s = \sum_{k=1}^{d} \frac{1}{N^k} \sum_{i,j} \left\| \partial_x F_{ij}^k \right\| e^{-\left\| \partial_x I_{t,ij}^k \right\|} + \left\| \partial_y F_{ij}^k \right\| e^{-\left\| \partial_y I_{t,ij}^k \right\|} \qquad (7)$$

Finally, the loss function l_{RRL} and $l_{refinement}$ are defined as follow, the parameters are empirically set as $\lambda_r = 1$, $\lambda_s = 0.01$, $d = 3$.

$$l_{RRL} = \lambda_r l_{r1} + \lambda_s l_s \qquad (8)$$

$$l_{refinement} = l_{r2} \qquad (9)$$

4 Experiments

4.1 Training

Training Dataset. For training, we collect 60-fps videos with a resolution of 1280×720 from YouTube, which contain a great variety of scenes. Then videos are split into triplets of three frames and all frames are resized to have a shortest dimension of 480. For each triplet, the middle frame serves as the ground truth while the other two are inputs. To have more challenging samples for training, we only select triplets with useful information, especially large motion. Hence we calculate optical flow between input frames using DIS flow [18] to drop samples with no or little motion. Finally, approximately 80,000 triplets are selected, 4000 samples are used for validation and 4000 samples are used as testing data for model analysis among them. We augment the training data by randomly cropping patches with a size of 352×352, flip each patch vertically or horizontally, and swap the temporal order.

Implementation Details. We pre-train the RRL and refinement network in turn, and then fine-tune the entire model. Adam [17] is used to optimize the proposed network. We set the β_1 and β_2 to 0.9 and 0.999 and use a batch size of 8. The learning rate is initialized to be $1e-4$, $1e-5$ for pre-train stage and fine-tune stage respectively, and decreased by a factor of 10 every 15 epochs. Batch normalization [14] is adopted on RRL for accelerating convergence. We train our network to interpolate intermediate frame at t = 0.5 temporal location in all experiments. Moreover, we train our model on an NVIDIA Tesla V100 GPU, which takes about one day to converge.

4.2 Evaluation Datasets and Metrics

The proposed method is evaluated on several independent datasets with different resolutions, including UCF101 (240P), Middlebury benchmark (480P), our testing data (480P), Thumos15 (720P), ActivityNet (1080P) and H.266 4K test sequences [5, 35].

UCF101 (240P). Videos from UCF101 are low resolution and relatively easy to interpolate intermediate frames. So we select videos with obvious motion using DIS flow, which are more difficult than that used in DVF [21].

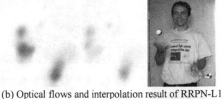

(b) Optical flows and interpolation result of RRPN-L1

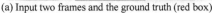

(a) Input two frames and the ground truth (red box)

(c) Optical flows and interpolation result of RRPN-L3

Fig. 7. Examples for the effectiveness of customizing the number of pyramid levels.

Table 1. Impact of the number of pyramid layer.

		PSNR	SSIM	IE
UCF101(240P)	RRPN-L1 w/o R	34.64	0.960	6.06
	RRPN-L2 w/o R	**34.72**	**0.962**	**5.98**
Our test set(480P)	RRPN-L1 w/o R	30.74	0.878	8.62
	RRPN-L2 w/o R	31.75	**0.913**	7.95
	RRPN-L3 w/o R	**31.80**	**0.913**	**7.92**
Thumos15(720P)	RRPN-L1 w/o R	33.56	0.936	7.89
	RRPN-L2 w/o R	34.50	0.946	7.04
	RRPN-L3 w/o R	34.65	**0.951**	6.83
	RRPN-L4 w/o R	**34.69**	**0.951**	**6.78**

Table 2. Effectiveness of the refinement network (test on 480P).

	PSNR	SSIM	IE
RRPN-L2 w/o R	31.75	0.913	7.95
RRPN-L2 (basic R)	31.78	0.910	7.93
RRPN-L2 (edge R)	31.83	0.913	7.89
RRPN-L2 (context R)	31.86	0.915	**7.85**
RRPN-L2 (whole R)	**31.90**	**0.916**	7.86

Middlebury Benchmark (480P). Since the interpolation category of the Middlebury optical flow benchmark is typically used for assessing frame interpolation methods, we submit our frame interpolation results to its website.

Thumos15 (720P), ActivityNet (1080P) and H.266 Test Sequences (4K). To verify the performance of our approach in high-resolution videos, we select 25 720P videos from Thumos15 test data, 20 1080P videos from ActivityNet data and all 6 4K (3840×2160) test sequences of VVC (H.266) video codec standard. These high-resolution videos contain a variety of situations, such as small and large movement, motion blur, global motion, and occlusion.

Metrics. PSNR, SSIM [38] and the interpolation error (IE) [2], which is defined as root-mean-square difference between the ground-truth and the prediction, are used to evaluate the quality of interpolated video frame. Lower IE indicate better performance.

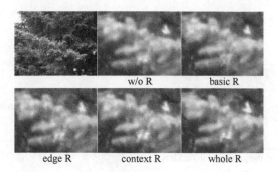

Fig. 8. Examples ('Evergreen' on the Middlebury set) for the effectiveness of refinement network. The context and edge maps can help produce sharper results in the highly textured region.

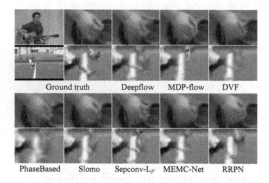

Fig. 9. Challenging sample results from our selected UCF101 dataset.

Table 3. Comparison on our UCF101 dataset (*Top*) and the UCF101 dataset (256 × 256) used in DVF [21] (*Bottom*).

	PSNR	SSIM	IE
MDP-Flow2 [41]	34.49	0.959	6.37
DeepFlow [39]	34.40	0.957	6.44
Phase-Based [24]	33.65	0.946	6.83
SepConv-L_F [27]	34.62	0.959	6.30
DVF [21]	34.13	0.956	6.35
Slomo [15]	34.59	0.960	6.06
DAIN [3]	34.75	**0.963**	**5.93**
MEMC-Net [4]	34.70	**0.963**	5.95
RRPN-L1 (Match for 240P)	34.73	0.962	5.95
RRPN-L2	**34.76**	0.962	**5.93**

	DVF [21]	ToFlow [42]	DAIN [3]	RRPN-L1
PSNR	34.12	34.58	34.99	34.76

4.3   Model Analysis

We analyze the contribution of the two key components in the proposed model: recurrent residual pyramid architecture and refinement network. UCF101 (240P), our testing data (480P), and Thumos15 (720P) are used here.

Customizing the Number of Pyramid Layers for the RRPN. To analyze the flexibility and effectiveness of the RRPN, we customize a series of RRPNs with different number of pyramid layers and then evaluate their performance on several datasets with various resolutions. Note that refinement network is not used for all these models in this testing. Table 1 shows the impact of the number of pyramid layers on interpolation performance. '-Lx' indicates the number of pyramid layers.

We can see that the quality of the interpolation can be improved by means of more pyramid layers, although each layer of the pyramid is with same network and weights. Moreover, when facing with large resolution (large motion) cases on Thumos15 (720p) dataset, using four RRLs can continue to increase the

Inputs   MDP-flow   CtxSyn   SepConv   SloMo   ToFlow   MEMC-Net   RRPN-L2

Fig. 10. Visual comparisons on the Middlebury benchmark. The proposed method reconstructs a clear shape of the ball.

Table 4. Evaluation on the Middlebury(480P). The RRPN-L2 has comparable performance with DAIN in terms of IE and NIE but with fewer parameters and calculation.

	AVERAGE		Mequon		Schefflera		Urban		Teddy		Backyard		Basketball		Dumptruck		Evergreen	
	IE	NIE	IE	NIE	IE	NIE	IE	NIE	IE	NIE	IE	NIE	IE	NIE	IE	NIE	IE	NIE
SepConv [27]	5.61	0.83	2.52	0.54	3.56	0.67	4.17	1.07	5.41	1.03	10.2	0.99	5.47	0.96	6.88	0.68	6.63	0.70
ToFlow [42]	5.49	0.84	2.54	0.55	3.70	0.72	3.43	0.92	5.05	0.96	9.84	0.97	5.34	0.98	6.88	0.72	7.14	0.90
Slomo [15]	5.31	0.78	2.51	0.59	3.66	0.72	2.91	0.74	5.05	0.98	9.56	0.94	5.37	0.96	6.69	0.60	6.73	0.69
CtxSyn [25]	5.28	0.82	2.24	0.50	2.96	0.55	4.32	1.42	4.21	0.87	9.59	0.95	5.22	0.94	7.02	0.68	6.66	0.67
MEMC-Net [4]	5.24	0.83	2.47	0.60	3.49	0.65	4.63	1.42	4.94	0.88	8.91	0.93	4.70	0.86	6.46	0.66	6.35	0.64
DAIN [3]	4.86	0.71	2.38	0.58	3.28	0.60	3.32	0.69	4.65	0.86	7.88	0.87	4.73	0.85	6.36	0.59	6.25	0.66
RRPN-L2	4.93	0.75	2.38	0.53	3.70	0.69	3.29	0.87	5.05	0.94	8.20	0.88	4.38	0.88	6.50	0.65	6.00	0.62

performance although this RRL is originally trained on a 3-level RRPN. These verify the core idea of the RRPN and indicate our approach can flexibly deal with large motion. Figure 7 provides a visualization of optical flows and interpolated frames for large motion cases. We can observe that the single RRL can only detect small displacements, so there are obvious artifacts in the hand and ball with large motion in Fig. 7(b). But it can divide large displacement prediction into multiple simple small displacement predictions in pyramid recurrent way to gradually capture large motion, as shown in Fig. 7(c).

However, the performance improvement brought by increasing the numbers of pyramid layers would gradually reaches saturation. As the Table 1 shows, one layer is sufficient for 240P frames, but the 480P and 720P frames may require 2 and 3 layers, respectively. Therefore, the flexibility of the RRPN is not only reflected in large motion cases, but also in making trade-offs between calculations and quality for cases of different difficulty levels.

Impact of the Refinement Network. In this part, four variants of refinement networks: whole refinement network (whole R), refinement network without context and edge maps (basic R), refinement network without context maps (edge R) and refinement network without edge maps (context R), are added behind RRPN-L2 to test our 480P test set. The quantitative results and interpolated images are shown in Table 2 and Fig. 8, which demonstrate context and edge maps can improve the performance and reproduce sharper results.

4.4 Comparison with State-of-the-Art Methods

In this section, our approach is compared with state-of-the-art methods published on Middlebury benchmark, including MDP-Flow2 [41], DeepFlow [39],

Table 5. Results on the Thumos15 720P (*Left*) and ActivityNet 1080P (*Right*).

	PSNR	SSIM	IE
DeepFlow [39]	33.65	0.946	7.67
Phase-Based [24]	32.77	0.927	8.42
SepConv-L_F [27]	33.73	0.940	7.79
DVF [21]	33.46	0.937	8.03
Slomo [15]	33.81	0.943	7.98
MEMC-Net [4]	33.96	0.948	6.99
DAIN [3]	34.53	0.950	7.02
RRPN-L3	**34.77**	**0.951**	**6.73**

	PSNR	SSIM	IE
SepConv-L_F [27]	28.86	0.883	12.00
DVF [21]	28.88	0.874	12.98
Slomo [15]	29.04	0.891	11.71
MEMC-Net [4]	29.20	0.890	11.57
DAIN [3]	29.29	0.892	11.44
RRPN-L3	**30.13**	0.898	10.93
RRPN-L4	30.08	**0.902**	**10.68**

Table 6. Results on the H.266(VVC) 4K (3840 × 2160) test sequences.

	PSNR	SSIM	IE
SepConv-L_F [27]	32.74	0.939	7.48
DVF [21]	32.81	0.937	7.41
Slomo [15]	33.54	0.948	6.98
MEMC-Net [4]	33.62	0.947	6.94
RRPN-L4	34.86	0.960	6.25
RRPN-L5 (Match for the resolution)	**35.28**	**0.961**	**6.11**

Table 7. Comparisons on parameter and runtime (test on 480P).

	#Parameters (million)	Runtime (seconds)
SepConv [27]	21.6	0.15
MEMC-net [4]	70.3	0.10
Slomo [15]	39.6	0.14
RRPN-L2	6.1	0.12
RRPN-L2 w/o R	4.8	0.06
RRPN-L3	6.1	0.12
RRPN-L3 w/o R	4.8	0.07

Phase based approach from [24], SepConv [27], DVF [21], recent Super-Slomo [15], MEMC-Net [4] and DAIN [3]. For all these methods, we use the source code or pre-trained models from the original papers. For optical flow methods, we apply the interpolation algorithm presented in [2]. UCF101 (240P), Middlebury (480P), Thumos15 (720P), ActivityNet (1080P) and H.266 test sequences (4K) are adopted for evaluation here.

UCF101. In this part, we utilize RRPN with one layer (RRPN-L1) to compare with other state-of-the-art methods on our UCF101 dataset. The quantitative results are shown in Table 3. RRPN-L1 has comparable performance and outperforms most methods in low resolution cases with fewer parameters. Moreover, the performance of RRPN-L1 on the UCF101 dataset (256 × 256) used in DVF [21] is consistent with results of our UCF101 dataset, while samples in our UCF101 dataset have larger motion. Sample interpolation results from our UCF101 can be found at Fig. 9.

Middlebury. The image resolution in Middlebury is around 640 × 480 pixels. Therefore, we use RRPN with just two layers (RRPN-L2) to test eight sequences provided by the Middlebury benchmark, and submit our frame interpolation results to its website. Normalized Interpolation Error (NIE) is also used on the

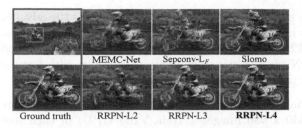

Fig. 11. Sample interpolation results from ActivityNet (**1080P**) videos. The proposed method can better restore the shapeof the motorcycle, which is an challenging example with large motion.

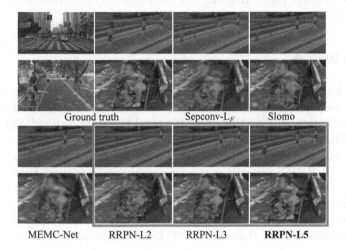

Fig. 12. Sample interpolation results from H.266 (**4K**) test data. Our method can gradually capture large motion for the 4K video examples, in which the pole and the baby carriage closer to the camera have larger motion. While other approaches produce significant artifacts on these super large motion cases that are not considered. Please see supplementary material for more image and video comparison.

Middlebury. In Table 4, we show the comparisons on the EVALUATION set of the benchmark. The proposed model not only outperforms representative non-neural methods based on optical flow, such as Deep flow, MDP-flow2, Epicflow [31], but also performs favorably against recent CNN-based approaches, like CtxSyn [25], ToFlow [42], Slomo, Sepconv, MEMC-Net. Our network with just two pyramid layers here balance calculations and quality well, which has comparable performance with DAIN [3] but with fewer parameters. Sample interpolation results from 'Backyard' sequences are shown Fig. 10.

High Resolution Videos. For Thumos15 (720P), ActivityNet (1080P) and H.266 (4K) test data, we use RRPN with three layers (RRPN-L3), four layers (RRPN-L4) and five layers (RRPN-L5) to interpolate intermediate frames, respectively. As reported in Table 5 and 6, our approach can achieve superior performance in higher resolution videos, which reflects the advantages of custom pyramid layers in dealing with large motion. Qualitative comparisons are shown in Fig. 11 and 12. For super large motion cases that have not included in training data, the RRPN can produce visually pleasing results with fewer artifacts, while other methods tend to produce significant artifacts.

Computational Efficiency. We list the number of model parameters and execution time (640×480 image, a Tesla V100 GPU) of each method in Table 7. Please see supplementary material for more network details. Compared with representative state-of-the-art methods, the proposed model is more compact and run faster. The RRPN-L2 has 71% fewer parameters than SepConv and save 20% execution time. Morover, the RRPN-L2 w/o refinement network can further save 21% parameters and 50% runtime.

5   Conclusion

Motivated by classical pyramid energy minimization optical flow algorithm, this paper proposed a compact and flexible network to handle large motion for video frame interpolation, named Recurrent Residual Pyramid Network (RRPN). The proposed RRPN adopts the same Recurrent Residual Layer (RRL) with shared weights at each pyramid layer to predict residual flows in between warped images. Therefore, the RRPN can customize the number of pyramid layers according to different video resolutions and thus make trade-offs between complexity and visual quality. Moreover, a refinement network is introduced to further enhancing details of the interpolated frame. Experiments demonstrate that the RRPN is more flexible and efficient than current SOTA methods but has fewer parameters.

Acknowledgement. Thanks to National Natural Science Foundation of China 61672063 and 61972129, Shenzhen Research Projects of JCYJ20180503182128089 and 2018060-80921419290.

References

1. van Amersfoort, J., et al.: Frame interpolation with multi-scale deep loss functions and generative adversarial networks. arXiv preprint arXiv:1711.06045 (2017)
2. Baker, S., Scharstein, D., Lewis, J., Roth, S., Black, M.J., Szeliski, R.: A database and evaluation methodology for optical flow. Int. J. Comput. Vis. **92**(1), 1–31 (2011). https://doi.org/10.1007/s11263-010-0390-2
3. Bao, W., Lai, W.S., Ma, C., Zhang, X., Gao, Z., Yang, M.H.: Depth-aware video frame interpolation. In: Proceedings of the IEEE Conference on Computer Vision and Pattern Recognition, pp. 3703–3712 (2019)
4. Bao, W., Lai, W.S., Zhang, X., Gao, Z., Yang, M.H.: MEMC-Net: motion estimation and motion compensation driven neural network for video interpolation and enhancement. arXiv preprint arXiv:1810.08768 (2019)
5. Bross, B., Chen, J., Liu, S.: Versatile video coding (draft 2). In: JVET-J1001 (2018)

6. Brox, T., Bruhn, A., Papenberg, N., Weickert, J.: High accuracy optical flow estimation based on a theory for warping. In: Pajdla, T., Matas, J. (eds.) ECCV 2004. LNCS, vol. 3024, pp. 25–36. Springer, Heidelberg (2004). https://doi.org/10.1007/978-3-540-24673-2_3
7. Dosovitskiy, A., et al.: FlowNet: learning optical flow with convolutional networks. In: Proceedings of the IEEE International Conference on Computer Vision, pp. 2758–2766 (2015)
8. Heilbron, F.C., Escorcia, V., Ghanem, B., Niebles, J.C.: ActivityNet: a large-scale video benchmark for human activity understanding. In: Proceedings of the IEEE Conference on Computer Vision and Pattern Recognition, pp. 961–970 (2015)
9. Flynn, J., Neulander, I., Philbin, J., Snavely, N.: DeepStereo: learning to predict new views from the world's imagery. In: Proceedings of the IEEE Conference on Computer Vision and Pattern Recognition, pp. 5515–5524 (2016)
10. Godard, C., Mac Aodha, O., Brostow, G.J.: Unsupervised monocular depth estimation with left-right consistency. In: Proceedings of the IEEE Conference on Computer Vision and Pattern Recognition, pp. 270–279 (2017)
11. Horn, B.K., Schunck, B.G.: Determining optical flow. Artif. Intell. 17(1–3), 185–203 (1981)
12. Hur, J., Roth, S.: Iterative residual refinement for joint optical flow and occlusion estimation. In: Proceedings of the IEEE Conference on Computer Vision and Pattern Recognition, pp. 5754–5763 (2019)
13. Ilg, E., Mayer, N., Saikia, T., Keuper, M., Dosovitskiy, A., Brox, T.: FlowNet 2.0: evolution of optical flow estimation with deep networks. In: IEEE Conference on Computer Vision and Pattern Recognition (CVPR), vol. 2, p. 6 (2017)
14. Ioffe, S., Szegedy, C.: Batch normalization: Accelerating deep network training by reducing internal covariate shift. arXiv preprint arXiv:1502.03167 (2015)
15. Jiang, H., Sun, D., Jampani, V., Yang, M.H., Learned-Miller, E., Kautz, J.: Super SloMo: high quality estimation of multiple intermediate frames for video interpolation. arXiv preprint arXiv:1712.00080 (2018)
16. Jiang, Y., et al.: Thumos challenge: action recognition with a large number of classes (2014)
17. Kingma, D.P., Ba, J.: Adam: a method for stochastic optimization. arXiv preprint arXiv:1412.6980 (2014)
18. Kroeger, T., Timofte, R., Dai, D., Van Gool, L.: Fast optical flow using dense inverse search. In: Leibe, B., Matas, J., Sebe, N., Welling, M. (eds.) ECCV 2016. LNCS, vol. 9908, pp. 471–488. Springer, Cham (2016). https://doi.org/10.1007/978-3-319-46493-0_29
19. Liu, P., Lyu, M.R., King, I., Xu, J.: SelFlow: self-supervised learning of optical flow. In: CVPR (2019)
20. Liu, Y.L., Liao, Y.T., Lin, Y.Y., Chuang, Y.Y.: Deep video frame interpolation using cyclic frame generation. In: AAAI Conference on Artificial Intelligence (2019)
21. Liu, Z., Yeh, R.A., Tang, X., Liu, Y., Agarwala, A.: Video frame synthesis using deep voxel flow. In: ICCV, pp. 4473–4481 (2017)
22. Long, G., Kneip, L., Alvarez, J.M., Li, H., Zhang, X., Yu, Q.: Learning image matching by simply watching video. In: Leibe, B., Matas, J., Sebe, N., Welling, M. (eds.) ECCV 2016. LNCS, vol. 9910, pp. 434–450. Springer, Cham (2016). https://doi.org/10.1007/978-3-319-46466-4_26
23. Meister, S., Hur, J., Roth, S.: UnFlow: unsupervised learning of optical flow with a bidirectional census loss. In: Thirty-Second AAAI Conference on Artificial Intelligence (2018)

24. Meyer, S., Wang, O., Zimmer, H., Grosse, M., Sorkine-Hornung, A.: Phase-based frame interpolation for video. In: Proceedings of the IEEE Conference on Computer Vision and Pattern Recognition, pp. 1410–1418 (2015)
25. Niklaus, S., Liu, F.: Context-aware synthesis for video frame interpolation. arXiv preprint arXiv:1803.10967 (2018)
26. Niklaus, S., Mai, L., Liu, F.: Video frame interpolation via adaptive convolution. In: IEEE Conference on Computer Vision and Pattern Recognition, vol. 1, p. 3 (2017)
27. Niklaus, S., Mai, L., Liu, F.: Video frame interpolation via adaptive separable convolution. arXiv preprint arXiv:1708.01692 (2017)
28. Perazzi, F., Pont-Tuset, J., McWilliams, B., Van Gool, L., Gross, M., Sorkine-Hornung, A.: A benchmark dataset and evaluation methodology for video object segmentation. In: Computer Vision and Pattern Recognition (2016)
29. Ranjan, A., Black, M.J.: Optical flow estimation using a spatial pyramid network. In: IEEE Conference on Computer Vision and Pattern Recognition (CVPR), vol. 2, p. 2. IEEE (2017)
30. Ren, Z., Yan, J., Ni, B., Liu, B., Yang, X., Zha, H.: Unsupervised deep learning for optical flow estimation. In: Thirty-First AAAI Conference on Artificial Intelligence (2017)
31. Revaud, J., Weinzaepfel, P., Harchaoui, Z., Schmid, C.: EpicFlow: edge-preserving interpolation of correspondences for optical flow. In: Proceedings of the IEEE Conference on Computer Vision and Pattern Recognition, pp. 1164–1172 (2015)
32. Ronneberger, O., Fischer, P., Brox, T.: U-Net: convolutional networks for biomedical image segmentation. In: Navab, N., Hornegger, J., Wells, W.M., Frangi, A.F. (eds.) MICCAI 2015. LNCS, vol. 9351, pp. 234–241. Springer, Cham (2015). https://doi.org/10.1007/978-3-319-24574-4_28
33. Simonyan, K., Zisserman, A.: Very deep convolutional networks for large-scale image recognition. arXiv preprint arXiv:1409.1556 (2014)
34. Soomro, K., Zamir, A.R., Shah, M.: UCF101: a dataset of 101 human actions classes from videos in the wild. arXiv preprint arXiv:1212.0402 (2012)
35. Suehring, K., Li, X.: JVET common test conditions and software reference configurations. JVET-B1010 (2016)
36. Sun, D., Yang, X., Liu, M.Y., Kautz, J.: PWC-Net: CNNs for optical flow using pyramid, warping, and cost volume. In: Proceedings of the IEEE Conference on Computer Vision and Pattern Recognition, pp. 8934–8943 (2018)
37. Wang, Y., Yang, Y., Yang, Z., Zhao, L., Wang, P., Xu, W.: Occlusion aware unsupervised learning of optical flow. In: Proceedings of the IEEE Conference on Computer Vision and Pattern Recognition, pp. 4884–4893 (2018)
38. Wang, Z., Bovik, A.C., Sheikh, H.R., Simoncelli, E.P.: Image quality assessment: from error visibility to structural similarity. IEEE Trans. Image Process. 13(4), 600–612 (2004)
39. Weinzaepfel, P., Revaud, J., Harchaoui, Z., Schmid, C.: DeepFlow: large displacement optical flow with deep matching. In: Proceedings of the IEEE International Conference on Computer Vision, pp. 1385–1392 (2013)
40. Xie, S., Tu, Z.: Holistically-nested edge detection. In: Proceedings of the IEEE International Conference on Computer Vision, pp. 1395–1403 (2015)
41. Xu, L., Jia, J., Matsushita, Y.: Motion detail preserving optical flow estimation. IEEE Trans. Pattern Anal. Mach. Intell. 34(9), 1744–1757 (2012)

42. Xue, T., Chen, B., Wu, J., Wei, D., Freeman, W.T.: Video enhancement with task-oriented flow. Int. J. Comput. Vis. **127**(8), 1106–1125 (2019). https://doi.org/10.1007/s11263-018-01144-2
43. Zhang, H., Wang, R., Zhao, Y.: Multi-frame pyramid refinement network for video frame interpolation. IEEE Access **7**, 130610–130621 (2019)

Learning Enriched Features for Real Image Restoration and Enhancement

Syed Waqas Zamir[1]([⊠]), Aditya Arora[1], Salman Khan[1,2], Munawar Hayat[1,2], Fahad Shahbaz Khan[1,2], Ming-Hsuan Yang[3,4], and Ling Shao[1,2]

[1] Inception Institute of Artificial Intelligence, Abu Dhabi, UAE
waqas.zamir@inceptioniai.org
[2] Mohamed bin Zayed University of Artificial Intelligence, Abu Dhabi, UAE
[3] University of California, Merced, USA
[4] Google Research, Merced, USA

Abstract. With the goal of recovering high-quality image content from its degraded version, image restoration enjoys numerous applications, such as in surveillance, computational photography and medical imaging. Recently, convolutional neural networks (CNNs) have achieved dramatic improvements over conventional approaches for image restoration task. Existing CNN-based methods typically operate either on full-resolution or on progressively low-resolution representations. In the former case, spatially precise but contextually less robust results are achieved, while in the latter case, semantically reliable but spatially less accurate outputs are generated. In this paper, we present an architecture with the collective goals of maintaining spatially-precise high-resolution representations through the entire network and receiving strong contextual information from the low-resolution representations. The core of our approach is a multi-scale residual block containing several key elements: (a) parallel multi-resolution convolution streams for extracting multi-scale features, (b) information exchange across the multi-resolution streams, (c) spatial and channel attention mechanisms for capturing contextual information, and (d) attention based multi-scale feature aggregation. In a nutshell, our approach learns an enriched set of features that combines contextual information from multiple scales, while simultaneously preserving the high-resolution spatial details. Extensive experiments on five real image benchmark datasets demonstrate that our method, named as MIRNet, achieves state-of-the-art results for image denoising, super-resolution, and image enhancement. The source code and pre-trained models are available at https://github.com/swz30/MIRNet.

Keywords: Image denoising · Super-resolution · Image enhancement

Electronic supplementary material The online version of this chapter (https://doi.org/10.1007/978-3-030-58595-2_30) contains supplementary material, which is available to authorized users.

1   Introduction

Image content is exponentially growing due to the ubiquitous presence of cameras on various devices. During image acquisition, degradations are often introduced because of the physical limitations of cameras and inappropriate lighting conditions. For instance, smartphone cameras have narrow aperture and small sensors with limited dynamic range. Consequently, they frequently generate noisy and low-contrast images. Similarly, images captured under unsuitable lighting are either too dark or too bright. The art of recovering the original image from its corrupted measurements is studied under the image restoration task.

Recently, deep learning models have made significant advancements for image restoration and enhancement, as they can learn strong (generalizable) priors from large-scale datasets. Existing CNNs typically follow one of the two architecture designs: 1) an encoder-decoder, or 2) high-resolution (single-scale) feature processing. The encoder-decoder models [17,59,84,124] first progressively map the input to a low-resolution representation, and then apply a gradual reverse mapping to the original resolution. Although these approaches learn a broad context by spatial-resolution reduction, on the downside, the fine spatial details are lost, making it extremely hard to recover them in the later stages. On the other side, the high-resolution (single-scale) networks [27,50,120,127] do not employ any downsampling operation, and thereby produce images with spatially more accurate details. However, these networks are less effective in encoding contextual information due to their limited receptive field.

Image restoration is a position-sensitive procedure, where pixel-to-pixel correspondence from the input image to the output image is needed. Therefore, it is important to remove only the undesired degraded image content, while carefully preserving the desired fine spatial details (such as true edges and texture). Such functionality for segregating the degraded content from the true signal can be better incorporated into CNNs with the help of large context, *e.g.*, by enlarging the receptive field. Towards this goal, we develop a new *multi-scale* approach that maintains the original high-resolution features along the network hierarchy, thus minimizing the loss of precise spatial details. Simultaneously, our model encodes multi-scale context by using *parallel convolution streams* that process features at lower spatial resolutions. The multi-resolution parallel branches operate in a manner that is complementary to the main high-resolution branch, thereby providing us more precise and contextually enriched feature representations.

The main difference between our method and existing multi-scale image processing approaches is the way we aggregate contextual information. First, the existing methods [37,71,97] process each scale in isolation, and exchange information only in a top-down manner. In contrast, we progressively fuse information across all the scales at each resolution-level, allowing both top-down and bottom-up information exchange. Simultaneously, both fine-to-coarse and coarse-to-fine knowledge exchange is laterally performed on each stream by a new *selective kernel* fusion mechanism. Different from existing methods that employ a simple concatenation or averaging of features coming from multi-resolution branches, our fusion approach dynamically selects the useful set of kernels from each branch representations using a self-attention approach. More importantly, the proposed fusion block combines features with varying receptive fields, while preserving their distinctive complementary characteristics. Our main contributions include:

- A novel feature extraction model that obtains a complementary set of features across multiple spatial scales, while maintaining the original high-resolution features to preserve precise spatial details.
- A regularly repeated mechanism for information exchange, where the features across multi-resolution branches are progressively fused together for improved representation learning.
- A new approach to fuse multi-scale features using a selective kernel network that dynamically combines variable receptive fields and faithfully preserves the original feature information at each spatial resolution.
- A recursive residual design that progressively breaks down the input signal to simplify the learning process, and allows building very deep networks.
- Comprehensive experiments are performed on five real image benchmark datasets for different image processing tasks including, image denoising, super-resolution and image enhancement. Our method achieves state-of-the-results on *all* five datasets. Furthermore, we extensively evaluate our approach on practical challenges, such as generalization ability across datasets.

2   Related Work

With the rapidly growing image content, there is a pressing need to develop effective image restoration and enhancement algorithms. In this paper, we propose a new method capable of performing image denoising, super-resolution and image enhancement. Unlike existing works for these problems, our approach processes features at the original resolution in order to preserve spatial details, while effectively fuses contextual information from multiple parallel branches. Next, we briefly describe the representative methods for each of the studied problems.

Image Denoising. Classic denoising methods are mainly based on modifying transform coefficients [30,90,115] or averaging neighborhood pixels [78,86,91, 98]. Although the classical methods perform well, the self-similarity [31] based algorithms, *e.g.*, NLM [10] and BM3D [21], demonstrate promising denoising performance. Numerous patch-based algorithms that exploit redundancy (self-similarity) in images are later developed [28,38,43,70]. Recently, deep learning-based approaches [5,9,11,35,39,80,119–121] make significant advances in image denoising, yielding favorable results than those of the hand-crafted methods.

Super-Resolution (SR). Prior to the deep-learning era, numerous SR algorithms have been proposed based on the sampling theory [53,55], edge-guided interpolation [4,122], natural image priors [58,110], patch-exemplars [15,33] and sparse representations [113,114]. Currently, deep-learning techniques are actively being explored, as they provide dramatically improved results over conventional algorithms. The data-driven SR approaches differ according to their architecture designs [6,13,106]. Early methods [26,27] take a low-resolution (LR) image as

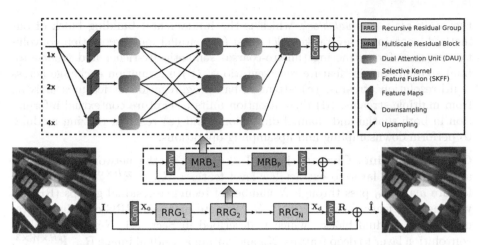

Fig. 1. The proposed network MIRNet is based on a recursive residual design. In the core of MIRNet is the multi-scale residual block (MRB) whose main branch is dedicated to maintaining spatially-precise high-resolution representations through the entire network and the complimentary set of parallel branches provide better contextualized features. It also allows information exchange across parallel streams via selective kernel feature fusion (SKFF) in order to consolidate the high-resolution features with the help of low-resolution features, and vice versa.

input and learn to directly generate its high-resolution (HR) version. In contrast to directly producing a latent HR image, recent SR networks [48,56,94,95] employ the residual learning framework [42] to learn the high-frequency image detail, which is later added to the input LR image to produce the final super-resolved result. Other networks designed to perform SR include recursive learning [3,41,57], progressive reconstruction [60,105], dense connections [99,104,127], attention mechanisms [23,125,126], multi-branch learning [22,60,64,66], and generative adversarial networks (GANs) [63,76,87,104].

Image Enhancement. Oftentimes, cameras generate images that are less vivid and lack contrast. For image enhancement, histogram equalization is the most commonly used approach. However, it frequently produces under- or over-enhanced images. Motivated by the Retinex theory [61], several enhancement algorithms mimicking human vision have been proposed in the literature [8,54,74,83]. Recently, CNNs have been successfully applied to general, as well as low-light, image enhancement problems [52]. Notable works employ Retinex-inspired networks [89,107,124], encoder-decoder networks [18,68,81], and GANs [19,25,51].

3   Proposed Method

In this section, we first present an overview of the proposed MIRNet for image restoration and enhancement, illustrated in Fig. 1. We then provide details of the *multi-scale residual block*, which is the fundamental building block of our method, containing several key elements: (a) parallel multi-resolution convolution streams for extracting (fine-to-coarse) semantically-richer and (coarse-to-fine) spatially-precise feature representations, (b) information exchange across multi-resolution streams, (c) attention-based aggregation of features arriving from multiple streams, (d) dual-attention units to capture contextual information in both spatial and channel dimensions, and (e) residual resizing modules to perform downsampling and upsampling operations.

Overall Pipeline. Given an image $\mathbf{I} \in \mathbb{R}^{H \times W \times 3}$, the network first applies a convolutional layer to extract low-level features $\mathbf{X_0} \in \mathbb{R}^{H \times W \times C}$. Next, the feature maps $\mathbf{X_0}$ pass through N number of recursive residual groups (RRGs), yielding deep features $\mathbf{X_d} \in \mathbb{R}^{H \times W \times C}$. We note that each RRG contains several multi-scale residual blocks, which is described in Sect. 3.1. Next, we apply a convolution layer to deep features $\mathbf{X_d}$ and obtain a residual image $\mathbf{R} \in \mathbb{R}^{H \times W \times 3}$. Finally, the restored image is obtained as $\hat{\mathbf{I}} = \mathbf{I} + \mathbf{R}$. We optimize the proposed network using the Charbonnier loss [16]:

$$\mathcal{L}(\hat{\mathbf{I}}, \mathbf{I}^*) = \sqrt{\left\| \hat{\mathbf{I}} - \mathbf{I}^* \right\|^2 + \varepsilon^2}, \tag{1}$$

where $\mathbf{I}^*$ denotes the ground-truth image, and ε is a constant which we empirically set to 10^{-3} for all the experiments.

3.1   Multi-scale Residual Block (MRB)

In order to encode context, existing CNNs [7,72,73,77,84,109] typically employ the following architecture design: (a) the receptive field of neurons is fixed in *each* layer/stage, (b) the spatial size of feature maps is *gradually* reduced to generate a semantically strong low-resolution representation, and (c) a high-resolution representation is *gradually* recovered from the low-resolution representation. However, it is well-understood in vision science that in the primate visual cortex, the sizes of the local receptive fields of neurons in the same region are different [47,49,82,88]. Therefore, such a mechanism of collecting multi-scale spatial information in the same layer needs to be incorporated in CNNs [32,46,92,93]. In this paper, we propose the multi-scale residual block (MRB), as shown in Fig. 1. It is capable of generating a spatially-precise output by maintaining high-resolution representations, while receiving rich contextual information from low-resolutions. The MRB consists of multiple (three in this paper) fully-convolutional streams connected in parallel. It allows information exchange across parallel streams in order to consolidate the high-resolution features with the help of low-resolution features, and vice versa. Next, we describe the individual components of MRB.

Selective Kernel Feature Fusion (SKFF). One fundamental property of neurons present in the visual cortex is to be able to change their receptive fields according to the stimulus [65]. This mechanism of adaptively adjusting receptive fields can be incorporated in CNNs by using multi-scale feature generation (in the same layer) followed by feature aggregation and selection. The most commonly

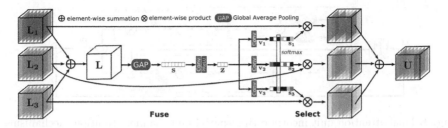

Fig. 2. Schematic for selective kernel feature fusion (SKFF). It operates on features from multiple convolutional streams, and performs aggregation based on self-attention.

used approaches for feature aggregation include simple concatenation or summation. However, these choices provide limited expressive power to the network, as reported in [65]. In MRB, we introduce a nonlinear procedure for fusing features coming from multiple resolutions using a self-attention mechanism. Motivated by [65], we call it selective kernel feature fusion (SKFF).

The SKFF module performs dynamic adjustment of receptive fields via two operations –*Fuse* and *Select*, as illustrated in Fig. 2. The *fuse* operator generates global feature descriptors by combining the information from multi-resolution streams. The *select* operator uses these descriptors to recalibrate the feature maps (of different streams) followed by their aggregation. Next, we provide details of both operators for the three-stream case, but one can easily extend it to more streams. **(1) Fuse:** SKFF receives inputs from three parallel convolution streams carrying different scales of information. We first combine these multi-scale features using an element-wise sum as: $\mathbf{L} = \mathbf{L_1} + \mathbf{L_2} + \mathbf{L_3}$. We then apply global average pooling (GAP) across the spatial dimension of $\mathbf{L} \in \mathbb{R}^{H \times W \times C}$ to compute channel-wise statistics $\mathbf{s} \in \mathbb{R}^{1 \times 1 \times C}$. Next, we apply a channel-downscaling convolution layer to generate a compact feature representation $\mathbf{z} \in \mathbb{R}^{1 \times 1 \times r}$, where $r = \frac{C}{8}$ for all our experiments. Finally, the feature vector $\mathbf{z}$ passes through three parallel channel-upscaling convolution layers (one for each resolution stream) and provides us with three feature descriptors $\mathbf{v_1}, \mathbf{v_2}$ and $\mathbf{v_3}$, each with dimensions $1 \times 1 \times C$. **(2) Select:** this operator applies the softmax function to $\mathbf{v_1}, \mathbf{v_2}$ and $\mathbf{v_3}$, yielding attention activations $\mathbf{s_1}, \mathbf{s_2}$ and $\mathbf{s_3}$ that we use to adaptively recalibrate multi-scale feature maps $\mathbf{L_1}, \mathbf{L_2}$ and $\mathbf{L_3}$, respectively. The overall process of feature recalibration and aggregation is defined as: $\mathbf{U} = \mathbf{s_1} \cdot \mathbf{L_1} + \mathbf{s_2} \cdot \mathbf{L_2} + \mathbf{s_3} \cdot \mathbf{L_3}$. Note that the SKFF uses $\sim 6\times$ fewer parameters than aggregation with concatenation but generates more favorable results.

Dual Attention Unit (DAU). While the SKFF block fuses information across multi-resolution branches, we also need a mechanism to share information within a feature tensor, both along the spatial and the channel dimensions. Motivated by the advances of recent low-level vision methods [5,23,125,126] based on the attention mechanisms [44,103], we propose the dual attention unit (DAU) to extract features in the convolutional streams. The schematic of DAU is shown in Fig. 3. The DAU suppresses less useful features and only allows more informative

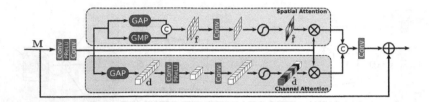

Fig. 3. Dual attention unit incorporating spatial and channel attention mechanisms.

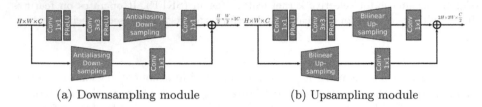

(a) Downsampling module   (b) Upsampling module

Fig. 4. Residual resizing modules to perform downsampling and upsampling.

ones to pass further. This feature recalibration is achieved by using channel attention [44] and spatial attention [108] mechanisms. **(1) Channel attention (CA)** branch exploits the inter-channel relationships of the convolutional feature maps by applying *squeeze* and *excitation* operations [44]. Given a feature map $\mathbf{M} \in \mathbb{R}^{H \times W \times C}$, the squeeze operation applies global average pooling across spatial dimensions to encode global context, thus yielding a feature descriptor $\mathbf{d} \in \mathbb{R}^{1 \times 1 \times C}$. The excitation operator passes $\mathbf{d}$ through two convolutional layers followed by the sigmoid gating and generates activations $\hat{\mathbf{d}} \in \mathbb{R}^{1 \times 1 \times C}$. Finally, the output of CA branch is obtained by rescaling $\mathbf{M}$ with the activations $\hat{\mathbf{d}}$. **(2) Spatial attention (SA)** branch is designed to exploit the inter-spatial dependencies of convolutional features. The goal of SA is to generate a spatial attention map and use it to recalibrate the incoming features $\mathbf{M}$. To generate the spatial attention map, the SA branch first independently applies global average pooling and max pooling operations on features $\mathbf{M}$ along the channel dimensions and concatenates the outputs to form a feature map $\mathbf{f} \in \mathbb{R}^{H \times W \times 2}$. The map $\mathbf{f}$ is passed through a convolution and sigmoid activation to obtain the spatial attention map $\hat{\mathbf{f}} \in \mathbb{R}^{H \times W \times 1}$, which we then use to rescale $\mathbf{M}$.

Residual Resizing Modules. MIRNet employs a recursive residual design (with skip connections) to ease the flow of information during the learning process. In order to maintain the residual nature of our architecture, we introduce residual resizing modules to perform downsampling (Fig. 4a) and upsampling (Fig. 4b) operations. In MRB, the size of feature maps remains constant along convolution streams; but across streams it changes depending on the input resolution index i and the output resolution index j. If $i < j$, the feature tensor is downsampled, and if $i > j$, the feature map is upsampled. To perform $2\times$ downsampling (halving the spatial dimension and doubling the channel dimension), we apply the module in Fig. 4a only once. For $4\times$ downsampling, the module is applied twice. Similarly, one can perform 2× and 4× upsampling by applying the module in Fig. 4b once and twice, respectively. Note in Fig. 4a, we integrate anti-aliasing downsampling [123] to improve the shift-equivariance of our network.

4   Experiments

We perform qualitative and quantitative assessment of the results produced by our MIRNet and compare it with the previous best methods. Next, we describe the datasets, and then provide the implementation details. Finally, we report results for (a) image denoising, (b) super-resolution and (c) image enhancement.

4.1   Real Image Datasets

Image Denoising. (1) **DND** [79] consists of 50 images. Since the images are of very high-resolution, the dataset providers extract 20 crops of size 512×512 from each image, yielding 1000 patches in total. All these patches are used for testing (as DND does not contain training or validation sets). The ground-truth noise-free images are not released publicly, therefore the PSNR and SSIM scores can only be obtained through an online server [24]. (2) **SIDD** [1] is particularly collected with smartphone cameras. Due to the small sensor and high-resolution, the noise levels in smartphone images are much higher than those of DSLRs. SIDD contains 320 image pairs for training and 1280 for validation.

Super-Resolution. RealSR [14] dataset contains real-world LR-HR image pairs of the same scene captured by adjusting the focal-length of the cameras. RealSR has both indoor and outdoor images taken with two cameras. The number of training image pairs for scale factors ×2, ×3 and ×4 are 183, 234 and 178, respectively. For each scale factor, 30 test images are also provided in RealSR.

Image Enhancement. (1) **LoL** [107] is created for low-light image enhancement problem. It provides 485 images for training and 15 for testing. Each image pair in LoL consists of a low-light input image and its corresponding well-exposed reference image. (2) **MIT-Adobe FiveK** [12] contains 5000 images captured with DSLR cameras. The tonal attributes of all images are manually adjusted by five trained photographers (labelled as experts A to E). Same as in [45,75,100], we also consider the enhanced images of expert C as the ground-truth. Moreover, the first 4500 images are used for training and the last 500 for testing.

4.2   Implementation Details

The proposed architecture is end-to-end trainable and requires no pre-training of sub-modules. We train three different networks for three different restoration tasks. The training parameters, common to all experiments, are the following. We use 3 RRGs, each of which further contains 2 MRBs. The MRB consists of 3 parallel streams with channel dimensions of $64, 128, 256$ at resolutions $1, \frac{1}{2}, \frac{1}{4}$,

Table 1. Denoising comparisons on the SIDD dataset [1].

Method	DnCNN [120]	MLP [11]	GLIDE [96]	TNRD [20]	FoE [85]	BM3D [21]	WNNM [38]	NLM [10]	KSVD [2]	EPLL [128]	CBDNet [39]	RIDNet [5]	VDN [118]	MIRNet (Ours)
PSNR ↑	23.66	24.71	24.71	24.73	25.58	25.65	25.78	26.76	26.88	27.11	30.78	38.71	39.28	**39.72**
SSIM ↑	0.583	0.641	0.774	0.643	0.792	0.685	0.809	0.699	0.842	0.870	0.754	0.914	0.909	**0.959**

Table 2. Denoising comparisons on the DND dataset [79].

Method	EPLL [128]	TNRD [20]	MLP [11]	BM3D [21]	FoE [85]	WNNM [38]	KSVD [2]	MCWNNM [112]	FFDNet+ [121]	TWSC [111]	CBDNet [39]	RIDNet [5]	VDN [118]	MIRNet (Ours)
PSNR ↑	33.51	33.65	34.23	34.51	34.62	34.67	36.49	37.38	37.61	37.94	38.06	39.26	39.38	**39.88**
SSIM ↑	0.824	0.831	0.833	0.851	0.885	0.865	0.898	0.929	0.942	0.940	0.942	0.953	0.952	**0.956**

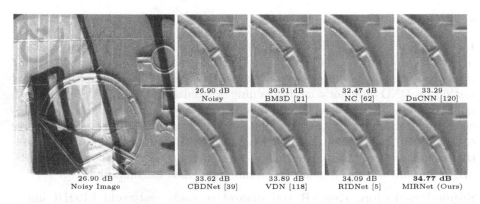

Fig. 5. Denoising example from DND [79].

respectively. Each stream has 2 DAUs. The models are trained with the Adam optimizer ($\beta_1 = 0.9$, and $\beta_2 = 0.999$) for 7×10^5 iterations. The initial learning rate is set to 2×10^{-4}. We employ the cosine annealing strategy [69] to steadily decrease the learning rate from initial value to 10^{-6} during training. We extract patches of size 128×128 from training images. The batch size is set to 16 and, for data augmentation, we perform horizontal and vertical flips.

4.3 Image Denoising

In this section, we demonstrate the effectiveness of the proposed MIRNet for image denoising. We train our network only on the training set of the SIDD [1] and directly evaluate it on the test images of both SIDD and DND [79] datasets. The PSNR and SSIM scores are summarized in Table 1 and Table 2 for SIDD and DND, respectively. Both tables show that our MIRNet performs favourably against the data-driven, as well as conventional, denoising algorithms. Specifically, when compared to the recent best method VDN [118], our algorithm demonstrates a gain of 0.44 dB on SIDD and 0.50 dB on DND. Furthermore, it

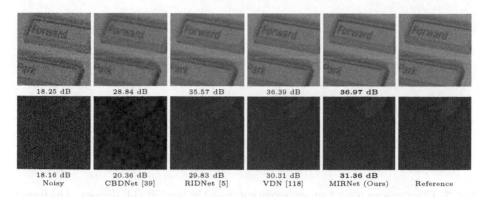

Fig. 6. Denoising examples from SIDD [1]. Our method effectively removes real noise from challenging images, while better recovering structural content and fine texture.

Table 3. Super-resolution evaluation on the RealSR [14] dataset. Compared to the state-of-the-art, our method consistently yields significantly better image quality scores.

Scale	Bicubic		VDSR [56]		SRResNet [63]		RCAN [125]		LP-KPN [14]		MIRNet (Ours)	
	PSNR	SSIM	PSNR	SSIM	PSNR	SSIM	PSNR	SSIM	PSNR	SSIM	PSNR	SSIM
×2	32.61	0.907	33.64	0.917	33.69	0.919	33.87	0.922	33.90	0.927	**34.35**	**0.935**
×3	29.34	0.841	30.14	0.856	30.18	0.859	30.40	0.862	30.42	0.868	**31.16**	**0.885**
×4	27.99	0.806	28.63	0.821	28.67	0.824	28.88	0.826	28.92	0.834	**29.14**	**0.843**

is worth noting that CBDNet [39] and RIDNet [5] use additional training data, yet our method provides significantly better results (8.94 dB improvement over CBDNet [39] on the SIDD dataset and 1.82 dB on DND).

In Fig. 5 and Fig. 6, we present visual comparisons of our results with those of other competing algorithms. It can be seen that our MIRNet is effective in removing real noise and produces perceptually-pleasing and sharp images. Moreover, it is capable of maintaining the spatial smoothness of the homogeneous regions without introducing artifacts. In contrast, most of the other methods either yield over-smooth images and thus sacrifice structural content and fine textural details, or produce images with chroma artifacts and blotchy texture.

Generalization Capability. The DND and SIDD datasets are acquired with different cameras having different noise characteristics. Since the DND benchmark does not provide training data, setting a new state-of-the-art on DND with our SIDD trained network indicates the good generalization of our approach.

4.4 Super-Resolution (SR)

We compare our MIRNet against the state-of-the-art SR algorithms (VDSR [56], SRResNet [63], RCAN [125], LP-KPN [14]) on the testing images of the RealSR [14] for upscaling factors of ×2, ×3 and ×4. Note that all the benchmarked algorithms are trained on the RealSR [14] dataset for a fair comparison.

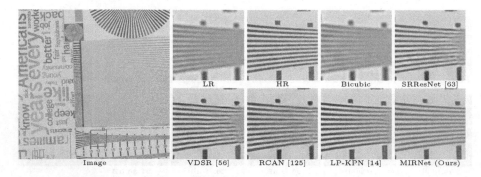

Fig. 7. Comparisons for ×4 super-resolution from the RealSR [14] dataset. The image produced by our MIRNet is more faithful to the ground-truth than other competing methods (see lines near the right edge of the crops).

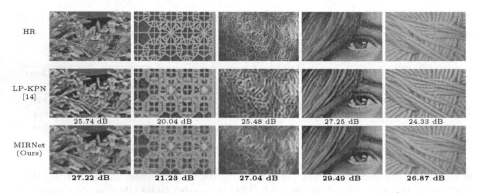

Fig. 8. Additional examples for ×4 super-resolution, comparing our MIRNet against the previous best approach [14]. All example crops are taken from different images.

In the experiments, we also include bicubic interpolation [55], which is the most commonly used method for generating super-resolved images. Here, we compute the PSNR and SSIM scores using the Y channel (in YCbCr color space), as it is a common practice in the SR literature [6,14,106,125]. The results in Table 3 show that the bicubic interpolation provides the least accurate results, thereby indicating its low suitability for dealing with real images. Moreover, the same table shows that the recent method LP-KPN [14] provides marginal improvement of only ∼ 0.04 dB over the previous best method RCAN [125]. In contrast, our method significantly advances state-of-the-art and consistently yields better image quality scores than other approaches for all three scaling factors. Particularly, compared to LP-KPN [14], our method provides performance gains of 0.45 dB, 0.74 dB, and 0.22 dB for scaling factors ×2, ×3 and ×4, respectively. The trend is similar for the SSIM metric as well.

Visual comparisons in Fig. 7 show that our MIRNet recovers content structures effectively. In contrast, VDSR [56], SRResNet [63] and RCAN [125] repro-

Table 4. Cross-camera generalization test for super-resolution. Networks trained for one camera are tested on the other camera. Our MIRNet shows good generalization.

Tested on	Scale	Bicubic	RCAN [125] Canon	(Trained on) Nikon	LP-KPN [14] Canon	(Trained on) Nikon	MIRNet Canon	(Trained on) Nikon
Canon	×2	33.05	34.34	34.11	34.38	34.18	**35.41**	**35.14**
	×3	29.67	30.65	30.28	30.69	30.33	**31.97**	**31.56**
	×4	28.31	29.46	29.04	29.48	29.10	**30.35**	**29.95**
Nikon	×2	31.66	32.01	32.30	32.05	32.33	**32.58**	**33.19**
	×3	28.63	29.30	29.75	29.34	29.78	**29.71**	**30.05**
	×4	27.28	27.98	28.12	28.01	28.13	**28.16**	**28.37**

Table 5. Low-light image enhancement evaluation on the LoL dataset [107]. The proposed method significantly advances the state-of-the-art.

Method	BIMEF [116]	CRM [117]	Dong [29]	LIME [40]	MF [34]	RRM [67]	SRIE [34]	Retinex-Net [107]	MSR [54]	NPE [101]	GLAD [102]	KinD [124]	MIRNet (Ours)
PSNR	13.86	17.20	16.72	16.76	18.79	13.88	11.86	16.77	13.17	16.97	19.72	20.87	**24.14**
SSIM	0.58	0.64	0.58	0.56	0.64	0.66	0.50	0.56	0.48	0.59	0.70	0.80	**0.83**

Table 6. Image enhancement comparisons on the MIT-Adobe FiveK dataset [12].

Method	HDRNet [36]	W-Box [45]	DR [75]	DPE [19]	DeepUPE [100]	MIRNet (Ours)
PSNR	21.96	18.57	20.97	22.15	23.04	**23.73**
SSIM	0.866	0.701	0.841	0.850	0.893	**0.925**

duce results with noticeable artifacts. Furthermore, LP-KPN [14] is not able to preserve structures (see near the right edge of the crop). Several more examples are provided in Fig. 8 to further compare the image reproduction quality of our method against the previous best method [14]. It can be seen that LP-KPN [14] has a tendency to over-enhance the contrast (cols. 1, 3, 4) and in turn causes loss of details near dark and high-light areas. In contrast, the proposed MIRNet successfully reconstructs structural patterns and edges (col. 2) and produces images that are natural (cols. 1, 4) and have better color reproduction (col. 5).

Cross-Camera Generalization. The RealSR [14] dataset consists of images taken with Canon and Nikon cameras at three scaling factors. To test the cross-camera generalizability of our method, we train the network on the training images of one camera and directly evaluate it on the test set of the other camera. Table 4 demonstrates the generalization of competing methods for four possible cases: (a) training and testing on Canon, (b) training on Canon, testing on Nikon, (c) training and testing on Nikon, and (d) training on Nikon, testing on Canon. It can be seen that, for all scales, LP-KPN [14] and RCAN [125] shows comparable performance. In contrast, our MIRNet exhibits more promising generalization.

Fig. 9. Comparison of low-light enhancement approaches on the LoL [107] dataset.

Fig. 10. Image enhancement results on the MIT-Adobe FiveK [12] dataset. Compared to the state-of-the-art, MIRNet makes better color and contrast adjustments.

4.5   Image Enhancement

In this section, we demonstrate the effectiveness of our algorithm by evaluating it for the image enhancement task. We report PSNR/SSIM values of our method and several other techniques in Table 5 and Table 6 for the LoL [107] and MIT-Adobe FiveK [12] datasets, respectively. It can be seen that our MIRNet achieves significant improvements over previous approaches. Notably, when compared to the recent best methods, MIRNet obtains 3.27 dB performance gain over KinD [124] on the LoL dataset and 0.69 dB improvement over DeepUPE [100] on the Adobe-Fivek dataset.

We show visual results in Fig. 9 and Fig. 10. Compared to other techniques, our method generates enhanced images that are natural and vivid in appearance and have better global and local contrast.

Table 7. Impact of individual components of MRB.

Skip connections		✓	✓	✓	✓
DAU	✓		✓		✓
SKFF intermediate	✓	✓			✓
SKFF final	✓	✓	✓	✓	✓
PSNR (in dB)	27.91	30.97	30.78	30.57	**31.16**

Table 8. Feature aggregation. Our SKFF uses ∼ 6× fewer parameters than concat, but generates better results.

Method	Sum	Concat	SKFF
PSNR (in dB)	30.76	30.89	**31.16**
Parameters	0	12,288	2,049

Table 9. Ablation study on different layouts of MRB. *Rows* denote the number of parallel resolution streams, and *Cols* represent the number of columns containing DAUs.

	Rows = 1			Rows = 2			Rows = 3		
	Cols = 1	Cols = 2	Cols = 3	Cols = 1	Cols = 2	Cols = 3	Cols = 1	Cols = 2	Cols = 3
PSNR	29.92	30.11	30.17	30.15	30.83	30.92	30.24	31.16	31.18

5   Ablation Studies

We study the impact of each of our architectural components and design choices on the final performance. All the ablation experiments are performed for the super-resolution task with ×3 scale factor. Table 7 shows that removing skip connections causes the largest performance drop. Without skip connections, the network finds it difficult to converge and yields high training errors, and consequently low PSNR. Furthermore, the information exchange among parallel convolution streams via SKFF is helpful and leads to improved performance. Similarly, DAU also makes a positive influence to the final image quality.

Next, we analyze the feature aggregation strategy in Table 8. It shows that the proposed SKFF generates favorable results compared to summation and concatenation. Moreover, our SKFF uses ∼ 6× fewer parameters than concatenation. Finally, in Table 9 we study how the number of convolutional streams and columns (DAU blocks) of MRB affect the image restoration quality. We note that increasing the number of streams provides significant improvements, thereby justifying the importance of multi-scale features processing. Moreover, increasing the number of columns yields better scores, thus indicating the significance of information exchange among parallel streams for feature consolidation.

6   Concluding Remarks

Conventional image restoration and enhancement pipelines either stick to the full resolution features along the network hierarchy or use an encoder-decoder architecture. The first approach helps retain precise spatial details, while the latter one provides better contextualized representations. However, these methods can satisfy only one of the above two requirements, although real-world image restoration tasks demand a combination of both conditioned on the given input sample. In this work, we propose a novel architecture whose main branch is dedicated to full-resolution processing and the complementary set of parallel branches provides better contextualized features. We propose novel mechanisms to learn relationships between features within each branch as well as across multi-scale branches. Our feature fusion strategy ensures that the receptive field can be dynamically adapted without sacrificing the original feature details. Consistent achievement of state-of-the-art results on five datasets for three image restoration and enhancement tasks corroborates the effectiveness of our approach.

Acknowledgment. Ming-Hsuan Yang is supported by the NSF CAREER Grant 1149783.

References

1. Abdelhamed, A., Lin, S., Brown, M.S.: A high-quality denoising dataset for smartphone cameras. In: CVPR (2018)
2. Aharon, M., Elad, M., Bruckstein, A.: K-SVD: an algorithm for designing over-complete dictionaries for sparse representation. Trans. Sig. Proc. (2006)
3. Ahn, N., Kang, B., Sohn, K.-A.: Fast, accurate, and lightweight super-resolution with cascading residual network. In: Ferrari, V., Hebert, M., Sminchisescu, C., Weiss, Y. (eds.) ECCV 2018. LNCS, vol. 11214, pp. 256–272. Springer, Cham (2018). https://doi.org/10.1007/978-3-030-01249-6_16
4. Allebach, J., Wong, P.W.: Edge-directed interpolation. In: ICIP (1996)
5. Anwar, S., Barnes, N.: Real image denoising with feature attention. ICCV (2019)
6. Anwar, S., Khan, S., Barnes, N.: A deep journey into super-resolution: a survey. arXiv (2019)
7. Badrinarayanan, V., Kendall, A., Cipolla, R.: SegNet: a deep convolutional encoder-decoder architecture for image segmentation. TPAMI (2017)
8. Bertalmío, M., Caselles, V., Provenzi, E., Rizzi, A.: Perceptual color correction through variational techniques. TIP (2007)
9. Brooks, T., Mildenhall, B., Xue, T., Chen, J., Sharlet, D., Barron, J.T.: Unprocessing images for learned raw denoising. In: CVPR (2019)
10. Buades, A., Coll, B., Morel, J.M.: A non-local algorithm for image denoising. In: CVPR (2005)
11. Burger, H.C., Schuler, C.J., Harmeling, S.: Image denoising: can plain neural networks compete with BM3D? In: CVPR (2012)
12. Bychkovsky, V., Paris, S., Chan, E., Durand, F.: Learning photographic global tonal adjustment with a database of input/output image pairs. In: CVPR (2011)
13. Cai, J., Gu, S., Timofte, R., Zhang, L.: Ntire 2019 challenge on real image super-resolution: methods and results. In: CVPRW (2019)
14. Cai, J., Zeng, H., Yong, H., Cao, Z., Zhang, L.: Toward real-world single image super-resolution: a new benchmark and a new model. In: ICCV (2019)
15. Chang, H., Yeung, D.Y., Xiong, Y.: Super-resolution through neighbor embedding. In: CVPR (2004)
16. Charbonnier, P., Blanc-Feraud, L., Aubert, G., Barlaud, M.: Two deterministic half-quadratic regularization algorithms for computed imaging. In: ICIP (1994)
17. Chen, C., Chen, Q., Xu, J., Koltun, V.: Learning to see in the dark. In: CVPR (2018)

18. Chen, L.-C., Zhu, Y., Papandreou, G., Schroff, F., Adam, H.: Encoder-decoder with atrous separable convolution for semantic image segmentation. In: Ferrari, V., Hebert, M., Sminchisescu, C., Weiss, Y. (eds.) ECCV 2018. LNCS, vol. 11211, pp. 833–851. Springer, Cham (2018). https://doi.org/10.1007/978-3-030-01234-2_49
19. Chen, Y.S., Wang, Y.C., Kao, M.H., Chuang, Y.Y.: Deep photo enhancer: unpaired learning for image enhancement from photographs with GANs. In: CVPR (2018)
20. Chen, Y., Yu, W., Pock, T.: On learning optimized reaction diffusion processes for effective image restoration. In: CVPR (2015)
21. Dabov, K., Foi, A., Katkovnik, V., Egiazarian, K.: Image denoising by sparse 3-D transform-domain collaborative filtering. TIP (2007)
22. Dahl, R., Norouzi, M., Shlens, J.: Pixel recursive super resolution. In: ICCV (2017)
23. Dai, T., Cai, J., Zhang, Y., Xia, S.T., Zhang, L.: Second-order attention network for single image super-resolution. In: CVPR (2019)
24. https://noise.visinf.tu-darmstadt.de/benchmark/ (2017). Accessed 29 Feb 2020
25. Deng, Y., Loy, C.C., Tang, X.: Aesthetic-driven image enhancement by adversarial learning. In: ACM Multimedia (2018)
26. Dong, C., Loy, C.C., He, K., Tang, X.: Learning a deep convolutional network for image super-resolution. In: Fleet, D., Pajdla, T., Schiele, B., Tuytelaars, T. (eds.) ECCV 2014. LNCS, vol. 8692, pp. 184–199. Springer, Cham (2014). https://doi.org/10.1007/978-3-319-10593-2_13
27. Dong, C., Loy, C.C., He, K., Tang, X.: Image super-resolution using deep convolutional networks. TPAMI (2015)
28. Dong, W., Shi, G., Li, X.: Nonlocal image restoration with bilateral variance estimation: a low-rank approach. TIP (2012)
29. Dong, X., et al.: Fast efficient algorithm for enhancement of low lighting video. In: ICME (2011)
30. Donoho, D.L.: De-noising by soft-thresholding. Trans. Inf. Theor. (1995)
31. Efros, A.A., Leung, T.K.: Texture synthesis by non-parametric sampling. In: ICCV (1999)
32. Fourure, D., Emonet, R., Fromont, É., Muselet, D., Trémeau, A., Wolf, C.: Residual conv-deconv grid network for semantic segmentation. In: BMVC (2017)
33. Freedman, G., Fattal, R.: Image and video upscaling from local self-examples. TOG (2011)
34. Fu, X., Zeng, D., Huang, Y., Zhang, X.P., Ding, X.: A weighted variational model for simultaneous reflectance and illumination estimation. In: CVPR (2016)
35. Gharbi, M., Chaurasia, G., Paris, S., Durand, F.: Deep joint demosaicking and denoising. TOG (2016)
36. Gharbi, M., Chen, J., Barron, J.T., Hasinoff, S.W., Durand, F.: Deep bilateral learning for real-time image enhancement. TOG (2017)
37. Gu, S., Li, Y., Gool, L.V., Timofte, R.: Self-guided network for fast image denoising. In: ICCV (2019)
38. Gu, S., Zhang, L., Zuo, W., Feng, X.: Weighted nuclear norm minimization with application to image denoising. In: CVPR (2014)
39. Guo, S., Yan, Z., Zhang, K., Zuo, W., Zhang, L.: Toward convolutional blind denoising of real photographs. In: CVPR (2019)
40. Guo, X., Li, Y., Ling, H.: Lime: Low-light image enhancement via illumination map estimation. TIP (2016)
41. Han, W., Chang, S., Liu, D., Yu, M., Witbrock, M., Huang, T.S.: Image super-resolution via dual-state recurrent networks. In: CVPR (2018)

508   S. W. Zamir et al.

42. He, K., Zhang, X., Ren, S., Sun, J.: Deep residual learning for image recognition. In: CVPR (2016)
43. Hedjam, R., Moghaddam, R.F., Cheriet, M.: Markovian clustering for the nonlocal means image denoising. In: ICIP (2009)
44. Hu, J., Shen, L., Sun, G.: Squeeze-and-excitation networks. In: CVPR (2018)
45. Hu, Y., He, H., Xu, C., Wang, B., Lin, S.: Exposure: A white-box photo postprocessing framework. TOG (2018)
46. Huang, G., Chen, D., Li, T., Wu, F., van der Maaten, L., Weinberger, K.Q.: Multi-scale dense networks for resource efficient image classification. In: ICLR (2018)
47. Hubel, D.H., Wiesel, T.N.: Receptive fields, binocular interaction and functional architecture in the cat's visual cortex. J. Physiol. (1962)
48. Hui, Z., Wang, X., Gao, X.: Fast and accurate single image super-resolution via information distillation network. In: CVPR (2018)
49. Hung, C.P., Kreiman, G., Poggio, T., DiCarlo, J.J.: Fast readout of object identity from macaque inferior temporal cortex. Science (2005)
50. Ignatov, A., Kobyshev, N., Timofte, R., Vanhoey, K., Van Gool, L.: DSLR-quality photos on mobile devices with deep convolutional networks. In: ICCV (2017)
51. Ignatov, A., Kobyshev, N., Timofte, R., Vanhoey, K., Van Gool, L.: WESPE: weakly supervised photo enhancer for digital cameras. In: CVPRW (2018)
52. Ignatov, A., Timofte, R.: NTIRE 2019 challenge on image enhancement: methods and results. In: CVPRW (2019)
53. Irani, M., Peleg, S.: Improving resolution by image registration. CVGIP (1991)
54. Jobson, D.J., Rahman, Z.U., Woodell, G.A.: A multiscale retinex for bridging the gap between color images and the human observation of scenes. TIP (1997)
55. Keys, R.: Cubic convolution interpolation for digital image processing. TASSP (1981)
56. Kim, J., Kwon Lee, J., Mu Lee, K.: Accurate image super-resolution using very deep convolutional networks. In: ICCV (2016)
57. Kim, J., Kwon Lee, J., Mu Lee, K.: Deeply-recursive convolutional network for image super-resolution. In: CVPR (2016)
58. Kim, K.I., Kwon, Y.: Single-image super-resolution using sparse regression and natural image prior. TPAMI (2010)
59. Kupyn, O., Martyniuk, T., Wu, J., Wang, Z.: DeblurGAN-v2: deblurring (orders-of-magnitude) faster and better. In: ICCV (2019)
60. Lai, W.S., Huang, J.B., Ahuja, N., Yang, M.H.: Deep Laplacian pyramid networks for fast and accurate superresolution. In: CVPR (2017)
61. Land, E.H.: The retinex theory of color vision. Sci. Am. (1977)
62. Lebrun, M., Colom, M., Morel, J.M.: The noise clinic: a blind image denoising algorithm. IPOL (2015)
63. Ledig, C., et al.: Photo-realistic single image super-resolution using a generative adversarial network. In: CVPR (2017)
64. Li, J., Fang, F., Mei, K., Zhang, G.: Multi-scale residual network for image super-resolution. In: Ferrari, V., Hebert, M., Sminchisescu, C., Weiss, Y. (eds.) ECCV 2018. LNCS, vol. 11212, pp. 527–542. Springer, Cham (2018). https://doi.org/10.1007/978-3-030-01237-3_32
65. Li, X., Wang, W., Hu, X., Yang, J.: Selective kernel networks. In: CVPR (2019)
66. Lim, B., Son, S., Kim, H., Nah, S., Mu Lee, K.: Enhanced deep residual networks for single image super-resolution. In: CVPRW (2017)
67. Liu, Y., Wang, R., Shan, S., Chen, X.: Structure inference net: object detection using scene-level context and instance-level relationships. In: CVPR (2018)

68. Lore, K.G., Akintayo, A., Sarkar, S.: LLNet: a deep autoencoder approach to natural low-light image enhancement. Pattern Recogn. (2017)
69. Loshchilov, I., Hutter, F.: SGDR: stochastic gradient descent with warm restarts. In: ICLR (2017)
70. Mairal, J., Bach, F., Ponce, J., Sapiro, G., Zisserman, A.: Non-local sparse models for image restoration. In: ICCV (2009)
71. Nah, S., Kim, T.H., Lee, K.M.: Deep multi-scale convolutional neural network for dynamic scene deblurring. In: CVPR (2017)
72. Newell, A., Yang, K., Deng, J.: Stacked hourglass networks for human pose estimation. In: Leibe, B., Matas, J., Sebe, N., Welling, M. (eds.) ECCV 2016. LNCS, vol. 9912, pp. 483–499. Springer, Cham (2016). https://doi.org/10.1007/978-3-319-46484-8_29
73. Noh, H., Hong, S., Han, B.: Learning deconvolution network for semantic segmentation. In: ICCV (2015)
74. Palma-Amestoy, R., Provenzi, E., Bertalmío, M., Caselles, V.: A perceptually inspired variational framework for color enhancement. TPAMI (2009)
75. Park, J., Lee, J.Y., Yoo, D., So Kweon, I.: Distort-and-recover: Color enhancement using deep reinforcement learning. In: CVPR (2018)
76. Park, S.-J., Son, H., Cho, S., Hong, K.-S., Lee, S.: SRFeat: single image super-resolution with feature discrimination. In: Ferrari, V., Hebert, M., Sminchisescu, C., Weiss, Y. (eds.) ECCV 2018. LNCS, vol. 11220, pp. 455–471. Springer, Cham (2018). https://doi.org/10.1007/978-3-030-01270-0_27
77. Peng, X., Feris, R.S., Wang, X., Metaxas, D.N.: A recurrent encoder-decoder network for sequential face alignment. In: Leibe, B., Matas, J., Sebe, N., Welling, M. (eds.) ECCV 2016. LNCS, vol. 9905, pp. 38–56. Springer, Cham (2016). https://doi.org/10.1007/978-3-319-46448-0_3
78. Perona, P., Malik, J.: Scale-space and edge detection using anisotropic diffusion. TPAMI (1990)
79. Plotz, T., Roth, S.: Benchmarking denoising algorithms with real photographs. In: CVPR (2017)
80. Plötz, T., Roth, S.: Neural nearest neighbors networks. In: NeurIPS (2018)
81. Ren, W., et al.: Low-light image enhancement via a deep hybrid network. TIP (2019)
82. Riesenhuber, M., Poggio, T.: Hierarchical models of object recognition in cortex. Nat. Neurosci. (1999)
83. Rizzi, A., Gatta, C., Marini, D.: From retinex to automatic color equalization: issues in developing a new algorithm for unsupervised color equalization. J. Electron. Imaging (2004)
84. Ronneberger, O., Fischer, P., Brox, T.: U-Net: convolutional networks for biomedical image segmentation. In: Navab, N., Hornegger, J., Wells, W.M., Frangi, A.F. (eds.) MICCAI 2015. LNCS, vol. 9351, pp. 234–241. Springer, Cham (2015). https://doi.org/10.1007/978-3-319-24574-4_28
85. Roth, S., Black, M.J.: Fields of experts. IJCV (2009)
86. Rudin, L.I., Osher, S., Fatemi, E.: Nonlinear total variation based noise removal algorithms. Physica D (1992)
87. Sajjadi, M.S., Scholkopf, B., Hirsch, M.: EnhanceNet: single image super-resolution through automated texture synthesis. In: ICCV (2017)
88. Serre, T., Wolf, L., Bileschi, S., Riesenhuber, M., Poggio, T.: Robust object recognition with cortex-like mechanisms. TPAMI (2007)
89. Shen, L., Yue, Z., Feng, F., Chen, Q., Liu, S., Ma, J.: MSR-net: low-light image enhancement using deep convolutional network. arXiv (2017)

90. Simoncelli, E.P., Adelson, E.H.: Noise removal via Bayesian wavelet coring. In: ICIP (1996)
91. Smith, S.M., Brady, J.M.: SUSAN-a new approach to low level image processing. IJCV (1997)
92. Sun, K., Xiao, B., Liu, D., Wang, J.: Deep high-resolution representation learning for human pose estimation. In: CVPR (2019)
93. Szegedy, C., et al.: Going deeper with convolutions. In: CVPR (2015)
94. Tai, Y., Yang, J., Liu, X.: Image super-resolution via deep recursive residual network. In: CVPR (2017)
95. Tai, Y., Yang, J., Liu, X., Xu, C.: MemNet: a persistent memory network for image restoration. In: ICCV (2017)
96. Talebi, H., Milanfar, P.: Global image denoising. TIP (2013)
97. Tao, X., Gao, H., Shen, X., Wang, J., Jia, J.: Scale-recurrent network for deep image deblurring. In: CVPR (2018)
98. Tomasi, C., Manduchi, R.: Bilateral filtering for gray and color images. In: ICCV (1998)
99. Tong, T., Li, G., Liu, X., Gao, Q.: Image super-resolution using dense skip connections. In: ICCV (2017)
100. Wang, R., Zhang, Q., Fu, C.W., Shen, X., Zheng, W.S., Jia, J.: Underexposed photo enhancement using deep illumination estimation. In: CVPR (2019)
101. Wang, S., Zheng, J., Hu, H.M., Li, B.: Naturalness preserved enhancement algorithm for non-uniform illumination images. TIP (2013)
102. Wang, W., Wei, C., Yang, W., Liu, J.: GLADNet: low-light enhancement network with global awareness. In: FG (2018)
103. Wang, X., Girshick, R., Gupta, A., He, K.: Non-local neural networks. In: CVPR (2018)
104. Wang, X., et al.: ESRGAN: enhanced super-resolution generative adversarial networks. In: ECCVW (2018)
105. Wang, Z., Liu, D., Yang, J., Han, W., Huang, T.: Deep networks for image super-resolution with sparse prior. In: ICCV (2015)
106. Wang, Z., Chen, J., Hoi, S.C.: Deep learning for image super-resolution: a survey. TPAMI (2019)
107. Wei, C., Wang, W., Yang, W., Liu, J.: Deep retinex decomposition for low-light enhancement. BMVC (2018)
108. Woo, S., Park, J., Lee, J.-Y., Kweon, I.S.: CBAM: convolutional block attention module. In: Ferrari, V., Hebert, M., Sminchisescu, C., Weiss, Y. (eds.) ECCV 2018. LNCS, vol. 11211, pp. 3–19. Springer, Cham (2018). https://doi.org/10.1007/978-3-030-01234-2_1
109. Xiao, B., Wu, H., Wei, Y.: Simple baselines for human pose estimation and tracking. In: Ferrari, V., Hebert, M., Sminchisescu, C., Weiss, Y. (eds.) ECCV 2018. LNCS, vol. 11210, pp. 472–487. Springer, Cham (2018). https://doi.org/10.1007/978-3-030-01231-1_29
110. Xiong, Z., Sun, X., Wu, F.: Robust web image/video super-resolution. TIP (2010)
111. Xu, J., Zhang, L., Zhang, D.: A trilateral weighted sparse coding scheme for real-world image denoising. In: Ferrari, V., Hebert, M., Sminchisescu, C., Weiss, Y. (eds.) ECCV 2018. LNCS, vol. 11212, pp. 21–38. Springer, Cham (2018). https://doi.org/10.1007/978-3-030-01237-3_2
112. Xu, J., Zhang, L., Zhang, D., Feng, X.: Multi-channel weighted nuclear norm minimization for real color image denoising. In: ICCV (2017)
113. Yang, J., Wright, J., Huang, T., Ma, Y.: Image super-resolution as sparse representation of raw image patches. In: CVPR (2008)

114. Yang, J., Wright, J., Huang, T.S., Ma, Y.: Image super-resolution via sparse representation. TIP (2010)
115. Yaroslavsky, L.P.: Local adaptive image restoration and enhancement with the use of DFT and DCT in a running window. In: Wavelet Applications in Signal and Image Processing IV (1996)
116. Ying, Z., Li, G., Gao, W.: A bio-inspired multi-exposure fusion framework for low-light image enhancement. arXiv preprint arXiv:1711.00591 (2017)
117. Ying, Z., Li, G., Ren, Y., Wang, R., Wang, W.: A new image contrast enhancement algorithm using exposure fusion framework. In: CAIP (2017)
118. Yue, Z., Yong, H., Zhao, Q., Meng, D., Zhang, L.: Variational denoising network: Toward blind noise modeling and removal. In: NeurIPS (2019)
119. Zamir, S.W., et al.: CycleISP: real image restoration via improved data synthesis. In: CVPR (2020)
120. Zhang, K., Zuo, W., Chen, Y., Meng, D., Zhang, L.: Beyond a gaussian denoiser: Residual learning of deep CNN for image denoising. TIP (2017)
121. Zhang, K., Zuo, W., Zhang, L.: FFDNet: toward a fast and flexible solution for CNN-based image denoising. TIP (2018)
122. Zhang, L., Wu, X.: An edge-guided image interpolation algorithm via directional filtering and data fusion. TIP (2006)
123. Zhang, R.: Making convolutional networks shift-invariant again. In: ICML (2019)
124. Zhang, Y., Zhang, J., Guo, X.: Kindling the darkness: a practical low-light image enhancer. In: MM (2019)
125. Zhang, Y., Li, K., Li, K., Wang, L., Zhong, B., Fu, Y.: Image super-resolution using very deep residual channel attention networks. In: Ferrari, V., Hebert, M., Sminchisescu, C., Weiss, Y. (eds.) ECCV 2018. LNCS, vol. 11211, pp. 294–310. Springer, Cham (2018). https://doi.org/10.1007/978-3-030-01234-2_18
126. Zhang, Y., Li, K., Li, K., Zhong, B., Fu, Y.: Residual non-local attention networks for image restoration. In: ICLR (2019)
127. Zhang, Y., Tian, Y., Kong, Y., Zhong, B., Fu, Y.: Residual dense network for image restoration. TPAMI (2020)
128. Zoran, D., Weiss, Y.: From learning models of natural image patches to whole image restoration. In: ICCV (2011)

Detail Preserved Point Cloud Completion via Separated Feature Aggregation

Wenxiao Zhang[1], Qingan Yan[2], and Chunxia Xiao[1(✉)]

[1] School of Computer Science, Wuhan University, Wuhan, China
wenxxiao.zhang@gmail.com, cxxiao@whu.edu.cn
[2] JD.com American Technologies Corporation, Mountain View, CA, USA
qingan.yan@jd.com

Abstract. Point cloud shape completion is a challenging problem in 3D vision and robotics. Existing learning-based frameworks leverage encoder-decoder architectures to recover the complete shape from a highly encoded global feature vector. Though the global feature can approximately represent the overall shape of 3D objects, it would lead to the loss of shape details during the completion process. In this work, instead of using a global feature to recover the whole complete surface, we explore the functionality of multi-level features and aggregate different features to represent the known part and the missing part separately. We propose two different feature aggregation strategies, named global & local feature aggregation (GLFA) and residual feature aggregation (RFA), to express the two kinds of features and reconstruct coordinates from their combination. In addition, we also design a refinement component to prevent the generated point cloud from non-uniform distribution and outliers. Extensive experiments have been conducted on the ShapeNet and KITTI dataset. Qualitative and quantitative evaluations demonstrate that our proposed network outperforms current state-of-the art methods especially on detail preservation.

Keywords: Point cloud · Shape completion · Deep learning

1 Introduction

As the low-cost sensors like depth camera and LIDAR are becoming increasingly available, 3D data has gained large attention in vision and robotics community. However, viewpoint occlusion and low sensor resolution in 3D scans always lead to incomplete shapes, which can not be directly used in practical applications. To this end, it is desired to recover a complete 3D model from a partial shape, which has significant values in variety of tasks such as 3D reconstruction [4,7,8,45], robotics [38], scene understanding [3,46] and autonomous driving [26].

Electronic supplementary material The online version of this chapter (https:// doi.org/10.1007/978-3-030-58595-2_31) contains supplementary material, which is available to authorized users.

© Springer Nature Switzerland AG 2020
A. Vedaldi et al. (Eds.): ECCV 2020, LNCS 12370, pp. 512–528, 2020.
https://doi.org/10.1007/978-3-030-58595-2_31

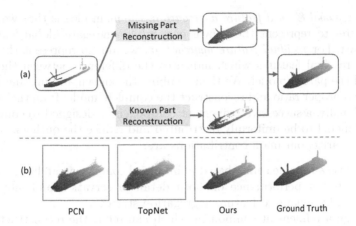

Fig. 1. (a) Given a partial input, the proposed network reconstructs the complete shape from known and missing parts using separated feature representation. (b) Compared with PCN [51] and TopNet [36], our method performs better in both detail preservation and latent shape prediction.

Recent learning-based works succeed in performing shape completion on volumetric representation of 3D objects, such as occupied grids or TSDF volume, where convolution operations can be applied directly [4,11,19,43,47]. However, volumetric representation always leads to expensive memory cost and low shape fidelity. In contrast, point cloud is a more compact and finer representation of 3D data than voxel but is harder to incorporate in the neural network due to its irregular properties. Recently, several network architectures have been designed for direct point cloud shape completion, such as PCN [51], TopNet [36], RL-GAN-Net [31], demonstrating the advantage of point cloud shape completion through learning-based methods. These methods are all based on encoder-decoder networks, where the completed 3D model is recovered via a global feature vector obtained from the encoder. Though the encoded vector is able to represent the overall shape, merely considering it in shape completion will lead to the loss of geometric details existing in original point clouds.

To address this problem, rather than using only a global feature vector to generate the whole complete model, we extract multi-level features and aggregate different-level features to represent the known and missing parts separately, which contributes to both existing detail preservation and missing shape prediction, as illustrated in Fig. 1(a).

We first extract multi-level features for each point by a hierarchical feature learning architecture. These features can present the existing details well, but they do not involve enough missing part cues. If we directly use these features for shape completion, the generated results are likely tangled into the existing partial input. To this end, we consider aggregating diverse features for the known and missing parts separately. We propose two feature aggregation strategies, *i.e., global & local feature aggregation (GLFA)* and *residual feature aggregation*

(RFA). For *global & local feature aggregation*, the main idea is that we leverage local features to represent the known part while aggregate global features for missing part. For *residual feature aggregation*, we aim to represent the missing part with residual features which indicates the difference between the holistic shape and the partial model. We then combine the known and missing part features with a proper ratio and reconstruct the complete model from the combined features. Finally, a successive refinement component is designed to converge the generated model to be uniformly distributed and reduce the outliers.

To summarize, our main contributions are:

- We propose a novel learning based point cloud completion architecture which achieves better performance on both detail preservation and latent shape prediction by separated feature aggregation strategy.
- We design a refinement component which can refine the reconstructed coordinates to be uniformly distributed and reduce the noises and outliers.
- Extensive experiments demonstrate our proposed network outperforms state-of-the-art 3D point cloud completion methods both quantitatively and qualitatively.

2   Related Work

Deep Learning on Point Cloud. Qi *et al.* [28] first introduced a deep learning network PointNet which uses symmetric function to directly process point cloud. PointNet++ [29] captures point cloud local structure from neighborhoods at multiple scales. FoldingNet [49] uses a novel folding-based decoder which deforms a canonical 2D grid onto the underlying shape surface. A series of network architectures on point cloud have been proposed in succession for point cloud analysis [2,13,14,18,20,22,30,35,39,40,42,44,53,54], and related applications such as object detection [5,10,17,26,27,32,41,52] and reconstruction [12,39,48].

Non-learning Based Shape Completion. Shape completion has long been a popular problem on interest in the graphics and vision field. Some effective descriptors have been developed in the early years, such as [15,24,34], which leverages geometric cues to fill the missing parts in the surface. These methods are usually limited to fill only the small holes. Another way to complete the shape is to find the symmetric structure as priors to achieve the completion [23, 25,37]. However, these methods work well only when the missing part can be inferred from the existing partial model. Some researchers proposed data-driven methods [16,21,33] which usually retrieve the most likely model based on the partial input from a large 3D shape database. Though convincing results can be obtained, these methods are time-consuming in matching process according to the database size.

Learning Based Shape Completion. Recently more researchers tend to solve 3D vision tasks using learning methods. Learning based methods on shape completion usually use deep neural network with a encoder-decoder architecture to directly map the partial input to a complete shape. Most pioneering works

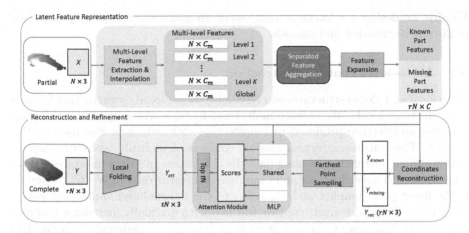

Fig. 2. Overall network architecture. Given a partial point cloud of N points with XYZ coordinates, our network extracts multi-level features and interpolates each level feature to the same size $N \times C_m$ (implemented with PointNet++ [29] layers). Multi-level features are then aggregated to represent known and missing parts separately with feature aggregation strategy. A high-resolution completion result Y_{rec} of size $rN \times 3$ is reconstructed from the expanded features where r is the expansion factor. The reconstructed results are finally refined by a refinement component.

[4, 11, 19, 43, 47] rely on volumetric representations where convolution operations can be directly applied. Volumetric representations lead to large computation and memory costs, thus most works operate on low dimension voxel grids leading to details missing. To avoid these limitations, Yuan *et al.* proposed PCN [51] which directly generates complete shape with partial point cloud as input. PCN recovers the complete point cloud in a two-stage process which first generates a coarse result with low resolution and then recovers the final output using the coarse one. TopNet [36] explores hierarchical rooted tree structure as decoder to generate arbitrary grouping of points in completion task. RL-GAN-Net [31] presents a completion framework using reinforcement learning agent to control the GAN generator. All these approaches generate the complete point cloud by feeding a encoded global feature vector to a decoder network. Though the global feature can almost represent the underlying holistic surface, it discards many details existing in the partial input.

3   Network Architecture

The overall architecture of our network is shown in Fig. 2. First, the multi-level features are extracted via a hierarchical feature learning to efficiently represent both local and global properties. Then we aggregate features for known and missing parts of the point set separately to provide explicit cues for detail preservation and shape prediction. After that, we expand the features and reconstruct the coordinates from the expanded features to obtain a high-resolution result.

Finally, we design a refinement component to make the complete point cloud uniformly distributed and smooth.

3.1 Multi-level Features Extraction

Both local and global structures can be efficiently explored by extracting features from different levels. We extract multi-level features via a hierarchical feature learning architecture proposed in PointNet++ [29], which is also used in PU-Net[50]. The feature extraction module consists of multiple layers of sampling and grouping operation to embed multi-level features and then interpolates each level feature to have the same point number and feature size of $N \times C_m$, where N is the input point number and C_m refers to the interpolated multi-level feature dimension. We progressively capture features with gradually increasing grouping radius. The features at the i-th level is defined as f_i. Different from the PU-Net [50], we extract a global feature f_{global} from the last-level feature. The global feature f_{global} have the same size $1 \times C_m$ and we duplicate it to $N \times C_m$.

3.2 Separated Feature Aggregation

If we directly concatenate the multi-level features for completion, a main problem is that these features can preserve the existing details, but it does not capture enough information to complete the missing shape. The generated points are easier to be tangled at the original partial input even if we add a repulsion loss on the generated results. We discuss this problem in experiments (Sect. 4.4).

To this end, we consider providing explicit cues for the network to balance detail preservation and shape prediction. We separately represent the known and missing parts with diverse features. For known part features, denoted as f_{known}, we want to ensure the propagation of local structure of the input. The missing part features, denoted as $f_{missing}$, can be regarded as the features predicted from global structure, or features indicating the difference between the complete shape and the existing partial structure.

Taking the advantages of multi-level features, we propose and compare two different types of feature aggregation strategies namely GLFA and RFA, which is illustrated in Fig. 3(a) (b).

Global & Local Feature Aggregation (GLFA). Intuitively, the known part should be represented with more local features to keep the original details, whereas the missing part should be expressed with a more global feature to predict the latent underlying surface for the completion task. Generally, lower-level features layers in a network correspond to local features in smaller scales, while higher level features are more related to the global features. To this end, we represent the f_{known} and $f_{missing}$ as:

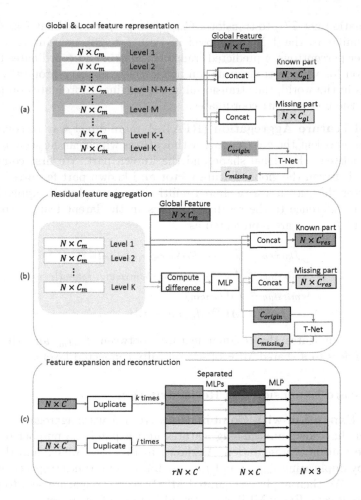

Fig. 3. Illustration of the proposed feature aggregation strategies and the process of feature expansion and reconstruction.

$$f_{known} = [f_1, \ldots, f_m, C_{origin}, f_{global}],$$
$$f_{missing} = [f_{n-m+1}, \ldots, f_n, C_{missing}, f_{global}],$$
$$C_{missing} = \mathcal{T}(C_{origin}), \tag{1}$$
$$m = \lfloor \frac{n}{2} \rfloor + 1,$$

where n is the total level number. We aggregate the first m levels features $[f_1, \ldots, f_m]$ to f_{known} and last m level features $[f_{n-m+1}, \ldots, f_n]$ to $f_{missing}$.

C_{origin} is the original points coordinates in the partial point cloud. $C_{missing}$ indicates the possible coordinates of the missing part. At first, we just use the C_{origin} as $C_{missing}$, but we find the network can converge faster if we set $C_{missing}$ with more proper initial coordinates. To this end, we leverage a learnable transformation net $\mathcal{T}(\cdot)$ to transform C_{origin} to proper coordinates as $C_{missing}$. $\mathcal{T}(\cdot)$ is similar to the T-Net proposed in Pointnet [28], containing a series of multi-layer perceptrons, a predicted transform matrix and coordinates bias. Our observation for using a transformation net is the symmetry properties of most of objects in the world, thus transforming the original coordinates properly can better fit the missing part coordinates.

Residual Feature Aggregation (RFA). A more direct way to consider this issue is to represent the missing part with features which can be seen as residual features between the global shape and the known part. We first compute the difference between the global feature vector and known part features in feature space. After that, a successive shared multi-layer perceptron is applied to generalize the difference to the residual features in the latent feature space. The f_{known} and $f_{missing}$ are represented as:

$$
\begin{aligned}
f_{known} &= [f_1, \ldots, f_n, C_{origin}, f_{global}], \\
f_{missing} &= [f_{res_i}, \ldots, f_{res_n}, C_{missing}, f_{global}], \\
C_{missing} &= \mathcal{T}(C_{origin}), \\
f_{res_i} &= \mathbf{MLP}([f_{global} - f_i]),
\end{aligned}
\tag{2}
$$

where f_{res_i} indicates the residual features between f_{global} and the f_i, and $\mathbf{MLP}(\cdot)$ refers to a shared MLP of several fully connected layers.

3.3 Feature Expansion and Reconstruction

Feature Expansion with Combination. After feature aggregation, we combine both the known and missing features and expand the number of features to high-resolution representation. As shown in Fig. 3(c), we expand the feature number by duplicating f_{known} and $f_{missing}$ for j and k times respectively, where $j + k = r$. We then apply r separated MLPs to the r feature sets to generate diverse point sets. Every MLP shares weights in the feature set.

An important factor is how we define the combination ratio of j and k. In our experiments, we define $j : k = 1 : 1$, as the visible part is often about a half of the whole object. We discuss the effect of the ratio in the supplementary material.

Coordinates Reconstruction. We reconstruct a coarse model Y_{rec} from the expanded features via a sharded MLP and the output is point coordinates $rN \times 3$. The corresponding reconstructed coordinates from the known part and missing part are denoted as Y_{known} and $Y_{missing}$.

3.4 Refinement Component

In practice, we notice that the reconstructed points are easy to locate too close to each other due to the high correlation of the duplicated features, and suffer from noises and outliers. Thus, we design a refinement component to enhance the distribution uniformity and reduce useless points.

We first apply farthest point sampling (FPS) to get a relatively uniformly subsampled $\frac{r}{2}N$ point set. However, FPS algorithm is random and the subsampling depends on which point is selected first, which will not get rid of the noises and outliers in the point set.

We apply a following attention module to reduce the incorrect points. The attention module comprises a shared MLP of 3 stacking fully connected layers with softplus activation function applied on the last layer to produce a score map. It selects the top tN features and points as shown in Fig. 2. The input to the attention module is the corresponding $\frac{r}{2}N \times C$ features to the selected points, and the output is the indexes of the most significant tN points. The selected points are denoted as Y_{att}.

Finally, we apply a local folding unit [49] to approximate a smooth surface of high resolution, which is proposed in PCN [51]. The input to the local folding unit is the $tN \times (3 + C)$ points and corresponding features. For each point, a patch of u^2 points is generated in the local coordinates centered at x_i via the folding operation, and transformed into the global coordinates by adding x_i to the output. The final output is the refined point coordinates $rN \times 3$.

3.5 Loss Function

To measure the differences between two point clouds (S_1, S_2), Chamfer Distance (CD) and Earth Mover's Distance (EMD) are introduced in recent work [6]. We choose the Chamfer distance like [31,36], due to its efficiency over EMD.

$$\mathcal{L}_{CD}(S_1, S_2) = \frac{1}{|S_1|} \sum_{x \in S_1} \min_{y \in S_2} \|x - y\|_2 + \frac{1}{|S_2|} \sum_{y \in S_2} \min_{x \in S_1} \|y - x\|_2. \qquad (3)$$

Besides FPS algorithm, we also explicitly ensure the distribution uniformity of the attention module output in the loss function to reduce the incorrect points. We apply the repulsion loss proposed in PU-Net [50] which is defined as:

$$\mathcal{L}_{rep}(S) - \sum_{x_i \in S} \sum_{x_{i'} \in K(x_i)} \eta(\|x_{i'} - x_i\|) w(\|x_{i'} - x_i\|), \qquad (4)$$

where $\eta(\cdot)$ and $w(\cdot)$ are two repulsion term to penalize x_i if x_i is too close to its neighboring point $x_{i'}$.

We jointly train the network by minimizing the following loss function:

$$\begin{aligned} L_{sum} = &\alpha \mathcal{L}_{CD}(Y_{rec}, Y_{gt}) + \mathcal{L}_{CD}(Y_{att}, Y_{gt}) \\ &+ \mathcal{L}_{CD}(Y_{final}, Y_{gt}) + \beta \mathcal{L}_{rep}(Y_{att}), \end{aligned} \qquad (5)$$

where we set $\alpha = 0.5$ as we do not need Y_{rec} to be an very accurate result, and $\beta = 0.2$ in our experiments. Note that we apply repulsion loss only on Y_{att}, as local folding unit can approximate a smooth surface which represents the local geometry of a shape, so we just need to ensure Y_{att} to be uniformly distributed.

We do not explicitly constrain Y_{known} and $Y_{missing}$ in the loss function to be close to the known part and missing points respectively. If we supervise Y_{known}

Table 1. Quantitative comparison on known categories with state-of-the-art methods with the metric as Chamfer Distance multiplied by 10^4.

Method	Airplane	Cabinet	Car	Chair	Lamp	Sofa	Table	Vessel	Average
FC	5.69	11.02	8.77	10.96	11.13	11.75	9.32	9.72	9.79
Folding	5.96	10.83	9.27	11.24	12.17	11.63	9.45	10.02	10.07
PCN	5.50	10.625	8.69	10.99	11.33	11.67	8.59	9.66	9.63
TopNet	5.85	10.78	8.84	10.80	11.15	11.41	8.79	9.17	9.60
NSFA-RFA	**4.76**	**10.18**	**8.63**	**8.53**	**7.03**	10.53	7.35	7.48	**8.06**
NSFA-GLFA	4.85	10.31	8.92	8.99	7.24	**10.28**	**7.33**	**7.15**	8.14

Table 2. Quantitative comparison on novel categories with state-of-the-art methods with the metric as Chamfer Distance multiplied by 10^4.

Method	Similar					Dissimilar				
	Bus	Bed	Bookshelf	Bench	Avg	Guitar	Motor	Skateboard	Pistol	Avg
FC	9.82	21.23	15.12	10.81	14.20	9.92	14.56	12.00	14.97	12.90
Folding	10.58	19.08	14.88	10.55	13.80	9.06	15.56	11.91	13.13	12.40
PCN	9.46	21.63	14.79	11.02	14.20	10.40	14.75	12.04	14.23	12.90
TopNet	9.31	20.38	14.12	10.16	13.40	9.88	14.30	9.26	12.86	11.50
NSFA-RFA	9.43	18.21	12.50	9.83	12.40	**7.49**	11.41	9.09	**9.09**	**9.20**
NSFA-GLFA	**9.26**	**15.43**	**11.92**	**9.26**	**11.40**	7.71	**9.94**	**9.06**	10.16	**9.20**

with partial input, it will leave the whole completion task to the missing part features reconstruction. We expect the network itself to learn to reconstruct diverse coordinates according to the different feature representation for known and missing parts, which makes the completion can process in both Y_{known} and $Y_{missing}$. Our experiments demonstrate this in Sect. 4.3.

4   Experiments

Training Set. We conduct our experiments on the dataset used by PCN [51] which is a subset of the Shapenet dataset. The ground truth contains 16384 points uniformly sampled from the mesh, and the partial inputs with 2048 points are generated by back-projecting 2.5D depth images into 3D. The training set contains 28974 different models from 8 categories. Each model contains a complete point cloud with about 7 partial point clouds taken from different viewpoint for data augmentation. The validation set contains 100 models.

Testing Set from ShapeNet. The testing set from ShapeNet [1] are divided into two sets: one contains 8 known object categories on which the models are trained; another contains 8 novel categories that are not in the training set. The novel categories are also divided into two groups: one that is visually similar

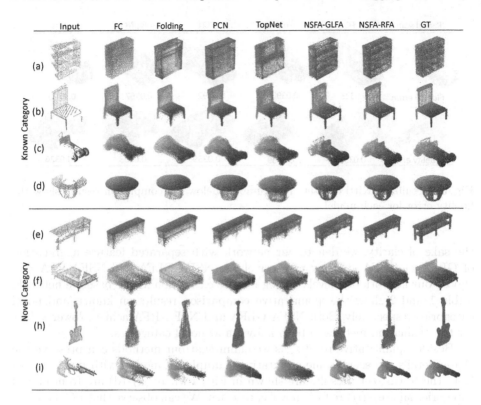

Fig. 4. Qualitative comparisons on both known and novel categories.

to the known categories, and another that is visually dissimilar. There are 150 models in each category.

Testing Set from Kitti. We also test our methods on real-world scans from Kitti dataset [9]. The testing scans are cars which are extracted from each frame according to the ground truth object bounding boxes. The testing set contains 2483 partial point clouds labeled as cars.

Training Setup. We train our model for 30 epochs with a batch size of 8. The initial learning rate is set to be 0.0007 which is decayed by 0.7 for every 50,000 iterations. We set other parameters $r = 8$, $t = 2$, $u = 2$ in our implements.

4.1   Completion Results on ShapeNet

We qualitatively and quantitatively compare our network on both known categories and novel categories with several state-of-the-art point cloud completion methods: FC (Pointnet auto-encoder) [28], FoldingNet [49], PCN [51], and TopNet [36]. For FC, Folding, PCN, we use the pre-trained model and evaluation codes released in the public project of PCN on github. For TopNet, we use their public code and retrain their network using the training set in PCN. For

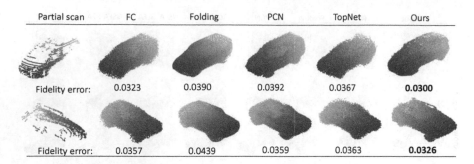

Fig. 5. Results on Kitti dataset. The numbers below the completion results show the fidelity error for each model.

the sake of clarity, we denote our network with separated feature aggregation of GLFA and RFA strategy respectively as NSFA-GLFA and NSFA-RFA. We choose our network of 5 levels during feature extraction as the baseline network. Table 1 and 2 show the quantitative comparison results on known and novel categories respectively. Both NSFA-GLFA and NSFA-RFA achieve lower values for the evaluation metrics in both known and novel categories.

Besides quantitative results, as we claim that our methods can preserve the shape details, we select some qualitative examples of models with much details from the testing set. Results are shown in Fig. 4 where (a)–(d) are from known categories and (e)–(i) are from novel categories. We can observe that FC, Folding, PCN and TopNet can predict a overall shape but most details of the model are lost. In contrast, NSFA-GLFA and NSFA-RFA show their outperformance in both detail preservation and missing shape prediction.

4.2   Completion Results on Kitti

As there are no complete ground truth point clouds for Kitti, we use two metrics proposed in PCN to quantitatively evaluate the performance: 1) Fidelity error, which is the average distance from each point in the input to its nearest neighbour in the output. This measures how well the input is preserved; 2) Minimal Matching Distance (MMD), which is the Chamfer Distance between the output and the car point cloud from ShapeNet that is closest to the output point cloud in terms of CD. This measures how much the output resembles a typical car.

Table 3. Quantitative comparison on known categories with state-of-the-art methods with the metric as Chamfer Distance.

Method	FC	Folding	TopNet	PCN	Ours
Fidelity error	0.0331	0.0361	0.0308	0.0335	**0.0261**
MMD	0.0148	**0.0146**	0.0158	0.0151	0.0154

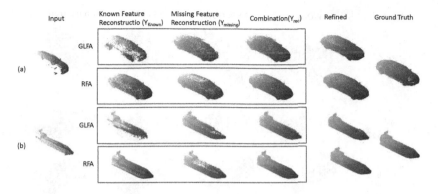

Fig. 6. Reconstructed coordinates visualization from known and missing part features.

The quantitative and qualitative results are shown in Table 3 and Fig. 5 respectively. The fidelity error of each model is also attached in qualitative results. We use NSFA-RFA as our method for comparison as NSFA-RFA performs better than NSFA-GLFA on car category on ShapeNet.

From both quantitative and qualitative results, it can be observed that our method achieves lowest fidelity error, which meets our claim that our network can preserve the existing details better. In Fig. 5, we can see other methods also present reasonable results, but some details in the partial model seems to be lost. Besides, the performances of all the methods on MMD metric are very close, indicating the results from all methods can resemble typical cars.

4.3 Reconstructed Coordinates Visualization

As we consider the known and missing parts separately, we visualize the reconstructed coordinates Y_{known} and $Y_{missing}$ in Y_{rec} from the known part and missing part features to validate our method. Figure 6 shows the visualization examples of both NSFA-GLFA and NSFA-RFA. In general, Y_{known} is closer to the partial input, and $Y_{missing}$ is closer to the missing shape. Meanwhile, there are also completion effects for the Y_{known}, and $Y_{missing}$ also has some original points. This is reasonable as we aggregate global feature to both part features, so the completion can progress in both parts. Specifically, the completion effects on Y_{known} of NSFA-RFA is more significant than NSFA-GLFA. The reason may be that we concatenate all level features to f_{known} of NSFA-RFA but only low-level local features in NSFA-GLFA, thus the completion effects are more apparent on the Y_{known} of NSFA-RFA.

4.4 Feature Aggregation Strategy Evaluation

As we mentioned in Sect. 3.2, directly concatenating the multi-level features for completion will lead to imbalance between detail preservation and shape

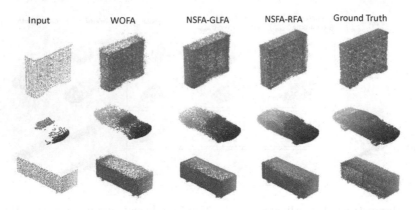

Input   WOFA   NSFA-GLFA   NSFA-RFA   Ground Truth

Fig. 7. Qualitative evaluation of the proposed feature aggregation strategies.

Table 4. Quantitative evaluation of the proposed refinement component on known and novel categories.

Method	NSFA-RFA		NSFA-GLFA	
	Known	Novel	Known	Novel
Without Refine	8.65	10.09	9.38	10.70
With Refine	**8.06**	**10.08**	**8.14**	**9.98**

Table 5. Quantitative evaluation of the proposed feature aggregation strategies.

Method	Known	Novel
NWoSFA	8.74	10.02
NSFA-RFA	**8.06**	10.08
NSFA-GLFA	8.14	**9.98**

completion. We denote our network without feature aggregation strategies as NWoSFA. We evaluate the proposed feature aggregation strategies with qualitative examples shown in Fig. 7. It can be seen that the generated points of NWoSFA are more likely to be gathered at the original input. This effect is released in NSFA-GLFA and the generated points of NSFA-RFA seems can be well spread on the surface. The reason why NSFA-RFA performs better than NSFA-GLFA may due to its more significant completion effects on the known part as mentioned in Sect. 4.3. The completion effects on the known part can help fill the missing shape better. The quantitative results are shown in Table 5. It is notable that NSFA-RFA and NSFA-GLFA significantly boost the performance on the known categories. For novel categories, NSFA-GLFA achieves the lowest Chamfer Distance but NSFA-RFA seems not work well. This indicates that it is hard to generate missing part features using the residual feature aggregation for a totally unseen category. In contrast, NSFA-GLFA uses the global feature to represent the missing part, which is more suitable for novel category.

4.5   Effectiveness of Refinement Component

We also evaluate the effectiveness of the refinement component. Some intermediate results produced by NSFA-GLFA are shown in Fig. 8. The FPS algorithm

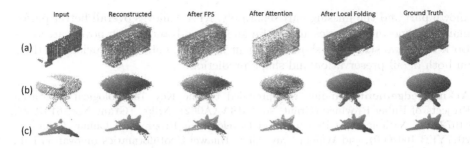

Fig. 8. Effectiveness of the refinement component. FPS module makes the result to be more uniformly distributed and the attention module reduces the invalid points. The local folding unit spread the points to a smooth surface.

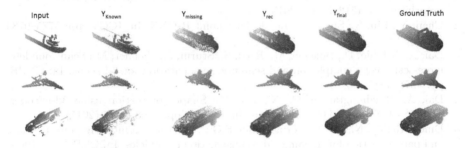

Fig. 9. Symmetrical characteristic during the completion.

enhances the point set distribution uniformity, but it can not get rid of the incorrect points. With the attention module, the generated points are more uniformly distributed with fewer outliers and noises. Finally, the local folding unit spread the points to a high-resolution result with smooth surface. The quantitative results are also shown in Table 4.

4.6 Symmetrical Characteristic During Completion

During the completion process, we find our network try to learn the symmetrical characteristic of the object to complete the model. As shown in Fig. 9, it can be seen that the $Y_{missing}$ is close to the partial input after a proper transformation. This indicates that the details can be preserved not only in the partial input but also in the predicted symmetrical part taking advantages of the symmetrical characteristic.

5 Conclusion

In this work we have proposed a network for point cloud completion via with two separated feature aggregation namely GLFA and RFA, considers the existing known part and the missing part separately. RFA achieves overall better performance on known categories and GLFA shows its advantages on novel categories. Both these two strategies show significant improvements over previous methods on both detail preservation and shape prediction.

Acknowledgement. Funding was provided by the Key Technological Innovation Projects of Hubei Province (Grant No. 2018AAA062), NSFC (Grant Nos. 61972298, 61672390), National Key Research and Development Program of China (Grant No. 2017YFB 1002600), and Wuhan University - Huawei GeoInformatics Innovation Lab.

References

1. Chang, A.X., et al.: ShapeNet: an information-rich 3D model repository. arXiv preprint arXiv:1512.03012 (2015)
2. Chen, Y., Liu, S., Shen, X., Jia, J.: Fast point R-CNN. In: ICCV, pp. 9775–9784 (2019)
3. Dai, A., Ritchie, D., Bokeloh, M., Reed, S., Sturm, J., Nießner, M.: ScanComplete: large-scale scene completion and semantic segmentation for 3d scans. In: CVPR, pp. 4578–4587 (2018)
4. Dai, A., Ruizhongtai Qi, C., Nießner, M.: Shape completion using 3d-encoder-predictor CNNs and shape synthesis. In: CVPR, pp. 5868–5877 (2017)
5. Dinesh Reddy, N., Vo, M., Narasimhan, S.G.: CarFusion: combining point tracking and part detection for dynamic 3d reconstruction of vehicles. In: CVPR, pp. 1906–1915 (2018)
6. Fan, H., Su, H., Guibas, L.J.: A point set generation network for 3D object reconstruction from a single image. In: CVPR, pp. 605–613 (2017)
7. Fu, Y., Yan, Q., Liao, J., Xiao, C.: Joint texture and geometry optimization for RGB-D reconstruction. In: Proceedings of the IEEE/CVF Conference on Computer Vision and Pattern Recognition, pp. 5950–5959 (2020)
8. Fu, Y., Yan, Q., Yang, L., Liao, J., Xiao, C.: Texture mapping for 3D reconstruction with RGB-D sensor. In: Proceedings of the IEEE Conference on Computer Vision and Pattern Recognition (CVPR), pp. 4645–4653. IEEE (2018)
9. Geiger, A., Lenz, P., Stiller, C., Urtasun, R.: Vision meets robotics: the KITTI dataset. Int. J. Rob. Res. **32**(11), 1231–1237 (2013)
10. Giancola, S., Zarzar, J., Ghanem, B.: Leveraging shape completion for 3D Siamese tracking. In: CVPR, pp. 1359–1368 (2019)
11. Han, X., Li, Z., Huang, H., Kalogerakis, E., Yu, Y.: High-resolution shape completion using deep neural networks for global structure and local geometry inference. In: ICCV, pp. 85–93 (2017)
12. Han, Z., Wang, X., Liu, Y.S., Zwicker, M.: Multi-angle point cloud-VAE: unsupervised feature learning for 3D point clouds from multiple angles by joint self-reconstruction and half-to-half prediction. arXiv preprint arXiv:1907.12704 (2019)
13. He, T., et al.: GeoNet: deep geodesic networks for point cloud analysis. In: CVPR, pp. 6888–6897 (2019)
14. Hua, B.S., Tran, M.K., Yeung, S.K.: Pointwise convolutional neural networks. In: CVPR, pp. 984–993 (2018)
15. Kazhdan, M., Hoppe, H.: Screened Poisson surface reconstruction. TOG **32**(3), 29 (2013)

16. Kim, Y.M., Mitra, N.J., Yan, D.M., Guibas, L.: Acquiring 3D indoor environments with variability and repetition. TOG **31**(6), 138 (2012)

17. Lang, A.H., Vora, S., Caesar, H., Zhou, L., Yang, J., Beijbom, O.: PointPillars: fast encoders for object detection from point clouds. In: CVPR, pp. 12697–12705 (2019)

18. Le, T., Duan, Y.: PointGrid: a deep network for 3d shape understanding. In: CVPR, pp. 9204–9214 (2018)

19. Li, D., Shao, T., Wu, H., Zhou, K.: Shape completion from a single RGBD image. TVCG **23**(7), 1809–1822 (2016)

20. Li, J., Chen, B.M., Hee Lee, G.: So-Net: self-organizing network for point cloud analysis. In: CVPR, pp. 9397–9406 (2018)

21. Li, Y., Dai, A., Guibas, L., Nießner, M.: Database-assisted object retrieval for real-time 3D reconstruction. In: CGF, vol. 34, pp. 435–446. Wiley Online Library (2015)

22. Liu, Y., Fan, B., Xiang, S., Pan, C.: Relation-shape convolutional neural network for point cloud analysis. In: CVPR, pp. 8895–8904 (2019)

23. Mitra, N.J., Guibas, L.J., Pauly, M.: Partial and approximate symmetry detection for 3D geometry. TOG **25**, 560–568 (2006)

24. Nealen, A., Igarashi, T., Sorkine, O., Alexa, M.: Laplacian mesh optimization. In: Proceedings of the 4th International Conference on Computer Graphics and Interactive Techniques in Australasia and Southeast Asia, pp. 381–389. ACM (2006)

25. Pauly, M., Mitra, N.J., Wallner, J., Pottmann, H., Guibas, L.J.: Discovering structural regularity in 3D geometry. TOG **27**, 43 (2008)

26. Qi, C.R., Litany, O., He, K., Guibas, L.J.: Deep hough voting for 3D object detection in point clouds. In: ICCV, pp. 9277–9286 (2019)

27. Qi, C.R., Liu, W., Wu, C., Su, H., Guibas, L.J.: Frustum PointNets for 3D object detection from RGB-D data. In: CVPR, pp. 918–927 (2018)

28. Qi, C.R., Su, H., Mo, K., Guibas, L.J.: PointNet: deep learning on point sets for 3D classification and segmentation. In: CVPR, vol. 1, no. 2, p. 4 (2017)

29. Qi, C.R., Yi, L., Su, H., Guibas, L.J.: PointNet++: deep hierarchical feature learning on point sets in a metric space. In: NeurIPS, pp. 5099–5108 (2017)

30. Rethage, D., Wald, J., Sturm, J., Navab, N., Tombari, F.: Fully-convolutional point networks for large-scale point clouds. In: Ferrari, V., Hebert, M., Sminchisescu, C., Weiss, Y. (eds.) ECCV 2018. LNCS, vol. 11208, pp. 625–640. Springer, Cham (2018). https://doi.org/10.1007/978-3-030-01225-0_37

31. Sarmad, M., Lee, H.J., Kim, Y.M.: RL-GAN-Net: a reinforcement learning agent controlled GAN network for real-time point cloud shape completion. In: CVPR, pp. 5898–5907 (2019)

32. Shi, S., Wang, X., Li, H.: PointRCNN: 3D object proposal generation and detection from point cloud. In: CVPR, pp. 770–779 (2019)

33. Shi, Y., Long, P., Xu, K., Huang, H., Xiong, Y.: Data-driven contextual modeling for 3d scene understanding. Comput. Graph. **55**, 55–67 (2016)

34. Sorkine, O., Cohen-Or, D.: Least-squares meshes. In: Proceedings Shape Modeling Applications, pp. 191–199. IEEE (2004)

35. Su, H., et al.: SPLATNet: sparse lattice networks for point cloud processing. In: CVPR, pp. 2530–2539 (2018)

36. Tchapmi, L.P., Kosaraju, V., Rezatofighi, H., Reid, I., Savarese, S.: TopNet: structural point cloud decoder. In: Proceedings of the IEEE Conference on Computer Vision and Pattern Recognition, pp. 383–392 (2019)

37. Thrun, S., Wegbreit, B.: Shape from symmetry. In: ICCV, vol. 2, pp. 1824–1831. IEEE (2005)

38. Varley, J., DeChant, C., Richardson, A., Ruales, J., Allen, P.: Shape completion enabled robotic grasping. In: IROS, pp. 2442–2447. IEEE (2017)
39. Wang, C., Samari, B., Siddiqi, K.: Local spectral graph convolution for point set feature learning. In: Ferrari, V., Hebert, M., Sminchisescu, C., Weiss, Y. (eds.) ECCV 2018. LNCS, vol. 11208, pp. 56–71. Springer, Cham (2018). https://doi.org/10.1007/978-3-030-01225-0_4
40. Wang, S., Suo, S., Ma, W.C., Pokrovsky, A., Urtasun, R.: Deep parametric continuous convolutional neural networks. In: CVPR, pp. 2589–2597 (2018)
41. Wang, Y., Chao, W.L., Garg, D., Hariharan, B., Campbell, M., Weinberger, K.Q.: Pseudo-lidar from visual depth estimation: bridging the gap in 3D object detection for autonomous driving. In: CVPR, pp. 8445–8453 (2019)
42. Wu, W., Qi, Z., Fuxin, L.: PointConv: deep convolutional networks on 3D point clouds. In: CVPR, pp. 9621–9630 (2019)
43. Wu, Z., et al.: 3D ShapeNets: a deep representation for volumetric shapes. In: CVPR, pp. 1912–1920 (2015)
44. Xu, Y., Fan, T., Xu, M., Zeng, L., Qiao, Yu.: SpiderCNN: deep learning on point sets with parameterized convolutional filters. In: Ferrari, V., Hebert, M., Sminchisescu, C., Weiss, Y. (eds.) ECCV 2018. LNCS, vol. 11212, pp. 90–105. Springer, Cham (2018). https://doi.org/10.1007/978-3-030-01237-3_6
45. Yan, Q., Yang, L., Liang, C., Liu, H., Hu, R., Xiao, C.: Geometrically based linear iterative clustering for quantitative feature correspondence. Comput. Graph. Forum **35**, 1–10 (2016)
46. Yan, Q., Yang, L., Zhang, L., Xiao, C.: Distinguishing the indistinguishable: exploring structural ambiguities via geodesic context. In: Proceedings of the IEEE Conference on Computer Vision and Pattern Recognition, pp. 3836–3844 (2017)
47. Yang, B., Wen, H., Wang, S., Clark, R., Markham, A., Trigoni, N.: 3D object reconstruction from a single depth view with adversarial learning. In: ICCV, pp. 679–688 (2017)
48. Yang, G., Huang, X., Hao, Z., Liu, M.Y., Belongie, S., Hariharan, B.: PointFlow: 3D point cloud generation with continuous normalizing flows. In: ICCV, pp. 4541–4550 (2019)
49. Yang, Y., Feng, C., Shen, Y., Tian, D.: FoldingNet: point cloud auto-encoder via deep grid deformation. In: CVPR, pp. 206–215 (2018)
50. Yu, L., Li, X., Fu, C.W., Cohen-Or, D., Heng, P.A.: PU-Net: point cloud upsampling network. In: CVPR, pp. 2790–2799 (2018)
51. Yuan, W., Khot, T., Held, D., Mertz, C., Hebert, M.: PCN: point completion network. In: 3DV, pp. 728–737. IEEE (2018)
52. Zhang, W., Xiao, C.: PCAN: 3D attention map learning using contextual information for point cloud based retrieval. In: CVPR, pp. 12436–12445 (2019)
53. Zhao, H., Jiang, L., Fu, C.W., Jia, J.: PointWeb: enhancing local neighborhood features for point cloud processing. In: CVPR, pp. 5565–5573 (2019)
54. Zhao, Y., Birdal, T., Deng, H., Tombari, F.: 3D point capsule networks. In: CVPR, pp. 1009–1018 (2019)

LabelEnc: A New Intermediate Supervision Method for Object Detection

Miao Hao[1], Yitao Liu[2], Xiangyu Zhang[3(✉)], and Jian Sun[3]

[1] Beijing University of Posts and Telecommunications, Beijing, China
haomiao@bupt.edu.cn
[2] Tongji University, Shanghai, China
att@tongji.edu.cn
[3] MEGVII Technology, Beijing, China
{zhangxiangyu,sunjian}@megvii.com

Abstract. In this paper we propose a new intermediate supervision method, named LabelEnc, to boost the training of object detection systems. The key idea is to introduce a novel label encoding function, mapping the ground-truth labels into latent embedding, acting as an auxiliary intermediate supervision to the detection backbone during training. Our approach mainly involves a two-step training procedure. First, we optimize the label encoding function via an AutoEncoder defined in the label space, approximating the "desired" intermediate representations for the target object detector. Second, taking advantage of the learned label encoding function, we introduce a new auxiliary loss attached to the detection backbones, thus benefiting the performance of the derived detector. Experiments show our method improves a variety of detection systems by around 2% on COCO dataset, no matter one-stage or two-stage frameworks. Moreover, the auxiliary structures only exist during training, i.e. it is completely cost-free in inference time.

Keywords: Object detection · Auxiliary supervision · AutoEncoder

1 Introduction

Object detection is one of the fundamental problems in computer vision. In deep learning era, modern object detection networks [11,14,23,24,30–32,38] are composed of two main components: one is the *backbone* part $f(\cdot; \theta_f)$, which

---

M. Hao and Y. Liu–Equal contribution. This work is done during Miao Hao and Yitao Liu's internship at MEGVII Technology and is supported by The National Key Research and Development Program of China (No. 2017YFA0700800) and Beijing Academy of Artificial Intelligence (BAAI).

Electronic supplementary material The online version of this chapter (https://doi.org/10.1007/978-3-030-58595-2_32) contains supplementary material, which is available to authorized users.

© Springer Nature Switzerland AG 2020
A. Vedaldi et al. (Eds.): ECCV 2020, LNCS 12370, pp. 529–545, 2020.
https://doi.org/10.1007/978-3-030-58595-2_32

generates the intermediate embedding from each image; the other part is the *detection head* $d(\cdot; \theta_d)$, to extract instance information (i.e. class label as well as the corresponding bounding box) from the intermediate representation. To learn the parameters θ_f and θ_d, earlier work like [15] proposes to optimize them separately on different datasets respectively. However, most of recent state-of-the-art detection frameworks [11,23,26,30,32] suggest **joint optimization** of the backbones and detection heads for simpler pipeline and better performance, formulated as follows:

$$\theta_f^*, \theta_d^* = \arg\min_{\theta_f, \theta_d} \mathbb{E}_{(I,y)\sim\mathcal{D}} \quad \mathcal{L}_{det}\left(d(f(I; \theta_f); \theta_d), y\right), \tag{1}$$

where (I, y) stands for a pair of image and ground-truth label; $\mathcal{D}$ is the dataset distribution; and $\mathcal{L}_{det}(\cdot, \cdot)$ represents the detection loss, which is usually composed of classification terms and bounding-box regression terms [32].

Typically, the backbone part $f(\cdot; \theta_f)$ contains too many parameters, thus may be nontrivial or very costly to be directly optimized in the detection dataset [13,22,34,46]. A common practice is to introduce *pretraining*, for instance, initializing θ_f in Eq. 1 with *ImageNet* pretrained [23,24,26,30–32] or self-supervised [7,12] weights. Though such *pretraining-then-finetuning* paradigm has been demonstrated to achieve state-of-the-art performances [4,14], however, we find that only pretraining backbone weights θ_f may be suboptimal for the optimization. Since the weights in detection head θ_d are still randomly initialized, during training, gradient passed from the detection head to the backbone could be very noisy, especially in the very beginning. The noisy gradient may significantly harm the pretrained weights, causing slower convergence or poorer performance. Actually, such degradation has been observed in many codebases and a few workarounds are also proposed. For example, a well-known workaround is to freeze a few weight layers in the backbone during finetuning to avoid unstable optimization [11,32]; however, it seems still insufficient to fully address the issue.

In this paper, we propose to deal with the problem from a new direction – introducing an auxiliary intermediate supervision *directly* to the backbone. The key motivation is, if we can provide a feasible supervision in the training phase, the backbone part could be effectively optimized even before the detection head converges. We formulate our method as follows:

$$\theta_f^*, \theta_d^* = \arg\min_{\theta_f, \theta_d} \mathbb{E}_{(I,y)\sim\mathcal{D}} \quad \mathcal{L}_{det}\left(d(f(I; \theta_f); \theta_d), y\right) + \lambda\mathcal{R}(f(I; \theta_f), y), \tag{2}$$

where $\mathcal{R}(f(I; \theta_f), y)$ means the auxiliary loss attached to the outputs of the backbone, which is *independent* to the detection head $d(\cdot, \theta_d)$ thus not affected by the latter's convergence progress. λ is the balanced coefficient.

The core of our approach thus includes the design of $\mathcal{R}(\cdot, \cdot)$. Intuitively, the auxiliary supervision aims to minimize the distance between latent feature representation and some "ideal" embedding of the corresponding training sample. However, how to define and calculate the desired representation? Some previous works, especially *Knowledge Distillation* [17] methods, suggest acquiring the intermediate supervision from more powerful *teacher models*; nevertheless, whose representations are not guaranteed to be optimal. Instead in this work, for the first time, we point that the *inverse* of the *underlying optimal* detection head (i.e. $d^{-1}(y; \theta_d^*)$) could be the feasible embedding, which traces the ground-truth label y back to the corresponding latent feature. More discussion will be referred in Sect. 3.

Motivated by the analyses, in our proposed method **LabelEnc**, we introduce a novel *label encoding function* to realize $\mathcal{R}(\cdot, \cdot)$ in Eq. 2, which maps the ground-truth labels into the latent embedding space thus providing an auxiliary intermediate supervision to the detector's training. Label encoding function is designed to approximate $d^{-1}(y; \theta_d^*)$, since the *underlying optimal* parameters θ_d^* and the "*inverse form*" $d^{-1}(\cdot)$ in the latter's formulation are nontrivial to be directly derived in mathematics. Thus our method in general involves a *two-step* training pipeline. **First**, to learn the *label encoding function*, we train an *AutoEncoder* architecture, embedding the ground-truth labels into the latent space according to the (approximated) optimal detection head. **Second**, with the help of the learned label encoding function, we optimize Eq. 2 under the auxiliary supervision $\mathcal{R}(f(I; \theta_f), y)$; in addition, initial weights in the detection head θ_d can also inherit from the AutoEncoder instead of random values for more stable optimization.

We evaluate our method on various object detection systems. Under different backbones (e.g. *ResNet*-50, *ResNet*-101 [16] and *Deformable Convolutional Networks* [9,47]) or detection frameworks (e.g. *RetinaNet* [24], *FCOS* [38] and *FPN* [23]), on each of them our training pipeline achieves significant performance gains consistently, e.g. ~**2%** improvements on *COCO* [25] dataset. More importantly, our method is completely cost-free in inference time, as the auxiliary structures only exist during training. Please refer to Sect. 4 for detailed results.

In conclusion, the major contributions of our paper are as follows:

- We propose a new auxiliary intermediate supervision method named **LabelEnc**, to boost the training of object detection systems. With the novel *label encoding function*, our method can effectively overcome the drawbacks of randomly initialized detection heads, leading to more stable optimization and better performance.
- Our method is demonstrated to be generally applicable in most of modern object detection systems. Compared with previous methods like [21,34,47], though various auxiliary losses are also introduced, usually those methods rely on specified backbone architectures or detection frameworks. Furthermore, though the underlying formulations appear to be somewhat complex, the implementation of our approach is relatively simple. Code will be released soon.

2   Related Work

Auxiliary Supervision. *Auxiliary Supervision* is a common technique to improve the performance of the model in indirect ways, e.g., *weight decay, Center*

Loss [41], etc. Among various auxiliary supervision methods, *Multi-task Learning* (MTL) [5] methods are used commonly. MTL solves multiple tasks using a single model. By sharing parameters between the tasks, inductive bias is transferred and better generalization is gained. In object detection, *Mask R-CNN* [14] combines object detection with instance segmentation by adding a simple mask branch to *Faster R-CNN* model [32]. The MTL strategy can improve the performance of the detection branch efficiently, but it requires additional mask annotation. [20], on the contrary, does not need additional annotations, but it requires carefully-designed auxiliary tasks.

Deeply Supervise is another common method of auxiliary supervise. Instead of introducing additional tasks, Deeply Supervise introduces supervision on additional layers. *DSN* [19] first proposes the concept by adding additional supervision on the hidden layers. *Inception* [36] also uses similar auxiliary classifiers on lower stages of the network. In semantic segmentation, *PSPNet* [45] and *ExFuse* [44] adopt Deeply Supervise in order to improve the low-level features. In object detection, *DSOD* [34] utilizes Deeply Supervise with dense connections to enable from-scratch training. In our method, we adopt the idea of Deeply Supervise by proposing a label encoding function, with which we can map the labels into latent embedding for auxiliary intermediate supervision.

Knowledge Distillation. our method shares some common inspiration with *Knowledge Distillation* [17,33,40,43]. In Knowledge Distillation, the training is a two-step process. A large teacher model is trained first. Then its predictions are used to supervise a smaller student model. Knowledge Distillation has been used in several fields, e.g., face [27], speech [37], re-id [8]. There are several works focusing on object detection as well: [6] uses balanced loss on classification, bounded loss on regression and $L2$ loss on feature; [21,47] propose their distillation methods based on RoIs; [39] so that distillation focuses on object-local areas.

From the distillation perspective, the *label encoding function* is the teacher model in our pipeline. It is trained in the first step and utilized for supervision in Step 2. But it is a relatively simple architecture and does not involve feature in real world. On the contrary, traditional distillation models rely heavily on a big teacher model. Usually, the stronger the teacher model is, the better distillation performance it can give. However, teacher models with high performance are not always available in practice. The state-of-the-art models are the best teachers we can find. This limits the performance of traditional distillation.

Label Encoding. There are several works that use label encoding to boost training [1,3,35,42]. However, few evaluate in supervised object detection task. Among them, our method is most similar to [28]. [28] uses an AutoEncoder to model the labels of semantic segmentation. The AutoEncoder is then used to perform auxiliary supervision. Compared with our method, there are two main differences: first, in object detection, label structures hardly exist. Segmentation has rich information in label structures thanks to the outline of regions in annotation, e.g. a cat has a long tail, a thick body and a small head. Whereas in object detection, such structures are very limited, since all objects are just boxes with different scales and aspect ratios. Second, we propose a joint optimization scheme that introduces auxiliary structures for training AutoEncoder, which we empirically find vital to the performance. Whereas in [28], the AutoEncoder is trained independently.

3 Method

3.1 Intermediate Auxiliary Supervision

As mentioned in the introduction, the core of our method is to define the supervision term $\mathcal{R}(\cdot,\cdot)$ in Eq. 2, which is expected to provide feasible supervision to the backbone training. Intuitively, the auxiliary loss should encourage the latent feature generated by the backbone network to be close to some "ideal" embedding $\mathcal{T}(I, y)$ for each training sample:

$$\mathcal{R}(f(I; \theta_f), y) = \mathcal{L}_{dis}(f(I; \theta_f), \mathcal{T}(I, y)), \tag{3}$$

where $\mathcal{L}_{dis}(\cdot, \cdot)$ represents the distance measurement. Therefore, a problem rises: how to define the so-called "ideal" feature $\mathcal{T}(I, y)$? Obviously, the calculation of $\mathcal{T}(I, y)$ **cannot** directly rely on the training of the detection head $d(\cdot; \theta_d)$, otherwise it may be unstable and redundant to the existing detection loss $\mathcal{L}_{det}$.

Let us think for a further step. If we have finished the optimization in Eq. 2 via some way, i.e. the corresponding optimal weights θ_f^* and θ_d^* have been obtained, we can intuitively define the inverse of the detection head $d^{-1}(y; \theta_d^*)$ as the "optimal" intermediate embedding. So,

$$\mathcal{R}(f(I; \theta_f), y) = \mathcal{L}_{dis}(f(I; \theta_f), d^{-1}(y; \theta_d^*)). \tag{4}$$

We argue that the definition of $\mathcal{R}(\cdot, \cdot)$ is feasible because if the auxiliary loss tends to zero, it is easy to verify that the detector will predict the ground truth y exactly. Unfortunately, Eq. 4 cannot be directly used in the optimization. **First**, to substitute Eq. 4 into Eq. 2, we find θ_d^* exists in both side of the equation – we cannot determine the value in advance. **Second**, even though θ_d^* is given, the inverse form $d^{-1}(\cdot; \theta_d^*)$ is still difficult to be calculated due to the high nonlinearity of neural networks (actually the inverse is generally not unique).

We deal with the second problem firstly. Notice that for any y, we have $d^{-1} \circ d(y; \theta_d^*) \equiv y$. Motivated by this, to approximate $d^{-1}(\cdot; \theta_d^*)$ we introduce a new network $h(\cdot; \psi)$, whose parameters are learned by the optimization:

$$\psi^* = \arg\min_{\psi} \mathbb{E}_{(I,y) \sim \mathcal{D}} \quad \mathcal{L}_{det}(d(h(y; \psi); \theta_d^*), y). \tag{5}$$

Here, $\mathcal{L}_{det}(\cdot, \cdot)$ is the detection loss, following the definition in Eq. 1. Intuitively, $h(\cdot; \psi^*)$ maps the ground truth label y into the latent feature space and $d(\cdot; \theta_d^*)$

recovers the label from the latent representation. So, we say that $h(\cdot; \psi^*)$ approximates the "inverse" of $d(\cdot; \theta_d^*)$. It is worth noting that the composite function $(h \circ d)(\cdot; \psi^*, \theta_d^*)$ actually represents an **AutoEncoder** defined in the *label space*. Thus we name $h(\cdot)$ as *label encoding function*. Thanks to the approximation, we rewrite Eq. 4 as follows:

$$\mathcal{R}(f(I; \theta_f), y) = \mathcal{L}_{dis}(f(I; \theta_f), h(y; \psi^*)). \tag{6}$$

Then we come back to the first problem. In Eq. 6, note that the optimization of ψ^* still implies θ_d^* (Eq. 5). So, in our formulations (Eq. 2, 6 and 5) there still exists the recursive dependence on θ_d^*. To get out of the dilemma, we use an *unrolling* trick, i.e. recursively substituting Eq. 6 and Eq. 5 into Eq. 2. Thus we obtain the final formulations (please refer to the appendix for the detailed derivation):

$$\theta_f^*, \theta_d^* = \arg \min_{\theta_f, \theta_d} \mathbb{E}_{(I,y) \sim \mathcal{D}} \quad \mathcal{L}_{det}(d(f(I; \theta_f); \theta_d), y) + \lambda \mathcal{L}_{dis}(f(I; \theta_f), h(y; \psi^*)), \tag{7}$$

where

$$\psi^* = \arg \min_{\psi} \mathbb{E}_{(I,y) \sim \mathcal{D}} \quad \mathcal{L}_{det}(d(h(y; \psi); \hat{\theta}_d), y),$$

$$s.t. \quad \hat{\theta}_d = \arg \min_{\theta_d'} \left[\min_{\theta_f'} \mathbb{E}_{(I,y) \sim \mathcal{D}} \mathcal{L}_{det}(\theta_f', \theta_d') + \lambda \mathcal{L}_{dis}(f(I; \theta_f'), h(y; \psi)) \right]. \tag{8}$$

Here $\mathcal{L}_{det}(\theta_f', \theta_d')$ is short for $\mathcal{L}_{det}(d(f(I; \theta_f'); \theta_d'), y)$.

Equation 7 and Eq. 8 compose the core idea of our method. The formulations actually imply a **two-step** training pipeline. In the first step, by optimizing the auxiliary *AutoEncoder* defined in Eq. 8, we obtain an encoding function $h(\cdot; \psi^*)$ mapping the ground-truth label map y into the latent space. Then in the second step, we train the detection framework with the intermediate supervision of $h(y; \psi^*)$, as described in Eq. 7. In the next subsections, we will introduce the optimization details.

3.2 Step 1: AutoEncoder Training

In this subsection we aim to derive the *label encoding function* $h(\cdot; \psi^*)$ via Eq. 8. However, directly solving Eq. 8 is not easy – since ψ exists in both the target and the constraint, it is actually a *bilevel optimization* problem, which seems nontrivial to be implemented with current deep learning tools. Therefore, we propose to relax the formulation into *joint optimization* scheme, as follows:

$$\psi^*, \hat{\theta}_d = \arg \min_{\psi, \theta_d'} \min_{\theta_f'} \mathbb{E}_{(I,y) \sim \mathcal{D}} \quad \mathcal{L}_{det}(d(h(y; \psi); \theta_d'), y)$$

$$+ \lambda_1 \mathcal{L}_{det}(d(f(I; \theta_f'); \theta_d'), y) + \lambda_2 \mathcal{L}_{dis}(f(I; \theta_f'), h(y; \psi)), \tag{9}$$

where λ_1 and λ_2 are balanced coefficients, while in our experiment we just trivially set them to 1. It is clear that Eq. 9 simply corresponds to a multi-task training paradigm with three loss terms: the first one is *reconstruction loss* (**L1**) for the label's AutoEncoder; the second term is the common detection loss (**L2**), which enforces $d(\cdot; \theta'_d)$ to be a *valid* detection head; the third loss (**L3**) minimizes the gap between the two latent spaces (namely the outputs of the backbone $f(\cdot; \theta'_f)$ and label encoding function $h(\cdot; \psi)$ respectively).

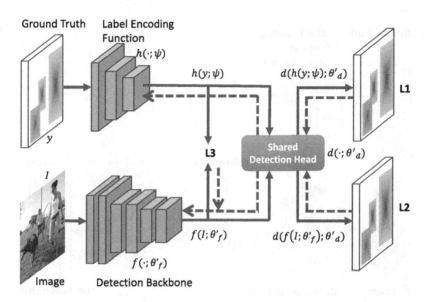

Fig. 1. Step 1: AutoEncoder training. **L1** – AutoEncoder reconstruction loss; **L2** – detection loss; **L3** – distance minimization loss; please refer to Eq. 9 for details. The solid and dashed lines indicate the forward and backward flows respectively

Figure 1 illustrates the implementation and optimization of Eq. 9. According to Eq. 9, the same detection head $d(\cdot; \theta'_d)$ is applied in both **L1** and **L2** terms – which is why we mark "shared detection head" in Fig. 1. It is also worth noting that we forbid the gradient flow from **L3** to the label encoding function $h(\cdot; \psi)$. The motivation is, in Eq. 8 (which is the original form of Eq. 9), the optimization of θ'_d does not directly affect ψ, thus we follow the property in the implementation. We empirically find the above details are critical to improve the final performance.

Initialization. Before optimization, we follows the common practice of initialization method, i.e. using pretrained weights (e.g. pretrained on *ImageNet* [10]) for backbone parameters θ'_f and Gaussian random weights for ψ and θ'_d. One may argue that according to the introduction, randomly initialized detection head $d(\cdot; \theta'_d)$ may cause unstable training. But actually, since this training step mainly aims to learn the label encoding function $h(\cdot; \psi)$, the detection backbone $f(\cdot; \theta'_f)$ and the detection head $d(\cdot; \theta'_d)$ are thus "auxiliary structures" in this step, whose performances are not that important. Furthermore, as we will introduce, the architecture of $h(\cdot; \psi)$ is relatively simple, so the optimization seems not difficult.

3.3 Step 2: Detector Training with Intermediate Supervision

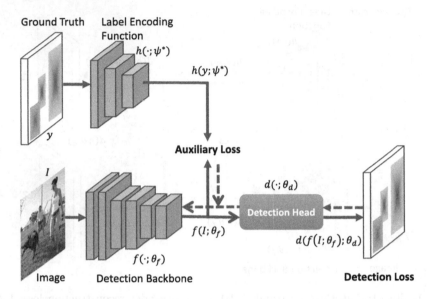

Fig. 2. Step 2: Detector training with intermediate supervision. Please refer to Eq. 7 for the detailed definitions. The solid and dashed lines indicate the forward and backward flows respectively

After the *label encoding function* $h(\cdot; \psi^*)$ has been learned, we then use it as the intermediate supervision to improve object detector training, according to Eq. 7. Figure 2 illustrates the implementation. In addition to the common detection loss, we introduce an auxiliary loss $\lambda \mathcal{L}_{dis}(f(I; \theta_f), h(y; \psi^*))$ to *directly* supervise the detection backbone. The coefficient λ is also trivially set to 1. Besides, Eq. 7 also suggests that ψ^* is fixed rather than optimization variable. So, we block the gradient flow from the auxiliary loss to $h(\cdot; \psi^*)$, as shown in the figure. After training, the auxiliary structure – $h(\cdot; \psi^*)$ – is then removed. The resulted $(f \circ d)(\cdot; \theta_f^*, \theta_d^*)$ is the learned object detector we expected.

Another important detail on the implementation is *initialization*. From Eq. 7 and Eq. 8 we know that in the two training steps, the detection backbones $f(\cdot)$ and the detection heads $d(\cdot)$ shares the same network architecture respectively, however, whose parameters are not necessarily the same. So, in Step 2, we *reinitialize* the backbone parameters θ_f (using *ImageNet* pretrained weights, for instance) before training. As for the detection head parameters θ_d, empirically we find that initializing them with the corresponding parameters $\hat{\theta}_d$ learned in

Step 1 (see Eq. 9) results in better performance and stable convergence. It may be because the pretrained detection head can provide less gradient noise to the backbone, compared with the randomly initialized heads.

3.4 Implementation Details and Remarks

Ground-Truth Label Representation. As mentioned above, in both two training steps the *label encoding function* $h(\cdot)$ needs to take ground-truth labels y as the network inputs. It is nontrivial because in detection task, each image contains different numbers of instances, each of which may have various class labels and bounding boxes. We have to produce a fixed-length label map that contains all the ground-truth information for each image.

We propose to use a $C \times H \times W$ tensor to represent the ground-truth objects in one image, where $H \times W$ equals to the image size and C is the number of classes in the dataset (e.g. 80 for $COCO$ [25] dataset). For an object of the c-th class, we fill the corresponding region (according to the bounding box) in the c-th channel with positive values: the value ranges from 1 at the object center to 0.5 in the box boundary, which decays linearly. Figure 1 and Fig. 2 visualize the encoding. Specially, if two bounding boxes of the same class overlap with each other, the joint region is filled with larger values of those calculated separately. Additionally, in training, the boxes are augmented by multiplying a random number between 0 and 1 with a probability of 0.5. Other values in the tensor remain to be zeros.

Architecture of Label Encoding Function. For ease of optimization, we use relatively simple architecture to implement $h(\cdot)$. The design of the structure is inspired by *ResNet* [16], while the number of residual blocks in each stage reduces to $\{1, 2, 2, 1\}$ respectively. In addition, the *Max Pooling* layer is replaced by stride convolution. The input channels is set to 80 to satisfy the number of classes in $COCO$ [25] dataset. *Batch Normalization* [18] is **not** used here. We use the same architecture for all experiments in the paper. Please refer to the appendix for details.

Multi-scale Intermediate Supervision. Recently, state-of-the-art detection frameworks like [23,24,38] usually introduce *Feature Pyramid Networks* (FPNs) to generate multi-scale feature maps, which greatly improves the capacity to detect objects of various sizes. Our approach can be easily generalized to multi-scale cases. First, we attach one *FPN* structure to the label encoding function $h(\cdot)$ so that it can produce multi-resolution representations. Then in both Step 1 and Step 2, we make the intermediate supervision terms $\mathcal{L}_{dis}(f(I), h(y))$ (see Eq. 9 and Eq. 7) applied on all the scale levels. As shown in the following experiments, our method can effectively boost the detection frameworks with FPNs.

Distance Measurement. In Eq. 7 and Eq. 9, the *distance measurement* term $\mathcal{L}_{dis}(\cdot,\cdot)$ is used to minimize the difference between two feature maps. One simple alternative is to use $L2$-distance directly. However, there are several issues as follows: 1) the sizes of the two feature maps may be different; 2) since the feature maps are generated from different domains respectively, directly minimizing their difference may suffer from very large gradient. So, we propose to introduce a *feature adaption* block into the distance measurement, which is defined as follows:

$$\mathcal{L}_{dis}(\mathbf{x}_f, \mathbf{x}_h) \triangleq \min_{\phi} \|LN(\mathcal{A}(\mathbf{x}_f; \phi)) - LN(\mathbf{x}_h)\|^2, \tag{10}$$

where $LN(\cdot)$ means *Layer Normalization* [2]; $\|\cdot\|$ is $L2$-distance; $\mathbf{x}_f$ and $\mathbf{x}_h$ are feature maps derived from the backbone and the *label encoding function* respectively. $\mathcal{A}(\cdot)$ represents *feature adaption network*, which acts as the transformer between the two domains. We implement $\mathcal{A}(\cdot)$ with three convolution layers, whose kernel size is 3×3 and number of channels is 256. The parameters ϕ are learned jointly with the outer optimization. Similar to $h(\cdot)$, $\mathcal{A}(\cdot)$ is also an auxiliary structure thus will be discarded after training.

4   Experiment

4.1   Setup

All our experiments are done with *PyTorch* [29]. We use *COCO* [25] dataset to evaluate our method. Following the common practice [23,24], we train our models with the union of 80k train images and a subset of 35k validation images (*trainval35k*). We test our models in the rest 5k of validation images (*minival*). All results are evaluated with mmAP, i.e. mAP@[0.5,0.95], using common single-scale test protocol. For both training and inference, we resize each images to 800 pixels on the shorter edge. The training batch size is a total of 16 in 8 GPUs. We mainly use so-called 1× schedule for training, which refers to 90k iterations with two learning rate decays at 60k and 80k iteration. We use almost the same training protocol for our Step 1 and Step 2 training, as well as all the counterpart baseline models respectively, with two exceptions: for Step 1, we find that adding L3 from the beginning cause L3 to be nearly zero. The network somehow finds a way to cheat, causing terrible results. So we add an additional 30k warmup iterations without L3, which we find sufficient to solve the problem; for Step 2, we remove the auxiliary loss in the last 10k iterations, which results in minor improvements. Since our training pipeline involves two steps, the total number of the iterations thus doubles. For fair comparison, we provide 2× schedule for baseline models as well, which refers to 180k iterations with two learning rate decays at 120k and 160k iteration.

4.2   Main Results

In order to show the effectiveness of our model on different detection frameworks, we evaluate our method on *RetinaNet* [24], *FCOS* [38] and *FPN* [23],

Table 1. Experiments on various baselines (mmAP/%)

Model	Backbone	Baseline(1x)	Baseline(2x)	Ours
RetinaNet [24] (*our impl.*)	ResNet50	36.1	36.4	**38.4**
	ResNet101	38.1	38.6	**40.3**
	Res101-DCN	40.6	41.1	**42.1**
FCOS [38] (*our impl.*)	ResNet50	36.7	37.0	**38.9**
	ResNet101	38.8	39.2	**41.2**
	Res101-DCN	41.9	41.9	**43.2**
FPN [23] (*our impl.*)	ResNet50	36.8	37.3	**38.8**
	ResNet101	38.9	39.6	**40.9**
	Res101-DCN	41.8	42.7	**43.2**

which are representative baselines of one-stage detectors, anchor-free methods and two-stage frameworks respectively. We also evaluate our method on various commonly-used backbones, including *ResNet*-50, *ResNet*-101 [16] and *Deformable Convolutional Networks* (DCNs) [9].

Results are presented in Table 1. Compared with the counterparts with 1× schedule, our method achieves performance gains of over 2% on both ResNet-50 and ResNet-101 backbones. On ResNet-101-DCN, there are still relative improvements of ∼1.4% in average. Compared with the baselines of 2× schedule, the gap becomes closer but still remains considerable, which suggests that our improvements are not mainly brought by more training iterations. It is worth noting that although our training pipeline doubles the total number of iterations, we argue that our *label encoding function* can usually be reused among different backbones (see the next subsection). Therefore in practice, we usually only need to run Step 1 only once for different models.

4.3 Ablation Study

Step 1: Is Joint Optimization Required? In Sect. 3.2, to optimize Eq. 9 we propose a *joint optimization* scheme to take all the three loss terms into account. Recall that in Step 1, only the learned *label encoding function* will be reserved into the next stage. As a result, one may argue that whether the auxiliary structure, i.e. the detection backbone, is really necessary in training. In other words, the question is, can we only use **L1** (*AutoEncoder reconstruction loss*) in Eq. 9 for this step? If it is true, the training step can be further simplified. Unfortunately, we find it not the case.

To validate the argument, we conduct a comparison by removing **L2** and **L3** in Eq. 9 to derive the *label encoding function*. Other settings such as Step 2 keep unchanged. The results are listed in Table 2, while the modified counterparts are marked with "reconstruction loss only". We compare them on RetinaNet with ResNet-50 and ResNet-101 backbones. It is clear that, without the auxiliary backbone, our method (although still outperforms baseline models) shows significant degradation in precision.

Table 2. Ablation study of removing the auxiliary structures in Step 1

Backbone	Methods	mmAP (%)
ResNet50	Baseline (1×)	36.1
	Baseline (2×)	36.4
	Ours (reconstruction loss only)	36.9
	Ours	**38.4**
ResNet101	Baseline (1×)	38.1
	Baseline (2×)	38.6
	Ours (reconstruction loss only)	39.0
	Ours	**40.3**

Table 3. Comparisons of different detection backbones in Step 1

Step 1 backbone	Step 2 backbone	mmAP (%)
ResNet50	ResNet101	**40.3**
ResNet101		**40.3**

Discussion and Remarks. In Step 1, although the existence of auxiliary structures is vital, we find the exact weights in the backbone are actually less important. From Eq. 7 and Eq. 8, we know that θ'_f does not affect the optimization of θ_f directly. It only contributes to the optimization of ψ^*. Also, unlike θ_d which is inherited from $\hat{\theta}_d$ for initialization, θ_f is reinitialized exactly in Step 2. Therefore, the trained auxiliary detection backbone $f(\cdot; \theta'_f)$ in Step 1 is completely discarded.

The observation inspires an interesting assumption: is the final performance actually insensitive to the detailed backbone architecture in Step 1? We try to verify the guess by using different backbones in Step 1 and Step 2. As reported in Table 3, we use ResNet-50 as the auxiliary backbone in the first step. Whereas in Step 2, the final detection backbone is ResNet-101. Compared with the model whose backbones in both stages are ResNet-101, the performances almost keep the same. The new finding thus suggests another advantage of our method in practice. The *label encoding function* $h(\cdot; \psi^*)$ can be **pretrained once but reused for multiple detectors with different backbones,** as long as they have the same detection head. This property of our method greatly reduces the cost of the practical applications.

Is Step 1 Alone Sufficient? In Step 1, we only aim to solve the *label encoding function* for later intermediate supervision. However, the training framework in Step 1 is quite similar to that in Step 2, and there is a detection model (the auxiliary structure) that can be proceeded for testing. Intuitively, the detection model in Step 1 should improve as well. One may even guess that Step 1 alone is sufficient. We show the ablation in Table 4. We only use Step 1 and test the performance of the detection model (the auxiliary structure). We compare them on multiple models with ResNet50 backbone. Step1-only can indeed improve the detection model over baseline, but clearly it alone is not sufficient.

Table 4. Results of only using Step 1

Model	Backbone	Method	mmAP (%)
RetinaNet	ResNet50	Step1-only	37.9
		Ours	**38.4**
FCOS	ResNet50	Step1-only	38.0
		Ours	**38.9**
FPN	ResNet50	Step1-only	37.3
		Ours	**38.8**

Step 2: Do Intermediate Supervision and Initialization Matter? In Step 2, we use two methods to facilitate the optimization, i.e. *intermediate supervision* on the backbone as well as the *initialization* of the detection head. In Table 5, we show the ablation studies on them. The baseline framework is *RetinaNet* [24] with ResNet-50 backbone. We also make the combinational studies of the case that using reconstruction loss only in Step 1 (please refer to Table 2). The results suggest that both methods contribute to the final performance.

Table 5. Intermediate supervision and initialization in Step 2

Step 1	Supervision	Initialization	mmAP (%)
ResNet50 Baseline			36.1
Ours (reconstruction loss only)	✓		**36.9**
		✓	35.8
	✓	✓	**36.9**
Ours	✓		36.8
		✓	37.3
	✓	✓	**38.4**

4.4 Comparison with Knowledge Distillation

Our two-step pipeline resembles *Knowledge Distillation* (KD). Actually, if we train an object detector alone in Step 1 instead of our *label encoding function* with a joint framework, and use it in Step 2 for supervision, the method becomes KD. In Table 6 we show comparison between our method and the alternative mentioned above, denoted as "Vanilla KD". On a lightweight backbone, i.e. MobileNet, our method can reach similar performance to Knowledge Distillation, although we only use a label encoding function instead of a heavy ResNet-50 that extracts "real" features. On a heavier backbone, i.e. ResNet-50, our method outperforms KD with ResNet-50 and ResNet-101 as teachers, whose improvements are limited due to the small performance gap between teacher and student. Knowledge distillation requires a teacher network that is strong enough, which is usually not easy to find when the student network is already strong. Our method, on the other hand, is not limited by it.

Table 6. Comparison with knowledge distillation (%)

Backbone	Method	Teacher network	mmAP
MobileNet	Baseline	–	27.7
	Vanilla KD	ResNet50	29.7
	Ours	Label encoding function	**29.8**
ResNet50	Baseline	–	36.1
	Vanilla KD	ResNet50	36.8
	Vanilla KD	ResNet101	36.5
	Ours	Label encoding function	**38.4**

Table 7. Experiments on MaskRCNN (mmAP/%)

Backbone	Method	Box	Mask
ResNet50	Baseline (1×)	37.4	34.2
	Baseline (2×)	38.2	34.6
	Ours	**39.1**	**35.6**
ResNet101	Baseline (1×)	40.0	36.0
	Baseline (2×)	40.6	36.4
	Ours	**41.7**	**37.6**

4.5 Performance on Mask Prediction

Above we mainly focus on object detection. However, our previous discussion when proposing the method (Sect. 1 and Sect. 3) is based on the structure and optimization of detection networks, not object detection task itself. Thus it is likely that our method can be extended to other tasks with similar framework. We tested our method on Mask R-CNN [14], which produces mask prediction in instance segmentation, but has a similar framework to FPN. It is worth noting that for Mask R-CNN, we use masks instead of boxes as the input for label encoding function. Results are presented in Table 7. It indicates our method improves mask prediction as well.

5   Conclusions

In this paper, we propose a new training pipeline for object detection systems. We design a feature encoding function and utilize it to introduce intermediate supervision on the detection backbone. Our method is generally applicable and efficient, adding no extra cost in inference time. To show its ability, we evaluate it on a variety of detection models and gain consistent improvement.

References

1. Akata, Z., Perronnin, F., Harchaoui, Z., Schmid, C.: Label-embedding for attribute-based classification. In: Proceedings of the IEEE Conference on Computer Vision and Pattern Recognition, pp. 819–826 (2013)
2. Ba, J.L., Kiros, J.R., Hinton, G.E.: Layer normalization. arXiv preprint arXiv:1607.06450 (2016)
3. Bengio, S., Weston, J., Grangier, D.: Label embedding trees for large multi-class tasks. In: Advances in Neural Information Processing Systems, pp. 163–171 (2010)
4. Cai, Z., Vasconcelos, N.: Cascade R-CNN: delving into high quality object detection. In: Proceedings of the IEEE Conference on Computer Vision and Pattern Recognition, pp. 6154–6162 (2018)
5. Caruana, R.: Multitask learning. Mach. Learn. **28**(1), 41–75 (1997)
6. Chen, G., Choi, W., Yu, X., Han, T., Chandraker, M.: Learning efficient object detection models with knowledge distillation. In: Advances in Neural Information Processing Systems, pp. 742–751 (2017)
7. Chen, T., Kornblith, S., Norouzi, M., Hinton, G.: A simple framework for contrastive learning of visual representations. arXiv preprint arXiv:2002.05709 (2020)
8. Chen, Y., Wang, N., Zhang, Z.: DarkRank: accelerating deep metric learning via cross sample similarities transfer. In: Thirty-Second AAAI Conference on Artificial Intelligence (2018)
9. Dai, J., et al.: Deformable convolutional networks. In: Proceedings of the IEEE International Conference on Computer Vision, pp. 764–773 (2017)
10. Deng, J., Dong, W., Socher, R., Li, L.J., Li, K., Fei-Fei, L.: ImageNet: a large-scale hierarchical image database. In: 2009 IEEE Conference on Computer Vision and Pattern Recognition, pp. 248–255. IEEE (2009)
11. Girshick, R.: Fast R-CNN. In: Proceedings of the IEEE International Conference on Computer Vision, pp. 1440–1448 (2015)
12. He, K., Fan, H., Wu, Y., Xie, S., Girshick, R.: Momentum contrast for unsupervised visual representation learning. arXiv preprint arXiv:1911.05722 (2019)

13. He, K., Girshick, R., Dollár, P.: Rethinking ImageNet pre-training. In: Proceedings of the IEEE International Conference on Computer Vision, pp. 4918–4927 (2019)
14. He, K., Gkioxari, G., Dollár, P., Girshick, R.: Mask R-CNN. In: Proceedings of the IEEE International Conference on Computer Vision, pp. 2961–2969 (2017)
15. He, K., Zhang, X., Ren, S., Sun, J.: Spatial pyramid pooling in deep convolutional networks for visual recognition. IEEE Trans. Pattern Anal. Mach. Intell. **37**(9), 1904–1916 (2015)
16. He, K., Zhang, X., Ren, S., Sun, J.: Deep residual learning for image recognition. In: Proceedings of the IEEE Conference on Computer Vision and Pattern Recognition, pp. 770–778 (2016)
17. Hinton, G., Vinyals, O., Dean, J.: Distilling the knowledge in a neural network. arXiv preprint arXiv:1503.02531 (2015)
18. Ioffe, S., Szegedy, C.: Batch normalization: accelerating deep network training by reducing internal covariate shift. arXiv preprint arXiv:1502.03167 (2015)
19. Lee, C.Y., Xie, S., Gallagher, P., Zhang, Z., Tu, Z.: Deeply-supervised nets. In: Artificial Intelligence and Statistics, pp. 562–570 (2015)
20. Lee, W., Na, J., Kim, G.: Multi-task self-supervised object detection via recycling of bounding box annotations. In: Proceedings of the IEEE Conference on Computer Vision and Pattern Recognition, pp. 4984–4993 (2019)
21. Li, Q., Jin, S., Yan, J.: Mimicking very efficient network for object detection. In: Proceedings of the IEEE Conference on Computer Vision and Pattern Recognition, pp. 6356–6364 (2017)
22. Li, Z., Peng, C., Yu, G., Zhang, X., Deng, Y., Sun, J.: DetNet: a backbone network for object detection. arXiv preprint arXiv:1804.06215 (2018)
23. Lin, T.Y., Dollár, P., Girshick, R., He, K., Hariharan, B., Belongie, S.: Feature pyramid networks for object detection. In: Proceedings of the IEEE Conference on Computer Vision and Pattern Recognition, pp. 2117–2125 (2017)
24. Lin, T.Y., Goyal, P., Girshick, R., He, K., Dollár, P.: Focal loss for dense object detection. In: Proceedings of the IEEE International Conference on Computer Vision, pp. 2980–2988 (2017)
25. Lin, T.-Y., et al.: Microsoft COCO: common objects in context. In: Fleet, D., Pajdla, T., Schiele, B., Tuytelaars, T. (eds.) ECCV 2014. LNCS, vol. 8693, pp. 740–755. Springer, Cham (2014). https://doi.org/10.1007/978-3-319-10602-1_48
26. Liu, W., et al.: SSD: single shot MultiBox detector. In: Leibe, B., Matas, J., Sebe, N., Welling, M. (eds.) ECCV 2016. LNCS, vol. 9905, pp. 21–37. Springer, Cham (2016). https://doi.org/10.1007/978-3-319-46448-0_2
27. Luo, P., Zhu, Z., Liu, Z., Wang, X., Tang, X.: Face model compression by distilling knowledge from neurons. In: Thirtieth AAAI Conference on Artificial Intelligence (2016)
28. Mostajabi, M., Maire, M., Shakhnarovich, G.: Regularizing deep networks by modeling and predicting label structure. In: Proceedings of the IEEE Conference on Computer Vision and Pattern Recognition, pp. 5629–5638 (2018)
29. Paszke, A., et al.: PyTorch: an imperative style, high-performance deep learning library. In: Advances in Neural Information Processing Systems, pp. 8024–8035 (2019)
30. Redmon, J., Divvala, S., Girshick, R., Farhadi, A.: You only look once: unified, real-time object detection. In: Proceedings of the IEEE Conference on Computer Vision and Pattern Recognition, pp. 779–788 (2016)
31. Redmon, J., Farhadi, A.: Yolo9000: better, faster, stronger. In: Proceedings of the IEEE Conference on Computer Vision and Pattern Recognition, pp. 7263–7271 (2017)

32. Ren, S., He, K., Girshick, R., Sun, J.: Faster R-CNN: towards real-time object detection with region proposal networks. In: Advances in Neural Information Processing Systems, pp. 91–99 (2015)
33. Romero, A., Ballas, N., Kahou, S.E., Chassang, A., Gatta, C., Bengio, Y.: FitNets: hints for thin deep nets. arXiv preprint arXiv:1412.6550 (2014)
34. Shen, Z., Liu, Z., Li, J., Jiang, Y.G., Chen, Y., Xue, X.: DSOD: learning deeply supervised object detectors from scratch. In: Proceedings of the IEEE International Conference on Computer Vision, pp. 1919–1927 (2017)
35. Sun, X., Wei, B., Ren, X., Ma, S.: Label embedding network: learning label representation for soft training of deep networks. arXiv preprint arXiv:1710.10393 (2017)
36. Szegedy, C., et al.: Going deeper with convolutions. In: Proceedings of the IEEE Conference on Computer Vision and Pattern Recognition, pp. 1–9 (2015)
37. Tang, Z., Wang, D., Zhang, Z.: Recurrent neural network training with dark knowledge transfer. In: 2016 IEEE International Conference on Acoustics, Speech and Signal Processing (ICASSP), pp. 5900–5904. IEEE (2016)
38. Tian, Z., Shen, C., Chen, H., He, T.: FCOS: fully convolutional one-stage object detection. In: Proceedings of the IEEE International Conference on Computer Vision, pp. 9627–9636 (2019)
39. Wang, T., Yuan, L., Zhang, X., Feng, J.: Distilling object detectors with fine-grained feature imitation. In: Proceedings of the IEEE Conference on Computer Vision and Pattern Recognition, pp. 4933–4942 (2019)
40. Wang, X., Zhang, R., Sun, Y., Qi, J.: KDGAN: knowledge distillation with generative adversarial networks. In: Advances in Neural Information Processing Systems, pp. 775–786 (2018)
41. Wen, Y., Zhang, K., Li, Z., Qiao, Yu.: A discriminative feature learning approach for deep face recognition. In: Leibe, B., Matas, J., Sebe, N., Welling, M. (eds.) ECCV 2016. LNCS, vol. 9911, pp. 499–515. Springer, Cham (2016). https://doi.org/10.1007/978-3-319-46478-7_31
42. Xie, S., Huang, X., Tu, Z.: Top-down learning for structured labeling with convolutional Pseudoprior. In: Leibe, B., Matas, J., Sebe, N., Welling, M. (eds.) ECCV 2016. LNCS, vol. 9908, pp. 302–317. Springer, Cham (2016). https://doi.org/10.1007/978-3-319-46493-0_19
43. Zagoruyko, S., Komodakis, N.: Paying more attention to attention: improving the performance of convolutional neural networks via attention transfer. arXiv preprint arXiv:1612.03928 (2016)
44. Zhang, Z., Zhang, X., Peng, C., Xue, X., Sun, J.: ExFuse: enhancing feature fusion for semantic segmentation. In: Ferrari, V., Hebert, M., Sminchisescu, C., Weiss, Y. (eds.) ECCV 2018. LNCS, vol. 11214, pp. 273–288. Springer, Cham (2018). https://doi.org/10.1007/978-3-030-01249-6_17
45. Zhao, H., Shi, J., Qi, X., Wang, X., Jia, J.: Pyramid scene parsing network. In: Proceedings of the IEEE Conference on Computer Vision and Pattern Recognition, pp. 2881–2890 (2017)
46. Zhu, R., et al.: ScratchDet: training single-shot object detectors from scratch. In: Proceedings of the IEEE Conference on Computer Vision and Pattern Recognition, pp. 2268–2277 (2019)
47. Zhu, X., Hu, H., Lin, S., Dai, J.: Deformable convnets v2: more deformable, better results. In: Proceedings of the IEEE Conference on Computer Vision and Pattern Recognition, pp. 9308–9316 (2019)

Unsupervised Learning of Category-Specific Symmetric 3D Keypoints from Point Sets

Clara Fernandez-Labrador[1,2,3]([✉]), Ajad Chhatkuli[3], Danda Pani Paudel[3], Jose J. Guerrero[1], Cédric Demonceaux[2], and Luc Van Gool[3,4]

[1] I3A, University of Zaragoza, Zaragoza, Spain
{cfernandez,josechu.guerrero}@unizar.es
[2] VIBOT ERL CNRS 6000, ImViA, Université de Bourgogne Franche-Comté, Dijon, France
cedric.demonceaux@u-bourgogne.fr
[3] Computer Vision Lab, ETH Zürich, Zürich, Switzerland
{ajad.chhatkuli,paudel,vangool}@vision.ee.ethz.ch
[4] VISICS, ESAT/PSI, KU Leuven, Leuven, Belgium

Abstract. Automatic discovery of category-specific 3D keypoints from a collection of objects of a category is a challenging problem. The difficulty is added when objects are represented by 3D point clouds, with variations in shape and semantic parts and unknown coordinate frames. We define keypoints to be category-specific, if they meaningfully represent objects' shape and their correspondences can be simply established order-wise across all objects. This paper aims at learning such 3D keypoints, in an unsupervised manner, using a collection of misaligned 3D point clouds of objects from an unknown category. In order to do so, we model shapes defined by the keypoints, within a category, using the symmetric linear basis shapes without assuming the plane of symmetry to be known. The usage of symmetry prior leads us to learn stable keypoints suitable for higher misalignments. To the best of our knowledge, this is the first work on learning such keypoints directly from 3D point clouds for a general category. Using objects from four benchmark datasets, we demonstrate the quality of our learned keypoints by quantitative and qualitative evaluations. Our experiments also show that the keypoints discovered by our method are geometrically and semantically consistent.

1 Introduction

A set of keypoints representing any object is historically of large interest for geometric reasoning, due to their simplicity and ease of handling. Keypoints-based methods [1–3] have been crucial to the success of many vision applications.

Electronic supplementary material The online version of this chapter (https://doi.org/10.1007/978-3-030-58595-2_33) contains supplementary material, which is available to authorized users.

Fig. 1. Category-specific 3D Keypoints. The predicted keypoints follow the symmetric linear shape basis prior modeling all instances in a category under a common framework. They not only are consistent across different instances, but also are ordered and correspond to semantically meaningful locations.

A few examples include; 3D reconstruction [4–6], registration [7–10], human body pose [11–14], recognition [15,16], and generation [17,18]. That being said, many keypoints are defined manually, while considering their semantic locations such as facial landmarks and human body joints, to address the problem at hand. To further benefit from their widespread utility, several attempts have been made on learning to detect keypoints [19–23], as well as on automatically discovering them [24–27]. In this regard, the task of learning to detect keypoints from several supervision examples, has achieved many successes [20,28]. However, discovering them automatically from unlabeled 3D data –such that they meaningfully represent shapes and semantics– so as to have a similar utility as those of manually defined, has received only limited attention due to its difficulty.

As objects of interest reside in the 3D space, it is not surprising that 3D keypoints are preferred for geometric reasoning. For the given 3D keypoints, their counterparts in 2D images can be associated by merely using camera projection models [29–31]. However, being able to directly predict keypoints on provided 3D data (point clouds) has the advantage that the task can be achieved when multiple camera views or images are not available. In this work, we are interested on learning keypoints using only 3D structures. In fact, 3D structures with keypoints suffice for several applications including, registration [32], shape completion [33], and shape modeling [34]; without requiring their 2D counterparts.

When 3D objects go through shape variations, due to deformation or when two different objects of a category are compared, consistent keypoints are desired for meaningful geometric reasoning. Recall the examples of semantic keypoints such as facial landmarks and body joints. To serve a similar purpose, *can we automatically find kepoints that are consistent over inter-subject shape variations and intra-subject deformations in a category?* This is the primary question that we are interested to answer in this paper. Furthermore, we wish to discover such keypoints directly from 3D point sets, in an unsupervised manner. We call these keypoints "category-specific", which are expected to meaningfully represent objects' shape and offer their correspondence order-wise across all objects. More formally, we define the desired properties of category-specific keypoints as: i) generalizability over different shape instances and alignments in a category,

ii) one-to-one ordered correspondences and semantic consistency, iii) representative of the shape as well as the category while preserving shape symmetry. These properties not only make the representation meaningful, but also tend to enhance the usefulness of keypoints. Learning category-specific keypoints on point clouds, however, is a challenging problem because not all the object parts are always present in a category. The challenges are exacerbated when the practical cases of misaligned data and unsupervised learning are considered. Related works do not address all these problems, but instead opt for; dropping category-specificity and using aligned data [26], employing manual supervision on 2D images [20], or using aligned 3D and multiple 2D images with known pose [27]. The latter method achieves category-specificity without explicitly reasoning on the shapes. Yet another work leverages predefined local shape descriptors and a template model [35] specifically on faces.

In this paper, we show that the category-specific keypoints with the listed properties can be learned unsupervised by modeling them with non-rigidity, based on unknown linear basis shapes. We further impose an unknown reflective symmetry on the deformation model, when considering categories with instance-wise symmetry. For categories where instance-wise symmetry is not applicable, we propose the use of symmetric linear basis shapes in order to better model, what we define as symmetric deformation spaces, e.g., human body deformations. This allows us to better constrain the pose and the shape coefficients prediction. Our proposed learning method does not assume aligned shapes [27], pre-computed basis shapes [20] or known planes of symmetry [36] and all quantities are learned in an end-to-end manner. Our symmetry modeling is powerful and more flexible compared to that of previous NRSfM methods [36,37]. We achieve this by considering the shape basis for a category and the reflective plane of symmetry as the neural network weight variables, optimized during the training process. The training is done on a single input, circumventing the Siamese-like architecture used in [7,26]. At inference time, the network predicts the basis coefficients and the pose in order to estimate the instance-specific keypoints. Using multiple categories from four benchmark datasets, we evaluate the quality of our learned keypoints both quantitatively and with qualitative visualization. Our experiments show that the keypoints discovered by our method are geometrically and semantically consistent, which are measured respectively by intra-category registration and semantic part-wise assignments. We further show that symmetric basis shapes can be used to model symmetric deformation space of categories such as the human body.

2   Related Work

Category-specific keypoints on objects have been extensively used in NRSfM methods, however, only few methods have tackled the problem of estimating them. In terms of the outcome, our work is closest to [27], which learns category-specific 3D keypoints by solving an auxiliary task of rigid registration between multiple renders of the same shape and by considering the category instances to be pre-aligned. Although the method shows promising results on 2D and 3D, it does so without explicitly modeling the shapes. Consequently, it requires renders of different instances to be pre-aligned to reason on keypoint correspondences between instances. A similar task is also solved in [20] for 6-degrees of freedom (DoF) estimation which uses low-rank shape prior to condition keypoints in 3D. Although, the low-rank shape modeling is a powerful tool, [20] requires supervision for heatmap prediction and relies on aligned shapes and pre-computed shape basis. [28] also predicts keypoints for categories with low-rank shape prior but the method is again trained on fully supervised manner. Moreover, all of the mentioned methods learn keypoints on images as heatmaps and thereafter lift them to 3D. Different from the other works, [35] exploits deformation model and symmetry to directly predict keypoints on 3D but requires a face template, aligned shapes and known basis. Shape modeling of category shape instances has been widely explored in NRSfM works. Linear low-rank shape basis[5,38,39], low-rank trajectory basis [40], isometry or piece-wise rigidity [41,42] are some of the different methods used for NRSfM. Recently, a few number of works have used low-rank shape basis in order to devise learned methods [4,28,36,43]. Another useful tool in modeling shape category is the reflective symmetry, which is also directly related to the object pose. Although [37] showed that the low-rank shape basis can be formulated with unknown reflective symmetry, its adaptation to learned NRSfM methods is not trivial. Recent methods, in fact, assume that the plane of symmetry is one among a few known planes [44]. Moreover, none of the methods formulate symmetry applicable for non-rigidly deforming objects such as the human body. A parallel work [45] on this regard models symmetry probabilistically in a warped canonical space to reconstruct 3D of different objects.

While shape modeling is a key aspect of our work, another challenge is to infer ordered keypoints by learning on unordered point sets. Despite several advances on deep neural networks for point sets [46–48], current achievements of learning on images dwarf those of learning on point sets. A related work learns to predict 3D keypoints unsupervised by again solving the auxiliary task of correctly estimating rotations in a Siamese architecture [49]. The keypoint prediction is done without order by pooling features of certain point neighborhoods. Another previous work [7] proposes learning point features for matching, again using alignment as the auxiliary task. Matching such keypoints across shapes is not an easy task as the keypoints are not predicted in any order. In the following sections we show how one can model shape instances using the low-rank symmetric shape basis and use the shape modeling to predict ordered category-specific keypoints.

3 Background and Theory

Notations. We represent sets and matrices with special Latin characters (e.g., $\mathcal{V}$) or bold Latin characters (e.g., $\mathbf{V}$). Lower or uppercase normal fonts, e.g., K denote scalars. Lowercase bold Latin letters represent vectors as in $\mathbf{v}$. We use lowercase Latin letters to represent indices (e.g., i). Uppercase Greek letters represent mappings or functions (e.g., Π). We use $\mathcal{L}$ to denote loss functions. Finally the operator mat(.) converts a vector $v \in \mathbb{R}^{3N \times 1}$ to a matrix $M \in \mathbb{R}^{3 \times N}$.

3.1 Category-Specific Shape and Keypoints

We represent shapes as point clouds, defined as an unordered set of points $S = \{s_1, s_2, \ldots, s_M\}$, $s_j \in \mathbb{R}^3$, $j \in \{1, 2, \ldots, M\}$. The set of all such shapes in a category defines the category shape space $\mathcal{C}$. We write a particular i-th category-specific shape instance in $\mathcal{C}$ as S_i. For convenience, we will use the terms category-specific shape and shape interchangeably. The category shape space $\mathcal{C}$ can be anything from a set of discrete shapes to a smooth manifold of category-specific shapes spanned by a deformation function $\Psi_{\mathcal{C}}$. The focus of the work is on learning meaningful 3D keypoints from the point set representation of S_i. To that end, this section defines category-specific keypoints and develops their modeling.

Category-Specific Keypoints. We represent category-specific keypoints of a shape S_i as a sparse tuple of points, $P_i = (p_{i1}, p_{i2}, \ldots, p_{iN})$, $p_{ij} \in \mathbb{R}^3$, $j \in \{1, 2, \ldots, N\}$. Unlike the shape, its keypoints are represented as ordered points. Our objective is to learn a mapping $\Pi_{\mathcal{C}} : S_i \to P_i$ in order to obtain the category-specific keypoints from an input shape S_i in $\mathcal{C}$. Although not completely unambiguous, we can define the category-specific keypoints using the properties listed in Sect. 1. In mathematical notations they are:

(i) Generalization: $\Pi_{\mathcal{C}}(S_i) = P_i$, $\forall S_i \in \mathcal{C}$.
(ii) Corresponding points and semantic consistency: Given $S_a, S_b \in \mathcal{C}$, we want $p_{aj} \Leftrightarrow p_{bj}$. Similarly, p_{aj} and p_{bj} should have the same semantics.
(iii) Representative-ness: $\text{vol}(S_i) = \text{vol}(P_i)$ and $p_{ij} \in S_i$, where $\text{vol}(.)$ is the Volume operator for a shape. If $S_i \in \mathcal{C}$ has a reflective symmetry, P_i should have the same symmetry.

3.2 Category-Specific Shapes as Instances of Non-rigidity

Several recent works have modeled shapes in a category as instances of non-rigid deformations [4,28,36,43]. The motivation lies in the fact that such shapes often share geometric similarities. Consequently, there likely exists a deformation function $\Psi_{\mathcal{C}} : S_T \to S_i$, which can map a global shape property S_T (shape template or basis shapes) to a category shape instance S_i. However, we argue that modeling $\Psi_{\mathcal{C}}$ is not trivial and in fact a convenient representation of $\Psi_{\mathcal{C}}$ may not exist in many cases. This observation, in fact, is what makes the dense Non-Rigid Structure-from-Motion (NRSfM) so challenging. On the other hand, one can imagine a deformation function $\Phi_{\mathcal{C}} : P_T \to P_i$, going from a global keypoints property P_T to the category-specific keypoints P_i. The deformation function $\Phi_{\mathcal{C}}$ thus satisfies: $p_{ij} \in \Phi_{\mathcal{C}}$ implies $p_{ij} \in \Psi_{\mathcal{C}}$ and effectively, $\Phi_{\mathcal{C}} \subset \Psi_{\mathcal{C}}$, if the set order in P_i is ignored. Unlike $\Psi_{\mathcal{C}}$, the deformation function $\Phi_{\mathcal{C}}$ may be simple enough to model and use for estimating the category-specific keypoints P_i. We therefore, choose to seek the non-rigidity modeling in the space of keypoints

$\mathcal{P} = \{P_1, P_2, \ldots, P_L\}$, which functions as an abstraction of the space $\mathcal{C}$. Non-rigidity can be used to define the prediction function $\Pi_{\mathcal{C}}$ as below:

$$\Pi_{\mathcal{C}}(S_i; \theta) = \Phi_{\mathcal{C}}(r_i; \theta) = P_i \qquad (1)$$

where θ denotes the constant function parameters of $\Pi_{\mathcal{C}}$ and r_i is the predicted instance specific vector parameter. In our problem, we want to learn θ from the example shapes in $\mathcal{C}$ without using the ground-truth labels, supervised by $\Phi_{\mathcal{C}}$. In the NRSfM literature, two common approaches of modeling shape deformations are the low-rank shape prior [5,38–40] and the isometric prior [41,42]. In this paper, we investigate the modeling using the low-rank shape prior, with instance-wise symmetry as well as symmetry of the deformation space.

3.3   Low-Rank Non-rigid Representation of Keypoints

The NRSfM approach of low-rank shape basis comes as a natural extension of the rigid orthographic factorization prior [50] and was introduced by Bregler et al. [38]. The key idea is that a large number of object deformations can be explained by linearly combining a smaller K number of basis shapes at some pose. In the rigid case, this number is one, hence the rank is 3. In the non-rigid case, it can be higher, while the exact value depends on the complexity of the deformations. Consider F shape instances in $\mathcal{C}$ and N points in each keypoints instance P_i. The following equation describes the projection with shape basis.

$$P_i = \Phi_{\mathcal{C}}(r_i; \theta) = R_i \, \mathrm{mat}(\mathcal{B}_{\mathcal{C}} \, c_i) \qquad (2)$$

where $\mathcal{B}_{\mathcal{C}} = (B_1, \ldots, B_K), \mathcal{B}_{\mathcal{C}} \in \mathbb{R}^{3N \times K}$ forms the low-rank shape basis. The rank is lower than the maximum possible rank of $3F$ or N for $3K < 3F$ or $3K < N$. The vector $c_i \in \mathbb{R}^K$ denotes the coefficients that linearly combines different basis for the keypoints instance i. Each keypoints instance is then completely parametrized by the basis $\mathcal{B}_{\mathcal{C}}$ and the coefficients c_i. Next, the projection matrix $R_i \in SO_3$ is simply the rotation matrix for the shape instance i.

Unlike in NRSfM, the problem of computing the category-specific keypoints, has P_i as unknown. Similar to NRSfM, the rest of the quantities in Eq. (2) – c_i, $\mathcal{B}_{\mathcal{C}}$ and R_i are also unknown. This fact makes our problem doubly hard. First the problem becomes more than just lifting the 2D keypoints to 3D and second, the order of keypoints present in the NRSfM measurements matrix is not available. We intend to solve the aforementioned problems by learning based on Eq. (2), which is related to the deformation representation of $\Phi_{\mathcal{C}}$ in Eq. (1). Here, θ includes the global parameters or basis $\mathcal{B}_{\mathcal{C}}$ and r_i includes the instance-wise pose R_i and coefficients c_i. To further reduce ambiguities on pose, we propose to also compute the reflective plane of symmetry for a category.

3.4   Modeling Symmetry with Non-rigidity

Many object categories have shapes which exhibit a fixed reflective symmetry over the whole category. To discover and use symmetry, we consider two different priors: instance-wise symmetry and symmetric deformation space.

Instance-wise symmetry. Instance-wise reflective symmetry about a fixed plane is observed in a large number of rigid object categories (e.g. ShapeNet [51] and ModelNet [52]). Such a symmetry has been previously combined with the shape basis prior in NRSfM [37], however, a convenient representation for learning both the symmetry and the shapes have not been explored yet. A recent learning-based method [36,44] uses the symmetry prior by performing an exhaustive search over a few planes in order to predict symmetric dense non-rigid shapes. However, such a strategy may not work when the shapes are not perfectly aligned. Instance-wise symmetry can be included by re-writing Eq. (2) as follows:

$$\mathsf{P}_{i\frac{1}{2}} = \mathsf{R}_i \, \mathrm{mat}(\mathcal{B}_{\mathcal{C}\frac{1}{2}} \mathsf{c}_i), \quad \mathsf{P}_i = \left[\mathsf{P}_{i\frac{1}{2}} \; A_{\mathcal{C}}\mathsf{P}_{i\frac{1}{2}}\right] \tag{3}$$

where $\mathsf{P}_{i\frac{1}{2}} \in \mathbb{R}^{3 \times N/2}$ represents one half of the category-specific keypoints. $\mathsf{P}_{i\frac{1}{2}}$ is reflected using $A_{\mathcal{C}} \in \mathbb{R}^{3 \times 3}$ and concatenated to obtain the final keypoints. Due to the exact instance-wise symmetry, we similarly can parametrize the basis as $\mathcal{B}_{\mathcal{C}\frac{1}{2}} \in \mathbb{R}^{3N/2 \times K}$ to denote the shape basis for the first half of the keypoints. The reflection operator $A_{\mathcal{C}}$ is parametrized by a unit normal vector $n_{\mathcal{C}} \in \mathbb{R}^3$ of the plane of symmetry passing through the origin. The advantage of going from Eq. (2) to Eq. (3) should be apparent from the reduced dimensionality of the unknowns in $\mathcal{B}_{\mathcal{C}}$ as well as the additional second equality constraint of Eq. (3), which reduces the ambiguities in NRSfM [37].

Symmetric Deformation Space. In many non-rigid objects, shape instances are not symmetric. However, symmetry may still exist in the deformation space, e.g., in a human body. Suppose that a particular shape instance $\mathsf{S}_k \in \mathcal{C}$ has the reflective symmetry about $n_{\mathcal{C}}$, which allows us to define its two halves: $\mathsf{S}_{k\frac{1}{2}}$ and $\mathsf{S}'_{k\frac{1}{2}}$ and thus correspondingly for all shape instances.

Definition 1 (Symmetric deformation space). *$\mathcal{C}$ is a symmetric deformation space if for every half shape deformation instance $\mathsf{S}_{i\frac{1}{2}}$, there exists any shape instance $\mathsf{S}_j \in \mathcal{C}$ such that the $\mathsf{S}'_{j\frac{1}{2}}$ is symmetric to $\mathsf{S}_{i\frac{1}{2}}$.*

The above definition also applies for the keypoints shape space $\mathcal{P}$. The instance-wise symmetric space is a particular case of the above. However, Eq. (3) cannot model the keypoints instances in the symmetric deformation space. We model such keypoints by introducing symmetric basis that can be weighted asymmetrically, thereby, obtaining the following:

$$\mathsf{P}_i = \mathsf{R}_i \left[\mathrm{mat}(\mathcal{B}_{\mathcal{C}\frac{1}{2}} \mathsf{c}_i) \; \mathrm{mat}(\mathcal{B}'_{\mathcal{C}\frac{1}{2}} \mathsf{c}'_i)\right] \tag{4}$$

where $\mathcal{B}'_{\mathcal{C}\frac{1}{2}}$ is obtained by reflecting $\mathcal{B}_{\mathcal{C}\frac{1}{2}}$ with $A_{\mathcal{C}}$ and $\mathsf{c}'_i \in \mathbb{R}^K$ forms the coefficients for the second half of the basis. Although Eq. (4) increases the dimension of the unknowns in the coefficients over Eq. (2), the added modeling of the symmetry of the deformation space and the reduced dimensionality of the basis can improve the final keypoints estimate. This brings us to the following proposition.

Proposition 1. *Provided that $\mathcal{B}_{c\frac{1}{2}}$ and $\mathcal{B}'_{c\frac{1}{2}}$ are symmetric about a plane, Eq. (4) models a symmetric deformation space if the estimates of c_i and c'_i come from the same probabilistic distribution.*

Proof. The proof is straightforward and provided in the supplementary material.

As a consequence of Proposition 1, we can model keypoints in non-rigid symmetric objects with Eq. (4), while also tightly modeling the symmetry as long as we maintain the distribution of c and c' to be the same.

4 Learning Category-Specific Keypoints

In this section, we use the modeling of Φ_C to describe the unsupervised learning process of the category-specific keypoints. More precisely, we want to learn the function $\Pi_C : S_i \rightarrow P_i$ as a neural network of parameters θ, using the supervisory signal from Φ_C. In regard to learning keypoints on point sets, recent work [26] trains a Siamese network to predict order-agnostic keypoints stable to rotations for rigid objects [26]. Part of our network architecture is inspired from [26], which is based on PointNet [46]. However, we use a single input avoiding the expensive Siamese training. The network architecture is shown in Fig. 2, whose input consists of a single shape S_i misaligned in SO_2. This is reasonable since point clouds are usually aligned to the vertical direction. We describe the different components of the network architecture below.

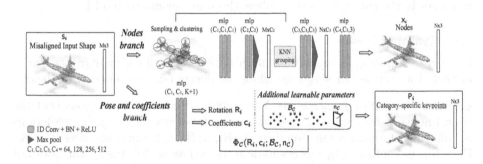

Fig. 2. Network architecture: The *pose and coefficients branch* and the *additional learnable parameters* generate the output category-specific keypoints. The *nodes branch* estimates the nodes that guide the learning process. "mlp" stands for multi-layer perceptron. Refer to Sect. 3 for the modeling, Sect. 4 for learning.

Node Branch. This branch estimates a sparse tuple of nodes that are potentially category-specific keypoints but are not ordered. We denote them as $X_i = \{x_{i1}, x_{i2}, \ldots, x_{iN}\}, x_{ij} \in \mathbb{R}^3$ and $j \in \{1, 2, \ldots, N\}$. Initially, a predefined number of nodes N are sampled from the input shape using the Farthest Point

Sampling (FPS) and a local neighborhood of points is built for each node with point-to-node grouping [26,53], creating N clusters which are mean normalized inside the network. Every point in S_i is associated with one of these nodes. The branch consists of two PointNet-like [46] networks followed by a kNN grouping layer that uses the initial sampled nodes to achieve hierarchical information aggregation. Finally, the local feature vectors are fed into a Multi-Layer Perceptron (MLP) that outputs the nodes.

Pose and Coefficients Branch. We predict the quantities R_i and c_i with this branch. We use a single rotation angle to parametrize R_i. The branch consists of an MLP that estimates the mentioned parameters. The output size varies depending on whether we are interested in symmetric shape instances as in Eq. (3) or symmetric basis as in Eq. (4), the size being double in the latter.

Additional Learnable Parameters. Several unknown quantities in Eq. (3) or (4) are constant for a category shape space $\mathcal{C}$. Such quantities need not be predicted instance-wise. We rather choose to optimize them as part of the network parameters θ. They are the shape basis $\mathcal{B_C} \in \mathbb{R}^{3N \times K}$ and the unit normal of the plane of symmetry $n_{\mathcal{C}} \in \mathbb{R}^3$. We observed that a good choice for the number of shape basis is $5 \leq K \leq 10$. In fact, the generated keypoints are not very sensitive to the choice of K, as a large K tends to generate sparser shape coefficients and similar keypoints. Depending upon the problem, alternate parametrization can be considered for $n_{\mathcal{C}}$, e.g., Euler angles.

At inference time, we apply Non-Maximal Suppression obtaining the final N' number of keypoints. Our method consistently provides N' keypoints for all instances in the category, as they follow the same geometric model.

4.1   Training Losses

In order to adhere to the definitions of the category-specific keypoints introduced in Sect. 1 as well as our shape modeling, we design our loss functions as below.

Chamfer Loss with Symmetry and Non-rigidity. Equation (1) suggests that the neural network $\Pi_{\mathcal{C}}$ can be trained with an ℓ_2 loss between the node predictions X_i and the deformation function $P_i = \Phi_{\mathcal{C}}(R_i, c_i; \mathcal{B_C}, n_{\mathcal{C}})$, thus obtaining $P_i = X_i$. However, as confirmed by our evaluations as well as in [26], the ℓ_2 loss does not converge as the network is unable to predict the point order. Alternatively, the Chamfer loss [54] does converge, minimizing the distance between each point x_{ik} in the first set X_i and its nearest neighbor p_{ij} in the second set P_i and vice versa.

$$\mathcal{L}_{chf} = \sum_{k=1}^{N} \min_{p_{ij} \in P_i} \|x_{ik} - p_{ij}\|_2^2 + \sum_{j=1}^{N} \min_{x_{ik} \in X_i} \|x_{ik} - p_{ij}\|_2^2, \tag{5}$$

The Chamfer loss in Eq. (5) ensures that the learned keypoints follow a generalizable category-specific property – that they are a linear combination of common basis learned specifically for the category. To additionally model symmetry, Eq. (3) or (4) is directly used in Eq. (5). Therefore, two different Chamfer losses are possible modeling two different types of symmetries.

Coverage and Inclusivity Loss. The Chamfer loss in Eq. (5) does not ensure that the keypoints follow the object shape. However, one can add the following conditions: a) the keypoints cover the whole category shape (coverage loss), b) the keypoints are not far from the point cloud (inclusivity loss). The coverage loss can be defined as a Huber loss between the volume of the nodes X_i and that of the input shape S_i, using the product of the singular values. However, we instead approximate the volume using the 3D bounding box defined by the points. This improves the training speed and, based on our initial evaluations, also does not harm performance. The coverage loss is thus given by:

$$\mathcal{L}_{cov} = \|\mathrm{vol}(X_i) - \mathrm{vol}(S_i)\| \tag{6}$$

The inclusivity loss is formulated as a single side Chamfer loss [55] which penalizes nodes in X_i that are far from the original shape S_i, similarly to Eq. (5):

$$\mathcal{L}_{inc} = \sum_{k=1}^{N} \min_{s_{ij} \in S_i} \|x_{ik} - s_{ij}\|_2^2. \tag{7}$$

5   Experimental Results

We conduct experiments to evaluate the desired properties of the proposed category-specific keypoints and show their generalization over indoor/outdoor objects and rigid/non-rigid objects with four different datasets in total (Sect. 5.1, 5.2). All these properties are also compared with a proposed baseline. We then evaluate the practical use of our keypoints for intra-category shapes registration (Sect. 5.3), analyzing the influence of symmetry. Additional qualitative results are shown in Fig. 1 and the supplementary material.

Datasets. We use four main datasets. They are ModelNet10 [52], ShapeNet parts [51], Dynamic FAUST [56] and Basel Face Model 2017 [57]. Since our method is category-specific, we require separate training data for each class in the datasets. For indoor rigid objects, we choose three categories from Model-Net10 [52]; chair, table and bed. Three outdoor rigid object categories: airplane, car and motorbike, are evaluated from ShapeNet parts [51]. For non-rigid objects, we randomly choose a sequence of the Dynamic Faust [56], that provides high-resolution 4D scans of human subjects in motion. Finally, we generate shape models of faces using the Basel Face Model 2017 [57] combining 50 different shapes and 20 different expressions. All models are normalized in the range -1 to 1 and are randomly misaligned within $\pm 45°$.

Baseline. Since this is the first work computing category-specific keypoints from point sets, we construct our own baseline based on the recent work USIP [26]. The method detects stable interest points in 3D point clouds under arbitrary transformations and is also unsupervised, which makes it the closest method for comparison. The USIP detector is not category-based, so we train the network per category to create the baseline. Additionally, we adapt the number of predicted keypoints so that the results are directly comparable to ours. While training with some of the categories, specifically car and bed, we observe that predicting lower number of keypoints can lead to some degeneracies [26].

Implementation Details. Input point clouds of dimension 3×2000 are used. We implement the network in Pytorch [58] and train it end-to-end from scratch using the Adam optimizer [59]. The initial learning rate is 10^{-3}, which is exponentially decayed by a rate of 0.5 every 40 epochs. We use a batch size of 32 and train each model until convergence, for 200 epochs. The final loss function combines the three training losses, Eqs. (5), (6) and (7), and are weighted as follows: $w_{chf} = w_{cov} = 1$ and $w_{inc} = 2$. For ModelNet10 and ShapeNet parts, we use the training and testing split provided by the authors. For the Basel Face Model 2017, we follow the common practice and split the 1000 generated faces in 85% training and 15% test. We use the same split strategy for the sequence '50009_jiggle_on_toes' of Dynamic Fuaust, which contains 244 examples.

Table 1. *Properties Analysis:* Top (ours) and bottom (baseline [26]). For coverage, correspondence and inclusivity *higher is better*, and for model and symmetry error *lower is better*. We empirically show the desired properties of our keypoints, as well as the generalization of our method over indoor/outdoor and rigid/non-rigid objects. Best results are in bold.

Category	Coverage	Model Err	Correspondence	Inclusivity	Sym Err	Definition
	%	%	%	%	°	
Chair	**88.83**	0.72	**100**	90.46	0.40	10
Table	**93.33**	0.99	**100**	93.38	2.86	6
Bed	**80.31**	0.94	**100**	**95.33**	0.13	6
Airplane	**89.15**	0.64	**100**	**96.35**	0.20	8
Car	**92.39**	0.72	**100**	**97.77**	2.21	8
Motorbike	**96.13**	0.79	**100**	90.53	1.42	8
Human body	**85.59**	0.72	**100**	97.73	33.30	11
Faces	**97.93**	0.41	**100**	**100**	0.15	9
Chair	79.73	–	55.6	**98.50**	–	10
Table	79.72	–	34.5	**99.83**	–	6
Bed	42.18	–	49.33	70.00	–	6
Airplane	69.24	–	47.5	87.13	–	8
Car	26.87	–	32.18	74.0	–	8
Motorbike	75.29	–	48.14	84.57	–	8
Human body	72.66	–	50.45	**100**	–	11
Faces	42.98	–	30.11	**100**	–	9

5.1   Desired Properties Analysis

As described in Sect. 1 and 3, the category-specific keypoints satisfy certain desired properties. We propose six different metrics to evaluate the properties which are also used for comparison against the baseline. All the results are presented in Table 1, and are averaged across the test samples.

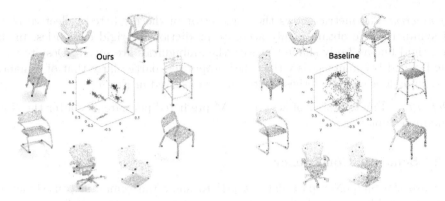

Fig. 3. Keypoints correspondence/repeatability across instances. We cluster the predicted keypoints for all the instances in the category to show their geometric consistency. Note how our keypoints are neatly clustered as they are consistently predicted in the corresponding geometric locations, unlike the baseline keypoints. (Note: cluster colors do not correspond to keypoint colors.)

Coverage: According to property *iii)*, we seek keypoints that are representative of each instance shape as well as of the category itself. To measure it, we calculate the percentage of the input shape covered by the keypoints' 3D bounding box. On average, we achieve a 29.4% more coverage than the baseline.

Model Error: This metric refers to the Chamfer distance between the estimated nodes and the learned category-specific keypoints, normalized by the model's scale. We obtain less than 1% of error in all the categories, meaning that the network satisfactorily manages to generalize, describing the nodes with the symmteric non-rigidity modeling (Properties *i)* and *iii)*).

Correspondence/Repeatability: We measure the ability of the model to find the same set of keypoints on different instances of a given category (Property *ii)*). For our method, we cluster the keypoints using their inherent order whereas for the baseline, we use K-means clustering to evaluate and compare this property. We show the evaluation in Fig. 3, the rest of the categories are provided in the supplementary material. One can see at a glance how our keypoints are well clustered, unlike the baseline keypoints. Numerically, we show the % occurrence of each specific keypoint belonging to the same cluster across instances. Our keypoints satisfy 100% the correspondence/repeatability test thanks to our geometric non-rigidity modelling.

Inclusivity: We measure the percentage of keypoints that lie inside the point cloud (of scale 2) within a chosen threshold of 0.15, which also proves property *iii)*. This is the only metric in which our method doesn't outperform the baseline in all cases. On average, our method achieves ~ 95% inclusivity compared to ~ 89% for the baseline.

Symmetry: The metric shows the angle error of the predicted reflective plane of symmetry. We obtain highly accurate prediction for rigid categories. In the non-rigid human body shape however, the ambiguities are severe. Despite that, the learned keypoints satisfy the other properties, particularly that of semantic correspondence. Both of these facts can be observed in Fig. 1.

Definition: Final number of keypoints N' predicted per category after the Non-Maximal Suppression.

5.2 Semantic Consistency

We use the ShapeNet part dataset [51] to show the semantic consistency of the proposed keypoints. Following the low-rank non-rigidity modelling, the keypoints lie on geometrically corresponding locations. The idea of the experiment is to measure keypoint-semantics relationship for every keypoint across instances of the category. The results are presented in Fig. 4 as covariance matrices, along with keypoint visualizations per category for our method. On average, the proposed keypoints have a high semantic consistency of 93% across instances, despite the large intra-category variability. The same experiment is performed for the baseline and presented in bottom of Fig. 4. Here, the degeneracy causes all the keypoints to approach the object centroid for 'Car'. Nonetheless, we observe no semantic consistency even for 'Airplane' without degeneracies. Our model, aiming for a common representation for all the instances of the category, avoids placing keypoints in less representative parts or unique parts, e.g., arm rests in chairs (in Fig. 1), engines in airplanes or gas tank in motorbikes. This highlights significant robustness achieved in modelling and learning the keypoints.

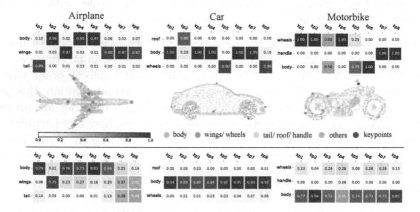

Fig. 4. Semantic part correspondence. Top to bottom: the semantic correspondence for the proposed keypoints, qualitative results and the baseline semantic correspondence. Our predicted keypoints show the correct semantic correspondence across the category.

5.3   Object Pose and Intra-category Registration

Previous methods do not handle misaligned data due to the obvious difficulty it poses to unsupervised learning. This deserves special attention since real data is never aligned. In this section we evaluate the intra-category registration performance of our model and show the impact of the different symmetry models proposed. These results implicitly measure the object poses estimated as well.

Rotation Ambiguities. Recent unsupervised approaches for keypoint detection actually self-supervise rotation during training, e.g., [26,27], and highlight that it is crucial for achieving a good performance. In our case, we do not directly supervise the rotations. Therefore, the different combination of basis shapes can result in different alignments. This implies that computing P_i with the deformation function Φ_C will give the correct set of keypoints along with the correct plane of symmetry, but the predicted rotation alone is not meaningful for registration.

Experimental Setup. Despite the above ambiguity, an important characteristic of the proposed keypoints is that they are ordered, which empowers direct inter-instances registration since no extra descriptors are needed for matching. We perform experiments for the chair category, using 10 keypoints (Table 1) and a misalignment of $\pm 45°$. Three different models are compared. The first one is trained without symmetry awareness following Eq. (2). A second one uses shape symmetry during training as shown in Eq. (3). The last model is trained with basis symmetry as in Eq. (4). We attempt to register keypoints in each instance to those of randomly chosen three aligned templates by computing a similarity transformation and observe the mean error. Figure 5 shows that symmetry helps to have more control over the rotations and tackle higher misalignment. More results and analysis are provided in the supplementary.

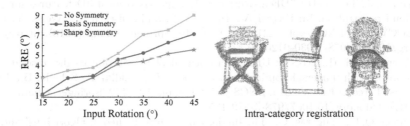

Fig. 5. Left: Relative rotation error for different symmetry modelings. Right: 3 examples of registration between different instances of the same category.

6   Conclusions

This paper investigates automatic discovery of kepoints in 3D misaligned point clouds that are consistent over inter-subject shape variations and intra-subject deformations in a category. We find that this can be solved, with unsupervised learning, by modeling keypoints with non-rigidity, based on symmetric linear basis shapes. Additionally, the proposed category-specific keypoints have one-to-one ordered correspondences and semantic consistency. Applications for the learned keypoints include registration, recognition, generation, shape completion and many more. Our experiments showed that high quality keypoints can be obtained using the proposed methods and that the method can be extended to complex non-rigid deformations. Future work could focus on better modeling complex deformations with non-linear approaches.

Acknowledgements. This research was funded by the EU Horizon 2020 research and innovation program under grant agreement No. 820434. This work was also supported by Project RTI2018-096903-B-I00 (AEI/FEDER, UE) and Regional Council of Bourgogne Franche-Comté (2017-9201AAO048S01342).

References

1. Lowe, D.G.: Distinctive image features from scale-invariant keypoints. Int. J. Comput. Vision **60**(2), 91–110 (2004)
2. Tola, E., Lepetit, V., Fua, P.: DAISY: an efficient dense descriptor applied to wide-baseline stereo. IEEE Trans. Pattern Anal. Mach. Intell. **32**(5), 815–830 (2009)
3. Bay, H., Ess, A., Tuytelaars, T., Van Gool, L.: Speeded-up robust features (SURF). Comput. Vis. Image Underst. **110**(3), 346–359 (2008)
4. Novotny, D., Ravi, N., Graham, B., Neverova, N., Vedaldi, A.: C3DPO: canonical 3D pose networks for non-rigid structure from motion. In: Proceedings of the IEEE International Conference on Computer Vision, pp. 7688–7697 (2019)
5. Dai, Y., Li, H., He, M.: A simple prior-free method for non-rigid structure-from-motion factorization. In: CVPR (2012)
6. Snavely, N., Seitz, S.M., Szeliski, R.: Modeling the world from internet photo collections. Int. J. Comput. Vision **80**(2), 189–210 (2007)
7. Yew, Z.J., Lee, G.H.: 3DFeat-Net: weakly supervised local 3D features for point cloud registration. In: Ferrari, V., Hebert, M., Sminchisescu, C., Weiss, Y. (eds.) ECCV 2018. LNCS, vol. 11219, pp. 630–646. Springer, Cham (2018). https://doi.org/10.1007/978-3-030-01267-0_37
8. Kneip, L., Li, H., Seo, Y.: UPnP: an optimal $O(n)$ solution to the absolute pose problem with universal applicability. In: Fleet, D., Pajdla, T., Schiele, B., Tuytelaars, T. (eds.) ECCV 2014. LNCS, vol. 8689, pp. 127–142. Springer, Cham (2014). https://doi.org/10.1007/978-3-319-10590-1_9
9. Luong, Q.T., Faugeras, O.: The fundamental matrix: theory, algorithms, and stability analysis. Int. J. Comput. Vision **17**, 43–75 (1995)
10. Loper, M., Mahmood, N., Romero, J., Pons-Moll, G., Black, M.J.: SMPL: a skinned multi-person linear model. ACM Trans. Graph. (Proc. SIGGRAPH Asia) **34**(6), 248:1–248:16 (2015)
11. Shotton, J., et al.: Real-time human pose recognition in parts from single depth images. In: CVPR 2011, pp. 1297–1304. IEEE (2011)
12. Moreno-Noguer, F.: 3D human pose estimation from a single image via distance matrix regression. In: Proceedings of the IEEE Conference on Computer Vision and Pattern Recognition, pp. 2823–2832 (2017)

13. Cao, Z., Simon, T., Wei, S.E., Sheikh, Y.: Realtime multi-person 2d pose estimation using part affinity fields. In: Proceedings of the IEEE Conference on Computer Vision and Pattern Recognition, pp. 7291–7299 (2017)
14. Bogo, F., Kanazawa, A., Lassner, C., Gehler, P., Romero, J., Black, M.J.: Keep it SMPL: automatic estimation of 3D human pose and shape from a single image. In: Leibe, B., Matas, J., Sebe, N., Welling, M. (eds.) ECCV 2016. LNCS, vol. 9909, pp. 561–578. Springer, Cham (2016). https://doi.org/10.1007/978-3-319-46454-1_34
15. He, K., Gkioxari, G., Dollár, P., Girshick, R.: Mask R-CNN. In: Proceedings of the IEEE International Conference on Computer Vision, pp. 2961–2969 (2017)
16. Sattler, T., Leibe, B., Kobbelt, L.: Fast image-based localization using direct 2D-to-3D matching. In: 2011 International Conference on Computer Vision, pp. 667–674. IEEE (2011)
17. Tang, H., Xu, D., Liu, G., Wang, W., Sebe, N., Yan, Y.: Cycle in cycle generative adversarial networks for keypoint-guided image generation. In: Proceedings of the 27th ACM International Conference on Multimedia, pp. 2052–2060 (2019)
18. Zafeiriou, S., Chrysos, G.G., Roussos, A., Ververas, E., Deng, J., Trigeorgis, G.: The 3D menpo facial landmark tracking challenge. In: Proceedings of the IEEE International Conference on Computer Vision Workshops, pp. 2503–2511 (2017)
19. Huang, S., Gong, M., Tao, D.: A coarse-fine network for keypoint localization. In: Proceedings of the IEEE International Conference on Computer Vision, pp. 3028–3037 (2017)
20. Pavlakos, G., Zhou, X., Chan, A., Derpanis, K.G., Daniilidis, K.: 6-DoF object pose from semantic keypoints. In: ICRA (2017)
21. Zhang, Z., Luo, P., Loy, C.C., Tang, X.: Facial landmark detection by deep multi-task learning. In: Fleet, D., Pajdla, T., Schiele, B., Tuytelaars, T. (eds.) ECCV 2014. LNCS, vol. 8694, pp. 94–108. Springer, Cham (2014). https://doi.org/10.1007/978-3-319-10599-4_7
22. Dong, X., Yan, Y., Ouyang, W., Yang, Y.: Style aggregated network for facial landmark detection. In: Proceedings of the IEEE Conference on Computer Vision and Pattern Recognition, pp. 379–388 (2018)
23. Yu, X., Zhou, F., Chandraker, M.: Deep deformation network for object landmark localization. In: Leibe, B., Matas, J., Sebe, N., Welling, M. (eds.) ECCV 2016. LNCS, vol. 9909, pp. 52–70. Springer, Cham (2016). https://doi.org/10.1007/978-3-319-46454-1_4
24. Alahi, A., Ortiz, R., Vandergheynst, P.: FREAK: fast retina keypoint. In: 2012 IEEE Conference on Computer Vision and Pattern Recognition, pp. 510–517. IEEE (2012)
25. Li, Y.: A novel fast retina keypoint extraction algorithm for multispectral images using geometric algebra. IEEE Access 7, 167895–167903 (2019)
26. Li, J., Lee, G.H.: USIP: unsupervised stable interest point detection from 3D point clouds. In: Proceedings of the IEEE International Conference on Computer Vision, pp. 361–370 (2019)
27. Suwajanakorn, S., Snavely, N., Tompson, J.J., Norouzi, M.: Discovery of latent 3D keypoints via end-to-end geometric reasoning. In: Advances in Neural Information Processing Systems, pp. 2059–2070 (2018)
28. Wu, J., et al.: Single image 3D interpreter network. In: Leibe, B., Matas, J., Sebe, N., Welling, M. (eds.) ECCV 2016. LNCS, vol. 9910, pp. 365–382. Springer, Cham (2016). https://doi.org/10.1007/978-3-319-46466-4_22
29. Yang, H., Carlone, L.: In perfect shape: certifiably optimal 3D shape reconstruction from 2D landmarks. arXiv preprint arXiv:1911.11924 (2019)

30. Hejrati, M., Ramanan, D.: Analyzing 3D objects in cluttered images. In: Advances in Neural Information Processing Systems, pp. 593–601 (2012)
31. Wang, C., Wang, Y., Lin, Z., Yuille, A.L., Gao, W.: Robust estimation of 3D human poses from a single image. In: Proceedings of the IEEE Conference on Computer Vision and Pattern Recognition, pp. 2361–2368 (2014)
32. Persad, R.A., Armenakis, C.: Automatic 3D surface co-registration using keypoint matching. Photogram. Eng. Remote Sens. **83**(2), 137–151 (2017)
33. Mitra, N.J., Wand, M., Zhang, H., Cohen-Or, D., Kim, V., Huang, Q.X.: Structure-aware shape processing. In: ACM SIGGRAPH 2014 Courses, pp. 1–21 (2014)
34. Reed, M.P.: Modeling body shape from surface landmark configurations. In: Duffy, V.G. (ed.) DHM 2013. LNCS, vol. 8026, pp. 376–383. Springer, Heidelberg (2013). https://doi.org/10.1007/978-3-642-39182-8_44
35. Creusot, C., Pears, N., Austin, J.: 3D landmark model discovery from a registered set of organic shapes. In: 2012 IEEE Computer Society Conference on Computer Vision and Pattern Recognition Workshops, pp. 57–64. IEEE (2012)
36. Sridhar, S., Rempe, D., Valentin, J., Sofien, B., Guibas, L.J.: Multiview aggregation for learning category-specific shape reconstruction. In: Advances in Neural Information Processing Systems, pp. 2348–2359 (2019)
37. Gao, Y., Yuille, A.L.: Symmetric non-rigid structure from motion for category-specific object structure estimation. In: Leibe, B., Matas, J., Sebe, N., Welling, M. (eds.) ECCV 2016. LNCS, vol. 9906, pp. 408–424. Springer, Cham (2016). https://doi.org/10.1007/978-3-319-46475-6_26
38. Bregler, C., Hertzmann, A., Biermann, H.: Recovering non-rigid 3D shape from image streams. In: CVPR (2000)
39. Torresani, L., Hertzmann, A., Bregler, C.: Nonrigid structure-from-motion: estimating shape and motion with hierarchical priors. IEEE Trans. Pattern Anal. Mach. Intell. **30**(5), 878–892 (2008)
40. Akhter, I., Sheikh, Y., Khan, S., Kanade, T.: Nonrigid structure from motion in trajectory space. In: NIPS (2008)
41. Taylor, J., Jepson, A.D., Kutulakos, K.N.: Non-rigid structure from locally-rigid motion. In: CVPR (2010)
42. Parashar, S., Pizarro, D., Bartoli, A.: Isometric non-rigid shape-from-motion in linear time. In: CVPR (2016)
43. Kong, C., Lucey, S.: Deep non-rigid structure from motion. In: Proceedings of the IEEE International Conference on Computer Vision, pp. 1558–1567 (2019)
44. Wang, H., Sridhar, S., Huang, J., Valentin, J., Song, S., Guibas, L.J.: Normalized object coordinate space for category-level 6D object pose and size estimation. In: Proceedings of the IEEE Conference on Computer Vision and Pattern Recognition, pp. 2642–2651 (2019)
45. Wu, S., Rupprecht, C., Vedaldi, A.: Unsupervised learning of probably symmetric deformable 3D objects from images in the wild. In: CVPR (2020)
46. Qi, C.R., Su, H., Mo, K., Guibas, L.J.: PointNet: deep learning on point sets for 3D classification and segmentation. In: CVPR (2017)
47. Qi, C.R., Yi, L., Su, H., Guibas, L.J.: PointNet++: deep hierarchical feature learning on point sets in a metric space. In: Advances in Neural Information Processing Systems (2017)
48. Verma, N., Boyer, E., Verbeek, J.: FeastNet: feature-steered graph convolutions for 3D shape analysis. In: CVPR (2018)
49. Bromley, J., Guyon, I., LeCun, Y., Säckinger, E., Shah, R.: Signature verification using a "siamese" time delay neural network. In: Advances in Neural Information Processing Systems, pp. 737–744 (1994)

50. Tomasi, C., Kanade, T.: Shape and motion from image streams under orthography: a factorization method. Int. J. Comput. Vision **9**(2), 137–154 (1992)
51. Yi, L., et al.: A scalable active framework for region annotation in 3D shape collections. ACM Trans. Graph. (TOG) **35**(6), 1–12 (2016)
52. Wu, Z., et al.: 3D ShapeNets: a deep representation for volumetric shapes. In: CVPR, pp. 1912–1920 (2015)
53. Li, J., Chen, B.M., Hee Lee, G.: SO-Net: self-organizing network for point cloud analysis. In: Proceedings of the IEEE Conference on Computer Vision and Pattern Recognition, pp. 9397–9406 (2018)
54. Fan, H., Su, H., Guibas, L.J.: A point set generation network for 3D object reconstruction from a single image. In: Proceedings of the IEEE Conference on Computer Vision and Pattern Recognition, pp. 605–613 (2017)
55. Besl, P.J., McKay, N.D.: Method for registration of 3-D shapes. In: Sensor fusion IV: Control Paradigms and Data Structures, vol. 1611, pp. 586–606. International Society for Optics and Photonics (1992)
56. Bogo, F., Romero, J., Pons-Moll, G., Black, M.J.: Dynamic FAUST: registering human bodies in motion. In: CVPR, pp. 6233–6242 (2017)
57. Gerig, T., et al.: Morphable face models-an open framework. In: 2018 13th IEEE International Conference on Automatic Face & Gesture Recognition (FG 2018), pp. 75–82. IEEE (2018)
58. Paszke, A., et al.: PyTorch: an imperative style, high-performance deep learning library. In: NIPS (2019)
59. Kingma, D.P., Ba, J.: Adam: a method for stochastic optimization. arXiv preprint arXiv:1412.6980 (2014)

PAMS: Quantized Super-Resolution via Parameterized Max Scale

Huixia Li[1], Chenqian Yan[1], Shaohui Lin[2], Xiawu Zheng[1], Baochang Zhang[3], Fan Yang[4], and Rongrong Ji[5(✉)]

[1] Media Analytics and Computing Lab, Department of Artificial Intelligence, School of Informatics, Xiamen University, Xiamen, China
{hxlee,zhengxiawu}@stu.xmu.edu.cn, im.cqyan@gmail.com
[2] National University of Singapore, Singapore, Singapore
shaohuilin007@gmail.com
[3] Beihang University, Beijing, China
bczhang@buaa.edu.cn
[4] Huawei Technologies Co., Ltd., Shenzhen, China
yangfan74@huawei.com
[5] Peng Cheng Laboratory, Shenzhen, China
rrji@xmu.edu.cn

Abstract. Deep convolutional neural networks (DCNNs) have shown dominant performance in the task of super-resolution (SR). However, their heavy memory cost and computation overhead significantly restrict their practical deployments on resource-limited devices, which mainly arise from the floating-point storage and operations between weights and activations. Although previous endeavors mainly resort to fixed-point operations, quantizing both weights and activations with fixed coding lengths may cause significant performance drop, especially on low bits. Specifically, most state-of-the-art SR models without batch normalization have a large dynamic quantization range, which also serves as another cause of performance drop. To address these two issues, we propose a new quantization scheme termed PArameterized Max Scale (PAMS), which applies the trainable truncated parameter to explore the upper bound of the quantization range adaptively. Finally, a structured knowledge transfer (SKT) loss is introduced to fine-tune the quantized network. Extensive experiments demonstrate that the proposed PAMS scheme can well compress and accelerate the existing SR models such as EDSR and RDN. Notably, 8-bit PAMS-EDSR improves PSNR on Set5 benchmark from 32.095 dB to 32.124 dB with 2.42× compression ratio, which achieves a new state-of-the-art.

Keywords: Super resolution · Network quantization

H. Li and C. Yan—Equal contribution.

A. Vedaldi et al. (Eds.): ECCV 2020, LNCS 12370, pp. 564–580, 2020.
https://doi.org/10.1007/978-3-030-58595-2_34

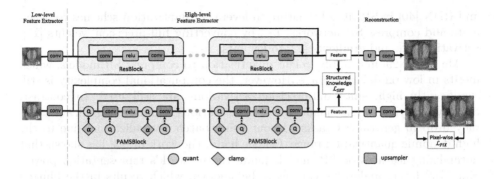

Fig. 1. The framework of our approach. The super-resolution operation is split into three modules, *i.e.*, low-level feature extractor, high-level feature extractor and reconstruction. We deploy PAMS with different α on each activation layer in the high-level feature extractor. *quant* denotes the quantization operation and *clamp* represents the clamp function of quantization. Dash lines denote the weights are quantized with the maximum. Here, we illustrate EDSR as backbone.

1   Introduction

Single image super-resolution (SISR) aims to recover a high-resolution (HR) image from the corresponding low-resolution (LR) one, which has been a research hot spot in computer vision for decades. Coming with the advances of deep learning, deep convolutional neural networks (DCNNs) [7,18,23] have dominated SR in recent years. These networks commonly use an extraction module to extract a series of feature maps from the LR image, cascaded with the up-sampling module, which stepwisely increases the resolution to reconstruct the HR image.

As one of the pioneering works for deep learning based SR, Dong *et al.* [7] introduce three convolution layers to achieve high visual perception. After that, Kim *et al.* [18] design a deep network VDSR by stacking 20 convolutional layers. Subsequent works mainly resort to increasing the network depth to improve SR performance. For instance, Lim *et al.* [23] propose the enhanced deep residual networks (*e.g.* EDSR and MDSR) and remove batch normalization (BN) [16] to reduce the memory consumption, which however still requires at least 64 convolution layers (more than 160 layers for MDSR). A channel attention mechanism equipped into the RCAN model [39] requires more than 400 layers with about 30B FLOPs and 13M parameters. Such significant computation and memory overheads restrict their applications in scenarios where only limited memory and computation resources are available. Consequently, compressing deep SR networks has attracted increasing attention recently [29].

Beyond SR, neural network compression and acceleration have been widely studied in the literature. Representative works include parameter pruning [11–13,22,26,27], low-rank approximation [6,24,25], compact networks [28,34], knowledge distillation (KD) [14,33], neural architecture search (NAS) [41,44] and quantization [5,17]. Considering the unique structures such as EDSR [23] and RDN [40] in SR, it is by nature to leverage quantization schemes to accelerate and compress SR networks, *i.e.*, by converting full-precision weights [17], activations [2], and gradients [42] to low bits.

Ma *et al.* [29] first apply weight quantization to compress SR models, which merits in low on-device storage. However, the computational complexity is still significantly high, since full-precision activations are still used. In contrast, directly applying weight quantization to activations will incur significant accuracy drop in general SR tasks without using batch normalization, due to the high dynamic quantization range. On one hand, the work in [23] has shown that normalizing features on SR models limits the network's representation power. Since BN layers make the features to be smooth, which results in the blurred reconstructed HR images with artifacts. To this end, recent SOTA SR models (*e.g.* EDSR [23], RDN [40]) have already removed BN layers to obtain better reconstructed HR images. On the other hand, the absence of BN causes a severe dynamic range problem when quantizing the activations by using the SOTA quantization methods [3,17]. For example, the work [17] simply set the upper scale of activations to their max value, which causes significant performance degeneration in SR task. This is due to the fixed max scale that may be an outlier as the upper scale. Although Choi *et al.* [3] propose PACT to clip and quantize activations by learnable parameters, it only concentrates on the positive range while neglecting the gradient information in the negative range. In addition, the novel regularization term [4] is added to automatically learn quantized controlling parameters and then obtain an accurate low-precision model. However, it leads to the increase of additional computation burdens and memory footprint, which is not runtime friendly for practical applications.

To address the above issues, a novel quantization scheme, termed PArameterized Max Scale (PAMS), is proposed to compress and accelerate SR models. Different from the previous works that focus on quantizing activations in a fixed manner, PAMS adaptively explores the upper bound of quantization range based on the gradients using a trainable clamp function, which significantly improves the model generality. Furthermore, structured knowledge transfer (SKT) is introduced to transfer structured knowledge from the full-precision network to the quantized one, which enables the latter to gain better visual perception. Figure 1 presents the flowchart of our method. We first replace each basic block in the SR model with PAMS block. In each PAMS block, weights are quantized before they are convolved with the inputs and activations are quantized after the outputs of convolutional layer with its own learnable max scale. To further improve the performance of the quantized model, we align the high-level features between full-precision model and the corresponding low-precision quantized one among pixels. Finally, we employ stochastic gradient descent (SGD) method to minimize the objective function, which leverages the distillation loss to pixel-wise loss.

We evaluate our method on several benchmarks over widely-used deep SR models like EDSR [23] and RDN [40]. Quantitative and qualitative results demonstrate that PAMS can well quantize various SR models with a significantly high compression ratio, as well as nearly identical accuracy to the full-precision

SR models. The proposed PAMS also well outperforms most existing alternatives such as Dorefa [42], Tensorflow Lite [17] and PACT [3]. For instance, on BSD100, the 4-bit PAMS-EDSR outperforms 4-bit Dorefa-EDSR by 0.828 dB with a scale factor of ×4. Extended experiments also show that SKT is more effective for the quantized SR models with lower-bit operations.

2 Related Work

Deep SR Models with Light Weights. Most recent SR models are built based upon DCNNs, for instance, MDSR [23] and RDN [40]. Such networks are typically deep with heavy computation cost and memory footprint, which restrict their applications in resource-limited devices. Recent advances in SR network compression mostly focus on redesigning light-weight networks. For instance, DRRN [35] and DRCN [19] have been proposed to share parameters for reducing network parameters. However, the cost of computation and memory storage in these networks are still very large, due to the floating-point operations during inference and the sufficient parameters to ensure the model capability.

Network Quantization. Previous works in network quantization mainly focus on quantizing weights [32], while maintaining the full-precision activations to ensure the model performance. Joint quantization of activations and weights are explored in HWGQ [2] and PACT [3]. However, these methods mainly concentrate on object classification [10, 20], which is easier than the complex pixel-wise or patch-wise SR tasks. The work in [29] serves as the first to extend quantization to compress SR models, which quantizes only weights to be binary. However, the operations between activations and quantized weights are still floating-point, which cannot largely reduce the FLOPs towards the practical speedup. Different from the previous work [29], we optimize the SR network with both low-bit quantized weights and activations by introducing a learnable parameter, which achieves the bound of the quantization range.

Knowledge Distillation. Knowledge distillation [14] aims to transfer the knowledge from a cumbersome network (teacher) to a compact network (student). It has been widely applied to various computer vision tasks by using the softened output knowledge [14] and intermediate feature representations [24, 38]. In line with our work, Zhuang et al. [43] proposed a guidance loss to jointly optimize the full-precision network and the low-precision model. However, it is not suitable to directly use such probability-based loss for SR, as the outputs of SR are reconstructed HR images. Different from these methods, our approach adopts structured knowledge based on the implicit information of a pre-trained network, which concentrates on aligning the spatial correlation between the low-precision and full-precision features to be more suitable for pixel-wise SR task.

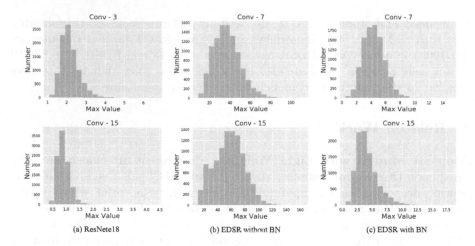

Fig. 2. Max value of activations from different layers and samples of ResNet-18 on ImageNet, EDSR [23] w./wo. BN on DIV2K. The absence of BN causes more dynamic range problem in SR models.

3 The Proposed Method

3.1 A Close Look at SR Model Quantization

Current practice [29] only quantizes the weights in deep SR models, which does reduce the storage cost but unfortunately ignores the computational efficiency caused by the full-precision multiplication between weights and activations. Moreover, the conversion between low-precision weights and full-precision activations aggravates the training time. It is not runtime-friendly to deploy such quantization scheme in real scenarios. Note that some quantization methods quantize the activations based on the premise of batch normalization [16]. In this way, the activations are supposed to stay in a stable range.

However, prior work [23] has shown that batch normalization layers get rid of range flexibility by normalizing the features, and simply removing them can make a big margin of improvements while reducing GPU memory cost. This modification can be effectively extended to the recent state-of-the-art SR models (*e.g.* RDN [40], RCAN [39], DBPN [9]) for ensuring range flexibility and reducing artifacts. Figure 2 shows the statistics collected from pre-trained ResNet-18 on ImageNet, EDSR with and without BN on DIV2K. We can see that the max value of activations varies a lot in different samples in the same layer, and the activation range is more dynamic of SR model (EDSR) than that in classification model (ResNet-18). It indicates the dynamic range problem is more severe in the SR model than that of the classification model. Moreover, the absence of BN causes a more severe dynamic range problem. Compared to EDSR with BN (Fig. 2(b)), the max value of activations in EDSR without BN has a wider max value range and shows a more even distribution, which indicates that removing BN in current SR models causes activations in a more dynamic range, so as to be difficult to manually decide the quantization range. We argue that this quantization range is vital to the performance: If its maximum tends to a tiny value, the upper bound of the quantization range will be very small. And as reflected in the reconstructed HR images, the details will be mostly lost, which thus causes significant quality degradation. In contrast, if its maximum is abnormally large, the quantization range may include outliers that contain redundant information and decrease the accuracy of quantized DNNs.

3.2 Parameterized Max Scale (PAMS)

The proposed PAMS quantizes both activations and weights of deep SR models. In this subsection, we first elaborate on our overall quantization approach. Then we describe how to leverage trainable truncated parameters to adaptively learn the upper bound of activations. To efficiently use the pre-trained network and improve the performance, we further introduce a structured knowledge transfer (SKT) loss. The overall framework is presented in Fig. 1.

Quantization Function. As shown in [2], distributions on different layers of activations tend to be symmetric. This characteristic can help to improve the model accuracy of a quantized network with extremely low-bit weights and activations, as validated in [8]. Therefore, given a specific full-precision model with a parameter set $\mathcal{X}$ ($\mathcal{X}$ denotes either weights or activations of a specific layer), we quantize every element x ($x \in \mathcal{X}$) by using the following point-wise quantization function Q with a symmetric mode:

$$Q(x, n) = \lfloor \frac{f(x)}{s(n)} \rceil s(n), \tag{1}$$

where $f(x)$ is the clamp function that limits the inputs range and $s(n)$ is the map function that scales the higher precision inputs to their lower bit reflections, which can be formulated by $f(x) = max(min(x, a), -a)$ and $s(n) = \frac{a}{2^{n-1}-1}$, respectively. n denotes the number of quantization level. a represents the maximum of the absolute value of $\mathcal{X}$ and $\lfloor \cdot \rceil$ rounds the value to the nearest integer.

For quantizing weights, previous work [17] has shown that simply set $a := max(|w|)$ only has a negligible effect on the performance, which is therefore adopted in our approach. As for activations, the quantization range depends on the inputs, which leads to a dynamic range. This instability is unfavorable to the performance and model generality, which is designed in the following.

Trainable Upper Bound. In the previous work [3], the dynamic range of activations can be partially alleviated by using a parameterized clipping activation function to replace the Rectified Linear Unit (ReLU), which limits the application scope. In this paper, we propose a novel activation quantization scheme, in which the clamp function $f^*(\cdot)$ has the trainable parameter α to dynamically adjust the upper bound of the quantization range. We can directly employ the stochastic gradient descent to update this parameter, which is able to minimize the performance degradation arising from the quantization. For a given activation, the corresponding value will be quantized to n bits by:

$$x_q = Q(x, n) = \frac{\alpha}{2^{n-1} - 1} \times \lfloor \tilde{x} \times \frac{2^{n-1} - 1}{\alpha} \rceil, \tag{2}$$

where $\tilde{x} = f^*(x) = max(min(x, \alpha), -\alpha)$. The dynamic range is limited to $[-\alpha, \alpha]$. The advantages of our quantization function lie in that $Q(x, n)$ directly involves in the back-propagation process based on only one learnable parameter α, based upon which we can train the quantized SR network in an end-to-end manner. Extensive experiments in Sect. 4 demonstrate that Eq. 2 can introduce more effectiveness comparing to several state-of-the-art quantization methods [3,17,42].

Back-Propagation with Quantization. In back-propagation, $\frac{\partial x_q}{\partial \tilde{x}}$ can be approximated to 1 based on the straight-through estimator (STE) [5]. Inspired by [3], the gradient of α is calculated as follows:

$$\frac{\partial x_q}{\partial \alpha} \approx \frac{\partial x_q}{\partial \tilde{x}} \frac{\partial \tilde{x}}{\partial \alpha} = \begin{cases} -1, & x \in (-\infty, -\alpha], \\ 0, & x \in (-\alpha, \alpha), \\ 1, & x \in [\alpha, +\infty). \end{cases} \tag{3}$$

Note that, the work in [3] cuts off the gradients in the regions satisfied with $x < 0$, while PAMS can adaptively adjust α based on the gradients in both $x \geq \alpha$ and $x \leq \alpha$ areas. It is important for the post-training quantization, since the gradients of the pre-trained model tend to 0. In other words, PAMS can retain more gradient information for updating α.

Initializing α. To avoid gradients vanishing or exploding, non-convex optimization on DCNNs heavily depends on the initialization of parameters. Instead of manually designing the initial value of α, initialization based on the statistics from a pre-trained network can achieve better performance. Therefore, we resort to task-related statistical methods based on the pre-trained network to calibrate the quantization error. In particular, given the l-th layer with m input activations $x_1^{(l,t)}, ..., x_m^{(l,t)}$, $\alpha^{(l)}$ is calculated by the redefined exponential moving average (EMA) function at the start of training:

$$\alpha^{(l,t)} = \beta \cdot \alpha^{(l,t-1)} + (1 - \beta) \cdot avg(max(x_1^{(l,t)}), .., max(x_m^{(l,t)}), \tag{4}$$

where t is the iteration number and β denotes the smoothing parameter of EMA, which is set to be 0.9997. Specially, we set β to 0 when t is 0.

3.3 Optimization

Pixel-Wise Loss. Given a training dataset $D = \{I_{LR}^i, I_{HR}^i\}_{i=1}^n$ with n LR input images and their corresponding HR counterparts, SR models are commonly

Algorithm 1. Quantization SR Model

Input: Training dataset D, full-precision model T, quantization level n;
Output: The quantized model S;
 1: Define the low-precision model S by replacing convolution layers of T by n-bit PAMS;
 2: Initialize $\alpha^{(l)}$ of each layer l with Eq. (4);
 3: **for** $i = 1, ..., N$ epoch **do**
 4:    Forward pass by applying clamp function to weights and activations using Eq. (1) and Eq. (2);
 5:    Update all parameters in Eq. (7) via SGD;
 6: **end for**
 7: **return** S;

---

optimized by minimizing the conventional pixel-wise L_1 loss between the output I_{SR} and the ground truth image I_{HR}:

$$L_{PIX} = \frac{1}{n} \sum_{i=1}^{n} ||I_{HR}^i - I_{SR}^i||_1, \qquad (5)$$

where $|| \cdot ||_1$ denotes the L_1 norm. A better SR model needs to infer the high-frequency textures from a low-resolution input. However, it is hard to obtain by only using Eq. 5 based on low-bit quantization, which is due to the accumulated quantization error.

Structured Knowledge Transfer (SKT). Inspired by [38], we consider that the full-precision model has learned high-level representation, which provides knowledge to the low-precision one about where it concentrates. More specifically, instead of using the soft probability in the classification task, we align the structured features between the cumbersome network and the quantized one by minimizing their pixel-wise distance. Therefore, the loss function for our SKT is defined as:

$$L_{SKT} = ||\frac{F_S'}{||F_S'||_2} - \frac{F_T'}{||F_T'||_2}||_p, \qquad (6)$$

where F_T', F_S' are a pair of structure features after the spatial mapping of activations from the full-precision network and the correspond low-precision one, respectively. The spatial mapping defined by $F' = \sum_{i=1}^{C} |F_i|^2 \in \mathbb{R}^{H \times W}$, where $F \in \mathbb{R}^{C \times H \times W}$ denotes the activations after the last layer in the high-level feature extractor. We set $p = 2$ for p-norm in our experiments. In sum, SKT enhances the learning process of spatial correlation in the low-precision model which effectively improves the performance of the quantized network and provides an additional constraint to avoid producing over-smoothed images.

The Overall Loss Function. Given an SR model, as consistent with the distillation term mentioned above, the whole objective function is given as:

$$L_{SR} = \lambda_p L_{PIX} + \lambda_s L_{SKT}, \qquad (7)$$

Table 1. Comparison between quantizing EDSR [23] and RDN [40] by deploying PAMS with low-bit weights and activations on the public benchmark (PSNR(dB)/SSIM). The higher PSNR and higher SSIM, the better performance the methods achieve. EDSR is based on the residual block and RDN is based on the dense block. RDN* denotes the results based on our implementation.

Dataset	Scale	Bicubic	EDSR	PAMS-EDSR (8-bit)	PAMS-EDSR (4-bit)	RDN*	PAMS-RDN (8-bit)	PAMS-RDN (4-bit)
Set5	×2	33.66/0.9299	37.985/0.9604	37.946/0.9603	37.665/0.9588	38.027/0.9606	38.060/0.9606	36.528/0.9527
	×4	28.42/0.8104	32.095/0.8938	32.124/0.8940	31.591/0.8851	32.244/0.8959	32.340/0.8966	30.441/0.8624
Set14	×2	30.24/0.8688	33.568/0.9175	33.564/0.9175	33.196/0.9146	33.604/0.9174	33.732/0.9189	32.392/0.9050
	×4	26.00/0.7027	28.576/0.7813	28.585/0.7811	28.199/0.7725	28.669/0.7838	28.721/0.7848	27.536/0.7530
BSD100	×2	29.56/0.8431	32.155/0.8993	32.157/0.8994	31.936/0.8966	32.187/0.8999	32.215/0.9000	31.268/0.8853
	×4	25.96/0.6675	27.562/0.7355	27.565/0.7352	27.322/0.7282	27.627/0.7379	27.644/0.7382	26.869/0.7097
Urban100	×2	26.88/0.8403	31.977/0.9272	32.003/0.9274	31.100/0.9194	32.084/0.9284	32.262/0.9298	29.703/0.8976
	×4	23.14/0.6577	26.035/0.7848	26.016/0.7843	25.321/0.7624	26.293/0.7924	26.367/0.7955	24.523/0.7256

where λ_p and λ_s are coefficients to control the balance of the corresponding loss. We set λ_p to 1 and λ_s to 10^3. The overall optimized process is summarized in Algorithm 1.

4   Experiments

4.1   Experimental Settings

Datasets and Metrics. DIV2K [36] contains 800 training images, 100 validating images and 100 testing images. We train all models with DIV2K training images. For testing, we use four standard benchmark datasets: Set5 [1], Set14 [21], BSD100 [30] and Urban100 [15]. For the evaluation metrics, we use PSNR and SSIM [37] over the Y channel between the output quality image and the original HR image.

SR Models and Alternative Approaches. Both residual block and dense block are widely used in SR models, like VDSR [18], EDSR [23] and RDN [40]. To validate the superiority of our approach, we choose EDSR and RDN as backbones and use 8-bit and 4-bit quantization on them. As most parameters exist in the high-level feature extraction module, we do not quantize weights and activations in low-level feature extraction and reconstruction modules, which ensures a trade-off between performance and model size. The qualitative comparisons are generated by the publicly available source code in EDSR [23].

Training Setting. The model is implemented by using PyTorch [31]. Following the setting of [23], we pre-process all images in the DIV2K training dataset by subtracting the mean RGB and adopt a normal data augmentation during training, which includes random horizontal flips and vertical rotations. The mini-batch size is set to 16. We deploy the ADAM optimizer with $\beta_1 = 0.9$, $\beta_2 = 0.999$ and $\epsilon = 10^{-8}$ to the model, which is trained for 30 epochs. The learning rate is initialized by 10^{-4} and is halved at every 10 epochs.

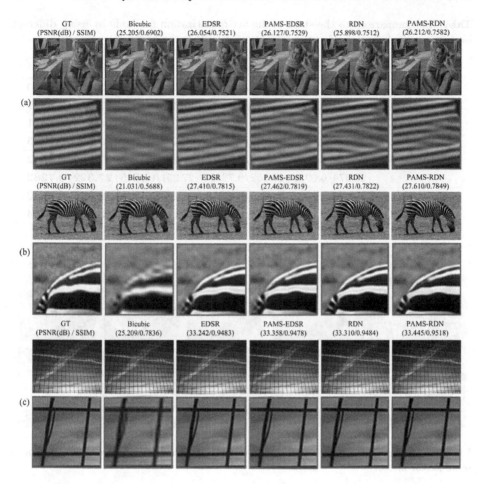

Fig. 3. Qualitative comparison between 8-bit and full-precision models with a scale factor of ×4. (a) and (b) are the results of "barbara" and "zebra" from Set14, respectively. (c) is the results of "img055" from Urban100. Note that the quantized models with PAMS produce extremely similar or even better SR images to their full-precision counterparts, while the former has a significant reduction of model size and computational complexity.

4.2 Quantitative and Qualitative Results

As shown in Table 1, the proposed PAMS with 8-bit weights and activations achieves competitive or even better results on different backbones. For instance, 8-bit PAMS-RDN outperforms the full-precision RDN by 0.178 dB PSNR and 0.074 dB PSNR on Urban100 with scale factors of ×2 and ×4, respectively. The 4-bit PAMS-EDSR only suffers 0.24 dB PSNR loss on BSD100 for a scale factor of ×4 compared to its full-precision model. Quantizing RDN leads to a significant improvement over EDSR in 8-bit, which indicates that dense blocks may produce more redundancy than residual blocks. We provide more qualitative evaluations

Table 2. Comparison to the state-of-the-art quantization methods by using different bits on a scale factor of ×4 super-resolution. EDSR is the backbone network.

Dataset	Bits	Dorefa-EDSR	TF Lite-EDSR	PACT-EDSR	PAMS-EDSR
Set5	8	30.194/0.8556	31.910/0.8906	31.520/0.8853	**32.124/0.8940**
	4	29.569/0.8369	31.380/0.8812	31.393/0.8834	**31.591/0.8851**
Set14	8	27.297/0.7492	28.416/0.7779	28.181/0.7712	**28.585/0.7811**
	4	26.817/0.7352	28.109/0.7690	28.104/0.7695	**28.199/0.7725**
BSD100	8	26.767/0.7079	27.470/0.7329	27.288/0.7261	**27.565/0.7352**
	4	26.474/0.6971	27.252/0.7239	27.251/0.7245	**27.322/0.7282**
Urban100	8	24.220/0.7128	25.739/0.7760	25.245/0.7570	**26.016/0.7843**
	4	23.753/0.6898	25.198/0.7551	25.148/0.7535	**25.321/0.7624**

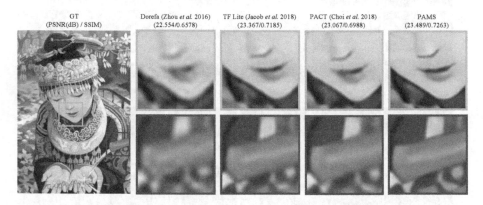

Fig. 4. Qualitative comparison of our method with other quantization methods on a scale factor of ×4.

on the 8-bit quantization in Fig. 3. The models with PAMS produce more visually natural images than the bicubic interpolation, and are extremely similar to their full-precision counterparts. Considering that residual-based models are widely used, the results also indicate the generality of the proposed method.

For a better comparison, we re-implement Dorefa [42], Tensorflow Lite [17] and PACT [3] on EDSR. We use the same initialization method and quantize both weights and activations in each residual block as PAMS-EDSR. For Dorefa, we do not quantize gradients for a fair comparison. Table 2 shows the results of 8-bit and 4-bit EDSR. Our method achieves better performance, compared to all baselines. For example, 8-bit PAMS-EDSR outperforms 8-bit Dorefa-EDSR by 1.288 dB PSNR and 1.796 dB PSNR on Set14 and Urban100, respectively. The reconstruction results are further shown in Fig. 4. Compared to other methods. The output (SR images) using PAMS are better-looking with sharp edges and rich details. In conclusion, PAMS with trainable truncated parameters rely on the backward which achieves much better generalization ability.

Table 3. Comparison of EDSR and RDN with different bits on BSD100. W and A represent the number of bits of weights and activations, respectively.

Model	W/A	StorageSize (r_{comp})	PSNR(dB)/SSIM
EDSR (32-bit)	32/32	1.518M (0%)	27.562/0.7355
PAMS-EDSR (8-bit)	8/8	0.631M (58.4%)	27.565/0.7352
PAMS-EDSR (4-bit)	4/4	0.484M (68.1%)	27.322/0.7282
RDN (32-bit)	32/32	22.27M (0%)	27.627/0.7379
PAMS-RDN (8-bit)	8/8	5.82M (73.9%)	27.644/0.7382
PAMS-RDN (4-bit)	4/4	3.08M (86.2%)	26.869/0.7097

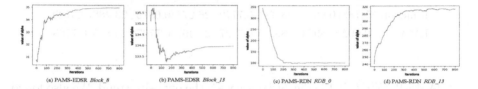

(a) PAMS-EDSR *Block_8* (b) PAMS-EDSR *Block_13* (c) PAMS-RDN *RDB_0* (d) PAMS-RDN *RDB_13*

Fig. 5. Convergence curves of α for 8-bit PAMS-EDSR and 8-bit PAMS-RDN.

4.3 Compression Ratio

The model size and compression ratio of EDSR and RDN are presented in Table 3. In particular, the full-precision network is represented by using single precision floating point. The model size of the full-precision network considerably decreases after quantization. Note that, we only quantize the weights and activations in the high-level feature extractor module, such that the compression ratios are calculated based on the total parameters of the network and the parameters in the high-level feature extractor. Although PAMS introduces a trainable parameter α, it still yields a 50%–90% compression ratio, since it directly depends on the backbone and the number of bits. It can be seen that 4-bit weights and activations cause more performance degradation than the 8-bit model. But lower-bit quantized networks can significantly reduce storage requirement.

4.4 Convergence of the α

To demonstrate the convergence of our method, we directly validate the convergence on α during training. The results are presented in Fig. 5. The first and second columns show the α of PAMS-EDSR on the layer of *Block_8* and *Block_13*, respectively. The third and fourth columns show the α of PAMS-RDN in *RDB_0* and *RDB_13*, respectively (*RDB* denotes the Residual Dense Block). It illustrates that α in different layers not only have different values but also have different evolving directions.

For instance, PAMS-EDSR *Block_8* (Fig. 5(a)) and PAMS-RDN *RDB_0* (Fig. 5(c)) act in the same direction, while PAMS-EDSR *Block_13* (Fig. 5(b))

Table 4. Comparison of the performance gap between the singe-precision EDSR, 8-bit PACT-EDSR w./wo. BN and 8-bit PAMS wo. BN. (PSNR(dB)/SSIM).

Model	With BN	Set5	Set14	BSD100	Urban100
PACT-EDSR	✓	0.531/0.0083	0.273/0.0068	0.166/0.0056	0.354/0.0125
PACT-EDSR	✗	0.575/0.0085	0.395/0.0101	0.274/0.0094	0.790/0.0278
PAMS-EDSR	✗	0.029/0.0002	0.009/−0.0002	0.003/−0.0003	−0.019/−0.0005

Table 5. Results about different initialization methods of α on EDSR with ×4 scale factor (PSNR(dB)/SSIM).

Init.	Set5	Set14	BSD100	Urban100
Random	31.782/0.8896	28.383/0.7779	26.273/0.6879	23.488/0.6780
EMA	32.002/0.8923	28.497/0.7797	28.497/0.7797	25.806/0.7788

and PAMS-RDN RDB_13 (Fig. 5(d)) are with the opposite trend. We also found that α can promote the convergence to a stable value for both EDSR and RDN, which indicates the effectiveness of our method.

4.5   Ablation Study

Effect of BN in SR Models. To investigate the effect of quantizing normalized features, we use PACT to quantize EDSR with BN and without BN. As shown in Table 4, the performance gap between the quantized EDSR without BN is larger than the quantized EDSR with BN. For example, The gap of 8-bit PACT-EDSR without BN is 0.790 dB PSNR on Urban100, which is larger than PACT-EDSR with BN (0.354 dB PSNR). It shows that the performance degradation of unnormalized features is more pronounced in lower-precision SR models, Moreover, PAMS-EDSR can save more important information for unnormalized weights and activations which largely decrease the performance gaps.

Effect of the Learnable α. We compare our learnable max scale (PAMS) with the fixed maximum (TF Lite) for quantizing activations. Quantitative and qualitative results are represented in Table 2 and Fig. 4, respectively. Compared to TF Lite-EDSR, PAMS-EDSR achieves a better score as it produces sharper images and more realistic textures. It indicates that our method can learn a more suitable quantization range which contains more information about the full-precision model and reduces the quantization error.

Effect of the Initialization of α. We evaluate our EMA initialization with random initialization on EDSR with a scale factor of ×4. For the random mode, we initialize α in the activation quantization layer with a random number ranges from 0 to 128, which ensures that α can be initialized to a larger value in different layers independently. As illustrated in Table 5, EMA initialization achieves

Table 6. Results of PAMS-EDSR w./wo. L_{SKT} on 8-bit and 4-bit settings (PSNR(dB)/SSIM).

Dataset	bits	without L_{SKT}	with L_{SKT}	metrics. ↑
Set5	8	32.127/0.8939	32.124/0.8940	−0.003/0.0001
	4	31.538/0.8842	31.591/0.8851	**0.053/0.0009**
Set14	8	28.541/0.7807	28.585/0.7811	**0.044/0.0004**
	4	28.177/0.7723	28.199/0.7725	0.022/0.0002
BSD100	8	27.550/0.7352	27.565/0.7352	0.015 /0.0000
	4	27.302/0.7280	27.322/0.7282	**0.020/0.0002**
Urban100	8	25.984/0.7835	26.016/0.7843	0.032/0.0008
	4	25.250/0.7607	25.321/0.7624	**0.071/0.0017**

better performance on all benchmark datasets. To explain, EMA achieves better statistical distribution by α that can further help improve SR performance.

Investigating SKT Loss. To investigate the effectiveness of SKT, we further compare the quantized model with and without SKT. As shown in Table 6, PAMS-EDSR which is optimized with the SKT outperforms the corresponding counterpart. Especially, our method obtains much better performance on lower bits. For instance, compared to the PAMS-EDSR without L_{SKT} on Urban100, 4-bit PAMS-EDSR with L_{SKT} gains 0.071 dB PSNR while 8-bit PAMS-EDSR with the same optimization gains only 0.032 dB PSNR. It also indicates that the feature maps from the full-precision model can help the low-precision model to better capture the spatial correlation from images.

5 Conclusion

In this paper, we propose a novel symmetric quantization scheme, termed PArameterized Max Scale (PAMS), to effectively quantize both weights and activations of the full-precision network for SR tasks. The proposed method adopts a truncated parameter α to adaptively adjust the upper bound of quantization range. This technique alleviates the negative effect of dynamic range caused by the absence of batch normalization layers and helps to reduce the quantization error. To further approximate the full-precision network, we employ structured knowledge transfer (SKT) to retrain the quantized network in a few epochs. We have comprehensively evaluated the performance of the proposed approach on EDSR and RDN over public benchmarks, which demonstrates the superior performance gains and significant reduction in model size and computational complexity.

Acknowledgements. This work is supported by the Nature Science Foundation of China (No. U1705262, No. 61772443, No. 61572410, No. 61802324 and No. 61702136), National Key R&D Program (No. 2017YFC0113000, and No. 2016Y FB1001503), Key R&D Program of Jiangxi Province (No. 20171ACH80022) and Natural Science Foundation of Guangdong Provice in China No. 2019B1515120049).

References

1. Bevilacqua, M., Roumy, A., Guillemot, C., Alberimorel, M.L.: Low-complexity single-image super-resolution based on nonnegative neighbor embedding. In: BMVC (2012)
2. Cai, Z., He, X., Sun, J., Vasconcelos, N.: Deep learning with low precision by half-wave Gaussian quantization. In: CVPR (2017)
3. Choi, J.: PACT: parameterized clipping activation for quantized neural networks. In: CVPR (2018)
4. Choi, Y., El-Khamy, M., Lee, J.: Learning low precision deep neural networks through regularization. arXiv preprint arXiv:1809.00095 (2018)
5. Courbariaux, M., Hubara, I., Soudry, D., El-Yaniv, R., Bengio, Y.: Binarized neural networks: Training deep neural networks with weights and activations constrained to +1 or −1. CoRR abs/1602.02830 (2016)
6. Denton, E.L., Zaremba, W., Bruna, J., LeCun, Y., Fergus, R.: Exploiting linear structure within convolutional networks for efficient evaluation. In: NeurIPS (2014)
7. Dong, C., Loy, C.C., He, K., Tang, X.: Learning a deep convolutional network for image super-resolution. In: Fleet, D., Pajdla, T., Schiele, B., Tuytelaars, T. (eds.) ECCV 2014. LNCS, vol. 8692, pp. 184–199. Springer, Cham (2014). https://doi.org/10.1007/978-3-319-10593-2_13
8. Faraone, J., Fraser, N., Blott, M., Leong, P.: SYQ: learning symmetric quantization for efficient deep neural networks. In: CVPR (2018)
9. Haris, M., Shakhnarovich, G., Ukita, N.: Deep back-projection networks for super-resolution. In: CVPR (2018)
10. He, K., Zhang, X., Ren, S., Sun, J.: Deep residual learning for image recognition. In: CVPR (2016)
11. He, Y., Zhang, X., Sun, J.: Channel pruning for accelerating very deep neural networks. In: ICCV (2017)
12. He, Y., Kang, G., Dong, X., Fu, Y., Yang, Y.: Soft filter pruning for accelerating deep convolutional neural networks. arXiv preprint arXiv:1808.06866 (2018)
13. He, Y., Liu, P., Wang, Z., Hu, Z., Yang, Y.: Filter pruning via geometric median for deep convolutional neural networks acceleration. In: Proceedings of the IEEE Conference on Computer Vision and Pattern Recognition, pp. 4340–4349 (2019)
14. Hinton, G., Vinyals, O., Dean, J.: Distilling the knowledge in a neural network. In: NeurIPS 2014 Workshops
15. Huang, J., Singh, A., Ahuja, N.: Single image super-resolution from transformed self-exemplars. In: CVPR (2015)
16. Ioffem, S., Szegedy, C.: Batch normalization: accelerating deep network training by reducing internal covariate shift. In: ICML (2015)
17. Jacob, B., et al.: Quantization and training of neural networks for efficient integer-arithmetic-only inference. In: CVPR (2018)
18. Kim, J., Lee, J.K., Lee, K.M.: Accurate image super-resolution using very deep convolutional networks. In: CVPR (2016)

19. Kim, J.W., Lee, J.K., Lee, K.M.: Deeply-recursive convolutional network for image super-resolution. In: CVPR (2016)
20. Krizhevsky, A., Sutskever, I., Hinton, G.E.: ImageNet classification with deep convolutional neural networks. In: NeurIPS (2012)
21. Ledig, C., et al.: Photo-realistic single image super-resolution using a generative adversarial network. In: CVPR (2017)
22. Li, Y., et al.: Exploiting kernel sparsity and entropy for interpretable CNN compression. In: Proceedings of the IEEE Conference on Computer Vision and Pattern Recognition, pp. 2800–2809 (2019)
23. Lim, B., Son, S., Kim, H., Nah, S., Lee, K.M.: Enhanced deep residual networks for single image super-resolution. In: CVPR (2017)
24. Lin, S., Ji, R., Chen, C., Tao, D., Luo, J.: Holistic CNN compression via low-rank decomposition with knowledge transfer. TPAMI **41**(12), 2889–2905 (2018)
25. Lin, S., Ji, R., Guo, X., Li, X.: Towards convolutional neural networks compression via global error reconstruction. In: IJCAI (2016)
26. Lin, S., et al.: Towards optimal structured CNN pruning via generative adversarial learning. In: CVPR (2019)
27. Lin, S., Ji, R., Li, Y., Wu, Y., Huang, F., Zhang, B.: Accelerating convolutional networks via global & dynamic filter pruning. In: IJCAI, pp. 2425–2432 (2018)
28. Ma, N., Zhang, X., Zheng, H.-T., Sun, J.: ShuffleNet V2: practical guidelines for efficient CNN architecture design. In: Ferrari, V., Hebert, M., Sminchisescu, C., Weiss, Y. (eds.) Computer Vision – ECCV 2018. LNCS, vol. 11218, pp. 122–138. Springer, Cham (2018). https://doi.org/10.1007/978-3-030-01264-9_8
29. Ma, Y., Xiong, H., Hu, Z., Ma, L.: Efficient super resolution using binarized neural network. In: CVPR (2018)
30. Martin, D., Fowlkes, C.C., Tal, D., Malik, J.: A database of human segmented natural images and its application to evaluating segmentation algorithms and measuring ecological statistics. In: ICCV (2001)
31. Paszke, A., et al.: Automatic differentiation in PyTorch. In: NeurIPS 2017 Workshops
32. Rastegari, M., Ordonez, V., Redmon, J., Farhadi, A.: XNOR-Net: ImageNet classification using binary convolutional neural networks. CoRR abs/1603.05279, arXiv preprint arXiv:1603.05279 (2016)
33. Romero, A., Ballas, N., Kahou, S.E., Chassang, A., Gatta, C., Bengio, Y.: FitNets: hints for thin deep nets. arXiv preprint arXiv:1412.6550 (2014)
34. Sandler, M., Howard, A., Zhu, M., Zhmoginov, A., Chen, L.: MobileNetV2: inverted residuals and linear bottlenecks. In: CVPR (2018)
35. Tai, Y., Yang, J., Liu, X.: Image super-resolution via deep recursive residual network. In: CVPR (2017)
36. Timofte, R., Agustsson, E., Van Gool, L., Yang, M., Zhang, L., et al.: NTIRE 2017 challenge on single image super-resolution: methods and results. In: CVPR 2017 Workshops
37. Wang, Z., Bovik, A.C., Sheikh, H.R., Simoncelli, E.P., et al.: Image quality assessment: from error visibility to structural similarity. TIP **13**(4), 600–612 (2004)
38. Zagoruyko, S., Komodakis, N.: Paying more attention to attention: improving the performance of convolutional neural networks via attention transfer. In: ICLR (2017)
39. Zhang, Y., Li, K., Li, K., Wang, L., Zhong, B., Fu, Y.: Image super-resolution using very deep residual channel attention networks. In: Ferrari, V., Hebert, M., Sminchisescu, C., Weiss, Y. (eds.) ECCV 2018. LNCS, vol. 11211, pp. 294–310. Springer, Cham (2018). https://doi.org/10.1007/978-3-030-01234-2_18

40. Zhang, Y., Tian, Y., Kong, Y., Zhong, B., Fu, Y.: Residual dense network for image super-resolution. In: CVPR (2018)
41. Zheng, X., Ji, R., Tang, L., Zhang, B., Liu, J., Tian, Q.: Multinomial distribution learning for effective neural architecture search. In: Proceedings of the IEEE International Conference on Computer Vision, pp. 1304–1313 (2019)
42. Zhou, S., Ni, Z., Zhou, X., Wen, H., Wu, Y., Zou, Y.: DoReFa-Net: training low bitwidth convolutional neural networks with low bitwidth gradients. CoRR abs/1606.06160 (2016)
43. Zhuang, B., Shen, C., Tan, M., Liu, L., Reid, I.: Towards effective low-bitwidth convolutional neural networks. In: CVPR (2018)
44. Zoph, B., Le, Q.V.: Neural architecture search with reinforcement learning. In: ICCV (2016)

SSN: Shape Signature Networks for Multi-class Object Detection from Point Clouds

Xinge Zhu[1]($\boxtimes$), Yuexin Ma[3], Tai Wang[1], Yan Xu[1], Jianping Shi[2], and Dahua Lin[1]

[1] The Chinese University of Hong Kong, Sha Tin, Hong Kong
{zx018,wt019,xy019,dhlin}@ie.cuhk.edu.hk
[2] SenseTime Research, Sha Tin, Hong Kong
shijianping@sensetime.com
[3] Hong Kong Baptist University, Kowloon Tong, Hong Kong
yuexinma@comp.hkbu.edu.hk

Abstract. Multi-class 3D object detection aims to localize and classify objects of multiple categories from point clouds. Due to the nature of point clouds, *i.e.* unstructured, sparse and noisy, some features benefitting multi-class discrimination are underexploited, such as shape information. In this paper, we propose a novel 3D shape signature to explore the shape information from point clouds. By incorporating operations of symmetry, convex hull and Chebyshev fitting, the proposed shape signature is not only compact and effective but also robust to the noise, which serves as a soft constraint to improve the feature capability of multi-class discrimination. Based on the proposed shape signature, we develop the shape signature networks (SSN) for 3D object detection, which consist of pyramid feature encoding part, shape-aware grouping heads and explicit shape encoding objective. Experiments show that the proposed method performs remarkably better than existing methods on two large-scale datasets. Furthermore, our shape signature can act as a plug-and-play component and ablation study shows its effectiveness and good scalability (Source code at SSN and also available at mmdetection3d soon.).

1 Introduction

The success of autonomous vehicles in urban scene heavily relies on the ability to handle the complex environments, where the accurate and robust perception is the foundation. To achieve this, autonomous vehicles are equipped with various sensors, including camera, radar and lidar, in which lidar is considered as the most critical one. The lidar sensor could provide the accurate depth information which is a significant advantage than image and thus lidar-based object detection [13,36,37,40] also achieves greatly better performance than image-based

---

Electronic supplementary material The online version of this chapter (https://doi.org/10.1007/978-3-030-58595-2_35) contains supplementary material, which is available to authorized users.

A. Vedaldi et al. (Eds.): ECCV 2020, LNCS 12370, pp. 581–597, 2020.
https://doi.org/10.1007/978-3-030-58595-2_35

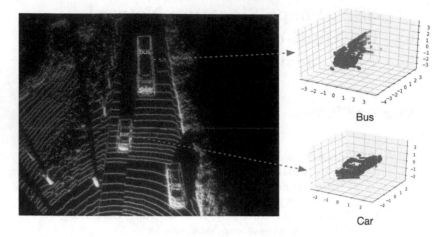

Fig. 1. We show an example of the point clouds of two objects belonging to different categories. It is noted that they have different shapes and scales.

methods [4, 14, 19, 32]. The mainstream 3D detection frameworks often focus on the single-category detection, such as car or pedestrian, while in the real world the autonomous vehicles need to detect multi-class objects simultaneously. In this way, how to distinguish heterogeneous categories plays an indispensable role in the success of multi-class 3D object detection.

A natural idea to handle this challenge is to utilize the difference on appearance or texture to distinguish different objects. Unfortunately, this approach is not feasible for point clouds, due to its point-based representation lacking of texture or appearance. An appealing alternative is to explore the shape information to guide the discriminative feature learning. Figure 1 shows an example that demonstrates the shape difference between two categories. From the teaser, we can find that the shape and scale vary with the categories. However, due to the sparsity and noise of the point cloud, how to build the effective and robust shape encoding remains a widely open question.

In this paper, we propose a novel shape signature for shape encoding, which possesses two appealing properties, *i.e.* **compact** (effective and short as the objective) and **robust** (robust against the sparsity and noise). Specifically, as the scan of lidar often covers parts of object (*e.g.* two or three faces), we first use the *symmetry* operation to complete the sparse points. Then we *project* the points to three views of the object, including bird view, side view and front view, for thoroughly modeling the shape information. Furthermore, the *convex hull* is introduced to represent the shape of three views, making it robust to the inner-sparsity. Based on the convex hull, we use an *angle-radius strategy* to form the function of convex hull, in which each separate angle corresponds to a radius from inner-center to contour. Finally, to make the shape encoding compacter and more robust, we apply the *Chebyshev fitting* to perform the approximation on the function of angle-radius strategy, and then the final shape encoding is formed by the coefficients of Chebyshev approximation. Note that the proposed shape signature aims to keep the shape information **consistent** (not same) within the same category and separate the shape distributions across different categories, which enables the shape signature serve as a soft constraint for learning discriminative and class-specific features.

Based on the proposed shape signature, we develop the shape signature networks for multi-class 3D object detection. The basic idea is to incorporate the shape information to better distinguish multiple categories. Specifically, SSN consists of four components, point-to-structure, pyramid feature encoding part, shape-aware grouping heads and shape signature objective. Here, shape-aware grouping heads bring the objects with similar shape together, so as to share weights based on the object size (*e.g.* bus and truck need a heavier head than car); while shape signature acts as an auxiliary objective, thus benefitting the feature capability of multi-category discrimination.

We tested the proposed framework on two large-scale datasets, nuScenes [3] and Lyft [1] dataset, which contain multi-class objects, including car, bus, pedestrian, motorcycle and *etc*. On these experiments, SSN yields considerable improvement over existing methods, about **10%** in NDS and **5%** in mAP-3D, respectively. We also make an in-depth investigation on the proposed shape signature, showing its good scalability with different backbone networks on different datasets. TSNE visualization of shape signature vector also verifies its role of soft constraint.

The contributions of this work mainly lie in four aspects: (1) We propose a novel shape signature to explicitly explore the 3D shape information from point clouds, which is compact but contains sufficient information, and robust against the noise and sparsity. (2) We develop the shape signature networks (SSN) for object detection from point clouds, which effectively perform the multi-class detection through shape-aware heads grouping and shape signature investigation. (3) We conduct extensive experiments to compare the proposed methods with others on various benchmarks, where it consistently yields notable performance gains. (4) The proposed 3D shape signature could act as a plug-and-play component and be independent to the backbone. Experiments on different backbone networks show its good scalability.

2   Related Work

Shape Representation. Numerous works processing on this research area have been made in recent decades. Johnson *et al.* [10] introduced a local shape based descriptors on 3D point clouds called spin images. Based on spin image, Golovinskiy *et al.* [8] incorporated the contextual features into shape descriptor. While these local descriptors construct encoding resorting to the local neighborhood, global descriptors [2,6,11,21] encode the geometric and structured information of the whole 3D point cloud. IS [9] introduced an implicit shape signature for instance segmentation by using the auto-encoder to learn a low-dimensional shape embedding space. Viewpoint Feature Histogram (VFH) [27] used the viewpoint direction component and surface shape component to bin the point cloud for shape encoding. However, most of them do not pursue the compact representation and the robustness to the sparsity, which is the major difference between our shape signature and theirs. The proposed shape signature performs the symmetry for completion, convex hull for inner sparsity and Chebyshev fitting for short vector. The cooperation of these operations leads to the compact and robust shape encoding.

3D Object Detection. Most 3D object detection methods can be divided into two groups: image-based methods and lidar-based methods. For the image-based methods, the key insight is to estimate the reliable depth information to replace lidar [14,19,32]. Monocular or stereo based depth estimation methods [35] have greatly pushed forward the-state-of-art in this field. [33] introduced a multi-level fusion method by concatenating the image and generated depth map. [22] incorporated depth features including disparity map and distance to the ground into the detection framework. However, although the image-based methods have made significant progress, the performance of this type of methods still lags far behind lidar-based methods.

Lidar-based methods are the mainstream of 3D detection task as lidar provides accurate 3D information. Most lidar-based methods process the unstructured point input in different representations. In [31,36,40], point cloud were converted into voxels and a SSD [20] based convolution network was used for detection. PointPillar [13] used the pillar to encode the point cloud with Point-Net [26]. [5,12,15,16,34,38] converted point cloud data into a BEV representation and then fed them into the structured convolution network. [24,28,39] introduced the two-stage detector into 3D detection, where coarse proposals were first generated and then refine stage was used to get the final predictions. [25] used the raw point cloud as input and extracted the frustum region reasoned from 2D object detection to localize 3D objects. However, most of them focus on the single-class detection, while neglecting to explore the multi-class discrimination. Compared to these works, our proposed method differs essentially in that it effectively explores the shape information, which plays a crucial role in distinguishing multi-class objects.

3   Methodology

3.1   Overview

Given a point cloud, our goal is to localize and classify the multi-class target objects. Unlike the single-class detectors, we desire to obtain a detector which could effectively distinguish the objects from multiple categories. To this end, we propose a multi-class 3D detection framework based on shape information exploration. The basic idea is to utilize the shape information via two key ingredients, *i.e.* shape signature objective and shape-aware grouping heads, to benefit the multi-class classification.

As shown in Fig. 3, our framework consists of four components, *i.e.* point-to-structure, pyramid feature encoding, shape-aware grouping heads and multi-task objectives, where point-to-structure and pyramid feature encoding are flexible (*i.e.* multiple options are available). The key components of SSN are the shape signature objective and the shape-aware grouping heads. Particularly, during the training the shape signature objective could guide the learning of discriminative features via back-propagation, benefitting the multi-class discrimination. After training, the shape signature objective is no longer needed. In what follows, we will present the details of shape signature and SSN.

3.2 Shape Signature

Given the ground truth points of object, we parameterize the shape information of the object with the proposed shape signature, then apply the obtained shape signature vector as a soft constraint to improve the feature capability of multi-class discrimination. As mentioned above, the desired shape signature should carry two properties: 1) compact and effective as a part of objective; 2) robust to the sparsity and noise. To achieve this, we introduce several operations to handle the issue of point clouds. As shown in Fig. 2, the shape signature contains two components, shape completion and shape embedding, where shape completion consists of Transform and Symmetry, and shape encoding involves Projection, Convex Hull, Angle-Radius and Chebyshev Fitting.

Shape Completion. Since the scan of lidar sensor only covers the partial observation, this property limits the shape investigation. We thus introduce the shape completion to tackle this issue, which consists of following steps.

Transform. The points of target object are located in the scene. We first transform the center of ground truth box to the origin point, and use the forwarding direction as the reference axis.

Symmetry. Lidar scans could only cover two or three faces of object, thus this partial observation would affect the investigation of shape. We introduce the centro-symmetry to complete the partial view. From Fig. 2(b), we can find that after symmetry, the points of target object become more dense and the observation gets complete.

Shape Embedding. We then introduce following operations to achieve the compact and effective shape embedding.

Projection. Given the completed points, we project the 3D points to three 2D views, *i.e.* bird view, front view and side view. Based on the projection, the 3D points are decoupled into several 2D planes, which could thoroughly describe the 3D shape and benefit the reduction of parameters.

Convex Hull. After projection, we get 2D points of different views. However, it can be found that the organization of 2D points is limited to effectively represent the shape and there still exists the inner-sparsity. Hence, the convex hull is introduced to characterize these 2D points and emphasize the contour of views,

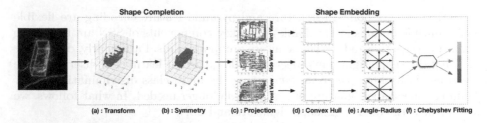

Fig. 2. We show the workflow of the proposed shape signature. Two major components, *i.e.* Shape Completion and Shape Embedding, are illustrated with two dashed rectangles. Specifically, step (a) is to transform the center of box to the origin point. (b) is the symmetry for completing the partial observation. (c) is to project the 3D points into three views. (d) is to extract the convex hull to enhance the robustness to sparsity. (e) is the Angle-Radius and step (f) is the Chebyshev fitting to get the final shape vector. (Best viewed in color). (Color figure online)

thus being robust to the inner-sparsity. Furthermore, the contour of 2D points also maintains the scale information, which is an important factor for multi-class discrimination (see Fig. 2(d)).

Angle-Radius. To describe the convex hull and highlight the contour shape and scale, we design an angle-radius parametric function $f(\theta)$. We use the center of ground truth box as the origin point σ and densely sample some angles θ. In this way, the function $f(\theta) = dist(\sigma \xrightarrow{\theta} \mathbb{C})$, where $\mathbb{C}$ is the convex hull and *dist* indicates the distance between origin point and intersection point (*i.e.* radius). In the implementation, we sample 360 angles and calculate the radius accordingly.

From Fig. 2(e) (see the aspect ratios), it is noted that the function $f(\theta)$ involving the angle and radius does well in maintaining the shape and scale of contour. However, the dense sampling also introduces the long vector (360 dimensions) which is not desired for the objective. Hence, to shorten the long vector representation and further enhance the robustness against the noise (*e.g.* some outliers in the 2D points), we introduce the Chebyshev Fitting to process the angle-radius function $f(\theta)$.

Chebyshev Fitting. Chebyshev Polynomials Fitting [23] provides an approximation that is close to the polynomial of best approximation to a function under the maximum norm. Our goal is to apply the Chebyshev polynomials to approximate the angle-radius function, and then use their coefficients to serve as the final shape vector.

There are two kinds of Chebyshev polynomials fitting [23], and we use the Chebyshev polynomials of first kind. The first kind $T_n(x)$ is defined by the recurrence relation:

$$T_0(x) \quad = 1, T_1(x) = x, \tag{1}$$
$$T_{n+1}(x) = 2xT_n(x) - T_{n-1}(x). \tag{2}$$

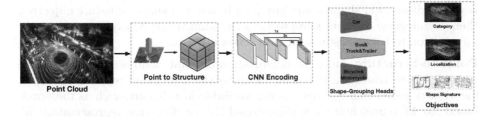

Fig. 3. The pipeline of our framework SSN. Four major components are illustrated with four dashed rectangles. The first one is the Point-to-Structure part, which converts the raw points into the structured representation, such as voxels [36,40] or pillars [13]. The second is the pyramid feature encoding part. The third one is the shape-aware grouping heads, which consist of multiple branches for objects with similar shape and scale. The final part is the objective, including classification, localization and shape signature regression. (Best viewed in color). (Color figure online)

Hence, the generic formulation of Chebyshev approximation can be written as a sum of $T_n(x)$.

$$f(x) \approx \sum_{n=0}^{N} \alpha_n T_n(x), \tag{3}$$

where α are the coefficients. These coefficients can be computed with the formulas:

$$\alpha_0 = \frac{1}{N+1} \sum_{n=0}^{N} f(x_n) T_0(x_n) \tag{4}$$

$$\alpha_j = \frac{2}{N+1} \sum_{n=0}^{N} f(x_n) T_j(x_n) \tag{5}$$

Since the number of coefficients in $f(x)$ is 2^{N-1}, we truncate α with top k terms. For each view, top k coefficients are the shape vector. The final shape signature is $[\underbrace{\alpha_1, \ldots, \alpha_k}_{\text{Birdview}}, \underbrace{\alpha_1, \ldots, \alpha_k}_{\text{Sideview}}, \underbrace{\alpha_1, \ldots, \alpha_k}_{\text{Frontview}}]$. In the implementation, we use $k = 3$ and the dimension of final shape signature vector is 9, which is suitable to serve as an objective for the network.

Some Extreme Cases. Due to the limitation of Lidar sensor and human annotators, some ground truth boxes contain less than or equal to 5 points, even 0 point for incorrect labeling. For these boxes, it is hard to model the shape information, and we thus use the average encoding of that category to represent their shape vectors.

3.3   SSN: Shape Signature Networks

Based on the proposed shape signature, we design the SSN to achieve the effective multi-class 3D detection. We first describe each component, especially two key ingredients, *i.e.* shape-aware grouping heads and shape signature objective, then we integrate different parts to form the unified target: exploring the shape information to better distinguish multi-class objects.

Point-to-Structure. Since the organization of point cloud is unstructured, the first step is to transform the point cloud to the structured representation. As mentioned above, multiple options are available in this part, such as the voxel-based [36,40] representation or pillar-based [13] or Bird-view representation [5]. After obtaining the structured representation, the subsequent 2D convolution or 3D convolution networks can be applied. In the implementation, we choose the pillar-based representation to structure the point clouds. Furthermore, we also test the shape signature with other structure representation (voxel-based) and the proposed shape signature shows good scalability.

Pyramid Feature Encoding. We follow the idea of FPN [17] to perform the feature encoding. A top-down convolutional network is first applied to extract the feature from multiple spatial resolutions. Then all features are fused together through upsampling and concatenation.

Shape-aware Grouping Heads. Since multi-class target objects vary significantly in scale and shape, we propose the shape-aware grouping heads to adapt this ideology for multi-class discrimination. The basic idea is to create multiple heads, in which objects with similar scale and shape share the weights. The reasons mainly lie in the following: 1) objects with different scale and shape should have different heads. For example, the head of bus needs to be heavier (or more deep) than the head of bike due to its large scale, because heavier head, larger receptive field. 2) shape grouping heads could perform the coarse shape exploration and also alleviate the effect from other groups.

As shown in Fig. 3, the design of shape-aware grouping heads follows the spirit of "larger object, heavier head". Based on the shape and scale of target objects, we group the bus, truck and trailer together with a heavier head, and gather bicycle and motorcycle with a lighter head, and treat the car with a medium head. Each head only covers the prediction of corresponding categories. By integrating above components, a SSD-based detection framework is formed.

3.4   Multi-task Objectives

In our framework, there are three objectives, *i.e.* multi-class classification, localization regression and shape vector regression. For the multi-class classification, we follow the previous work [36] to use the focal loss [18]

$$\mathcal{L}_{cls} = -\alpha_t(1 - p_t)^\gamma \log(p_t), \tag{6}$$

where p_t is the class probability of the default box and we use $\alpha = 0.25$ and $\gamma = 2$.

For the localization loss, we use the smooth L1 loss to minimize the distance between predictions and localization residuals [36].

$$\mathcal{L}_{loc} = \text{SmoothL1}(\triangle b), \tag{7}$$

where $\triangle b$ are the localization residuals, including the center (x, y, z), scale (w, h, l) and rotation (θ).

Unlike regressing the residuals in localization, the network is trained to directly regress the shape vector. For the shape regression, we also apply the smooth L1 loss.

$$\mathcal{L}_{shape} = \text{SmoothL1}(\mathbb{S}), \tag{8}$$

where $\mathbb{S}$ is the shape vector.

The total objective of three tasks is therefore:

$$\mathcal{L} = \beta_1 \mathcal{L}_{cls} + \beta_2 \mathcal{L}_{loc} + \beta_3 \mathcal{L}_{shape}, \tag{9}$$

where β are the constant factors of loss terms. As the shape loss is much larger than localization and classification loss, we set $\beta_1 = 1.0$, $\beta_2 = 1.0$ and $\beta_3 = 0.5$ to balance the value scale.

4   Experiments

4.1   Datasets

Two large-scale datasets, nuScenes dataset and Lyft dataset, are applied in experiments. The details of two datasets are shown in the following.

NuScenes Dataset [3]. It collects 1000 scenes of 20s duration with 32 beams lidar sensor. The number of total frames is 40,000, which is sampled 2 Hz, and total 3D boxes are about 1.4 million. 10 categories are annotated for 3D detection, including Car, Pedestrian, Bus, Barrier, and *etc.* (details in the experimental results). They also officially split the data into training and validation set, and the test results are evaluated at EvalAI[1]. Furthermore, a new metric is also introduced in nuScenes dataset, namely nuScenes detection score (NDS) [3], which quantifies the quality of detections in terms of average classification precision, box location, size, orientation, attributes, and velocity. The mean average precision (mAP) is based on the distance threshold (*i.e.* 0.5 m, 1.0 m, 2.0 m and 4.0 m). The whole range is about 100 m, and we mainly use the range of 0–50 in full 360°.

Lyft Dataset [1]. It contains one 40-beam roof lidar and two 40-beam bumper lidars, and in the experiments, we only use the data from roof lidar. The data format is similar to the nuScenes dataset. Total 9 categories are annotated for detection, including car, emergency_vehicle, motorcycle, bus, truck, and *etc.* Total 22,680 frames are used as the training data, and test set contains 27,468 frames while 30% of the test data is for validation in Kaggle competition[2]. The evaluation metric is the mean average precision, which is similar to the metric of COCO dataset but calculates the 3D IoU (with the threshold of 0.5, 0.55, 0.6, 0.65, ..., 0.95). Hence, we name it as **mAP-3D**, and it is worthy to note that mAP-3D is much strict than mAP in nuScenes and Kitti [7].

---

[1] https://evalai.cloudcv.org/web/challenges/challenge-page/356/overview.

[2] https://www.kaggle.com/c/3d-object-detection-for-autonomous-vehicles.

4.2   Implementation Details

In our implementation, we use the pillar based [13] method to convert the point cloud to the structured representation. For nuScenes dataset, the x, y, z range is ([−49.6, 49.6], [−49.6, 49.6], [−5, 3]) and the pillar size is [0.2, 0.2, 8]. The max number of pillars is 30,000 and max number of points per pillar is 20. For Lyft dataset, the range is ([−89.6, 89.6], [−89.6, 89.6], [−5, 3]) and the pillar size is [0.2, 0.2, 8] too. The max number of pillars is 60,000 and max number of points per pillar is 12.

For the anchors, we calculate the mean width, length and height of each class and use birdview 2D IoU (width and length) as the matching metric; when the matching between anchors and ground truth is larger than the positive threshold, these anchors are positive, otherwise if the matching is smaller than negative threshold, they are negative anchors. The matching threshold is different for different categories. During inference, the multi-class and rotational NMS is employed, where multi-class NMS indicates applying NMS for each class independently. For a **fair comparison**, no multi-scale training/testing, SyncBN and ensemble are applied. For nuScenes dataset, online ground truth sampling [36] is not used.

Network Details. For the point-to-structure, we follow the network in [13], where a simplified PointNet is used. It contains a linear layer, BatchNorm and ReLU layer to handle the features of pillars. For the CNN feature encoding, the FPN based module is introduced to extract the fused features. Three levels of features are first upsampled with the transposed 2D convolution, and then concatenated. For the shape-aware grouping heads, objects with similar shape and scale share the same head. For bus, truck and trailer, a heavier head is applied, where two downsample blocks process the features from FPN. Each downsample block consists of 3×3 2D convolution layer with stride = 2, followed by BatchNorm and ReLU. For the lighter head (such as bicycle, motorcycle), the block with stride = 1 is used. For the medium head, one downsample block is applied. Note that another block with stride = 1 is followed in each downsample block.

Optimization. We use the Adam optimizer with cycle learning decay. The maximum learning rate is 3e−3 and weight decay is 0.001. We train 60 epochs and 80 epochs for nuScenes dataset and Lyft dataset, respectively; the batch size is 2 for nuScenes and 1 for Lyft dataset.

4.3   Results

Results on nuScenes Dataset. In this experiment, we test our model on nuScenes dataset and report the performance on the test set from official evaluation server. The results are shown in Table 1. We give the detailed AP of each category and other metrics. It can be found that SSN achieves about 15% improvement in mAP and 10% in NDS compared to these lidar-based methods, even for some small objects, such as pedestrian and traffic cone. Even compared

Table 1. Results of multi-class 3D detection on nuScenes dataset. "Trail", "CV", "Ped", "MC", "Bicy", "TC", "Bar" indicates the trailer, construction vehicle, pedestrian, motorcycle, bicycle, traffic cone, and barrier respectively. Bold-face and underline numbers denote the best and second-best respectively for single model

Methods	Modality	Car	Truck	Bus	Trail	CV	Ped	MC	Bicy	TC	Bar	mAP	NDS
Mono [29]	RGB	47.8	22.0	18.8	17.6	7.4	37.0	29.0	**24.5**	48.7	51.1	30.4	38.4
Second [36]	Lidar	73.1	25.2	30.5	31.5	8.5	59.3	21.7	4.9	18.0	43.3	31.6	46.8
PP [13]	Lidar	68.4	23.0	28.2	23.4	4.1	59.7	27.4	1.1	30.8	38.9	30.5	45.3
Painting [30]	Lidar& RGB	<u>77.9</u>	<u>35.8</u>	<u>36.1</u>	<u>37.3</u>	**15.8**	**73.3**	<u>41.5</u>	<u>24.1</u>	**62.4**	**60.2**	**46.4**	**58.1**
SSN	Lidar	**80.7**	**37.5**	**39.9**	**43.9**	<u>14.6</u>	<u>72.3</u>	**43.7**	20.1	<u>54.2</u>	<u>56.3</u>	<u>46.3</u>	<u>56.9</u>
SSN + TTA	Lidar	82.4	41.8	46.1	48.1	17.5	75.6	49.0	24.6	60.1	61.2	51.0	61.7

with the Lidar&RGB fusion method [30], our lidar-based model also achieves comparable performance and performs better in the main categories of traffic scenarios, such as Car, Truck, Bus and Motorcycle, *etc.* Note that the results of PointPillar and Painting [30] are copied from the original papers and for Second, we re-implement it under our setting and hyper-parameters are followed with SSN. For bicycle, due to its sparsity and low height, it is difficult to specify in the point cloud while it can be accessed in the image, thus the result of Bicycle in image detection is better than the 3D detection. We further use the Test Time Augmentation (TTA) to boost results, where we flip the input in x-axis, y-axis and x-y-axis and fuse all four inputs to obtain the final results.

Results on Lyft Dataset. For Lyft dataset, there is no official split of training set and validation set. Hence, we report the results on Kaggle competition (30% test data is used for public validation but the host does not provide the ground truth. We submit the outputs of SSN and our baseline model to obtain the results). As Lyft dataset is a very new dataset, there is no official implementation. We re-implement PointPillar and Second to perform experiment on Lyft dataset, and optimization method and anchor matching strategy follow the SSN. Table 2 shows the results of SSN and other existing methods on the test set. SSN consistently achieves the better performance with about 5% improvement compared to existing methods. Due to the strict metric (mAP-3D under IoU 0.5 to 0.95), the result on Lyft dataset is lower than nuScenes. Note that we only report the results of single model with single-scale training. The result on the official websites is 18.1% which is applied with multi-scale training.

TSNE Visualization. We use the TSNE to visualize the distribution of shape signature in Fig. 4. Four categories in nuScenes, including Car, Truck, Motorcycle and Ped, are sampled to display for a clearly visual effect. We sample 50 instances for each category, where 25 of them are with distance <40 m and others are with distance >40 m. It can be observed that the discrepancy across different classes is clear, which indicates the capability of our shape signature to separate the shape distribution across different categories. Meanwhile, the distribution of shape signature within the same class differs with different distance (points with distance <40 m and points with distance >40 m cluster at different regions accordingly), which demonstrates the shape signature acts as a soft (not hard) constraint and keeps the shape distribution consistent (not same).

Table 2. Results on test set of Lyft dataset

Methods	Modality	mAP-3D
PointPillar [13]	Lidar	13.4
Second [36]	Lidar	13.0
SSN	Lidar	**17.9**
SSN + TTA	Lidar	20.1

Table 3. Experimental results of ablation studies on two key components on nuScenes dataset

Methods	mAP	NDS
PointPillar [13]	29.4	44.9
+ Shape-aware Grouping Heads	40.6	51.3
+ Shape Signature	45.3	57.0

4.4 Ablation Studies

In this section, we perform the thorough ablation experiments to investigate the effect of different components in our method, including shape-aware grouping heads and shape signature, the scalability of the proposed shape signature with various backbone networks, and comparison with other shape signature.

Effect of Different Components. In this experiment, we choose the PointPillar as the backbone, and perform the ablation study by adding the components step-by-step. Due to the limited submissions in the evaluation server, we report the results on the official validation set of nuScenes dataset. As shown in Table 3, it can be found that two key components, shape-aware grouping heads and shape signature, achieve the significant performance gain, with 6.4% and 5.7% improvements in NDS respectively, which demonstrates that the shape information does improve the multi-class detection.

Scalability of Shape Signature. To investigate the scalability of the proposed shape signature, we perform a thorough study, where the shape signature is combined with different backbone networks and tested on different datasets. The detailed results are shown in Table 4. For different backbone networks, we use PointPillar and Second, which utilize the 2D convolution and 3D convolution networks, respectively, and cover the mainstream in 3D object detection. It can be found that the shape signature could greatly improve the performance for different backbone networks on various datasets. Furthermore, it also achieves the consistent performance gain across different datasets, *i.e.* nuScenes, Lyft and Kitti [7] dataset. Note that the mAP-3D in Lyft is similar to COCO dataset, which is much difficult than mAP in nuScenes and Kitti. From these two perspectives, we can find that the proposed shape signature does possess good scalability and the exploration of shape information does improve the capability of detection networks in the discrimination of multiple categories.

Shape-Aware Grouping Heads *v.s.* One-to-One Heads. To verify the effectiveness of the shape-aware grouping heads, we compare the shape-aware

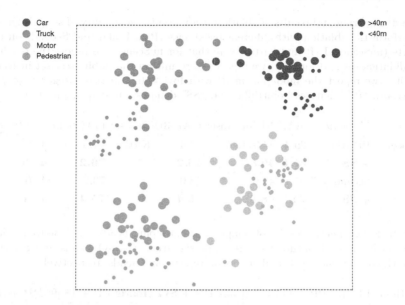

Fig. 4. We show the distribution of our shape signature via TSNE. (Best viewed in color). (Color figure online)

heads to the one-to-one heads, in which each head covers one category. The difference between two types of heads is the shape information investigation. From the results shown in Table 5, it can be found that the shape-aware grouping heads perform much better than one-to-one heads in both metric terms, which further demonstrates the shape information benefits the multi-class discrimination. Moreover, the shape grouping strategy is also more effective than the one-to-one strategy, which groups the objects with similar shape and scale to aid the exploration of shape information.

Comparison with other Shape Signature. The previous work [9] provides an implicit shape representation for instance segmentation. We adapt this approach into the point cloud segmentation and obtain the implicit shape signature with same dimension ("IS" is the notation). We compare the "IS" with our shape signature ("SS") in Table 5. It can be found that our shape signature outperforms the implicit shape signature with a large margin because "SS" better handles difficulties from point cloud by completion and robustness enhancement.

Dimension of Shape Signature. We use top 3 coefficients of Chebyshev approximation, because they principally and effectively cover the shape function. For example, for the bird-view shape vector of a car (we show full coefficients), $[1.93, -0.65, 0.083, 4.68e-03, 1.064e-05, \ldots]$, it can be found that top 3 coefficients contain the main knowledge and are appropriate as objective.

Table 4. Experimental results of ablation studies on the scalability of shape signature. We perform the ablation with different backbones (PointPollar and Second) on three datasets (nuScenes, Lyft and Kitti). Note that for nuScenes, we report the results on the validation set and for Lyft, we report the results on the public test set in Kaggle. For Kitti, we report the moderate mAP with IoU = 0.7 on two categories (car and pedestrian). "PP" denotes PointPillar and "SS" denotes our shape signature

Dataset	Methods	mAP	NDS	Dataset	mAP-3D	Dataset	mAP@car	mAP@ped
nuScenes	PP [13]	29.4	44.9	Lyft	13.4	Kitti	74.3	41.9
	+ SS	**36.6**	**49.8**		**16.2**		**76.2**	**43.5**
	Second [36]	31.1	46.9		13.0		73.7	42.6
	+ SS	**34.3**	**48.9**		**15.4**		**75.4**	**44.1**

Table 5. Experimental results of Shape-aware grouping heads *v.s.* One-to-one heads and Implicit shape signature *v.s.* our shape signature. O-to-O Heads and SG Heads denote the one-to-one heads and shape-aware grouping heads, respectively

Methods	PP [13]	PP + O-to-O Heads	**PP + SG Heads**	PP + IS [9]	**PP + SS**
mAP	29.4	32.0	**39.1**	31.4	**36.6**
NDS	44.9	46.2	**51.0**	46.7	**49.8**

5   Conclusion

In this paper, we design a novel shape signature which acts as a soft constraint, and thus aid the feature capability of multi-class discrimination. Two appealing properties are carried, *i.e.* compact and effective as the objective and robust against the sparsity and noise. Based on the proposed shape signature, we develop the shape signature networks for object detection from point clouds, which makes use of shape information to promote the multi-class detection, through shape-aware heads and shape signature objective. We conduct extensive experiments and ablation studies, which demonstrate our model achieves state-of-the-art and the proposed shape signature keeps good scalability on various backbones.

Acknowledgement. This work is partially supported by the SenseTime Collaborative Grant on Large-scale Multi-modality Analysis (CUHK Agreement No. TS1610626 & No. TS1712093), the General Research Fund (GRF) of Hong Kong (No. 14236516 & No. 14203518).

References

1. Lyft level 5 dataset. https://level5.lyft.com/dataset/
2. Belongie, S., Malik, J., Puzicha, J.: Shape context: a new descriptor for shape matching and object recognition. In: Advances in Neural Information Processing Systems, pp. 831–837 (2001)

3. Caesar, H., et al.: nuScenes: a multimodal dataset for autonomous driving. arXiv preprint arXiv:1903.11027 (2019)
4. Chen, X., Kundu, K., Zhang, Z., Ma, H., Fidler, S., Urtasun, R.: Monocular 3D object detection for autonomous driving. In: Proceedings of the IEEE Conference on Computer Vision and Pattern Recognition, pp. 2147–2156 (2016)
5. Chen, X., Ma, H., Wan, J., Li, B., Xia, T.: Multi-view 3D object detection network for autonomous driving. In: Proceedings of the IEEE Conference on Computer Vision and Pattern Recognition, pp. 1907–1915 (2017)
6. Frome, A., Huber, D., Kolluri, R., Bülow, T., Malik, J.: Recognizing objects in range data using regional point descriptors. In: Pajdla, T., Matas, J. (eds.) ECCV 2004. LNCS, vol. 3023, pp. 224–237. Springer, Heidelberg (2004). https://doi.org/10.1007/978-3-540-24672-5_18
7. Geiger, A., Lenz, P., Stiller, C., Urtasun, R.: Vision meets robotics: the KITTI dataset. Int. J. Rob. Res. **32**, 1231–1237 (2013)
8. Golovinskiy, A., Kim, V.G., Funkhouser, T.: Shape-based recognition of 3D point clouds in urban environments. In: 2009 IEEE 12th International Conference on Computer Vision, pp. 2154–2161. IEEE (2009)
9. Jetley, S., Sapienza, M., Golodetz, S., Torr, P.H.S.: Straight to shapes: real-time detection of encoded shapes. In: CVPR, pp. 4207–4216 (2016)
10. Johnson, A.E., Hebert, M.: Surface matching for object recognition in complex three-dimensional scenes. Image Vis. Comput. **16**(9–10), 635–651 (1998)
11. Kasaei, S.H., Tomé, A.M., Lopes, L.S., Oliveira, M.: Good: a global orthographic object descriptor for 3D object recognition and manipulation. Pattern Recogn. Lett. **83**, 312–320 (2016)
12. Ku, J., Mozifian, M., Lee, J., Harakeh, A., Waslander, S.L.: Joint 3D proposal generation and object detection from view aggregation. In: 2018 IEEE/RSJ International Conference on Intelligent Robots and Systems (IROS), pp. 1–8. IEEE (2018)
13. Lang, A.H., Vora, S., Caesar, H., Zhou, L., Yang, J., Beijbom, O.: PointPillars: fast encoders for object detection from point clouds. In: Proceedings of the IEEE Conference on Computer Vision and Pattern Recognition, pp. 12697–12705 (2019)
14. Li, P., Chen, X., Shen, S.: Stereo R-CNN based 3D object detection for autonomous driving. In: Proceedings of the IEEE Conference on Computer Vision and Pattern Recognition, pp. 7644–7652 (2019)
15. Liang, M., Yang, B., Chen, Y., Hu, R., Urtasun, R.: Multi-task multi-sensor fusion for 3D object detection. In: CVPR, pp. 7337–7345 (2019)
16. Liang, M., Yang, B., Wang, S., Urtasun, R.: Deep continuous fusion for multi-sensor 3D object detection. In: Ferrari, V., Hebert, M., Sminchisescu, C., Weiss, Y. (eds.) ECCV 2018. LNCS, vol. 11220, pp. 663–678. Springer, Cham (2018). https://doi.org/10.1007/978-3-030-01270-0_39
17. Lin, T.Y., Dollár, P., Girshick, R., He, K., Hariharan, B., Belongie, S.: Feature pyramid networks for object detection. In: Proceedings of the IEEE Conference on Computer Vision and Pattern Recognition, pp. 2117–2125 (2017)
18. Lin, T.Y., Goyal, P., Girshick, R., He, K., Dollár, P.: Focal loss for dense object detection. In: Proceedings of the IEEE International Conference on Computer Vision, pp. 2980–2988 (2017)
19. Liu, L., Lu, J., Xu, C., Tian, Q., Zhou, J.: Deep fitting degree scoring network for monocular 3D object detection. In: Proceedings of the IEEE Conference on Computer Vision and Pattern Recognition, pp. 1057–1066 (2019)

20. Liu, W., et al.: SSD: single shot multibox detector. In: Leibe, B., Matas, J., Sebe, N., Welling, M. (eds.) ECCV 2016. LNCS, vol. 9905, pp. 21–37. Springer, Cham (2016). https://doi.org/10.1007/978-3-319-46448-0_2

21. Marton, Z.C., Pangercic, D., Blodow, N., Beetz, M.: Combined 2D–3D categorization and classification for multimodal perception systems. Int. J. Rob. Res. **30**(11), 1378–1402 (2011)

22. Pham, C.C., Jeon, J.W.: Robust object proposals re-ranking for object detection in autonomous driving using convolutional neural networks. Sig. Process. Image Commun. **53**, 110–122 (2017)

23. Chebyshev polynomials. https://en.wikipedia.org/wiki/chebyshev_polynomials

24. Qi, C.R., Litany, O., He, K., Guibas, L.J.: Deep Hough voting for 3D object detection in point clouds. arXiv preprint arXiv:1904.09664 (2019)

25. Qi, C.R., Liu, W., Wu, C., Su, H., Guibas, L.J.: Frustum PointNets for 3D object detection from RGB-D data. In: Proceedings of the IEEE Conference on Computer Vision and Pattern Recognition, pp. 918–927 (2018)

26. Qi, C.R., Su, H., Mo, K., Guibas, L.J.: PointNet: deep learning on point sets for 3D classification and segmentation. In: Proceedings of the IEEE Conference on Computer Vision and Pattern Recognition, pp. 652–660 (2017)

27. Rusu, R.B., Bradski, G., Thibaux, R., Hsu, J.: Fast 3D recognition and pose using the viewpoint feature histogram. In: 2010 IEEE/RSJ International Conference on Intelligent Robots and Systems, pp. 2155–2162. IEEE (2010)

28. Shi, S., Wang, X., Li, H.: PointRCNN: 3D object proposal generation and detection from point cloud. In: Proceedings of the IEEE Conference on Computer Vision and Pattern Recognition, pp. 770–779 (2019)

29. Simonelli, A., Bulò, S.R.R., Porzi, L., López-Antequera, M., Kontschieder, P.: Disentangling monocular 3D object detection. arXiv preprint arXiv:1905.12365 (2019)

30. Vora, S., Lang, A.H., Helou, B., Beijbom, O.: PointPainting: sequential fusion for 3D object detection. arXiv abs/1911.10150 (2019)

31. Wang, T., Zhu, X., Lin, D.: Reconfigurable voxels: a new representation for lidar-based point clouds. arXiv preprint arXiv:2004.02724 (2020)

32. Wang, Y., Chao, W.L., Garg, D., Hariharan, B., Campbell, M., Weinberger, K.Q.: Pseudo-lidar from visual depth estimation: bridging the gap in 3D object detection for autonomous driving. In: Proceedings of the IEEE Conference on Computer Vision and Pattern Recognition, pp. 8445–8453 (2019)

33. Xu, B., Chen, Z.: Multi-level fusion based 3D object detection from monocular images. In: Proceedings of the IEEE Conference on Computer Vision and Pattern Recognition, pp. 2345–2353 (2018)

34. Xu, D., Anguelov, D., Jain, A.: PointFusion: deep sensor fusion for 3D bounding box estimation. In: CVPR, pp. 244–253 (2017)

35. Xu, Y., Zhu, X., Shi, J., Zhang, G., Bao, H., Li, H.: Depth completion from sparse lidar data with depth-normal constraints. In: Proceedings of the IEEE International Conference on Computer Vision, pp. 2811–2820 (2019)

36. Yan, Y., Mao, Y., Li, B.: Second: sparsely embedded convolutional detection. Sensors **18**(10), 3337 (2018)

37. Yang, B., Liang, M., Urtasun, R.: HDNET: exploiting HD maps for 3D object detection. In: Conference on Robot Learning, pp. 146–155 (2018)

38. Yang, B., Luo, W., Urtasun, R.: PIXOR: real-time 3D object detection from point clouds. In: Proceedings of the IEEE Conference on Computer Vision and Pattern Recognition, pp. 7652–7660 (2018)

39. Yang, Z., Sun, Y., Liu, S., Shen, X., Jia, J.: STD: sparse-to-dense 3D object detector for point cloud. arXiv preprint arXiv:1907.10471 (2019)
40. Zhou, Y., Tuzel, O.: VoxelNet: end-to-end learning for point cloud based 3D object detection. In: Proceedings of the IEEE Conference on Computer Vision and Pattern Recognition, pp. 4490–4499 (2018)

OID: Outlier Identifying and Discarding in Blind Image Deblurring

Liang Chen[1], Faming Fang[1(✉)], Jiawei Zhang[2], Jun Liu[3], and Guixu Zhang[1]

[1] Shanghai Key Laboratory of Multidimensional Information Processing, School of Computer Science and Technology, East China Normal University, Shanghai, China
liangchen527@gmail.com, fmfang@cs.ecnu.edu.cn
[2] SenseTime Research, Shenzhen, China
[3] Key Laboratory of Applied Statistics of MOE, School of Mathematics and Statistics, Northeast Normal University, Changchun, China

Abstract. Blind deblurring methods are sensitive to outliers, such as saturated pixels and non-Gaussian noise. Even a small amount of outliers can dramatically degrade the quality of the estimated blur kernel, because the outliers are not conforming to the linear formation of the blurring process. Prior arts develop sophisticated edge-selecting steps or noise filtering pre-processing steps to deal with outliers (i.e. indirect approaches). However, these indirect approaches may fail when massive outliers are presented, since informative details may be polluted by outliers or erased during the pre-processing steps. To address these problems, this paper develops a simple yet effective Outlier Identifying and Discarding (OID) method, which alleviates limitations in existing Maximum A Posteriori (MAP)-based deblurring models when significant outliers are presented. Unlike previous indirect outlier processing methods, OID tackles outliers directly by explicitly identifying and discarding them, when updating both the latent image and the blur kernel during the deblurring process, where the outliers are detected by using the sparse and entropy-based modules. OID is easy to implement and extendable for non-blind restoration. Extensive experiments demonstrate the superiority of OID against recent works both quantitatively and qualitatively.

Keywords: Blind deblurring · Outliers · Identifying and discarding

1 Introduction

Single image blind deblurring is a well-known and ill-posed problem. It has drawn a lot of attention due to large requirements in digital image processing. Image blurring can be seen as a low-pass filtering process, resulting in distortion as well as irreversible degradation of high-frequency information in images such as edges

Electronic supplementary material The online version of this chapter (https://doi.org/10.1007/978-3-030-58595-2_36) contains supplementary material, which is available to authorized users.

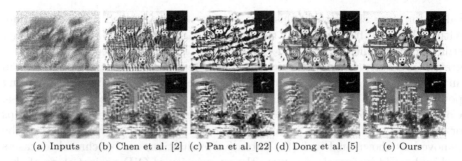

(a) Inputs   (b) Chen et al. [2] (c) Pan et al. [22] (d) Dong et al. [5]   (e) Ours

Fig. 1. Comparisons of deblurring results when outliers are presented. Inputs in the first and second rows contain impulsive noise and saturated pixels respectively. State-of-the-art method [2] is ineffective encounter outliers. Recent outlier handling methods [5,22] can ease the blur to some extent, but they are not as effective as our approach. (Note that the input with impulsive noise is preprocessed with Gaussian filter for (b) before the deblurring process as reported in their paper.)

and details [27]. Recent studies have shown promising results to deal with the deblurring problem [2,3,7,8,13,14,17,18,20,23–25,28–30], which mainly focus on two aspects including the MAP-based models that explore statistical priors for natural images, and other models that select informative edges. Despite the effectiveness of these methods, they are not able to recover blurred images that contain significant amounts of outliers, as presented in Fig. 1. The main reasons are that extracting edges in the presence of massive outliers is difficult, and outliers tend to violate the linear formation assumption of the blurring process [4,22] given by,

$$B = I \otimes K + \eta, \tag{1}$$

where B, I, K, and η represent the blurred image, latent sharp image, blur kernel, and additive Gaussian noise, respectively. We use $\otimes$ to denote the convolution operator.

There are two main types of outliers remain to be solved, including non-Gaussian noise (e.g. impulsive noise) [1] and saturated pixels. Recent state-of-the-art outlier-handling models [5,22] develop sophisticated edge-selecting skills or designed specific fidelity term to cope with outliers. These techniques showed their effectiveness in many cases. However, when the informative edges in the images are difficult to extract, the edge-selecting approach will eventually fail (Fig. 1 (c)). In the meantime, specially designed fidelity functions may not be appropriate to fit the additive noise, which would lead to artifacts in the estimated latent images when the noise is not properly handled [25]. This explains the ineffectiveness of the method from [5] in the given examples (Fig. 1 (d)).

Instead of seeking useful edges or designing indirect functions to deal with outliers, we solve the problem by resorting to a more effective framework, namely outlier identifying and discarding (OID). To completely and precisely avoid the side-effect brought by outliers, OID explicitly targets at polluted elements in the fidelity term during the deblurring process and assigns predefined minimum values for these elements. In this way, outliers are guaranteed not to contribute within the MAP-framework. At the same time, the additive Gaussian noise can still be properly fitted using an l_2 noise model. To be more specific, OID is integrated into both the updating steps of the latent image and the blur kernel in an iterative manner during the deblurring process. OID is capable of revealing potential outliers as well as neutralizing them during the deblurring process. Compared to prior arts, OID does not require complicated pre-processing steps or heuristic goodness-of-fit in function, and it enables massive outliers to be removed as shown in Fig. 1 (f). Extensive evaluations on benchmark datasets and real-world images demonstrate the superiority of OID against state-of-the-art outlier deblurring methods, especially when the blurred image contains significant outliers. The contributions of this work are three-fold.

- We propose outlier identifying and discarding (OID), a new strategy that iteratively identifies and discards outliers in both the processes of updating the latent image and the blur kernel. Further theoretical explanation validates the rationality of OID.
- OID employs continuous weights to indicate the probabilities of outliers, which can well target at polluted pixels without sacrificing a proper noise fitting model.
- OID can be effectively extended to the non-blind deblurring task. Extensive experiments demonstrate the superiority of OID against state-of-the-art methods in benchmark datasets and real-world blurry images.

2   Related Works

Outlier-handling Blind Deblurring Methods. Many works [4–6,10,22,26] have been proposed to deal with outliers in the deblurring task. We review some highly related blind deblurring approaches in this section.

Pan et al. [22] adopt a specially designed edge selecting strategy to find informative edges during image estimation step, and they also propose to cover more potentially polluted areas after outliers are detected. However, problems come with these strategies. When there exist massive outliers, selecting useful edges turns out to be quiet difficult, and this method tends to overcover unpolluted areas, leaving insufficient details to reveal the correct kernel. To avoid detecting outliers directly, Dong et al. [5] develop a sophisticated data fidelity term to suppress the side effect brought by outliers during deblurring steps. However, this scheme neglects the contribution of a decent noise fitting model, which will result in ringing artifacts in the estimated latent images [25]. In contrast to pioneer works, OID does not require any heuristic designs or strong regularization priors, and it shows comparable or even better performance confronting outliers.

Outlier Detection Skills. Locating outliers in the deblurring process is not as challenging as removing the side-effects brought by which. Intuitively, outliers are highly correlated with residuals between blurred images and convolution results of latent images and blur kernels: the higher the residuals values, the more likely the corresponding elements are outliers. In this work, we propose to indicate inliers and outliers in a more reliable approach. To be more specific, elements are not assigned with binary weights, but positive weights ranging from 0 to 1, which can equally be viewed as probabilities of entries classified as inliers. To predict the probabilities more faithfully, we employ a maximum entropy regularization term, which serves to minimize the prediction bias [9]. The final sigmoid alike weighting function complies with the intuitional assumption, and it is replaceable with more potential outlier detecting methods.

3   Our Approach

In the real-world, blurry images are frequently degraded by other gross corruptions besides small additive noise. The most common degradations are saturated pixels and non-Gaussian noise [4]. While outliers often have significant effects on the goodness-of-fit in (1) [5], both the kernel and latent image updating processes will be misled by the incorrect elements in the fidelity term, the overall framework is destined to fail ultimately. Meanwhile, the edge selecting work may also fail since the edges of outliers are often more remarkable than inliers.

To make the MAP-based framework workable, a reasonable approach is to explicitly exclude the polluted elements in the fidelity term. This idea can be fulfilled by assigning different weights to elements: those classified as outliers are assigned with weights equal to zero to make sure they do not contribute to the deblurring process and vise versa for inliers. To avoid the overall optimization framework to be stuck in bad local minima, we propose to use a continuous weighting strategy instead of binary weights. The proposed strategy can also be viewed as classifying with probabilities.

With regularization terms imposed on the latent variables, the solutions can be obtained by optimizing the following equation,

$$\{I, K, W\} = \arg min \sum_i W_i |B_i - (I \otimes K)_i|^2 + R_I(I) + R_K(K) + R_W(W), \quad (2)$$

where W denotes the weighting matrix, and i represents pixel location; $R_I(\cdot)$, $R_K(\cdot)$ and $R_W(\cdot)$ are regularization terms imposed on latent images, blur kernels and weighting masks respectively. Here we use the l_2 norm to fit the additive noise same as the strategies from [2, 19, 23, 29]. Compared to existing arts [5, 22], the formulation of OID is more simple, and it enables the additive noise to be well modeled by an l_2 function. Taking the straightforward formation of OID, questions may be raised about its effectiveness. We show in the next subsection that this model can easily fail unless it is solved with a proper updating strategy.

3.1   Observations

In this subsection, we show that locating outliers is not the only factor that leads to the success of OID. Different updating strategies will result in totally different results. A naive approach to solve (2) is

(a)   (b)   (c)   (d)   (e)   (f)   (g)

Fig. 2. Illustration of the proposed updating strategy and a naive approach mentioned in Sect. 3.1. (a) Blurry input. (b)-(c) Intermediate outputs using the naive approach and the proposed strategy. (d)-(e) Detected outliers (dark pixels) corresponding to (b) and (c). (f)-(g) Outputs of the last updating sequence using the naive approach and the proposed strategy. The naive approach detects incorrect outliers with multiple useful edges, which accordingly leads to the failure case for the final results.

by updating the three variables in a sequence (i.e. $\{I, K, W\}$) until converge. This approach can be equally viewed as adding an outlier detecting step within the conventional MAP framework. However, this naive strategy has an intrinsic defect. Take the step of updating I for example, every optimization step will lead to the change of the convolution output (i.e. $I \otimes K$). Consequently, the residual (i.e. $B - I \otimes K$) and the corresponding outlier information (i.e. W) change with the convolution output, because the outlier information is highly associated with the residual as mentioned in Sect. 2. Thus, the outdated outlier information is not applicable for the next updating step (i.e. updating K). As a result, the kernel misled by the incorrect outliers can be entirely different from the ground truth. Worse still, the overall deblurring process may fail with its output kernel in a delta function form. An example in Fig. 2 shows the limitation of this naive approach, where the detected outliers (Fig. 2 (d)) deviates from what is correct, and the overall process results in a delta kernel in the end (Fig. 2 (f)). More explanations of this strategy are presented in Sect. 4.1.

Based on the findings, we propose to remove the side-effects of outliers with a new updating approach. Especially, outliers should be re-identified in both steps of kernel and image updating processes, and they are calculated as soon as the latent variables (i.e. I and K) are updated. Moreover, because the re-identified outliers may reversely lead to the change of the latent variables, we propose to iteratively update the latent variables and outliers until convergence. The overall updating strategy can be viewed as iteratively updating two inner loops (i.e. $\{\{W, I\}, \{W, K\}\},$). Note that with this strategy, the outliers can be initialized to be any value. The example shown in Fig. 2 illustrates the effectiveness of our observations, in which outliers in the blurry image are detected substantially correct (Fig. 2 (e)), and the final outputs (Fig. 2 (g)) are barely affected by the outliers. Additionally, we give an extensive explanation to validate the rationality of the proposed updating strategy in Sect. 4.1.

3.2   Proposed Method

Regularization terms for the image and blur kernel are not influential factors to the problem. For a fair comparison, we impose the hyper-Laplacian prior [15] on latent image the same as [5,22], and we use a smooth constraint on the blur kernel for computational simplicity. As for the weighting mask (i.e. W), we assume that the corresponding classification probability should follow the maximum entropy rule [9], and outliers (i.e. elements with small weights) are sparse. The final OID model can be expressed as follows,

$$\min_{I,K,W} \sum_i W_i |B_i - (I \otimes K)_i|^2 + \lambda \|\nabla I\|_{0.8} + \theta \|K\|_2^2 + \alpha \|\overline{W}\|_1 + \beta \sum_i (W_i \log W_i + \overline{W}_i \log \overline{W}_i),$$

$$\text{s.t.} \quad W_i + \overline{W}_i = 1, \quad \left\{ W_i, \overline{W}_i \right\} \in [0,1],$$

(3)

where ∇ denotes gradient operator in horizontal and vertical dimensions (i.e., $\nabla = \{\nabla_h, \nabla_v\}$); λ, θ, α and β are weighting parameters.

OID is developed to take advantage of clean elements while discarding elements polluted by outliers during the deblurring process, and it can benefit both kernel and latent image updating processes. Questions may be raised about the selection of sparse constraint on outliers. Although l_0 norm is ideal for hosting outliers, we use the l_1 norm in our formulation with reasonable modification and the computation complexity consideration. Please refer to our supplementary material for more illustrations.

3.3   Optimization

As described in Sect. 3.1, the optimization process of OID is carried out by iteratively minimizing following models,

$$\begin{cases} \min_{I,W} \sum_i W_i |B_i - (I \otimes K)_i|^2 + R_I(I) + R_W(W), & (4) \\[2ex] \min_{K,W} \sum_i W_i |B_i - (I \otimes K)_i|^2 + R_K(K) + R_W(W). & (5) \end{cases}$$

We solve (4) by alternatively updating I and W while fixing the other, and K is fixed during the phase. We use the same updating strategy to solve (5). The overall process contains three individual optimization parts: the problems referring to update I, K and W, respectively. We give a description for the optimization details in the following subsections.

Optimizing the Problem Referring to I. While fixing K and W, the problem referring to I is given by,

$$\min_I \sum_i W_i |B_i - (I \otimes K)_i|^2 + \lambda |(\nabla I)_i|^{0.8}.$$

(6)

Fig. 3. Main steps of the proposed algorithm. The red and black dash lines denote outer and inner iteration during the process, respectively. Note the weight map in the kernel estimation step is different with which in the image updating step because it is calculated in the gradient domain. We only show the map in the horizontal dimension. (Color figure online)

We use the iteratively reweighted least squares (IRLS) method [15] to minimize (6) for simplicity. At each iteration, we have the following equation to solve,

$$\min_{I^t} \sum_i W_i |B_i - (I^t \otimes K)_i|^2 + \lambda P_i |(\nabla I^t)_i|^2, \tag{7}$$

where $P_i = \min\{|(\nabla I^{t-1})_i|^{-1.2}, \epsilon\}$, the constant ϵ here is used to prevent 0 in the denominator, and t represents the iteration index. When P_i are fixed, (7) becomes a quadratic function, and we can efficiently solve it with a conjugate gradient (CG) method. The whole process of IRLS can be seen as iteratively updating weights (P_i) and the latent image.

Optimizing the Problem Referring to K. To improve the accuracy of the estimated kernel [3,25,29], we replace the intensity domain in the data fidelity term by gradient domain. Removing the irrelevant terms, the blur kernel can be obtained by solving the following equation,

$$\min_K \sum_i W_i |(\nabla B - \nabla I \otimes K)_i|^2 + \theta \|K\|_2^2. \tag{8}$$

We use the CG method to solve the problem. We set its negative elements of K to be 0 and normalize it after obtaining the kernel.

Optimizing the Problem Referring to W. Picking out the terms relevant to W and $\overline{W}$ results in the following optimization problem,

$$\min_{W, \overline{W}} \sum_i W_i |B_i - (I \otimes K)_i|^2 + \alpha \|\overline{W}\|_1 + \beta \sum_i (W_i \log W_i + \overline{W}_i \log \overline{W}_i), \tag{9}$$

$$\text{s.t.} \quad W_i + \overline{W}_i = 1, \quad \{W_i, \overline{W}_i\} \in [0, 1].$$

Decomposing (9) into a set of independent sub-problems, and meeting the first constraint (i.e. replacing $\overline{W}_i$ with $1 - W_i$), we have,

$$\min_{W_i} W_i |B_i - (I \otimes K)_i|^2 + \alpha(1 - W_i) + \beta(W_i \log W_i + (1 - W_i) \log(1 - W_i)). \tag{10}$$

Algorithm 1: Blind image deblurring with massive outliers

Input: Image pyramid $\{B_1, B_2, ..., B_n\}$ obtained by down-sampling the input image B which is severely corrupted, and $B_1 = B$.

1: Estimate coarse kernels (from K_n to K_2) by iteratively updating latent image and blur kernel without weighting matrix updating steps.

2: Upsample K_2 as an initial kernel for the full resolution deblurring process.

while *iter = 1:maxiter* **do**

    repeat

        3: Updating latent image using (6)

        4: Updating weighting matrix using (9)

    until I_1 *converges*;

    repeat

        5: Updating blur kernel using (8)

        6: Updating weighting matrix using (9)

    until K_1 *converges*;

end

7: With blur kernel K, we use the proposed non-blind deblurring method to recover the final image I (i.e. conducting step 3 and 4 iteratively).

Output: Blur kernel K and sharp image I.

The closed-form solution of (10) can be given as,

$$W_i = \left(\exp \left(\frac{|B_i - (I \otimes K)_i|^2 - \alpha}{\beta} \right) + 1 \right)^{-1}. \tag{11}$$

Note that the solution in (11) meets the second constraint in (9) (i.e. $W_i \in [0,1]$), and it is in a standard sigmoid function form, which complies with our intuitive assumption that the probabilities of elements being outliers vary inversely with their corresponding residuals.

3.4 Overall Algorithm

Our algorithm is implemented in a coarse-to-fine framework [3]. Since the outliers are largely removed by the down-sampling procedure, handling outliers in coarse Image pyramids is unnecessary [31], and thus we deblur the coarse image pyramids without the outlier detecting step. Only for the original resolution pyramid B_1, we apply the OID method. After the blur kernel is obtained, the sharp image is recovered by our non-blind deblurring method. The overall deblurring steps are described in Algorithm 1. Our non-blind deblurring method is by iteratively updating the latent image and weighting matrix as described in steps 3 and 4. Main steps of the proposed algorithm are illustrated in Fig. 3.

4 Analysis

In this section, we give more explanations of the proposed updating strategy and further provide an analysis of the effectiveness of the outlier handling method. Please refer to our supplementary material for further analyses.

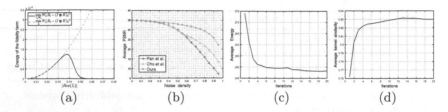

(a)   (b)   (c)   (d)

Fig. 4. (a) Energies of the data fidelity term correspond to different residua value (i.e. $Res(I) = B - I \otimes K$) from different updating strategies. (b) Evaluations of different outlier handling methods [4,22] on the dataset [16] with increasing impulsive noise (density from 0 to 0.95). (c) Average energy of (4). (d) Average kernel similarity [11]. (Color figure online)

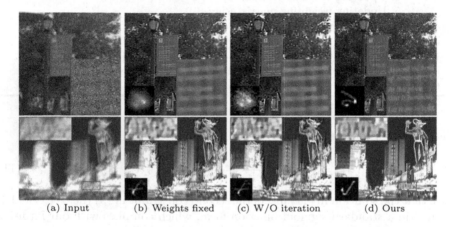

(a) Input   (b) Weights fixed   (c) W/O iteration   (d) Ours

Fig. 5. Deblurring results of different updating strategies. (b) is the naive approach that iterates $\{I, K, W\}$ in a sequence. (c) is the proposed approach without inner iteration which iterates $\{W, I, W, K\}$ in a sequence.

4.1   Explanation of the Updating Strategy

As described in Sect. 3.1, our proposed updating strategy is the main reason that leads to the success of this method. Besides the intuitive explanation provided in Sect. 3.1, we here analyze the intrinsic differences between different strategies.

Taking the process of solving (4) for an instance. For an individual element, we here only focus on the fidelity term because it is most affected by the outlier. Replacing W_i with its formation in (11), we have,

$$\min_{I_i, W_i} W_i |B_i - (I \otimes K)_i|^2 = \min_{I_i} \frac{|B_i - (I \otimes K)_i|^2}{\exp(\frac{|B_i - (I \otimes K)_i|^2 - \alpha}{\beta}) + 1}$$

$$= \min_{Res(I_i)} \frac{|Res(I_i)|^2}{\exp(\frac{|Res(I_i)|^2 - \alpha}{\beta}) + 1} \tag{12}$$

$$\text{s.t.}\quad Res(I_i) = B_i - (I \otimes K)_i.$$

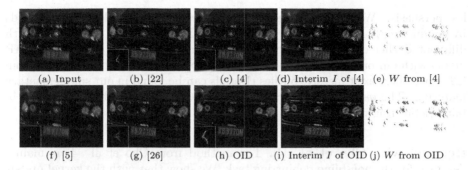

(a) Input   (b) [22]   (c) [4]   (d) Interim I of [4] (e) W from [4]

(f) [5]   (g) [26]   (h) OID   (i) Interim I of OID (j) W from OID

Fig. 6. Comparison of different outlier handling methods. Here the methods from [4] and [26] are originally designed for the non-blind deblurring task, and we extend them using the kernel updating strategy from OID.

As shown in Fig. 4 (a) (black line), when the value of the residual (i.e. $Res(\cdot)$) is large enough, which is the case for salient outliers, the corresponding energy stabilizes at a small value. In this case, the polluted element does not affect the deblurring process. In another view, minimizing the energy of (12) will lead to two different solutions, for the inlier, the minimizing procedure reduces the residual to 0, which serves to smooth the residual; for the potential outlier, the solution amplifies the residual towards $+\infty$, and this solution can promote the saliency of potential outliers. These properties guarantee that inliers contribute fully while outliers are discarded during the deblurring process.

In comparison, if the updating process is conducted while the weighting matrix is fixed, the outlier will cause a large offset for the fidelity term. As illustrated in Fig. 4 (red dot), this approach is incapable of identifying pixels according to their types (e.g. inlier or outlier) intrinsically. Besides the example given in Fig. 2, we here present another example with impulsive noise in Fig. 5. We note that both the results generated from the naive approach and the proposed method without inner iteration contain significant artifacts and residuals, while the proposed strategy generates results with clearer details and sharper edges. The results validate the effectiveness of the proposed strategy.

4.2 Differences from Other Outlier Handling Methods

Relation with Dong et al. [5]. The differences between OID and [5] are as follows. First, compared with OID, the method [5] uses a more sophisticated fidelity function to inexplicitly cope with outliers. Despite the complicated formation of this strategy, it may not be appropriate for the additive noise, which will affect both the latent image and kernel updating processes during deblurring [25]. In contrast, OID adopts a more reasonable l_2 norm to fit the additive Gaussian noise. A real-world example in Fig. 6 shows the limitation of this model, where their result contains significant artifacts and blur residue compared to ours.

Second, this method uses the outlier detection method from [22]. Compared to the proposed outlier identifying scheme, their function is more complex yet less persuasive. We verify the effectiveness of these two outlier detecting methods by conducting non-blind deblurring experiments on the given dataset [16] with different outlier detecting strategies. As shown in Fig. 4 (b), the same MAP model with our outlier detecting skill performs more efficiently than which from [22] when there exist massive outlies (Details can be found in our supplementary material). The results explain the reason why OID performs better than [5] in blind deblurring with outliers.

Relation with Cho et al. [4]. The method from Cho et al. [4] is mainly designed for the non-blind deblurring task. We show that with the kernel updating strategy presented in (4), this method can be easily extended for blind deblurring. As shown in Fig. 7 (b), the extension of [4] performs favorably against state-of-the-art outlier handling methods [5,22], which validates the effectiveness of the proposed kernel updating strategy.

The main difference between our approach and the extension of [4] is the selection of different outlier detecting methods. The approach [4] uses an Expectation-Maximization (EM) method to estimate outliers in the residual. Although effective on most occasions as it is, this method requires an evaluation of the outlier density before the deblurring process, which may encounter setbacks in some scenarios. Figure 6 shows one example where the extension of [4] does not perform well. The main reason is that the outliers are not correctly detected (Fig. 6 (c)). In contrast, the proposed method detects correct outliers and generates results with fine details. Moreover, the results in Fig. 4 (b) also show that the outlier detection method from [4] is less effective than which from OID when massive outliers exist. The results validate the superiority of OID over the extension of [4].

Relation with Other Outlier Handling Methods [22,26]. Although Pan et al. [22] propose to explicitly identify outliers during deblurring, they only conduct the detecting process once in an iteration sequence. Their method can be viewed as the naive approach we introduce in Sect. 3.1. To mitigate the problem, they use an ad-hoc edge-selecting step during latent image estimation step, and they also suggest to cover more potential outlier regions during kernel estimation. Example in Fig. 6 (b) shows the ineffectiveness of this approach compared to OID when salient edges are difficult to extract.

The non-blind deblurring method from Whyte et al. [26] extends the Richardson-Lucy algorithm by specific functions, and it is designed for saturated images. We note that this method can be straightforwardly extended to blind deblurring with the kernel updating strategy from OID, where the intermediate latent image estimation derives from their proposed non-blind deconvolution methods. As shown in Fig. 6 (g), although the extension can ease the blur to some extent, it is less effective than OID.

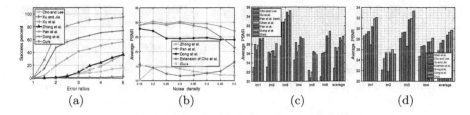

(a)   (b)   (c)   (d)

Fig. 7. Quantitative evaluations with state-of-the-art methods on synthetic datasets. (a) Dataset with impulsive noise. (b) Robustness to impulsive noise. (c) Dataset with saturated pixels [21]. (d) Dataset without outliers [12].

4.3   Convergence of the Proposed Algorithm

As our algorithm involves the non-convex optimization of l_p norm, a natural question is whether the model converges. We empirically evaluate the convergence property using the dataset from [16]. We compute the values of the objective function (4) and average kernel similarity [11] at the finest image scales. Results shown in Fig. 4 (b) and (c) demonstrate that our algorithm converges less than 20 iterations.

5   Experimental Results

The method is implemented in the MATLAB platform on a computer with an Intel Core i5 CPU and 12 GB RAM. We set λ and θ in (3) as 0.008 and 5, while α and β are fixed as 0.0018 and 0.0002 (analyses are given in supplementary material). We empirically set the maximum iteration number (i.e. *maxiter* in Algorithm 1) to be 4 as a trade-off between speed and accuracy).

We evaluate the performance of OID on both synthetic and real images and compare it with different state-of-the-art methods. We first evaluate OID on two synthetic image datasets with different types of outliers. Then, we quantitatively test OID on two benchmark datasets [12,16] which does not contain outliers. Finally, we examine OID on real captured images with significant outliers. To ensure fair comparisons, we use the same non-blind deblurring method introduced in Sect. 3.4 for all methods unless otherwise mentioned. For more examples, please refer to our supplementary material.

Blurry Images with Impulsive Noise: To better demonstrate the superiority of OID, we provide a challenging image set containing 15 sharp images with a size of 800×800 and 8 blur kernels from [16], and in which we add impulsive noise with a density of 10%. Thus, a total of 120 blurry and noisy images are used to evaluate the effectiveness of different methods. Several state-of-the-art algorithms [3,28,29] are compared including the outlier handling methods [5,22] and the method tailored to noise [31]. The cumulative ssd error ratio [16] is illustrated in Fig. 7 (a). OID takes lead with 69% of the results under error ration 2, while the figure for the second-best [5] is 47%.

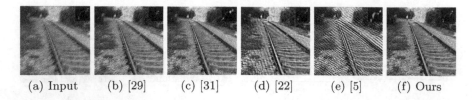

(a) Input   (b) [29]   (c) [31]   (d) [22]   (e) [5]   (f) Ours

Fig. 8. An example with impulsive noise.

(a)   (b)   (c)   (d)

Fig. 9. Deblurring results of images with increasing impulsive noises. (a) GT. (b)-(d) Images with noise densities of 0.1, 0.3, 0.5 and their corresponding results using OID.

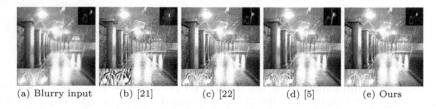

(a) Blurry input   (b) [21]   (c) [22]   (d) [5]   (e) Ours

Fig. 10. Comparison on a synthetic saturated regions. Results generate by our method contain finer details.

An example from this dataset is shown in Fig. 8. Due to the effect of outliers, the conventional deblurring method [29] fails to estimate the blur kernel (Fig. 8 (b)). The method from [31] uses different filters for noise, but it is less effective when massive noise is presented (Fig. 8 (c)). Moreover, because of the significant amount of outliers, state-of-the-art outlier handling methods [5,22] are also unable to estimate the correct blur kernels, which leads to lots of ringing artifacts in the final recovered latent images (Fig. 8 (d) and (e)). In contrast, the blur kernel estimated by OID is visually closer to the ground truth, and the restored sharp image contains clearer details and fewer ringing artifacts (Fig. 8 (f)).

We also evaluate the proposed method using images with different densities of noise. We add impulsive noise to the dataset from [16] with increasing noise density (from 15% to 50%). Note in this test, only three methods that can handle outliers [5,22,31] are compared. Figure 7 (b) shows that OID is more robust to outliers. Deblurring examples using OID are shown in Fig. 9.

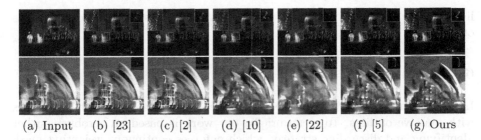

(a) Input   (b) [23]   (c) [2]   (d) [10]   (e) [22]   (f) [5]   (g) Ours

Fig. 11. Real examples contain significant outliers. The kernels estimated by our method are visually closer to the motion trajectories shown in the images (Parts eclosed in green boxes contain artifacts, best viewed on high-resolution displays with zoom-in).

Blurry Images with Saturated Pixels: To further evaluate the proposed method, we test OID on a provided saturated dataset [21], which contains 6 low-light images and 8 blur kernels from [16]. We add 1% random noise to the blurry images the same as the steps in [5,22]. We compare with 6 generic image deblurring methods [2,3,5,21,22,29]. Note that although the method from [10] can deal with images containing saturated pixels in many cases, we do not compare with it since most images from this dataset do not contain detectable light streaks. Average PSNR values are illustrated in Fig. 7 (c). OID achieves favorable results against the state-of-the-art methods.

We also use a challenging synthetic example to demonstrate the effectiveness of the proposed method intuitively. As shown in Fig. 10, the conventional method [21] fails to deal with the blurry image contains outliers, and state-of-the-art outlier handling methods [5,22] perform not well when given the vast scope of saturated regions. Both of these methods fail to generate blur kernels approximate to the ground truth. Consequently, the corresponding deblurring results contain lots of artifacts. In contrast, our method generates a high-quality blur kernel, and the final recovered image is more visually pleasing.

Images Without Outliers: OID can also be applied to images without outliers. We verify the effectiveness of OID by conducting experiments on the benchmark dataset [12]. Average PSNR values are taken as a comparison criterion for the dataset, and the final result is shown in Fig. 7 (d). Although OID is focused on the outlier deblurring area, it also achieves comparable results against several state-of-the-art methods. Evaluation result on another benchmark dataset [16] is given in our supplementary material.

Real-world Images: As shown in Fig. 11, state-of-the-art deblurring methods [2,23] fail to recover sharp images due to the outliers. Although the method from [10] can extract informative light streaks in these cases, some detrimental trajectories bring side-effects to the kernel estimation processes at the same time, resulting in artifacts in final recovered images. Moreover, the outlier-handling methods [5,22] are less effective than OID when there contain massive saturated regions. In contrast, the kernels estimated by OID are visually more similar to the light streaks appear in the blurry images, which demonstrates the effectiveness of OID.

6 Conclusion

In this paper, we introduce an effective framework for deblurring blurry images with massive outliers. To recap briefly, our work is based on a robust outlier identifying and discarding strategy, which enforces continuous weighting mask on elements to indicate their types. By integrating the weighting mask updating process into both the latent image and the blur kernel updating steps in an iterative manner, this strategy shows its effectiveness in identifying and penalizing outliers intrinsically. In contrast to recent art, our model does not require any heuristic edge selecting steps or sophisticated noise filtering preprocesses. Extensive evaluations on provided datasets and real images demonstrate the effectiveness of the proposed method against state-of-the-art methods.

Acknowledgement. This work has been sponsored in part by the NSFC (No. 61731009, 61871185 and 11701079), the "Chenguang Program" supported by Shanghai Education Development Foundation and Shanghai Municipal Education Commission (17CG25), the ˙Fundamental Research Funds for the Central Universities (No.2412020FZ023).

References

1. Bar, L., Kiryati, N., Sochen, N.: Image deblurring in the presence of impulsive noise. Int. J. Comput. Vis. **70**(3), 279–298 (2006)
2. Chen, L., Fang, F., Wang, T., Zhang, G.: Blind image deblurring with local maximum gradient prior. In: IEEE CVPR (2019)
3. Cho, S., Lee, S.: Fast motion deblurring. ACM Trans. Graph. **28**(5), 145 (2009)
4. Cho, S., Wang, J., Lee, S.: Handling outliers in non-blind image deconvolution. In: IEEE ICCV (2011)
5. Dong, J., Pan, J., Su, Z., Yang, M.H.: Blind image deblurring with outlier handling. In: IEEE ICCV (2017)
6. Dong, J., Pan, J., Sun, D., Su, Z., Yang, M.: Learning data terms for non-blind deblurring. In: ECCV (2018)
7. Fergus, R., Singh, B., Hertzmann, A., Roweis, S.T., Freeman, W.T.: Removing camera shake from a single photograph. ACM Trans. Graph. **25**(3), 787–794 (2006)
8. Gong, D., Tan, M., Zhang, Y., van den Hengel, A., Shi, Q.: Blind image deconvolution by automatic gradient activation. In: IEEE CVPR (2016)
9. Guo, X., Lin, Z.: ROUTE: robust outlier estimation for low rank matrix recovery. In: International Joint Conference on Artificial Intelligence (2017)
10. Hu, Z., Cho, S., Wang, J., Yang, M.H.: Deblurring low-light images with light streaks. In: IEEE CVPR (2014)
11. Hu, Z., Yang, M.H.: Good regions to deblur. In: Fitzgibbon, A., Lazebnik, S., Perona, P., Sato, Y., Schmid, C. (eds.) ECCV 2012. LNCS, vol. 7576, pp. 59–72. Springer, Heidelberg (2012). https://doi.org/10.1007/978-3-642-33715-4_5

12. Köhler, R., Hirsch, M., Mohler, B., Schölkopf, B., Harmeling, S.: Recording and playback of camera shake: benchmarking blind deconvolution with a real-world database. In: Fitzgibbon, A., Lazebnik, S., Perona, P., Sato, Y., Schmid, C. (eds.) ECCV 2012. LNCS, vol. 7578, pp. 27–40. Springer, Heidelberg (2012). https://doi.org/10.1007/978-3-642-33786-4_3

13. Krishnan, D., Tay, T., Fergus, R.: Blind deconvolution using a normalized sparsity measure. In: IEEE CVPR (2011)

14. Lai, W., Ding, J., Lin, Y., Chuang, Y.: Blur kernel estimation using normalized color-line priors. In: IEEE CVPR (2015)

15. Levin, A., Fergus, R., Durand, F., Freeman, W.T.: Image and depth from a conventional camera with a coded aperture. ACM Trans. Graph. 26(3), 70 (2007)

16. Levin, A., Weiss, Y., Durand, F., Freeman, W.T.: Understanding and evaluating blind deconvolution algorithms. In: IEEE CVPR (2009)

17. Levin, A., Weiss, Y., Durand, F., Freeman, W.T.: Efficient marginal likelihood optimization in blind deconvolution. In: IEEE CVPR (2011)

18. Li, L., Pan, J., Lai, W.S., Gao, C., Sang, N., Yang, M.H.: Learning a discriminative prior for blind image deblurring. In: IEEE CVPR (2018)

19. Liu, J., Yan, M., Zeng, T.: Surface-aware blind image deblurring. IEEE Trans. Pattern Anal. Mach. Intell. (2019)

20. Michaeli, T., Irani, M.: Blind deblurring using internal patch recurrence. In: Fleet, D., Pajdla, T., Schiele, B., Tuytelaars, T. (eds.) ECCV 2014. LNCS, vol. 8691, pp. 783–798. Springer, Cham (2014). https://doi.org/10.1007/978-3-319-10578-9_51

21. Pan, J., Hu, Z., Su, Z., Yang, M.H.: l_0-regularized intensity and gradient prior for deblurring text images and beyond. IEEE Trans. Pattern Anal. Mach. Intell. 39(2), 342–355 (2017)

22. Pan, J., Lin, Z., Su, Z., Yang, M.H.: Robust kernel estimation with outliers handling for image deblurring. In: IEEE CVPR (2016)

23. Pan, J., Sun, D., Pfister, H., Yang, M.H.: Blind image deblurring using dark channel prior. In: IEEE CVPR (2016)

24. Ren, W., Cao, X., Pan, J., Guo, X., Zuo, W., Yang, M.H.: Image deblurring via enhanced low-rank prior. IEEE Trans. Image Process. 25(7), 3426–3437 (2016)

25. Shan, Q., Jia, J., Agarwala, A.: High-quality motion deblurring from a single image. ACM Trans. Graph. 27(3), 73 (2008)

26. Whyte, O., Sivic, J., Zisserman, A.: Deblurring shaken and partially saturated images. Int. J. Comput. Vis. 110(2), 185–201 (2014)

27. Wipf, D.P., Zhang, H.: Revisiting bayesian blind deconvolution. J. Mach. Learn. Res. 15(1), 3595–3634 (2014)

28. Xu, L., Jia, J.: Two-phase kernel estimation for robust motion deblurring. In: Daniilidis, K., Maragos, P., Paragios, N. (eds.) ECCV 2010. LNCS, vol. 6311, pp. 157–170. Springer, Heidelberg (2010). https://doi.org/10.1007/978-3-642-15549-9_12

29. Xu, L., Zheng, S., Jia, J.: Unnatural l_0 sparse representation for natural image deblurring. In: IEEE CVPR (2013)

30. Yan, Y., Ren, W., Guo, Y., Wang, R., Cao, X.: Image deblurring via extreme channels prior. In: IEEE CVPR (2017)

31. Zhong, L., Cho, S., Metaxas, D., Paris, S., Wang, J.: Handling noise in single image deblurring using directional filters. In: IEEE CVPR (2013)

Few-Shot Single-View 3-D Object Reconstruction with Compositional Priors

Mateusz Michalkiewicz[1]([✉]), Sarah Parisot[2,5], Stavros Tsogkas[3,4],
Mahsa Baktashmotlagh[1], Anders Eriksson[1], and Eugene Belilovsky[2]

[1] University of Queensland, Saint Lucia, Australia
{m.michalkiewicz,m.baktashmotlagh,a.eriksson}@uq.net.au
[2] Mila, University of Montreal, Montreal, Canada
eugene.belilovsky@umontreal.ca
[3] University of Toronto, Toronto, Canada
tsogkas@cs.toronto.edu
[4] Samsung AI Research Center, Toronto, Canada
[5] Huawei Noah's Ark Lab., London, UK
sarah.parisot@huawei.com

Abstract. The impressive performance of deep convolutional neural networks in single-view 3D reconstruction suggests that these models perform non-trivial reasoning about the 3D structure of the output space. Recent work has challenged this belief, showing that complex encoder-decoder architectures perform similarly to nearest-neighbor baselines or simple linear decoder models that exploit large amounts of per-category data, in standard benchmarks. A more realistic setting, however, involves inferring 3D shapes for categories with few available training examples; this requires a model that can successfully *generalize* to novel object classes. In this work we experimentally demonstrate that naive baselines fail in this *few-shot* learning setting, where the network must learn informative shape priors for inference of new categories. We propose three ways to learn a class-specific global shape prior, directly from data. Using these techniques, our learned prior is able to capture multi-scale information about the 3D shape, and account for intra-class variability by virtue of an implicit compositional structure. Experiments on the popular ShapeNet dataset show that our method outperforms a zero-shot baseline by over 50% and the current state-of-the-art by over 10% in terms of relative performance, in the few-shot setting.

Keywords: 3D reconstruction · Few-shot learning · Compositionality

Stavros Tsogkas and Sarah Parisot contributed to this article in their personal capacity as an Adjunct Professor at the University of Toronto and Visiting Scholar at Mila, respectively. The views expressed (or the conclusions reached) are their own and do not necessarily represent the views of Samsung Research America, Inc. and Huawei Technologies Co., Ltd.

Electronic supplementary material The online version of this chapter (https://doi.org/10.1007/978-3-030-58595-2_37) contains supplementary material, which is available to authorized users.

© Springer Nature Switzerland AG 2020
A. Vedaldi et al. (Eds.): ECCV 2020, LNCS 12370, pp. 614–630, 2020.
https://doi.org/10.1007/978-3-030-58595-2_37

1   Introduction

Inferring the 3D geometry of an object, or a scene, from its 2D projection on the image plane is a classical computer vision problem with a plethora of applications, including object recognition, scene understanding, medical diagnosis, animation, and more. After decades of research this problem remains challenging as it is inherently ill-posed: there are many valid 3D objects shapes (or scenes) that correspond to the same 2D projection (Fig. 1).

Traditional multi-view geometry and shape-from-X methods try to resolve this ambiguity by using multiple images of the same object/scene from different viewpoints to find a mathematical solution to the inverse 2D-to-3D reconstruction mapping. Notable examples of such methods include [10,11,14,27,36].

In contrast to the challenges faced by all these methods, humans can solve this ill-posed problem relatively easily, even using *just a single image*. Through experience and interaction with objects, people accumulate prior knowledge about their 3D structure, and develop mental models of the world that allow them to accurately predict how a 2D scene could be "lifted" in 3D, or how an object would look from a different viewpoint.

The question then becomes: "how can we incorporate similar priors into our models?". Some early works rely on CAD models[13,24,33,37], while Xu et al. [40] use low-level priors and mid-level Gestalt principles such as curvature, symmetry, and parallelism, to regularize the 3D reconstruction of a 2D sketch. The downside of such methods is that they require an extremely specific specification of the model priors, which often limits their applicability.

Motivated by the success of deep convolutional networks (CNN) in multiple domains, the community has recently switched to an alternative paradigm, where more sophisticated priors are directly *learned from data*. The idea is straightforward: given a an appropriate set of paired 2D-3D data, one can train a model that takes as input a 2D image and outputs a 3D shape. Most of these works rely on an encoder-decoder architecture, where the encoder extracts a latent representation of the object depicted in the image, and the decoder maps that representation into a 3D shape [3,16,26]. Many works have studied ways to make the 3D decoder more efficient and improve shape representation. The high quality outputs obtained suggest that, indeed, these models learn to perform non-trivial reasoning about 3D object structure.

Surprisingly, recent works [17,31] have shown that this is not the case. Tatarchenko et al. [31] argue that, because of the way current benchmarks are constructed, even the most sophisticated learning methods end up finding shortcuts, and rely primarily on recognition to solve single-view 3D reconstruction. Their experiments show that modern CNNs for 3D reconstruction are outperformed by simple nearest neighbor (NN) or classification baselines, both quantitatively, and qualitatively. Similarly, [17] showed that simple linear decoder models, learned by PCA, are sufficient to achieve competitive performance. There is one caveat though: to achieve good performance with these baselines, having a large dataset is crucial. More importantly, true 3D shape understanding implies good *generalization* to new object classes. This is trivial to humans –we reason about the

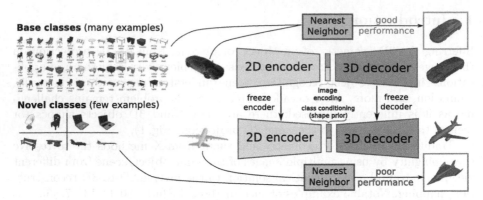

Fig. 1. We tackle the problem of single-view 3D reconstruction in the few-shot learning setup. [31] showed that naive baselines such as nearest neighbor, can outperform complicated models when data is abundant. However, such baselines cannot generalize to new classes for which only few training examples are available. We propose to use a deep encoder-decoder architecture whose output is conditioned on *learned* category-specific shape embeddings; our shape priors capture intra-class variability more effectively than previous works, significantly improving generalization.

3D structure of unknown objects, drawing on our inductive bias from *similar* objects we have seen– but still remains an open computer vision problem.

Based on this observation, we argue that single-view 3D reconstruction is of particular interest in the few-shot learning setting. Our hypothesis is that learning to recover 3D shapes using few examples, while promoting generalization to novel classes, provides a good setup for the development and evaluation of models that go beyond simple categorization and actually learn about shape.

To the best of our knowledge, the first work of that kind is by Wallace and Hariharan [32]. Instead of directly learning a mapping from 2D images to 3D shapes, they train a model that uses features extracted from 2D images to refine an input *shape prior* into a final 3D output. Their framework allows one to easily adapt the shape prior and use it when inferring new classes. However, their approach has several restrictions. First, the shape prior for an object class is computed either by i) averaging the available examples for that class or ii) randomly selecting one of them. Both of these operations collapse intra-class variability, failing to fully exploit the already limited available training data. Second, the method does not explicitly force inter-class concepts to be learned.

In this work, we first demonstrate empirically that naive baselines that are quite effective for general single-view object reconstruction [31] come up short when generalizing to novel classes in a few-shot learning setup [32], highlighting the importance of this setup for the design and evaluation of methods with generalization capability. Furthermore, we address the shortcomings of [32] by introducing three strategies for constructing the shape prior, focusing on modelling intra-class variability, compositionality and multi-scale conditioning. More specifically, we first learn a shape prior that captures intra-class variability by solving an optimization problem involving all shapes available for the new class. We then introduce a compositional bias in the shape prior that allows learning concepts that can be shared across different classes or transferred to new ones. Finally, we make use of conditional batch normalisation [22] to impose class conditioning explicitly at multiple scales of the decoding process.

In summary, we make the following contributions:

- We investigate the few-shot learning setting for 3D shape reconstruction and demonstrate that this setup constitutes an ideal testbed for the development of methods that reason about shapes.
- We introduce three strategies for shape prior modelling, including a compositional approach that successfully exploits similarities across classes.
- We conduct experiments demonstrating that we outperform the state of the art by a significant margin, while generalizing to new classes more accurately.

2   Related Work

2.1   Single-view 3D Reconstruction

Single- and multi-view 3D reconstruction have recently focused on improving learning efficiency and generation quality by finding better alternatives to the typically used 3D CNN decoder and voxelized shape representation [3,8,38,41, 42]. Such alternatives include point clouds [5], meshes [34], and representations based on the signed distance transform [2,18,21]. Although each one of these representations has its pros and cons, [17,31] showed that they do not beat naive baselines such as nearest neighbor (NN) or linear decoder.

2.2   Few-shot Learning

Few-shot learning has become a highly popular research topic in computer vision and machine learning [7,25]. Most works focus on the classification task, with few investigating more complex problems such as segmentation [29] or object detection [35,39]. Our work considers the few-shot setting in the practical 3-d shape reconstruction which has only been considered in [32]. Existing methods can be divided into two categories: meta-learning/meta-gradient based approaches [6], and metric-learning/prototype based approaches [23,30]. The former aims to teach models to adapt quickly, in a few gradient updates, to new unseen classes, while the latter learns a distance metric such that the distance of a query image to the few annotated examples of the same class is minimal.

3   Methods

Let $\mathcal{D}_b = \{(I_i^b, S_i^b)\}$ be a set of image-shape pairs, belonging to one of N_b base object classes. We assume that $|\mathcal{D}_b|$ is *large*, i.e., $\mathcal{D}_b$ contains enough training examples for our purposes. We also consider a *much smaller* set of *novel* classes, $\mathcal{D}_n^K$. Each class in $\mathcal{D}_n^K$ comprises only a small set of K image-shape pairs $\{(I_1^n, S_1^n), \ldots, (I_K^n, S_K^n)\}$, and a large set of test or query images.

Our objective is to use the abundant data in $\mathcal{D}_b$ to train a model that takes a 2D input image I, containing a single object, and outputs its 3D reconstruction, $\bar{S}$. The model should also be able to leverage the limited data in $\mathcal{D}_n^K$ to successfully generalize to novel categories. Similar to previous works employing an encoder-decoder architecture, we choose voxels as our 3D shape representation (facilitating comparison to [32]) and propose *three* strategies to achieve this.

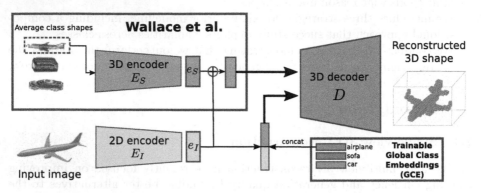

Fig. 2. Comparison of [32] to GCE. The former collapses variability of new classes by averaging. GCE is able to obtain a global shape representation for each class. Note that we combine e_I and e_S by concatenation, instead of element-wise sum.

3.1 Shape Encoding and Global Class Embedding

Consider an encoder-decoder framework involving

- an encoder E_I that takes a 2D image, I, and outputs its embedding, e_I;
- a category-specific shape embedding, e_S;
- a decoder D that takes the image and shape embeddings and outputs the reconstructed 3D shape in the form of a voxelized 3D grid, $\bar{S}$:

$$\bar{S} = D\left(e_I, e_S\right) = D\left(E_I(I), e_S\right). \tag{1}$$

This model can be trained using a binary cross-entropy loss between the predicted occupancy confidence p_i at voxel i, and the respective label $y_i \in \{0, 1\}$ from a ground truth shape S with N_v voxels:

$$\mathcal{L}(S, \bar{S}) = -\frac{1}{N_v} \sum_i^{N_v} y_i \log(p_i) + (1 - y_i) \log(1 - p_i). \tag{2}$$

In the rest of the text, we drop S for notational simplicity.

Figure 2 (top) illustrates the pipeline of [32]. e_S^i is computed with a shape encoder E_S that takes a category-specific shape prior, S_i^p, as input; i.e., $e_S = E_S(S_i^p)$. For base class training, E_I, E_S, and D are learned by minimizing (2). For inference on new classes, the 3D shape is recovered simply by feeding the image and class specific prior (e_S) to the trained network. The shape prior S_i^p is defined either as a randomly selected shape from the training set $\mathcal{D}_n^K$ associated with class i, or the average, in voxel space, of all training shapes of class i.

Both choices have severe limitations: they cannot account for intra-class variability and are, therefore, intrinsically sub-optimal when more than one training examples are available. To address this limitation, we propose to *learn* a global class embedding (GCE), e_S^i, that conditions the network for object class-i, but is dependent non-linearly on all available shapes. We expect this conditioning vector that is a derived from all shapes to capture nuances (like intra-class variability) more accurately than simple shape averaging.

Our framework is illustrated in Fig. 2 (bottom). We first train the model on base classes, jointly optimizing the parameters of the encoder E_I, the decoder D, and the base class embeddings e_S^i, by minimizing the objective in Eq. (2). For novel classes with a small training set $\{(I_i^n, S_i^n)\}_{i=1}^K$, all model parameters of E_I and D are fixed, and class specific embeddings e_S^i are obtained by solving

$$\hat{e}_S^i = \arg\min_{e_S^i} \sum_{j=1}^K \mathcal{L}(D(E_I(I_j), e_S^i)). \tag{3}$$

Our approach enjoys the following practical advantages: First, the optimization problem in Eq. (3) can be solved in just a few iterations since it only involves a small set of parameters (e_S^i) and a small number of novel category samples. Second, the model can continually learn implicit shape priors for novel classes, *without compromising performance on the base classes*, by construction, since the weights of E_I and D are frozen. Finally, we note that we combine e_I and e_S by concatenation, instead of the element-wise sum used in [32].

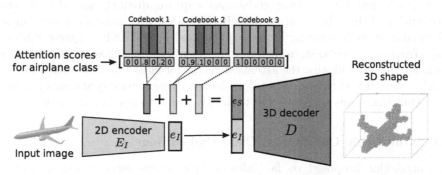

Fig. 3. Compositional GCE constructs a code by a composition of codes from different codebooks, applying a different attention to each codebook based on the class.

3.2   Compositional Global Class Embeddings

GCE allows us to exploit all available training shapes to learn a representative shape prior for a specific object class. However, the learned global embeddings do not explicitly exploit similarities across different classes, which may result in sub-optimal, and potentially redundant representations. As a result, exploring inductive biases for sharing representations across classes has the potential to increase robustness in the lowest data regimes. To this end, we introduce an extension of the GCE model, which we call Compositional Global Class Embeddings (CGCE), aiming to learn compositional representations between classes. This model is illustrated in Fig. 3.

Our objective is to explicitly encourage the model to discover "concepts", representing geometric or semantic parts, that are shared across different object categories. Taking inspiration from work on compressing word embeddings [28], we propose to decompose our class representation into a linear combination of learned vectors that are shared across classes. More specifically, we learn a set of M codebooks (or embedding tables), with each codebook $\mathbf{C}_j$ containing m individual embedding vectors (*codes*) $\mathbf{C}_j = \{\mathbf{c}_{j,1}, \ldots, \mathbf{c}_{j,m}\}$, where $\mathbf{c}_{j,m} \in \mathbb{R}^D$. Intuitively, each codebook can be interpreted as the representation of an abstract concept which can be shared across multiple classes.

For each class i, we learn an attention vector $\boldsymbol{\alpha}_i$ that selects the most relevant code(s) from each codebook. A weighted sum of all codes yields the final embedding: $e_S^i = \sum_{k=1}^{M} \sum_{j=1}^{m} a_i^{k,j} c_{k,j}$, where $a_i^{j,k}$ is the scalar attention on code j at codebook k, while $c_{j,k}$ corresponds to the jth code of codebook k. During base class training we learn both $\boldsymbol{\alpha}_i$ and $c_{j,k}$. We highlight that codebooks are shared across classes and therefore need only be trained on base classes. As a result, $\boldsymbol{\alpha}_i$ is the only class-specific variable we need to infer for novel classes:

$$\hat{\boldsymbol{\alpha}}_i = \arg\min_{\boldsymbol{\alpha}_i} \sum_{j=1}^{N} \mathcal{L}(D(E_I(I_j), e_S^i)).$$

A desirable property is that codebooks capture distinct and diverse class attributes and that they contain meaningful codes, with minimal redundancies. We encourage such behavior by having the model select only a sparse subset of codes from each codebook, using a form of attention that relies on the sparsemax operator [15]. Specifically, the attention vector for class i at codebook j is given by $\boldsymbol{a}_i^j = \text{SPARSEMAX}(\boldsymbol{w}_i^j)$, where $\boldsymbol{w}_i^j$ are learned parameters; sparsemax produces an output that sums to 1, but will typically attend to just a few outputs.

3.3   Multi-scale Conditional Class Embeddings

The strategies proposed so far influence the shape reconstruction stage at the input level by combining the 2D image embedding with a learned shape prior. Another approach we propose to investigate is multi-scale conditioning throughout the decoding process. An elegant way to do this is by applying the conditional batch normalization technique [22] to the 3D decoder model.

Conditional batch normalization replaces the affine parameters in all batch-normalization layers with layer-specific learned embeddings. Since 3D decoders have an inherently multi-scale structure with layers producing features at progressively higher resolutions, each layer's batch-norm parameters can be seen as conditioning/constraining the reconstruction process at different scales. Similarly to GCE, class-specific conditional batch normalization parameters are learned by fine-tuning the model on novel classes, keeping the encoder and decoder frozen. We refer to this approach as Multi-scale Conditional Class Embeddings (MCCE).

3.4 Nearest Neighbor Oracle, Zero-Shot and All-Shot Baselines

We introduce three simple baselines we use in our experiments. First, we consider an *oracle nearest neighbor (ONN)* [31] baseline. Given a query 3D shape, ONN exhaustively searches a shape database for the most similar entry with respect to a given metric (Intersection over Union in this case). Although this method cannot be applied in practice, it provides an upper bound on how well a retrieval method can perform on the task.

We also consider a zero-shot (ZS), and all-shot (AS) baseline. For the *ZS baseline*, we train the encoder-decoder model as described in Eq. (1) and use it to infer 3D shapes for novel classes, *without* using the category-specific shape prior e_S. We expect this to give a lower bound of performance, since it does not make any use of shape prior information. For the *AS baseline*, we merge the base class and novel class datasets, train the model on this joint dataset, and then test only on novel class examples. We expect that this baseline will set an upper bound on the performance of the vanilla encoder-decoder architecture, since the model also has access to the examples from the novel classes in $\mathcal{D}_n^K$.

4   Experiments

4.1   Dataset and Evaluation Protocol

For our experiments we use the ShapeNetCore_v1.0 [1] dataset and the few-shot generalization benchmark of [32]. As in [32], we use 7 categories as our *base classes*: **plane, car, chair, display, phone, speaker, table**; and 10 categories as our *novel classes*: **bench, cabinet, lamp, rifle, sofa, watercraft, knife, bathtub, guitar, laptop**. Note that we have added additional categories to the standard benchmark, for a more extensive evaluation. Out data comes in the form of pairs of 128×128 images rendered using Blender [4], and $32 \times 32 \times 32$ voxelized representations obtained using Binvox [19,20]. Each 3D model has 24 associated images, rendered from random viewpoints. For evaluation, we use the standard Intersection over Union (IoU) score to compare predicted shapes $\bar{S}$ to ground truth shapes S: $\text{IoU} = |S \cap \bar{S}|/|S \cup \tilde{S}|$.

4.2 Implementation Details

All methods are trained on the 7 base classes except for the AS-baseline which is trained on all 17 categories. All methods share the same 2D encoder and 3D decoder architectures. We use the same 2D encoder as in [26,32], a ResNet [9] that takes a 128×128 image as input, and outputs a 128-dimensional embedding. Our 3D decoder consists of 7 convolutional layers, followed by batch-normalization, and ReLU activations. For training, we use the same 80–20 train-test split as in R2N2 [3,32]. Unless otherwise stated, we use $l_r = 0.0001$ as the learning rate and ADAM [12] as the optimizer. All networks are trained with binary cross entropy on the predicted voxel presence probabilities in the output 3D grid.

ZS-Baseline is trained on the 7 base categories for 25 epochs. We use the trained model to make predictions for novel classes without further adaptations.

AS-baseline is trained on *all* 17 categories for 25 epochs. We do not use any pre-trained weights, but train this baseline model from a random initialization.

Wallace et al. [32]. To ensure a fair comparison, we re-implemented this framework, using the exact same settings reported in [32]. In the supplemental material we include a comparison only on the subset of classes used in [32], validating that our implementation yields practically identical results.

GCE. We use the same architecture as in the baseline models in [32]. Contrary to the element-wise addition used in [32], we concatenate the 128-d embeddings from the 2D encoder and the conditional branch, and we feed the resulting 256-d embedding into the 3D decoder. The class conditioning vectors are initialized randomly from a normal distribution $\sim \mathcal{N}(0, 1)$. After training the GCE on the base classes, we freeze the parameters of E_I and D and initialize the *novel class* embeddings as the average of the learned base class encodings. We then optimize them using stochastic gradient descent (SGD) with momentum set to 0.9.

CGCE. The conditional branch is composed of 5 codebooks, each containing 6 codes of dimension 128, and an attention array of size $17 \times 5 \times 6$; i.e., one attention value per $(class, codebook, code)$ triplet. The codes and attention values are initialized using a uniform distribution $U(-0.4, 0.4)$. During training, we push the attention array to focus on meaningful codes by employing *sparsemax* [15]. After training the CGCE on the base classes, we freeze the parameters of E_I and D, as well as the codebook entries $\mathbf{c}_{j,k}$. We initialize the *novel class* attentions $\boldsymbol{\alpha}_i$ from a uniform distribution $U(-0.4, 0.4)$. We then optimize $\boldsymbol{\alpha}_i$ using stochastic gradient descent (SGD) with momentum set to 0.9.

MCCE. We replace all batch normalization (bnorm) layers in the 3D decoder with *conditional* batch normalization (cond-bnorm) [22]. More precisely, the affine parameters γ_i and β_i are initialized from a normal distribution $\sim \mathcal{N}(1, 0.2)$, and conditioned on the class i. For novel class adaptation only the aforementioned γ_i and β_i for new classes are learned. We use SGD as optimizer with momentum set to 0.9 for this novel class adaptation.

Table 1. Zero-shot (ZS), All-shot (AS), and Oracle Nearest Neighbor (ONN-K) IoU results for different number of shots, K. ONN outperforms an encoder-decoder model when the full dataset is available. However, in the low-shot regime, even the zero-shot variant shows better generalization, outperforming ONN.

Cat	ZS-Baseline	AS-baseline	ONN-1	ONN-2	ONN-3	ONN-4	ONN-5	ONN-10	ONN-25	ONN-full
Bench	0.366	0.524	0.238	0.240	0.245	0.271	0.276	0.360	0.420	0.708
Cabinet	0.686	0.753	0.400	0.458	0.460	0.461	0.480	0.495	0.631	0.842
Lamp	0.186	0.368	0.153	0.162	0.177	0.189	0.194	0.223	0.282	0.515
Firearm	0.133	0.561	0.377	0.396	0.420	0.425	0.434	0.510	0.550	0.707
Sofa	0.519	0.692	0.445	0.458	0.459	0.530	0.534	0.579	0.616	0.791
Watercraft	0.283	0.560	0.259	0.286	0.317	0.354	0.372	0.479	0.527	0.697
Mean_novel	0.362	0.576	0.312	0.333	0.346	0.371	0.381	0.441	0.504	0.710

4.3   Comparing Baselines in the Few-Shot Regime

Tatarchenko et al. [31] showed that naive 3D reconstruction baselines not only perform well, but manage to surpass in performance more complicated, state of the art approaches. We show that such baselines, however, perform poorly in a few-shot learning setup [32], where a more nuanced understanding of 3D shape is required for generalization to novel examples. In Table 1 we compare the ONN, ZS, and AS baselines, described in Sect. 3.4. We consider several versions of ONN, with access to varying numbers of examples in the few-shot spectrum, ranging from a "1-shot" (ONN-1) to "full-shot" (ONN-full - access to all shapes for that class). We observe that ONN-full outperforms AS, which has been trained on all available data, supporting the findings of [32]. However, once the number of shots decreases, performance for ONN quickly deteriorates, and drops below that of even the ZS baseline.

Note that the ZS baseline already achieves relatively high performance on select classes (`sofa` and `cabinet`). We hypothesize that this is due to the similarity of these classes to some of the base categories. To test the validity of our hypothesis, we compute a similarity score between each novel class and the base class set. Let $\mathcal{C}$ be the set of all shapes S in a novel class. We compute its nearest neighbor with respect to *all* base classes: $\text{IoU}(S, \mathcal{D}_b) = \max_{S_b \in \mathcal{D}_b} \text{IoU}(S, S_b)$. We then compute an *inter-class proximity* between $\mathcal{C}$ and all base classes as the average of these IoU scores: $P(\mathcal{C}, \mathcal{D}_b) = \frac{1}{|\mathcal{C}|} \sum_{S_i \in \mathcal{C}} \text{IoU}(S_i, \mathcal{D}_b)$.

Figure 4 shows the IoU scores of novel classes, sorted by decreasing proximity scores to the base set. To better study the effect of proximity to IoU performance, we have included four (4) additional novel classes from ShapeNet, highlighted in blue. Note that ZS performs better for classes with higher proximity to base classes, supporting our original hypothesis. This also means that novel classes with low proximity have much higher potential for improvement using few-shot learning, with respect to ZS.

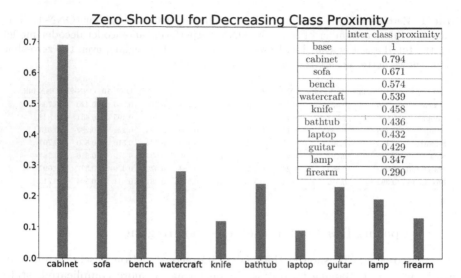

Fig. 4. Zero-shot IoU for decreasing proximity between ot the base set. The higher the proximity of a novel class to the base set, the better ZS performs. To make this point clear, we add more classes of low proximity (blue color) to our evaluation. (Color figure online)

4.4   Evaluating Few Shot-Generalization

In Table 2 we evaluate the three methods described in Sect. 3, on 1-shot reconstruction. We report both the IOU as well as the relative improvement over the ZS baseline. Note that as the ZS-baseline provides strong performance for easy classes, the average IOU is dominated by these, thus relative improvement is a more meaningful metric for aggregation across classes. Please note that GCE improves performance over [32], particularly for classes with low proximity to the base set, obtaining 45% relative improvement over ZS, overall, compared to [32]. The compositional and multiscale priors lead to further improvements of 54% and 52%, respectively, compared to the simple shape prior of [32].

In Table 3 we evaluate the CGCE variant (which performs best in 1-shot evaluation) on the 10- and 25-shot settings, and compare to [32]. We observe that, similarly to the 1-shot case, most methods do not significantly improve the performance for classes with high proximity to the base set. For distant classes, on the other hand, we see substantial performance improvements (sometimes 200%+ in IoU). Table 3 also shows the increased gap in performance between CGCE and [32], as the number of shots increases, supporting our argument that the global conditional embedding can better capture intra-class variability and thus remains effective beyond the 1-shot setting.

Validating the Contribution of the Shape Prior. To validate that our GCE framework (and by extension, CGCE and MCCE) does not simply ignore

Table 2. IoU scores for single-image 3D reconstruction in the 1-shot setting. Numbers in parentheses indicate *relative* performance gains over ZS. Note the marked improvement, especially for novel classes with low proximity to the base set, indicating much better generalization of our method.

Cat	Zero-shot	All-shot	1 shot			
	ZS	AS	Wallace [32]	GCE	CGCE	MCCE
Cabinet	0.69	0.75	0.69 (0.00)	0.69 (0.01)	**0.71 (0.03)**	0.69 (0.01)
Sofa	0.52	0.69	0.54 (0.04)	0.52 (0.00)	**0.54 (0.04)**	**0.54 (0.03)**
Bench	0.37	0.52	0.37 (0.00)	0.37 (0.00)	**0.37 (0.00)**	**0.37 (0.00)**
Watercraft	0.28	0.56	0.33 (0.16)	0.34 (0.19)	**0.39 (0.39)**	0.37 (0.29)
Knife	0.12	0.60	0.30 (1.47)	0.26 (1.13)	**0.31 (1.5)**	0.27 (1.19)
Bathtub	0.24	0.46	0.26 (0.05)	0.27 (0.09)	**0.28 (0.13)**	0.27 (0.11)
Llaptop	0.09	0.56	0.21 (1.30)	0.27 (1.85)	**0.29 (2.10)**	0.27 (1.87)
Guitar	0.23	0.69	0.31 (0.38)	0.30 (0.31)	**0.32 (0.42)**	0.30 (0.31)
Lamp	0.19	0.37	0.20 (0.05)	0.20 (0.07)	0.20 (0.05)	**0.22 (0.16)**
Firearm	0.13	0.56	0.21 (0.58)	0.24 (0.83)	0.23 (0.70)	**0.30 (1.26)**
Mean (relative to ZS)			40.2%	44.7%	**53.7%**	52.2%

Table 3. IoU scores for K-shot evaluation ($K \in \{10, 25\}$). Numbers in parentheses are performance gains over ZS. Improvements for CGCE widen as K increases.

Cat	Zero-shot	All-shot	10 shot		25 shot	
	ZS	AS	Wallace	CGCE	Wallace	CGCE
Cabinet	0.69	0.75	0.69 (0.00)	**0.71 (0.03)**	0.69 (0.01)	**0.71 (0.04)**
Sofa	0.52	0.69	0.54 (0.04)	0.54 (0.04)	0.54(0.04)	**0.55 (0.06)**
Bench	0.37	0.52	0.36 (−0.01)	**0.37 (0.03)**	0.36 (−0.01)	**0.38 (0.04)**
Watercraft	0.28	0.56	0.36 (0.26)	**0.41 (0.45)**	0.37 (0.29)	**0.43 (0.53)**
Knife	0.12	0.60	0.31 (1.52)	**0.32 (1.62)**	0.31 (1.57)	**0.35 (1.87)**
Bathtub	0.24	0.46	0.26 (0.05)	**0.28 (0.16)**	0.26 (0.06)	**0.30 (0.23)**
Laptop	0.09	0.56	0.24 (1.53)	**0.30 (2.24)**	0.27 (1.85)	**0.32 (2.45)**
Guitar	0.23	0.69	0.32 (0.39)	**0.33 (0.47)**	0.32 (0.42)	**0.37 (0.62)**
Lamp	0.19	0.37	0.19 (0.04)	**0.20 (0.05)**	0.19 (0.03)	**0.20 (0.07)**
Firearm	0.13	0.56	**0.24 (0.83)**	0.23 (0.75)	0.26 (0.95)	**0.28 (1.08)**
Mean (relative to ZS)			46.5%	**58.3%**	51.9%	**69.8%**

the conditioning on the shape prior, we perform a simple ablation in which we randomly select the class of the corresponding global embedding for a given input; we call this variant GCE-rand. As shown in Table 4, performance drops drastically, validating that the model learns to use the class-specific shape priors (Fig. 5).

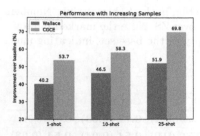

Fig. 5. Percentage gains for 1, 10 and 25 shot over ZS baseline. The gains of our method increase, relative to [32], with greater number of shots (larger intra-class variability).

Table 4. Performance drops significantly when the class embedding is randomly selected, validating that the class conditioning is being used by the GCE model.

Cat	ZS	AS	GCE	GCE_rand
Plane	0.580	0.572	0.582	0.198
Car	0.835	0.830	0.837	0.412
Chair	0.504	0.500	0.510	0.284
Monitor	0.516	0.508	0.520	0.346
Cellphone	0.704	0.689	0.710	0.497
Speaker	0.648	0.659	0.670	0.505
Table	0.536	0.537	0.540	0.376

Fig. 6. 3D reconstructions with our compositional GCE (CGCE) model. Eliminating the contribution of a selected codebook in the shape prior (CGCE-cb) deletes object parts, such as table legs or plane wings, from the reconstructed shape, indicating that the learned codebooks capture meaningful semantic attributes.

Analysis of the Compositional GCE. We analyze the CGCE codes learned by our model through visualizations that unveil associations of codebook entries with object parts. Given a 2D input image, we generate its 3D reconstruction, after randomly removing the contribution of selected codebook entries in the compositional shape prior. Figure 6 shows the results. We observe that removing certain codes results in the removal of semantically meaningful portions of the reconstructed object, such as table legs or plane wings.

We also explicitly analyze the learned attention over the codebook entries. We start by using the IOU-based class proximity metric described in Sect. 4.3 to associate each novel class to its closest base classes (see Fig. 7). We observe a positive correlation of high proximity scores and alignment of the attention distribution over codes for novel and base classes. Finally, in Fig. 8 we visually compare CGCE reconstructions to those of [32], in the 25-shot case, confirming that numerical performance gains translate into higher reconstruction quality for our approach. For more visualizations we refer to the supplementary material.

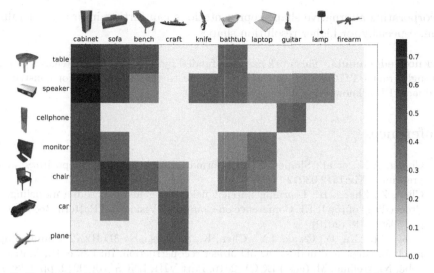

Fig. 7. Proximity between base classes (y-axis) and novel classes (x-axis). Distance is measured, as a mean IoU of nearest neighbors.

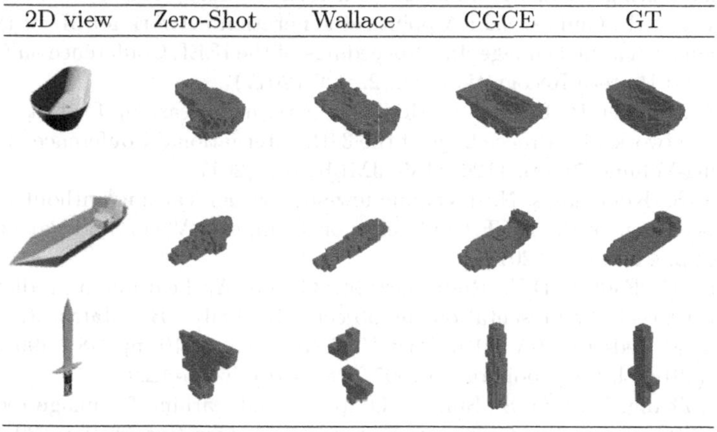

2D view	Zero-Shot	Wallace	CGCE	GT

Fig. 8. Qualitative analysis on 3 different examples using novel classes with 25-shots. We show predictions by different models and the ground truth (GT). Our model exhibits qualitatively better reconstructions than [32] and the Zero-Shot baseline.

5 Conclusions

We have identified few-shot 3D reconsruction as an ideal benchmark for studying 3D deep learning models and their ability to reason about object shapes and generalize to new categories. We have addressed several key weaknesses of previously proposed models in this setting, particularly in capturing intra-class variability, and have proposed compositional and multi-scale shape priors that improve performance and interpretability. Plans for future work in this area include whether incorporating alternative shape representations can further improve generalization, especially for higher resolution shapes.

Acknowledgements. This work has been funded by the Australian Research Council through grant FT170100072. Authors would like to thank Ming Xu for constructive feedback. EB acknowledges funding from IVADO.

References

1. Chang, A.X., et al.: Shapenet: An information-rich 3D model repository. arXiv preprint arXiv:1512.03012 (2015)
2. Chen, Z., Zhang, H.: Learning implicit fields for generative shape modeling. In: Proceedings of the IEEE Conference on Computer Vision and Pattern Recognition, pp. 5939–5948 (2019)
3. Choy, C.B., Xu, D., Gwak, J.Y., Chen, K., Savarese, S.: 3D-R2N2: a unified approach for single and multi-view 3D object reconstruction. In: Leibe, B., Matas, J., Sebe, N., Welling, M. (eds.) ECCV 2016, Part VIII. LNCS, vol. 9912, pp. 628–644. Springer, Cham (2016). https://doi.org/10.1007/978-3-319-46484-8_38
4. Community, B.O.: Blender - a 3D Modelling and Rendering Package. Blender Foundation. Stichting Blender Foundation, Amsterdam (2018). http://www.blender.org
5. Fan, H., Su, H., Guibas, L.J.: A point set generation network for 3D object reconstruction from a single image. In: Proceedings of the IEEE Conference on Computer Vision and Pattern Recognition, vol. 2, p. 6 (2017)
6. Finn, C., Abbeel, P., Levine, S.: Model-agnostic meta-learning for fast adaptation of deep networks. In: Proceedings of the 34th International Conference on Machine Learning-Volume 70. pp. 1126–1135. JMLR. org (2017)
7. Gidaris, S., Komodakis, N.: Dynamic few-shot visual learning without forgetting. In: Proceedings of the IEEE Conference on Computer Vision and Pattern Recognition, pp. 4367–4375 (2018)
8. Girdhar, R., Fouhey, D.F., Rodriguez, M., Gupta, A.: Learning a predictable and generative vector representation for objects. In: Leibe, B., Matas, J., Sebe, N., Welling, M. (eds.) ECCV 2016, Part VI. LNCS, vol. 9910, pp. 484–499. Springer, Cham (2016). https://doi.org/10.1007/978-3-319-46466-4_29
9. He, K., Zhang, X., Ren, S., Sun, J.: Deep residual learning for image recognition. In: IEEE Conference on Computer Vision and Pattern Recognition (2016)
10. Hoiem, D., Efros, A.A., Hebert, M.: Automatic photo pop-up. In: ACM SIGGRAPH 2005 Papers, pp. 577–584. ACM (2005)
11. Horn, B.K.: Shape from shading: A method for obtaining the shape of a smooth opaque object from one view. Technical report, CSAIL, USA (1970)
12. Kingma, D.P., Ba, J.: Adam: A method for stochastic optimization. arXiv preprint arXiv:1412.6980 (2014)
13. Kong, C., Lin, C.H., Lucey, S.: Using locally corresponding cad models for dense 3D reconstructions from a single image. In: Proceedings of the IEEE Conference on Computer Vision and Pattern Recognition, pp. 4857–4865 (2017)
14. Kutulakos, K.N., Seitz, S.M.: A theory of shape by space carving. Int. J. Comput. Vis. **38**(3), 199–218 (2000). https://doi.org/10.1023/A:1008191222954
15. Martins, A., Astudillo, R.: From softmax to sparsemax: a sparse model of attention and multi-label classification. In: International Conference on Machine Learning, pp. 1614–1623 (2016)

16. Mescheder, L., Oechsle, M., Niemeyer, M., Nowozin, S., Geiger, A.: Occupancy networks: Learning 3D reconstruction in function space (2018)
17. Michalkiewicz, M., Belilovsky, E., Baktashmotlagh, M., Eriksson, A.: A simple and scalable shape representation for 3d reconstruction. arXiv preprint arXiv:2005.04623 (2020)
18. Michalkiewicz, M., Pontes, J.K., Jack, D., Baktashmotlagh, M., Eriksson, A.P.: Deep level sets: implicit surface representations for 3D shape inference. In: Proceedings of the International Conference on Computer Vision (ICCV) (2019)
19. Min, P.: binvox. http://www.patrickmin.com/binvox or https://www.google.com/search?q=binvox (2004–2019). Accessed 05 Mar 2020
20. Nooruddin, F.S., Turk, G.: Simplification and repair of polygonal models using volumetric techniques. IEEE Trans. Visual. Comput. Graphics 9(2), 191–205 (2003)
21. Park, J.J., Florence, P., Straub, J., Newcombe, R., Lovegrove, S.: DeepSDF: learning continuous signed distance functions for shape representation. In: Proceedings of the IEEE Conference on Computer Vision and Pattern Recognition, pp. 165–174 (2019)
22. Perez, E., Strub, F., De Vries, H., Dumoulin, V., Courville, A.: Film: visual reasoning with a general conditioning layer. In: Thirty-Second AAAI Conference on Artificial Intelligence (2018)
23. Qi, H., Brown, M., Lowe, D.G.: Low-shot learning with imprinted weights. In: Proceedings of the IEEE Conference on Computer Vision and Pattern Recognition, pp. 5822–5830 (2018)
24. Ramakrishna, V., Kanade, T., Sheikh, Y.: Reconstructing 3D human pose from 2D image landmarks. In: Fitzgibbon, A., Lazebnik, S., Perona, P., Sato, Y., Schmid, C. (eds.) ECCV 2012, Part IV. LNCS, vol. 7575, pp. 573–586. Springer, Heidelberg (2012). https://doi.org/10.1007/978-3-642-33765-9_41
25. Ravi, S., Larochelle, H.: Optimization as a model for few-shot learning. In: ICLR (2017)
26. Richter, S.R., Roth, S.: Matryoshka networks: predicting 3D geometry via nested shape layers. In: CVPR, pp. 1936–1944. IEEE Computer Society (2018)
27. Savarese, S., Andreetto, M., Rushmeier, H., Bernardini, F., Perona, P.: 3D reconstruction by shadow carving: theory and practical evaluation. Int. J. Comput. Vis. 71(3), 305–336 (2007)
28. Shu, R., Nakayama, H.: Compressing word embeddings via deep compositional code learning. arXiv preprint arXiv:1711.01068 (2017)
29. Siam, M., Oreshkin, B., Jagersand, M.: Adaptive masked proxies for few-shot segmentation. arXiv preprint arXiv:1902.11123 (2019)
30. Snell, J., Swersky, K., Zemel, R.: Prototypical networks for few-shot learning. In: Advances in Neural Information Processing Systems, pp. 4077–4087 (2017)
31. Tatarchenko, M., Richter, S.R., Ranftl, R., Li, Z., Koltun, V., Brox, T.: What do single-view 3D reconstruction networks learn? In: Proceedings of the IEEE Conference on Computer Vision and Pattern Recognition, pp. 3405–3414 (2019)
32. Wallace, B., Hariharan, B.: Few-shot generalization for single-image 3D reconstruction via priors. In: Proceedings of the IEEE International Conference on Computer Vision, pp. 3818–3827 (2019)
33. Wang, C., Wang, Y., Lin, Z., Yuille, A.L., Gao, W.: Robust estimation of 3D human poses from a single image. In: Proceedings of the IEEE Conference on Computer Vision and Pattern Recognition, pp. 2361–2368 (2014)

34. Wang, N., Zhang, Y., Li, Z., Fu, Y., Liu, W., Jiang, Y.-G.: Pixel2Mesh: generating 3D mesh models from single RGB images. In: Ferrari, V., Hebert, M., Sminchisescu, C., Weiss, Y. (eds.) ECCV 2018, Part XI. LNCS, vol. 11215, pp. 55–71. Springer, Cham (2018). https://doi.org/10.1007/978-3-030-01252-6_4

35. Wang, X., Huang, T.E., Darrell, T., Gonzalez, J.E., Yu, F.: Frustratingly simple few-shot object detection. arXiv preprint arXiv:2003.06957 (2020)

36. Witkin, A.P.: Recovering surface shape and orientation from texture. Artif. Intell. **17**(1–3), 17–45 (1981)

37. Wu, J., et al.: Single image 3D Interpreter Network. In: Leibe, B., Matas, J., Sebe, N., Welling, M. (eds.) ECCV 2016, Part VI. LNCS, vol. 9910, pp. 365–382. Springer, Cham (2016). https://doi.org/10.1007/978-3-319-46466-4_22

38. Wu, J., Zhang, C., Xue, T., Freeman, B., Tenenbaum, J.: Learning a probabilistic latent space of object shapes via 3D generative-adversarial modeling. In: Advances in Neural Information Processing Systems, pp. 82–90 (2016)

39. Wu, X., Sahoo, D., Hoi, S.C.: Meta-R-CNN: Meta learning for few-shot object detection. arXiv preprint arXiv:1909.13032 (2019)

40. Xu, B., Chang, W., Sheffer, A., Bousseau, A., McCrae, J., Singh, K.: True2form: 3D curve networks from 2D sketches via selective regularization. ACM Trans. Graph (TOG) **33**(4), 1–13 (2014)

41. Yan, X., Yang, J., Yumer, E., Guo, Y., Lee, H.: Perspective transformer nets: Learning single-view 3d object reconstruction without 3d supervision. In: Advances in Neural Information Processing Systems, pp. 1696–1704 (2016)

42. Zhu, R., Kiani Galoogahi, H., Wang, C., Lucey, S.: Rethinking reprojection: closing the loop for pose-aware shape reconstruction from a single image. In: The IEEE International Conference on Computer Vision (ICCV), October 2017

Enhanced Sparse Model for Blind Deblurring

Liang Chen[1], Faming Fang[1(✉)], Shen Lei[2], Fang Li[3], and Guixu Zhang[1]

[1] Shanghai Key Laboratory of Multidimensional Information Processing, School of Computer Science and Technology, East China Normal University, Shanghai, China
liangchen527@gmail.com, fmfang@cs.ecnu.edu.cn
[2] School of Software Engineering, East China Normal University, Shanghai, China
[3] School of Mathematical Sciences, East China Normal University, Shanghai, China

Abstract. Existing arts have shown promising efforts to deal with the blind deblurring task. However, most of the recent works assume the additive noise involved in the blurring process to be simple-distributed (i.e. Gaussian or Laplacian), while the real-world case is proved to be much more complicated. In this paper, we develop a new term to better fit the complex natural noise. Specifically, we use a combination of a dense function (i.e. l_2) and a newly designed enhanced sparse model termed as l_e, which is developed from two sparse models (i.e. l_1 and l_0), to fulfill the task. Moreover, we further suggest using l_e to regularize image gradients. Compared to the widely-adopted l_0 sparse term, l_e can penalize more insignificant image details (Fig. 1). Based on the half-quadratic splitting method, we provide an effective scheme to optimize the overall formulation. Comprehensive evaluations on public datasets and real-world images demonstrate the superiority of the proposed method against state-of-the-art methods in terms of both speed and accuracy.

Keywords: Blind deblurring · Noise model · Enhanced sparse model

1 Introduction

Assuming the image is degraded by a spatially-invariant blur kernel, the blurry image y can be obtained by convolving a sharp image x and a blur kernel k:

$$y = x * k + n, \tag{1}$$

where n denote the unavoidable noise. We use $*$ to represent the convolution operator. In the blind deblurring task, we aim to estimate x and k with only y.

Electronic supplementary material The online version of this chapter (https://doi.org/10.1007/978-3-030-58595-2_38) contains supplementary material, which is available to authorized users.

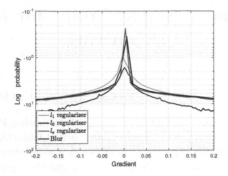

Fig. 1. Average gradient distribution of blurred images and intermediate latent images obtained from different sparse regularizers. We use the imageset from Köhler et al. [12]. The proposed l_e model shows stronger sparsity than others.

In order to solve the highly ill-posed problem, effective priors must be imposed to regularize the solution space:

$$\{x, k\} = argmin_{x,k}F(y - x * k) + R_1(x) + R_2(k), \tag{2}$$

where the fidelity term $F(\cdot)$ is used to model the noise n in (1); $R_1(\cdot)$ and $R_2(\cdot)$ are used as regularization terms for x and k. It can be observed that the deblurring result can benefit from a decent noise modeling step. In fact, the inappropriate noise modeling step is proved to be a major cause of the ringing artifacts appeared in the recovered image [25]. Most of former maximum a posterior (MAP)-based methods [1,3,13,20,23,24,28] assume the noise to follow the Gaussian or Laplacian distribution. As a result, they adopt l_2 or l_1 norm on the basic fidelity term. However, previous study has demonstrated that the noise model in natural images should be much more complex [32], assuming the distribution of noise either to follow Gaussian or Laplacian is far from convincing. Thus, in order to recover sharper images, a more reasonable noise model is required.

Inspired by the success in previous work [6] that combines a dense and a sparse model (i.e. l_2 and l_1) to model unknown noise, we conjecture if it helps to replace the l_1 model with an enhanced one. Presumably, the combination with the enhanced sparse model should be able to meet wider range of distributions, thus can better fit the complex natural noise.

To this end, we design an enhanced sparse model termed as l_e, which is based on a simple combination of the l_1 and l_0 sparse models. Surprisingly, a simple combination of these two models turns out to be sparser than either single one in practice as shown in Fig. 1, which plots the statics of the gradients of the intermediate latent images obtained by different regularizers. We observe that using the l_e model helps obtain more small gradients than that of l_0 and l_1, which demonstrates the sparseness of the proposed model. We further give an intuitive explanation for the reason in Sect. 3.1.

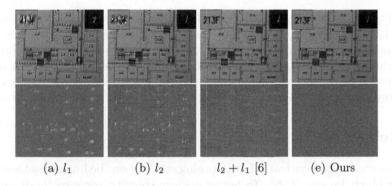

(a) l_1 (b) l_2 $l_2 + l_1$ [6]   (e) Ours

Fig. 2. Comparison between existing noise modeling strategies. The first and second row show intermediate results and corresponding noise maps from different models. Our noise map contains fewer image structures, which leads to better deblurring results. (Color figure online)

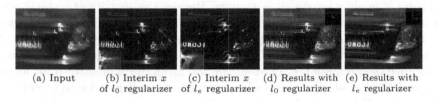

(a) Input   (b) Interim x (c) Interim x (d) Results with   (e) Results with
of l_0 regularizer   of l_e regularizer l_0 regularizer l_e regularizer

Fig. 3. Deblurring results with l_0 regularizer and l_e regularizer on latent image. The part enclosed in the red box from (b) contain insignificant pixels. (Color figure online)

By combining the l_e and l_2 models and considering the spatial randomness of natural noise [25], we can develop a new noise fitting function (please refer to Sect. 3.2 for detailed description). As shown in Fig. 2, we note that the proposed noise fitting term performs more effectively than other models, and the corresponding results contain fewer artifacts as illustrated in the red boxes.

Revisiting the regularization term for the latent image. Recall that sparse priors are often adopted to penalize fine details [29] which are proved to be harmful to the deblurring process [28]. In this work, we use the proposed enhanced sparse model to regularize the image. Besides the statistical illustration given in Fig. 1, we provide an example in Fig. 3, which shows that l_e model is able to prune more insignificant pixels than that of l_0, and the method based on l_e also generates a better result.

Optimizing the overall non-convex formulation is challenging. We address the problem by adopting an effective half-quadratic splitting method. The whole framework is carried out in a MAP-based coarser-to-fine [3] manner. The following analysis illustrates the convergence of our model.

Contributions of this work are three-fold. (1) We propose a novel term to better fit the unknown natural noise in the blurring process. Specifically, we take advantage of a dense model (i.e. l_2) and a newly designed enhanced sparse model (i.e. l_e) to fulfill the task, in which l_e is developed from two sparse functions (i.e. l_1 and l_0). (2) We further propose to use l_e to regularize image gradients. With an unnatural representation approach [29], l_e can better penalize insignificant edges than other models. (3) Through experimental results on the benchmark datasets [12,14,16] and real-world images demonstrate that our method performs favorably against state-of-the-art methods both quantitatively and qualitatively.

2 Related Work

Previous studies demonstrate that imposing sparsity on the image gradient helps recover blurry images [4,29]. To better achieve sparsity, some methods use specially designed regularizers to promote sparsity. Shan et al. [25] use an l_1 norm on image gradient, and incorporate it with a ringing removal term. Krishnan et al. [13] adopt a special l_1/l_2 regularization to model sparse constraint. Furthermore, Xu et al. [29] propose an unnatural l_0 sparse regularization on image gradients, and solve it in an approximation manner. Besides the sparsity of images, other statistic priors are also developed to solve the problem. For example, Pan et al. [23] introduce the dark channel prior to deblur natural images. Yan et al. [30] further propose a combination of dark channel and the opposite bright channel to improve the performance. Li et al. [18] learned a discriminative prior for the task, and Chen et al. [1] develop a local maximum gradient prior to reveal more information hidden in the blurry images.

Instead of exploring the statistical distribution of natural images, some methods select salient edges for kernel estimation. Specifically, Joshi et al. [11] extract sharp edges from blurry images by locating step edges first, and they further propagate the extrema values along the edge profile. Cho and Lee [3] adopt both bilateral and shock filtering for edge prediction. Xu and Jia [28] suggest that insignificant edges may have adverse effects on kernel estimation, and they propose a criterion for selecting informative edges. Lai et al. [14] use both filtering and data-driven prior to predict sharp edges. However, these methods will fail if there are few strong edges [23]. Thus, Gong et al. [5] propose to automatically select a subset of edges by a gradient activation method. Despite the effectiveness of these methods, they neglect the contribution of a proper noise modeling step. In this paper, we show that the proposed noise modeling strategy can boost the accuracy of the estimated kernel.

3 Proposed Method

3.1 Enhanced Sparse Model

The proposed enhanced sparse model is based on a combination of l_0 and l_1 sparse models given by,

$$\| \cdot \|_e = \| \cdot \|_0 + \| \cdot \|_1. \tag{3}$$

We show in the following that the l_e model can lead to a sparser solution than the widely-used unnatural l_0 approach [29] under the same condition.

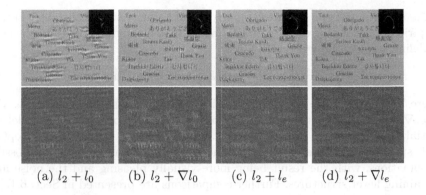

(a) $l_2 + l_0$ (b) $l_2 + \nabla l_0$ (c) $l_2 + l_e$ (d) $l_2 + \nabla l_e$

Fig. 4. Example with possible combinations of noise-fitting functions. First and second rows present deblurring results and corresponding noise maps of each noise modeling strategies. The model with $l_2 + \nabla l_e$ (i.e. proposed) generates better results and the corresponding noise map contain fewer image structure.

Given a corrupted signal $\mathcal{A}$, assuming the latent signal $\mathcal{B}$ is sparse which can be obtained by being imposed with the enhanced sparse model. With a basic quadratic penalty, the objective energy function can be expressed as following,

$$\min_{\mathcal{B}} \frac{1}{4\sigma^2}\|\mathcal{A} - \mathcal{B}\|_2^2 + \|\mathcal{B}\|_e, \tag{4}$$

where σ is the regularization parameter. Decomposing the above formulation into a set of independent sub-problems, we can rewrite (4) into,

$$\min_{\mathcal{B}_i} \frac{1}{4\sigma^2} \sum_i |\mathcal{A}_i - \mathcal{B}_i|^2 + |\mathcal{B}_i|^e, \tag{5}$$

where i denotes the location of an element. The equation above has a closed form solution,

$$\mathcal{B}_i = \begin{cases} \mathcal{A}_i + 2\sigma^2, & \text{if } \mathcal{A}_i + 2\sigma^2 < -2\sigma \\ \mathcal{A}_i - 2\sigma^2, & \text{if } \mathcal{A}_i - 2\sigma^2 > 2\sigma \\ 0, & \text{Otherwise.} \end{cases} \tag{6}$$

Proof can be found in our supplementary material. Note that in this case the value of the latent signal $\mathcal{B}$ will be sparser (i.e. more likely to be 0 under the same conditions) compared to the case when minimizing l_0 norm (see our supplementary file for detailed illustration), which explains the reason why l_e model is more effective at penalizing fine details. We provide further evaluation of these two models in Sect. 6.1.

3.2 Improved Noise Modeling

Instead of adopting complicate noise modeling skills, such as the mixture of Gaussian [19] or continuous mixed p norm [10], we suggest a simple combination of the l_2 norm and the enhanced sparse model to fit natural noise distribution. Empirically, our model can fit any continuous distribution in between. The noise modeling step can be written as follow,

$$F(y - x * k) = \|y - x * k\|_2^2 + \beta\|\nabla y - \nabla x * k\|_e, \tag{7}$$

where ∇ is the derivate operator in vertical and horizontal dimensions (i.e. $\nabla = \{\nabla_h, \nabla_v\}$). For simplicity, we use one order derivative operators to model the spatial randomness [25] of natural noise. As shown in Fig. 4, the model adopting both spatial randomness prior and l_e norm performs the best among possible combinations, with the result being more visually pleasing and the noise map containing fewer structures. Further comparisons are presented in Sect. 6.1.

3.3   Model and Optimization

Analogous to previous works [5,23,29], we use an l_2 norm to encourage the smoothness of blur kernels. The overall deblurring model is given by,

$$\min_{x,k} \|y - x * k\|_2^2 + \beta\|\nabla y - \nabla x * k\|_e + \theta\|\nabla x\|_e + \gamma\|k\|_2^2, \tag{8}$$

where β, θ and γ are weight parameters. We obtain the solution of (8) by alternatively updating x and k with the other one fixed. The sub-problems referring to x and k are given by,

$$\begin{cases} \min_{x} \|y - x * k\|_2^2 + \beta\|\nabla y - \nabla x * k\|_e + \theta\|\nabla x\|_e, & (9) \\ \min_{k} \|y - x * k\|_2^2 + \beta\|\nabla y - \nabla x * k\|_e + \gamma\|k\|_2^2. & (10) \end{cases}$$

Update Latent Image. With the intrusion of l_0 in the l_e norm, (9) becomes highly non-convex. We thus use the half-quadratic splitting method for the task. Variables u and g are introduced corresponding to $\nabla(y - x * k)$ and ∇x, respectively. Thus, (9) can be transformed into,

$$\min_{x,u,g} \|y - x * k\|_2^2 + \beta\|u\|_e + \theta\|g\|_e + \lambda_1\|u - \nabla(y - x * k)\|_2^2 + \lambda_2\|g - \nabla x\|_2^2, \tag{11}$$

where λ_1 and λ_2 are penalty parameters. We solve (11) by updating x, u and g separately.

(1) **Solving** x. The objective function referring to x is a quadratic problem:

$$\min_{x} \|y - x * k\|_2^2 + \lambda_1\|u - \nabla(y - x * k)\|_2^2 + \lambda_2\|g - \nabla x\|_2^2. \tag{12}$$

We can use a Fast Fourier Transform (FFT) to solve the above equation [1].

(2) **Solving** u. The subproblem referring to u is given by,

$$\min_{u} \beta\|u\|_e + \lambda_1\|u - \nabla(y - x * k)\|_2^2. \tag{13}$$

Algorithm 1: Enhanced sparse model for blur kernel estimation

Input: Blurry image y, initialized k from the coarser level.
for $iter = 1:maxiter$ **do**
    repeat
        Updating x, u and g using Eq. (12), (13) and (15), respectively;
        $\lambda_1 \leftarrow 2\lambda_1, \lambda_2 \leftarrow 2\lambda_2$.
    until x *converges*;
    repeat
        Updating k and p using Eq. (17) and (18); $\lambda_3 \leftarrow 2\lambda_3$.
    until k *converges*;
end
Output: Blur kernel k and latent image x.

Referring to (6), the solution can be written as,

$$
u = \begin{cases} \{s1 | s1 = \nabla(y - x * k) - \frac{\beta}{2\lambda_1}\}, s1 > \sqrt{\frac{\beta}{\lambda_1}} \\ \{s2 | s2 = \nabla(y - x * k) + \frac{\beta}{2\lambda_1}\}, s2 < -\sqrt{\frac{\beta}{\lambda_1}} \\ \qquad\qquad 0, \qquad\qquad \text{Otherwise.} \end{cases} \tag{14}
$$

(3) **Solving** g. With x and u fixed, we can update g by the following equation,

$$
\min_g \theta \|g\|_e + \lambda_2 \|g - \nabla x\|_2^2. \tag{15}
$$

The solution of (15) is analogous to that of (13), and we omit it here.

Update Blur Kernel. The objective function $w.r.t.$ k also involveing nonconvex optimization. We use the same strategy as (11) by introducing new variable p for $\nabla(y - x * k)$. To boost the accuracy of the estimated kernel, we use the gradient domain instead of the intensity domain [3,17]. Thus, (10) is reformulated to,

$$
\min_{k,p} \|\nabla y - \nabla x * k\|_2^2 + \beta \|p\|_e + \gamma \|k\|_2^2 + \lambda_3 \|p - \nabla(y - x * k)\|_2^2, \tag{16}
$$

where λ_3 is the weight parameter. We solve (16) by splitting it into two subproblems referring to k, p respectively. The solution can be obtained by alternatively updating following formulations,

$$
\begin{cases} \min_k \|\nabla y - \nabla x * k\|_2^2 + \lambda_3 \|p - \nabla(y - x * k)\|_2^2 + \gamma \|k\|_2^2, & (17) \\[2mm] \min_p \beta \|p\|_e + \lambda_3 \|p - \nabla(y - x * k)\|_2^2. & (18) \end{cases}
$$

The solution of (17) can be efficiently obtained by FFT, and the problem in (18) is similar to (14). Both solutions are uncomplicated and will not be reproduced here. After obtaining k, we set the negative elements of k to 0, and normalize it to make it equal to 1. Same to existing methods, the overall kernel estimation process is implemented in a coarse-to-fine manner using an image pyramid [3]. The main steps from one pyramid level are shown in Algorithm 1.

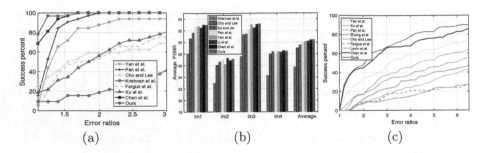

Fig. 5. Quantitative evaluations on benchmark datasets [12, 15, 16]. Our method performs competitively against existing models.

4   Extension to Non-uniform Deblurring

The proposed model can be directly extended to non-uniform deblurring where the blur kernel across an image scale is spatially-variant. Based on the geometric model of camera motion [26, 27], the blurry image can be modeled as a weighted sum of the latent image under geometry transformations,

$$y = \sum_t k_t h_t x + n, \tag{19}$$

where y, x and n denote blurry image, latent image and noise in vector form, respectively; t is the index of camera pose samples, and k_t is the corresponding weight; H_t denotes a homography matrix. Similar to [27], we rewrite (19) as,

$$y = Hx + n = zk + n, \tag{20}$$

where $H = \sum_t k_t h_t$, $z = [h_1 x, h_1 x, ..., h_t x]$, and $k = [k_1, k_2, ..., k_t]^T$. Based on (20), the non-uniform deblurring problem is solved by alternatively minimizing,

$$\begin{cases} \min_x \|Hx - y\|_2^2 + \beta \|H\nabla x - \nabla y\|_e + \theta \|\nabla x\|_e, & (21) \\[2mm] \min_k \|zk - y\|_2^2 + \beta \|\nabla zk - \nabla y\|_e + \gamma \|k\|_2^2. & (22) \end{cases}$$

The updating details are similar to the uniform deblurring case, and latent image x and the weight k are estimated by the fast forward approximation [7].

5   Experimental Results

For the hyper-parameters used in the model, we set $\beta = \theta = 0.004$ and $\gamma = 2$. We first evaluate our method on three benchmark datasets [12, 15, 16] and compare it with several state-of-the-art algorithms. Then, we examine our method on domain-specific images including text [22], face [21] and low-illumination [8] images. Similar to conventional practice, we use a non-blind deblurring method to recover final images after kernels are obtained, and we use the method from

(a) Input   (b) Pan et al. [23]   (c) Yan et al. [30]   (d) Chen et al. [1]   (e)Ours

Fig. 6. A challenging example from dataset [15]. Parts enclosed in red boxes contain moderate artifacts. (Color figure online)

(a) Input   (b) Krishnan [13]   (c) Xu [29]   (d) Pan [22]   (e) Chen [1]   (f) Ours

Fig. 7. Deblurring results from real-world blur images. Here we use the same non-blind deconvolution method from [2].

[22] unless otherwise mentioned. We implement our model in Matlab and assess the efficiency on an Intel Core i5-7400 CPU with 12 GB RAM. More examples are demonstrated in our supplementary material.

5.1   Evaluation on Natural Images

We first evaluate our model on the dataset from Levin et al. [16] which contains 32 blurry images generated by 4 images filtered with 8 blur kernels. The images are all of size 255×255. We compare our model with 7 generic image deblurring methods $[1,3,4,13,23,29,30]$ in term of SSD error ratio [16]. As shown in Fig. 5 (a), our method performs favorbly among state-of-the-art methods.

Next, we examine the proposed method on the natural image dataset from Köhler et al. [12] which contains 12 blur kernels and 4 images. We compare our result with a total of 7 recent deblurring methods $[1,3,13,18,23,29,30]$ in term of average PSNR. We compare the PSNR values by using the protocol used in [12]. As shown in Fig. 5 (b), our method performs favorably against state-of-the-art algorithms.

We also evaluate our method on the dataset from Lai et al. [15], which contains 100 images including face, text, and low-illumination images. We compare our results to several state-of-the-art methods $[1,3,4,17,22,29–31]$. For fair comparison, we use the same non-blind algorithm from [2] to generate final results after acquiring blur kernels. The overall error ratios are shown in Fig. 5 (c), and

Table 1. Results on the text dataset [22]. Our method performs favorably among existing methods.

	Cho and Lee [3]	Xu and Jia [28]	Levin et al. [17]	Xu et al. [29]	Pan et al. [23]	Li et al. [18]	Pan et al. [22]	Ours
Avg. PSNR	23.80	26.21	24.90	26.21	27.94	28.10	28.80	28.83

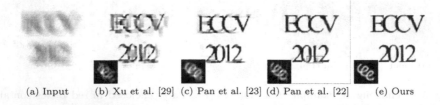

(a) Input   (b) Xu et al. [29] (c) Pan et al. [23] (d) Pan et al. [22]   (e) Ours

Fig. 8. Deblurring results of a text blurred image.

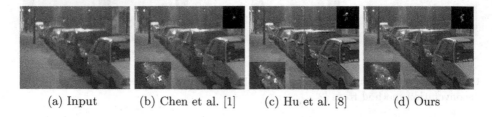

(a) Input   (b) Chen et al. [1]   (c) Hu et al. [8]   (d) Ours

Fig. 9. Deblurring results of real-world low-illumination blur image.

our method performs the best among compared methods. A challenging example from the dataset is shown in Fig. 6, in which most state-of-the-art methods generate results with moderate ringing artifacts. In contrast, our method generates images with fewer artifacts and clearer details.

We further have our method tested in real-world blur images. In this place, we use the non-blind deconvolution method from Cho et al. [2] after obtaining the kernels of each compared method. As shown in Fig. 7, images restored by state-of-the-art methods [1,13,23,29] contain strong artifacts, while our model generates clearer edges, and is more visually pleasing.

5.2   Evaluation on Domain-Specific Images

Text images: We evaluate the effectiveness of our method on text blurry images by conducting experiments on the dataset provided by Pan et al. [22], which contains 15 images and 8 blur kernels from [16]. Table 1 shows the average PSNR values of each method. The proposed method performs favorably against the method specially designed for text deblurring [22]. Visually, the proposed model generated comparable results to that by [22] (Fig. 8).

Low-illumination images: As shown in Fig. 9, state-of-the-art method [1] fails to estimate the kernel due to the saturated regions. Although the method designed for low-illumination can ease the blur to some extent, their results contain residuals because the light streak is difficult to extract in this case. In contrast, our method generates results containing fewer artifacts. Note that our method is only effective with small saturated regions. Images with large saturated regions is still a challenging problem to solve.

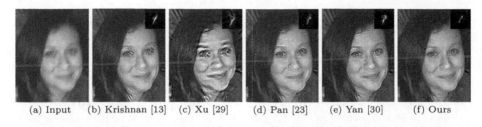

(a) Input   (b) Krishnan [13]   (c) Xu [29]   (d) Pan [23]   (e) Yan [30]   (f) Ours

Fig. 10. Deblurring results of a real-world face blur image.

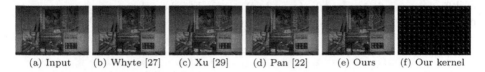

(a) Input   (b) Whyte [27]   (c) Xu [29]   (d) Pan [22]   (e) Ours   (f) Our kernel

Fig. 11. Deblurring results on a non-uniform blurred image.

Face images: Face blurred images are also challenging for methods that are aimed for natural images, because they often contain fewer edges or structures [21] which play a vital role in the kernel estimation process. Figure 10 shows the final recovered results of a face blurred image by several methods. Our result has sharper edges and fewer ringing artifacts than the sate-of-the-art methods [13, 23, 29, 30].

5.3 Non-uniform Deblurring

As discussed in Sect. 4, the proposed model can also be extended to the non-uniform deblurring task. We provide deblurring results on an image degraded by spatially-variant blur in Fig. 11. As shown in the figure, the proposed method can estimate blur kernels in every image tile and produces a comparable result with sharp edges.

6 Analysis and Discussion

6.1 Effectiveness of the Proposed Model

The novelties of our model lie in two aspects, the l_e sparse norm and the improved noise modeling step.

We first evaluate the effectiveness of the l_e norm. We conduct ablation study on the dataset from [16]. Note in this step, the fidelity term is fixed as l_e norm while the regularization term uses different settings. As shown in Fig. 12 (a), the model with l_e imposed on regularization term is more effective than which with l_0 regularized. An example is shown in Fig. 13 (b) and (d). The proposed model with l_e (Fig. 13 (d)) generates a more visually pleasing result than that with l_0 (Fig. 13 (b)).

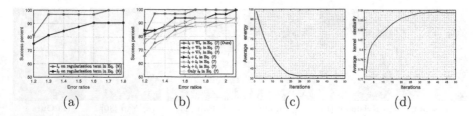

| (a) | (b) | (c) | (d) |

Fig. 12. (a) and (b) are ablation studies for the proposed model on the benchmark dataset [16]. (a) Effects of different sparse models for the regularization term. (b) Effects of different noise-fitting models. (c) and (d) are used to show the convergence property of the model. (c) The energy value of the objective function (9). (d) Average kernel similarity [9].

In (7), we impose l_2 on noise intensity domain and l_e on noise gradient (abbr. as $l_2 + \nabla l_e$) to fit natural noise while also considering its spatial randomness. We conduct ablation study on the benchmark dataset [16] to verify the effectiveness of the proposed strategy. There are a total of 6 combinations that we compare (i.e. abbr. $l_2 + \nabla l_0$, $l_2 + \nabla l_1$, $l_2 + l_e$, $l_2 + l_0$, $l_2 + l_1$ and l_2). As shown in Fig. 12 (b), the proposed setting performs the best among different combinations. Note that the noise modeling step is not as effective as others when uses only l_2 term, while with a sparse model, it performs more effectively. In another view, the performance has positive correlation with the sparsity of the sparse component (from l_1 to l_e), this phenomenon validates the rationality of our assumption. We also show that l_e on gradient domain can be more effective than that on intensity domain (black line in Fig. 12 (b)). The noise maps over iterations shown in Fig. 13 (h) and (i) also illustrate the effectiveness of the proposed noise modeling step.

6.2 Parameter Analysis

The proposed model involves 3 main parameters, β, θ and γ. We evaluate the effects of these parameters on image deblurring in the dataset from [16] by varying one and keeping others fixed. Average PSNR is taken as an evaluation criterion. The parameter β is used to balance dense and sparse distribution in the noise model, which can benefit deblurring if it is set in a reasonable range (from 0.001 to 0.005 as shown in Fig. 14 (a)). Moreover, the best range for θ is

Table 2. Running time comparisons on varying sizes of images. Codes are implemented in MATLAB unless mentioned.

	Xu (C++) [29]	Krishnan [13]	Pan [23]	Chen [1]	Ours
600×600	3.61	50.02	130.10	649.65	38.51
800×800	6.90	90.94	233.58	1680.18	70.17

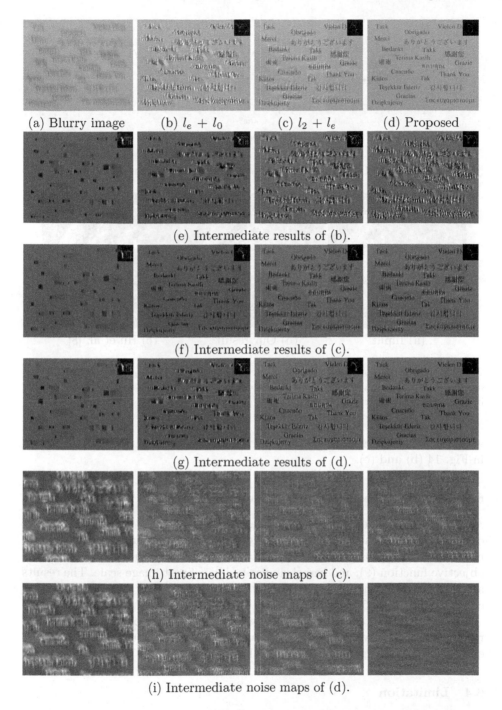

(a) Blurry image   (b) $l_e + l_0$ (c) $l_2 + l_e$ (d) Proposed

(e) Intermediate results of (b).

(f) Intermediate results of (c).

(g) Intermediate results of (d).

(h) Intermediate noise maps of (c).

(i) Intermediate noise maps of (d).

Fig. 13. Effectiveness of the proposed model. (b) Results from the proposed noise fitting model and an l_0 model to regularize image gradient. (c) Results from an l_2 model to fit noise and the proposed sparse term to regularize image gradient. The noise map using the proposed model containing fewer image structure over iterations than that without it.

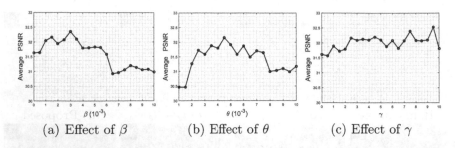

(a) Effect of β (b) Effect of θ (c) Effect of γ

Fig. 14. Effects of the parameters used in our model.

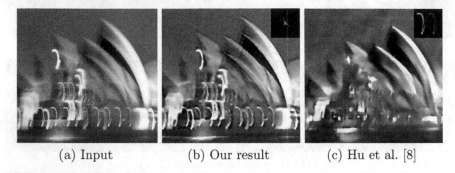

(a) Input   (b) Our result   (c) Hu et al. [8]

Fig. 15. Limitation of the proposed model. The specially designed method [8] can handle the blurry image with large saturated regions, while our method is ineffective in this situation.

within 0.002 to 0.008, while the value of γ has little effect on the model as shown in Fig. 14 (b) and (c).

6.3   Convergence Property and Running Time

As our model involves non-convex regularizations, a natural question is whether our optimization scheme converges. We quantitatively evaluate the convergence property of our algorithm using the dataset [16]. We measure the values of the objective function (9), and kernel similarity [9] at finest image scale. The results are demonstrated in Fig. 12 (c) and (d), which indicates that our algorithm converges less than 50 iterations.

In addition, we test several models with different sizes of images in term of running time. The overall result is summarised in Table 2. Our method conducts one of the fastest running time among these methods.

6.4   Limitation

Although our method is effective in deblurring various kinds of blur images, we find its limitation in directly applying in images with large saturated areas. Figure 15 shows an example of deblurring image with multiple saturated regions.

Our method performs poorly when directly applied in this situation, while methods designed for these tasks [8] generate a clearer result.

7 Conclusion

In this paper, we propose a new perspective for improving the blind deblurring task. In brief, we first present an enhanced sparse model, and combined it with an l_2 model to fit the complex natural noise. Then, we use the enhanced sparse model to penalize more insignificant details. To restore images regularized by the non-convex settings, we develop an effective optimization scheme based on the half-quadric splitting method. Extensive evaluations on benchmark datasets and real-world images demonstrate that the proposed method performs favorably against state-of-the-art methods in terms of both accuracy and speed, and it works well in most given specific scenarios.

Acknowledgement. This work has been sponsored by the National Natural Science Foundation of China (No. 61731009, 61871185, 61731009, and 11671002), the "Chenguang Program" supported by Shanghai Education Development Foundation and Shanghai Municipal Education Commission (17CG25), the Fundamental Research Funds for the Central Universities, and Science and Technology Commission of Shanghai Municipality (No. 19JC1420102 and 18dz2271000).

References

1. Chen, L., Fang, F., Wang, T., Zhang, G.: Blind image deblurring with local maximum gradient prior. In: CVPR (2019)
2. Cho, S., Wang, J., Lee, S.: Handling outliers in non-blind image deconvolution. In: ICCV (2011)
3. Cho, S., Lee, S.: Fast motion deblurring. ACM T. Graph. **28**(5), 145 (2009)
4. Fergus, R., Singh, B., Hertzmann, A., Roweis, S.T., Freeman, W.T.: Removing camera shake from a single photograph. ACM T. Graph. **25**(3), 787–794 (2006)
5. Gong, D., Tan, M., Zhang, Y., van den Hengel, A., Shi, Q.: Blind image deconvolution by automatic gradient activation. In: CVPR (2016)
6. Gong, Z., Shen, Z., Toh, K.C.: Image restoration with mixed or unknown noises. Multiscale Model. Simul. **12**(2), 458–487 (2014)
7. Hirsch, M., Schuler, C.J., Harmeling, S., Schölkopf, B.: Fast removal of non-uniform camera shake. In: ICCV (2011)
8. Hu, Z., Cho, S., Wang, J., Yang, M.H.: Deblurring low-light images with light streaks. In: CVPR (2014)
9. Hu, Z., Yang, M.-H.: Good regions to deblur. In: Fitzgibbon, A., Lazebnik, S., Perona, P., Sato, Y., Schmid, C. (eds.) ECCV 2012, Part V. LNCS, vol. 7576, pp. 59–72. Springer, Heidelberg (2012). https://doi.org/10.1007/978-3-642-33715-4_5
10. Javaheri, A., Zayyani, H., Figueiredo, M.A.T., Marvasti, F.: Robust sparse recovery in impulsive noise via continuous mixed norm. IEEE Signal Process. Lett. **25**(8), 1146–1150 (2018)
11. Joshi, N., Szeliski, R., Kriegman, D.: PSF estimation using sharp edge prediction. In: CVPR (2008)

12. Köhler, R., Hirsch, M., Mohler, B., Schölkopf, B., Harmeling, S.: Recording and playback of camera shake: benchmarking blind deconvolution with a real-world database. In: Fitzgibbon, A., Lazebnik, S., Perona, P., Sato, Y., Schmid, C. (eds.) ECCV 2012, Part VII. LNCS, vol. 7578, pp. 27–40. Springer, Heidelberg (2012). https://doi.org/10.1007/978-3-642-33786-4_3

13. Krishnan, D., Tay, T., Fergus, R.: Blind deconvolution using a normalized sparsity measure. In: CVPR (2011)

14. Lai, W., Ding, J., Lin, Y., Chuang, Y.: Blur kernel estimation using normalized color-line priors. In: CVPR (2015)

15. Lai, W.S., Huang, J.B., Hu, Z., Ahuja, N., Yang, M.H.: A comparative study for single image blind deblurring. In: CVPR (2016)

16. Levin, A., Weiss, Y., Durand, F., Freeman, W.T.: Understanding and evaluating blind deconvolution algorithms. In: CVPR (2009)

17. Levin, A., Weiss, Y., Durand, F., Freeman, W.T.: Efficient marginal likelihood optimization in blind deconvolution. In: CVPR (2011)

18. Li, L., Pan, J., Lai, W.S., Gao, C., Sang, N., Yang, M.H.: Learning a discriminative prior for blind image deblurring. In: CVPR (2018)

19. Meng, D., la Torre, F.D.: Robust matrix factorization with unknown noise. In: ICCV (2013)

20. Michaeli, T., Irani, M.: Blind deblurring using internal patch recurrence. In: Fleet, D., Pajdla, T., Schiele, B., Tuytelaars, T. (eds.) ECCV 2014, Part III. LNCS, vol. 8691, pp. 783–798. Springer, Cham (2014). https://doi.org/10.1007/978-3-319-10578-9_51

21. Pan, J., Hu, Z., Su, Z., Yang, M.-H.: Deblurring face images with exemplars. In: Fleet, D., Pajdla, T., Schiele, B., Tuytelaars, T. (eds.) ECCV 2014, Part VII. LNCS, vol. 8695, pp. 47–62. Springer, Cham (2014). https://doi.org/10.1007/978-3-319-10584-0_4

22. Pan, J., Hu, Z., Su, Z., Yang, M.H.: l_0-regularized intensity and gradient prior for deblurring text images and beyond. IEEE TPAMI **39**(2), 342–355 (2017)

23. Pan, J., Sun, D., Pfister, H., Yang, M.H.: Blind image deblurring using dark channel prior. In: CVPR (2016)

24. Ren, W., Cao, X., Pan, J., Guo, X., Zuo, W., Yang, M.H.: Image deblurring via enhanced low-rank prior. IEEE TIP **25**(7), 3426–3437 (2016)

25. Shan, Q., Jia, J., Agarwala, A.: High-quality motion deblurring from a single image. ACM Trans. Graph. **27**(3), 73 (2008)

26. Tai, Y., Tan, P., Brown, M.S.: Richardson-lucy deblurring for scenes under a projective motion path. IEEE TPAMI **33**(8), 1603–1618 (2011)

27. Whyte, O., Sivic, J., Zisserman, A., Ponce, J.: Non-uniform deblurring for shaken images. IJCV **98**(2), 168–186 (2012). https://doi.org/10.1007/s11263-011-0502-7

28. Xu, L., Jia, J.: Two-phase kernel estimation for robust motion deblurring. In: Daniilidis, K., Maragos, P., Paragios, N. (eds.) ECCV 2010, Part I. LNCS, vol. 6311, pp. 157–170. Springer, Heidelberg (2010). https://doi.org/10.1007/978-3-642-15549-9_12

29. Xu, L., Zheng, S., Jia, J.: Unnatural l_0 sparse representation for natural image deblurring. In: CVPR (2013)

30. Yan, Y., Ren, W., Guo, Y., Wang, R., Cao, X.: Image deblurring via extreme channels prior. In: CVPR (2017)

31. Zhong, L., Cho, S., Metaxas, D., Paris, S., Wang, J.: Handling noise in single image deblurring using directional filters. In: CVPR (2013)

32. Zhu, F., Chen, G., Heng, P.: From noise modeling to blind image denoising. In: CVPR (2016)

SumGraph: Video Summarization
via Recursive Graph Modeling

Jungin Park[1], Jiyoung Lee[1], Ig-Jae Kim[2], and Kwanghoon Sohn[1(✉)]

[1] Yonsei University, Seoul, Korea
{newrun,easy00,khsohn}@yonsei.ac.kr
[2] Korea Institute of Science and Technology (KIST), Seoul, Korea
drjay@kist.re.kr

Abstract. The goal of video summarization is to select keyframes that are visually diverse and can represent a whole story of an input video. State-of-the-art approaches for video summarization have mostly regarded the task as a frame-wise keyframe selection problem by aggregating all frames with equal weight. However, to find informative parts of the video, it is necessary to consider how all the frames of the video are related to each other. To this end, we cast video summarization as a graph modeling problem. We propose recursive graph modeling networks for video summarization, termed SumGraph, to represent a relation graph, where frames are regarded as nodes and nodes are connected by semantic relationships among frames. Our networks accomplish this through a recursive approach to refine an initially estimated graph to correctly classify each node as a keyframe by reasoning the graph representation via graph convolutional networks. To leverage SumGraph in a more practical environment, we also present a way to adapt our graph modeling in an unsupervised fashion. With SumGraph, we achieved state-of-the-art performance on several benchmarks for video summarization in both supervised and unsupervised manners.

Keywords: Video summarization · Graph convolutional networks · Recursive graph refinement

1 Introduction

Over the years, the growth of online video platforms has made it difficult for users to access the video data they want. Moreover, the length of the uploaded videos is getting more extended every day, and it can be impractical for people to watch these videos in full to obtain useful information. In response to these issues,

---

J. Park and J. Lee—Both authors contributed equally to this work.

Electronic supplementary material The online version of this chapter (https://doi.org/10.1007/978-3-030-58595-2_39) contains supplementary material, which is available to authorized users.

A. Vedaldi et al. (Eds.): ECCV 2020, LNCS 12370, pp. 647–663, 2020.
https://doi.org/10.1007/978-3-030-58595-2_39

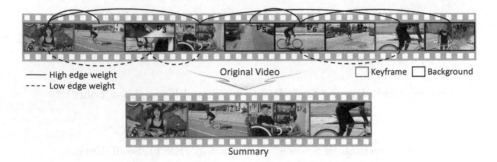

Fig. 1. Illustration of SumGraph. We regard video summarization as a graph modeling problem. We obtain a richer video summary by constructing the graph represents relationships between frames in a video and recursively refining the graph.

computer vision techniques have attracted intense attention in recent years for efficient browsing of the enormous video data. In particular, the research topic, which automatically selects a simple yet informative summary that succinctly depicts the contents of the original video, has become a prominent research topic as a promising tool to cope with the overwhelming amount of video data [21,40].

Inspired by the great successes of deep learning in recent years, current approaches [10,21,37,41] have commonly treated video summarization as a sequence labeling or scoring problem to solve it with variant of recurrent neural networks (RNNs). Although RNNs efficiently captures long-range dependencies among frames, the operations of RNNs are applied repeatedly, propagating signals progressively through the frames. It causes optimization difficulties that need to be carefully addressed [9], as well as multihop dependency modeling, which makes it difficult to deliver messages back and forth [34]. To tackle these limitations, Rochan *et al.* [30] proposed fully convolutional sequence networks (SUM-FCN), in which video summarization is considered as a sequence labeling problem. However, it inevitably neglects semantic relevance between keyframes with varying time distances.

Graphical models have been used to specifically model semantic interactions [2,11,16,17,25,39]. These approaches have been recently revisited with graph convolutional networks (GCNs) [16], which generalize convolutions from grid-like data to non-grid structures. GCNs have therefore been the subject of increasing interest in various computer vision applications, such as object detection [38], video classification [35], video object tracking [5], and action localization [39]. These works model knowledge graphs based on the relationships between different entities, such as images, objects, and proposals. Although GCNs have shown promising results, they generally use a fixed graph directly obtained from the affinity of feature representations [12], where nodes are strongly connected when they have similar entities. These approaches are therefore difficult to be directly employed for video summarization. It requires to

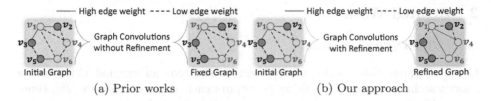

Fig. 2. Comparison of our approach with prior works using GCNs. The red circle and black circle represent node features of keyframes and background, respectively: (a) methods using GCNs without graph refinement and (b) SumGraph, which refines an initial graph by recursively estimating the graph. With the graph refinement, Sum-Graph leverages semantic relationships. (Color figure online)

extract the comprehensive semantic relationships between frames which identify the connections of the whole story in the video to infer the summary.

In this paper, we cast video summarization as a relation graph modeling problem. We present a novel framework, referred as SumGraph, to incorporate the advantages of graph modeling into a deep learning framework, which is suited to the modeling of frame-to-frame interactions. As illustrated in Fig. 1, we regard a video frame as a node of a relation graph. Nodes are connected by edges representing semantic affinities between nodes to represent the relationships over frames in a video. If a node is included in a summary, it is connected to other keyframe nodes with high affinity weights, so that the semantic connections between frames can be modeled through graph convolutions. We additionally formulate SumGraph to recursively estimate the relation graph, which is used for iterative reasoning of graph representations. As shown in Fig. 2, our approach leverages semantic relationships between nodes by recursively estimating and refining the relation graph. In contrast to prior works using a fixed graph without refinement, SumGraph enhances the graph and refines the feature representations according to the updated graph. The proposed method is extensively examined through an ablation study, and comparison with previous methods in both a supervised and an unsupervised manner on two benchmarks including SumMe [8] and TVSum [31].

Our contributions are as follow:

- To the best of our knowledge, this work is the first attempt to exploit deep graph modeling to perform relationship reasoning between frames for video summarization.
- Our model recursively refines the relation graph to obtain the optimal relation graph of an input video, and leverages the estimated graph to classify whether a node is a keyframe.
- The experimental results show that the presented approach achieves state-of-the-art performance in both supervised and unsupervised manner.

2   Related Work

2.1   Video Summarization

Given an input video, video summarization shortens an original video into a short watchable synopsis, resulting in outputs such as video synopses [28], time-lapses [13,26], montages [14,32], or storyboards [6,7]. Early video summarization relied primarily on handcrafted criteria [14,18–20,22,27], including importance, relevance, representativeness and diversity to produce a summary video.

Deep networks have recently been applied with considerable success, CNN based approaches have made significant progress [30,41,42]. Recurrent models are widely used for video summarization capturing variable range dependencies between frames [41,42]. Although recurrent network based approaches have been applied to video data, recurrent operations are sequential, limiting the processing all the frames simultaneously. To overcome this limitation, Rochan *et al.* [30] considered video summarization as a binary label prediction problem, by establishing a connection between semantic segmentation and video summarization. However, consideration of modeling the relationship amongst frames, which provides significant cues as to how best to summarize the video, is not addressed in these approaches. Fajtl *et al.* [4] proposed a self-attention based video summarization method that modeled pairwise relations between frames. While they showed significant performance improvements, they considered visual similarity only without considering semantic similarity (*i.e.*, keyframe and background).

Existing methods have been extended into an unsupervised training scheme [21,29,37]. Mahasseni *et al.* [21] extended an LSTM based framework with a discriminator network without human annotated summary videos. Their frame selector uses a variational auto encoder LSTM to decode the output for reconstruction through selected frames, and the discriminator is an other LSTM network that learns to distinguish between the input video and its reconstruction. Rochan *et al.* [29] trained a network from unpaired data using adversarial learning. While He *et al.* [10] produced weighted frame features to predict importance scores with attentive conditional GANs, Yuan *et al.* [37] proposed a cycle consistent learning objective to relieve the difficulty of unsupervised learning. Although these approaches resolved the problem of insufficient data, the locality of recurrent and convolutional operations, which does not directly compute relevance between any two frames, is still problematic.

2.2   Graphical Models

Our notion of modeling a graph from video is partly related to recent research in graphical models. One popular direction is using conditional random fields (CRF) [17], especially for semantic segmentation [2,17], where the CRF model is applied to all pairs of pixels in an image to infer mean-field with high confidence.

An attempt at modeling pairwise spatiotemporal relations has been made in the non-local neural networks [34]. However, the model is not explicitly defined on graphs. Moreover, the non-local operator is applied to every pixel in the

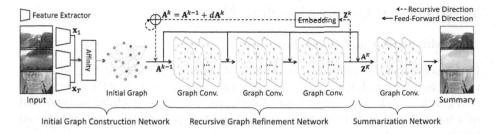

Fig. 3. Network configuration of SumGraph, consisting of a initial graph construction network, recursive graph refinement network, and summarization network in a recurrent structure.

feature space, from lower to higher layers incurring a high computational cost. Graph convolutional networks (GCNs) [16] have been used in several areas of computer vision such as skeleton-based action recognition [36], video classification [11,35], visual object tracking [5], and temporal action localization [39]. They have demonstrated the effectiveness of GCNs by exploiting the relations between input data, and have shown satisfactory performance on each task. However, an initial graph obtained directly from the affinity of input feature representations is suboptimal graph [12]. Rather than using the initially obtained graph as a fixed form in GCNs, we recursively refine the graph model by learning the relationship between keyframes to obtain the optimal relation graph.

3   Preliminaries

Here we present a brief review of GCNs [16]. Given a graph $\mathcal{G}$ represented by a tuple $\mathcal{G} = (\mathcal{V}, \mathcal{E})$ where $\mathcal{V}$ is the set of unordered vertices and $\mathcal{E}$ is the set of edges representing the connectivity between vertices $v \in \mathcal{V}$. GCNs aim to extract richer features at a vertex by aggregating the features of vertices from its neighborhood. The vertices v_i and v_j are connected to each other with an edge $e_{ij} \in \mathcal{E}$. GCNs represent vertices by associating each vertex v with a feature representation h_v. The adjacency matrix $\mathbf{A}$ is derived as a $T \times T$ matrix with $A_{ij} = 1$ if $e_{ij} \in \mathcal{E}$, and $A_{ij} = 0$ if $e_{ij} \notin \mathcal{E}$.

In standard GCNs, the output of the graph convolution operation is as follows:

$$\mathbf{Z} = \sigma(\mathbf{D}^{-1/2}\hat{\mathbf{A}}\mathbf{D}^{-1/2}\mathbf{X}\mathbf{W}), \tag{1}$$

where $\sigma(\cdot)$ denotes an activation function such as the ReLU, $\mathbf{X}$ and $\mathbf{Z}$ are input and output features, $\hat{\mathbf{A}} = \mathbf{A} + \mathbf{I}$, where $\mathbf{I}$ is the identity matrix, $\mathbf{D}$ is a diagonal matrix in which a diagonal entry is the sum of the row elements of $\hat{\mathbf{A}}$, and $\mathbf{W}$ is a trainable weight matrix in the graph convolution layer, respectively. Given the graph representation, we can perform reasoning on the graph by applying the GCNs, rather than applying CNNs or RNNs, which have limited capability to represent relationships between features.

4   Recursive Graph Modeling Networks

4.1   Motivation and Overview

In this section, we describe the formulation of recursive graph modeling networks, termed SumGraph. Inspired by [22], our networks learn to model the input video as a graph $\mathcal{G} = (\mathcal{V}, \mathcal{E})$ to select a set of keyframes, $\mathcal{S}$, where each frame is treated as a node, $v \in \mathcal{V}$, and each edge, $e \in \mathcal{E}$, is used to represent the relation between frames.

In conventional GCNs, the input graph is constructed and fixed through input data with explicit graphical modeling. However, we seek to iteratively refine an initial graph in order that the nodes are connected by the story of the video, not the similarity between entities. To realize this, we formulate recursive graph modeling networks which gradually complete the optimal graph, by repeatedly estimating the adjacency matrix $\mathbf{A}$. Our networks are split into three parts, including an *initial graph construction network* to build the initial graph $\mathcal{G}$, a *recursive graph refinement network* to infer the optimal graph incorporating the semantic relationships between frames, and a *summarization network* to classify the node features into keyframes for the summary video, as shown in Fig. 3.

4.2   Network Architecture

Initial Graph Construction Network. To obtain an initial graph, we first compute the affinity between every pair of frame features. The edge weights of the initial graph are set using the affinity scores. The affinity between two frame features is computed as their cosine similarity:

$$f(\mathbf{x}_i, \mathbf{x}_j) = \frac{\mathbf{x}_i^T \mathbf{x}_j}{||\mathbf{x}_i||_2 \cdot ||\mathbf{x}_j||_2}, \tag{2}$$

where $\mathbf{x} \in \mathbf{X}$ is a node feature of $\mathcal{V}$. We assign $f(\mathbf{x}_i, \mathbf{x}_j)$ to the (i,j)-th entry in the adjacency matrix of the initial graph $\mathbf{A}^0$. The initial graph is passed to a subsequent graph convolution layer with input feature $\mathbf{X}$,

$$\mathbf{X}^0 = \sigma(\tilde{\mathbf{A}}^0 \mathbf{X} \mathbf{W}_C), \tag{3}$$

where $\tilde{\mathbf{A}} = \mathbf{D}^{-1/2}(\mathbf{A} + \mathbf{I})\mathbf{D}^{-1/2}$ and $\mathbf{W}_C$ is the learnable weight matrix of the graph convolution layer. The output of the graph convolution layer is an aggregated feature from its neighborhoods for each node. We denote the node number as T, thus the adjacency matrix dimension has dimensionality $T \times T$.

Recursive Graph Refinement Network. Constructing edges by linking all frames with each other will aggregate the redundant and noisy information for video summarization. Therefore, the connection between semantically unrelated frames should be disconnected. Formally, given the graph and features, an intermediate feature denoted as $\mathbf{Z}^k$ is extracted by a feed-forward graph convolution process such that, $\mathbf{Z}^k = \mathcal{F}(\mathbf{Z}^{k-1}, \mathbf{A}^{k-1} | \mathbf{W}_R)$ with the network parameters

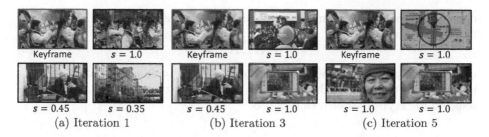

(a) Iteration 1   (b) Iteration 3   (c) Iteration 5

Fig. 4. Convergence of SumGraph: Frames which have top3 affinity value with a selected keyframe at (a) iteration 1; (b) iteration 3; and (c) iteration 5, where s denotes the normalized and averaged user-annotated importance scores which range from 0 to 1. As the graph refinement repeats in SumGraph, the keyframes are progressively connected with high affinity value.

$\mathbf{W}_R$. The recursive graph refinement network repeatedly estimates the residual between the previous and current adjacency matrix as

$$\mathbf{A}^k - \mathbf{A}^{k-1} = d\mathbf{A}^k$$
$$= \frac{(\mathbf{W}_\theta \mathbf{Z}^k)^T (\mathbf{W}_\phi \mathbf{Z}^k)}{||\mathbf{W}_\theta \mathbf{Z}^k||_2 \cdot ||\mathbf{W}_\phi \mathbf{Z}^k||_2}, \tag{4}$$

where $\mathbf{W}_\theta$ and $\mathbf{W}_\phi$ are two different weight matrices to be learned in the network, that enable to compute the affinity in a linear embedding space. The final adjacency matrix is then estimated in a recurrent manner as follows:

$$\mathbf{A}^K = \mathbf{A}^0 + \sum_{k=1}^{K} d\mathbf{A}^k, \tag{5}$$

where K denotes the maximum iteration and $\mathbf{A}^0$ is an initial adjacency matrix from the initial graph construction network.

In contrast to [35], in which the affinity scores of input features were considered as a fixed adjacency matrix, we obtain the optimal adjacency matrix using an iterative refinement procedure with output feature representations. Repeatedly inferring the residuals of the adjacency matrix facilitates fast convergence for video summarization. Moreover, frames initially connected by the visual similarity are progressively linked into the subset of frames based on the semantic connection. As shown in Fig. 4, the edge weights between semantically connected frames (i.e., keyframes) become progressively higher through iterative estimation.

Summarization Network. As illustrated in Fig. 3, the updated node features of the refined optimal graph after the recursive graph refinement network are fed into a summarization network for graph reasoning. Our final goal is to classify each node in the optimal graph that is linked by the semantic relationships between frames. We append a graph convolutional layer, followed by a sigmoid operation to obtain a summary score $\mathbf{Y}$ indicating whether each node is included in summary such that:

$$\mathbf{Y} = \mathcal{F}(\mathbf{Z}^K, \mathbf{A}^K | \mathbf{W}_S) \tag{6}$$

with matrix parameters $\mathbf{W}_S$. Similar to the binary node classification tasks, if the summary score of each node $y_i \in \mathbf{Y}$ is higher than 0.5, the i-th node is selected for keyframes such that $v_i \in \mathcal{S}$.

4.3   Loss Functions

To deal with the imbalance between the number of keyframes and the number of background frames, we design two loss functions., node classification loss and sparsity loss. We define node classification loss as a weighted binary cross entropy loss for supervised learning [30]:

$$\mathcal{L}_c = -\frac{1}{T} \sum_{t=1}^{T} w_t [y_t^* \log(y_t) + (1 - y_t^*) \log(1 - y_t)], \tag{7}$$

where y_t^* is the groundtruth label of the t-th frame. Each node is weighted by $w_t = median\_freq/freq(c)$ for the t-th frame. In our work, $freq(c)$ is $\frac{|\mathcal{S}_v|}{T}$ for keyframes and $1 - \frac{|\mathcal{S}_v|}{T}$ for background, where $|\mathcal{S}_v|$ is the number of keyframes in video v. Since the number of classes is 2 (keyframe or not), $median\_freq$ is set to 0.5.

In practice, a long video can be summarized into a sparse subset of keyframes. Based on this intuition, SumGraph learns parameters with which to construct sparse connections between graph nodes for video summarization. To enforce this constraint, the sparsity loss is given by an L_1 normalization that measures the sparsity of node connections on the final adjacency graph as follows [23]:

$$\mathcal{L}_s = \sum_{i=1}^{T} \sum_{j=1}^{T} ||a_{ij}||_1, \tag{8}$$

where $a_{ij} \in \mathbf{A}^K$ is the affinity between two nodes, v_i and v_j.

For diverse keyframe selection [30,41], we use additional loss functions such as reconstruction and diversity loss. We apply additional graph convolutions to selected keyframes $\mathbf{Y}_\mathcal{S}$ to reconstruct the original features $\mathbf{X}_\mathcal{S}$. We use two graph convolution layers so that the dimensionality of the reconstructed features is the same as that of the original features. The reconstruction loss $\mathcal{L}_r$ is defined as the mean squared error between the reconstructed features and the original features, such that:

$$\mathcal{L}_r = \frac{1}{|\mathcal{S}|} \sum_{i \in \mathcal{S}} ||\mathbf{x}_i - \hat{\mathbf{y}}_i||_2^2, \tag{9}$$

where $\hat{\mathbf{y}}$ denotes the reconstructed features.

Table 1. Comparison of our algorithm with other recent supervised techniques on the SumMe [8] and TVSum [31] datasets, with various data configurations including standard data, augmented data, and transfer data settings.

Method	SumMe			TVSum		
	Standard	Augment	Transfer	Standard	Augment	Transfer
Zhang et al. [40]	40.9	41.3	38.5	–	–	–
Zhang et al. [41]	38.6	42.9	41.8	54.7	59.6	58.7
Mahasseni et al. [21] (SUM-GAN$_{sup}$)	41.7	43.6	–	56.3	61.2	–
Rochan et al. [30] (SUM-FCN)	47.5	51.1	44.1	56.8	59.2	58.2
Rochan et al. [30] (SUM-DeepLab)	48.8	50.2	45.0	58.4	59.1	57.4
Zhou et al. [44]	42.1	43.9	42.6	58.1	59.8	58.9
Zhang et al. [42]	–	44.9	–	–	63.9	–
Fajtl et al. [4]	49.7	51.1	–	61.4	62.4	–
Rochan et al. [29]	–	48.0	41.6	–	56.1	55.7
He et al. [10]	47.2	–	–	59.4	–	–
Ours	**51.4**	**52.9**	**48.7**	**63.9**	**65.8**	**60.5**

Table 2. Comparison of our algorithm with other recent unsupervised techniques on the SumMe [8] and TVSum [31] datasets with standard data, augmented data, and transfer data configurations.

Method	SumMe			TVSum		
	Standard	Augment	Transfer	Standard	Augment	Transfer
Mahasseni et al. [21]	39.1	43.4	–	51.7	59.5	–
Yuan et al. [37]	41.9	–	–	57.6	–	–
Rochan et al. [30] (SUM-FCN$_{unsup}$)	41.5	–	39.5	52.7	–	–
Rochan et al. [29]	47.5	–	41.6	55.6	–	55.7
He et al. [10]	46.0	47.0	44.5	58.5	58.9	**57.8**
Ours	**49.8**	**52.1**	**47.0**	**59.3**	**61.2**	57.6

From [29, 30], we employ a repelling regularizer [43] as the diversity loss, $\mathcal{L}_d$, to enforce the diversity of selected keyframes:

$$\mathcal{L}_d = \frac{1}{|\mathcal{S}|(|\mathcal{S}| - 1)} \sum_{i \in \mathcal{S}} \sum_{j \in \mathcal{S}, j \neq i} f(\hat{\mathbf{z}}_i, \hat{\mathbf{z}}_j), \tag{10}$$

where $f(\cdot)$ is the affinity function in (2), $\hat{\mathbf{z}}_i$ and $\hat{\mathbf{z}}_j$ denote the reconstructed feature vectors of the i-th and j-th node.

The final loss function for supervised learning is then,

$$\mathcal{L}_{sup} = \mathcal{L}_c + \lambda \cdot \mathcal{L}_s + \alpha \cdot \mathcal{L}_d + \beta \cdot \mathcal{L}_r, \tag{11}$$

where λ, α and β control the trade-off between the four loss functions. The graph modeling scheme in SumGraph has also been extended for unsupervised video summarization with simple modifications to the loss functions. Since the

Table 3. Summarization performance (%) on the SumMe [8] and TVSum [31] in terms of three standard metrics: Precision, Recall, and F-score. † denotes an unsupervised method and ‡ denotes supervised method. * is taken from [29].

Method	SumMe			TVSum		
	Precision	Recall	F-score	Precision	Recall	F-score
Rochan *et al.* [30]†* (SUM-FCN$_{unsup}$)	43.9	46.2	44.8	59.1	49.1	53.6
Rochan *et al.* [29]†* (UnpairedVSN)	46.3	49.4	46.5	61.1	50.9	55.6
Rochan *et al.* [29]‡* (UnpairedVSN$_{psup}$)	46.7	49.9	48.0	61.7	51.4	56.1
Ours†	48.2	51.1	49.6	59.7	58.9	59.3
Ours‡	**50.6**	**52.3**	**51.4**	**64.3**	**63.5**	**63.9**

Table 4. Kendall's τ [15] and Spearman's ρ [45] correlation coefficients computed on the TVSum benchmark [31].

Method	Kendall's τ	Spearman's ρ
Zhang *et al.* [41]	0.042	0.055
Zhou *et al.* [44]	0.020	0.026
Human	0.177	0.204
Ours	0.094	0.138

groundtruth summary cannot be used for supervision in an unsupervised manner, the final loss function for unsupervised learning is represented as:

$$\mathcal{L}_{unsup} = \mathcal{L}_s + \alpha \cdot \mathcal{L}_d + \beta \cdot \mathcal{L}_r, \tag{12}$$

where α and β are balancing parameters to control the trade-off between the three terms.

5   Experimental Results

5.1   Implementation Details

To train SumGraph, we uniformly sample frames for every video at 2 fps, as described in [41]. For feature extraction, we use the ImageNet-pretrained GoogleNet [33], where the 1024-dimensional activations are extracted from the 'pool5' layer. Note that our feature extraction follows prior work [30, 42], in order to ensure fair comparisons.

Since different datasets provide groundtruth annotations in various formats, we follow [6, 30, 41] to generate single keyframe based annotations. If a frame is selected for summary video, label it 1; otherwise, label it 0. During testing, we follow [30, 41] to convert predicted keyframes to keyshots, to allow fair comparison with other methods.

We train our model for 50 epochs using Adam optimizer with a batch size of 5. The learning rate is set to 10^{-3} and decayed by a factor of 0.1 for every 20 epochs.

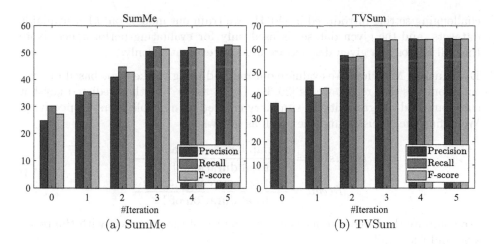

Fig. 5. Convergence analysis with respect to the number of iterations on (a) SumMe benchmark [8] and (b) TVSum benchmark [31].

We set $\lambda = 0.001$, $\alpha = 10$ and $\beta = 1$ in (11) for supervised learning, and $\alpha = 100$ and $\beta = 10$ in (12) for unsupervised learning. The maximum iteration number K is fixed to 5 throughout the ablation study. All experiments are conducted five times on five random splits of the data, and we report the average performance. Details of the implementation and training of our system are provided in the supplemental material. Our code will be made publicly available.

5.2 Experimental Settings

Datasets. We evaluate our approach on two standard video summarization datasets: SumMe [8] and TVSum [31]. SumMe dataset consists of 25 videos capturing multiple events such as cooking and sports, and the lengths of the videos vary from 1.5 to 6.5 min. The TVSum dataset contains 10 categories from the MED task, and samples 5 videos per category from YouTube. The contents of the videos are diverse, similar to SumMe, and the video lengths vary from one to five minutes. Those datasets provide frame-level importance scores annotated by several users. We use additional datasets, the YouTube [3] and the OVP [1] datasets, to augment the training data.

Data Configuration. We conduct experiments using different three data configurations: standard supervision, augmented data setting, and transfer data setting. In standard data setting, the training and testing videos are from the same dataset. We randomly select 20% of videos for testing and the rest of the videos are used for training and validation. For the augmented data setting, we used the other three datasets to augment the training data. By augmenting the training data, recent works [30,42] showed improved performance, and our experimental results derived similar conclusion. In the transfer data setting, which is a more challenging setting introduced in [40,41], we train our models on other available datasets, and the given dataset is used only for evaluating performance. Note that all videos in a given dataset are used for evaluation only.

Evaluation Metrics. We evaluate our method using the keyshot-based metrics commonly used in recent works [29,30]. Let Y and Y^* be the predicted keyshot summary and the groundtruth summary created by multiple users, respectively. We define the precision and the recall as follows:

$$
Precision = \frac{\text{overlap between } Y \text{ and } Y^*}{\text{total duration of } Y},
$$
$$
Recall = \frac{\text{overlap between } Y \text{ and } Y^*}{\text{total duration of } Y^*}
$$

(13)

We compute the F-score to measure the quality of the summary with the precision and the recall:

$$
F\text{-}score = \frac{2 \times Precision \times Recall}{Presion + Recall}.
$$

(14)

For datasets with multiple groundtruth summaries, we follow standard approaches [7,8,41] to calculate the metrics for the videos.

We also evaluate our method using the rank based metrics, Kendall's τ [15] and Spearman's ρ [45] correlation coefficients, following [24]. To compute the correlation coefficients, we first rank the video frames according to their probability of being a keyframe and the annotated importance scores. And we compare the generated ranking with each annotated ranking. The correlation scores are then computed by averaging over the individual results.

5.3   Results

In Table 1, we show our results in comparison to supervised video summarization methods [4,10,21,29,30,40–42] in terms of F-score on the SumMe and TVSum datasets. We observed a significant boost in performance over the state-of-the-art methods in various data configuration settings. Our model achieves state-of-the-art performance of 52.9% on the SumMe and 65.8% on the TVSum datasets in the data augmented setting.

We compare our results trained in an unsupervised manner with recent unsupervised approaches for video summarization [10,21,29–31,37] in Table 2. While the results showed inferior performance to the supervised approaches, the use of our relation graph improved the performance without unpaired data. The results show that our sparsity and diversity losses are sufficient to learn the graphical model for video summarization in unsupervised manner.

Table 3 shows the performance according to precision, recall, and F-score. Our method outperforms supervised approaches for video summarization on all evaluation metrics. Especially, results show that the improvement in recall is greater than the improvement in precision, as SumGraph provides a more accurate summary. Surprisingly, the performance of our unsupervised approach

Table 5. Ablation study for the various combination of loss functions in SumGraph on the TVSum benchmark [31].

Classification	Sparsity	Diversity + Reconstruction	F-Score
✓			62.8
✓	✓		63.6
✓		✓	63.5
✓	✓	✓	63.9

even outperforms the approach using partial supervision (UnpairedVSN$_{psup}$). The comparison studies demonstrate that graphical modeling using SumGraph is an effective approach to the development summary video in comparison with CNNs and RNNs based approaches.

The results for the correlation coefficients are shown in Table 4. We compare our results with those results of two methods, deepLSTM [41] and DR-DSN [44], reported in [24]. Although we use the probabilities of the keyframes, not the importance scores, our model outperforms the existing models by 0.052 for Kendall's τ and 0.083 for Spearman's ρ.

5.4   Ablation Study

Number of Iterations. All ablation studies are investigated with standard supervision configuration with the TVSum benchmark [31]. To validate the effectiveness of the recursively estimate relation graph used in SumGraph, we examined the F-score corresponding to the number of iterations. With increasing numbers of iterations, the accuracies of all evaluation metrics gradually improved. SumGraph converges in three to five iterations as shown in Fig. 5. The additional results of ablation study for the number of iterations are provided in the supplemental material.

Loss Functions. We conducted an additional experiment to investigate the effectiveness of the loss functions. When we trained our model in a supervised manner, four loss terms were employed, classification, sparsity, reconstruction, and diversity losses. The reconstruction loss forces the reconstructed features to be similar to the original features, and the diversity loss enforces the diversity of reconstructed features. We analyzed the effectiveness of the reconstruction and diversity losses together. To verify the effectiveness of each loss function, we applied the diversity and the reconstruction losses, and compared their results in a supervised setting. As shown in Table 5, we observed that both the sparsity loss and the sum of the diversity and the reconstruction loss improve the performance by 0.8% and 0.7%, respectively, on the TVSum benchmark. The full usage of loss functions contributes a performance improvement of 1.1%.

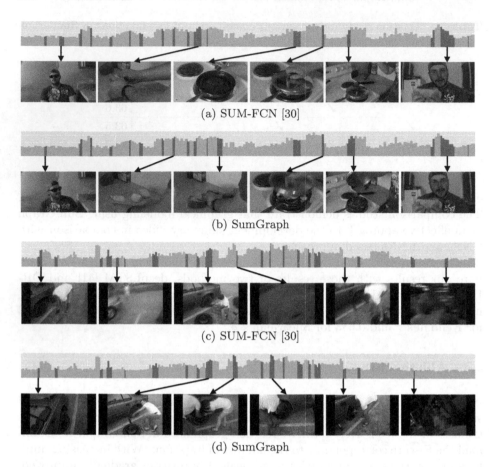

(a) SUM-FCN [30]

(b) SumGraph

(c) SUM-FCN [30]

(d) SumGraph

Fig. 6. Qualitative results on the TVSum benchmark [31]: (a) SUM-FCN [30], (b) SumGraph for video number 18, and (c) SUM-FCN [30], (d) SumGraph for video number 3. Brown bars show frame level user annotation. Red bars are selected subset shots. Best viewed in color. (Color figure online)

5.5   Qualitative Analysis

In Fig. 6, we present the groundtruth importance scores and selected frames produced by [30] and SumGraph. For the visualization of the summaries, we sampled six frames which had been selected for summary. The red bars on brown backgrounds are the frames selected as summaries. The summary generated by SumGraph is visually more diverse, and captures almost all of the peak regions of the groundtruth scores. This observation indicates that SumGraph is able to estimate semantic relationships and connects informative frames for generating optimal and meaningful summaries.

6   Conclusion

In this paper, we have proposed SumGraph to formulate video summarization as a graphical modeling problem. The key idea of our approach is to solve the problem of video summarization by constructing and recursively estimating a relation graph to embed the frame-to-frame semantic interactions. With Sum-Graph, the obtained relation graph is exploited to infer a summary video based on semantic understanding of the whole frames in both supervised and unsupervised fashion. Our model showed significant improvement of performance over other approaches. We hope that the results of this study will facilitate further advances in video summarization and its related tasks.

Acknowledgement. This research was supported by R&D program for Advanced Integrated-intelligence for Identification (AIID) through the National Research Foundation of KOREA(NRF) funded by Ministry of Science and ICT (NRF-2018M3E3A1057289).

References

1. Open video project. https://open-video.org/
2. Chen, L.C., Papandreou, G., Kokkinos, I., Murphy, K., Yuille, A.L.: DeepLab: semantic image segmentation with deep convolutional nets, atrous convolution, and fully connected CRFs. In: TPAMI (2018)
3. De Avila, S.E.F., Lopes, A.P.B., da Luz Jr, A., de Albuquerque Araújo, A.: VSUMM: a mechanism designed to produce static video summaries and a novel evaluation method. Patt. Rec. Lett. **32**(1), 56–68 (2011)
4. Fajtl, J., Sokeh, H.S., Argyriou, V., Monekosso, D., Remagnino, P.: Summarizing videos with attention. In: ACCVW (2018)
5. Gao, J., Zhang, T., Xu, C.: Graph convolutional tracking. In: CVPR (2019)
6. Gong, B., Chao, W.L., Grauman, K., Sha, F.: Diverse sequential subset selection for supervised video summarization. In: NeurIPS (2014)
7. Gygli, M., Grabner, H., Gool, L.V.: Video summarization by learning submodular mixtures of objectives. In: CVPR (2015)
8. Gygli, M., Grabner, H., Riemenschneider, H., Van Gool, L.: Creating summaries from user videos. In: Fleet, D., Pajdla, T., Schiele, B., Tuytelaars, T. (eds.) ECCV 2014. LNCS, vol. 8695, pp. 505–520. Springer, Cham (2014). https://doi.org/10.1007/978-3-319-10584-0_33
9. He, K., Zhang, X., Ren, S., Sun, J.: Deep residual learning for image recognition (2016)
10. He, X., et al.: Unsupervised video summarization with attentive conditional generative adversarial networks. In: ACMMM (2019)
11. Jain, A., Zamir, A.R., Savarese, S., Saxena, A.: Structural-RNN: deep learning on spatio-temporal graphs. In: CVPR (2016)
12. Jiang, B., Zhang, Z., Lin, D., Tang, J., Luo, B.: Semi-supervised learning with graph learning-convolutional networks. In: CVPR (2019)
13. Joshi, N., Kienzle, W., Toelle, M., Uyttendaele, M., Cohen, M.F.: Real-time hyperlapse creation via optimal frame selection. ACM Trans. Graph. **34**(4), 1–9 (2015)

14. Kang, H.W., Matsushita, Y., Tang, X., Chen, X.Q.: Space-time video montage. In: CVPR (2006)
15. Kendall, M.G.: The treatment of ties in ranking problems. Biometrika **33**(3), 239–251 (1945)
16. Kipf, T.N., Welling, M.: Semi-supervised classification with graph convolutional networks. In: ICLR (2017)
17. Krähenbühl, P., Koltun, V.: Efficient inference in fully connected CRFs with gaussian edge potentials. In: NIPS (2011)
18. Lee, Y.J., Ghosh, J., Grauman, K.: Discovering important people and objects for egocentric video summarization. In: CVPR (2012)
19. Liu, T., Kender, J.R.: Optimization algorithms for the selection of key frame sequences of variable length. In: Heyden, A., Sparr, G., Nielsen, M., Johansen, P. (eds.) ECCV 2002. LNCS, vol. 2353, pp. 403–417. Springer, Heidelberg (2002). https://doi.org/10.1007/3-540-47979-1_27
20. Lu, Z., Grauman, K.: Story-driven summarization for egocentric video. In: CVPR (2013)
21. Mahasseni, B., Lam, M., Todorovic, S.: Unsupervised video summarization with adversarial LSTM networks. In: CVPR (2017)
22. Ngo, C.W., Ma, Y.F., Zhang, H.J.: Automatic video summarization by graph modeling. In: ICCV (2003)
23. Nguyen, P., Liu, T., Prasad, G., Han, B.: Weakly supervised action localization by sparse temporal pooling network. In: CVPR (2018)
24. Otani, M., Nakashima, Y., Rahtu, E., Heikkilä, J.: Rethinking the evaluation of video summaries. In: CVPR (2019)
25. Park, J., Lee, J., Jeon, S., Kim, S., Sohn, K.: Graph regularization network with semantic affinity for weakly-supervised temporal action localization. In: ICIP (2019)
26. Poleg, Y., Halperin, T., Arora, C., Peleg, S.: Egosampling: fast-forward and stereo for egocentric videos. In: CVPR (2015)
27. Potapov, D., Douze, M., Harchaoui, Z., Schmid, C.: Category-specific video summarization. In: Fleet, D., Pajdla, T., Schiele, B., Tuytelaars, T. (eds.) ECCV 2014. LNCS, vol. 8694, pp. 540–555. Springer, Cham (2014). https://doi.org/10.1007/978-3-319-10599-4_35
28. Pritch, Y., Rav-Acha, A., Gutman, A., Peleg, S.: Webcam synopsis: peeking around the world. In: ICCV (2007)
29. Rochan, M., Wang, Y.: Video summarization by learning from unpaired data. In: CVPR (2019)
30. Rochan, M., Ye, L., Wang, Y.: Video summarization using fully convolutional sequence networks. In: Ferrari, V., Hebert, M., Sminchisescu, C., Weiss, Y. (eds.) ECCV 2018. LNCS, vol. 11216, pp. 358–374. Springer, Cham (2018). https://doi.org/10.1007/978-3-030-01258-8_22
31. Song, Y., Vallmitjana, J., Stent, A., Jaimes, A.: TVSum: summarizing web videos using titles. In: CVPR (2015)
32. Sun, M., Farhadi, A., Taskar, B., Seitz, S.: Salient montages from unconstrained videos. In: Fleet, D., Pajdla, T., Schiele, B., Tuytelaars, T. (eds.) ECCV 2014. LNCS, vol. 8695, pp. 472–488. Springer, Cham (2014). https://doi.org/10.1007/978-3-319-10584-0_31
33. Szegedy, C., et al.: Going deeper with convolutions. In: CVPR (2015)
34. Wang, X., Girshick, R., Gupta, A., He, K.: Non-local neural networks. In: CVPR (2018)

35. Wang, X., Gupta, A.: Videos as space-time region graphs. In: Ferrari, V., Hebert, M., Sminchisescu, C., Weiss, Y. (eds.) ECCV 2018. LNCS, vol. 11209, pp. 413–431. Springer, Cham (2018). https://doi.org/10.1007/978-3-030-01228-1_25
36. Yan, S., Xiong, Y., Lin, D.: Spatial temporal graph convolutional networks for skeleton-based action recognition. In: AAAI (2018)
37. Yuan, L., Tay, F.E., Li, P., Zhou, L., Feng, J.: Cycle-sum: cycle-consistent adversarial LSTM networks for unsupervised video summarization. In: AAAI (2019)
38. Yuan, Y., Liang, X., Wang, X., Yeung, D.Y., Gupta, A.: Temporal dynamic graph LSTM for action-driven video object detection. In: ICCV (2017)
39. Zeng, R., et al.: Graph convolutional networks for temporal action localization. In: ICCV (2019)
40. Zhang, K., Chao, W.L., Sha, F., Grauman, K.: Summary transfer: examplar-based subset selection for video summarization. In: CVPR (2016)
41. Zhang, K., Chao, W.-L., Sha, F., Grauman, K.: Video summarization with long short-term memory. In: Leibe, B., Matas, J., Sebe, N., Welling, M. (eds.) ECCV 2016. LNCS, vol. 9911, pp. 766–782. Springer, Cham (2016). https://doi.org/10.1007/978-3-319-46478-7_47
42. Zhang, K., Grauman, K., Sha, F.: Retrospective encoders for video summarization. In: Ferrari, V., Hebert, M., Sminchisescu, C., Weiss, Y. (eds.) ECCV 2018. LNCS, vol. 11212, pp. 391–408. Springer, Cham (2018). https://doi.org/10.1007/978-3-030-01237-3_24
43. Zhao, B., Li, X., Lu, X.: Hierarchical recurrent neural network for video summarization. In: ACMMM (2017)
44. Zhou, K., Qiao, Y., Xiang, T.: Deep reinforcement learning for unsupervised video summarization with diversity-representativeness reward. In: AAAI (2018)
45. Zwillinger, D., Kokoska, S.: CRC Standard Probability and Statistics Tables and Formulae. CRC Press (1999)

Feature Normalized Knowledge Distillation for Image Classification

Kunran Xu[1], Lai Rui[1(✉)], Yishi Li[1], and Lin Gu[2,3]

[1] School of Microelectronics, Xidian University, Xi'an, Shaanxi 710071, China
aazzttcc@gmail.com , rlai@mail.xidian.edu.cn , yshlee1994@outlook.com
[2] RIKEN AIP, Tokyo 103-0027, Japan
lin.gu@riken.jp
[3] The University of Tokyo, Tokyo, Japan

Abstract. Knowledge Distillation (KD) transfers the knowledge from a cumbersome teacher model to a lightweight student network. Since a single image may reasonably relate to several categories, the one-hot label would inevitably introduce the encoding noise. From this perspective, we systematically analyze the distillation mechanism and demonstrate that the L_2-norm of the feature in penultimate layer would be too large under the influence of label noise, and the temperature T in KD could be regarded as a correction factor for L_2-norm to suppress the impact of noise. Noticing different samples suffer from varying intensities of label noise, we further propose a simple yet effective feature normalized knowledge distillation which introduces the sample specific correction factor to replace the unified temperature T for better reducing the impact of noise. Extensive experiments show that the proposed method surpasses standard KD as well as self-distillation significantly on Cifar-100, CUB-200-2011 and Stanford Cars datasets. The codes are in https://github.com/aztc/FNKD

Keywords: Label noise · Knowledge distillation · Image classification

1 Introduction

Convolutional Neural Network (CNN) has achieved great success in the field of artificial intelligence in recent years, especially in computer vision [1,2,7,8,10,16,39]. However, this success is accompanied by high inference cost in computation and memory. Many works have devoted to reduce computational complexity, such as model pruning [5,9], lightweight network structure design [12,20,28] and automated architecture search [31,32]. One promising and widely used method for model lightweight is Knowledge Distillation (KD) proposed by Hinton et al. [11], which transfers'dark knowledge' from an ensemble or full model to a single compact model via soft-target cross entropy loss function. Through distillation, student model not only inherits better quality from the teacher, but also be more efficient for inference due to its compactness.

© Springer Nature Switzerland AG 2020
A. Vedaldi et al. (Eds.): ECCV 2020, LNCS 12370, pp. 664–680, 2020.
https://doi.org/10.1007/978-3-030-58595-2_40

Recently, KD has made huge success, some works have extended this effective idea to other application domains [13,18,39], others [17,24,37] improve the standard KD by kinds of techniques such as feature based distillation and achieve better results. Researchers also attempt to seek for better understanding about KD. For example, Lopez-Paz et al. [19] established the connection between KD and privileged information, Yuan et al. [38] regarded KD as an special case of Label Smoothing Regularization (LSD) which imposes constraint on student training and Tang et al. [33] broke down the effects of KD into label smoothing, example re-weighting and prior knowledge of optimal output layer geometry three aspects. In this paper, we systematically analyze the mechanism of temperature in KD from the perspective of label noise and introduce the L_2-norm of the feature in penultimate layer into soft-target to make a further improvement.

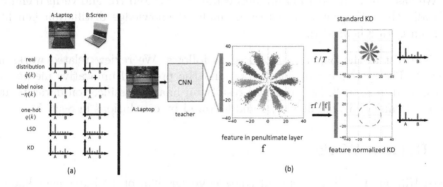

(a)   (b)

Fig. 1. The Overview for this paper. (a) Since there are visual similarities between images, one-hot label which assumes classes are independent can't always accurately describe image's real distribution over classes. The difference between one-hot label and real distribution is a kind of label noise. LSD and KD can provide better supervisions. (b) KD softens the label by reducing the L_2-norm of the feature in penultimate layer with a unified T while our method with a unique $\|\mathbf{f}\|$ for each sample.

Since there are visual similarities between images, one-hot label which assumes classes are independent can't always accurately describe image's real distribution over classes [23], as shown in Fig. 1(a). The difference between one-hot label and real distribution is a kind of label noise and harms model accuracy [6]. From the perspective of label noise, the methods like LSD [30] are actually introducing the priors to reduce this noise. We show that KD could be regarded that the teacher network learns noise information and produces better denoised labels (Fig. 1(a)). Then, we demonstrate that the L_2-norm of the feature in penultimate layer would be too large under the influence of label noise, and the temperature in KD could be regarded as a correction factor for L_2-norm to suppress the impact of noise. Since the L_2-norm also indicates the intensity of label noise, we introduce the L_2-norm into soft-target as the sample specific correction factor to replace the unified temperature T for better reducing the impact of noise (Fig. 1(b)). Finally, we empirically show that our proposed method combines the advantages of both KD and Hypersphere Embedding (HE) [26,35] which is another effective regularization.

In summary, we make the following contributions:

1) We systematically analyzed the mechanism of temperature in Knowledge Distillation from the novel perspective of one-hot label noise and verified that the higher temperature is actually a correction factor for L_2-norm of penultimate layer's feature which represents the intensity of label noise.
2) Based on our theoretical analysis and empirical findings, we proposed a simple yet effective innovative feature normalized KD for further refinement of temperature mechanism. Extensive experiments on image classification datasets support that our proposed method could improve over standard KD.
3) We has shown the relationship between KD, LSD and HE and verified empirically that the proposed feature normalized knowledge distillation benefits from both KD and HE.

The rest of the paper is organized as follows. We review related works in Sect. 2. The systematic demonstration and the proposed innovative method is introduced in Sect. 3. Experimental results on image classification datasets are presented and analyzed in Sect. 4 and followed by conclusions in Sect. 5.

2   Related Works

Since Hinton et al. [11] proposed Knowledge Distillation to implement knowledge transfer, many works have extended this approach to other domains. For example, by introducing KD, Zheng et al. [13] achieved fast and accurate super-resolution with a compact CNN. Zhang et al. [39] distilled the knowledge from multiple image parts into a single model to improve the performance of fine-grained visual classification. Li et al. [18] attempted to learn from noisy data with distillation which transfers the knowledge learned in small clean dataset.

In addition to exploring the application of KD in other fields, another important direction works on further improving the performance of knowledge distillation. Romero et al. [27] suggested that a student model could also imitate intermediate representations (feature maps) learned by teacher model and proposed to distill the knowledge by MSE loss and soft-label loss jointly. Guided by this work, feature based distillation has made impressive developments. Yim et al. [37] demonstrated that learning transform direction between two layers of the teacher model instead of just mimicking the features would be more efficient. Park et al. [24] introduced a novel approach that transfers relational properties of different sample's feature. Sun et al. [29] extended the FITNET [27] to minimise the mean-squared error between each individual layer of the student and teacher, which is effective for BERT model compression.

Except for feature based distillation, there are methods to improve the training procedure. Since KD requires a two-phase training procedure, Lan et al. [17] presented an On-the-fly Native Ensemble model learning strategy for one-stage online distillation to reduce the complexity of training phase. Yang et al. [36] extracted information from earlier epochs in the same generation to enable teacher-student optimization in one generation, which could further improve the efficiency of training. Mirzadeh et al. [21] found the student network performance degrades when the gap between student and teacher is large and introduced an assistant mechanism to bridge the gap.

Despite the large success of knowledge distillation, surprisingly few theoretical research has been done to better understand the mechanism of how it works. Phuong et al. [25] provided the first insights into the working mechanisms of distillation by studying the special case of deep linear classifiers and found three key factors that determine the success of distillation, which is data geometry, optimization bias and strong monotonicity. Müller et al. [22] found the conflict between KD and LSD and argued that the resemblances between instances of different classes is crucial for distillation. Moreover, Tang et al. [33] broke down the effects of KD into label smoothing, example re-weighting and prior knowledge of optimal output layer geometry three aspects which is similar to [25]. The most relevant work to ours is Yuan et al. [38], who also realized the relation ship between KD and LSD, however they did not further reveal the underlying causes of both methods. In addition, we are working on an improved KD while they aimed for a teacher-free framework.

3 Method

In this section, we provide a systematic analyses for the mechanisms behind our proposed method based on theoretical and empirical results. We start by introducing the ubiquitous label noise in one-hot label and analyzing the standard KD from the perspective of label denoising. After that, we propose our feature normalized knowledge distillation based on the finding that the L_2-norm of the feature in penultimate layer is a good estimation for label noise.

3.1 Noise in One-Hot Label

Label noise is a common problem in image classification. As suggested by Benoît [6], label noise has four main classes of potential sources. In this paper, we focus on label encoding noise.

Considering K-way image classification, for a given $\mathbf{x}$, the goal is to learn a parametric mapping function $\sigma(\psi(\mathbf{x}; \theta))$ which generates a class distribution $\mathbf{p}(k|\mathbf{x})$ to estimate the real distribution $\hat{\mathbf{q}}(k|\mathbf{x})$, where $k \in \{1...K\}$, σ is the *softmax* normalized function and $\psi(\mathbf{x}; \theta)$ denotes the CNN consisting of stacked convolution, pooling, relu, etc. In most cases, we don't know $\hat{\mathbf{q}}(k)$ exactly and use the ont-hot encoded label $\mathbf{q}(k) = \left\{ \begin{smallmatrix} 1 & k=t \\ 0 & k \neq t \end{smallmatrix} \right.$ to approximate it, where t is the ground-truth class of $\mathbf{x}$ and we omit $\mathbf{x}$ in conditional distribution for simplicity. However, the approximation by $\mathbf{q}(k)$ would introduce label noise. Here, we show some examples from datasets CUB-200-2011 [34] and ImageNet [4] in Fig. 2. From the top row, we can see that although images in "Black footed Albatross" are very similar to those in "Sooty Albatross", the probabilities that they are in class "Sooty Albatross" are still assigned 0 by one-hot label. In addition, the class "Black footed Albatross" looks much closer to "Sooty Albatross" than "Pileated Woodpecker", but one-hot label makes these two classes have the same "distance" to "Sooty Albatross". These phenomenons are more salient in ImageNet which contains 1000 categories with more visually similar subclasses. For instance, the images of the middle bottom row in Fig. 2 could be classified as either "Laptop Computer" or "Screen CRT", however, they are eventually assigned a hundred percent probability of being in category "Laptop Computer" out of some subjective reasons. This phenomenon is serious and common in this dataset.

Fig. 2. The visual examples for label noise. From the top row, we could see that although images belonging to "Black footed Albatross" are very similar to images of "Sooty Albatross", the probability that they are in class "Sooty Albatross" is still assigned 0 by one-hot label. The class "Black footed Albatross" looks much closer to "Sooty Albatross" than "Pileated Woodpecker", but these three classes have the same "distance" to each other hypothesized by one-hot label. Similar situation would be observed in the ImageNet.

According to the above analysis, we could see that one-hot label assumes that categories are independent of each other and every $\mathbf{x}$ has no correlation to non ground-truth classes. However, images belonging to different classes often have much visual similarities even though they are semantically independent. Therefore, the strong hypothesis of one-hot label will bring about noise between $\hat{\mathbf{q}}(k)$ and $\mathbf{q}(k)$ (Fig. 1(a)). In view of this, we introduce a compensation distribution $\eta(k)$ and let

$$\hat{\mathbf{q}}(k) = \mathbf{q}(k) + \eta(k). \tag{1}$$

The $-\eta(k)$ could be used to represent the noise caused by one-hot label, as shown in Fig. 1(a). Although datasets with one-hot label often contain noise, it is still difficult to find a more precise estimation for $\hat{\mathbf{q}}(k)$ than $\mathbf{q}(k)$ manually. So, the noise $-\eta(k)$ would be present widely to varying degrees and causes some troubles such as over-fitting.

In addition to qualitative analysis above, we perform a simple experiment on CUB-200-2011 to quantitatively measure the impact of label noise on model accuracy. Although we don't know the true $\hat{\mathbf{q}}(k)$ so the real noise $-\eta(k)$ can't be obtained, we can still introduce some priors to estimate it just like Label Smoothing Regularization (LSD) [30]. LSD is an effective regularization that softens one-hot label by mixing $\mathbf{q}(k)$ with an uniform distribution $u(k)$, which is mathematically formulated as

$$\mathbf{q}_{lsd}(k) = (1 - \epsilon_1)\mathbf{q}(k) + \epsilon_1 u(k), \tag{2}$$

where $\mathbf{q}_{lsd}(k)$ is the modified label and ϵ_1 controls its smoothness. Comparing Eq. 2 and Eq. 1, we can regard $\frac{\epsilon_1}{1-\epsilon_1}u(k)$ as an estimation for $\eta(k)$, so the LSD is actually a label denoising approach by using isotropic filtering to produce a distribution approximating $\hat{\mathbf{q}}(k)$. Considering that most images exhibit varying degrees of visual similarities within each category instead of uniform diversities hypothesized by LSD, we present an anisotropic LSD which introduces another non-uniform distribution $\rho(k)$ to estimate $\hat{\mathbf{q}}(k)$ better. The anisotropic LSD label $\mathbf{q}_{alsd}(k)$ can be expressed as:

$$\mathbf{q}_{alsd}(k) = (1 - \epsilon_1 - \epsilon_2)\mathbf{q}(k) + \epsilon_1 u(k) + \epsilon_2 \rho(k)$$
$$\rho(k) = \begin{cases} 1/|\mathcal{A}(\mathbf{x})| & k \in \mathcal{A}(\mathbf{x}), \\ 0 & k \notin \mathcal{A}(\mathbf{x}), \end{cases} \tag{3}$$

where $\mathcal{A}(\mathbf{x})$ denotes the set containing classes more 'closer' to the ground-truth class of $\mathbf{x}$. $\mathcal{A}(\mathbf{x})$ is decided by category's name provided by the dataset. For instance, CUB-200-2011 contains 5 different species of "Woodpecker", so the probability for each "Woodpecker" subclass will be $\epsilon_1/5$ more than other non ground-truth classes. Due to the introduction of meta-information about categories, we could presume that $\mathbf{q}_{alsd}(k)$ is a better estimation for $\hat{\mathbf{q}}(k)$ than $\mathbf{q}_{lsd}(k)$ and will result in higher model accuracy.

To verify this, we use LSD and anisotropic LSD with $\epsilon_1 = 0.2$ and $\epsilon_2 = 0.02$ to train Resnet [10] and then compare their performance as shown in Table 1. As expected, LSD outperforms one-hot label in terms of accuracy significantly which is consistent with that reporterd by Szegedy et al. [30], our anisotropic LSD further improves by introducing more information about $\hat{\mathbf{q}}(k)$. This experiment indicates that the noise in one-hot label indeed causes a decline in model accuracy, as the estimation for $\eta(k)$ becomes more accurate, we would obtain a more 'clean' target to alleviate the problem caused by one-hot label. Seeing that LSD suppresses label noise via a pre-defined prior, we argue that learning from data is another way to estimate the real distribution $\hat{\mathbf{q}}(k)$. In the following section, we will explain that KD is actually one of such methods.

3.2 Standard Knowledge Distillation

As suggested by Li et al. [38], KD is a special case of LSR. In this section, we will further discuss their relationship from the perspective of label denoising and argue that the teacher in KD provides a more accurate estimation for label noise,

Table 1. Training different architectures with different labels. LSD denotes the Label Smoothing Regularization and anisotropic LSD is its improved version. These two labels could be regarded as the denoised versions of original one-hot label and achieve much better model accuracy, which indicates that the noise in one-hot label have serious impact on model training. The last row shows the results of training by KD with a Resnet50 teacher and a Resnet152 teacher respectively.

Label	Resnet18 [10]	Resnet50 [10]
One-hot label	77.23	83.49
LSD [30]	77.85	84.05
Anisotropy LSD	78.21	84.45
KD $T = 1$	79.46	85.78

so KD could obtain a distribution approximating real distribution $\hat{\mathbf{q}}(k)$ better to help promote a student.

A CNN is usually trained by minimizing the cross-entropy loss $\mathcal{H}(\mathbf{q}, \mathbf{p}) = -\sum_{k=1}^{K} \mathbf{q}(k) log(\mathbf{p}(k))$ over the entire datasets. Instead of optimizing the $\mathcal{H}(\mathbf{q}, \mathbf{p})$, KD modified the objective by adding another regularization term. The optimizing objective is generally defined as

$$\mathcal{L}_{kd} = (1 - \alpha)\mathcal{H}(\mathbf{q}, \sigma(\psi(\mathbf{x}; \theta))) + \alpha\mathcal{H}(\mathbf{q}_{kd}, \sigma(\frac{\psi(\mathbf{x}; \theta)}{T})) \tag{4}$$

$$\mathbf{q}_{kd}(k) = \frac{exp(\mathbf{v}_k/T)}{\sum_{i=1}^{K} exp(\mathbf{v}_i/T)}, \tag{5}$$

where $\mathbf{q}_{kd}(k)$ is another label generated by the teacher model based on its logits $\mathbf{v} \in \mathbb{R}^K$ and α controls the balance between two terms. The temperature T introduced by Hinton et al. [11] acts as a factor to smooth both the outputs of teacher and student.

When $T = 1$, the Eq. 4 can be simplified to

$$\mathcal{L}_{kd}^{T=1} = \mathcal{H}(\mathbf{q}_t, \sigma(\psi(\mathbf{x}; \theta))) \tag{6}$$

$$\mathbf{q}_t(k) = (1 - \alpha)\mathbf{q}(k) + \alpha\mathbf{q}_{kd}(k). \tag{7}$$

Comparing Eq. 7 with Eq. 2 and Eq. 3, it is easy to find that these equations have the similar form. This implies that $\mathbf{q}_t(k)$ here plays the same role as $\mathbf{q}_{lsd}(k)$ and $\mathbf{q}_{alsd}(k)$. Based on the discussion above, we argue that $\frac{\alpha}{1-\alpha}\mathbf{q}_{kd}(k)$ is also a estimation for compensation distribution $\eta(k)$ and the only difference is that $u(k)$ and $\rho(k)$ is pre-defined while $\mathbf{q}_{kd}(k)$ is learned by another CNN from data. Therefore, from the perspective of label denoising, both LSD and KD aim to remove noise in one-hot label and produce distributions closer to real distribution $\hat{\mathbf{q}}(k)$. To further compare KD and LSD quantitatively, we use Resnet152 and Resnet50 as teachers to train Resnet50 and Resnet18 respectively using Eq. 6

with $\alpha = 0.5$. As shown in the bottom row in Table 1, KD outperforms LSD and anisotropic LSD with a large margin in both settings, which demonstrates that teacher could learn about label noise from training data and thus provide a better compensation $\mathbf{q}_{kd}(k)$ than the uniform prior $u(k)$.

To further suppress the noise's influence, Hinton et al. [11] introduced an simple yet effective way by raising the temperature T. With T increasing, the distribution computed by Eq. 5 is going to be softer. When $T \gg \mathbf{v}_k$, we can Taylor expand both numerator and denominator in Eq. 5 to approximate $\mathbf{q}_{kd}(k)$ as

$$\mathbf{q}_{kd}(k) \approx \frac{1 + \mathbf{v}_k/T}{K + \sum_i \mathbf{v}_i/T} \approx \frac{1}{K} = u(k). \tag{8}$$

Equation 8 illustrates that as temperature raises, $\mathbf{q}_{kd}(k)$ becomes gradually smooth until perfectly even. Previous works [11,17] have found empirically that a moderate T would yield a better student. From the perspective of label noise, we argue that this is because the $\mathbf{q}_{kd}(k)$ with small T is more noisy due to its less diversity from one-hot label while the higher temperature would filter out much noise's influence and help student better. To make this argument more clear, we will discuss what the logits $\mathbf{v}$ of teacher is and how it is affected by one-hot label noise in the next section.

3.3   Feature in Penultimate Layer

In this section, we will at first show that the L_2-norm of the feature in the penultimate layer could effectively indicate the one-hot label noise. We further demonstrate that the temperature T in KD could be regarded as an correction factor for this noise.

The last layer of a CNN for classification is usually a K-way fully-connected operation. It takes feature $\mathbf{f} \in \mathbb{R}^D$ as input and produces the logits $\mathbf{v}$ by a linear transform $\mathbf{v} = \mathbf{W}\mathbf{f}$, where $\mathbf{W} \in \mathbb{R}^{C \times D}$ is a parameter matrix. Note that

$$\mathbf{v}_i = \mathbf{W}_i \cdot \mathbf{f} = \|\mathbf{f}\| \|\mathbf{W}_i\| \cos(\theta_i), \tag{9}$$

where $\|\cdot\|$ denotes L_2-norm, $\mathbf{v}_i$ is the ith element of $\mathbf{v}$, $\mathbf{W}_i$ is the ith row of matrix $\mathbf{W}$ and θ_i is the angle between vector $\mathbf{f}$ and $\mathbf{W}_i$. Since $\mathbf{f}$ has the same influence on each $\mathbf{v}_i$, if we just want to know the class of a given sample, $\|\mathbf{W}_i\| \cos(\theta_i)$ is sufficient, so what is the role of $\|\mathbf{f}\|$? Wang et al. [35] has proven that a feature $\mathbf{f}$ with bigger L_2-norm could produce a harder distribution and fit one-hot label better. Since a *softmax* loss always encourages examples classified correctly to have higher probability, so the L_2-norm of the feature in penultimate layer would be larger and larger in the training. In brief, the larger the $\|\mathbf{f}\|$ is, the closer the output distribution will be to one-hot label. However, considering the fact that there exists label noise as illustrated above, the real distribution $\hat{\mathbf{q}}(k)$ is actually softer than one-hot label, so large $\|\mathbf{f}\|$ is partially caused by noise and a shorter $\mathbf{f}$ would be more appropriate. Therefore, we can see that why there is a $T > 1$ in KD, in fact, the temperature T could be regarded as an correction factor for L_2-norm, which abates $\|\mathbf{f}\|$ to weaken the impact of label noise.

Since $\|\mathbf{f}\|$ is partially decided by label noise, we argue that the $\|\mathbf{f}\|$ could be used to indicate the noise intensity. To study this empirically, we conduct a experiment on CUB-200-2011 to select three categories and exhibit the images with first two biggest and smallest $\|\mathbf{f}\|$ of each class. As shown in Fig. 3, the images with lower feature L_2-norm have similar angles, illuminations, backgrounds and very alike looking birds. Comparatively speaking, the images with larger $\|\mathbf{f}\|$ looks more characteristic and easier to tell apart. Rajeev [26] performed a similar experiment to divide the images from IJB-A [14] dataset into 3 sets based on the example's $\|\mathbf{f}\|$ and found that the images with smaller $\|\mathbf{f}\|$ have poor quality and are hard for model to classify correctly. These results demonstrate that although one-hot label encourages $\mathbf{f}$ to have large L_2-norm, these hard examples which contain more label noise would still remain relatively small L_2-norm on account of some model priors. Noticing different samples suffer from varying intensities of label noise, we propose a novel feature normalized KD by suppressing noise for each sample according to their L_2-norm instead of an identical T for all samples.

Fig. 3. Images with different feature L_2-norm. The bottom row shows these examples with lower feature L_2-norm, it could be seen that these images have similar angle, illumination, backgrounds and very similar looking birds. Comparatively speaking, the images with larger L_2-norm looks easier to tell apart. It indicates that the $\|\mathbf{f}\|$ could be used to represent the noise intensity in one-hot label.

3.4   Feature Normalized Knowledge Distillation

As previously mentioned, the L_2-norm of examples's feature represents the noise intensity in one-hot label, where the lower L_2-norm indicates stronger noise intensity. Therefore, we propose to weight every sample by the inverse of L_2-norm. With that in mind, we introduce a novel teacher's supervision distribution as

$$\mathbf{q}_{fn}(k) = \frac{exp(\frac{\tau \mathbf{v}_k}{\|\mathbf{f}\|})}{\sum_{i=1}^{K} exp(\frac{\tau \mathbf{v}_i}{\|\mathbf{f}\|})}, \tag{10}$$

where τ is a parameter controlling the smoothness of distribution $\mathbf{q}_{fn}(k)$ like the original temperature T. For students, we let them to compute a similar output following Eq. 10 to mimic the teacher, so the final feature normalized KD learning objective is

$$\mathcal{L}_{fn} = \mathcal{H}(\mathbf{q}, \sigma(\psi(\mathbf{x}; \theta))) + \lambda^2 \mathcal{H}(\mathbf{q}_{fn}, \sigma(\frac{\tau\psi(\mathbf{x}; \theta)}{\|\mathbf{f}\|})), \tag{11}$$

in which we take away the parameter α and add a new weight λ compared to original soft-target cross-entropy loss expressed in Eq. 4. To further illustrate, we compute the loss gradient, $\partial\mathcal{L}_{fn}/\partial\mathbf{z}_k$, with respect to each logit $\mathbf{z}_k$ of the distilled student model. This gradient is given by

$$\begin{aligned} \frac{\partial\mathcal{L}_{fn}}{\partial\mathbf{z}_k} &= \mathbf{p}(k) - \mathbf{q}(k) + \frac{\lambda^2\tau}{\|\mathbf{f}_s\|}(\mathbf{p}_{fn}(k) - \mathbf{q}_{fn}(k)) \\ &= \mathbf{p}(k) - \mathbf{q}(k) + \frac{\lambda^2\tau}{\|\mathbf{f}_s\|}(\frac{exp(\frac{\tau\mathbf{z}_k}{\|\mathbf{f}_s\|})}{\sum_i exp(\frac{\tau\mathbf{z}_i}{\|\mathbf{f}_s\|})} - \frac{exp(\frac{\tau\mathbf{v}_k}{\|\mathbf{f}_t\|})}{\sum_i exp(\frac{\tau\mathbf{v}_i}{\|\mathbf{f}_t\|})}). \end{aligned} \tag{12}$$

Using a similar proof technique as Hinton et al. [11], assuming that $\sum_i \mathbf{z}_i = \sum_i \mathbf{v}_i = 0$ and $\|\mathbf{f}_s\| = \|\mathbf{f}_t\| \gg \tau\mathbf{z}_k$, we Taylor expand both numerator and denominator in the last term and get

$$\frac{\partial\mathcal{L}_{fn}}{\partial\mathbf{z}_k} \approx \mathbf{p}(k) - \mathbf{q}(k) + \frac{\lambda^2\tau^2}{K\|\mathbf{f}_t\|^2}(\mathbf{z}_k - \mathbf{v}_k). \tag{13}$$

It is clear to see that Eq. 13 introduces a teacher's supervision $\mathbf{v}_k$ to balance the influence from the one-hot label and $\|\mathbf{f}_t\|$ helps to control the contribution of $\mathbf{z}_k - \mathbf{v}_k$ which represents how different the student is from teacher.

Comparing Eq. 13 and its counterpart in KD [11], we could find the biggest difference is the presence of $\|\mathbf{f}_t\|$ which assigns each sample a different weights between one-hot label and teacher instead of a same weight given by standard KD. When the noise in $\mathbf{q}(k)$ is strong, $\|\mathbf{f}_t\|$ is going to be small and the impact of $\mathbf{z}_k - \mathbf{v}_k$ will be relatively higher. In turn, if the one-hot label has less noise, $\|\mathbf{f}_t\|^2$ would reduce the effect of teacher to negligible and $\mathbf{p}(k) - \mathbf{q}(k)$ dominates. In brief, the feature normalized KD could determine adaptively how much a student needs to trust the teacher according to the intensity of label noise in examples.

As suggested by Hinton et al. [11], it is important to ensure that the relative contributions of the hard and soft targets remain roughly the same order of magnitude. Therefore, we keep $\lambda^2\tau^2/(\|\bar{\mathbf{f}}_t\|)^2 \approx 1$, where $\|\bar{\mathbf{f}}_t\|$ is the mean over the training set. To fairly compare with standard KD, we then let $\|\bar{\mathbf{f}}_t\|/\tau \approx T$. The specific parameter setting will be introduced in the following experiments section.

4   Experiments

In this section, we will conduct extensive experiments on Cifar-100, Cifar-10, CUB-200-2011 and Stanford Cars datasets to verify the effectiveness of our proposed feature normalized knowledge distillation (KD-fn) for varying image classification tasks. On this basis, we will further compare KD-fn with standard Knowledge Distillation (KD) and Hypersphere Embedding (HE) and discuss the relationship between them.

4.1 Results on Cifar

Cifar-100 and Cifar-10 are two widely studied datasets for image classification, both of which consist of 60000 32 × 32 color images. Cifar-100 involves 20 superclasses, each of which contains 5 subclasses, for a total of 100 classes while Cifar-10 only contains 10 distinct categories. To compare our approach with standard KD, we respectively utilize Resnet110 and Resnet56 as the teacher models to supervise the student models of Resnet56 and Resnet20. All models are trained on a single NVIDIA GeForce 1080Ti GPU using MXNet [3] for 200 epochs on the training set with 128 examples per minibatch, and evaluated on the test set. Learning rates start at 0.1 and are divided by 10 after 100 and 150 epochs for all models. We use SGD optimizer with momentum of 0.9, and weight decay is set to 1e-4. In addition to mean subtraction and standard deviation normalization, no more data augmentation or training strategies are used. We set $\alpha = 0.5$, $T = 3$ for KD and $\tau = 2$, $\lambda = 3$ for our method.

Table 2. Results on Cifar-100 and Ciar-10

Model	Method	Cifar-100	Cifar-10
Resnet56	Teacher	81.73	93.63
Resnet20	Student	78.30	92.11
	KD	80.34	**92.86**
	KD-fn	**81.19**	92.67
Resnet110	Teacher	82.01	94.29
Resnet56	Student	81.73	93.63
	KD	81.82	94.10
	KD-fn	**82.23**	**94.14**

As represented by the scores in Table 2, our proposed KD-fn achieves 81.19% high accuracy with Resnet20 student which surpasses KD with remarkable 0.85% in Cifar-100 set. When Resnet110 is utilized as the teacher, KD only brings student tiny improvement, by contrast, the student trained with KD-fn still achieves a promotion of 0.5% accuracy and even outperforms the teacher surprisingly. In Cifar-10, KD and KD-fn have very similar performances and both of them bring relatively less improvement when compared with results of Cifar-100. According to the description of this dataset, the classes in Cifar-10 are completely mutually exclusive. There is no overlap and less visual similarity between these 10 classes, which means one-hot label is already a good approximation for real distribution

$\hat{q}(k)$ and introduces less noise. Since both KD and KD-fn could be regarded as the method to suppress the noise in label based on our previous discussion, they perform less effectively in Cifar-10 relative to Cifar-100.

4.2 Results on Fine-Grained Visual Categorization

To verify the performance of our proposed KD-fn on fine-grained visual categorization (FGVC) tasks, we conduct experiments on two classical benchmarks of CUB-200-2011 [34] and Stanford Cars [15]. The CUB-200-2011 is a most widely studied bird's classification task with 5994 training images and 5794 test images from 200 wild bird species. It is one of the most competitive datasets since each category has only 30 images for training. The Stanford Cars dataset contains 8,144 training images and 8,041 test images over 196 classes.

During training, we set the batchsize to 72 and the initial learning rate as 0.05 with decay factor of 0.1 after every 30 epochs to train each model for 120 epoches. We use random cropping, brightness jitter and random flip data augmentations which are provided as standard training setting by MXNet [3], please refer to our code for more parameter settings. In the experiments, we set $\alpha = 0.5$, $T = 3$ for KD. Based on the principle of parameter setting discussed in Sect. 3 as well as the experimental result that $\|\mathbf{f}\|$ is roughly 24, we set $\tau = 8$ and $\lambda = 3$.

Considering that subordinate classes share most of the visual characteristics except for subtle differences in particular regions, the images from different classes always have more similarities than that in general image classification. Therefore, the difference between real distribution $\hat{q}(k)$ and one-hot label is much larger, i.e. the noise in one-hot label is stronger. In view of this, we could speculate that both KD and KD-fn would perform more effectively on FGVC datasets. This is supported by our experimental results, Table 3 shows that teacher always brings about much promotion (at least 1.95%) in terms of accuracy, which is consistent with our above speculation. Furthermore, this is also an evidence that the effectiveness of KD is the suppression of one-hot label noise.

It is more noteworthy, the proposed KD-fn outperforms KD in all settings. On the CUB-200-2011 with Resnet18 student and Resnet50 teacher, KD-fn achieves 81.52% accuracy which surpasses the KD with remarkable 1.15%. Although it's a little bit lower increasing (0.79%) of accuracy on Stanford Cars, the student eventually surpasses its teacher significantly. Since distilling the knowledge to a lightweight network is common and important in application, we compare the performance of our proposed method with KD to distill the knowledge from Resnet50 to Mobilenetv2 which is a typical lightweight model. It is obvious that our approach also achieves good results and surpasses KD 0.92% and 0.61% respectively on two datasets, which indicates that our approach also applies across model family. Moreover, we have also tested the performance of our method when there is a big gap between teacher and student. On CUB-200-2011, it can be seen that when changing the teacher model from Resnet50 to Resnet152, the student's accuracy obtained by KD only increases 0.09% while that trained with KD-fn improves 0.4%.

Table 3. Results on CUB-200-2011 and Stanford Cars

Model	Method	CUB-200-2011	Stanford Cars
Resnet50	Teacher	83.30	90.89
Resnet18	Student	77.23	88.10
	KD	80.37	90.74
	KD-fn	**81.52**	**91.53**
Resnet50	Teacher	83.30	90.89
Mobilenetv2	Student	79.53	87.09
	KD	81.48	90.49
	KD-fn	**82.40**	**91.10**
Resnet152	Teacher	83.76	92.13
Mobilenetv2	KD	81.57	90.71
	KD-fn	**82.80**	**91.42**

4.3 Self-distillation

Self-distillation refers to the special KD, where the student and teacher model share the same architecture. The idea is to feed in predictions of the trained model as teacher to provide new target values for retraining itself. When there are constraints on training resources or when it is hard to find a better teacher than the student, self-distillation is an effective option to obtain higher accuracy. From the perspective of label denosing, we argue that since student can also learn knowledge about the noise in one-hot label, it can use this knowledge to suppress the noise's influence and thus improve itself's learning. We compare self KD-fn and self KD on Cifar-100 and CUB-200-2011 with 5 different models. Table 4 shows that self KD-fn surpasses self KD in all settings, which further demonstrates the effectiveness of our proposed method.

Table 4. Results on self-distillation

Dataset	Model	Baseline	self KD	self KD-fn
Cifar-100	Resnet20	78.30	79.48	**80.16**
	Resnet56	81.73	83.33	**83.73**
CUB-200-2011	Resnet18	77.23	79.15	**79.61**
	Resnet50	83.30	83.92	**84.24**
	Mobilenetv2	79.53	80.32	**80.47**

4.4 The Relationship with Hypershpere Embedding

Hypershpere Embedding (HE) [26,35] is a method to restrict the feature of penultimate layer to lie on a hypersphere of a fixed radius, which is prevalent in face verification. The method usually fine-tune a well-trained model using cross-entropy loss with multiplying the L_2-norm of the feature in penultimate layer by $r/\|\mathbf{f}\|, r \in \mathcal{R}$. We directly write the gradient with respect to logit of this method as

$$\frac{\partial \mathcal{L}_{he}}{\partial \mathbf{z}_k} = \frac{r}{\|\mathbf{f}\|}(\mathbf{p}_{he}(k) - \mathbf{q}(k)) \tag{14}$$

where $\mathbf{p}_{he}(k)$ is the output computed following Eq. 10. We can find that this method is similar to KD-fn, which also weights each sample by $\|\mathbf{f}\|$ to pay more attention to those hard examples with much label noise. The difference with our method is that the $\mathbf{p}_{he}(k)$'s objective is still one-hot label while $\mathbf{p}_{fn}(k)$'s objective is another teacher. So, KD-fn combines the strengths of both teacher and $\|\mathbf{f}\|$ at the same time. Table 5 shows the comparison results. Due to the presence of teacher, KD-fn outperforms HE significantly.

Table 5. Comparison to Hypershpere Embedding

Dataset	Model (S+T)	HE (S)	KD-fn (S+T)
Cifar-100	Resnet20+Resnet56	78.96	**81.19**
	Resnet56+Resnet110	81.65	**82.23**
CUB-200-2011	Resnet18+Resnet50	80.25	**81.52**
	Mobilenetv2+Resnet50	80.55	**82.40**

5 Conclusions

In this paper, we propose a simple yet effective feature normalized distillation strategy for image classification. Based on the systematically analysis from the perspective of label denoising, we introduce the L_2-norm of the feature in penultimate layer into soft-target as the sample specific correction factor to replace the unified temperature of KD for better reducing the impact of noise in one-hot label. Comprehensive experiments show that the proposed method surpasses standard KD significantly on Cifar-100, CUB-200-2011 and Stanford Cars datasets.

Acknowledgement. This work was supported in part by the National Key R&D Program of China under Grant 2018YFE0202800, Natural Science Foundation of China (NSFC) (Grant Nos. 61674120, U1709218, 61672131), and JST, ACT-X Grant Number JPMJAX190D, Japan.

References

1. Chen, C., Liu, X., Qiu, T., Sangaiah, A.K.: A short-term traffic prediction model in the vehicular cyber-physical systems. Future Gener. Comput. Syst. **105**, 894–903 (2020)

2. Chen, C.C., Hu, J., Qiu, T.: CVCG: cooperative V2V-aided transmission scheme based on coalitional game for popular content distribution in vehicular ad-hoc networks. IEEE Trans. Mob. Comput. **18**(12), 2811–2828 (2019)
3. Chen, T., et al.: MXNet: a flexible and efficient machine learning library for heterogeneous distributed systems. CoRR abs/1512.01274 (2015)
4. Deng, J., Dong, W., Socher, R., Li, L., Li, K., Li, F.: Imagenet: A large-scale hierarchical image database. In: 2009 IEEE Computer Society Conference on Computer Vision and Pattern Recognition (CVPR 2009), 20–25 June 2009, Miami, Florida, USA. pp. 248–255 (2009)
5. Frankle, J., Carbin, M.: The lottery ticket hypothesis: finding sparse, trainable neural networks. In: 7th International Conference on Learning Representations, ICLR 2019, New Orleans, LA, USA, 6–9 May 2019 (2019)
6. Frénay, B., Verleysen, M.: Classification in the presence of label noise: a survey. IEEE Trans. Neural Netw. Learn. Syst. **25**(5), 845–869 (2014)
7. Guan, J., Lai, R., Xiong, A.: Wavelet deep neural network for stripe noise removal. IEEE Access **7**, 44544–44554 (2019)
8. Guan, J., Lai, R., Xiong, A., Liu, Z., Gu, L.: Fixed pattern noise reduction for infrared images based on cascade residual attention CNN. Neurocomputing **377**, 301–313 (2020)
9. Han, S., Pool, J., Tran, J., Dally, W.J.: Learning both weights and connections for efficient neural network. In: Advances in Neural Information Processing Systems 28: Annual Conference on Neural Information Processing Systems 2015, Montreal, Quebec, Canada, 7–12 December 2015, pp. 1135–1143 (2015)
10. He, K., Zhang, X., Ren, S., Sun, J.: Identity mappings in deep residual networks. In: Leibe, B., Matas, J., Sebe, N., Welling, M. (eds.) ECCV 2016. LNCS, vol. 9908, pp. 630–645. Springer, Cham (2016). https://doi.org/10.1007/978-3-319-46493-0_38
11. Hinton, G.E., Vinyals, O., Dean, J.: Distilling the knowledge in a neural network. CoRR abs/1503.02531 (2015)
12. Howard, A.G., et al.: MobileNets: efficient convolutional neural networks for mobile vision applications. CoRR abs/1704.04861 (2017)
13. Hui, Z., Wang, X., Gao, X.: Fast and accurate single image super-resolution via information distillation network. In: 2018 IEEE Conference on Computer Vision and Pattern Recognition, CVPR 2018, Salt Lake City, UT, USA, 18–22 June 2018, pp. 723–731 (2018)
14. Klare, B.F., et al.: Pushing the frontiers of unconstrained face detection and recognition: IARPA janus benchmark A. In: IEEE Conference on Computer Vision and Pattern Recognition, CVPR 2015, Boston, MA, USA, 7–12 June 2015, pp. 1931–1939 (2015)
15. Krause, J., Stark, M., Deng, J., Fei-Fei, L.: 3D object representations for fine-grained categorization. In: 4th International IEEE Workshop on 3D Representation and Recognition (3dRR-13), Sydney, Australia (2013)
16. Lai, R., Li, Y., Guan, J., Xiong, A.: Multi-scale visual attention deep convolutional neural network for multi-focus image fusion. IEEE Access **7**, 114385–114399 (2019)
17. Lan, X., Zhu, X., Gong, S.: Knowledge distillation by on-the-fly native ensemble. In: Advances in Neural Information Processing Systems 31: Annual Conference on Neural Information Processing Systems 2018, NeurIPS 2018, Montréal, Canada, 3–8 December 2018, pp. 7528–7538 (2018)
18. Li, Y., Yang, J., Song, Y., Cao, L., Luo, J., Li, L.: Learning from noisy labels with distillation. In: IEEE International Conference on Computer Vision, ICCV 2017, Venice, Italy, 22–29 October 2017, pp. 1928–1936 (2017)

19. Lopez-Paz, D., Bottou, L., Schölkopf, B., Vapnik, V.: Unifying distillation and privileged information. In: 4th International Conference on Learning Representations, ICLR 2016, San Juan, Puerto Rico, 2–4 May 2016. Conference Track Proceedings (2016)
20. Ma, N., Zhang, X., Zheng, H.-T., Sun, J.: ShuffleNet V2: practical guidelines for efficient CNN architecture design. In: Ferrari, V., Hebert, M., Sminchisescu, C., Weiss, Y. (eds.) Computer Vision – ECCV 2018. LNCS, vol. 11218, pp. 122–138. Springer, Cham (2018). https://doi.org/10.1007/978-3-030-01264-9_8
21. Mirzadeh, S., Farajtabar, M., Li, A., Ghasemzadeh, H.: Improved knowledge distillation via teacher assistant: bridging the gap between student and teacher. CoRR abs/1902.03393 (2019)
22. Müller, R., Kornblith, S., Hinton, G.E.: When does label smoothing help? In: Advances in Neural Information Processing Systems 32: Annual Conference on Neural Information Processing Systems 2019, NeurIPS 2019, Vancouver, BC, Canada, 8–14 December 2019. pp. 4696–4705 (2019)
23. Murphy, K.P.: Machine Learning - A Probabilistic Perspective. MIT Press, Cambridge (2012)
24. Park, W., Kim, D., Lu, Y., Cho, M.: Relational knowledge distillation. In: IEEE Conference on Computer Vision and Pattern Recognition, CVPR 2019, Long Beach, CA, USA, 16–20 June 2019, pp. 3967–3976 (2019)
25. Phuong, M., Lampert, C.: Towards understanding knowledge distillation. In: Proceedings of the 36th International Conference on Machine Learning, ICML 2019, Long Beach, California, USA, 9–15 June 2019, vol. 97, pp. 5142–5151 (2019)
26. Ranjan, R., Castillo, C.D., Chellappa, R.: L2-constrained softmax loss for discriminative face verification. CoRR abs/1703.09507 (2017)
27. Romero, A., Ballas, N., Kahou, S.E., Chassang, A., Gatta, C., Bengio, Y.: FitNets: hints for thin deep nets. In: 3rd International Conference on Learning Representations, ICLR 2015, San Diego, CA, USA, 7–9 May 2015. Conference Track Proceedings (2015)
28. Sandler, M., Howard, A.G., Zhu, M., Zhmoginov, A., Chen, L.: Mobilenetv 2: Inverted residuals and linear bottlenecks. In: 2018 IEEE Conference on Computer Vision and Pattern Recognition, CVPR 2018, Salt Lake City, UT, USA, 18–22 June 2018, pp. 4510–4520. IEEE Computer Society (2018)
29. Sun, S., Cheng, Y., Gan, Z., Liu, J.: Patient knowledge distillation for BERT model compression. In: Proceedings of the 2019 Conference on Empirical Methods in Natural Language Processing and the 9th International Joint Conference on Natural Language Processing, EMNLP-IJCNLP 2019, Hong Kong, China, 3–7 November 2019, pp. 4322–4331 (2019)
30. Szegedy, C., Vanhoucke, V., Ioffe, S., Shlens, J., Wojna, Z.: Rethinking the inception architecture for computer vision. In: 2016 IEEE Conference on Computer Vision and Pattern Recognition, CVPR 2016, Las Vegas, NV, USA, 27–30 June 2016, pp. 2818–2826 (2016)
31. Tan, M., et al.: MnasNet: platform-aware neural architecture search for mobile. In: IEEE Conference on Computer Vision and Pattern Recognition, CVPR 2019, Long Beach, CA, USA, 16–20 June 2019, pp. 2820–2828 (2019)
32. Tan, M., Le, Q.V.: EfficientNet: rethinking model scaling for convolutional neural networks. In: Proceedings of the 36th International Conference on Machine Learning, ICML 2019, 9–15 June 2019, Long Beach, California, USA, vol. 97, pp. 6105–6114 (2019)
33. Tang, J., et al.: Understanding and improving knowledge distillation. CoRR abs/2002.03532 (2020)

34. Wah, C., Branson, S., Welinder, P., Perona, P., Belongie, S.: The Caltech-UCSD Birds-200-2011 Dataset. Tech. rep. CNS-TR-2011-001, California Institute of Technology (2011)
35. Wang, F., Xiang, X., Cheng, J., Yuille, A.L.: Normface: L_2 hypersphere embedding for face verification. In: Liu, Q., et al. (eds.) Proceedings of the 2017 ACM on Multimedia Conference, MM 2017, Mountain View, CA, USA, 23–27 October 2017, pp. 1041–1049 (2017)
36. Yang, C., Xie, L., Su, C., Yuille, A.L.: Snapshot distillation: Teacher-student optimization in one generation. In: IEEE Conference on Computer Vision and Pattern Recognition, CVPR 2019, Long Beach, CA, USA, 16–20 June 2019, pp. 2859–2868 (2019)
37. Yim, J., Joo, D., Bae, J., Kim, J.: A gift from knowledge distillation: fast optimization, network minimization and transfer learning. In: 2017 IEEE Conference on Computer Vision and Pattern Recognition, CVPR 2017, Honolulu, HI, USA, 21–26 July 2017, pp. 7130–7138 (2017)
38. Yuan, L., Tay, F.E.H., Li, G., Wang, T., Feng, J.: Revisit knowledge distillation: a teacher-free framework. CoRR abs/1909.11723 (2019)
39. Zheng, H., Fu, J., Zha, Z., Luo, J.: Looking for the devil in the details: learning trilinear attention sampling network for fine-grained image recognition. In: IEEE Conference on Computer Vision and Pattern Recognition, CVPR 2019, Long Beach, CA, USA, 16–20 June 2019, pp. 5012–5021 (2019)

A Metric Learning Reality Check

Kevin Musgrave[1($\boxtimes$)], Serge Belongie[1], and Ser-Nam Lim[2]

[1] Cornell Tech, New York City, USA
tkm45@cornell.edu
[2] Facebook AI, New York City, USA

Abstract. Deep metric learning papers from the past four years have consistently claimed great advances in accuracy, often more than doubling the performance of decade-old methods. In this paper, we take a closer look at the field to see if this is actually true. We find flaws in the experimental methodology of numerous metric learning papers, and show that the actual improvements over time have been marginal at best. Code is available at github.com/KevinMusgrave/powerful-benchmarker.

Keyword: Deep metric learning

1 Metric Learning Overview

1.1 Why Metric Learning Is Important

Metric learning attempts to map data to an embedding space, where similar data are close together and dissimilar data are far apart. In general, this can be achieved by means of embedding and classification losses. Embedding losses operate on the relationships between samples in a batch, while classification losses include a weight matrix that transforms the embedding space into a vector of class logits.

In cases where a classification loss is applicable, why are embeddings used during test time, instead of the logits or the subsequent softmax values? Typically, embeddings are preferred when the task is some variant of information retrieval, where the goal is to return data that is most similar to a query. An example of this is image search, where the input is a query image, and the output is the most visually similar images in a database. Open-set classification is a variant of this, where test set and training set classes are disjoint. In this situation, query data can be classified based on a nearest neighbors vote, or verified based on distance thresholding in the embedding space. Some notable applications of this are face verification [47], and person re-identification [20]. Both have seen improvements in accuracy, largely due to the use of convnets, but also due to loss functions that encourage well-clustered embedding spaces.

Electronic supplementary material The online version of this chapter (https://doi.org/10.1007/978-3-030-58595-2_41) contains supplementary material, which is available to authorized users.

© Springer Nature Switzerland AG 2020
A. Vedaldi et al. (Eds.): ECCV 2020, LNCS 12370, pp. 681–699, 2020.
https://doi.org/10.1007/978-3-030-58595-2_41

Then there are cases where using a classification loss is not possible. For example, when constructing a dataset, it might be difficult or costly to assign class labels to each sample, and it might be easier to specify the relative similarities between samples in the form of pair or triplet relationships [64]. Pairs and triplets can also provide additional training signals for existing datasets [9]. In both cases, there are no explicit labels, so embedding losses become a suitable choice.

Recently, there has been significant interest in self-supervised learning. This is a form of unsupervised learning where pseudo-labels are applied to the data during training, often via clever use of data augmentations or signals from multiple modalities [6,18,39]. In this case, the pseudo-labels exist to indicate the similarities between data in a particular batch, and as such, they do not have any meaning across training iterations. Thus, embedding losses are favored over classification losses.

Other applications of embedding losses include learning 3D point cloud features [7], dimensionality reduction for visualization [1], imitation learning [48], sequence prediction [38], and even vanilla image classification [23].

In the computer vision domain, deep convnets have resulted in dramatic improvements in nearly every subfield, including classification [19,27], segmentation [32], object detection [42], and generative models [15]. It is no surprise, then, that deep networks have had a similar effect on metric learning. The combination of the two is often called deep metric learning, and this will be the focus of the remainder of the paper. The rest of this section will briefly review the recent advances in deep metric learning, as well as related work, and the contributions of this paper.

1.2 Embedding Losses

Pair and triplet losses provide the foundation for two fundamental approaches to metric learning. A classic pair based method is the contrastive loss [16], which attempts to make the distance between positive pairs (d_p) smaller than some threshold (m_{pos}), and the distance between negative pairs (d_n) larger than some threshold (m_{neg}):

$$L_{contrastive} = [d_p - m_{pos}]_+ + [m_{neg} - d_n]_+ \qquad (1)$$

(Note that in many implementations, m_{pos} is set to 0.) The theoretical downside of this method is that the same distance threshold is applied to all pairs, even though there may be a large variance in their similarities and dissimilarities.

The triplet margin loss [63] theoretically addresses this issue. A triplet consists of an anchor, positive, and negative sample, where the anchor is more similar to the positive than the negative. The triplet margin loss attempts to make the anchor-positive distances (d_{ap}) smaller than the anchor-negative distances (d_{an}), by a predefined margin (m):

$$L_{triplet} = [d_{ap} - d_{an} + m]_+ \qquad (2)$$

This theoretically places fewer restrictions on the embedding space, and allows the model to account for variance in interclass dissimilarities.

A wide variety of losses has since been built on these fundamental concepts. For example, the angular loss [60] is a triplet loss where the margin is based on the angles formed by the triplet vectors. The margin loss [65] modifies the contrastive loss by setting $m_{pos} = \beta - \alpha$ and $m_{neg} = \beta + \alpha$, where α is fixed, and β is learnable via gradient descent. More recently, Yuan et al. [70] proposed a variation of the contrastive loss based on signal to noise ratios, where each embedding vector is considered signal, and the difference between it and other vectors is considered noise. Other pair losses are based on the softmax function and LogSumExp, which is a smooth approximation of the maximum function. Specifically, the lifted structure loss [37] is the contrastive loss but with Log-SumExp applied to all negative pairs. The N-Pairs loss [50] applies the softmax function to each positive pair relative to all other pairs. (The N-Pairs loss is also known as InfoNCE [38] and NT-Xent [6].) The recent multi similarity loss [62] applies LogSumExp to all pairs, but is specially formulated to give weight to different relative similarities among each embedding and its neighbors. The tuplet margin loss [69] combines LogSumExp with an implicit pair weighting method, while the circle loss [52] weights each pair's similarity by its deviation from a pre-determined optimal similarity value. In contrast with these pair and triplet losses, FastAP [3] attempts to optimize for average precision within each batch, using a soft histogram binning technique.

1.3   Classification Losses

Classification losses are based on the inclusion of a weight matrix, where each column corresponds to a particular class. In most cases, training consists of matrix multiplying the weights with embedding vectors to obtain logits, and then applying a loss function to the logits. The most straightforward case is the normalized softmax loss [31,58,72], which is identical to cross entropy, but with the columns of the weight matrix L2 normalized. ProxyNCA [35] is a variation of this, where cross entropy is applied to the Euclidean distances, rather than the cosine similarities, between embeddings and the weight matrix. A number of face verification losses have modified the cross entropy loss with angular margins in the softmax expression. Specifically, SphereFace [31], CosFace [57,59], and ArcFace [11] apply multiplicative-angular, additive-cosine, and additive-angular margins, respectively. (It is interesting to note that metric learning papers have consistently left out face verification losses from their experiments, even though there is nothing face-specific about them.) The SoftTriple loss [41] takes a different approach, by expanding the weight matrix to have multiple columns per class, theoretically providing more flexibility for modeling class variances.

1.4   Pair and Triplet Mining

Mining is the process of finding the best pairs or triplets to train on. There are two broad approaches to mining: offline and online. Offline mining is performed before batch construction, so that each batch is made to contain the most informative samples. This might be accomplished by storing lists of hard negatives [49], doing a nearest neighbors search before each epoch [17], or before each iteration [51]. In contrast, online mining finds hard pairs or triplets within each randomly sampled batch. Using all possible pairs or triplets is an alternative, but this has two weaknesses: practically, it can consume a lot of memory, and theoretically, it has the tendency to include a large number of easy negatives and positives, causing performance to plateau quickly. Thus, one intuitive strategy is to select only the most difficult positive and negative samples [20], but this has been found to produce noisy gradients and convergence to bad local optima [65]. A possible remedy is semihard negative mining, which finds the negative samples in a batch that are close to the anchor, but still further away than the corresponding positive samples [47]. On the other hand, Wu *et al.* [65] found that semihard mining makes little progress as the number of semihard negatives drops. They claim that distance-weighted sampling results in a variety of negatives (easy, semihard, and hard), and improved performance. Online mining can also be integrated into the structure of models. Specifically, the hard-aware deeply cascaded method [71] uses models of varying complexity, in which the loss for the complex models only considers the pairs that the simpler models find difficult. Recently, Wang *et al.* [62] proposed a simple pair mining strategy, where negatives are chosen if they are closer to an anchor than its hardest positive, and positives are chosen if they are further from an anchor than its hardest negative.

1.5 Advanced Training Methods

To obtain higher accuracy, many recent papers have gone beyond loss functions or mining techniques. For example, several recent methods incorporate generator networks in their training procedure. Lin *et al.* [29] use a generator as part of their framework for modeling class centers and intraclass variance. Duan *et al.* [12] use a hard-negative generator to expose the model to difficult negatives that might be absent from the training set. Zheng *et al.* [73] follow up on this work by using an adaptive interpolation method that creates negatives of varying difficulty, based on the strength of the model. Other sophisticated training methods include HTL [14], ABE [25], MIC [43], and DCES [46]. HTL constructs a hierarchical class tree at regular intervals during training, to estimate the optimal per-class margin in the triplet margin loss. ABE is an attention based ensemble, where each model learns a different set of attention masks. MIC uses a combination of clustering and encoder networks to disentangle class specific properties from shared characteristics like color and pose. DCES uses a divide and conquer approach, by partitioning the embedding space, and training an embedding layer for each partition separately.

1.6 Related Work

Exposing hype and methodological flaws is not new. Papers of this type have been written for machine learning [30], image classification [4], neural network pruning [2], information retrieval [68], recommender systems [10], and generative adversarial networks [33]. Recently, Fehervari et al. [13] addressed the problem of unfair comparisons in metric learning papers, by evaluating loss functions on a more level playing field. However, they focused mainly on methods from 2017 or earlier, and did not address the issue of hyperparameter tuning on the test set. Concurrent with our work is Roth et al. [44], which addresses many of the same flaws that we find, and does an extensive analysis of various loss functions. But again, they do not address the problem of training with test set feedback, and their hyperparameters are tuned using a small grid search around values proposed in the original papers. In contrast, we use cross-validation and bayesian optimization to tune hyperparameters. We find that this significantly minimizes the performance differences between loss functions. See Sect. 3 for a complete explanation of our experimental methodology.

1.7 Contributions of This Paper

In the following sections, we examine flaws in the current literature, including the problem of unfair comparisons, the weaknesses of commonly used accuracy metrics, and the bad practice of training with test set feedback. We propose a training and evaluation protocol that addresses these flaws, and then run experiments on a variety of loss functions. Our results show that when hyperparameters are properly tuned via cross-validation, most methods perform similarly to one another. This opens up research questions regarding the relationship between hyperparameters and datasets, and the factors limiting open-set accuracy that may be inherent to particular dataset/architecture combinations. As well, by comparing algorithms using proper machine learning practices and a level playing field, the performance gains in future research will better reflect reality, and will be more likely to generalize to other high-impact fields like self-supervised learning.

2 Flaws in the Existing Literature

2.1 Unfair Comparisons

In order to claim that a new algorithm outperforms existing methods, it's important to keep as many parameters constant as possible. That way, we can be certain that it was the new algorithm that boosted performance, and not one of the extraneous parameters. This has not been the case with metric learning papers.

One of the easiest ways to improve accuracy is to upgrade the network architecture, yet this fundamental parameter has not been kept constant across papers. Some use GoogleNet, while others use BN-Inception, sometimes referred to as "Inception with Batch Normalization." Choice of architecture is important in metric learning, because the networks are typically pretrained on ImageNet, and then finetuned on smaller datasets. Thus, the initial accuracy on the smaller datasets varies depending on the chosen network. One widely-cited paper from 2017 used ResNet50, and then claimed huge performance gains. This is questionable, because the competing methods used GoogleNet, which has significantly lower initial accuracies (see Table 1). Therefore, much of the performance gain likely came from the choice of network architecture, and not their proposed method. In addition, papers have changed the dimensionality of the embedding space, and increasing dimensionality leads to increased accuracy. Therefore, varying this parameter further complicates the task of comparing algorithms.

Table 1. Recall@1 of models pretrained on ImageNet. Output embedding sizes were reduced to 512 using PCA and L2 normalized. For each image, the smaller side was scaled to 256, followed by a center-crop to 227×227.

	CUB200	Cars196	SOP
GoogleNet	41.1	33.9	45.2
BN-Inception	51.1	46.9	50.7
ResNet50	48.7	43.5	52.9

Another easy way to improve accuracy is to use more sophisticated image augmentations. In fact, image augmentation strategies have been central to several recent advances in supervised and self-supervised learning [6,8,18,53]. In the metric learning field, most papers claim to apply the following transformations: resize the image to 256×256, randomly crop to 227×227, and do a horizontal flip with 50% chance. But the official open-source implementations of some recent papers show that they are actually using the more sophisticated cropping method described in the original GoogleNet paper. This method randomly changes the location, size, and aspect ratio of each crop, which provides more variability in the training data, and helps combat overfitting.

Papers have also been inconsistent in their choice of optimizer (SGD, Adam, RMSprop etc.) and learning rate. The effect on test set accuracy is less clear in this case, as adaptive optimizers like Adam and RMSprop will converge faster, while SGD may lead to better generalization [34]. Regardless, varying the optimizer and learning rate makes it difficult to do apples-to-apples comparisons.

It is also possible for papers to omit small details that have a big effect on accuracy. For example, in the official open-source code for a 2019 paper, the pretrained ImageNet model has its BatchNorm parameters frozen during training. This can help reduce overfitting, and the authors explain in the code that it results in a 2 point performance boost on the CUB200 dataset. Yet this is not mentioned in their paper.

Finally, most papers do not present confidence intervals for their results, and improvements in accuracy over previous methods often range in the low single digits. Those small improvements would be more meaningful if the results were averaged over multiple runs, and confidence intervals were included.

2.2 Weakness of Commonly Used Accuracy Metrics

To report accuracy, most metric learning papers use Recall@K, Normalized Mutual Information (NMI), and the F1 score. But are these necessarily the best metrics to use? Fig. 1 shows three embedding spaces, and each one scores nearly 100% Recall@1, even though they have different characteristics. (Note that 100% Recall@1 means that Recall@K for any K >1 is also 100%.) More importantly, Fig. 1(c) shows a better separation of the classes than Fig. 1(a), yet they receive approximately the same score. F1 and NMI also return roughly equal scores for all three embedding spaces. Moreover, they require the embeddings to be clustered, which introduces two factors of variability: the choice of clustering algorithm, and the sensitivity of clustering results to seed initialization. Since we know the ground-truth number of clusters, k-means clustering is the obvious choice and is what is typically used. However, as Fig. 1 shows, this results in uninformative NMI and F1 scores. Other clustering algorithms could be considered, but each one has its own drawbacks and subtleties. Introducing a clustering algorithm into the evaluation process is simply adding a layer of complexity between the researcher and the embedding space. Instead, we would like an accuracy metric that operates directly on the embedding space, like Recall@K, but that provides more nuanced information.

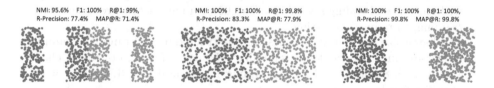

Fig. 1. How different accuracy metrics score on three toy examples.

NMI also tends to give high scores to datasets that have many classes, regardless of the model's true accuracy (see Table 2). Adjusted Mutual Information [55] removes this flaw, but still requires clustering to be done first.

2.3 Training with Test Set Feedback

The majority of papers split each dataset so that the first 50% of classes are used for the training set, and the remainder are used for the test set. Then during training, the test set accuracy of the model is checked at regular intervals, and the best test set accuracy is reported. In other words, there is no validation set, and model selection and hyperparameter tuning are done with direct feedback from the test set. Some papers do not check performance at regular intervals,

Table 2. NMI of embeddings from randomly initialized convnets. CUB200 and Cars196 have about 200 classes, while SOP has about 20,000.

	CUB200	Cars196	SOP
GoogleNet	23.6	19.1	81.2
BN-Inception	18.5	13.7	73.1
ResNet50	21.3	16.7	80.8

and instead report accuracy after training for a predetermined number of iterations. In this case, it is unclear how the number of iterations is chosen, and hyperparameters are still tuned based on test set performance. This breaks one of the most basic commandments of machine learning. Training with test set feedback leads to overfitting on the test set, and therefore brings into question the steady rise in accuracy over time, as presented in metric learning papers.

3   Proposed Evaluation Method

The following is an explanation of our experimental methodology, which fixes the flaws described in the previous section.

3.1   Fair Comparisons and Reproducibility

All experiments are run using PyTorch [40] with the following settings:

- The trunk model is an ImageNet [45] pretrained BN-Inception network [21], with output embedding size of 128. BatchNorm parameters are frozen during training, to reduce overfitting.
- The batch size is set to 32. Batches are constructed by first randomly sampling C classes, and then randomly sampling M images for each of the C classes. We set $C = 8$ and $M = 4$ for embedding losses, and $C = 32$ and $M = 1$ for classification losses.
- During training, images are augmented using the random resized cropping strategy. Specifically, we first resize each image so that its shorter side has length 256, then make a random crop that has a size between 40 and 256, and aspect ratio between 3/4 and 4/3. This crop is then resized to 227×227, and flipped horizontally with 50% probability. During evaluation, images are resized to 256 and then center cropped to 227.
- All network parameters are optimized using RMSprop with learning rate 1e–6. We chose RMSprop because it converges faster than SGD, and seems to generalize better than Adam, based on a small set of experiments. For loss functions that include their own learnable weights (e.g. ArcFace), we use RMSprop but leave the learning rate as a hyperparameter to be optimized.
- Embeddings are L2 normalized before computing the loss, and during evaluation.

Source code, configuration files, and other supplementary material are available at github.com/KevinMusgrave/powerful-benchmarker.

3.2   Informative Accuracy Metrics

We measure accuracy using Mean Average Precision at R (MAP@R), which combines the ideas of Mean Average Precision and R-precision.

- R-Precision is defined as follows: For each query[1], let R be the total number of references that are the same class as the query. Find the R nearest references to the query, and let r be the number of those nearest references that are the same class as the query. The score for the query is $\frac{r}{R}$.
- One weakness of R-precision is that it does not account for the ranking of the correct retrievals. So we instead use MAP@R, which is Mean Average Precision with a couple of modifications: 1) the number of nearest neighbors for each sample is set to R, and 2) the final divisor is set to R, rather than the number of correct retrievals. For a single query:

$$\text{MAP@R} = \frac{1}{R} \sum_{i=1}^{R} P(i) \tag{3}$$

$$P(i) = \begin{cases} \text{precision at } i, & \text{if the ith retrieval is correct} \\ 0, & \text{otherwise} \end{cases} \tag{4}$$

The benefits of MAP@R are that it is more informative than Recall@1 (see Fig. 1 and Table 3), it can be computed directly from the embedding space (no clustering step required), it is easy to understand, and it rewards well clustered embedding spaces. MAP@R is also more stable than Recall@1. Across our experiments, we computed the lag-one autocorrelation of the validation accuracy during training: Recall@1 = 0.73 and MAP@R = 0.81. Thus, MAP@R is less noisy, making it easier to select the best performing model checkpoints.

Table 3. Accuracy metrics on hypothetical retrieval results. The accuracy numbers represent percentages. Assume R = 10. Despite the clear differences, Recall@1 scores all four retrieval results at 100%, so it fails to capture important information.

Retrieval results	Recall@1	R-Precision	MAP@R
10 results, of which only the 1st is correct	100	10	10
10 results, of which the 1st and 10th are correct	100	20	12
10 results, of which the 1st and 2nd are correct	100	20	20
10 results, of which all 10 are correct	100	100	100

In our results tables in Sect. 4, we present R-precision and MAP@R. For the sake of comparisons to previous papers, we also show Precision@1 (also known as "Recall@1" in the previous sections and in metric learning papers).

---

[1] A query is an image for which we are trying to find similar images, and the references are the searchable database.

3.3   Hyperparameter Search via Cross Validation

To find the best loss function hyperparameters, we run 50 iterations of bayesian optimization. Each iteration consists of 4-fold cross validation:

- The first half of classes are used for cross validation, and the 4 partitions are created deterministically: the first 0–12.5% of classes make up the first partition, the next 12.5–25% of classes make up the second partition, and so on. The training set comprises 3 of the 4 partitions, and cycles through all leave-one-out possibilities. As a result, the training and validation sets are always class-disjoint, so optimizing for validation set performance should be a good proxy for accuracy on open-set tasks. Training stops when validation accuracy plateaus.
- The second half of classes are used as the test set. This is the same setting that metric learning papers have used for years, and we use it so that results can be compared more easily to past papers.

Hyperparameters are optimized to maximize the average validation accuracy. For the best hyperparameters, the highest-accuracy checkpoint for each training set partition is loaded, and its embeddings for the test set are computed and L2 normalized. Then we compute accuracy using two methods:

1. **Concatenated (512-dim)**: For each sample in the test set, we concatenate the 128-dim embeddings of the 4 models to get 512-dim embeddings, and then L2 normalize. We then report the accuracy of these embeddings.
2. **Separated (128-dim)**: For each sample in the test set, we compute the accuracy of the 128-dim embeddings separately, and therefore obtain 4 different accuracies, one for each model's embeddings. We then report the average of these accuracies.

We do 10 training runs using the best hyperparameters, and report the average across these runs, as well as confidence intervals. This way our results are less subject to random seed noise.

4   Experiments

4.1   Losses and Datasets

We ran experiments on 13 losses, and 1 loss+miner combination, and prioritized methods from recent conferences (see Table 7). For every loss, we used the settings described in Sect. 3, and we ran experiments on three widely used metric learning datasets: CUB200 [56], Cars196 [26], and Stanford Online Products (SOP) [37]. We chose these datasets because they have been the standard for several years, and we wanted our results to be easily comparable to prior papers. Tables 4, 5 and 6 show the mean accuracy across 10 training runs, as well as the 95% confidence intervals where applicable. Bold represents the best mean accuracy. We also include the accuracy of the pretrained model, the embeddings of which are reduced to 512 or 128, using PCA. In the supplementary material, we show results for CUB200 using a batch size of 256 instead of 32. The results are roughly the same, with the exception of FastAP, which gets a significant boost in accuracy, and performs on par with the rest of the methods.

Table 4. Accuracy on CUB200

	Concatenated (512-dim)			Separated (128-dim)		
	P@1	RP	MAP@R	P@1	RP	MAP@R
Pretrained	51.05	24.85	14.21	50.54	25.12	14.53
Contrastive	**68.13 ± 0.31**	37.24 ± 0.28	26.53 ± 0.29	59.73 ± 0.40	31.98 ± 0.29	21.18 ± 0.28
Triplet	64.24 ± 0.26	34.55 ± 0.24	23.69 ± 0.23	55.76 ± 0.27	29.55 ± 0.16	18.75 ± 0.15
NT-Xent	66.61 ± 0.29	35.96 ± 0.21	25.09 ± 0.22	58.12 ± 0.23	30.81 ± 0.17	19.87 ± 0.16
ProxyNCA	65.69 ± 0.43	35.14 ± 0.26	24.21 ± 0.27	57.88 ± 0.30	30.16 ± 0.22	19.32 ± 0.21
Margin	63.60 ± 0.48	33.94 ± 0.27	23.09 ± 0.27	54.78 ± 0.30	28.86 ± 0.18	18.11 ± 0.17
Margin/class	64.37 ± 0.18	34.59 ± 0.16	23.71 ± 0.16	55.56 ± 0.16	29.32 ± 0.15	18.51 ± 0.13
N. Softmax	65.65 ± 0.30	35.99 ± 0.15	25.25 ± 0.13	58.75 ± 0.19	31.75 ± 0.12	20.96 ± 0.11
CosFace	67.32 ± 0.32	**37.49 ± 0.21**	**26.70 ± 0.23**	59.63 ± 0.36	31.99 ± 0.22	21.21 ± 0.22
ArcFace	67.50 ± 0.25	37.31 ± 0.21	26.45 ± 0.20	**60.17 ± 0.32**	**32.37 ± 0.17**	**21.49 ± 0.16**
FastAP	63.17 ± 0.34	34.20 ± 0.20	23.53 ± 0.20	55.58 ± 0.31	29.72 ± 0.16	19.09 ± 0.16
SNR	66.44 ± 0.56	36.56 ± 0.34	25.75 ± 0.36	58.06 ± 0.39	31.21 ± 0.28	20.43 ± 0.28
MS	65.04 ± 0.28	35.40 ± 0.12	24.70 ± 0.13	57.60 ± 0.24	30.84 ± 0.13	20.15 ± 0.14
MS+Miner	67.73 ± 0.18	37.37 ± 0.19	26.52 ± 0.18	59.41 ± 0.30	31.93 ± 0.15	21.01 ± 0.14
SoftTriple	67.27 ± 0.39	37.34 ± 0.19	26.51 ± 0.20	59.94 ± 0.33	32.12 ± 0.14	21.31 ± 0.14

Table 5. Accuracy on Cars196

	Concatenated (512-dim)			Separated (128-dim)		
	P@1	RP	MAP@R	P@1	RP	MAP@R
Pretrained	46.89	13.77	5.91	43.27	13.37	5.64
Contrastive	81.78 ± 0.43	35.11 ± 0.45	24.89 ± 0.50	69.80 ± 0.38	27.78 ± 0.34	17.24 ± 0.35
Triplet	79.13 ± 0.42	33.71 ± 0.45	23.02 ± 0.51	65.68 ± 0.58	26.67 ± 0.36	15.82 ± 0.36
NT-Xent	80.99 ± 0.54	34.96 ± 0.38	24.40 ± 0.41	68.16 ± 0.36	27.66 ± 0.23	16.78 ± 0.24
ProxyNCA	83.56 ± 0.27	35.62 ± 0.28	25.38 ± 0.31	73.46 ± 0.23	28.90 ± 0.22	18.29 ± 0.22
Margin	81.16 ± 0.50	34.82 ± 0.31	24.21 ± 0.34	68.24 ± 0.35	27.25 ± 0.19	16.40 ± 0.20
Margin/class	80.04 ± 0.61	33.78 ± 0.51	23.11 ± 0.55	67.54 ± 0.60	26.68 ± 0.40	15.88 ± 0.39
N. Softmax	83.16 ± 0.25	36.20 ± 0.26	26.00 ± 0.30	72.55 ± 0.18	29.35 ± 0.20	18.73 ± 0.20
CosFace	**85.52 ± 0.24**	37.32 ± 0.28	27.57 ± 0.30	**74.67 ± 0.20**	29.01 ± 0.11	18.80 ± 0.12
ArcFace	85.44 ± 0.28	37.02 ± 0.29	27.22 ± 0.30	72.10 ± 0.37	27.29 ± 0.17	17.11 ± 0.18
FastAP	78.45 ± 0.52	33.61 ± 0.54	23.14 ± 0.56	65.08 ± 0.36	26.59 ± 0.36	15.94 ± 0.34
SNR	82.02 ± 0.48	35.22 ± 0.43	25.03 ± 0.48	69.69 ± 0.46	27.55 ± 0.25	17.13 ± 0.26
MS	85.14 ± 0.29	**38.09 ± 0.19**	**28.07 ± 0.22**	73.77 ± 0.19	**29.92 ± 0.16**	**19.32 ± 0.18**
MS+Miner	83.67 ± 0.34	37.08 ± 0.31	27.01 ± 0.35	71.80 ± 0.22	29.44 ± 0.21	18.86 ± 0.20
SoftTriple	84.49 ± 0.26	37.03 ± 0.21	27.08 ± 0.21	73.69 ± 0.21	29.29 ± 0.16	18.89 ± 0.16

4.2 Papers Versus Reality

First, let's consider the general trend of paper results. Figure 2(a) shows the inexorable rise in accuracy we have all come to expect in this field, with modern methods completely obliterating old ones.

Table 6. Accuracy on SOP

	Concatenated (512-dim)			Separated (128-dim)		
	P@1	RP	MAP@R	P@1	RP	MAP@R
Pretrained	50.71	25.97	23.44	47.25	23.84	21.36
Contrastive	73.12 ± 0.20	47.29 ± 0.24	44.39 ± 0.24	69.34 ± 0.26	43.41 ± 0.28	40.37 ± 0.28
Triplet	72.65 ± 0.28	46.46 ± 0.38	43.37 ± 0.37	67.33 ± 0.34	40.94 ± 0.39	37.70 ± 0.38
NT-Xent	74.22 ± 0.22	48.35 ± 0.26	45.31 ± 0.25	69.88 ± 0.19	43.51 ± 0.21	40.31 ± 0.20
ProxyNCA	75.89 ± 0.17	50.10 ± 0.22	47.22 ± 0.21	71.30 ± 0.20	44.71 ± 0.21	41.74 ± 0.21
Margin	70.99 ± 0.36	44.94 ± 0.43	41.82 ± 0.43	65.78 ± 0.34	39.71 ± 0.40	36.47 ± 0.39
Margin/class	72.36 ± 0.30	46.41 ± 0.40	43.32 ± 0.41	67.56 ± 0.42	41.37 ± 0.48	38.15 ± 0.49
N. Softmax	75.67 ± 0.17	50.01 ± 0.22	47.13 ± 0.22	**71.65 ± 0.14**	**45.32 ± 0.17**	**42.35 ± 0.16**
CosFace	75.79 ± 0.14	49.77 ± 0.19	46.92 ± 0.19	70.71 ± 0.19	43.56 ± 0.21	40.69 ± 0.21
ArcFace	**76.20 ± 0.27**	**50.27 ± 0.38**	**47.41 ± 0.40**	70.88 ± 1.51	44.00 ± 1.26	41.11 ± 1.22
FastAP	72.59 ± 0.26	46.60 ± 0.29	43.57 ± 0.28	68.13 ± 0.25	42.06 ± 0.25	38.88 ± 0.25
SNR	73.40 ± 0.09	47.43 ± 0.13	44.54 ± 0.13	69.45 ± 0.10	43.34 ± 0.12	40.31 ± 0.12
MS	74.50 ± 0.24	48.77 ± 0.32	45.79 ± 0.32	70.43 ± 0.33	44.25 ± 0.38	41.15 ± 0.38
MS+Miner	75.09 ± 0.17	49.51 ± 0.20	46.55 ± 0.20	71.25 ± 0.15	45.19 ± 0.16	42.10 ± 0.16
SoftTriple	76.12 ± 0.17	50.21 ± 0.18	47.35 ± 0.19	70.88 ± 0.20	43.83 ± 0.20	40.92 ± 0.20

Table 7. The losses covered in our experiments. Note that NT-Xent is the name we used in our code, but it is also known as N-Pairs or InfoNCE. For the Margin loss, we tested two versions: "Margin" uses the same β value for all training classes, and "Margin/class" uses a separate β for each training class. In both versions, β is learned during training. Face verification losses have been consistently left out of metric learning papers, so we included two losses (CosFace and ArcFace) from that domain. (We used only the loss functions from those two papers. We did not train on any face datasets or use any model trained on faces.)

Method	Year	Loss type
Contrastive [16]	2006	Embedding
Triplet [63]	2006	Embedding
NT-Xent [6,38,50]	2016	Embedding
ProxyNCA [35]	2017	Classification
Margin [65]	2017	Embedding
Margin/class [65]	2017	Embedding
Normalized Softmax (N. Softmax) [31,58,72]	2017	Classification
CosFace [57,59]	2018	Classification
ArcFace [11]	2019	Classification
FastAP [3]	2019	Embedding
Signal to Noise Ratio Contrastive (SNR) [70]	2019	Embedding
MultiSimilarity (MS) [62]	2019	Embedding
MS+Miner [62]	2019	Embedding
SoftTriple [41]	2019	Classification

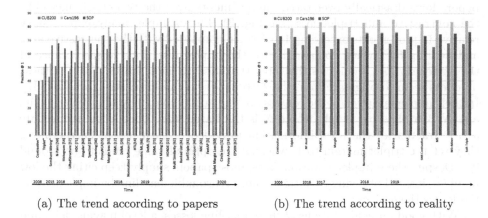

(a) The trend according to papers (b) The trend according to reality

Fig. 2. Papers versus Reality: the trend of Precision@1 of various methods over the years. In a), the baseline methods have * next to them, which indicates that their numbers are the average reported accuracy from all papers that included those baselines.

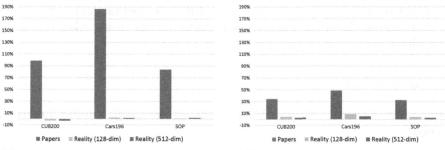

(a) Relative improvement over the contrastive loss (b) Relative improvement over the triplet loss

Fig. 3. Papers versus Reality: we look at the results tables of all methods presented in Fig. 2(a). 11 of these include the contrastive loss, and 12 include the triplet loss (without semihard mining). For each paper, we compute the relative percentage improvement of their proposed method over their reported result for the contrastive or triplet loss, and then take the average improvement across papers (grey bars in the above figures). The green and red bars are the average relative improvement that we obtain, in the separated 128-dim and concatenated 512-dim settings, respectively. For the "reality" numbers in (a) we excluded the FastAP loss from the calculation, since it was a poor performing outlier in our experiments, and we excluded the triplet loss since we consider it a baseline method. Likewise for the "reality" numbers in (b), we excluded the FastAP and contrastive losses from the calculation. (Color figure online)

But how do the claims made in papers stack up against reality? We find that papers have drastically overstated improvements over the two classic methods, the contrastive and triplet loss (see Fig. 3). For example, many papers show relative improvements exceeding 100% when compared with the contrastive loss, and nearing 50% when compared with the triplet loss. This arises because of the extremely low accuracies that are attributed to these losses. Some of these numbers seem to originate from the 2016 paper on the lifted structure loss [37]. In their implementation of the contrastive and triplet loss, they sample $N/2$ pairs and $N/3$ triplets per batch, where N is the batch size. Thus, they utilize only a tiny fraction of the total information provided in each batch. Furthermore, they set the triplet margin to 1, whereas the optimal value tends to be around 0.1. Despite these implementation flaws, most papers simply keep citing the low numbers instead of trying to obtain a more reasonable baseline by implementing the losses themselves.

With good implementations of those baseline losses, a level playing field, and proper machine learning practices, we obtain the trend as shown in Fig. 2(b). The trend appears to be a relatively flat line, indicating that the methods perform similarly to one another, whether they were introduced in 2006 or 2019. In other words, metric learning algorithms have not made the spectacular progress that they claim to have made. This brings into question the results of other cutting edge papers not covered in our experiments. It also raises doubts about the value of the hand-wavy theoretical explanations in metric learning papers. If a paper attempts to explain the performance gains of its proposed method, and it turns out that those performance gains are non-existent, then their explanation must be invalid as well.

5   Conclusion

In this paper, we uncovered several flaws in the current metric learning literature, namely:

- Unfair comparisons caused by changes in network architecture, embedding size, image augmentation method, and optimizers.
- The use of accuracy metrics that are either misleading, or do not a provide a complete picture of the embedding space.
- Training without a validation set, i.e. with test set feedback.

We then ran experiments with these issues fixed, and found that state of the art loss functions perform marginally better than, and sometimes on par with, classic methods. This is in stark contrast with the claims made in papers, in which accuracy has risen dramatically over time.

Future work could explore the relationship between optimal hyperparameters and dataset/architecture combinations, as well as the reasons for why different losses are performing similarly to one another. Of course, pushing the state-of-the-art in accuracy is another research direction. If proper machine learning practices are followed, and comparisons to prior work are done in a fair manner, the results of future metric learning papers will better reflect reality, and will be more likely to generalize to other high-impact areas like self-supervised learning.

Acknowledgements. This work is supported by a Facebook AI research grant awarded to Cornell University.

References

1. Amid, E., Warmuth, M.K.: TriMap: large-scale dimensionality reduction using triplets. arXiv preprint arXiv:1910.00204 (2019)
2. Blalock, D., Ortiz, J.J.G., Frankle, J., Guttag, J.: What is the state of neural network pruning? arXiv preprint arXiv:2003.03033 (2020)
3. Cakir, F., He, K., Xia, X., Kulis, B., Sclaroff, S.: Deep metric learning to rank. In: Proceedings of the IEEE Conference on Computer Vision and Pattern Recognition, pp. 1861–1870 (2019)
4. Chatfield, K., Simonyan, K., Vedaldi, A., Zisserman, A.: Return of the devil in the details: delving deep into convolutional nets. arXiv preprint arXiv:1405.3531 (2014)
5. Chen, B., Deng, W.: Hybrid-attention based decoupled metric learning for zero-shot image retrieval. In: Proceedings of the IEEE Conference on Computer Vision and Pattern Recognition, pp. 2750–2759 (2019)
6. Chen, T., Kornblith, S., Norouzi, M., Hinton, G.: A simple framework for contrastive learning of visual representations. arXiv preprint arXiv:2002.05709 (2020)
7. Choy, C., Park, J., Koltun, V.: Fully convolutional geometric features. In: Proceedings of the IEEE International Conference on Computer Vision, pp. 8958–8966 (2019)
8. Cubuk, E.D., Zoph, B., Mane, D., Vasudevan, V., Le, Q.V.: AutoAugment: learning augmentation strategies from data. In: Proceedings of the IEEE Conference on Computer Vision and Pattern Recognition, pp. 113–123 (2019)
9. Cui, Y., Zhou, F., Lin, Y., Belongie, S.: Fine-grained categorization and dataset bootstrapping using deep metric learning with humans in the loop. In: Computer Vision and Pattern Recognition (CVPR). Las Vegas, NV (2016). http://vision.cornell.edu/se3/wp-content/uploads/2016/04/1950.pdf
10. Dacrema, M.F., Cremonesi, P., Jannach, D.: Are we really making much progress? A worrying analysis of recent neural recommendation approaches. In: Proceedings of the 13th ACM Conference on Recommender Systems, pp. 101–109 (2019)
11. Deng, J., Guo, J., Xue, N., Zafeiriou, S.: ArcFace: additive angular margin loss for deep face recognition. In: Proceedings of the IEEE Conference on Computer Vision and Pattern Recognition, pp. 4690–4699 (2019)
12. Duan, Y., Zheng, W., Lin, X., Lu, J., Zhou, J.: Deep adversarial metric learning. In: Proceedings of the IEEE Conference on Computer Vision and Pattern Recognition, pp. 2780–2789 (2018)
13. Fehervari, I., Ravichandran, A., Appalaraju, S.: Unbiased evaluation of deep metric learning algorithms. arXiv preprint arXiv:1911.12528 (2019)
14. Ge, W., Huang, W., Dong, D., Scott, M.R.: Deep metric learning with hierarchical triplet loss. In: Ferrari, V., Hebert, M., Sminchisescu, C., Weiss, Y. (eds.) ECCV 2018. LNCS, vol. 11210, pp. 272–288. Springer, Cham (2018). https://doi.org/10.1007/978-3-030-01231-1_17

15. Goodfellow, I., et al.: Generative adversarial nets. In: Advances in Neural Information Processing Systems, pp. 2672–2680 (2014)
16. Hadsell, R., Chopra, S., LeCun, Y.: Dimensionality reduction by learning an invariant mapping. In: 2006 IEEE Computer Society Conference on Computer Vision and Pattern Recognition (CVPR 2006), vol. 2, pp. 1735–1742. IEEE (2006)
17. Harwood, B., Kumar, B., Carneiro, G., Reid, I., Drummond, T., et al.: Smart mining for deep metric learning. In: Proceedings of the IEEE International Conference on Computer Vision, pp. 2821–2829 (2017)
18. He, K., Fan, H., Wu, Y., Xie, S., Girshick, R.: Momentum contrast for unsupervised visual representation learning. arXiv preprint arXiv:1911.05722 (2019)
19. He, K., Zhang, X., Ren, S., Sun, J.: Deep residual learning for image recognition. In: Proceedings of the IEEE Conference on Computer Vision and Pattern Recognition, pp. 770–778 (2016)
20. Hermans, A., Beyer, L., Leibe, B.: In defense of the triplet loss for person re-identification. arXiv preprint arXiv:1703.07737 (2017)
21. Ioffe, S., Szegedy, C.: Batch normalization: accelerating deep network training by reducing internal covariate shift. In: International Conference on Machine Learning, pp. 448–456 (2015)
22. Jacob, P., Picard, D., Histace, A., Klein, E.: Metric learning with horde: high-order regularizer for deep embeddings. In: Proceedings of the IEEE International Conference on Computer Vision, pp. 6539–6548 (2019)
23. Khosla, P., et al.: Supervised contrastive learning. arXiv preprint arXiv:2004.11362 (2020)
24. Kim, S., Kim, D., Cho, M., Kwak, S.: Proxy anchor loss for deep metric learning. In: Proceedings of the IEEE/CVF Conference on Computer Vision and Pattern Recognition, pp. 3238–3247 (2020)
25. Kim, W., Goyal, B., Chawla, K., Lee, J., Kwon, K.: Attention-based ensemble for deep metric learning. In: Ferrari, V., Hebert, M., Sminchisescu, C., Weiss, Y. (eds.) ECCV 2018. LNCS, vol. 11205, pp. 760–777. Springer, Cham (2018). https://doi.org/10.1007/978-3-030-01246-5_45
26. Krause, J., Stark, M., Deng, J., Fei-Fei, L.: 3D object representations for fine-grained categorization. In: 4th International IEEE Workshop on 3D Representation and Recognition (3dRR-13), Sydney, Australia (2013)
27. Krizhevsky, A., Sutskever, I., Hinton, G.E.: ImageNet classification with deep convolutional neural networks. In: Advances in Neural Information Processing Systems, pp. 1097–1105 (2012)
28. Law, M.T., Urtasun, R., Zemel, R.S.: Deep spectral clustering learning. In: International Conference on Machine Learning, pp. 1985–1994 (2017)
29. Lin, X., Duan, Y., Dong, Q., Lu, J., Zhou, J.: Deep variational metric learning. In: Ferrari, V., Hebert, M., Sminchisescu, C., Weiss, Y. (eds.) ECCV 2018. LNCS, vol. 11219, pp. 714–729. Springer, Cham (2018). https://doi.org/10.1007/978-3-030-01267-0_42
30. Lipton, Z.C., Steinhardt, J.: Troubling trends in machine learning scholarship. arXiv preprint arXiv:1807.03341 (2018)
31. Liu, W., Wen, Y., Yu, Z., Li, M., Raj, B., Song, L.: SphereFace: deep hypersphere embedding for face recognition. In: Proceedings of the IEEE Conference on Computer Vision and Pattern Recognition, pp. 212–220 (2017)
32. Long, J., Shelhamer, E., Darrell, T.: Fully convolutional networks for semantic segmentation. In: Proceedings of the IEEE Conference on Computer Vision and Pattern Recognition, pp. 3431–3440 (2015)

33. Lucic, M., Kurach, K., Michalski, M., Gelly, S., Bousquet, O.: Are GANs created equal? a large-scale study. In: Advances in Neural Information Processing Systems, pp. 700–709 (2018)
34. Luo, L., Xiong, Y., Liu, Y.: Adaptive gradient methods with dynamic bound of learning rate. In: International Conference on Learning Representations (2019). https://openreview.net/forum?id=Bkg3g2R9FX
35. Movshovitz-Attias, Y., Toshev, A., Leung, T.K., Ioffe, S., Singh, S.: No fuss distance metric learning using proxies. In: Proceedings of the IEEE International Conference on Computer Vision, pp. 360–368 (2017)
36. Oh Song, H., Jegelka, S., Rathod, V., Murphy, K.: Deep metric learning via facility location. In: Proceedings of the IEEE Conference on Computer Vision and Pattern Recognition, pp. 5382–5390 (2017)
37. Oh Song, H., Xiang, Y., Jegelka, S., Savarese, S.: Deep metric learning via lifted structured feature embedding. In: Proceedings of the IEEE Conference on Computer Vision and Pattern Recognition, pp. 4004–4012 (2016)
38. Oord, A.V.d., Li, Y., Vinyals, O.: Representation learning with contrastive predictive coding. arXiv preprint arXiv:1807.03748 (2018)
39. Owens, A., Efros, A.A.: Audio-visual scene analysis with self-supervised multisensory features. In: Ferrari, V., Hebert, M., Sminchisescu, C., Weiss, Y. (eds.) ECCV 2018. LNCS, vol. 11210, pp. 639–658. Springer, Cham (2018). https://doi.org/10.1007/978-3-030-01231-1_39
40. Paszke, A., et al.: PyTorch: an imperative style, high-performance deep learning library. In: Advances in Neural Information Processing Systems, pp. 8024–8035 (2019)
41. Qian, Q., Shang, L., Sun, B., Hu, J., Li, H., Jin, R.: SoftTriple loss: deep metric learning without triplet sampling. In: Proceedings of the IEEE International Conference on Computer Vision, pp. 6450–6458 (2019)
42. Ren, S., He, K., Girshick, R., Sun, J.: Faster R-CNN: towards real-time object detection with region proposal networks. In: Advances in Neural Information Processing Systems, pp. 91–99 (2015)
43. Roth, K., Brattoli, B., Ommer, B.: Mic: Mining interclass characteristics for improved metric learning. In: Proceedings of the IEEE International Conference on Computer Vision, pp. 8000–8009 (2019)
44. Roth, K., Milbich, T., Sinha, S., Gupta, P., Ommer, B., Cohen, J.P.: Revisiting training strategies and generalization performance in deep metric learning (2020)
45. Russakovsky, O., et al.: ImageNet large scale visual recognition challenge. Int. J. Comput. Vis. 115(3), 211–252 (2015)
46. Sanakoyeu, A., Tschernezki, V., Buchler, U., Ommer, B.: Divide and conquer the embedding space for metric learning. In: Proceedings of the IEEE Conference on Computer Vision and Pattern Recognition, pp. 471–480 (2019)
47. Schroff, F., Kalenichenko, D., Philbin, J.: FaceNet: a unified embedding for face recognition and clustering. In: Proceedings of the IEEE Conference on Computer Vision and Pattern Recognition, pp. 815–823 (2015)
48. Sermanet, P., et al.: Time-contrastive networks: self-supervised learning from video. In: 2018 IEEE International Conference on Robotics and Automation (ICRA), pp. 1134–1141. IEEE (2018)
49. Smirnov, E., Melnikov, A., Novoselov, S., Luckyanets, E., Lavrentyeva, G.: Doppelganger mining for face representation learning. In: Proceedings of the IEEE International Conference on Computer Vision Workshops, pp. 1916–1923 (2017)
50. Sohn, K.: Improved deep metric learning with multi-class n-pair loss objective. In: Advances in Neural Information Processing Systems, pp. 1857–1865 (2016)

51. Suh, Y., Han, B., Kim, W., Lee, K.M.: Stochastic class-based hard example mining for deep metric learning. In: Proceedings of the IEEE Conference on Computer Vision and Pattern Recognition, pp. 7251–7259 (2019)
52. Sun, Y., et al.: Circle Loss: a unified perspective of pair similarity optimization. In: Proceedings of the IEEE/CVF Conference on Computer Vision and Pattern Recognition, pp. 6398–6407 (2020)
53. Tan, M., Le, Q.V.: EfficientNet: rethinking model scaling for convolutional neural networks. arXiv preprint arXiv:1905.11946 (2019)
54. Ustinova, E., Lempitsky, V.: Learning deep embeddings with histogram loss. In: Advances in Neural Information Processing Systems, pp. 4170–4178 (2016)
55. Vinh, N.X., Epps, J., Bailey, J.: Information theoretic measures for clusterings comparison: variants, properties, normalization and correction for chance. J. Mach. Learn. Res. **11**, 2837–2854 (2010)
56. Wah, C., Branson, S., Welinder, P., Perona, P., Belongie, S.: The Caltech-UCSD Birds-200-2011 Dataset. Tech. rep. CNS-TR-2011-001, California Institute of Technology (2011)
57. Wang, F., Cheng, J., Liu, W., Liu, H.: Additive margin softmax for face verification. IEEE Signal Process. Lett. **25**(7), 926–930 (2018)
58. Wang, F., Xiang, X., Cheng, J., Yuille, A.L.: NormFace: L2 hypersphere embedding for face verification. In: Proceedings of the 25th ACM International Conference on Multimedia, pp. 1041–1049 (2017)
59. Wang, H., et al.: CosFace: large margin cosine loss for deep face recognition. In: Proceedings of the IEEE Conference on Computer Vision and Pattern Recognition, pp. 5265–5274 (2018)
60. Wang, J., Zhou, F., Wen, S., Liu, X., Lin, Y.: Deep metric learning with angular loss. In: Proceedings of the IEEE International Conference on Computer Vision, pp. 2593–2601 (2017)
61. Wang, X., Hua, Y., Kodirov, E., Hu, G., Garnier, R., Robertson, N.M.: Ranked list loss for deep metric learning. In: Proceedings of the IEEE Conference on Computer Vision and Pattern Recognition, pp. 5207–5216 (2019)
62. Wang, X., Han, X., Huang, W., Dong, D., Scott, M.R.: Multi-similarity loss with general pair weighting for deep metric learning. In: Proceedings of the IEEE Conference on Computer Vision and Pattern Recognition, pp. 5022–5030 (2019)
63. Weinberger, K.Q., Blitzer, J., Saul, L.K.: Distance metric learning for large margin nearest neighbor classification. In: Advances in Neural Information Processing Systems, pp. 1473–1480 (2006)
64. Wilber, M., Kwak, S., Belongie, S.: Cost-effective hits for relative similarity comparisons. In: Human Computation and Crowdsourcing (HCOMP), Pittsburgh (2014). http://arxiv.org/abs/1404.3291
65. Wu, C.Y., Manmatha, R., Smola, A.J., Krahenbuhl, P.: Sampling matters in deep embedding learning. In: Proceedings of the IEEE International Conference on Computer Vision, pp. 2840–2848 (2017)
66. Xu, X., Yang, Y., Deng, C., Zheng, F.: Deep asymmetric metric learning via rich relationship mining. In: Proceedings of the IEEE Conference on Computer Vision and Pattern Recognition, pp. 4076–4085 (2019)
67. Xuan, H., Stylianou, A., Pless, R.: Improved embeddings with easy positive triplet mining. In: The IEEE Winter Conference on Applications of Computer Vision, pp. 2474–2482 (2020)

68. Yang, W., Lu, K., Yang, P., Lin, J.: Critically examining the "neural hype" weak baselines and the additivity of effectiveness gains from neural ranking models. In: Proceedings of the 42nd International ACM SIGIR Conference on Research and Development in Information Retrieval, pp. 1129–1132 (2019)
69. Yu, B., Tao, D.: Deep metric learning with tuplet margin loss. In: The IEEE International Conference on Computer Vision (ICCV), October 2019
70. Yuan, T., Deng, W., Tang, J., Tang, Y., Chen, B.: Signal-to-noise ratio: a robust distance metric for deep metric learning. In: Proceedings of the IEEE Conference on Computer Vision and Pattern Recognition, pp. 4815–4824 (2019)
71. Yuan, Y., Yang, K., Zhang, C.: Hard-aware deeply cascaded embedding. In: Proceedings of the IEEE International Conference on Computer Vision, pp. 814–823 (2017)
72. Zhai, A., Wu, H.Y.: Classification is a strong baseline for deep metric learning. arXiv preprint arXiv:1811.12649 (2018)
73. Zheng, W., Chen, Z., Lu, J., Zhou, J.: Hardness-aware deep metric learning. In: Proceedings of the IEEE Conference on Computer Vision and Pattern Recognition, pp. 72–81 (2019)

FTL: A Universal Framework for Training Low-Bit DNNs via Feature Transfer

Kunyuan Du[1], Ya Zhang[1(✉)], Haibing Guan[1], Qi Tian[2], Yanfeng Wang[1], Shenggan Cheng[1], and James Lin[1]

[1] Shanghai Jiao Tong University, Shanghai, China
{dukunyuan,ya_zhang,hbguan,wangyanfeng,chengshenggan,james}@sjtu.edu.cn
[2] Huawei Noah's Ark Lab, Shenzhen, China
tian.qi1@huawei.com

Abstract. Low-bit Deep Neural Networks (low-bit DNNs) have recently received significant attention for their high efficiency. However, low-bit DNNs are often difficult to optimize due to the saddle points in loss surfaces. Here we introduce a novel feature-based knowledge transfer framework, which utilizes a 32-bit DNN to guide the training of a low-bit DNN via feature maps. It is challenge because feature maps from two branches lie in continuous and discrete space respectively, and such mismatch has not been handled properly by existing feature transfer frameworks. In this paper, we propose to directly transfer information-rich continuous-space feature to the low-bit branch. To alleviate the negative impacts brought by the feature quantizer during the transfer process, we make two branches interact via centered cosine distance rather than the widely-used p-norms. Extensive experiments are conducted on Cifar10/100 and ImageNet. Compared with low-bit models trained directly, the proposed framework brings 0.5% to 3.4% accuracy gains to three different quantization schemes. Besides, the proposed framework can also be combined with other techniques, e.g. logits transfer, for further enhancement.

Keywords: Low-bit DNN · Feature Transfer · Space mismatch

1 Introduction

The gains of Deep Neural Networks (DNNs) in various pattern analysis tasks have been accompanied by dramatic increases in model complexity. To mitigate this problem, Network quantization [8,10,11,15,21,23,30,34], which converts 32-bit weights and activations into low-bit, has been proposed to deploy models to mobile platforms. For example, XNOR-net [21] can achieve 58× faster convolutional operations and 32× smaller model size. However, optimizing a low-bit DNN is often more difficult due to the noise in gradients [28] and the saddle points in its loss surface [23]. Various techniques have been developed to better train a low-bit model. Incremental quantization [33] gradually decreases the bit-width of the model to better adapt to the quantization noise. Logits Transfer [18,20] supervises low-bit DNNs with soft labels from 32-bit DNNs to make

© Springer Nature Switzerland AG 2020
A. Vedaldi et al. (Eds.): ECCV 2020, LNCS 12370, pp. 700–716, 2020.
https://doi.org/10.1007/978-3-030-58595-2_42

use of the correlation between labels. Attention Transfer [17] encourages low-bit DNNs to produce high quality attention maps for better training. And Feature Transfer [27, 35] guides low-bit DNNs via feature maps from 32-bit ones. Methods from different categories assist the optimization of low-bit DNNs from different aspects, and can be combined for further enhancement.

In this paper, we focus on the feature transfer approach. For non-quantized DNNs, a variety of feature transfer frameworks [1, 6, 14, 16, 25, 26] have been proposed, which directly minimizes the distance between feature maps from two DNN branches. Nevertheless, feature maps from low-bit DNNs lie in discrete space. Hence, the above studies cannot be directly applied to low-bit ones. To resolve this mismatch, [27, 35] quantizes the continuous knowledge to the same discrete space before transferring. However, transferring discrete knowledge has two main drawbacks. Firstly, regularization in discrete space introduces abrupt changes to gradients, especially for lower bit-width, which leads to unstable training process. Secondly, to convert 32-bit feature maps to discrete space, the specific form of the quantizer is needed. However the quantizer is adaptive for advanced quantization schemes [11, 30] and has no explicit expression. It is desired to design an universal framework, which can handle the mismatch problem for all low-bit DNNs.

To resolve the above problem, this paper explores to directly transfer knowledge from a 32-bit DNN to low-bit one without quantization. In other word, we propose to perform knowledge transfer before the quantizer. Since the quantizer is sensitive to distribution fluctuations during training, we introduce *centered cosine similarity* to replace the widely-used p-norms as the distance function, which focuses on the relative numerical relationship between feature elements and can better maintain the data distribution. We further reveal that the training of a low-bit DNN can be regarded as minimizing its distance to the corresponding 32-bit version. Because low-bit DNNs have much lower learning capacity than the 32-bit ones and may fail to follow its guidance, we further explore to relax the guidance of the 32-bit branch during training. It's worth noting that the proposed method is independent of the form of the quantizer. Therefore, it is an universal framework applicable to all low-bit DNNs.

To demonstrate the effectiveness of the proposed method in improving the performance of low-bit DNNs, we experiment with different benchmark datasets (i.e. Cifar-10/100 [13] and ImageNet [3]), different models (i.e. Alexnet, Vggnet and Resnet), different bit-width and different quantization algorithms (i.e. BNN [8], DoReFa-Net [34], LQ-Nets [30]). The proposed method consistently achieves 0.5% to 3.4% accuracy gains, and reaches *state-of-the-art* performance when taking LQ-Net [30] as the base model. Furthermore, experimental results show that FTL can be combined with other approaches, e.g. logits Transfer [7], for further enhancement.

Below we summary the main contributions of this paper.

- We propose to guide a low-bit DNN before its feature quantizer, which leads to more stable training process and more accurate guidance.

– We introduce centered cosine similarity for feature transfer, which ensures the consistency of guidance when going through the feature quantizer.
– We explore to relax the guidance when the learning capacities of the low-bit DNN prevent it from absorbing the knowledge from the 32-bit DNN.

2   Related Work

The proposed algorithm aims to enhance the classification performance of low-bit DNNs, leveraging a special case of knowledge transfer frameworks.

2.1   Low-Bit DNNs

For smaller model size and higher computational efficiency, both weights and activations of low-bit DNNs lie in discrete space [21]. According to bit-width, low-bit DNNs can be divided into two categories. With bit-width of 8 or 16, the low-bit DNNs can directly be obtained from the 32-bit DNN without additional training [10,19,32]. However, with bit-width equal or less than 4 bits [11,15,21,30,34], re-training considering quantization effect is required to mitigate accuracy degradation, namely quantization-aware training. In this paper, all low-bit DNNs refer to the second category unless otherwise specified. BNN [8] is one of the earliest work for extreme low-bit quantization. To improve the representational capacity of low-bit models, XNOR-Net [21] assigns scaling weights to each layer. Dorefanet [34] extends XNOR-Net from binarization to arbitrary bit-width. LQ-nets further adopt adaptive quantizer to enhance the flexibility of the model. In [11], network pruning technique is adopted to optimize the quantization interval. In order to prove that our method can be applied to various quantization algorithms, we choose BNN [8], DoReFa-net [34] and LQ-nets [30] as our base models.

2.2   Knowledge Transfer

DNNs learn 'knowledge' from training data, and the 'knowledge' can be transferred from one DNN to another. In logits-based Knowledge Transfer [7], knowledge can be viewed as the soft label from the pre-trained teacher DNN, which is absorbed by student DNN via minimizing the Kullback-Leibler divergence between outputs of two DNNs. Such process can be repeated for multiple times for further enhancement [4]. In mutual learning [31], DNNs can learn from each other, rather than one way transfer from teacher to student.

Knowledge can also be transferred via feature maps. Since feature maps have much higher dimensions, it is more challenging to align two DNNs in middle layer than logits. To transfer knowledge, previous frameworks empirically minimize the p-norms between feature maps from two DNNs, without further explanation. Some methods [14,26,27] add 'attention' to original feature maps, or directly transfer the attention maps between different DNNs [29]. And generative adversarial learning is adopted in [16] to better align different branches. However, most frameworks can not be applied to transfer feature-based knowledge from 32-bit DNNs to low-bit DNNs, because it is nontrivial to align feature maps with different numerical precision.

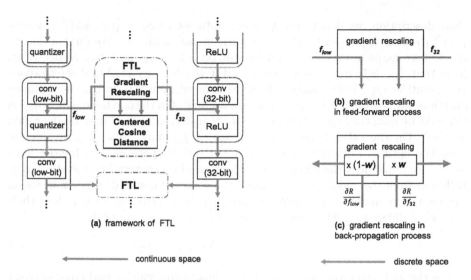

(a) framework of FTL

(b) gradient rescaling in feed-forward process

(c) gradient rescaling in back-propagation process

◀——————— continuous space

◀——————— discrete space

Fig. 1. Subfigure **(a)** is the overall framework of FTL. Subfigure **(b)** and **(c)** are further demonstration of gradient rescaling module in FTL.

3 Feature Transfer for Low-Bit DNNs

This section introduces the proposed method, which is specially designed for low-bit DNNs to overcome the space mismatch problem. Below we first introduce the overall framework, then the key components will be addressed in details.

3.1 Overall Framework

We attempt to utilize a 32-bit DNN to guide the training of a low-bit DNN via feature maps. Both two DNN branches are trained from scratch. This training scheme enables the low-bit DNN to learn the path to convergence [18]. For the sake of simplicity, the 32-bit DNN is constructed with the same hyper-parameters of the low-bit DNN. The only difference between two DNNs is that the low-bit one quantizes its weights and feature maps in each layer to discrete space.

Figure 1 shows the overall framework of FTL. Intuitively, the low-bit DNN should learn from multiple layers of the 32-bit DNN to achieve more accuracy gains. However, feature maps of the first few layers often have weaker semantic information and more redundant details, which makes interaction via these layers a universal challenge for Knowledge Transfer frameworks. Since the focus of this paper is to alleviate the problem caused by the mismatch between continuous space and discrete space, we only make two DNNs interact via the output of the last convolution layer, which follows the practice in previous frameworks [12,27]. We do not need to explicitly define the form of the quantizer $Q(\cdot)$ because the proposed framework is independent of $Q(\cdot)$. The interaction between two DNN branches is achieved by minimizing a distance function in continuous space. For clear description, we denote the training data set as $S_t = \{(x_i, y_i)\}_{i=1}^N$, where $\{x_i\}_{i=1}^N$ are the inputs and $\{y_i\}_{i=1}^N$ are corresponding targets. We further denote the feature maps in the 32-bit and low-bit branch as f_{32} and f_{low} respectively. Note that f_{low} is in continuous space. And it will be converted to discrete space via quantizer $Q(\cdot)$ before further forward computation. To design the distance function, two factors need to be taken into account. On the one hand, since f_{low} is followed by quantizer $Q(\cdot)$, the knowledge transferred to f_{low} may be degraded by $Q(\cdot)$. On the other hand, the guidance of f_{32} may cause f_{low} to deviate from the optimal numerical range for quantization operation. To handle both issues, we implement the distance function based on centered cosine similarity. Different from the widely-used p-norms, the centered cosine distance focuses on the relative numerical relationship between feature elements, rather than their numerical differences. The overall optimization object is to obtain:

$$\min \quad L_{C_{32}} + L_{C_{low}} + \lambda \cdot R(f_{low}, f_{32}), \tag{1}$$

where the first two terms $L_{C_{32}}$ and $L_{C_{low}}$ denote the widely-used cross entropy losses for the 32-bit DNN and the low-bit DNN respectively. The third term $R(f_{low}, f_{32})$ denotes the distance function, which is designed to add additional supervision on low-bit DNNs and can be viewed as regularization. $\lambda \geq 0$ is a balancing parameter.

In our framework, knowledge is transferred from f_{32} to f_{low}. It seems straightforward to make f_{32} not influenced by f_{low} (equivalent to set $\frac{\partial R}{\partial f_{32}} = 0$). However, due to its limited representational capacity, the low-bit DNN may fail to follow the strong guidance from the 32-bit DNN and the 32-bit DNN should 'realize' it and make some concessions, which in turn requires $\frac{\partial R}{\partial f_{32}} \neq 0$. To balance these two requirements, we should control how much $\frac{\partial R}{\partial f_{32}}$ is retained. Therefore, Gradient Rescaling Module is designed to balance the 'guidance' and 'concessions' from the 32-bit DNN. Next, we will introduce the design of regularization function in detail, and further combine it with Gradient Rescaling Module.

3.2   Distance Function

Definition. In this section, we explore the design of distance function for the low-bit branch. The goal is to transfer knowledge from f_{32} to $Q(f_{low})$, where $Q(\cdot)$ is the feature quantizer. Since f_{32} and $Q(f_{low})$ lies in continous space and discrete space respectively, it is nontrivial to minimize the distance between $Q(f_{low})$ and f_{32}. Previous methods [27,35] first quantize f_{32} and then utilize $Q(f_{32})$ to guide $Q(f_{low})$. However, minimizing the distance in discrete space brings abrupt changes to gradients, and quantization operation on f_{32} can lead to a loss of information for the knowledge. We instead directly minimize the distance between f_{low} and f_{32}, and focus on their mismatch probability [22,24]. To be specific, given any pair of feature elements $f_{32}^i \leq f_{32}^j$ in the 32-bit branch, it is desired that the low-bit branch produces $f_{low}^i \leq f_{low}^j$, so that feature elements in f_{low} and f_{32} have a high positive correlation. To achieve this purpose, we define the distance function based on centered cosine similarity, as shown in Eq. (2).

$$R(f_{32}, f_{low}) = 1 - \frac{(f_{low} - \overline{f_{low}}) \cdot (f_{32} - \overline{f_{32}})}{\left\| f_{low} - \overline{f_{low}} \right\|_2 \left\| f_{32} - \overline{f_{32}} \right\|_2},$$ (2)

The distance function defined by Eq. (2) enables f_{low} to produce a high centered cosine similarity with f_{32}. Note that due to the non-decreasing property of $Q(\cdot)$, if $f_{low}^i \leq f_{low}^j$, the quantized feature maps in the low-bit branch also satisfy $Q(f_{low}^i) \leq Q(f_{low}^j)$, which ensures the consistency of knowledge passing through $Q(\cdot)$. Compared with p-norms, centered cosine distance only constrains the relative numerical relationship between elements of f_{low} rather than the magnitude of each element, which brings negligible changes to the data distribution of f_{low} during training. Such property is beneficial for the low-bit branch to converge, because f_{low} should maintain certain distribution to match with the quantizer $Q(\cdot)$, and the distribution fluctuation will be amplified by $Q(f_{low})$ due to its coarse feature pixel values.

Relationship with Mutual Information. We assume that feature maps f_{low} and f_{32} are generated by variables v_{low} and v_{32} respectively. Since previous works [2,9] have shown that both f_{low} and f_{32} follow a data distribution similar to Gaussian, we model both v_{low} and v_{32} as Gaussian variables $v_{low} \sim \mathcal{N}(\mu_{low}, \sigma_{low}^2)$ and $v_{32} \sim \mathcal{N}(\mu_{32}, \sigma_{32}^2)$. On this basis, the Mutual Information between v_{low} and v_{32} can be explicit formulated as Eq. (3) [5], where ρ is the correlation coefficient between v_{low} and v_{32}, ranging from −1 to 1. Note that ρ can be estimated by the centered cosine similarity between f_{32} and f_{low}. Therefore, the minimizing the centered cosine distance can be viewed as to increase of Mutual Information between v_{low} and v_{32}.

$$MI(v_{low}, v_{32}) = -\frac{1}{2}log(1 - \rho^2).$$ (3)

The question arising naturally is that can we directly maximize the Mutual Information in Eq. (3) rather than centered cosine similarity for guidance? Below we demonstrate two main drawbacks of Eq. (3). The first is gradients explosion, which can lead to unstable training process, as is shown in Eq. (4). The second problem is that maximizing Eq. (3) may induce $\rho \to -1$, which indicates that v_{low} and v_{32} have a strong negative correlation. However, v_{low} and v_{32} should instead have a positive correlation to ensure both of them are activated (or clipped), because most quantizers and activation functions only activate larger values while clipping smaller ones. Therefore, it is inappropriate to directly utilize Eq. (3) to guide the low-bit DNN.

$$\lim_{|\rho| \to 1} \left| \frac{\partial \, log(1 - \rho^2)}{\partial \rho} \right| = +\infty.$$ (4)

3.3   Gradient Rescaling Module

In the field of knowledge transfer, two (or more) DNNs interact typically by two modes: teacher-student mode and mutual learning mode. The former transfers knowledge unidirectionally from 'teacher' DNN to 'student' DNN, while The latter allows DNNs to learn from each other.

Nevertheless, neither mode is optimal for the proposed algorithm. In this paper, we aim to transfer knowledge from the 32-bit DNN to the low-bit DNN, however, the latter may fail to absorb knowledge from the former due to its limited representational capacity and slow convergence speed. Simply with teacher-student mode, the 32-bit DNN cannot adjust itself according to the feedback from the low-bit DNN. Simply with mutual learning mode, the 32-bit DNN makes too many concessions and the noise from the low-bit DNN may worsen its performance, which in turn degrades its guidance for the low-bit DNN.

For the reasons above, Gradient Rescaling Module is designed to combine the advantages of both strategies, as is shown in Fig. 1(b)(c). In feed-forward process, Gradient Rescaling Module is simply an identity function and can be ignored. In back-propagation process, gradients of $R(f_{low}, f_{32})$ can be obtained, and Gradient Rescaling Module scales this gradients by the factor of $1 - w$ and w for the low-bit DNN and the 32-bit DNN respectively. w is a hyper-parameter, with the range of 0 to 0.5. Then the gradients of Eq. (1) with respect to f_{low} and f_{32} can be denoted as Eq. (5) and Eq. (6):

$$\Delta_{f_{low}} L = \frac{\partial L_{C_{low}}}{\partial f_{low}} + (1 - w) \cdot \lambda \cdot \frac{\partial R}{\partial f_{low}} \tag{5}$$

and

$$\Delta_{f_{32}} L = \frac{\partial L_{C_{32}}}{\partial f_{32}} + w \cdot \lambda \cdot \frac{\partial R}{\partial f_{32}}. \tag{6}$$

Following the same notation in Eq. (1), the low-bit DNN absorbs knowledge from the 32-bit DNN through $\frac{\partial R}{\partial f_{low}}$ in Eq. (5), while the latter receives feedback from the former via $\frac{\partial R}{\partial f_{32}}$ in Eq. (6). It can be seen that both teacher-student mode (when $w = 0$, f_{32} is not influenced by f_{low}.) and mutual learning mode (when $w = 0.5$, f_{32} and f_{low} affect each other to the same extent.) can be viewed as the extreme cases of Gradient Rescaling Module. With proper choice of hyper-parameter w (0 to 0.5), the 32-bit DNN can make 'appropriate' adjustments and concessions based on the feedback, which can relax its regularization on the low-bit DNN.

4   Experiments

In this section, we present experimental analysis on two widely used benchmark datasets, Cifar-10/100 [13] and ImageNet (ILSVRC12) [3]. Cifar-10 has 60,000 32×32 colour images in 10 classes, with 50,000 training images and 10,000 test images. Cifar-100 further divides Cifar-10 dataset to 100 classes. ImageNet (ILSVRC12) is a large scale dataset containing about 1.2 million training images and 50,000 validation images in 1,000 classes.

4.1 Implementation Details

To verify the effectiveness of the proposed algorithm, we experiment with three well-known low-bit DNNs: BNN [8], DoReFa-Net [34] and LQ-Nets [30]. To better expose the problem of space mismatch, we first experiment with simple quantization method BNN and Dorefa-Net, because simple methods suffer more from the mismatch problem. We further verify the performance on LQ-nets, one of the state-of-the-art quantization methods. All experiments are implemented based on the corresponding officially released source codes. To eliminate other distractions, we keep all experiment settings (e.g. network structure, data augmentation, hyper-parameters) consistent between standard low-bit DNNs (baseline) and guided low-bit DNNs (ours). The proposed algorithm has two hyper-parameters, i.e. λ and w. λ is a balancing parameter between empirical loss and regularization loss. We choose proper λ to make the gradients of the two loss functions comparable, so that both of them can contribute to the training. w in Gradient Rescaling Module controls the interaction mode between two DNNs, which ranges from 0 to 0.5. With a larger w, the low-bit DNN is more likely to converge while the 32-bit DNN suffers more noise from the low-bit DNN, which in turn degrades its guidance for the low-bit one. Thus, we start with $w = 0.5$ and reduce it by 10x each time until no significant performance degradation is observed for the 32-bit DNN. In fact, the significant performance of FTL is not due to excessive hyper-parameter adjustment. We set $w = 0.005$ (unless otherwise stated) for all experiments rather than searching for better choice for each model. And λ ranges from 1 to 3.

4.2 Performance Evaluation

The proposed algorithm aims to use the 32-bit DNN to guide training of the low-bit DNN. In this section, we evaluate the performance of the proposed algorithm on Cifar-10/100 [13] and ImageNet [3].

Performance on Cifar-10/100. Table 1 presents the experimental results of Resnet-small model and Vgg-small model. Since advanced low-bit DNNs (e.g. DoReFa-Net [34] and LQ-Nets [30]) have already achieved excellent performance on small scale datasets like Cifar-10/100, we only experiment with BNN [8], a naive quantization algorithm. Table 1 shows that the proposed algorithm brings 0.79% to 3.00% accuracy gains over the baseline for Cifar-10/100, where "W/A/G" denotes the bit-width of weights/activations/gradients.

Table 1. Top-1 accuracy (average of 5 runs) on Cifar10/100. "W/A/G" denotes the bit-width of weights/activations/gradients. "Full precision" denotes the classification accuracy of the 32-bit DNN. "Baseline" represents the low-bit DNN trained without guidance.

Dataset	Model	Bit-width(W/A/G)	Baseline	Ours	Accuracy gain	Full precision
Cifar10	Resnet-small	1/1/32	88.16	90.88	**+2.72**	93.7
	Vgg-small	1/1/32	88.98	89.82	**+0.84**	93.0
Cifar100	Resnet-small	1/1/32	61.20	64.20	**+3.00**	70.9
	Vgg-small	1/1/32	63.76	64.55	**+0.79**	69.1

Table 2. Top-1 accuracy on ImageNet. "Quantizer type" refers to the type of quantizer in certain quantization method. "Method" means different quantization algorithm. "W/A/G" denotes the bit-width of weights/activations/gradients. "Full precision" denotes the classification accuracy of the 32-bit DNN. "Baseline" represents the low-bit DNN trained without FTL.

Method	Model	Bit-width(W/A/G)	Baseline	Ours	Accuracy gain	Full precision
BNN	Alexnet	1/1/32	36.6	37.9	**+1.3**	60.6
	Resnet-18	1/1/32	46.3	46.9	**+0.6**	69.6
DoReFa-Net	Alexnet	1/2/32	52.6	54.0	**+1.4**	59.7
	Alexnet	1/2/4	41.5	44.9	**+3.4**	59.7
	Resnet-18	1/2/32	56.1	57.0	**+0.9**	69.6
	Resnet-18	1/2/4	52.1	53.7	**+1.6**	69.6
LQ-Net	Alexnet	1/2/32	55.7	56.3	**+0.6**	61.8
	Resnet-18	1/2/32	62.6	63.1	**+0.5**	70.3
	Resnet-34	1/2/32	66.3	67.4	**+1.1**	73.8
	Resnet-50	1/2/32	68.7	69.6	**+0.9**	76.4
	Resnet-50	2/2/32	70.3	71.4	**+1.1**	76.4

Table 3. Comparison between the state-of-the-art and ours on Cifar-10. "JGT" denotes the framework proposed in [35]. Since no experiment is conducted based on BNN in the original paper, we implement "JGT" ourselves. All results are average of 5 runs.

Model	Baseline	JGT	**Ours**
Resnet-small	88.16	88.89	**90.88**
Vgg-small	88.98	89.10	**89.82**

Performance on ImageNet. Table 2 presents the experimental results on the ImageNet. Though various quantization algorithms have been developed, low-bit DNNs still struggle to achieve satisfying performance on such large scale dataset. Hence, we conduct various experiments on ImageNet with different qunatization methods, different models and different bit-width. Experimental results show 0.5% to 3.4% accuracy gains. The enhancement for different models varies a little, which is mainly because we simply assign the same hyper-parameter value for all

Table 4. Comparison between the state-of-the-art and ours on ImageNet with Alexnet. "JGT" and "JGT*" denotes the guided framework proposed in [35] with different training strategy. We directly quote the experimental results for JGT and JGT* from the original paper.

	Top-1	Top-5		Top-1	Top-5
JGT	50.0	74.1	Baseline (JGT)	48.8	72.2
JGT*	51.6	76.2	Baseline (JGT*)	50.9	74.9
Ours	**54.0**	**77.2**	Baseline (Ours)	52.6	76.0

experiments without further tuning. Note that with quantized gradients of 4-bit (equivalent to adding more noise to gradients), the proposed algorithm can bring more accuracy gains. This phenomenon demonstrates that additional supervision on middle layers can alleviate the negative impact of noise in gradients [28].

Comparison with the State-of-the-Art. As is introduced above, various techniques have been proposed to better train a low-bit DNN, which can be divided into Incremental quantization [33], Logits Transfer [18,20], Attention Transfer [17] and Feature Transfer [27,35]. Since different kinds of methods can be applied simultaneously for further enhancement, it is proper to only make comparison within the same category. This paper focuses on the Feature Transfer approach. Jointly Guided training (JGT) proposed in [35] is the state-of-the-art framework to guide the low-bit DNN via feature maps. In this section, we make a comparison between JGT and FTL. There is no results related to TCO [27] because TCO is specially designed for object detection task. Table 3 and Table 4 demonstrate the results implemented on BNN [8] and DoReFa-Net [34] respectively. No experiment is conducted on LQ-nets [30] because JGT framework is not applicable to low-bit DNNs with adaptive quantizers (e.g. LQ-nets [30]), which is a serious limitation compared with our framework. More than that, experimental results show that FTL can even bring more accuracy gains when training BNN and DoReFa-Net. The gains are mainly from the information-rich continuous-space knowledge.

4.3 Ablation Study

FTL consists of Centered Cosine Distance and Gradient Rescaling Module. To verify their effectiveness, ablation study is conducted based on BNN [8].

Centered Cosine Distance

Results. To analyze the effectiveness of centered cosine distance implemented with centered cosine similarity, we make a comparison between the centered cosine distance and the widely used p-norm $\|\cdot\|_p$. Following [12,35], we take $p = 1$ for $\|\cdot\|_p$, denoted as L1 norm. Since the performance of each distance

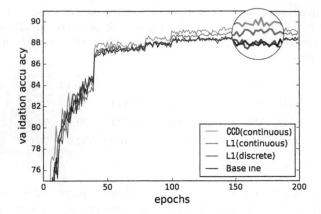

Fig. 2. Effectiveness of centered cosine distance. "CCD(continuous)" represents the proposed centered cosine distance, which is applied in continuous space. "L1(discrete)" and "L1(continuous)" curves represent L1 norm applied in discrete and continuous space, while "Baseline" is standard training of the low-bit DNN. Compared to "Baseline", "MIR(continuous)", "L1(continuous)" and "L1(discrete)" achieve 0.84%, +0.45% and −0.07% accuracy gains respectively.

function is greatly affected by the balancing parameter λ in Eq. (1), we search for the 'optimal' λ for L1 norm in {0.04, 0.2, 1, 5, 25, 100} and demonstrate the best performance. In order to reduce random fluctuations in training, each curve is obtained by averaging 5 runs. In our framework, centered cosine distance is applied in continuous space. So we also implement L1 norm in continuous space, which is denoted as "L1(continuous)" in Fig. 2. It can be seen that our centered cosine distance (CCD) obviously outperforms L1 norm when both applied in continuous space.

Besides that, in order to verify whether guiding the low-bit branch in continuous space can bring more performance gains, we also experiment with L1 norm in discrete space, which is represented as "L1(discrete)" in Fig. 2. It can be seen that "L1(discrete)" can hardly bring performance gains over "Baseline" while "L1(continuous)" achieve better performance, which is consistent with our analysis in Introduction section.

Further Analysis. Below we further analyze why centered cosine distance outperforms p-norm. The feature maps from the low-bit DNN and the 32-bit DNN are denoted as f_{low} and f_{32}, respectively. According to Eq. (2), centered cosine distance inclines f_{low} to mimic the relative numerical relationship in f_{32}. However, regularized by p-norm, f_{low} tends to learn the magnitude of each element in f_{32}, which is a stronger regularization than centered cosine distance. In consequence, p-norm may affect the overall distribution of f_{low}. In low-bit DNNs, the distribution of f_{low} is of vital importance and it should match the pre-defined quantizer. Otherwise the quantization noise will increase and degrade the performance of low-bit DNNs.

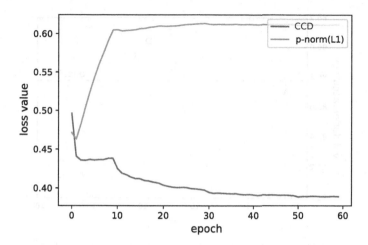

Fig. 3. Curves of centered cosine distance (CCD) and p-norm during fine-tuning. Gradients of both regularization are not back-propagated. Results are averaged of 5 runs.

An empirical experiment is conducted to demonstrate the difference between centered cosine distance and p-norm. We initialize a low-bit DNN with a pretrained 32-bit DNN, and fine-tune it without any feature guidance. Such initialization is to make f_{low} and f_{32} have certain similarities at the beginning. As the fine-tuning progresses, the low-bit DNN gradually adapts itself to the pre-defined quantizer. We report the loss value of centered cosine distance and p-norm between f_{low} and f_{32} at every epoch in Fig. 3. Note that no gradients of both guidance are back-propagated. We observe an interesting phenomenon that p-norm curve shows an upward trend, which suggests that p-norm negatively impacts the adaptation of low-bit DNNs to the pre-defined quantizer. In contrast, centered cosine distance decreases as the fine-tuning progresses. Since we do not back-propagate the gradients of the centered cosine distance (CCD), intuitively, the curve of CCD should increase or remain stable at best. However, only trained with empirical loss, the feature maps of the low-bit branch can also minimize its centered cosine distance with the 32-bit branch, which provides some insights for explaining the training of low-bit DNNs. In Fig. 3, the CCD between two branches is converged to ≈ 0.4. In the proposed framework, since we back-propagate the gradient of CCD, it can further decrease to ≈ 0.2. Due to their differences between CCD and p-norms, the former can bring more accuracy gains to low-bit DNNs.

Gradient Rescaling Module. In this section, we analyze whether Gradient Rescaling Module can explore better interaction modes between two DNNs than teacher-student mode [7] and mutual learning mode [31]. We conduct experiments on Cifar-10 with vgg-small variant (only **0.5×** channel numbers to save training time). All experimental results are average of 5 runs. As is shown in Fig. 4, we change w (hyper-parameter in Gradient Rescaling Module) from 1e–5

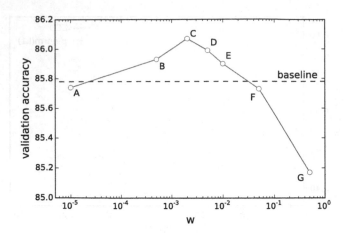

Fig. 4. Impact of Gradient Rescaling Module. The X-axis is the hyper-parameter w in Gradient Rescaling Module. A to G represent $w = $ 1e−5, 5e−4, 2e−3, 5e−3, 1e−2, 5e−2 and 5e−1 respectively. "Baseline" represents directly training for the low-bit DNN. Compared to "Baseline", "A" to "G" achieve −0.04%, +0.15%, +0.29%, +0.21%, +0.12%, −0.05%, −0.61% accuracy gains respectively.

to 5e−1 while other conditions remain unchanged, which corresponds to point "A" to point "G" respectively. Among them, G ($w = 0.5$) is equal to mutual learning mode, and A ($w \approx 0$) can be approximately considered as teacher-student mode. Both modes fail to bring performance gains. This can be explained from two aspects. On the one hand, low-bit DNNs have much smaller representational capacity than 32-bit DNNs. Merely with teacher-student mode ($w = 0$), the low-bit DNN fails to mimic the feature maps from the latter since the 32-bit one makes no concession and adjustments. On the other hand, with mutual learning mode ($w = 0.5$), the 32-bit DNN absorbs a large amount of feedback (can be viewed as noise) from the low-bit DNN, which in turn worsens its guidance to the latter. However, our Gradient Rescaling Module enables the exploration (different choices of w) for better interaction modes (e.g. point "C" and "D") instead of having to choose between "A" and "G".

4.4   Combination with Other Methods

Except the proposed algorithm, there exist other methods to assist training of low-bit DNNs such as Logits Transfer and fine-tuning from pre-trained 32-bit DNN. Since these techniques and our FTL enhance performance of low-bit DNNs from different aspects, we explore whether combining FTL with these methods leads to better performance. We conduct experiments on Cifar-10 with Vgg-small model, as is shown in Table 5. For "Fine-tuning" and "Fine-tuning + ours" method, we only train for 60 epochs (200 in others) since it has better initialization. All experimental results are average of 5 runs. It can be seen that the proposed algorithm can be combined with other methods for fast training or better performance.

Table 5. Combination with other methods. "Logits Transfer" denotes Knowledge Distillation propsed in [7]. "Fine-tuning" denotes fine-tuning from a pre-trained 32-bit DNN. All methods are trained for 200 epochs except "Fine-tuning" and "Fine-tuning + Ours".

Method	Validation accuracy
Baseline	88.98
Ours	**89.82**
Fine-tuning (60 epochs)	89.31
Fine-tuning + Ours (60 epochs)	**89.62**
Logits Transfer	89.49
Logits Transfer + Ours	**89.96**

5 Conclusion

We analyze the difficulty in optimizing low-bit DNNs and propose a universal framework named FTL to assist its training. In FTL, an auxiliary 32-bit DNN is constructed to provide middle layer supervision for the low-bit one. Different from traditional discrete space supervision, we make two DNNs interact in continuous space. Considering the quantization operation in the low-bit DNN, we guide the low-bit DNN with centered cosine distance, which has better performance compared to empirically used p-norms. Besides, Gradient Rescaling Module is designed to coordinate the training of two DNNs, which can combine the advantages of teacher-student mode and mutual learning mode.

Experimental results suggest that with FTL, the classification accuracy of three different low-bit DNNs increases by 0.5% to 3.4%. Moreover, our framework can be well combined with other existing methods (e.g. Knowledge Distillation) to train a more accurate low-bit DNN. For future work, we plan to provide supervision for multiple middle layers to better guide training. Furthermore, the 'attention' mechanism can also be considered to improve the quality of the guidance.

Acknowledgement. This work is supported by the National Key Research and Development Program of China (No. 2019YFB1804304), SHEITC (No. 2018-RGZN-02046), 111 plan (No. BP0719010), and STCSM (No. 18DZ2270700), and State Key Laboratory of UHD Video and Audio Production and Presentation. The computations in this paper were run on the p 2.0 cluster supported by the Center for High Performance Computing at Shanghai Jiao Tong University.

References

1. Ahn, S., Hu, S.X., Damianou, A., Lawrence, N.D., Dai, Z.: Variational information distillation for knowledge transfer. In: Proceedings of the IEEE Conference on Computer Vision and Pattern Recognition, pp. 9163–9171 (2019)

2. Cai, Z., He, X., Sun, J., Vasconcelos, N.: Deep learning with low precision by half-wave gaussian quantization. In: Proceedings of the IEEE Conference on Computer Vision and Pattern Recognition, pp. 5918–5926 (2017)
3. Deng, J., Dong, W., Socher, R., Li, L.J., Li, K., Fei-Fei, L.: ImageNet: a large-scale hierarchical image database. In: 2009 IEEE Conference on Computer Vision and Pattern Recognition, pp. 248–255. IEEE (2009)
4. Furlanello, T., Lipton, Z., Tschannen, M., Itti, L., Anandkumar, A.: Born again neural networks. In: International Conference on Machine Learning, pp. 1607–1616 (2018)
5. Gel'Fand, I., Yaglom, A.: About a random function contained in another such function. Eleven Pap. Anal. Probab. Topol. **12**, 199 (1959)
6. Heo, B., Kim, J., Yun, S., Park, H., Kwak, N., Choi, J.Y.: A comprehensive overhaul of feature distillation. In: Proceedings of the IEEE International Conference on Computer Vision, pp. 1921–1930 (2019)
7. Hinton, G., Vinyals, O., Dean, J.: Distilling the knowledge in a neural network. arXiv preprint arXiv:1503.02531 (2015)
8. Hubara, I., Courbariaux, M., Soudry, D., El-Yaniv, R., Bengio, Y.: Binarized neural networks. In: Advances in Neural Information Processing Systems, pp. 4107–4115 (2016)
9. Ioffe, S., Szegedy, C.: Batch normalization: accelerating deep network training by reducing internal covariate shift. In: International Conference on Machine Learning, pp. 448–456 (2015)
10. Jacob, B., et al.: Quantization and training of neural networks for efficient integer-arithmetic-only inference. In: Proceedings of the IEEE Conference on Computer Vision and Pattern Recognition, pp. 2704–2713 (2018)
11. Jung, S., et al.: Learning to quantize deep networks by optimizing quantization intervals with task loss. In: Proceedings of the IEEE Conference on Computer Vision and Pattern Recognition, pp. 4350–4359 (2019)
12. Kim, J., Park, S., Kwak, N.: Paraphrasing complex network: network compression via factor transfer. In: Advances in Neural Information Processing Systems, pp. 2760–2769 (2018)
13. Krizhevsky, A., Hinton, G., et al.: Learning multiple layers of features from tiny images. Technical report, Citeseer (2009)
14. Li, X., Xiong, H., Wang, H., Rao, Y., Liu, L., Huan, J.: Delta: deep learning transfer using feature map with attention for convolutional networks. In: International Conference on Learning Representations (2019). https://openreview.net/forum?id=rkgbwsAcYm
15. Lin, X., Zhao, C., Pan, W.: Towards accurate binary convolutional neural network. In: Advances in Neural Information Processing Systems, pp. 345–353 (2017)
16. Liu, Y., Chen, K., Liu, C., Qin, Z., Luo, Z., Wang, J.: Structured knowledge distillation for semantic segmentation. In: Proceedings of the IEEE Conference on Computer Vision and Pattern Recognition, pp. 2604–2613 (2019)
17. Martinez, B., Yang, J., Bulat, A., Tzimiropoulos, G.: Training binary neural networks with real-to-binary convolutions. In: International Conference on Learning Representations (2020). https://openreview.net/forum?id=BJg4NgBKvH
18. Mishra, A., Marr, D.: Apprentice: using knowledge distillation techniques to improve low-precision network accuracy. arXiv preprint arXiv:1711.05852 (2017)
19. Nagel, M., Baalen, M.v., Blankevoort, T., Welling, M.: Data-free quantization through weight equalization and bias correction. In: Proceedings of the IEEE International Conference on Computer Vision, pp. 1325–1334 (2019)

20. Polino, A., Pascanu, R., Alistarh, D.: Model compression via distillation and quantization. arXiv preprint arXiv:1802.05668 (2018)
21. Rastegari, M., Ordonez, V., Redmon, J., Farhadi, A.: XNOR-Net: ImageNet classification using binary convolutional neural networks. In: Leibe, B., Matas, J., Sebe, N., Welling, M. (eds.) ECCV 2016. LNCS, vol. 9908, pp. 525–542. Springer, Cham (2016). https://doi.org/10.1007/978-3-319-46493-0_32
22. Sakr, C., Kim, Y., Shanbhag, N.: Analytical guarantees on numerical precision of deep neural networks. In: Proceedings of the 34th International Conference on Machine Learning, vol. 70, pp. 3007–3016. JMLR. org (2017)
23. Sun, X., et al.: Hybrid 8-bit floating point (HFP8) training and inference for deep neural networks. In: Advances in Neural Information Processing Systems, pp. 4901–4910 (2019)
24. Sun, X., et al.: Hybrid 8-bit floating point (HFP8) training and inference for deep neural networks. In: Wallach, H., Larochelle, H., Beygelzimer, A., d'Alché-Buc, F., Fox, E., Garnett, R. (eds.) Advances in Neural Information Processing Systems, vol. 32, pp. 4900–4909. Curran Associates, Inc. (2019). http://papers.nips.cc/paper/8736-hybrid-8-bit-floating-point-hfp8-training-and-inference-for-deep-neural-networks.pdf
25. Tung, F., Mori, G.: Similarity-preserving knowledge distillation. In: Proceedings of the IEEE International Conference on Computer Vision, pp. 1365–1374 (2019)
26. Wang, T., Yuan, L., Zhang, X., Feng, J.: Distilling object detectors with fine-grained feature imitation. In: Proceedings of the IEEE Conference on Computer Vision and Pattern Recognition, pp. 4933–4942 (2019)
27. Wei, Y., Pan, X., Qin, H., Ouyang, W., Yan, J.: Quantization mimic: towards very tiny CNN for object detection. In: Ferrari, V., Hebert, M., Sminchisescu, C., Weiss, Y. (eds.) ECCV 2018. LNCS, vol. 11212, pp. 274–290. Springer, Cham (2018). https://doi.org/10.1007/978-3-030-01237-3_17
28. Yin, P., Lyu, J., Zhang, S., Osher, S., Qi, Y., Xin, J.: Understanding straight-through estimator in training activation quantized neural nets. arXiv preprint arXiv:1903.05662 (2019)
29. Zagoruyko, S., Komodakis, N.: Paying more attention to attention: improving the performance of convolutional neural networks via attention transfer. arXiv preprint arXiv:1612.03928 (2016)
30. Zhang, D., Yang, J., Ye, D., Hua, G.: LQ-Nets: learned quantization for highly accurate and compact deep neural networks. In: Ferrari, V., Hebert, M., Sminchisescu, C., Weiss, Y. (eds.) ECCV 2018. LNCS, vol. 11212, pp. 373–390. Springer, Cham (2018). https://doi.org/10.1007/978-3-030-01237-3_23
31. Zhang, Y., Xiang, T., Hospedales, T.M., Lu, H.: Deep mutual learning. In: Proceedings of the IEEE Conference on Computer Vision and Pattern Recognition, pp. 4320–4328 (2018)
32. Zhao, R., Hu, Y., Dotzel, J., De Sa, C., Zhang, Z.: Improving neural network quantization without retraining using outlier channel splitting. In: International Conference on Machine Learning, pp. 7543–7552 (2019)
33. Zhou, A., Yao, A., Wang, K., Chen, Y.: Explicit loss-error-aware quantization for low-bit deep neural networks. In: The IEEE Conference on Computer Vision and Pattern Recognition (CVPR), June 2018

34. Zhou, S., Wu, Y., Ni, Z., Zhou, X., Wen, H., Zou, Y.: DoReFa-Net: training low bitwidth convolutional neural networks with low bitwidth gradients. arXiv preprint arXiv:1606.06160 (2016)
35. Zhuang, B., Shen, C., Tan, M., Liu, L., Reid, I.: Towards effective low-bitwidth convolutional neural networks. In: Proceedings of the IEEE Conference on Computer Vision and Pattern Recognition, pp. 7920–7928 (2018)

XingGAN for Person Image Generation

Hao Tang[1,2(✉)], Song Bai[2], Li Zhang[2], Philip H. S. Torr[2], and Nicu Sebe[1,3]

[1] University of Trento, Trento, Italy
hao.tang@unitn.it
[2] University of Oxford, Oxford, UK
[3] Huawei Research Ireland, Dublin, Ireland

Abstract. We propose a novel Generative Adversarial Network (Xing-GAN or CrossingGAN) for person image generation tasks, *i.e.*, translating the pose of a given person to a desired one. The proposed Xing generator consists of two generation branches that model the person's appearance and shape information, respectively. Moreover, we propose two novel blocks to effectively transfer and update the person's shape and appearance embeddings in a crossing way to mutually improve each other, which has not been considered by any other existing GAN-based image generation work. Extensive experiments on two challenging datasets, *i.e.*, Market-1501 and DeepFashion, demonstrate that the proposed XingGAN advances the state-of-the-art performance both in terms of objective quantitative scores and subjective visual realness. The source code and trained models are available at https://github.com/Ha0Tang/XingGAN.

Keywords: Generative Adversarial Networks (GANs) · Person image generation · Appearance cues · Shape cues

1 Introduction

The problem of person image generation aims to generate photo-realistic person images conditioned on an input person image and several desired poses. This task has a wide range of applications such as person image/video generation [2,9,11,19,41] and person re-identification [28,45]. Exiting methods such as [21,22,31,35,45] have achieved promising performance on this challenging task. For example, Zhu *et al.* [45] recently proposed a conditional GAN model that comprises a sequence of pose-attentional transfer blocks. Wherein, each block transfers certain regions it attends to and progressively generates the desired person image.

Although [45] performed an interesting exploration, we still observe unsatisfactory aspects and visual artifacts in the generated person images due to several reasons. First, [45] stacks several convolution layers to generate the attention maps of the shape features, then the generated attention maps are used

Electronic supplementary material The online version of this chapter (https://doi.org/10.1007/978-3-030-58595-2_43) contains supplementary material, which is available to authorized users.

© Springer Nature Switzerland AG 2020
A. Vedaldi et al. (Eds.): ECCV 2020, LNCS 12370, pp. 717–734, 2020.
https://doi.org/10.1007/978-3-030-58595-2_43

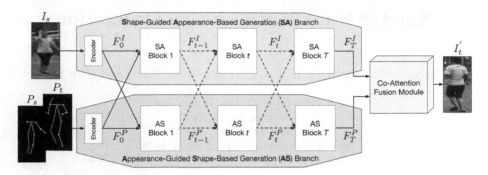

Fig. 1. Overview of the proposed Xing generator. Both the Shape-guided Appearance-based generation (SA) and the Appearance-guided Shape-based generation (AS) branches consist of a sequence of SA and AS blocks in a crossing way. All these components are trained in an end-to-end fashion so that the SA branch and AS branch can benefit from each other to generate more shape-consistent and appearance-consistent person images.

to attentively highlight the appearance features. Since convolutional operations are building blocks that process one local neighborhood at a time, this means that they cannot capture the joint influence between the appearance and the shape features. Second, the attention maps in [45] are only produced by using one single modality, *i.e.*, the pose, leading to insufficiently accurate correlations for both modalities (*i.e.*, the pose and the image modality), and thus misguiding the image generation.

Based on these observations, we propose a novel Generative Adversarial Network (XingGAN or CrossingGAN), which consists of a Xing generator, a shape-guided discriminator, and an appearance-guided discriminator. The overall framework is shown in Fig. 1. The Xing generator consists of three parts, *i.e.*, a Shape-guided Appearance-based generation (SA) branch, an Appearance-guided Shape-based generation (AS) branch, and a co-attention fusion module. Specifically, the proposed SA branch contains a sequence of SA blocks, which aim to progressively update the appearance representation under the guidance of the shape representation, while the proposed AS branch contains a sequence of AS blocks, which aim to progressively update the shape representation under the guidance of the appearance representation. We also present a novel crossing operation in both SA and AS blocks to capture the joint influence between the image modality and the pose modality by creating attention maps jointly produced by both modalities. Moreover, we introduce a co-attention fusion model to better fuse the final appearance and shape features to generate the desired person images. We present an appearance-guided discriminator and a shape-guided discriminator to jointly judge how likely is that the generated image contains the same person in the input image and how well the generated image aligns with the targeted pose, respectively. The proposed XingGAN is trained in an end-to-end fashion so that the generation branches can enjoy the mutually improved benefits from each other.

We conduct extensive experiments on two challenging datasets, *i.e.*, Market-1501 [44] and DeepFashion [20]. Qualitative and quantitative results demonstrate that XingGAN achieves better results than state-of-the-art methods, regarding both visual fidelity and alignment with targeted person poses.

To summarize, the contributions of our paper are three-fold:

- We propose a novel XingGAN (or CrossingGAN) for person image generation. It explores cascaded guidance with two different generation branches, and aims at progressively producing a more detailed synthesis from both person shape and appearance embeddings.
- We propose SA and AS blocks, which effectively transfer and update person shape and appearance features in a crossing way to mutually improve each other, and are able to significantly boost the quality of the final outputs.
- Extensive experiments clearly demonstrate the effectiveness of XingGAN, and show new state-of-the-art results on two challenging datasets, *i.e.*, Market-1501 [44] and DeepFashion [20].

2 Related Work

Generative Adversarial Networks (GANs) [8] consist of a generator and a discriminator where the goal of the generator is to produce photo-realistic images so that the discriminator cannot tell the generated images apart from real images. GANs have shown the capability of generating photo-realistic images [3,14,30]. However, it is still hard for vanilla GANs to generate images in a controlled setting. To fix this limitation, Conditional GANs (CGANs) [23] have been proposed.

Image-to-Image Translation aims to learning the translation mapping between target and input images. CGANs have achieved decent results in pixel-wise aligned image-to-image translation tasks [1,12,34]. For example, Isola *et al.* propose Pix2pix [12], which adopts CGANs to generate the target domain images based on the input domain images, such as photo-to-map, sketch-to-image, and night-to-day. However, pixel-wise alignment is not suitable for person image generation tasks due to the shape deformation between the input person image and target person image.

Person Image Generation. To remedy this, several works started to use poses to guide person image generation [7,21,22,31,35,45]. For example, Ma *et al.* first present PG2 [21], which is a two-stage model to generate the target person images based on an input image and the target poses. Moreover, Siarohin *et al.* propose PoseGAN [31], which requires an extensive affine transformation computation to deal with the input-output misalignment caused by pose differences. Zhu *et al.* propose Pose-Transfer [45], which contains a sequence of pose-attentional transfer blocks to generate the target person image progressively. Besides the aforementioned supervised methods, several works focus on solving this task in an unsupervised setting [27,33]. For instance, Pumarola *et al.* propose an unsupervised framework [27] to generate person images, which induces some geometric errors as revealed in their paper.

Note that the aforementioned methods adopt human keypoints or skeleton as pose guidance, which are usually extracted by using OpenPose [4]. In addition, several works adopt DensePose [24], 3D pose [18], and segmented pose [6] to generate person images because they contain more information about body depth and part segmentation, producing better results with more texture details. However, the keypoint-based pose representation is much cheaper and more flexible than the DensePose, 3D pose, segmented pose representations, and can be more easily applied to practical applications. Therefore, we favor keypoint-based pose representation in this paper.

Image-Guidance Conditioning Schemes. Recently, there were proposed many schemes to incorporate the extra guidance (*e.g.*, human poses [21,45], segmentation maps [25,36,37], facial landmarks [35,42], *etc*) into an image-to-image translation model, which can be divided into four categories, *i.e.*, input concatenation [35,40,43], feature concatenation [7,16–18,21,22], one-way guidance-to-image interaction [10,25,26,31], two-way guidance-and-image interaction [1,5,45].

The most straightforward way of conditioning the guidance is to concatenate the input image and the guidance along the channel dimension. For example, C2GAN [35] takes the input person image and the targeted poses as input to output the corresponding targeted person images. Instead of concatenating the guidance and the image at the input, several works [7,21,22] concatenate their feature representations at a certain layer. For instance, PG2 [21] concatenates the embedded pose feature with the embedded image feature at the bottleneck fully connected layer. Another more general scheme is to use the guidance to guide the generation of the image. For example, Siarohin *et al.* [31] first learn an affine transformation between the input and the target pose, then they use it to 'move' the feature maps between the input image and the targeted image. Unlike existing one-way guidance-to-image interaction schemes that allow information flow only from the guidance to the input image, a recent scheme, *i.e.*, two-way guidance-and-image interaction, also considers the information flow from the input image back to the guidance [1,45]. For example, Zhu *et al.* [45] propose an attention-based GAN model to simultaneously update the person's appearance and shape features under the guidance of each other, and show that the proposed two-way guidance-and-image interaction strategy leads to better performance on person image generation tasks.

Contrary to the existing two-way guidance-and-image interaction schemes [1, 45] that allow both the image and guidance to guide and update each other in a local way, we show that the proposed cross-conditioning strategy can further improve the performance of person image generation tasks.

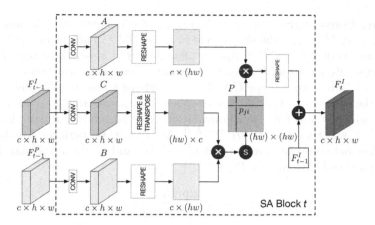

Fig. 2. Structure of the proposed SA block which takes the previous appearance code F_{t-1}^I and the previous shape code F_{t-1}^P as input and obtains the appearance code F_t^I in a crossed non-local way. The symbols $\oplus$, $\otimes$ and ⓢ and ⓒ denote element-wise addition, element-wise multiplication, Softmax activation, and channel-wise concatenation, respectively.

3   Xing Generative Adversarial Networks

We start by presenting the details of the proposed XingGAN (Fig. 1) consisting of three parts, *i.e.*, a Shape-guided Appearance-based generation (SA) branch modeling the person shape representation, an Appearance-guided Shape-based generation (AS) branch modeling the person appearance representation, and a Co-Attention Fusion (CAF) module for fusing these two branches. In the following, we first present the design of the two proposed generation branches, and then introduce the co-attention fusion module. Lastly, we present the proposed two discriminators, the overall optimization objective and implementation details.

The inputs of the proposed Xing generator are the source image I_s, the source pose P_s, and the target pose P_t. The goal is to translate the pose of the person in the source image I_s from the source pose P_s to the target pose P_t, thus synthesizing a photo-realistic person image I_t'. In this way, the source image I_s provides the appearance information and the poses (P_s, P_t) provide the shape information to the Xing generator for synthesizing the desired person image.

Shape-Guided Appearance-Based Generation. The proposed Shape-guided Appearance-based generation (SA) branch consists of an image encoder and a series of the proposed SA blocks. The source image I_s is first fed into the image encoder to produce the appearance code F_0^I, as shown in Fig. 1. The encoder consists of two convolutional layers in our experiments. The SA branch contains several cascaded SA blocks which progressively update the initial appearance code F_0^I to the final appearance code F_T^I under the guidance of the AS branch. As we can see in Fig. 1, all SA blocks have an identical network structure. Consider the t-th block in Fig. 2, whose inputs are the appearance code $F_{t-1}^I \in \mathbb{R}^{c \times h \times w}$ and the shape code $F_{t-1}^P \in \mathbb{R}^{c \times h \times w}$. The output is the refined appearance code $F_t^I \in \mathbb{R}^{c \times h \times w}$. Specifically, given the appearance code F_{t-1}^I, we first feed it into a convolution layer to generate a new appearance code C, where $C \in \mathbb{R}^{c \times h \times w}$. Then we reshape C to $\mathbb{R}^{c \times (hw)}$, where $n = hw$ is the number of pixels. At the same time, the SA block receives the shape code F_{t-1}^P from the AS branch, which is also fed into a convolution layer to produce a new shape code $B \in \mathbb{R}^{c \times h \times w}$ and then reshape to $\mathbb{R}^{c \times (hw)}$. After that, we perform a matrix multiplication between the transpose of C and B, and apply a Softmax layer to produce a correlation matrix $P \in \mathbb{R}^{(hw) \times (hw)}$,

$$p_{ji} = \frac{\exp(B_i C_j)}{\sum_{i=1}^n \exp(B_i C_j)}, \tag{1}$$

where p_{ji} measures the impact of the i-th position of B on the j-th position of the appearance code C. In this crossing way, the SA branch can capture more joint influence between the appearance code F_{t-1}^I and shape code F_{t-1}^P, producing a richer appearance code F_t^I.

Note that Eq. (1) has a close relationship with the non-local operator proposed by Wang et al. [38]. The major difference is that the non-local operator in [38] computes the pairwise similarity within the same feature map to incorporate global information, whereas the proposed crossing way computes the pairwise similarity between different feature maps, i.e., the person appearance and shape feature maps.

After that, we feed F_{t-1}^I into a convolution layer to produce a new appearance code $A \in \mathbb{R}^{c \times h \times w}$ and reshape it to $\mathbb{R}^{c \times (hw)}$. We then perform a matrix multiplication between A and the transpose of P and reshape the result to $\mathbb{R}^{c \times h \times w}$. Finally, we multiply the result by a scale parameter α and conduct an element-wise sum operation with the original appearance code F_{t-1}^I to obtain the refined appearance code $F_t^I \in \mathbb{R}^{c \times h \times w}$,

$$F_t^I = \alpha \sum_{i=1}^n (p_{ji} A_i) + F_{t-1}^I, \tag{2}$$

where α is 0 in the beginning and but is gradually updated. By doing so, each position of the refined appearance code F_t^I is a weighted sum of all positions of the shape code F_{t-1}^P and the previous appearance code F_{t-1}^I. Thus, it has a global contextual view between F_{t-1}^P and F_{t-1}^I, and it selectively aggregates useful contexts according to the correlation matrix P.

Appearance-Guided Shape-Based Generation. In our preliminary experiments, we observe that only the SA generation branch is not sufficient to learn such a complex deformable translation process. Intuitively, since the shape features can guide the appearance features, we believe the appearance features can also be used to guide the shape features in turn. Therefore, we also propose an Appearance-guided Shape-based generation (AS) branch. The proposed AS

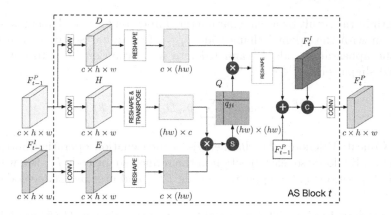

Fig. 3. Structure of the proposed AS block, which takes the previous shape code F_{t-1}^P and the previous appearance code F_{t-1}^I as inputs and obtains the shape code F_t^P in a crossing way. The symbols $\oplus$, $\otimes$ and $\circledS$ and $\copyright$ denote element-wise addition, element-wise multiplication, Softmax activation, and channel-wise concatenation, respectively.

branch mainly consists of a pose encoder and a sequence of AS blocks, as shown in Fig. 1. The source pose P_s and target pose P_t are first concatenated along the channel dimension and then fed into the pose encoder to produce the initial shape representation F_0^P. The pose encoder has the same network structure as the image encoder. Note that to capture the dependency between the two poses, we only adopt one pose encoder.

The AS branch contains several cascaded AS blocks, which progressively update the initial shape code F_0^P to the final shape code F_T^P under the guidance of the SA branch. All AS blocks have the same network structure, as illustrated in Fig. 1. Consider the t-th block in Fig. 3, whose inputs are the shape code $F_{t-1}^P \in \mathbb{R}^{c \times h \times w}$ and the appearance code $F_{t-1}^I \in \mathbb{R}^{c \times h \times w}$. The output is the refined shape code $F_t^P \in \mathbb{R}^{c \times h \times w}$.

Specifically, given the shape code F_{t-1}^P, we first feed it into a convolution layer to generate a new shape code H, where $H \in \mathbb{R}^{c \times h \times w}$. We then reshape H to $\mathbb{R}^{c \times (hw)}$. At the same time, the AS block receives the appearance code F_{t-1}^I from the SA branch, which is also fed into a convolution layer to produce a new appearance code E and then reshape it to $\mathbb{R}^{c \times (hw)}$. After that, we perform a matrix multiplication between the transpose of H and E, and apply a Softmax layer to produce another correlation matrix $Q \in \mathbb{R}^{(hw) \times (hw)}$,

$$q_{ji} = \frac{\exp(E_i H_j)}{\sum_{i=1}^{n} \exp(E_i H_j)}, \tag{3}$$

where q_{ji} measures the impact of i-th position of E on the j-th position of the shape code H. $n = hw$ is the number of pixels.

Meanwhile, we feed F_{t-1}^P into a convolution layer to produce a new shape code $D \in \mathbb{R}^{c \times h \times w}$ and reshape it to $\mathbb{R}^{c \times (hw)}$. We then perform a matrix multiplication between D and the transpose of Q and reshape the result to $\mathbb{R}^{c \times h \times w}$. Finally, we multiply the result by a scale parameter β and conduct an element-wise sum operation with the original shape code F_{t-1}^P. The result is then concatenated with the appearance code F_t^I and fed into a convolution layer to obtain the updated shape code $F_t^P \in \mathbb{R}^{c \times h \times w}$,

$$F_t^P = \text{Concat}(\beta \sum_{i=1}^{n} (q_{ji} D_i) + F_{t-1}^P, F_t^I), \tag{4}$$

where $\text{Concat}(\cdot)$ denotes the channel-wise concatenation operation and β is a parameter. By doing so, each position in the refined shape code F_t^P is a weighted sum of all positions in the appearance code F_{t-1}^I and previous shape code F_{t-1}^P.

Co-Attention Fusion. The proposed Co-Attention Fusion (CAF) module consists of two parts, *i.e.*, generating intermediate results and co-attention maps. These co-attention maps are used to spatially select from both the intermediate generations and the input image, and are combined to synthesize a final output. This idea of the proposed CAF module comes from the multi-channel attention selection module in SelectionGAN [36]. However, there are three differences: (i) We use two generation branches to generate intermediate results, *i.e.*, SA branch and AS branch. (ii) Attention maps are generated by the combination of both shape and appearance features, so the model learns more correlations between the two features. (iii) We also produce the input attention map, which aims to select useful content from the input image for generating the final image.

We consider two directions to generate intermediate results. One is generating multiple intermediate image synthesis results from the final appearance code F_T^I, and the other is generating multiple intermediate image synthesis results from the final shape code F_T^P. Specifically, the appearance code F_T^I is fed into a decoder to generate N intermediate results $I^I = \{I_i^I\}_{i=1}^N$, and followed by a Tanh activation function. Meanwhile, the final shape code F_T^P is fed into another decoder to generate another N intermediate results $I^P = \{I_i^P\}_{i=1}^N$, and also followed by a Tanh activation function. Both can be formulated as,

$$\begin{aligned} I_i^I &= \text{Tanh}(F_T^I W_i^I + b_i^I), && \text{for } i = 1, \cdots, N \\ I_i^P &= \text{Tanh}(F_T^P W_i^P + b_i^P), && \text{for } i = 1, \cdots, N \end{aligned} \tag{5}$$

where two convolution operations are performed with N convolutional filters $\{W_i^I, b_i^I\}_{i=1}^N$ and $\{W_i^P, b_i^P\}_{i=1}^N$. Thus, the $2N$ intermediate results and the input image I_s can be regarded as the candidate image pool.

To generate the co-attention map which reflects the correlation between the appearance F_T^I and shape F_T^P codes, we first stack both F_T^I and F_T^P along the channel axes, and then feed them into a group of filters $\{W_i^A, b_i^A\}_{i=1}^{2N+1}$ to generate the corresponding $2N+1$ co-attention maps,

$$I_i^A = \text{Softmax}(\text{Concat}(F_T^I, F_T^P) W_i^A + b_i^A), \quad \text{for } i = 1, \cdots, 2N+1 \tag{6}$$

where Softmax is a channel-wise Softmax function used for the normalization, and $\text{Concat}(\cdot)$ denotes the channel-wise concatenation operation. Finally, the learned co-attention maps are used to perform a channel-wise selection from each intermediate generation and the input image as follows,

$$I_t' = (I_1^A \otimes I_1^I) \oplus \cdots (I_{2N}^A \otimes I_{2N}^P) \oplus (I_{2N+1}^A \otimes I_s), \tag{7}$$

where I_t' represents the final synthesized person image selected from the multiple diverse results and the input image. $\otimes$ and $\oplus$ denote the element-wise multiplication and addition, respectively.

Optimization Objective. We use three different losses as our full optimization objective, *i.e.*, adversarial loss $\mathcal{L}_{gan}$, pixel loss $\mathcal{L}_{l1}$, and perceptual loss $\mathcal{L}_p$,

$$\min_G \max_{D_I, D_P} \mathcal{L} = \lambda_{gan}\mathcal{L}_{gan} + \lambda_{l1}\mathcal{L}_{l1} + \lambda_p\mathcal{L}_p, \tag{8}$$

where λ_{gan}, λ_{l1} and λ_p are the weights, measuring corresponding contributions of each loss to the total loss $\mathcal{L}$. The total adversarial loss is derived from the appearance-guided discriminator D_I and the shape-guided discriminator D_P, which aims to judge how likely is that I_t' contains the same person in I_s and how well I_t' aligns with the target pose P_t, respectively. The $L1$ pixel loss is used to compute the difference between the generated image I_t' and the real target image I_t, *i.e.*, $\mathcal{L}_{l1}=||I_t - I_t'||_1$. The perceptual loss $\mathcal{L}_p$ is used to reduce pose distortions and make the generated images look more natural and smooth, *i.e.*, $\mathcal{L}_p=||\phi(I_t) - \phi(I_t')||_1$, where ϕ denotes the outputs of several layers in the pre-trained VGG19 network [32].

Implementation Details. We follow the training procedures of GANs and alternatively train the proposed Xing generator G and two discriminators (D_I, D_P). During training, G takes I_s, P_s and P_t as input and outputs a translated person image I_t' with target pose P_t. Specifically, I_s is fed to the SA branch, and P_s, P_t are fed to the AS branch. For the adversarial training, (I_s, I_t) and (I_s, I_t') are fed to the appearance-guided discriminator D_P for ensuring appearance consistency. (P_t, I_t) and (P_t, I_t') are fed to the shape-guided discriminator D_P for ensuring shape consistency.

Adam optimizer [15] is used to train the proposed XingGAN for around 90 K iterations with $\beta_1 = 0.5$ and $\beta_2 = 0.999$. We set $T = 9$ in the proposed Xing generator and $N = 10$ in the proposed co-attention fusion module on both datasets. λ_{gan}, λ_{l1} and λ_p in Eq. (8) are set to 5, 50 and 50, respectively. For the decoders, the kernel size of convolutions for generating the intermediate images and co-attention maps are 3×3 and 1×1, respectively.

4   Experiments

Datasets. We follow [21,31,45] and conduct experiments on two challenging datasets, *i.e.*, Market-1501 [44] and DeepFashion [20]. Images on Market-1501 and DeepFashion are rescaled to 128×64 and 256×256, respectively. To generate human skeletons as training data, we employ OpenPose [4] to extract human joints. In this way, both P_s and P_t consist of an 18-channel heat map encoding the positions of 18 joints of a human body. We also filter out images where no human is detected. Thus, we collect 101,966 training pairs and 8,570 testing pairs on DeepFashion. For Market-1501, we have 263,632 training and 12,000 testing pairs. Note that to better evaluate the proposed XingGAN, the person identities of the training set do not overlap with those of the testing set.

Evaluation Metrics. We follow [21,31,45] and adopt Structure Similarity (SSIM) [39], Inception Score (IS) [29], and their masked versions, *i.e.*, Mask-SSIM and Mask-IS, as the evaluation metrics. Moreover, we adopt the PCKh score proposed in [45] to explicitly assess the shape consistency.

Quantitative Comparisons. We compare the proposed XingGAN with several leading methods, *i.e.*, PG2 [21], DPIG [22], VUnet [7], PoseGAN [31], Pose-Warp [2], CMA [5], C2GAN [35], BTF [1] and Pose-Transfer [45]. Quantitative results measured by SSIM, IS, Mask-SSIM, Mask-IS, and PCKh metrics are shown in Table 1. Note that previous works [21,31] did not release the train/test split, thus we use their well-trained models and re-evaluate their performance on our testing set as in Pose-Transfer [45]. Although our testing set inevitably includes some of their training samples, XingGAN still achieves the best results in terms of SSIM, IS, Mask-SSIM, and Mask-IS metrics on both datasets. For the PCKh metric, [45] obtains slightly better results than XingGAN. However, we observe that the images generated by XingGAN are more realistic and have less visual artifacts than those generated by [45] (see Fig. 4 and 5).

Qualitative Comparisons. Results compared with PG2 [21], VUnet [7] and PoseGAN [31] are shown on the left of Fig. 4 and 5. We can see that the proposed XingGAN achieves much better results than PG2, VUnet, and PoseGAN on both datasets, especially at appearance details and the integrity of generated persons. Moreover, to evaluate the effectiveness of XingGAN, we compare it with a stronger baseline, *i.e.*, Pose-Transfer [45]. Results are shown on the right of Fig. 4 and 5. We can see that XingGAN also generates much better person images having fewer visual artifacts than Pose-Transfer. For instance, Pose-Transfer [45] always generates a lot of visual artifacts in the background as shown in Fig. 5.

Human Evaluation. We follow the evaluation protocol of [21,31,45] and recruited 30 volunteers to conduct a user study. Participants were shown a sequence of images and asked to give an instant judgment about each image

Table 1. Quantitative results on Market-1501 and DeepFashion. For all metrics, higher is better. (∗) denotes the results tested on our testing set.

Method	Market-1501					DeepFashion		
	SSIM	IS	Mask-SSIM	Mask-IS	PCKh	SSIM	IS	PCKh
PG2 [21]	0.253	3.460	0.792	3.435	–	0.762	3.090	–
DPIG [22]	0.099	3.483	0.614	3.491	–	0.614	3.228	–
PoseGAN [31]	0.290	3.185	0.805	3.502	–	0.756	3.439	–
C2GAN [35]	0.282	3.349	0.811	3.510	–	–	–	–
BTF [1]	–	–	–	–	–	0.767	3.220	–
PG2* [21]	0.261	3.495	0.782	3.367	0.73	0.773	3.163	0.89
PoseGAN* [31]	0.291	3.230	0.807	3.502	**0.94**	0.760	3.362	0.94
VUnet* [7]	0.266	2.965	0.793	3.549	0.92	0.763	3.440	0.93
PoseWarp* [2]	–	–	–	–	–	0.764	3.368	0.93
CMA* [5]	–	–	–	–	–	0.768	3.213	0.92
Pose-Transfer* [45]	0.311	3.323	0.811	3.773	**0.94**	0.773	3.209	**0.96**
XingGAN (Ours)	**0.313**	**3.506**	**0.816**	**3.872**	0.93	**0.778**	**3.476**	0.95
Real Data	1.000	3.890	1.000	3.706	1.00	1.000	4.053	1.00

within a second. Specifically, we randomly select 55 real and 55 fake images (generated by our model) and shuffle them. The first 10 of them are used for practice and the remaining 100 images are used for evaluation. Results compared with PG2 [21], PoseGAN [31], Pose-Transfer [45] and C2GAN [35] are shown in Table 2. We observe that the proposed XingGAN achieves the best results on all measurements compared with the leading methods, further validating that the generated images by our model are more sharp and photo-realistic.

Variants of XingGAN. We conduct extensive ablation studies on Market-1501 [44] to evaluate different components of our XingGAN. XingGAN has four baselines as shown in Table 3. (i) 'SA' means only using the proposed Shape-guided Appearance-based generation branch. (ii) 'AS' means only adopting the proposed Appearance-guided Shape-based generation branch. (iii) 'SA+AS' combines both branches to produce the final person images. (iv) 'SA+AS+CAF' is our full model and employs the proposed Co-Attention Fusion module.

Effect of Dual-Branch Generation. The results of the ablation study are shown in Table 3. We see that the proposed SA branch achieves only 0.239 and 0.768 in SSIM and Mask-SSIM, respectively. When we only use the proposed AS branch, the values of SSIM and Mask-SSIM are improved to 0.286 and 0.798, respectively. Thus we conclude that the AS branch is more effective than the SA branch for generating photo-realistic person images. The AS branch takes the person poses as input and aims to learn person appearance representations, while the SA branch takes the person image as input and targets to learn person shape representations. Learning the appearance representations is much easier than

| I_s | P_s | P_t | I_t | PG2 | VUNet | Pose GAN | Xing GAN | I_s | P_s | P_t | I_t | Pose-Transfer | Xing GAN |

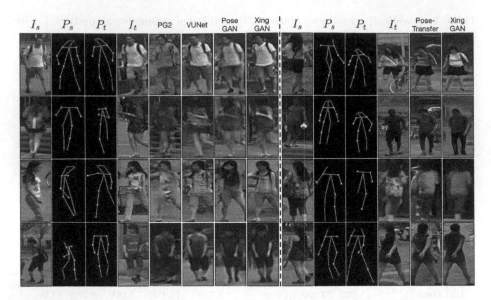

Fig. 4. Qualitative comparison with PG2 [21], VUnet [7], PoseGAN [31] and Pose-Transfer [45] on Market-1501.

Table 2. User study of person image generation (%). R2G means the percentage of real images rated as generated w.r.t. all real images. G2R means the percentage of generated images rated as real w.r.t. all generated images. The results of other methods are reported from their papers.

Method	Market-1501		DeepFashion	
	R2G	G2R	R2G	G2R
PG2 [21]	11.2	5.5	9.2	14.9
PoseGAN [31]	22.67	50.24	12.42	24.61
C2GAN [35]	23.20	46.70	–	–
Pose-Transfer [45]	32.23	63.47	19.14	31.78
XingGAN (Ours)	**35.28**	**65.16**	**21.61**	**33.75**

learning the shape representations since there are shape deformations between the input person image and the desired person image, leading the AS branch to achieve better results than the SA branch.

Next, when adopting the combination of the proposed SA and AS branches, the performance in terms of SSIM and Mask-SSIM further boosts. However, the results in terms of IS and Mask-IS do not decline too much. Moreover, Fig. 6 (*left*) shows some qualitative examples of the ablation study. We observe that the visualization results of 'SA', 'AS', and 'SA+AS' are consistent with the quantitative results. Therefore, both quantitative and qualitative results confirm the effectiveness of the proposed dual-branch generation strategy.

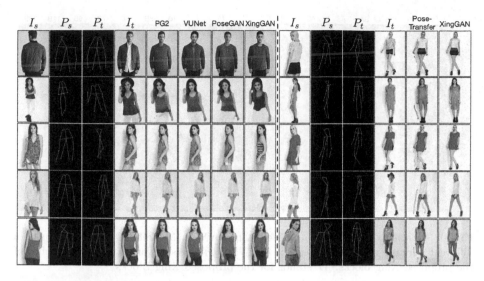

Fig. 5. Qualitative comparison with PG2 [21], VUnet [7], PoseGAN [31] and Pose-Transfer [45] on DeepFashion.

Table 3. Quantitative comparison of different variants of the proposed XingGAN on Market-1501. For all metrics, higher is better. 'SA', 'AS' and 'CAF' stand for the proposed SA branch, AS branch and co-attention fusion module, respectively.

Variants of XingGAN	IS	Mask-IS	SSIM	Mask-SSIM
SA	**3.849**	3.645	0.239	0.768
AS	3.796	3.810	0.286	0.798
SA + AS	3.558	3.807	0.310	0.807
SA + AS + CAF (Full)	3.506	**3.872**	**0.313**	**0.816**

Effect of Co-attention Fusion. 'SA+AS+CAF' outperforms the 'SA+AS' baseline with around 0.065, 0.003, and 0.009 gain on Mask-IS, SSIM, and Mask-SSIM, respectively. This means that the proposed co-attention fusion model indeed learns more correlations between the appearance and shape representations for generating the targeted person images, confirming our design motivation. Moreover, the proposed CAF module obviously improves the quality of the visualization results, as shown in the column 'Full' of Fig. 6.

Lastly, we show the learned co-attention maps and the generated intermediate results. These co-attention maps are complementary, which could be qualitatively verified by visualizing the results in Fig. 7. It is clear that they have learned different activated content between the generated intermediate results and the input image for generating the final person images.

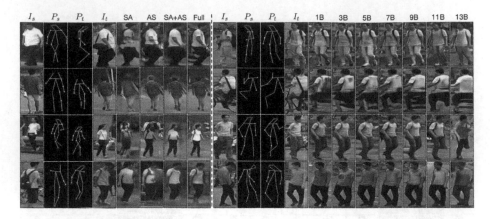

Fig. 6. Ablation study of the proposed XingGAN on Market-1501. (*left*) Results of different variants of the proposed XingGAN. (*right*) Results of varying the number of the proposed Xing blocks. 'B' stands for the proposed Xing Blocks.

Table 4. Quantitative comparison and ablation study of the proposed Xing generator on Market-1501. For all metrics, higher is better.

Method	IS	Mask-IS	SSIM	Mask-SSIM
Xing generator (1 blocks)	3.378	3.713	0.310	0.812
Xing generator (3 blocks)	3.241	3.866	**0.316**	0.813
Xing generator (5 blocks)	3.292	3.860	0.313	0.812
Xing generator (7 blocks)	3.293	3.871	0.310	0.810
Xing generator (9 blocks)	3.506	**3.872**	0.313	**0.816**
Xing generator (11 blocks)	3.428	3.712	0.286	0.793
Xing generator (13 blocks)	**3.708**	3.679	0.257	0.774
Resnet generator (5 blocks)	3.236	3.807	0.297	0.802
Resnet generator (9 blocks)	3.077	3.862	0.301	0.802
Resnet generator (13 blocks)	3.134	3.731	0.300	0.797
PATN generator (5 blocks)	3.273	3.870	0.309	0.809
PATN generator (9 blocks)	3.323	3.773	0.311	0.811
PATN generator (13 blocks)	3.274	3.797	0.314	0.808

Effect of the Xing Generator. The proposed Xing generator has two important network designs. One is the carefully designed Xing block, consisting of two sub-blocks, *i.e.*, SA block and AS block. The Xing blocks jointly model both shape and appearance representations in a crossing way and enjoying the mutually improved benefits from each other. The other one is the cascaded network design, which deals with the complex and deformable translation problem progressively. Thus, we further conduct two experiments, one is to show the advantage of the progressive generation strategy by varying the number of the

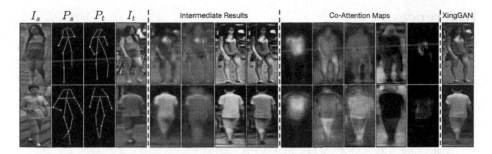

I_s P_s P_t I_t | Intermediate Results | Co-Attention Maps | XingGAN

Fig. 7. Visualization of intermediate results and co-attention maps generated by the proposed XingGAN on Market-1501. We randomly show four intermediate results, the corresponding four co-attention maps and the input attention map. Attention maps are normalized for better visualization.

proposed Xing blocks, and the other is to explore the advantage of the Xing block by replacing it with the residual block [13] and PATB [45] resulting in two generators named Resnet generator and PATN generator in Table 4, respectively.

Quantitative and qualitative results are shown in Table 4 and Fig. 6 (*right*). We observe that the proposed Xing generator with 9 blocks works the best. However, increasing the number of blocks further reduces generation performance. This could be attributed to the proposed Xing block. Only a few blocks are needed to capture the useful appearance and shape representations and the connection between them. Thus, we adopt 9 Xing blocks as default in our experiments for both datasets. Moreover, we see that the proposed Xing generator with only 5 Xing blocks outperforms both ResNet and PATN generators with 13 blocks on most metrics, which further certifies that our Xing generator has a good appearance and shape modeling capabilities with a very few blocks.

5   Conclusions

We propose a novel XingGAN for the challenging person image generation task. It uses cascaded guidance with two different generation branches, and learns a deformable translation mapping from both person shape and appearance features. Moreover, we propose two novel blocks to effectively update person shape and appearance features in a crossing way. Extensive experiments based on human judgments and automatic evaluation metrics show that Xing-GAN achieves new state-of-the-art results on two challenging datasets. Lastly, we believe that the proposed blocks and the XingGAN framework can be easily extended to address other GAN-based generation and even multi-modality fusion tasks.

Acknowledgment. This work has been partially supported by the Italy-China collaboration project TALENT.

References

1. AlBahar, B., Huang, J.B.: Guided image-to-image translation with bi-directional feature transformation. In: ICCV (2019)
2. Balakrishnan, G., Zhao, A., Dalca, A.V., Durand, F., Guttag, J.: Synthesizing images of humans in unseen poses. In: CVPR (2018)
3. Brock, A., Donahue, J., Simonyan, K.: Large scale GAN training for high fidelity natural image synthesis. In: ICLR (2019)
4. Cao, Z., Simon, T., Wei, S.E., Sheikh, Y.: Realtime multi-person 2D pose estimation using part affinity fields. In: CVPR (2017)
5. Chi, L., Tian, G., Mu, Y., Tian, Q.: Two-stream video classification with cross-modality attention. In: ICCV Workshops (2019)
6. Dong, H., Liang, X., Gong, K., Lai, H., Zhu, J., Yin, J.: Soft-gated warping-GAN for pose-guided person image synthesis. In: NeurIPS (2018)
7. Esser, P., Sutter, E., Ommer, B.: A variational U-Net for conditional appearance and shape generation. In: CVPR (2018)
8. Goodfellow, I., et al.: Generative adversarial nets. In: NeurIPS (2014)
9. Grigorev, A., Sevastopolsky, A., Vakhitov, A., Lempitsky, V.: Coordinate-based texture inpainting for pose-guided human image generation. In: CVPR (2019)
10. Huang, X., Belongie, S.: Arbitrary style transfer in real-time with adaptive instance normalization. In: ICCV (2017)
11. Lakhal, M.I., Lanz, O., Cavallaro, A.: Pose guided human image synthesis by view disentanglement and enhanced weighting loss. In: Leal-Taixé, L., Roth, S. (eds.) ECCV 2018. LNCS, vol. 11130, pp. 380–394. Springer, Cham (2019). https://doi.org/10.1007/978-3-030-11012-3_30
12. Isola, P., Zhu, J.Y., Zhou, T., Efros, A.A.: Image-to-image translation with conditional adversarial networks. In: CVPR (2017)
13. Johnson, J., Alahi, A., Fei-Fei, L.: Perceptual losses for real-time style transfer and super-resolution. In: Leibe, B., Matas, J., Sebe, N., Welling, M. (eds.) ECCV 2016. LNCS, vol. 9906, pp. 694–711. Springer, Cham (2016). https://doi.org/10.1007/978-3-319-46475-6_43
14. Karras, T., Laine, S., Aila, T.: A style-based generator architecture for generative adversarial networks. In: CVPR (2019)
15. Kingma, D.P., Ba, J.: Adam: a method for stochastic optimization. In: ICLR (2015)
16. Lai, W.-S., Huang, J.-B., Wang, O., Shechtman, E., Yumer, E., Yang, M.-H.: Learning blind video temporal consistency. In: Ferrari, V., Hebert, M., Sminchisescu, C., Weiss, Y. (eds.) ECCV 2018. LNCS, vol. 11219, pp. 179–195. Springer, Cham (2018). https://doi.org/10.1007/978-3-030-01267-0_11
17. Li, Y., Huang, J.B., Ahuja, N., Yang, M.H.: Joint image filtering with deep convolutional networks. IEEE TPAMI 41(8), 1909–1923 (2019)
18. Li, Y., Huang, C., Loy, C.C.: Dense intrinsic appearance flow for human pose transfer. In: CVPR (2019)
19. Liu, W., Piao, Z., Min, J., Luo, W., Ma, L., Gao, S.: Liquid warping GAN: a unified framework for human motion imitation, appearance transfer and novel view synthesis. In: ICCV (2019)
20. Liu, Z., Luo, P., Qiu, S., Wang, X., Tang, X.: DeepFashion: powering robust clothes recognition and retrieval with rich annotations. In: CVPR (2016)
21. Ma, L., Jia, X., Sun, Q., Schiele, B., Tuytelaars, T., Van Gool, L.: Pose guided person image generation. In: NeurIPS (2017)

22. Ma, L., Sun, Q., Georgoulis, S., Van Gool, L., Schiele, B., Fritz, M.: Disentangled person image generation. In: CVPR (2018)
23. Mirza, M., Osindero, S.: Conditional generative adversarial nets. arXiv preprint arXiv:1411.1784 (2014)
24. Neverova, N., Alp Güler, R., Kokkinos, I.: Dense pose transfer. In: Ferrari, V., Hebert, M., Sminchisescu, C., Weiss, Y. (eds.) ECCV 2018. LNCS, vol. 11207, pp. 128–143. Springer, Cham (2018). https://doi.org/10.1007/978-3-030-01219-9_8
25. Park, T., Liu, M.Y., Wang, T.C., Zhu, J.Y.: Semantic image synthesis with spatially-adaptive normalization. In: CVPR (2019)
26. Perez, E., Strub, F., De Vries, H., Dumoulin, V., Courville, A.: Film: Visual reasoning with a general conditioning layer. In: AAAI (2018)
27. Pumarola, A., Agudo, A., Sanfeliu, A., Moreno-Noguer, F.: Unsupervised person image synthesis in arbitrary poses. In: CVPR (2018)
28. Qian, X., et al.: Pose-normalized image generation for person re-identification. In: Ferrari, V., Hebert, M., Sminchisescu, C., Weiss, Y. (eds.) ECCV 2018. LNCS, vol. 11213, pp. 661–678. Springer, Cham (2018). https://doi.org/10.1007/978-3-030-01240-3_40
29. Salimans, T., Goodfellow, I., Zaremba, W., Cheung, V., Radford, A., Chen, X.: Improved techniques for training GANs. In: NeurIPS (2016)
30. Shaham, T.R., Dekel, T., Michaeli, T.: SinGAN: learning a generative model from a single natural image. In: ICCV (2019)
31. Siarohin, A., Sangineto, E., Lathuilière, S., Sebe, N.: Deformable GANs for pose-based human image generation. In: CVPR (2018)
32. Simonyan, K., Zisserman, A.: Very deep convolutional networks for large-scale image recognition. In: ICLR (2015)
33. Song, S., Zhang, W., Liu, J., Mei, T.: Unsupervised person image generation with semantic parsing transformation. In: CVPR (2019)
34. Tang, H., Wang, W., Xu, D., Yan, Y., Sebe, N.: GestureGAN for hand gesture-to-gesture translation in the wild. In: ACM MM (2018)
35. Tang, H., Xu, D., Liu, G., Wang, W., Sebe, N., Yan, Y.: Cycle in cycle generative adversarial networks for keypoint-guided image generation. In: ACM MM (2019)
36. Tang, H., Xu, D., Sebe, N., Wang, Y., Corso, J.J., Yan, Y.: Multi-channel attention selection GAN with cascaded semantic guidance for cross-view image translation. In: CVPR (2019)
37. Tang, H., Xu, D., Yan, Y., Torr, P.H., Sebe, N.: Local class-specific and global image-level generative adversarial networks for semantic-guided scene generation. In: CVPR (2020)
38. Wang, X., Girshick, R., Gupta, A., He, K.: Non-local neural networks. In: CVPR (2018)
39. Wang, Z., Bovik, A.C., Sheikh, H.R., Simoncelli, E.P.: Image quality assessment: from error visibility to structural similarity. IEEE TIP 13(4), 600–612 (2004)
40. Xian, W., et al.: TextureGAN: controlling deep image synthesis with texture patches. In: CVPR (2018)
41. Yang, C., Wang, Z., Zhu, X., Huang, C., Shi, J., Lin, D.: Pose guided human video generation. In: Ferrari, V., Hebert, M., Sminchisescu, C., Weiss, Y. (eds.) ECCV 2018. LNCS, vol. 11214, pp. 204–219. Springer, Cham (2018). https://doi.org/10.1007/978-3-030-01249-6_13
42. Zakharov, E., Shysheya, A., Burkov, E., Lempitsky, V.: Few-shot adversarial learning of realistic neural talking head models. In: ICCV (2019)
43. Zhang, R., et al.: Real-time user-guided image colorization with learned deep priors. ACM Trans. Graph. 36(4), 119 (2017)

44. Zheng, L., Shen, L., Tian, L., Wang, S., Wang, J., Tian, Q.: Scalable person re-identification: a benchmark. In: ICCV (2015)
45. Zhu, Z., Huang, T., Shi, B., Yu, M., Wang, B., Bai, X.: Progressive pose attention transfer for person image generation. In: CVPR (2019)

GATCluster: Self-supervised Gaussian-Attention Network for Image Clustering

Chuang Niu[1], Jun Zhang[2], Ge Wang[3], and Jimin Liang[1(✉)]

[1] School of Electronic Engineering, Xidian University, Xi'an, Shaanxi 710071, China
jiminliang@gmail.com
[2] Tencent AI Lab, Shenzhen, Guangdong 518057, China
[3] Rensselaer Polytechnic Institute, Troy, NY 12180, USA

Abstract. We propose a self-supervised Gaussian ATtention network for image Clustering (GATCluster). Rather than extracting intermediate features first and then performing traditional clustering algorithms, GATCluster directly outputs semantic cluster labels without further post-processing. We give a Label Feature Theorem to guarantee that the learned features are one-hot encoded vectors and the trivial solutions are avoided. Based on this theorem, we design four self-learning tasks with the constraints of transformation invariance, separability maximization, entropy analysis, and attention mapping. Specifically, the transformation invariance and separability maximization tasks learn the relations between samples. The entropy analysis task aims to avoid trivial solutions. To capture the object-oriented semantics, we design a self-supervised attention mechanism that includes a Gaussian attention module and a soft-attention loss. Moreover, we design a two-step learning algorithm that is memory-efficient for clustering large-size images. Extensive experiments demonstrate the superiority of our proposed method in comparison with the state-of-the-art image clustering benchmarks.

1 Introduction

Clustering is the process of separating data into groups according to sample similarity, which is a fundamental unsupervised learning task with numerous applications. Similarity or discrepancy measurement between samples plays a critical role in data clustering. Specifically, the similarity or discrepancy is determined by both data representation and distance function.

Before the extensive application of deep learning, handcrafted features, such as SIFT [30] and HoG [8], and domain-specific distance functions are often used to measure the similarity. Based on the similarity measurement, various rules were developed for clustering. These include space-partition based (e.g., k-means

Electronic supplementary material The online version of this chapter (https://doi.org/10.1007/978-3-030-58595-2_44) contains supplementary material, which is available to authorized users.

© Springer Nature Switzerland AG 2020
A. Vedaldi et al. (Eds.): ECCV 2020, LNCS 12370, pp. 735–751, 2020.
https://doi.org/10.1007/978-3-030-58595-2_44

(a)   **(b)**

Fig. 1. Clustering results on STL10. Each column represents a cluster. (a) Sample images clustered by the proposed model without attention, where the clustering principles focus on trivial cues, such as texture (first column), color (second column), or background (fifth column); and (b) Sample images clustered by the proposed model with attention, where the object concepts are well captured.

[31] and spectral clustering [34]) and hierarchical methods (e.g., BIRCH [53]). With the development of deep learning techniques, researchers have been dedicated to leverage deep neural networks for joint representation learning and clustering, which is commonly referred to as deep clustering. Although significant advances have been witnessed, deep clustering still suffers from an inferior performance for natural images (e.g., ImageNet [38]) in comparison with that for simple handwritten digits in MNIST.

Various challenges arise when applying deep clustering on natural images. *First*, many deep clustering methods use stacked auto-encoders (SAE) [2] to extract clustering-friendly intermediate features by imposing some constraints on the hidden layer and the output layer respectively. However, pixel-level reconstruction is not an effective constraint for extracting discriminative semantic features of natural images, since these images usually contain much more instance-specific details that are unrelated to semantics. Recent progress [5,13,21,45] has demonstrated that it is an effective way to directly map data to label features just as in the supervised classification task. However, training such a model in an unsupervised manner is difficult to extract clustering-related discriminative features. *Second*, clusters are expected to be defined by appropriate semantics while current methods tend to group the images by alternative principles (such as colors, textures, or background), as shown in Fig. 1. *Third*, the dynamic change between different clustering principles during the training process tends to make the model unstable and easily get trapped in trivial solutions that assign all samples to a single or very few clusters. *Fourth*, the existing methods were usually evaluated on small images (32×32 to 96×96). This is mainly due to the large batch of samples required for training the deep clustering model preventing us from processing large images on memory-limited devices.

To tackle these problems, we propose a self-supervised Gaussian attention network for clustering (GATCluster) that directly outputs discriminative semantic label features. Theoretically, we introduce a Label Feature Theorem, ensuring that the learned features are one-hot encoded vectors and the trivial solutions can be avoided. Accordingly, we design four self-learning tasks with the constraints of transformation invariance, separability maximization, entropy analysis, and attention mapping. GATCluster is trained in a completely unsupervised manner, as all the guiding signals for clustering are self-generated during training. Specifically, 1) the transformation invariance maximizes the similarity between a sample and its random transformations. 2) The separability maximization task explores both similarity and discrepancy of each paired samples to guide the model learning. 3) The entropy analysis task helps avoid trivial solutions. 4) To capture object-orientated semantics, an attention mechanism is proposed based on the observation that the discriminative information of objects is usually presented on local regions.

For processing large-size images, we develop an efficient two-step learning algorithm. First, the pseudo-targets over a large batch of samples are computed statistically in a split-and-merge manner. Second, the model is iteratively trained on the same batch in a supervised learning manner using the pseudo-targets. It should be noted that GATCluster is trained by optimizing all loss functions simultaneously instead of alternately. Our learning algorithm is memory-efficient and thus easy to process large images.

To summarize, the contributions of this paper include

(1) We introduce a Label Feature Theorem ensuring that the learned features are one-hot encoded vectors and trivial solutions can be avoided.
(2) We propose an attention module with a Gaussian kernel and a soft-attention loss to capture object-oriented semantics. To our best knowledge, this is the first attempt in exploring the attention mechanism for unsupervised learning.
(3) Our two-step learning algorithm that is memory-efficient makes it possible to perform the clustering on large-size images.
(4) Extensive experimental results demonstrate that the proposed GATCluster significantly outperforms or is comparable to the state-of-the-art methods on image clustering datasets. Our code has been made publicly available at https://github.com/niuchuangnn/GATCluster.

2   Related Work

2.1   Deep Clustering

We divide the deep clustering methods into two categories: 1) intermediate-feature-based deep clustering and 2) semantic deep clustering. The first category extracts intermediate features and then conducts conventional clustering. The second one directly constructs a nonlinear mapping between original data and cluster labels. By doing so, the samples are clustered just as in the supervised classification task, without any need for additional processing.

Some intermediate-feature-based deep clustering methods usually employ the SAE [2,15] or its variants [23,32,33,43] to extract intermediate features, and then conduct k-means [6,18] or spectral clustering [20]. Instead of performing representation learning and clustering separately, some studies integrate these two stages into a unified framework [9,10,22,25,41,46,47,51,55]. However, as applied to complex natural images, the reconstruction loss of SAE tends to overestimate the importance of low-level features. In contrast to the SAE-based methods, some methods [16,17,48] directly use the convolutional neural network (CNN) or multi-layer perceptron (MLP) for representation learning by designing specific loss functions. Unfortunately, the high-dimensional nature of intermediate features are too abundant to effectively reveal the discriminative semantic information of natural images.

Semantic deep clustering methods have recently shown a great promise for clustering. To train such models in the unsupervised manner, various rules have been designed for supervision. DAC [5] recasts clustering into a binary pairwise-classification problem, and the supervised labels are adaptively generated by thresholding the similarity matrix. As an extension to DAC, DCCM [45] investigates both pair-wise sample relations and triplet mutual information between deep and shallow layers. However, these two methods are practically susceptible to trivial solutions. IIC [21] directly trains a classification network by maximizing the mutual information between original data and their transformations. However, the computation of mutual information requires a very large batch size in the training process, which is challenging to apply on large images.

2.2 Self-supervised Learning

Self-supervised learning can learn general features by optimizing cleverly designed objective functions of some pretext tasks, in which all supervised pseudo labels are automatically generated from the input data without manual annotations. Various pretext tasks were proposed, including image completion [37], image colorization [52], jigsaw puzzle [35], counting [36], rotation [12], clustering [4,51], etc. For the pretext task of clustering, cluster assignments are often used as pseudo labels, which can be obtained by k-means or spectral clustering algorithms. In our study, both the self-generated relation of paired samples and object attention are used as the guiding signals for clustering.

2.3 Attention

In recent years, the attention mechanism has been successfully applied to various tasks in machine learning and computer vision, such as machine translation [42], image captioning and visual question answering [1], GAN [50], person re-identification [28], visual tracking [44], crowd counting [29], weakly- and semi-supervised semantic segmentation [26], and text detection and recognition [14]. Given the ground-truth labels, the attention weights are learned to scale-up more related local features for better predictions. However, it is still not explored for deep clustering models that are trained without human-annotated labels. In this work, we design a Gaussian-kernel-based attention module and a soft-attention loss to learn the attention weights in a self-supervised manner.

2.4   Learning Algorithm of Deep Clustering

Various of learning algorithms are designed for training deep clustering models. Most existing deep clustering models are alternatively trained between updating cluster assignments and network parameters [46], or between different clustering heads [21]. Some of them need pre-training in an unsupervised [46,47,51] or supervised manner [16,17]. On the other hand, some studies [5,45] directly train the deep clustering models by optimizing all component objective functions simultaneously. However, they do not consider the statistical constraint and are susceptible to trivial solutions. In this work, we propose a two-step self-supervised learning algorithm that is memory-efficient for processing the large batch training with large-size images.

3   Method

3.1   Label Feature Theorem and Problem Formulation

Given a set of samples $\mathcal{X} = \{x_i\}_{i=1}^N$ and the predefined number of clusters k, this work aims to automatically divide $\mathcal{X}$ into k groups by predicting the label features $l_i \in R^k$ of each sample x_i, where N is the total number of samples.

We first review the theorem introduced by DAC [5]. Clustering can be recast as a binary classification problem that measures the similarity and discrepancy between two samples and then determines whether they belong to the same cluster. For each sample x_i, the label feature $l_i = f(x_i; w)$ is computed, where $f(\cdot, w)$ is a mapping function with parameters w. The parameters w are obtained by minimizing the following objective function:

$$\min_{w} \mathbf{E}(w) = \sum_{i,j}^{N} L(r_{ij}, l_i \cdot l_j), \tag{1}$$

$$s.t. \ \forall i \ \|l_i\|_2 = 1, l_{ih} \geq 0, h = 1, \cdots, k,$$

where r_{ij} is the ground-truth relation between samples x_i and x_j, i.e., $r_{ij} = 1$ indicates that x_i and x_j belong to the same cluster and $r_{ij} = 0$ otherwise. In the unsupervised setting, r_{ij} can be estimated by thresholding [5,45] or the approach introduced in Sect. 3.3; the inner product $l_i \cdot l_j$ is the cosine distance between two samples as the label feature is constrained with $\|l_i\|_2 = 1$; L is a loss function instantiated by the binary cross entropy; and k is the predefined number of clusters. The theorem proved in [5] claimed that if the optimal value of Eq. (1) is attained, the learned label features will be k diverse one-hot vectors. Thus, the cluster identification c_i of image x_i can be directly obtained by selecting the maximum of label features, i.e., $c_i = argmax_h \ l_{ih}$. However, it practically tends to obtain trivial solutions that assign all samples to a single or a few clusters. In the supplementary, we give a theoretical analysis of why it will get trapped in the trivial solutions when optimizing Eq. (1).

Based on the above analysis, we formulate the clustering as the following optimization problem with a probability and a nonempty cluster constraint:

$$\min_w \mathbf{E}(w) = \sum_{i,j}^{N} L(r_{ij}, \frac{l_i}{\|l_i\|_2} \cdot \frac{l_j}{\|l_j\|_2}) - \sum_{i=1}^{N} l_i \cdot l_i,$$

$$s.t. \, \forall i \, \|l_i\|_1 = 1, 0 \leq l_{ih} \leq 1, h = 1, \cdots, k. (probability) \qquad (2)$$

$$\forall h \, p_h > 0, p_h = \frac{1}{N} \sum_{i=1}^{N} l_{ih}. (nonempty \ cluster)$$

Although DCCM [45] also implements the probability constraint, it cannot guarantee the trivial solutions being avoided. However, our probability constraint is necessary for the nonempty cluster constraint and computing the entropy loss to avoid trivial solutions. In the nonempty cluster constraint, p_h denotes the frequency of assigning N samples into the hth cluster. And we have a Label Feature Theorem (the proof of this theorem can be found in the supplementary) as follows:

Label Feature Theorem. *If the optimal value of Eq. (2) is attained, for $\forall i, j, l_i \in E^k, l_i \neq l_j \Leftrightarrow r_{ij} = 0, l_i = l_j \Leftrightarrow r_{ij} = 1,$ and $|\{l_i\}_{i=1}^{N}| = k,$ where $|\cdot|$ denotes the cardinality of a set.*

Label Feature Theorem ensures that the learned features are one-hot encoded vectors in which each bit represents a cluster, and all predefined k clusters are nonempty. However, the learned features may focus on various of cues for clustering as introduced in Sect. 1. To capture the object-oriented semantics in the unsupervised setting, we propose a Gaussian attention mechanism with a soft-attention loss. By incorporating the Label Feature Theorem with the attention mechanism, we formulate clustering as the following optimization problem,

$$\min_w \mathbf{E}(w) = \sum_{i,j=1}^{N} L_R(r_{ij}, l_i, l_j) + \sum_{i=1}^{N} (\alpha_1 L_T(l_i) + \alpha_2 L_E(l_i) + \alpha_3 L_A(l_i, l_i^a)), \quad (3)$$

where L_R and L_T correspond to the first and second items in the objective function of Eq. (2), L_E is to satisfy the nonempty cluster constraint, L_A represents the attention loss, which is described in Sect. 3.3, and $\alpha_1, \alpha_2, \alpha_3$ are the hyper-parameters to balance the importance of different losses. In practice, the probability constraint is always satisfied by setting the label features as the outputs of the softmax function. To optimize the problem of Eq. (3) for unsupervised clustering, we propose a GATCluster model with four self-learning tasks as introduced in the following sections.

3.2 Framework

GATCluster consists of the following three components: 1) an image feature module, 2) a label feature module, and 3) an attention module, as shown in

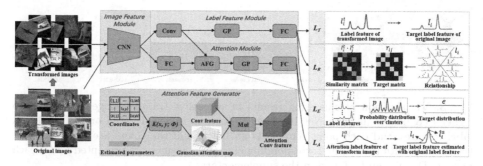

Fig. 2. GATCluster framework. *CNN* is a convolutional network, *GP* means global pooling, *Mul* represents channel-independent multiplication, *Conv* is a convolution layer, *FC* is a fully connected layer, and *AFG* represents an attention feature generator.

Fig. 2. The image feature module extracts convolutional features of images with a fully convolutional network. The label feature module, which contains a convolutional layer, a global pooling layer and a fully-connected layer, aims to map the convolutional features to semantic label features. The attention module makes the model focus on discriminative local regions automatically, facilitating the capture of object-oriented semantics. The attention module consists of three submodules, including a fully connected layer for estimating the parameters of Gaussian kernel, an attention feature generator, and a global pooling layer followed by another fully connected layer for computing the attention label features. The attention feature generator has three inputs, i.e., the estimated Gaussian parameters Φ, the convolutional features from the label feature module, and the two-dimensional coordinates of the attention map that are self-generated according to the attention map size H and W.

In the training stage, we design four learning tasks driven by the transformation invariance, separability maximization, entropy analysis and attention mapping. Specifically, the transformation invariance and separability maximization losses are computed with respect to the predicted label features, the attention loss is evaluated with the attention module outputs, and the entropy loss is used to supervise both the label feature module and the attention module. For inference, only the image feature module and label feature module are combined as a classifier to suggest the cluster assignments. The clustering results in successive training stages are visualized in Fig. 3.

3.3   Self-learning Tasks

Transformation Invariance Task. An image after any practically reasonable transformations still reflect the same object. Hence, these transformed images should have similar feature representations. To learn such a similarity, the label feature l_i of original sample x_i is constrained to be close to its transformed counterpart l_i^t of $T(x_i)$, where T is a practically reasonable transformation function.

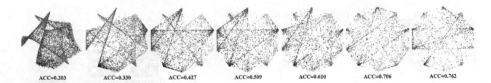

ACC=0.203   ACC=0.330   ACC=0.427   ACC=0.509   ACC=0.610   ACC=0.706   ACC=0.762

Fig. 3. Visualization of clustering results in successive training stages (from left to right) 13 K images in ImageNet-10. The results are visualized based on the predicted label features, and each point represents an image and the colors are rendered with the ground-truth label. The corresponding clustering accuracy is presented under each picture. Details can be found in the supplementary.

In this work, the transformation function is predefined as the composition of random flipping, random affine transformation, and random color jittering, see Fig. 2. Specifically, the loss function is defined as

$$L_T(l_i^t, \hat{l}_i) = -l_i^t \cdot \hat{l}_i, \tag{4}$$

where $\hat{l}_i$ is the target label feature of an original image x_i that is recomputed as:

$$\hat{l}_{ih} = \frac{l_{ih}/z_h}{\sum_{h'} l_{ih'}/z_{h'}}, \quad z_h = \sum_{j=1}^{M} l_{jh}, h = 1, 2, \cdots, k, \tag{5}$$

where M is the number of samples, i.e., the batch size used in the training process. Eq. (5) can balance the sample assignments by dividing the cluster assignment frequency z_h, preventing the empty clusters.

Separability Maximization Task. If the relations between all pairs of samples are well captured, the label features will be one-hot encoded vectors as introduced in Sect. 3.1. However, the ground-truth relations cannot be obtained in the unsupervised learning environment. Therefore, we evaluate the relationships of a batch of samples as follows:

$$r_{ij} = \begin{cases} 1, & c_i = c_j \ or \ i = j, \\ 0, & otherwise, \end{cases} \tag{6}$$

where $c_i = c_j$ indicates that the samples x_i and x_j belong to the same cluster, $i = j$ indicates that the similarity of a sample to itself is 1. To get the cluster identification c_i, k-means algorithm is conducted on a set of samples based on the predicted label features. Instead of estimating r_{ij} with a high pre-defined threshold as in [5, 45], our approach can determine it adaptively.

The separability maximization task is to improve the purity of clusters by encouraging samples that are similar to be closer to each other while dissimilar samples to be further away from each other. The loss function is defined as:

$$L_R(r_{ij}, l_i, l_j) = -r_{ij} \log(d(l_i, l_j)) - (1 - r_{ij}) \log(1 - d(l_i, l_j)), \tag{7}$$

where $d(l_i, l_j) = \frac{l_i}{\|l_i\|_2} \cdot \frac{l_j}{\|l_j\|_2}$ is the cosine distance.

Entropy Analysis Task. The entropy analysis task is designed to avoid trivial solutions by satisfying the nonempty cluster constraint in Eq. (2). We maximize the entropy of the empirical probability distribution p over k cluster assignments. Thus, the loss function is defined as

$$L_E(l_1, \cdots, l_m) = \sum_{h=1}^{k} p_h \log(p_h),$$

$$p_h = \frac{1}{m} \sum_{i=1}^{m} l_{ih}, h = 1, \cdots, k,$$

$$(8)$$

where $p = [p_1, \cdots, p_k]$ is estimated with the predicted label features of m samples, which can be a subset of the whole batch. Actually, maximizing the entropy will steer p towards a uniform distribution (denoted by e in Fig. 2), i.e., $\forall h, p_h \to \frac{1}{m} > 0$, and thus the nonempty constraint is satisfied so that the trivial solutions are avoided according to the **Label Feature Theorem**.

Attention Mapping Task. The attention mapping task aims to make the model recognize the most discriminative local regions concerning the whole image semantic. The basic idea is that the response to the discriminative local regions should be more intense than that to the entire image. To this end, there are two problems to be solved: 1) how to design the attention module for localizing the discriminative local regions? and 2) how to train the attention module in a self-supervised manner?

With regard to the first problem, we design a two-dimensional Gaussian kernel $K(u; \Phi)$ to generate an attention map A as:

$$A(x, y) = K(u; \Phi) = e^{-\frac{1}{\alpha}(u-\mu)^T \Sigma^{-1}(u-\mu)},$$

$$x = 1, \cdots, H, \ and \ y = 1, \cdots, W,$$

$$(9)$$

where $u = [x, y]^T$ denotes the coordinate vector, $\Phi = [\mu, \Sigma]$ denotes the parameters of the Gaussian kernel, $\mu = [\mu_x, \mu_y]^T$ is the mean vector that defines the most discriminative location, $\Sigma \in \mathbf{R}^{2 \times 2}$ is the covariance matrix that defines the shape and size of a local region, α is a predefined hyper parameter, and H and W are the height and width of the attention map. In our implementation, the coordinates are normalized over $[0, 1]$. Taking CNN features as the input, a fully connected layer is used to estimate the parameter Φ. Then, the model can focus on the discriminative local region by multiplying each channel of convolutional features with the attention map. The weighted features are mapped to the attention label features using a global pooling layer and a fully connected layer, as shown in Fig. 2. It should be noted that there are also alternative designs of the attention module to generate attention maps, such as a convolution layer followed by a sigmoid function. However, we obtained better results with the parameterized Gaussian attention module due to that it has a much less number of parameters to be estimated, and the Gaussian attention prior fits for capturing the local object in the unsupervised learning setting.

With regard to the second problem, we define a soft-attention loss as

$$L_A(l_i^a, \hat{l}_i^a) = \frac{1}{k} \sum_{h=1}^{k} -\hat{l}_{ih}^a \log(l_{ih}^a) - (1 - \hat{l}_{ih}^a) \log(1 - l_{ih}^a), \tag{10}$$

$$\hat{l}_{ih}^a = \frac{l_{ih}^2/z_h}{\sum_{h'} l_{ih'}^2/z_{h'}}, h = 1, \cdots, k, \tag{11}$$

where l_i^a is the output of the attention module, $\hat{l}_i^a$ is the target label feature for regression, and z_h is the same as in Eq. (5) to balance the cluster assignments. As defined in Eq. (11), the target label feature $\hat{l}_i^a$ encourages the current high scores and suppresses low scores of the whole image label feature l_i, thus making $\hat{l}_i^a$ a more confident version of the whole image label feature l_i, see Fig. 2 for demonstration. By doing so, the local image region, which is localized by the attention module, is discriminative in terms of the whole image semantics. In practice, the local region usually presents the expected object or the discriminative part as shown in Fig. 4.

Algorithm 1: GATCluster learning algorithm.

Input: Dataset $\mathcal{X} = \{x_i\}_{i=1}^{N}$, k, M, m_1, m_2
Output: Cluster label c_i of $x_i \in \mathcal{X}$

1 Randomly initialize network parameters w ;
2 Initialize $e = 0$;
3 **while** $e < total\ epoch\ number$ **do**
4   **for** $b \in \{1, 2, \ldots, \lfloor \frac{N}{M} \rfloor\}$ **do**
5   Select M samples as $\mathcal{X}_b$ from $\mathcal{X}$;
6   *Step-1:*
7   **for** $u \in \{1, 2, \ldots, \lfloor \frac{M}{m_1} \rfloor\}$ **do**
8   Select m_1 samples as $\mathcal{X}_u$ from $\mathcal{X}_b$;
9   Calculate the label features of $\mathcal{X}_u$;
10   **end**
11   Concatenate all label features of M samples ;
12   Calculate pseudo targets $T_b = \{(\hat{l}_i, r_{ij}, \hat{l}_i^a)\}$ of $\mathcal{X}_b$ with Eqs. (5), (6), and (11);
13   *Step-2:*
14   Randomly transform samples in $\mathcal{X}_b$ as $\mathcal{X}_b^t$;
15   **for** $v \in \{1, 2, \ldots, \lfloor \frac{M}{m_2} \rfloor\}$ **do**
16   Randomly select m_2 samples as $[\mathcal{X}_v; T_v]$ from $[\mathcal{X}_b^t; T_b]$;
17   Optimize w on $[\mathcal{X}_v; T_v]$ by minimizing Eq. (3) using Adam ;
18   **end**
19   **end**
20     $e := e + 1$
21 **end**
22 **foreach** $x_i \in \mathcal{X}$ **do**
23     $l_i := f(l_i; w)$;
24     $c_i := \arg\max_h (l_{ih})$;
25 **end**

3.4 Learning Algorithm

We develop a two-step learning algorithm that combines all the self-learning tasks to train GATCluster in an unsupervised learning manner. The total loss function is defined by Eq. (3), in which the entropy loss is computed with the label features l_i and l_i^a predicted by the label feature module and attention module respectively, i.e., $L_E = L_E(l_1, \cdots, l_M) + L_E(l_1^a, \cdots, l_M^a)$.

The proposed two-step learning algorithm is presented in Algorithm 1. Since deep clustering methods usually require a large batch of samples for training, it is difficult to process large images with a memory-limited device. To tackle this problem, we divide the large-batch-based training process into two steps for each iteration. The first step is the forward process that statistically calculates the pseudo-targets for a large batch of M samples using the model trained in the last iteration. To achieve this with a memory-limited device, we further split the large batch into sub-batches and calculate the label features for each sub-batch of m_1 samples independently. Then, all label features of M samples are concatenated for computing their pseudo labels. Given these samples with pseudo labels, the second step is the supervised training process that trains the model with a sub-batch of m_2 samples iteratively.

4 Experiments and Results

4.1 Data

We evaluated the proposed and the compared deep clustering methods on five datasets, including STL10 [7] that contains 13K 96×96 images of 10 clusters, ImageNet-10 [5] that 13 K images of 10 clusters, ImageNet-Dog [5] that 19.5 K images of 15 dog subcategories, Cifar10 and Cifar100-20 [24]. The image size of ImageNet-10 and ImageNet-Dog is around 500×300. Cifar10 and Cifar100-20 both contain 60K 32×32 images, and have 10 and 20 clusters.

4.2 Implementation Details

At the training stage, especially at the beginning, samples tend to be clustered by color cues. Therefore, we took grayscale images as inputs except for ImageNet-Dog, as the color plays an important role in differentiating the sub-categories of dogs. It is noted that the images are converted to grayscale after applying the random color jittering during training. For simplicity, we assume $\Sigma = \begin{bmatrix} \delta & 0 \\ 0 & \delta \end{bmatrix}$, and there are only three parameters for Gaussian kernel to be estimated, i.e., $[\mu_x, \mu_y; \delta]$. We used Adam to optimize the network parameters and the base learning rate was set to 0.001. We set the batch size M to 1000 for STL10 and ImageNet-10, 1500 for ImageNet-Dog, 4000 for Cifar10, and 6000 for Cifar100-20. The sub-batch size m_1 in calculating pseudo targets can be adjusted according to the device memory and will not affect the results. The sub-batch size m_2 was 32 for all experiments. Hyper parameters α, α_1, α_2, and α_3 were empirically set to 0.05, 5, 5, and 3 respectively.

In all experiments, we used the VGG-style convolutional network with batch normalization to implement the image feature extraction module. The architecture details of different experiments can be found in the supplementary.

4.3   Evaluation Metrics

We used three popular metrics to evaluate the performance of the involved clustering methods, including Adjusted Rand Index (ARI) [19], Normalized Mutual Information (NMI) [40] and clustering Accuracy (ACC) [27].

Table 1. Comparison with the existing methods. GATCluster-128 resizes input images to 128×128 for ImageNet-10 and ImageNet-Dog while other models take 96×96 images as inputs. On Cifar10 and Cifar100, the input size is 32×32. The best three results are highlighted in **bold**.

Method	STL10			ImageNet-10			ImageNet-dog			Cifar10			Cifar100-20		
	ACC	NMI	ARI	ACC	NMI	ARI	ACC	NMI	ARI	ACC	NMI	ARI	ACC	NMI	ARI
k-means [31]	0.192	0.125	0.061	0.241	0.119	0.057	0.105	0.055	0.020	0.229	0.087	0.049	0.130	0.084	0.028
SC [34]	0.159	0.098	0.048	0.274	0.151	0.076	0.111	0.038	0.013	0.247	0.103	0.085	0.136	0.090	0.022
AC [11]	0.332	0.239	0.140	0.242	0.138	0.067	0.139	0.037	0.021	0.228	0.105	0.065	0.138	0.098	0.034
NMF [3]	0.180	0.096	0.046	0.230	0.132	0.065	0.118	0.044	0.016	0.190	0.081	0.034	0.118	0.079	0.026
AE [2]	0.303	0.250	0.161	0.317	0.210	0.152	0.185	0.104	0.073	0.314	0.239	0.169	0.165	0.100	0.048
SAE [2]	0.320	0.252	0.161	0.335	0.212	0.174	0.183	0.113	0.073	0.297	0.247	0.156	0.157	0.109	0.044
SDAE [43]	0.302	0.224	0.152	0.304	0.206	0.138	0.190	0.104	0.078	0.297	0.251	0.163	0.151	0.111	0.046
DeCNN [49]	0.299	0.227	0.162	0.313	0.186	0.142	0.175	0.098	0.073	0.282	0.240	0.174	0.133	0.092	0.038
SWWAE [54]	0.270	0.196	0.136	0.324	0.176	0.160	0.159	0.094	0.076	0.284	0.233	0.164	0.147	0.103	0.039
CatGAN [39]	0.298	0.210	0.139	0.346	0.225	0.157	N/A	N/A	N/A	0.315	0.265	0.176	N/A	N/A	N/A
GMVAE [9]	0.282	0.200	0.146	0.334	0.193	0.168	N/A	N/A	N/A	0.291	0.245	0.167	N/A	N/A	N/A
JULE-SF [48]	0.274	0.175	0.162	0.293	0.160	0.121	N/A	N/A	N/A	0.264	0.192	0.136	N/A	N/A	N/A
JULE-RC [48]	0.277	0.182	0.164	0.300	0.175	0.138	0.138	0.054	0.028	0.272	0.192	0.138	0.137	0.103	0.033
DEC [46]	0.359	0.276	0.186	0.381	0.282	0.203	0.195	0.122	0.079	0.301	0.257	0.161	0.185	0.136	0.050
DAC* [5]	0.434	0.347	0.235	0.503	0.369	0.284	0.246	0.182	0.095	0.498	0.379	0.280	0.219	0.162	0.078
DAC [5]	0.470	**0.366**	**0.257**	0.527	0.394	0.302	0.275	0.219	0.111	0.522	**0.396**	**0.306**	0.238	**0.185**	**0.088**
IIC [21]	**0.499**	N/A	N/A	N/A	N/A	N/A	N/A	N/A	N/A	**0.617**	N/A	N/A	**0.257**	N/A	N/A
DCCM [45]	**0.482**	**0.376**	**0.262**	**0.710**	**0.608**	**0.555**	**0.383**	**0.321**	**0.182**	**0.623**	**0.496**	**0.408**	**0.327**	**0.285**	**0.173**
GATCluster	**0.583**	**0.446**	**0.363**	**0.739**	**0.594**	**0.552**	**0.322**	**0.281**	**0.163**	**0.610**	**0.475**	**0.402**	**0.281**	**0.215**	**0.116**
GATCluster-128	N/A	N/A	N/A	**0.762**	**0.609**	**0.572**	**0.333**	**0.322**	**0.200**	N/A	N/A	N/A	N/A	N/A	N/A

4.4   Comparison with Existing Methods

Table 1 presents a comparison with the existing methods. Under the same conditions, the proposed method significantly improves the clustering performance by 8%, 7%, and 10% approximately compared with the best of the others in terms of ACC, NMI and ARI on STL10. On ImageNet-10, ACC is improved by 5% compared with the strong baseline that is set by the most recently proposed DCCM [45]. On the sub-category dataset ImageNet-Dog, our method achieves results comparable to that of DCCM. Moreover, our method is capable of processing large images, and in that case the clustering results are further improved. On the small image datasets, i.e., Cifar10 and Cifar100-20, the proposed method also achieves comparable performance relative to the state-of-the-art. Importantly, our GATCluster has the interpretability to the learned cluster semantics by presenting the corresponding local regions. The above results strongly demonstrate the superiority of our proposed method.

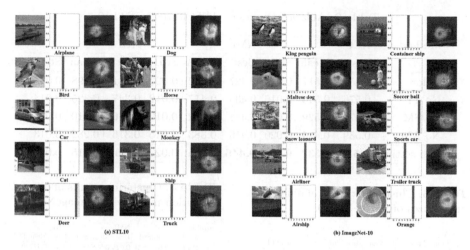

Fig. 4. Visualization of GATCluster on STL10 and ImageNet10. For each class, an example image, the predicted label feature, and the attention map overlaid on the image are shown from left to right.

4.5 Ablation Study

To validate the effectiveness of each component, we conducted the ablation studies as shown in Table 2. Similar to [13], each variant was evaluated ten times and the best accuracy, average accuracy and the standard deviation are reported. Table 2 demonstrates that the best accuracy is achieved when all learning tasks are used with grayscale images. Particularly, the attention mapping (AP) improves the accuracy by up to 4.4 % for the best accuracy and 4.3 % for average accuracy. This is attributed to that the attention module has the ability to localize the discriminative regions with respect to the whole image semantic, and thus it can well capture the expected object-oriented semantics, as shown in Fig. 4. In addition, the color information is a strong distraction for object clustering, and better clustering results can be obtained after the color images are changed to grayscale. We do not show the results of ablated entropy loss, as it is easy to get trapped at trivial solutions in our experiments.

4.6 Effectiveness of Image Size

The biggest image size used by most of the existing unsupervised clustering methods is not larger than 96×96 (e.g., in STL10). However, images in the modern datasets usually have much larger sizes, which are not effectively explored by unsupervised deep clustering methods. With the proposed two-step learning algorithm, we are able to process large images. An interesting question then arises: will large images help produce a better clustering accuracy? To answer this question, we explored the effect of image size on clustering results. Specifically, we evaluated four input image sizes, i.e., 96×96, 128×128, 160×160, and 192×192 by simply resizing the original images on ImageNet-10. We conducted

Table 2. Ablation studies of GATCluster on STL10.

Method	ACC			NMI			ARI		
	Best	Mean	Std	Best	Mean	Std	Best	Mean	Std
Color	0.556	0.517	0.034	0.427	0.402	0.022	0.341	0.298	0.031
No TI	0.576	0.546	0.016	0.435	0.417	0.012	0.347	0.325	0.014
No SM	0.579	0.529	0.029	0.438	0.412	0.019	0.356	0.310	0.024
No AM	0.539	0.494	0.020	0.416	0.383	0.015	0.316	0.282	0.013
Full setting	**0.583**	0.537	0.033	**0.446**	0.415	0.022	**0.363**	0.315	0.032

Table 3. Clustering results of different image sizes on ImageNet-10.

Size	ACC			NMI			ARI		
	Best	Mean	Std	Best	Mean	Std	Best	Mean	Std
96	0.739	0.708	0.031	0.594	0.581	0.012	0.552	0.529	0.019
128	**0.762**	0.735	0.020	0.609	0.592	0.013	0.572	0.544	0.023
160	0.712	0.669	0.033	0.567	0.511	0.043	0.500	0.453	0.039
192	0.738	0.608	0.067	0.612	0.474	0.071	0.559	0.405	0.079

Table 4. Clustering results of different attention map sizes on ImageNet-10.

Size	ACC			NMI			ARI		
	Best	Mean	Std	Best	Mean	Std	Best	Mean	Std
2	0.746	0.666	0.050	0.625	0.538	0.050	0.569	0.477	0.045
4	0.706	0.678	0.017	0.539	0.528	0.012	0.486	0.473	0.014
6	**0.762**	0.735	0.020	0.609	0.592	0.013	0.571	0.544	0.023
8	0.742	0.719	0.018	0.618	0.594	0.019	0.561	0.536	0.018
10	0.671	0.645	0.020	0.549	0.520	0.021	0.478	0.450	0.020

five experimental trails for each image size and report the best and average accuracies as well as the standard deviation in Table 3. The results show that the clustering performance is significantly improved when the image size is increased from 96 × 96 to 128 × 128. It is demonstrated that taking the larger images as inputs can benefit the clustering.

Practically, our proposed methods can be performed on much larger size of images. The clustering results are not further improved when the image size is larger than 128 × 128. It may be due to that networks become deepened with an increased image size, and thus there is a trade-off between the number of network parameters and the size of the training dataset. However, it is valuable to explore larger size of images for clustering in the future.

4.7   Effectiveness of Attention Map Size

A high-resolution attention map will provide precise location but weaken the global semantics. We evaluated the effect of the attention map size on the clustering results for ImageNet-10. We set the size of input image in this experiment to 128 × 128, and evaluate five sizes of attention map (in pixels): 2 × 2, 4 × 4, 6 × 6, 8 × 8, and 10 × 10 as shown in Table 4. It shows that the 6 × 6 attention map achieves the best results.

5   Conclusion

For deep unsupervised clustering, we introduce a Label Feature Theorem that guarantees the learned features are one-hot encoded and all pre-defined clusters are nonempty. Based on this theorem, we formulate the clustering problem with four self learning tasks. Particulary, the attention mechanism can facilitate the formation of object semantics during the training process. We design a memory-efficient learning algorithm for processing large images. GATCluster model has a great potential for clustering the images with complex contents and discovering discriminative local regions in the unsupervised setting.

Acknowledgments. The research was supported by the National Natural Science Foundation of China (61976167, U19B2030, 61571353) and the Science and Technology Projects of Xi'an, China (201809170CX11JC12).

References

1. Anderson, P., et al.: Bottom-up and top-down attention for image captioning and visual question answering. In: CVPR (2018)
2. Bengio, Y., Lamblin, P., Popovici, D., Larochelle, H., Montreal, U.: Greedy layer-wise training of deep networks. NeurIPS **19**, 153–160 (2007)
3. Cai, D., He, X., Wang, X., Bao, H., Han, J.: Locality preserving nonnegative matrix factorization. In: IJCAI, pp. 1010–1015 (2009)
4. Caron, M., Bojanowski, P., Joulin, A., Douze, M.: Deep clustering for unsupervised learning of visual features. In: ECCV, vol. 11218, pp. 139–156 (2018)
5. Chang, J., Wang, L., Meng, G., Xiang, S., Pan, C.: Deep adaptive image clustering. In: ICCV, pp. 5880–5888 (2017)
6. Chen, D., Lv, J., Zhang, Y.: Unsupervised multi-manifold clustering by learning deep representation. In: AAAI Workshops. AAAI Workshops, vol. WS-17. AAAI Press (2017)
7. Coates, A., Ng, A.Y., Lee, H.: An analysis of single-layer networks in unsupervised feature learning. In: AISTATS, vol. 15, pp. 215–223 (2011)
8. Dalal, N., Triggs, B.: Histograms of oriented gradients for human detection. In: CVPR, vol. 1, pp. 886–893 (2005)
9. Dilokthanakul, N., et al.: Deep unsupervised clustering with gaussian mixture variational autoencoders. ArXiv abs/1611.02648 (2017)
10. Dizaji, K.G., Herandi, A., Deng, C., Cai, W., Huang, H.: Deep clustering via joint convolutional autoencoder embedding and relative entropy minimization. In: ICCV, pp. 5747–5756 (2017)
11. Franti, P., Virmajoki, O., Hautamaki, V.: Fast agglomerative clustering using a k-nearest neighbor graph. IEEE Trans. Pattern Anal. Mach. Intell. **28**(11), 1875–1881 (2006)
12. Gidaris, S., Singh, P., Komodakis, N.: Unsupervised representation learning by predicting image rotations. In: ICLR. OpenReview.net (2018)
13. Haeusser, P., Plapp, J., Golkov, V., Aljalbout, E., Cremers, D.: Associative deep clustering: training a classification network with no labels. In: Brox, T., Bruhn, A., Fritz, M. (eds.) Pattern Recognition, pp. 18–32 (2019)
14. He, T., Tian, Z., Huang, W., Shen, C., Qiao, Y., Sun, C.: An end-to-end textspotter with explicit alignment and attention. In: CVPR (2018)
15. Hinton, G.E., Salakhutdinov, R.R.: Reducing the dimensionality of data with neural networks. Science **313**(5786), 504–507 (2006)

16. Hsu, C., Lin, C.: Cnn-based joint clustering and representation learning with feature drift compensation for large-scale image data. IEEE Trans. Multimedia **20**(2), 421–429 (2018)
17. Hu, W., Miyato, T., Tokui, S., Matsumoto, E., Sugiyama, M.: Learning discrete representations via information maximizing self-augmented training. In: ICML, vol. 70, pp. 1558–1567 (2017)
18. Huang, P., Huang, Y., Wang, W., Wang, L.: Deep embedding network for clustering. In: ICPR, pp. 1532–1537 (2014)
19. Hubert, L., Arabie, P.: Comparing partitions. J. Classif. **2**(1), 193–218 (1985)
20. Ji, P., Zhang, T., Li, H., Salzmann, M., Reid, I.: Deep subspace clustering networks. In: NeurIPS, pp. 23–32 (2017)
21. Ji, X., Henriques, J.F., Vedaldi, A.: Invariant information clustering for unsupervised image classification and segmentation. In: ICCV (2019)
22. Jiang, Z., Zheng, Y., Tan, H., Tang, B., Zhou, H.: Variational deep embedding: an unsupervised and generative approach to clustering. In: IJCAI, pp. 1965–1972 (2017)
23. Kingma, D.P., Welling, M.: Auto-encoding variational bayes (2013)
24. Krizhevsky, A.: Learning multiple layers of features from tiny images. University of Toronto, Technical report (2009)
25. Li, F., Qiao, H., Zhang, B.: Discriminatively boosted image clustering with fully convolutional auto-encoders. Pattern Recogn. **83**, 161–173 (2018)
26. Li, K., Wu, Z., Peng, K.C., Ernst, J., Fu, Y.: Tell me where to look: guided attention inference network. In: CVPR (2018)
27. Li, T., Ding, C.H.Q.: The relationships among various nonnegative matrix factorization methods for clustering. In: ICDM, pp. 362–371. IEEE Computer Society (2006)
28. Li, W., Zhu, X., Gong, S.: Harmonious attention network for person re-identification. In: CVPR (2018)
29. Liu, J., Gao, C., Meng, D., Hauptmann, A.G.: Decidenet: counting varying density crowds through attention guided detection and density estimation. In: CVPR (2018)
30. Lowe, D.G.: Object recognition from local scale-invariant features. In: ICCV (1999)
31. Macqueen, J.: Some methods for classification and analysis of multivariate observations. In: In 5-th Berkeley Symposium on Mathematical Statistics and Probability, pp. 281–297 (1967)
32. Makhzani, A., Shlens, J., Jaitly, N., Goodfellow, I.J.: Adversarial autoencoders. CoRR abs/1511.05644 (2015)
33. Masci, J., Meier, U., Cireşan, D., Schmidhuber, J.: Stacked convolutional auto-encoders for hierarchical feature extraction. In: Honkela, T., Duch, W., Girolami, M., Kaski, S. (eds.) Artificial Neural Networks and Machine Learning, pp. 52–59 (2011)
34. Ng, A.Y., Jordan, M.I., Weiss, Y.: On spectral clustering: analysis and an algorithm. In: Dietterich, T.G., Becker, S., Ghahramani, Z. (eds.) NeurIPS, pp. 849–856 (2002)
35. Noroozi, M., Favaro, P.: Unsupervised learning of visual representations by solving jigsaw puzzles. In: ECCV, vol. 9910, pp. 69–84 (2016)
36. Noroozi, M., Pirsiavash, H., Favaro, P.: Representation learning by learning to count. In: ICCV, pp. 5899–5907. IEEE Computer Society (2017)
37. Pathak, D., Krahenbuhl, P., Donahue, J., Darrell, T., Efros, A.A.: Context encoders: feature learning by inpainting. In: 2016 IEEE Conference on Computer Vision and Pattern Recognition (CVPR), pp. 2536–2544 (2016)

38. Russakovsky, O., et al.: Imagenet large scale visual recognition challenge. Int. J. Comput. Vis. **115**(3), 211–252 (2015)
39. Springenberg, J.T.: Unsupervised and semi-supervised learning with categorical generative adversarial networks. In: Bengio, Y., LeCun, Y. (eds.) ICLR (2016)
40. Strehl, A., Ghosh, J.: Cluster ensembles - a knowledge reuse framework for combining multiple partitions. J. Mach. Learn. Res. (JMLR) **3**, 583–617 (2002)
41. Tian, K., Zhou, S., Guan, J.: DeepCluster: a general clustering framework based on deep learning. In: Ceci, M., Hollmén, J., Todorovski, L., Vens, C., Džeroski, S. (eds.) ECML PKDD 2017. LNCS (LNAI), vol. 10535, pp. 809–825. Springer, Cham (2017). https://doi.org/10.1007/978-3-319-71246-8_49
42. Vaswani, A., et al.: Attention is all you need. In: Guyon, I., et al. (eds.) NeurIPS, pp. 5998–6008 (2017)
43. Vincent, P., Larochelle, H., Lajoie, I., Bengio, Y., Manzagol, P.A.: Stacked denoising autoencoders: learning useful representations in a deep network with a local denoising criterion. J. Mach. Learn. Res. **11**(12), 3371–3408 (2010)
44. Wang, Q., Teng, Z., Xing, J., Gao, J., Hu, W., Maybank, S.: Learning attentions: residual attentional siamese network for high performance online visual tracking. In: CVPR (2018)
45. Wu, J., et al.: Deep comprehensive correlation mining for image clustering. In: ICCV (2019)
46. Xie, J., Girshick, R., Farhadi, A.: Unsupervised deep embedding for clustering analysis. In: ICML, pp. 478–487 (2016)
47. Yang, B., Fu, X., Sidiropoulos, N.D., Hong, M.: Towards k-means-friendly spaces: simultaneous deep learning and clustering. In: Precup, D., Teh, Y.W. (eds.) ICML, vol. 70, pp. 3861–3870 (2017)
48. Yang, J., Parikh, D., Batra, D.: Joint unsupervised learning of deep representations and image clusters. In: CVPR (2016)
49. Zeiler, M.D., Krishnan, D., Taylor, G.W., Fergus, R.: Deconvolutional networks. In: Computer Vision and Pattern Recognition (2010)
50. Zhang, H., Goodfellow, I.J., Metaxas, D.N., Odena, A.: Self-attention generative adversarial networks. ArXiv abs/1805.08318 (2018)
51. Zhang, J., Li, C.G., You, C., Qi, X., Zhang, H., Guo, J., Lin, Z.: Self-supervised convolutional subspace clustering network. In: CVPR (2019)
52. Zhang, R., Isola, P., Efros, A.A.: Colorful image colorization. In: Leibe, B., Matas, J., Sebe, N., Welling, M. (eds.) ECCV 2016. LNCS, vol. 9907, pp. 649–666. Springer, Cham (2016). https://doi.org/10.1007/978-3-319-46487-9_40
53. Zhang, T., Ramakrishnan, R., Livny, M.: Birch: an efficient data clustering method for very large databases. In: SIGMOD Conference (1996)
54. Zhao, J.J., Mathieu, M., Goroshin, R., LeCun, Y.: Stacked what-where autoencoders. CoRR abs/1506.02351 (2015)
55. Zhou, P., Hou, Y., Feng, J.: Deep adversarial subspace clustering. In: CVPR (2018)

VCNet: A Robust Approach to Blind Image Inpainting

Yi Wang[1(✉)], Ying-Cong Chen[2], Xin Tao[3], and Jiaya Jia[1,4]

[1] The Chinese University of Hong Kong, Sha Tin, Hong Kong
{yiwang,leojia}@cse.cuhk.edu.hk
[2] MIT CSAIL, Cambridge, USA
ycchen@csail.mit.edu
[3] Kuaishou Technology, Beijing, China
jiangsutx@gmail.com
[4] SmartMore, Sha Tin, Hong Kong

Abstract. Blind inpainting is a task to automatically complete visual contents without specifying masks for missing areas in an image. Previous work assumes known missing-region-pattern, limiting the application scope. We instead relax the assumption by defining a new blind inpainting setting, making training a neural system robust against various unknown missing region patterns. Specifically, we propose a two-stage visual consistency network (VCN) to estimate where to fill (via masks) and generate what to fill. In this procedure, the unavoidable potential mask prediction errors lead to severe artifacts in the subsequent repairing. To address it, our VCN predicts semantically inconsistent regions first, making mask prediction more tractable. Then it repairs these estimated missing regions using a new spatial normalization, making VCN robust to mask prediction errors. Semantically convincing and visually compelling content can be generated. Extensive experiments show that our method is effective and robust in blind image inpainting. And our VCN allows for a wide spectrum of applications.

Keywords: Blind image inpainting · Visual consistency · Spatial normalization · Generative adversarial networks

1 Introduction

Image inpainting aims to complete missing regions of an image based on its context. Generally, it takes a corrupted image as well as a mask that indicates missing pixels as input, and restore it based on the semantics and textures of uncorrupted regions. It serves applications of object removal, image restoration, etc. We note the requirement of having accurate masks makes it difficult to

Electronic supplementary material The online version of this chapter (https://doi.org/10.1007/978-3-030-58595-2_45) contains supplementary material, which is available to authorized users.

A. Vedaldi et al. (Eds.): ECCV 2020, LNCS 12370, pp. 752–768, 2020.
https://doi.org/10.1007/978-3-030-58595-2_45

Fig. 1. Our blind inpainting method on raindrop removal (**left**, from [29]), face (**top right**, from FFHQ [17]), and animal (**bottom right**, from ImageNet [6]). *No* masks are provided during inference, and these filling patterns are not included in our training.

be practical in several scenarios where masks are not available, *e.g.*, graffiti and raindrop removal (Fig. 1). Users need to carefully locate corrupted regions manually, where inaccurate masks may lead to inferior results. We in this paper analyze blind inpainting that automatically finds pixels to complete, and propose a suitable solution based on image context understanding. Existing work [3, 24] on blind inpainting assumes that the missing areas are filled with constant values or Gaussian noise. Thus the corrupted areas can be identified easily and almost perfectly based on noise patterns. This oversimplified assumption could be problematic when corrupted areas are with unknown content. To improve the applicability, we relax the assumption and propose the *versatile blind inpainting* task. We solve it by taking deeper semantics of the input image into overall consideration and detecting more semantically meaningful *inconsistency* based on the context in contrast to previous blind inpainting.

Note that blind inpainting without assuming the damage patterns is highly ill-posed. This is because the unknown degraded regions need to be located based on their difference from the intact ones instead of their known characteristics, and the uncertainties in this prediction make the further inpainting challenging. We address it in two aspects, i.e., a new data generation approach and a novel network architecture.

For training data collection, if we only take common black or noise pixels in damaged areas as input, the network may detect these patterns as features instead of utilizing the contextual semantics as we need. In this scenario, the damage for training should be diverse and complicated enough so that the contextual inconsistency instead of the pattern in damage can be extracted. Our first contribution, therefore, is the new strategy to generate diverse training data where natural images are adopted as the filling content with random strokes.

For model design, our framework consists of two stages of mask prediction and robust inpainting. A discriminative model is used to conduct binary pixel-wise classification to predict inconsistent areas. With the mask estimated, we use it to guide the inpainting process. Though this framework is intuitive, its specific designs to address the biggest issue in this framework are non-trivial: *how to neutralize the generation degradation brought by inevitable mask estimation errors* in the first stage. To cope with this challenge, we propose a probabilistic context normalization (PCN) to spatially transfers contextual information in different neural layers, enhancing information aggregation of the inpainting network based on the mask prediction probabilities. We experimentally validate that it outperforms other existing approaches exploiting masks, e.g., concatenating mask with the input image and using convolution variants (like Partial Convolution [22] or Gated Convolution [44]) to employ masks, in evaluation.

Though trained without seeing any graffiti or trivial noise patterns (*e.g.* constant color or Gaussian noise), our model can automatically remove them without manually annotated marks, even for complex damages introduced by real images. This is validated in several benchmarks like FFHQ [17], ImageNet [6], and Places2 [49]. Besides, we find our predicted mask satisfyingly focuses on visual inconsistency in images as expected instead of inherent damage patterns when these two stages are jointly trained in an adversarial manner. This further improves robustness for this very challenging task, and leads to the application of exemplar-guided face-swap (Sec. 4.3). Also, such blind inpainting ability can be transferred to other removal tasks such as severe raindrop removal as exemplified in Fig. 1 and Sec. 4.2. Many applications are enabled.

Our contribution is twofold. First, we propose the first relativistic generalized blind inpainting system. It is robust against various unseen degradation patterns and mask prediction errors. We jointly model mask estimation and inpainting procedure, and address error propagation from the computed masks to the subsequent inpainting via new spatial normalization. Second, effective tailored training data synthesis for this new task is presented with comprehensive analysis. It makes our blind inpainting system robust to visual inconsistency, which is beneficial for various inpainting tasks.

2   Related Work

Blind Image Inpainting. Conventional inpainting methods employ external or internal image local information to fill missing regions [2,4,5,14,18,19,32]. For the blind image setting, existing research [3,7,24,36,41,47] assumes contamination with simple data distributions, *e.g.* text-shaped or thin stroke masks filled with constant values. This setting makes even a simple model applicable by only considering local information, without understanding the semantics of the input.

Generative Image Inpainting. Recent advancement [1,26,34,46] in the conditional generative models makes it possible to fill large missing areas in images [13,20,23,28,31,35,37–39,39,40,42,43,45,48,48]. Pathak *et al.* [28] learned an inpainting encoder-decoder network using both reconstruction and adversarial losses. Iizuka *et al.* [13] proposed the global and local discriminators for the adversarial training scheme. To obtain more vivid texture, coarse-to-fine [40,42,43] or multi-branch [37] network architecture, and non-local patch-match-like losses [37,42] or network layer [43] were introduced.

Specifically, Yang *et al.* [42] applied style transfer in an MRF manner to post-process the output of the inpainting network, creating crisp textures at the

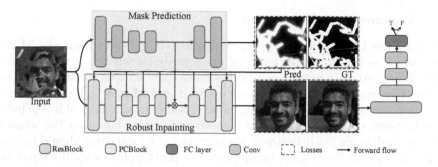

Fig. 2. Our framework. It consists of sequentially connected mask prediction and robust inpainting networks, trained in an adversarial fashion.

cost of heavy iterative optimization during testing. Further, Yu *et al.* [43] conducted the neural patch copy-paste operation with full convolutions, enabling texture generation in one forward pass. Instead of forcing copy-paste in the testing phase, Wang *et al.* [37] gave MRF-based non-local loss to encourage the network to model it implicitly. To better handle the generation of the missing regions, various types of intermediate representations (*e.g.* edges [27] and foreground segmentation [40]) are exploited to guide the final fine detail generation in a two-stage framework. Meanwhile, some researches focus on generating pluralistic results [48] or improving generation efficiency [31].

Also, research exists to study convolution variants [22,30,33,44]. They exploit the mask more explicitly than simple concatenation with the input. Generally, the crafted networks learn upon known pixels indicated by the mask.

Other Removal Tasks. A variety of removal tasks are related to blind inpainting, *e.g.* raindrop removal [29]. Their assumptions are similar regarding the condition that some pixels are clean or useful. The difference is on feature statistics of noisy areas subject to various strong priors.

3 Robust Blind Inpainting

For this task, the input is only a degraded image $\mathbf{I} \in \mathbb{R}^{h \times w \times c}$ (contaminated by unknown visual signals), and the output is expected to be a plausible image $\hat{\mathbf{O}} \in \mathbb{R}^{h \times w \times c}$, approaching ground truth $\mathbf{O} \in \mathbb{R}^{h \times w \times c}$ of $\mathbf{I}$.

The degraded image $\mathbf{I}$ in the blind inpainting setting is formulated as

$$\mathbf{I} = \mathbf{O} \odot (\mathbf{1} - \mathbf{M}) + \mathbf{N} \odot \mathbf{M}, \tag{1}$$

where $\mathbf{M} \in \mathbb{R}^{h \times w \times 1}$ is a binary region mask (with value 0 for known pixels and 1 otherwise), and $\mathbf{N} \in \mathbb{R}^{h \times w \times c}$ is a noisy visual signal. $\odot$ is the Hadamard product operator. Given $\mathbf{I}$, we predict $\hat{\mathbf{O}}$ (an estimate of $\mathbf{O}$) with latent variables $\mathbf{M}$ and $\mathbf{N}$. Also, Eq. (1) is the means to produce training tuples $< \mathbf{I}_i, \mathbf{O}_i, \mathbf{M}_i, \mathbf{N}_i >_{|i=1,\dots,m}$.

3.1   Training Data Generation

How to define the possible image contamination ($\mathbf{N}$ indicates what and $\mathbf{M}$ indicates where in Eq. (1)) is the essential prerequisite for whether a neural system could be robust to a variety of possible image contamination. Setting $\mathbf{N}$ as a constant value or certain kind of noise makes it and $\mathbf{M}$ easy to be distinguished by a deep neural net or even a simple linear classifier from a natural image patch. This prevents the model to predict inconsistent regions based on the semantic context, as drawing prediction with the statistics of a local patch should be much easier. It converts the original blind inpainting problem into a vanilla inpainting one with a nearly perfect prediction of $\mathbf{M}$. It becomes solvable with the existing techniques. But its assumption generally does not hold in the real-world scenarios, $e.g.$, graffiti removal shown in Fig. 1.

In this regard, the key for defining $\mathbf{N}$ is to make it indistinguishable as much as possible from $\mathbf{I}$ on image pattern, so that the model cannot decide if a local patch is corrupted without seeing the image context. Then a neural system trained with such data has the potential to work on unknown contamination.

In this paper, we use real-world image patches to form $\mathbf{N}$. This ensures that local patches between $\mathbf{N}$ and $\mathbf{I}$ are indistinguishable, enforcing the model to draw an inference based on contextual information, which eventually improves the generalization ability for real-world data. Further, we alleviate any priors introduced by $\mathbf{M}$ in training via employing free-form strokes [44]. Existing blind or non-blind inpainting methods often generate the arbitrary size of a rectangle or text-shaped masks. However, this is not suitable for our task, because it may encourage the model to locate the corrupted part based on the rectangle shape. Free-form masks can largely diversify the shape of masks, making the model harder to infer corrupted regions with shape information.

Also, we note that direct blending image $\mathbf{O}$ and $\mathbf{N}$ using Eq. (1) would lead to noticeable edges, which are strong indicators to distinguish among noisy areas. This will inevitably sacrifice the semantic understanding capability of the used model. Thus, we dilate the $\mathbf{M}$ into $\tilde{\mathbf{M}}$ by the iterative Gaussian smoothing in [37] and employ alpha blending in the contact regions between $\mathbf{O}$ and $\mathbf{N}$.

3.2   Our Method

We propose an end-to-end framework, named Visual Consistent Network (VCN) (Fig. 2). VCN has two sub-modules, $i.e.$ Mask Prediction Network (MPN) and Robust Inpainting Network (RIN). MPN is to predict potential visually inconsistent areas of a given image, while RIN is to inpaint inconsistent parts based on the predicted mask and the image context. Note that these two submodules are correlated. MPN provides an inconsistency mask $\hat{\mathbf{M}} \in \mathbb{R}^{h \times w \times 1}$, where $\hat{\mathbf{M}}_p \in [0, 1]$, helping RIN locate inconsistent regions. On the other hand, by leveraging local and global semantic context, RIN largely regularizes MPN, enforcing it to focus on these regions instead of simply fitting our generated data.

Our proposed VCN is robust to blind image inpainting in the given relativistic generalized setting. Its robustness is shown in two aspects. MPN of VCN can predict the regions to be repaired with decent performance even the contamination patterns are new to the trained model. More importantly, RIN of VCN synthesizes plausible and convincing visual content for the predicted missing regions, robust against mask prediction errors. Their designs are detailed below.

Mask Prediction Network (MPN). MPN aims to learn a mapping F where $F(\mathbf{I}) \rightarrow \mathbf{M}$. MPN is with an encoder-decoder structure using residual blocks [11], and takes binary cross-entropy loss between $\hat{\mathbf{M}}$ and $\mathbf{M}$ as the optimization goal. To stabilize its learning, a self-adaptive loss is introduced to balance positive- and negative-sample classification, because clear pixels outnumber the damages ones ($|\{p|\mathbf{M}_p = 1\}| = \rho|\{p|\mathbf{M}_p = 0\}|$ where $\rho = 0.56 \pm 0.17$). This self-adaptive loss is expressed as

$$\mathcal{L}_m(\hat{\mathbf{M}}, \mathbf{M}) = -\tau \sum_p \mathbf{M}_p \cdot \log(\hat{\mathbf{M}}_p) - (1 - \tau) \sum_q (1 - \mathbf{M}_q) \cdot \log(1 - \hat{\mathbf{M}}_q), \quad (2)$$

where $p \in \{p|\mathbf{M}_p = 1\}$, $q \in \{q|\mathbf{M}_q = 0\}$, and $\tau = |\{p|\mathbf{M}_p = 0\}|/(h \times w)$.

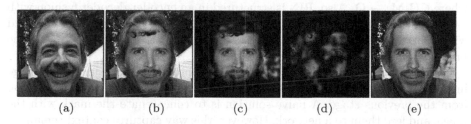

(a)	(b)	(c)	(d)	(e)

Fig. 3. Visualization of learned masks with different training strategies. (a) Input ground truth. (b) Input face image whose central part is replaced by another face with the rectangle mask. (c) Estimated mask with training MPN alone. (d) Estimated mask with joint training with inpainting network. (e) Output image of VCN. The used MPN is trained with free-form stroke masks [44].

Note that $\hat{\mathbf{M}}$ is an estimated soft mask where $0 \leq \hat{\mathbf{M}}_p \leq 1$ for $\forall p$, although we employ a binary version for $\mathbf{M}$ in Eq. (1). It means the damaged pixels are not totally abandoned in the following inpainting process. The softness of $\hat{\mathbf{M}}$ enables the differentiability of the whole network. Additionally, it lessens error accumulation caused by pixel misclassification, since pixels whose status (damaged or not) MPN are uncertain about are still utilized in the later process.

Note that the objective of MPN is to detect all corrupted regions. Thus it tends to predict large corrupted regions for an input corrupted image, which is shown in Fig. 3(c). As a result, it makes the subsequent inpainting task too difficult to achieve. To make the task more tractable, we instead propose to detect the *inconsistency* region of the image, as shown in Fig. 3(d), which is much smaller. If these regions are correctly detected, other corrupted regions can be naturally blended to the image, leading to realistic results. In the following,

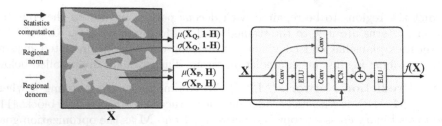

Fig. 4. Left: $\mathcal{T}(\cdot)$ in probabilistic context normalization (PCN, defined in Eq. (3)). Right: probabilistic contextual block (PCB). $\mathbf{X}$ and $\hat{\mathbf{M}}$ denote the input feature map and the predicted mask, respectively. $\mathbf{X_P} = \mathbf{X} \odot \hat{\mathbf{M}}$ and $\mathbf{X_Q} = \mathbf{X} \odot (\mathbf{I} - \hat{\mathbf{M}})$.

we show that by jointly learning MPN with RIN, the MPN eventually locates *inconsistency* regions instead of all corrupted ones.

Robust Inpainting Network (RIN). With the $\hat{\mathbf{M}}$ located by MPN, RIN corrects them and produces a realistic result $\mathbf{O}$ – that is, RIN learns a mapping G where $G(\mathbf{I}|\hat{\mathbf{M}}) \rightarrow \mathbf{O}$. Also, RIN is structured in an encoder-decoder fashion with probabilistic contextual blocks (PCB). PCB is a residual block variant armed with a new normalization (Fig. 4), incorporating spatial information with the predicted mask.

With the predicted mask $\hat{\mathbf{M}}$, repairing corrupted regions requires knowledge inference from context, and being skeptical to the mask for error propagation from the previous stage. A naive solution is to concatenate the mask with the image and feed them to a network. However, this way captures context semantics only in deeper layers, and does not consider the mask prediction error explicitly. To improve contextual modeling and minimize mask error propagation, it would be better if the transfer is done in all building blocks, driven by the estimated mask confidence. Hence, we propose a probabilistic context normalization (PCN, Fig. 4) to transfer contextual information in different layers.

Our PCN module is composed of the context feature transfer term and feature preserving term. The former transfers mean and variance from known features to unknown areas, both indicated by the estimated soft mask $\hat{\mathbf{M}}$ ($\mathbf{H}$ defined below is its downsampled version). It is a learnable convex combination of feature statistics from the predicted known areas and unknowns ones. Feature preserving term keeps the features in the known areas (of high confidence) intact. The formulation of PCN is given as

$$\mathrm{PCN}(\mathbf{X}, \mathbf{H}) = \underbrace{[\beta \cdot \mathcal{T}(\mathbf{X}, \mathbf{H}) \odot \mathbf{H} + (1-\beta)\mathbf{X} \odot \mathbf{H}]}_{\text{Context feature transfer}} + \underbrace{\mathbf{X} \odot \bar{\mathbf{H}}}_{\text{Feature preserving}}, \qquad (3)$$

and the operator $\mathcal{T}(\cdot)$ is to conduct instance internal statistics transfer as

$$\mathcal{T}(\mathbf{X}, \mathbf{H}) = \frac{\mathbf{X_P} - \mu(\mathbf{X_P}, \mathbf{H})}{\sigma(\mathbf{X_P}, \mathbf{H})} \cdot \sigma(\mathbf{X_Q}, \bar{\mathbf{H}}) + \mu(\mathbf{X_Q}, \bar{\mathbf{H}}), \qquad (4)$$

where $\mathbf{X}$ is the input feature map of PCN, and $\mathbf{H}$ is nearest-neighbor down-sampled from $\hat{\mathbf{M}}$, which shares the same height and width with $\mathbf{X}$. $\bar{\mathbf{H}} = 1 - \mathbf{H}$ indicates the regions that MPN considers clean. $\mathbf{X_P} = \mathbf{X} \odot \mathbf{H}$ and $\mathbf{X_Q} = \mathbf{X} \odot \bar{\mathbf{H}}$. β is a learnable channel-wise vector ($\beta \in \mathcal{R}^{1 \times 1 \times c}$ and $\beta \in [0,1]$) computed from $\mathbf{X}$ by a squeeze-and-excitation module [12] as

$$\beta = f(\bar{x}), \quad \text{and} \quad \bar{x}_k = \frac{1}{h' \times w'} \sum_{i=1}^{h'} \sum_{j=1}^{w'} \mathbf{X}_{i,j,k}, \tag{5}$$

where $\bar{x} \in \mathcal{R}^{1 \times 1 \times c}$ is also a channel-wise vector computed by average pooling $\mathbf{X}$, and $f(\cdot)$ is the excitation function composed by two fully-connected layers with activation functions (ReLU and Sigmoid, respectively).

$\mu(\cdot, \cdot)$ and $\sigma(\cdot, \cdot)$ in Eq. (4) compute the weighted average and standard deviation respectively in the following manner:

$$\mu(\mathbf{Y}, \mathbf{T}) = \frac{\sum_{i,j} (\mathbf{Y} \odot \mathbf{T})_{i,j}}{\epsilon + \sum_{i,j} \mathbf{T}_{i,j}}, \sigma(\mathbf{Y}, \mathbf{T}) = \sqrt{\frac{\sum_{i,j} (\mathbf{Y} \odot \mathbf{T} - \mu(\mathbf{Y}, \mathbf{T}))_{i,j}^2}{\epsilon + \sum_{i,j} \mathbf{T}_{i,j}}} + \epsilon, \tag{6}$$

where $\mathbf{Y}$ is a feature map, $\mathbf{T}$ is a soft mask with the same size of $\mathbf{Y}$, and ϵ is a small positive constant. i and j are the indexes of height and width, respectively.

Prior work [8,15] showed that feature mean and variance from an image are related to its semantics and texture. The feature statistics propagation by PCN helps regenerate inconsistent areas by leveraging contextual mean and variance. This is intrinsically different from existing methods that implicitly achieve this goal in deep layers, as we explicitly accomplish it in each building block. Thus PCN is beneficial to the learning and performance of blind inpainting. More importantly, RIN keeps robust considering potential errors in $\hat{\mathbf{M}}$ from MPN, although RIN is guided by $\hat{\mathbf{M}}$ for repairing. This is validated in Sect. 4.3.

Other special design in RIN includes feature fusion and a comprehensive optimization target. Feature fusion denotes concatenating the discriminative feature (bottleneck of MPN) to the bottleneck of RIN. This not only enriches the given features to be transformed into a natural image by introducing potential spatial information, but also enhances the discriminative learning for the location problem based on the gradients from the generation procedure.

The learning objective of RIN considers pixel-wise reconstruction errors, the semantic and texture consistency, and a learnable optimization target by fooling a discriminator via generated images as

$$\mathcal{L}_g(\hat{\mathbf{O}}, \mathbf{O}) = \underbrace{\lambda_r ||\hat{\mathbf{O}} - \mathbf{O}||_1}_{\text{reconstruction}} + \underbrace{\lambda_s ||V_{\hat{\mathbf{O}}}^l - V_{\mathbf{O}}^l||_1}_{\text{semantic consistency}} + \underbrace{\lambda_f \mathcal{L}_{mrf}(\hat{\mathbf{O}}, \mathbf{O})}_{\text{texture consistency}} + \underbrace{\lambda_a \mathcal{L}_{adv}(\hat{\mathbf{O}}, \mathbf{O})}_{\text{adversarial term}}, \tag{7}$$

where $\hat{\mathbf{O}} = G(\mathbf{I}|\hat{\mathbf{M}})$. V is a pre-trained VGG19 network. $V_{\mathbf{O}}^l$ means we extract the feature layer l (ReLU3_2) of the input $\mathbf{O}$ when $\mathbf{O}$ is passed into V. Besides, λ_r, λ_s, λ_f, and λ_a are regularization coefficients to adjust each term influence, and they are set to 1.4, $1e-4$, $1e-3$, and $1e-3$ in our experiments, respectively.

ID-MRF loss [25,37] is employed as our texture consistency term. It computes the sum of the patch-wise difference between neural patches from the generated content and those from the corresponding ground truth using a relative similarity measure. It enhances generated image details by minimizing discrepancy with its most similar patch from the ground truth.

For the adversarial term, WGAN-GP [1,10] is adopted as

$$\mathcal{L}_{adv}(\hat{\mathbf{O}}, \mathbf{O}) = -E_{\hat{\mathbf{O}} \sim \mathbb{P}_{\hat{\mathbf{O}}}}[D(\hat{\mathbf{O}})], \tag{8}$$

where $\mathbb{P}$ denotes data distribution, and D is a discriminator for the adversarial training. Its corresponding learning objective for the discriminator is given as

$$\mathcal{L}_D(\hat{\mathbf{O}}, \mathbf{O}) = E_{\hat{\mathbf{O}} \sim \mathbb{P}_{\hat{\mathbf{O}}}}[D(\hat{\mathbf{O}})] - E_{\mathbf{O} \sim \mathbb{P}_{\mathbf{O}}}[D(\mathbf{O})] + \lambda_{gp} E_{\tilde{\mathbf{O}} \sim \mathbb{P}_{\tilde{\mathbf{O}}}}[(\|\nabla_{\tilde{\mathbf{O}}} D(\tilde{\mathbf{O}})\|_2 - 1)^2], \tag{9}$$

where $\tilde{\mathbf{O}} = t\hat{\mathbf{O}} + (1 - t)\mathbf{O}$, $t \in [0, 1]$, and $\lambda_{gp} = 10$.

3.3   Training Procedure

Generation of training data is given in Eq. (1), where production of $\mathbf{M}$ is adopted from [44] as free-form strokes. The final prediction of our model is $G(\mathbf{I}|F(\mathbf{I}))$. All input and output are linearly scaled within range $[-1, 1]$.

There are two training stages. MPN and RIN are separately trained at first. After both networks are converged, we jointly optimize $\min_{\theta_F, \theta_G} \lambda_m \mathcal{L}_m(F(\mathbf{I}), \mathbf{M}) + \mathcal{L}_g(G(\mathbf{I}|F(\mathbf{I})), \mathbf{O})$ with $\lambda_m = 2.0$.

4   Experimental Results and Analysis

Our model and baselines are implemented using Tensorflow (v1.10.1). The evaluation platform is a Linux server with an Intel Xeon E5 (2.60GHz) CPU and an NVidia TITAN X GPU. Our full model (MPN + RIN) has 3.79M parameters and costs around 41.64ms to process a 256×256-size RGB image.

The datasets include FFHQ (faces) [17], CelebA-HQ (faces) [16], ImageNet (objects) [6], and Places2 (scenes) [49]. Our training images are all with size 256×256 unless otherwise specified. For FFHQ, images are downsampled from the original 1024×1024. For ImageNet and Places2, central cropping and padding are applied. When training on FFHQ, its corresponding noisy images are drawn from the training sets of CelebA-HQ and ImageNet. For training on ImageNet and Places2, these two datasets are the noisy source for each other.

Our baselines are all based on GAN [9] frameworks. We construct four alternative models to show the influence brought by the network architecture and module design. For a fair comparison, they are all equipped with mask prediction network (MPN) in front of their input, and are trained from scratch (MPNs are trained in the same way explained in Sect. 3.3). The first two alternatives are built upon the contextual attention (CA) model [43] and generative multi-column (GMC) model [37]. The input of these two inpainting variants is the concatenation of the estimated soft mask and the noisy image. The last two baselines are by employing the partial convolution (PC) [22] and gated convolution (GC) [44] as their basic building blocks, respectively, to construct the network, intending to explore how the used neural unit affects this blind inpainting. Compared with our VCN (3.79M), the model complexity of these CA, GMC, PC, and GC baselines is high as 4.86M, 13.7M, 4.69M, and 6.06M, respectively. All these numbers already include the model complexity of MPN (1.96M).

Table 1. Quantitative results on the testing sets from different methods.

Method	FFHQ-2K			Places2-4K			ImageNet-4K		
	BCE↓	PSNR↑	SSIM↑	BCE↓	PSNR↑	SSIM↑	BCE↓	PSNR↑	SSIM↑
CA [43]	1.297	16.56	0.5509	0.574	18.12	0.6018	0.450	17.68	0.5285
GMC [37]	0.766	20.06	0.6675	0.312	20.38	0.6956	0.312	19.56	**0.6467**
PC [22]	**0.400**	20.19	0.6795	0.273	19.73	0.6682	0.229	19.53	0.6277
GC [44]	0.660	17.16	0.5915	0.504	18.42	0.6423	0.410	18.35	0.6416
Our VCN	**0.400**	**20.94**	**0.6999**	**0.253**	**20.54**	**0.6988**	**0.226**	**19.58**	0.6339

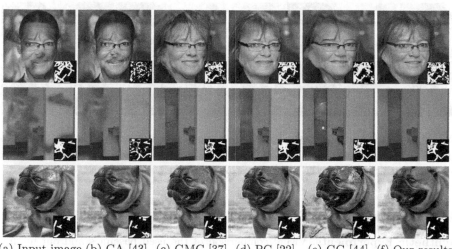

(a) Input image (b) CA [43] (c) GMC [37] (d) PC [22] (e) GC [44] (f) Our results

Fig. 5. Visual comparison on synthetic data from FFHQ (top), Places2 (middle), and ImageNet (bottom). The ground truth masks (shown in the first column) and the estimated ones (in binary form) are shown on the bottom right corner of each image.

4.1 Mask Estimation Evaluation

We evaluate the mask prediction performance of all used methods based on their computed binary cross-entropy (BCE) loss (the lower the better) on the testing sets. As shown in Table 1, our VCN achieves superior performance compared to GC [44], PC [22], GMC [37], and CA [43], except that our SSIM in ImageNet-4K is slightly lower than GMC. It shows that different generative structures and modules affect not only generation but also the relevant mask estimation performance. Clearly, VCN with spatial normalization works decently, benefiting mask prediction by propagating clean pixels to the damaged areas.

Partial convolution (in PC [22]) yields relatively lower performance, and direct concatenation between the estimated mask and the input image (used in CA [43] and GMC [37]) is least effective. Visual comparison of the predicted masks of different methods is included in Fig. 5, where the results from PC and VCN are comparable. They look better than those of CA, GMC, and GC.

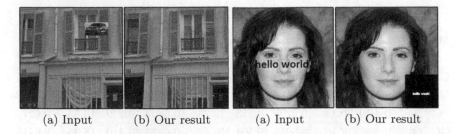

(a) Input   (b) Our result   (a) Input   (b) Our result

Fig. 6. Our results on facades and faces with other shaped masks.

Fig. 7. Visual results on FFHQ with masks filled with different contents. First row: input; second row: corresponding results from our model. Last two images are filled with content drawn from the testing sets of CelebA-HQ and ImageNet respectively.

4.2   Blind Inpainting Evaluation

Synthetic Experiments. Visual comparison of the used baselines and our method on the synthetic data (composed in the way we describe in Sec. 3.1) are given in Fig. 5. Our method produces more visually convincing results with fewer artifacts, which are not much disturbed by the unknown contamination areas. On the other hand, the noisy areas from CA and GMC baselines manifest that concatenation of mask and input to learn the ground truth is not an effective way for blind inpainting setting. More cases are given in the supplementary file.

About randomly inserted patches or text shape masks, Fig. 6 shows that our method can locate the inserted car, complete the facade (train/test on Paris Streetview [28]), and restore text-shape corrupted regions on the testing image from FFHQ.

Robustness against Various Degradation Patterns. Our training scheme makes the proposed model robust to fill content, as shown in Fig. 7. It can deal with Gaussian noise or constant color filling directly, while these patterns are not included in our training. This also shows such a training scheme makes the model learn to tell and inpaint visual inconsistency instead of memorizing synthetic missing data distribution.

PSNR and SSIM index evaluated on the testing sets of the used datasets are given in Table 1 for reference. Generally, VCN yields better or comparable results compared with baselines, verifying the effectiveness of spatial normalization about image fidelity restoration in this setting.

Further, pairwise A/B tests are adopted for blind user studies using Google Forms. 50 participants are invited for evaluating 12 questionnaires. Each has 40 pairwise comparisons, and every comparison shows results predicted from two different methods

Table 2. User studies. Each entry gives the percentage of cases where results by our approach are judged as more realistic than another solution. The observation and decision time for users is unlimited.

Methods	VCN > CA	VCN > GMC	VCN > PC	VCN > GC
FFHQ	99.64%	80.83%	77.66%	92.15%
Places2	81.39%	51.63%	70.49%	78.15%
ImageNet	91.20%	50.09%	77.92%	83.30%

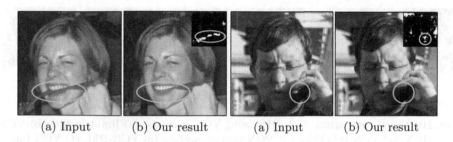

(a) Input   (b) Our result   (a) Input   (b) Our result

Fig. 8. Blind inpainting on the real occluded faces from COCO dataset with VCN. Red ellipses in the pictures highlight the regions to be edited.

Fig. 9. Visual evaluation on raindrop removal dataset. Left: Input image. Middle: AttentiveGAN [29]. Right: Ours (Best view in original resolution).

based on the same input, randomized in the left-right order. As given in Table 2, our method outperforms the CA, PC, and GC in all datasets and GMC in FFHQ, and yields comparable visual performance with GMC on ImageNet and Places2 with a much smaller model size (3.79M vs. 13.70M).

Blind Inpainting on Real Cases. Fig. 8 gives blind inpainting (trained on FFHQ) on the occluded face from COCO dataset [21]. Note VCN can automatically, and at least partially, restore these detected occlusions. The incomplete removal with red strip bit in the mouth may be caused by similar patterns in FFHQ, as mentioned that the detected visual inconsistency is inferred upon the learned distribution from the training data.

Model Generalization. We evaluate the generality of our model on raindrop removal with a few training data. The dataset in [29] gives paired data (noisy and clean ones) without masks. Our full model (pre-trained on Places2 with random strokes) achieves promising qualitative results (Fig. 9) on the testing set, which is trained with a few

Table 3. Quantitative results of component ablation of VCN on FFHQ (ED: Encoder-decoder; fusion: the bottleneck connection between MPN and RIN; -RM: removing the estimated contamination as $G(\mathbf{I} \odot (\mathbf{1} - \hat{\mathbf{M}})|\hat{\mathbf{M}})$; SC: semantic consistency term).

Model	ED	VCN w/o MPN	VCN w/o fusion	VCN w/o SC	VCN-RM	VCN full
PSNR↑	19.43	18.88	20.06	20.56	20.87	**20.94**
SSIM↑	0.6135	0.6222	0.6605	0.6836	**0.7045**	0.6999
BCE↓	-	-	0.560	0.653	0.462	**0.400**

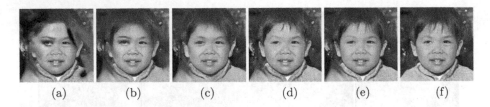

(a)   (b)   (c)   (d)   (e)   (f)

Fig. 10. Visual comparison on FFHQ using VCN variants. (a) Input image. (b) VCN w/o MPN. (c) VCN w/o skip. (d) VCN w/o semantics. (e) VCN-RM. (f) VCN full.

Fig. 11. Visual editing (face-swap) on FFHQ. First row: image with coarse editing where a new face (from CelebA-HQ) is pasted at the image center; Second row: corresponding results from our model. Best viewed with zoom-in.

training images (20 RGB images of resolution 480×720, around 2.5% training data). In the same training setting, testing results by AttentiveGAN [29] (a raindrop removal method) yield 24.99dB while ours is 26.22dB. It proves the learned visual consistency ability can be transferred to other similar removal tasks with a few target data.

4.3   Ablation Studies

w and w/o MPN. Without MPN, fidelity restoration of VCN degrades a lot in Table 3. The comparison in Fig. 10(b) shows VCN w/o MPN finds obvious artifacts like blue regions. But it fails to completely remove the external introduced woman face. Thus our introduced task decomposition and joint training strategy are effective. Compared with the performance of ED, VCN variants show the superiority of the module design in our solution.

Fusion of Discriminative and Generative Bottlenecks. Improvement of such modification on mask prediction (BCE), PSNR, and SSIM is limited. But this visual improvement shown in Fig. 10(c) and (f) is notable. Such a shortcut significantly enhances detail generation.

Input for Inpainting. Since the filling mask is estimated instead of given, removing possible contamination areas may degrade the generation performance due to the mask prediction error. Figure 10(e) validates our consideration.

Loss Discussion. Significance of the semantic consistency term that affects VCN is given in Fig. 10. It shows that this term benefits the discrimination ability and fidelity restoration of the model since removing it leads to a decrease of PSNR (from 20.94 to 20.56) and SSIM (from 0.6999 to 0.6836), and increase of BCE (from 0.4 to 0.653). Removing this term leads to hair and texture artifacts as shown in Fig. 10(d). Other terms have been discussed in [37,43].

Study of PCN. In the testing phase, we adjust ρ (instead of using the trained one) manually in PCN to show its flexibility in controlling interference of possible contamination (in the supplementary file). With increasing ρ, VCN tends to generate missing parts based on context instead of blending the introduced 'noise'.

Applications on Image Blending. Our blind inpainting system also finds applications on image editing, especially on blending user-fed visual material with the given image automatically. Our method can utilize the filling content to edit the original ones. The given material from external datasets is adjusted on its shape, color, shadow, and even its semantics to appeal to its new context, as given in Fig. 11. The editing results are natural and intriguing. Note the estimated masks mainly highlight the outlines of the pasted rectangle areas, which are just inconsistent regions according to context.

Limitation and Failure Cases. If contaminated areas in images are large enough to compromise main semantics, our model cannot decide which part is dominant and the performance would degrade dramatically. Some failure cases are given in the supplementary file. Moreover, if users want to remove a certain object from an image, it would be better to feed the user's mask into the robust inpainting network to complete the target regions. On the other hand, our method cannot repair the common occlusion problems (like human body occlusion) because our model does not regard this as an inconsistency.

5   Conclusion

We have proposed a robust blind inpainting framework with promising restoration ability on several benchmark datasets. We designed a new way of data preparation, which relaxes missing data assumptions, as well as an end-to-end model for joint mask prediction and inpainting. A novel probabilistic context normalization is used for better context learning. Our model can detect incompatible visual signals and transform them into contextual consistent ones. It is suitable to automatically repair images when manually labeling masks is hard. Our future work will be to explore the transition between common inpainting and blind inpainting, *e.g.* using coarse masks or weakly supervised hints to guide the process.

References

1. Arjovsky, M., Chintala, S., Bottou, L.: Wasserstein generative adversarial networks. In: ICML, pp. 214–223 (2017)

2. Barnes, C., Shechtman, E., Finkelstein, A., Goldman, D.B.: PatchMatch: a randomized correspondence algorithm for structural image editing. TOG **28**(3), 24 (2009)

3. Cai, N., Su, Z., Lin, Z., Wang, H., Yang, Z., Ling, B.W.-K.: Blind inpainting using the fully convolutional neural network. The Visual Computer **33**(2), 249–261 (2015). https://doi.org/10.1007/s00371-015-1190-z

4. Criminisi, A., Pérez, P., Toyama, K.: Region filling and object removal by exemplar-based image inpainting. TIP **13**(9), 1200–1212 (2004)

5. Darabi, S., Shechtman, E., Barnes, C., Goldman, D.B., Sen, P.: Image melding: combining inconsistent images using patch-based synthesis. TOG **31**(4), 82 (2012)

6. Deng, J., Dong, W., Socher, R., Li, L.J., Li, K., Fei-Fei, L.: ImageNet: a large-scale hierarchical image database. In: CVPR, pp. 248–255 (2009)

7. Dong, B., Ji, H., Li, J., Shen, Z., Xu, Y.: Wavelet frame based blind image inpainting. Appl. Comput. Harmonic Anal. **32**(2), 268–279 (2012)

8. Gatys, L.A., Ecker, A.S., Bethge, M.: Image style transfer using convolutional neural networks. In: CVPR, pp. 2414–2423 (2016)

9. Goodfellow, I., et al.: Generative adversarial nets. In: NeurIPS, pp. 2672–2680 (2014)

10. Gulrajani, I., Ahmed, F., Arjovsky, M., Dumoulin, V., Courville, A.C.: Improved training of Wasserstein GANs. In: NeurIPS, pp. 5769–5779 (2017)

11. He, K., Zhang, X., Ren, S., Sun, J.: Deep residual learning for image recognition. In: CVPR, pp. 770–778 (2016)

12. Hu, J., Shen, L., Sun, G.: Squeeze-and-excitation networks. In: CVPR, pp. 7132–7141 (2018)

13. Iizuka, S., Simo-Serra, E., Ishikawa, H.: Globally and locally consistent image completion. TOG **36**(4), 107 (2017)

14. Jia, J., Tang, C.K.: Image repairing: robust image synthesis by adaptive nd tensor voting. In: CVPR (2003)

15. Johnson, J., Alahi, A., Fei-Fei, L.: Perceptual Losses for Real-Time Style Transfer and Super-Resolution. In: Leibe, B., Matas, J., Sebe, N., Welling, M. (eds.) ECCV 2016. LNCS, vol. 9906, pp. 694–711. Springer, Cham (2016). https://doi.org/10.1007/978-3-319-46475-6_43

16. Karras, T., Aila, T., Laine, S., Lehtinen, J.: Progressive growing of GANs for improved quality, stability, and variation. arXiv preprint arXiv:1710.10196 (2017)

17. Karras, T., Laine, S., Aila, T.: A style-based generator architecture for generative adversarial networks. arXiv preprint arXiv:1812.04948 (2018)

18. Kopf, J., Kienzle, W., Drucker, S., Kang, S.B.: Quality prediction for image completion. TOG **31**(6), 131 (2012)

19. Levin, A., Zomet, A., Weiss, Y.: Learning how to inpaint from global image statistics. In: ICCV (2003)

20. Li, Y., Liu, S., Yang, J., Yang, M.H.: Generative face completion. In: CVPR, pp. 3911–3919 (2017)

21. Lin, T.-Y., Maire, M., Belongie, S., Hays, J., Perona, P., Ramanan, D., Dollár, P., Zitnick, C.L.: Microsoft COCO: Common Objects in Context. In: Fleet, D., Pajdla, T., Schiele, B., Tuytelaars, T. (eds.) ECCV 2014. LNCS, vol. 8693, pp. 740–755. Springer, Cham (2014). https://doi.org/10.1007/978-3-319-10602-1_48

22. Liu, G., Reda, F.A., Shih, K.J., Wang, T.-C., Tao, A., Catanzaro, B.: Image Inpainting for Irregular Holes Using Partial Convolutions. In: Ferrari, V., Hebert, M., Sminchisescu, C., Weiss, Y. (eds.) ECCV 2018. LNCS, vol. 11215, pp. 89–105. Springer, Cham (2018). https://doi.org/10.1007/978-3-030-01252-6_6

23. Liu, H., Jiang, B., Xiao, Y., Yang, C.: Coherent semantic attention for image inpainting. In: ICCV, pp. 4170–4179 (2019)
24. Liu, Y., Pan, J., Su, Z.: Deep blind image inpainting. arXiv preprint arXiv:1712.09078 (2017)
25. Mechrez, R., Talmi, I., Zelnik-Manor, L.: The contextual loss for image transformation with non-aligned data. arXiv preprint arXiv:1803.02077 (2018)
26. Miyato, T., Kataoka, T., Koyama, M., Yoshida, Y.: Spectral normalization for generative adversarial networks. arXiv preprint arXiv:1802.05957 (2018)
27. Nazeri, K., Ng, E., Joseph, T., Qureshi, F., Ebrahimi, M.: EdgeConnect: generative image inpainting with adversarial edge learning. arXiv preprint arXiv:1901.00212 (2019)
28. Pathak, D., Krahenbuhl, P., Donahue, J., Darrell, T., Efros, A.A.: Context encoders: feature learning by inpainting. In: CVPR, pp. 2536–2544 (2016)
29. Qian, R., Tan, R.T., Yang, W., Su, J., Liu, J.: Attentive generative adversarial network for raindrop removal from a single image. In: CVPR, pp. 2482–2491 (2018)
30. Ren, J.S., Xu, L., Yan, Q., Sun, W.: Shepard convolutional neural networks. In: NeurIPS, pp. 901–909 (2015)
31. Sagong, M.C., Shin, Y.G., Kim, S.w., Park, S., Ko, S.J.: Pepsi: Fast image inpainting with parallel decoding network. In: CVPR, pp. 11360–11368 (2019)
32. Sun, J., Yuan, L., Jia, J., Shum, H.Y.: Image completion with structure propagation. TOG **24**, 861–868 (2005)
33. Uhrig, J., Schneider, N., Schneider, L., Franke, U., Brox, T., Geiger, A.: Sparsity invariant CNNs. In: 3DV, pp. 11–20 (2017)
34. Wang, T.C., Liu, M.Y., Zhu, J.Y., Tao, A., Kautz, J., Catanzaro, B.: High-resolution image synthesis and semantic manipulation with conditional GANs. In: CVPR, pp. 8798–8807 (2018)
35. Wang, Y., Chen, Y.C., Zhang, X., Sun, J., Jia, J.: Attentive normalization for conditional image generation. In: CVPR, pp. 5094–5103 (2020)
36. Wang, Y., Szlam, A., Lerman, G.: Robust locally linear analysis with applications to image denoising and blind inpainting. SIAM J. Imaging Sci. **6**(1), 526–562 (2013)
37. Wang, Y., Tao, X., Qi, X., Shen, X., Jia, J.: Image inpainting via generative multi-column convolutional neural networks. In: NeurIPS (2018)
38. Wang, Y., Tao, X., Shen, X., Jia, J.: Wide-context semantic image extrapolation. In: CVPR, pp. 1399–1408 (2019)
39. Xie, C., et al.: Image inpainting with learnable bidirectional attention maps. arXiv preprint arXiv:1909.00968 (2019)
40. Xiong, W., et al.: Foreground-aware image inpainting. In: CVPR, pp. 5840–5848 (2019)
41. Yan, M.: Restoration of images corrupted by impulse noise and mixed gaussian impulse noise using blind inpainting. SIAM J. Imaging Sci. **6**(3), 1227–1245 (2013)
42. Yang, C., Lu, X., Lin, Z., Shechtman, E., Wang, O., Li, H.: High-resolution image inpainting using multi-scale neural patch synthesis. In: CVPR, p. 3 (2017)
43. Yu, J., Lin, Z., Yang, J., Shen, X., Lu, X., Huang, T.S.: Generative image inpainting with contextual attention. arXiv preprint arXiv:1801.07892 (2018)
44. Yu, J., Lin, Z., Yang, J., Shen, X., Lu, X., Huang, T.S.: Free-form image inpainting with gated convolution. In: ICCV, pp. 4471–4480 (2019)
45. Zeng, Y., Fu, J., Chao, H., Guo, B.: Learning pyramid-context encoder network for high-quality image inpainting. In: CVPR, pp. 1486–1494 (2019)
46. Zhang, H., Goodfellow, I., Metaxas, D., Odena, A.: Self-attention generative adversarial networks. arXiv preprint arXiv:1805.08318 (2018)

47. Zhang, S., He, R., Sun, Z., Tan, T.: DeMeshNet: blind face inpainting for deep MeshFace verification. IEEE Trans. Inf. Forensics Secur. **13**(3), 637–647 (2017)
48. Zheng, C., Cham, T.J., Cai, J.: Pluralistic image completion. In: CVPR, pp. 1438–1447 (2019)
49. Zhou, B., Lapedriza, A., Khosla, A., Oliva, A., Torralba, A.: Places: a 10 million image database for scene recognition. TPAMI **40**, 1452–1464 (2017)

Learning to Predict Context-Adaptive Convolution for Semantic Segmentation

Jianbo Liu[1], Junjun He[2], Yu Qiao[2], Jimmy S. Ren[3], and Hongsheng Li[1(✉)]

[1] CUHK-SenseTime Joint Laboratory, The Chinese University of Hong Kong,
Hong Kong, China
liujianbo@link.cuhk.edu.hk, hsli@ee.cuhk.edu.hk
[2] Shenzhen Key Lab of Computer Vision and Pattern Recognition, Shenzhen
Institutes of Advanced Technology, Chinese Academy of Sciences, Beijing, China
[3] SenseTime Research, Hong Kong, China

Abstract. Long-range contextual information is essential for achieving high-performance semantic segmentation. Previous feature re-weighting methods demonstrate that using global context for re-weighting feature channels can effectively improve the accuracy of semantic segmentation. However, the globally-sharing feature re-weighting vector might not be optimal for regions of different classes in the input image. In this paper, we propose a Context-adaptive Convolution Network (CaC-Net) to predict a spatially-varying feature weighting vector for each spatial location of the semantic feature maps. In CaC-Net, a set of context-adaptive convolution kernels are predicted from the global contextual information in a parameter-efficient manner. When used for convolution with the semantic feature maps, the predicted convolutional kernels can generate the spatially-varying feature weighting factors capturing both global and local contextual information. Comprehensive experimental results show that our CaC-Net achieves superior segmentation performance on three public datasets, PASCAL Context, PASCAL VOC 2012 and ADE20K.

Keywords: Semantic segmentation · Dynamic filter · Feature weighting

1 Introduction

Semantic segmentation aims at estimating a category label for each pixel of an input image, which is a fundamental problem in computer vision. It plays an important role in many applications including autonomous driving, image editing, computer-aided diagnosis, etc. Recently, state-of-the-art approaches leverage the Fully Convolutional Network (FCN) [23] as a base network to encode dense semantic representations from the input image and predict the class label for each pixel [4,5,11,30,34,37]. However, the significant scale variations of objects belonging to the same class and the similar appearances of objects belonging to different classes pose great challenges for semantic segmentation methods.

© Springer Nature Switzerland AG 2020
A. Vedaldi et al. (Eds.): ECCV 2020, LNCS 12370, pp. 769–786, 2020.
https://doi.org/10.1007/978-3-030-58595-2_46

To overcome these challenges, many works have been proposed to exploit the long-range contextual information from the dense semantic representations [4,11,34,37] to better distinguish scale and appearance ambiguity. One common solution is to aggregate the local context from different locations or subregions. The contextual information is collected by taking a fixed or an adaptively weighted aggregation from the local neighborhoods [7,16,34,35,37].

In contrast to encoding the relationship of local spatial context, another category of methods attempted to capture the global contextual information for estimating the channel-wise feature importances and using it to re-weight the feature channels for improving the segmentation accuracy. As illustrated in Fig. 1, the feature weighting can automatically highlight the features that are more relevant to the given scene and suppresses the irrelevant feature. For instance, boats usually appear in the sea or rivers but not in indoor environments. With the global context of a water scene, water-related feature channels should be higher weighted to increase the probability of predicting boat pixels. SE-Net [13] proposed the squeeze-excitation operation to learn a global feature weighting vector for weighting feature maps to improve image classification, detection and segmentation. EncNet [34] designed a global context encoding layer to weight features for improving semantic segmentation. Although this strategy has shown improved accuracy on segmentation, one of its key problems is that all the spatial locations share a common channel-wise weighting vector to calibrate the contributions of feature channels. For instance, features in the sky regions and the water regions of a water scene should be weighted differently.

To tackle this challenge, as shown in Fig. 1, we propose a novel segmentation framework, which properly weights feature channels with the global context but in a spatially varying manner, $i.e.$, feature channels at different spatial locations are modulated differently based on predictable and input-variant convolutions. Although there is a naive solution that simply generates kernels with a large number of parameters to conduct dot-product with the original feature maps, such strategies introduce too many parameters and cannot be used in practice. We propose a novel approach, which learns to predict Context-adaptive Convolution (CaC) kernels from the global context for generating the spatially-varying feature weighting factors. To reduce the parameters and the computational burden, we do not predict all CAC kernel parameters with fully-connected (FC) layers as previous dynamic kernels [15] do, which need too many learnable FC parameters. We instead propose an efficient context-adaptive kernel learning scheme that generates the CaC kernel parameters via simple matrix multiplication. The CaC kernels not only fully encode global context of the input feature maps but also generate context-aware spatially-varying feature weighting factors for each spatial location via depth-wise convolution with the input feature maps. In addition, we utilize a series of dilated depth-wise convolutions with different dilation factors to effectively capture information of multiple scales.

Our main contributions can be summarized as threefold: (1) To better regularize the semantic segmentation with global contextual information, we propose to estimate spatially-varying feature weighting factors for properly weighting

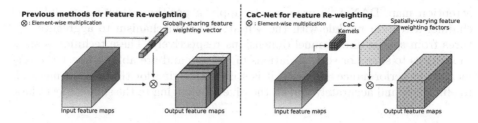

Fig. 1. (Left): Previous feature re-weighting methods [13,34] used a globally-sharing weighting vector to improve the performance of semantic segmentation, but ignores the spatially varying characteristics of the input image. (Right): Our CaC-Net learns to predict context-adaptive convolution kernels from the global context for weighting feature channels in a spatially-varying manner

features at different spatial locations to improve the semantic segmentation performance. (2) We train an efficient deep network to predict the context-adaptive convolution kernels from the global context of the input image. The proposed CaC kernel prediction is both computation and memory efficient, which can effectively generate spatially-varying weights based on both global context and local information. (3) With the proposed CaC module, our proposed approach achieves state-of-the-art performance on multiple public benchmarks, including PASCAL-Context, PASCAL VOC 2012, and ADE20K.

2   Related Work

Context Aggregation.   Fully convolution network [23] based methods have made great achievements in semantic segmentation. With a series of convolution and down-sampling operations, the features of deeper layers gradually capture information with larger receptive fields. However, they still have limited receptive fields and cannot effectively take advantages of the global or long-range context. Global or long-range contextual information aggregation has been shown their effectiveness on improving the segmentation accuracy of large homogeneous semantic regions or objects with large scale variations. ParseNet [20] proposed to capture the global context by concatenating a global pooling feature with the original feature maps. PSPNet [37] designed a Spatial Pyramid Pooling (SPP) module to collect contextual information of different scales. Atrous Spatial Pyramid Pooling (ASPP) [4,5] applied a set of different dilated convolutions to capture multi-scale contextual information. However, these methods treat all pixels in each sub-region with uniform or fixed weights for feature aggregation.

To achieve adaptive and flexible feature aggregations, APCNet [11] proposed an adaptive context module (ACM) to leverage local and global representations to estimate inter-pixel affinity weights for feature aggregation. CFNet [35] designed an aggregated co-occurrent feature (ACF) module to aggregate the co-occurrent context using the pair-wise similarities in the feature space. PSANet[38] aggregated contextual information for each pixel with a predicted attention map. DANet [7] proposed to apply a position attention module and channel attention module with the self-attention mechanism to aggregate features from spatial and channel dimensions respectively. These techniques show robustness to shape or scale variations of objects and are able to boost the segmentation performance. However, it is still challenging for this kind of methods to efficiently and accurately find all the pixels belonging to the same object class.

Channel-wise Feature Re-weighting. To take advantages of the global contextual information of the input images, some pioneering methods [13,34] have been proposed to re-weight different channels of the 2D feature maps with a scaling vector learned from the global context feature vector. Both SE-Net [13] and EncNet [34] learned a globally-sharing attention vector from the global context. SE-Net [13] proposed to learn feature weighting factors by the squeeze-excitation operation. The squeeze operation aggregates the feature maps across all spatial locations to produce a global context-encoded feature vector. Then the excitation operation learns the weighting factors from the global-context features. EncNet [34] predicted one globally-sharing feature re-weighting vector using a context encoding module. This module integrates dictionary learning and residual encoding components to learn a global context encoded feature vector, based on which, the feature weighting factor vector is predicted. However, both methods only consider the global context and output a feature re-weighting vector that is shared across all spatial locations. Such a globally-sharing weighting scheme might not be suitable for different spatial regions belonging to different objects in the same scene. To tackle this challenge, we propose to predict learnable kernels for re-weighting the feature maps in a spatially-varying manner.

Dynamic Filters. Dynamic filters or kernels were proposed by [15] to generate content-aware filters, which are conditional on the input images. These filters are adaptive to the input and are predicted by the neural network. It has shown effectiveness in various computer vision applications. Some methods adopted the predicted dynamic filters for low-level vision and video understanding, *e.g.*, video interpolation [26], image synthesis [21] and image denoising [24]. Pixel-Adaptive Convolution (PAC) Network [29] was proposed to predict spatially-varying kernels for several computer vision applications including deep joint image upsampling, semantic segmentation and efficient CRF inference. SAC [36] utilized a scale regression layer to predict position-adaptive scale coefficients, which were used to automatically adjust the sizes of receptive fields for objects of different sizes. DMNet [10] exploited a set of dynamic filters of different sizes, which were generated from multi-scale neighborhoods for handling the scale variations of objects for semantic segmentation. The previous methods with dynamic filters directly predict all the filter parameters, which are time inefficient and occupy too much memory. In comparison, our work learns to predict the context-adaptive convolution kernels from global context in a parameter-efficient manner.

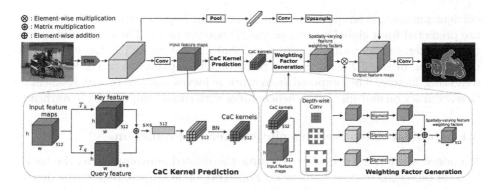

Fig. 2. Pipeline of Context-adaptive Convolution Network (CaC-Net). CaC-Net consists of a backbone convolution neural network (CNN), a Context-adaptive Convolution (CaC) kernel prediction module and a spatially-varying weight generation module. The key component, CaC kernel prediction, learns to predict a spatially-sharing context-aware convolution kernels. The weight generation module uses the predicted dynamic kernels to generate one spatially-varying feature weighting factor for each location in the input feature maps

3   Method

Feature re-weighting has proven to be a powerful approach to capture long-range semantic context by learning channel-wise weighting factors from the global contextual information. Although it has shown its effectiveness in various tasks including classification, detection and semantic segmentation [13,34], one of its key issues is that the weighting vector is shared by all spatial locations of the 2D feature map.

We argue that, for semantic segmentation, a globally-shared weighting vector is not an optimal solution, as different spatial locations generally belong to objects of different classes. Therefore, desirable feature weighting factors should still be learned from the global context but be spatially-varying to capture different locations' unique characteristics to achieve high segmentation accuracy. Predicting convolution kernels from the global context to generate the spatially-varying weights is a desirable solution. Compared with traditional convolutions on the feature maps, which only have local receptive fields and are input-invariant, predicted kernels from the global context are well aware of the overall scene structure for better weighting the features at different locations.

To achieve this goal, we propose a novel Context-adaptive Convolution (CaC) Network (see Fig. 2), which consists of a 2D Convolutional Neural Network (CNN)-based backbone for encoding the input images into 2D feature maps and a Context-adaptive Convolution (CaC) module for learning to channel-wisely re-weight the 2D feature maps with global context. A series of context-adaptive convolution kernels are predicted from the CaC module. Unlike the previous dynamic filters, which require using a large number of learnable parameters to predict the kernels, the proposed CaC kernels are predicted in a parameter-efficient manner via simple matrix multiplication. Importantly, the CaC kernels are predicted from global context of the 2D feature maps. The convolution with the CaC kernels can well integrate the global context as well as the multi-scale information of the 2D feature maps to predict the spatially-varying feature re-weighting factors. The proposed framework achieves state-of-the-art segmentation accuracy on multiple public benchmarks with small computational overhead.

3.1   Context-Adaptive Convolution Kernel Prediction

We adopt a pre-trained ResNet [12] with the dilated convolutions as the backbone of our segmentation framework. Following [4,33,34], we remove the downsampling operations and set the dilation rates to be 2 and 4 at the last two ResNet-blocks to generate an output feature map of $1/8$ spatial size of the input image. It encodes each input 2D image into a 2D feature map $X \in \mathbb{R}^{h \times w \times c}$, where h, w, c are the height, width, and feature channels of the feature map. The feature map can roughly capture semantic information of the input image. Properly re-weighting the feature map X in a sptially-varying manner according to the global context can boost the segmentation performance.

To conduct spatially-varying feature re-weighting via kernel prediction, there are two naive solutions: (1) one can directly predict c sets of $s \times s \times c$ convolutional kernels (where $s \times s$ is the kernel spatial size) following dynamic filters [15] and then conducting convolution of the input feature map X with the kernels to generate the c sets of feature weighting maps. However, this solution requires a fully connected (FC) layer to predict the kernel weights, which has too many $(s^2 c^3)$ learnable parameters and computation cost. (2) One can also predict the kernels from the global average pooled features of the input feature map with an FC layer to capture the global context. Feature weighting maps can be obtained by conducting convolution on the input feature map with the predicted kernels. However, such a solution loses all spatial information during kernel prediction and show inferior performance in our experiments.

To tackle the challenges, our proposed Context-adaptive Convolution module predicts a series of $s \times s \times c$ CaC convolution kernels from the global context in a parameter-efficient manner. The input feature map $X \in \mathbb{R}^{h \times w \times c}$ is first transformed into the 2D query feature map $Q \in \mathbb{R}^{h \times w \times s^2}$ and the key feature map $K \in \mathbb{R}^{h \times w \times c}$ by two independent transformations T_k and T_q, respectively. The transformations T_k and T_q are independently implemented by 1×1 convolutions. Generally, the key feature $K \in \mathbb{R}^{h \times w \times c}$ captures c different characteristics of the input feature map X via its c-dimensional feature maps, while the query feature $Q \in \mathbb{R}^{h \times w \times s^2}$ is used to capture the global spatial distributions of K, where s^2 sets of global spatial characteristics would be captured by Q.

To achieve the goal, the query feature and key feature are first reshaped to obtain $\bar{Q} \in \mathbb{R}^{n \times s^2}$ and $\bar{K} \in \mathbb{R}^{n \times c}$, where $n = h \times w$. For the ith column $\bar{Q}(:, i) \in \mathbb{R}^n$ of query feature, it can be used to capture the overall spatial distribution of each feature channel j of the key feature $\bar{K}(:, j) \in \mathbb{R}^n$ over all $n = h \times w$ spatial locations via the dot product $\langle \bar{Q}(:, i), \bar{K}(:, j) \rangle$. The result would be a scalar to measure the similarity between the spatial distributions $\bar{Q}(:, i)$ and $\bar{K}(:, j)$. If we repeat the procedure for all c feature channels of K, we obtain a c-dimensional vector to characterize the spatial distributions of each feature channel of $\bar{K}$ with a query vector $\bar{Q}(:,i)$. Since we have s^2 query vectors in total, we can capture s^2 characteristics of the overall spatial distributions of the c-dimensional key feature map K as

$$\bar{D} = \bar{Q}^\top \bar{K}, \tag{1}$$

where $\bar{D} \in \mathbb{R}^{s^2 \times c}$.

We then reshape $\bar{D}$ into the size of $s \times s \times c$ and use a batch normalization to modulate it to obtain the predicted $D \in \mathbb{R}^{s \times s \times c}$ as our CaC kernels, which are used to convolved with the input feature map X to generate the spatially-varying feature re-weighting factors for all $h \times w$ spatial locations.

Note that the CaC kernels are predicted and would therefore be adaptive to different inputs to capture their different global context. There are two distinct advantages of the predicted convolution kernel D. 1) The CaC kernels are able to capture the global context of the input feature map X, since the matrix multiplication in Eq. (1) considers all spatial locations for kernel prediction. 2) The CaC kernels are generated in a parameter-efficient manner, where only $c^2 + s^2 c$ learnable parameters are needed with an inference time complexity of $O(c^2 + s^2 c)$ for kernel prediction, which is significantly lower than $O(s^2 c^3)$ parameters and complexity of dynamic filters.

3.2   Spatially-Varying Weight Generation

We use the predicted CaC kernels to produce the spatially-varying weighting map for weighting each pixel of the input feature maps. The predicted kernels $D \in \mathbb{R}^{s \times s \times c}$ are used in a depth-wise convolution. Therefore, each channel of D is responsible for modulating one channel of the input feature maps independently. To further encourage the predicted kernel D being scale invariant as well as capturing multi-scale context of the input feature map. We denote the original predicted kernels D with dilation 1 as D_1, and create another two CaC kernels with shared parameters of D but with different dilation rates 2 and 3, which are denoted as D_2 and D_3.

As shown in Fig. 2, for each set of predicted CaC kernels of D_1, D_2, D_3, they are used to separately perform depth-wise convolution on the input feature map X followed by the sigmoid function. Each of them would generate an independent spatially-varying weighting map $W_1, W_2, W_3 \in \mathbb{R}^{h \times w \times c}$, which are added to generate the overall spatially-varying weighting map W,

$$W = W_1 \oplus W_2 \oplus W_3, \tag{2}$$

where the symbol $\oplus$ denotes the element-wise addition.

Given W, we re-weight the input feature maps as $X^\star = X \odot W$, where $\odot$ represents the element-wise multiplication. In this manner, we develop a computationally efficient way to predict the spatially-varying feature weighting factors for each spatial location of the input feature map X. For each predicted feature weighting vector at the spatial location $W(i,j) \in \mathbb{R}^c$, it re-weights the features $X(i,j)$ according to the global contextual information. Intuitively, the larger values in the $W(i,j)$ vector highlight more target class-related features while the smaller values suppress non-target-class-related features according to the global context.

3.3   Global Pooling and Multi-head Ensembles

Following state-of-the-art segmentation frameworks [35,37], we also integrate a global pooling branch in our framework, which globally averages the feature vectors of all spatial locations and replicates the vector to all spatial locations. This replicated global-pooling feature maps are channel-wise concatenated with the re-weighted feature maps $X^\star$ to obtain the final feature maps for segmentation.

The multi-head ensembling strategy is implemented by performing multiple proposed CaC modules in parallel and producing multiple output feature maps. Since the different head modules operate on the different subspace of the input feature maps, some previous works [10,31,35] show that the multi-head ensembling strategy is able to further increase the performance. In our work, we apply this strategy to improve the capability of our CaC-Net by concatenating two output feature maps from our CaC modules.

4   Experiments

In this section, we first introduce the implementation details, training strategies and evaluation metrics of the experiments. Then, to evaluate the proposed CaC-Net, we conduct comprehensive experiments on three public datasets, Pascal Context [25], Pascal VOC 2012 [6] and ADE20K [40]. The ablation study of our CaC-Net is carried out on the Pascal Context dataset. Finally, we report the overall results on PASCAL Context, PASCAL VOC 2012 and ADE20K.

4.1   Implementation Details

Network Structure.   We adopt ResNet [12] as our backbone. The stride of the last two stages of the backbone networks is removed and these dilation rates are set as 2 and 4 respectively. Thus the size of the feature maps is $8\times$ smaller than that of the input image. To predict a semantic label for each pixel, the output of our CaC-Net is upscaled to the size of input image by bilinear interpolation. The ImageNet [28] pre-trained weights are adopted to initialize the backbone networks.

Training Setting.   A poly learning rate policy [4], $lr = initial\_lr \times (1 - \frac{iter}{total\_iter})^{power}$ is used. We set the initial learning rate as 0.001 for PASCAL Context [25], 0.002 for PASCAL VOC 2012 [6] and 0.004 for ADE20K [40].

Table 1. Ablation study of CaC-Net on PASCAL Context dataset. CaC represents our proposed CaC module. GP indicates the global pooling

Method	Backbone	CaC	GP	pixAcc%	mIoU%
FCN	ResNet50			76.0	45.8
CaC-Net	ResNet50	✓		79.8	52.0
CaC-Net	ResNet50	✓	✓	80.2	52.5
CaC-Net	ResNet101	✓	✓	81.5	55.4

Table 2. Ablation study of different setting in training and evaluation strategies. DS: Deep supervision loss strategy [37]. Flip: horizontally flipping the input image for evaluation. MS: Multi-scale evaluation

Backbone	DS	Flip	MS	pixAcc%	mIoU%
ResNet50				79.4	50.7
ResNet50	✓			79.7	51.5
ResNet50	✓	✓		79.9	51.8
ResNet50	✓	✓	✓	80.2	52.5

The power of poly learning rate policy is set as 0.9. The optimizer is stochastic gradient descent (SGD) [3] with momentum 0.9 and weight decay 0.0001. We train our CaC-Net for 120 epochs for PASCAL Context dataset, 80 epochs for PASCAL 2012 dataset and 180 epochs for ADE20K dataset. We set the crop size to 512×512 on PASCAL Context and PASCAL 2012. Due to the average image size is larger than the other two datasets, we use 576×576 as the crop size on ADE20K. For data augmentation, we only randomly flip the input image and scale it randomly in the range from 0.5 to 2.0. As the prior work [34,35], we adopt an auxiliary segmentation loss, which is added after Res-4. We adopt Sync-BN [34] for normalization and set the batch size as 16 for all experiments.

Evaluation Metrics. We choose the standard evaluation metrics of pixel accuracy (pixAcc) and mean Intersection of Union (mIoU) as the evaluation metrics in this experiments. Following the best practice [7,11,34], we apply the strategy of averaging the network predictions in multiple scales for evaluation. For multi-scale evaluation, we first resize the input image to multiple scales and horizontally flip them. Then the predictions are averaged as final predictions.

4.2 Results on PASCAL Context

PASCAL Context dataset [25] is a challenging scene understanding dataset, which provides the semantic labels for the images. There are 4,998 images for training and 5,105 images for validation on PASCAL Context dataset. Following previous work [34,35], the 59 most frequent categories are used for training our CaC-Net and all the other classes are considered as the background class.

Ablation Study on CaC-Net. We conduct experiments with different settings to evaluate the performance of our proposed CaC-Net using a ResNet-50 [12] backbone on the PASCAL Context dataset. The baseline is a ResNet-50 based FCN [23] by removing the proposed CaC modules and the global pooling

Table 3. The results of different numbers of our CaC module exploited in the CaC-Net

	$H=1$	$H=2$	$H=3$	$H=4$
pixAcc	79.9	80.2	79.9	80.0
mIoU	51.7	52.5	52.3	52.1

Table 4. The results of different kernel sizes used in our proposed CaC module

	$3+3$	$3+5$	$3+7$
pixAcc	80.2	80.2	80.1
mIoU	52.5	52.3	52.3

Table 5. The results of different dilation rate sets for generating the weighting factors in CaC-Net

	{1}	{1,2}	{1,2,3}	{1,2,3,4}
pixAcc	79.9	80.1	80.2	79.7
mIoU	51.9	52.1	52.5	51.6

Table 6. Results of alternative ways to generate weighting map and dynamic kernels.

	Fixed	FC	GAP	SEHead	EncHead	Ours
pixAcc	79.7	79.8	79.8	79.7	79.7	80.0
mIoU	51.3	51.5	51.6	50.9	51.2	52.5

Table 7. Parameters and FLOPS of backbone and segmentation heads from APCNet [11], DMNet [10], and our CaC-Net.

Methods	Backbone	APCNet	DMNet	Ours
Parameters	56M	+10M	+9M	+5M
FLOPS	225G	+22G	+20G	+21G

branch in our CaC-Net. We choose the pixAcc and mIoU for 60 classes on the PASCAL Context dataset as our evaluation metrics for the ablation study.

We first evaluate the individual components, which are added into the baseline FCN one at a time. The size of predicted CaC kernels is 3×3 and we use two CaC modules in all experiments. As shown in Table 1, the baseline FCN with a ResNet50 backbone achieves 76.0% pixAcc and 45.8% mIoU. With our proposed CaC, the results of pixACC and mIoU are increased by 3.8% and 6.2% respectively. The global pooling branch results in a further 0.5% mIoU improvement. We can see that our proposed CaC module can significantly improve the segmentation results.

We also conduct experiments to explore training and evaluation strategies, other plausible ways of generating the weighting maps, the influence of the number of our proposed CaC modules for feature concatenation as introduced in Sect. 3, the kernel size of our predicted CaC kernels, and the dilation rates in the feature weighting factor generation.

Ablation Study on Training and Evaluation Strategies. We conduct experiments to explore the effects of training and evaluation strategies and the results are shown in Table 2. We use a deep supervision strategy by adding an FCN head to the output of ResNet-4 as an auxiliary loss. From the table, we observe that the deep supervision training strategy results in a 0.8% mIOU improvement. We adopt the image flipping and multi-scale evaluation strategy during inference. These two evaluation strategies can further boost the performance of segmentation.

Ablation Study on the Alternative Ways to Generate Weighting Maps and Dynamic Kernels. To investigate other possible ways to generate spatially-varying weighting maps, we keep our overall framework unchanged but replace our CaC modules with alternative approaches to generate the feature weighting maps. The first intuitive way is to directly predict the feature weighting maps via traditional convolutions on the input feature maps, whose parameters are still learned during training but are fixed to different inputs during testing. If our CaC kernels are replaced by the input-invariant convolutions of the same kernel sizes and different dilation rates. Denoted by "Fixed" in Table 6, the performance of the fixed-kernel channel weighting prediction declines dramatically, which demonstrates that the predicted CaC kernels can generate context-aware feature weighting maps to boost the performance of semantic segmentation.

Meanwhile, there have some other possible ways to predict the dynamic filters. If we directly generate the dynamic kernel weights by one FC layer, the parameter overhead of this FC layer is $h \times w \times s^2 \times c^2$, which are about hw times more parameters than our method and occupy too much GPU memory to be implemented in practice. If we instead adopt a depth-wise FC layer on the input feature map to generate the dynamic kernel weights. The parameters of the depth-wise FC layer reduce to $h \times w \times s^2 \times c$, which are the same as our CaC module. However, the mIoU on PASCAL Context decreases to 51.7% ("FC" in Table 6) with a ResNet-50 backbone, which is lower than our CaC-Net (52.5%).

The third alternative way is to use the global average pooling (GAP) features of the input feature maps to predict the dynamic kernels. In this way, the dynamic kernels can also capture global context. The input feature maps is first average pooled to a c-d vector followed by an FC layer to predict the $s \times s \times c$ dynamic kernels. However, the parameters of this scheme would be s^2c^2, significantly more than our CaC module's $c^2 + s^2c$ parameters. In addition, since the input feature map is average pooled first, the image spatial structure is lost, which limits its capacity on predicting spatially-aware dynamic kernels. If replacing our CaC kernels with such dynamic kernels from GAP features, the mIoU on PASCAL Context decreases to 51.9% ("GAP" in Table 6) on PASCAL Context.

Ablation Study on Comparison with the Globally-Sharing Feature Re-weighting Methods. To compare with globally-sharing feature re-weighting methods, we conduct two experiments by replacing the proposed CaC modules in our CaC-Net with SE-Head [13] and EncHead [34] for globally-sharing feature re-weighting. The results are shown in Table 6, which demonstrate the proposed spatially-varying feature re-weighting method shows superior performance than the globally-sharing feature re-weighting methods for semantic segmentation.

Ablation Study on the Number of CaC Modules. Table 3 illustrates the effects of different number of CaC modules for multi-head ensemble in our proposed CaC-Net, which shows that two CaC modules is optimal for achieving the best performance for semantic segmentation for our designed CaC-Net. The

Table 8. Segmentation results of state-of-the-art methods on PASCAL Context dataset

Method	Backbone	mIoU%
FCN-8S [23]		37.8
CRF-RNN [39]		39.3
ParseNet [20]		40.4
HO_CRF [1]		41.3
Piecewise [19]		43.3
DeepLab-v2 [4]	ResNet101-COCO	45.7
RefineNet [18]	ResNet152	47.3
MSCI [17]	ResNet152	50.3
EncNet [34]	ResNet101	51.7
DANet [7]	ResNet101	52.6
APCNet [11]	ResNet101	54.7
CFNet [35]	ResNet101	54.0
ACNet [8]	ResNet101	54.1
APNB [41]	ResNet101	52.8
DMNet [10]	ResNet101	54.4
Ours	ResNet50	52.5
Ours	ResNet101	**55.4**

Table 9. Segmentation results of state-of-the-art methods on ADE20K validation set

Method	Backbone	mIoU%
FCN [23]		29.39
SegNet [2]		21.64
RefineNet [18]	ResNet152	40.7
PSPNet [37]	ResNet101	43.29
EncNet [34]	ResNet101	44.65
SAC [36]	ResNet101	44.30
PSANet [38]	ResNet101	43.77
UperNet [40]	ResNet101	42.66
APCNet [11]	ResNet101	45.38
CFNet [35]	ResNet101	44.89
CCNet [14]	ResNet101	45.22
APNB [41]	ResNet101	45.24
ACNet [8]	ResNet101	45.90
DMNet [10]	ResNet101	45.50
Ours	ResNet101	**46.12**

results are getting worse when H is larger than 2 because the larger H introduces additional parameters and model capacity, which might overfit the data if H is too large. We therefore fix the number of CaC module to be 2.

Ablation Study on Kernel Size. In following experiments, the influence of the kernel size of the predicted dynamic CaC kernels is investigated. We report results of three sets of kernel sizes, $3 + 3$, $3 + 5$, $3 + 7$, of the two CaC modules respectively in Table 4. We first set the kernel size of one CaC module as 3×3 according to the experience that 3×3 kernels is usually sufficient to obtain good performance and is computationally efficient. By increasing the kernel size of another CaC module from 3×3, 5×5, 7×7, we observe that the performance of our proposed CaC-Net decreases slightly. The reason might be increasing the kernel size also requires many additional FC parameters, which causes the models to be difficult to train. To reduce the computational cost and achieve the optimal performance, we set the kernel size of both CaC modules to 3×3.

Ablation Study on Dilation Rates. For the spatially-varying feature weighting factor generation, we exploit a set of dilated depth-wise convolutions in each predicted CaC kernel to increase the ability of capturing multi-scale contextual

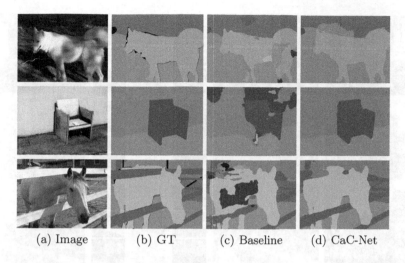

(a) Image	(b) GT	(c) Baseline	(d) CaC-Net

Fig. 3. Visualization examples from the PASCAL Context dataset

Table 10. Results of each category on PASCAL VOC 2012 test set. Our CaC-Net achieves 85.1% without MS COCO dataset pre-training.

Method	Aero	Bike	Bird	Boat	Bottle	Bus	Car	Cat	Chair	Cow	Table	Dog	Horse	mbike	Person	Plant	Sheep	Sofa	Train	Tv	mIoU%
FCN [23]	76.8	34.2	68.9	49.4	60.3	75.3	74.7	77.6	21.4	62.5	46.8	71.8	63.9	76.5	73.9	45.2	72.4	37.4	70.9	55.1	62.2
DeepLabv2 [4]	84.4	54.5	81.5	63.6	65.9	85.1	79.1	83.4	30.7	74.1	59.8	79.0	76.1	83.2	80.8	59.7	82.2	50.4	73.1	63.7	71.6
CRF-RNN [39]	87.5	39.0	79.7	64.2	68.3	87.6	80.8	84.4	30.4	78.2	60.4	80.5	77.8	83.1	80.6	59.5	82.8	47.8	78.3	67.1	72.0
DeconvNet [27]	89.9	39.3	79.7	63.9	68.2	87.4	81.2	86.1	28.5	77.0	62.0	79.0	80.3	83.6	80.2	58.8	83.4	54.3	80.7	65.0	72.5
DPN [22]	87.7	59.4	78.4	64.9	70.3	89.3	83.5	86.1	31.7	79.9	62.6	81.9	80.0	83.5	82.3	60.5	83.2	53.4	77.9	65.0	74.1
Piecewise [19]	90.6	37.6	80.0	67.8	74.4	92	85.2	86.2	39.1	81.2	58.9	83.8	83.9	84.3	84.8	62.1	83.2	58.2	80.8	72.3	75.3
ResNet38 [32]	94.4	72.9	94.9	68.8	78.4	90.6	90.0	92.1	40.1	90.4	71.7	89.9	93.7	91.0	89.1	71.3	90.7	61.3	87.7	78.1	82.5
PSPNet [37]	91.8	71.9	94.7	71.2	75.8	95.2	89.9	95.9	39.3	90.7	71.7	90.5	94.5	88.8	89.6	72.8	89.6	**64.0**	85.1	76.3	82.6
EncNet [34]	94.1	69.2	**96.3**	76.7	**86.2**	96.3	90.7	94.2	38.8	90.7	73.3	90.0	92.5	88.8	87.9	68.7	92.6	59.0	86.4	73.4	82.9
APCNet [11]	95.8	75.8	84.5	76.0	80.6	**96.9**	90.0	96.0	**42.0**	93.7	75.4	91.6	95.0	90.5	**89.3**	75.8	92.8	61.9	88.9	79.6	84.2
CFNet [35]	95.7	71.9	95.0	76.3	**82.8**	94.8	90.0	95.9	37.1	92.6	73.0	**93.4**	94.6	89.6	88.4	74.9	**95.2**	63.2	**89.7**	78.2	84.2
DMNet [10]	96.1	77.3	94.1	72.8	78.1	**97.1**	**92.7**	96.4	39.8	91.4	75.5	92.7	**95.8**	91.0	**90.3**	**76.6**	94.1	62.1	85.5	77.6	84.4
Ours	**96.3**	76.2	95.3	**78.1**	80.8	96.5	91.8	**96.9**	40.7	**96.3**	**76.4**	**94.3**	**95.8**	**91.3**	89.1	73.1	93.3	62.2	86.7	**80.2**	**85.1**

information. The different dilation rates are explored here. Table 5 shows the results of different dilation rates adopted in our CaC-Net. We found that the dilated convolution could boost the performance of our proposed CaC-Net as the dilated convolution increase the receptive fields. However, the performance of the dilated rate sets $\{1, 2, 3, 4\}$ is lower than that of $\{1, 2, 3\}$ because of two aspects: (a) The receptive field of the dilation rate 3 is enough for the size of feature maps in our proposed CaC-Net for the PASCAL Context dataset. (b) Too many dilation rates bring too large computational complexity. Based on this observation, the dilation set that we choose is $\{1, 2, 3\}$ in all experiments.

Comparisons with the State-of-the-Art Methods. The results are shown in Table 8. APCNet [11] and CFNet [35] both exploit a dynamic or adaptive manner to globally aggregate features, which has expensive computational and memory cost. Our proposed CaC-Net with ResNet101 backbone surpasses other

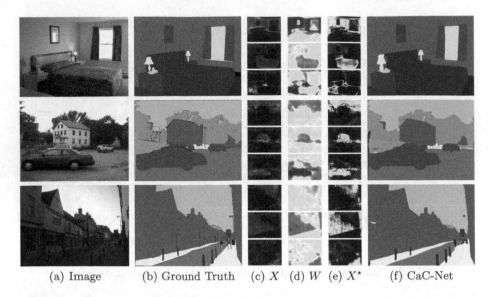

(a) Image   (b) Ground Truth   (c) X (d) W (e) $X^\star$ (f) CaC-Net

Fig. 4. Visualization results on ADE20K dataset. (a) The input images. (b) Ground truth label maps. (c)-(e) Some representative channels of the input feature maps X, the output feature maps $X^\star$ and the produced spatially-varying weighting factors W. In our CaC-Net, $X^\star = X \odot W$. (f) Results of our proposed CaC-Net

approaches by significant margins with a light-weight head. Meanwhile, the performance of CaC-Net with ResNet50 backbone even achieves better performance than most previous methods with a deeper backbone. Especially, by learning to predict the spatially-varying feature weighting factors for each location, the performance of our proposed CaC-Net significantly outperforms EncNet [34], which predicts a globally-sharing weight factor for re-weighting feature maps. In Fig. 3, we illustrate the visual improvements of our approach over the baseline FCN network on the PASCAL Context. It can be seen that our proposed method boosts the performance of semantic segmentation in some challenging scenarios.

Meanwhile, with the dilated ResNet-101 backbone and input image size 512×512, the computational and parameter overheads of the backbone, the heads of APCNet, DMNet and our CaC-Net are provided in Table 7. Compared with the backbone, the proposed CaC-Net brings less than 10% extra cost. Compared with the two other segmentation heads with two times more parameters, our CaC-Net has a $> 1\%$ mIoU improvement on the PASCAL Context dataset.

4.3   Results on PASCAL VOC 2012

The PASCAL VOC 2012 dataset [6] is one of the most competitive semantic segmentation benchmarks, which contains 20 foreground object classes and 1 background class. There are $1,464$ images for training, $1,449$ images for validation and $1,456$ images for testing in the original PASCAL VOC 2012 dataset.

Following the best practice [11,34,35], the augmented training set of PASCAL VOC2012 [9] is adopted as our training set, which includes 10,582 training images. The training strategy is the same as [11,34,35], we first train our CaC-Net on the augmented training set, and then fine-tune on the original training and validation sets. In Table 10, we illustrate the results of our CaC-Net and state-of-the-art methods on PASCAL VOC 2012 benchmark. We can observe that our CaC-Net yields mIOU 85.1% ont the test set, which outperforms other methods without COCO pre-training and achieves superior performance on most categories.

4.4   Results on ADE20K

ADE20K dataset [40] is a large-scale scene parsing dataset which provides 150 class categories, and consists 20 K training images, 2K validation 3 K test samples. In this subsection, we carry out experiments on ADE20K to evaluate the effectiveness of our proposed CaC-Net. We train our CaC-Net with a ResNet101 backbone on the training set and evaluate the models on the validation set. Results of state-of-the-art methods on ADE20K are shown in Table 9. Our CaC-Net with a ResNet101 backbone achieves 46.12% mIOU and outperforms all previous methods in mIoU with the same backbone. In Fig. 4, we show some results of our predicted results and randomly select some representative channels of their feature maps in CaC-Net. In the visualized feature maps, the darker colors represent the larger values. We can observe that the spatially-varying weights produced by our CaC-Net can efficiently highlight the class-dependent regions.

5   Conclusion

In this paper, we propose a novel network, CaC-Net, for semantic segmentation. The key innovation lies in the prediction of context-adaptive convolutional kernels to integrate both global context of the input semantic feature maps. Convolution with the predicted kernels leads to feature re-weighting maps that can effectively re-weight the feature maps in a spatially-varying manner. Extensive experiments demonstrate the outstanding performance of our proposed CaC-Net, surpassing state-of-the-art segmentation methods on multiple datasets.

Acknowledgements. This work is supported in part by SenseTime Group Limited, in part by the General Research Fund through the Research Grants Council of Hong Kong under Grants CUHK 14202217/14203118/14205615/14207814/14213616/14208417/14239816, in part by CUHK Direct Grant.

References

1. Arnab, A., Jayasumana, S., Zheng, S., Torr, P.H.S.: Higher order conditional random fields in deep neural networks. In: Leibe, B., Matas, J., Sebe, N., Welling, M. (eds.) ECCV 2016. LNCS, vol. 9906, pp. 524–540. Springer, Cham (2016). https://doi.org/10.1007/978-3-319-46475-6_33

2. Badrinarayanan, V., Kendall, A., Cipolla, R.: Segnet: A deep convolutional encoder-decoder architecture for image segmentation. arXiv preprint arXiv:1511.00561 (2015)
3. Bottou, L.: Large-scale machine learning with stochastic gradient descent. In: Proceedings of COMPSTAT'2010, pp. 177–186. Springer, Heidelberg (2010). https://doi.org/10.1007/978-3-7908-2604-3_16
4. Chen, L.C., Papandreou, G., Kokkinos, I., Murphy, K., Yuille, A.L.: Deeplab: semantic image segmentation with deep convolutional nets, atrous convolution, and fully connected crfs. IEEE Trans. Pattern Anal. Mach. Intell. **40**(4), 834–848 (2017)
5. Chen, L.C., Papandreou, G., Schroff, F., Adam, H.: Rethinking atrous convolution for semantic image segmentation. arXiv preprint arXiv:1706.05587 (2017)
6. Everingham, M., Van Gool, L., Williams, C.K., Winn, J., Zisserman, A.: The pascal visual object classes (voc) challenge. Int. J. Comput. Visi. **88**(2), 303–338 (2010)
7. Fu, J., Liu, J., Tian, H., Li, Y., Bao, Y., Fang, Z., Lu, H.: Dual attention network for scene segmentation. In: Proceedings of the IEEE Conference on Computer Vision and Pattern Recognition, pp. 3146–3154 (2019)
8. Fu, J., et al.: Adaptive context network for scene parsing. In: The IEEE International Conference on Computer Vision (ICCV) (2019)
9. Hariharan, B., Arbeláez, P., Girshick, R., Malik, J.: Hypercolumns for object segmentation and fine-grained localization. In: Proceedings of the IEEE Conference on Computer Vision and Pattern Recognition, pp. 447–456 (2015)
10. He, J., Deng, Z., Qiao, Y.: Dynamic multi-scale filters for semantic segmentation. In: Proceedings of the IEEE International Conference on Computer Vision, pp. 3562–3572 (2019)
11. He, J., Deng, Z., Zhou, L., Wang, Y., Qiao, Y.: Adaptive pyramid context network for semantic segmentation. In: Proceedings of the IEEE Conference on Computer Vision and Pattern Recognition, pp. 7519–7528 (2019)
12. He, K., Zhang, X., Ren, S., Sun, J.: Deep residual learning for image recognition. In: Proceedings of the IEEE Conference on Computer Vision and Pattern Recognition, pp. 770–778 (2016)
13. Hu, J., Shen, L., Sun, G.: Squeeze-and-excitation networks. In: Proceedings of the IEEE Conference on Computer Vision and Pattern Recognition, pp. 7132–7141 (2018)
14. Huang, Z., Wang, X., Huang, L., Huang, C., Wei, Y., Liu, W.: CCnet: criss-cross attention for semantic segmentation. In: The IEEE International Conference on Computer Vision (ICCV) (2019)
15. Jia, X., De Brabandere, B., Tuytelaars, T., Gool, L.V.: Dynamic filter networks. In: Advances in Neural Information Processing Systems, pp. 667–675 (2016)
16. Li, X., Zhong, Z., Wu, J., Yang, Y., Lin, Z., Liu, H.: Expectation-maximization attention networks for semantic segmentation. In: The IEEE International Conference on Computer Vision (ICCV) (2019)
17. Lin, D., Ji, Y., Lischinski, D., Cohen-Or, D., Huang, H.: Multi-scale context intertwining for semantic segmentation. In: Proceedings of the European Conference on Computer Vision (ECCV), pp. 603–619 (2018)
18. Lin, G., Milan, A., Shen, C., Reid, I.: Refinenet: multi-path refinement networks for high-resolution semantic segmentation. In: Proceedings of the IEEE conference on computer vision and pattern recognition. pp. 1925–1934 (2017)
19. Lin, G., Shen, C., Van Den Hengel, A., Reid, I.: Efficient piecewise training of deep structured models for semantic segmentation. In: Proceedings of the IEEE Conference on Computer Vision and Pattern Recognition, pp. 3194–3203 (2016)

20. Liu, W., Rabinovich, A., Berg, A.C.: Parsenet: Looking wider to see better. arXiv preprint arXiv:1506.04579 (2015)
21. Liu, X., Yin, G., Shao, J., Wang, X., Li, H.: Learning to predict layout-to-image conditional convolutions for semantic image synthesis. In: Advances in Neural Information Processing Systems, pp. 570–580 (2019)
22. Liu, Z., Li, X., Luo, P., Loy, C.C., Tang, X.: Semantic image segmentation via deep parsing network. In: Proceedings of the IEEE International Conference on Computer Vision, pp. 1377–1385 (2015)
23. Long, J., Shelhamer, E., Darrell, T.: Fully convolutional networks for semantic segmentation. In: Proceedings of the IEEE Conference on Computer Vision and Pattern Recognition, pp. 3431–3440 (2015)
24. Mildenhall, B., Barron, J.T., Chen, J., Sharlet, D., Ng, R., Carroll, R.: Burst denoising with kernel prediction networks. In: Proceedings of the IEEE Conference on Computer Vision and Pattern Recognition, pp. 2502–2510 (2018)
25. Mottaghi, R., et al.: The role of context for object detection and semantic segmentation in the wild. In: Proceedings of the IEEE Conference on Computer Vision and Pattern Recognition, pp. 891–898 (2014)
26. Niklaus, S., Mai, L., Liu, F.: Video frame interpolation via adaptive separable convolution. In: Proceedings of the IEEE International Conference on Computer Vision, pp. 261–270 (2017)
27. Noh, H., Hong, S., Han, B.: Learning deconvolution network for semantic segmentation. In: Proceedings of the IEEE International Conference on Computer Vision, pp. 1520–1528 (2015)
28. Russakovsky, O., et al.: Imagenet large scale visual recognition challenge. Int. J. Comput. Vis. **115**(3), 211–252 (2015)
29. Su, H., Jampani, V., Sun, D., Gallo, O., Learned-Miller, E., Kautz, J.: Pixel-adaptive convolutional neural networks. In: Proceedings of the IEEE Conference on Computer Vision and Pattern Recognition, pp. 11166–11175 (2019)
30. Takikawa, T., Acuna, D., Jampani, V., Fidler, S.: Gated-SCNN: gated shape cnns for semantic segmentation. In: Proceedings of the IEEE International Conference on Computer Vision, pp. 5229–5238 (2019)
31. Vaswani, A., et al.: Attention is all you need. In: Advances in Neural Information Processing Systems, pp. 5998–6008 (2017)
32. Wu, Z., Shen, C., Hengel, A.V.d.: Wider or deeper: Revisiting the resnet model for visual recognition. arXiv preprint arXiv:1611.10080 (2016)
33. Yu, F., Koltun, V., Funkhouser, T.: Dilated residual networks. In: Proceedings of the IEEE Conference on Computer Vision and Pattern Recognition, pp. 472–480 (2017)
34. Zhang, H., et al.: Context encoding for semantic segmentation. In: The IEEE Conference on Computer Vision and Pattern Recognition (CVPR) (2018)
35. Zhang, H., Zhang, H., Wang, C., Xie, J.: Co-occurrent features in semantic segmentation. In: The IEEE Conference on Computer Vision and Pattern Recognition (CVPR) (2019)
36. Zhang, R., Tang, S., Zhang, Y., Li, J., Yan, S.: Scale-adaptive convolutions for scene parsing. In: Proceedings of the IEEE International Conference on Computer Vision, pp. 2031–2039 (2017)
37. Zhao, H., Shi, J., Qi, X., Wang, X., Jia, J.: Pyramid scene parsing network. In: Proceedings of the IEEE Conference on Computer Vision and Pattern Recognition, pp. 2881–2890 (2017)

38. Zhao, H., et al.: PSANet: point-wise spatial attention network for scene parsing. In: Proceedings of the European Conference on Computer Vision (ECCV), pp. 267–283 (2018)
39. Zheng, S., et al.: Conditional random fields as recurrent neural networks. In: Proceedings of the IEEE International Conference on Computer Vision, pp. 1529–1537 (2015)
40. Zhou, B., Zhao, H., Puig, X., Fidler, S., Barriuso, A., Torralba, A.: Scene parsing through ade20k dataset. In: Proceedings of the IEEE Conference on Computer Vision and Pattern Recognition, pp. 633–641 (2017)
41. Zhu, Z., Xu, M., Bai, S., Huang, T., Bai, X.: Asymmetric non-local neural networks for semantic segmentation. In: Proceedings of the IEEE International Conference on Computer Vision, pp. 593–602 (2019)

Author Index

Printed in the United States
By Bookmasters